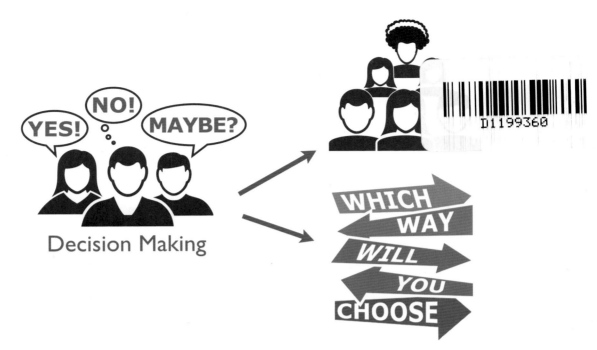

Decision Making

D1199360

WHICH WAY WILL YOU CHOOSE

- **Decision making simulations** – place your students in the role of a key decision-maker where they are asked to make a series of decisions. The simulation will change and branch based on the decisions students make, providing a variation of scenario paths. Upon completion of each simulation, students receive a grade, as well as a detailed report of the choices they made during the simulation and the associated consequences of those decisions.

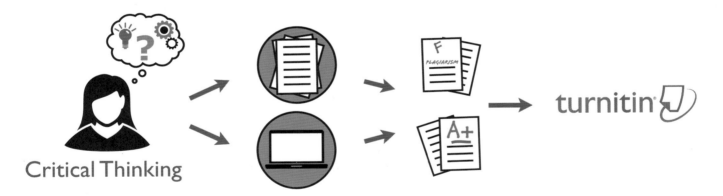

Critical Thinking

turnitin

- **Writing Space** – better writers make great learners—who perform better in their courses. Providing a single location to develop and assess concept mastery and critical thinking, the Writing Space offers automatic graded, assisted graded and create your own writing assignments; allowing you to exchange personalized feedback with students quickly and easily.

  Writing Space can also check students' work for improper citation or plagiarism by comparing it against the world's most accurate text comparison database available from **Turnitin**.

http://www.pearsonmylabandmastering.com

PEARSON

STRATEGIC MANAGEMENT
Concepts and Cases

A COMPETITIVE ADVANTAGE APPROACH

STRATEGIC MANAGEMENT
Concepts and Cases

FIFTEENTH EDITION

A COMPETITIVE ADVANTAGE APPROACH

Fred R. David

Francis Marion University
Florence, South Carolina

Forest R. David

Strategic Planning Consultant

PEARSON

Boston   Columbus   Indianapolis   New York   San Francisco   Upper Saddle River
Amsterdam   Cape Town   Dubai   London   Madrid   Milan   Munich   Paris   Montréal   Toronto
Delhi   Mexico City   São Paulo   Sydney   Hong Kong   Seoul   Singapore   Taipei   Tokyo

Editor in Chief: Stephanie Wall
Program Management Lead: Ashely Santora
Program Manager: Sarah Holle
Editorial Assistant: Bernard Ollila
Marketing Director: Maggie Moylan
Senior Marketing Manager: Erin Gardner
Project Management Lead: Judy Leale
Project Manager: Ann Pulido
Procurement Specialist: Michelle Klein
Art Director, Interior: Kenny Beck
Designer, Interior: Laura Ierardi
Creative Director, Cover: Jayne Conte
Designer, Cover: Bruce Kenselaar
VP, Director of Digital Strategy & Assessment: Paul Gentile
Brian Surette: Digital Editor
Robin Lazrus: Digital Development Manager
Alana Coles: Digital Project Manager
Joan Waxman: MyLab Product Manager
Digital Production Project Manager: Lisa Rinaldi
Full-Service Project Management and Composition: Integra
Printer/Binder: Courier/Kendallville
Cover Printer: Lehigh-Phoenix Color / Hagerstown
Text Font: 10/12 Times

Credits and acknowledgments borrowed from other sources and reproduced, with permission, in this textbook appear on the appropriate page within text with the exception of the Pepsi logo that appears throughout the text and is credited to PSL Images/Alamy.

Microsoft® and Windows® are registered trademarks of the Microsoft Corporation in the U.S.A. and other countries. Screen shots and icons reprinted with permission from the Microsoft Corporation. This book is not sponsored or endorsed by or affiliated with the Microsoft Corporation.

Copyright © 2015, 2013, 2011, 2009, 2007 by Pearson Education, Inc. All rights reserved. Manufactured in the United States of America. This publication is protected by Copyright, and permission should be obtained from the publisher prior to any prohibited reproduction, storage in a retrieval system, or transmission in any form or by any means, electronic, mechanical, photocopying, recording, or likewise. To obtain permission(s) to use material from this work, please submit a written request to Pearson Education, Inc., Permissions Department, One Lake Street, Upper Saddle River, New Jersey 07458, or you may fax your request to 201-236-3290.

Many of the designations by manufacturers and sellers to distinguish their products are claimed as trademarks. Where those designations appear in this book, and the publisher was aware of a trademark claim, the designations have been printed in initial caps or all caps.

Library of Congress Cataloging-in-Publication Data
David, Fred R.
   Strategic management : concepts and cases : a competitive advantage approach/ Fred R. David and Forest R. David
Francis Marion University, Florence, South Carolina.—Fifteenth edition.
      pages cm
   ISBN-13: 978-0-13-344479-7
   ISBN-10: 0-13-344479-1
   1. Strategic planning.   2. Strategic planning—Case studies.   I. David, Forest R.   II. Title.
HD30.28.D385 2015
658.4'012—dc23
                                                                    2013041984

10 9 8 7 6 5 4 3

ISBN 10:   0-13-344479-1
ISBN 13: 978-0-13-344479-7

Brief Contents

Contents

Chapter 4 The Internal Assessment   89

Chapter 5 Strategies in Action   127

Chapter 6 Strategy Analysis and Choice   165

Cases

USA Headquartered

Outside-USA Headquartered

Welcome Forest, and Thank You:

- For joining me as a coauthor on this 15th edition
- For preparing the *Case Instructor's Manual* for this textbook and five previous editions
- For writing 29 new, excellent cases included in this edition, and many cases in prior editions
- For publishing many strategic management papers and articles with me and other authors
- For your wise strategic-management counsel over many years as this textbook has evolved
- For assisting students for many years through the Strategy Club (www.strategyclub.com) that now also offers your free Excel Student Template
- For developing an outstanding Case MyLab testing feature for this edition
- For preparing the *Chapter Instructor's Manual* for this edition

Preface

Why Adopt This Text?

This textbook is trusted around the world to provide managers the latest skills and concepts needed to effectively formulate and efficiently implement a strategic plan—a game plan, if you will—that can lead to sustainable competitive advantage for any type of business. The Association to Advance Collegiate Schools of Business (AACSB) increasingly advocates a more skills-oriented, practical approach in business books, which the David text provides, rather than a theory-based approach. This textbook meets all AACSB-International guidelines for the strategic-management course at both the graduate and undergraduate levels, and previous editions have been used at more than 500 colleges and universities around the world. We believe you will find this edition to be the best textbook available for communicating both the excitement and value of strategic management. Concise and exceptionally well organized, this text is now published in English, Chinese, Spanish, Thai, German, Japanese, Farsi, Indonesian, Indian, and Arabic. A version in Russian is being negotiated. Not only universities, but also hundreds of companies, organizations, and governmental bodies use this text as a management guide.

In contrast to many other strategic-management textbooks, the David book provides:

1. An effective process for developing a clear strategic plan, rather than simply presenting seminal theories in strategy, and
2. An effective model or flow for actually doing strategic planning.

Eric N. Sims, a professor who in 2013 adopted the David book for his classes at Sonoma State University in California, says:

> "I have read many strategy books. I am going to use the David book. What I like—to steal a line from Alabama coach Nick Saban—is your book teaches 'a process.' I believe at the end of your book, you can actually help a company do strategic planning. In contrast, the other books teach a number of near and far concepts related to strategy."

A recent reviewer of this textbook says:

> "One thing I admire most about the David text is that it follows the fundamental sequence of strategy formulation, implementation, and evaluation. There is a basic flow from vision/ mission to internal/external environmental scanning, to strategy development, selection, implementation, and evaluation. This has been, and continues to be, a hallmark of the David text. Many other strategy texts are more disjointed in their presentation, and thus confusing to the student, especially at the undergraduate level."

New Chapter Features

1. The fifteenth edition is 40 percent new and improved from the prior edition.
2. Chapter 11, Global and International Issues, is expanded 30 percent with new coverage of cultural and conceptual strategic-management differences across countries. Doing business globally has become a necessity in most industries. Nearly all strategic decisions today are affected by global issues and concerns.
3. Chapter 10, Business Ethics, Social Responsibility, and Environmental Sustainability, is expanded 30 percent, providing extensive new coverage of ethics, workplace romance, and sustainability. This text emphasizes that "good ethics is good business." Unique to strategic-management texts, the sustainability discussion is strengthened in this edition to promote and encourage firms to conduct operations in an environmentally sound manner. Respect for the natural environment has become an important concern for consumers, companies, society, and AACSB-International.

4. A brand new Cohesion Case on PepsiCo, Inc. (2013) is provided. PepsiCo is one of the most successful, well-known, and best-managed global companies in the world. Students apply strategy concepts to PepsiCo at the end of each chapter through brand new Assurance of Learning Exercises.

5. Fifty percent new or improved Assurance of Learning Exercises appear at the end of all chapters to apply chapter concepts. The exercises prepare students for strategic-management case analysis.

6. A new boxed insert at the beginning of each chapter showcases a company doing strategic management exceptionally well.

7. There are all new examples in all the chapters.

8. There is new narrative on strategic-management theory and concepts in every chapter.

9. On average, 10 new review questions are provided at the end of each chapter.

10. Twenty-two brand new color photographs bring this new edition to life and illustrate "the practice of strategic management."

11. All current readings at the end of all chapters are new, as new research and theories of seminal thinkers are included. However, practical aspects of strategic management are center stage and the trademark of this text.

12. For the first time ever, the Excel Student Template is provided free at **www.strategyclub.com** to all students who use this textbook. Widely used for more than a decade by both students and businesses, and improved dramatically just for this edition, the free Excel Student Template enables students to more easily apply strategic-management concepts while engaging in assurance of learning exercises or case analysis. Using the Template, students can devote more time to applying strategy concepts and less time to the mechanics of formatting strategy matrices, tables, and PowerPoints.

13. Every sentence and paragraph has been scrutinized, modified, clarified, deleted, streamlined, updated, and improved to enhance the content and caliber of presentation.

New Case Features

1. All 29 cases have a 2013 time setting, offering students up-to-date issues to evaluate;

2. All 29 cases are on student-friendly, well-known companies, thus exciting and effective for applying strategy concepts;

3. Ten of the 29 case companies (such as BMW and L'Oréal) are headquartered outside the USA; the only strategy text with such a global offering;

4. All 29 cases are undisguised, featuring real organizations in real industries using real names (nothing is fictitious in any case);

5. All 29 cases feature an organization and industry undergoing strategic change;

6. All 29 cases provide ample, excellent quantitative information, so students can prepare a defensible strategic plan;

7. All 29 cases are written in a lively, concise writing style that captures the reader's interest;

8. All 29 cases are "comprehensive," focusing on multiple business functions, rather than a single problem or issue;

9. All 29 cases include current financial statements for the firm, so students can show the impact of a proposed strategic plan;

10. All 29 cases provide an organizational chart and a vision and mission statement— important strategy concepts;

11. All 29 cases are supported by an excellent teacher's note, provided to professors in a new *Case Instructor's Manual*;

12. All 29 cases are available for inclusion in a customized tailored text to meet the special needs of some professors;

13. All 29 cases facilitate coverage of all strategy concepts, but as revealed in the new Concepts by Cases Matrix, some cases especially exemplify some concepts, enabling professors to effectively use various cases with various chapters in the text;

14. All 29 cases have been class-tested to ensure that they are interesting, challenging, and effective for illustrating strategy concepts;

15. All 29 cases appear in no other textbooks, thus offering a truly fresh, new, up-to-date, learning platform;

16. The 29 case companies provide an excellent mix of firms performing really well and some performing very poorly, including 13 service-based and 16 manufacturing-based firms, and a good mix of small cap to large cap firms.

17. All 29 case companies have excellent websites in English that provide detailed financial information, history, sustainability statements, ethics statements, and press releases, so students can easily access current information to apply strategy concepts.

18. For the first time ever with this textbook, all 29 cases are written by the authors, to ensure maximum control and effectiveness in applying strategic-management concepts through case analysis.

19. For the first time ever with any strategic-management text, a Case MyLab testing feature has been carefully developed and designed specifically to apply strategic-management concepts through case analysis. The Case MyLab product assures that the cases apply the concepts, simplifies grading for professors, and achieves AACSB's key assurance of learning objectives—even in purely or partly online class settings. The new Case MyLab testing feature enables professors to use the cases to monitor student learning of strategy concepts, as revealed in the Concepts by Cases Matrix given below.

Time-Tested Features

1. This text meets all AACSB-International guidelines that support a practitioner orientation rather than a theory/research approach. This text offers a skills-oriented process for developing a vision and mission statement; performing an external audit; conducting an internal assessment; and formulating, implementing, and evaluating strategies.

2. The author's writing style is concise, conversational, interesting, logical, lively, and supported by numerous current examples.

3. A simple, integrative strategic-management model appears in all chapters and on the inside front cover. The model is widely used by strategic planning consultants and companies worldwide.

4. An exciting, new Cohesion Case on PepsiCo, Inc. follows Chapter 1 and is revisited at the end of each chapter, allowing students to apply strategic-management concepts and techniques to a real company as chapter material is covered, thus preparing students for case analysis as the course evolves.

5. End-of-chapter Assurance of Learning Exercises apply chapter concepts and techniques in a challenging, meaningful, and enjoyable manner. Seventeen exercises apply text material to the Cohesion Case; 11 exercises apply textual material to a college or university; another 9 exercises send students into the business world to explore important strategy topics.

6. There is excellent pedagogy, including learning objectives opening each chapter and key terms, current readings, discussion questions, and assurance of learning exercises ending each chapter.

7. There is excellent coverage of strategy formulation issues, such as business ethics, global versus domestic operations, vision and mission, matrix analysis, partnering, joint venturing, competitive analysis, value chain analysis, governance, and matrices for assimilating and evaluating information.

8. There is excellent coverage of strategy implementation issues such as corporate culture, organizational structure, outsourcing, marketing concepts, financial analysis, business ethics, whistleblowing, bribery, pay and performance linkages, and workplace romance.

9. A systematic, analytical "process" is presented that includes nine matrices: IFEM, EFEM, CPM, SWOT, BCG, IE, GRAND, SPACE, and QSPM.

10. Both the chapter material and case material is published in four colors.

11. Chapters-only paperback and e-book versions of the text are available.

12. Custom-case publishing is available whereby an instructor can combine chapters from this text with cases from a variety of sources or select any number of the 29 cases provided.

13. For the chapter material, an outstanding ancillary package includes a comprehensive *Instructor's Manual,* Test Bank, TestGen, and Chapter PowerPoints.

Instructor Supplements

At **www.pearsonhighered.com/irc**, instructors can access a variety of resources that accompany this new edition. Registration is easy, please contact your Pearson Sales Representative who will provide you with the access information you need.

If you ever need assistance, our dedicated technical support team is ready to help with the media supplements that accompany this text. Visit **http://247.pearsoned.com/** for answers to frequently asked questions and toll-free user support phone numbers.

The following supplements are available to adopting instructors:

- *Chapter Instructor's Manual*
- *Case Instructor's Manual*
- **Chapter PowerPoints**
- **Test Bank**
- **TestGen**

CourseSmart Textbooks Online

CourseSmart eTextbooks were developed for students looking to save the cost on required or recommended textbooks. Students simply select their eText by title or author and purchase immediate access to the content for the duration of the course using any major credit card. With a CourseSmart eText, students can search for specific keywords or page numbers, take notes online, print reading assignments that incorporate lecture notes, and bookmark important passages for later review. For more information or to purchase a CourseSmart eTextbook, visit **www.coursesmart.com**.

Sample of Universities Recently Using This Textbook

Abraham Baldwin Agricultural College

Adelphi University

Akron Institute

Albany State University

Albertus Magnus College

Albright College

Alcorn State University

Alvernia University

Ambassador College

Amberton University

American Intercontinental University—Weston

American International College

American International Continental (AIU) University—Houston

American International University

American University

Anderson University

Angelo State University

Aquinas College

Arizona State University—Polytechnic Campus

Art Institute of California

Averett University

Avila University

Azusa Pacific University

Baker College—Flint

Baldwin Wallace College

Barry University

Belhaven University—Jackson

Bellevue University

Belmont Abbey College

Benedictine University

Black Hills State University

Bloomsburg University

Briar Cliff University

Brooklyn College

Broward College—Central

Broward College—North

Broward College—South

Bryant & Stratton—Orchard Park

Buena Vista University—Storm Lake

Caldwell College

California Polytechnic State University

California State University—Sacramento

California State University—San Bernadino

California University of PA

Calumet College

Capella University

Carlow University

Carson-Newman College

Catawba College

Catholic University of America

Cedar Crest College

Central Connecticut State University

Central Michigan University

Central New Mexico Community College

Central Washington University

Chatham University

Chestnut Hill College

Chicago State University

Christian Brothers University

Claflin University

Clarion University of Pennsylvania

Clarkson College

Clatsop Community College

Cleveland State University

College of William & Mary

Colorado State University—Pueblo

Columbia College

Columbia Southern University—Online

Concordia University

Concordia University Wisconsin

Curry College

Cuyahoga Community College

Daniel Webster College

Davis & Elkins College

Delaware State University

Delaware Technology & Community College—Dover

Delaware Technology & Community College—Wilmington

DePaul University—Loop Campus

East Stroudsburg University

Eastern Michigan University

Eastern Oregon University

Eastern Washington University

ECPI College of Technology—Charleston

ECPI Computer Institute

Elmhurst College

Embry-Riddle Aero University—Prescott

Ferrum College

Florida Agricultural & Mechanical University

Florida Southern College

Florida State University

Florida Technical College—Deland

Florida Technical College—Kissimmee

Florida Technical College—Orlando

Fort Valley State College

Francis Marion University

Fresno Pacific University

Frostburg State University

George Fox University

Georgetown College

Georgia Southern University

Georgia Southwestern State University

Hampton University

Harding University

Harris Stowe State University

Herzing College—Madison

Herzing College—New Orleans

Herzing College—Winter Park

Herzing University—Atlanta

High Point University

Highline Community College

Hofstra University

Hood College

Hope International University

Houghton College

Huntingdon College

Indiana University Bloomington

Indiana Wesleyan CAPS

Iona College

Iowa Lakes Community College—Emmetsburg

Jackson Community College

Jackson State University

John Brown University

Johnson & Wales—Charlotte

Johnson & Wales—Colorado

Johnson & Wales—Miami

Johnson & Wales—Rhode Island

Johnson C. Smith University

Kalamazoo College

Kansas State University

Keene State College

Kellogg Community College

La Salle University

Lake Michigan College

Lebanon Valley College

Lee University

Lehman College of CUNY

Liberty University

Limestone College—Gaffney

Lincoln Memorial University

Loyola College Business Center

Loyola College—Chennai

Loyola University—Maryland

Lyndon State College

Madonna University

Manhattan College

Manhattanville College

Marian University—Indiana

Marshall University

Marshall University Graduate College

Marymount University—Arlington

Medgar Evers College

Medical Careers Institute/Newport News

Mercer University—Atlanta

Mercer University—Macon

Miami-Dade College—Homestead

Miami-Dade College—Kendal

Miami-Dade College—North

Miami-Dade College—Wolfson

Michigan State University

Mid-America Christian

Millersville University

Mississippi University for Women

Morgan State University

Morrison College of Reno

Mount Marty College—South Dakota

Mount Mercy University

Mount Wachusett Community College

Mt. Hood Community College

Mt. Vernon Nazarene

MTI Western Business College

Muhlenberg College

Murray State University

New England College

New Mexico State University

New York University

North Carolina Wesleyan College

North Central College

North Central State College

Northwest Arkansas Community College

Northwestern College

Northwood University—Cedar Hill

Notre Dame of Maryland University

Nyack College

Oakland University

Ohio Dominican University

Oklahoma Christian University

Oklahoma State University

Olivet College

Oral Roberts University

Pace University—Pleasantville

Park University

Penn State University—Abington

Penn State University—Hazleton

Pensacola State College

Philadelphia University

Point Park University

Prince George's Community College

Queens College of CUNY

Richard Stockton University

Rider University

Roger Williams University

Saint Edwards University

Saint Leo University

Saint Mary's College

Saint Mary's College—Indiana

Saint Xavier University

San Antonio College

Santa Fe College

Savannah State University

Shippensburg University

Siena Heights University

Southern Nazarene University

Southern New Hampshire University

Southern Oregon University

Southern University—Baton Rouge

Southern Wesleyan University

Southwest Baptist University

Southwest University

St. Bonaventure University

St. Francis University

St. Louis University

St. Martins University

Sterling College

Stevenson University

Strayer University—DC

Texas A&M University—Commerce

Texas A&M University—Texarkana

Texas A&M—San Antonio

Texas Tech University

The College of St. Rose

The Masters College

Tri-County Technical College

Trinity Christian College

Troy State University

Troy University—Dothan

Troy University—Main Campus

Troy University—Montgomery

University Alabama—Birmingham

University Maryland—College Park

University of Arkansas—Fayetteville

University of Findlay

University of Houston—Clearlake

University of Louisiana at Monroe

University of Maine at Augusta

University of Maine—Fort Kent

University of Maryland

University of Massachusetts—Boston Harbor

University of Massachusetts—Dartmouth

University of Miami

University of Michigan—Flint

University of Minnesota—Crookston

University of Mobile

University of Montevallo

University of Nebraska—Omaha

University of Nevada Las Vegas

University of New Orleans

University of North Texas

University of North Texas—Dallas

University of Pikeville

University of Sioux Falls

University of South Florida

University of St. Joseph

University of Tampa

University of Texas—Pan American

University of The Incarnate Word

University of Toledo

Upper Iowa University

Valley City State University

Virginia Community College System

Virginia State University

Virginia Tech

Wagner College

Wake Forest University

Washington University

Webber International University

Webster University

West Chester University

West Liberty University

West Valley College

West Virginia Wesleyan College

Western Connecticut State University

Western Kentucky University

Western Michigan University

Western Washington University

William Jewell College

Williams Baptist College

Winona State University

Winston-Salem State University

WSU Vancouver

Sample of Countries Outside the USA Where This Textbook is Very Widely Used

Mexico, China, Japan, Australia, Singapore, Canada, Indonesia, Pakistan, Iran, Kenya, Congo, Hong Kong, India, England, Argentina, Equador, Zambia, Guam, Italy, Cyprus, Colombia, Philippines, South Africa, Peru, Turkey, Malaysia, and Egypt

Acknowledgments

Many persons have contributed time, energy, ideas, and suggestions for improving this text over 15 editions. The strength of this text is largely attributed to the collective wisdom, work, and experiences of strategic-management professors, researchers, students, and practitioners. Names of particular individuals whose published research is referenced in this edition are listed alphabetically in the Name Index. To all individuals involved in making this text so popular and successful, we are indebted and thankful.

Many special persons and reviewers contributed valuable material and suggestions for this edition. We would like to thank our colleagues and friends at Auburn University, Mississippi State University, East Carolina University, the University of South Carolina, Campbell University, the University of North Carolina at Pembroke, and Francis Marion University. We have taught strategic management at all these universities. Scores of students and professors at these schools helped shape the development of this text. Many thanks go to the following reviewers whose comments shaped the fourteenth and fifteenth editions:

Moses Acquaah, University of North Carolina at Greensboro

Gary L. Arbogast, Glenville State College

Charles M. Byles, Virginia Commonwealth University

Charles J. Capps III, Sam Houston State University

Neil Dworkin, Western Connecticut State University

Jacalyn M. Florn, University of Toledo

John Frankenstein, Brooklyn College/City University of New York

Bill W. Godair, Landmark College, Community College of Vermont

Carol Jacobson, Purdue University

Susan M. Jensen, University of Nebraska at Kearney

Dmitry Khanin, California State University at Fullerton

Thomas E. Kulik, Washington University at St. Louis

Jerrold K. Leong, Oklahoma State University

Trina Lynch-Jackson, Indiana University

Elouise Mintz, Saint Louis University

Raza Mir, William Paterson University

Gerry N. Muuka, Murray State University

Braimoh Oseghale, Fairleigh Dickinson University

Lori Radulovich, Baldwin-Wallace College

Thomas W. Sharkey, University of Toledo

Frederick J. Slack, Indiana University of Pennsylvania

Daniel Slater, Union University

Demetri Tsanacas, Ferrum College

Jill Lynn Vihtelic, Saint Mary's College

Michael W. Wakefield, Colorado State University–Pueblo

Don Wicker, Brazosport College

We want to thank you, the reader, for investing the time and effort to read and study this text. It will help you formulate, implement, and evaluate strategies for any organization with which you become associated. We hope you come to share our enthusiasm for the rich subject area of strategic management and for the systematic learning approach taken in this text. We want to welcome and invite your suggestions, ideas, thoughts, comments, and questions regarding any part of this text or the ancillary materials. Please contact Dr. Fred R. David at the following e-mail freddavid9@gmail.com, or write him at the School of Business, Francis Marion University, Florence, SC 29501. We sincerely appreciate and need your input to continually improve this text in future editions. Your willingness to draw my attention to specific errors or deficiencies in coverage or exposition will especially be appreciated.

Thank you for using this text.

Fred R. David and Forest R. David

About the Authors

Fred R. and Forest R. David, a father–son team, have published more than 50 journal articles in outlets such as *Academy of Management Review, Academy of Management Executive, Journal of Applied Psychology, Long Range Planning, International Journal of Management, Journal of Business Strategy,* and *Advanced Management Journal.* Fred and Forest's February 2011 *Business Horizons* article titled "What are Business Schools Doing for Business Today?" is changing the way many business schools view their curricula.

Fred and Forest are coauthors of *Strategic Management: Concepts and Cases* that has been on a two-year revision cycle since 1986 when the first edition was published. This text is among the best-selling strategic-management textbooks in the world. This text has led the field of strategic management for more than two decades in providing an applications, practitioner-approach to the discipline. More than 500 colleges and universities have used this textbook over the years, including Harvard University, Duke University, Carnegie-Mellon University, Johns Hopkins University, the University of Maryland, University of North Carolina, University of Georgia, San Francisco State University, University of South Carolina, Wake Forest University, and countless universities in Japan, China, Australia, Mexico, and the Middle East. For six editions of this book, Forest has been sole author of the *Case Instructor's Manual,* having developed extensive teachers' notes (solutions) for all the cases. Forest is author of the Case MyLab ancillary and the free Excel Student Template that accompany this fifteenth edition.

Fred R. David

Fred and Forest actively assist businesses globally in doing strategic planning. They have written and published more than 100 strategic management cases. Fred and Forest were recently keynote speakers at the Pearson International Forum in Monterrey, Mexico. With a PhD in Management from the University of South Carolina, Fred is the TranSouth Professor of Strategic Planning at Francis Marion University (FMU) in Florence, South Carolina. Forest has taught strategic-management courses at Mississippi State University, Campbell University, and FMU.

Forest R. David

The Case Rationale

Case analysis remains the primary learning vehicle used in most strategic-management classes, for five important reasons:

1. Analyzing cases gives students the opportunity to work in teams to evaluate the internal operations and external issues facing various organizations and to craft strategies that can lead these firms to success. Working in teams gives students practical experience solving problems as part of a group. In the business world, important decisions are generally made within groups; strategic-management students learn to deal with overly aggressive group members and also timid, noncontributing group members. This experience is valuable because strategic-management students are near graduation and soon enter the working world full-time.
2. Analyzing cases enables students to improve their oral and written communication skills as well as their analytical and interpersonal skills by proposing and defending particular courses of action for the case companies.
3. Analyzing cases allows students to view a company, its competitors, and its industry concurrently, thus simulating the complex business world. Through case analysis, students learn how to apply concepts, evaluate situations, formulate strategies, and resolve implementation problems.
4. Analyzing cases allows students to apply concepts learned in many business courses. Students gain experience dealing with a wide range of organizational problems that impact all the business functions.
5. Analyzing cases gives students practice in applying concepts, evaluating situations, formulating a "game plan," and resolving implementation problems in a variety of business and industry settings.

Case MyLab Testing Feature

New to this edition is an enhanced MyLab with new cases that include gradeable outcomes. As revealed in the new Concepts x Cases matrix below, student learning of 29 key strategic-management concepts can easily be tested by using the 29 fifteenth edition cases. This feature assures that the cases are excellent for testing student learning of the key strategic-management concepts, thus serving as a great mechanism for professors to achieve AACSB's Assurance of Learning Objectives. This new testing feature simplifies grading for professors in both traditional and online class settings.

The Case MyLab testing feature includes 25 multiple choice questions for each case, comprised of 10 *Basic* questions that simply test whether the student read the case before class, and 15 *Applied* questions that test the student's ability to apply various strategic-management concepts. In addition, there are 2 *Discussion* questions per case. This testing feature enables professors to determine, before class if desired, whether students 1) read the case in *Basic* terms, and/ or 2) are able to *Apply* strategy concepts to resolve issues in the case. For example, the MyLab case *Basic* question may be: In what country is BMW headquartered? Whereas, a MyLab case *Applied* question may be: What are three aspects of the organizational chart given in the BMW case that violate strategic-management guidelines? The Answers to these questions can be found in the *Case Instructor's Manual*.

The New Concepts by Cases Matrix

All 29 cases facilitate coverage of all strategy concepts, but as revealed below by purple cells, some cases especially exemplify some key strategy concepts. The purple cells reveal which concepts are tested with multiple choice questions in the MyLab. The Concepts by Cases matrix enables professors to effectively utilize various cases to assure student learning of various chapter concepts. Note from the purple boxes that two, three, or four cases are used to test each strategic-management concept. This new, innovative ancillary promises to elevate the case learning method to new heights in teaching strategic management.

Case Number	USA Headquartered	Key Strategic-Management Concepts	Strategy Model/Process	Vision/Mission Statements	Competitive Profile Matrix	Porter's Five Forces Model	EFE Matrix	Resource Based View	Financial Ratios & Breakeven	Value Chain Analysis	IFE Matrix	Strategy Types	Porter's Five Generic Strategies
USA-Based Service Companies													
Case 1	Domino's Pizza, Inc.					▓						▓	
Case 2	Spirit Airlines, Inc.												
Case 3	Buffalo Wild Wings, Inc.				▓				▓				
Case 4	Rite Aid Corp.			▓									
Case 5	Best Buy Co.						▓						
Case 6	Publix Super Markets, Inc.						▓						
Case 7	JPMorgan Chase & Co.												
Case 8	Walt Disney Company							▓			▓		
Case 9	Lowe's Companies, Inc.					▓					▓		
Case 10	United Parcel Service, Inc.												
Case 11	United States Postal Service												
USA-Based Manufacturing Companies													
Case 12	Crocs, Inc.			▓	▓								
Case 13	Snyder's-Lance, Inc.		▓								▓		▓
Case 14	Netgear, Inc.								▓				
Case 15	Polaris Industries, Inc.		▓										
Case 16	Under Armour, Inc.												▓
Case 17	Avon Products, Inc.												
Case 18	Exxon Mobil Corporation										▓		
Case 19	Microsoft Corporation												
	Outside-USA Headquartered												
Case 20	The Emirates Group											▓	
Case 21	Royal Bank of Canada												
Case 22	Embraer S.A.										▓		
Case 23	Bayerische Motoren Werke (BMW) Group		▓			▓	▓						
Case 24	Davide Campari-Milano S.p.A.												▓
Case 25	L'Oréal Group			▓	▓								
Case 26	Nikon Corporation												
Case 27	Grupo Modelo S.A.B.				▓							▓	
Case 28	Pearson PLC							▓					
Case 29	Lenovo Group Limited								▓				

First Mover Advantages

Outsourcing

SWOT Matrix

SPACE Matrix

BCG & IE Matrices

Grand Strategy Matrix & QSPM

Governance

Organizational Structure

Organizational Culture

Human Resource Management

Market Segmentation & Product Position

EPS-EBIT Analysis

Projected Financial Statements

Company Valuation

Balanced Scorecard

Business Ethics

Environmental Sustainability

Foreign Business Culture

The Case Synopses

USA-Based Service Companies

1. **Domino's Pizza, Inc. (DPZ)**

   Headquartered in Ann Arbor, Michigan, Domino's is the second-largest pizza chain in the USA behind Pizza Hut. Domino's has over 9,700 delivery-only stores in about 65 countries and all 50 USA states. Among the 5,000 Domino's in the USA, only about 400 are company-owned, while the others are franchised. Domino's offers a gluten free crust in all its USA restaurants, the first national pizza delivery chain to offer such a product. Domino's has about 10,000 full-time employees.

2. **Spirit Airlines (SAVE)**

   Headquartered in Miramar, Florida, Spirit Airlines is a rapidly growing, low-cost airline that serves many locations in the Bahamas, Caribbean, Latin America, as well as about a dozen USA cities. With an average fleet age of 4.4 years old, Spirit has the third youngest Airbus fleet in the Americas after Virgin America and the Mexican airline Volaris. Spirit has on order 108 Airbus A320s, including 45 A320neo (new engine option) aircraft, to be delivered between 2012 and 2021. Spirit has about 2,600 full-time employees.

3. **Buffalo Wild Wings (BWLD)**

   Headquartered in Minneapolis, Minnesota, Buffalo Wild Wings (BWW) is a casual dining restaurant and sports bar that operates about 835 restaurants in 48 states in the USA and Canada. BWW offers chicken wings and legs with many signature sauces and seasonings as well as bottled beer, wine, and liquor. Only about 320 BWW restaurants are company-owned; the remaining are franchised. BWW plans to acquire other restaurant firms (maybe Denny's or Nathan's Famous) and has about 2,700 full-time employees.

4. **Rite Aid Corporation (RAD)**

   Headquartered in Camp Hill, Pennsylvania, Rite Aid is a distant third (behind CVS and Walgreen) in the USA retail drugstore business. Rite Aid operates 4,700 drugstores in 31 states, fills prescriptions (about two-thirds of sales), and sells health and beauty aids, convenience foods, greeting cards, and 3,000 Rite Aid brand products. About 60% of Rite Aid stores are freestanding; about 50% have drive-through pharmacies. With 51,300 employees, Rite Aid has a strategic alliance with GNC to operate GNC stores within Rite Aid stores.

5. **Best Buy Company (BBY)**

   Headquartered in Richfield, Minnesota, Best Buy is a mass retailer of consumer electronics products and services, including installation, maintenance, and technical support of movies, computers, and phones. With over 1,400 stores in the USA and Canada and another 2,600 stores in Europe and China, Best Buy recently sold Napster to online mp3 store Rhapsody. With 167,000 employees well trained and wearing the trademark blue shirts, Best Buy has a problem in that many customers go to Best Buy, get educated, and then leave and purchase online.

6. **Publix Super Markets, Inc. (Employee Owned)**

   Headquartered in Lakeland, Florida, Publix is the largest ESOP (employee stock ownership plan) in the USA; employees own 31% of Publix. More than two-thirds of all Publix's are in Florida, but some are in Alabama, Georgia, South Carolina, and Tennessee. Publix makes some of its own bakery, deli, dairy goods, and fresh prepared foods. Many Publix's include a pharmacy and bank. Publix has about 140,000 employees, 1,086 supermarkets, cooking schools, 8 distribution centers, and 9 manufacturing facilities.

7. **JPMorgan Chase & Co. (JPM)**

   Headquartered in New York City, JPMorgan Chase is the USA's largest bank holding company with more than $2 trillion in assets, 5,500 branches in thirty states, and 260,000 employees. JPM is also among the nation's top mortgage lenders and credit card issuers (it holds some $132 billion in credit card loans). Founded in 1823 and now active in over 60 countries, JPM owns private equity firm One Equity Partners.

8. Walt Disney Company (DIS)

Headquartered in Burbank, California, Disney competes in the family entertainment and media broadcasting industry. Serving customers for nearly 100 years, Disney is a diversified conglomerate, owning ABC, ESPN, theme parks, cruise boats, cable networks, and more. As a member of the DOW 30, Disney owns 8 television stations and 35 radio stations, as well as Walt Disney Studios that produces films through Walt Disney Pictures, Disney Animation, and Pixar.

9. Lowe's Companies, Inc. (LOW)

Headquartered in Mooresville, North Carolina, Lowe's is a nationwide chain of home improvement superstores that plans to expand internationally. Lowe's has more than 1,745 stores in 50 states and more than 30 locations in Canada and Mexico, second only to Home Depot. With over 160,000 employees that focus on home maintenance, repair, remodeling and decorating, Lowe's is the second largest U.S. home appliance retailer after Sears.

10. United Parcel Service, Inc. (UPS)

Headquartered in Atlanta, Georgia, UPS is the world's largest package delivery company transporting more than 15 million packages and documents per business day in the USA and 220 countries and territories. UPS operates a fleet of about 100,000 "brown" trucks, vans, tractors, and motorcycles as well as 525 aircraft. UPS also offers logistics and freight forwarding, and less-than-truckload (LTL) and truckload (TL) freight transportation through UPS Freight. With 222,000 employees, UPS is acquiring TNT Express for $6.8 billion.

11. United States Postal Service (nonprofit)

The United States Postal Service (USPS) is an independent agency of the United States government responsible for delivering mail. With over 574,000 workers and 218,000 vehicles, the USPS operates the largest vehicle fleet in the world. The USPS is legally obligated to serve all Americans, regardless of geography, at uniform price and quality. The USPS competes with UPS and FedEx, but is closing 252 of its 461 mail processing centers, eliminating 28,000 jobs, ending overnight delivery of first-class mail, and closing 3,700 local post offices.

USA-Based Manufacturing Companies

12. Crocs, Inc. (CROX)

Headquartered in Niwot, Colorado, Crocs is a footwear company that offers colorful slip-on, casual and athletic shoes made of closed-cell resin (Croslite); Jibbitz are Crocs' decorative add-on charms. Crocs designs, develops, manufactures, markets, and distributes boots, sandals, sneakers, mules, and flats in more than 90 countries. With manufacturing facilities in Mexico, Italy, and China and distribution centers worldwide, Crocs has 4,150 employees. Crocs, Inc. owns 180 retail stores, 92 outlet stores, 42 Web stores, and 158 kiosks in malls worldwide.

13. Snyder's-Lance, Inc. (LNCE)

Headquartered in Charlotte, North Carolina, Snyder's-Lance manufactures and markets snack foods such as Toastchee, Nipchee, and Captain's Wafers. Snyder's-Lance products include pretzels, cookies, crackers, nuts, potato chips, cakes, and candy sold under the Lance, Cape Cod, Tom's, Archway, and Snyder's brands at food retailers, mass merchants, and convenience and club stores in the USA. Snyder's-Lance primarily does business in the USA and has 6,100 employees.

14. Netgear (NTGR)

Headquartered in San Jose, California, Netgear designs and produces Internet networking equipment, such as adapters, hubs, routers, Ethernet switches, wireless controllers, media servers, and interfaces. NETGEAR sells products through distributors such as Ingram Micro and Tech Data, retailers such as Best Buy and RadioShack, as well as through 29,000 retail locations around the globe and 36,000 value-added resellers. With offices in 25 countries and 810 employees, Netgear generates about half of its revenue from outside the USA.

15. Polaris Industries, Inc. (PII)

    Headquartered in Medina, Minnesota, Polaris designs, manufactures, and markets off-road, all-terrain vehicles (ATVs), recreational and utility RANGER-brand vehicles, snowmobiles, and even the Victory brand motorcycle. Polaris also produces and sells replacement parts and accessories such as covers, tow hitches, cargo racks, saddlebags, helmets, and also recreational apparel such as jackets, bibs, pants, and hats. With 3,900 employees and 30% of its revenue derived from outside the USA, Polaris partners with Fuji Heavy Industries to build engines.

16. Under Armour, Inc. (UA)

    Headquartered in Baltimore, Maryland, Under Armour (UA) is a producer and marketer of compression, fitted, and loose sports apparel, including athletic footwear; UA is the official footwear supplier of Major League Baseball. UA dresses athletes from head (COLDGEAR) to toe (Team Sock) with products are made from the company's patented moisture wicking and heat-dispersing fabrics that keeps athletes dry during workouts. With 1,800 employees, UA sells its products online, by catalog, in company-owned and sporting goods stores, worldwide.

17. Avon Products (AVP)

    Headquartered in New York City, Avon Products is the world's largest direct seller firm, and by far the largest direct seller of cosmetics and beauty-related items. Avon is the fifth-largest cosmetics and fragrance firm in the world. The company receives sales from catalogs and online, but the vast majority of its sales come from about six million independent sales representatives in 110 countries. Since 1892, Avon has empowered women to be their own boss and become leaders in communities and business. Avon is struggling to recover from poor management and global bribery investigations.

18. Exxon Mobil Corporation (XOM)

    Headquartered in Irving, Texas, Exxon Mobil is the world's largest oil company and engages in oil and gas exploration, production, supply, transportation, and marketing worldwide. With 24.9 billion barrels of proven oil reserves, Exxon's 36 refineries in 20 countries have a capacity of more than 6.2 million barrels per day. Exxon supplies refined products to more than 25,000 gas stations in 100 countries. With operations on all continents except Antarctica, Exxon has 82,000 employees and operates over 30,000 oil wells around the world.

19. Microsoft Corporation (MSFT)

    Headquartered in Redmond, Washington, Microsoft is the world's largest software firm with its core product being the Windows PC operating system and Office business productivity application suite sold in part through PC makers. Selling online and through resellers, Microsoft also designs and manufactures video game consoles (Xbox 360), enterprise applications (Microsoft Dynamics), server and storage software, and digital music players (Zune). With 90,000 employees, Microsoft also engages in online advertising and consulting services.

Outside USA-Based

Service Firms	**Country HQ**

20. The Emirates Group   UAE

    Headquartered in Dubai in the United Arab Emirates, The Emirates Group is the parent of Emirates, the largest airline in the Middle East, operating over 2,500 flights per week from its hub at Dubai International Airport. Emirates flies to 120 cities in 70 countries and operates four of the world's 10 longest non-stop commercial flights. With 50,000 employees and 50 subsidiaries, The Emirates Group is wholly owned by the government of Dubai and controlled by the Investment Corp. of Dubai. Emirates is very profitable and growing over 20% annually.

21. Royal Bank of Canada   Canada

    Headquartered in Toronto, Canada, Royal Bank of Canada (RBC) is Canada's largest bank. RBC provides a full range of services from commercial banking and wealth management to insurance and capital markets services. With more than 1,000 locations in Canada and operations in more than 50 countries, RBC sold its RBC Bank unit in the Southeast USA to PNC Financial in 2012, but still owns investment bank RBC Dominion Securities and RBC Wealth Management in the USA. Founded in 1864, RBC has about 68,000 full-time employees.

Manufacturing Firms

22. Embraer S.A.   Brazil
Headquartered in Sao Paulo, Brazil, Embraer is one of the world's top four aircraft manufacturers, making commercial jets (55%) that seat between 30–120 passengers, 7 models of executive jets (20%), and military aircraft (12%). About 40% of its Embraer sales are in North and South America. With 17,200 employees, Embraer is Brazil's largest exporter of industrial products. Embraer's CEO, Frederico Curado, received the 2012 Tony Jannus Award, given annually for distinguished contributions to commercial aviation.

23. Bayerische Motoren Werke (BMW) AG   Germany
Headquartered in Munich, Bavaria, Germany, BMW is a large automobile, motorcycle and engine manufacturing company founded in 1917. BMW is the parent company of Rolls-Royce Motor Cars. With about 100,000 employees, BMW produces motorcycles under the Motorrad and Husqvarna brands and is the sponsor of the 2012 Olympics in London. Financial services bolster BMW's bottom line, including purchase financing and leasing, asset management, dealer financing, and corporate fleets. About 3,000 dealers worldwide sell BMWs.

24. Campari Group S.p.A   Italy
Headquartered in Milan, Italy, Gruppo Campari is the sixth largest producer of alcoholic and non-alcoholic beverages worldwide. Campari owns a portfolio of over 40 brands, including Wild Turkey bourbon. Campari markets and distributes drinks in more than 190 countries. With 2,270 employees, Campari is structured into three segments: spirits, wines, and soft drinks. The Garavoglia family owns 51% of Campari, which is expanding through acquisitions (it owns U.S. vodka maker Skyy Spirits) and by entering growing markets in Asia and South America.

25. L'Oréal Group   France
Headquartered outside of Paris in Clichy, Hauts-de-Seine, France, L'Oréal is the world's largest cosmetics and beauty company. Specializing in hair color, skin care, sun protection, make-up, perfumes, and hair care, L'Oréal is the leading nanotechnology patent-holder in the USA. L'Oréal recently opened a huge new factory in Indonesia. L'Oréal is a listed company with 66,000 employees, but the founder's daughter Liliane Bettencourt and the Swiss food company Nestle each control over a quarter of the shares and voting rights.

26. Nikon Corporation   Japan
Headquartered in Tokyo, Japan, Nikon develops, produces, and markets cameras, binoculars, microscopes, measurement instruments, imaging lenses, photographic enlargers, and other imaging products such as Nikonos underwater film cameras. Nikon competes with Canon, Casio, Kodak, Sony, Pentax, Panasonic, Fujifilm, and Olympus. With 24,000 employees and founded in 1917, Nikon is part of the huge Mitsubishi *keiretsu*, a group of businesses linked by cross-ownership.

27. Grupo Modelo, S.A.B. de C.V.   Mexico
Headquartered in Mexico, Mexico, Grupo Modelo is among the largest beer producing, distributing, and marketing firms in the world. Some of Modelo's 13 beer brands include Corona Extra, the number one Mexican beer sold in the world, Barrilito, Victoria, Estrella, Medelo, and Paciffico. With 37,300 employees, Modelo also produces bottled water and operates 960 convenience stores under the Extra name. With more than a 60% share of the Mexican beer market and operating 8 breweries, Modelo was recently acquired by Anheuser-Busch InBev.

28. Pearson plc   England

    Headquartered in London, England, Pearson is the largest education company and the largest book publisher in the world. Pearson publishes market-leading books and newspapers in education (Prentice Hall, Longman & FT Press), consumer markets (Penguin, Dorling Kindersley, and Ladybird), and business information (*Financial Times*). With about 40,000 employees, Pearson has two operating divisions: 1) Pearson Education, and 2) The Financial Times Group. Pearson's major competitor is McGraw-Hill.

29. Lenovo Group Limited   China

    Headquartered in Beijing, China, Lenovo designs, produces, and markets personal computers, workstations, servers, electronic storage, IT management software, and other related products and services. The world's second-largest PC vendor (behind HP), Lenovo markets the ThinkPad line of notebook computers and ThinkCentre line of desktops. With 26,300 employees, Lenovo sells directly to consumers and businesses, as well as through online sales, company-owned stores, chain retailers, and major technology distributors and vendors.

STRATEGIC MANAGEMENT
Concepts and Cases

A COMPETITIVE ADVANTAGE APPROACH

## PART 1

OVERVIEW OF STRATEGIC MANAGEMENT

Source: Pixland/Thinkstock

MyManagementLab®
⭐ **Improve Your Grade!**

Over 10 million students improved their results using the Pearson MyLabs.
Visit **mymanagementlab.com** for simulations, tutorials, and end-of-chapter problems.

The Nature of Strategic Management

CHAPTER OBJECTIVES

After studying this chapter, you should be able to do the following:

1. Discuss the nature and role of a chief strategy officer (CSO).
2. Describe the strategic-management process.
3. Explain the need for integrating analysis and intuition in strategic management.
4. Define and give examples of key terms in strategic management.
5. Discuss the nature of strategy formulation, implementation, and evaluation activities.
6. Describe the benefits of good strategic management.
7. Discuss the relevance of Sun Tzu's *The Art of War* to strategic management.
8. Discuss how a firm may achieve sustained competitive advantage.

ASSURANCE OF LEARNING **EXERCISES**

The following exercises are found at the end of this chapter.

EXERCISE 1A Compare Business Strategy with Military Strategy
EXERCISE 1B Gather Strategy Information for PepsiCo
EXERCISE 1C Update the PepsiCo Cohesion Case
EXERCISE 1D Strategic Planning for Your University
EXERCISE 1E Strategic Planning at a Local Company
EXERCISE 1F Get Familiar With the Strategy Club Website
EXERCISE 1G Get Familiar With the Case MyLab

When CEOs from the big three U.S. automakers—Ford, General Motors (GM), and Chrysler—showed up a few years ago without a clear strategic plan to ask congressional leaders for bailout monies, they were sent home with instructions to develop a clear strategic plan for the future. Austan Goolsbee, one of President Barack Obama's top economic advisers, said, "Asking for a bailout without a convincing business plan was crazy." Goolsbee also said, "If the three auto CEOs need a bridge, it's got to be a bridge to somewhere, not a bridge to nowhere."[1] This textbook gives the instructions on how to develop a clear strategic plan—a bridge to somewhere rather than nowhere.

This chapter provides an overview of strategic management. It introduces a practical, integrative model of the strategic-management process; it defines basic activities and terms in strategic management.

This chapter also introduces the notion of boxed inserts. A boxed insert at the beginning of each chapter reveals how some firms are doing really well competing in a growing economy. The firms showcased are utilizing excellent strategic management to prosper as their rivals weaken. Each boxed insert examines the strategies of firms doing great amid rising consumer demand and intense price competition. The first company featured for excellent performance is the popular hamburger place, Five Guys Enterprises. Note that there are more than 1,000 Five Guys grills in the United States and Canada.

PepsiCo is featured as the new Cohesion Case because it is a well-known global firm undergoing strategic change and is well managed. By working through the PepsiCo–related Assurance of Learning Exercises at the end of each chapter, you will be well prepared to develop an effective strategic plan for any company assigned to you this semester. The end-of-chapter exercises apply chapter tools and concepts.

EXCELLENT STRATEGIC MANAGEMENT SHOWCASED

Five Guys Enterprises

Have you ever eaten at a Five Guys grill? Headquartered in Lorton, Virginia, Five Guys Enterprises has grown every year for 25 years and still is growing, thanks to excellent strategic management (and great hamburgers served with all the peanuts you can eat). Five Guys Burgers and Fries is a quick-service restaurant company that offers a simple menu of burgers, fries, and hot dogs. With more than 1,000 stores in the United States and Canada, Five Guys prides itself on using only top-notch ingredients, the best ground beef, rolls, and fries, and uses only peanut oil; in keeping with the peanut theme, its restaurants serve peanuts in bulk. Founded in 1986 by Jerry Murrell, his wife, and their five sons (Jim, Matt, Chad, Ben, and Tyler), Five Guys grill succeeds every day in taking business from all the larger fast food hamburger chains.

Five Guys' strategy has always been to use only the best ingredients, do no advertising or marketing except by word-of-mouth, "treat people right," provide great employee pay and benefits, and offer outstanding customer service. All 30,000-plus Five Guys employees have access to the company's Secret Shopper Bonus program in which employees anonymously go check on operations at other stores. All employees receive additional store-level bonuses to ensure that every store provides great burgers with great service. Five Guys employees all have a sense of ownership in their store because their compensation package is tied to how well their store performs. Five Guys employees are determined to "make your day" every time you visit their restaurant. Five Guys burgers are a bit pricey, but customers keep coming back daily to eat the freshly prepared product in an upscale décor with exceptional service.

Another Five Guys strategy is franchising (discussed in Chapter 5). About 800 Five Guys grills are owned by franchisees. All of the territory in both the USA and Canada has been sold to franchisees, and Five Guys plans to open its first restaurant in Great Britain in 2013, with plans to open four in the UK in 2013. Murrell says in starting a business, do not rely on banks, but rather rely on venture capitalists that include friends and family. With more than $1 billion in revenue in 2013, Murrell, now 62, gives this advice to all current and future businesspersons: "Treat your employees and customers right. Find something you love to do and just do it. Make sure your heart is in it. You can't be everything to everybody. You've got to be what you are. That's all you can do." Do a Google search for "Jerry Murrell Video" to watch a 2-minute excellent video of Murrell sharing lessons he learned in building Five Guys.

Source: Based on Lottie Joiner, "Five Guys Family Keeps It Simple," *USA Today* (July 30, 2012): 3B.

What Is Strategic Management?

Once there were two company presidents who competed in the same industry. These two presidents decided to go on a camping trip to discuss a possible merger. They hiked deep into the woods. Suddenly, they came upon a grizzly bear that rose up on its hind legs and snarled. Instantly, the first president took off his knapsack and got out a pair of jogging shoes. The second president said, "Hey, you can't outrun that bear." The first president responded, "Maybe I can't outrun that bear, but I surely can outrun you!" This story captures the notion of strategic management, which is to achieve and maintain competitive advantage.

Defining Strategic Management

Strategic management can be defined as the art and science of formulating, implementing, and evaluating cross-functional decisions that enable an organization to achieve its objectives. As this definition implies, strategic management focuses on integrating management, marketing, finance and accounting, production and operations, research and development, and information systems to achieve organizational success. The term *strategic management* in this text is used synonymously with the term **strategic planning**. The latter term is more often used in the business world, whereas the former is often used in academia. Sometimes the term *strategic management* is used to refer to strategy formulation, implementation, and evaluation and *strategic planning* referring only to strategy formulation. The purpose of strategic management is to exploit and create new and different opportunities for tomorrow; **long-range planning**, in contrast, tries to optimize for tomorrow the trends of today.

The term *strategic planning* originated in the 1950s and was popular between the mid-1960s and the mid-1970s. During these years, strategic planning was widely believed to be the answer for all problems. At the time, much of corporate America was "obsessed" with strategic planning. Following that boom, however, strategic planning was cast aside during the 1980s as various planning models did not yield higher returns. The 1990s, however, brought the revival of strategic planning, and the process is widely practiced today in the business world. Many companies today have a *chief strategy officer (CSO)*.

A strategic plan is, in essence, a company's game plan. Just as a football team needs a good game plan to have a chance for success, a company must have a good strategic plan to compete successfully. Profit margins among firms in most industries are so slim that there is little room for error in the overall strategic plan. A strategic plan results from tough managerial choices among numerous good alternatives, and it signals commitment to specific markets, policies, procedures, and operations in lieu of other, "less desirable" courses of action.

The term *strategic management* is used at many colleges and universities as the title for the capstone course in business administration. This course integrates material from all business courses, and, in addition, introduces new strategic management concepts and techniques being widely used by firms in strategic planning.

Stages of Strategic Management

The **strategic-management process** consists of three stages: strategy formulation, strategy implementation, and strategy evaluation. **Strategy formulation** includes developing a vision and mission, identifying an organization's external opportunities and threats, determining internal strengths and weaknesses, establishing long-term objectives, generating alternative strategies, and choosing particular strategies to pursue. Strategy-formulation issues include deciding what new businesses to enter, what businesses to abandon, whether to expand operations or diversify, whether to enter international markets, whether to merge or form a joint venture, and how to avoid a hostile takeover.

Because no organization has unlimited resources, strategists must decide which alternative strategies will benefit the firm most. Strategy-formulation decisions commit an organization to specific products, markets, resources, and technologies over an extended period of time. Strategies determine long-term competitive advantages. For better or worse, strategic decisions have major multifunctional consequences and enduring effects on an organization. Top managers have the best perspective to understand fully the ramifications of strategy-formulation decisions; they have the authority to commit the resources necessary for implementation.

Strategy implementation requires a firm to establish annual objectives, devise policies, motivate employees, and allocate resources so that formulated strategies can be executed. Strategy implementation includes developing a strategy-supportive culture, creating an effective organizational structure, redirecting marketing efforts, preparing budgets, developing and using information systems, and linking employee compensation to organizational performance.

Strategy implementation often is called the "action stage" of strategic management. Implementing strategy means mobilizing employees and managers to put formulated strategies into action. Often considered to be the most difficult stage in strategic management, strategy implementation requires personal discipline, commitment, and sacrifice. Successful strategy implementation hinges on managers' ability to motivate employees, which is more an art than a science. Strategies formulated but not implemented serve no useful purpose.

Interpersonal skills are especially critical for successful strategy implementation. Strategy-implementation activities affect all employees and managers in an organization. Every division and department must decide on answers to questions such as "What must we do to implement our part of the organization's strategy?" and "How best can we get the job done?" The challenge of implementation is to stimulate managers and employees throughout an organization to work with pride and enthusiasm toward achieving stated objectives.

Strategy evaluation is the final stage in strategic management. Managers desperately need to know when particular strategies are not working well; strategy evaluation is the primary means for obtaining this information. All strategies are subject to future modification because external and internal factors are constantly changing. Three fundamental strategy-evaluation activities are (1) reviewing external and internal factors that are the bases for current strategies, (2) measuring performance, and (3) taking corrective actions. Strategy evaluation is needed because success today is no guarantee of success tomorrow! Success always creates new and different problems; complacent organizations experience demise.

Formulation, implementation, and evaluation of strategy activities occur at three hierarchical levels in a large organization: corporate, divisional or strategic business unit, and functional. By fostering communication and interaction among managers and employees across hierarchical levels, strategic management helps a firm function as a competitive team. Most small businesses and some large businesses do not have divisions or strategic business units; they have only the corporate and functional levels. Nevertheless, managers and employees at these two levels should be actively involved in strategic-management activities.

Peter Drucker says the prime task of strategic management is thinking through the overall mission of a business:

> that is, of asking the question, "What is our business?" This leads to the setting of objectives, the development of strategies, and the making of today's decisions for tomorrow's results. This clearly must be done by a part of the organization that can see the entire business; that can balance objectives and the needs of today against the needs of tomorrow; and that can allocate resources of men and money to key results.[2]

Integrating Intuition and Analysis

Edward Deming once said, *"In God we trust. All others bring data."* The strategic-management process can be described as an objective, logical, systematic approach for making major decisions in an organization. It attempts to organize qualitative and quantitative information in a way that allows effective decisions to be made under conditions of uncertainty. Yet strategic management is not a pure science that lends itself to a nice, neat, one-two-three approach.

Based on past experiences, judgment, and feelings, most people recognize that **intuition** is essential to making good strategic decisions. Intuition is particularly useful for making decisions in situations of great uncertainty or little precedent. It is also helpful when highly interrelated variables exist or when it is necessary to choose from several plausible alternatives. Some managers and owners of businesses profess to have extraordinary abilities for using intuition alone in devising brilliant strategies. For example, Will Durant, who organized GM, was described by Alfred Sloan as "a man who would proceed on a course of action guided solely, as far as I could tell, by some intuitive flash of brilliance. He never felt obliged to make an engineering hunt for the facts. Yet at times, he was astoundingly correct in his judgment."[3] Albert Einstein acknowledged the importance of intuition when he said, "I believe in intuition and inspiration. At times I feel certain that I am right while not knowing the reason. Imagination is more important than knowledge, because knowledge is limited, whereas imagination embraces the entire world."[4]

Although some organizations today may survive and prosper because they have intuitive geniuses managing them, most are not so fortunate. Most organizations can benefit from strategic management, which is based on integrating intuition and analysis in decision making. Choosing an intuitive or analytic approach to decision making is not an either-or proposition. Managers at all levels in an organization inject their intuition and judgment into strategic-management analyses. Analytical thinking and intuitive thinking complement each other.

Operating from the I've-already-made-up-my-mind-don't-bother-me-with-the-facts mode is not management by intuition; it is management by ignorance.[5] Drucker says, "I believe in intuition only if you discipline it. 'Hunch' artists, who make a diagnosis but don't check it out with the facts, are the ones in medicine who kill people, and in management kill businesses."[6] As Henderson notes:

> The accelerating rate of change today is producing a business world in which customary managerial habits in organizations are increasingly inadequate. Experience alone was an adequate guide when changes could be made in small increments. But intuitive and experience-based management philosophies are grossly inadequate when decisions are strategic and have major, irreversible consequences.[7]

In a sense, the strategic-management process is an attempt to duplicate what goes on in the mind of a brilliant, intuitive person who knows the business and assimilates and integrates that knowledge using analysis to formulate effective strategies.

Adapting to Change

The strategic-management process is based on the belief that organizations should continually monitor internal and external events and trends so that timely changes can be made as needed. The rate and magnitude of changes that affect organizations are increasing dramatically, as evidenced by how the global economic recession caught so many firms by surprise. Firms, like organisms, must be "adept at adapting" or they will not survive.

One company trying hard to adapt is the Washington Post Company, best known as publisher of the *Washington Post* newspaper that has a circulation of 525,000 in the Washington, DC area. But the newspaper industry is in decline globally, so the Washington Post Company recently diversified by acquiring Celtic Healthcare, a provider of hospice and home health care facilities in Pennsylvania and Maryland. Treating patients at home instead of paying for hospital stays is a much faster growing industry than selling newspapers. The Washington Post Company also owns Kaplan, a well-known source of test preparation materials, and six TV stations.

To survive, all organizations must astutely identify and adapt to change. The strategic-management process is aimed at allowing organizations to adapt effectively to change over the long run. As Waterman has noted:

> In today's business environment, more than in any preceding era, the only constant is change. Successful organizations effectively manage change, continuously adapting their bureaucracies, strategies, systems, products, and cultures to survive the shocks and prosper from the forces that decimate the competition.[8]

On a political map, the boundaries between countries may be clear, but on a competitive map showing the real flow of financial and industrial activity, the boundaries have largely disappeared. The speedy flow of information has eaten away at national boundaries so that people worldwide readily see for themselves how other people live and work. We have become a borderless world with global citizens, global competitors, global customers, global suppliers, and global distributors! U.S. firms are challenged by large rival companies in many industries. For example, Samsung recently surpassed Apple and Lenovo surpassed HP and Dell in revenues.

The need to adapt to change leads organizations to key strategic-management questions, such as "What kind of business should we become?" "Are we in the right field(s)?" "Should we reshape our business?" "What new competitors are entering our industry?" "What strategies should we pursue?" "How are our customers changing?" "Are new technologies being developed that could put us out of business?"

The Internet promotes endless comparison shopping, which thus enables consumers worldwide to band together to demand discounts. The Internet has transferred power from businesses to individuals. Buyers used to face big obstacles when attempting to get the best price and service, such as limited time and data to compare, but now consumers can quickly scan hundreds of vendor offerings. Both the number of people shopping online and the average amount they spend is increasing dramatically. Digital communication has become the name of the game in marketing. Consumers today are flocking to blogs, sending tweets, watching and posting videos on YouTube, and spending hours on Tumbler, Facebook, Reddit, Instagram, and LinkedIn instead of watching television, listening to the radio, or reading newspapers, and magazines. Facebook and Myspace recently unveiled features that further marry these social sites to the wider Internet. Users on these social sites now can log on to many business shopping sites from their social site so their friends can see what items they have purchased on various shopping sites. Both of these social sites want their members to use their identities to manage *all* their online identities. Most traditional retailers have learned that their online sales can boost in-store sales if they use their websites to promote in-store promotions.

Key Terms in Strategic Management

Before we further discuss strategic management, we should define nine key terms: competitive advantage, strategists, vision and mission statements, external opportunities and threats, internal strengths and weaknesses, long-term objectives, strategies, annual objectives, and policies.

Competitive Advantage

Strategic management is all about gaining and maintaining **competitive advantage**. This term can be defined as "anything that a firm does especially well compared to rival firms." When a firm can do something that rival firms cannot do or owns something that rival firms desire, that can represent a competitive advantage. For example, having ample cash on the firm's balance sheet can provide a major competitive advantage. Some cash-rich firms are buying distressed rivals. Examples of cash-rich (cash as a percentage of total assets) companies today include Priceline. com (63%), Altera (80%), Franklin Resources (51%), Gilead Sciences (57%), and Lorillard (54%). Microsoft, Apple, and Samsung are cash rich, as is the Cohesion Case company, PepsiCo.

Having less fixed assets than rival firms also can provide major competitive advantages. For example, Apple has no manufacturing facilities of its own, and rival Sony has 57 electronics factories. Apple relies exclusively on contract manufacturers for production of all of its products, whereas Sony owns its own plants. Less fixed assets has enabled Apple to remain financially lean with virtually no long-term debt. Sony, in contrast, has built up massive debt on its balance sheet.

CEO Paco Underhill of Envirosell says, "Where it used to be a polite war, it's now a 21st-century bar fight, where everybody is competing with everyone else for the customers' money." Shoppers are "trading down," so Nordstrom is taking customers from Neiman Marcus and Saks Fifth Avenue, TJ Maxx and Marshalls are taking customers from most other stores in the mall, and Family Dollar is taking revenues from Walmart.[9] Getting and keeping competitive advantage is essential for long-term success in an organization. In mass retailing, big-box companies such as Walmart, Best Buy, and Sears are losing competitive advantage to smaller stores, so there is a dramatic shift in mass retailing to becoming smaller. As customers shift more to online purchases, less brick and mortar is definitely better for sustaining competitive advantage in retailing. Walmart Express stores of less than 40,000 square feet each, rather than 185,000-square-foot Supercenters, and Office Depot's new 5,000-square-foot stores are examples of smaller is better.

Normally, a firm can sustain a competitive advantage for only a certain period because of rival firms imitating and undermining that advantage. Thus, it is not adequate to simply obtain competitive advantage. A firm must strive to achieve **sustained competitive advantage** by (1) continually adapting to changes in external trends and events and internal capabilities, competencies, and resources; and by (2) effectively formulating, implementing, and evaluating strategies that capitalize on those factors.

An increasing number of companies are gaining a competitive advantage by using the Internet for direct selling and for communication with suppliers, customers, creditors, partners, shareholders, clients, and competitors who may be dispersed globally. E-commerce allows firms to sell products, advertise, purchase supplies, bypass intermediaries, track inventory, eliminate paperwork, and share information. In total, e-commerce is minimizing the expense and cumbersomeness of time, distance, and space in doing business, thus yielding better customer service, greater efficiency, improved products, and higher profitability.

Strategists

Strategists are the individuals most responsible for the success or failure of an organization. Strategists have various job titles, such as chief executive officer, president, owner, chair of the board, executive director, chancellor, dean, or entrepreneur. Jay Conger, professor of organizational behavior at the London Business School and author of *Building Leaders*, says, "All strategists have to be chief learning officers. We are in an extended period of change. If our leaders aren't highly adaptive and great models during this period, then our companies won't adapt either, because ultimately leadership is about being a role model."

Strategists help an organization gather, analyze, and organize information. They track industry and competitive trends, develop forecasting models and scenario analyses, evaluate corporate and divisional performance, spot emerging market opportunities, identify business threats, and develop creative action plans. Strategic planners usually serve in a support or staff role. Usually found in higher levels of management, they typically have considerable authority for decision making in the firm. The CEO is the most visible and critical strategic manager. Any manager who has responsibility for a unit or division, responsibility for profit and loss outcomes, or direct authority over a major piece of the business is a strategic manager (strategist). In the last few years, the position of CSO has emerged as a new addition to the top management ranks of many organizations, including Sun Microsystems, Network Associates, Clarus, Lante, Marimba, Sapient, Commerce One, BBDO, Cadbury Schweppes, General Motors, Ellie Mae, Cendant, Charles Schwab, Tyco, Campbell Soup, Morgan Stanley, and Reed-Elsevier. This corporate officer title represents recognition of the growing importance of strategic planning in business. Franz Koch, the CSO of German sportswear company Puma AG, was recently promoted to CEO of Puma. When asked about his plans for the company, Koch said on a conference call "I plan to just focus on the long-term strategic plan."

Strategists differ as much as organizations themselves, and these differences must be considered in the formulation, implementation, and evaluation of strategies. Some strategists will not consider some types of strategies because of their personal philosophies. Strategists differ in their attitudes, values, ethics, willingness to take risks, concern for social responsibility, concern for profitability, concern for short-run versus long-run aims, and management style. The founder of Hershey Foods, Milton Hershey, built the company to manage an orphanage. From corporate profits, Hershey Foods today cares for about 900 boys and 1,000 girls in its boarding school for pre-K through 12 grade.

Several CSOs who spoke at the CSO Summit in May 2013 in San Francisco were:

Roland Pan at Skype

Mark Achler at Redbox

Jon Berlin at Wells Fargo

Drew Aldrich at Trans-Lux

Ann Neir at Cisco Systems

Jennifer Scott at Virgin Media

Gina Copeland at Mitsubishi Electric

Raj Ratnaker at Tyco Electronics

Tim Johnsone at Hopelink

Nhat Ngo at Omnicell

Daniel Gastel at UBS

Clarence So at Salesforce

Barry Margerum at Plantronics

Vision and Mission Statements

Many organizations today develop a **vision statement** that answers the question "What do we want to become?" Developing a vision statement is often considered the first step in strategic planning, preceding even development of a mission statement. Many vision statements are a single sentence. For example, the vision statement of Stokes Eye Clinic in Florence, South Carolina, is "Our vision is to take care of your vision."

Mission statements are "enduring statements of purpose that distinguish one business from other similar firms. A mission statement identifies the scope of a firm's operations in product and market terms."[10] It addresses the basic question that faces all strategists: "What is our business?" A clear mission statement describes the values and priorities of an organization. Developing a mission statement compels strategists to think about the nature and scope of present operations and to assess the potential attractiveness of future markets and activities. A mission statement broadly charts the future direction of an organization. A mission statement is a constant reminder to its employees of why the organization exists and what the founders envisioned when they put their fame and fortune at risk to breathe life into their dreams.

External Opportunities and Threats

External opportunities and **external threats** refer to economic, social, cultural, demographic, environmental, political, legal, governmental, technological, and competitive trends and events that could significantly benefit or harm an organization in the future. Opportunities and threats are largely beyond the control of a single organization—thus the word *external*. A few opportunities and threats that face many firms are listed here:

- Availability of capital can no longer be taken for granted.
- Consumers expect green operations and products.
- Marketing is moving rapidly to the Internet.
- Commodity food prices are increasing.
- Political unrest in the Middle East is raising oil prices.
- Computer hacker problems are increasing.
- Intense price competition is plaguing most firms.
- Unemployment and underemployment rates remain high globally.
- Interest rates are rising.
- Product life cycles are becoming shorter.
- State and local governments are financially weak.
- Drug cartel-related violence in Mexico.
- Winters are colder and summers hotter than usual.
- Home prices remain exceptionally low.
- Global markets offer the highest growth in revenues.

These types of changes are creating a different type of consumer and consequently a need for different types of products, services, and strategies. Many companies in many industries face the severe external threat of online sales capturing increasing market share in their industry.

Other opportunities and threats may include the passage of a law, the introduction of a new product by a competitor, a national catastrophe, or the declining value of the Euro. A competitor's strength could be a threat. A growing middle class in Africa, rising energy costs, or social media networking could represent an opportunity or a threat.

A basic tenet of strategic management is that firms need to formulate strategies to take advantage of external opportunities and avoid or reduce the impact of external threats. For this reason, identifying, monitoring, and evaluating external opportunities and threats are essential for success. This process of conducting research and gathering and assimilating external information is sometimes called **environmental scanning** or industry analysis. Lobbying is one activity that some organizations use to influence external opportunities and threats.

Internal Strengths and Weaknesses

Internal strengths and **internal weaknesses** are an organization's controllable activities that are performed especially well or poorly. They arise in the management, marketing, finance/accounting, production/operations, research and development (R&D), and management information systems (MIS) activities of a business. Identifying and evaluating organizational strengths and weaknesses in the functional areas of a business is an essential strategic-management activity. Organizations strive to pursue strategies that capitalize on internal strengths and eliminate internal weaknesses.

Strengths and weaknesses are determined relative to competitors. *Relative deficiency or superiority is important information.* Also, strengths and weaknesses can be determined by elements of being rather than performance. For example, a strength may involve ownership of natural resources or a historic reputation for quality. Strengths and weaknesses may be determined relative to a firm's own objectives. For example, high levels of inventory turnover may not be a strength for a firm that seeks never to stock-out.

In performing a strategic-management case analysis, it is important to be as divisional as possible when determining and stating internal strengths and weaknesses. In other words, for a company such as Walmart saying that Sam Club's revenues grew 11 percent in the recent quarter, rather than Walmart couching all of their internal factors in terms of Walmart as a *whole*. This practice will enable strategies to be more effectively formulated because in strategic planning, firms must allocate resources among divisions (segments) of the firm (that is, by product, region, customer, or whatever the various units of the firm are), such as Sam's Club versus Supercenters or Mexico versus Europe at Walmart.

Both internal and external factors should be stated in specific terms to the extent possible, using numbers, percentages, dollars, and ratios, as well as comparisons over time and to rival firms. *Specificity is important because strategies will be formulated and resources allocated based on this information.* The more specific the underlying external and internal factors, the more effectively strategies can be formulated and resources allocated. Determining the numbers takes more time, but survival of the firm often is at stake, so identifying and estimating numbers associated with key factors is essential.

Internal factors can be determined in a number of ways, including computing ratios, measuring performance, and comparing to past periods and industry averages. Various types of surveys also can be developed and administered to examine internal factors such as employee morale, production efficiency, advertising effectiveness, and customer loyalty.

Long-Term Objectives

Objectives can be defined as specific results that an organization seeks to achieve in pursuing its basic mission. Long-term means more than one year. Objectives are essential for organizational success because they provide direction; aid in evaluation; create synergy; reveal priorities; focus coordination; and provide a basis for effective planning, organizing, motivating, and controlling activities. Objectives should be challenging, measurable, consistent, reasonable, and clear. In a multidimensional firm, objectives should be established for the overall company and for each division.

Strategies

Strategies are the means by which **long-term objectives** will be achieved. Business strategies may include geographic expansion, diversification, acquisition, product development, market penetration, retrenchment, divestiture, liquidation, and joint ventures. Strategies currently being pursued by some companies are described in Table 1-1

Strategies are potential actions that require top management decisions and large amounts of the firm's resources. In addition, strategies affect an organization's long-term prosperity, typically for at least five years, and thus are future-oriented. Strategies have multifunctional or multidivisional consequences and require consideration of both the external and internal factors facing the firm.

Annual Objectives

Annual objectives are short-term milestones that organizations must achieve to reach long-term objectives. Like long-term objectives, annual objectives should be measurable, quantitative, challenging, realistic, consistent, and prioritized. They should be established at the corporate, divisional, and functional levels in a large organization. Annual objectives should be stated in terms of management, marketing, finance/accounting, production/operations, R&D, and MIS accomplishments.

TABLE 1-1 Sample Strategies in Action in 2013

Walgreen Company

Do you prefer Walgreen's or CVS? Headquartered in Deerfield, Illinois, Walgreen's is deepening its penetration into the southeastern portion of the USA by acquiring firms such as USA Drug, May's Drug, Med-X, Drug Warehouse, and Super D Drug. At the same time, Walgreen's is expanding globally through acquisition of firms such as U.K pharmacy-led health-and-beauty retailer Alliance Boots GmbH. Perhaps a reason Walgreen's is acquiring firms is that its same-store pharmacy sales have dropped 15 percent in the last year, mainly as a result of selling more generic rather than prescription drugs, and their same-store-overall sales have dropped 10 percent, mainly because of the chain's exit from pharmacy-benefit manager Express Scripts Holding. Of course, their major rival firm, CVS, could also be a key reason why Walgreen's is acquiring other firms—to show net growth, despite lower organic (internal) revenue declines.

Netflix Inc.

Based in Los Gatos, California, the long-time DVD-by-mail provider is struggling to survive as the firm switches from the DVD business to (a) providing Internet-delivered streaming content and (b) expanding to overseas markets. Major rivals to Netflix include News Corp.'s Hulu and Coinstar's Redbox, who are growing rapidly, in the USA. Netflix's overseas efforts are not going well because that strategy requires country-by-country deals to line up video content. In a recent quarter, Netflix lost 850,000 DVD subscribers and added 530,000 movie and TV-show streaming customers. Netflix's international streaming business lost about $400 million in 2012.

Microsoft

Based in Redmond, Washington, Microsoft added 35 retail "pop-up stores" in late 2012 to go with its 30 existing retail stores in the United States and one store in Toronto. This forward integration strategy coincided with Microsoft introducing its first tablet computer, Surface, which unlike Apple's iPad, runs popular Microsoft Office apps such as Word and Excel. The Surface also has an innovative keyboard cover that makes typing easier. In addition to its new retail stores, Microsoft is also selling its new Surface tablet online, but many customers want to touch and see before buying such a product online.

A set of annual objectives is needed for each long-term objective. Annual objectives are especially important in strategy implementation, whereas long-term objectives are particularly important in strategy formulation. Annual objectives represent the basis for allocating resources.

Policies

Policies are the means by which annual objectives will be achieved. Policies include guidelines, rules, and procedures established to support efforts to achieve stated objectives. Policies are guides to decision making and address repetitive or recurring situations.

Policies are most often stated in terms of management, marketing, finance/accounting, production/operations, R&D, and MIS activities. Policies can be established at the corporate level and apply to an entire organization at the divisional level and apply to a single division, or they can be established at the functional level and apply to particular operational activities or departments. Policies, like annual objectives, are especially important in strategy implementation because they outline an organization's expectations of its employees and managers. Policies allow consistency and coordination within and between organizational departments.

Substantial research suggests that a healthier workforce can more effectively and efficiently implement strategies. Smoking has become a heavy burden for Europe's state-run social welfare systems, with smoking-related diseases costing more than $100 billion a year. Smoking also is a huge burden on companies worldwide, so firms are continually implementing policies to curtail smoking. Starbucks in mid-2013 banned smoking within 25 feet of its 7,000 stores not located inside another retail establishment.

Hotel and motels in the United States are rapidly going "smoke-free throughout" with more than 13,000 now having this policy. The American Hotel and Lodging Association says there are 50,800 hotel/motels in the USA with 15 or more rooms. All Marriotts are now nonsmoking. Almost all (except Hertz) car rental companies are exclusively nonsmoking, including Avis, Dollar, Thrifty, and Budget. Most rental car companies charge a $250 cleaning fee if a customer smokes in their rental vehicle. More cigarettes are smoked in Russia per capita (2,786) than any other country in the world, but that country in 2013 instituted strict, mandatory new antismoking policies among all restaurants and bars and government facilities.[11] Sixty percent of men in Russia smoke. Other heavily smoking countries per capita include Japan (1,841), China (1,711), and Indonesia (1,085), compared to the USA (1,028). Excise taxes in Russia on tobacco products are set to rise 135 percent by 2015. About 400,000 Russians die each year as a result of smoking, costing the country 1.5 trillion rubles ($48.1 billion) annually in health-care costs.

The Strategic-Management Model

The strategic-management process can best be studied and applied using a model. Every model represents some kind of process. The framework illustrated in Figure 1-1 with white shading is a widely accepted, comprehensive model of the strategic-management process.[12] This model does not guarantee success, but it does represent a clear and practical approach for formulating, implementing, and evaluating strategies. Relationships among major components of the strategic-management process are shown in the model, which appears in all subsequent chapters with appropriate areas

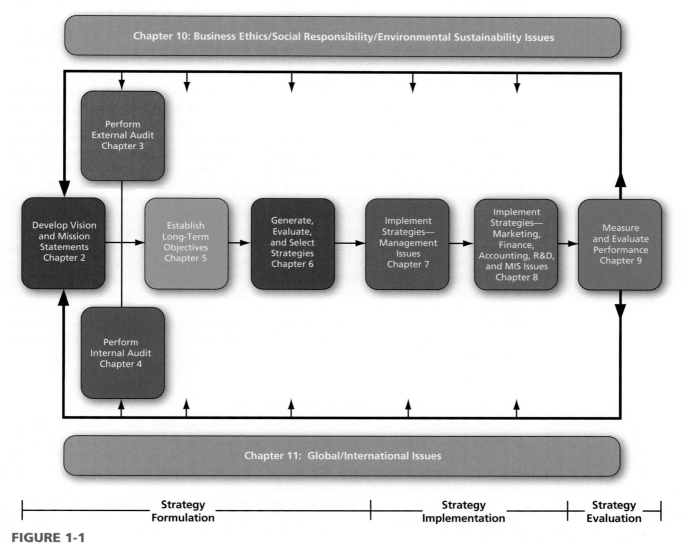

FIGURE 1-1

A Comprehensive Strategic-Management Model

Source: Fred R. David, "How Companies Define Their Mission," *Long Range Planning* 22, no. 3 (June 1988): 40.

shaped to show the particular focus of each chapter. These are three important questions to answer in developing a strategic plan:

Where are we now?

Where do we want to go?

How are we going to get there?

Identifying an organization's existing vision, mission, objectives, and strategies is the logical starting point for strategic management because a firm's present situation and condition may preclude certain strategies and may even dictate a particular course of action. Every organization has a vision, mission, objectives, and strategy, even if these elements are not consciously designed, written, or communicated. The answer to where an organization is going can be determined largely by where the organization has been!

The strategic-management process is dynamic and continuous. A change in any one of the major components in the model can necessitate a change in any or all of the other components. For instance, African countries coming online could represent a major opportunity and require a change in long-term objectives and strategies; a failure to accomplish annual objectives could require a change in policy; or a major competitor's change in strategy could require a change in the firm's mission. Therefore, strategy formulation, implementation, and evaluation activities should be performed on a continual basis, not just at the end of the year or semiannually. The strategic-management process never really ends.

Note in the **strategic-management model** that business ethics, social responsibility, and environmental sustainability issues impact all activities in the model as discussed in Chapter 10. Also, note in the model that global and international issues also impact virtually all strategic decisions today, as described in detail in Chapter 11.

The strategic-management process is not as cleanly divided and neatly performed in practice as the strategic-management model suggests. Strategists do not go through the process in lockstep fashion. Generally, there is give-and-take among hierarchical levels of an organization. Many organizations conduct formal meetings semiannually to discuss and update the firm's vision, mission, opportunities, threats, strengths, weaknesses, strategies, objectives, policies, and performance. These meetings are commonly held off-premises and are called **retreats**. The rationale for periodically conducting strategic-management meetings away from the work site is to encourage more creativity and candor from participants. Good communication and feedback are needed throughout the strategic-management process.

Application of the strategic-management process is typically more formal in larger and well-established organizations. Formality refers to the extent that participants, responsibilities, authority, duties, and approach are specified. Smaller businesses tend to be less formal. Firms that compete in complex, rapidly changing environments, such as technology companies, tend to be more formal in strategic planning. Firms that have many divisions, products, markets, and technologies also tend to be more formal in applying strategic-management concepts. Greater formality in applying the strategic-management process is usually positively associated with the cost, comprehensiveness, accuracy, and success of planning across all types and sizes of organizations.[13]

Benefits of Strategic Management

Strategic management allows an organization to be more proactive than reactive in shaping its own future; it allows an organization to initiate and influence (rather than just respond to) activities—and thus to exert control over its own destiny. Small business owners, chief executive officers, presidents, and managers of many for-profit and nonprofit organizations have recognized and realized the benefits of strategic management.

Historically, the principal benefit of strategic management has been to help organizations formulate better strategies through the use of a more systematic, logical, and rational approach to strategic choice. This certainly continues to be a major benefit of strategic management, but research studies now indicate that the process, rather than the decision or document, is the more important contribution of strategic management.[14] *Communication is a key to successful strategic management.* Through involvement in the process, in other words, through dialogue

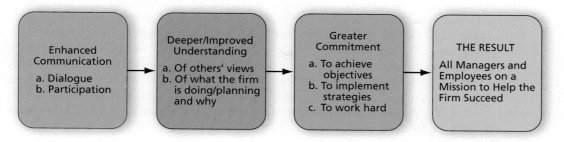

FIGURE 1-2

Benefits to a Firm That Does Strategic Planning

and participation, managers and employees become committed to supporting the organization. Figure 1-2 illustrates this intrinsic benefit of a firm engaging in strategic planning. Note that all firms need all employees "on a mission" to help the firm succeed. Dale McConkey said "plans are less important than planning."

The manner in which strategic management is carried out is thus exceptionally important. A major aim of the process is to achieve understanding and commitment from all managers and employees. Understanding may be the most important benefit of strategic management, followed by commitment. When managers and employees understand what the organization is doing and why, they often feel a part of the firm and become committed to assisting it. This is especially true when employees also understand links between their own compensation and organizational performance. Managers and employees become surprisingly creative and innovative when they understand and support the firm's mission, objectives, and strategies. A great benefit of strategic management, then, is the opportunity that the process provides to empower individuals. **Empowerment** is the act of strengthening employees' sense of effectiveness by encouraging them to participate in decision making and to exercise initiative and imagination, and rewarding them for doing so. William Fulmer said "you want your people to run the business as it if were their own."

Strategic planning is a learning, helping, educating, and supporting process, not merely a paper-shuffling activity among top executives. Strategic-management dialogue is more important than a nicely bound strategic-management document.[15] The worst thing strategists can do is develop strategic plans themselves and then present them to operating managers to execute. Through involvement in the process, line managers become "owners" of the strategy. Ownership of strategies by the people who have to execute them is a key to success!

Although making good strategic decisions is the major responsibility of an organization's owner or chief executive officer, both managers and employees must also be involved in strategy formulation, implementation, and evaluation activities. Participation is a key to gaining commitment for needed changes.

An increasing number of corporations and institutions are using strategic management to make effective decisions. But strategic management is not a guarantee for success; it can be dysfunctional if conducted haphazardly.

Financial Benefits

Research indicates that organizations that use strategic-management concepts are more profitable and successful than those that do not.[16] Businesses using strategic-management concepts show significant improvement in sales, profitability, and productivity compared to firms without systematic planning activities. High-performing firms tend to do systematic planning to prepare for future fluctuations in their external and internal environments. Firms with planning systems more closely resembling strategic-management theory generally exhibit superior long-term financial performance relative to their industry.

High-performing firms seem to make more informed decisions with good anticipation of both short- and long-term consequences. In contrast, firms that perform poorly often engage in activities that are shortsighted and do not reflect good forecasting of future conditions. Strategists of low-performing organizations are often preoccupied with solving internal problems and meeting paperwork deadlines. They typically underestimate their competitors' strengths and overestimate their own firm's strengths. They often attribute weak performance to uncontrollable factors such as a poor economy, technological change, or foreign competition.

More than 100,000 businesses in the USA fail annually. Business failures include bankruptcies, foreclosures, liquidations, and court-mandated receiverships. Although many factors besides a lack of effective strategic management can lead to business failure, the planning concepts and tools described in this text can yield substantial financial benefits for any organization. The business failure rate in the USA fell dramatically in 2012/2013, but rates rose significantly throughout Europe.

Nonfinancial Benefits

Besides helping firms avoid financial demise, strategic management offers other tangible benefits, such as an enhanced awareness of external threats, an improved understanding of competitors' strategies, increased employee productivity, reduced resistance to change, and a clearer understanding of performance–reward relationships. Strategic management enhances the problem-prevention capabilities of organizations because it promotes interaction among managers at all divisional and functional levels. Firms that have nurtured their managers and employees, shared organizational objectives with them, empowered them to help improve the product or service, and recognized their contributions can turn to them for help in a pinch because of this interaction.

In addition to empowering managers and employees, strategic management often brings order and discipline to an otherwise floundering firm. It can be the beginning of an efficient and effective managerial system. Strategic management may renew confidence in the current business strategy or point to the need for corrective actions. The strategic-management process provides a basis for identifying and rationalizing the need for change to all managers and employees of a firm; it helps them view change as an opportunity rather than as a threat. Some nonfinancial benefits of a firm utilizing strategic management, according to Greenley, are increased discipline, improved coordination, enhanced communication, reduced resistance to change, increased forward thinking, improved decision-making, increased synergy, and more effective allocation of time and resources.[17]

Why Some Firms Do No Strategic Planning

Some firms do no strategic planning, and some firms do strategic planning but receive no support from managers and employees. Ten reasons (excuses) often given for poor or no strategic planning in a firm are as follows:

1. No formal training in strategic management
2. No understanding of or appreciation for the benefits of planning
3. No monetary rewards for doing planning
4. No punishment for not planning
5. Too busy "firefighting" (resolving internal crises) to plan ahead
6. To view planning as a waste of time, since no product/service is made
7. Laziness; effective planning takes time and effort; time is money
8. Content with current success; failure to realize that success today is no guarantee for success tomorrow; even Apple Inc. is an example
9. Overconfident
10. Prior bad experience with strategic planning done sometime/somewhere

Pitfalls in Strategic Planning

Strategic planning is an involved, intricate, and complex process that takes an organization into uncharted territory. It does not provide a ready-to-use prescription for success; instead, it takes the organization through a journey and offers a framework for addressing questions and solving problems. Being aware of potential pitfalls and being prepared to address them is essential to success.

Some pitfalls to watch for and avoid in strategic planning are these:

- Using strategic planning to gain control over decisions and resources
- Doing strategic planning only to satisfy accreditation or regulatory requirements
- Too hastily moving from mission development to strategy formulation
- Failing to communicate the plan to employees, who continue working in the dark
- Top managers making many intuitive decisions that conflict with the formal plan
- Top managers not actively supporting the strategic-planning process
- Failing to use plans as a standard for measuring performance
- Delegating planning to a "planner" rather than involving all managers
- Failing to involve key employees in all phases of planning
- Failing to create a collaborative climate supportive of change
- Viewing planning as unnecessary or unimportant
- Becoming so engrossed in current problems that insufficient or no planning is done
- Being so formal in planning that flexibility and creativity are stifled[18]

Guidelines for Effective Strategic Management

Failing to follow certain guidelines in conducting strategic management can foster criticisms of the process and create problems for the organization. Issues such as "Is strategic management in our firm a people process or a paper process?" should be addressed. Some organizations spend an inordinate amount of time developing a strategic plan, but then fail to follow through with effective implementation. Change and results in a firm come through implementation, not through formulation, although effective formulation is critically important for successful implementation. Continual evaluation of strategies is also essential because the world changes so rapidly that existing strategies can need modifying often.

Strategic management must not become a self-perpetuating bureaucratic mechanism. Rather, it must be a self-reflective learning process that familiarizes managers and employees in the organization with key strategic issues and feasible alternatives for resolving those issues. Strategic management must not become ritualistic, stilted, orchestrated, or too formal, predictable, and rigid. Words supported by numbers, rather than numbers supported by words, should represent the medium for explaining strategic issues and organizational responses. A key role of strategists is to facilitate continuous organizational learning and change.

R. T. Lenz offers six guidelines for effective strategic management:

1. Keep the process simple and easily understandable.
2. Eliminate vague planning jargon.
3. Keep the process nonroutine, so vary assignments, team membership, meeting formats, settings, and even the planning calendar.
4. Welcome bad news and encourage devil's advocate thinking.
5. Do not allow technicians to monopolize the planning process.
6. To the extent possible, involve managers from all areas of the firm.[19]

An important guideline for effective strategic management is open-mindedness. A willingness and eagerness to consider new information, new viewpoints, new ideas, and new possibilities is essential; all organizational members must share a spirit of inquiry and learning. Strategists such as chief executive officers, presidents, owners of small businesses, and heads of government agencies must commit themselves to listen to and understand managers' positions well enough to be able to restate those positions to the managers' satisfaction. In addition, managers and employees throughout the firm should be able to describe the strategists' positions to the satisfaction of the strategists. This degree of discipline will promote understanding and learning.

No organization has unlimited resources. No firm can take on an unlimited amount of debt or issue an unlimited amount of stock to raise capital. Therefore, no organization can pursue all the strategies that potentially could benefit the firm. Strategic decisions thus always have to be made to eliminate some courses of action and to allocate organizational resources among others. Most organizations can afford to pursue only a few corporate-level strategies at any given time.

TABLE 1-2 Seventeen Guidelines for the Strategic-Planning Process to Be Effective

1. It should be a people process more than a paper process.
2. It should be a learning process for all managers and employees.
3. It should be words supported by numbers rather than numbers supported by words.
4. It should be simple and nonroutine.
5. It should vary assignments, team memberships, meeting formats, and even the planning calendar.
6. It should challenge the assumptions underlying the current corporate strategy.
7. It should welcome bad news.
8. It should welcome open-mindness and a spirit of inquiry and learning.
9. It should not be a bureaucratic mechanism.
10. It should not become ritualistic, stilted, or orchestrated.
11. It should not be too formal, predictable, or rigid.
12. It should not contain jargon or arcane planning language.
13. It should not be a formal system for control.
14. It should not disregard qualitative information.
15. It should not be controlled by "technicians."
16. Do not pursue too many strategies at once.
17. Continually strengthen the "good ethics is good business" policy.

It is a critical mistake for managers to pursue too many strategies at the same time, thereby spreading the firm's resources so thin that all strategies are jeopardized.

Strategic decisions require trade-offs such as long-range versus short-range considerations or maximizing profits versus increasing shareholders' wealth. There are ethics issues too. Strategy trade-offs require subjective judgments and preferences. In many cases, a lack of objectivity in formulating strategy results in a loss of competitive posture and profitability. Most organizations today recognize that strategic-management concepts and techniques can enhance the effectiveness of decisions. Subjective factors such as attitudes toward risk, concern for social responsibility, and organizational culture will always affect strategy-formulation decisions, but organizations need to be as objective as possible in considering qualitative factors. Table 1-2 summarizes important guidelines for the strategic-planning process to be effective.

Comparing Business and Military Strategy

A strong military heritage underlies the study of strategic management. Terms such as *objectives, mission, strengths*, and *weaknesses* first were formulated to address problems on the battlefield. According to *Webster's New World Dictionary*, strategy is "the science of planning and directing large-scale military operations, of maneuvering forces into the most advantageous position prior to actual engagement with the enemy"[20]. The word *strategy* comes from the Greek *strategos*, which refers to a military general and combines *stratos* (the army) and *ago* (to lead). The history of strategic planning began in the military. A key aim of both business and military strategy is "to gain competitive advantage." In many respects, business strategy is like military strategy, and military strategists have learned much over the centuries that can benefit business strategists today. Both business and military organizations try to use their own strengths to exploit competitors' weaknesses. If an organization's overall strategy is wrong (ineffective), then all the efficiency in the world may not be enough to allow success. Business or military success is generally not the happy result of accidental strategies. Rather, success is the product of both continuous attention to changing external and internal conditions and the formulation and implementation of insightful adaptations to those conditions. The element of surprise provides great competitive advantages in both military and business strategy; information systems that provide data on opponents' or competitors' strategies and resources are also vitally important.

Of course, a fundamental difference between military and business strategy is that business strategy is formulated, implemented, and evaluated with an assumption of *competition*, whereas military strategy is based on an assumption of *conflict*. Nonetheless, military conflict and business competition are so similar that many strategic-management techniques apply equally to both. Business strategists have access to valuable insights that military thinkers have refined over time. Superior strategy formulation and implementation can overcome an opponent's superiority in numbers and resources.

Born in Pella in 356 B.C.E., Alexander the Great was king of Macedon, a state in northern ancient Greece. Tutored by Aristotle until the age of 16, Alexander had created one of the largest empires of the ancient world by the age of 30, stretching from the Ionian Sea to the Himalayas. Alexander was undefeated in battle and is considered one of history's most successful commanders. He became the measure against which military leaders even today compare themselves, and military academies throughout the world still teach his strategies and tactics. Alexander the Great once said: *"Greater is an army of sheep led by a lion, than an army of lions led be a sheep."* This quote reveals the overwhelming importance of an excellent strategic plan for any organization to succeed. The legendary Alabama football coach Bear Bryant once said: *I will defeat the opposing coach's team with my players, but if given a week's notice, I could defeat the opposing coach's team with his players and he take my players.*

Both business and military organizations must adapt to change and constantly improve to be successful. Too often, firms do not change their strategies when their environment and competitive conditions dictate the need to change. Gluck offered a classic military example of this:

> When Napoleon won, it was because his opponents were committed to the strategy, tactics, and organization of earlier wars. When he lost—against Wellington, the Russians, and the Spaniards—it was because he, in turn, used tried-and-true strategies against enemies who thought afresh, who were developing the strategies not of the last war but of the next.[21]

Similarities can be construed from Sun Tzu's writings to the practice of formulating and implementing strategies among businesses today. Table 1-3 provides narrative excerpts from *The Art of War*. As you read through the table, consider which of the principles of war apply to business strategy as companies today compete aggressively to survive and grow.

The Art of War has been applied to many fields well outside of the military. Much of the text is about how to fight wars without actually having to do battle: it gives tips on how to outsmart one's opponent so that physical battle is not necessary. As such, it has found application as a training guide for many competitive endeavors that do not involve actual combat, such as in devising courtroom trial strategy or acquiring a rival company. There are business books applying its lessons to office politics and corporate strategy. Many Japanese companies make the book required reading for their top executives. The book is a popular read among Western business managers who have turned to it for inspiration and advice on how to succeed in competitive business situations.

The Art of War has also been applied in the world of sports. NFL coach Bill Belichick is known to have read the book and used its lessons to gain insights in preparing for games. Australian cricket, as well as Brazilian association football coaches Luis Felipe Scolari and Carolos Alberto Parreira, embraced the text. Scolari made the Brazilian World Cup squad of 2002 study the ancient work during their successful campaign.

Special Note to Students

In performing strategic-management case analysis, emphasize throughout your project, beginning with the first page or slide, where your firm has competitive advantages and disadvantages. More importantly, emphasize throughout how you recommend the firm sustain and grow its competitive advantages and how you recommend the firm overcome its competitive disadvantages. Begin paving the way early for what you ultimately recommend your firm should do over the next three years. The notion of competitive advantage should be integral to the discussion of every page or PowerPoint slide. Therefore, avoid being merely *descriptive* in your written or oral analysis; rather, be *prescriptive*, insightful, and forward-looking throughout your project.

TABLE 1-3 Excerpts from Sun Tzu's *The Art of War* Writings

- War is a matter of vital importance to the state: a matter of life or death, the road either to survival or ruin. Hence, it is imperative that it be studied thoroughly.
- Warfare is based on deception. When near the enemy, make it seem that you are far away; when far away, make it seem that you are near. Hold out baits to lure the enemy. Strike the enemy when he is in disorder. Avoid the enemy when he is stronger. If your opponent is of choleric temper, try to irritate him. If he is arrogant, try to encourage his egotism. If enemy troops are well prepared after reorganization, try to wear them down. If they are united, try to sow dissension among them. Attack the enemy where he is unprepared, and appear where you are not expected. These are the keys to victory for a strategist. It is not possible to formulate them in detail beforehand.
- A speedy victory is the main object in war. If this is long in coming, weapons are blunted and morale depressed. When the army engages in protracted campaigns, the resources of the state will fall short. Thus, while we have heard of stupid haste in war, we have not yet seen a clever operation that was prolonged.
- Generally, in war the best policy is to take a state intact; to ruin it is inferior to this. To capture the enemy's entire army is better than to destroy it; to take intact a regiment, a company, or a squad is better than to destroy it. For to win one hundred victories in one hundred battles is not the epitome of skill. To subdue the enemy without fighting is the supreme excellence. Those skilled in war subdue the enemy's army without battle.
- The art of using troops is this: When ten to the enemy's one, surround him. When five times his strength, attack him. If double his strength, divide him. If equally matched, you may engage him with some good plan. If weaker, be capable of withdrawing. And if in all respects unequal, be capable of eluding him.
- Know your enemy and know yourself, and in a hundred battles you will never be defeated. When you are ignorant of the enemy but know yourself, your chances of winning or losing are equal. If ignorant both of your enemy and of yourself, you are sure to be defeated in every battle.
- He who occupies the field of battle first and awaits his enemy is at ease, and he who comes later to the scene and rushes into the fight is weary. And therefore, those skilled in war bring the enemy to the field of battle and are not brought there by him. Thus, when the enemy is at ease, be able to tire him; when well fed, be able to starve him; when at rest, be able to make him move.
- Analyze the enemy's plans so that you will know his shortcomings as well as his strong points. Agitate him to ascertain the pattern of his movement. Lure him out to reveal his dispositions and to ascertain his position. Launch a probing attack to learn where his strength is abundant and where deficient. It is according to the situation that plans are laid for victory, but the multitude does not comprehend this.
- An army may be likened to water, for just as flowing water avoids the heights and hastens to the lowlands, so an army should avoid strength and strike weakness. And as water shapes its flow in accordance with the ground, so an army manages its victory in accordance with the situation of the enemy. And as water has no constant form, there are in warfare no constant conditions. Thus, one able to win the victory by modifying his tactics in accordance with the enemy situation may be said to be divine.
- If you decide to go into battle, do not announce your intentions or plans. Project "business as usual."
- Unskilled leaders work out their conflicts in courtrooms and battlefields. Brilliant strategists rarely go to battle or to court; they generally achieve their objectives through tactical positioning well in advance of any confrontation.
- When you do decide to challenge another company (or army), much calculating, estimating, analyzing, and positioning bring triumph. Little computation brings defeat.
- Skillful leaders do not let a strategy inhibit creative counter-movement. Nor should commands from those at a distance interfere with spontaneous maneuvering in the immediate situation.
- When a decisive advantage is gained over a rival, skillful leaders do not press on. They hold their position and give their rivals the opportunity to surrender or merge. They do not allow their forces to be damaged by those who have nothing to lose.
- Brilliant strategists forge ahead with illusion, obscuring the area(s) of major confrontation, so that opponents divide their forces in an attempt to defend many areas. Create the appearance of confusion, fear, or vulnerability so the opponent is helplessly drawn toward this illusion of advantage.

Note: Substitute the words *strategy* or *strategic planning* for *war* or *warfare*.

Conclusion

All firms have a strategy, even if it is informal, unstructured, and sporadic. All organizations are heading somewhere, but unfortunately some organizations do not know where they are going. The old saying "If you do not know where you are going, then any road will lead you there!" accents the need for organizations to use strategic-management concepts and techniques. The strategic-management process is becoming more widely used by small firms, large companies, nonprofit institutions, governmental organizations, and multinational conglomerates alike. The process of empowering managers and employees has almost limitless benefits.

Organizations should take a proactive rather than a reactive approach in their industry, and they should strive to influence, anticipate, and initiate rather than just respond to events. The strategic-management process embodies this approach to decision making. It represents a logical, systematic, and objective approach for determining an enterprise's future direction. The stakes are generally too high for strategists to use intuition alone in choosing among alternative courses of action. Successful strategists take the time to think about their businesses, where they are with their businesses, and what they want to be as organizations—and then they implement programs and policies to get from where they are to where they want to be in a reasonable period of time.

It is a known and accepted fact that people and organizations that plan ahead are much more likely to become what they want to become than those that do not plan at all. A good strategist plans and controls his or her plans, whereas a bad strategist never plans and then tries to control people! This textbook is devoted to providing you with the tools necessary to be a good strategist.

MyManagementLab®

Go to **mymanagementlab.com** to complete the problems marked with this icon .

Key Terms and Concepts

annual objectives (p. 11)
competitive advantage (p. 8)
empowerment (p. 15)
environmental scanning (p. 10)
external opportunities (p. 10)
external threats (p. 10)
internal strengths (p. 10)
internal weaknesses (p. 10)
intuition (p. 6)
long-range planning (p. 5)
long-term objectives (p. 11)
mission statements (p. 10)
policies (p. 12)

retreats (p. 14)
strategic management (p. 5)
strategic-management model (p. 14)
strategic-management process (p. 5)
strategic planning (p. 5)
strategies (p. 11)
strategists (p. 9)
strategy evaluation (p. 6)
strategy formulation (p. 5)
strategy implementation (p. 6)
sustained competitive advantage (p. 8)
vision statement (p. 10)

Issues for Review and Discussion

1-1. Strengths and weaknesses should be determined relative to competitors, or by elements of being or relative to a firm's own objectives. Explain.

1-2. Explain why internal strengths and weaknesses should be stated in divisional terms to the extent possible.

1-3. Explain why both internal and external factors should be stated in specific terms (that is, using numbers, percents, money ratios, and comparisons over time) to the extent possible.

1-4. Compare and contrast the near-end-of-chapter quotes by Alexander the Great and Bear Bryant regarding the importance of strategic planning in military or athletic settings. How applicable are those quotes in a business setting? Discuss

1-5. Are "strategic management" and "strategic planning" synonymous terms? Explain.

1-6. What are the three stages in strategic management? Which stage is more analytical? Which relies most on empowerment to be successful? Which relies most on statistics? Justify your answers.

1-7. Why do many firms move too hastily from vision and mission development to devising alternative strategies?

1-8. Why are strategic planning retreats often conducted away from the work site? How often should firms have a retreat, and who should participate in them?

1-9. Distinguish between long-range planning and strategic planning.

1-10. Compare a company's strategic plan with a football team's game plan.

1-11. Describe the three activities that comprise strategy evaluation.

1-12. How important do you feel "being adept at adapting" is for business firms? Explain.

1-13. Compare the opossum and turtle to the woolly mammoth and saber-toothed tiger in terms of being adept at adapting. What can we learn from the opossum and turtle?

1-14. As cited in the chapter, Edward Deming, a famous businessman, once said, "*In God we trust. All others bring data.*" What did Deming mean in terms of developing a strategic plan?

1-15. What strategies do you believe can save newspaper companies from extinction?

1-16. Distinguish between the concepts of vision and mission.

1-17. Your university has fierce competitors. List three external opportunities and three external threats that face your university.

1-18. List three internal strengths and three internal weaknesses that characterize your university.

1-19. List reasons why objectives are essential for organizational success.

1-20. List four strategies and a hypothetical example of each.

1-21. List six characteristics of annual objectives.

1-22. Why are policies especially important in strategy implementation?

1-23. What is a "retreat," and why do firms take the time and spend the money to have these?

⭐ **1-24.** Discuss the notion of strategic planning being more formal versus informal in an organization. On a 1- to 10-scale from formal to informal, what number best represents your view of the most effective approach? Why?

1-25. List 10 guidelines for making the strategic-planning process effective. Arrange your guidelines in prioritized order of importance in your opinion.

1-26. List what you feel are the five most important lessons for business that can be garnered from *The Art of War* book.

1-27. What is the fundamental difference between business strategy and military strategy in terms of basic assumptions?

1-28. Explain why the strategic management class is often called a "capstone course".

1-29. What aspect of strategy formulation do you think requires the most time? Why?

1-30. Why is strategy implementation often considered the most difficult stage in the strategic-management process?

1-31. Why is it so important to integrate intuition and analysis in strategic management?

1-32. Explain the importance of a vision and a mission statement.

⭐ **1-33.** Discuss relationships among objectives, strategies, and policies.

⭐ **1-34.** Why do you think some chief executive officers fail to use a strategic-management approach to decision making?

1-35. Discuss the importance of feedback in the strategic-management model.

1-36. How can strategists best ensure that strategies will be effectively implemented?

1-37. Give an example of a recent political development that changed the overall strategy of an organization.

1-38. Who are the major competitors of your college or university? What are their strengths and weaknesses? What are their strategies? How successful are these institutions compared to your college?

1-39. Would strategic-management concepts and techniques benefit foreign businesses as much as domestic firms? Justify your answer.

1-40. What do you believe are some potential pitfalls or risks in using a strategic-management approach to decision making?

1-41. In your opinion, what is the single major benefit of using a strategic-management approach to decision making? Justify your answer.

1-42. Compare business strategy and military strategy.

1-43. Why is it important for all business majors to study strategic management because most students will never become a chief executive officer nor even a top manager in a large company?

1-44. Describe the content available at the Strategy Club website at www.strategyclub.com.

1-45. List four financial and four nonfinancial benefits of a firm engaging in strategic planning.

1-46. Why is it that a firm can normally sustain a competitive advantage for only a limited period of time?

1-47. Why it is not adequate to simply obtain competitive advantage?

1-48. How can a firm best achieve sustained competitive advantage?

MyManagementLab®

Go to **mymanagementlab.com** for Auto-graded writing questions as well as the following Assisted-graded writing questions:

1-49. Strengths and weaknesses should be determined relative to competitors, or by elements of being, or relative to a firm's own objectives. Explain.

1-50. What are the three stages in strategic management? Which stage is more analytical? Which relies most on empowerment to be successful? Which relies most on statistics? Justify your answers.

1-51. Mymanagementlab Only—comprehensive writing assignment for this chapter.

Current Readings

Foote, Nathaniel, Russell Eisenstat, and Tobias Fredberg. "The Higher-Ambition Leader." *Harvard Business Review* (September 2011): 94.

Frisch, Bob. "Who Really Makes the Big Decisions in Your Company?" *Harvard Business Review* (December 2011): 104.

Gavetti, Giovanni. "The New Psychology of Strategic Leadership." *Harvard Business Review* (July–August 2011): 118.

Isaacson, Walter. "The Real Leadership Lessons of Steve Jobs." *Harvard Business Review* (April 2012): 92.

Lafley, A. G. and Noel M. Tichy. "The Art and Science of Finding the Right CEO." *Harvard Business Review* (October 2011): 66.

Leavy, Brian. "Michael Beer—Higher Ambition Leadership." *Strategy and Leadership* 40, no. 4 (2012): 5–11.

Reeves, Martin and Mike Deimler. "Adaptability: The New Competitive Advantage." *Harvard Business Review* (July–August 2011): 134.

Reeves, Martin, Claire Love, and Philipp Tillmanns. "Your Strategy Needs a Strategy." *Harvard Business Review* (September 2012): 56.

Ronda-Pupo, Guillermo Armando, and Luis Ángel Guerras. "Dynamics of the Evolution of the Strategy Concept 1962–2008: A Co-word Analysis." *Strategic Management Journal* 33, no. 2 (February 2012): 162–188.

Stieger, Daniel, Kurt Matzler, Sayan Chatterjee, and Florian Ladstaetter-Fussenegger. "Democratizing Strategy: How Crowdsourcing Can Be Used for Strategy Dialogues." *Inside CMR* 54, no. 4 (Summer 2012): 44.

Zachary, Miles A., Aaron F. McKenny, Jeremy C. Short, and David J. Ketchen. "Strategy in Motion: Using Motion Pictures to Illustrate Strategic Management Concepts." *Business Horizons* 55, no. 1 (January 2012): 5–10.

Zahra, Shaker A., and Satish Nambisan. "Entrepreneurship and Strategic Thinking in Business Ecosystems." *Business Horizons* 55, no. 3 (May 2012): 219–229.

Zook, Chris, and James Allen. "The Great Repeatable Business Model." *Harvard Business Review* (November 2011): 106.

PepsiCo, Inc.—2014

www.pepsico.com, PEP

Headquartered in Purchase, New York, PepsiCo is the second largest carbonated soft-drink maker in the world, behind Coca-Cola Company. In North America, PepsiCo is the largest food and beverage company, having soft-drink brands that include Pepsi-Cola, Mountain Dew, and Diet Pepsi, as well as Tropicana orange juice, Gatorade sports drink, SoBe tea, and Aquafina bottled water. Unlike Coca-Cola, PepsiCo is diversified, owning Frito-Lay and Quaker Foods. Frito-Lay is the largest salty snack provider in the USA, having brands that include Lay's, Ruffles, Doritos, Cheetos, and Fritos; Quaker Foods offers breakfast cereals (Life, Quaker Oats), rice (Rice-A-Roni), and side dishes (Near East).

Pepsi's products are available in more than 200 countries and the company specializes in innovating/changing products to match local tastes and cultures. For example, in Jordan, Bario, a nonalcoholic malt drink is popular, and Tropicana Pulp Sacs are popular in China. Fifty percent of company revenue comes from outside the USA and that percentage is increasing. PepsiCo is the largest food and beverage business in Russia, India, and the Middle East, is number two in Mexico, and is in the top five in Brazil, Turkey, and many other emerging markets like Vietnam, the Philippines, Thailand.

PepsiCo is forward integrated, owning its two largest bottlers, Pepsi Bottling Group and PepsiAmericas. Pepsi products are available worldwide through a variety of systems, including direct store delivery (DSD), broker-warehouse, food service, and vending machines. Twenty-two of PepsiCo's products have generated retail sales of more than $1 billion, including three brands that recently reached this milestone: Diet Mountain Dew, Brisk, and Starbucks ready-to-drink beverages.

PepsiCo made a deal with Burger King in 2013 for Pepsi products to replace Coke products sold at all Burger Kings in China. The world's second largest hamburger chain, Burger King has fewer than 100 locations in China but is expanding rapidly there. Fountain soda accounts for about a quarter of soft-drink sales volume in China, according to the market researcher Euromonitor International. Also in China, PepsiCo recently swapped its holdings in its bottling operations for a stake in Tingyi, a Chinese beverage maker. In Shanghai, China, PepsiCo recently opened its largest food and beverage R&D center outside North America. The new facility is an advanced culinary center with test kitchens focused on developing and tailoring PepsiCo food and beverage brands for distinct, locally relevant taste preferences throughout Asia.

In mid-2013, Trian Fund Management LP, headed by Nelson Peltz, purchased $1.4 billion in stock of both PepsiCo and snacks rival, Mondelez International. Mr. Peltz wants to see PepsiCo acquire Mondelez or divest its snack divisions to Mondelez. PepsiCo is presently engaged in talks with Mr. Peltz.

History

The secret formula for Pepsi was developed in the 1880s by Caleb Bradham, a pharmacist in Newbern, North Carolina. Caleb named his product "Pepsi-Cola" in 1898. As his product gained popularity, he created the Pepsi-Cola Company in 1902 and registered a patent for his recipe in 1903. Interestingly, the formula for Coca-Cola was developed in 1886 by pharmacist John Pemberton in Columbus, Georgia. The Coca-Cola formula and brand was bought in 1889 by Asa Candler who incorporated The Coca-Cola Company in 1892. Pepsi-Cola Company was first incorporated in Delaware in 1919.

In 1965, the Pepsi-Cola Company merged with Frito-Lay, Inc. to become PepsiCo, Inc., as the company is known today. Between the late 1970s and the mid-1990s, PepsiCo expanded via acquisition of restaurant and other businesses outside of its core focus of packaged food and beverage brands. This was a big strategic mistake and the company exited these noncore business lines largely in 1997, selling some and spinning off others into a new company that became known as Yum! Brands. A few brands formerly owned by PepsiCo include Pizza Hut, Taco Bell, Kentucky Fried Chicken, D'Angelo Sandwich Shops, Wilson Sporting Goods, North American Van Lines, and Stolichnaya. In December 2005, PepsiCo surpassed Coca-Cola Company in market value for the first time in 112 years since both companies began to compete.

PepsiCo's divestments concluded in 2007 but ironically were followed by many new large acquisitions, as the company began to extend its operations beyond soft drinks and snack foods into other lines of foods and beverages. PepsiCo purchased Tropicana Products in 1998 and acquired Quaker Oats Company in 2001. In 2010, PepsiCo acquired its two largest bottlers in North America: Pepsi Bottling Group and PepsiAmericas. In 2011, PepsiCo made its largest international acquisition by purchasing

Wimm-Bill-Dann Foods, a Russian food company that produces milk, yogurt, fruit juices, and dairy products. This acquisition made PepsiCo the largest food and beverage company in Russia. This acquisition boosted PepsiCo's nutrition portfolio. In late 2011, Pepsi acquired privately held Grupo Mabel, a Brazilian cookie company, for about $500 million.

In January 2012, PepsiCo hired its first female CEO, Indra Nooyi. A month later, CEO Nooyi said PepsiCo planned to cut 8,700 jobs or about 3 percent of the company's global workforce and boost marketing spending by as much as $600 million. With the cuts, PepsiCo expected to save about $1.5 billion by 2014.

PepsiCo and Theo Muller Group (Muller), the privately-held dairy business in Germany, have a USA joint venture named Muller Quaker Dairy, which in July 2012 began selling European-style premium yogurt products in the United States. These products—Muller Corner, Muller Greek Corner and Muller FrutUp—mark the first entry by either PepsiCo or Muller into U.S. dairy aisles. With this joint venture, PepsiCo is trying to boost its nutrition portfolio.

For Q1 of 2013, PepsiCo's earnings fell to $1.08 billion from $1.13 billion the year earlier, but revenues rose 1.2 percent to $12.58 billion. As beverage industry growth shifts away from soda to healthier beverages, both PepsiCo and Coca-Cola have turned toward emerging markets in Asia, the Middle East, and Africa, where sales rose by 12 percent and 15 percent, respectively, for the two companies in Q1 of 2013. PepsiCo is also trying to increase its cola sales by adding Novel natural sweetener in its cola drinks without sacrificing the taste. Novel is under the Food and Drug Administration review process, and as soon as it gets approval, PepsiCo will launch new cola products.

Vision and Mission

PepsiCo's vision is stated on the company website to be as follows: "PepsiCo's responsibility is to continually improve all aspects of the world in which we operate—environment, social, economic— creating a better tomorrow than today."

PepsiCo's mission is also given on the website as follows: "to be the world's premier consumer products company focused on convenient foods and beverages. We seek to produce financial rewards to investors as we provide opportunities for growth and enrichment to our employees, our business partners and the communities in which we operate. And in everything we do, we strive for honesty, fairness and integrity." (www.pepsico.com)

Organizational Structure

PepsiCo is organized into four business units (PAF, PAB, Europe, and AMEA) as indicated below:

1. PepsiCo Americas Foods (PAF)—includes Frito-Lay North America (FLNA), Quaker Foods North America (QFNA), and Latin American Foods (LAF)
2. PepsiCo Americas Beverages (PAB)
3. PepsiCo Europe (includes South Africa)
4. PepsiCo Asia, Middle East & Africa (AMEA)

Note that PepsiCo breaks down their business in the Americas by foods versus beverages, but their Europe business unit includes beverages, foods, and snacks, as does their AMEA business unit.

PepsiCo's top executives are listed in Exhibit 1 along with an organizational chart. The top Frito-Lay North America executive as well as the top Quaker Foods North America executive report to the CEO, PepsiCo Americas Foods.

Segments

From the four business units listed and described previously, PepsiCo monitors and reports results of their operations in six segments as given below. Note again that outside North America, PepsiCo's beverages and snacks are combined as segments (Europe or ASEA).

Inside North America

1. PepsiCo Americas Beverages (PAB)—sample products include Pepsi, Gatorade, Mountain Dew, Aquafina, 7UP (outside the United States), and Tropicana
2. Frito-Lay North America (FLNA)—sample products include Doritos, Cheetos, Tostitos, Ruffles, Fritos, SunChips, and Santitas
3. Quaker Foods North America (QFNA)—sample products include Quaker oatmeal, Aunt Jemima mixes and syrups, Quaker Chewy granola bars, Quaker grits, Cap'n Crunch cereal, Life cereal, Rice-a-Roni side dishes
4. Latin America Foods (LAF)—includes many of the Frito-Lay and Quaker products

EXHIBIT 1 PepsiCo's Organizational Chart

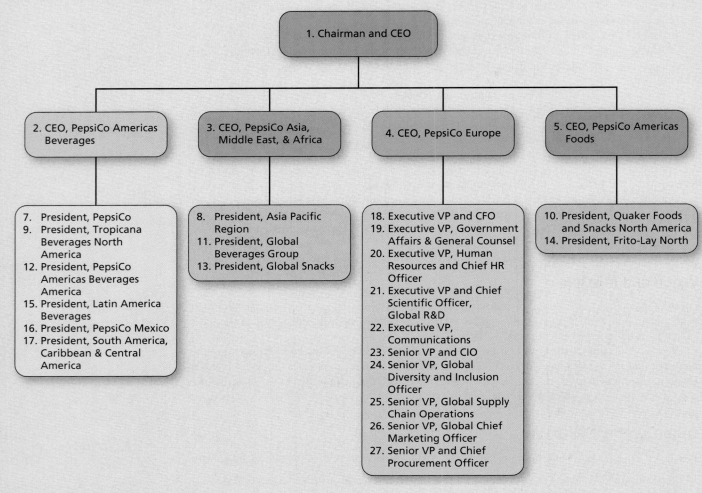

Source: Company documents.

Outside North America

5. Europe—includes many of the beverages and foods listed in inside North America with many modified to match particular country culture and desires

6. Asia, Middle East & Africa (AMEA)—includes many of the beverages and foods listed in inside North America with many modified to match particular country culture and desires

Note in Exhibit 2 that PepsiCo Americas Foods (PAF) segment has the nicest percentage increase (1.8%) in revenue in 2012 verus the prior year, whereas the PepsiCo Americas Beverages (PAB) has the largest decline (1%).

EXHIBIT 2 PepsiCo Revenues (%)

	2012	2011
AMEA	10.2	11.1
Europe	20.5	20.4
PepsiCo Americas Beverages (PAB)	32.7	33.7
PepsiCo Americas Foods (PAF)	36.6	34.8
	100.0	100.0

Source: Company documents.

Note in Exhibit 3 the alarming drop in PepsiCo revenues in 2012 in Mexico, Canada, and "all other countries." The best revenue results were reported from Russia.

Note in Exhibit 4 that AMEA's profit declined 15.9 percent in 2012. Note also in Exhibit 4 that the only real bring spot for PepsiCo in terms of their 2012 operating profit was the 9.9 percent increase in the Europe segment. Most segments reported a decrease.

Note in Exhibit 5 that PepsiCo generates most of their revenue from its PepsiCo Americas Beverages (PAB) segment, followed by its Europe and FLNA. However, note the 2012 decrease in PAB, Europe, and AMEA.

EXHIBIT 3 PepsiCo's Revenue by Country (in millions of $)

Revenue	2012	2011	% Change
USA	33,348	33,053	0.89
Russia	4,861	4,749	2.36
Mexico	3,955	4,782	−17.29
Canada	3,290	3,364	−2.20
UK	2,102	2,075	1.30
Brazil	1,866	1,838	1.52
All Other Countries	16,070	16,643	−3.44

Source: Company documents.

EXHIBIT 4 Recent Trends in PepsiCo's Operating Profit

	2012	2011	2010	2009	% Change 2012	2011
NORTH AMERICA						
FLNA	3,646	3,621	3,376	3,105	0.7	7.3
QFNA	695	797	741	781	−12.8	7.6
LAF	1,059	1,078	1,004	904	−1.8	7.3
PAB	2,937	3,273	2,776	2,172	−10.3	17.9
OUTSIDE NORTH AMERICA						
Europe	1,330	1,210	1,054	948	9.9	14.8
AMEA	747	887	708	700	−15.9	25.3
Total	9,667	9,633	8,332	8,044	0.4	15.6
Operating profit margin	13.9%	14.5%	14.4%	18.6%	−0.6	0.1

Source: Based on company documents.

EXHIBIT 5 PepsiCo's 2012/2011/2010 Revenue/Assets by Segment (in millions of $)

REVENUE	FLNA	QFNA	LAF	PAB	EUROPE	AMEA	TOTAL
2012	13,574	2,636	7,780	21,408	13,441	6,653	65,492
2011	13,322	2,656	7,156	22,418	13,560	7,392	66,504
2010	12,573	2,656	6,315	20,401	9,602	6,291	57,838
TOTAL ASSETS							
2012	5,332	966	4,993	30,899	19,218	5,738	67,146
2011	5,384	1,024	4,721	31,142	18,461	6,038	66,770

Source: Based on company documents.

EXHIBIT 6 PepsiCo v. Coca-Cola, Revenue Results for Q1 2013

PepsiCo v. Coca-Cola: Revenue Contribution: Their Two Biggest Operating Segments

	Q1 2012	Q1 2013	Total Revenue (%)	Change yr. over yr. (%)
PepsiCo				
Frito-Lay North America (FLNA)	$3.01B	$3.12B	24.8%	3.8%
PepsiCo Americas Beverages (PAB)	$4.44B	$4.42B	35.1%	−0.6%
Coca-Cola				
North America	$4.92B	$4.89B	44.3%	−0.7%
Bottling Investments	$2.10B	$2.04B	18.5%	−3.1%

Source: Company documents.

Finance

For Q1 of 2013, PepsiCo's total volume for Snacks and Beverages increased 4 percent and 3 percent, respectively. In international markets, PepsiCo's snacks volume increased 5 percent and beverage volume grew by 6 percent. However, PepsiCo's noncarbonated drink volume (Gatorade and Tropicana juices) dropped by 1 percent, whereas Coca-Cola's comparable products rose 6 percent. PepsiCo's beverages volume increased 1 percent in Latin America, but declined 1 percent in North America. For Q1 of 2013, PepsiCo's European revenues rose 5 percent to $1.94 billion, whereas in Asia, Middle East, and Africa (AMEA) region revenue dropped 14 percent to $1.10 billion (largely as a result of PepsiCo refranchising its beverage business in China), which hurt segment's revenue by 27 percentage points (organic revenue rose 15%).

Comparative information for PepsiCo versus Coca-Cola for Q1 of 2013 is provided in Exhibit 6. Note the 0.6 percent decline in PAB.

Income Statement

PepsiCo's income statements are provided in Exhibit 7. Note the 1.52 percent drop in revenue.

Balance Sheets

PepsiCo's recent balance sheets are provided in Exhibit 8. Note the 2.85 percent decline in property, plant, and equipment, yet a 14.47 percent increase in long-term debt.

Marketing

PepsiCo sales to Walmart Stores, including Sam's Club, represented about 11 percent of total company revenue. PepsiCo's top five retail customers comprise about 30 percent of the firm's North American revenue, with Walmart (including Sam's) representing approximately 17 percent.

CBS's 2013 30-second Super Bowl advertising spots sold for a record $3.7 to $3.8 million each, compared with an average $3.5 million during the 2012 broadcast on NBC. The biggest repeat advertisers were Anheuser-Busch, Coca-Cola Co., PepsiCo, Frito-Lay, and Hyundai. PepsiCo is spending $600 million more in 2013 than 2012 to advertise its beverage brands, with a focus on North America.

Anheuser-Busch InBev and PepsiCo did joint television and retail store promotions leading up to the 2013 Super Bowl on February 3. New in-store signs showed bottles of Pepsi and Bud Light, along with bags of Doritos and the Super Bowl logo. A-B InBev and PepsiCo spend a combined $1.17 billion on measured media annually in the United States. There are rumors that Anheuser-Busch may be interested in purchasing PepsiCo's beverage division.

R&D

PepsiCo's revenue from emerging and developing markets has grown more than 10 percent in the last six years. To meet the needs of varied customers around the world, PepsiCo has ramped up its emphasis on innovation and R&D, increasing their investment in natural sweeteners, packaging, and nutrition platforms. For example, PepsiCo recently launched Quaker Real Medleys, Quaker Congee,

EXHIBIT 7 PepsiCo's Recent Income Statements (in millions of $)

	2012	2011	2010	2009
Revenue	65,492.0	66,504.0	57,838.0	43,251.0
Other Revenue, Total	0.0	0.0	0.0	0.0
Total Revenue	**65,492.0**	**66,504.0**	**57,838.0**	**43,251.0**
Cost of Revenue, Total	31,291.0	31,593.0	26,575.0	20,351.0
Gross Profit	**34,201.0**	**34,911.0**	**31,263.0**	**22,900.0**
Selling/General/Administrative Expenses, Total	24,675.0	24,433.0	21,770.0	15,489.0
Research & Development	0.0	0.0	0.0	388.0
Depreciation/Amortization	119.0	133.0	117.0	64.0
Interest Expense (Income), Net Operating	0.0	0.0	0.0	0.0
Unusual Expense (Income)	295.0	712.0	1,044.0	0.0
Other Operating Expenses, Total	0.0	0.0	0.0	0.0
Operating Income	**9,112.0**	**9,633.0**	**8,332.0**	**6,959.0**
Interest Income (Expense), Net Non-Operating	0.0	0.0	0.0	0.0
Gain (Loss) on Sale of Assets	0.0	0.0	0.0	0.0
Other, Net	0.0	0.0	0.0	0.0
Income Before Tax	**8,304.0**	**8,834.0**	**8,232.0**	**7,045.0**
Income Tax, Total	2,090.0	2,372.0	1,894.0	1,879.0
Income After Tax	**6,214.0**	**6,462.0**	**6,338.0**	**5,166.0**
Minority Interest	−(36.0)	−(19.0)	−(18.0)	−24.0
Equity In Affiliates	0.0	0.0	0.0	0.0
U.S. GAAP Adjustment	0.0	0.0	0.0	0.0
Net Income Before Extra Items	**6,178.0**	**6,443.0**	**6,320.0**	**5,142.0**
Total Extraordinary Items	0.0	0.0	0.0	0.0
Net Income	**6,178.0**	**6,443.0**	**6,320.0**	**5,142.0**

Source: Based on company documents.

breakfast product in China, Tropicana Farmstand, which is a fruit and vegetable juice, Tropicana Fruits in the Middle East, Mountain Dew Kickstart and Doritos Locos Tacos with their key important distributor Taco Bell. New products and new innovation over the past three years accounted for about 8 percent and of PepsiCo's 2012 revenue.

Sustainability

First Lady Michelle Obama heads a campaign to end childhood obesity (titled Let's Move!). Mrs. Obama desires to encourage healthier food options in public schools, improved food nutrition labeling, and increased exercise for children. In response to this initiative, PepsiCo, along with several food manufacturers, formed an alliance called "Healthy Weight Commitment Foundation" whose goal is to collectively cut one trillion calories from their products sold by the end of 2012 and 1.5 trillion calories by the end of 2015. Rival Coca-Cola has recently launched a massive anti-obesity marketing campaign.

PepsiCo recently unveiled the world's first plant-based PET bottle. The bottle is made from plant-based materials, such as switch grass, corn husks, and pine bark, and is 100 percent recyclable. PepsiCo plans to use more by-products (of their manufacturing processes) such as orange peels and oat hulls in the bottles. PepsiCo has identified methods to create a molecular structure that is the same as normal petroleum-based PET—which will make the new bottle technology, dubbed "Green Bottle," feel the same as normal PET. PepsiCo will pilot production in 2012, and on successful completion of the pilot, intends moving to full-scale commercialization.

Coca-Cola has developed the PlantBottle, which is 70 percent petroleum-based and 30 percent sugar cane-based. Coca-Cola plans to transition all of its plastic packaging to PlantBottle by 2020. Coca-Cola's Dasani water brand is provided in PlantBottles.

In September 2012, PepsiCo was recognized by the Dow Jones Sustainability Index (DJSI) and the Carbon Disclosure Project (CDJ) for the company's leadership in promoting sustainable business

EXHIBIT 8 PepsiCo's Recent Balance Sheets (in millions of $)

	2012	2011	2010	2009
Assets				
Cash and Short-Term Investments	6,619.0	4,425.0	6,369.0	2,277.0
Total Receivables, Net	7,041.0	6,912.0	6,323.0	4,683.0
Total Inventory	3,581.0	3,827.0	3,372.0	2,522.0
Prepaid Expenses	1,479.0	2,277.0	1,505.0	1,324.0
Other Current Assets, Total	0.0	0.0	0.0	0.0
Total Current Assets	**18,720.0**	**17,441.0**	**17,569.0**	**10,806.0**
Property/Plant/Equipment, Total, Net	19,136.0	19,698.0	19,058.0	11,663.0
Goodwill, Net	16,971.0	16,800.0	14,661.0	5,124.0
Intangibles, Net	16,525.0	16,445.0	13,808.0	1,860.0
Long-Term Investments	2,351.0	1,566.0	2,021.0	3,883.0
Note Receivable, Long-Term	136.0	159.0	165.0	115.0
Other Long-Term Assets, Total	799.0	773.0	871.0	2,543.0
				0.0
Total Assets	**74,638.0**	**72,882.0**	**68,153.0**	**35,994.0**
Liabilities and SEquity				
Accounts Payable	4,451.0	4,083.0	3,865.0	2,846.0
Payable/Accrued	0.0	0.0	0.0	0.0
Accrued Expenses	3,892.0	3,876.0	3,620.0	2,843.0
Notes Payable/Short-Term Debt	4,815.0	6,205.0	4,898.0	369.0
Current Port. of LT Debt/Capital Leases	0.0	0.0	0.0	0.0
Other Current Liabilities, Total	3,931.0	3,990.0	3,509.0	2,729.0
Total Current Liabilities	**17,089.0**	**18,154.0**	**15,892.0**	**8,787.0**
Total Long-Term Debt	23,544.0	20,568.0	19,999.0	7,858.0
Deferred Income Tax	5,063.0	4,995.0	4,057.0	226.0
Minority Interest	105.0	311.0	312.0	476.0
Other Liabilities, Total	6,543.0	8,266.0	6,729.0	6,541.0
Total Liabilities	**52,344.0**	**52,294.0**	**46,989.0**	**23,888.0**
Redeemable Preferred Stock	0.0	0.0	0.0	0.0
Preferred Stock, Non Redeemable, Net	−(123.0)	−(116.0)	−(109.0)	−97.0
Common Stock	26.0	26.0	31.0	30.0
Additional Paid-In Capital	4,178.0	4,461.0	4,527.0	351.0
Retained Earnings	43,158.0	40,316.0	37,090.0	30,638.0
Treasury Stock, Common	−(19,458.0)	−(17,870.0)	−(16,745.0)	−14,122.0
ESOP Debt Guarantee	0.0	0.0	0.0	0.0
Unrealized Gain (Loss)	0.0	0.0	0.0	0.0
Other SEquity, Total	−(5,487.0)	−(6,229.0)	−(3,630.0)	−4,694.0
Total SEquity	**22,294.0**	**20,588.0**	**21,164.0**	**12,106.0**
Total Liabilities & SEquity	**74,638.0**	**72,882.0**	**68,153.0**	**35,994.0**
Total Common Shares Outstanding	1,544.0	1,565.0	1,581.0	1,553.0
Total Preferred Shares Outstanding	0.8	0.8	0.8	0.8

Source: Based on company documents.

practices. DJSI is comprised of companies across all industries that outperform their peers in numerous sustainability metrics. PepsiCo has been named a member of the Dow Jones Sustainability North America Index seven times and the World Index six times. CDP represents 655 institutional investors with $78 trillion in assets, and its indices highlight companies that have displayed a strong approach to information disclosure regarding climate change. It's the second consecutive year that PepsiCo has been named to the CDP Global and S&P 500 Leadership Indices.

"PepsiCo's Performance with Purpose strategy is built on sustainable business practices that optimize our near-term operating efficiency and profitability while ensuring that we are well positioned to deliver long-term business growth," said Indra Nooyi, Chairman and CEO of PepsiCo.

PepsiCo recently received the Stockholm Industry Water Award in recognition of the company's innovative and outstanding water stewardship initiatives. PepsiCo's fleet of all-electric trucks introduced by its Frito-Lay North America division recently surpassed one million miles driven. These trucks have eliminated the need for approximately 200,000 gallons of diesel fuel.

Both Coca-Cola and PepsiCo have recently changed the ingredients in their cola after a California warning that would link certain ingredients in cola with cancer. Both companies' products contain caramel, which is used to give them a brown color and contains 4-Methylimidazole, which may cause cancer, so both firms have reduced the level of 4-Methy.

Competitors

Although Coca-Cola is PepsiCo's major competitor, other huge firms such as Nestle S.A., Kraft Foods, Kellogg's, Mondelez, Monster, and Dr Pepper Snapple are also major rivals. In 2012, Kellogg acquired Procter & Gamble's Pringles business for about $2.7 billion. This acquisition significantly expanded Kellogg's snack food business that competes with PepsiCo. Pringles is the world's second largest snacks product doing about $1.5 billon annually in sales across more than 140 countries. PepsiCo's plan is to soon produce one half of its snacks sold in the United States with only natural ingredients by, for example, removing monosodium glutamate and about three dozen other artificial ingredients in more than 60 PepsiCo snacks such as Lay's, Tostitos, SunChips, and Rold Gold.

Note in Exhibit 9 that PepsiCo lags Coca-Cola in several important financial measures, including revenue per employee, return on investment, and long-term debt. Note also that PepsiCo has more than 14 times the number of employees as Dr Pepper/Snapple and almost twice Coca-Cola's.

As indicated in Exhibit 10, PepsiCo's packaged food and beverage sales declined 1.52 percent in 2012, but four rival firms all had increases.

EXHIBIT 9 Comparative Information for PepsiCo v. Rivals

	PepsiCo	Dr Pepper/Snapple	Coca-Cola
Employees (#)	280,000	19,000	150,000
Net income ($)	6.12 billion	630 million	8.72 billion
Revenue ($)	66 billion	6 billion	48 billion
Revenue ($)/Employees (#)	225,000	316,000	320,000
EPS (%)	3.90	3.10	1.91
Stock Price ($)	83	49	42
Return on investment (%)	8.3	7.1	10.1
Total long-term debt ($)	23.5 billion	2.55 billion	14.7 billion

Source: Company documents.

EXHIBIT 10 Sales of Packaged Food and Beverages in 2012 (in millions of $)

Company	2012 Sales	2011 Sales	% Change
PepsiCo Inc.	65,492	66,504	−1.52
Kraft Foods	18,339	18,655	−1.69
Coca-Cola Co.	48,017	46,542	+ 3.17
Tyson Foods	33,278	32,266	+ 3.14
General Mills	16,657	14,880	+11.94
Kellogg Co.	14,197	13,198	+ 7.56

Source: Company documents.

Coca-Cola Company

Headquartered in Atlanta, Georgia, Coca-Cola is the leading manufacturer and marketer of nonalcoholic beverages in the world, selling more than 500 nonalcoholic beverage brands globally. Coca-Cola produces and distributes soft drinks, fruit juices, sports/energy drinks, ready-to-drink teas/coffees, and bottled water to customers in more than 200 countries. Coca-Cola brands include four of the world's top five nonalcoholic sparkling beverage products, Coke, Diet Coke, Sprite and Fanta. Coca-Cola has a dominating presence in juices, owning the Minute Maid, Simply and POWERade brands. Coca-Cola possesses one of the largest distribution networks in the world and leverages this to gain and sustain competitive advantage. Coca-Cola generates 70 percent of its revenue and about 80 percent of its operating profit from outside the United States. Coke owns about 80 percent of its distribution in North America.

Because carbonated beverage consumption is at near-zero growth in North America and developed markets, Coca-Cola is rapidly expanding in the emerging markets of India, Russia, and China. Company reports indicate that 43 percent of Coca-Cola's business is generated in the developed markets (USA, Western Europe, Australia, Japan), 37 percent in developing nations and 20 percent in the emerging markets. The company's top management team expects that each of these geographic segments will contribute 33 percent of the company's business by the end of 2020. That is a 10 percent drop in revenue from developed markets. Coca-Cola recently paid $980 million to acquire a roughly 50 percent stake in Aujan Industries, a Middle Eastern beverage company that sells Rani, Vimto (a fruity drink), and malted beverage Barbican. Coca-Cola plans to invest more than $4 billion in China between 2012 and 2015, doubling its revenue from China. As of mid-2012 there were 41 Coca-Cola bottling plants in China.

Some analysts contend that Coca-Cola needs to increase its advertising spending in North America because of PepsiCo's increased focus on North American beverages. Factors that hamper both Coca-Cola and PepsiCo are a slow economic recovery, strained consumer discretionary spending, changing consumer preferences, and increasing health consciousness.

Coca-Cola's Q1 of 2013 revenues and profits were down year-over-year. Coke's profit fell by 15 percent to $1.75 billion and its revenue fell from $11.14 billion to $11.04 billion. For Q1 of 2013, Coca-Cola's International operations reported strong 5 percent volume growth, coming mostly from emerging markets. India and Russia each showed growth of 8 percent whereas Thailand saw the highest growth numbers at 18 percent. Also for Q1 2013, Coca-Cola's sparkling beverage volume growth grew by 3 percent throughout the world, led by Russia where volume grew 15 percent, India 30 percent, Thailand 38 percent, China 6 percent, and Brazil 2 percent.

For Q1 of 2013, Coca-Cola's Latin America and Eurasia & Africa were the only regions where its revenues increased. The company's revenues in North America were down 1 percent to $4.8 billion, in Europe down 2 percent to $1.17 billion, in the Pacific down 4 percent to $1.39 billion, whereas Latin America increased 4 percent to $1.2 billion. Coca-Cola gets more than 40 percent of its revenue from North America where the firm is showing little to no growth; Coca-Cola's bottling investments are its second biggest revenue source, also showing little to no growth.

Dr Pepper Snapple Group (DPS)

Headquartered in Plano, Texas, DPS is the bottler and distributor of drinks in the United States, Canada, and Mexico. DPS offers many popular nonalcoholic beverages including flavored, carbonated soft drinks and noncarbonated soft drinks, along with ready-to-drink noncarbonated teas, juices, juice drinks, and mixers. Among DPS's most popular brands are Dr Pepper, Snapple, A&W Root Beer, 7UP, Hawaiian Punch, Mott's, Schweppes, Vernors, Squirt, Canada Dry, Country Time, Sun Drop, Sun Kist, Yoo-hoo, and Royal Crown (RC) Cola. DPS is the number 3 soft drink company in North America after Coke and Pepsi.

DPS derives 90 percent of its revenue from North America and, 70 percent of that amount comes from carbonated drinks—mostly from 7UP, Sunkist, A&W, and Canada Dry. Given current industry trends, DPS is and must expand globally. DPS has just repurchased distribution rights in its South Asia and Pacific regions, and thus now distribute its products in Australia, China, Japan, South Korea and Malaysia. DPS sales derived from 7/11 stores rose 70 percent in January 2013 compared to the prior year.

Dr Pepper has a strong position in the flavored carbonated soft drinks (CSD) market. Dr Pepper owns some of the most popular CSD and noncarbonated beverages (NCB) brands. DPS also holds the number-1 position in the flavored non-cola CSD market in the USA with a market share of 40 percent. Dr Pepper soft drink, the most popular CSD brand, holds the number-2 position in the flavored CSD market in the USA. DPS makes regular marketing investments to build brand value. Over the last three years, the company has spent more than $100 million of marketing investment in its popular brands.

When it comes to snack foods, investors typically think PepsiCo's Frito-Lay division is dominant with its 40 percent share of the global salty snack market. Frito-Lay does dominate the U.S. snack market with more than 64 percent market share in the salty snack market. Frito-Lay is PepsiCo's most profitable segment, accounting for 40 percent of operating profits. However, Frito-Lay is not nearly as profitable outside the USA, primarily because of a key rival firm, Mondelez International (NASDAQ: MDLZ). Mondelez has the leading market share in every category and every region in which it competes outside the USA. Mondelez owns famous brands such as Oreo, Nabisco, Cadbury, Wheat Thins, Nabisco, and Trident.

Mondelez International

Headquartered in Deerfield, Illinois, Mondelez is number one in the $80 billion market for cookies and crackers, providing food and beverages to consumers in 165 countries around the world. Mondelez produces biscuits, chocolate, candy and powdered beverages as well as gum and coffee, including Oreo, Nabisco and LU biscuits; Milka, Cadbury Dairy Milk and Cadbury chocolates; Trident gum; Jacobs coffee; and Tang powdered beverage. In late 2012, Mondelez completed the spin-off of its North American grocery business, Kraft Foods Group, Inc. (Kraft Foods Group).

Rumors are that Mondelez's top management would support a sale to PepsiCo, whose $7 billion in cash makes it capable of such an acquisition. Acquiring Mondelez would boost earnings at PepsiCo and may even spur the firm to go ahead and spin off its slower-growing beverage unit, which rumors indicate might happen anyway. Such a two-prong (acquisition/divestiture) PepsiCo strategy would enable the firm to repackage itself as a purely snacks firm and would get rid of its major snacks rival (Mondelez) outside the USA. Mondelez would benefit because it does not have PepsiCo's vast direct-store-delivery network, which allows PepsiCo to maintain direct relationships with retailers, which increases its bargaining power. PepsiCo maintains excellent control over its distribution and can deliver both snacks and carbonated soft drinks in a cost-efficient manner.

Monster Beverage Corp.

Headquartered in Corona, California, Monster (NASDAQ: MNST) recently posted 8 percent growth in the energy drinks category of the beverage industry, but that was down in comparison to previous years, primarily as a result of strong competition from rival Red Bull, which reported 7.5 percent growth in February 2013. For Monster, the consumer preference shift from carbonated drinks to energy drinks is a huge opportunity, so the firm is adding "rehab" drinks and flavors to its product portfolio. The company's energy drinks comprise 90 percent of its overall revenue. Monster's sales outside the USA are growing rapidly. Monster posted more than 35 percent sales growth year-over-year in Q4 of 2012 by selling its products in more than 90 countries globally, excluding the USA. "Monster Energy" is one of its top-selling products. During Q1 of 2013, Monster began distribution in Slovenia, Peru, Chile, Korea, Singapore, India, Romania, Albania, and Croatia, with additional markets in Central/Eastern Europe being served by mid-2013. Monster expects to deliver earning growth of 20 percent year-over-year starting from 2013.

External Issues

Per capita soda consumption in the USA has been declining for years and is now 44 gallons per person, down from 54 gallons in 1998, mainly as a result of increasing health concerns about sugary, carbonated drinks. However, recent research by the U.S. Food and Beverage Industry indicates that the food and beverage industry will see substantial growth in 2013 from new health/wellness products (51%), increased selling prices (40%), and new customers (59%). These changes are resultant of consumer's preference shift from soda drinks to juice, tea and flavored water.

A few statistics about the U.S. soft drinks industry, reported in January 2013 at http://beta.fool.com/ronchat/2012/12/27/which-one-you-should-go-coca-cola-or-pepsico/19668/?ticker=PEP&source=eogyholnk0000001, are given here:

1. "The soft drink sector earns $60 billion in annual revenue and produces 15 billion gallons of soft drinks a year.
2. The average 12-19 year-old age drinks the equivalent of 868 cans a year.
3. 56% of 8-year-olds drink at least one can of soda pop daily.
4. Soft drink purchases by teenagers in schools surged by 1,100% over the past 20 years, while dairy product purchases dropped by 30%.
5. Soft drinks account for more than 25% of all drinks consumed in the USA."

The IGD, a U.K.-based industry group, reported in April 2012 that the Chinese retail grocery market was estimated at 607 billion, followed by the USA at 572 billion, Japan at 254 billion, India at 244 billion, and Brazil at 212 billion. The Chinese market is expected by 2015 to be worth 918 billion, followed by the USA at 675 billion, but then comes India, Russia, and Brazil.

Consumers are trying to eat fresher, healthier snacks, beverages, and food. The volume of packaged food consumed is declining whereas the volume of fresh food is increasing. Firms like PepsiCo are actively developing a variety of healthier foods and beverages that focus on such areas as nutrition, weight management, improved digestion, disease prevention, and allergy remedies. These new products generally contain fewer calories, less fat, low carbohydrates, or less sugar and sodium. Many new products are gluten-free or whole-fiber.

The effort to eat and drink healthier generally increases with age, so there is a growing overlap among food and beverage industry with the healthcare and cosmetics industries. PepsiCo has a new zero-calorie sweetener called Stevia and Coca-Cola has a similar product call Truvia, both aimed at reducing the obesity concerns of consumers and governments. PepsiCo is used in PepsiCo's new Gatorade product, G2 Natural, and is its SoBe Lifewater and in reduced-calorie Tropicana 50. PepsiCo recently launched Sierra Mist as Sierra Mist Natural, made with real sugar rather than high-fructose corn syrup.

As indicated in Exhibit 11, consumers are drinking less carbonated beverages. In the United States, consumption is declining 1 percent annually compared to an increase of 1 percent for all refreshment beverages.

Note in Exhibit 12 that the relative market share of Pepsi-Cola and Diet Pepsi-Cola slipped more than other carbonated soft drink brands in 2011. Note also that Coca-Cola has the two best selling products and that PepsiCo's market share did not increase for any of their products.

Increasingly, beverage companies are offering smaller containers to meet consumer preference for lower price, less sugar, fewer calories, and smaller households. About 28 percent of USA adults live alone, with retired empty nesters comprising the largest part of that number. Coca-Cola has reduced the size of its cans in the eight-can pack from 8.0 ounces to 7.5 ounces to bring the calorie count below 100.

EXHIBIT 11 Percent Change in U.S. Consumption in 2011 v. 2010

Category	Change (%)
Carbonated beverages	−1.0
Energy drinks	+ 14.4
Ready-to-drink coffee	+ 9.4
Sports drinks	+ 8.8
Bottled water	+ 4.1

Source: Based on Beverage marketing Corp. information.

EXHIBIT 12 The Best Selling Carbonated Soft Drinks in the USA (2011)

Brand	Company	Market Share (%)	Change from 2010 (%)
Coke	Coca-Cola	17.0	0.0
Diet Coke	Coca-Cola	9.9	−0.3
Pepsi-Cola	PepsiCo	9.2	−0.3
Mt. Dew	PepsiCo	6.7	−0.1
Dr Pepper	Dr Pepper/Snapple	6.4	+0.1
Sprite	Coca-Cola	5.7	+0.1
Diet Pepsi	PepsiCo	4.9	−0.4
Diet Mt. Dew	PepsiCo	2.0	0.0
Fanta	Coca-Cola	1.9	+0.1
Diet Dr Pepper	Dr Pepper/Snapple	1.8	−0.1

Source: Based on information at *Beverage Digest*.

As a result of rising concern for healthy drinking and eating, especially in the USA and developed countries, companies are promoting both what their products contain (e.g., antioxidants) and what they do not contain (e.g., trans fats). The dramatic shift away from carbonated soft drinks and flavored water and to energy drinks, sports drinks, and bottled water is significant. Coca-Cola is more vulnerable than PepsiCo to the shift away from carbonated beverages. Regarding energy drinks, Coca-Cola has tried to sell Full Throttle, NOS, Surge, and Vault—without much success. Similarly, PepsiCo has tried to sell Amp and Kickstart. Leading energy drinks are Red Bull, Monster, and 5-Hour Energy. A privately-held firm, Living Essentials, owns both Red Bull and 5-Hour Energy.

Labeling Issues

Beverage companies are increasingly being required to disclose on their packages the contents of their products, especially in terms of calories, sugar, chemicals, caffeine, sweeteners, etc. For example, corn sugar cannot be used for the ingredient "high-fructose corn syrup," which has been aligned with the national obesity problem. Many consumers prefer sugar to high-fructose corn syrup, believing sugar is healthier.

Currency Exchange Rates

A strong U.S. dollar is generally unfavorable to sales and earnings of PepsiCo and Coca-Cola, because a strong dollar makes U.S. goods less affordable for markets with weak currencies. Also, a stronger dollar causes international revenues/profits of U.S. multinational firms to be translated back (based on currency exchange rates) into a smaller amount of U.S. dollars.

The Future

PepsiCo, Coca-Cola, and feisty smaller rivals continue to battle daily for shelf space at millions of retail outlets globally. Beverage and snack companies continue to expand aggressively globally because the U.S. market offers minimal to no growth in sugary, carbonated beverages.

There is speculation among analysts that PepsiCo will split into two separate companies, and that Anheuser-Busch may in interested in the beverage segment. Another speculation is that PepsiCo will try to acquire Mondelez International or Monster Beverage. Pepsi is also in talks to buy Soda Stream, an Israeli company that makes machines that convert tap water into carbonated drinks. That deal could be worth $2 billion, but PepsiCo is denying the rumor.

ASSURANCE OF LEARNING EXERCISES

EXERCISE 1A
Compare Business Strategy with Military Strategy

Purpose

This exercise will enable you to compare and contrast military strategy with business strategy because in many ways, operating a business is similar to conducting a military campaign. Many strategic-management concepts evolved out of the military. Napoleon Bonaparte listed 115 maxims for military strategy. U.S. Civil War General Nathan Bedford Forrest, however, had only one strategic principle: "to git thar furst with the most men" (to get there first with the most men). The strategy concepts given as essential in the United States Army's Field Manual (FM-3-0) of Military Operations (sections 4–32 to 4–39) says there are nine key military strategy maxims:

1. Objective—direct every military operation towards a clearly defined, decisive, and attainable objective
2. Offensive—seize, retain, and exploit the initiative
3. Mass—concentrate combat power at the decisive place and time
4. Economy of Force—allocate minimum essential combat power to secondary efforts

5. Maneuver—place the enemy in a disadvantageous position through the flexible application of combat power
6. Unity of Command—for every objective, ensure unity of effort under one responsible commander
7. Security—never permit the enemy to acquire an unexpected advantage
8. Surprise—strike the enemy at a time, at a place, or in a manner for which he is unprepared
9. Simplicity—prepare clear, uncomplicated plans and clear, concise orders to ensure thorough understanding

Instructions

Step 1   Consider the extent to which each of the nine maxims listed are applicable in formulating and implementing strategies in a business setting.

Step 2   Rank order the nine maxims above, from 1 = most important to 9 = least important in formulating and implementing strategies in a business setting.

Step 3   Provide a rationale for each of your rankings in Step 2.

EXERCISE 1B
Gather Strategy Information for PepsiCo

Purpose

The purpose of this exercise is to get you familiar with strategy terms introduced and defined in this chapter. Let's apply these terms to PepsiCo, Inc. (stock symbol = PEP).

Instructions

Step 1   Go to www.pepsico.com (PepsiCo's website). Along the top of the site, click on Relations. Then click on 2012 *Annual Report* and print that document. The *Form 10K* or *Annual Report* document contains excellent information for developing a list of PepsiCo's internal strengths and weaknesses.

Step 2   Go to your college library and make a copy of Standard & Poor's Industry Surveys for the snacks/beverages industry. This document will contain excellent information for developing a list of external opportunities and threats facing PEP.

Step 3   Go to the www.finance.yahoo.com website. Enter PEP. Note the wealth of information on PepsiCo that may be obtained by clicking any item along the left column. Click on Competitors down the left column. Then print out the resultant tables and information. Note that PepsiCo's major competitors are Coca-Cola Company, Kraft Foods, and Dr Pepper Snapple.

Step 4   Using the Cohesion Case, the www.finance.yahoo.com information, the *Annual Report*, and the Industry Survey document, on a separate sheet of paper list what you consider to be PepsiCo's ten major strengths, ten major weaknesses, ten major opportunities, and ten major threats. Each factor listed for this exercise must include a percent, number, dollar, or ratio to reveal some quantified fact or trend. These factors provide the underlying basis for a strategic plan because a firm strives to take advantage of strengths, improve weaknesses, avoid threats, and capitalize on opportunities.

Step 5   Through class discussion, compare your lists of external and internal factors to those developed by other students and add to your lists of factors. Keep this information for use in later exercises at the end of other chapters.

Step 6   Whatever case company is assigned to you this semester, update the information on your company by following the steps listed in this Exerise 1B.

EXERCISE 1C
Update the PepsiCo Cohesion Case

Purpose

Every week PepsiCo updates its website with News Releases of important strategic decisions and information. Since the time this text was published, more than 50 PepsiCo News Releases have been posted. In performing strategic planning and classroom strategic-management case analysis, it is important to have the latest information possible on which to base decisions and processes.

Instructions

Step 1   Go to the www.pepsico.com website and near the bottom of the page, click on News & Press Releases. Read the most recent PepsiCo Press Releases.

Step 2   Type a two-page Executive Summary of PepsiCo's newest strategies being formulated and implemented.

Step 3   Submit your report to your professor.

 EXERCISE 1D
Strategic Planning for Your University

Purpose

External and internal factors are the underlying bases of strategies formulated and implemented by organizations. Your college or university faces numerous external opportunities and threats and has many internal strengths and weaknesses. The purpose of this exercise is to illustrate the process of identifying critical external and internal factors.

External influences include trends in the following areas: economic, social, cultural, demographic, environmental, technological, political, legal, governmental, and competitive. External factors could include declining numbers of high school graduates; population shifts; community relations; increased competitiveness among colleges and universities; rising numbers of adults returning to college; decreased support from local, state, and federal agencies; increasing numbers of foreign students attending U.S. colleges; and a rising number of Internet courses.

Internal factors of a college or university include faculty, students, staff, alumni, athletic programs, physical plant, grounds and maintenance, student housing, administration, fund-raising, academic programs, food services, parking, placement, clubs, fraternities, sororities, and public relations.

Instructions

Step 1   On a separate sheet of paper, write four headings: External Opportunities, External Threats, Internal Strengths, and Internal Weaknesses.

Step 2   As related to your college or university, list five factors under each of the four headings.

Step 3   Discuss the factors as a class. Write the factors on the board.

Step 4   What new things did you learn about your university from the class discussion? How could this type of discussion benefit an organization?

 EXERCISE 1E
Strategic Planning at a Local Company

Purpose

This activity is aimed at giving you practical knowledge about how organizations in your city or town are doing strategic planning. This exercise also will give you experience interacting on a professional basis with local business leaders.

Instructions

Step 1   Use the telephone to contact business owners or top managers. Find an organization that does strategic planning. Make an appointment to visit with the strategist (president, chief executive officer, or owner) of that business.

Step 2   Seek answers to the following questions during the interview:
- How does your firm formally conduct strategic planning? Who is involved in the process? Does the firm hold planning retreats? If yes, how often and where?
- Does your firm have a written mission statement? How was the statement developed? When was the statement last changed?
- What are the benefits of engaging in strategic planning?
- What are the major costs or problems in doing strategic planning in your business?
- Do you anticipate making any changes in the strategic-planning process at your company? If yes, please explain.

Step 3   Report your findings to the class.

EXERCISE 1F
Get Familiar With the Strategy Club Website

Purpose

You may use for free all the resources provided at the author website, www.strategyclub.com, including the downloadable Excel student template. Thousands of students have found this template to be immensely useful in preparing a strategic management case analysis.

Instructions

Step 1   Go to the www.strategyclub.com website. Review the following free resources:
1. Excel student template
2. sample case analysis PowerPoints
3. live case analysis presentations
4. chapter updates

Step 2   Prepare to give your class an overview of your impression of the website.

EXERCISE 1G
Get Familiar with the Case MyLab

Purpose

The Case MyLab testing feature that accompanies this textbook may be used by your professor to help apply chapter concepts using various of the 29 cases found in this text. This exercise gets you familiar with this new feature.

Instructions

Step 1   Find in the Preface of this textbook the section that describes the Case MyLab testing feature. Read this material.

Step 2   Be able to describe for your professor the purpose and nature of the Case MyLab.

Step 3   For your assigned case company, identify three strategic management concepts represented in your case.

Step 4   Be able to describe for your professor how your assigned case company is performing on the three concepts.

Endnotes

1. Kathy Kiely, "Officials Say Auto CEOs Must Be Specific on Plans," *USA Today*, November 24, 2008, 3B.
2. Peter Drucker, *Management: Tasks, Responsibilities, and Practices* (New York: Harper & Row, 1974), 611.
3. Alfred Sloan, Jr., *Adventures of the White Collar Man* (New York: Doubleday, 1941), 104.
4. Quoted in Eugene Raudsepp, "Can You Trust Your Hunches?" *Management Review* 49, no. 4 (April 1960): 7.
5. Stephen Harper, "Intuition: What Separates Executives from Managers," *Business Horizons* 31, no. 5 (September–October 1988): 16.
6. Ron Nelson, "How to Be a Manager," *Success*, July–August 1985, 69.
7. Bruce Henderson, *Henderson on Corporate Strategy* (Boston: Abt Books, 1979), 6.
8. Robert Waterman, Jr., *The Renewal Factor: How the Best Get and Keep the Competitive Edge* (New York: Bantam, 1987). See also *BusinessWeek*, September 14, 1987, 100. Also, see *Academy of Management Executive* 3, no. 2 (May 1989): 115.
9. Jayne O'Donnell, "Shoppers Flock to Discount Stores," *USA Today*, February 25, 2009, B1.
10. John Pearce II and Fred David, "The Bottom Line on Corporate Mission Statements," *Academy of Management Executive* 1, no. 2 (May 1987): 109.
11. Lukas Alpert, "Kremlin Cracks Down on Big Tobacco," *Wall Street Journal* (October 16, 2012): B1.
12. Fred R. David, "How Companies Define Their Mission," *Long Range Planning* 22, no. 1 (February 1989): 91.
13. Jack Pearce and Richard Robinson, *Strategic Management,* 7th ed. (New York: McGraw-Hill, 2000), 8.
14. Ann Langley, "The Roles of Formal Strategic Planning," *Long Range Planning* 21, no. 3 (June 1988): 40.
15. Bernard Reimann, "Getting Value from Strategic Planning," *Planning Review* 16, no. 3 (May–June 1988): 42.
16. G. L. Schwenk and K. Schrader, "Effects of Formal Strategic Planning in Financial Performance in Small Firms: A Meta-Analysis," *Entrepreneurship and Practice* 3, no. 17 (1993): 53–64. Also, C. C. Miller and L. B. Cardinal, "Strategic Planning and Firm

Performance: A Synthesis of More Than Two Decades of Research," *Academy of Management Journal* 6, no. 27 (1994): 1649–1665; Michael Peel and John Bridge, "How Planning and Capital Budgeting Improve SME Performance," *Long Range Planning* 31, no. 6 (October 1998): 848–856; Julia Smith, "Strategies for Start-Ups," *Long Range Planning* 31, no. 6 (October 1998): 857–872.

17. Gordon Greenley, "Does Strategic Planning Improve Company Performance?" *Long Range Planning* 19, no. 2 (April 1986): 106.

18. Adapted from www.des.calstate.edu/limitations.html and www.entarga.com/stratplan/purposes.html

19. R. T. Lenz, "Managing the Evolution of the Strategic Planning Process," *Business Horizons* 30, no. 1 (January–February 1987): 39.

20. *Webster's New World Dictionary*, Year: 1998. Publisher: Pearson plc. Edition: 4th. Edited by Victoria Neufeldt. Pearson purchased this Dictionary from Simon & Schuster in 1998, but sold it to IDG Books in 1999.

21. Frederick Gluck, "Taking the Mystique out of Planning," *Across the Board*, July–August 1985, 59.

## PART 2

STRATEGY FORMULATION

2

Source: Pressmaster/Shutterstock

MyManagementLab®

⭐ **Improve Your Grade!**

Over 10 million students improved their results using the Pearson MyLabs.
Visit **mymanagementlab.com** for simulations, tutorials, and end-of-chapter problems.

The Business Vision and Mission

CHAPTER OBJECTIVES

After studying this chapter, you should be able to do the following:

1. Describe the nature and role of vision and mission statements in strategic management.

2. Discuss why the process of developing a mission statement is as important as the resulting document.

3. Identify the components of mission statements.

4. Discuss how clear vision and mission statements can benefit other strategic-management activities.

5. Evaluate mission statements of different organizations.

6. Write good vision and mission statements.

ASSURANCE OF LEARNING EXERCISES

The following exercises are found at the end of this chapter.

This chapter focuses on the concepts and tools needed to evaluate and write business vision and mission statements. A practical framework for developing mission statements is provided. Actual mission statements from large and small organizations and for-profit and nonprofit enterprises are presented and critically examined. The process of creating a vision and mission statement is discussed. The recent economic recession resulted in many firms changing direction and thereby altering their entire vision and mission. For example, Microsoft entered the smartphone business with Nokia, and IBM is focusing more on business analytics.

The boxed insert company examined in this chapter is J. Crew, which has a clear strategic plan. Note that J. Crew has more than 400 stores in the USA and Canada.

We can perhaps best understand vision and mission by focusing on a business when it is first started. In the beginning, a new business is simply a collection of ideas. Starting a new business rests on a set of beliefs that the new organization can offer some product or service to some customers in some geographic area using some type of technology at a profitable price. A new business owner typically believes that the management philosophy of the new enterprise will result in a favorable public image and that this concept of the business can be communicated to, and will be adopted by, important constituencies. When the set of beliefs about a business at its inception is put into writing, the resulting document mirrors the same basic ideas that underlie the vision and mission statements. As a business grows, owners or managers find it necessary to revise the founding set of beliefs, but those original ideas usually are reflected in the revised statements of vision and mission.

Vision and mission statements often can be found in the front of annual reports. They often are displayed throughout a firm's premises and are distributed with company information sent to constituencies. The statements are part of numerous internal reports, such as loan requests, supplier agreements, labor relations contracts, business plans, and customer service agreements.

EXCELLENT **STRATEGIC MANAGEMENT** SHOWCASE

J. Crew Group, Inc.

Do you wear J. Crew apparel? Headquartered in New York City, J. Crew is clothing retailer known for its cashmere cardigans, Capri pants, jeans, khakis, and other basic (but pricey) items sold to young professionals through its catalogs, websites, and more than 360 retail and factory stores in the USA and Canada under the J. Crew, crewcuts (for kids), and Madewell brand names. Madewell is a women's-only collection of hip, casual clothes. J. Crew's CEO Millard Drexler in recent years has presided over excellent strategic management as his company aggressively expands both in the USA and in Asia. J. Crew debuted its fashions in Hong Kong and Beijing in late 2012 at Lane Crawford, Asia's version of Barney's New York. Armed with new strategies and enthusiasm, Drexler also wants to return J. Crew to Japan where it faltered four years ago.

Another recent, effective strategy for J. Crew has been their shipping online orders to more than 100 countries as a way to test the markets. Australia, Japan, and Hong Kong are now among J. Crew's top five international e-commerce markets. J. Crew does not plan to expand globally with local partners as the company did unsuccessfully in Japan a few years ago. Drexler says: "We like control. We have the capital to do it, and I don't want to visit a store where I have to discuss with my partner what I like or don't like about my store."

J. Crew opened 42 new stores in the USA in 2012. Drexler says: "Unlike many of our competitors, we are not in Asia because we are running out of places to go in America. We have so much organic growth there." Drexler is delighted that Asian and Australian customers are attracted to his company's high-quality apparel, and he intends to serve them both with online orders and slowly with free-standing stores. J. Crew was taken private by TPG Capital and Leonard Green & Partners in 2011, and since then has been doing well.

Although not given at the company website (**www.jcrew.com**), J. Crew's mission statement may include the following phrase that the firm uses often: "Quality is our highest priority. Always has been, always will be."

Source: Based on Jeffrey Mg and Mariko Sanchanta, "J. Crew Brings Its Brand to China," *Wall Street Journal* (August 1, 2012): B8.

What Do We Want to Become?

It is especially important for managers and executives in any organization to agree on the basic vision that the firm strives to achieve in the long term. A vision statement should answer the basic question, "What do we want to become?" A clear vision provides the foundation for developing a comprehensive mission statement. Many organizations have both a vision and mission statement, but the vision statement should be established first and foremost. The vision statement should be short, preferably one sentence, and as many managers as possible should have input into developing the statement. Where there is no vision, the people perish (Proverbs 29: 18)

Several example vision statements are provided in Table 2-1.

What Is Our Business?

Current thought on mission statements is based largely on guidelines set forth in the mid-1970s by Peter Drucker, who is often called "the father of modern management" for his pioneering studies at General Motors and for his 22 books and hundreds of articles. *Harvard Business Review* has called Drucker "the preeminent management thinker of our time."

Drucker says that asking the question "What is our business?" is synonymous with asking the question "What is our mission?" An enduring statement of purpose that distinguishes one organization from other similar enterprises, the **mission statement** is a declaration of an organization's "reason for being." It answers the pivotal question "What is our business?" A clear mission statement is essential for effectively establishing objectives and formulating strategies.

Sometimes called a **creed statement**, a statement of purpose, a statement of philosophy, a statement of beliefs, a statement of business principles, or a statement "defining our business," a mission statement reveals what an organization wants to be and whom it wants to serve. All organizations have a reason for being, even if strategists have not consciously transformed this reason into writing. As illustrated with white shading in Figure 2-1, carefully prepared statements of vision and mission are widely recognized by both practitioners and academicians as the first step in strategic management. Drucker has the following to say about mission statements (paraphrased):

TABLE 2-1   Vision Statement Examples

Tyson Foods' vision is to be the world's first choice for protein solutions while maximizing shareholder value. *(Author comment: Good statement, unless Tyson provides nonprotein products)*

General Motors' vision is to be the world leader in transportation products and related services. *(Author comment: Good statement)*

PepsiCo's responsibility is to continually improve all aspects of the world in which we operate—environment, social, economic—creating a better tomorrow than today. *(Author comment: Statement is too vague; it should reveal beverage and food business)*

Dell's vision is to create a company culture where environmental excellence is second nature. *(Author comment: Statement is too vague; it should reveal computer business in some manner; the word environmental is generally used to refer to natural environment so is unclear in its use here)*

The vision of First Reliance Bank is to be recognized as the largest and most profitable bank in South Carolina. *(Author comment: This is a small new bank headquartered in Florence, South Carolina, so this goal is not achievable in five years; the statement is too futuristic)*

Samsonite's vision is to provide innovative solutions for the traveling world. *(Author comment: Statement needs to be more specific, perhaps mention luggage; statement as is could refer to air carriers or cruise lines, which is not good)*

Royal Caribbean's vision is to empower and enable our employees to deliver the best vacation experience for our guests, thereby generating superior returns for our shareholders and enhancing the well-being of our communities. *(Author comment: Statement is good but could end after the word "guests")*

Procter & Gamble's vision is to be, and be recognized as, the best consumer products company in the world. *(Author comment: Statement is too vague and readability is not that good)*

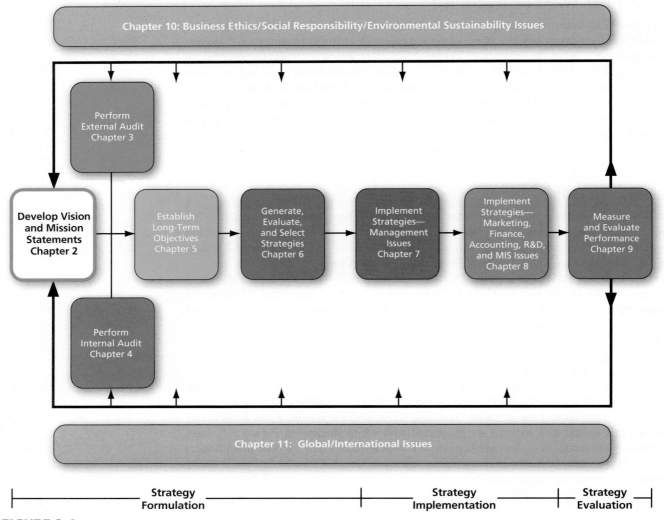

FIGURE 2-1

A Comprehensive Strategic-Management Model

Source: Fred R. David, "How Companies Define Their Mission," *Long Range Planning* 22, no. 3 (June 1988): 40.

A mission statement is the foundation for priorities, strategies, plans, and work assignments. It is the starting point for the design of jobs and organizational structures. Nothing may seem simpler or more obvious than to know what a company's business is. A lumber mill makes lumber, an airline carries passengers and freight, and a bank lends money. But "What is our business?" is almost always a difficult question and the right answer is usually anything but obvious. The answer to this question is the first responsibility of strategists.[1]

Some strategists spend almost every moment of every day on administrative and tactical concerns, and strategists who rush quickly to establish objectives and implement strategies often overlook the development of a vision and mission statement. This problem is widespread even among large organizations. Many corporations in the USA have not yet developed a formal vision or mission statement. An increasing number of organizations are developing these statements.

Some companies develop mission statements simply because they feel it is fashionable, rather than out of any real commitment. However, as described in this chapter, firms that develop and systematically revisit their vision and mission statements, treat them as living documents, and consider them to be an integral part of the firm's culture realize great benefits. Johnson & Johnson (J&J) is an example firm. J&J managers meet regularly with employees to review, reword, and reaffirm the firm's vision and mission. The entire J&J workforce recognizes the value that top management places on this exercise, and these employees respond accordingly.

Vision versus Mission

Many organizations develop both a mission statement and a vision statement. Whereas the mission statement answers the question "What is our business?" the **vision statement** answers the question "What do we want to become?" Many organizations have both a mission and vision statement.

For many if not most corporations, profit rather than mission or vision is the primary motivator. But profit alone is not enough to motivate people. Profit is perceived negatively by many stakeholders of a firm. For example, employees may see profit as something that they earn and management then uses and even gives away to shareholders. Although this perception is undesired and disturbing to management, it clearly indicates that both profit and vision are needed to motivate a workforce effectively.

When employees and managers together shape or fashion the vision and mission statements for a firm, the resultant documents can reflect the personal visions that managers and employees have in their hearts and minds about their own futures. Shared vision creates a commonality of interests that can lift workers out of the monotony of daily work and put them into a new world of opportunity and challenge.

Vision Statement Analysis

A vision statement should at a minimum reveal the type of business the firm engages. For example, to have a vision that says "to become the best retailing firm in the USA" is not good, because that firm could be selling anything from boats to bunnies.

STARBUCKS PROPOSED VISION STATEMENT

"Starbucks strives to ethically find and roast the highest quality Arabica coffee in the world. With stores around the world, we are the premier roaster and retailer of specialty coffee globally."

STARBUCKS "IMPROVED" VISION STATEMENT

Starbucks' vision is to be the most well-known, specialty coffee, tea, and pastry restaurant in the world, offering sincere customer service, a welcoming atmosphere, and unequaled quality.

STARBUCKS VISION STATEMENT ANALYSIS

- The existing vision statement does not state what the company wants to become. Nor does it acknowledge the firm's movement into specialty tea offerings.
- The improved vision statement reveals the company's aspirations for the future and acknowledges that upscale tea and pastries complement their premium coffee offerings.

The Process of Developing Vision and Mission Statements

As indicated in the strategic-management model, clear vision and mission statements are needed before alternative strategies can be formulated and implemented. As many managers as possible should be involved in the process of developing these statements because, through involvement, people become committed to an organization.

A widely used approach to developing a vision and mission statement is first to select several articles about these statements and ask all managers to read these as background information. Then ask managers themselves to prepare a vision and mission statement for the organization. A facilitator or committee of top managers should then merge these statements into a single document and distribute the draft statements to all managers. A request for modifications, additions, and deletions is needed next, along with a meeting to revise the document. To the extent that all managers have input into and support the final documents, organizations can more easily obtain managers' support for other strategy formulation, implementation, and evaluation activities. Thus, the process of developing a vision and mission statement represents a great opportunity for strategists to obtain needed support from all managers in the firm.

During the process of developing vision and mission statements, some organizations use discussion groups of managers to develop and modify existing statements. Some organizations hire an outside consultant or facilitator to manage the process and help draft the language. Sometimes an outside person with expertise in developing such statements, who has unbiased views, can manage the process more effectively than an internal group or committee of managers. Decisions on how best to communicate the vision and mission to all managers, employees, and external constituencies of an organization are needed when the documents are in final form. Some organizations even develop a videotape to explain the statements and how they were developed.

An article by Campbell and Yeung emphasizes that the process of developing a mission statement should create an "emotional bond" and "sense of mission" between the organization and its employees.[2] Commitment to a company's strategy and intellectual agreement on the strategies to be pursued do not necessarily translate into an emotional bond; hence, strategies that have been formulated may not be implemented. These researchers stress that an emotional bond comes when an individual personally identifies with the underlying values and behavior of a firm, thus turning intellectual agreement and commitment to strategy into a sense of mission. Campbell and Yeung also differentiate between the terms *vision* and *mission*, saying that vision is "a possible and desirable future state of an organization" that includes specific goals, whereas mission is more associated with behavior and the present.

Importance (Benefits) of Vision and Mission Statements

The importance (benefits) of vision and mission statements to effective strategic management is well documented in the literature, although research results are mixed. Rarick and Vitton found that firms with a formalized mission statement have twice the average return on shareholders' equity than those firms without a formalized mission statement have; Bart and Baetz found a positive relationship between mission statements and organizational performance; *BusinessWeek* reports that firms using mission statements have a 30 percent higher return on certain financial measures than those without such statements; however, some studies have found that having a mission statement does not directly contribute positively to financial performance.[3] The extent of manager and employee involvement in developing vision and mission statements can make a difference in business success. This chapter provides guidelines for developing these important documents. In actual practice, wide variations exist in the nature, composition, and use of both vision and mission statements. King and Cleland recommend that organizations carefully develop a written mission statement in order to reap the following benefits:

1. To make sure all employees/managers understand the firm's purpose or reason for being.
2. To provide a basis for prioritization of key internal and external factors utilized to formulate feasible strategies.
3. To provide a basis for the allocation of resources.
4. To provide a basis for organizing work, departments, activities, and segments around a common purpose.[4]

Reuben Mark, former CEO of Colgate, maintains that a clear mission increasingly must make sense internationally. Mark's thoughts on vision are as follows:

> When it comes to rallying everyone to the corporate banner, it's essential to push one vision globally rather than trying to drive home different messages in different cultures. The trick is to keep the vision simple but elevated: "We make the world's fastest computers" or "Telephone service for everyone." You're never going to get anyone to charge the machine guns only for financial objectives. It's got to be something that makes people feel better, feel a part of something.[5]

A Resolution of Divergent Views

Another benefit of developing a comprehensive mission statement is that divergent views among managers can be revealed and resolved through the process. The question "What is our business?" can create controversy. Raising the question often reveals differences among strategists in the organization. Individuals who have worked together for a long time and who think they know each other suddenly may realize that they are in fundamental disagreement.

For example, in a college or university, divergent views regarding the relative importance of teaching, research, and service often are expressed during the mission statement development process. Negotiation, compromise, and eventual agreement on important issues are needed before people can focus on more specific strategy-formulation activities.

Considerable disagreement among an organization's strategists over vision and mission statements can cause trouble if not resolved. For example, unresolved disagreement over the business mission was one of the reasons for W. T. Grant's bankruptcy and eventual liquidation. Top executives of the firm, including Ed Staley and Lou Lustenberger, were firmly entrenched in opposing positions that W. T. Grant should be like Kmart or JC Penney respectively. W.T. Grant decided to become a bit like both Kmart and JC Penney; this compromise was a huge strategic mistake. In other words, top executives of W. T. Grant never resolved their vision/mission issue, which ultimately led to the firm's disappearance.[6]

Too often, strategists develop vision and business mission statements only when the organization is in trouble. Of course, it is needed then. Developing and communicating a clear mission during troubled times indeed may have spectacular results and even may reverse decline. However, to wait until an organization is in trouble to develop a vision and mission statement is a gamble that characterizes irresponsible management. According to Drucker, the most important time to ask seriously, "What do we want to become?" and "What is our business?" is when a company has been successful:

> Success always obsoletes the very behavior that achieved it, always creates new realities, and always creates new and different problems. Only the fairy tale story ends, "They lived happily ever after." It is never popular to argue with success or to rock the boat. It will not be long before success will turn into failure. Sooner or later, even the most successful answer to the question "What is our business?" becomes obsolete.[7]

In multidivisional organizations, strategists should ensure that divisional units perform strategic-management tasks, including the development of a statement of vision and mission. Each division should involve its own managers and employees in developing a vision and mission statement that is consistent with and supportive of the corporate mission. Ten benefits of having a clear mission and vision are provided in Table 2-2.

An organization that fails to develop a vision statement as well as a comprehensive and inspiring mission statement loses the opportunity to present itself favorably to existing and potential stakeholders. All organizations need customers, employees, and managers, and most firms need creditors, suppliers, and distributors. The vision and mission statements are effective vehicles for communicating with important internal and external stakeholders. The principal benefit of these statements as tools of strategic management is derived from their specification of the ultimate aims of a firm. Vision and mission statements reveal the firm's shared expectations internally among all employees and managers. For external constituencies, the statements reveal the firm's long-term commitment to responsible, ethical action in providing a needed product and/or service for customers.

TABLE 2-2   Ten Benefits of Having a Clear Mission and Vision

1. Achieve clarity of purpose among all managers and employees.
2. Provide a basis for all other strategic planning activities, including internal and external assessment, establishing objectives, developing strategies, choosing among alternative strategies, devising policies, establishing organizational structure, allocating resources, and evaluating performance.
3. Provide direction.
4. Provide a focal point for all stakeholders of the firm.
5. Resolve divergent views among managers.
6. Promote a sense of shared expectations among all managers and employees.
7. Project a sense of worth and intent to all stakeholders.
8. Project an organized, motivated organization worthy of support.
9. Achieve higher organizational performance.
10. Achieve synergy among all managers and employees.

Characteristics of a Mission Statement

A Declaration of Attitude

A mission statement is more than a statement of specific details; it is a declaration of attitude and outlook. It usually is broad in scope for at least two major reasons. First, a good mission statement allows for the generation and consideration of a range of feasible alternative objectives and strategies without unduly stifling management creativity. Excess specificity would limit the potential of creative growth for the organization. However, an overly general statement that does not exclude any strategy alternatives could be dysfunctional. Apple Computer's mission statement, for example, should not open the possibility for diversification into pesticides—or Ford Motor Company's into food processing.

Second, a mission statement needs to be broad to reconcile differences effectively among, and appeal to, an organization's diverse **stakeholders**, the individuals and groups of individuals who have a special stake or claim on the company. Thus, a mission statement should be **reconcilatory**. Stakeholders include employees, managers, stockholders, boards of directors, customers, suppliers, distributors, creditors, governments (local, state, federal, and foreign), unions, competitors, environmental groups, and the general public. Stakeholders affect and are affected by an organization's strategies, yet the claims and concerns of diverse constituencies vary and often conflict. For example, the general public is especially interested in social responsibility, whereas stockholders are more interested in profitability. Claims on any business literally may number in the thousands, and they often include clean air, jobs, taxes, investment opportunities, career opportunities, equal employment opportunities, employee benefits, salaries, wages, clean water, and community services. All stakeholders' claims on an organization cannot be pursued with equal emphasis. A good mission statement indicates the relative attention that an organization will devote to meeting the claims of various stakeholders.

The fine balance between specificity and generality is difficult to achieve, but it is well worth the effort. George Steiner offers the following insight on the need for a mission statement to be broad in scope:

> Most business statements of mission are expressed at high levels of abstraction. Vagueness nevertheless has its virtues. Mission statements are not designed to express concrete ends, but rather to provide motivation, general direction, an image, a tone, and a philosophy to guide the enterprise. An excess of detail could prove counterproductive since concrete specification could be the base for rallying opposition. Precision might stifle creativity in the formulation of an acceptable mission or purpose. Once an aim is cast in concrete, it creates a rigidity in an organization and resists change. Vagueness leaves room for other managers to fill in the details.[8]

As indicated in Table 2-3, in addition to being broad in scope, an effective mission statement should not be too lengthy; recommended length is less than 250 words. An effective mission statement should arouse positive feelings and emotions about an organization; it should be inspiring in the sense that it motivates readers to action. A mission statement should be enduring. All of these are desired characteristics of a statement. An effective mission statement

---

TABLE 2-3 Characteristics of a Mission Statement

1. Broad in scope; do not include monetary amounts, numbers, percentages, ratios, or objectives
2. Less than 250 words in length
3. Inspiring
4. Identify the utility of a firm's products
5. Reveal that the firm is socially responsible
6. Reveal that the firm is environmentally responsible
7. Include nine components customers, products or services, markets, technology, concern for survival/growth/profits, philosophy, self-concept, concern for public image, concern for employees
8. Reconciliatory
9. Enduring

generates the impression that a firm is successful, has direction, and is worthy of time, support, and investment—from all socioeconomic groups of people.

It reflects judgments about future growth directions and strategies that are based on forward-looking external and internal analyses. A business mission should provide useful criteria for selecting among alternative strategies. A clear mission statement provides a basis for generating and screening strategic options. The statement of mission should be dynamic in orientation, allowing judgments about the most promising growth directions and those considered less promising.

A Customer Orientation

A good mission statement describes an organization's purpose, customers, products or services, markets, philosophy, and basic technology. According to Vern McGinnis, a mission statement should (a) define what the organization is and what the organization aspires to be, (b) be limited enough to exclude some ventures and broad enough to allow for creative growth, (c) distinguish a given organization from all others, (d) serve as a framework for evaluating both current and prospective activities, and (e) be stated in terms sufficiently clear to be widely understood throughout the organization.[9]

A good mission statement reflects the anticipations of customers. Rather than developing a product and then trying to find a market, the operating philosophy of organizations should be to identify customers' needs and then provide a product or service to fulfill those needs.

Good mission statements identify the utility of a firm's products to its customers. This is why AT&T's mission statement focuses on communication rather than on telephones; it is why ExxonMobil's mission statement focuses on energy rather than on oil and gas; it is why Union Pacific's mission statement focuses on transportation rather than on railroads; it is why Universal Studios' mission statement focuses on entertainment rather than on movies. A major reason for developing a business mission statement is to attract customers who give meaning to an organization.

The following utility statements are relevant in developing a mission statement:

Do not offer me things.

Do not offer me clothes. Offer me attractive looks.

Do not offer me shoes. Offer me comfort for my feet and the pleasure of walking.

Do not offer me a house. Offer me security, comfort, and a place that is clean and happy.

Do not offer me books. Offer me hours of pleasure and the benefit of knowledge.

Do not offer me CDs. Offer me leisure and the sound of music.

Do not offer me tools. Offer me the benefits and the pleasure that come from making beautiful things.

Do not offer me furniture. Offer me comfort and the quietness of a cozy place.

Do not offer me things. Offer me ideas, emotions, ambience, feelings, and benefits.

Please, do not offer me *things*.

Mission Statement Components

Mission statements can and do vary in length, content, format, and specificity. Most practitioners and academicians of strategic management feel that an effective statement should include these nine **mission statement components**. Because a mission statement is often the most visible and public part of the strategic-management process, it is important that it includes the nine characteristics as summarized in Table 2-3, as well as the following nine components:

1. *Customers*—Who are the firm's customers?
2. *Products or services*—What are the firm's major products or services?
3. *Markets*—Geographically, where does the firm compete?
4. *Technology*—Is the firm technologically current?
5. *Concern for survival, growth, and profitability*—Is the firm committed to growth and financial soundness?
6. *Philosophy*—What are the basic beliefs, values, aspirations, and ethical priorities of the firm?
7. *Self-concept*—What is the firm's distinctive competence or major competitive advantage?
8. *Concern for public image*—Is the firm responsive to social, community, and environmental concerns?
9. *Concern for employees*—Are employees a valuable asset of the firm?[10]

TABLE 2-4   Examples of the Nine Essential Components of a Mission Statement

1. **Customers**

   We believe our first responsibility is to the doctors, nurses, patients, mothers, and all others who use our products and services. (Johnson & Johnson)

   To earn our customers' loyalty, we listen to them, anticipate their needs, and act to create value in their eyes. (Lexmark International)

2. **Products or Services**

   AMAX's principal products are molybdenum, coal, iron ore, copper, lead, zinc, petroleum and natural gas, potash, phosphates, nickel, tungsten, silver, gold, and magnesium. (AMAX Engineering Company)

   Standard Oil Company (Indiana) is in business to find and produce crude oil, natural gas, and natural gas liquids; to manufacture high-quality products useful to society from these raw materials; and to distribute and market those products and to provide dependable related services to the consuming public at reasonable prices. (Standard Oil Company)

3. **Markets**

   We are dedicated to the total success of Corning Glass Works as a worldwide competitor. (Corning Glass Works)

   Our emphasis is on North American markets, although global opportunities will be explored. (Blockway)

4. **Technology**

   Control Data is in the business of applying micro-electronics and computer technology in two general areas: computer-related hardware; and computing-enhancing services, which include computation, information, education, and finance. (Control Data)

   We will continually strive to meet the preferences of adult smokers by developing technologies that have the potential to reduce the health risks associated with smoking. (RJ Reynolds)

5. **Concern for Survival, Growth, and Profitability**

   In this respect, the company will conduct its operations prudently and will provide the profits and growth which will assure Hoover's ultimate success. (Hoover Universal)

   To serve the worldwide need for knowledge at a fair profit by adhering, evaluating, producing, and distributing valuable information in a way that benefits our customers, employees, other investors, and our society. (McGraw-Hill)

6. **Philosophy**

   Our world-class leadership is dedicated to a management philosophy that holds people above profits. (Johnson Company)

   It's all part of the Mary Kay philosophy—a philosophy based on the golden rule.
   A spirit of sharing and caring where people give cheerfully of their time, knowledge, and experience. (Mary Kay Cosmetics)

7. **Self-Concept**

   Crown Zellerbach is committed to leapfrogging ongoing competition within 1,000 days by unleashing the constructive and creative abilities and energies of each of its employees. (Crown Zellerbach)

8. **Concern for Public Image**

   To share the world's obligation for the protection of the environment. (Dow Chemical)

   To contribute to the economic strength of society and function as a good corporate citizen on a local, state, and national basis in all countries in which we do business. (Pfizer)

9. **Concern for Employees**

   To recruit, develop, motivate, reward, and retain personnel of exceptional ability, character, and dedication by providing good working conditions, superior leadership, compensation on the basis of performance, an attractive benefit program, opportunity for growth, and a high degree of employment security. (Barnes Corporation)

   To compensate its employees with remuneration and fringe benefits competitive with other employment opportunities in its geographical area and commensurate with their contributions toward efficient corporate operations. (Public Service Electric & Gas Company)

Excerpts from the mission statements of different organizations are provided in Table 2-4 to exemplify the nine essential mission statement components.

Writing and Evaluating Mission Statements

Perhaps the best way to develop a skill for writing and evaluating mission statements is to study actual company missions. Therefore, the mission statements presented in Table 2-5 are evaluated based on the nine desired components. Note in Table 2-5 that numbers provided in each statement reveal what components are included in the respective documents. Among the statements in Table 2-5, note that the Dell mission statement is the best because it lacks only one component, whereas the L'Oreal statement is the worst, lacking six of the nine recommended components.

There is no one best mission statement for a particular organization, so good judgment is required in evaluating mission statements. Realize that some individuals are more demanding than others in assessing mission statements in this manner. For example, if a statement merely includes the word "customers" without specifying who the customers are, is that satisfactory?

TABLE 2-5 Example Mission Statements

Fleetwood Enterprises will lead the recreational vehicle and manufactured housing industries (2, 7) in providing quality products, with a passion for customer-driven innovation (1). We will emphasize training, embrace diversity and provide growth opportunities for our associates and our dealers (9). We will lead our industries in the application of appropriate technologies (4). We will operate at the highest levels of ethics and compliance with a focus on exemplary corporate governance (6). We will deliver value to our shareholders, positive operating results and industry-leading earnings (5). *(Author comment: Statement lacks two components: Markets and Concern for Public Image)*

We aspire to make **PepsiCo** the world's (3) premier consumer products company, focused on convenient foods and beverages (2) We seek to produce healthy financial rewards for investors (5) as we provide opportunities for growth and enrichment to our employees, (9) our business partners and the communities (8) in which we operate. And in everything we do, we strive to act with honesty, openness, fairness and integrity (6). *(Author comment: Statement lacks three components: Customers, Technology, and Self-Concept)*

We are loyal to **Royal Caribbean** and **Celebrity** and strive for continuous improvement in everything we do. We always provide service with a friendly greeting and a smile (7). We anticipate the needs of our customers and make all efforts to exceed our customers' expectations (1). We take ownership of any problem that is brought to our attention. We engage in conduct that enhances our corporate reputation and employee morale (9). We are committed to act in the highest ethical manner and respect the rights and dignity of others. (6). *(Author comment: Statement lacks five components: Products/Services, Markets, Technology, Concern for Survival/Growth/Profits, Concern for Public Image)*

Dell's mission is to be the most successful computer company (2) in the world (3) at delivering the best customer experience in markets we serve (1). In doing so, Dell will meet customer expectations of highest quality; leading technology (4); competitive pricing; individual and company accountability (6); best-in-class service and support (7); flexible customization capability (7); superior corporate citizenship (8); financial stability (5). *(Author comment: Statement lacks only one component: Concern for Employees)*

Procter & Gamble will provide branded products and services of superior quality and value (7) that improve the lives of the world's (3) consumers. As a result, consumers (1) will reward us with industry leadership in sales, profit (5), and value creation, allowing our people (9), our shareholders, and the communities (8) in which we live and work to prosper. *(Author comment: Statement lacks three components: Products/Services, Technology, and Philosophy)*

At **L'Oreal**, we believe that lasting business success is built upon ethical (6) standards which guide growth and on a genuine sense of responsibility to our employees (9), our consumers, our environment and to the communities in which we operate (8). *(Author comment: Statement lacks six components: Customers, Products/Services, Markets, Technology, Concern for Survival/Growth/Profits, Concern for Public Image)*

Note: The numbers in parentheses correspond to the nine components listed on page 50; author comments also refer to those components.

Ideally a statement would provide more than simply inclusion of a single word such as "products" or "employees" regarding a respective component. Why? Because the statement should be informative, inspiring, enduring, and serve to motivate stakeholders to action. Evaluation of a mission statement regarding inclusion of the nine components is just the beginning of the process to assess a statement's overall effectiveness.

Special Note to Students

Recall that gaining and sustaining competitive advantage is the essence of strategic management, so when presenting your vision or mission analysis for the firm, be sure to address the "self-concept" or "distinctive competence" component. Compare your recommended vision or mission statement both with the firm's existing statements and with rival firms' statements to clearly reveal how your recommendations or strategic plan enables the firm to gain and sustain competitive advantage. Thus, your proposed mission statement should certainly include the nine components and nine characteristics, but in your vision or mission discussion, focus on competitive advantage. In other words, be prescriptive, forward-looking, and insightful— couching your vision/mission overview in terms of how you believe the firm can best gain and sustain competitive advantage. Do not be content with merely showing a nine-component comparison of your proposed statement with rival firms' statements, although that would be nice to include in your analysis.

Conclusion

Every organization has a unique purpose and reason for being. This uniqueness should be reflected in vision and mission statements. The nature of a business vision and mission can represent either a competitive advantage or disadvantage for the firm. An organization achieves a heightened sense of purpose when strategists, managers, and employees develop and communicate a clear business vision and mission. Drucker says that developing a clear business vision and mission is the "first responsibility of strategists."

A good mission statement reveals an organization's customers; products or services; markets; technology; concern for survival, growth, and profitability; philosophy; self-concept; concern for public image; and concern for employees. These nine basic components serve as a practical framework for evaluating and writing mission statements. As the first step in strategic management, the vision and mission statements provide direction for all planning activities.

Well-designed vision and mission statements are essential for formulating, implementing, and evaluating strategy. Developing and communicating a clear business vision and mission are the most commonly overlooked tasks in strategic management. Without clear statements of vision and mission, a firm's short-term actions can be counterproductive to long-term interests. Vision and mission statements always should be subject to revision, but, if carefully prepared, they will require infrequent major changes. Organizations usually reexamine their vision and mission statements annually. Effective mission statements stand the test of time.

Vision and mission statements are essential tools for strategists, a fact illustrated in a short story told by Porsche's former CEO Peter Schultz (paraphrased):

> Three guys were at work building a large church. All were doing the same job, but when each was asked what his job was, the answers varied: "Pouring cement," the first replied; "Earning a paycheck," responded the second; "Helping to build a cathedral," said the third. Few of us can build cathedrals. But to the extent we can see the cathedral in whatever cause we are following, the job seems more worthwhile. Good strategists and a clear mission help us find those cathedrals in what otherwise could be dismal issues and empty causes.[11]

MyManagementLab®

Go to **mymanagementlab.com** to complete the problems marked with this icon ⭐.

Key Terms and Concepts

concern for employees (p. 49)
concern for public image (p. 49)
concern for survival, growth, and profitability (p. 49)
creed statement (p. 43)
customers (p. 49)
markets (p. 49)
mission statement (p. 43)
mission statement components (p. 49)

philosophy (p. 49)
products or services (p. 49)
reconciliatory (p. 48)
self-concept (p. 49)
stakeholders (p. 48)
technology (p. 49)
vision statement (p. 45)

Issues for Review and Discussion

2-1. List four components and four characteristics that the J. Crew mission statement fails to exhibit. Write a new and improved mission for J. Crew.

2-2. Note at the www.jcrew.com website, a vision statement is not given. Write a recommended vision statement for J. Crew given their strategies.

2-3. Explain how it a firm such as J. Crew can be doing well, but does not have an effective vision or mission statement.

2-4. Some excellent nine-component mission statements consist of just two sentences. Write a two-sentence mission statement for a company of your choice.

2-5. How do you think an organization can best align company mission with employee mission?

2-6. What are some different names for "mission statement," and where will you likely find a firm's mission statement?

2-7. If your company does not have a vision or mission statement, describe a good process for developing these documents.

⭐ **2-8.** Explain how developing a mission statement can help resolve divergent views among managers in a firm.

2-9. Drucker says the most important time to seriously reexamine the firm's vision or mission is when the firm is successful. Why is this?

2-10. Explain why a mission statement should not include monetary amounts, numbers, percentages, ratios, goals, or objectives.

⭐ **2-11.** Discuss the meaning of the following statement: "Good mission statements identify the utility of a firm's products to its customers."

2-12. Distinguish between the "self-concept" and the "philosophy" components in a mission statement. Give an example of each for your university.

2-13. When someone or some company is "on a mission" to achieve something, many times they cannot be stopped.

List three things in prioritized order that you are on a mission to achieve in life.

2-14. Compare and contrast vision statements with mission statements in terms of composition and importance.

2-15. Do local service stations need to have written vision and mission statements? Why or why not?

2-16. Why do you think organizations that have a comprehensive mission tend to be high performers? Does having a comprehensive mission cause high performance?

2-17. Explain why a mission statement should not include strategies and objectives.

2-18. What is your college or university's self-concept? How would you state that in a mission statement?

2-19. Explain the principal value of a vision and a mission statement.

2-20. Why is it important for a mission statement to be reconciliatory?

2-21. In your opinion, what are the three most important components that should be included when writing a mission statement? Why?

2-22. How would the mission statements of a for-profit and a nonprofit organization differ?

2-23. Write a vision and mission statement for an organization of your choice.

2-24. Conduct a search on the Internet with the keywords *vision statement* and *mission statement*. Find various company vision and mission statements and evaluate the documents. Write a one-page, single-spaced report on your findings.

2-25. Who are the major stakeholders of the bank that you do business with locally? What are the major claims of those stakeholders?

2-26. List seven characteristics of a mission statement.

2-27. List eight benefits of having a clear mission statement.

⭐ **2-28.** How often do you think a firm's vision and mission statements should be changed?

MyManagementLab®

Go to **mymanagementlab.com** for Auto-graded writing questions as well as the following Assisted-graded writing questions:

2-29. Explain why a mission statement should not include strategies and objectives.

2-30. List seven characteristics of a mission statement.

2-31. Mymanagementlab Only—comprehensive writing assignment for this chapter.

Current Readings

Bartkus, Barbara, Myron Glassman, and R. Bruce McAfee. "Mission Statements: Are They Smoke and Mirrors?" *Business Horizons* 43, no. 6 (November–December 2000): 23.

Church Mission Statements, http://www.missionstatements.com/church_mission_statements.html.

Collins, David J., and Michael G. Rukstad. "Can You Say What Your Strategy Is?" *Harvard Business Review*, April 2008, 82.

Company Mission Statements, http://www.missionstatements.com/company_mission_statements.html.

Conger, Jay A., and Douglas A. Ready. "Enabling Bold Visions." *MIT Sloan Management Review* 49, no. 2 (Winter 2008): 70.

Day, George S., and Paul Schoemaker. "Peripheral Vision: Sensing and Acting on Weak Signals." *Long Range Planning* 37, no. 2 (April 2004): 117.

Ibarra, Herminia, and Otilia Obodaru. "Women and the Vision Thing." *Harvard Business Review*, January 2009, 62–71.

Lissak, Michael, and Johan Roos. "Be Coherent, Not Visionary." *Long Range Planning* 34, no. 1 (February 2001): 53.

Newsom, Mi Kyong, David A. Collier, and Eric O. Olsen. "Using 'Biztainment' to Gain Competitive Advantage." *Business Horizons*, March–April 2009, 167–166.

Nonprofit Organization Mission Statements, http://www.missionstatements.com/nonprofit_mission_statements.html.

Restaurant Mission Statements, http://www.missionstatements.com/restaurant_mission_statements.html.

School Mission Statements, http://www.missionstatements.com/school_mission_statements.html.

ASSURANCE OF LEARNING EXERCISES

EXERCISE 2A
Develop an Improved Mission Statement for J. Crew

Purpose

As showcased at the beginning of this chapter, J. Crew goes toe-to-toe every day competing against Gap and Limited brands.

Instructions

Step 1   Develop and improved mission statement for J. Crew that complies with (a) the nine components and (b) the nine characteristics presented in this chapter.

Step 2   Turn your work in for a classwork grade.

EXERCISE 2B
Evaluate Mission Statements

Purpose

A business mission statement is an integral part of strategic management. It provides direction for formulating, implementing, and evaluating strategic activities. This exercise will give you practice evaluating mission statements, a skill that is a prerequisite to writing a good mission statement.

Instructions

Step 1   On a clean sheet of paper, prepare a 9 × 6 matrix. Place the nine mission statement components down the left column and the following six companies across the top of your paper.

Step 2   Write *Yes* or *No* in each cell of your matrix to indicate whether you feel the particular mission statement includes the respective component.

Step 3   Turn your paper in to your instructor for a classwork grade.

Mission Statements
Advance Auto Parts

It is the Mission of Advance Auto Parts to provide personal vehicle owners and enthusiasts with the vehicle related products and knowledge that fulfill their wants and needs at the right price. Our friendly, knowledgeable and professional staff will help inspire, educate and problem-solve for our customers.

Barnes & Noble

Our mission is to operate the best specialty retail business in America, regardless of the product we sell. Because the product we sell is books, our aspirations must be consistent with the promise and the ideals of the volumes which line our shelves. To say that our mission exists independent of the product we sell is to demean the importance and the distinction of being booksellers. As booksellers we are determined to be the very best in our business, regardless of the size, pedigree or inclinations of our competitors. We will continue to bring our industry nuances of style and approaches to bookselling which are consistent with our evolving aspirations. Above all, we expect to be a credit to the communities we serve, a valuable resource to our customers, and a place where our dedicated booksellers can grow and prosper. Toward this end we will not only listen to our customers and booksellers but embrace the idea that the Company is at their service.

Estée Lauder

The guiding vision of The Estée Lauder Companies is "Bringing the best to everyone we touch." By "The best," we mean the best products, the best people and the best ideas. These three pillars have been the hallmarks of our Company since it was founded by Mrs. Estée Lauder in 1946. They remain the foundation upon which we continue to build our success today.

Family Dollar Stores

For Our Customers A compelling place to shop...by providing convenience and low prices For Our Associates A compelling place to work...by providing exceptional opportunities and rewards for achievement For Our Investors A compelling place to invest...by providing outstanding returns.

FedEx

FedEx will produce superior financial returns for shareowners by providing high value-added supply chain, transportation, business and related information services through focused operating companies. Customer requirements will be met in the highest quality manner appropriate to each market segment served. FedEx will strive to develop mutually rewarding relationships with its employees, partners and suppliers. Safety will be the first consideration in all operations. Corporate activities will be conducted to the highest ethical and professional standards.

Ford Motor Company

We are a global family with a proud heritage passionately committed to providing personal mobility for people around the world.

Source: Based on http://www.missionstatements.com/fortune_500_mission_statements.html.

EXERCISE 2C
Write a Vision and Mission Statement for PepsiCo

Purpose

There is always room for improvement in regard to an existing vision and mission statement. PepsiCo has a vision statement and mission statement, but this exercise asks you to develop improved statements. But first, go to the PepsiCo website. Look down the left column and click on Company Overview. Read this material because some of that narrative may be good to include in your proposed PepsiCo vision and mission statement.

Instructions

Step 1	Refer back to the Cohesion Case to see PepsiCo's vision and mission statements
Step 2	On a clean sheet of paper, write a one-sentence new and improved vision statement for PepsiCo.
Step 3	On that same sheet of paper, write a new and improved mission statement for PepsiCo.

EXERCISE 2D

Compare Your College or University's Vision Statement to a Leading Rival University

Purpose

Most universities have a vision and mission statement. The purpose of this exercise is to give you practice comparing the effectiveness of a vision and mission statement for a university with the statements from a competing university.

Instructions

Step 1   Determine whether your institution has a vision or mission statement. Look in the front of the college handbook. If your institution has a written statement, contact an appropriate administrator of the institution to inquire as to how and when the statement was prepared. Share this information with the class. Analyze your college's vision and mission statement in light of the concepts presented in this chapter.

Step 2   Compare the vision statement and a mission statement of your college or university to a leading institution.

Step 3   Write a one-page analysis comparing the statements.

EXERCISE 2E

Conduct Mission Statement Research

Purpose

This exercise gives you the opportunity to study the nature and role of vision and mission statements in strategic management.

Instructions

Step 1   Visit the websites of various organizations in your city or county to identify firms that have developed a formal vision or mission statement. Include some websites of nonprofit organizations and government agencies in addition to small and large businesses. Ask to speak with the director, owner, or chief executive officer of several organization. Explain that you are studying vision and mission statements in class and are conducting research as part of a class activity.

Step 2   Ask several executives the following four questions, and record their answers.
1. When did your organization first develop its vision or mission statement? Who was primarily responsible for its development?
2. How long have your current statements existed? When were they last modified? Why were they modified at that time?
3. By what process are your firm's vision and mission statements altered?
4. How are your vision and mission statements used in the firm?

Step 3   Provide an overview of your findings to the class.

EXERCISE 2F

Evaluate a Mission Proposal for Delta Airlines

Purpose

Delta Air Lines actual mission statement is given here. An employee recently proposed an improved mission statement for Delta. The employee's proposed new statement is also given. This exercise gives you practice evaluating a new employee's proposal.

Instructions

Step 1   Review and analyze the actual and proposed vision/mission statements for Delta Air Lines.

Step 2   Respond to the employee's proposal with a one-page written assessment. Turn your analysis in to your professor.

Delta Air Lines' Actual Mission Statement

"We—Delta's employees, customers, and community partners together form a force for positive local and global change, dedicated to bettering standards of living and the environment where we and our customers live and work."

A Proposed Mission Statement for Delta Air Lines

Delta has a vested interest in employees, customers, shareholders, local and global environments, by promoting diversity, superior customer service, maintaining profitability, and continually investing in the improvement of the environment. We encourage positive partnerships and understand that the ability to continually progress, transform, and expand our business is vital for continued sustainability as a leader in the global airline industry.

Your New and Improved Mission Statement for Delta Air Lines

Notes

1. Peter Drucker, *Management: Tasks, Responsibilities, and Practices* (New York: Harper & Row, 1974), 61.
2. Andrew Campbell and Sally Yeung, "Creating a Sense of Mission," *Long Range Planning* 24, no. 4 (August 1991): 17.
3. Charles Rarick and John Vitton, "Mission Statements Make Cents," *Journal of Business Strategy* 16 (1995): 11. Also, Christopher Bart and Mark Baetz, "The Relationship Between Mission Statements and Firm Performance: An Exploratory Study," *Journal of Management Studies* 35 (1998): 823; "Mission Possible," *Business Week* (August 1999): F12.
4. W. R. King and D. I. Cleland, *Strategic Planning and Policy* (New York: Van Nostrand Reinhold, 1979), 124.
5. Brian Dumaine, "What the Leaders of Tomorrow See," *Fortune,* July 3, 1989, 50.
6. "How W. T. Grant Lost $175 Million Last Year," *Business Week,* February 25, 1975, 75.
7. Drucker, *Management,* 88.
8. John Pearce II, "The Company Mission as a Strategic Tool," *Sloan Management Review* 23, no. 3 (Spring 1982): 74.
9. George Steiner, *Strategic Planning: What Every Manager Must Know* (New York: The Free Press, 1979), 160.
10. Vern McGinnis, "The Mission Statement: A Key Step in Strategic Planning," *Business* 31, no. 6 (November–December 1981): 41.
11. http://ezinearticles.com/?Elements-of-a-Mission-Statement&id=3846671.

## 3

Source: Fuse/Thinkstock

MyManagementLab®

⭐ Improve Your Grade!

Over 10 million students improved their results using the Pearson MyLabs.
Visit **mymanagementlab.com** for simulations, tutorials, and end-of-chapter problems.

The External Assessment

CHAPTER OBJECTIVES

After studying this chapter, you should be able to do the following:

1. Discuss the nature and role of labor unions in the USA as a corporate strategic issue.

2. Describe how to conduct an external strategic-management audit.

3. Discuss 10 major external forces that affect organizations: economic, social, cultural, demographic, environmental, political, governmental, legal, technological, and competitive.

4. Describe key sources of external information.

5. Discuss important forecasting tools used in strategic management.

6. Discuss the importance of monitoring external trends and events.

7. Explain how to develop an EFE Matrix.

8. Explain how to develop a Competitive Profile Matrix.

9. Discuss the importance of gathering competitive intelligence.

10. Discuss market commonality and resource similarity in relation to competitive analysis.

ASSURANCE OF LEARNING EXERCISES

The following exercises are found at the end of this chapter.

This chapter examines the tools and concepts needed to conduct an external strategic management audit (sometimes called **environmental scanning** or **industry analysis**). An **external audit** focuses on identifying and evaluating trends and events beyond the control of a single firm, such as increased foreign competition, population shifts to coastal areas of the USA, an aging society, and taxing Internet sales. An external audit reveals key opportunities and threats confronting an organization so that managers can formulate strategies to take advantage of the opportunities and avoid or reduce the impact of threats. This chapter presents a practical framework for gathering, assimilating, and analyzing external information. The Industrial Organization (I/O) view of strategic management is introduced.

The Chapter 3 boxed insert company pursuing strategies based on an excellent external strategic analysis is PetSmart, Inc. Note that PetSmart has more than 1,200 stores in the USA and Canada.

The Nature of an External Audit

The purpose of an external audit is to develop a finite list of opportunities that could benefit a firm and threats that should be avoided. As the term *finite* suggests, the external audit is not aimed at developing an exhaustive list of every possible factor that could influence the business; rather, it is aimed at identifying key variables that offer actionable responses. Firms should be able to respond either offensively or defensively to the factors by formulating strategies that take advantage of external opportunities or that minimize the impact of potential threats. Figure 3-1 illustrates with white shading how the external audit fits into the strategic-management process.

EXCELLENT STRATEGIC MANAGEMENT SHOWCASE

PetSmart Inc.

Do you own a dog or cat or pet of any kind? If yes, you may be interested to know that PetSmart is the top pet company in the industry. PetSmart is the number-one U.S. specialty retailer of pet food and supplies, with 1,270 stores in the USA and Canada. PetSmart has become profitable and is growing rapidly as a result of excellent strategies based on a "humanization of pets" mission whereby the company treats pet owners as pet parents and treats pets and children.

CEO Bob Moran at PetSmart says his company does not ask customers "How can I help you?" but rather says "Please tell me about your pet." PetSmart plans to open 50 new stores each year between 2012 and 2022. A key advantage for PetSmart is its excellent strategic transition from being a pet-supply store to being a pet-service center.

Ranging from 12,000 to 20,000 square feet in size, PetSmart stores offer more than 10,000 products, ranging from scratching posts to iguana harnesses and all sold under national brands and PetSmart's own private labels. Most of these stores include a pet hotel and pet hospital. The company also sells products through its PetSmart website. Stores also provide in-store boarding facilities (PetsHotels), grooming services, day camps (Doggie Day Camps), and obedience training. Veterinary services are available, as well, in about 800 shops through pet hospital operator Medical Management International (known as Banfield), of which PetSmart owns about 20 percent.

Because there are more cats in urban areas because of size constraints, urban PetSmart stores focus more on cats and cat customers, whereas nonurban stores focus more on dog customers. But all PetSmart stores are meeting places because Moran says customers come in with their pets and just want to talk about their pets and then buy products or services offered. He says the trend toward providing more natural, organic foods and products for pets is a rapidly growing trend and PetSmart provides the latest and greatest organic products and services.

In 2013, PetSmart began letting customers reserve pet rooms and services online after extensively improving their website in prior years. The company takes full advantage of seasonal holidays by, for example, providing numerous Halloween toys and costumes in different colors and makes during October each year. But the overriding competitive advantage for PetSmart is their overarching philosophy to treat pet owners like parents and to treat pets like children, providing tender loving care of both.

Facing thousands of mom-and-pop pet stores nationwide as well as mass retailers such as Walmart and Target, PetSmart's major competitor is privately held PETCO Animal Supplies, which has more than 1,000 stores in the USA and is headquartered in San Diego, California.

Source: Based on Emily Glazer, "PetSmart Thrives Treating Owners Like Parents," *Wall Street Journal* (9-12-12): B7.

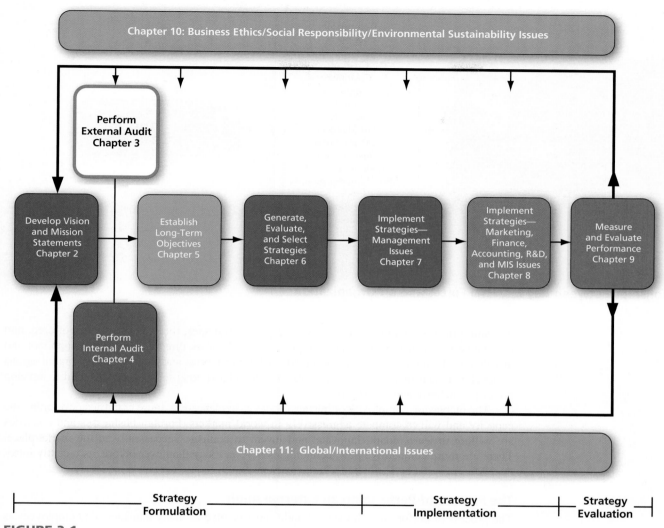

FIGURE 3-1

A Comprehensive Strategic-Management Model

Source: Fred R. David, "How Companies Define Their Mission," *Long Range Planning* 22, no. 3 (June 1988): 40.

Key External Forces

External forces can be divided into five broad categories: (1) economic forces; (2) social, cultural, demographic, and natural environment forces; (3) political, governmental, and legal forces; (4) technological forces; and (5) competitive forces. Relationships among these forces and an organization are depicted in Figure 3-2. External trends and events, such as rising food prices and people in African countries coming online, significantly affect products, services, markets, and organizations worldwide. IMPORTANT NOTE: WHEN IDENTIFYING AND PRIORITIZING KEY EXTERNAL FACTORS IN STRATEGIC PLANNING, MAKE SURE THE FACTORS SELECTED ARE SPECIFIC, IE QUANTIFIED TO THE EXTENT POSSIBLE; PERHAPS MORE IMPORTANTLY MAKE SURE THE FACTORS SELECTED ARE *ACTIONABLE*, IE MEANINGFUL IN TERMS OF HAVING STRATEGIC IMPLICATIONS. For example, regarding *actionable*, to say "the stock market is rising" is not actionable because there is no apparent strategy that the firm could formulate to capitalize on that factor. In contrast, a factor such as "the GDP of Brazil is 6.8 percent" is actionable because the firm should perhaps open 100 new stores in Brazil. In other words, select factors that will be helpful in deciding what to recommend the firm to do, rather than selecting nebulous factors.

Changes in external forces translate into changes in consumer demand for both industrial and consumer products and services. External forces affect the types of products developed,

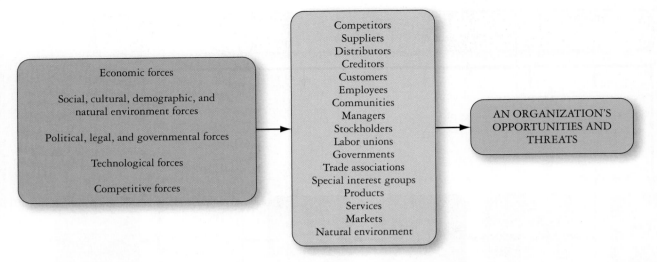

FIGURE 3-2
Relationships Between Key External Forces and an Organization

the nature of positioning and market segmentation strategies, the type of services offered, and the choice of businesses to acquire or sell. External forces directly affect both suppliers and distributors. Identifying and evaluating external opportunities and threats enables organizations to develop a clear mission, to design strategies to achieve long-term objectives, and to develop policies to achieve annual objectives.

The increasing complexity of business today is evidenced by more countries developing the capacity and will to compete aggressively in world markets. Foreign businesses and countries are willing to learn, adapt, innovate, and invent to compete successfully in the marketplace. There are more competitive new technologies in Asia today than ever before, as recently introduced for example by Lenovo in China and Samsung in South Korea.

The Process of Performing an External Audit

The process of performing an external audit must involve as many managers and employees as possible. As emphasized in previous chapters, involvement in the strategic-management process can lead to understanding and commitment from organizational members. Individuals appreciate having the opportunity to contribute ideas and to gain a better understanding of their firm's industry, competitors, and markets.

To perform an external audit, a company first must gather competitive intelligence and information about economic, social, cultural, demographic, environmental, political, governmental, legal, and technological trends. Individuals can be asked to monitor various sources of information, such as key magazines, trade journals, and newspapers. These persons can submit periodic scanning reports to a committee of managers charged with performing the external audit. This approach provides a continuous stream of timely strategic information and involves many individuals in the external-audit process. The Internet provides another source for gathering strategic information, as do corporate, university, and public libraries. Suppliers, distributors, salespersons, customers, and competitors represent other sources of vital information.

Once information is gathered, it should be assimilated and evaluated. A meeting or series of meetings of managers is needed to collectively identify the most important opportunities and threats facing the firm. These key external factors should be listed on flip charts or a chalkboard. A prioritized list of these factors could be obtained by requesting that all managers rank the factors identified, from 1 for the most important opportunity or threat to 20 for the least important opportunity or threat. These key external factors can vary over time and by industry. Relationships with suppliers or distributors are often a critical success factor. Other variables commonly used include market share, breadth of competing products, world economies, foreign affiliates, proprietary and key account advantages, price competitiveness, technological advancements, population shifts, interest rates, and pollution abatement.

Freund emphasized that these key external factors should be (a) important to achieving long-term and annual objectives, (b) measurable, (c) applicable to all competing firms, and (d) hierarchical in the sense that some will pertain to the overall company and others will be more narrowly focused on functional or divisional areas. A final list of the most important key external factors should be communicated and distributed widely in the organization. Both opportunities and threats can be key external factors.[1]

The Industrial Organization (I/O) View

The **Industrial Organization (I/O)** approach to competitive advantage advocates that external (industry) factors are more important than internal factors in a firm for achieving competitive advantage. Proponents of the I/O view, such as Michael Porter, contend that organizational performance will be primarily determined by industry forces. Porter's Five-Forces Model, presented later in this chapter, is an example of the I/O perspective, which focuses on analyzing external forces and industry variables as a basis for getting and keeping competitive advantage. Competitive advantage is determined largely by competitive positioning within an industry, according to I/O advocates. Managing strategically from the I/O perspective entails firms striving to compete in attractive industries, avoiding weak or faltering industries, and gaining a full understanding of key external factor relationships within that attractive industry. I/O research provides important contributions to our understanding of how to gain competitive advantage.

I/O theorists contend that external factors and the industry in which a firm competes has a stronger influence on the firm's performance than do the internal functional issues in marketing, finance, and the like. Firm performance, they contend, is based more on industry properties such as economies of scale, barriers to market entry, product differentiation, the economy, and level of competitiveness than on internal resources, capabilities, structure, and operations. The USA's recent economic recovery having such a positive impact on both strong and weak firms adds credence to the notion that external forces are more important than internal.

The I/O view has enhanced the understanding of strategic management. However, it is not a question of whether external or internal factors are more important in gaining and maintaining competitive advantage. Effective integration and understanding of *both* external and internal factors is the key to securing and keeping a competitive advantage. In fact, as discussed in Chapter 6, matching key external opportunities and threats with key internal strengths and weaknesses provides the basis for successful strategy formulation.

Economic Forces

The lingering high underemployment rate in the USA bodes well for discount firms ranging from Dollar Tree to TJ Maxx to Walmart to Subway, but hurts thousands of traditional priced retailers in many industries. The Dow Jones Industrial Average is over 15,000, corporate profits are high, dividend increases are up sharply, and emerging markets are growing. Yet, job growth is still stymied, home prices remain low, and millions of people work for minimum wages or are either unemployed or underemployed. As a result of droughts, commodity prices are up sharply, especially food, which is contributing to rising inflation fears. Many firms are switching to the extent possible to part-time rather than full-time employees to avoid having to pay health benefits. Consumer spending is rebounding. Much of Europe lingers in a recession.

Economic factors have a direct impact on the potential attractiveness of various strategies. For example, with interest rates, funds needed for capital expansion are less costly. As interest rates rise, discretionary income declines, and the demand for discretionary goods falls. When stock prices increase, the desirability of equity as a source of capital for market development increases. When the market rises, consumer and business wealth expands. A summary of economic variables that often represent opportunities and threats for organizations is provided in Table 3-1.

To take advantage of Canada's robust economy and eager-to-spend people, many firms are aggressively expanding operations into Canada, including TJX opening many Marshalls stores, Target opening stores, Walmart opening supercenters, and Tanger Outlet Factory Centers

TABLE 3-1 Key Economic Variables to Be Monitored

Shift to a service economy in the USA	Import/export factors
Availability of credit	Demand shifts for different categories of goods and services
Level of disposable income	Income differences by region and consumer groups
Propensity of people to spend	Price fluctuations
Interest rates	Export of labor and capital from the USA
Inflation rates	Monetary policies
Money market rates	Fiscal policies
Federal government budget deficits	Tax rates
Gross domestic product trend	European Economic Community (EEC) policies
Consumption patterns	Organization of Petroleum Exporting Countries (OPEC) policies
Unemployment trends	Coalitions of Lesser Developed Countries (LDC) policies
Worker productivity levels	
Value of the dollar in world markets	
Stock market trends	
Foreign countries' economic conditions	

opening new stores. "Canada is one of the most economically prosperous countries in the world," said Howard Davidowitz, chairman of Davidowitz & Associates, a retail consultancy and investment banking firm. "It has a stable currency, it did not have a banking crisis and it did not spend itself into insanity."

Trends in the dollar's value have significant and unequal effects on companies in different industries and in different locations. For example, the pharmaceutical, tourism, entertainment, motor vehicle, aerospace, and forest products industries benefit greatly when the dollar falls against the yen and euro. Agricultural and petroleum industries are hurt by the dollar's rise against the currencies of Mexico, Brazil, Venezuela, and Australia. Generally, a strong or high dollar makes U.S. goods more expensive in overseas markets. This worsens the U.S. trade deficit. When the value of the dollar falls, tourism-oriented firms benefit because Americans do not travel abroad as much when the value of the dollar is low; rather, foreigners visit and vacation more in the United States.

A low value of the dollar means lower imports and higher exports; it helps U.S. companies' competitiveness in world markets. A falling dollar makes U.S. goods cheaper to foreign consumers and combats deflation by pushing up prices of imports. A low value of the dollar benefits the U.S. economy in many ways. First, it helps stave off the risks of deflation in the USA and also reduces the U.S. trade deficit. In addition, a low value of the dollar raises the foreign sales and profits of domestic firms, thanks to dollar-induced gains, and encourages foreign countries to lower interest rates and loosen fiscal policy, which stimulates worldwide economic expansion. Some sectors, such as consumer staples, energy, materials, technology, and health care, especially benefit from a low value of the dollar. Manufacturers in many domestic industries in fact benefit because of a weak dollar, which forces foreign rivals to raise prices and extinguish discounts. Domestic firms with big overseas sales, such as McDonald's, greatly benefit from a weak dollar. Table 3-2 lists some advantages and disadvantages of a weak U.S. dollar for U.S. firms.

In contrast to rivals Nissan Motor and Honda Motor, Mazda Motor Corp. based in Hiroshima, Japan, has a strategy to produce more than 80 percent of its vehicles in Japan and export them rather than building manufacturing plants globally. Even if the value of the dollar weakens to 77 yen, Mazda says it can make a profit on its CX-5 vehicles. But with the dollar at 79 yen, Honda and Nissan say they must keep moving production abroad and will do so until or unless the dollar climbs back to at least 100 yen. Thus, value of the dollar versus the Japanese yen is an important factor in strategic planning among Japanese firms.

The value of the dollar changes some every day, but generally in 2012–2013 the value of the dollar was strong and thus profits of U.S. companies with revenue from abroad were lowered on average 6 to 7 percent. Why the lowered profits? Because, for example, 100 euros earned in Europe, when translated back to U.S. dollars for reporting purposes, the 100 euros is worth

TABLE 3-2 Advantages and Disadvantages of a Weak Dollar for Domestic Firms

Advantages	Disadvantages
1. Leads to more exports	1. Can lead to inflation
2. Leads to lower imports	2. Can cause rise in oil prices
3. Makes U.S. goods cheaper to foreign consumers	3. Can weaken U.S. government
4. Combats deflation by pushing up prices of imports	4. Makes it unattractive for Americans to travel globally
5. Can contribute to rise in stock prices in short run	5. Can contribute to fall in stock prices in long run
6. Encourages foreign countries to lower interest rates	
7. Raises the revenues and profits of firms that do business outside the USA	
8. Forces foreign firms to raise prices	
9. Reduces the U.S. trade deficit	
10. Encourages firms to globalize	
11. Encourages foreigners to visit the United States	

maybe $75. To combat this "loss," some companies try to raise prices in their European or Mexican stores, but that carries a risk of alienating shoppers, angering retailers, and giving local competitors a price edge. Some advantages of a strong dollar however are that companies with substantial outside U.S. operations see their overseas expenses, such as salaries paid in euros, become cheaper. Another advantage of a strong dollar is that it gives U.S. companies greater firepower for international acquisitions. Another advantage of a strong dollar is that companies that import benefit from greater buying power because their dollars now go further overseas.

A recent *Wall Street Journal* article (12-4-12, B4) explains the unfavorable foreign-exchange rate environment plaguing U.S. firms. For example, the starch and sweetener maker Ingredion Inc.'s earnings were reduced by 20 cents per share recently by weakness in the Brazilian real, Argentine peso, British pound, and the euro. Similarly, General Motors reported that its third quarter 2012 sales were reduced by about $1.3 billion as a result of weakness in the European euro, Russian ruble, Hungarian forint, South Korean won, South African rand, Canadian dollar, and Mexican pesos.

Social, Cultural, Demographic, and Natural Environment Forces

Asian Americans are now the best-educated, highest-earning, and fastest-growing racial group in the United States.[2] The number of Asian Americans in the United States grew by 46 percent between 2000 and 2010, with Chinese Americans becoming by far the largest group. The median U.S. household income is $49.8K, with Asian American's median being $66K, compared to whites $54K, Hispanics $40K, and African Americans $33.3K.[3]

The U.S. Fish and Wildlife Service reported in late 2012 that 11 percent more Americans (ages 16 and older) fished and 9 percent more hunted in 2011 than in 2006. The report also revealed that among children aged 6 to 15, 13 percent more hunted and 2 percent more fished during the same period. A variety of reasons account for the shift back to "doing outdoor things," but this trend is excellent news for thousands of sporting goods companies.

Social, cultural, demographic, and environmental changes have a major impact on virtually all products, services, markets, and customers. Small, large, for-profit, and nonprofit organizations in all industries are being staggered and challenged by the opportunities and threats arising from changes in social, cultural, demographic, and environmental variables. In every way, the United States is much different today than it was yesterday, and tomorrow promises even greater changes.

The USA is getting older and less white. The oldest among the 76 million baby boomers in the USA plan to retire soon, and this has lawmakers and younger taxpayers deeply concerned about who will pay their Social Security, Medicare, and Medicaid. Individuals age 65 and older in the USA as a percentage of the population, will rise to 18.5 percent by 2025. The oldest USA veteran is Richard Everton of East Austin, Texas, who is 108; the oldest USA woman is 114, Teralean Talley of Inkster, Michigan.

By 2075, the USA will have no racial or ethnic majority. This forecast is aggravating tensions over issues such as immigration and affirmative action. Hawaii, California, and New Mexico already have no majority race or ethnic group

The population of the world recently surpassed 7 billion; the USA has slightly more than 310 million people. That leaves billions of people outside the USA who may be interested in the products and services produced through domestic firms. Remaining solely domestic is an increasingly risky strategy, especially as the world population continues to grow to an estimated 8 billion in 2028 and 9 billion in 2054.

Social, cultural, demographic, and environmental trends are shaping the way Americans live, work, produce, and consume. New trends are creating a different type of consumer and, consequently, a need for different products, different services, and different strategies. There are now more U.S. households with people living alone or with unrelated people than there are households consisting of married couples with children. U.S. households are making more and more purchases online.

The trend toward an older USA is good news for restaurants, hotels, airlines, cruise lines, tours, resorts, theme parks, luxury products and services, recreational vehicles, home builders, furniture producers, computer manufacturers, travel services, pharmaceutical firms, automakers, and funeral homes. Older Americans are especially interested in health care, financial services, travel, crime prevention, and leisure. The world's longest-living people are the Japanese, with Japanese women living to 86.3 years and men living to 80.1 years on average. By 2050, the Census Bureau projects that the number of Americans age 100 and older will increase to over 834,000 from just under 100,000 centenarians in the USA in 2000. Americans age 65 and over will increase from 12.6 percent of the U.S. population in 2000 to 20.0 percent by the year 2050. The aging U.S. population affects the strategic orientation of nearly all organizations.

The historical trend of people moving from the Northeast and Midwest to the Sunbelt and West has dramatically slowed. Hard number data related to this trend can represent key opportunities for many firms and thus can be essential for successful strategy formulation, including where to locate new plants and distribution centers and where to focus marketing efforts.

A summary of important social, cultural, demographic, and environmental variables that represent opportunities or threats for virtually all organizations is given in Table 3-3.

Political, Governmental, and Legal Forces

Figure 3-3 reveals the USA county-by-county presidential election results for the 2012 Barack Obama versus Mitt Romney election, with the red being Republican and the blue being Democratic. The red indicates counties that had a Republican majority vote result, but much of this land is sparsely inhabited. President Obama and the Democrats won both the popular vote and the Electoral College count. Various industries, such as aerospace, and all their supplier firms, typically support and lobby for Republicans, whereas other industries, such as automotive and all their supplier firms, generally support Democrats. National, state, and local elections impact businesses, with ongoing healthy debate concerning the pros and cons of each party's agenda for business. Should firms take stances on political issues?

Political issues and stances do matter for business, especially in today's world of instant tweeting and e-mailing. For example, Starbucks' recent support of same-sex marriage in its home state of Washington was praised by a number of prominent rights activists. Maine, Maryland, Minnesota, Washington, Massachusetts, New York, California, and a few other states all allow same-sex marriage. But the Seattle-based coffee chain's outspoken opponents, such as the National Organization for Marriage (NOM), has vowed to make Starbucks (along with other companies that support same-sex marriage) pay a "price" for this stance. "Middle Eastern countries are hostile to lesbian, gay, bisexual and transgender (LGBT)

TABLE 3-3 Key Social, Cultural, Demographic, and Natural Environment Variables

Childbearing rates	Attitudes toward retirement
Number of special-interest groups	Attitudes toward leisure time
Number of marriages	Attitudes toward product quality
Number of divorces	Attitudes toward customer service
Number of births	Pollution control
Number of deaths	Attitudes toward foreign peoples
Immigration and emigration rates	Energy conservation
Social Security programs	Social programs
Life expectancy rates	Number of churches
Per capita income	Number of church members
Location of retailing, manufacturing, and service businesses	Social responsibility
Attitudes toward business	Attitudes toward careers
Lifestyles	Population changes by race, age, sex, and level of affluence
Traffic congestion	Attitudes toward authority
Inner-city environments	Population changes by city, county, state, region, and country
Average disposable income	Value placed on leisure time
Trust in government	Regional changes in tastes and preferences
Attitudes toward government	Number of women and minority workers
Attitudes toward work	Number of high school and college graduates by geographic area
Buying habits	Recycling
Ethical concerns	Waste management
Attitudes toward saving	Air pollution
Sex roles	Water pollution
Attitudes toward investing	Ozone depletion
Racial equality	Endangered species
Use of birth control	
Average level of education	
Government regulation	

rights. So for example, in Qatar, in the Middle East, we've begun working to make sure that there's some price to be paid for this," Brian Brown of the NOM said. "These are not countries that look kindly on same-sex marriage. And this is where Starbucks wants to expand, as well as India." In essence, the question needs to be asked, should firms take stances on contentious social issues?

Beginning in 2014, U.S. businesses will have to offer workers a minimum level in medical insurance or pay a penalty starting at $2,000 for each worker. This is part of the so-called Obamacare legislation. So, thousands of U.S. businesses, such as Pillar Hotels & Resorts, are transitioning to having a larger percentage of their workforce being comprised of part-time workers rather than full-time employees. Pillar Hotels owns Sheraton, Fairfield Inns, Hampton Inns, and Holiday Inns.

A political debate still rages in the USA regarding sales taxes on the Internet. Walmart, Target, and other large retailers are pressuring state governments to collect sales taxes from Amazon.com. Big brick-and-mortar retailers are backing a coalition called the Alliance for Main Street Fairness, which is leading political efforts to change sales-tax laws in more than a dozen states. Walmart's executive Raul Vazquez says, "The rules today don't allow brick-and-mortar retailers to compete evenly with online retailers, and that needs to be addressed."

Federal, state, local, and foreign governments are major regulators, deregulators, subsidizers, employers, and customers of organizations. Political, governmental, and legal factors, therefore, can represent key opportunities or threats for both small and large organizations. Political unrest in the Middle East threatens to raise oil prices globally, which could cause inflation. The political

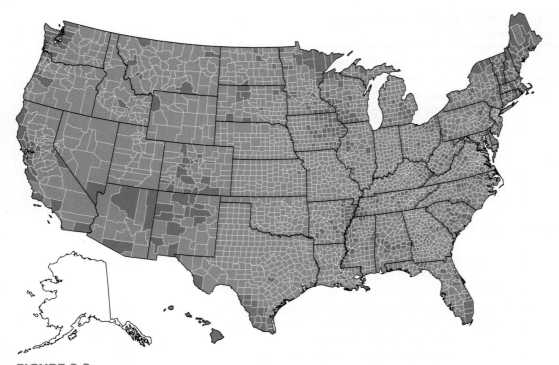

FIGURE 3-3

County-by County USA 2012 Presidential Results (red = Republican; blue = Democrat)

overthrow of monarchies in Egypt, Tunisia, Yemen, and Libya has spread to Syria and even Turkey because people in all nations desire liberty and freedom rather than oppression and suppression.

For industries and firms that depend heavily on government contracts or subsidies, political forecasts can be the most important part of an external audit. Changes in patent laws, antitrust legislation, tax rates, and lobbying activities can affect firms significantly. The increasing global interdependence among economies, markets, governments, and organizations makes it imperative that firms consider the possible impact of political variables on the formulation and implementation of competitive strategies.

The Marketplace Fairness Act (MFA) in the U.S. Senate and the Marketplace Equity Act (MEA) in the U.S. House are likely to pass in 2013, basically reversing the 1992 Supreme Court decision exempting many online retailers from collecting state sales taxes unless they had a physical presence in the state, such as a warehouse. But as online sales boom, states continue to suffer severe budget shortfalls and brick-and-mortar companies cannot compete with online firms, so legislation to tax online sales is expected to pass soon.

Many countries worldwide are resorting to protectionism to safeguard their own industries. European Union (EU) nations, for example, have tightened their own trade rules and resumed subsidies for various of their own industries while barring imports from certain other countries. The EU recently restricted imports of U.S. chicken and beef. India is increasing tariffs on foreign steel. Russia perhaps has instituted the most protectionist measures by raising tariffs on most imports and subsidizing its own exports. Russia even imposed a new toll on trucks from the EU, Switzerland, and Turkmenistan. Despite these measures taken by other countries, the USA has largely refrained from "Buy American" policies and protectionist measures, although there are increased tariffs on French cheese and Italian water. Many economists say trade constraints will make it harder for global economic growth.

Labor Unions

The extent that a state is unionized can be a significant political factor in strategic planning decisions as related to manufacturing plant location and other operational matters. The size of U.S. labor unions has fallen sharply in the last decade as a result in large part of erosion of the U.S. manufacturing base.

Huge declines of late in receipts of federal, state, and municipal governments has contributed to a sharp decline in the membership of public-sector unions. Organized public-sector labor issues are being debated in many state legislatures. State governments seek concessions, the most drastic of which may be the abolition of collective bargaining rights. Wisconsin recently passed a law eliminating most collective-bargaining rights for the state's public-employee unions. That law sets a precedent that many other states may follow to curb union rights as a way to help state budgets become solvent. Ohio is close to passing a similar bill curbing union rights for 400,000 public workers.

According to the U.S. Bureau of Labor Statistics, the union membership rate (the percent of wage and salary workers who were members of a union) in the USA was 11.8 percent in 2011, down slightly from 11.9 percent the prior year. The number of wage and salary workers belonging to unions, at 14.8 million, also showed little movement over the year. By comparison, in 1983, the union membership rate was 20.1 percent and there were 17.7 million union workers. Highlights from the Bureau's 2011 data are as follows:

- Public-sector workers had a union membership rate (37.0 percent) more than five times higher than that of private-sector workers (6.9 percent).
- Workers in education, training, and library occupations had the highest unionization rate, at 36.8 percent, whereas the lowest rate occurred in sales and related occupations (3.0 percent).
- Black workers were more likely to be union members than were white, Asian, or Hispanic workers.
- Among states, New York continued to have the highest union membership rate (24.1 percent) and North Carolina again had the lowest rate (2.9 percent).

In Europe, German-based Lufthansa AG recently cancelled two-thirds of its airline flights as a result of an anticipated strike by its cabin crew. The union UFO represents 18,000 Lufthansa cabin-crew members who want higher wages, but Lufthansa says their average flight attendant' salary is 52,492 euros compared with 23,680 euros at rival firm Air Berlin PLC. Similarly, British Airways recently was hammered by the cabin-crew union Unite, costing the airline about $250 million.

Local, state, and federal laws; regulatory agencies; and special-interest groups can have a major impact on the strategies of small, large, for-profit, and nonprofit organizations. Many companies have altered or abandoned strategies in the past because of political or governmental actions. In the academic world, as state budgets have dropped in recent years, so too has state support for colleges and universities. Resulting from the decline in monies received from the state, many institutions of higher learning are doing more fund-raising on their own—naming buildings and classrooms, for example, for donors. A summary of political, governmental, and legal variables that can represent key opportunities or threats to organizations is provided in Table 3-4.

TABLE 3-4 Some Political, Governmental, and Legal Variables

Government regulations or deregulations	Sino American relationships
Changes in tax laws	Russian American relationships
Special tariffs	European American relationships
Political action committees	African American relationships
Voter participation rates	Import–export regulations
Number, severity, and location of government protests	Government fiscal and monetary policy changes
Number of patents	Political conditions in foreign countries
Changes in patent laws	Special local, state, and federal laws
Environmental protection laws	Lobbying activities
Level of defense expenditures	Size of government budgets
Legislation on equal employment	World oil, currency, and labor markets
Level of government subsidies	Location and severity of terrorist activities
Antitrust legislation	Local, state, and national elections

Technological Forces

The **Internet** has changed the nature of opportunities and threats by altering the life cycles of products, increasing the speed of distribution, creating new products and services, erasing limitations of traditional geographic markets, and changing the historical trade-off between production standardization and flexibility. The Internet has lowered entry barriers and redefined the relationship between industries and various suppliers, creditors, customers, and competitors.

Papa John's International a few years ago received more than 50 percent of all its pizza orders through its website, up from 30 percent in 2011 and far more than the industry average of 10 percent. Technology is a key to Papa John's success as it strives to compete with Domino's Pizza and Pizza Hut. Papa John's new website is interactive, where customers can see a picture of their pizza as they decide upon toppings. Papa John's new loyalty program, called Papa Points, is promoted heavily through its new website.

Google's Nexus 7 tablet computer and Apple's iPhone 5 released in late 2012 worldwide provide a reminder of the kind of competition that has left Japan's consumer electronics makers struggling to survive. Japanese firms such as Sony Corp., Panasonic Corp. and Sharp Corp. once dominated the electronics business. Sharp's new restructuring plan involves the firm cutting more than 10,000 jobs, cutting wages, and selling plants in Mexico, China, and Malaysia.

According to media consultant BIA/Kelsey, small and midsize businesses in the USA spent about $1.3 billion in 2011 on online reputation management tools and services. Those figures grew to about $1.6 billion in 2012 and are expected to grow to $2.5 billion by 2016 according to the firm. Further, the firm says about 57 percent of small and midsize businesses in the USA monitor online content about their businesses, with 71 percent using free, do-it-yourself software. In general, monitoring of online reviews about your business, large or small, has become a burdensome but an essential task, especially given emergence of social-media channels, such as Twitter, that empowers opinionated customers. Research is clear that benign neglect of a company's online reputation could quickly hurt sales, especially given the new normal behavior of customers consulting their smartphones for even the smallest of purchases.[4]

To effectively capitalize on e-commerce, a number of organizations are establishing two new positions in their firms: **chief information officer (CIO)** and **chief technology officer (CTO)**. This trend reflects the growing importance of **information technology (IT)** in strategic management. A CIO and CTO work together to ensure that information needed to formulate, implement, and evaluate strategies is available where and when it is needed. These individuals are responsible for developing, maintaining, and updating a company's information database. The CIO is more a manager, managing the firm's relationship with stakeholders; the CTO is more a technician, focusing on technical issues such as data acquisition, data processing, decision-support systems, and software and hardware acquisition.

Technological forces represent major opportunities and threats that must be considered in formulating strategies. Technological advancements can dramatically affect organizations' products, services, markets, suppliers, distributors, competitors, customers, manufacturing processes, marketing practices, and competitive position. Technological advancements can create new markets, result in a proliferation of new and improved products, change the relative competitive cost positions in an industry, and render existing products and services obsolete. Technological changes can reduce or eliminate cost barriers between businesses, create shorter production runs, create shortages in technical skills, and result in changing values and expectations of employees, managers, and customers. Technological advancements can create new competitive advantages that are more powerful than existing advantages. No company or industry today is insulated against emerging technological developments. In high-tech industries, identification and evaluation of key technological opportunities and threats can be the most important part of the external strategic-management audit.

Organizations that traditionally have limited technology expenditures to what they can fund after meeting marketing and financial requirements urgently need a reversal in thinking. The pace of technological change is increasing and literally wiping out businesses every day. An emerging consensus holds that technology management is one of the key responsibilities of strategists. Firms should pursue strategies that take advantage of technological opportunities to achieve sustainable, competitive advantages in the marketplace.

In practice, critical decisions about technology too often are delegated to lower organizational levels or are made without an understanding of their strategic implications. Many strategists spend countless hours determining market share, positioning products in terms of features and price, forecasting sales and market size, and monitoring distributors; yet too often, technology does not receive the same respect.

Not all sectors of the economy are affected equally by technological developments. The communications, electronics, aeronautics, and pharmaceutical industries are much more volatile than the textile, forestry, and metals industries.

Competitive Forces

An important part of an external audit is identifying rival firms and determining their strengths, weaknesses, capabilities, opportunities, threats, objectives, and strategies. George Salk said: "If you're not faster than your competitor, you're in a tenuous position, and if you're only half as fast, you're terminal."

Collecting and evaluating information on competitors is essential for successful strategy formulation. Identifying major competitors is not always easy because many firms have divisions that compete in different industries. Many multidivisional firms do not provide sales and profit information on a divisional basis for competitive reasons. Also, privately-held firms do not publish any financial or marketing information. Addressing questions about competitors such as those presented in Table 3-5 is important in performing an external audit.

Competition in virtually all industries can be described as intense—and sometimes as cutthroat. For example, Walgreens and CVS pharmacies are located generally across the street from each other and battle each other every day on price and customer service. Most automobile dealerships also are located close to each other. Dollar General, based in Goodlettsville, Tennessee, and Family Dollar, based in Matthews, North Carolina, compete intensely on price to attract customers away from each other and away from Walmart.

Seven characteristics describe the most competitive companies:

1. Strive to continually increase market share.
2. Use the vision/mission as a guide for all decisions.
3. Realize that the old adage "if it's not broke, don't fix it" has been replaced by "whether its broke or not, fix it;" in other words, continually strive to improve everything about the firm
4. Continually adapt, innovate, improve – especially when the firm is successful.
5. Strive to grow through acquisition whenever possible
6. Hire and retain the best employees and managers possible
7. Strive to stay cost-competitive on a global basis.[5]

TABLE 3-5 Key Questions About Competitors

1. What are the major competitors' strengths?
2. What are the major competitors' weaknesses?
3. What are the major competitors' objectives and strategies?
4. How will the major competitors most likely respond to current economic, social, cultural, demographic, environmental, political, governmental, legal, technological, and competitive trends affecting our industry?
5. How vulnerable are the major competitors to our alternative company strategies?
6. How vulnerable are our alternative strategies to successful counterattack by our major competitors?
7. How are our products or services positioned relative to major competitors?
8. To what extent are new firms entering and old firms leaving this industry?
9. What key factors have resulted in our present competitive position in this industry?
10. How have the sales and profit rankings of major competitors in the industry changed over recent years? Why have these rankings changed that way?
11. What is the nature of supplier and distributor relationships in this industry?
12. To what extent could substitute products or services be a threat to competitors in this industry?

Competitive Intelligence Programs

What is competitive intelligence? **Competitive intelligence (CI)**, as formally defined by the Society of Competitive Intelligence Professionals (SCIP), is a systematic and ethical process for gathering and analyzing information about the competition's activities and general business trends to further a business's own goals (SCIP website).

Good competitive intelligence in business, as in the military, is one of the keys to success. The more information and knowledge a firm can obtain about its competitors, the more likely it is that it can formulate and implement effective strategies. Major competitors' weaknesses can represent external opportunities; major competitors' strengths may represent key threats.

Various legal and ethical ways to obtain competitive intelligence include the following:

- Hire top executives from rival firms
- Reverse engineer rival firms' products
- Use surveys and interviews of customers, suppliers, and distributors
- Conduct drive by and on-site visits to rival firm operations
- Search online databases
- Contact government agencies for public information about rival firms
- Systematically monitor relevant trade publications, magazines, and newspapers
- Include gathering competitive intelligence in the job description of salespersons

Many U.S. executives grew up in times when U.S. firms dominated foreign competitors so much that gathering CI did not seem worth the effort. Too many of these executives still cling to these attitudes—to the detriment of their organizations today. Even most MBA programs do not offer a course in competitive and business intelligence, thus reinforcing this attitude. As a consequence, three strong misperceptions about business intelligence prevail among U.S. executives today:

1. Running an intelligence program requires lots of people, computers, and other resources.
2. Collecting intelligence about competitors violates antitrust laws; business intelligence equals espionage.
3. Intelligence gathering is an unethical business practice.[6]

Any discussions with a competitor about price, market, or geography intentions could violate antitrust statutes. However, this fact must not lure a firm into underestimating the need for and benefits of systematically collecting information about competitors for strategic planning purposes. The Internet is an excellent medium for gathering CI. Information gathering from employees, managers, suppliers, distributors, customers, creditors, and consultants also can make the difference between having superior or just average intelligence and overall competitiveness.

Firms need an effective CI program. The three basic objectives of a CI program are (1) to provide a general understanding of an industry and its competitors, (2) to identify areas in which competitors are vulnerable and to assess the impact strategic actions would have on competitors, and (3) to identify potential moves that a competitor might make that would endanger a firm's position in the market.[7] Competitive information is equally applicable for strategy formulation, implementation, and evaluation decisions. An effective CI program allows all areas of a firm to access consistent and verifiable information in making decisions. All members of an organization—from the CEO to custodians—are valuable intelligence agents and should feel themselves to be a part of the CI process. Special characteristics of a successful CI program include flexibility, usefulness, timeliness, and cross-functional cooperation.

The increasing emphasis on **competitive analysis** in the USA is evidenced by corporations putting this function on their organizational charts under job titles such as Director of Competitive Analysis, Competitive Strategy Manager, Director of Information Services, or Associate Director of Competitive Assessment. The responsibilities of a **director of competitive analysis** include planning, collecting data, analyzing data, facilitating the process of gathering and analyzing data, disseminating intelligence on a timely basis, researching special issues, and recognizing what information is important and who needs to know. CI is not corporate espionage because 95 percent of the information a company needs to make strategic decisions is available and accessible to the public. Sources of competitive information include trade journals, want ads, newspaper articles, and government filings, as well as customers, suppliers, distributors, competitors themselves, and the Internet.

Unethical tactics such as bribery, wiretapping, and computer hacking should never be used to obtain information. All the information you could wish for can be collected without resorting to unethical tactics.

Market Commonality and Resource Similarity

By definition, competitors are firms that offer similar products and services in the same market. Markets can be geographic or product areas or segments. For example, in the insurance industry the markets are broken down into commercial/consumer, health/life, or Europe/Asia. Researchers use the terms *market commonality* and *resource similarity* to study rivalry among competitors. **Market commonality** can be defined as the number and significance of markets that a firm competes in with rivals.[8] **Resource similarity** is the extent to which the type and amount of a firm's internal resources are comparable to a rival.[9] One way to analyze competitiveness between two or among several firms is to investigate market commonality and resource similarity issues while looking for areas of potential competitive advantage along each firm's value chain.

Competitive Analysis: Porter's Five-Forces Model

Wayne Calloway said: "Nothing focuses the mind better than the constant sight of a competitor that wants to wipe you off the map." As illustrated in Figure 3-4, **Porter's Five-Forces Model** of competitive analysis is a widely used approach for developing strategies in many industries. The intensity of competition among firms varies widely across industries. Table 3-6 reveals the average gross profit margin and earnings per share for firms in different industries. Note the substantial variation among industries. For example, note that industry profit margins range from 20.5 to 2.3 percent, whereas industry return on equity (ROE) values range from 23.2 to 8.9. Note that bookstores have the lowest average profit margin (2.3), which implies fierce competition in that industry. Intensity of competition is highest in lower-return industries. The collective impact of competitive forces is so brutal in some industries that the market is clearly "unattractive" from a profit-making standpoint. Rivalry among existing firms is severe, new rivals can enter the industry with relative ease, and both suppliers and customers can exercise considerable bargaining leverage. According to Porter, the nature of competitiveness in a given industry can be viewed as a composite of five forces:

1. Rivalry among competing firms
2. Potential entry of new competitors
3. Potential development of substitute products
4. Bargaining power of suppliers
5. Bargaining power of consumers

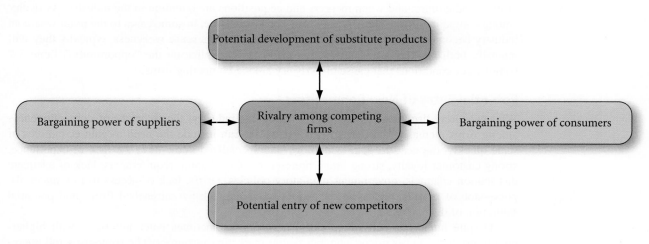

FIGURE 3-4

The Five-Forces Model of Competition

TABLE 3-6 Competitiveness Across a Few Industries (late 2013 data)

	Profit Margin (%)	EPS ($)
Pharmaceutical	20.5	20.3
Telecommunications	8.0	14.1
Fragrances/Cosmetics	9.8	22.6
Banking	16.1	8.9
Bookstores	2.3	10.5
Food Manufacturers	6.6	19.3
Oil and Gas	6.1	15.7
Airlines	2.5	23.2
Machinery/Construction	7.2	21.6
Paper Products	7.6	10.6

Source: Based on information at www.finance.yahoo.com retrieved on May 10, 2011.

The following three steps for using Porter's Five-Forces Model can indicate whether competition in a given industry is such that the firm can make an acceptable profit:

1. Identify key aspects or elements of each competitive force that impact the firm.
2. Evaluate how strong and important each element is for the firm.
3. Decide whether the collective strength of the elements is worth the firm entering or staying in the industry.

Rivalry Among Competing Firms

Rivalry among competing firms is usually the most powerful of the five competitive forces. The strategies pursued by one firm can be successful only to the extent that they provide competitive advantage over the strategies pursued by rival firms. Changes in strategy by one firm may be met with retaliatory countermoves, such as lowering prices, enhancing quality, adding features, providing services, extending warranties, and increasing advertising.

The intensity of rivalry among competing firms tends to increase as the number of competitors increases, as competitors become more equal in size and capability, as demand for the industry's products declines, and as price cutting becomes common. Rivalry also increases when consumers can switch brands easily; when barriers to leaving the market are high; when fixed costs are high; when the product is perishable; when consumer demand is growing slowly or declines such that rivals have excess capacity or inventory; when the products being sold are commodities (not easily differentiated, such as gasoline); when rival firms are diverse in strategies, origins, and culture; and when mergers and acquisitions are common in the industry. As rivalry among competing firms intensifies, industry profits decline, in some cases to the point where an industry becomes inherently unattractive. When rival firms sense weakness, typically they will intensify both marketing and production efforts to capitalize on the "opportunity." Table 3-7 summarizes conditions that cause high rivalry among competing firms.

Potential Entry of New Competitors

Whenever new firms can easily enter a particular industry, the intensity of competitiveness among firms increases. Barriers to entry, however, can include the need to gain economies of scale quickly, the need to gain technology and specialized know-how, the lack of experience, strong customer loyalty, strong brand preferences, large capital requirements, lack of adequate distribution channels, government regulatory policies, tariffs, lack of access to raw materials, possession of patents, undesirable locations, counterattack by entrenched firms, and potential saturation of the market.

Despite numerous barriers to entry, new firms sometimes enter industries with higher-quality products, lower prices, and substantial marketing resources. The strategist's job, therefore, is to identify potential new firms entering the market, to monitor the new rival firms' strategies, to counterattack as needed, and to capitalize on existing strengths and opportunities.

TABLE 3-7 Conditions That Cause High Rivalry Among Competing Firms

1. High number of competing firms
2. Similar size of firms competing
3. Similar capability of firms competing
4. Falling demand for the industry's products
5. Falling product or service prices in the industry
6. When consumers can switch brands easily
7. When barriers to leaving the market are high
8. When barriers to entering the market are low
9. When fixed costs are high among firms competing
10. When the product is perishable
11. When rivals have excess capacity
12. When consumer demand is falling
13. When rivals have excess inventory
14. When rivals sell similar products/services
15. When mergers are common in the industry

When the threat of new firms entering the market is strong, incumbent firms generally fortify their positions and take actions to deter new entrants, such as lowering prices, extending warranties, adding features, or offering financing specials.

Walt Disney is rapidly building its Shanghai Disneyland $4.4 billion complex set to open in China in 2016, complete with hotels, restaurants, retail shops and other amenities. However, a rival firm, DreamWorks Animation SKG, is now building a $3.1 billion entertainment district named Dream Center in Shanghai right beside Disneyland and says its facility will also open in 2016. Although expensive to build, theme parks are becoming more popular globally. Time Warner's Warner Brothers is building Harry Potter attractions around the world, including a converted movie studio outside London.

Potential Development of Substitute Products

In many industries, firms are in close competition with producers of substitute products in other industries. Examples are plastic container producers competing with glass, paperboard, and aluminum can producers, and acetaminophen manufacturers competing with other manufacturers of pain and headache remedies. The presence of substitute products puts a ceiling on the price that can be charged before consumers will switch to the substitute product. Price ceilings equate to profit ceilings and more intense competition among rivals. Producers of eyeglasses and contact lenses, for example, face increasing competitive pressures from laser eye surgery. Producers of sugar face similar pressures from artificial sweeteners. Newspapers and magazines face substitute-product competitive pressures from the Internet and 24-hour cable television. The magnitude of competitive pressure derived from the development of substitute products is generally evidenced by rivals' plans for expanding production capacity, as well as by their sales and profit growth numbers.

Competitive pressures arising from substitute products increase as the relative price of substitute products declines and as consumers' costs of switching decrease. The competitive strength of substitute products is best measured by the inroads into the market share those products obtain, as well as those firms' plans for increased capacity and market penetration.

For example, circulation of U.S. newspapers continues to drop drastically, with the exception of the *Wall Street Journal, USA Today,* and a few others. The growing popularity of free news on the web and more timely news online are two key factors negatively impacting traditional papers such as the *New York Times*, *Los Angeles Times*, and others.

Bargaining Power of Suppliers

The bargaining power of suppliers affects the intensity of competition in an industry, especially when there are few suppliers, when there are few good substitute raw materials, or when the cost of switching raw materials is especially high. It is often in the best interest of both suppliers and producers to assist each other with reasonable prices, improved quality, development of new services, just-in-time deliveries, and reduced inventory costs, thus enhancing long-term profitability for all concerned.

Firms may pursue a backward integration strategy to gain control or ownership of suppliers. This strategy is especially effective when suppliers are unreliable, too costly, or not capable of meeting a firm's needs on a consistent basis. Firms generally can negotiate more favorable terms with suppliers when backward integration is a commonly used strategy among rival firms in an industry.

However, in many industries it is more economical to use outside suppliers of component parts than to self-manufacture the items. This is true, for example, in the outdoor power equipment industry, where producers of lawn mowers, rotary tillers, leaf blowers, and edgers such as Murray generally obtain their small engines from outside manufacturers such as Briggs & Stratton that specialize in such engines and have huge economies of scale.

In more and more industries, sellers are forging strategic partnerships with select suppliers in efforts to (a) reduce inventory and logistics costs (e.g., through just-in-time deliveries); (b) speed the availability of next-generation components; (c) enhance the quality of the parts and components being supplied and reduce defect rates; and (d) squeeze out important cost savings for both themselves and their suppliers.[10]

Bargaining Power of Consumers

When customers are concentrated or large in number or buy in volume, their bargaining power represents a major force affecting the intensity of competition in an industry. Rival firms may offer extended warranties or special services to gain customer loyalty whenever the bargaining power of consumers is substantial. Bargaining power of consumers also is higher when the products being purchased are standard or undifferentiated. When this is the case, consumers often can negotiate selling price, warranty coverage, and accessory packages to a greater extent.

The bargaining power of consumers can be the most important force affecting competitive advantage. Consumers gain increasing bargaining power under the following circumstances:

1. If they can inexpensively switch to competing brands or substitutes
2. If they are particularly important to the seller
3. If sellers are struggling in the face of falling consumer demand
4. If they are informed about sellers' products, prices, and costs
5. If they have discretion in whether and when they purchase the product[11]

Sources of External Information

A wealth of strategic information is available to organizations from both published and unpublished sources. Unpublished sources include customer surveys, market research, speeches at professional and shareholders' meetings, television programs, interviews, and conversations with stakeholders. Published sources of strategic information include periodicals, journals, reports, government documents, abstracts, books, directories, newspapers, and manuals. A company website is usually an excellent place to start to find information about a firm, particularly on the Investor Relations web pages.

There are many excellent websites for gathering strategic information, but five that the author uses routinely are:

1. www.money.msn.com
2. http://finance.yahoo.com
3. www.hoovers.com
4. http://globaledge.msu.edu/industries/
5. www.monrningstar.com

An excellent source of industry information is provided by Michigan State University at http://globaledge.msu.edu/industries/. Industry Profiles provided at that site are an excellent source for information, news, events, and statistical data for any industry. In addition to a wealth of indices, risk assessments, and interactive trade information, a wide array of global resources are provided.

Most college libraries subscribe to Standard & Poor's (S&P's) *Industry Surveys*. These documents are exceptionally up-to-date and give valuable information about many different industries. Each report is authored by a Standard & Poor's industry research analyst and includes the following sections:

1. Current Environment
2. Industry Trends
3. How the Industry Operates
4. Key Industry Ratios and Statistics
5. How to Analyze a Company
6. Glossary of Industry Terms
7. Additional Industry Information
8. References
9. Comparative Company Financial Analysis

Forecasting Tools and Techniques

Forecasts are educated assumptions about future trends and events. Forecasting is a complex activity because of factors such as technological innovation, cultural changes, new products, improved services, stronger competitors, shifts in government priorities, changing social values, unstable economic conditions, and unforeseen events. Managers often must rely on published forecasts to effectively identify key external opportunities and threats.

A sense of the future permeates all action and underlies every decision a person makes. People eat expecting to be satisfied and nourished in the future. People sleep assuming that in the future they will feel rested. They invest energy, money, and time because they believe their efforts will be rewarded in the future. They build highways assuming that automobiles and trucks will need them in the future. Parents educate children on the basis of forecasts that they will need certain skills, attitudes, and knowledge when they grow up. The truth is we all make implicit forecasts throughout our daily lives. The question, therefore, is not whether we should forecast but rather how we can best forecast to enable us to move beyond our ordinarily unarticulated assumptions about the future. Can we obtain information and then make educated assumptions (forecasts) to better guide our current decisions to achieve a more desirable future state of affairs? Assumptions must be made based on facts, figures, trends, and research. Strive for the firm's assumptions to be more accurate than rival firm's assumptions.

Sometimes organizations must develop their own projections. Most organizations forecast (project) their own revenues and profits annually. Organizations sometimes forecast market share or customer loyalty in local areas. Because forecasting is so important in strategic management and because the ability to forecast (in contrast to the ability to use a forecast) is essential, selected forecasting tools are examined further here.

Forecasting tools can be broadly categorized into two groups: quantitative techniques and qualitative techniques. Quantitative forecasts are most appropriate when historical data are available and when the relationships among key variables are expected to remain the same in the future. **Linear regression**, for example, is based on the assumption that the future will be just like the past—which, of course, it never is. As historical relationships become less stable, quantitative forecasts become less accurate.

No forecast is perfect, and some forecasts are even wildly inaccurate. This fact accents the need for strategists to devote sufficient time and effort to study the underlying bases for published forecasts and to develop internal forecasts of their own. Key external opportunities and threats can be effectively identified only through good forecasts. Accurate forecasts can provide major competitive advantages for organizations. Accurate forecasts are vital to the strategic-management process and to the success of organizations.

Making Assumptions

Planning would be impossible without assumptions. McConkey defines assumptions as the "best present estimates of the impact of major external factors, over which the manager has little if any control, but which may exert a significant impact on performance or the ability to achieve desired results."[12] Strategists are faced with countless variables and imponderables that can be neither controlled nor predicted with 100 percent accuracy. Wild guesses should never be made in formulating strategies, but reasonable assumptions based on available information must *always* be made.

By identifying future occurrences that could have a major effect on the firm and by making reasonable assumptions about those factors, strategists can carry the strategic-management process forward. Assumptions are needed only for future trends and events that are most likely to have a significant effect on the company's business. Based on the best information at the time, assumptions serve as checkpoints on the validity of strategies. If future occurrences deviate significantly from assumptions, strategists know that corrective actions may be needed. Without reasonable assumptions, the strategy-formulation process could not proceed effectively. Firms that have the best information generally make the most accurate assumptions, which can lead to major competitive advantages.

Industry Analysis: The External Factor Evaluation Matrix

An **external factor evaluation (EFE) matrix** allows strategists to summarize and evaluate economic, social, cultural, demographic, environmental, political, governmental, legal, technological, and competitive information. Illustrated in Table 3-8, the EFE Matrix can be developed in five steps:

1. List key external factors as identified in the external-audit process. Include a total of 20 factors, including both opportunities and threats that affect the firm and its industry. List the opportunities first and then the threats. Be as specific as possible, using percentages, ratios, and comparative numbers whenever possible. Recall that Edward Deming said: "In God we trust. Everyone else bring data." In addition, utilize "*actionable*" factors as defined earlier in this chapter.
2. Assign to each factor a weight that ranges from 0.0 (not important) to 1.0 (very important). The weight indicates the relative importance of that factor to being successful in the firm's industry. Opportunities often receive higher weights than threats, but threats can receive high weights if they are especially severe or threatening. Appropriate weights can be determined by comparing successful with unsuccessful competitors or by discussing the factor and reaching a group consensus. The sum of all weights assigned to the factors must equal 1.0.
3. Assign a rating between 1 and 4 to each key external factor to indicate how effectively the firm's current strategies respond to the factor, where 4 = *the response is superior*, 3 = *the response is above average*, 2 = *the response is average*, and 1 = *the response is poor.* Ratings are based on effectiveness of the firm's strategies. Ratings are thus company-based, whereas the weights in Step 2 are industry-based. It is important to note that both threats and opportunities can receive a 1, 2, 3, or 4.
4. Multiply each factor's weight by its rating to determine a weighted score.
5. Sum the weighted scores for each variable to determine the total weighted score for the organization.

Regardless of the number of key opportunities and threats included in an EFE Matrix, the highest possible total weighted score for an organization is 4.0 and the lowest possible total weighted score is 1.0. The average total weighted score is 2.5. A total weighted score of 4.0 indicates that an organization is responding in an outstanding way to existing opportunities and threats in its industry. In other words, the firm's strategies effectively take advantage of existing opportunities and minimize the potential adverse effects of external threats. A total score of 1.0 indicates that the firm's strategies are not capitalizing on opportunities or avoiding external threats.

An example of an EFE Matrix is provided in Table 3-8 for a local 10-theater cinema complex. Note that the most important factor to being successful in this business is "Trend toward healthy eating eroding concession sales" as indicated by the 0.12 weight. Also note that the local cinema is doing excellent in regard to handling two factors, "TDB University is expanding 6 percent annually" and "Trend toward healthy eating eroding concession sales." Perhaps the cinema is placing flyers on campus and also adding yogurt and healthy drinks to its concession menu. Note that you may have a 1, 2, 3, or 4 anywhere down the Rating column. Note also that the factors are stated in quantitative terms to the extent possible, rather than being stated in vague terms. Quantify the factors as much as possible in constructing an EFE Matrix. Note also that all the factors are "actionable" instead of being something like "the economy is bad." Finally, note that the total weighted score of 2.58 is above the average (midpoint) of 2.5, so this cinema business is doing pretty well, taking advantage of the

TABLE 3-8 EFE Matrix for a Local 10-Theater Cinema Complex

Key External Factors	Weight	Rating	Weighted Score
Opportunities			
1. Rowan County is growing 8 percent annually in population	0.05	3	0.15
2. TDB University is expanding 6 percent annually	0.08	4	0.32
3. Major competitor across town recently ceased operations	0.08	3	0.24
4. Demand for going to cinema growing 10 percent annually	0.07	2	0.14
5. Two new neighborhoods being developed within 3 miles	0.09	1	0.09
6. Disposable income among citizens grew 5 percent in prior year	0.06	3	0.18
7. Unemployment rate in county declined to 3.1 percent	0.03	2	0.06
Threats			
8. Trend toward healthy eating eroding concession sales	0.12	4	0.48
9. Demand for online movies and DVDs growing 10 percent annually	0.06	2	0.12
10. Commercial property adjacent to cinemas for sale	0.06	3	0.18
11. TDB University installing an on-campus movie theater	0.04	3	0.12
12. County and city property taxes increasing 25 percent this year	0.08	2	0.16
13. Local religious groups object to R-rated movies being shown	0.04	3	0.12
14. Movies rented from local Blockbuster store up 12 percent	0.08	2	0.16
15. Movies rented last quarter from Time Warner up 15 percent	0.06	1	0.06
Total	**1.00**		**2.58**

external opportunities and avoiding the threats facing the firm. There is definitely room for improvement, though, because the highest total weighted score would be 4.0. As indicated by ratings of 1, this business needs to capitalize more on the "two new neighborhoods nearby" opportunity and the "movies rented from Time Warner" threat. Note also that there are many percentage-based factors among the group. Be quantitative to the extent possible! Note also that the ratings range from 1 to 4 on both the opportunities and threats.

An EFEMatrix for Netflix is provided in Table 3-9. Note that the most important external factors for Netflix were the growth in Internet users globally as indicated by a weight of 0.08. Netflix's total weighted score of 2.73 is good but not excellent.

The Competitive Profile Matrix

The **Competitive Profile Matrix (CPM)** identifies a firm's major competitors and its particular strengths and weaknesses in relation to a sample firm's strategic position. The weights and total weighted scores in both a CPM and an EFE have the same meaning. However, *critical success factors* in a CPM include both internal and external issues; therefore, the ratings refer to strengths and weaknesses, where 4 = major strength, 3 = minor strength, 2 = minor weakness, and 1 = major weakness. The critical success factors in a CPM are not grouped into opportunities and threats as they are in an EFE. In a CPM, the ratings and total weighted scores for rival firms can be compared to the sample firm. This comparative analysis provides important internal strategic information. Avoid assigning the same rating to firms included in your CPM analysis.

A sample CPM is provided in Table 3-10. In this example, the two most important factors to being successful in the industry are "advertising" and "global expansion," as indicated by weights of 0.20. If there were no weight column in this analysis, note that each factor then would be equally important. Thus, having a weight column makes for a more robust analysis because it enables the analyst to assign higher and lower numbers to capture perceived or actual levels of importance. Note in Table 3-10 that Company 1 is strongest on "product quality," as indicated by a rating of 4, whereas Company 2 is strongest on "advertising." Overall, Company 1 is strongest, as indicated by the total weighted score of 3.15 and Company 3 is weakest.

TABLE 3-9 An Actual EFE Matrix for Netflix

Opportunities	Weight	Rating	WScore
1. Netflix has 30 million members globally. Millions more would like Netflix.	0.07	2	.14
2. Movie ticket prices rose 3 percent in 2012.	0.04	2	.08
3. Blockbuster closed 30 percent of its stores in 2012.	0.06	4	.24
Number of Internet users globally increased from 2.4 billion in mid-2012 to over 3.0 billion in 2013.	0.08	4	.32
4. The introduction of smart TVs is enabling online content to be viewed faster and without gaming consoles.	0.06	3	.18
5. Average cable bills nationwide increased 5.8 percent.	0.05	2	.10
6. The average price of a DVD is $25 and rising.	0.04	2	.08
7. Percentage of Americans who play computer & video games is 72 percent.	0.03	3	.09
8. Once you start a movie stream on Blockbuster, you only have 24 hours to watch as any number of times.	0.05	4	.20
9. Smartphone usage is growing 20 percent annually.	0.02	3	.06
Threats			
1. Unemployment exceeds 10 percent in many areas.	0.04	2	.08
2. Blockbuster has new movie and television titles available 28 days before Redbox and Netflix.	0.05	4	.20
3. Blockbuster offers disc-only plans, stream-only plans, and combination plans.	0.04	3	.12
4. Blockbuster offers unlimited rentals-by-mail *and* in-store exchanges.	0.06	2	.12
5. Redbox installed about 6,000 kiosks in Canada in 2012.	0.05	3	.15
6. Netflix's streaming content licensing costs rose from $180 million in 2010 to a huge $1.98 billion in 2012.	0.06	4	.24
7. Coinstar is partnering with Verizon to enter the streaming market.	0.07	2	.14
8. YouTube has an agreement with Paramount to stream movies through their website.	0.05	2	.10
9. Increase in online activity increases the threat of identity theft.	0.03	1	.04
10. Amazon, Apple, and Hulu enter the movie streaming business.	0.05	3	.15
Total	**1.00**		**2.73**

Other than the critical success factors listed in the example CPM, factors often included in this analysis include breadth of product line, effectiveness of sales distribution, proprietary or patent advantages, location of facilities, production capacity and efficiency, experience, union relations, technological advantages, and e-commerce expertise.

Just because one firm receives a 3.20 overall rating and another receives a 2.80 in a CPM, it does not necessarily follow that the first firm is precisely 14.3 percent better than the second, but it does suggest that the first firm is better in some areas. Regarding weights in a CPM, EFEM, or IFEM, 0.08 is 33 percent higher than 0.06, so even small differences can reveal important perceptions regarding the relative importance of various factors. The aim with numbers is to assimilate and evaluate information in a meaningful way that aids in decision-making.

Another CPM is provided in Table 3-11. Note that Company 2 has the best product quality and management experience; Company 3 has the best market share and inventory system; and Company 1 has the best price as indicated by the ratings. Again, avoid assigning duplicate ratings on any row in a CPM.

TABLE 3-10 An Example Competitive Profile Matrix

Critical Success Factors	Weight	Company 1 Rating	Score	Company 2 Rating	Score	Company 3 Rating	Score
Advertising	0.20	1	0.20	4	0.80	3	0.60
Product Quality	0.10	4	0.40	3	0.30	2	0.20
Price Competitiveness	0.10	3	0.30	2	0.20	1	0.10
Management	0.10	4	0.40	3	0.20	1	0.10
Financial Position	0.15	4	0.60	2	0.30	3	0.45
Customer Loyalty	0.10	4	0.40	3	0.30	2	0.20
Global Expansion	0.20	4	0.80	1	0.20	2	0.40
Market Share	0.05	1	0.05	4	0.20	3	0.15
Total	**1.00**		**3.15**		**2.50**		**2.20**

Note: The ratings values are as follows: 1 = major weakness, 2 = minor weakness, 3 = minor strength, 4 = major strength. As indicated by the total weighted score of 2.50, Competitor 2 is weakest. Only eight critical success factors are included for simplicity; this is too few in actuality.

An example CPM for Royal Caribbean Cruises (RCC) is provided in Table 3-12. Note that RCC's main rival is Carnival Corporation. Having 40 ships in its fleet, RCC is the world's second-largest cruise line operator, after Carnival, which has 100 ships. RCC owns Celebrity Cruises, Pullmantur Cruises, Azamara Club Cruises, and CDF Croisieres de France. Carnival recently ordered a brand new ship (being built by Fincantieri) to be the largest cruise ship ever built, having a passenger capacity of 4,000 and a tonnage of 135,000, and scheduled for delivery in 2016. Note in the CPM that Carnival has a much better financial position than RCC, but RCC has the nicest ships as of year 2013, led by its Oasis ship.

Special Note To Students

In developing and presenting your external assessment for the firm, be mindful that gaining and sustaining competitive advantage is the overriding purpose of developing the opportunity and threat lists, value chain, EFEM, and CPM. During this section of your written or oral project, emphasize how and why particular factors can yield competitive advantage for the firm. In

TABLE 3-11 Another Example Competitive Profile Matrix

Critical Success Factors	Weight	Company 1 Rating	Weighted Score	Company 2 Rating	Weighted Score	Company 3 Rating	Weighted Score
Market Share	0.15	3	0.45	2	0.30	4	0.60
Inventory System	0.08	2	0.16	1	0.08	4	0.32
Financial Position	0.10	2	0.20	3	0.30	4	0.40
Product Quality	0.08	3	0.24	4	0.32	2	0.16
Consumer Loyalty	0.02	3	0.06	1	0.02	4	0.08
Sales Distribution	0.10	3	0.30	2	0.20	4	0.40
Global Expansion	0.15	3	0.45	2	0.30	4	0.60
Organization Structure	0.05	3	0.15	4	0.20	2	0.10
Production Capacity	0.04	3	0.12	2	0.08	4	0.16
E-commerce	0.10	3	0.30	1	0.10	4	0.40
Customer Service	0.10	3	0.30	2	0.20	4	0.40
Price Competitive	0.02	4	0.08	1	0.02	3	0.06
Management Experience	0.01	2	0.02	4	0.04	3	0.03
Total	**1.00**		**2.83**		**2.16**		**3.69**

TABLE 3-12 A Competitive Profile Matrix for Royal Caribbean Cruises

		RCC		Carnival Corp	
Critical Success Factors	Weight	Rating	Score	Rating	Score
Advertising	0.20	2	0.40	4	0.80
Quality of Ships	0.20	4	0.80	2	0.40
Price Competitiveness	0.15	3	0.45	4	0.60
Management	0.15	3	0.45	2	0.30
Financial Position	0.05	1	0.05	4	0.20
Customer Loyalty	0.15	2	0.30	4	0.60
Global Expansion	0.05	.	.15	3	0.15
Market Share	0.05	1	0.05	4	0.20
Total	**1.00**		**2.65**		**3.25**

other words, instead of robotically going through the weights and ratings (which by the way are critically important), highlight various factors in light of where you are leading the firm. Make it abundantly clear in your discussion how your firm, with your suggestions, can subdue rival firms or at least profitably compete with them. Showcase during this section of your project the key underlying reasons how and why your firm can prosper among rivals. Remember to be *prescriptive*, rather than *descriptive*, in the manner that you present your entire project. If presenting your project orally, be self-confident and passionate rather than timid and uninterested. Definitely "bring the data" throughout your project because "vagueness" is the most common downfall of students in case analyses.

Conclusion

Increasing turbulence in markets and industries around the world means the external audit has become an explicit and vital part of the strategic-management process. This chapter provides a framework for collecting and evaluating economic, social, cultural, demographic, environmental, political, governmental, legal, technological, and competitive information. Firms that do not mobilize and empower their managers and employees to identify, monitor, forecast, and evaluate key external forces may fail to anticipate emerging opportunities and threats and, consequently, may pursue ineffective strategies, miss opportunities, and invite organizational demise. Firms not taking advantage of e-commerce and social media networks are technologically falling behind.

A major responsibility of strategists is to ensure development of an effective external-audit system. This includes using information technology to devise a competitive intelligence system that works. The external-audit approach described in this chapter can be used effectively by any size or type of organization. Typically, the external-audit process is more informal in small firms, but the need to understand key trends and events is no less important for these firms. The EFE Matrix and Porter's Five-Forces Model can help strategists evaluate the market and industry, but these tools must be accompanied by good intuitive judgment. Multinational firms especially need a systematic and effective external-audit system because external forces among foreign countries vary so greatly.

MyManagementLab®

Go to **mymanagementlab.com** to complete the problems marked with this icon ⭐.

Key Terms and Concepts

actionable factors (p. 61)
chief information officer (CIO) (p. 70)
chief technology officer (CTO) (p. 70)

competitive analysis (p. 72)
competitive intelligence (CI) (p. 72)
competitive profile matrix (CPM) (p. 79)

director of competitive analysis (p. 72)
environmental scanning (p. 60)
external audit (p. 60)
external factor evaluation (EFE)
    matrix (p. 78)
external forces (p. 61)
Industrial Organization (I/O) (p. 63)

industry analysis (p. 60)
information technology (IT) (p. 70)
Internet (p. 70)
linear regression (p. 77)
market commonality (p. 73)
Porter's Five-Forces Model (p. 73)
resource similarity (p. 73)

Issues for Review and Discussion

3-1. Should firms take stances on contentious social issues? Discuss.

3-2. Should firms take stances on political issues?

3-3. Describe union membership trends in the United States. What are implications for strategic planning in firms such as Boeing or Heinz or Caterpillar.

3-4. List some legal or ethical ways to gather competitive intelligence. List some illegal or unethical ways.

3-5. As value of the dollar rises, U.S. firms doing business abroad see their profits fall, so some firms raise prices of their products to offset the decrease in profits. What are some risks of raising price?

3-6. In your opinion, what are the four major external threats facing PetSmart, and the four major opportunities? Realizing the importance of quantification in stating key factors, how could your factors be quantified? Identify specific estimates (numbers) for your factors.

3-7. Does McDonald's Corp. benefit from a low or high value of the dollar? Explain why.

3-8. Explain how Facebook, Twitter, and Instagram can represent a major threat or opportunity for a company.

3-9. Rate the five websites provided under the "Sources of External Information" section of the chapter from best to worst for finding information about a company.

3-10. If your CPM has three firms and they all end up with the same total weighted score, would the analysis still be useful? Why?

3-11. Describe the "process of performing an external audit" in an organization doing strategic planning for the first time.

3-12. The global recession forced thousands of firms into bankruptcy. Does this fact alone confirm that "external factors are more important than internal factors" in strategic planning? Discuss.

3-13. Do the advantages of a low value of the dollar offset the disadvantages for (a) a firm that derives 60 percent of its revenues from foreign countries and (b) a firm that derives 10 percent of its revenues from foreign countries? Justify your answers.

3-14. The migration of people has slowed from (a) region to region across the USA, from (b) city to suburb worldwide, and from (c) country to country across the globe. What are the strategic implications of these trends for companies?

3-15. Governments worldwide are turning to "nationalization of companies" to cope with economic problems. What are the strategic implications of this trend for firms that compete with these nationalized firms?

3-16. Governments worldwide are turning to "protectionism" to cope with economic problems, imposing tariffs and subsidies on foreign goods and restrictions and incentives on their own firms to keep jobs at home. What are the strategic implications of this trend for international commerce?

3-17. Compare and contrast the duties and responsibilities of a CIO with a CTO in a large firm.

3-18. What are the three basic objectives of a CI program?

3-19. Distinguish between market commonality and resource similarity. Apply these concepts to two rival firms that you are familiar with.

3-20. Let's say you work for McDonald's and you applied Porter's Five-Forces Model to study the fast-food industry. Would information in your analysis provide factors more readily to an EFE Matrix, a CPM, or to neither matrix? Justify your answer.

3-21. Explain why it is appropriate for ratings in an EFE Matrix to be 1, 2, 3, or 4 for any opportunity or threat.

3-22. Why is inclusion of about 20 factors recommended in the EFE Matrix rather than about 10 factors or about 40 factors?

3-23. In developing an EFE Matrix, would it be advantageous to arrange your opportunities according to the highest weight, and do likewise for your threats? Explain.

3-24. In developing an EFE Matrix, would it be best to have 10 opportunities and 10 threats, or would 17 opportunities (or threats) be fine with 3 of the other to achieve a total of 20 factors as desired?

3-25. Could or should critical success factors in a CPM include external factors? Explain.

3-26. Explain how to conduct an external strategic-management audit.

3-27. Identify a recent economic, social, political, or technological trend that significantly affects the local Pizza Hut.

3-28. Discuss the following statement: Major opportunities and threats usually result from an interaction among key environmental trends rather than from a single external event or factor.

3-29. Identify two industries experiencing rapid technological changes and three industries that are experiencing little technological change. How does the need for technological forecasting differ in these industries? Why?

3-30. Use Porter's Five-Forces Model to evaluate competitiveness within the U.S. banking industry.

3-31. How does the external audit affect other components of the strategic-management process?

3-32. As the owner of a small business, explain how you would organize a strategic-information scanning system. How would you organize such a system in a large organization?

3-33. Construct an EFE Matrix for an organization of your choice.

3-34. What is your forecast for interest rates and the stock market in the next several months? As the stock market moves up, do interest rates always move down? Why? What are the strategic implications of these trends?

3-35. Let's say your boss develops an EFE Matrix that includes 62 factors. How would you suggest reducing the number of factors to 20?

 3-36. Discuss the ethics of gathering CI.

3-37. Discuss the ethics of cooperating with rival firms.

3-38. Do you agree with I/O theorists that external factors are more important than internal factors to a firm's achieving competitive advantage? Explain both your and their position.

3-39. Define, compare, and contrast the weights versus ratings in an EFE Matrix.

3-40. Develop a CPM for your university. Include six factors.

3-41. List the 10 external areas that give rise to opportunities and threats.

MyManagementLab®

Go to **mymanagementlab.com** for Auto-graded writing questions as well as the following Assisted-graded writing questions:

3-42. Describe the "process of performing an external audit" in an organization doing strategic planning for the first time.

3-43. Compare and contrast the duties and responsibilities of a CIO with a CTO in a large firm.

3-44. Mymanagementlab Only—comprehensive writing assignment for this chapter.

Current Readings

Allio, Robert J. and Liam Fahey. "Joan Magretta: What Executives can Learn from Revisiting Michael Porter." *Strategy and Leadership* 40, no. 3 (2012): 5–10.

Berchicci, Luca, Glen Dowell, and Andrew A. King. "Environmental Capabilities and Corporate Strategy: Exploring Acquisitions Among US Manufacturing Firms." *Strategic Management Journal* 33, no. 9 (September 2012): 1053–1071.

Berman, Saul J. "Digital Transformation: Opportunities to Create New Business Models." *Strategy and Leadership* 40, no. 3 (2012): 16–24.

Kim, Kwang-Ho and Wenpin Tsai. "Social Comparison Among Competing Firms." *Strategic Management Journal* 33, no. 2 (February 2012): 115–136.

Pacheco-de-Almeida, Gonçalo and Peter B. Zemsky. "Some Like it Free: Innovators' Strategic Use of Disclosure to Slow Down Competition." *Strategic Management Journal* 33, no. 7 (July 2012): 773–793.

ASSURANCE OF LEARNING EXERCISES

 EXERCISE 3A
Competitive Intelligence (CI) Certification

Purpose

This exercise will enhance your knowledge of CI, which is the action of defining, gathering, analyzing, and distributing information about products, customers, and competitors as needed to support executives and managers in making strategic decisions for an organization. With the right information, organizations can avoid unpleasant surprises by anticipating competitors' moves and decreasing response time. CI information is available in newspapers and magazines, such as the *Wall Street Journal*, *Business Week*, and *Fortune*. The Internet has made gathering CI information easier. However, because the Internet is mostly public domain material, information gathered is less likely to be good CI. In fact, there is a risk that information gathered from the Internet may be misinformation and mislead users, so CI researchers are often wary of such information. Many therefore spend their time and budget gathering intelligence using primary research, which includes networking with industry experts, attending trade shows and conferences, gathering information from their own customers and suppliers, and so on. The Internet is primarily used to gather information on what the company says about itself and its online presence (in the form of links to other companies, its strategy regarding search engines and online advertising, mentions in discussion forums and on blogs, etc.). Also important in CI are online subscription databases and news aggregation sources, which have simplified the secondary source collection process. Social media sources also have become important—providing potential interviewee names, as well as opinions and attitudes, and sometimes breaking news.

Instructions

Step 1   Do a Google search for the following five CI topics and write a short overview of each item.
1. Strategic & Competitive Intelligence Professionals
2. The *Journal of Competitive Intelligence and Management*
3. The Institute for Competitive Intelligence
4. The Fuld-Gilad-Herring Academy of Competitive Intelligence
5. Competitive Intelligence Ethics: Navigating the Gray Zone

EXERCISE 3B
Develop Divisional PepsiCo EFE Matrices

Purpose

PepsiCo faces fierce but different competitors in its snacks versus beverages segment as described in the Cohesion Case. The external opportunities and threats that PepsiCo faces are different in each segment, so each division prepares its own list of critical external success factors. This external analysis is critically important in strategic planning because a firm needs to exploit opportunities and avoid or at least mitigate threats.

Instructions

Step 1   Conduct research to determine what you believe are the four major threats and the four major opportunities critical to strategic planning within PepsiCo's snacks versus beverages business segments. Focus solely on North America because outside North America, PepsiCo combines these product segments in (a) Europe and (b) AMEA. Review the relevant S&P Industry Survey documents for *Annual Report* and Cohesion Case.

Step 2   Based on the information from Step 1, develop divisional EFE matrices for PepsiCo. Work within a team of students if your instructor so requests, but you will need an EFE Matrix for the (a) snacks and (b) beverage segments of PepsiCo.

Step 3   Discuss how PepsiCo could combine your two EFE matrices to develop a corporate EFE Matrix.

EXERCISE 3C
Develop an EFE Matrix for PepsiCo

Purpose

This exercise will give you practice developing an EFE matrix. An EFE Matrix summarizes the results of an external audit. This is an important tool widely used by strategists.

Instructions

Step 1   Join with two other students in class, and jointly prepare an EFE Matrix for PepsiCo. Refer back to the Cohesion Case (p. 24) and to Exercise 1B (p. 36), if necessary, to identify external opportunities and threats. Make sure the factors you include are both specific and actionable. Use the information in the S&P Industry Surveys that you copied as part of Assurance of Learning Exercise 1B. Be sure not to include strategies as opportunities, but do include as many monetary amounts, percentages, numbers, and ratios as possible.

Step 2   All three-person teams participating in this exercise should record their EFE total weighted scores on the board. Put your initials after your score to identify it as your team's.

Step 3   Compare the total weighted scores. Which team's score came closest to the instructor's answer? Discuss reasons for variation in the scores reported on the board.

EXERCISE 3D
Perform an External Assessment

Purpose

This exercise will give you practice doing an external assessment. A key part of preparing an external audit is searching the Internet and examining published sources of information for relevant economic, social, cultural, demographic, environmental, political, governmental, legal, technological, and competitive trends and events. External opportunities and threats must be identified and evaluated before strategies can be formulated effectively.

Instructions

Step 1   Select a company or business where you currently or previously have worked. Conduct an external audit for this company. Find opportunities and threats in recent issues of newspapers and magazines. Search for information using the Internet. Use the following five websites:

www.hoovers.com
www.money.msn.com
http://finance.yahoo.com
www.morning.star.com
http://globaledge.msu.edu/industries/

Step 2   On a separate sheet of paper, list 10 opportunities and 10 threats that face this company. Be specific in stating each factor.

Step 3   Include a bibliography to reveal where you found the information.

Step 4   Write a three-page summary of your findings, and submit it to your instructor.

 ### EXERCISE 3E
Develop an EFE Matrix for Your University

Purpose

Most colleges and universities do strategic planning. Institutions are consciously and systematically identifying and evaluating external opportunities and threats facing higher education in your state, the nation, and the world.

Instructions

Step 1   Join with two other individuals in class and jointly prepare an EFE Matrix for your institution.

Step 2   Go to the board and record your total weighted score in a column that includes the scores of all three-person teams participating. Put your initials after your score to identify it as your team's.

Step 3   Which team viewed your college's strategies most positively? Which team viewed your college's strategies most negatively? Discuss the nature of the differences.

 ### EXERCISE 3F
Comparing PetSmart With PETCO Animal Supplies

Purpose

The company featured at the beginning of this chapter, PetSmart, competes with PETCO in thousands of cities across the USA and Canada. Gaining and sustaining competitive advantage is something that both firms strive to do every day. This exercise gives you practice identifying competitive advantages that could provide a basis for strategic action.

Instructions

Step 1   Using the Internet sites described in this chapter as well as other sources of information including an on-site visit, conduct research aimed at comparing PetSmart with PETCO.

Step 2   Identify four competitive advantages that PetSmart has over PETCO and four competitive advantages that PETCO has over PetSmart. Give a rationale and source for each of your identified factors.

Step 3   Discuss or write up how PetSmart can best sustain and promote its competitive advantages while at the same time minimizing PETCO's competitive advantages.

 ### EXERCISE 3G
Develop a Competitive Profile Matrix for PepsiCo

Purpose

Monitoring competitors' performance and strategies is a key aspect of an external audit. This exercise is designed to give you practice evaluating the competitive position of organizations in a given industry and assimilating that information in the form of a CPM.

Instructions

Step 1   Gather your information from Assurance of Learning Exercise 1B. Also, turn back to the Cohesion Case and review the section on competitors (page 31).

Step 2   On a separate sheet of paper, prepare a CPM that includes PepsiCo and Coca-Cola Company.

Step 3   Turn in your CPM for a classwork grade.

 EXERCISE 3H

Develop a Competitive Profile Matrix for Your University

Purpose

Your college or university competes with all other educational institutions in the world, especially those in your own state. State funds, students, faculty, staff, endowments, gifts, and federal funds are areas of competitiveness. Other areas include athletic programs, dorm life, academic reputation, location, and career services. The purpose of this exercise is to give you practice thinking competitively about the business of education in your state.

Instructions

Step 1   Identify two colleges or universities in your state that compete directly with your institution for students. Interview several persons, perhaps classmates, who are aware of particular strengths and weaknesses of those universities. Record information about the two competing universities.

Step 2   Prepare a CPM that includes your institution and the two competing institutions. Include at least the following 10 factors in your analysis:

1. Tuition costs
2. Quality of faculty
3. Academic reputation
4. Average class size
5. Campus landscaping
6. Athletic programs
7. Quality of students
8. Graduate programs
9. Location of campus
10. Campus culture

Step 3   Submit your CPM to your instructor for evaluation.

Notes

1. York Freund, "Critical Success Factors," *Planning Review* 16, no. 4 (July–August 1988): 20.
2. Lee Siegel, "Rise of the Tiger Nation," *Wall Street Journal* (October 27, 2012): C1.
3. Siegel, "Rise of the Tiger Nation."
4. Roger Yu, "Online Rep Crucial for Small Companies," USA Today (October 30, 2012): 5B.
5. Bill Saporito, "Companies That Compete Best," Fortune, May 22, 1989, 36.
6. Kenneth Sawka, "Demystifying Business Intelligence," *Management Review* (October 1996): 49.
7. John Prescott and Daniel Smith, "The Largest Survey of 'Leading-Edge' Competitor Intelligence Managers," *Planning Review* 17, no. 3 (May–June 1989): 6–13.
8. M. J. Chen, "Competitor Analysis and Interfirm Rivalry: Toward a Theoretical Integration," *Academy of Management Review* 21 (1996): 106.
9. S. Jayachandran, J. Gimeno, and P. R. Varadarajan, "Theory of Multimarket Competition: A Synthesis and Implications for Marketing Strategy," *Journal of Marketing* 63, 3 (1999): 59; and M. J. Chen. "Competitor Analysis and Interfirm Rivalry: Toward a Theoretical Integration," *Academy of Management Review* 21 (1996): 107–108.
10. Arthur Thompson, Jr., A. J. Strickland III, and John Gamble, Crafting and Executing Strategy: Text and Readings (New York: McGraw-Hill/Irwin, 2005), 63.
11. Michael E. Porter, Competitive Strategy: Techniques for Analyzing Industries and Competitors (New York: Free Press, 1980), 24–27.
12. Dale McConkey, "Planning in a Changing Environment," Business Horizons 31, no. 5 (September–October 1988): 67.

Source: Andy Dean Photography/Shutterstock

4

MyManagementLab®

⭐ **Improve Your Grade!**

More than 10 million students improved their results using the Pearson MyLabs.
Visit **mymanagementlab.com** for simulations, tutorials, and end-of-chapter problems.

The Internal Assessment

CHAPTER OBJECTIVES

After studying this chapter, you should be able to do the following:

1. Explain how the nature and role of chief marketing officer has changed.

2. Be able to work out breakeven analysis business problems.

3. Describe how to perform an internal strategic-management audit.

4. Discuss the resource-based view (RBV) in strategic management.

5. Discuss key interrelationships among the functional areas of business.

6. Identify the basic functions or activities that make up management, marketing, finance and accounting, production and operations, research and development, and management information systems.

7. Explain how to determine and prioritize a firm's internal strengths and weaknesses.

8. Explain the importance of financial ratio analysis.

9. Discuss the nature and role of management information systems in strategic management.

10. Develop an internal factor evaluation (IFE) matrix.

11. Explain cost/benefit analysis, value chain analysis, and benchmarking as strategic-management tools.

ASSURANCE OF LEARNING **EXERCISES**

The following exercises are found at the end of this chapter.

This chapter focuses on identifying and evaluating a firm's strengths and weaknesses in the functional areas of business, including management, marketing, finance and accounting, production and operations, research and development (R&D), and management information systems (MIS). Relationships among these areas of business are examined. Strategic implications of important functional area concepts are examined. The process of performing an internal audit is described. The resource-based view (RBV) of strategic management is introduced as is the value chain analysis (VCA) concept. Priceline.com does an excellent job using its strengths to capitalize on external opportunities. Priceline is showcased in the opening chapter boxed insert.

The Nature of an Internal Audit

All organizations have strengths and weaknesses in the functional areas of business. No enterprise is equally strong or weak in all areas. Maytag, for example, is known for excellent production and product design, whereas Procter & Gamble is known for superb marketing. Internal strengths and weaknesses, coupled with external opportunities and threats and clear vision and mission statements, provide the basis for establishing objectives and strategies. Objectives and strategies are established with the intention of capitalizing on internal strengths and overcoming weaknesses. The internal-audit part of the strategic-management process is illustrated in Figure 4-1 with white shading.

EXCELLENT STRATEGIC MANAGEMENT SHOWCASED

Priceline.com, Inc.

Do you prefer Priceline or Expedia to find low travel prices? Headquartered in Norwalk, Connecticut, Priceline.com Inc. is the leading online travel company where buyers "name their own price" for airline tickets, hotel rooms, rental cars, cruises, and vacation packages. Founded in 1997 with a patented business model, Priceline.com operates through the Booking.com, Priceline.com, TravelJigsaw, and Agoda brand names. Priceline.com uses excellent strategic management to dominate the online travel business. For example, the company generates annual sales of more than $4 billion and has an EPS of more than $30. Priceline's common stock (PCLN) had the best five-year (2007–2011) performance of all companies in the S&P 500: a total return of 972 percent. Many analysts have a $750.00/share price target for Priceline stock. In the last 12 months, PCLN's return on assets was 23.08 percent, compared to its competitors Expedia (EXPE)'s 4.19 percent and Orbitz World Wide (OWW)'s 2.60. PCLN's return on equity was 48.41 percent, much higher than EXPE's 13.44 percent and Orbitz World Wide OWW's negative 21.25. PCLN's profit margin for the last 12 months was 25.58 percent, compared to EXPE's 10.42 percent and OWW's negative 4.83.

With more than 5,000 employees, Priceline's customers can choose set-price options. For airline tickets and hotel reservations, Priceline.com generates sales on the margin, keeping the difference between the price paid by the individual and what Priceline.com paid for the ticket or hotel room. Priceline's recent success has been especially driven by international travel, particularly to emerging market destinations. About

65 percent of Priceline.com hotel room bookings are expected to be non-European going forward, up from 42 percent the prior year.

Priceline provides price-disclosed hotel and rental car reservation services on a worldwide basis with approximately 185,000 hotels and accommodations in 160 countries. The company's rental car services operate through its Name Your Own Price demand-collection system, as well as vacation packages consisting of airfare, hotel, and rental car components; cruise trips; and destination services, including parking, event tickets, ground transfers, and tours in the USA. Priceline provides an optional travel insurance package that covers trip cancellation, trip interruption, medical expenses, and emergency evacuation, as well as for loss of baggage, property, and travel documents for air, hotel, and vacation package customers; and collision damage waiver insurance for rental car customers in the USA.

Priceline's major competitor, Expedia, was founded in 1996, a year before Priceline. Priceline has four times the volume of revenues of Expedia, but the two firms aggressively compete every day for customers worldwide.

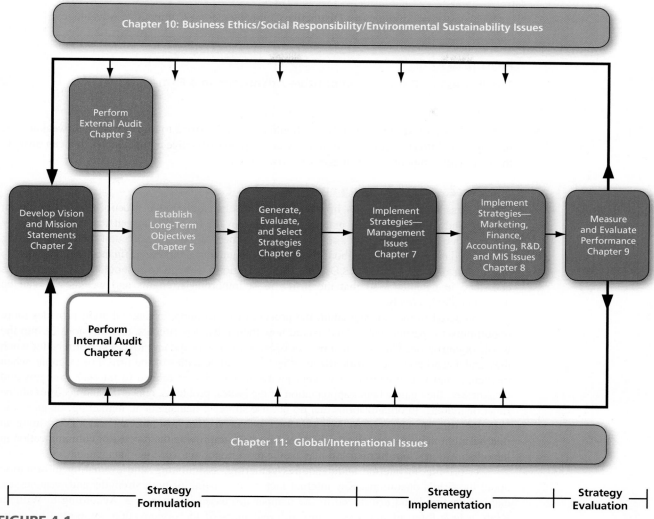

FIGURE 4-1

A Comprehensive Strategic-Management Model

Source: Fred R. David, "How Companies Define Their Mission," *Long Range Planning* 22, no. 3 (June 1988): 40.

Key Internal Forces

It is not possible in a strategic-management text to review in depth all the material presented in courses such as marketing, finance, accounting, management, management information systems, and production and operations; there are many subareas within these functions, such as customer service, warranties, advertising, packaging, and pricing under marketing. But strategic planning must include a detailed assessment of how the firm is doing in all internal areas.

For different types of organizations, such as hospitals, universities, and government agencies, the functional business areas, of course, differ. In a hospital, for example, functional areas may include cardiology, hematology, nursing, maintenance, physician support, and receivables. Functional areas of a university can include athletic programs, placement services, housing, fund-raising, academic research, counseling, and intramural programs. Within large organizations, each division has certain strengths and weaknesses.

A firm's strengths that cannot be easily matched or imitated by competitors are called **distinctive competencies.** Building competitive advantages involves taking advantage of distinctive competencies. Strategies are designed in part to improve on a firm's weaknesses, turning them into strengths—and maybe even into distinctive competencies.

Weaknesses ⇒ Strenghts ⇒ Distinctive Competencies ⇒ Competitive Advantage

FIGURE 4-2

The Process of Gaining Competitive Advantage in a Firm

Figure 4-2 illustrates that all firms should continually strive to improve on their weaknesses, turning them into strengths, and ultimately developing distinctive competencies that can provide the firm with competitive advantages over rival firms.

The Process of Performing an Internal Audit

The process of performing an **internal audit** closely parallels the process of performing an external audit. Representative managers and employees from throughout the firm need to be involved in determining a firm's strengths and weaknesses. The internal audit requires gathering and assimilating information about the firm's management, marketing, finance and accounting, production and operations, R&D, and MIS operations. Key factors should be prioritized as described in Chapter 3 so that the firm's most important strengths and weaknesses can be determined collectively.

Compared to the external audit, the process of performing an internal audit provides more opportunity for participants to understand how their jobs, departments, and divisions fit into the whole organization. This is a great benefit because managers and employees perform better when they understand how their work affects other areas and activities of the firm. For example, when marketing and manufacturing managers jointly discuss issues related to internal strengths and weaknesses, they gain a better appreciation of the issues, problems, concerns, and needs of all the functional areas. In organizations that do not use strategic management, marketing, finance, and manufacturing managers often do not interact with each other in significant ways. Performing an internal audit thus is an excellent vehicle or forum for improving the process of communication in the organization. **Communication** may be the most important word in management.

Performing an internal audit requires gathering, assimilating, and evaluating information about the firm's operations. Key internal factors, consisting of both strengths and weaknesses, can be identified and prioritized in the manner discussed in Chapter 3. According to William King, a task force of managers from different units of the organization, supported by staff, should be charged with determining the 20 most important strengths and weaknesses that should influence the future of the organization. He says:

> The development of conclusions on the 20 most important organizational strengths and weaknesses can be, as any experienced manager knows, a difficult task, when it involves managers representing various organizational interests and points of view. Developing a 20-page list of strengths and weaknesses could be accomplished relatively easily, but a list of the 20 most important ones involves significant analysis and negotiation. This is true because of the judgments that are required and the impact which such a list will inevitably have as it is used in the formulation, implementation, and evaluation of strategies.[1]

Strategic management is a highly interactive process that requires effective coordination among management, marketing, finance and accounting, production and operations, R&D, and MIS managers. Although the strategic-management process is overseen by strategists, success requires that managers and employees from all functional areas work together to provide ideas and information. Financial managers, for example, may need to restrict the number of feasible options available to operations managers, or R&D managers may develop products for which marketing managers need to set higher objectives. A key to organizational success is effective coordination and understanding among managers from all functional business areas. Through involvement in performing an internal strategic-management audit, managers from different departments and divisions of the firm come to understand the nature and effect of decisions in other functional business areas in their firm. Knowledge of these relationships is critical for effectively establishing objectives and strategies.

A failure to recognize and understand relationships among the functional areas of business can be detrimental to strategic management, and the number of those relationships that must be managed increases dramatically with a firm's size, diversity, geographic dispersion, and the number of products or services offered. Governmental and nonprofit enterprises traditionally have not placed sufficient emphasis on relationships among the business functions. Some firms place too great an emphasis on one function at the expense of others. Ansoff explained:

> During the first fifty years, successful firms focused their energies on optimizing the performance of one of the principal functions: production/operations, R&D, or marketing. Today, due to the growing complexity and dynamism of the environment, success increasingly depends on a judicious combination of several functional influences. This transition from a single function focus to a multifunction focus is essential for successful strategic management.[2]

Financial ratio analysis exemplifies the complexity of relationships among the functional areas of business. A declining return on investment or profit margin ratio could be the result of ineffective marketing, poor management policies, R&D errors, or a weak MIS. The effectiveness of strategy formulation, implementation, and evaluation activities hinges on a clear understanding of how major business functions affect one another. For strategies to succeed, a coordinated effort among all the functional areas of business is needed. In the case of planning, George wrote:

> We may conceptually separate planning for the purpose of theoretical discussion and analysis, but in practice, neither is it a distinct entity nor is it capable of being separated. The planning function is mixed with all other business functions and, like ink once mixed with water, it cannot be set apart. It is spread throughout and is a part of the whole of managing an organization.[3]

The Resource-Based View

Some researchers emphasize the importance of the internal audit part of the strategic-management process by comparing it to the external audit. Robert Grant concluded that the internal audit is more important, saying:

> In a world where customer preferences are volatile, the identity of customers is changing, and the technologies for serving customer requirements are continually evolving, an externally focused orientation does not provide a secure foundation for formulating long-term strategy. When the external environment is in a state of flux, the firm's own resources and capabilities may be a much more stable basis on which to define its identity. Hence, a definition of a business in terms of what it is capable of doing may offer a more durable basis for strategy.[4]

The **resource-based view (RBV)** approach to competitive advantage contends that internal resources are more important for a firm than external factors in achieving and sustaining competitive advantage. In contrast to the Industrial Organization (I/O) theory presented in the previous chapter, proponents of the RBV view contend that organizational performance will primarily be determined by internal resources that can be grouped into three all-encompassing categories: physical resources, human resources, and organizational resources.[5] Physical resources include all plant and equipment, location, technology, raw materials, machines; human resources include all employees, training, experience, intelligence, knowledge, skills, abilities; and organizational resources include firm structure, planning processes, information systems, patents, trademarks, copyrights, databases, and so on. RBV theory asserts that resources are actually what helps a firm exploit opportunities and neutralize threats.

The basic premise of the RBV is that the mix, type, amount, and nature of a firm's internal resources should be considered first and foremost in devising strategies that can lead to sustainable competitive advantage. Managing strategically according to the RBV involves developing and exploiting a firm's unique resources and capabilities, and continually maintaining and strengthening those resources. The theory asserts that it is advantageous for a firm to pursue a strategy that is not currently being implemented by any competing firm. When other firms are unable to duplicate a particular strategy, then the focal firm has a sustainable competitive advantage, according to RBV theorists.

For a resource to be valuable, it must be either (a) rare, (b) hard to imitate, or (c) not easily substitutable. Often called **empirical indicators**, these three characteristics of resources enable a firm to implement strategies that improve its efficiency and effectiveness and lead to a sustainable competitive advantage. The more a resource(s) is rare, nonimitable, and nonsubstitutable, the stronger a firm's competitive advantage will be and the longer it will last.

Rare resources are resources that other competing firms do not possess. If many firms have the same resource, then those firms will likely implement similar strategies, thus giving no one firm a sustainable competitive advantage. This is not to say that resources that are common are not valuable; they do indeed aid the firm in its chance for economic prosperity. However, to sustain a competitive advantage, it is more advantageous if the resource(s) is also rare.

It is also important that these same resources be difficult to imitate. If firms cannot easily gain the resources, say RBV theorists, then those resources will lead to a competitive advantage more so than resources easily imitable. Even if a firm employs resources that are rare, a sustainable competitive advantage may be achieved only if other firms cannot easily obtain these resources.

The third empirical indicator that can make resources a source of competitive advantage is substitutability. Borrowing from Porter's Five-Forces Model, to the degree that there are no viable substitutes, a firm will be able to sustain its competitive advantage. However, even if a competing firm cannot perfectly imitate a firm's resource, it can still obtain a sustainable competitive advantage of its own by obtaining resource substitutes.

RBV has continued to grow in popularity and continues to seek a better understanding of the relationship between resources and sustained competitive advantage in strategic management. However, as alluded to in Chapter 3, one cannot say with any degree of certainty that either external or internal factors will always or even consistently be more important in seeking competitive advantage. Understanding both external and internal factors, and more importantly, understanding the relationships among them, will be the key to effective strategy formulation (discussed in Chapter 6). Because both external and internal factors continually change, strategists seek to identify and take advantage of positive changes and buffer against negative changes in a continuing effort to gain and sustain a firm's competitive advantage. This is the essence and challenge of strategic management, and oftentimes survival of the firm hinges on this work.

Integrating Strategy and Culture

Relationships among a firm's functional business activities perhaps can be exemplified best by focusing on organizational culture, an internal phenomenon that permeates all departments and divisions of an organization. **Organizational culture** can be defined as "a pattern of behavior that has been developed by an organization as it learns to cope with its problem of external adaptation and internal integration, and that has worked well enough to be considered valid and to be taught to new members as the correct way to perceive, think, and feel."[6] This definition emphasizes the importance of matching external with internal factors in making strategic decisions.

Organizational culture captures the subtle, elusive, and largely unconscious forces that shape a workplace. Remarkably resistant to change, culture can represent a major strength or weakness for the firm. It can be an underlying reason for strengths or weaknesses in any of the major business functions.

Defined in Table 4-1, **cultural products** include values, beliefs, rites, rituals, ceremonies, myths, stories, legends, sagas, language, metaphors, symbols, heroes, and heroines. These products or dimensions are levers that strategists can use to influence and direct strategy formulation, implementation, and evaluation activities. An organization's culture compares to an individual's personality in the sense that no two organizations have the same culture and no two individuals have the same personality. Both culture and personality are enduring and can be warm, aggressive, friendly, open, innovative, conservative, liberal, harsh, or likable.

At Google, the culture is informal. Employees are encouraged to wander the halls on employee-sponsored scooters and brainstorm on public whiteboards provided everywhere. In contrast, the culture at Procter & Gamble (P&G) is so rigid that employees jokingly call

TABLE 4-1 Example Cultural Products Defined

Rites	Planned sets of activities that consolidate various forms of cultural expressions into one event.
Ceremonial	Several rites connected together.
Ritual	A standardized set of behaviors used to manage anxieties.
Myth	A narrative of imagined events, usually not supported by facts.
Saga	A historical narrative describing the unique accomplishments of a group and its leaders.
Legend	A handed-down narrative of some wonderful event, usually not supported by facts.
Story	A narrative usually based on true events.
Folktale	A fictional story.
Symbol	Any object, act, event, quality, or relation used to convey meaning.
Language	The manner in which members of a group communicate.
Metaphors	Shorthand of words used to capture a vision or to reinforce old or new values.
Values	Life-directing attitudes that serve as behavioral guidelines.
Belief	An understanding of a particular phenomenon.
Heroes/Heroines	Individuals greatly respected.

Source: Based on H. M. Trice and J. M. Beyer, "Studying Organizational Cultures through Rites and Ceremonials," *Academy of Management Review* 9, no. 4 (October 1984): 655.

themselves "Proctoids." Despite this difference, the two companies are swapping employees and participating in each other's staff training sessions. Why? Because P&G spends more money on advertising than any other company and Google desires more of P&G's $8.7 billion in annual advertising expenses; P&G has come to realize that the next generation of laundry-detergent, toilet-paper, and skin-cream customers now spend more time online than watching TV.

Dimensions of organizational culture permeate all the functional areas of business. It is something of an art to uncover the basic values and beliefs that are deeply buried in an organization's rich collection of stories, language, heroes, and rituals, but cultural products can represent both important strengths and weaknesses. Culture is an aspect of an organization that can no longer be taken for granted in performing an internal strategic-management audit because culture and strategy must work together.

Table 4-2 provides some example (possible) aspects of an organization's culture. Note you could ask employees and managers to rate the degree that the dimension characterizes the firm. When one firm acquires another firm, integrating the two cultures can be important. For example, in Table 4-2, one firm may score mostly 1's (low) and the other firm may score mostly 5's (high), which would present a challenging strategic problem.

The strategic-management process takes place largely within a particular organization's culture. Lorsch found that executives in successful companies are emotionally committed to the firm's culture, but he concluded that culture can inhibit strategic management in two basic ways. First, managers frequently miss the significance of changing external conditions because they are blinded by strongly held beliefs. Second, when a particular culture has been effective in the past, the natural response is to stick with it in the future, even during times of major strategic change.[7] An organization's culture must support the collective commitment of its people to a common purpose. It must foster competence and enthusiasm among managers and employees.

Organizational culture significantly affects business decisions and thus must be evaluated during an internal strategic-management audit. If strategies can capitalize on cultural strengths, such as a strong work ethic or highly ethical beliefs, then management often can swiftly and easily implement changes. However, if the firm's culture is not supportive, strategic changes may be ineffective or even counterproductive. A firm's culture can become antagonistic to new strategies, with the result being confusion and disorientation.

TABLE 4-2 Fifteen Example (Possible) Aspects of an Organization's Culture

Dimension	Low	Degree			High
1. Strong work ethic; arrive early and leave late	1	2	3	4	5
2. High ethical beliefs; clear code of business ethics followed	1	2	3	4	5
3. Formal dress; shirt and tie expected	1	2	3	4	5
4. Informal dress; many casual dress days	1	2	3	4	5
5. Socialize together outside of work	1	2	3	4	5
6. Do not question supervisor's decision	1	2	3	4	5
7. Encourage whistle-blowing	1	2	3	4	5
8. Be health conscious; have a wellness program	1	2	3	4	5
9. Allow substantial "working from home"	1	2	3	4	5
10. Encourage creativity, innovation, and open-mindness	1	2	3	4	5
11. Support women and minorities; no glass ceiling	1	2	3	4	5
12. Be highly socially responsible; be philanthropic	1	2	3	4	5
13. Have numerous meetings	1	2	3	4	5
14. Have a participative management style	1	2	3	4	5
15. Preserve the natural environment; have a sustainability program	1	2	3	4	5

An organization's culture should infuse individuals with enthusiasm for implementing strategies. Allarie and Firsirotu emphasized the need to understand culture:

Culture provides an explanation for the insuperable difficulties a firm encounters when it attempts to shift its strategic direction. Not only has the "right" culture become the essence and foundation of corporate excellence, it is also claimed that success or failure of reforms hinges on management's sagacity and ability to change the firm's driving culture in time and in time with required changes in strategies.[8]

The potential value of organizational culture has not been realized fully in the study of strategic management. Ignoring the effect that culture can have on relationships among the functional areas of business can result in barriers to communication, lack of coordination, and an inability to adapt to changing conditions. Some tension between culture and a firm's strategy is inevitable, but the tension should be monitored so that it does not reach a point at which relationships are severed and the culture becomes antagonistic. The resulting disarray among members of the organization would disrupt strategy formulation, implementation, and evaluation. In contrast, a supportive organizational culture can make managing much easier.

Internal strengths and weaknesses associated with a firm's culture sometimes are overlooked because of the interfunctional nature of this phenomenon. It is important, therefore, for strategists to understand their firm as a sociocultural system. Success is often determined by linkages between a firm's culture and strategies. The challenge of strategic management today is to bring about the changes in organizational culture and individual mind-sets that are needed to support the formulation, implementation, and evaluation of strategies.

Management

The **functions of management** consist of five basic activities: planning, organizing, motivating, staffing, and controlling. An overview of these activities is provided in Table 4-3. These activities are important to assess in strategic planning because an organization should continually capitalize on its management strengths and improve on its management weak areas.

Planning

The only thing certain about the future of any organization is change, and **planning** is the essential bridge between the present and the future that increases the likelihood of achieving desired results. Planning is the process by which one determines whether to attempt a task, works out the most effective way of reaching desired objectives, and prepares to overcome

TABLE 4-3 **The Basic Functions of Management**

Function	Description	Stage of Strategic-Management Process When Most Important
Planning	Planning consists of all those managerial activities related to preparing for the future. Specific tasks include forecasting, establishing objectives, devising strategies, developing policies, and setting goals.	Strategy Formulation
Organizing	Organizing includes all those managerial activities that result in a structure of task and authority relationships. Specific areas include organizational design, job specialization, job descriptions, job specifications, span of control, unity of command, coordination, job design, and job analysis.	Strategy Implementation
Motivating	Motivating involves efforts directed toward shaping human behavior. Specific topics include leadership, communication, work groups, behavior modification, delegation of authority, job enrichment, job satisfaction, needs fulfillment, organizational change, employee morale, and managerial morale.	Strategy Implementation
Staffing	Staffing activities are centered on personnel or human resource management. Included are wage and salary administration, employee benefits, interviewing, hiring, firing, training, management development, employee safety, affirmative action, equal employment opportunity, union relations, career development, personnel research, discipline policies, grievance procedures, and public relations.	Strategy Implementation
Controlling	Controlling refers to all those managerial activities directed toward ensuring that actual results are consistent with planned results. Key areas of concern include quality control, financial control, sales control, inventory control, expense control, analysis of variances, rewards, and sanctions.	Strategy Evaluation

unexpected difficulties with adequate resources. Planning is the start of the process by which an individual or business may turn empty dreams into achievements. Planning enables one to avoid the trap of working extremely hard but achieving little.

Planning is an up-front investment in success. Planning helps a firm achieve maximum effect from a given effort. Planning enables a firm to take into account relevant factors and focus on the critical ones. Planning helps ensure that the firm can be prepared for all reasonable eventualities and for all changes that will be needed. Planning enables a firm to gather the resources needed and carry out tasks in the most efficient way possible. Planning enables a firm to conserve its own resources, avoid wasting ecological resources, make a fair profit, and be seen as an effective, useful firm. Planning enables a firm to identify precisely what is to be achieved and to detail precisely the who, what, when, where, why, and how needed to achieve desired objectives. Planning enables a firm to assess whether the effort, costs, and implications associated with achieving desired objectives are warranted.[9] Planning is the cornerstone of effective strategy formulation. But even though it is considered the foundation of management, it is commonly the task that managers neglect most. Planning is essential for successful strategy implementation and strategy evaluation, largely because organizing, motivating, staffing, and controlling activities depend on good planning.

The process of planning must involve managers and employees throughout an organization. The time horizon for planning decreases from two to five years for top-level to less than six months for lower-level managers. The important point is that all managers do planning and should involve subordinates in the process to facilitate employee understanding and commitment.

Planning can have a positive impact on organizational and individual performance. Planning allows an organization to identify and take advantage of external opportunities as well as minimize the impact of external threats. Planning is more than extrapolating from the past and present into the future (long-range planning). It also includes developing a mission, forecasting future events and trends, establishing objectives, and choosing strategies to pursue (strategic planning).

An organization can develop synergy through planning. **Synergy** exists when everyone pulls together as a team that knows what it wants to achieve; synergy is the $2 + 2 = 5$ effect. By establishing and communicating clear objectives, employees and managers can work together toward desired results. Synergy can result in powerful competitive advantages. The strategic-management process itself is aimed at creating synergy in an organization.

Planning allows a firm to adapt to changing markets and thus to shape its own destiny. Strategic management can be viewed as a formal planning process that allows an organization to pursue proactive rather than reactive strategies. Successful organizations strive to control their own futures rather than merely react to external forces and events as they occur. Historically, organisms and organizations that have not adapted to changing conditions have become extinct. Swift adaptation is needed today more than ever because changes in markets, economies, and competitors worldwide are accelerating. Many firms did not adapt to the global recession of late and went out of business.

Organizing

The purpose of **organizing** is to achieve coordinated effort by defining task and authority relationships. Organizing means determining who does what and who reports to whom. There are countless examples in history of well-organized enterprises successfully competing against— and in some cases defeating—much stronger but less-organized firms. A well-organized firm generally has motivated managers and employees who are committed to seeing the organization succeed. Resources are allocated more effectively and used more efficiently in a well-organized firm than in a disorganized firm.

The organizing function of management can be viewed as consisting of three sequential activities: breaking down tasks into jobs (work specialization), combining jobs to form departments (departmentalization), and delegating authority. Breaking down tasks into jobs requires the development of job descriptions and job specifications. These tools clarify for both managers and employees what particular jobs entail. In *The Wealth of Nations*, published in 1776, Adam Smith cited the advantages of work specialization in the manufacture of pins:

> One man draws the wire, another straightens it, a third cuts it, a fourth points it, a fifth grinds it at the top for receiving the head. Ten men working in this manner can produce 48,000 pins in a single day, but if they had all wrought separately and independently, each might at best produce twenty pins in a day.[10]

Combining jobs to form departments results in an organizational structure, span of control, and a chain of command. Changes in strategy often require changes in structure because positions may be created, deleted, or merged. Organizational structure dictates how resources are allocated and how objectives are established in a firm. Allocating resources and establishing objectives geographically, for example, is much different from doing so by product or customer.

The most common forms of departmentalization are functional, divisional, strategic business unit, and matrix. These types of structure are discussed further in Chapter 7.

Delegating authority is an important organizing activity, as evidenced in the old saying "You can tell how good a manager is by observing how his or her department functions when he or she isn't there." Employees today are more educated and more capable of participating in organizational decision making than ever before. In most cases, they expect to be delegated authority and responsibility and to be held accountable for results. Delegation of authority is embedded in the strategic-management process.

Motivating

Motivating can be defined as the process of influencing people to accomplish specific objectives.[11] Motivation explains why some people work hard and others do not. Objectives, strategies, and policies have little chance of succeeding if employees and managers are not motivated to implement strategies once they are formulated. The motivating function of management includes at least four major components: leadership, group dynamics, communication, and organizational change.

When managers and employees of a firm strive to achieve high levels of productivity, this indicates that the firm's strategists are good leaders. Good leaders establish rapport with subordinates, empathize with their needs and concerns, set a good example, and are trustworthy and fair. Leadership includes developing a vision of the firm's future and inspiring people to work hard to achieve that vision. Kirkpatrick and Locke reported that certain traits also characterize effective leaders: knowledge of the business, cognitive ability, self-confidence, honesty, integrity, and drive.[12] Sun Tzu said: "Weak leadership can wreck the soundest strategy."

Research suggests that democratic behavior on the part of leaders results in more positive attitudes toward change and higher productivity than does autocratic behavior. Drucker said:

Leadership is not a magnetic personality. That can just as well be demagoguery. It is not "making friends and influencing people." That is flattery. Leadership is the lifting of a person's vision to higher sights, the raising of a person's performance to a higher standard, the building of a person's personality beyond its normal limitations.[13]

Group dynamics play a major role in employee morale and satisfaction. Informal groups or coalitions form in every organization. The norms of coalitions can range from being positive to negative toward management. It is important, therefore, that strategists identify the composition and nature of informal groups in an organization to facilitate strategy formulation, implementation, and evaluation. Leaders of informal groups are especially important in formulating and implementing strategy changes.

Communication, perhaps the most important word in management, is a major component in motivation. An organization's system of communication determines whether strategies can be implemented successfully. Good two-way communication is vital for gaining support for departmental and divisional objectives and policies. Top-down communication can encourage bottom-up communication. The strategic-management process becomes a lot easier when subordinates are encouraged to discuss their concerns, reveal their problems, provide recommendations, and give suggestions. A primary reason for instituting strategic management is to build and support effective communication networks throughout the firm.

The manager of tomorrow must be able to get his people to commit themselves to the business, whether they are machine operators or junior vice-presidents. The key issue will be empowerment, a term whose strength suggests the need to get beyond merely sharing a little information and a bit of decision making.[14]

Staffing

The management function of **staffing**, also called **personnel management** or **human resource management**, includes activities such as recruiting, interviewing, testing, selecting, orienting, training, developing, caring for, evaluating, rewarding, disciplining, promoting, transferring, demoting, and dismissing employees, as well as managing union relations.

Staffing activities play a major role in strategy-implementation efforts, and for this reason, human resource managers are becoming more actively involved in the strategic-management process. It is important to identify strengths and weaknesses in the staffing area.

The complexity and importance of human resource activities have increased to such a degree that all but the smallest organizations now need a full-time human resource manager. Numerous court cases that directly affect staffing activities are decided each day. Organizations and individuals can be penalized severely for not following federal, state, and local laws and guidelines related to staffing. Line managers simply cannot stay abreast of all the legal developments and requirements regarding staffing. The human resources department coordinates staffing decisions in the firm so that an organization as a whole meets legal requirements. This department also provides needed consistency in administering company rules, wages, policies, and employee benefits as well as collective bargaining with unions.

Human resource management is particularly challenging for international companies. For example, the inability of spouses and children to adapt to new surroundings can be a staffing problem in overseas transfers. The problems include premature returns, job performance slumps, resignations, discharges, low morale, marital discord, and general discontent. Firms such as Ford Motor and ExxonMobil screen and interview spouses and children before assigning persons to overseas positions. 3M Corporation introduces children to peers in the target country and offers spouses educational benefits.

Controlling

The **controlling** function of management includes all of those activities undertaken to ensure that actual operations conform to planned operations. All managers in an organization have controlling responsibilities, such as conducting performance evaluations and taking necessary action to minimize inefficiencies. The controlling function of management is particularly important for effective strategy evaluation. Controlling consists of four basic steps:

1. Establishing performance standards
2. Measuring individual and organizational performance
3. Comparing actual performance to planned performance standards
4. Taking corrective actions

Measuring individual performance is often conducted ineffectively or not at all in organizations. Some reasons for this shortcoming are that evaluations can create confrontations that most managers prefer to avoid, can take more time than most managers are willing to give, and can require skills that many managers lack. No single approach to measuring individual performance is without limitations. For this reason, an organization should examine various methods, such as the graphic rating scale, the behaviorally anchored rating scale, and the critical incident method, and then develop or select a performance-appraisal approach that best suits the firm's needs. Increasingly, firms are striving to link organizational performance with managers' and employees' pay. This topic is discussed further in Chapter 7.

Management Audit Checklist of Questions

The following checklist of questions can help determine specific strengths and weaknesses in the functional area of business. An answer of *no* to any question could indicate a potential weakness, although the strategic significance and implications of negative answers, of course, will vary by organization, industry, and severity of the weakness. Positive or *yes* answers to the checklist questions suggest potential areas of strength.

1. Does the firm use strategic-management concepts?
2. Are company objectives and goals measurable and well communicated?
3. Do managers at all hierarchical levels plan effectively?
4. Do managers delegate authority well?
5. Is the organization's structure appropriate?
6. Are job descriptions and job specifications clear?
7. Is employee morale high?
8. Are employee turnover and absenteeism low?
9. Are organizational reward and control mechanisms effective?

Marketing

Marketing can be described as the process of defining, anticipating, creating, and fulfilling customers' needs and wants for products and services. There are seven basic **functions of marketing**: (1) customer analysis, (2) selling products and services, (3) product and service planning, (4) pricing, (5) distribution, (6) marketing research, and (7) opportunity analysis.[15] Understanding these functions helps strategists identify and evaluate marketing strengths and weaknesses.

Customer Analysis

Customer analysis—the examination and evaluation of consumer needs, desires, and wants—involves administering customer surveys, analyzing consumer information, evaluating market positioning strategies, developing customer profiles, and determining optimal market segmentation strategies. The information generated by customer analysis can be essential in developing an effective mission statement. Customer profiles can reveal the demographic characteristics of an organization's customers. Buyers, sellers, distributors, salespeople, managers, wholesalers, retailers, suppliers, and creditors can all participate in gathering information to successfully identify customers' needs and wants. Successful organizations continually monitor present and potential customers' buying patterns.

Selling Products and Services

Successful strategy implementation generally rests on the ability of an organization to sell some product or service. **Selling** includes many marketing activities, such as advertising, sales promotion, publicity, personal selling, sales force management, customer relations, and dealer relations. These activities are especially critical when a firm pursues a market penetration strategy. The effectiveness of various selling tools for consumer and industrial products varies. Personal selling is most important for industrial goods companies, whereas advertising is most important for consumer goods companies.

For example, the J.M. Smucker Company has $5.5 and 4.8 billion in revenue in 2012 and 2011, respectively, and spent $119 and $115 million in advertising during those two years, comprising 2.1 and 2.4 percent of revenues, respectively. About 3 percent of revenues is normal for companies to spend on advertising although this can vary across industries. J.M. Smucker has a product portfolio that includes coffee, peanut butter, fruit spreads, jams, shortening and oils, baking mixes, canned milk, flour, syrups, pickles, and more. One aspect of ads recently is that they generally take more direct aim at competitors, and this marketing practice is holding true in our bad economic times. Nick Brien at Mediabrands says, "Ads have to get combative in bad times. It's a dog fight, and it's about getting leaner and meaner." Ads are less lavish and glamorous today and are also more interactive. Table 4-4 lists specific characteristics of ads in response to the economic hard times many people nationwide and worldwide are facing.

Marketers spent about $3 million per 30-second advertising spot during the 2012 Super Bowl. Advertising can be expensive, and that is why marketing is a major business function to be studied carefully. Without marketing, even the best products and services have little chance of being successful.

Chief marketing officers (CMOs) such as Eduardo Conrado at Motorola now spend more than 50 percent of their budget on technology to manage activities like online marketing and social media.[16] Marketing is becoming technical with software to track and target customers and manage customer relationships, predict consumer behavior, run online storefronts, analyze social media, manage websites, and craft targeted advertisements. IBM in response to this trend is shifting its attention from CIOs to CMOs as their primary clients.

TABLE 4-4 Desirable Characteristics of Ads Today

1. Take direct aim at competitors; so leaner, meaner, and to the point.
2. Be less lavish and glamorous, requiring less production dollars to develop.
3. Be short and sweet, mostly 10- and 15-second ads rather than longer than 30 seconds.
4. "Make you feel good" or "put you in a good mood" because (a) ads can be more easily avoided than ever and (b) people are experiencing hard times and seek comfort.
5. Be more pervasive such as on buses, elevators, cell phones, and trucks.
6. Appear less on websites as banner ads become the new junk mail.
7. Red will overtake the color orange as the most popular ad color.
8. More than ever emphasize low price and value versus rivals.
9. More than ever emphasize how the product or service will make your life better.

Source: Based on Suzanne Vranica, "Ads to Go Leaner, Meaner in '09," *Wall Street Journal,* January 5, 2009, B8.

The world's largest social network, Facebook may epitomize where the advertising industry is going. Facebook allows a company to "leverage the loyalty" of its best customers. If you have recently gotten engaged and updated your Facebook status, you may start seeing ads from local jewelers who have used Facebook's automated ad system to target you. Facebook enables any firm today to effectively target their exact audience with perfect advertising.[17] In performing a strategic planning analysis, in addition to comparing rival firms' websites, it is important to compare rival firms' Facebook page.

One of the last off-limit advertising outlets has historically been books, but with the proliferation of e-books, marketers are experimenting more and more with advertising to consumers as they read e-books. New ads are being targeted based on the book's content and the demographic profile of the reader. Digital e-book companies such as Wowio and Amazon are trying to insert ads between chapters and along borders of digital pages. Random House says its e-books will soon include ads, but only with author approval.

Determining organizational strengths and weaknesses in the selling function of marketing is an important part of performing an internal strategic-management audit. With regard to advertising products and services on the Internet, a new trend is to base advertising rates exclusively on sales rates. This new accountability contrasts sharply with traditional broadcast and print advertising, which bases rates on the number of persons expected to see a given advertisement. The new cost-per-sale online advertising rates are possible because any website can monitor which user clicks on which advertisement and then can record whether that consumer actually buys the product. If there are no sales, then the advertisement is free.

Product and Service Planning

Product and service planning includes activities such as test marketing; product and brand positioning; devising warranties; packaging; determining product options, features, style, and quality; deleting old products; and providing for customer service. Product and service planning is particularly important when a company is pursuing product development or diversification.

One of the most effective product and service planning techniques is **test marketing.** Test markets allow an organization to test alternative marketing plans and to forecast future sales of new products. In conducting a test market project, an organization must decide how many cities to include, which cities to include, how long to run the test, what information to collect during the test, and what action to take after the test has been completed. Test marketing is used more frequently by consumer goods companies than by industrial goods companies. Test marketing can allow an organization to avoid substantial losses by revealing weak products and ineffective marketing approaches before large-scale production begins.

After extensive test marketing, the chocolate maker Hershey recently launched its first candy in China, a condensed milk candy. The company also opened a new Shanghai-based Asia Innovation Center to test market many potential premium milk type chocolate candies in various Asian countries. Hershey increased its number of stores in China by 32 percent and its sales force by 60 percent in 2013.

Pricing

In late 2012, J.C. Penney abandoned its month-long specials that cut prices of select items by 20 to 29 percent, and instead implemented permanent price cuts on a large amount of merchandise in their stores. Penney's pricing strategy gave consumers two options: everyday low prices and clearance sales on certain items. Penney's price change strategy came as the company's stock price had dropped 40 percent in recent months. To support the new pricing strategy, Penney's began offering free haircuts every Sunday for children aged 5 to 12. Free is a good price and this program exists in 949 of Penney's 1,100 stores totaling about 1 million haircuts per month. "It definitely drove new people and reintroduced J.C. Penney to existing customers who didn't know about the latest changes," said Jan Hodges, senior vice president of Penney's salon services. But in an about-face after losses, Penney's fired CEO Ron Johnson, brought back his predecessor Myron "Mike" Ullman, and began a "we're listening" campaign on Facebook to woo customers back into the stores.

Five major stakeholders affect **pricing** decisions: consumers, governments, suppliers, distributors, and competitors. Sometimes an organization will pursue a forward integration strategy primarily to gain better control over prices charged to consumers. Governments can impose constraints on price fixing, price discrimination, minimum prices, unit pricing, price advertising, and price controls. For example, the Robinson-Patman Act prohibits manufacturers and wholesalers from discriminating in price among channel member purchasers (suppliers and distributors) if competition is injured.

Competing organizations must be careful not to coordinate discounts, credit terms, or condition of sale; not to discuss prices, markups, and costs at trade association meetings; and not to arrange to issue new price lists on the same date, to rotate low bids on contracts, or to uniformly restrict production to maintain high prices. Strategists should view price from both a short-run and a long-run perspective because competitors can copy price changes with relative ease. Often a dominant firm will aggressively match all price cuts by competitors.

With regard to pricing, as the value of the dollar increases, U.S. multinational companies have a choice. They can raise prices in the local currency of a foreign country or risk losing sales and market share. Alternatively, multinational firms can keep prices steady and face reduced profit when their export revenue is reported in the United States in dollars.

Intense price competition, coupled with Internet price-comparative shopping, has reduced profit margins to bare minimum levels for most companies. For example, when Toys 'R' Us introduced its first tablet for kids (the Tabeo) in late 2012 for $149.99, the company's three main competitors instantly reduced their tablet for kids: the Kurlo 7 by Techno Source, the Lexibook by Lexibook Ltd., and the Meep by Oregon Scientific. To help combat Internet comparative shopping, the Tabeo is available only at Toys 'R' Us stores.

Nike raised its shoe and clothing prices by 5 to 10 percent in late 2012 when the company introduced its new LeBron James basketball shoe that sells for $315. That shoe features embedded motion sensors that can measure how high players jump. Even the price of Nike's venerable Converse All-Star sneaker increased to just slightly more than $50. Nike faces rising labor costs in China, where it manufactures a third of its products.

Target Corp. recently joined Best Buy in offering to match online prices of rival retailers. Both companies are seeking to combat "showrooming" by shoppers who check out products in their stores but buy them on rival's websites. Both Target and Best Buy are matching prices from Amazon.com and Walmart.com and Toysrus.com.

Distribution

Distribution includes warehousing, distribution channels, distribution coverage, retail site locations, sales territories, inventory levels and location, transportation carriers, wholesaling, and retailing. Most producers today do not sell their goods directly to consumers. Various marketing entities act as intermediaries; they bear a variety of names such as wholesalers, retailers, brokers, facilitators, agents, vendors—or simply distributors.

Distribution becomes especially important when a firm is striving to implement a market development or forward integration strategy. Some of the most complex and challenging decisions facing a firm concern product distribution. Intermediaries flourish in our economy because many producers lack the financial resources and expertise to carry out direct marketing. Manufacturers who could afford to sell directly to the public often can gain greater returns by expanding and improving their manufacturing operations.

Successful organizations identify and evaluate alternative ways to reach their ultimate market. Possible approaches vary from direct selling to using just one or many wholesalers and retailers. Strengths and weaknesses of each channel alternative should be determined according to economic, control, and adaptive criteria. Organizations should consider the costs and benefits of various wholesaling and retailing options. They must consider the need to motivate and control channel members and the need to adapt to changes in the future. Once a marketing channel is chosen, an organization usually must adhere to it for an extended period of time.

Marketing Research

Marketing research is the systematic gathering, recording, and analyzing of data about problems relating to the marketing of goods and services. Marketing research can uncover critical strengths and weaknesses, and marketing researchers employ numerous scales, instruments, procedures, concepts, and techniques to gather information. Marketing research activities support all of the major business functions of an organization. Organizations that possess excellent marketing research skills have a definite strength in pursuing generic strategies. The president of PepsiCo said,

Looking at the competition is the company's best form of market research. The majority of our strategic successes are ideas that we borrow from the marketplace, usually from a small regional or local competitor. In each case, we spot a promising new idea, improve on it, and then out-execute our competitor.[18]

Cost/Benefit Analysis

The seventh function of marketing is **cost/benefit analysis,** which involves assessing the costs, benefits, and risks associated with marketing decisions. Three steps are required to perform a cost/benefit analysis: (1) compute the total costs associated with a decision, (2) estimate the total benefits from the decision, and (3) compare the total costs with the total benefits. When expected benefits exceed total costs, an opportunity becomes more attractive. Sometimes the variables included in a cost/benefit analysis cannot be quantified or even measured, but usually reasonable estimates can be made to allow the analysis to be performed. One key factor to be considered is risk. Cost/benefit analysis should also be performed when a company is evaluating alternative ways to be socially responsible.

The practice of cost/benefit analysis differs among countries and industries. Some of the main differences include the types of impacts that are included as costs and benefits within appraisals, the extent to which impacts are expressed in monetary terms, and differences in the discount rate. Government agencies across the world rely on a basic set of key cost/benefit indicators, including the following:

1. net present value (NPV)
2. present value of benefits (PVB)
3. present value of costs (PVC)
4. benefit cost ratio (BCR) = PVB / PVC
5. Net benefit = PVB – PVC
6. NPV/k (where k is the level of funds available)[19]

Marketing Audit Checklist of Questions

The following questions about marketing must be examined in strategic planning:

1. Are markets segmented effectively?
2. Is the organization positioned well among competitors?
3. Has the firm's market share been increasing?
4. Are present channels of distribution reliable and cost effective?
5. Does the firm have an effective sales organization?
6. Does the firm conduct market research?
7. Are product quality and customer service good?
8. Are the firm's products and services priced appropriately?
9. Does the firm have an effective promotion, advertising, and publicity strategy?
10. Are marketing, planning, and budgeting effective?
11. Do the firm's marketing managers have adequate experience and training?
12. Is the firm's Internet presence excellent as compared to rivals?

Finance and Accounting

Financial condition is often considered the single best measure of a firm's competitive position and overall attractiveness to investors. Determining an organization's financial strengths and weaknesses is essential to effectively formulating strategies. A firm's liquidity, leverage, working capital, profitability, asset utilization, cash flow, and equity can eliminate some strategies as being feasible alternatives. Financial factors often alter existing strategies and change implementation plans.

Especially good websites from which to obtain financial information about firms are provided in Table 4-5.

Finance and Accounting Functions

According to James Van Horne, the **functions of finance/accounting** comprise three decisions: the investment decision, the financing decision, and the dividend decision.[20] Financial ratio analysis is the most widely used method for determining an organization's strengths and weaknesses

TABLE 4-5 Excellent Websites to Obtain Information on Companies, Including Financial Ratios

1. www.money.msn.com
2. http://finance.yahoo.com
3. www.morningstar.com
4. www.hoovers.com
5. http://globaledge.msu.edu/industries/

in the investment, financing, and dividend areas. Because the functional areas of business are so closely related, financial ratios can signal strengths or weaknesses in management, marketing, production, R&D, and MIS activities. Financial ratios are equally applicable in for-profit and nonprofit organizations. Even though nonprofit organizations obviously would not have return-on-investment or earnings-per-share ratios, they would routinely monitor many other special ratios. For example, a church would monitor the ratio of dollar contributions to number of members, whereas a zoo would monitor dollar food sales to number of visitors. A university would monitor number of students divided by number of professors. Therefore, be creative when performing ratio analysis for nonprofit organizations because they strive to be financially sound just as for-profit firms do. Nonprofit organizations need strategic planning just as much as for-profit firms.

The **investment decision,** also called **capital budgeting,** is the allocation and reallocation of capital and resources to projects, products, assets, and divisions of an organization. Once strategies are formulated, capital budgeting decisions are required to successfully implement strategies. The **financing decision** determines the best capital structure for the firm and includes examining various methods by which the firm can raise capital (for example, by issuing stock, increasing debt, selling assets, or using a combination of these approaches). The financing decision must consider both short-term and long-term needs for working capital. Two key financial ratios that indicate whether a firm's financing decisions have been effective are the debt-to-equity ratio and the debt-to-total-assets ratio.

Dividend decisions concern issues such as the percentage of earnings paid to stockholders, the stability of dividends paid over time, and the repurchase or issuance of stock. Dividend decisions determine the amount of funds that are retained in a firm compared to the amount paid out to stockholders. Three financial ratios that are helpful in evaluating a firm's dividend decisions are the earnings-per-share ratio, the dividends-per-share ratio, and the price-earnings ratio. The benefits of paying dividends to investors must be balanced against the benefits of internally retaining funds, and there is no set formula on how to balance this trade-off. For the reasons listed here, dividends are sometimes paid out even when funds could be better reinvested in the business or when the firm has to obtain outside sources of capital:

1. Paying cash dividends is customary. Failure to do so could be thought of as a stigma. A dividend change is considered a signal about the future.
2. Dividends represent a sales point for investment bankers. Some institutional investors can buy only dividend-paying stocks.
3. Shareholders often demand dividends, even in companies with great opportunities for reinvesting all available funds.
4. A myth exists that paying dividends will result in a higher stock price.

In the second quarter of 2012 alone, 505 U.S. companies boosted their dividends, after 677 firms boosted their dividends in the first quarter. In fact, 70 percent of the stocks in the S&P 500 raised their dividend in 2012. S&P companies are on average today paying out 31 percent of their earnings in the form of dividends, but that is down from 52 percent of earnings in some years.[21] For calendar 2013, companies in the S&P 500 are expected to pay at least $300 billion in dividends, topping 2012's $282 billion. Companies are also buying back their own stock (called Treasury stock) at record levels.

Unlike most firms, RadioShack Corp. recently suspended its 12.5 cents-a-share quarterly dividend, saving $50 million annually to avoid a liquidity crunch as the company seeks to lower its debt. The 91-year-old company has 4,700 stores in towns and cities across the United States and Mexico, but RadioShack is struggling to compete with online-only rivals such as Amazon because customers increasingly order electronics online.

Based in London, BP PLC recently boosted its quarterly dividend 13 percent to $0.09 a share. BP's board, in announcing the increase, said the company has a bright future with its recent $26.8 billion cash-and-shares deal to acquire a 20 percent stake in Russia's state-controlled OAO Rosneft. Despite not yet settling lawsuits related to the Gulf of Mexico Deepwater Horizons oil spill, BP posted a net profit for the three months ended September, 30, 2012, of $5.43 billion, up from $5.04 billion the prior year.

Costco in late 2012 borrowed $3.5 billion just to pay its shareholders a $7 dividend per share, totaling $3 billion. The dividend payout, without the borrowing, would have depleted Costco's cash account. Many companies near the end of 2012 paid "special" dividends, 175 in November 2012 alone or firms paid dividends early, to avoid the expected 2013 substantial increase in taxes on dividends.

Basic Types of Financial Ratios

Financial ratios are computed from an organization's income statement and balance sheet. Computing financial ratios is like taking a picture because the results reflect a situation at just one point in time. Comparing ratios over time and to industry averages is more likely to result in meaningful statistics that can be used to identify and evaluate strengths and weaknesses. Trend analysis, illustrated in Figure 4-3, is a useful technique that incorporates both the time and industry average dimensions of financial ratios. Note that the dotted lines reveal projected ratios. Some websites, such as those provided in Table 4-5, calculate financial ratios and provide data with charts.

Table 4-6 provides a summary of key financial ratios showing how each ratio is calculated and what each ratio measures. However, all the ratios are not significant for all industries and companies. For example, accounts receivable turnover and average collection period are not meaningful to a company that primarily does a cash receipts business. Key financial ratios can be classified into the following five types:

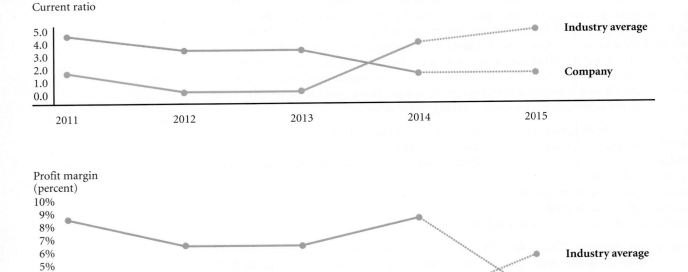

FIGURE 4-3

A Financial Ratio Trend Analysis

1. **Liquidity ratios** measure a firm's ability to meet maturing short-term obligations.

   Current ratio

   Quick (or acid-test) ratio

2. **Leverage ratios** measure the extent to which a firm has been financed by debt.

   Debt-to-total-assets ratio

   Debt-to-equity ratio

   Long-term debt-to-equity ratio

   Times-interest-earned (or coverage) ratio

3. **Activity ratios** measure how effectively a firm is using its resources.

   Inventory turnover

   Fixed assets turnover

   Total assets turnover

   Accounts receivable turnover

   Average collection period

4. **Profitability ratios** measure management's overall effectiveness as shown by the returns generated on sales and investment.

   Gross profit margin

   Operating profit margin

   Net profit margin

   Return on total assets (ROA)

   Return on stockholders' equity (ROE)

   Earnings per share (EPS)

   Price-earnings ratio

5. **Growth ratios** measure the firm's ability to maintain its economic position in the growth of the economy and industry.

   Sales

   Net income

   Earnings per share

   Dividends per share

Financial ratio analysis must go beyond the actual calculation and interpretation of ratios. The analysis should be conducted on three separate fronts:

1. *How has each ratio changed over time?* This information provides a means of evaluating historical trends. It is important to note whether each ratio has been historically increasing, decreasing, or nearly constant. For example, a 10 percent profit margin could be bad if the trend has been down 20 percent each of the last three years. But a 10 percent profit margin could be excellent if the trend has been up, up, up. Therefore, calculate the percentage change in each ratio from one year to the next to assess historical financial performance on that dimension. Identify and examine large percent changes in a financial ratio from one year to the next.

2. *How does each ratio compare to industry norms?* A firm's inventory turnover ratio may appear impressive at first glance but may pale when compared to industry standards or norms. Industries can differ dramatically on certain ratios. For example grocery companies, such as Kroger, have a high inventory turnover whereas automobile dealerships have a lower turnover. Therefore, comparison of a firm's ratios within its particular industry can be essential in determining strength and weakness.

TABLE 4-6 A Summary of Key Financial Ratios

Ratio	How Calculated	What It Measures
Liquidity Ratios		
Current Ratio	$\dfrac{\text{Current assets}}{\text{Current liabilities}}$	The extent to which a firm can meet its short-term obligations
Quick Ratio	$\dfrac{\text{Current assets minus inventory}}{\text{Current liabilities}}$	The extent to which a firm can meet its short-term obligations without relying on the sale of its inventories
Leverage Ratios		
Debt-to-Total-Assets Ratio	$\dfrac{\text{Total debt}}{\text{Total assets}}$	The percentage of total funds that are provided by creditors
Debt-to-Equity Ratio	$\dfrac{\text{Total debt}}{\text{Total stockholders' equity}}$	The percentage of total funds provided by creditors versus by owners
Long-Term Debt-to-Equity Ratio	$\dfrac{\text{Long-term debt}}{\text{Total stockholders' equity}}$	The balance between debt and equity in a firm's long-term capital structure
Times-Interest-Earned Ratio	$\dfrac{\text{Profits before interest and taxes}}{\text{Total interest charges}}$	The extent to which earnings can decline without the firm becoming unable to meet its annual interest costs
Activity Ratios		
Inventory Turnover	$\dfrac{\text{Sales}}{\text{Inventory of finished goods}}$	Whether a firm holds excessive stocks of inventories and whether a firm is slowly selling its inventories compared to the industry average
Fixed Assets Turnover	$\dfrac{\text{Sales}}{\text{Fixed assets}}$	Sales productivity and plant and equipment utilization
Total Assets Turnover	$\dfrac{\text{Sales}}{\text{Total assets}}$	Whether a firm is generating a sufficient volume of business for the size of its asset investment
Accounts Receivable Turnover	$\dfrac{\text{Annual credit sales}}{\text{Accounts receivable}}$	The average length of time it takes a firm to collect credit sales (in percentage terms)
Average Collection Period	$\dfrac{\text{Accounts receivable}}{\text{Total credit sales/365 days}}$	The average length of time it takes a firm to collect on credit sales (in days)
Profitability Ratios		
Gross Profit Margin	$\dfrac{\text{Sales minus cost of goods sold}}{\text{Sales}}$	The total margin available to cover operating expenses and yield a profit
Operating Profit Margin	$\dfrac{\text{Earnings before interest and taxes EBIT}}{\text{Sales}}$	Profitability without concern for taxes and interest
Net Profit Margin	$\dfrac{\text{Net income}}{\text{Sales}}$	After-tax profits per dollar of sales
Return on Total Assets (ROA)	$\dfrac{\text{Net income}}{\text{Total assets}}$	After-tax profits per dollar of assets; this ratio is also called return on investment (ROI)
Return on Stockholders' Equity (ROE)		After-tax profits per dollar of stockholders' investment in the firm
Earnings Per Share (EPS)	$\dfrac{\text{Net income}}{\text{Number of shares of common stock outstanding}}$	Earnings available to the owners of common stock
Price-Earnings Ratio	$\dfrac{\text{Market price per share}}{\text{Earnings per share}}$	Attractiveness of firm on equity markets
Growth Ratios		
Sales	Annual percentage growth in total sales	Firm's growth rate in sales
Net Income	Annual percentage growth in profits	Firm's growth rate in profits
Earnings Per Share	Annual percentage growth in EPS	Firm's growth rate in EPS
Dividends Per Share	Annual percentage growth in dividends per share	Firm's growth rate in dividends per share

3. *How does each ratio compare with key competitors?* Oftentimes competition is more intense between several competitors in a given industry or location than across all rival firms in the industry. When this is true, financial ratio analysis should include comparison to those key competitors. For example, if a firm's profitability ratio is trending up over time and compares favorably to the industry average, but it is trending down relative to its leading competitor, there may be reason for concern.

Financial ratio analysis is not without some limitations. First of all, financial ratios are based on accounting data, and firms differ in their treatment of such items as depreciation, inventory valuation, R&D expenditures, pension plan costs, mergers, and taxes. Also, seasonal factors can influence comparative ratios. Therefore, conformity to industry composite ratios does not establish with certainty that a firm is performing normally or that it is well managed. Likewise, departures from industry averages do not always indicate that a firm is doing especially well or badly. For example, a high inventory turnover ratio could indicate efficient inventory management and a strong working capital position, but it also could indicate a serious inventory shortage and a weak working capital position.

Another limitation of financial ratios in terms of including them as key internal factors in the upcoming IFE Matrix is that financial ratios are not very "actionable" in terms of revealing potential strategies needed, i.e. since they generally are based on performance of the overall firm. For example, to include as a key internal factor that the firm's "current ratio increased from 1.8 to 2.1" is not as "actionable" as "the firm's fragrance division revenues increased 18 percent in Africa in 2013." Recall from the prior chapter the importance of selecting "actionable" key factors, both externally and internally, upon which to formulate strategies. Selecting "actionable" key factors, both externally and internally, upon which to formulate strategies is important.

A firm's financial condition depends not only on the functions of finance, but also on many other factors that include (1) management, marketing, management production and operations, R&D, and MIS; (2) actions by competitors, suppliers, distributors, creditors, customers, and shareholders; and (3) economic, social, cultural, demographic, environmental, political, governmental, legal, and technological trends.

Breakeven Analysis

Because consumers remain price sensitive, many firms have lowered prices to compete. As a firm lowers prices, its **breakeven (BE) point** in terms of units sold increases, as illustrated in Figure 4-4. The breakeven point can be defined as the quantity of units that a firm must sell for its total revenues (TR) to equal its total costs (TC). Note that the before and after chart in Figure 4-4 reveals that the TR line rotates to the right with a decrease in price, thus increasing the quantity (Q) that must be sold just to break even. Increasing the breakeven point is thus a huge drawback of lowering prices. Of course when rivals are lowering prices, a firm may have to lower prices anyway to compete. However, the breakeven concept should be kept in mind because it is so important, especially in recessionary times.

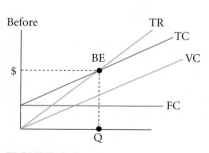
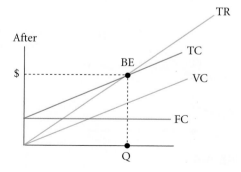

FIGURE 4-4

A Before and After Breakeven Chart When Prices Are Lowered

Notice in Figure 4-5 that increasing fixed costs (FC) also raises a firm's breakeven quantity. Note the before and after chart in Figure 4-5 reveals that adding fixed costs such as more stores, or more plants, or even more advertising as part of a strategic plan raises the TC line, which makes the intersection of the TC and TR lines at a point farther down the Quantity axis. Increasing a firm's FC thus significantly raises the quantity of goods that must be sold to break even. This is not just theory for the sake of theory. Firms with less fixed costs, such as Apple and Amazon.com, have lower breakeven points, which give them a decided competitive advantage in harsh economic times. Figure 4-5 reveals that adding **fixed costs (FC),** such as plant, equipment, stores, advertising, and land, may be detrimental whenever there is doubt that significantly more units can be sold to offset those expenditures.

Firms must be cognizant of the fact that lowering prices and adding fixed costs could be a catastrophic double whammy because the firm's breakeven quantity needed to be sold is increased dramatically. Figure 4-6 illustrates this double whammy. Note how far the breakeven point shifts with both a price decrease and an increase in fixed costs. If a firm does not break-even, then it will of course incur losses, and losses are not good, especially sustained losses.

Finally, note in Figures 4-4, 4-5, and 4-6 that **variable costs (VC),** such as labor and materials, when increased, have the effect of raising the breakeven point, too. Raising VC is reflected by the VC line shifting left or becoming steeper. When the TR line remains constant, the effect of increasing VC is to increase TC, which increases the point at which TR = TC = BE.

The formula for calculating breakeven point is BE Quantity = TFC divided by (price – VC). In other words, the quantity or units of product that need to be sold for a firm to breakeven is total fixed costs divided by (price per unit – variable costs per unit). A breakeven problem is given in Table 4-7.

Suffice it to say here that various strategies can have dramatically beneficial or harmful effects on the firm's financial condition because of the concept of breakeven analysis.

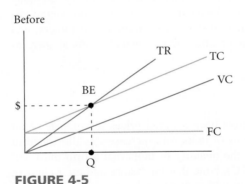
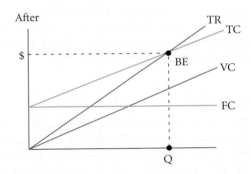

FIGURE 4-5

A Before and After Breakeven Chart When Fixed Costs Are Increased

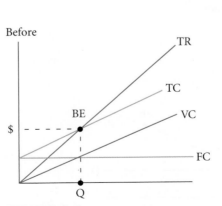
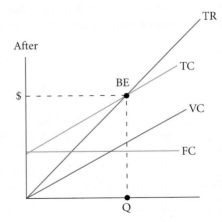

FIGURE 4-6

A Before and After Breakeven Chart When Prices Are Lowered and Fixed Costs Are Increased

TABLE 4-7 Applying Breakeven Analysis for Joy's Day Care

Seeing a need for childcare in her town, Joy is considering opening her own day-care service. Joy's Day Care needs to be affordable, so Joy would like to care for each child for $12 a day. But Joy also wants to make money. Joy needs to know how many children she will have to watch per day to make money. Joy gathered the following information about her potential new business.

- The month of June has 20 workdays, Monday through Friday for 4 weeks.
- Insurance and rent on her business will be $200 and $400, respectively, per month.
- Expenses per student per day will be snacks (2 @ $1.00) + meals (2 @ $3.00).

Joy's Analysis

Breakeven = Operating Expenses ÷ ($12.00 – $8.00)

Breakeven = $600 ÷ $4.00 Breakeven = 150 units (children) in June.

Because there are 20 days in June, Joy must watch 150 ÷ 20 = 7.5 kids, or 8 children every day to make a profit.

Joy's Conclusion

Thanks to breakeven analysis, Joy is pondering whether or not she can care for 8 children daily. Instead of abruptly opening the business, Joy is now considering adding a helper for $50 per day and charging $20 per student per day. How many students now would Joy have to care for to make a profit under this scenario? (Answer 6.6 = 7) What do you think would be an ideal scenario for Joy in planning for her new business?

There are some limitations of breakeven analysis, including the following points:

1. Breakeven analysis is only a supply side (i.e., costs only) analysis because it tells you nothing about what sales are likely to be for the product at various prices.
2. It assumes that fixed costs are constant. Although this is true in the short run, an increase in the scale of production will cause fixed costs to rise.
3. It assumes average variable costs are constant per unit of output, at least in the range of likely quantities of sales.
4. It assumes that the quantity of goods produced is equal to the quantity of goods sold (i.e., there is no change in beginning or ending inventory).
5. In multiproduct companies, it assumes that the relative proportions of each product sold and produced are constant (i.e., the sales mix is constant).[22]

Finance and Accounting Audit Checklist

The following finance and accounting questions, like the similar questions about marketing and management previously, should be examined:

1. Where is the firm financially strong and weak as indicated by financial ratio analyses?
2. Can the firm raise needed short-term capital?
3. Can the firm raise needed long-term capital through debt or equity?
4. Does the firm have sufficient working capital?
5. Are capital budgeting procedures effective?
6. Are dividend payout policies reasonable?
7. Does the firm have good relations with its investors and stockholders?
8. Are the firm's financial managers experienced and well trained?
9. Is the firm's debt situation excellent?

Production and Operations

The extent to which a manufacturing plant's output reaches its potential output is called **capacity utilization,** a key strategic variable. The higher the capacity utilization the better because otherwise equipment may sit idle. The estimated plant capacity utilization in Europe for the major auto producers is Volkswagen (84%), Renault (77%), Peugeot (73%), Ford (66%), GM (60%), and Fiat (55%).[23]

The **production/operations function** of a business consists of all those activities that transform inputs into goods and services. Production and operations management deals with inputs, transformations, and outputs that vary across industries and markets. A manufacturing operation transforms or converts inputs such as raw materials, labor, capital, machines, and facilities into finished goods and services. As indicated in Table 4-8, Roger Schroeder suggested

TABLE 4-8 The Basic Functions (Decisions) Within Production/Operations

Decision Areas	Example Decisions
1. Process	These decisions include choice of technology, facility layout, process flow analysis, facility location, line balancing, process control, and transportation analysis. Distances from raw materials to production sites to customers are a major consideration.
2. Capacity	These decisions include forecasting, facilities planning, aggregate planning, scheduling, capacity planning, and queuing analysis. Capacity utilization is a major consideration.
3. Inventory	These decisions involve managing the level of raw materials, work-in-process, and finished goods, especially considering what to order, when to order, how much to order, and materials handling.
4. Workforce	These decisions involve managing the skilled, unskilled, clerical, and managerial employees by caring for job design, work measurement, job enrichment, work standards, and motivation techniques.
5. Quality	These decisions are aimed at ensuring that high-quality goods and services are produced by caring for quality control, sampling, testing, quality assurance, and cost control.

Source: Based on R. Schroeder, *Operations Management* (New York: McGraw-Hill, 1981), 12.

that production and operations management comprises five functions or decision areas: process, capacity, inventory, workforce, and quality.

Production and operations activities often represent the largest part of an organization's human and capital assets. In most industries, the major costs of producing a product or service are incurred within operations, so production and operations can have great value as a competitive weapon in a company's overall strategy. Strengths and weaknesses in the five functions of production can mean the success or failure of an enterprise.

Many production and operations managers are finding that cross-training of employees can help their firms respond faster to changing markets. Cross-training of workers can increase efficiency, quality, productivity, and job satisfaction. For example, at General Motors' Detroit gear and axle plant, costs related to product defects were reduced 400 percent in 2 years as a result of cross-training workers. As shown in Table 4-9, James Dilworth outlined implications of several types of strategic decisions that a company might make.

A magazine that had been printed since 1933, *Newsweek*, ended its print edition of the magazine on December 31, 2012, after suffering through years of declining profits and falling subscriptions. Now only an all digital-tablet version, *Newsweek Global*, is available with a paid subscription. As a result of this strategic decision, *Newsweek* is laying off employees and closing production facilities both in the USA and abroad. Among the USA's three icon weekly magazines, *Time, Newsweek*, and *U.S. News and World Report*, only *Time* now remains in print version. The weekly cost to publish and distribute the print version of *Newsweek* was $42 million. The top 10 print magazines by circulation in 2012 are:

1. *AARP Magazine* (22,528,478)
2. *AARP Bulletin* (22,283,411)
3. *Game Informer* (8,169,524)
4. *Better Homes and Gardens* (7,617,038)
5. *Reader's Digest* (5,577,717)
6. *Good Housekeeping* (4,346,757)
7. *National Geographic* (4,232,205)
8. *Family Circle* (4,100,977)
9. *People* (3,563,035)
10. *Woman's Day* (3,449,692)

A current trend that is accelerating among U.S. manufacturers is to extend the payment term on monies owed to suppliers. Procter & Gamble is leading the way on this trend, freeing

TABLE 4-9 Implications of Various Strategies on Production and Operations

Various Strategies	Implications
1. Low-cost provider	Creates high barriers to entry
	Creates larger market
	Requires longer production runs and fewer product changes
2. A high-quality provider	Requires more quality-assurance efforts
	Requires more expensive equipment
	Requires highly skilled workers and higher wages
3. Provide great customer service	Requires more service people, service parts, and equipment
	Requires rapid response to customer needs or changes in customer tastes
	Requires a higher inventory investment
4. Be the first to introduce new products	Has higher research and development costs
	Has high retraining and tooling costs
5. Become highly automated	Requires high capital investment
	Reduces flexibility
	May affect labor relations
	Makes maintenance more crucial
6. Minimize layoffs	Serves the security needs of employees and may develop employee loyalty
	Helps to attract and retain highly skilled employees

Source: Based on: J. Dilworth, *Production and Operations Management: Manufacturing and Nonmanufacturing,* 2nd ed. Copyright © 1983 by Random House, Inc.

up nearly $2 billion in cash annually by delaying payments to suppliers. Hundreds of other firms are doing the same, including Unilever and even retailers such as Walmart and Kohl's.

Another trend among U.S. manufacturers and retailers regarding suppliers is to quit doing business with unsafe factories, such as the one in Bangladesh that recently collapsed and killed 1,100 people. Walmart has publicly blacklisted 250 Bangladeshi suppliers found to have safety problems.

Production and Operations Audit Checklist

Questions such as the following should be examined:

1. Are supplies of raw materials, parts, and subassemblies reliable and reasonable?
2. Are facilities, equipment, machinery, and offices in good condition?
3. Are inventory-control policies and procedures effective?
4. Are quality-control policies and procedures effective?
5. Are facilities, resources, and markets strategically located?
6. Does the firm have technological competencies?

Research and Development

The fifth major area of internal operations that should be examined for specific strengths and weaknesses is **research and development (R&D).** Many firms today conduct no R&D, and yet many other companies depend on successful R&D activities for survival. Firms pursuing a product development strategy especially need to have a strong R&D orientation. Founded in 1897 and headquartered in Orrville, Ohio, J.M. Smucker Company had $5.5 and 4.8 billion in revenue in 2012 and 2011, and spent $21.9 and $20.9 million in R&D during those two years, comprising 0.39 and 0.43 percent of revenues, respectively. In contrast, Microsoft had revenues of $73.7 and $69.9 billion in 2012 and 2011 and spent $9.8 and $9.0 billion on R&D, comprising 13.3 and 12.9 percent of revenues respectively. High-tech firms such as Microsoft spend a much larger proportion of their revenues on R&D.

Huawei Technologies, the world's largest supplier of telecom equipment, increased its R&D spending by 25 percent in 2012 to $4.7 billion, almost equal to rival Ericsson's R&D expenditures of $4.8 billion. A key decision for many firms is whether to be a "first mover" or a "late follower," i.e. spending heavily on R&D to be the first to develop radically new products, or alternatively spending less on R&D by imitating/duplicating/improving upon products once rival firms develop them.

Organizations invest in R&D because they believe that such an investment will lead to a superior product or service and will give them competitive advantages. R&D expenditures are directed at developing new products before competitors do, at improving product quality, or at improving manufacturing processes to reduce costs.

Effective management of the R&D function requires a strategic and operational partnership between R&D and the other vital business functions. A spirit of partnership and mutual trust between general and R&D managers is evident in the best-managed firms today. Managers in these firms jointly explore; assess; and decide the what, when, where, why, and how much of R&D. Priorities, costs, benefits, risks, and rewards associated with R&D activities are discussed openly and shared. The overall mission of R&D thus has become broad based, including supporting existing businesses, helping launch new businesses, developing new products, improving product quality, improving manufacturing efficiency, and deepening or broadening the company's technological capabilities.[24]

The best-managed firms today seek to organize R&D activities in a way that breaks the isolation of R&D from the rest of the company and promotes a spirit of partnership between R&D managers and other managers in the firm. R&D decisions and plans must be integrated and coordinated across departments and divisions by having the departments share experiences and information. The strategic-management process facilitates this cross-functional approach to managing the R&D function.

R&D spending in the USA was $418.6 billion in 2012 and is expected to increase only 1.2 percent to $423.7 billion in 2013. The inflation-adjusted R&D spending for 2013 actually is expected to decline 0.7 percent. In comparison, the number-2 R&D spending country, China, spent $197.3 billion in 2012, but it is annually increasing its expenditure 10 to 12 percent. According to the Battelle Memorial Institute, China will achieve parity with the USA in R&D spending in 2022.

Internal and External Research and Development

Cost distributions among R&D activities vary by company and industry, but total R&D costs generally do not exceed manufacturing and marketing start-up costs. Four approaches to determining R&D budget allocations commonly are used: (1) financing as many project proposals as possible, (2) using a percentage-of-sales method, (3) budgeting about the same amount that competitors spend for R&D, or (4) deciding how many successful new products are needed and working backward to estimate the required R&D investment.

R&D in organizations can take two basic forms: (1) internal R&D, in which an organization operates its own R&D department, or (2) contract R&D, in which a firm hires independent researchers or independent agencies to develop specific products. Many companies use both approaches to develop new products. A widely used approach for obtaining outside R&D assistance is to pursue a joint venture with another firm. R&D strengths (capabilities) and weaknesses (limitations) play a major role in strategy formulation and strategy implementation.

Most firms have no choice but to continually develop new and improved products because of changing consumer needs and tastes, new technologies, shortened product life cycles, and increased domestic and foreign competition. A shortage of ideas for new products, increased global competition, increased market segmentation, strong special-interest groups, and increased government regulations are several factors making the successful development of new products more and more difficult, costly, and risky. In the pharmaceutical industry, for example, only one out of every few thousand drugs created in the laboratory ends up on pharmacists' shelves. Scarpello, Boulton, and Hofer emphasized that different strategies require different R&D capabilities:

> The focus of R&D efforts can vary greatly depending on a firm's competitive strategy. Some corporations attempt to be market leaders and innovators of new products, while others are satisfied to be market followers and developers of currently available products. The basic skills required to support these strategies will vary, depending on whether R&D becomes the driving force behind competitive strategy. In cases where new product introduction is the driving force for strategy, R&D activities must be extensive.[25]

Research and Development Audit

Questions such as the following should be asked in performing an R&D audit:

1. Does the firm have R&D facilities? Are they adequate?
2. If outside R&D firms are used, are they cost-effective?
3. Are the organization's R&D personnel well qualified?
4. Are R&D resources allocated effectively?
5. Are management information and computer systems adequate?
6. Is communication between R&D and other organizational units effective?
7. Are present products technologically competitive?

Management Information Systems

Billions of bits of information are now "in the cloud." Information ties all business functions together and provides the basis for all managerial decisions. It is the cornerstone of all organizations. Information represents a major source of competitive management advantage or disadvantage. Assessing a firm's internal strengths and weaknesses in information systems is a critical dimension of performing an internal audit.

A MIS's purpose is to improve the performance of an enterprise by improving the quality of managerial decisions. An effective information system thus collects, codes, stores, synthesizes, and presents information in such a manner that it answers important operating and strategic questions. The heart of an information system is a database containing the kinds of records and data important to managers.

A **management information system (MIS)** receives raw material from both the external and internal evaluation of an organization. It gathers data about marketing, finance, production, and personnel matters internally, and social, cultural, demographic, environmental, economic, political, governmental, legal, technological, and competitive factors externally. Data are integrated in ways needed to support managerial decision making.

There is a logical flow of material in an information system, whereby data are input to the system and transformed into output. Outputs include computer printouts, written reports, tables, charts, graphs, checks, purchase orders, invoices, inventory records, payroll accounts, and a variety of other documents. Payoffs from alternative strategies can be calculated and estimated. **Data** becomes **information** only when it is evaluated, filtered, condensed, analyzed, and organized for a specific purpose, problem, individual, or time.

Management Information Systems Audit

Questions such as the following should be asked when conducting this audit:

1. Do all managers in the firm use the information system to make decisions?
2. Is there a chief information officer or director of information systems position in the firm?
3. Are data in the information system updated regularly?
4. Do managers from all functional areas of the firm contribute input to the information system?
5. Are there effective passwords for entry into the firm's information system?
6. Are strategists of the firm familiar with the information systems of rival firms?
7. Is the information system user-friendly?
8. Do all users of the information system understand the competitive advantages that information can provide firms?
9. Are computer training workshops provided for users of the information system?
10. Is the firm's information system continually being improved in content and user-friendliness?

Value Chain Analysis

According to Porter, the business of a firm can best be described as a value chain, in which total revenues minus total costs of all activities undertaken to develop and market a product or service yields value. All firms in a given industry have a similar value chain, which includes activities such as obtaining raw materials, designing products, building manufacturing facilities, developing cooperative agreements, and providing customer service. A firm will be profitable as long as total revenues exceed the total costs incurred in creating and delivering the product or service. Firms should strive to understand not only their own value chain operations but also their competitors', suppliers', and distributors' value chains.

Value chain analysis (VCA) refers to the process whereby a firm determines the costs associated with organizational activities from purchasing raw materials to manufacturing product(s) to marketing those products. VCA aims to identify where low-cost advantages or disadvantages exist anywhere along the value chain from raw material to customer service activities. VCA can enable a firm to better identify its own strengths and weaknesses, especially as compared to competitors' value chain analyses and their own data examined over time.

Substantial judgment may be required in performing a VCA because different items along the value chain may impact other items positively or negatively, so there exist complex interrelationships. For example, exceptional customer service may be especially expensive yet may reduce the costs of returns and increase revenues. Cost and price differences among rival firms can have their origins in activities performed by suppliers, distributors, creditors, or even shareholders. Despite the complexity of VCA, the initial step in implementing this procedure is to divide a firm's operations into specific activities or business processes. Then the analyst attempts to attach a cost to each discrete activity, and the costs could be in terms of both time and money. Finally, the analyst converts the cost data into information by looking for competitive cost strengths and weaknesses that may yield competitive advantage or disadvantage. Conducting a VCA is supportive of the RBV's examination of a firm's assets and capabilities as sources of distinctive competence.

When a major competitor or new market entrant offers products or services at low prices, this may be because that firm has substantially lower value chain costs or perhaps the rival firm is just waging a desperate attempt to gain sales or market share. Thus, VCA can be critically important for a firm in monitoring whether its prices and costs are competitive. An example value chain is illustrated in Figure 4-7. There can be more than a hundred particular value-creating activities associated with the business of producing and marketing a product or service, and each one of the activities can represent a competitive advantage or disadvantage for the firm. The combined costs of all the various activities in a company's value chain define the firm's cost of doing business. Firms should determine where cost advantages and disadvantages in their value chain occur *relative* to the value chain of rival firms.

Value chains differ immensely across industries and firms. Whereas a paper products company, such as Stone Container, would include on its value chain timber farming, logging, pulp mills, and papermaking, a company such as Hewlett-Packard would include programming, peripherals, software, hardware, and laptops. A motel would include food, housekeeping, check-in and check-out operations, website, reservations system, and so on. However, all firms should use VCA to develop and nurture a core competence and convert this competence into a distinctive competence. A **core competence** is a VCA that a firm performs especially well. When a core competence evolves into a major competitive advantage, then it is called a distinctive competence. Figure 4-8 illustrates this process.

More and more companies are using VCA to gain and sustain competitive advantage by being especially efficient and effective along various parts of the value chain. For example, Walmart has built powerful value advantages by focusing on exceptionally tight inventory control and volume purchasing of products. Computer companies in contrast compete aggressively along the distribution end of the value chain. Price competitiveness is a key component of competitiveness for both mass retailers and computer firms.

Benchmarking

Benchmarking is an analytical tool used to determine whether a firm's VCA are competitive compared to rivals and thus conducive to winning in the marketplace. Benchmarking entails measuring costs of value chain activities across an industry to determine "best practices" among competing firms for the purpose of duplicating or improving on those best practices. Benchmarking enables a firm to take action to improve its competitiveness by identifying (and improving on) value chain activities where rival firms have comparative advantages in cost, service, reputation, or operation.

Supplier Costs
    Raw materials
    Fuel
    Energy
    Transportation
    Truck drivers
    Truck maintenance
    Component parts
    Inspection
    Storing
    Warehouse
Production Costs
    Inventory system
    Receiving
    Plant layout
    Maintenance
    Plant location
    Computer
    R&D
    Cost accounting
Distribution Costs
    Loading
    Shipping
    Budgeting
    Personnel
    Internet
    Trucking
    Railroads
    Fuel
    Maintenance
Sales and Marketing Costs
    Salespersons
    Website
    Internet
    Publicity
    Promotion
    Advertising
    Transportation
    Food and lodging
Customer Service Costs
    Postage
    Phone
    Internet
    Warranty
Management Costs
    Human resources
    Administration
    Employee benefits
    Labor relations
    Managers
    Employees
    Finance and legal

FIGURE 4-7

An Example Value Chain for a Typical Manufacturing Firm

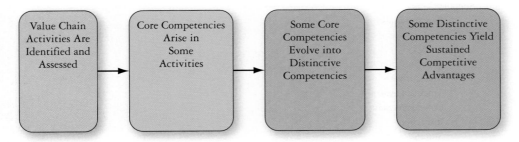

FIGURE 4-8

Transforming Value Chain Activities into Sustained Competitive Advantage

A comprehensive survey on benchmarking was recently commissioned by the Global Benchmarking Network, a network of benchmarking centers representing 22 countries. More than 450 organizations responded from over 40 countries. The results showed that:

1. Mission and vision statements along with customer (client) surveys are the most used (77 percent of organizations) of 20 improvement tools, followed by SWOT analysis (72 percent), and informal benchmarking (68 percent). Performance benchmarking was used by 49 percent and best practice benchmarking by 39 percent.
2. The tools that are likely to increase in popularity the most over the next three years are performance benchmarking, informal benchmarking, SWOT, and best practice benchmarking. More than 60 percent of organizations not currently using these tools indicated they are likely to use them in the next three years.[26]

The hardest part of benchmarking can be gaining access to other firms' VCA with associated costs. Typical sources of benchmarking information, however, include published reports, trade publications, suppliers, distributors, customers, partners, creditors, shareholders, lobbyists, and willing rival firms. Some rival firms share benchmarking data. However, the International Benchmarking Clearinghouse provides guidelines to help ensure that restraint of trade, price fixing, bid rigging, bribery, and other improper business conduct do not arise between participating firms.

Because of the popularity of benchmarking today, numerous consulting firms such as Accenture, AT Kearney, Best Practices Benchmarking & Consulting, as well as the Strategic Planning Institute's Council on Benchmarking, gather benchmarking data, conduct benchmarking studies, and distribute benchmark information without identifying the sources.

The Internal Factor Evaluation Matrix

A summary step in conducting an internal strategic-management audit is to construct an **Internal Factor Evaluation (IFE) Matrix**. This strategy-formulation tool summarizes and evaluates the major strengths and weaknesses in the functional areas of a business, and it also provides a basis for identifying and evaluating relationships among those areas. Intuitive judgments are required in developing an IFE Matrix, so the appearance of a scientific approach should not be interpreted to mean this is an all-powerful technique. A thorough understanding of the factors included is more important than the actual numbers. Similar to the EFE Matrix and CPM described in Chapter 3, an IFE Matrix can be developed in five steps:

1. List key internal factors as identified in the internal-audit process. Use a total of 20 internal factors, including both strengths and weaknesses. List strengths first and then weaknesses. Be as specific as possible, using percentages, ratios, and comparative numbers. Recall that Edward Deming said: "In God we trust. Everyone else bring data." Include "actionable" factors that can provide insight regarding strategies to pursue. For example, the factor "our Quick Ratio is 2.1 vs. industry average of 1.8" is not actionable, whereas the factor "our chocolate division's ROI increased from 8 to 15 percent in South America" is actionable.
2. Assign a weight that ranges from 0.0 (not important) to 1.0 (all-important) to each factor. The weight assigned to a given factor indicates the relative importance of the factor to being successful in the firm's industry. Regardless of whether a key factor is an internal strength

or weakness, factors considered to have the greatest effect on organizational performance should be assigned the highest weights. The sum of all weights must equal 1.0.

3. Assign a 1-to-4 rating to each factor to indicate whether that factor represents a major weakness (rating = 1), a minor weakness (rating = 2) a minor strength (rating = 3), or a major strength (rating = 4). Note that strengths must receive a 3 or 4 rating and weaknesses must receive a 1 or 2 rating. Ratings are thus company-based, whereas the weights in step 2 are industry-based.
4. Multiply each factor's weight by its rating to determine a weighted score for each variable.
5. Sum the weighted scores for each variable to determine the total weighted score for the organization.

Regardless of how many factors are included in an IFE Matrix, the total weighted score can range from a low of 1.0 to a high of 4.0, with the average score being 2.5. Total weighted scores well below 2.5 characterize organizations that are weak internally, whereas scores significantly above 2.5 indicate a strong internal position. Like the EFE Matrix, an IFE Matrix should include 20 key factors. The number of factors has no effect on the range of total weighted scores because the weights always sum to 1.0.

When a key internal factor is both a strength and a weakness, the factor may be included twice in the IFE Matrix, and a weight and rating assigned to each statement. For example, the Playboy logo both helps and hurts Playboy Enterprises; the logo attracts customers to *Playboy* magazine, but it keeps the Playboy cable channel out of many markets. Be as quantitative as possible when stating factors. Use monetary amounts, percentages, numbers, and ratios to the extent possible.

An example IFE Matrix is provided in Table 4-10 for a retail computer store. Note that the two most important factors to be successful in the retail computer store business are "revenues from repair/service in the store" and "location of the store." Also note that the store is doing best on "average customer purchase amount" and "in-store technical support." The store is having major problems with its carpet, bathroom, paint, and checkout procedures. Note also that the matrix contains substantial quantitative data rather than vague statements; this is excellent. Overall, this store

TABLE 4-10 A Sample Internal Factor Evaluation Matrix for a Retail Computer Store

Key Internal Factors	Weight	Rating	Weighted Score
Strengths			
1. Inventory turnover increased from 5.8 to 6.7	0.05	3	0.15
2. Average customer purchase increased from $97 to $128	0.07	4	0.28
3. Employee morale is excellent	0.10	3	0.30
4. In-store promotions resulted in 20 percent increase in sales	0.05	3	0.15
5. Newspaper advertising expenditures increased 10 percent	0.02	3	0.06
6. Revenues from repair/service segment of store up 16 percent	0.15	3	0.45
7. In-store technical support personnel have MIS college degrees	0.05	4	0.20
8. Store's debt-to-total assets ratio declined to 34 percent	0.03	3	0.09
9. Revenues per employee up 19 percent	0.02	3	0.06
Weaknesses			
1. Revenues from software segment of store down 12 percent	0.10	2	0.20
2. Location of store negatively impacted by new Highway 34	0.15	2	0.30
3. Carpet and paint in store somewhat in disrepair	0.02	1	0.02
4. Bathroom in store needs refurbishing	0.02	1	0.02
5. Revenues from businesses down 8 percent	0.04	1	0.04
6. Store has no website	0.05	2	0.10
7. Supplier on-time delivery increased to 2.4 days	0.03	1	0.03
8. Often customers have to wait to check out	0.05	1	0.05
Total	**1.00**		**2.50**

TABLE 4-11 An Actual IFE Matrix for Fresenius, Inc.

Strengths	Weight	Rating	WScore
1. Sales and earnings per share have not declined a single year for 10 years	0.09	4	0.36
2. Fresenius Medical Care is the market leader in dialysis services and products	0.09	4	0.36
3. Trading volume increased by 17 percent in 2011	0.05	3	0.15
4. Dividends were just raised for the 20th consecutive year	0.06	4	0.24
5. Financial analysts ratings show 23 "buy," 2 "hold," and no "sell"	0.06	3	0.18
6. Has a renown training school for nurses and other health workers	0.03	3	0.09
7. DAX30 ranking in market capitalization steadily improving	0.05	4	0.20
8. Fresenius Medical increased worldwide clinics by 6 percent	0.03	3	0.09
9. Fresenius Helios is the second largest private hospital operators in Germany	0.06	3	0.18
10. Diversified 4 business segments in different healthcare sectors	0.05	3	0.15
Weaknesses			
1. Quick Ratio of 0.65 shows a lack of ability to cover cash needs	0.07	2	0.14
2. Group sales decreased by 4 percent in North America	0.03	2	0.06
3. Group debt increased by 9 percent	0.05	1	0.05
4. Fresenius Biotech has a negative EBIT of approx. $–38.6 million	0.05	2	0.10
5. Decrease of 21% in operating cash flow from 2010 to 2011	0.08	1	0.08
6. Fresenius Helios dropped 3.1 billion euro takeover of rival Rhoen-Klinikum on September 3, 2012, because of rival hospital operators blocking the merger	0.01	2	0.02
7. Fresenius Vamed made no material acquisitions	0.02	2	0.04
8. No racial diversity on management and supervisory boards	0.04	2	0.08
9. Healthcare Group board members and committees comprised of all males	0.04	1	0.04
10. Only one female in all top management	0.04	1	0.04
Total	**1.0**		**2.65**

receives a 2.5 total weighted score, which on a 1-to-4 scale is exactly average/halfway, indicating there is definitely room for improvement in store operations, strategies, policies, and procedures.

The IFE Matrix provides important information for strategy formulation. For example, this retail computer store might want to hire another checkout person and repair its carpet, paint, and bathroom problems. Also, the store may want to increase advertising for its repair/services, because that is a really important (weight 0.15) factor to being successful in this business.

Headquartered in Germany and specializing in kidney dialysis, Fresenius provides healthcare products and services in about 100 countries. Fresenius owns and operates 2,800 dialysis clinics and many other healthcare facilities. Table 4-11 provides an actual IFE matrix created for Fresenius in late 2012. As indicated in Table 4-11, Fresenius is financially strong, but needs to include women and minorities in its management.

In multidivisional firms, each autonomous division or strategic business unit should construct an IFE Matrix. Divisional matrices then can be integrated to develop an overall corporate IFE Matrix. Be as divisional as possible when developing a corporate IFE Matrix. Also, in developing an IFE Matrix, do not allow more than 30 percent of the key factors to be financial ratios because financial ratios are generally the result of many other factors so it is difficult to know what particular strategies should be considered based on financial ratios. For example, a firm would have no insight on whether to sell in Brazil or South Africa to take advantage of a high corporate ROI ratio.

Special Note to Students

It can be debated whether external or internal factors are more important in strategic planning, but there is no debate regarding the fact that gaining and sustaining competitive advantage is the essence or purpose of strategic planning. In the internal portion of your case analysis, emphasize how and why your internal strengths and weaknesses can be leveraged to both gain competitive advantage and overcome competitive disadvantage, in light of the direction you are taking the firm. Maintain your project's upbeat, insightful, and forward-thinking demeanor during the internal assessment, rather than being mundane, descriptive, and vague. Focus on how your firm's resources, capabilities, structure, and strategies, with your recommended improvements, can lead the firm to prosperity. Although the numbers absolutely must be there, must be accurate, and must be reasonable, do not bore a live audience or class with overreliance on numbers. Periodically throughout your presentation or written analysis, refer to your recommendations, explaining how your plan of action will improve the firm's weaknesses and capitalize on strengths in light of anticipated competitor countermoves. Keep your audience's attention, interest, and suspense, rather than "reading" to them or "defining" ratios for them.

Conclusion

Management, marketing, finance and accounting, production and operations, R&D, and MIS represent the core operations of most businesses. A strategic-management audit of a firm's internal operations is vital to organizational health. Many companies still prefer to be judged solely on their bottom-line performance. However, an increasing number of successful organizations are using the internal audit to gain competitive advantages over rival firms.

Systematic methodologies for performing strength-weakness assessments are not well developed in the strategic-management literature, but it is clear that strategists must identify and evaluate internal strengths and weaknesses to effectively formulate and choose among alternative strategies. The EFE Matrix, CPM, IFE Matrix, and clear statements of vision and mission provide the basic information needed to successfully formulate competitive strategies. The process of performing an internal audit represents an opportunity for managers and employees throughout the organization to participate in determining the future of the firm. Involvement in the process can energize and mobilize managers and employees.

MyManagementLab®

Go to **mymanagementlab.com** to complete the problems marked with this icon .

Key Terms and Concepts

activity ratios (p. 108)
benchmarking (p. 116)
breakeven (BE) point (p. 109)
capacity utilization (p. 111)
capital budgeting (p. 105)
communication (p. 92)
controlling (p. 100)
core competence (p. 116)
cost/benefit analysis (p. 104)
cultural products (p. 94)
customer analysis (p. 101)
data (p. 115)
distinctive competencies (p. 91)
distribution (p. 103)
dividend decisions (p. 105)
empirical indicators (p. 94)
financial ratio analysis (p. 93)
fixed costs (FC) (p. 110)
financing decision (p. 105)
functions of finance/accounting (p. 104)
functions of management (p. 96)
functions of marketing (p. 100)
growth ratios (p. 108)
human resource management (p. 99)
information (p. 115)

internal audit (p. 92)
internal factor evaluation (IFE) matrix (p. 118)
investment decision (p. 105)
leverage ratios (p. 108)
liquidity ratios (p. 108)
management information system
    (MIS) (p. 115)
marketing research (p. 103)
motivating (p. 99)
organizational culture (p. 94)
organizing (p. 98)
personnel management (p. 99)
planning (p. 96)
pricing (p. 102)
product and service planning (p. 102)
production/operations function (p. 111)
profitability ratios (p. 108)
research and development (R&D) (p. 113)
resource-based view (RBV) (p. 93)
selling (p. 101)
staffing (p. 99)
synergy (p. 98)
test marketing (p. 102)
value chain analysis (VCA) (p. 116)
variable costs (VC) (p. 110)

Issues for Review and Discussion

4-1. Marketing is becoming much more technical as are the duties and responsibilities of chief marketing officers (CMOs). Give four examples of increasing technical aspects of marketing.

4-2. S&P companies are on average today paying out 31 percent of their earnings in the form of dividends, but that is down from 52 percent of earnings in some years. What are the pros and cons of reinvesting earnings as opposed to paying dividends?

4-3. Is a capacity utilization rate of 50 percent good? Why?

4-4. If Priceline.com increases its advertising expenses by 30 percent while keeping its price and variable costs the same, does that mean the company's breakeven point will increase 30 percent? Show this calculation for a hypothetical firm.

4-5. What are the limitations of breakeven analysis?

4-6. In the Joy's Daycare breakeven example in the chapter, how would a $1,000 annual advertising expenditure impact the business breakeven point?

4-7. Explain cost/benefit analysis.

4-8. Explain why "communication" may be the most important word in management. What do you think is the most important word in marketing? In finance? In accounting?

4-9. Discuss how the nature of advertisements have changed in the last few years.

4-10. Rate the five websites in Table 4-5 from best to worst for finding comparative financial ratio information about a company.

4-11. Explain why it is best not to have more than 30 percent of the factors in an IFE matrix be financial ratios.

4-12. List three firms you are familiar with and give a distinctive competence for each firm.

4-13. Give some key reasons why prioritizing strengths and weaknesses are essential.

4-14. Why may it be easier in performing an internal assessment to develop a list of 80 strengths and weaknesses than to decide on the top 20 to use in formulating strategies?

4-15. Think of an organization you are familiar with. List three resources of that entity that are empirical indicators.

4-16. Think of an organization you are familiar with. Rate that entity's organizational culture on the 15 example dimensions listed in Table 4-2.

4-17. If you and a partner were going to visit a foreign country where you have never been before, how much planning would you do ahead of time? What benefit would you expect that planning to provide?

4-18. Even though planning is considered the foundation of management, why do you think it is commonly the task that managers neglect most?

4-19. Are you more organized than the person sitting beside you in class? If not, what problems could that present in terms of your performance and rank in the class? How analogous is this situation to rival companies?

4-20. List the three ways that financial ratios should be compared or used. Which of the three comparisons do you feel is most important? Why?

4-21. Illustrate how value chain activities can become core competencies and eventually distinctive competencies. Give an example for an organization you are familiar with.

4-22. In an IFE Matrix, would it be advantageous to list your strengths, and then your weaknesses, in order of increasing "weight"? Why?

4-23. In an IFE Matrix, a critic may say there is no significant difference between a "weight" of 0.08 and 0.06. How would you respond?

4-24. List six desirable characteristics of advertisements in recessionary times.

4-25. Why are so many firms raising their dividend payout amounts?

4-26. When someone says dividends paid are double taxed, what are they referring to?

4-27. Draw a breakeven chart to illustrate a drop in labor costs.

4-28. Draw a breakeven chart to illustrate an increase in advertising expenses.

4-29. Draw a breakeven chart to illustrate closing stores.

4-30. Draw a breakeven chart to illustrate lowering price.

4-31. Explain why prioritizing the relative importance of strengths and weaknesses in an IFE matrix is an important strategic-management activity.

4-32. How can delegation of authority contribute to effective strategic management?

4-33. Which of the three basic functions of finance and accounting do you feel is most important in a small electronics manufacturing concern? Justify your position.

4-34. Do you think aggregate R&D expenditures for U.S. firms will increase or decrease next year? Why?

4-35. Explain how you would motivate managers and employees to implement a major new strategy.

4-36. Why do you think production and operations managers often are not directly involved in strategy-formulation activities? Why can this be a major organizational weakness?

4-37. Give two examples of staffing strengths and two examples of staffing weaknesses of an organization with which you are familiar.

4-38. Would you ever pay out dividends when your firm's annual net profit is negative? Why? What effect could this have on a firm's strategies?

4-39. If a firm has zero debt in its capital structure, is that always an organizational strength? Why or why not?

4-40. Describe the production and operations system in a police department.

4-41. After conducting an internal audit, a firm discovers a total of 100 strengths and 100 weaknesses. What procedures then could be used to determine the most important of these? Why is it important to reduce the total number of key factors?

4-42. Why do you believe cultural products affect all the functions of business?

4-43. Do you think cultural products affect strategy formulation, implementation, or evaluation the most? Why?

4-44. Identify cultural products at your college or university. Do these products, viewed collectively or separately, represent a strength or weakness for the organization?

4-45. Explain the difference between data and information in terms of each being useful to strategists.

4-46. What are the most important characteristics of an effective management information system?

4-47. Do you agree or disagree with the resource-based view theorists that internal resources are more important for a firm than external factors in achieving and sustaining competitive advantage? Explain your and their position.

4-48. Define and discuss "empirical indicators."

4-49. Define and discuss the "spam" problem in the USA.

4-50. Define and explain value chain analysis.

4-51. List five financial ratios that may be used by your university to monitor operations.

4-52. Explain benchmarking.

MyManagementLab®

Go to **mymanagementlab.com** for Auto-graded writing questions as well as the following Assisted-graded writing questions:

4-53. List three ways that financial ratios should be compared or used. Which of the three comparisons do you feel is most important? Why?

4-54. Would you ever pay out dividends when your firm's annual net profit is negative? Why? What effect could this have on a firm's strategies?

4-55. Mymanagementlab Only—comprehensive writing assignment for this chapter.

Current Readings

Arora, Ashish and Anand Nandkumar. "Insecure Advantage? Markets for Technology and the Value of Resources for Entrepreneurial Ventures." *Strategic Management Journal* 33, no. 3 (March 2012): 231–251.

Browning, Tyson R., Sanders, and Nada R. "Can Innovation Be Lean?" *California Management Review* 54, no. 4 (Summer 2012): 5–19.

Knott, Anne Marie. "The Trillion-Dollar R&D Fix." *Harvard Business Review* (May 2012): 76.

Lemper, Timothy A. "The Critical Role of Timing in Managing Intellectual Property." *Business Horizons* 55, no. 4 (July 2012): 339–347.

Lindenberg, Siegwart, and Nicolai J. Foss. "Managing Joint Production Motivation: The Role of Goal Framing and Governance Mechanisms." *The Academy of Management Review* 36, no. 3 (July 2011): 500.

Mossholder, Kevin W., Hettie A. Richardson, and Randall P. Settoon. "Human Resource Systems and Helping in Organizations: A Relational Perspective." *The Academy of Management Review* 36, no. 1 (January 2011): 33.

Rader, David. "How Cloud Computing Maximizes Growth Opportunities for a Firm Challenging Established Rivals." *Strategy and Leadership* 40, no. 4 (2012): 36–43.

Turner, Karynne L., and Mona V. Makhija. "The Role of Individuals in the Information Processing Perspective." *Strategic Management Journal* 33, no. 6 (June 2012): 661–680.

Watkins, Michael D. "How Managers Become Leaders." *Harvard Business Review* (June 2012): 64.

ASSURANCE OF LEARNING EXERCISES

EXERCISE 4A
Apply Breakeven Analysis

Purpose

Breakeven analysis is one of the simplest yet underused analytical tools in management. It helps to provide a dynamic view of the relationships among sales, costs, and profits. A better understanding of breakeven analysis can enable an organization to formulate and implement strategies more effectively. This exercise will show you how to calculate breakeven points mathematically.

The formula for calculating breakeven point is BE Quantity = TFC/P–VC. In other words, the quantity (Q) or units of product that need to be sold for a firm to break even is total fixed costs (TFC) divided by (Price per Unit – Variable Costs per Unit).

Instructions

Step 1   Lets say an airplane company has fixed costs of $100 million and variable costs per unit of $2 million. Planes sell for $3 million each. What is the company's breakeven point in terms of the number of planes that need to be sold just to break even?

Step 2   If the airplane company wants to make a profit of $99 million annually, how many planes will it have to sell?

Step 3   If the company can sell 200 airplanes in a year, how much annual profit will the firm make?

 EXERCISE 4B
Comparing Priceline.com with Expedia.com

Purpose

Showcased at the beginning of this chapter, Priceline and rival Expedia rely almost exclusively on their website for business. Thus, it is obviously essential in this industry to have the most effective, efficient, and user-friendly website possible. This exercise gives you practice identifying key strengths and weaknesses for two rival firms.

Instructions

Step 1   Visit the priceline.com and the expedia.com websites and study their features, prices, ease of navigation, user friendliness, and general layout.

Step 2   Identify four strengths and four weaknesses of the Priceline.com website as compared to its major rival Expedia's website.

Step 3   Prepare an analysis and report for Priceline's website manager to reveal how her company can improve its performance by improving its website.

 EXERCISE 4C
Perform a Financial Ratio Analysis for PepsiCo

Purpose

Financial ratio analysis is one of the best techniques for identifying and evaluating internal strengths and weaknesses. Potential investors and current shareholders look closely at firms' financial ratios, making detailed comparisons to industry averages and to previous periods of time. Financial ratio analyses provide vital input information for developing an IFE Matrix.

Instructions

Step 1   On a separate sheet of paper, number from 1 to 20. Referring to PepsiCo's income statement and balance sheet (pp. 29–30), calculate 20 financial ratios for 2012 for the company. Use Table 4-6 as a reference.

Step 2   In a second column, indicate whether you consider each ratio to be a strength, a weakness, or a neutral factor for PepsiCo.

Step 3   Go to the websites in Table 4-5 that calculate PepsiCo's financial ratios, without your having to pay a subscription (fee) for the service. Make a copy of the ratio information provided and record the source. Report this research to your classmates and your professor.

 EXERCISE 4D
Construct an IFE Matrix for PepsiCo

Purpose

This exercise will give you experience in developing an IFE Matrix. Identifying and prioritizing factors to include in an IFE Matrix fosters communication among functional and divisional managers. Preparing an IFE Matrix allows human resource, marketing, production and operations, finance and accounting, R&D, and MIS managers to articulate their concerns and thoughts regarding the business condition of the firm. This results in an improved collective understanding of the business.

Instructions

Step 1   Join with two other individuals to form a three-person team. Develop a team IFE matrix for PepsiCo. Use information from Exercise 1B on page 36.

Step 2   Compare your team's IFE Matrix to other teams' IFE matrices. Discuss any major differences.

Step 3   What strategies do you think would allow PepsiCo to capitalize on its major strengths? What strategies would allow PepsiCo to improve on its major weaknesses?

 EXERCISE 4E

Construct an IFE Matrix for Your University

Purpose

This exercise gives you the opportunity to evaluate your university's major strengths and weaknesses. As will become clearer in the next chapter, an organization's strategies are largely based on striving to take advantage of strengths and improving upon weaknesses.

Instructions

Step 1   Join with two other individuals to form a three-person team. Develop a team IFE Matrix for your university. You may use the strengths and weaknesses determined in Assurance of Learning Exercise 1D on page 37.

Step 2   Go to the board and diagram your team's IFE Matrix.

Step 3   Compare your team's IFE Matrix to other teams' IFE matrices. Discuss any major differences.

Step 4   What strategies do you think would allow your university to capitalize on its major strengths? What strategies would allow your university to improve upon its major weaknesses?

Notes

1. Reprinted by permission of the publisher from "Integrating Strength–Weakness Analysis into Strategic Planning," by William King, *Journal of Business Research* 2, no. 4: 481. Copyright 1983 by Elsevier Science Publishing Co., Inc.

2. Igor Ansoff, "Strategic Management of Technology" *Journal of Business Strategy* 7, no. 3 (Winter 1987): 38.

3. Claude George Jr., *The History of Management Thought*, 2nd ed. (Upper Saddle River, NJ: Prentice-Hall, 1972), 174.

4. Robert Grant, "The Resource-Based Theory of Competitive Advantage: Implications for Strategy Formulation," *California Management Review*, Spring 1991, 116.

5. J. B. Barney, "Firm Resources and Sustained Competitive Advantage," *Journal of Management* 17 (1991): 99–120; J. B. Barney, "The Resource-Based Theory of the Firm," *Organizational Science* 7 (1996): 469; J. B. Barney, "Is the Resource-Based 'View' a Useful Perspective for Strategic Management Research? Yes." *Academy of Management Review* 26, no. 1 (2001): 41–56.

6. Edgar Schein, *Organizational Culture and Leadership* (San Francisco: Jossey-Bass, 1985), 9.

7. John Lorsch, "Managing Culture: The Invisible Barrier to Strategic Change," *California Management Review* 28, no. 2 (1986): 95–109.

8. Y. Allarie and M. Firsirotu, "How to Implement Radical Strategies in Large Organizations," *Sloan Management Review* (Spring 1985): 19.

9. www.mindtools.com/plfailpl.html

10. Adam Smith, *The Wealth of Nations* (New York: Modern Library, 1937), 3–4.

11. Richard Daft, *Management*, 3rd ed. (Orlando, FL: Dryden Press, 1993), 512.

12. Shelley Kirkpatrick and Edwin Locke, "Leadership: Do Traits Matter?" *Academy of Management Executive* 5, no. 2 (May 1991): 48.

13. Peter Drucker, *Management Tasks, Responsibilities, and Practice* (New York: Harper & Row, 1973), 463.

14. Brian Dumaine, "What the Leaders of Tomorrow See," *Fortune*, July 3, 1989, 51.

15. J. Evans and B. Bergman, *Marketing* (New York: Macmillan, 1982), 17.

16. Spencer Ante, "As Economy Cools, IBM Furthers Focus on Marketers," *Wall Street Journal* (July 18, 2012): B3.

17. Brad Stone, "See Your Friends," *Bloomberg Businessweek* (September 27–October 3, 2010): 65–69.

18. Quoted in Robert Waterman, Jr., "The Renewal Factor," *BusinessWeek*, September 14, 1987, 108.

19. http://en.wikipedia.org/wiki/Cost-benefit_analysis

20. J. Van Horne, *Financial Management and Policy* (Upper Saddle River, N.J.: Prentice-Hall, 1974), 10.

21. Matt Krantz, "Today's Fat Dividends are Getting Even Heftier," *Wall Street Journal* (August 6, 2012): 3B.

22. http://en.wikipedia.org/wiki/Break-even_(economics).

23. Andrew Peaple, "Fiat's Struggle With Italian Job Threatens American Promise," *Wall Street Journal* (September 28, 2012): C10.

24. Philip Rousebl, Kamal Saad, and Tamara Erickson, "The Evolution of Third Generation R&D," *Planning Review* 19, no. 2 (March–April 1991): 18–26.

25. Vida Scarpello, William Boulton, and Charles Hofer, "Reintegrating R&D into Business Strategy," *Journal of Business Strategy* 6, no. 4 (Spring 1986): 50–51.

26. http://en.wikipedia.org/wiki/Benchmarking.

## 5

Source: CandyBox Images/Shutterstock

MyManagementLab®

⭐ Improve Your Grade!

Over 10 million students improved their results using the Pearson MyLabs.
Visit **mymanagementlab.com** for simulations, tutorials, and end-of-chapter problems.

Strategies in Action

CHAPTER OBJECTIVES

After studying this chapter, you should be able to do the following:

1. Define and discuss secondary buyouts and dividend recapitalizations.

2. Identify the benefits and drawbacks of merging with another firm.

3. Discuss the value of establishing long-term objectives.

4. Identify 16 types of business strategies.

5. Identify numerous examples of organizations pursuing different types of strategies.

6. Discuss guidelines when particular strategies are most appropriate to pursue.

7. Discuss Porter's five generic strategies.

8. Describe strategic management in nonprofit, governmental, and small organizations.

9. Discuss the nature and role of joint ventures in strategic planning.

10. Compare and contrast financial with strategic objectives.

11. Discuss the levels of strategies in large versus small firms.

12. Explain the first mover advantages concept.

13. Discuss recent trends in outsourcing and reshoring.

ASSURANCE OF LEARNING **EXERCISES**

The following exercises are found at the end of this chapter.

EXERCISE 5A   Develop Hypothetical PepsiCo Strategies

EXERCISE 5B   Barilla's Actual Strategies

EXERCISE 5C   What Strategies Should PepsiCo Pursue in 2014?

EXERCISE 5D   Examine Strategy Articles

EXERCISE 5E   Classify Some Year 2013 Strategies

EXERCISE 5F   How Risky Are Various Alternative Strategies?

EXERCISE 5G   Develop Alternative Strategies for Your University

EXERCISE 5H   Lessons in Doing Business Globally

Hundreds of companies today, including IBM, Wells Fargo, and General Electric, have embraced strategic planning fully in their quest for higher revenues and profits. Kent Nelson, former chair of UPS, explains why his company has created a new strategic-planning department: "Because we're making bigger bets on investments in technology, we can't afford to spend a whole lot of money in one direction and then find out five years later it was the wrong direction."[1]

This chapter brings strategic management to life with many contemporary examples. Sixteen types of strategies are defined and exemplified, including Michael Porter's generic strategies: cost leadership, differentiation, and focus. Guidelines are presented for determining when each strategy is most appropriate to pursue. An overview of strategic management in non-profit organizations, governmental agencies, and small firms is provided. As showcased below, Barilla SpA is an example company that for many years has exemplified excellent strategic management.

Long-Term Objectives

Long-term objectives represent the results expected from pursuing certain strategies. Strategies represent the actions to be taken to accomplish long-term objectives. The time frame for objectives and strategies should be consistent, usually from two to five years.

The Nature of Long-Term Objectives

Objectives should be quantitative, measurable, realistic, understandable, challenging, hierarchical, obtainable, and congruent among organizational units. Each objective should also be associated with a timeline. Objectives are commonly stated in terms such as *growth in assets*, *growth in sales*, *profitability*, *market share*, *degree and nature of diversification*, *degree and nature of vertical integration*, *earnings per share*, and *social responsibility*. Clearly established objectives

---

EXCELLENT STRATEGIC MANAGEMENT SHOWCASED

Barilla SpA

Do you like pasta? If yes, you may have a box of Barilla pasta in your kitchen cabinet. A long-time supplier of pasta to U.S. (and European) supermarkets, Barilla SpA, the Italian food company based in Parma, Italy, is opening a new chain of Barilla-branded restaurants in 2013 in the USA. Chairman Guido Barilla, 54 years old and great grandson of the company's founder, says: "Most Americans eat pasta, but not very often; there is undoubtedly potential for expansion in the USA." Mr. Barilla may be right because on average, Americans eat 19.4 pounds of pasta each year, compared to 57.3 pounds for Italians and 28.7 pounds in for example Venezuela.

Barilla SpA is pursuing excellent strategies by shedding its non-core assets, such as its German bread maker and its Spanish bakery-products producer, and redeploying those funds into pasta-related businesses globally. Pasta is considerably less expensive than meat and many other foods, a primary reason why Barilla believes pasta has a bright future. Many global economies still struggle and many families globally are cutting back on all but the basics. Pasta sales in finance-troubled Greece for example grew 3.5 percent in 2012. CEO Claudio Colzani of Barilla is also building up Barilla's ready-made sauce footprint around the world.

In conjunction with the planned new chain of Italian restaurants, Barilla is also building up its stable of bottled sauces. The company has reopened a plant that produces sauces near its Parma headquarters in northern Italy. Barilla's main competitor in Italy is De Cecco brand, based near Chieti in the region of Abruzzo, but Barilla is convinced that its brand is better than all rival firms. The world's leading pasta maker, Barilla has about 40 percent of the market in Italy and about 25 percent of the pasta market in the USA.

Barilla's bakery business now comprises less than 60 percent of company revenues, whereas the company's pasta sauces and flour now account for nearly 40 percent of revenues, which is up from 26 percent in 2006. Barilla believes that a forward integration strategy of opening its own Italian restaurants will complement nicely its already existing name recognition in millions of households worldwide.

Source: Based on Manuela Mesco, "Barilla Makes U.S. Pasta Push," *Wall Street Journal* (August 1, 2012): B6.

TABLE 5-1 Varying Performance Measures by Organizational Level

Organizational Level	Basis for Annual Bonus or Merit Pay
Corporate	75% based on long-term objectives
	25% based on annual objectives
Division	50% based on long-term objectives
	50% based on annual objectives
Function	25% based on long-term objectives
	75% based on annual objectives

offer many benefits. They provide direction, allow synergy, aid in evaluation, establish priorities, reduce uncertainty, minimize conflicts, stimulate exertion, and aid in both the allocation of resources and the design of jobs. Objectives provide a basis for consistent decision making by managers whose values and attitudes differ. Objectives serve as standards by which individuals, groups, departments, divisions, and entire organizations can be evaluated.

Long-term objectives are needed at the corporate, divisional, and functional levels of an organization. They are an important measure of managerial performance. Many practitioners and academicians attribute a significant part of U.S. industry's competitive decline to the short-term, rather than long-term, strategy orientation of managers in the USA. Arthur D. Little argues that bonuses or merit pay for managers today must be based to a greater extent on long-term objectives and strategies. An example framework for relating objectives to performance evaluation is provided in Table 5-1. A particular organization could tailor these guidelines to meet its own needs, but incentives should be attached to both long-term and annual objectives.

Without long-term objectives, an organization would drift aimlessly toward some unknown end. It is hard to imagine an organization or individual being successful without clear objectives. You probably have worked hard the last few years striving to achieve an objective to graduate with a business degree. Success only rarely occurs by accident; rather, it is the result of hard work directed toward achieving certain objectives. Table 5-2 reveals the desired characteristics of objectives, while Table 5-3 summarizes the benefits of having clear objectives.

Financial versus Strategic Objectives

Two types of objectives are especially common in organizations: financial and strategic objectives. **Financial objectives** include those associated with growth in revenues, growth in earnings, higher dividends, larger profit margins, greater return on investment, higher earnings per share, a rising stock price, improved cash flow, and so on; whereas **strategic objectives** include things such as a larger market share, quicker on-time delivery than rivals, shorter design-to-market times than rivals, lower costs than rivals, higher product quality than rivals, wider geographic coverage than rivals, achieving technological leadership, consistently getting new or improved products to market ahead of rivals, and so on.

Although financial objectives are especially important in firms, oftentimes there is a trade-off between financial and strategic objectives such that crucial decisions have to be made.

TABLE 5-2 The Desired Characteristics of Objectives

1. Quantitative
2. Measurable
3. Realistic
4. Understandable
5. Challenging
6. Hierarchical
7. Obtainable
8. Congruent across departments

TABLE 5-3 The Benefits of Having Clear Objectives

1. Provide direction by revealing expectations
2. Allow synergy
3. Aid in evaluation by serving as standards
4. Establish priorities
5. Reduce uncertainty
6. Minimize conflicts
7. Stimulate exertion
8. Aid in allocation of resources
9. Aid in design of jobs
10. Provide basis for consistent decision making

For example, a firm can do certain things to maximize short-term financial objectives that would harm long-term strategic objectives. To improve financial position in the short run through higher prices may, for example, jeopardize long-term market share. The dangers associated with trading off long-term strategic objectives with near-term bottom-line performance are especially severe if competitors relentlessly pursue increased market share at the expense of short-term profitability. And there are other trade-offs between financial and strategic objectives, related to riskiness of actions, concern for business ethics, need to preserve the natural environment, and social responsibility issues. Both financial and strategic objectives should include both annual and long-term performance targets. Ultimately, the best way to sustain competitive advantage over the long run is to relentlessly pursue strategic objectives that strengthen a firm's business position over rivals. Financial objectives can best be met by focusing first and foremost on achieving strategic objectives that improve a firm's competitiveness and market strength.

Not Managing by Objectives

An unidentified educator once said, "If you think education is expensive, try ignorance." The idea behind this saying also applies to establishing objectives. Strategists should avoid the following alternative ways of "not managing by objectives."

- *Managing by Extrapolation*—adheres to the principle "If it ain't broke, don't fix it." The idea is to keep on doing the same things in the same ways because things are going well.
- *Managing by Crisis*—based on the belief that the true measure of a really good strategist is the ability to solve problems. Because there are plenty of crises and problems to go around for every person and every organization, strategists ought to bring their time and creative energy to bear on solving the most pressing problems of the day. Managing by crisis is actually a form of reacting rather than acting and of letting events dictate the what and when of management decisions.
- *Managing by Subjectives*—built on the idea that there is no general plan for which way to go and what to do; just do the best you can to accomplish what you think should be done. In short, "Do your own thing, the best way you know how" (sometimes referred to as *the mystery approach to decision making* because subordinates are left to figure out what is happening and why).
- *Managing by Hope*—based on the fact that the future is laden with great uncertainty and that if we try and do not succeed, then we hope our second (or third) attempt will succeed. Decisions are predicated on the hope that they will work and that good times are just around the corner, especially if luck and good fortune are on our side![2]

Types of Strategies

The model illustrated in Figure 5-1 provides a conceptual basis for applying strategic management. Defined and exemplified in Table 5-4, alternative strategies that an enterprise could pursue can be categorized into 11 actions: forward integration, backward integration, horizontal integration, market penetration, market development, product development, related diversification,

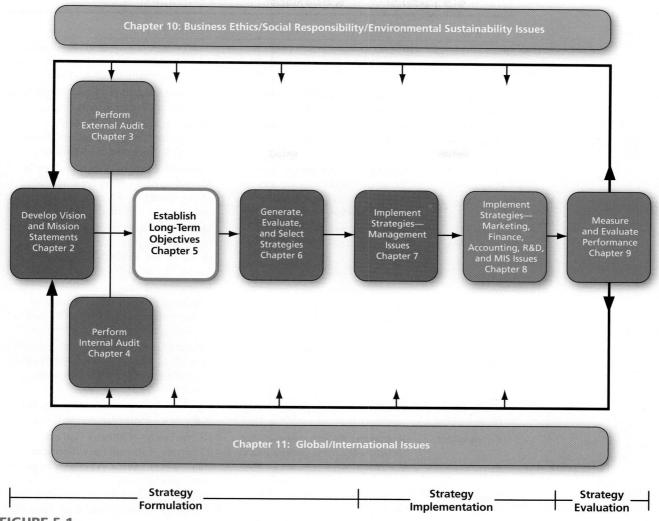

FIGURE 5-1

A Comprehensive Strategic-Management Model

Source: Fred R. David, "How Companies Define Their Mission," *Long Range Planning* 22, no. 3 (June 1988): 40.

unrelated diversification, retrenchment, divestiture, and liquidation. Each alternative strategy has countless variations. For example, market penetration can include adding salespersons, increasing advertising expenditures, couponing, and using similar actions to increase market share in a given geographic area.

Many, if not most, organizations simultaneously pursue a combination of two or more strategies, but a **combination strategy** can be exceptionally risky if carried too far. No organization can afford to pursue all the strategies that might benefit the firm. Difficult decisions must be made. Priority must be established. Organizations, like individuals, have limited resources. Both organizations and individuals must choose among alternative strategies and avoid excessive indebtedness.

Hansen and Smith explain that strategic planning involves "choices that risk resources" and "trade-offs that sacrifice opportunity." In other words, if you have a strategy to go north, then you must buy snowshoes and warm jackets (spend resources) and forgo the opportunity of "faster population growth in southern states." You cannot have a strategy to go north and then take a step east, south, or west "just to be on the safe side." Firms spend resources and focus on a finite number of opportunities in pursuing strategies to achieve an uncertain outcome in the future. Strategic planning is much more than a roll of the dice; it is a wager based on predictions

TABLE 5-4 Alternative Strategies Defined and Exemplified

Strategy	Definition	Examples
Forward Integration	Gaining ownership or increased control over distributors or retailers	Forward Integration—PayPal is pushing its service off the Web and into stores via an agreement with Discover card.
Backward Integration	Seeking ownership or increased control of a firm's suppliers	Backward Integration—Fancy Motels Inc. acquiring a furniture manufacturer.
Horizontal Integration	Seeking ownership or increased control over competitors	Horizontal Integration—Britain's GlaxoSmithKline PLC acquired Human Genome Sciences Inc. for $3 billion.
Market Penetration	Seeking increased market share for present products or services in present markets through greater marketing efforts	Market Penetration—PepsiCo is heavily advertising its new Diet Pepsi special-edition silver cans featuring the blue-and-red Pepsi logo in a heart shape.
Market Development	Introducing present products or services into new geographic area	Market Development—China Petrochemical purchased three Canadian oil companies, Daylight Energy, Tanganyika Oil, and Syncrude Canada.
Product Development	Seeking increased sales by improving present products or services or developing new ones	Product Development—General Electric is building new composite material jet engines, whereas rival Pratt & Whitney is developing newly designed jet engines.
Related Diversification	Adding new but related products or services	Related Diversification—The toy retailer, Toys 'R' Us developed a new Wi-Fi tablet computer for children (the Tabeo for $149.99).
Unrelated Diversification	Adding new, unrelated products or services	Unrelated Diversification—Retailer IKEA is opening a chain of motels in Europe.
Retrenchment	Regrouping through cost and asset reduction to reverse declining sales and profit	Retrenchment—Callaway Golf cut 12 percent of its workforce; Deutsche Bank AG cut 1,000 jobs from its investment bank segment.
Divestiture	Selling a division or part of an organization	Divestiture—Dean Foods sold off its WhiteWave-Alpro organic dairy business.
Liquidation	Selling all of a company's assets, in parts, for their tangible worth	Liquidation—Big Sky Farms, one of Canada's biggest hog-producing firms, liquidated.

and hypotheses that are continually tested and refined by knowledge, research, experience, and learning. Survival of the firm itself may hinge on your strategic plan.[3]

Organizations cannot do too many things well because resources and talents get spread thin and competitors gain advantage. In large, diversified companies, a combination strategy is commonly employed when different divisions pursue different strategies. Also, organizations struggling to survive may simultaneously employ a combination of several defensive strategies, such as divestiture, liquidation, and retrenchment.

Levels of Strategies

Strategy making is not just a task for top executives. Middle-and lower-level managers also must be involved in the strategic-planning process to the extent possible. In large firms, there are actually four levels of strategies: corporate, divisional, functional, and operational—as illustrated in Figure 5-2. However, in small firms, there are actually three levels of strategies: company, functional, and operational.

In large firms, the persons primarily responsible for having effective strategies at the various levels include the CEO at the corporate level; the president or executive vice president at the divisional level; the respective chief finance officer (CFO), chief information officer (CIO),

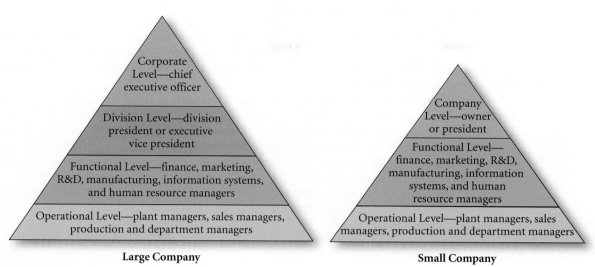

FIGURE 5-2

Levels of Strategies With Persons Most Responsible

human resource manager (HRM), chief marketing officer (CMO), and so on at the functional level; and the plant manager, regional sales manager, and so on at the operational level. In small firms, the persons primarily responsible for having effective strategies at the various levels include the business owner or president at the company level and then the same range of persons at the lower two levels, as with a large firm.

It is important that all managers at all levels participate and understand the firm's strategic plan to help ensure coordination, facilitation, and commitment while avoiding inconsistency, inefficiency, and miscommunication. Plant managers, for example, need to understand and be supportive of the overall strategic plan (game plan), whereas the president and the CEO need to be knowledgeable of strategies being employed in various sales territories and manufacturing plants.

Integration Strategies

The exclusively online men's pants company, Bonobos, now sells menswear wholesale to Nordstrom and in addition is opening its own stores in New York, Palo Alto, Chicago, and other cities. However, shoppers do not walk out of Bonobos stores with anything; the stores are simply for customers to try on the clothing before ordering online.

Forward integration, backward integration, and horizontal integration are sometimes collectively referred to as **vertical integration** strategies. Vertical integration strategies allow a firm to gain control over distributors, suppliers, or competitors.

Forward Integration

Forward integration involves gaining ownership or increased control over distributors or retailers. Increasing numbers of manufacturers (suppliers) today are pursuing a forward integration strategy by establishing websites to directly sell products to consumers. This strategy is causing turmoil in some industries. For example, Amazon is doubling down on forward integration by quietly installing large metal cabinets, called Amazon Lockers, in hundreds of grocery, 7-Eleven, and drugstores that accept the packages for customers for later pickup. This strategy dispels the concern of urban apartment dwellers who fear they will miss an Amazon delivery or have their item stolen. This strategy also combats a growing problem of thieves following UPS and FedEx trucks and stealing packages at doorsteps. Amazon has lockers in the USA and United Kingdom. This strategy entails Amazon emailing customers a code to open the locker holding their merchandise. Curtailing failed deliveries is essential for Amazon because otherwise consumers call customer service, switch to a competitor, or get a replacement item. Amazon pays a small fee each month to store owners where it has lockers.

To combat Amazon's forward integration, Walmart too is pursuing forward integration by launching its Walmart-to-go service in which the company promises same-day delivery in many cities for orders placed online. With that new service, Walmart ships products from its company's stores rather than a warehouse or distribution center. The new Walmart service costs $10 regardless of size of the order.

Ford Motor in 2014–2015 is opening a nationwide network of exclusive Lincoln dealers in China to promote an image of "luxury with simplicity" to compete with China's heavyweight luxury brands, Volkswagen AG's Audi, BMW AG, and Daimler AG's Mercedes-Benz. Jim Farley, Ford Group VP for Global Marketing Sales and Service says that through extensive interviews and surveys the company knows that: "China is changing. Chinese wants to show off less. They want to consume for themselves, not for other people." Ford is hunting for new dealers in China. The new Lincolns will have large back seats, a must in the Chinese luxury-car market where owners often employ drivers. Ford added 115 new dealers in China in 2012 and will increase its total to 500 by 2015.

Samsung in mid-2013 began adding upfront boutiques in all Best Buy stores. For the first time ever, Samsung is recruiting and training thousands of retail workers to staff their new boutiques. This forward integration strategy is a big move for Samsung, who unlike rivals Apple and Microsoft, currently own no retail stores of their own. Samsung is one of Best Buy's top five vendors (suppliers). Also using forward integration, IKEA, the huge furniture retailer, has recently agreed to begin building hotels, i.e. the Moxy brand, with Marriott. Most Moxy hotels will feature rooms prefabricated offsite and then assembled with IKEA furniture.

An effective means of implementing forward integration is **franchising**. Approximately 2,000 companies in about 50 different industries in the USA use franchising to distribute their products or services. Businesses can expand rapidly by franchising because costs and opportunities are spread among many individuals. Total sales by franchises in the United States are annually about $1 trillion.

The International Franchise Association Educational Foundations reports that there are about 800,000 franchise businesses in the USA. However, a growing trend is for franchisees, who for example may operate 10 franchised restaurants, stores, or whatever, to buy out their part of the business from their franchiser (corporate owner). There is a growing rift between franchisees and franchisers as the segment often outperforms the parent. McDonald's today owns only 67 percent of its restaurants, up from 20 percent a decade ago. Restaurant chains are increasingly being pressured to own fewer of their locations. Companies such as McDonald's are using proceeds from the sale of company stores and restaurants to franchisees to buy back company stock, pay higher dividends, and make other investments to benefit shareholders.

Also, McDonald's franchisees in 2012–2013 are opposing the company's remodeling investments, marketing campaigns, and discounting. Mark Kalinowski, lead restaurant analyst at Janney Capital Markets, recently asked 30 McDonald's franchisees to gauge how they felt about what's going on, and some comments were as follows:

- "We are bankrupting the system in the name of 'rebranding' the system!"
- "Major remodel projects are wiping out our cash flow and our equity."
- "Cash flow is trending up, but not as fast as McDonald's cash flow is."
- "We cannot absorb all these costs, do all this discounting, and still pay to remodel our landlord's (McDonald's) building."

McDonald's ironically gets 67 percent of its sales from company-owned restaurants. However, rival fast-food chain Burger King is converting virtually all of its company-owned outlets to franchised operations, with revenue from franchisees going from 30 percent of sales in 2011 to 90 percent in 2015. This change results in more than a 60 percent drop in Burger King revenues in two years since franchisees show revenues on their own personal income statements, but Burger King's operating profit more than doubled during this time. Burger King already has 45 percent of its stores outside the USA, and the company plans to increase that percentage dramatically. Rival Yum Brands owns virtually all of its outside-U.S. restaurants and says that policy gives greater control and benefits if things go well (or bad). In contrast, Burger King has so much long-term debt it has to rely on franchisees for capital.

The following six guidelines indicate when forward integration may be an especially effective strategy:[4]

- When an organization's present distributors are especially expensive, unreliable, or incapable of meeting the firm's distribution needs.
- When the availability of quality distributors is so limited as to offer a competitive advantage to those firms that integrate forward.
- When an organization competes in an industry that is growing and is expected to continue to grow markedly; this is a factor because forward integration reduces an organization's ability to diversify if its basic industry falters.
- When an organization has both the capital and human resources needed to manage the new business of distributing its own products.
- When the advantages of stable production are particularly high; this is a consideration because an organization can increase the predictability of the demand for its output through forward integration.
- When present distributors or retailers have high profit margins; this situation suggests that a company could profitably distribute its own products and price them more competitively by integrating forward.

Backward Integration

In March 2013, Starbucks purchased its first coffee farm—a 600 acre property in Costa Rica. This backward integration strategy was utilized primarily to develop new coffee varieties and to test methods to combat a fungal disease known as coffee rust that plagues the industry. Both manufacturers and retailers purchase needed materials from suppliers. **Backward integration** is a strategy of seeking ownership or increased control of a firm's suppliers. This strategy can be especially appropriate when a firm's current suppliers are unreliable, too costly, or cannot meet the firm's needs.

Campbell Soup recently acquired one of its primary suppliers, Bolthouse Farms, headquartered in Bakersfield, California, for $1.55 billion in an effort to move more aggressively into fresher foods rather than relying so heavily on canned foods. Canned foods, including Campbell's famous soups, are full of preservatives so they will last a long time on shelves, but for an increasing number of consumers, freshness trumps longevity.

Starbucks in early 2014 will open its first company-owned factory to make soluble products such as its VIA Ready Brew and the coffee base for Frappuccinos and many of the company's ready-to-drink beverages. These products are currently made in Colombia, South America, and in Switzerland by third-party manufacturers. Starbucks says this backward integration strategy will enable the company to save on transportation and ensure better quality. The new Starbucks plant is being built in Augusta, Georgia. In addition, Starbucks recently began producing and selling a single-cup coffee brewing machine that will brew coffee, lattes, and espresso in one machine. Some analysts are concerned that consumers may now make their own Starbucks drink at home for one dollar, rather than going to a Starbucks and buying that drink for four dollars.

Priceline.com Inc., recently acquired Kayak Software for $1.8 billion, representing a 29 percent premium over Kayak's closing stock price. Priceline wanted Kayak because that company makes money by referring customers to online travel agencies such as Priceline and rival Expedia. Kayak operated websites and mobile applications for travelers to compare prices for airline, hotel, and rental-car bookings.

Some industries in the USA, such as the automotive and aluminum industries, are reducing their historical pursuit of backward integration. Instead of owning their suppliers, companies negotiate with several outside suppliers. Ford and Chrysler buy more than half of their component parts from outside suppliers such as TRW, Eaton, General Electric (GE), and Johnson Controls. **De-integration** makes sense in industries that have global sources of supply. Companies today shop around, play one seller against another, and go with the best deal.

Global competition is also spurring firms to reduce their number of suppliers and to demand higher levels of service and quality from those they keep. Although traditionally relying on many suppliers to ensure uninterrupted supplies and low prices, U.S. firms now are following the lead of Japanese firms, which have far fewer suppliers and closer, long-term relationships with those few. "Keeping track of so many suppliers is onerous," says Mark Shimelonis, formerly of Xerox.

Seven guidelines when backward integration may be an especially effective strategy are:[5]

- When an organization's present suppliers are especially expensive, unreliable, or incapable of meeting the firm's needs for parts, components, assemblies, or raw materials.
- When the number of suppliers is small and the number of competitors is large.
- When an organization competes in an industry that is growing rapidly; this is a factor because integrative-type strategies (forward, backward, and horizontal) reduce an organization's ability to diversify in a declining industry.
- When an organization has both capital and human resources to manage the new business of supplying its own raw materials.
- When the advantages of stable prices are particularly important; this is a factor because an organization can stabilize the cost of its raw materials and the associated price of its product(s) through backward integration.
- When present suppliers have high profit margins, which suggests that the business of supplying products or services in the given industry is a worthwhile venture.
- When an organization needs to quickly acquire a needed resource.

Horizontal Integration

Horizontal integration refers to a strategy of seeking ownership of or increased control over a firm's competitors. One of the most significant trends in strategic management today is the increased use of horizontal integration as a growth strategy. Mergers, acquisitions, and takeovers among competitors allow for increased economies of scale and enhanced transfer of resources and competencies. Kenneth Davidson makes the following observation about horizontal integration:

> The trend towards horizontal integration seems to reflect strategists' misgivings about their ability to operate many unrelated businesses. Mergers between direct competitors are more likely to create efficiencies than mergers between unrelated businesses, both because there is a greater potential for eliminating duplicate facilities and because the management of the acquiring firm is more likely to understand the business of the target.[6]

Pearson PLC's Penguin book publishing business recently merged with Bertelsmann SE's Random House book publishing division to create a new company named Penguin Random House. This horizontal integration strategy for the two parent firms combines Penguin's 10 percent U.S. book market share with Random House's 20 percent market share into the new joint-venture company. Combining forces allows the new firm to gain more heft in negotiating terms with retailers such as Amazon. Combining forces in the publishing industry is also deemed necessary because publishers' revenue coming from e-books is growing rapidly, to about 18 percent now, compared to 6.3 percent in 2010.

Based in Frankfurt, Germany, Bayer AG actively pursues horizontal integration, having just recently acquired vitamins maker Schiff Nutrition for $1.2 billion, as well as AgraQuest, a maker of biological crop protection and Teva Pharmaceutical Industries' U.S. animal health business. Based in Salt Lake City, Utah, Schiff produces Airborne, as well as many vitamin supplements and nutrition bars.

Sherwin-Williams recently acquired Mexico-based coatings maker Consorcio Comex SA for about $2.34 billion. Sherwin-Williams CEO Chris Connor said: "The transaction will significantly increase our presence in markets where our store count is low and it builds upon our strategy to grow our architectural paint business in the Americas."

Two rival Canadian furniture and appliance retailers, Leon's Furniture Ltd. and Brick Ltd, recently merged. Leon's CEO said: "During these economic times where we have seen multiple American corporations make inroads into our country through acquisitions, it is a pleasure to see two successful Canadian retailers reach an agreement that will better serve Canadian consumers."

In the kidney-dialysis market, the second largest manufacturer, Baxter International, recently acquired the third largest manufacturer, Gambro, based in Sweden, for $4 billion. More than two million patients globally receive some form of kidney dialysis, with treatment rates increasing more than 5 percent annually.

These five guidelines indicate when horizontal integration may be an especially effective strategy:[7]

- When an organization can gain monopolistic characteristics in a particular area or region without being challenged by the federal government for "tending substantially" to reduce competition.
- When an organization competes in a growing industry.
- When increased economies of scale provide major competitive advantages.
- When an organization has both the capital and human talent needed to successfully manage an expanded organization.
- When competitors are faltering as a result of a lack of managerial expertise or a need for particular resources that an organization possesses; note that horizontal integration would not be appropriate if competitors are doing poorly because in that case overall industry sales are declining.

Intensive Strategies

Market penetration, market development, and product development are sometimes referred to as **intensive strategies** because they require intensive efforts if a firm's competitive position with existing products is to improve.

Market Penetration

A **market penetration** strategy seeks to increase market share for present products or services in present markets through greater marketing efforts. This strategy is widely used alone and in combination with other strategies. Market penetration includes increasing the number of salespersons, increasing advertising expenditures, offering extensive sales promotion items, or increasing publicity efforts. Chrysler Group LLC recently launched a new marketing campaign for its redesigned Ram pickup truck that features new technology and improved fuel economy. Chrysler desires to make inroads into the market share of the truck sales leader F-150. Chrysler's new ads feature gruff-voiced actor Sam Elliott promoting Ram trucks over the Chevrolet Silverado and the GMC Sierra trucks.

General Motors in 2013 rolled out its global advertising campaign for its Chevrolet brand in hopes of improving the brand's image globally and halting its market-share slide in the United States. The new tagline for the GM campaign is "Find New Roads" that replaces the lackluster "Chevy Runs Deep" slogan. The new ad campaign is designed to support GM introducing 13 new or refreshed Chevrolet vehicles in the United States in 2013 and another 12 in different regions around the world.

In the 2013 Super Bowl, Anheuser-Busch InBev launched a huge new advertising campaign to coincide with its new Black Crown brand of beer. The prior year, the company had used the Super Bowl to launch its Bud Light Platinum brand. The company believes the Super Bowl is the ideal venue to launch something new because viewers of the game surpass 110 million annually. Black Crown is a golden amber lager that is a little bit darker and a little bit more flavorful than tradition Budweiser lager, and Black Crown has a 6 percent alcohol content rather than 5 percent. Anheuser is especially targeting the 21- to 34-year-old-age group with the new ads and brand.

These five guidelines indicate when market penetration may be an especially effective strategy:[8]

- When current markets are not saturated with a particular product or service.
- When the usage rate of present customers could be increased significantly.
- When the market shares of major competitors have been declining while total industry sales have been increasing.
- When the correlation between dollar sales and dollar marketing expenditures historically has been high.
- When increased economies of scale provide major competitive advantages.

Market Development

Market development involves introducing present products or services into new geographic areas. India is a target for numerous firms to expand geographically. For example, Coca-Cola Company and its bottling partners are investing $5 billion in India between 2013 and 2020 because that country has 1.2 billion people who on average only consume 12 eight-ounce bottles of Coke a year compared with 240 in Brazil and 90 bottles globally. PepsiCo is also expanding aggressively into India (the CEO of PepsiCo is Indra Nooyi who was born in India). The Swedish furniture company, IKEA Group, is investing $1.9 billion in India to open 25 new stores between 2013 and 2018. Seattle-based Starbucks Corp. opened its first store in India in late 2012.

PepsiCo is also expanding aggressively into China and just opened its sixth snack plant in that country, in China's landlocked city of Wuhan. CEO Nooyi at Pepsi said: "China will be the largest consumer market in the next decade, and PepsiCo aims to be the largest food-and-beverage company in that market." The snack-food market in China was about $12 billion in 2012, up 44 percent from 2008. PepsiCo's revenue from emerging markets increased from $8 billion in 2008 to over $25 billion in 2013.

China's Dalian Wanda Group Corp. recently acquired all 346 AMC (AMC Entertainment Holdings) multiplex theaters in the USA and Canada. Valued at $2.6 billion, the acquisition was the largest ever between a Chinese company and the U.S. film industry. AMC was the second-largest theater chain in the USA behind Regal Entertainment. Carmike is another competitor in the theater industry.

These six guidelines indicate when market development may be an especially effective strategy:[9]

- When new channels of distribution are available that are reliable, inexpensive, and of good quality.
- When an organization is successful at what it does.
- When new untapped or unsaturated markets exist.
- When an organization has the needed capital and human resources to manage expanded operations.
- When an organization has excess production capacity.
- When an organization's basic industry is rapidly becoming global in scope.

Product Development

Product development is a strategy that seeks increased sales by improving or modifying present products or services. Product development usually entails large research and development expenditures. Walt Disney Company is quickly developing a Disney Baby line of products and services that it expects to become a powerful baby brand for customers ages zero to two. Bob Chapek, president of Disney Consumer Products, recently said: "This gives Disney the opportunity to reach out to moms when magical moments begin; there is no more special occasion than the birth of a baby." The company plans to create Disney Baby sections in its 200-plus Disney Stores in the USA. Disney Baby online will sell everything from $14 Disney Cuddly Bobysuits to $69 Peeking Pooh Premiere Crib Bumpers.

Microsoft Corp. just released Office 365, an Internet-based (or cloud), subscription-based office system, in conjunction with its new Office 2013. Office 365 represents a culture shift for Microsoft, as web-based software such as Google's Chrome, Android, and Doc and mobile devices undermine the strategic importance of PCs and programs install on them.

Ford Motor is set to release its aluminum body F-150 in 2014, which will cut the weight of that truck by 15 percent or 800 pounds and enable 25 percent lower gas mileage and use of a smaller engine. This is a huge strategic bet by Ford because the F-150 truck accounts for up to a third of their $8 billion operating profit globally. The F-250 and F-350 do not fall under the new emission guidelines so are not being redesigned. Aluminum is more expensive than steel and harder to work with, so Ford is betting that this strategy will work, rather than having the vehicle shut down at stoplights to conserve fuel, or investing as GM is doing for its trucks, in designing more efficient engines. GM and Ford rarely take such divergent strategic paths, but in this case they are. Ford is betting on aluminum and GM is not. The F-Series pickup is Ford's top money-maker and has been the top-selling vehicle of any kind in the USA for 30 years.

Merck is testing a new cancer drug that can unleash the body's immune system's power to fight malignancies. The new drug, known as MK-3475, is among a new class of agents called PD-1 inhibitors, than enable the immune system to destroy cancer cells. Also using product development, Burger King is doubling its offerings of coffee, to include ten items, such as flavored iced coffee and vanilla lattes. Burger King is trying to catch up with rival McDonald's whose specialty coffee line, McCafé, is growing rapidly. Burger King also wants to regain the #2 burger chain in the USA in sales, having lost that ranking to Wendy's.

These five guidelines indicate when product development may be an especially effective strategy to pursue:[10]

- When an organization has successful products that are in the maturity stage of the product life cycle; the idea here is to attract satisfied customers to try new (improved) products as a result of their positive experience with the organization's present products or services.
- When an organization competes in an industry that is characterized by rapid technological developments.
- When major competitors offer better-quality products at comparable prices.
- When an organization competes in a high-growth industry.
- When an organization has especially strong research and development capabilities.

Diversification Strategies

For the first time its 129-year history, Cincinnati-based Kroger began adding clothing to its lineup of products. The new Kroger apparel section in its store in Mansfield, Ohio, includes branded shoes, jewelry, outerwear, and undergarments from Levi, Carhartt, Carter, Skechers, Hanes, Maidenform, and other apparel producers. There is only about a 1 percent profit margin in the grocery business, so Kroger is trying to diversify.

There are two general types of **diversification strategies**: **related diversification** and **unrelated diversification**. Businesses are said to be related when their value chains possesses competitively valuable cross-business strategic fits; businesses are said to be unrelated when their value chains are so dissimilar that no competitively valuable cross-business relationships exist.[11] Most companies favor related diversification strategies to capitalize on synergies as follows:

- Transferring competitively valuable expertise, technological know-how, or other capabilities from one business to another.
- Combining the related activities of separate businesses into a single operation to achieve lower costs.
- Exploiting common use of a well-known brand name.
- Cross-business collaboration to create competitively valuable resource strengths and capabilities.[12]

Diversification strategies are becoming less popular because organizations are finding it more difficult to manage diverse business activities. In the 1960s and 1970s, the trend was to diversify to avoid being dependent on any single industry, but the 1980s saw a general reversal of that thinking. Diversification is now on the retreat. Michael Porter, of the Harvard Business School, says, "Management found it couldn't manage the beast." Hence businesses are selling, or closing, less profitable divisions to focus on core businesses. Although many firms are successful operating in a single industry, new technologies, new products, or fast-shifting buyer preferences can decimate a single business.

Diversification must do more than simply spread business risk across different industries, because shareholders could accomplish this by simply purchasing equity in different firms across different industries or by investing in mutual funds. Diversification makes sense only to the extent the strategy adds more to shareholder value than what shareholders could accomplish acting individually. Thus, the chosen industry for diversification must be attractive enough to yield consistently high returns on investment and offer potential across the operating divisions for synergies greater than those entities could achieve alone.

A few companies today, however, pride themselves on being conglomerates, from small firms such as Pentair Inc. and Blount International to huge companies such as Textron, Allied Signal, Emerson Electric, GE, Viacom, and Samsung. Conglomerates prove that focus and diversity are not always mutually exclusive.

Many strategists contend that firms should "stick to the knitting" and not stray too far from the firms' basic areas of competence. However, diversification is still sometimes an appropriate strategy, especially when the company is competing in an unattractive industry. Hamish Maxwell, Philip Morris's former CEO, says, "We want to become a consumer-products company." Diversification makes sense for Philip Morris because cigarette consumption is declining, product liability suits are a risk, and some investors reject tobacco stocks on principle.

Related Diversification

Firms are generally moving away from diversification to focus. For example, ITT recently divided itself into three separate, specialized companies. ITT once owned everything from Sheraton hotels and Hartford Insurance to the maker of Wonder bread and Hostess Twinkies. About the ITT breakup, analyst Barry Knap said, "Companies generally are not very efficient diversifiers; investors usually can do a better job of that by purchasing stock in a variety of companies."

Bucking the trend however is Berkshire Hathaway, a holding company for diverse companies that include Dairy Queen, Burlington Northern Santa Fe Railroad, and Geico Insurance. Also bucking the trend, Amazon.com continues to diversify and is expected in 2013 to enter the smartphone business, to complement its Kindle e-reader and tablet devices. About 675 smartphones were sold in 2012, up 39 percent from 2011, whereas tablet sales increased 75 percent to 113 million. In another related diversification move in 2012, Amazon acquired mapping app maker UpNext. In addition, analysts expect Amazon to soon enter the mobile payments business and compete with offerings from eBay and Square.

Google in late 2012 entered the cable operator business by providing high-speed Internet and TV service in Kansas City, Missouri, and beyond. This new service entails Google supplying Web connections rather than the services that run on them. Google plans to expand this new service to all markets that Verizon has not entered. Google's new service costs $120 a month and provides 100 times faster Internet service than Time Warner. Google provides less money options but the $120 gets users online file storage space and a Nexus 7 computer tablet that they can use as a remote control, as well as DVR storage of 500 hours of shows, including eight shows simultaneously that can be watched on demand, and more.

IBM recently paid a 42 percent premium (42 percent more than the book value) to acquire Kenexa Corp. for about $1.3 billion, to move more deeply into the online business software applications business. Kenexa was a leading supplier of human-resources software and consulting services that help about 9,000 customers recruit, retain, and develop their employees. This acquisition moved IBM into competition with enterprise-software makers such as SAP AG, that recently acquired a company named Success Factors that competes with Kenexa, and with Oracle Corp., that recently bought human-resources software maker Taleo for $1.9 billion.

Starbucks recently made its largest acquisition ever, acquiring Atlanta-based tea retailer Teavana Holdings for a 54 percent premium over Teavana's closing stock price. Teavana customers tend to be to aficionados, so Starbucks plans to bring its tried-and-true strategy to Teavana, with a tea bar offering customized hot and cold tea drinks. Teavana currently sells most of its tea in loose-leaf form for home consumption.

Six guidelines for when related diversification may be an effective strategy are as follows.[13]

- When an organization competes in a no-growth or a slow-growth industry.
- When adding new, but related, products would significantly enhance the sales of current products.
- When new, but related, products could be offered at highly competitive prices.
- When new, but related, products have seasonal sales levels that counterbalance an organization's existing peaks and valleys.
- When an organization's products are currently in the declining stage of the product's life cycle.
- When an organization has a strong management team.

Unrelated Diversification

Based in Memphis, Tennessee, the huge overnight delivery firm FedEx recently entered the computer repair business offering major corporations with overnight computer repair. FedEx's Todd Taylor, manager of the company's TechConnect computer repair division says "What we offer is unparalleled turnaround time." FedEx's new computer repair service is initially focused on the enterprise market, but the company plans to expand the services to small businesses and consumers in the new future.

An unrelated diversification strategy favors capitalizing on a portfolio of businesses that are capable of delivering excellent financial performance in their respective industries, rather than striving to capitalize on value chain strategic fits among the businesses. Firms that employ unrelated diversification continually search across different industries for companies that can be acquired for a deal and yet have potential to provide a high return on investment. Pursuing unrelated diversification entails being on the hunt to acquire companies whose assets are undervalued, companies that are financially distressed, or companies that have high growth prospects but are short on investment capital. An obvious drawback of unrelated diversification is that the parent firm must have an excellent top management team that plans, organizes, motivates, delegates, and controls effectively. It is much more difficult to manage businesses in many industries than in a single industry. However, some firms are successful pursuing unrelated diversification, such as Walt Disney, which owns ABC, and GE, which owns NBC Universal. GE also produces locomotives, airplanes, appliances, and MRI machines and offers consumer finance, media, entertainment, oil, gas, and lighting products and services.

Numerous hotels are entering the beer brewing business to offer their guests a unique experience at "social" and "happy" hours. Specialty (or craft) beer sales are increasing about 15 percent annually. Four Fairmont hotels for example recently created their own microbrews using honey from on-site beehives. The Four Points by Sheraton in Los Angeles has a new director of brewer relations, a new beer advisory board, and customized in-room beer fridges.

Speaking of hotels and unrelated diversification, perhaps the first underwater hotel on the planet is being built in Dubai by Drydocks World in cooperation with BIG InvestConsult AG. The hotel is to be completed in 2015 and will offer 21 underwater rooms, with big windows looking out into the Persian Gulf, and disc-shaped luxury hotel attached above the water line.

Best Buy recently introduced its own tablet computer, the Insignia Flex, for $250. The new product is available only at Best Buy, the new product is 9.7 inches wide, putting it in the same size category as Apple's iPad and Microsoft's Surface. This is Best Buy's first foray into manufacturing its own electronic devices.

Deutsche Bank recently opened the $4 billion, 3,000-room Cosmopolitan casino on the Las Vegas Strip. The huge German bank was originally just funding the project, but when developers defaulted on their loans, Deutsche decided to finish the last two years of work on the project and own and operate the new casino themselves. The Cosmopolitan features a three-story, crystal-strewn bar meant to evoke the inside of a chandelier. Other financial institutions worldwide perhaps should consider unrelated diversification also by taking over some of their gone-bad projects rather than taking huge losses. Many more firms have failed at unrelated diversification than have succeeded as a result of immense management challenges.

Ten guidelines for when unrelated diversification may be an especially effective strategy are:[14]

- When revenues derived from an organization's current products or services would increase significantly by adding the new, unrelated products.
- When an organization competes in a highly competitive or a no-growth industry, as indicated by low industry profit margins and returns.
- When an organization's present channels of distribution can be used to market the new products to current customers.
- When the new products have countercyclical sales patterns compared to an organization's present products.
- When an organization's basic industry is experiencing declining annual sales and profits.
- When an organization has the capital and managerial talent needed to compete successfully in a new industry.
- When an organization has the opportunity to purchase an unrelated business that is an attractive investment opportunity.

- When there exists financial synergy between the acquired and acquiring firm. (Note that a key difference between related and unrelated diversification is that the former should be based on some commonality in markets, products, or technology, whereas the latter is based more on profit considerations.)
- When existing markets for an organization's present products are saturated.
- When antitrust action could be charged against an organization that historically has concentrated on a single industry.

Defensive Strategies

In addition to integrative, intensive, and diversification strategies, organizations also could pursue retrenchment, divestiture, or liquidation.

Retrenchment

Retrenchment occurs when an organization regroups through cost and asset reduction to reverse declining sales and profits. Sometimes called a *turnaround* or *reorganizational strategy*, retrenchment is designed to fortify an organization's basic distinctive competence. During retrenchment, strategists work with limited resources and face pressure from shareholders, employees, and the media. Retrenchment can entail selling off land and buildings to raise needed cash, pruning product lines, closing marginal businesses, closing obsolete factories, automating processes, reducing the number of employees, and instituting expense control systems.

Cosmetic company Revlon, whose brands include Almay and Mitchum, is closing its manufacturing plant in France and laying off 5 percent of its workforce in 2013 to combat high raw material costs, weakness in Europe, and a slowdown in China. Avon Products Inc. is presently exiting the South Korea and Vietnam markets and laying off 1,500 employees, as new CEO Sheri McCoy tries to stabilize the company, reeling from bribery allegations and falling sales.

In some cases, **bankruptcy** can be an effective type of retrenchment strategy. Bankruptcy can allow a firm to avoid major debt obligations and to void union contracts. There are five major types of bankruptcy: Chapter 7, Chapter 9, Chapter 11, Chapter 12, and Chapter 13.

Chapter 7 bankruptcy is a liquidation procedure used only when a corporation sees no hope of being able to operate successfully or to obtain the necessary creditor agreement. All the organization's assets are sold in parts for their tangible worth. Chapter 7 is also the bankruptcy provision most frequently used by individuals to wipe out many types of unsecured debt. Strauss Auto in 2012 filed Chapter 7 liquidation bankruptcy, after five previous times in its history filing and coming out of Chapter 11 reorganization bankruptcy. This time however, the auto-repair chain is closing its 46 remaining stores and selling its assets for their tangible worth.

Chapter 9 bankruptcy applies to municipalities. Stockton, a river port city of 290,000 in the Central Valley of California, declared Chapter 9 bankruptcy in 2012, to avoid having to close key functions such as their police and fire departments. A judge now, rather than city officials, has control over Stockton's debt-management problems. Stockton has twice in recent years toped *Forbes* magazine's list of "America's most miserable cities." However, the largest municipal (Chapter 9) bankruptcy in U.S. history occurred in 2011 in Birmingham, Alabama (Jefferson County). There were 13 municipal bankruptcies filed in 2011. Detroit, Michigan is eyeing the situation in Stockton to see if it needs to file for bankruptcy.

Chapter 11 bankruptcy allows organizations to reorganize and come back after filing a petition for protection. The Santa Ysabel Resort and Casino located 50 miles north of San Diego filed for Chapter 11 protection in mid-2012 to avoid having to shut down totally. Owned by the local Indian tribe Lipay Nation of Santa Ysabel, the casino owes $9 million to the Yavapai Apache Nation and that tribe needs to collect on their investment. Two military transport airlines declared bankruptcy in 2012, Southern Air and Global Aviation Holdings. Both firms cited the U.S. withdrawal of forces from Afghanistan as the primary reason for their demise.

Based in Mechanicsville, Virginia, the world's largest operator of bowling alleys, AMF Bowling Worldwide, filed for bankruptcy-court protection in late 2012 as the company failed to adapt to customers who shifted from being "blue-collar bowlers in leagues" to middle-class bowlers averse to leagues but who desire attractive amenities and facilities. AMF the last few years was too heavily burdened by debt to financially afford to refurbish its 262 bowling centers in the USA. Mom-and-pop operators and small bowling chains now operate more than 5,000 bowling alleys in the U.S.

Chapter 12 bankruptcy was created by the Family Farmer Bankruptcy Act of 1986. This law became effective in 1987 and provides special relief to family farmers with debt equal to or less than $1.5 million.

Chapter 13 bankruptcy is a reorganization plan similar to Chapter 11, but it is available only to small businesses owned by individuals with unsecured debts of less than $100,000 and secured debts of less than $350,000. The Chapter 13 debtor is allowed to operate the business while a plan is being developed to provide for the successful operation of the business in the future.

Five guidelines for when retrenchment may be an especially effective strategy to pursue are as follows:[15]

- When an organization has a clearly distinctive competence but has failed consistently to meet its objectives and goals over time.
- When an organization is one of the weaker competitors in a given industry.
- When an organization is plagued by inefficiency, low profitability, poor employee morale, and pressure from stockholders to improve performance.
- When an organization has failed to capitalize on external opportunities, minimize external threats, take advantage of internal strengths, and overcome internal weaknesses over time; that is, when the organization's strategic managers have failed (and possibly will be replaced by more competent individuals).
- When an organization has grown so large so quickly that major internal reorganization is needed.

Divestiture

Selling a division or part of an organization is called **divestiture**. Divestiture often is used to raise capital for further strategic acquisitions or investments. Divestiture can be part of an overall retrenchment strategy to rid an organization of businesses that are unprofitable, that require too much capital, or that do not fit well with the firm's other activities. Divestiture has also become a popular strategy for firms to focus on their core businesses and become less diversified. For example, United Technologies recently sold two divisions of its Hamilton Sundstrand pump and air compressor subsidiary to help pay for the company's $16.5 billion acquisition of Goodrich Corp. Owner of the Atlanta Braves baseball team, Liberty Media Corp., recently divested its Starz television network, but retains its large investments in Sirius XM Radio, Live Nation Entertainment, and Barnes & Noble.

New York Times Company (NYTC) recently sold its About.com how-to-website to a rival company, Answers.com, for $270 million. NYTC divested nearly 20 regional newspapers in the last twelve months and also divested its remaining stake in the Boston Red Sox. In addition, NYTC plans to divest *The Boston Globe*, the twenty third largest newspaper in the USA.

Bank of America just sold its overseas wealth-management operations for $880 million to Swiss private-banking specialist Julius Baer Group AG. Since Brian Moynihan became CEO of Bank of America in 2010, he divested more than $50 billion in what he calls noncore assets, dropping Bank of America below J.P. Morgan Chase as the largest bank in the USA.

Time Warner recently divested its magazine division, soon after News Corp. divested its publishing division. The year 2013 exceeded the prior two years in divestitures as firms used the strategy to increase stock price and overall value.

Six guidelines for when divestiture may be an especially effective strategy to pursue follow:[16]

- When an organization has pursued a retrenchment strategy and failed to accomplish needed improvements.
- When a division needs more resources to be competitive than the company can provide.
- When a division is responsible for an organization's overall poor performance.
- When a division is a misfit with the rest of an organization; this can result from radically different markets, customers, managers, employees, values, or needs.
- When a large amount of cash is needed quickly and cannot be obtained reasonably from other sources.
- When government antitrust action threatens an organization.

Liquidation

Selling all of a company's assets, in parts, for their tangible worth is called **liquidation**. Liquidation is a recognition of defeat and consequently can be an emotionally difficult strategy. However, it may be better to cease operating than to continue losing large sums of money. For example, the New York City–based discount retailer of designer clothing, Daffy's, recently liquidated, closing all its 19 stores and selling all its inventory. A family-run business based in Secaucus, New Jersey and founded in 1961, Daffy's decided it could not compete with T.J. Maxx and Marshalls, which had expanded aggressively into New York City. All 1,300 employees of Daffy's received severance pay of 60 days worth of work.

Delta Airlines recently liquidated its 35-year-old regional carrier Comair and sent termination notices to Comair's 1,700 remaining employees. More than 1,000 Comair employees were in the Cincinnati and northern Kentucky region, some 700 of those in Kentucky. Comair had slashed its fleet, flights and workforce in the last seven years and was down to 290 flights a day. Delta decided however that small regional planes are too expensive to fly because they are not as fuel-efficient and are more costly to maintain as the fleet ages. "We just really couldn't get the cost structure to where we wanted to get it," said Don Bornhorst, senior vice president of Delta Connection and a former Comair president. "It ultimately was a cost issue; it wasn't a quality issue with Comair. They're a good airline, great employees, very innovative...we just could not solve the cost issues."

Based in Waltham, Massachusetts, A123 Systems, the electric-car battery manufacturer, filed for bankruptcy recently and then sold all its tangible assets to Johnson Controls. Similarly, solar-panel manufacturer, Solyndra LLC, recently liquidated.

Based in Irving, Texas, Hostess Brands in late 2012 told all 18,000 of its workers that the firm will liquidate in five days unless the union-striking employees returned to work. The union work stoppage basically shut down two-thirds of Hostess' 36 manufacturing plants. Four unions were involved: (1) bakery, (2) confectionary, (3) tobacco workers, and (4) grain millers. The largest union's president, Frank Hurt, said: "I am well aware of the possibility of a liquidation, but our people will only take so much when it comes to cuts to their wages and benefits." The following brands were predicted by the *Wall Street Journal* in May 2013 to disappear in 2014:

J.C. Penney

Barnes & Noble's Nook

Martha Stewart's *Living Magazine*

Living Social (a daily deals website)

Volvo

Olympus cameras

Women's National Basketball Association (WNBA)

Leap Wireless International

Mitsubishi Motors

Road & Track (the automotive magazine)

Thousands of small businesses in Europe and the USA liquidate annually without ever making the news. It is tough to start and successfully operate a small business. In China and Russia, thousands of government-owned businesses liquidate annually as those countries try to privatize and consolidate industries.

These three guidelines indicate when liquidation may be an especially effective strategy to pursue:[17]

- When an organization has pursued both a retrenchment strategy and a divestiture strategy, and neither has been successful.
- When an organization's only alternative is bankruptcy. Liquidation represents an orderly and planned means of obtaining the greatest possible cash for an organization's assets. A company can legally declare bankruptcy first and then liquidate various divisions to raise needed capital.
- When the stockholders of a firm can minimize their losses by selling the organization's assets.

Michael Porter's Five Generic Strategies

Probably the three most widely read books on competitive analysis in the 1980s were Michael Porter's *Competitive Strategy* (1980), *Competitive Advantage* (1985), and *Competitive Advantage of Nations* (1989). According to Porter, strategies allow organizations to gain competitive advantage from three different bases: cost leadership, differentiation, and focus. Porter calls these bases **generic strategies**.

Cost leadership emphasizes producing standardized products at a low per-unit cost for consumers who are price-sensitive. Two alternative types of cost leadership strategies can be defined. Type 1 is a *low-cost* strategy that offers products or services to a wide range of customers at the lowest price available on the market. Type 2 is a *best-value* strategy that offers products or services to a wide range of customers at the best price-value available on the market; the best-value strategy aims to offer customers a range of products or services at the lowest price available compared to a rival's products with similar attributes. Both Type 1 and Type 2 strategies target a large market.

Porter's Type 3 generic strategy is **differentiation**, a strategy aimed at producing products and services considered unique industrywide and directed at consumers who are relatively price-insensitive.

Focus means producing products and services that fulfill the needs of small groups of consumers. Two alternative types of focus strategies are Type 4 and Type 5. Type 4 is a low-cost focus strategy that offers products or services to a small range (niche group) of customers at the lowest price available on the market. Examples of firms that use the Type 4 strategy include Jiffy Lube International and Pizza Hut, as well as local used car dealers and hot dog restaurants. Type 5 is a best-value focus strategy that offers products or services to a small range of customers at the best price-value available on the market. Sometimes called "focused differentiation," the best-value focus strategy aims to offer a niche group of customers products or services that meet their tastes and requirements better than rivals' products do. Both Type 4 and Type 5 focus strategies target a small market. However, the difference is that Type 4 strategies offer products or services to a niche group at the lowest price, whereas Type 5 offers products and services to a niche group at higher prices but loaded with features so the offerings are perceived as the best value. Examples of firms that use the Type 5 strategy include Cannondale (top-of-the-line mountain bikes), Maytag (washing machines), and Lone Star Restaurants (steakhouse), as well as bed-and-breakfast inns and local retail boutiques.

Porter's five strategies imply different organizational arrangements, control procedures, and incentive systems. Larger firms with greater access to resources typically compete on a cost leadership or differentiation basis, whereas smaller firms often compete on a focus basis. Porter's five generic strategies are illustrated in Figure 5-3. Note that a differentiation strategy (Type 3) can be pursued with either a small target market or a large target market. However, it is not effective to pursue a cost leadership strategy in a small market because profits margins are generally too small. Likewise, it is not effective to pursue a focus strategy in a large market because economies of scale would generally favor a low-cost or best-value cost leadership strategy to gain or sustain competitive advantage.

Porter stresses the need for strategists to perform cost-benefit analyses to evaluate "sharing opportunities" among a firm's existing and potential business units. Sharing activities and resources enhances competitive advantage by lowering costs or increasing differentiation. In addition to prompting sharing, Porter stresses the need for firms to effectively "transfer" skills and expertise among autonomous business units to gain competitive advantage. Depending on factors such as type of industry, size of firm, and nature of competition, various strategies could yield advantages in cost leadership, differentiation, and focus.

Cost Leadership Strategies (Type 1 and Type 2)

A primary reason for pursuing forward, backward, and horizontal integration strategies is to gain low-cost or best-value cost leadership benefits. But cost leadership generally must be pursued in conjunction with differentiation. A number of cost elements affect the relative attractiveness of generic strategies, including economies or diseconomies of scale achieved, learning and experience curve effects, the percentage of capacity utilization achieved, and linkages with

Type 1: Cost Leadership—Low Cost
Type 2: Cost Leadership—Best Value
Type 3: Differentiation
Type 4: Focus—Low Cost
Type 5: Focus—Best Value

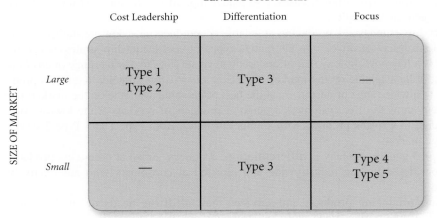

FIGURE 5-3

Porter's Five Generic Strategies

Source: Based on Michael E. Porter, *Competitive Strategy: Techniques for Analyzing Industries and Competitors* (New York: Free Press, 1980), 35–40.

suppliers and distributors. Other cost elements to consider in choosing among alternative strategies include the potential for sharing costs and knowledge within the organization, research and development (R&D) costs associated with new product development or modification of existing products, labor costs, tax rates, energy costs, and shipping costs.

Striving to be the low-cost producer in an industry can be especially effective when the market is composed of many price-sensitive buyers, when there are few ways to achieve product differentiation, when buyers do not care much about differences from brand to brand, or when there are a large number of buyers with significant bargaining power. The basic idea is to underprice competitors and thereby gain market share and sales, entirely driving some competitors out of the market. Companies employing a low-cost (Type 1) or best-value (Type 2) cost leadership strategy must achieve their competitive advantage in ways that are difficult for competitors to copy or match. If rivals find it relatively easy or inexpensive to imitate the leader's cost leadership methods, the leaders' advantage will not last long enough to yield a valuable edge in the marketplace. Recall that for a resource to be valuable, it must be either rare, hard to imitate, or not easily substitutable. To employ a cost leadership strategy successfully, a firm must ensure that its total costs across its overall value chain are lower than competitors' total costs. There are two ways to accomplish this:[18]

1. Perform value chain activities more efficiently than rivals and control the factors that drive the costs of value chain activities. Such activities could include altering the plant layout, mastering newly introduced technologies, using common parts or components in different products, simplifying product design, finding ways to operate close to full capacity year-round, and so on.
2. Revamp the firm's overall value chain to eliminate or bypass some cost-producing activities. Such activities could include securing new suppliers or distributors, selling products online, relocating manufacturing facilities, avoiding the use of union labor, and so on.

When employing a cost leadership strategy, a firm must be careful not to use such aggressive price cuts that their own profits are low or nonexistent. Constantly be mindful of cost-saving technological breakthroughs or any other value chain advancements that could erode or destroy the firm's competitive advantage. A Type 1 or Type 2 cost leadership strategy can be especially effective under the following conditions:[19]

1. When price competition among rival sellers is especially vigorous.
2. When the products of rival sellers are essentially identical and supplies are readily available from any of several eager sellers.
3. When there are few ways to achieve product differentiation that have value to buyers.
4. When most buyers use the product in the same ways.
5. When buyers incur low costs in switching their purchases from one seller to another.
6. When buyers are large and have significant power to bargain down prices.
7. When industry newcomers use introductory low prices to attract buyers and build a customer base.

A successful cost leadership strategy usually permeates the entire firm, as evidenced by high efficiency, low overhead, limited perks, intolerance of waste, intensive screening of budget requests, wide spans of control, rewards linked to cost containment, and broad employee participation in cost control efforts. Some risks of pursuing cost leadership are that competitors may imitate the strategy, thus driving overall industry profits down; that technological breakthroughs in the industry may make the strategy ineffective; or that buyer interest may swing to other differentiating features besides price. Several example firms that are well known for their low-cost leadership strategies are Walmart, BIC, McDonald's, Black & Decker, Lincoln Electric, and Briggs & Stratton.

Differentiation Strategies (Type 3)

Different strategies offer different degrees of differentiation. Differentiation does not guarantee competitive advantage, especially if standard products sufficiently meet customer needs or if rapid imitation by competitors is possible. Durable products protected by barriers to quick copying by competitors are best. Successful differentiation can mean greater product flexibility, greater compatibility, lower costs, improved service, less maintenance, greater convenience, or more features. Product development is an example of a strategy that offers the advantages of differentiation.

A differentiation strategy should be pursued only after a careful study of buyers' needs and preferences to determine the feasibility of incorporating one or more differentiating features into a unique product that features the desired attributes. A successful differentiation strategy allows a firm to charge a higher price for its product and to gain customer loyalty because consumers may become strongly attached to the differentiation features. Special features that differentiate one's product can include superior service, spare parts availability, engineering design, product performance, useful life, gas mileage, or ease of use.

A risk of pursuing a differentiation strategy is that the unique product may not be valued highly enough by customers to justify the higher price. When this happens, a cost-leadership strategy easily will defeat a differentiation strategy. Another risk of pursuing a differentiation strategy is that competitors may quickly develop ways to copy the differentiating features. Firms thus must find durable sources of uniqueness that cannot be imitated quickly or cheaply by rival firms.

Common organizational requirements for a successful differentiation strategy include strong coordination among the R&D and marketing functions and substantial amenities to attract scientists and creative people. Firms can pursue a differentiation (Type 3) strategy based on many different competitive aspects. For example, Mountain Dew and root beer have a unique taste; Lowe's, Home Depot, and Walmart offer wide selection and one-stop shopping; Dell Computer and FedEx offer superior service; BMW and Porsche offer engineering design and performance; IBM and Hewlett-Packard offer a wide range of products; and E*Trade and Ameritrade offer Internet convenience. Differentiation opportunities exist or can potentially be developed anywhere along the firm's value chain, including supply chain activities, product R&D activities, production and technological activities, manufacturing activities, human resource management activities, distribution activities, or marketing activities.

The most effective differentiation bases are those that are hard or expensive for rivals to duplicate. Competitors are continually trying to imitate, duplicate, and outperform rivals along any differentiation variable that has yielded competitive advantage. For example, when U.S. Airways cut its prices, Delta quickly followed suit. When Caterpillar instituted its quick-delivery-of-spare-parts policy, John Deere soon followed suit. To the extent that differentiating attributes are tough for rivals to copy, a differentiation strategy will be especially effective, but the sources of uniqueness must be time-consuming, cost prohibitive, and simply too burdensome for rivals to match. A firm, therefore, must be careful when employing a differentiation (Type 3) strategy. Buyers will not pay the higher differentiation price unless their perceived value exceeds the price they are paying.[20] Based on such matters as attractive packaging, extensive advertising, quality of sales presentations, quality of website, list of customers, professionalism, size of the firm, or profitability of the company, perceived value may be more important to customers than actual value.

A Type 3 differentiation strategy can be especially effective under the following conditions:[21]

1. When there are many ways to differentiate the product or service and many buyers perceive these differences as having value.
2. When buyer needs and uses are diverse.
3. When few rival firms are following a similar differentiation approach.
4. When technological change is fast paced and competition revolves around rapidly evolving product features.

Focus Strategies (Type 4 and Type 5)

A successful focus strategy depends on an industry segment that is of sufficient size, has good growth potential, and is not crucial to the success of other major competitors. Strategies such as market penetration and market development offer substantial focusing advantages. Midsize and large firms can effectively pursue focus-based strategies only in conjunction with differentiation or cost leadership–based strategies. All firms in essence follow a differentiated strategy. Because only one firm can differentiate itself with the lowest cost, the remaining firms in the industry must find other ways to differentiate their products.

Focus strategies are most effective when consumers have distinctive preferences or requirements and when rival firms are not attempting to specialize in the same target segment. For example, Clorox Company, which obtains 80 percent of its revenue from the United States, is focusing on brands viewed as environmentally friendly. To refocus, Clorox just sold its auto-care business and acquired personal care company, Burt's Bees, and expanded its Green Works line of household cleaners and Brita water filters. Clorox's CEO Don Knauss loves the United States and is avoiding a costly push into China, Brazil, or India. Knauss's focus is on natural cleaning products, including bleaches and peroxide-based disinfectants for both consumers and hospitals.

Marriott continues to focus on is hotel business by announcing plans to double its hotels in Asia to 260 by 2016, especially growing its China-based hotels to about 125 from 60 and covering nearly 75 percent of Chinese provinces. Reasoning for Marriott's strategy is than Chinese tourists are traveling at home and abroad in dramatically increased numbers, up 21 percent on average year-over-year.

Risks of pursuing a focus strategy include the possibility that numerous competitors will recognize the successful focus strategy and copy it or that consumer preferences will drift toward the product attributes desired by the market as a whole. An organization using a focus strategy may concentrate on a particular group of customers, geographic markets, or on particular product-line segments to serve a well-defined but narrow market better than competitors who serve a broader market.

A low-cost (Type 4) or best-value (Type 5) focus strategy can be especially attractive under the following conditions:[22]

1. When the target market niche is large, profitable, and growing.
2. When industry leaders do not consider the niche to be crucial to their own success.
3. When industry leaders consider it too costly or difficult to meet the specialized needs of the target market niche while taking care of their mainstream customers.
4. When the industry has many different niches and segments, thereby allowing a focuser to pick a competitively attractive niche suited to its own resources.
5. When few, if any, other rivals are attempting to specialize in the same target segment.

Strategies for Competing in Turbulent, High-Velocity Markets

The world is changing more and more rapidly, and consequently industries and firms themselves are changing faster than ever. Some industries are changing so fast that researchers call them **turbulent, high-velocity markets**, such as telecommunications, medical, biotechnology, pharmaceuticals, computer hardware, software, and virtually all Internet-based industries. High-velocity change is clearly becoming more and more the rule rather than the exception, even in such industries as toys, phones, banking, defense, publishing, and communication.

Meeting the challenge of high-velocity change presents the firm with a choice of whether to react, anticipate, or lead the market in terms of its own strategies. To primarily react to changes in the industry would be a defensive strategy used to counter, for example, unexpected shifts in buyer tastes and technological breakthroughs. The react-to-change strategy would not be as effective as the anticipate-change strategy, which would entail devising and following through with plans for dealing with the expected changes. However, firms ideally strive to be in a position to lead the changes in high-velocity markets, whereby they pioneer new and better technologies and products and set industry standards. Being the leader or pioneer of change in a high-velocity market is an aggressive, offensive strategy that includes rushing next-generation products to market ahead of rivals and being continually proactive in shaping the market to one's own benefit. Although a lead-change strategy is best whenever the firm has the resources to pursue this approach, on occasion even the strongest firms in turbulent industries have to employ the react-to-the-market strategy and the anticipate-the-market strategy.

An example turbulent, high-velocity market is the U.S. defense industry, especially with dramatic cuts looming and a shift to higher technology and space defense systems. Based in Hartford, Connecticut, United Technologies, which produces Blackhawk helicopters and a diverse array of other products such as Carrier air conditioners and Otis elevators, recently reduced is sales forecasts. One strategy to compete in a high turbulent industry is to diversify into less turbulent industries. United Technologies continues to diversify, recently acquiring Goodrich Corp. for $16.5 billion, as well as Rolls Royce Holdings PLC's stake in the company's engine joint venture.

Means for Achieving Strategies

Cooperation Among Competitors

In a recent *Wall Street Journal* article titled "Facebook, Yahoo Kiss and Make-Up," these two rival firms, locked for years in bitter patent litigation, revealed what they called a new strategic alliance, which included a patent cross-license, a new advertising partnership, expanded joint distribution, and joint media event coverage.[23]

Strategies that stress cooperation among competitors are being used more. For collaboration between competitors to succeed, both firms must contribute something distinctive, such as technology, distribution, basic research, or manufacturing capacity. But a major risk is that unintended transfers of important skills or technology may occur at organizational levels below where the deal was signed.[24] Information not covered in the formal agreement often gets traded in the day-to-day interactions and dealings of engineers, marketers, and product developers. Firms often give away too much information to rival firms when operating under cooperative agreements! Tighter formal agreements are needed.

Perhaps the best example of rival firms in an industry forming alliances to compete against each other is the airline industry. Today there are three major alliances: Star, SkyTeam, and Oneworld, but other alliances are forming, such as the trans-Atlantic joint venture among American Air, British Air, and Iberia Air formed by Oneworld. There is also a trans-Pacific joint venture among American, Japan Air, United Continental, and All Nippon Air.

The idea of joining forces with a competitor is not easily accepted by Americans, who often view cooperation and partnerships with skepticism and suspicion. Indeed, joint ventures and cooperative arrangements among competitors demand a certain amount of trust if companies are to combat paranoia about whether one firm will injure the other. However, multinational firms are becoming more globally cooperative, and increasing numbers of domestic firms are joining forces with competitive foreign firms to reap mutual benefits. Kathryn Harrigan at Columbia University says, "Within a decade, most companies will be members of teams that compete against each other." Once major rivals, Google's YouTube and Vivendi SA's Universal Music Group have formed a partnership called Vevo to provide a new music-video service. Google provides the technology and Universal Music provides the content, and both firms share the revenues. The two firms now operate the stand-alone site Vevo.com.

U.S. companies often enter alliances primarily to avoid investments, being more interested in reducing the costs and risks of entering new businesses or markets than in acquiring new skills. In contrast, *learning from the partner* is a major reason why Asian and European firms enter into cooperative agreements. U.S. firms, too, should place learning high on the list of reasons to be cooperative with competitors. U.S. companies often form alliances with Asian firms to gain an understanding of their manufacturing excellence, but Asian competence in this area is not easily transferable. Manufacturing excellence is a complex system that includes employee training and involvement, integration with suppliers, statistical process controls, value engineering, and design. In contrast, U.S. know-how in technology and related areas can be imitated more easily. U.S. firms thus need to be careful not to give away more intelligence than they receive in cooperative agreements with rival Asian firms.

Joint Venture and Partnering

Renault SA and British racing-car company Caterham Cars recently developed a joint venture to design, develop, and manufacture a family of sports cars that will be available in 2015. The partnership, named Societe des Automobiles Alpine Caterham, gives the British Formula One race-car maker access to Renault's manufacturing clout.

Joint venture is a popular strategy that occurs when two or more companies form a temporary partnership or consortium for the purpose of capitalizing on some opportunity. Often, the two or more sponsoring firms form a separate organization and have shared equity ownership in the new entity. Other types of **cooperative arrangements** include research and development partnerships, cross-distribution agreements, cross-licensing agreements, cross-manufacturing agreements, and joint-bidding consortia.

Joint ventures and cooperative arrangements are being used increasingly because they allow companies to improve communications and networking, to globalize operations, and to minimize risk. Joint ventures and partnerships are often used to pursue an opportunity that is too complex, uneconomical, or risky for a single firm to pursue alone. Such business creations also are used when achieving and sustaining competitive advantage when an industry requires a broader range of competencies and know-how than any one firm can marshal. Kathryn Rudie Harrigan, summarizes the trend toward increased joint venturing:

> In today's global business environment of scarce resources, rapid rates of technological change, and rising capital requirements, the important question is no longer "Shall we form a joint venture?" Now the question is "Which joint ventures and cooperative arrangements are most appropriate for our needs and expectations?" followed by "How do we manage these ventures most effectively?"[25]

In a global market tied together by the Internet, joint ventures, partnerships, and alliances are proving to be a more effective way to enhance corporate growth than mergers and acquisitions.[26] Strategic partnering takes many forms, including outsourcing, information sharing, joint marketing, and joint research and development. Many companies, such as Eli Lilly, now host partnership training classes for their managers and partners. There are today more than 10,000 joint ventures formed annually, more than all mergers and acquisitions. There are countless examples of successful strategic alliances, such as Internet coverage.

A major reason why firms are using partnering as a means to achieve strategies is globalization. Walmart's successful joint venture with Mexico's Cifra is indicative of how a domestic firm can benefit immensely by partnering with a foreign company to gain substantial presence in that new country. Technology also is a major reason behind the need to form strategic alliances, with the Internet linking widely dispersed partners. The Internet paved the way and legitimized the need for alliances to serve as the primary means for corporate growth. Neiman Marcus and Target recently announced a partnership whereby both firms will offer a limited collection of 50 items from stationery to sporting goods at the same price with all the items carrying both the Target bulls-eye logo and the Neiman Marcus logo. This unusual partnership between a high-end and low-end retailer benefits Neiman by expanding its reach and notoriety, while benefiting Target by raising its overall perceived quality.

Evidence is mounting that firms should use partnering as a means for achieving strategies. However, the sad fact is that most U.S. firms in many industries—such as financial services, forest products, metals, and retailing—still operate in a merger or acquire mode to obtain growth. Partnering is not yet taught at most business schools and is often viewed within companies as a financial issue rather than a strategic issue. However, partnering has become a core competency, a strategic issue of such importance that top management involvement initially and throughout the life of an alliance is vital.[27]

Joint ventures among once rival firms are commonly being used to pursue strategies ranging from retrenchment to market development. Although ventures and partnerships are preferred over mergers as a means for achieving strategies, certainly they are not all successful. The good news is that joint ventures and partnerships are less risky for companies than mergers, but the bad news is that many alliances fail. There are countless examples of failed joint ventures. A few common problems that cause joint ventures to fail are as follows:

1. Managers who must collaborate daily in operating the venture are not involved in forming or shaping the venture.
2. The venture may benefit the partnering companies but may not benefit customers, who then complain about poorer service or criticize the companies in other ways.
3. The venture may not be supported equally by both partners. If supported unequally, problems arise.
4. The venture may begin to compete more with one of the partners than the other.[28]

Six guidelines for when a joint venture may be an especially effective means for pursuing strategies are:[29]

- When a privately-owned organization is forming a joint venture with a publicly-owned organization; there are some advantages to being privately held, such as closed ownership; there are some advantages of being publicly held, such as access to stock issuances as a source of capital. Sometimes, the unique advantages of being privately and publicly held can be synergistically combined in a joint venture.
- When a domestic organization is forming a joint venture with a foreign company; a joint venture can provide a domestic company with the opportunity for obtaining local management in a foreign country, thereby reducing risks such as expropriation and harassment by host country officials.
- When the distinct competencies of two or more firms complement each other especially well.
- When some project is potentially profitable but requires overwhelming resources and risks.
- When two or more smaller firms have trouble competing with a large firm.
- When there exists a need to quickly introduce a new technology.

Merger/Acquisition

As of December 2012, there were 10,346 merger-and-acquisition deals in the USA for the year, a 9 percent increase over the prior year, but an 8 percent decline in terms of the dollar volume. Late in 2012, ConAgra bought Ralcorp for $5 billion and Equity Residential (and AvalonBay) bought Archstone for $6.5 billion.

Merger and acquisition are two commonly used ways to pursue strategies. A **merger** occurs when two organizations of about equal size unite to form one enterprise. An **acquisition** occurs when a large organization purchases (acquires) a smaller firm, or vice versa. When a merger or acquisition is not desired by both parties, it can be called a **takeover** or **hostile takeover**. In contrast, if the acquisition is desired by both firms, it is termed a **friendly merger**. Most mergers are friendly. For example, two Japanese steel producers, Nippon Steel Corp. and Sumitomo Metal Industries Ltd., recently merged in friendly fashion to form the world's second largest steel producer behind ArcelorMittal.

Despite many investment bankers predicting the demise of hostile takeovers because it is difficult to pull off, the number of hostile takeovers are on the rise. For example, Glaxo recently gave Human Genome a deadline to accept their offer or face a hostile takeover. Genomma recently

TABLE 5-5 Key Reasons Why Many Mergers and Acquisitions Fail

- Integration difficulties
- Inadequate evaluation of target
- Large or extraordinary debt
- Inability to achieve synergy
- Too much diversification
- Managers overly focused on acquisitions
- Too large an acquisition
- Difficult to integrate different organizational cultures
- Reduced employee morale due to layoffs and relocations

made an unsolicited offer to acquire Prestige at $16.60 a share and nominated a full slate of directors for election at Prestige's annual shareholder meeting. Prestige's board is not staggered, so Genomma has the chance to push out a majority of Prestige's board, clearing the way for a takeover. Other recent hostile takeovers or attempts include Martin Marietta trying to takeover Vulcan Materials and Westlake Chemical trying to take over Georgia Gulf and Roche's bid for Illumina.

In a rare example of a Chinese company engaging in a hostile takeover, Shanghai-based Cathy Fortune recently bypassed the board of cooper miner Discovery Metals Ltd. with an offer of 830 million Australian dollars. This was a 51 percent premium over the value of Sydney-based Discovery Metals' common stock. China consumes about 40 percent of the world's copper output but historically avoids hostile takeovers altogether.

White knight is a term that refers to a firm that agrees to acquire another firm when that other firm is facing a hostile takeover by some company. For example, Palo Alto, California–based CV Thereapeutics Inc., a heart-drug maker, was fighting a hostile takeover bid by Japan's Astellas Pharma. Then CVT struck a friendly deal to be acquired by Forest City, California–based Gilead Sciences at a higher price of $1.4 billion in cash. Gilead is known for its HIV drugs, so its move into the heart-drug business surprised many analysts.

Not all mergers are effective and successful. For example, even 12 months after PulteGroup bought rival Centex Corp., for $1.3 billion in stock, creating the largest home builder in the USA, PulteGroup's profits were still negative and the company's stock price was 30 percent lower than the week of the acquisition. PulteGroup's dismal performance is in sharp contrast to rival firms such as Toll Brothers and Lennar Corp., whose stock price is up 22 percent during the same period. So a merger between two firms can yield great benefits, but the price and reasoning must be right. Some key reasons why many mergers and acquisitions fail are provided in Table 5-5.

Among mergers, acquisitions, and takeovers in recent years, same-industry combinations have predominated. A general market consolidation is occurring in many industries, especially banking, insurance, defense, and health care, but also in pharmaceuticals, food, airlines, accounting, publishing, computers, retailing, financial services, and biotechnology. For example, there are many potential benefits of merging with or acquiring another firm, as indicated in Table 5-6.

The volume of mergers completed annually worldwide is growing dramatically and exceeds $1 trillion. There are annually more than 10,000 mergers in the USA that total more

TABLE 5-6 Potential Benefits of Merging With or Acquiring Another Firm

- To provide improved capacity utilization
- To make better use of the existing sales force
- To reduce managerial staff
- To gain economies of scale
- To smooth out seasonal trends in sales
- To gain access to new suppliers, distributors, customers, products, and creditors
- To gain new technology
- To reduce tax obligations

than $700 billion. The proliferation of mergers is fueled by companies' drive for market share, efficiency, and pricing power, as well as by globalization, the need for greater economies of scale, reduced regulation and antitrust concerns, the Internet, and e-commerce.

A **leveraged buyout (LBO)** occurs when a corporation's shareholders are bought (hence *buyout*) by the company's management and other private investors using borrowed funds (hence *leverage*). Besides trying to avoid a hostile takeover, other reasons for initiating an LBO are senior management decisions that particular divisions do not fit into an overall corporate strategy, must be sold to raise cash, or receipt of an attractive offering price. An LBO takes a corporation private.

Private-Equity Acquisitions

As stock prices increased and companies became cash-rich in 2012–2013, private-equity (PE) firms such as Kohlberg Kravis Roberts (KKR) jumped aggressively back into the business of acquiring and selling firms. PE firms have unleashed a wave of new initial public offerings (IPO). Apollo Global Management is a large private-equity firm that owns many companies.

The intent of virtually all PE acquisitions is to buy firms at a low price and sell them later at a high price, arguably just good business. Par Pharmaceutical was recently acquired by PE firm TPG for $184 million in cash. Based in Woodcliff Lake, New Jersey, Par's shareholders received $50 in cash for each share, a premium of about 37 percent over the firm's closing stock price.

PE firms increasingly are buying companies from other PE firms, such as Clayton, Dubilier & Rice recently buying David's Bridal from Leonard Green & Partners LP for $1.05 billion. Such PE to PE acquisitions, called **secondary buyouts**, totaled $30 billion in 2012 in the USA compared to $10.5 billion in 2011.

PE firms especially, but other firms also, in 2012 extensively borrowed money, more than $70 billion, at record low interest rates, simply to fund dividend payouts to themselves, a controversial practice known as **dividend recapitalizations**. The previous annual record for dividend recapitalizations, according to S&P's Capital IQ LCD data service, was $40.5 billion in 2010. Critics say dividend recapitalization saddles a company with debt, burdening its operations. One reason for the high 2012 number was the expectation that taxes on dividends would increase in 2013, so the thinking was pay me now.

For all of 2012, the value of private-equity deals by country of investment is given below (in millions $) for the top seven:

1. USA (99.3)
2. UK (23.9)
3. Germany (9.8)
4. China (9.7)
5. Australia (5.2)
6. Canada (4.1)
7. France (4.1)

First Mover Advantages

First mover advantages refer to the benefits a firm may achieve by entering a new market or developing a new product or service prior to rival firms. As indicated in Table 5-7, some advantages of being a first mover include securing access to rare resources, gaining new knowledge of key factors and issues, and carving out market share and a position that is easy to defend and costly for rival firms to overtake. First mover advantages are analogous to taking the high ground first, which puts one in an excellent strategic position to launch aggressive campaigns and to defend territory. Being the first mover can be an excellent strategy when such actions (a) build a firm's image and reputation with buyers, (b) produce cost advantages over rivals in terms of new technologies, new components, new distribution channels, and so on, (c) create strongly loyal customers, and (d) make imitation or duplication by a rival hard or unlikely.

To sustain the competitive advantage gained by being the first mover, a firm needs to be a fast learner. There are, however, risks associated with being the first mover, such as unexpected and unanticipated problems and costs that occur from being the first firm doing business in the new market. Therefore, being a slow mover (also called *fast follower* or *late mover*) can be effective when a firm can easily copy or imitate the lead firm's products or services. If technology is advancing rapidly, slow movers can often leapfrog a first mover's products with improved

TABLE 5-7 Benefits of a Firm Being the First Mover

1. Secure access and commitments to rare resources
2. Gain new knowledge of critical success factors and issues
3. Gain market share and position in the best locations
4. Establish and secure long-term relationships with customers, suppliers, distributors, and investors
5. Gain customer loyalty and commitments

second-generation products. Samsung is an example in the smartphone business. Apple has always been a good example of a first mover firm, although of late Apple is stumbling a bit as Samsung gains momentum.

First mover advantages tend to be greatest when competitors are roughly the same size and possess similar resources. If competitors are not similar in size, then larger competitors can wait while others make initial investments and mistakes and then respond with greater effectiveness and resources. Lenovo has done this of late, as has Volkswagen.

Outsourcing and Reshoring

Business-process outsourcing (BPO) involves companies hiring other companies to take over various parts of their the functional operations, such as human resources, information systems, payroll, accounting, customer service, and even marketing. Companies choose to outsource their functional operations for several reasons: (a) it is less expensive, (b) it allows the firm to focus on its core businesses, and (c) it enables the firm to provide better services. Other advantages of outsourcing are that the strategy (a) allows the firm to align itself with "best-in-world" suppliers who focus on performing the special task, (b) provides the firm flexibility should customer needs shift unexpectedly, and (c) allows the firm to concentrate on other internal value chain activities critical to sustaining competitive advantage. BPO is a means for achieving strategies that are similar to partnering and joint venturing.

Reshoring is the new term that refers to U.S. companies planning to move some of their manufacturing back to the USA. About 14 to 37 percent of U.S. companies plan to *reshore* in 2012–2014 for the following reasons: a desire to get products to market faster and respond rapidly to customer orders; savings from reduced transportation and warehousing; improved quality and protection of intellectual property; pressure to increase U.S. jobs.[30] For example, Google's new Nexus Q music and video player is being manufactured in the USA, something unusual for consumer electronics. GE's website has an "American Jobs Map" that gives details of 14,500 new GE jobs in the USA. A bill named the "Bring Jobs Home Act" is being considered in Congress.

"Made in the USA" is making a comeback. Even Walmart, which pioneered looking globally for the lowest-cost suppliers, is increasing by $50 billion its spending with U.S. suppliers in this decade. U.S. manufacturing is leading the way on superautomated factories that require less labor but more high-tech machines. For example, the 200,000 sq. ft. GE battery plant in Schenectady, NY has only 370 full-time employees but ships batteries around the world. New, high-tech, U.S. factories are leading to extensive "reshoring" in America.

Many firms, such as Dearborn, Michigan–based Visteon Corp. and J.P. Morgan Chase & Co., outsource their computer operations to IBM, which competes with firms such as Electronic Data Systems and Computer Sciences Corp. in the computer outsourcing business. 3M Corp. is outsourcing all of its manufacturing operations to Flextronics International Ltd. of Singapore or Jabil Circuit in Florida. 3M is also outsourcing all design and manufacturing of low-end standardized volume products by building a new design center in Taiwan.

U.S. and European companies for more than a decade have been outsourcing their manufacturing, tech support, and back-office work, but most insisted on keeping research and development activities in-house. However, an ever-growing number of firms today are outsourcing their product design to Asian developers. China and India are becoming increasingly important suppliers of intellectual property.

The details of what work to outsource, to whom, where, and for how much can challenge even the biggest, most sophisticated companies. And some outsourcing deals do not work out, such as the J.P. Morgan Chase deal with IBM and Dow Chemical's deal with Electronic Data Systems. Both outsourcing deals were abandoned after several years. Lehman Brothers Holdings and Dell Inc. both recently reversed decisions to move customer call centers to India after a customer rebellion. India has become a booming place for outsourcing. Outsourcing generally aims to achieve one or more of the following benefits:

- Cost savings: Access lower wages in foreign countries.
- Focus on core business: Focus resources on developing the core business rather than being distracted by other functions.
- Cost restructuring: Outsourcing changes the balance of fixed costs to variable costs by moving the firm more to variable costs. Outsourcing also makes variable costs more predictable.
- Improve quality: Improve quality by contracting out various business functions to specialists.
- Knowledge: Gain access to intellectual property and wider experience and knowledge.
- Contract: Gain access to services within a legally binding contract with financial penalties and legal redress. This is not the case with services performed internally.
- Operational expertise: Gain access to operational best practice that would be too difficult or time consuming to develop in-house.
- Access to talent: Gain access to a larger talent pool and a sustainable source of skills, especially science and engineering.
- Catalyst for change: Use an outsourcing agreement as a catalyst for major change that cannot be achieved alone.
- Enhance capacity for innovation: Use external knowledge to supplement limited in-house capacity for product innovation.
- Reduce time to market: Accelerate development or production of a product through additional capability brought by the supplier.
- Risk management: Manage risk by partnering with an outside firm.
- Tax benefit: Capitalize on tax incentives to locate manufacturing plants to avoid high taxes in various countries.

Strategic Management in Nonprofit and Governmental Organizations

Nonprofit organizations are basically just like for-profit companies except for two major differences: (1) nonprofits do not pay taxes and (2) nonprofits do not have shareholders to provide capital. In virtually all other ways, nonprofits are just like for-profits. Nonprofits have competitors that want to put them out of business. Nonprofits have employees, customers, creditors, suppliers, and distributors as well as financial budgets, income statements, balance sheets, cash flow statements, and so on. Nonprofit organizations embrace strategic planning just as much as for-profit firms, and perhaps even more, because equity capital is not an alternative source of financing.

The strategic-management process is being used effectively by countless nonprofit and governmental organizations, such as the Girl Scouts, Boy Scouts, the Red Cross, chambers of commerce, educational institutions, medical institutions, public utilities, libraries, government agencies, and churches. The nonprofit sector, surprisingly, is by far the largest employer in the USA. Many nonprofit and governmental organizations outperform private firms and corporations on innovativeness, motivation, productivity, and strategic management.

Compared to for-profit firms, nonprofit and governmental organizations may be totally dependent on outside financing. Especially for these organizations, strategic management provides an excellent vehicle for developing and justifying requests for needed financial support.

Educational Institutions

The world of higher education is rapidly moving to massive open online courses (MOOC), with many of the courses being free to anyone with an Internet connection. The American Council on Education, an association for higher education presidents, is considering allowing free, online courses to be eligible for credit toward a degree and eligible for transfer credit. Several companies, including edX, Udacity, Coursera, and the Jack Welch Management Institute, are most associated with MOOCs, but the list is growing weekly.

Educational institutions are more frequently using strategic-management techniques and concepts. Richard Cyert, former president of Carnegie Mellon University, said, "I believe we do a far better job of strategic management than any company I know." Population shifts nationally from the Northeast and Midwest to the Southeast and West are but one factor causing trauma for educational institutions that have not planned for changing enrollments. Ivy League schools in the Northeast are recruiting more heavily in the Southeast and West. This trend represents a significant change in the competitive climate for attracting the best high school graduates each year.

Online college degrees are commonplace and represent a threat to traditional colleges and universities. "You can put the kids to bed and go to law school," says Andrew Rosen, chief operating officer of Kaplan Education Centers, a subsidiary of the Washington Post Company.

Many U.S. colleges and universities have now established campuses outside the USA. For example, Yale University and the National University of Singapore established a joint campus in Singapore in 2013. The institution is Singapore's first liberal-arts college and Yale's first campus outside the Ivy League institution in New Haven, Connecticut.

Medical Organizations

The $200 billion U.S. hospital industry is experiencing declining margins, excess capacity, bureaucratic overburdening, poorly planned and executed diversification strategies, soaring health-care costs, reduced federal support, and high administrator turnover. The seriousness of this problem is accented by a 20 percent annual decline in use by inpatients nationwide. Declining occupancy rates, deregulation, and accelerating growth of health maintenance organizations, preferred provider organizations, urgent care centers, outpatient surgery centers, diagnostic centers, specialized clinics, and group practices are other major threats facing hospitals today. Many private and state-supported medical institutions are in financial trouble as a result of traditionally taking a reactive rather than a proactive approach in dealing with their industry.

Hospitals—originally intended to be warehouses for people dying of tuberculosis, smallpox, cancer, pneumonia, and infectious diseases—are creating new strategies today as advances in the diagnosis and treatment of chronic diseases are undercutting that previous mission. Hospitals are beginning to bring services to the patient as much as bringing the patient to the hospital; health care is more and more being concentrated in the home and in the residential community, not on the hospital campus. Chronic care will require day-treatment facilities, electronic monitoring at home, user-friendly ambulatory services, decentralized service networks, and laboratory testing. A successful hospital strategy for the future will require renewed and deepened collaboration with physicians, who are central to hospitals' well-being, and a reallocation of resources from acute to chronic care in home and community settings.

Current strategies being pursued by many hospitals include creating home health services, establishing nursing homes, and forming rehabilitation centers. Backward integration strategies that some hospitals are pursuing include acquiring ambulance services, waste disposal services, and diagnostic services. Millions of persons annually research medical ailments online, which is causing a dramatic shift in the balance of power between doctor, patient, and hospitals. The number of persons using the Internet to obtain medical information is skyrocketing. A motivated patient using the Internet can gain knowledge on a particular subject far beyond his or her doctor's knowledge because no person can keep up with the results and implications of billions of dollars' worth of medical research reported weekly. Patients today often walk into the doctor's office with a file folder of the latest articles detailing research and treatment options for their ailments.

Governmental Agencies and Departments

Federal, state, county, and municipal agencies and departments, such as police departments, chambers of commerce, forestry associations, and health departments, are responsible for formulating, implementing, and evaluating strategies that use taxpayers' dollars in the most cost-effective way to provide services and programs. Strategic-management concepts are generally required and thus widely used to enable governmental organizations to be more effective and efficient.

Strategists in governmental organizations operate with less strategic autonomy than their counterparts in private firms. Public enterprises generally cannot diversify into unrelated businesses or merge with other firms. Governmental strategists usually enjoy little freedom in altering the organizations' missions or redirecting objectives. Legislators and politicians often have direct or indirect control over major decisions and resources. Strategic issues get discussed and debated in the media and legislatures. Issues become politicized, resulting in fewer strategic choice alternatives. There is now more predictability in the management of public sector enterprises.

Government agencies and departments are finding that their employees get excited about the opportunity to participate in the strategic-management process and thereby have an effect on the organization's mission, objectives, strategies, and policies. In addition, government agencies are using a strategic-management approach to develop and substantiate formal requests for additional funding.

Strategic Management in Small Firms

The reason why "becoming your own boss" has become a national obsession is that entrepreneurs are role models in the USA. Almost everyone wants to own a business—from teens and college students, who are signing up for entrepreneurial courses in record numbers, to those older than age 65, who are forming more companies every year.

Strategic management is vital for large firms' success, but what about small firms? The strategic-management process is just as vital for small companies. From their inception, all organizations have a strategy, even if the strategy just evolves from day-to-day operations. Even if conducted informally or by a single owner or entrepreneur, the strategic-management process can significantly enhance small firms' growth and prosperity. Because an ever-increasing number of men and women in the United States are starting their own businesses, more individuals are becoming strategists. Widespread corporate layoffs have contributed to an explosion in small businesses and new ideas.

Numerous magazine and journal articles have focused on applying strategic-management concepts to small businesses. A major conclusion of these articles is that a lack of strategic-management knowledge is a serious obstacle for many small business owners. Other problems often encountered in applying strategic-management concepts to small businesses are a lack of both sufficient capital to exploit external opportunities and a day-to-day cognitive frame of reference. Research also indicates that strategic management in small firms is more informal than in large firms, but small firms that engage in strategic management outperform those that do not.

Special Note to Students

There are numerous alternative strategies that could benefit any firm, but your strategic management case analysis should result in specific recommendations that you decide will best provide the firm competitive advantages. Because company recommendations with costs comprise the most important pages or slides in your case project, introduce bits of that information early in the presentation as relevant supporting material is presented to justify your expenditures. Your recommendations page(s) itself should therefore be a summary of suggestions mentioned throughout your paper or presentation, rather than being a surprise shock to your reader or audience. You may even want to include with your recommendations insight as to why certain other feasible strategies were not chosen for implementation. That information too should be anchored in the notion of competitive advantage and disadvantage with respect to perceived costs and benefits. If someone asks "what is the difference between recommendations and strategies," respond saying: "Recommendations are alternative strategies actually selected for implementation."

Conclusion

The main appeal of any managerial approach is the expectation that it will enhance organizational performance. This is especially true of strategic management. Through involvement in strategic-management activities, managers and employees achieve a better understanding of an organization's priorities and operations. Strategic management allows organizations to be efficient, but more important, it allows them to be effective. Although strategic management does not guarantee organizational success, the process allows proactive rather than reactive decision making. Strategic management may represent a radical change in philosophy for some organizations, so strategists must be trained to anticipate and constructively respond to questions and issues as they arise. The strategies discussed in this chapter can represent a new beginning for many firms, especially if managers and employees in the organization understand and support the plan for action.

MyManagementLab®

Go to **mymanagementlab.com** to complete the problems marked with this icon ★.

Key Terms and Concepts

acquisition (p. 151)
backward integration (p. 135)
bankruptcy (p. 142)
business-process outsourcing (BPO) (p. 154)
combination strategy (p. 131)
cooperative arrangements (p. 150)
cost leadership (p. 145)
de-integration (p. 135)
differentiation (p. 145)
diversification strategies (p. 139)
divestiture (p. 143)
dividend recapitalizations (p. 153)
financial objectives (p. 129)
first mover advantages (p. 153)
focus (p. 145)
forward integration (p. 133)
franchising (p. 134)
friendly merger (p. 151)
generic strategies (p. 145)
horizontal integration (p. 136)
hostile takeover (p. 151)

integration strategies (p. 133)
intensive strategies (p. 137)
joint venture (p. 150)
leveraged buyout (LBO) (p. 153)
liquidation (p. 144)
long-term objectives (p. 128)
market development (p. 138)
market penetration (p. 137)
merger (p. 151)
product development (p. 138)
related diversification (p. 139)
reshoring (p. 154)
retrenchment (p. 142)
secondary buyouts (p. 153)
strategic objectives (p. 129)
takeover (p. 151)
turbulent, high-velocity markets (p. 149)
unrelated diversification (p. 139)
vertical integration (p. 133)
white knight (p. 152)

Issues for Review and Discussion

5-1. Define and give an example of *reshoring*. What are three reasons why reshoring is becoming more popular? What are three reasons many companies expect "never" to reshore (as Steve Jobs once told President Obama)?

5-2. Define and give an example of a *secondary buyout*. Why did secondary buyouts triple in total dollar value in 2012 versus 2011?

5-3. The number and dollar value of *hostile takeovers* are on the rise. Give two reasons for this trend.

5-4. Kroger is adding clothing to its line of products. Give two reasons why this may be a good strategy and two reasons why it may be a bad strategy.

5-5. What do you believe are the five most important benefits of outsourcing?

5-6. Define and give an example of a *dividend recapitalization*. List some pros and cons of doing this in a business.

5-7. How are for-profit firms different from nonprofit firms in terms of business? What are the implications for strategic planning?

5-8. If the CEO of a beverage company such as Dr Pepper/Snapple asked you whether backward or forward integration would be better for the firm, how would you respond?

5-9. In order of importance, list six "characteristics of objectives."

5-10. In order of importance, list six "benefits of objectives."

5-11. Called de-integration, there appears to be a growing trend for firms to become less forward integrated. Discuss why.

5-12. Called de-integration, there appears to be a growing trend for firms to become less backward integrated. Discuss why.

5-13. If a company has $1 million to spend on a new strategy and is considering market development versus product development, what determining factors would be most important to consider?

5-14. What conditions, externally and internally, would be desired or necessary for a firm to diversify?

5-15. Could a firm simultaneously pursue focus, differentiation, and cost leadership? Should firms do that? Discuss.

5-16. There is a growing trend of increased collaboration among competitors. List the benefits and drawbacks of this practice.

5-17. List four major benefits of forming a joint venture to achieve desired objectives.

5-18. List six major benefits of acquiring another firm to achieve desired objectives.

5-19. List five reasons why many mergers or acquisitions historically have failed.

5-20. Can you think of any reasons why not-for-profit firms would benefit less from doing strategic planning than for-profit companies?

5-21. Discuss how important it is for a college football or basketball team to have a good game plan for the big rival game this coming weekend. How much time and effort do you feel the coaching staff puts into developing that game plan? Why is such time and effort essential?

5-22. Define and give a hypothetical example of a "white knight" in the fast-food industry.

5-23. How does strategy formulation differ for a small versus a large organization? How does it differ for a for-profit versus a nonprofit organization?

5-24. Give recent examples of market penetration, market development, and product development.

5-25. Give recent examples of forward integration, backward integration, and horizontal integration.

5-26. Give recent examples of related and unrelated diversification.

5-27. Give recent examples of joint venture, retrenchment, divestiture, and liquidation.

5-28. Do you think hostile takeovers are unethical? Why or why not?

5-29. What are the major advantages and disadvantages of diversification?

5-30. What are the major advantages and disadvantages of an integrative strategy?

5-31. How does strategic management differ in for-profit and nonprofit organizations?

5-32. Why is it not advisable to pursue too many strategies at once?

5-33. Consumers can purchase tennis shoes, food, cars, boats, and insurance on the Internet. Are there any products today than cannot be purchased online? What is the implication for traditional retailers?

5-34. What are the pros and cons of a firm merging with a rival firm?

5-35. Compare and contrast financial objectives with strategic objectives. Which type is more important in your opinion? Why?

5-36. How do the levels of strategy differ in a large firm versus a small firm?

5-37. List 11 types of strategies. Give a hypothetical example of each strategy listed.

5-38. Discuss the nature of as well as the pros and cons of a "friendly merger" versus "hostile takeover" in acquiring another firm. Give an example of each.

5-39. Define and explain "first mover advantages."

5-40. Define and explain "outsourcing."

5-41. Give some advantages and disadvantages of cooperative versus competitive strategies.

MyManagementLab®

Go to **mymanagementlab.com** for Auto-graded writing questions as well as the following Assisted-graded writing questions:

5-42. What are the pros and cons of a firm merging with a rival firm?

5-43. Discuss the nature of as well as the pros and cons of a "friendly merger" versus "hostile takeover" in acquiring another firm. Give an example of each.

5-44. Mymanagementlab Only—comprehensive writing assignment for this chapter.

Current Readings

Ashkenas, Suzanne Francis, and Rick Heinick. "The Merger Dividend." *Harvard Business Review* (July-August 2011): 126.

Barczak, Gloria, and Kenneth B. Kahn. "Identifying New Product Development Best Practice." *Business Horizons* 55, no. 3 (May 2012): 293–305.

Bouchikhi, Hamid, and John R. Kimberly. "Making Mergers Work." *MITSloan Management Review* 54, no. 1 (Fall 2012): 63.

Fieldstad, Øystein D., Charles C. Snow, and Raymond E. Miles. "The Architecture of Collaboration." *Strategic Management Journal* 33, no. 6 (June 2012): 734–750.

Haleblian, Jerayr, Gerry McNamara, Kalin Kolev, and Bernadine J. Dykes. "Exploring Firm Characteristics that Differentiate Leaders from Followers in Industry Merger Waves: A Competitive Dynamics Perspective." *Strategic Management Journal* 33, no. 9 (September 2012): 1037–1052.

Holweg, Matthias, and Frits K. Pil. "Outsourcing Complex Business Processes: Lessons From An Enterprise Partnership." *California Management Review* 54, no. 3 (Spring 2012): 98–115.

Honeycutt Jr., Earl D., Vincent P. Magnini, and Shawn T. Thelen. "Solutions for customer complaints about offshoring and outsourcing services." *Business Horizons* 55, no. 1 (January–February 2012): 33.

Leavy, Brian. "Collaborative Innovation as the New Imperative—Design Thinking, Value Co-creation and the Power of Pull." *Strategy and Leadership* 40, no. 3 (2012): 25–34.

Muehlfeld, Katrin, Padma Rao Sahib, and Arien Van Witteloostuijn. "A Contextual Theory of Organizational Learning from Failures and Successes: A Study of Acquisition Completion in the Global Newspaper Industry, 1981–2008." *Strategic Management Journal* 33, no. 8 (August 2012): 938–964.

Thomke, Stefan, and Donald Reinertsen. "Six Myths of
Product Development." *Harvard Business Review*
(May 2012): 84.

Tsai, Wenpin, Kuo-Hsien Su, and Ming-Jer Chen. "Seeing
Through the Eyes of a Rival: Competitor Acumen
Based on Rival-Centric Perceptions." *The Academy of
Management Review 54*, no. 4 (August 2011): 761.

Souder, David, Zeki Simsek, and Scott G. Johnson. "The
Differing Effects of Agent and Founder CEOs on the

Firm's Market Expansion." *Strategic Management
Journal 33*, no. 1 (January 2012): 23–41.

Weigelt, Carmen, and MB Sarkar. "Performance Implications
of Outsourcing for Technological Innovations: Managing
the Efficiency and Adaptability Trade-off." *Strategic
Management Journal 33*, no. 2 (February 2012): 189–216.

Wunker, Stephen. "Better Growth Decisions: Early Mover, Fast
Follower or Late Follower?" *Strategy and Leadership 40*,
no. 3 (2012): 43–48.

ASSURANCE OF LEARNING **EXERCISES**

EXERCISE 5A
Develop Hypothetical PepsiCo Strategies

Purpose

Table 5-4 identifies, defines, and exemplifies 11 key types of strategies available to firms. This exercise will give you practice formulating possible strategies within each broad category.

Instructions

Step 1	On a clear sheet of paper, develop an 11 × 2 matrix where PepsiCo's (1) beverages and (2) snack segments are along the top and the 11 strategies listed in Table 5-4 are along the left side of your paper.
Step 2	Review the text material related to Table 5-4. Also, review the PepsiCo divisional information provided in Cohesion Case.
Step 3	In each of the 22 cells within your 11 × 2 matrix, write in a hypothetical strategy for the respective business segment indicated.

EXERCISE 5B
Barilla's Actual Strategies

Purpose

As showcased at the beginning of this chapter, Barilla is successfully pursuing a variety of strategies. This exercise gives you practice identifying types of strategies, which is important, especially because in the next chapter important strategic management matrices recommend various types of strategies depending on various internal and external factors.

Instructions

Step 1	Review the material about Barilla at the beginning of this chapter. In addition, go to the www.barillagroup.com website and click on Media Relations and then review current news releases about Barilla.
Step 2	For the following eight types of strategies, give an actual example being pursued by Barilla: forward integration, market penetration, market development, market penetration, product development, related diversification, divestiture, and retrenchment.

EXERCISE 5C
What Strategies Should PepsiCo Pursue in 2014?

Purpose

In performing strategic management case analysis, you can find information about the respective company's actual and planned strategies. Comparing *what is planned* versus *what you recommend* is an important part of case analysis. Do not recommend what the firm actually plans, unless in-depth analysis of the situation reveals those strategies to be best among all feasible alternatives. This exercise gives you experience conducting library and Internet research to determine what PepsiCo is doing in 2013 and should do in 2014.

Instructions

Step 1   Go to the www.pepsico.com website and click on Media and then click on Press Releases. Read through the most recent 20 press releases.

Step 2   Determine three new strategies that PepsiCo is actually pursuing. Identify three proposed strategies that you feel would be excellent for PepsiCo to pursue. Give a rationale for each of your proposed strategies.

EXERCISE 5D
Examine Strategy Articles

Purpose

Strategy articles can be found weekly in journals, magazines, and newspapers. By reading and studying strategy articles, you can gain a better understanding of the strategic-management process. Several of the best journals in which to find corporate strategy articles are *Advanced Management Journal, Business Horizons, Long Range Planning, Journal of Business Strategy*, and *Strategic Management Journal*. These journals are devoted to reporting the results of empirical research in management. They apply strategic-management concepts to specific organizations and industries. They introduce new strategic-management techniques and provide short case studies on selected firms. Other good journals in which to find strategic-management articles are *Harvard Business Review, Sloan Management Review, California Management Review, Academy of Management Review, Academy of Management Journal, Academy of Management Executive, Journal of Management*, and *Journal of Small Business Management*.

In contrast to journals, several of the best magazines in which to find applied strategy articles are *Dun's Business Month, Fortune, Forbes, BusinessWeek, Inc.*, and *Industry Week*. Newspapers such as *USA Today, Wall Street Journal, New York Times*, and *Barrons* cover strategy events when they occur—for example, a joint venture announcement, a bankruptcy declaration, a new advertising campaign start, acquisition of a company, divestiture of a division, a chief executive officer's hiring or firing, or a hostile takeover attempt.

In combination, journal, magazine, and newspaper articles can make the strategic-management course more exciting. They allow current strategies of for-profit and nonprofit organizations to be identified and studied.

Instructions

Step 1   Go to your college library (or online) and find a recent journal article that focuses on a strategic-management topic. Select your article from one of the journals listed above (not from a magazine). Copy the article and bring it to class.

Step 2   Give a three-minute oral report summarizing the most important information in your journal article. Include comments giving your personal reaction to the article. Pass your article around in class.

EXERCISE 5E
Classify Some Year 2013 Strategies

Purpose

This exercise can improve your understanding of various strategies by giving you experience classifying strategies. This skill will help you use the strategy-formulation tools presented later. Consider the following 19 actual year-2013 strategies by various firms:

1. Nokia cut 10,000 jobs and closed some plants.
2. Starbucks opened its first Tazo tea shops that offer 80 varieties of loose-leaf tea.
3. Wynn Resorts Ltd. is building its first casino in Macau, China.
4. Best Buy eliminated 2,400 store jobs, including 600 Geek Squad positions.
5. Discount European airlines, Malev in Hungary and Spanair in Spain, ceased operations.
6. eBay's PayPal is expanding its card services to 7 million retail stores that accept Discover cards.
7. Kodak is selling its camera-film business to raise cash.
8. Walt Disney opened its first Disney Baby retail store in a mall in Glendale, California.
9. Amazon introduced a new low priced Kindle Fire tablet computer.
10. Dole Food, known for its bananas and pineapples, sold its Asia fresh-produce business to Itochu Corp. of Japan.

11. The number-2 import beer behind Corona Extra, Heineken introduced a new, longer neck, slimmer green bottle for its beer in January 2013.
12. Brazil sold all the assets of its Banco Cruzeiro do Sul SA and closed the bank.
13. Bank of America eliminated another 16,000 jobs.
14. Tyco Int. spun off ADT as well as its Flow control business.
15. Mattress maker Sealy Corp. was acquired by rival Tempur-Pedic International.
16. Toyota is rolling out 21 new or redesigned gasoline-electric vehicles in 2013–2015.
17. Philip Morris International, producer of the world's top selling cigarette, Marlboro, is developing a flu vaccine derived from a type of tobacco plant.
18. HP cut 27,000 jobs between 2012 and 2014.
19. Samsung developed plastic rather than glass mobile devices, making them bendable, lighter, and unbreakable.

Instructions

Step 1	On a separate sheet of paper, number from 1 to 19. These numbers correspond to the strategies described.
Step 2	What type of strategy best describes the 19 actions cited? Indicate your answers.
Step 3	Exchange papers with a classmate, and grade each other's paper as your instructor gives the right answers.

EXERCISE 5F
How Risky Are Various Alternative Strategies?

Purpose

This exercise focuses on how risky various alternative strategies are for organizations to pursue. Different degrees of risk are based largely on varying degrees of *externality*, defined as movement away from present business into new markets and products. In general, the greater the degree of externality, the greater the probability of loss resulting from unexpected events. High-risk strategies generally are less attractive than low-risk strategies.

Instructions

Step 1	On a separate sheet of paper, number vertically from 1 to 10. Think of 1 as "most risky," 2 as "next most risky," and so forth to 10, "least risky."
Step 2	Write the following strategies beside the appropriate number to indicate how risky you believe the strategy is to pursue: horizontal integration, related diversification, liquidation, forward integration, backward integration, product development, market development, market penetration, retrenchment, and unrelated diversification.
Step 3	Grade your paper as your instructor gives you the right answers and supporting rationale. Each correct answer is worth 10 points.

EXERCISE 5G
Develop Alternative Strategies for Your University

Purpose

It is important for representatives from all areas of a college or university to identify and discuss alternative strategies that could benefit faculty, students, alumni, staff, and other constituencies. As you complete this exercise, notice the learning and understanding that occurs as people express differences of opinion. Recall that *the process of planning is more important than the document.*

Instructions

Step 1	Recall or locate the external opportunity and threat and internal strength and weakness factors that you identified as part of Exercise 1D. If you did not do that exercise, discuss now as a class important external and internal factors facing your college or university.
Step 2	Identify and put on the chalkboard alternative strategies that you feel could benefit your college or university. Your proposed actions should allow the institution to capitalize on particular strengths, improve upon certain weaknesses, avoid external threats, or take advantage of particular external opportunities. List 10 possible strategies on the board. Number the strategies as they are written on the board.

Step 3	On a separate sheet of paper, number from 1 to 10. Everyone in class individually should rate the strategies identified, using a 1 to 3 scale, where 1 = *I do not support implementation*, 2 = *I am neutral about implementation*, and 3 = *I strongly support implementation*. In rating the strategies, recognize that your institution cannot do everything desired or potentially beneficial.
Step 4	Go to the board and record your ratings in a row beside the respective strategies. Everyone in class should do this, going to the board perhaps by rows in the class.
Step 5	Sum the ratings for each strategy so that a prioritized list of recommended strategies is obtained. This prioritized list reflects the collective wisdom of your class. Strategies with the highest score are deemed best.
Step 6	Discuss how this process could enable organizations to achieve understanding and commitment from individuals.
Step 7	Share your class results with a university administrator, and ask for comments regarding the process and top strategies recommended.

EXERCISE 5H

Lessons in Doing Business Globally

Purpose

The purpose of this exercise is to discover some important lessons learned by local businesses that do business internationally.

Instructions

Contact several local business leaders. Find at least three firms that engage in international or export operations. Visit the owner or manager of each business in person. Ask the businessperson to give you several important lessons that his or her firm has learned in globally doing business. Record the lessons on paper, and report your findings to the class.

Notes

1. John Byrne, "Strategic Planning—It's Back," *BusinessWeek*, August 26, 1996, 46.
2. Steven C. Brandt, *Strategic Planning in Emerging Companies* (Reading, MA: Addison-Wesley, 1981). Reprinted with permission of the publisher.
3. F. Hansen and M. Smith, "Crisis in Corporate America: The Role of Strategy," *Business Horizons* (January–February 2003, 9.
4. Adapted from F. R. David, "How Do We Choose Among Alternative Growth Strategies?" *Managerial Planning* 33, no. 4 (January–February 1985): 14–17, 22.
5. Ibid.
6. Kenneth Davidson, "Do Megamergers Make Sense?" *Journal of Business Strategy* 7, no. 3 (Winter 1987): 45.
7. David, "How Do We Choose."
8. Ibid.
9. Ibid.
10. Ibid.
11. Arthur Thompson Jr., A. J. Strickland III, and John Gamble, *Crafting and Executing Strategy: Text and Readings* (New York: McGraw-Hill/Irwin, 2005, 241.
12. Michael E. Porter, *Competitive Strategy: Techniques for Analyzing Industries and Competitors* (New York: Free Press, 1980), 53–57, 318–319.
13. David, "How Do We Choose."
14. Ibid.
15. Ibid.
16. Ibid.
17. Ibid.
18. Michael Porter, *Competitive Advantage* (New York: Free Press, 1985), 97. Also, Arthur Thompson Jr., A. J. Strickland III, and John Gamble, *Crafting and Executing Strategy: Text and Readings* (New York: McGraw-Hill/Irwin, 2005), 117.
19. Arthur Thompson Jr., A. J. Strickland III, and John Gamble, *Crafting and Executing Strategy: Text and Readings* (New York: McGraw-Hill/Irwin, 2005), 125–126.
20. Porter, *Competitive Advantage,* 160–162.
21. Thompson, Strickland, and Gamble, 129–130.
22. Ibid., 134.
23. John Letzing, "Facebook, Yahoo Kiss and Make-Up," *Wall Street Journal* (July 9, 2102): B3.
24. Gary Hamel, Yves Doz, and C. K. Prahalad, "Collaborate with Your Competitors—and Win," *Harvard Business Review* 67, no. 1 (January–February 1989): 133.
25. Kathryn Rudie Harrigan, "Joint Ventures: Linking for a Leap Forward," *Planning Review* 14, no. 4 (July–August 1986): 10.
26. Matthew Schifrin, "Partner or Perish," *Forbes* (May 21, 2001): 26.
27. Ibid., 28.
28. Ibid., 32.
29. David, "How Do We Choose."
30. James Hagerty, "Some Firms Opt to Bring Manufacturing Back to USA," *Wall Street Journal* (July 18, 2012): B8.

## 6

Source: jiawangkun/Fotolia

MyManagementLab®

⭐ Improve Your Grade!

Over 10 million students improved their results using the Pearson MyLabs.
Visit **mymanagementlab.com** for simulations, tutorials, and end-of-chapter problems.

Strategy Analysis and Choice

CHAPTER OBJECTIVES

After studying this chapter, you should be able to do the following:

1. Describe a three-stage framework for choosing among alternative strategies.

2. Explain how to develop a Strengths-Weaknesses-Opportunities-Threats (SWOT) Matrix, Strategic Position and Action Evaluation (SPACE) Matrix, Boston Consulting Group (BCG) Matrix, Internal-External (IE) Matrix, and Quantitative Strategic Planning Matrix (QSPM).

3. Identify important behavioral, political, ethical, and social responsibility considerations in strategy analysis and choice.

4. Discuss the role of intuition in strategic analysis and choice.

5. Discuss the role of organizational culture in strategic analysis and choice.

6. Discuss the role of a board of directors in choosing among alternative strategies.

ASSURANCE OF LEARNING **EXERCISES**

The following exercises are found at the end of this chapter.

Strategy analysis and choice largely involve making subjective decisions based on objective information. This chapter introduces important concepts that can help strategists generate feasible alternatives, evaluate those alternatives, and choose a specific course of action. Behavioral aspects of strategy formulation are described, including politics, culture, ethics, and social responsibility considerations. Modern tools for formulating strategies are described, and the appropriate role of a board of directors is discussed. As showcased below, General Electric is an example company pursuing an excellent strategic plan.

The Nature of Strategy Analysis and Choice

As indicated by Figure 6-1 with white shading, this chapter focuses on generating and evaluating alternative strategies, as well as selecting strategies to pursue. Strategy analysis and choice seek to determine alternative courses of action that could best enable the firm to achieve its mission and objectives. The firm's present strategies, objectives, vision, and mission, coupled with the external and internal audit information, provide a basis for generating and evaluating feasible alternative strategies. This systematic approach is the best way to avoid a crisis. Rudin's Law states: "When a crisis forces choosing among alternatives, most people choose the worst possible one."

Unless a desperate situation confronts the firm, alternative strategies will likely represent incremental steps that move the firm from its present position to a desired future position. Alternative strategies do not come out of the wild blue yonder; they are derived from the firm's vision, mission, objectives, external audit, and internal audit; they are consistent with, or build on, past strategies that have worked well.

The Process of Generating and Selecting Strategies

Strategists never consider all feasible alternatives that could benefit the firm because there are an infinite number of possible actions and an infinite number of ways to implement those actions. Therefore, a manageable set of the most attractive alternative strategies must be developed. The advantages, disadvantages, trade-offs, costs, and benefits of these strategies should be determined. This section discusses the process that many firms use to determine an appropriate set

EXCELLENT **STRATEGIC MANAGEMENT** SHOWCASED

General Electric (GE) Company

Headquartered in Fairfield, Connecticut, GE is one of the most diversified corporations in the world, producing a vast array of products, including aircraft engines, turbines, locomotives, household appliances, power plants, medical imaging equipment, and a variety of electrical control equipment. GE is also one of the pre-eminent financial services providers in the USA. GE Capital, comprising commercial finance, commercial aircraft leasing, real estate, and energy financial services, is its largest segment.

The GE business screen analysis provided a foundation for the IE Matrix discussed in this chapter. GE, with CEO Jack Welch, historically (and even today) has been used as a model for how diversified companies are supposed to be managed. GE operates through four segments (divisions): energy, technology infrastructure, capital finance, and consumer and industrial.

GE ranks number 6 among Fortune 500 firms and number 3 among Forbes Global 2000. Also in 2011–2012, GE ranks include number 7 company for leaders (*Fortune*), number 5 best global brand (*Interbrand*), number 63 green company (*Newsweek*), number 15 most admired company (*Fortune*), and number 19 most innovative company (*Fast Company*).

GE increased its investment in research and development by 16 percent in 2011 compared to the previous year, and international sales of U.S.-made products totaled $18 billion, a $1 billion increase from 2010. GE is currently investing $1 billion in its appliance business, modernizing their factories in the USA and moving parts of its manufacturing operations back to the USA from China and Mexico. GE is and always has been a model firm for strategic management in practice.

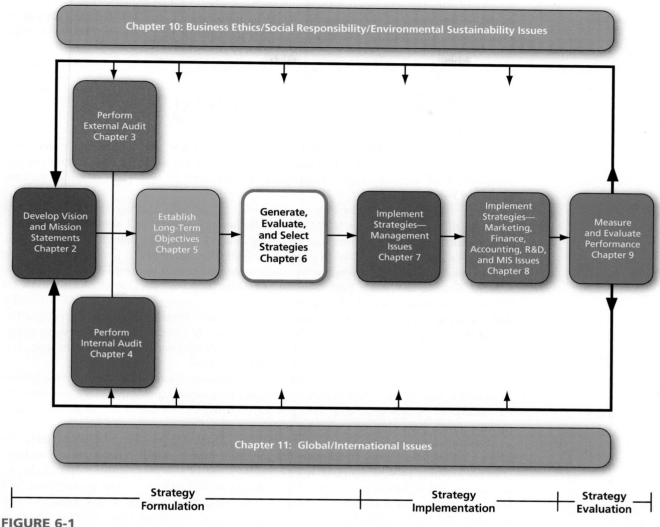

FIGURE 6-1

A Comprehensive Strategic-Management Model

Source: Fred R. David, "How Companies Define Their Mission," *Long Range Planning* 22, no. 3 (June 1988): 40.

of alternative strategies. Recommendations (strategies selected to pursue) come from alternative strategies formulated.

Identifying and evaluating alternative strategies should involve many of the managers and employees who previously assembled the organizational vision and mission statements, performed the external audit, and conducted the internal audit. Representatives from each department and division of the firm should be included in this process, as was the case in previous strategy-formulation activities. Recall that involvement provides the best opportunity for managers and employees to gain an understanding of what the firm is doing and why and to become committed to helping the firm accomplish its objectives.

All participants in the strategy analysis and choice activity should have the firm's external and internal audit information available. This information, coupled with the firm's mission statement, will help participants crystallize in their own minds particular strategies that they believe could benefit the firm most. Creativity should be encouraged in this thought process.

Alternative strategies proposed by participants should be considered and discussed in a meeting or series of meetings. Proposed strategies should be listed in writing. When all feasible strategies identified by participants are given and understood, the strategies should be ranked in order of attractiveness by all participants, with 1 = should not be implemented, 2 = possibly should be implemented, 3 = probably should be implemented, and 4 = definitely should be implemented. This process will result in a prioritized list of best strategies that reflects the collective wisdom of the group.

A Comprehensive Strategy-Formulation Analytical Framework

Important strategy-formulation techniques can be integrated into a three-stage decision-making framework, as shown in Figure 6-2. The tools presented in this framework are applicable to all sizes and types of organizations and can help strategists identify, evaluate, and select strategies.

Stage 1 of the formulation framework consists of the EFE Matrix, the IFE Matrix, and the Competitive Profile Matrix (CPM). Called the **input stage**, Stage 1 summarizes the basic input information needed to formulate strategies. Stage 2, called the **matching stage**, focuses on generating feasible alternative strategies by aligning key external and internal factors. Stage 2 techniques include the Strengths-Weaknesses-Opportunities-Threats (SWOT) Matrix, the Strategic Position and Action Evaluation (SPACE) Matrix, the Boston Consulting Group (BCG) Matrix, the Internal-External (IE) Matrix, and the Grand Strategy Matrix. Stage 3, called the **decision stage**, involves a single technique, the Quantitative Strategic Planning Matrix (QSPM). A QSPM uses input information from Stage 1 to objectively evaluate feasible alternative strategies identified in Stage 2. A QSPM reveals the relative attractiveness of alternative strategies and thus provides objective basis for selecting specific strategies.

All nine techniques included in the **strategy-formulation framework** require the integration of intuition and analysis. Autonomous divisions in an organization commonly use strategy-formulation techniques to develop strategies and objectives. Divisional analyses provide a basis for identifying, evaluating, and selecting among alternative corporate-level strategies.

Strategists themselves, not analytic tools, are always responsible and accountable for strategic decisions. Lenz emphasized that the shift from a words-oriented to a numbers-oriented planning process can give rise to a false sense of certainty; it can reduce dialogue, discussion, and argument as a means for exploring understandings, testing assumptions, and fostering organizational learning.[1] Strategists, therefore, must be wary of this possibility and use analytical tools to facilitate, rather than to diminish, communication. Without objective information and analysis, personal biases, politics, emotions, personalities, and **halo error** (the tendency to put too much weight on a single factor) unfortunately may play a dominant role in the strategy-formulation process.

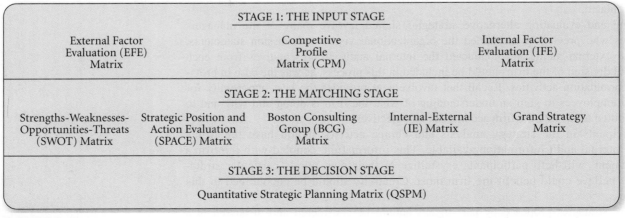

FIGURE 6-2

The Strategy-Formulation Analytical Framework

The Input Stage

Procedures for developing an EFE Matrix, an IFE Matrix, and a CPM were presented in Chapters 3 and 4. The information derived from these three matrices provides basic input information for the matching and decision stage matrices described later in this chapter.

The input tools require strategists to quantify subjectivity during early stages of the strategy-formulation process. Making small decisions in the input matrices regarding the relative importance of external and internal factors allows strategists to more effectively generate and evaluate alternative strategies. Good intuitive judgment is always needed in determining appropriate weights and ratings.

The Matching Stage

Strategy is sometimes defined as the match an organization makes between its internal resources and skills and the opportunities and risks created by its external factors.[2] The matching stage of the strategy-formulation framework consists of five techniques that can be used in any sequence: the SWOT Matrix, the SPACE Matrix, the BCG Matrix, the IE Matrix, and the Grand Strategy Matrix. These tools rely on information derived from the input stage to match external opportunities and threats with internal strengths and weaknesses. **Matching** external and internal critical success factors is the key to effectively generating feasible alternative strategies. For example, a firm with excess working capital (an internal strength) could take advantage of the cell phone industry's 20 percent annual growth rate (an external opportunity) by acquiring Cellfone, Inc., a firm in the cell phone industry. This example portrays simple one-to-one matching. In most situations, external and internal relationships are more complex, and the matching requires multiple alignments for each strategy generated. Successful matching of key external and internal factors depends upon those underlying key factors being both *specific* and *actionable*. The basic concept of matching is illustrated in Table 6-1.

Any organization, whether military, product-oriented, service-oriented, governmental, or even athletic, must develop and execute good strategies to win. A good offense without a good defense, or vice versa, usually leads to defeat. Developing strategies that use strengths to capitalize on opportunities could be considered an offense, whereas strategies designed to improve on weaknesses while avoiding threats could be termed defensive. Every organization has some external opportunities and threats and internal strengths and weaknesses that can be aligned to formulate feasible alternative strategies.

The SWOT Matrix

The **Strengths-Weaknesses-Opportunities-Threats (SWOT) Matrix** is an important matching tool that helps managers develop four types of strategies: SO (strengths-opportunities) strategies, WO (weaknesses-opportunities) strategies, ST (strengths-threats) strategies, and WT (weaknesses-threats) strategies.[3] Matching key external and internal factors is the most difficult part of developing a SWOT Matrix and requires good judgment—and there is no one best set of matches. Note in Table 6-1 that the first, second, third, and fourth strategies are SO, WO, ST, and WT strategies, respectively.

TABLE 6-1 Matching Key External and Internal Factors to Formulate Alternative Strategies

Key Internal Factor	Key External Factor	Resultant Strategy
Excess working capital (an internal strength)	+ 20 percent annual growth in the cell phone industry (an external opportunity)	= Acquire Cellfone, Inc.
Insufficient capacity (an internal weakness)	+ Exit of two major foreign competitors from the industry (an external opportunity)	= Pursue horizontal integration by buying competitors' facilities
Strong research and development expertise (an internal strength)	+ Decreasing numbers of younger adults (an external threat)	= Develop new products for older adults
Poor employee morale (an internal weakness)	+ Rising health-care costs (an external threat)	= Develop a new wellness program

SO strategies use a firm's internal strengths to take advantage of external opportunities. All managers would like their organization to be in a position in which internal strengths can be used to take advantage of external trends and events. Organizations generally will pursue WO, ST, or WT strategies to get into a situation in which they can apply SO strategies. When a firm has major weaknesses, it will strive to overcome them and make them strengths. When an organization faces major threats, it will seek to avoid them to concentrate on opportunities.

WO strategies aim at improving internal weaknesses by taking advantage of external opportunities. Sometimes key external opportunities exist, but a firm has internal weaknesses that prevent it from exploiting those opportunities. For example, there may be a high demand for electronic devices to control the amount and timing of fuel injection in automobile engines (opportunity), but a certain auto parts manufacturer may lack the technology required for producing these devices (weakness). One possible WO strategy would be to acquire this technology by forming a joint venture with a firm having competency in this area. An alternative WO strategy would be to hire and train people with the required technical capabilities.

ST strategies use a firm's strengths to avoid or reduce the impact of external threats. This does not mean that a strong organization should always meet threats in the external environment head-on. An example ST strategy occurred when Texas Instruments used an excellent legal department (a strength) to collect nearly $700 million in damages and royalties from nine Japanese and Korean firms that infringed on patents for semiconductor memory chips (threat). Rival firms that copy ideas, innovations, and patented products are a major threat in many industries. This is still a major problem for U.S. firms selling products in China.

WT strategies are defensive tactics directed at reducing internal weakness and avoiding external threats. An organization faced with numerous external threats and internal weaknesses may indeed be in a precarious position. In fact, such a firm may have to fight for its survival, merge, retrench, declare bankruptcy, or choose liquidation.

A schematic representation of the SWOT Matrix is provided in Figure 6-3. Note that a SWOT Matrix is composed of nine cells. As shown, there are four key factor cells, four strategy cells, and one cell that is always left blank (the upper-left cell). The four strategy cells, labeled *SO, WO, ST,* and *WT,* are developed after completing four key factor cells, labeled *S, W, O,* and *T.* There are eight steps involved in constructing a SWOT Matrix:

1. List the firm's key external opportunities.
2. List the firm's key external threats.
3. List the firm's key internal strengths.
4. List the firm's key internal weaknesses.
5. Match internal strengths with external opportunities, and record the resultant SO strategies in the appropriate cell.
6. Match internal weaknesses with external opportunities, and record the resultant WO strategies.
7. Match internal strengths with external threats, and record the resultant ST strategies.
8. Match internal weaknesses with external threats, and record the resultant WT strategies.

Some important aspects of a SWOT Matrix are evidenced in Figure 6-3. For example, note that both the internal and external factors and the SO, ST, WO, and WT strategies are stated in quantitative terms to the extent possible. This is important. For example, regarding the second SO number-2 and ST number-1 strategies, if the analyst just said, "Add new repair and service persons," the reader might think that 20 new repair and service persons are needed. Actually only two are needed. Always *be specific* to the extent possible in stating factors and strategies.

It is also important to include the "S1, O2" type notation after each strategy in a SWOT Matrix. This notation reveals the rationale for each alternative strategy. Strategies do not rise out of the blue. Note in Figure 6-3 how this notation reveals the internal and external factors that were matched to formulate desirable strategies. For example, note that this retail computer store business may need to "purchase land to build new store" because a new Highway 34 will make its location less desirable. The notation (W2, O2) and (S8, T3) in Figure 6-3 exemplifies this matching process.

The purpose of each Stage 2 matching tool is to generate feasible alternative strategies, not to select or determine which strategies are best. Not all of the strategies developed in the SWOT Matrix, therefore, will be selected for implementation.

The strategy-formulation guidelines provided in Chapter 5 can enhance the process of matching key external and internal factors. For example, when an organization has both the

	Strengths	Weaknesses
	1. Inventory turnover up 5.8 to 6.7	1. Software revenues in store down 12 percent
	2. Average customer purchase up $97 to $128	2. Location of store hurt by new Hwy 34
	3. Employee morale is excellent	3. Carpet and paint in store in disrepair
	4. In-store promotions = 20 percent increase in sales	4. Bathroom in store needs refurbishing
	5. Newspaper advertising expenditures down 10 percent	5. Total store revenues down 8 percent
	6. Revenues from repair and service in store up 16 percent	6. Store has no website
	7. In-store technical support persons have MIS degrees	7. Supplier on-time-delivery up to 2.4 days
	8. Store's debt-to-total-assets ratio down 34 percent	8. Customer checkout process too slow
		9. Revenues per employee up 19 percent
Opportunities	**SO Strategies**	**WO Strategies**
1. Population of city growing 10 percent	1. Add four new in-store promotions monthly (S4, O3)	1. Purchase land to build new store (W2, O2)
2. Rival computer store opening one mile away	2. Add two new repair and service persons (S6, O5)	2. Install new carpet, paint, and bath (W3, W4, O1)
3. Vehicle traffic passing store up 12 percent	3. Send flyer to all seniors over age 55 (S5, O5)	3. Up website services by 50 percent (W6, O7, O8)
4. Vendors average six new products a year		4. Launch mailout to all realtors in city (W5, O7)
5. Senior citizen use of computers up 8 percent		
6. Small business growth in area up 10 percent		
7. Desire for websites up 18 percent by realtors		
8. Desire for websites up 12 percent by small firms		
Threats	**ST Strategies**	**WT Strategies**
1. Best Buy opening new store in one year nearby	1. Hire two more repair persons and market these new services (S6, S7, T1)	1. Hire two new cashiers (W8, T1, T4)
2. Local university offers computer repair	2. Purchase land to build new store (S8, T3)	2. Install new carpet, paint, and bath (W3, W4, T1)
3. New bypass Hwy 34 in 1 year will divert traffic	3. Raise out-of-store service calls from $60 to $80 (S6, T5)	
4. New mall being built nearby		
5. Gas prices up 14 percent		
6. Vendors raising prices 8 percent		

FIGURE 6-3

A SWOT Matrix for a Retail Computer Store

capital and human resources needed to distribute its own products (internal strength) and distributors are unreliable, costly, or incapable of meeting the firm's needs (external threat), forward integration can be an attractive ST strategy. When a firm has excess production capacity (internal weakness) and its basic industry is experiencing declining annual sales and profits (external threat), related diversification can be an effective WT strategy.

Although the SWOT matrix is widely used in strategic planning, the analysis does have some limitations.[4] First, SWOT does not show how to achieve a competitive advantage, so it must not be an end in itself. The matrix should be the starting point for a discussion on how proposed strategies could be implemented as well as cost-benefit considerations that ultimately could lead to competitive advantage. Second, SWOT is a static assessment (or snapshot) in time.

A SWOT matrix can be like studying a single frame of a motion picture where you see the lead characters and the setting but have no clue as to the plot. As circumstances, capabilities, threats, and strategies change, the dynamics of a competitive environment may not be revealed in a single matrix. Third, SWOT analysis may lead the firm to overemphasize a single internal or external factor in formulating strategies. There are interrelationships among the key internal and external factors that SWOT does not reveal that may be important in devising strategies.

The Strategic Position and Action Evaluation (SPACE) Matrix

The **Strategic Position and Action Evaluation (SPACE) Matrix**, another important Stage 2 matching tool, is illustrated in Figure 6-4. Its four-quadrant framework indicates whether aggressive, conservative, defensive, or competitive strategies are most appropriate for a given organization. The axes of the SPACE Matrix represent two internal dimensions (**financial position [FP]** and **competitive position [CP]**) and two external dimensions (**stability position [SP]** and **industry position [IP]**). These four factors are perhaps the most important determinants of an organization's overall strategic position.[5]

It is helpful here to elaborate upon the difference between the SP and IP axes. SP refers to the volatility of profits and revenues for firms in a given industry. SP volatility (stability) is based on the expected impact of changes in core external factors such as technology, economy, demographic, seasonality, etc.) The higher frequency and magnitude of the changes the more unstable on SP. An industry can be stable or unstable on SP, yet high or low on IP. The smartphone industry for example would be unstable on SP yet high growth on IP, whereas the carbonated beverage industry would be stable on SP yet low growth on IP.

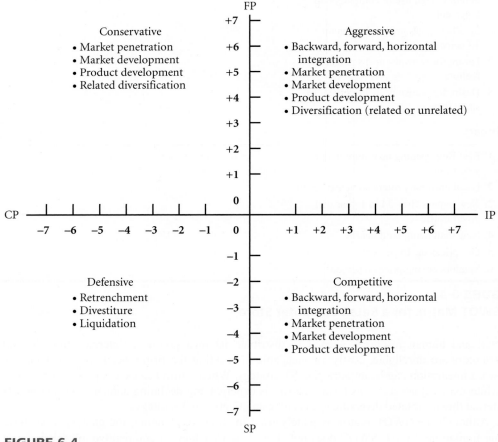

FIGURE 6-4

The SPACE Matrix

Source: Based on H. Rowe, R. Mason, and K. Dickel, *Strategic Management and Business Policy: A Methodological Approach* (Reading, MA: Addison-Wesley Publishing Co. Inc., © 1982), 155.

Depending on the type of organization, numerous variables could make up each of the dimensions represented on the axes of the SPACE Matrix. Factors that were included in the firm's EFE and IFE matrices should be considered in developing a SPACE Matrix. Other variables commonly included are given in Table 6-2. For example, return on investment, leverage, liquidity, working capital, and cash flow are commonly considered to be determining factors of an organization's financial strength. Like the SWOT Matrix, the SPACE Matrix should be both tailored to the particular organization being studied and based on factual information as much as possible.

The steps required to develop a SPACE Matrix are as follows:

1. Select a set of variables to define financial position (FP), competitive position (CP), stability position (SP), and industry position (IP).
2. Assign a numerical value ranging from +1 (worst) to +7 (best) to each of the variables that make up the FP and IP dimensions. Assign a numerical value ranging from –1 (best) to –7 (worst) to each of the variables that make up the SP and CP dimensions. On the FP and CP axes, make comparison to competitors. On the IP and SP axes, make comparison to other industries.
3. Compute an average score for FP, CP, IP, and SP by summing the values given to the variables of each dimension and then by dividing by the number of variables included in the respective dimension.
4. Plot the average scores for FP, IP, SP, and CP on the appropriate axis in the SPACE Matrix.
5. Add the two scores on the *x*-axis and plot the resultant point on X. Add the two scores on the *y*-axis and plot the resultant point on Y. Plot the intersection of the new *xy* point.
6. Draw a **directional vector** from the origin of the SPACE Matrix through the new intersection point. This vector reveals the type of strategies recommended for the organization: aggressive, competitive, defensive, or conservative.

Some examples of strategy profiles that can emerge from a SPACE analysis are shown in Figure 6-5. The directional vector associated with each profile suggests the type of strategies to pursue: aggressive, conservative, defensive, or competitive. When a firm's directional vector is located in the **aggressive quadrant** (upper-right quadrant) of the SPACE Matrix, an organization is in an excellent position to use its internal strengths to (a) take advantage of external opportunities, (b) overcome internal weaknesses, and (c) avoid external threats. Therefore, market penetration, market

TABLE 6-2 Example Factors That Make Up the SPACE Matrix Axes

Internal Strategic Position	External Strategic Position
Financial Position (FP)	*Stability Position (SP)*
Return on investment	Technological changes
Leverage	Rate of inflation
Liquidity	Demand variability
Working capital	Price range of competing products
Cash flow	Barriers to entry into market
Inventory turnover	Competitive pressure
Earnings per share	Ease of exit from market
Price earnings ratio	Price elasticity of demand
	Risk involved in business
Competitive Position (CP)	*Industry Position (IP)*
Market share	Growth potential
Product quality	Profit potential
Product life cycle	Financial stability
Customer loyalty	Extent leveraged
Capacity utilization	Resource utilization
Technological know-how	Ease of entry into market
Control over suppliers and distributors	Productivity, capacity utilization

Source: Based on H. Rowe, R. Mason, and K. Dickel, *Strategic Management and Business Policy: A Methodological Approach* (Reading, MA: Addison-Wesley Publishing Co. Inc., © 1982), 155–156.

development, product development, backward integration, forward integration, horizontal integration, or diversification, can be feasible, depending on the specific circumstances that face the firm.

When a particular company is known, the analyst must be much more specific in terms of recommended strategies. For example, instead of saying market penetration is a recommended

Aggressive Profiles

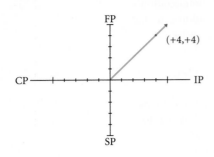

A financially strong firm that has achieved major competitive advantages in a growing and stable industry

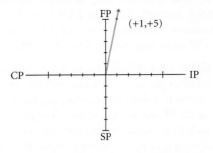

A firm whose financial strength is a dominating factor in the industry

Conservative Profiles

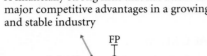

A firm that has achieved financial strength in a stable industry that is not growing; the firm has few competitive advantages

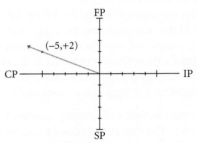

A firm that suffers from major competitive disadvantages in an industry that is technologically stable but declining in sales

Competitive Profiles

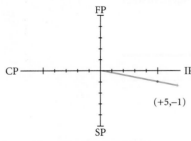

A firm with major competitive advantages in a high-growth industry

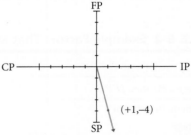

An organization that is competing fairly well in an unstable industry

Defensive Profiles

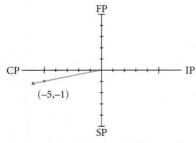

A firm that has a very weak competitive position in a negative growth, stable industry

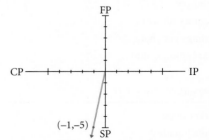

A financially troubled firm in a very unstable industry

FIGURE 6-5

Example Strategy Profiles

Source: Based on H. Rowe, R. Mason, and K. Dickel, *Strategic Management and Business Policy: A Methodological Approach* (Reading, MA: Addison-Wesley Publishing Co. Inc., © 1982), 155.

strategy when your vector goes in the conservative quadrant, say that adding 34 new stores in India is a recommended strategy. This is an important point for students doing case analyses because a particular company is generally known, and terms such as *market development* are too vague to use. That term could refer to adding a manufacturing plant in Thailand or Mexico or South Africa—*so students—be specific to the extent possible regarding implications of all the matrices presented in this chapter. Not being specific can be disastrous in this course. Avoid terms like expand, increase, decrease, grow—be much more specific than that!*

The directional vector may appear in the **conservative quadrant** (upper-left quadrant) of the SPACE Matrix, which implies staying close to the firm's basic competencies and not taking excessive risks. Conservative strategies most often include market penetration, market development, product development, and related diversification. The directional vector may be located in the lower-left or **defensive quadrant** of the SPACE Matrix, which suggests that the firm should focus on rectifying internal weaknesses and avoiding external threats. Defensive strategies include retrenchment, divestiture, liquidation, and related diversification. Finally, the directional vector may be located in the lower-right or **competitive quadrant** of the SPACE Matrix, indicating competitive strategies. Competitive strategies include backward, forward, and horizontal integration; market penetration; market development; and product development.

A SPACE Matrix analysis for a bank is provided in Table 6-3. Note that competitive type strategies are recommended. A SPACE Matrix for Hewlett-Packard (HP) is given in

TABLE 6-3 A SPACE Matrix for a Bank

Financial Position (FP)	Ratings
The bank's primary capital ratio is 7.23 percent, which is 1.23 percentage points over the generally required ratio of 6 percent.	1.0
The bank's return on assets is negative 0.77, compared to a bank industry average ratio of positive 0.70.	1.0
The bank's net income was $183 million, down 9 percent from a year previously.	3.0
The bank's revenues increased 7 percent to $3.46 billion.	4.0
	9.0

Industry Position (IP)	
Deregulation provides geographic and product freedom.	4.0
Deregulation increases competition in the banking industry.	2.0
Pennsylvania's interstate banking law allows the bank to acquire other banks in New Jersey, Ohio, Kentucky, the District of Columbia, and West Virginia.	4.0
	10.0

Stability Position (SP)	
Less-developed countries are experiencing high inflation and political instability.	−4.0
Headquartered in Pittsburgh, the bank historically has been heavily dependent on the steel, oil, and gas industries. These industries are depressed.	−5.0
Banking deregulation has created instability throughout the industry.	−4.0
	−13.0

Competitive Position (CP)	
The bank provides data processing services for more than 450 institutions in 38 states.	−2.0
Superregional banks, international banks, and nonbanks are becoming increasingly competitive.	−5.0
The bank has a large customer base.	−2.0
	−9.0

Conclusion

SP Average is −13.0 ÷ 3 = −4.33   IP Average is +10.0 ÷ 3 = 3.33

CP Average is −9.0 ÷ 3 = −3.00   FP Average is +9.0 ÷ 4 = 2.25

Directional Vector Coordinates: x-axis: −3.00 + (+3.33) = +0.33

y-axis: −4.33 + (+2.25) = −2.08

The bank should pursue competitive strategies.

TABLE 6-4 An Actual SPACE Matrix for Hewlett-Packard

Internal Analysis		External Analysis	
Financial Position (FP)		Stability Position (SP)	
Return on Investment (ROI)	1	Rate of Inflation	−2
Leverage	4	Technological Changes	−6
Liquidity	2	Price Elasticity of Demand	−3
Working Capital	1	Competitive Pressure	−7
Cash Flow	2	Barriers to Entry into Market	−4
Financial Position (FP) Average	**2**	**Stability Position (SP) Average**	**−4.4**
Internal Analysis		External Analysis	
Competitive Position (CP)		Industry Position (IP)	
Market Share	−7	Growth Potential	6
Product Quality	−2	Financial Stability	2
Customer Loyalty	−3	Ease of Entry into Market	4
Technological Know-how	−4	Resource Utilization	1
Control over Suppliers/Distributors	−5	Profit Potential	2
Competitive Position (CP) Average	**−4.2**	**Industry Position (IP) Average**	**3.0**

2.0 + (−4.4) = −2.4   y-axis
3.0 + (−4.2) = −1.2   x-axis
Coordinate (−1.2, −2.4)
Conclusion: Vector points in defensive quadrant

Table 6-4 followed by the Krispy Kreme Donuts SPACE diagram in Figure 6-6. Note that HP is in a precarious defensive position, struggling to compete against Apple, Dell, and Amazon.

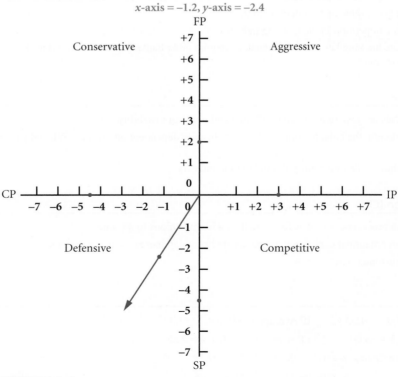

FIGURE 6-6

A SPACE Matrix for Krispy Kreme

The Boston Consulting Group (BCG) Matrix

Based in Boston and having 1,713 employees, the Boston Consulting Group (BCG) is a large consulting firm that endured the recent economic downturn without laying off any employees and in 2010 hired the most new consultants ever. BCG ranks number 2 in *Fortune*'s recent list of the "100 Best Companies To Work For."

Autonomous divisions (or profit centers) of an organization make up what is called a **business portfolio**. When a firm's divisions compete in different industries, a separate strategy often must be developed for each business. The Boston Consulting Group (BCG) Matrix and the Internal-External (IE) Matrix are designed specifically to enhance a multidivisional firm's efforts to formulate strategies. (BCG is a private management consulting firm based in Boston that currently employs about 4,400 consultants in 40 countries.)

In a *Form 10K* or *Annual Report*, some companies do not disclose financial information by segment, in which case a BCG portfolio analysis may not be possible by persons external to the firm. Reasons to disclose by-division financial information in the author's view, however, more than offset the reasons not to disclose, as indicated in Table 6-5.

The BCG Matrix graphically portrays differences among divisions in terms of relative market share position and industry growth rate. The BCG Matrix allows a multidivisional organization to manage its portfolio of businesses by examining the relative market share position and the industry growth rate of each division relative to all other divisions in the organization. **Relative market share position** is defined as the ratio of a division's own market share (or revenues) in a particular industry to the market share (or revenues) held by the largest rival firm in that industry. Note in Table 6-6 that other variables can be used in this analysis besides revenues. For example, number of stores, or number of restaurants, or in the airline industry number of airplanes could be used for comparative purposes to determine relative market share position. Relative market share position for Enterprise Rent-a-Car based on number of locations is $6,187/6,187 = 1.00$ as indicated in Table 6-6. Enterprise is the largest rental car company and its circle in a BCG Matrix would be somewhere along the far left axis.

Relative market share position is given on the *x*-axis of the BCG Matrix. The midpoint on the *x*-axis usually is set at 0.50, corresponding to a division that has half the market share of the leading firm in the industry. The *y*-axis represents the industry growth rate in sales, measured in percentage terms. The growth rate percentages on the *y*-axis could range from −20 to +20 percent, with 0.0 being the midpoint. The average annual increase in revenues for several leading firms in the industry would be a good estimate of the value. Also, various sources such as the S&P Industry Survey would provide this value. These numerical ranges on the *x*- and *y*-axes are often used, but other numerical values could be

TABLE 6-5 **Reasons to (or Not to) Disclose Financial Information by Segment (by Division)**

Reasons to Disclose	Reasons Not to Disclose
1. Transparency is a good thing in today's world of Sarbanes-Oxley	1. Can become free competitive information for rival firms
2. Investors will better understand the firm, which can lead to greater support	2. Can hide performance failures
3. Managers and employees will better understand the firm, which should lead to greater commitment	3. Can reduce rivalry among segments
4. Disclosure enhances the communication process both within the firm and with outsiders	

TABLE 6-6   Market Share Data for Selected Industries

Hard Cider (consumption growing rapidly; has about 5 percent alcohol; consumed 50/50 by men/women versus 80/20 men/women for beer; sweeter than beer); *WSJ*, 8-15-12, B9—Top hard cider brands in the USA in millions of liters sold in 2011.

Brand	Liters	Owner
Woodchuck Cider	14.1	Vermont Hard Cider
Strongbow Cider	6.9	Heineken NV
Hornsby's Cider	6.8	C&C Group PLC
Magners	6.2	C&C Group PLC
Ace Cider	2.1	California Cider Co.
Crispin Cider	1.0	MillerCoors LLC
Michelob Cider	1.0	Anheuser-Busch InBev NV
Angry Orchard Cider	1.0	Boston Beer Co. (maker of Sam Adams lager)
Other Ciders	60.9	
Total	100.0	

USA Car Rental Industry (*USA Today*, 8-28-12, p. 1B)

Brand	Number of Cars	Number of Locations	Airport Market Share (%)
Enterprise	920K	6,187	34
Hertz/Advantage/ Dollar Thrifty	438K	2,945	37
Avis/Budget	285K	2,300	26
Other	106K	978	03
TOTAL	1,749K	2,410	

Smartphones in the USA (*USA Today*, 10-18-12, p. 4B)

Brand	Market Share (%)
Apple	37.3
Samsung	27.0
LG	7.9
Motorola	6.7

Note: Ireland's C&C Group PLC is trying to acquire Vermont Hard Cider, maker of the best-selling Woodchuck cider. For many Americans until the mid-19th century, hard cider was the go-to alcoholic beverage, until drinkers turned to beer. Today in the USA, hard cider represents less than 0.5 percent of beer consumption, compared to the UK where it is closer to 15 percent. But hard cider, which has an alcohol content of about 5 percent like beer, is mounting a comeback in the USA.

established as deemed appropriate for particular organizations, such as -10 to +10 percent on the *y*-axis.

The basic BCG Matrix appears in Figure 6-7. Each circle represents a separate division. The size of the circle corresponds to the proportion of corporate revenue generated by that business unit, and the pie slice indicates the proportion of corporate profits generated by that division. Divisions located in Quadrant I of the BCG Matrix are called "Question Marks," those located in Quadrant II are called "Stars," those located in Quadrant III are called "Cash Cows," and those divisions located in Quadrant IV are called "Dogs."

- *Question Marks*—Divisions in Quadrant I have a low relative market share position, yet they compete in a high-growth industry. Generally these firms' cash needs are high and their cash generation is low. These businesses are called **question marks** because the organization must decide whether to strengthen them by pursuing an intensive

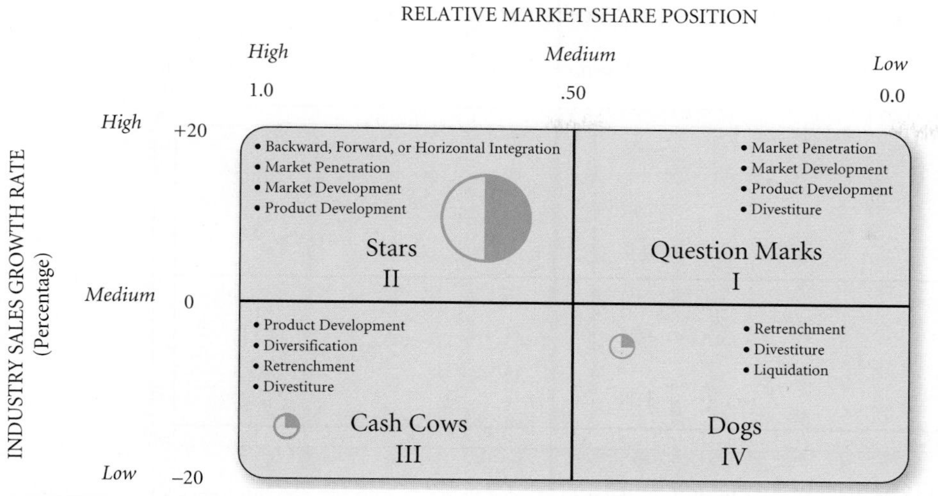

RELATIVE MARKET SHARE POSITION

FIGURE 6-7

The BCG Matrix

Source: Based on the BCG Portfolio Matrix from the Product Portfolio Matrix, © 1970, The Boston Consulting Group.

strategy (market penetration, market development, or product development) or to sell them.

- *Stars*—Quadrant II businesses (**stars**) represent the organization's best long-run opportunities for growth and profitability. Divisions with a high relative market share and a high industry growth rate should receive substantial investment to maintain or strengthen their dominant positions. Forward, backward, and horizontal integration; market penetration; market development; and product development are appropriate strategies for these divisions to consider, as indicated in Figure 6-7.
- *Cash Cows*—Divisions positioned in Quadrant III have a high relative market share position but compete in a low-growth industry. Called **cash cows** because they generate cash in excess of their needs, they are often milked. Many of today's cash cows were yesterday's stars. Cash cow divisions should be managed to maintain their strong position for as long as possible. Product development or diversification may be attractive strategies for strong cash cows. However, as a cash cow division becomes weak, retrenchment or divestiture can become more appropriate.
- *Dogs*—Quadrant IV divisions of the organization have a low relative market share position and compete in a slow- or no-market-growth industry; they are **dogs** in the firm's portfolio. Because of their weak internal and external position, these businesses are often liquidated, divested, or trimmed down through retrenchment. When a division first becomes a dog, retrenchment can be the best strategy to pursue because many Dogs have bounced back, after strenuous asset and cost reduction, to become viable, profitable divisions.

The major benefit of the BCG Matrix is that it draws attention to the cash flow, investment characteristics, and needs of an organization's various divisions. The divisions of many firms evolve over time: dogs become question marks, question marks become stars, stars become cash cows, and cash cows become dogs in an ongoing counterclockwise motion. Less frequently, stars become question marks, question marks become dogs, dogs become cash cows, and cash cows become stars (in a clockwise motion). In some organizations, no cyclical motion is apparent. Over time, organizations should strive to achieve a portfolio of divisions that are stars.

An example BCG Matrix is provided in Figure 6-8, which illustrates an organization composed of five divisions with annual sales ranging from $5,000 to $60,000. Division 1 has

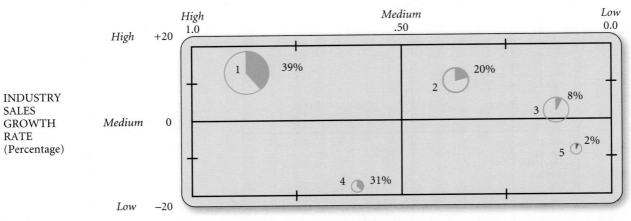

Division	Revenues	Percent Revenues	Profits	Percent Profits	Relative Market Share	Industry Growth Rate (%)
1	$60,000	37	$10,000	39	.80	+15
2	40,000	24	5,000	20	.40	+10
3	40,000	24	2,000	8	.10	+1
4	20,000	12	8,000	31	.60	−20
5	5,000	3	500	2	.05	−10
Total	**$165,000**	**100**	**$25,500**	**100**	—	—

FIGURE 6-8

An Example BCG Matrix

the greatest sales volume, so the circle representing that division is the largest one in the matrix. The circle corresponding to Division 5 is the smallest because its sales volume ($5,000) is least among all the divisions. The pie slices within the circles reveal the percent of corporate profits contributed by each division. As shown, Division 1 contributes the highest profit percentage, 39 percent, as indicated by 39 percent of the area within circle 1 being shaded. Notice in the diagram that Division 1 is considered a star, Division 2 is a question mark, Division 3 is also a question mark, Division 4 is a cash cow, and Division 5 is a dog.

The BCG Matrix, like all analytical techniques, has some limitations. For example, viewing every business as a star, cash cow, dog, or question mark is an oversimplification; many businesses fall right in the middle of the BCG Matrix and thus are not easily classified. Furthermore, the BCG Matrix does not reflect whether or not various divisions or their industries are growing over time; that is, the matrix has no temporal qualities, but rather it is a snapshot of an organization at a given point in time. Finally, other variables besides relative market share position and industry growth rate in sales, such as size of the market and competitive advantages, are important in making strategic decisions about various divisions.

An example BCG Matrix is provided in Figure 6-9. Note in Figure 6-9 that Division 5 had an operating loss of $188 million. Take note how the percent profit column is still calculated because oftentimes a firm will have a division that incurs a loss for a year. In terms of the pie slice in circle 5 of the diagram, note that it is a *different color* from the positive profit segments in the other circles.

The Internal-External (IE) Matrix

The **Internal-External (IE) Matrix** positions an organization's various divisions in a nine-cell display, illustrated in Figure 6-10. The IE Matrix is similar to the BCG Matrix in that both tools involve plotting organization divisions in a schematic diagram; this is why they are both called "portfolio matrices." Also, the size of each circle represents the percentage sales contribution of each division, and pie slices reveal the percentage profit contribution of each division in both the BCG and IE Matrix.

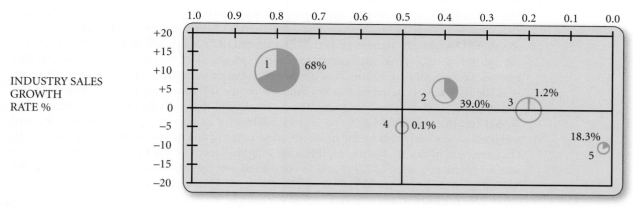

RELATIVE MARKET SHARE POSITION (RMSP)

Division	$ Sales (millions)	% Sales	$ Profits (millions)	% Profits	RMSP	IG Rate %
1.	$5,139	51.5	$799	68.0	0.8	10
2.	2,556	25.6	400	39.0	0.4	05
3.	1,749	17.5	12	1.2	0.2	00
4.	493	4.9	4	0.1	0.5	−05
5.	42	0.5	−188	(18.3)	.02	−10
Total	**$9,979**	**100.0**	**$1,027**	**100.0**		

FIGURE 6-9

An Example BCG Matrix

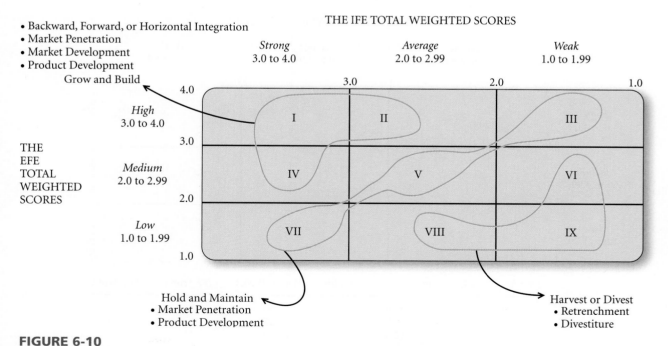

FIGURE 6-10

The Internal–External (IE) Matrix

Source: Based on: The IE Matrix was developed from the General Electric (GE) Business Screen Matrix. For a description of the GE Matrix, see Michael Allen, "Diagramming GE's Planning for What's WATT," in R. Allio and M. Pennington, eds., *Corporate Planning: Techniques and Applications* l par; New York: AMACOM, 1979.

But there are some important differences between the BCG Matrix and the IE Matrix. First, the axes are different. Also, the IE Matrix requires more information about the divisions than the BCG Matrix. Furthermore, the strategic implications of each matrix are different. For these reasons, strategists in multidivisional firms often develop both the BCG Matrix and the IE Matrix in formulating alternative strategies. A common practice is to develop a BCG Matrix and an IE Matrix for the present and then develop projected matrices to reflect expectations of the future. This before-and-after analysis forecasts the expected effect of strategic decisions on an organization's portfolio of divisions.

The IE Matrix is based on two key dimensions: the IFE total weighted scores on the *x*-axis and the EFE total weighted scores on the *y*-axis. Recall that each division of an organization should construct an IFE Matrix and an EFE Matrix for its part of the organization. The total weighted scores derived from the divisions allow construction of the corporate-level IE Matrix. On the *x*-axis of the IE Matrix, an IFE total weighted score of 1.0 to 1.99 represents a weak internal position; a score of 2.0 to 2.99 is considered average; and a score of 3.0 to 4.0 is strong. Similarly, on the *y*-axis, an EFE total weighted score of 1.0 to 1.99 is considered low; a score of 2.0 to 2.99 is medium; and a score of 3.0 to 4.0 is high.

The IE Matrix can be divided into three major regions that have different strategy implications. First, the prescription for divisions that fall into cells I, II, or IV can be described as *grow and build*. Intensive (market penetration, market development, and product development) or integrative (backward integration, forward integration, and horizontal integration) strategies can be most appropriate for these divisions. Second, divisions that fall into cells III, V, or VII can be managed best with *hold and maintain* strategies; market penetration and product development are two commonly employed strategies for these types of divisions. Third, a common prescription for divisions that fall into cells VI, VIII, or IX is *harvest or divest*. Successful organizations are able to achieve a portfolio of businesses positioned in or around cell I in the IE Matrix.

An example of a completed IE Matrix is given in Figure 6-11, which depicts an organization composed of four divisions. As indicated by the positioning of the circles, *grow and build* strategies are appropriate for Division 1, Division 2, and Division 3. Division 4 is a candidate for *harvest or divest*. Division 2 contributes the greatest percentage of company sales and thus is represented by the largest circle. Division 1 contributes the greatest proportion of total profits; it has the largest-percentage pie slice.

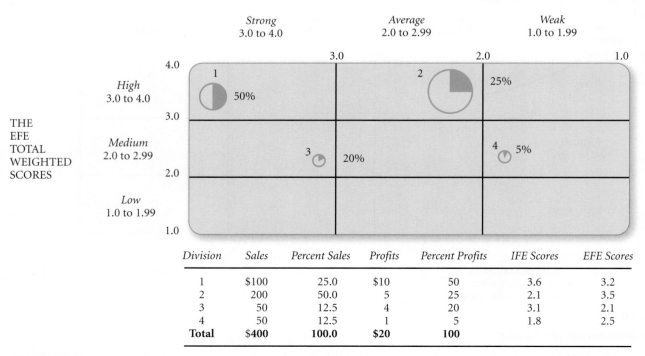

THE IFE TOTAL WEIGHTED SCORES

Division	Sales	Percent Sales	Profits	Percent Profits	IFE Scores	EFE Scores
1	$100	25.0	$10	50	3.6	3.2
2	200	50.0	5	25	2.1	3.5
3	50	12.5	4	20	3.1	2.1
4	50	12.5	1	5	1.8	2.5
Total	**$400**	**100.0**	**$20**	**100**		

FIGURE 6-11

An Example IE Matrix

THE IFE TOTAL WEIGHTED SCORES

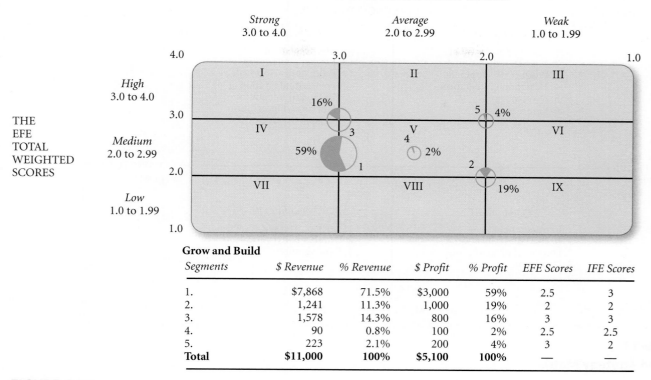

Grow and Build						
Segments	$ Revenue	% Revenue	$ Profit	% Profit	EFE Scores	IFE Scores
1.	$7,868	71.5%	$3,000	59%	2.5	3
2.	1,241	11.3%	1,000	19%	2	2
3.	1,578	14.3%	800	16%	3	3
4.	90	0.8%	100	2%	2.5	2.5
5.	223	2.1%	200	4%	3	2
Total	**$11,000**	**100%**	**$5,100**	**100%**	—	—

FIGURE 6-12
The IE Matrix

As indicated in Figure 6-12, the IE Matrix has five product segments. Note that Division 1 has the largest revenues (as indicated by the largest circle) and the largest profits (as indicated by the largest pie slice) in the matrix. It is common for organizations to develop both geographic and product-based IE Matrices to more effectively formulate strategies and allocate resources among divisions. In addition, firms often prepare an IE (or BCG) Matrix for competitors. Furthermore, firms will often prepare "before and after" IE (or BCG) Matrices to reveal the situation at present versus the expected situation after one year. This latter idea minimizes the limitation of these matrices being a "snapshot in time." In performing case analysis, feel free to estimate the IFE and EFE scores for the various divisions based upon your research into the company and industry—rather than preparing a separate IE Matrix for each division.

The Grand Strategy Matrix

In addition to the SWOT Matrix, SPACE Matrix, BCG Matrix, and IE Matrix, the **Grand Strategy Matrix** has become a popular tool for formulating alternative strategies. All organizations can be positioned in one of the Grand Strategy Matrix's four strategy quadrants. A firm's divisions likewise could be positioned. As illustrated in Figure 6-13, the Grand Strategy Matrix is based on two evaluative dimensions: competitive position and market (industry) growth. Any industry whose annual growth in sales exceeds 5 percent could be considered to have rapid growth. Appropriate strategies for an organization to consider are listed in sequential order of attractiveness in each quadrant of the matrix.

Firms located in Quadrant I of the Grand Strategy Matrix are in an excellent strategic position. For these firms, continued concentration on current markets (market penetration and market development) and products (product development) is an appropriate strategy. It is unwise for a Quadrant I firm to shift notably from its established competitive advantages. When a Quadrant I organization has excessive resources, then backward, forward, or horizontal integration may be effective strategies. When a Quadrant I firm is too heavily committed to a single product, then

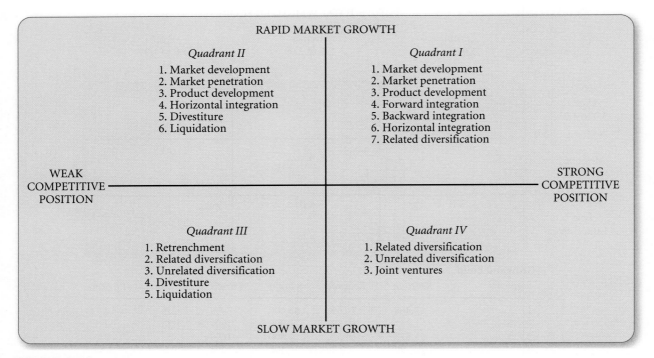

FIGURE 6-13

The Grand Strategy Matrix

Source: Based on Roland Christensen, Norman Berg, and Malcolm Salter, *Policy Formulation and Administration* (Homewood, IL: Richard D. Irwin, 1976), 16–18.

related diversification may reduce the risks associated with a narrow product line. Quadrant I firms can afford to take advantage of external opportunities in several areas. They can take risks aggressively when necessary.

Firms positioned in Quadrant II need to evaluate their present approach to the marketplace seriously. Although their industry is growing, they are unable to compete effectively, and they need to determine why the firm's current approach is ineffective and how the company can best change to improve its competitiveness. Because Quadrant II firms are in a rapid-market-growth industry, an intensive strategy (as opposed to integrative or diversification) is usually the first option that should be considered. However, if the firm is lacking a distinctive competence or competitive advantage, then horizontal integration is often a desirable alternative. As a last resort, divestiture or liquidation should be considered. Divestiture can provide funds needed to acquire other businesses or buy back shares of stock.

Quadrant III organizations compete in slow-growth industries and have weak competitive positions. These firms must make some drastic changes quickly to avoid further decline and possible liquidation. Extensive cost and asset reduction (retrenchment) should be pursued first. An alternative strategy is to shift resources away from the current business into different areas (diversify). If all else fails, the final options for Quadrant III businesses are divestiture or liquidation.

Finally, Quadrant IV businesses have a strong competitive position but are in a slow-growth industry. These firms have the strength to launch diversified programs into more promising growth areas: Quadrant IV firms have characteristically high cash-flow levels and limited internal growth needs and often can pursue related or unrelated diversification successfully. Quadrant IV firms also may pursue joint ventures.

Students: Even with the Grand Strategy Matrix, be sure to state your alternative strategies in *specific* terms whenever a particular company is known. Avoid using terms such as divestiture for example. Rather, specify the exact division to be sold. Also, be sure to use the free excel student template at www.strategyclub.com if you like.

The Decision Stage

Analysis and intuition provide a basis for making strategy-formulation decisions. The matching techniques just discussed reveal feasible alternative strategies. Many of these strategies will likely have been proposed by managers and employees participating in the strategy analysis and choice activity. Any additional strategies resulting from the matching analyses could be discussed and added to the list of feasible alternative options. As indicated previously in this chapter, participants could rate these strategies on a 1-to-4-scale so that a prioritized list of the best strategies could be achieved.

The Quantitative Strategic Planning Matrix (QSPM)

Other than ranking strategies to achieve the prioritized list, there is only one analytical technique in the literature designed to determine the relative attractiveness of feasible alternative actions. This technique is the **Quantitative Strategic Planning Matrix (QSPM)**, which comprises Stage 3 of the strategy-formulation analytical framework.[6] This technique objectively indicates which alternative strategies are best. The QSPM uses input from Stage 1 analyses and matching results from Stage 2 analyses to decide objectively among alternative strategies. That is, the EFE Matrix, IFE Matrix, and CPM that comprise Stage 1, coupled with the SWOT Matrix, SPACE Matrix, BCG Matrix, IE Matrix, and Grand Strategy Matrix that comprise Stage 2, provide the needed information for setting up the QSPM (Stage 3). The QSPM is a tool that allows strategists to evaluate alternative strategies objectively, based on previously identified external and internal key success factors. Like other strategy-formulation analytical tools, the QSPM requires good intuitive judgment.

The basic format of the QSPM is illustrated in Table 6-7. Note that the left column of a QSPM consists of key external and internal factors (from Stage 1), and the top row consists of feasible alternative strategies (from Stage 2). Specifically, the left column of a QSPM consists of information obtained directly from the EFE Matrix and IFE Matrix. In a column adjacent to the key success factors, the respective weights received by each factor in the EFE Matrix and the IFE Matrix are recorded.

The top row of a QSPM consists of alternative strategies derived from the SWOT Matrix, SPACE Matrix, BCG Matrix, IE Matrix, and Grand Strategy Matrix. These matching tools usually generate similar feasible alternatives. However, not every strategy suggested by the matching techniques has to be evaluated in a QSPM. Strategists should compare several viable alternative strategies in a QSPM. Make sure your strategies are stated in specific terms, such

TABLE 6-7   The Quantitative Strategic Planning Matrix—QSPM

Key Factors		Strategic Alternatives		
	Weight	Strategy 1	Strategy 2	Strategy 3
Key External Factors				
Economy				
Political/Legal/Governmental				
Social/Cultural/Demographic/Environmental				
Technological				
Competitive				
Key Internal Factors				
Management				
Marketing				
Finance/Accounting				
Production/Operations				
Research and Development				
Management Information Systems				

as "Open 275 new stores in Indonesia" rather than "Expand globally" or "Open new stores in Africa." In Chapter 8, you will see that a dollar value must be established for each recommended strategy; it would be impossible to establish a dollar value for "expand globally."

Conceptually, the QSPM determines the relative attractiveness of various strategies based on the extent to which key external and internal critical success factors are capitalized on or improved. The relative attractiveness of each strategy within a set of alternatives is computed by determining the cumulative impact of each external and internal critical success factor. Any number of sets of alternative strategies can be included in the QSPM, and any number of strategies can make up a given set, but only strategies within a given set are evaluated relative to each other. For example, one set of strategies may include diversification, whereas another set may include issuing stock and selling a division to raise needed capital. These two sets of strategies are totally different, and the QSPM evaluates strategies only within sets. Note in Table 6-7 that three strategies are included, and they make up just one set.

A QSPM for a retail computer store is provided in Table 6-8. This example illustrates all the components of the QSPM: strategic alternatives, key factors, weights, attractiveness scores (AS), total attractiveness scores (TAS), and the sum total attractiveness score. The three new terms just introduced—(1) attractiveness scores, (2) total attractiveness scores, and (3) the sum total attractiveness score—are defined and explained as the six steps required to develop a QSPM are discussed:

Step 1: ***Make a list of the firm's key external opportunities and threats and internal strengths and weaknesses in the left column of the QSPM.*** This information should be taken directly from the EFE Matrix and IFE Matrix. A minimum of 10 external key success factors and 10 internal key success factors should be included in the QSPM.

Step 2: ***Assign weights to each key external and internal factor.*** These weights are identical to those in the EFE Matrix and the IFE Matrix. The weights are presented in a straight column just to the right of the external and internal critical success factors.

Step 3: ***Examine the Stage 2 (matching) matrices, and identify alternative strategies that the organization should consider implementing.*** Record these strategies in the top row of the QSPM. Group the strategies into mutually exclusive sets if possible.

Step 4: ***Determine the Attractiveness Scores (AS)*** defined as numerical values that indicate the relative attractiveness of each strategy in a given set of alternatives. **Attractiveness Scores (AS)** are determined by examining each key external or internal factor, one at a time, and asking the question "Does this factor affect the choice of strategies being made?" If the answer to this question is yes, then the strategies should be compared relative to that key factor. Specifically, AS should be assigned to each strategy to indicate the relative attractiveness of one strategy over others, considering the particular factor. The range for AS is 1 = not attractive, 2 = somewhat attractive, 3 = reasonably attractive, and 4 = highly attractive. By attractive, we mean the extent that one strategy, compared to others, enables the firm to either capitalize on the strength, improve on the weakness, exploit the opportunity, or avoid the threat. Work row by row in developing a QSPM. If the answer to the previous question is *no*, indicating that the respective key factor has no effect upon the specific choice being made, then do not assign AS to the strategies in that set. Use a dash to indicate that the key factor does not affect the choice being made. *Note:* If you assign an AS score to one strategy, then assign an AS score(s) to the other. In other words, if one strategy receives a dash, then all others must receive a dash in a given row.

Step 5: ***Compute the Total Attractiveness Scores.*** **Total Attractiveness Scores (TAS)** are defined as the product of multiplying the weights (Step 2) by the AS (Step 4) in each row. The TAS indicate the relative attractiveness of each alternative strategy, considering only the impact of the adjacent external or internal critical success factor. The higher the TAS, the more attractive the strategic alternative (considering only the adjacent critical success factor).

TABLE 6-8   A QSPM for a Retail Computer Store

Key Factors	Weight	STRATEGIC ALTERNATIVES			
		1 Buy New Land and Build New Larger Store		2 Fully Renovate Existing Store	
		AS	TAS	AS	TAS
Opportunities					
1. Population of city growing 10 percent	0.10	4	0.40	2	0.20
2. Rival computer store opening one mile away	0.10	2	0.20	4	0.40
3. Vehicle traffic passing store up 12 percent	0.08	1	0.08	4	0.32
4. Vendors average six new products/year	0.05	—		—	
5. Senior citizen use of computers up 8 percent	0.05	—		—	
6. Small business growth in area up 10 percent	0.10	—		—	
7. Desire for websites up 18 percent by realtors	0.06	—		—	
8. Desire for websites up 12 percent by small firms	0.06	—		—	
Threats					
1. Best Buy opening new store nearby in one year	0.15	4	0.60	3	0.45
2. Local university offers computer repair	0.08	—		—	
3. New bypass for Hwy 34 in one year will divert traffic	0.12	4	0.48	1	0.12
4. New mall being built nearby	0.08	2	0.16	4	0.32
5. Gas prices up 14 percent	0.04	—		—	
6. Vendors raising prices 8 percent	0.03	—		—	
Total	**1.00**				
Strengths					
1. Inventory turnover increased from 5.8 to 6.7	0.05	—		—	
2. Average customer purchase increased from $97 to $128	0.07	2	0.14	4	0.28
3. Employee morale is excellent	0.10	—		—	
4. In-store promotions resulted in 20 percent increase in sales	0.05	—		—	
5. Newspaper advertising expenditures increased 10 percent	0.02	—		—	
6. Revenues from repair/service segment of store up 16 percent	0.15	4	0.60	3	0.45
7. In-store technical support personnel have MIS college degrees	0.05	—		—	
8. Store's debt-to-total-assets ratio declined to 34 percent	0.03	4	0.12	2	0.06
9. Revenues per employee up 19 percent	0.02	—		—	
Weaknesses					
1. Revenues from software segment of store down 12 percent	0.10	—		—	
2. Location of store negatively impacted by new Hwy 34	0.15	4	0.60	1	0.15
3. Carpet and paint in store somewhat in disrepair	0.02	1	0.02	4	0.08
4. Bathroom in store needs refurbishing	0.02	1	0.02	4	0.08
5. Revenues from businesses down 8%	0.04	3	0.12	4	0.16
6. Store has no website	0.05	—		—	
7. Supplier on-time delivery increased to 2.4 days	0.03	—		—	
8. Often customers have to wait to check out	0.05	2	0.10	4	0.20
Total	**1.00**		**3.64**		**3.27**

Step 6: *Compute the Sum Total Attractiveness Score.* Add TAS in each strategy column of the QSPM. The **Sum Total Attractiveness Scores (STAS)** reveal which strategy is most attractive in each set of alternatives. Higher scores indicate more attractive strategies, considering all the relevant external and internal factors that could affect the strategic decisions. The magnitude of the difference between the STAS in a given set of strategic alternatives indicates the relative desirability of one strategy over another.

In Table 6-8, two alternative strategies—(1) buy new land and build new larger store and (2) fully renovate existing store—are being considered by a computer retail store. Note by sum total attractiveness scores of 3.64 versus 3.27 that the analysis indicates the business should buy new land and build a new larger store. Note the use of dashes to indicate which factors do not affect the strategy choice being considered. If a particular factor affects one strategy but not the other, it affects the choice being made, so AS should be recorded for both strategies. Never rate one strategy and not the other. Note also in Table 6-8 that there are no double 1's, 2's, 3's, or 4's in a row. Never duplicate scores in a row. Never work column by column; always prepare a QSPM working row by row. If you have more than one strategy in the QSPM, then let the AS scores range from 1 to "the number of strategies being evaluated." This will enable you to have a different AS score for each strategy. These are all important guidelines to follow in developing a QSPM. In actual practice, the store did purchase the new land and build a new store; the business also did some minor refurbishing until the new store was operational.

There should be a rationale for each AS score assigned. Note in Table 6-8 in the first row that the "city population growing 10 percent annually" opportunity could be capitalized on best by Strategy 1, "building the new, larger store," so an AS score of 4 was assigned to Strategy 1. AS scores, therefore, are not mere guesses; they should be rational, defensible, and reasonable.

An example QSPM is given in Table 6-9. Note in the actual QSPM for Starbucks in Table 6-9 that many rows are not rated, indicating that the particular factor does not significantly impact the choice to be made. This is good procedure. Also, notice in Table 6-9 that the 3 and 4 ratings given to the Strategy 2 "Open 400 Stores in the Middle East, Asia/Africa" versus Strategy 1 and indicate that Strategy 2 is a better choice given most of the factors. Working row by row is also good procedure. In addition, notice in Table 6-9 that many rows are not rated at all, indicating the particular factor will not impact the choice between Strategy 1 and 2. Leaving perhaps half of the rows blank in this manner is also good procedure. Finally, note in Table 6-9, that Strategy 2 is better for Starbucks as indicated by a STAS of 2.41.

TABLE 6-9   An Actual QSPM for Starbucks (2013)

| | Strategy 1 | | | Strategy 2 | |
| | Open 100 Stores on U.S. College Campuses | | | Open 400 Stores in Middle East Asia/ Africa | |
	WT.	AS	TAS	AS	TAS
Strengths					
1. 22 percent of revenue comes from its international unit.	0.04	1	0.4	4	0.16
2. Net income grew to $333.1M for the recent quarter.	0.03	–	–	–	–
3. Total revenue grew to $3.30B from $2.92B.	0.04	–	–	–	–
4. Sales at global restaurants open at least 13 months rose 6 percent.	0.04	1	0.04	3	0.12
5. Starbucks earned a 100 percent HRC rating for the fourth consecutive year.	0.03	–	–	–	–
6. Starbucks global comparable store sales also increased 6 percent.	0.04	1	0.04	3	0.12
7. Starbucks revenues reached $166.9M in the Asian-Pacific region for 2011's last quarter (up 38 percent from a year earlier).	0.04	1	0.04	4	0.16
8. Starbucks only buys coffee grown at elevations higher than 2,600 feet because those beans are of better quality.	0.05	–	–	–	–
9. Starbucks employs more than 650 people to provide technology solutions.	0.04	–	–	–	–
10. Starbucks buys Evolution Fresh Inc. (a high end juice maker) for $30M.	0.05	–	–	–	–
11. Starbucks market share is 32.6 percent.	0.04	–	–	–	–
12. Starbucks sells 8.2 million coffee drinks on average each day in the United States.	0.04	4	0.16	1	0.04

(continued)

		Strategy 1		Strategy 2	
		Open 100 Stores on U.S. College Campuses		Open 400 Stores in Middle East Asia/ Africa	
	WT.	AS	TAS	AS	TAS

Weaknesses

13. Starbucks rose prices in the Northeast and Sunbelt by about 1 percent.	0.04	3	0.12	1	0.04
14. Starbucks rose prices in 500 Chinese mainland stores. Coffee prices will increase by 1 to 2 yuan (16 to 32 U.S. cents).	0.04	1	0.04	3	0.12
15. Starbucks reward cardholders protest firm charging for soy milk and flavored syrups.	0.05	–	–	–	–
16. Starbucks does not offer the same type and quality tea as would be served in India.	0.04	1	0.04	2	0.08
17. After 63 Starbucks were opened in France, the firm has never turned a profit there.	0.06	–	–	–	–
18. Sales for Starbucks in Europe open at least 13 months only rose 2 percent whereas in the United States had a 9 percent and Asia had a 20 percent growth.	0.06	–	–	–	–
19. Starbucks reputation takes a big hit among British consumers after a report showed they paid no tax on sales of 1.2 billion pounds in years past after telling the taxman it made no profit but told investors it was a profitable unit.	0.03	–	–	–	–
20. Starbucks comes in second place to Dunkin Donuts on Brand Keys 2012 Customer Loyalty Engagement Index.	0.04	–	–	–	–

Opportunities

21. 80 percent of U.S. adults are concerned about weight.	0.04	–	–	–	–
22. 45 percent of cell phone users have a smart phone.	0.04	–	–	–	–
23. China's projected GDP is $7.9 trillion.	0.02	2	0.04	4	0.08
24. U.S. projected GDP is $15.6 trillion.	0.02	4	0.08	2	0.04
25. Arabica coffee's futures price fell to a 17-month low after the likelihood of a record global crop in 2012–2013.	0.04	2	0.08	3	0.12
26. Since 2005 China's market for specialized coffee shops has tripled.	0.05	1	0.05	4	0.20
27. Tea is the second most consumed beverage in the world, behind bottled water.	0.04	1	0.04	4	0.16
28. India's tea industry accounts for 31 percent of global production.	0.04	1	0.04	4	0.16
29. Dunkin' Donuts comparable stores sales growth was 5.1 percent in 2011 versus Starbucks 8 percent.	0.02	–	–	–	–
30. The domestic coffee market in India is growing by 25 percent annually.	0.02	–	–	–	–

Threats

31. The European debt crisis causes the demand for coffee to falter in various countries; down 6.7 percent, 2.6 percent, and 1.6 percent in Britain, Spain, and Italy, respectively.	0.05	2	0.10	4	0.20
32. Consumer confidence index fell to 60.6 in August from 65.4 in July.	0.03	3	0.09	1	0.03
33. China's per capital GDP in 2011 was $5,184.	0.04	1	0.04	4	0.16
34. An estimated 30 to 50 million American adults are lactose intolerant.	0.04	–	–	–	–
35. Dunkin' Donuts opens outlets in the U.S. Northeast, South, and Mid-Atlantic at 10 college campuses.	0.03	4	0.12	1	0.03
36. Dunkin' Donuts announces its company's goal of doubling U.S. store presence over 20 years.	0.03	4	0.12	1	0.03
37. McDonald's Asia/Pacific, Middle East and Africa division had a 1.4 percent increase in comparable sales.	0.04	1	0.04	4	0.16
38. McDonald's had total revenues of $27B for fiscal 2011 compared to Starbucks $11.7B.	0.04	2	0.08	3	0.12
39. McDonald's takes 7th place in Interbrand's Best Global Brands 2012 while Starbucks comes in 88th place.	0.02	1	0.02	4	0.08
40. Select McDonald's stores in the United States and Europe are providing iPads for customers to use while they are in the store.	0.04	–	–	–	–
TOTAL	**1.00**		**1.82**		**2.41**

Positive Features and Limitations of the QSPM

A positive feature of the QSPM is that sets of strategies can be examined sequentially or simultaneously. For example, corporate-level strategies could be evaluated first, followed by division-level strategies, and then function-level strategies. There is no limit to the number of strategies that can be evaluated or the number of sets of strategies that can be examined at once using the QSPM.

Another positive feature of the QSPM is that it requires strategists to integrate pertinent external and internal factors into the decision process. Developing a QSPM makes it less likely that key factors will be overlooked or weighted inappropriately. A QSPM draws attention to important relationships that affect strategy decisions. Although developing a QSPM requires a number of subjective decisions, making small decisions along the way enhances the probability that the final strategic decisions will be best for the organization. A QSPM can be used by small and large, for-profit and nonprofit organizations.

The QSPM is not without some limitations. First, it always requires intuitive judgments and educated assumptions. The ratings and attractiveness scores require judgmental decisions, even though they should be based on objective information. Discussion among strategists, managers, and employees throughout the strategy-formulation process, including development of a QSPM, is constructive and improves strategic decisions. Constructive discussion during strategy analysis and choice may arise because of genuine differences of interpretation of information and varying opinions. Another limitation of the QSPM is that it can be only as good as the prerequisite information and matching analyses upon which it is based.

Cultural Aspects of Strategy Choice

All organizations have a culture. **Culture** includes the set of shared values, beliefs, attitudes, customs, norms, personalities, heroes, and heroines that describe a firm. Culture is the unique way an organization does business. It is the human dimension that creates solidarity and meaning, and it inspires commitment and productivity in an organization when strategy changes are made. All human beings have a basic need to make sense of the world, to feel in control, and to make meaning. When events threaten meaning, individuals react defensively. Managers and employees may even sabotage new strategies in an effort to recapture the status quo.

It is beneficial to view strategic management from a cultural perspective because success often rests on the degree of support that strategies receive from a firm's culture. If a firm's strategies are supported by cultural products such as values, beliefs, rites, rituals, ceremonies, stories, symbols, language, heroes, and heroines, then managers often can implement changes swiftly and easily. However, if a supportive culture does not exist and is not cultivated, then strategy changes may be ineffective or even counterproductive. A firm's culture can become antagonistic to new strategies, and the result of that antagonism may be confusion and disarray.

Strategies that require fewer cultural changes may be more attractive because extensive changes can take considerable time and effort. Whenever two firms merge, it becomes especially important to evaluate and consider culture-strategy linkages.

Culture provides an explanation for the difficulties a firm encounters when it attempts to shift its strategic direction, as the following statement explains:

> Not only has the "right" corporate culture become the essence and foundation of corporate excellence, but success or failure of needed corporate reforms hinges on management's sagacity and ability to change the firm's driving culture in time and in tune with required changes in strategies.[8]

The Politics of Strategy Choice

All organizations are political. Unless managed, political maneuvering consumes valuable time, subverts organizational objectives, diverts human energy, and results in the loss of some valuable employees. Sometimes political biases and personal preferences get unduly embedded in strategy choice decisions. Internal politics affect the choice of strategies in all organizations. The hierarchy of command in an organization, combined with the career aspirations of different people and the need to allocate scarce resources, guarantees the formation of coalitions of individuals who strive to take care of themselves first and the organization second, third, or fourth. Coalitions of individuals often form around key strategy issues that face an enterprise. A major responsibility of strategists is to guide the development of coalitions, to nurture an overall team concept, and to gain the support of key individuals and groups of individuals.

In the absence of objective analyses, strategy decisions too often are based on the politics of the moment. With development of improved strategy-formation tools, political factors become less important in making strategic decisions. In the absence of objectivity, political factors sometimes dictate strategies, and this is unfortunate. Managing political relationships is an integral part of building enthusiasm and esprit de corps in an organization.

A classic study of strategic management in nine large corporations examined the political tactics of successful and unsuccessful strategists.[9] Successful strategists were found to let weakly supported ideas and proposals die through inaction and to establish additional hurdles or tests for strongly supported ideas considered unacceptable but not openly opposed. Successful strategists kept a low political profile on unacceptable proposals and strived to let most negative decisions come from subordinates or a group consensus, thereby reserving their personal vetoes for big issues and crucial moments. Successful strategists did a lot of chatting and informal questioning to stay abreast of how things were progressing and to know when to intervene. They led strategy but did not dictate it. They gave few orders, announced few decisions, depended heavily on informal questioning, and sought to probe and clarify until a consensus emerged.

Successful strategists generously and visibly rewarded key thrusts that succeeded. They assigned responsibility for major new thrusts to **champions**, the individuals most strongly identified with the idea or product and whose futures were linked to its success. They stayed alert to the symbolic impact of their own actions and statements so as not to send false signals that could stimulate movements in unwanted directions.

Successful strategists ensured that all major power bases within an organization were represented in, or had access to, top management. They interjected new faces and new views into considerations of major changes. This is important because new employees and managers generally have more enthusiasm and drive than employees who have been with the firm a long time. New employees do not see the world the same old way; nor do they act as screens against changes. Successful strategists minimized their own political exposure on highly controversial issues and in circumstances in which major opposition from key power centers was likely. In combination, these findings provide a basis for managing political relationships in an organization.

Because strategies must be effective in the marketplace and capable of gaining internal commitment, the following tactics used by politicians for centuries can aid strategists:

1. Achieving desired results is more important that imposing a particular method, so consider various methods and choose, whenever possible, the one(s) that will afford the greatest commitment from employees/managers.
2. Achieving satisfactory results with a popular strategy is generally better than trying to achieve optimal results with an unpopular strategy.
3. An effective way to gain commitment and achieve desired results is oftentimes to shift from specific to general issues and concerns.
4. An effective way to gain commitment and achieve desired results is oftentimes to shift from short-term to long-term issues and concerns.
5. Middle level managers must be genuinely involved in and supportive of strategic decisions, because successful implementation will hinge on their support.[10]

Governance Issues

A "director," according to Webster's Dictionary, is "one of a group of persons entrusted with the overall direction of a corporate enterprise." A **board of directors** is a group of individuals who are elected by the ownership of a corporation to have oversight and guidance over management and who look out for shareholders' interests. The act of oversight and direction is referred to as **governance**. The National Association of Corporate Directors defines governance as "the characteristic of ensuring that long-term strategic objectives and plans are established and that the proper management structure is in place to achieve those objectives, while at the same time making sure that the structure functions to maintain the corporation's integrity, reputation, and responsibility to its various constituencies." Boards are being held accountable for the entire performance of the firm. Boards of directors are increasingly sued by shareholders for mismanaging their interests. New accounting rules in the USA and Europe now enhance corporate-governance codes and require much more extensive financial disclosure among publicly held firms. The roles and duties of a board of directors can be divided into four broad categories, as indicated in Table 6-10.

Shareholders today are wary of boards of directors. Shareholders of hundreds of firms are demanding that their boards do a better job of governing corporate America.[11] New compensation policies are needed as well as direct shareholder involvement in some director activities. For example, boards could require CEOs to groom possible replacements from inside the firm because exorbitant compensation is most often paid to new CEOs coming from outside the firm.

Most boards of directors globally have ended their image as rubber-stamping friends of CEOs. Boards are more autonomous than ever and continually mindful of and responsive to legal and institutional-investor scrutiny. Boards are more cognizant of auditing and compliance issues and more reluctant to approve excessive compensation and perks. Boards stay much more abreast today of public scandals that attract shareholder and media attention. Increasingly,

TABLE 6-10   Board of Director Duties and Responsibilities

1. CONTROL AND OVERSIGHT OVER MANAGEMENT
   a. Select the Chief Executive Officer (CEO).
   b. Sanction the CEO's team.
   c. Provide the CEO with a forum.
   d. Ensure managerial competency.
   e. Evaluate management's performance.
   f. Set management's salary levels, including fringe benefits.
   g. Guarantee managerial integrity through continuous auditing.
   h. Chart the corporate course.
   i. Devise and revise policies to be implemented by management.

2. ADHERENCE TO LEGAL PRESCRIPTIONS
   a. Keep abreast of new laws.
   b. Ensure the entire organization fulfills legal prescriptions.
   c. Pass bylaws and related resolutions.
   d. Select new directors.
   e. Approve capital budgets.
   f. Authorize borrowing, new stock issues, bonds, and so on.

3. CONSIDERATION OF STAKEHOLDERS' INTERESTS
   a. Monitor product quality.
   b. Facilitate upward progression in employee quality of work life.
   c. Review labor policies and practices.
   d. Improve the customer climate.
   e. Keep community relations at the highest level.
   f. Use influence to better governmental, professional association, and educational contacts.
   g. Maintain good public image.

4. ADVANCEMENT OF STOCKHOLDERS' RIGHTS
   a. Preserve stockholders' equity.
   b. Stimulate corporate growth so that the firm will survive and flourish.
   c. Guard against equity dilution.
   d. Ensure equitable stockholder representation.
   e. Inform stockholders through letters, reports, and meetings.
   f. Declare proper dividends.
   g. Guarantee corporate survival.

boards of directors monitor and review executive performance carefully without favoritism to executives, representing shareholders rather than the CEO. Boards are more proactive today, whereas in years past they were oftentimes merely reactive. These are all reasons why the chair of the board of directors should not also serve as the firm's CEO.[12]

Shareholders are also upset at boards for allowing CEOs to receive huge end-of-year bonuses when the firm's stock price drops drastically during the year.[13] For example, Chesapeake Energy Corp. and its board of directors came under fire from shareholders for paying Chairman and CEO Aubrey McClendon $112 million as the firm's stock price plummeted. Investor Jeffrey Bronchick wrote in a letter to the Chesapeake board that the CEO's compensation was a "near perfect illustration of the complete collapse of appropriate corporate governance."

Until recently, boards of directors did most of their work sitting around polished wooden tables. However, Hewlett-Packard's directors, among many others, now log on to their own special board website twice a week and conduct business based on extensive confidential briefing information posted there by the firm's top management team. Then the board members meet face-to-face and fully informed every two months to discuss the biggest issues facing the firm. Even the decision of whether to locate operations in countries with low corporate tax rates would be reviewed by a board of directors. New board involvement policies are aimed at curtailing lawsuits against board members. For example, there were 740 lawsuits filed in 2012 against directors regarding merger deals. The Federal Deposit Insurance Corporation (FDIC) filed 23 lawsuits against directors in 2012, compared to 16 in 2011 and just 2 in 2010.

Today, boards of directors are composed mostly of outsiders who are becoming more involved in organizations' strategic management. The trend in the USA is toward much greater board member accountability with smaller boards, now averaging 12 members rather than 18 as they did a few years ago. *BusinessWeek* recently evaluated the boards of most large U.S. companies and provided the following "principles of good governance":

1. Never have more than two of the firm's executives (current or past) on the board.
2. Never allow a firm's executives to be the board's audit, compensation, or nominating committees.
3. Require all board members to own a large amount of the firm's equity.
4. Require all board members to attend at least 75 percent of all meetings.
5. Require the board to meet annually to evaluate its own performance, without the CEO, COO, or top management in attendance.
6. Never allow the CEO to be Chairperson of the Board.
7. Never allow interlocking directorships (where a director or CEO sits on another director's board).[14]

Jeff Sonnerfeld, associate dean of the Yale School of Management, says, "Boards of directors are now rolling up their sleeves and becoming much more closely involved with management decision making." Company CEOs and boards are required to personally certify financial statements; company loans to company executives and directors are illegal; and there is faster reporting of insider stock transactions.

Just as directors place more emphasis on staying informed about an organization's health and operations, they are also taking a more active role in ensuring that publicly issued documents are accurate representations of a firm's status. Failure to accept responsibility for auditing or evaluating a firm's strategy is considered a serious breach of a director's duties. Stockholders, government agencies, and customers are filing legal suits against directors for fraud, omissions, inaccurate disclosures, lack of due diligence, and culpable ignorance about a firm's operations with increasing frequency. Liability insurance for directors has become exceptionally expensive and has caused numerous directors to resign.

The Sarbanes-Oxley Act resulted in scores of boardroom overhauls among publicly traded companies. The jobs of chief executive and chairman are now held by separate persons, and board audit committees must now have at least one financial expert as a member. Board audit committees now meet 10 or more times per year, rather than three or four times as they did prior to the act. The act put an end to the "country club" atmosphere of most boards and has shifted power from CEOs to directors. Although aimed at public companies, the act has also had a similar impact on privately owned companies.[15]

In Sweden, a new law requires 25 percent female representation in boardrooms. The Norwegian government has passed a similar law that requires 40 percent of corporate director seats to go to women. In the USA, women currently hold about 13 percent of board seats at S&P 500 firms and 10 percent at S&P 1,500 firms. The Investor Responsibility Research Center in Washington, D.C., reports that minorities hold just 8.8 percent of board seats of S&P 1,500 companies. Progressive firms realize that women and minorities ask different questions and make different suggestions in boardrooms than white men, which is helpful because women and minorities comprise much of the consumer base everywhere.

The European Union (EU) Justice Commissioner Viviane Reding introduced in late 2012 contentious legislation requiring publicly traded companies across the EU to fill at least 40 percent of board positions with women by 2020, or be hit with sanctions to be decided by the EU countries.

A direct response to increased pressure on directors to stay informed and execute their responsibilities is that audit committees are becoming commonplace. A board of directors should conduct an annual strategy audit in much the same fashion that it reviews the annual financial audit. In performing such an audit, a board could work jointly with operating management and/or seek outside counsel. Boards should play a role beyond that of performing a strategic audit. They should provide greater input and advice in the strategy-formulation process to ensure that strategists are providing for the long-term needs of the firm. This is being done through the formation of three particular board committees: nominating committees to propose candidates for the board and senior officers of the firm; compensation committees to evaluate the performance of top executives and determine the terms and conditions of their employment; and audit committees to give board-level attention to company accounting and financial policies and performance.

Special Note to Students

Your SWOT, SPACE, BCG, IE, Grand, and QSPM need to be developed accurately, but in covering those matrices in an oral presentation, focus more on the implications of those analyses than the nuts-and-bolts calculations. In other words, as you go through those matrices in a presentation, your goal is not to prove to the class that you did the calculations correctly. They expect accuracy and clarity and certainly you should have that covered. It is the implications of each matrix that your audience will be most interested in, so use these matrices to pave the way for your recommendations with costs, which generally come just a page or two deeper into the project. A good rule of thumb is to spend at least an equal amount of time on the implications as the actual calculations of each matrix when presented. This approach will improve the delivery aspect of your presentation or paper by maintaining the high interest level of your audience. Focusing on implications rather than calculations will also encourage questions from the audience when you finish. Questions on completion are a good thing. Silence on completion is a bad thing because silence could mean your audience was asleep, disinterested, or did not feel you did a good job. Also, utilize the free excel student template at www.strategyclub.com as needed.

Conclusion

The essence of strategy formulation is an assessment of whether an organization is doing the right things and how it can be more effective in what it does. Every organization should be wary of becoming a prisoner of its own strategy because even the best strategies become obsolete sooner or later. Regular reappraisal of strategy helps management avoid complacency. Objectives and strategies should be consciously developed and coordinated and should not merely evolve out of day-to-day operating decisions.

An organization with no sense of direction and no coherent strategy precipitates its own demise. When an organization does not know where it wants to go, it usually ends up some place it does not want to be. Every organization needs to consciously establish and communicate clear objectives and strategies.

Modern strategy-formulation tools and concepts are described in this chapter and integrated into a practical three-stage framework. Tools such as the SWOT Matrix, SPACE Matrix, BCG Matrix, IE Matrix, and QSPM can significantly enhance the quality of strategic decisions, but they should never be used to dictate the choice of strategies. Behavioral, cultural, and political aspects of strategy generation and selection are always important to consider and manage. Because of increased legal pressure from outside groups, boards of directors are assuming a more active role in strategy analysis and choice. This is a positive trend for organizations.

MyManagementLab®

Go to **mymanagementlab.com** to complete the problems marked with this icon ⭐.

Key Terms and Concepts

aggressive quadrant (p. 173)
attractiveness scores (AS) (p. 186)
board of directors (p. 191)
Boston Consulting Group (BCG) matrix (p. 177)
business portfolio (p. 177)
cash cows (p. 179)
champions (p. 191)
competitive position (CP) (p. 172)
competitive quadrant (p. 175)
conservative quadrant (p. 175)
culture (p. 190)
decision stage (p. 168)
defensive quadrant (p. 175)
directional vector (p. 173)
dogs (p. 179)
financial position (FP) (p. 172)
governance (p. 191)
Grand Strategy Matrix (p. 183)
halo error (p. 168)
industry position (IP) (p. 172)

input stage (p. 168)
internal-external (IE) matrix (p. 180)
matching (p. 169)
matching stage (p. 168)
Quantitative Strategic Planning Matrix (QSPM) (p. 185)
question marks (p. 178)
relative market share position (p. 177)
SO strategies (p. 170)
stability position (SP) (p. 172)
stars (p. 179)
Strategic Position and Action Evaluation (SPACE) Matrix (p. 172)
strategy-formulation analytical framework (p. 168)
Strengths-Weaknesses Opportunities-Threats (SWOT) Matrix (p. 169)
ST strategies (p. 170)
Sum Total Attractiveness Scores (STAS) (p. 188)
Total Attractiveness Scores (TAS) (p. 186)
WO strategies (p. 170)
WT strategies (p. 170)

Issues for Review and Discussion

6-1. Minorities and women each hold less than 15 percent of board seats of many S&P 500 companies. Why is this not good?

6-2. In developing a QSPM, if 10 strategies are being compared simultaneously, what would be a good scale for the AS scores? Why?

6-3. In developing a BCG or IE Matrix, what would be a good surrogate for revenues for Target Corp., Burger King, Bank of America, and Spirit Airlines.

6-4. In developing a SPACE Matrix, what would you expect the SP average to be for Apple, Heinz, Verizon, Amazon, and Kroger?

6-5. Rather than developing a QSPM, what is an alternative procedure for prioritizing the relative attractiveness of alternative strategies?

6-6. Overlay a BCG Matrix with a Grand Strategy Matrix and discuss similarities in terms of format and implications.

6-7. Walt Disney's Board of Directors consists of eight men and five women. Why should a board not consist of all men, or all women, or all whites, or all minorities?

6-8. Many multidivisional firms do not report revenues or profits by division or segment in their *Form 10K* or *Annual Report*. What are the pros and cons of this management practice? Discuss.

6-9. Define halo error. How can halo error inhibit selecting the best strategies to pursue?

6-10. List six drawbacks of using only subjective information in formulating strategies.

6-11. For a firm that you know well, give an example of SO strategy, showing how an internal strength can be matched with an external opportunity to formulate a strategy.

6-12. For a firm that you know well, give an example WT strategy, showing how an internal weakness can be matched with an external threat to formulate a strategy.

6-13. List three limitations of the SWOT matrix and analysis.

6-14. For the following three firms using the given factors, calculate a reasonable stability position (SP) coordinate to go on their SPACE Matrix axis, given what you know about the nature of those industries.

Factors	Winnebago	Apple	U.S. Postal Service
Barriers to entry into market			
Seasonal nature of business			
Technological changes SP Score			

6-15. Would the angle or degrees of the vector in a SPACE Matrix be important in generating alternative strategies? Explain.

6-16. On the competitive position (CP) axis of a SPACE Matrix, what level of capacity utilization would be necessary for you to give the firm a negative 1? Negative 7? Why?

6-17. If a firm has weak financial position and competes in an unstable industry, in which quadrant will the SPACE vector lie?

6-18. Describe a situation where the SPACE analysis would have no vector. In other words, describe a situation where the SPACE analysis coordinate would be (0,0). What should an analyst do in this situation?

6-19. Develop a BCG Matrix for your university. Because your college does not generate profits, what would be a good surrogate for the pie slice values? How many circles do you have and how large are they? Explain.

6-20. In a BCG Matrix, would the question mark quadrant or the cash cow quadrant be more desirable? Explain.

6-21. Would a BCG Matrix and analysis be worth performing if you do not know the profits of each segment? Why?

6-22. What major limitations of the BCG Matrix does the IE Matrix overcome?

6-23. In an IE Matrix, do you believe it is more advantageous for a division to be located in quadrant II or IV? Why?

6-24. Develop a $2 \times 2 \times 2 \times 2 \times 2$ QSPM for an organization of your choice (i.e., two strengths, two weaknesses, two opportunities, two threats, and two strategies). Follow all the QSPM guidelines presented in the chapter.

6-25. Give an example of "equifinality" as defined in the chapter.

6-26. Do you believe the reasons to disclose by-segment financial information offset the reasons not to disclose by-segment financial information? Explain why or why not.

6-27. How would application of the strategy-formulation analytical framework differ from a small to a large organization?

6-28. What types of strategies would you recommend for an organization that achieves total weighted scores of 3.6 on the IFE and 1.2 on the EFE Matrix?

6-29. Given the following information, develop a SPACE Matrix for the XYZ Corporation: FP = + 2; SP = − 6; CP = −2; IP = +4.

6-30. Given the information in the following table, develop a BCG Matrix and an IE Matrix:

Divisions	1	2	3
Profits	$10	$15	$25
Sales	$100	$50	$100
Relative Market Share	0.2	0.5	0.8
Industry Growth Rate	+.20	+.10	−.10
IFE Total Weighted Scores	1.6	3.1	2.2
EFE Total Weighted Scores	2.5	1.8	3.3

6-31. Explain the steps involved in developing a QSPM.

6-32. How would you develop a set of objectives for your school or business?

6-33. What do you think is the appropriate role of a board of directors in strategic management? Why?

6-34. Discuss the limitations of various strategy-formulation analytical techniques.

6-35. Explain why cultural factors should be an important consideration in analyzing and choosing among alternative strategies.

6-36. How are the SWOT Matrix, SPACE Matrix, BCG Matrix, IE Matrix, and Grand Strategy Matrix similar? How are they different?

6-37. How would for-profit and nonprofit organizations differ in their applications of the strategy-formulation analytical framework?

6-38. Develop a SPACE Matrix for a company that is weak financially and is a weak competitor. The industry for this company is pretty stable, but the industry's projected growth in revenues and profits is not good. Label all axes and quadrants.

6-39. List four limitations of a BCG Matrix.

6-40. Make up an example to show clearly and completely that you can develop an IE Matrix for a three-division company, where each division has $10, $20, and $40 in revenues and $2, $4, and $1 in profits. State other assumptions needed. Label axes and quadrants.

6-41. What procedures could be necessary if the SPACE vector falls right on the axis between the competitive and defensive quadrants?

6-42. In a BCG Matrix or the Grand Strategy Matrix, what would you consider to be a rapid market (or industry) growth rate?

6-43. How did the Sarbanes-Oxley Act of 2002 impact boards of directors?

6-44. Rank *BusinessWeek*'s "principles of good governance" from 1 to 14 (1 being most important and 14 least important) to reveal your assessment of these new rules.

6-45. Why is it important to work row by row instead of column by column in preparing a QSPM?

6-46. Why should one avoid putting double 4s in a row in preparing a QSPM?

6-47. Envision a QSPM with no weight column. Would that still be a useful analysis? Why or why not? What do you lose by deleting the weight column?

6-48. Prepare a BCG Matrix for a two-division firm with sales of $5 and $8 versus profits of $3 and $1, respectively. State assumptions for the RMSP and IGR axes to enable you to construct the diagram.

6-49. Consider developing a before-and-after BCG or IE Matrix to reveal the expected results of your proposed strategies. What limitation of the analysis would this procedure overcome somewhat?

6-50. If a firm has the leading market share in its industry, where on the BCG Matrix would the circle lie?

6-51. If a firm competes in a unstable industry, such as telecommunications, where on the SP axis of the SPACE Matrix would you plot the appropriate point?

6-52. Why do you think the SWOT Matrix is the most widely used of all strategy matrices?

MyManagementLab®

Go to **mymanagementlab.com** for Auto-graded writing questions as well as the following Assisted-graded writing questions:

6-53. Explain the steps involved in developing a QSPM.

6-54. How are the SWOT Matrix, SPACE Matrix, BCG Matrix, IE Matrix, and Grand Strategy Matrix similar? How are they different?

6-55. Mymanagementlab Only—comprehensive writing assignment for this chapter.

Current Readings

Arms, Hanjo, Mathias Wiecher, and Valeska Kleiderman. "Dynamic Models for Managing Big Decisions." *Strategy and Leadership* 40, no. 5 (2012): 39–46.

Blettner, Daniela P., Fernando R. Chaddad, and Richard A. Bettis. "The CEO Performance Effect: Statistical Issues and a Complex Fit Perspective." *Strategic Management Journal* 33, no. 8 (August 2012): 986–999.

Connelly, Brian L., and Erik J. Van Slyke. "The Power and Peril of Board Interlocks." *Business Horizons* 55, no. 5 (September 2012): 403–408.

Donaldson, Thomas. "The Epistemic Fault Line in Corporate Governance" *The Academy of Management Review* 37, no. 2 (April 2012): 256.

Fernhaber, Stephanie A., and Pankaj C. Patel. "How do young firms manage product portfolio complexity? The role of absorptive capacity and ambidexterity." *Strategic Management Journal* 33, no. 13 (December 2012): 1516–1539.

He, Jinyu, and Zhi Huang. "Board Informal Hierarchy and Firm Financial Performance: Exploring a Tacit Structure Guiding Boardroom Interactions." *The Academy of Management Journal* 54, no. 6 (December 2011): 1119.

Joseph, John, and William Ocasio. "Architecture, Attention, and Adaptation in the Multibusiness Firm: General Electric from 1951 to 2001." *Strategic Management Journal* 33, no. 6 (June 2012): 633–660.

Kiron, David, Pamela Kirk Prentice, and Renee Boucher Ferguson. "Innovating With Analytics." *MITSloan Management Review* 54, no. 1 (Fall 2012): 47.

Walls, Judith L., Pascual Berrone, and Phillip H. Phan. "Corporate Governance and Environmental Performance: Is There Really a Link?" *Strategic Management Journal* 33, no. 8 (August 2012): 885-913.

Walter, Jorge, Franz W. Kellermanns, and Christoph Lechner. "Decision Making Within and Between Organizations: Rationality, Politics and Alliance Performance." *Journal of Management* 38, no. 5 (September 2012): 1582.

ASSURANCE OF LEARNING EXERCISES

EXERCISE 6A
Perform a SWOT Analysis for PepsiCo

Purpose

SWOT is the most widely used of all strategic planning tools and techniques because it is conceptually simple and lends itself readily to discussion among executives and managers. SWOT is effective in formulating strategies because it clearly matches a firm's internal strengths and weaknesses with the firm's external opportunities and threats to generate feasible strategies that should be considered. The exercise gives you practice developing a SWOT for a large corporation.

Instructions

Step 1	Join with two other students in class. Together, develop a SWOT Matrix for PepsiCo. Follow all the SWOT guidelines provided in the chapter, including notation (for example, S4, T3) at the end of each strategy. Include three strategies in each of the four (SO, ST, WT, WO) quadrants. Be specific regarding your strategies, avoiding generic terms such as Forward Integration. Use the Cohesion Case material and your answers to Assurance of Learning Exercise 1A.
Step 2	Turn in your team-developed SWOT Matrix to your professor for a classwork grade.

EXERCISE 6B
Develop a SWOT Matrix for GE Capital

Purpose

Showcased at the beginning of this chapter for excellent strategic management, GE is a huge multidivisional firm. Each division (or segment or unit) of GE uses SWOT analysis to develop their matrix, and then submits their divisional matrix to corporate for the corporation to ultimately develop a unified SWOT Matrix for the firm. A division or segment of General Electric, GE Capital annually develops a SWOT Matrix to justify or request resources from the corporation that has numerous other divisions that also desire, request, and need resources. Realize that multidivisional firms such as GE (and PepsiCo) do not allocate resources evenly among divisions, but rather require each division annually to submit a SWOT Matrix as a basis for requesting funding. Then, a firm's top executives decide how best to allocate resources to benefit the firm most. The purpose of this exercise is to give you practice developing a divisional SWOT Matrix.

GE Capital is one of the world's largest providers of credit. For more than one million businesses, large and small, GE Capital provides financing to purchase, lease, and distribute equipment, as well as capital for real estate and corporate acquisitions, refinancings, and restructurings. GE Capital has more than 100 million consumer customers and offers them credit cards, sales finance programs, home, car, and personal loans, and credit insurance.

Instructions

Recall from Assurance of Learning Exercise 1A that you already may have determined Disney's external opportunities and threats and internal strengths and weaknesses. This information could be used to complete this exercise. Follow the steps outlined as follows:

Step 1	Do some research on GE Capital by going to www.ge.com and click on finance-business or go to www.gecapital.com. Also, review the narrative on GE Capital in the company's most recent *Annual Report* or *Form 10K*.
Step 2	On a separate sheet of paper, construct a large nine-cell diagram that will represent your SWOT Matrix. Appropriately label the cells.
Step 3	Appropriately record GE Capital's opportunities and threats and strengths and weaknesses in your diagram.
Step 4	Match external and internal factors to generate feasible alternative strategies for GE Capital. Record SO, WO, ST, and WT strategies in the appropriate cells of the SWOT Matrix. Use the proper notation to indicate the rationale for the strategies. You do not necessarily have to have strategies in all four strategy cells.
Step 5	Compare your SWOT Matrix to another student's SWOT Matrix. Discuss any major differences.

EXERCISE 6C
Develop a SPACE Matrix for PepsiCo

Purpose

The SPACE Matrix is one of five matching strategic management tools widely used to formulate feasible strategies. Used in conjunction with the SWOT, BCG, IE, and GRAND, the SPACE can be helpful in devising a strategic plan because hard choices normally must be made between attractive strategic options. This exercise gives you practice developing a SPACE Matrix.

Instructions

Step 1   Review PepsiCo business as described in the Cohesion Case as well as the company's most recent *Annual Report* and *Form 10K*.

Step 2   Review industry and competitive information pertaining to PepsiCo.

Step 3   Develop a SPACE Matrix for PepsiCo. Write a one-page executive overview summarizing strategies that you recommend for this business segment, given your SPACE analysis. Avoid generic, vague terms such as market development.

EXERCISE 6D

Develop a BCG Matrix for PepsiCo

Purpose

Portfolio matrices are widely used by multidivisional organizations to help identify and select strategies to pursue. A BCG analysis identifies particular divisions that should receive fewer resources than others. It may identify some divisions that need to be divested. This exercise can give you practice developing a BCG Matrix.

Instructions

Step 1   Place the following five column headings at the top of a separate sheet of paper: Divisions, Revenues, Profits, Relative Market Share Position, Industry Growth Rate. Down the far left of your page, list PepsiCo's geographic divisions. Now turn back to the Cohesion Case and find information to fill in all the cells in your data table from page 27.

Step 2   Complete a BCG Matrix for PepsiCo.

Step 3   Compare your BCG Matrix to other students' matrices. Discuss any major differences.

EXERCISE 6E

Develop a QSPM for PepsiCo

Purpose

This exercise can give you practice developing a QSPM to determine the relative attractiveness of various strategic alternatives.

Instructions

Step 1   Join with two other students in class to develop a joint QSPM for PepsiCo.

Step 2   Go to the blackboard and record your strategies and their STAS. Compare your team's strategies and STAS to those of other teams. Be sure not to assign the same AS score in a given row. Recall that dashes should be inserted all the way across a given row when used.

Step 3   Discuss any major differences.

EXERCISE 6F

Formulate Individual Strategies

Purpose

Individuals and organizations are alike in many ways. Each has competitors, and each should plan for the future. Every individual and organization faces some external opportunities and threats and has some internal strengths and weaknesses. Both individuals and organizations establish objectives and allocate resources. These and other similarities make it possible for individuals to use many strategic-management concepts and tools. This exercise is designed to demonstrate how the SWOT Matrix can be used by individuals to plan their futures. As one nears completion of a college degree and begins interviewing for jobs, planning can be particularly important.

Instructions

On a separate sheet of paper, construct a SWOT Matrix. Include what you consider to be your major external opportunities, your major external threats, your major strengths, and your major weaknesses. An internal weakness may be a low grade point average. An external opportunity may be that your university offers a graduate program that interests you. Match key external and internal factors by recording in the appropriate cell of the matrix alternative strategies or actions that would allow you to capitalize on your strengths, overcome your weaknesses, take advantage of your external opportunities, and minimize the impact of external threats. Be sure to use the appropriate matching notation in the strategy cells of the matrix. Because every individual (and organization) is unique, there is no one right answer to this exercise.

 EXERCISE 6G
The Mach Test

Purpose

The purpose of this exercise is to enhance your understanding and awareness of the impact that behavioral and political factors can have on strategy analysis and choice.

Instructions

Step 1   On a separate sheet of paper, number from 1 to 10. For each of the 10 statements given as follows, record a *1, 2, 3, 4,* or *5* to indicate your attitude, where

> 1 = I disagree a lot.
> 2 = I disagree a little.
> 3 = My attitude is neutral.
> 4 = I agree a little.
> 5 = I agree a lot.

1. The best way to handle people is to tell them what they want to hear.
2. When you ask someone to do something for you, it is best to give the real reason for wanting it, rather than a reason that might carry more weight.
3. Anyone who completely trusts anyone else is asking for trouble.
4. It is hard to get ahead without cutting corners here and there.
5. It is safest to assume that all people have a vicious streak, and it will come out when they are given a chance.
6. One should take action only when it is morally right.
7. Most people are basically good and kind.
8. There is no excuse for lying to someone else.
9. Most people forget more easily the death of their father than the loss of their property.
10. Generally speaking, people won't work hard unless they're forced to do so.

Step 2   Add up the numbers you recorded beside statements 1, 3, 4, 5, 9, and 10. This sum is Subtotal One. For the other four statements, reverse the numbers you recorded, so a *5* becomes a *1*, *4* becomes *2*, *2* becomes *4*, *1* becomes *5*, and *3* remains *3*. Then add those four numbers to get Subtotal Two. Finally, add Subtotal One and Subtotal Two to get your Final Score.

Your Final Score

Your Final Score is your Machiavellian Score. Machiavellian principles are defined in a dictionary as "manipulative, dishonest, deceiving, and favoring political expediency over morality." These tactics are not desirable, are not ethical, and are not recommended in the strategic-management process! You may, however, encounter some highly Machiavellian individuals in your career, so beware. It is important for strategists not to manipulate others in the pursuit of organizational objectives. Individuals today recognize and resent manipulative tactics more than ever before. J. R. Ewing (on *Dallas,* a television show in the 1980s) was a good example of someone who was a high Mach (score more than 30). The National Opinion Research Center used this short quiz in a random sample of U.S. adults and found the national average Final Score to be 25.[1] The higher your score, the more Machiavellian (manipulative) you tend to be. The following scale is descriptive of individual scores on this test:

- Below 16: Never uses manipulation as a tool.
- 16 to 20: Rarely uses manipulation as a tool.
- 21 to 25: Sometimes uses manipulation as a tool.
- 26 to 30: Often uses manipulation as a tool.
- Over 30: Always uses manipulation as a tool.

Test Development

The Mach (Machiavellian) test was developed by Dr. Richard Christie, whose research suggests the following tendencies:

1. Men generally are more Machiavellian than women.
2. There is no significant difference between high Machs and low Machs on measures of intelligence or ability.
3. Although high Machs are detached from others, they are detached in a pathological sense.

4. Machiavellian scores are not statistically related to authoritarian values.
5. High Machs tend to be in professions that emphasize the control and manipulation of individuals—for example, law, psychiatry, and behavioral science.
6. Machiavellianism is not significantly related to major demographic characteristics such as educational level or marital status.
7. High Machs tend to come from a city or have urban backgrounds.
8. Older adults tend to have lower Mach scores than younger adults.[2]

A classic book on power relationships, *The Prince,* was written by Niccolo Machiavelli. Several excerpts from *The Prince* follow:

Men must either be cajoled or crushed, for they will revenge themselves for slight wrongs, while for grave ones they cannot. The injury therefore that you do to a man should be such that you need not fear his revenge.

We must bear in mind...that there is nothing more difficult and dangerous, or more doubtful of success, than an attempt to introduce a new order of things in any state. The innovator has for enemies all those who derived advantages from the old order of things, while those who expect to be benefitted by the new institution will be but lukewarm defenders.

A wise prince, therefore, will steadily pursue such a course that the citizens of his state will always and under all circumstances feel the need for his authority, and will therefore always prove faithful to him.

A prince should seem to be merciful, faithful, humane, religious, and upright, and should even be so in reality, but he should have his mind so trained that, when occasion requires it, he may know how to change to the opposite.[3]

Notes

1. Richard Christie and Florence Geis, *Studies in Machiavellianism* (Orlando, FL: Academic Press, 1970). Material in this exercise adapted with permission of the authors and the Academic Press.
2. Ibid., 82–83.
3. Niccolo Machiavelli, *The Prince* (New York: The Washington Press, 1963).

EXERCISE 6H
Develop a BCG Matrix for Your University

Purpose

Developing a BCG Matrix for many nonprofit organizations, including colleges and universities, is a useful exercise. Of course, there are no profits for each division or department—and in some cases no revenues. However, be creative in performing a BCG Matrix. For example, the pie slice in the circles can represent the number of majors receiving jobs on graduation, the number of faculty teaching in that area, or some other variable that you believe is important to consider. The size of the circles can represent the number of students majoring in particular departments or areas.

Instructions

Step 1	On a separate sheet of paper, develop a BCG Matrix for your university. Include all academic schools, departments, or colleges.
Step 2	Diagram your BCG Matrix on the blackboard.
Step 3	Discuss differences among the BCG Matrices on the board.

EXERCISE 6I
The Role of Boards of Directors

Purpose

This exercise will give you a better understanding of the role of boards of directors in formulating, implementing, and evaluating strategies.

Instructions

Identify a person in your community who serves on a board of directors. Make an appointment to interview that person, and seek answers to the following questions. Summarize your findings in a five-minute oral report to the class.

- On what board are you a member?
- How often does the board meet?
- How long have you served on the board?
- What role does the board play in this company?
- How has the role of the board changed in recent years?
- What changes would you like to see in the role of the board?
- To what extent do you prepare for the board meeting?
- To what extent are you involved in strategic management of the firm?

EXERCISE 6J
Locate Companies in a Grand Strategy Matrix

Purpose
The Grand Strategy Matrix is a popular tool for formulating alternative strategies. All organizations can be positioned in one of the Grand Strategy Matrix's four strategy quadrants. The divisions of a firm likewise could be positioned. The Grand Strategy Matrix is based on two evaluative dimensions: competitive position and market growth. Appropriate strategies for an organization to consider are listed in sequential order of attractiveness in each quadrant of the matrix. This exercise gives you experience using a Grand Strategy Matrix.

Instructions
Using the year-end 2012 financial information provided, prepare a Grand Strategy Matrix on a separate sheet of paper. Write the respective company names in the appropriate quadrant of the matrix. Based on this analysis, what strategies are recommended for each company?

Company	Gross Margin % EPS	Industry	Gross Margin % EPS
The Boeing Company	17.0 5.79	Aerospace/Defense	27.0 1.41
Deere & Company	29.0 74.9	Farm & Machinery	27.0 1.64
Nestle	47.0 3.32	Confectioners	33.0 0.32
Pfizer Inc.	79.0 1.33	Drug Manufacturers	0.56 0.16
Books-A-Million	28.0 −0.05	Specialty Retail	33.0 0.11

Source: Based on information at www.finance.yahoo.com on 10-10-12.

Notes

1. R. T. Lenz, "Managing the Evolution of the Strategic Planning Process," *Business Horizons* 30, no. 1 (January–February 1987): 37.
2. Robert Grant, "The Resource-Based Theory of Competitive Advantage: Implications for Strategy Formulation," *California Management Review*, Spring 1991, 114.
3. Heinz Weihrich, "The TOWS Matrix: A Tool for Situational Analysis," *Long Range Planning* 15, no. 2 (April 1982): 61. *Note:* Although Dr. Weihrich first modified SWOT analysis to form the TOWS matrix,

the acronym SWOT is much more widely used than TOWS in practice.
4. Greg Dess, G. T. Lumpkin, and Alan Eisner, *Strategic Management: Text and Cases* (New York: McGraw-Hill/Irwin, 2006), 72.
5. Adapted from H. Rowe, R. Mason, and K. Dickel, *Strategic Management and Business Policy: A Methodological Approach* (Reading, MA: Addison-Wesley, 1982), 155–156.
6. Fred David, "The Strategic Planning Matrix—A Quantitative Approach," *Long Range Planning* 19, no. 5

(October 1986): 102; Andre Gib and Robert Margulies, "Making Competitive Intelligence Relevant to the User," *Planning Review* 19, no. 3 (May–June 1991): 21.

7. Fred David, "Computer-Assisted Strategic Planning in Small Businesses," *Journal of Systems Management* 36, no. 7 (July 1985): 24–34.

8. Y. Allarie and M. Firsirotu, "How to Implement Radical Strategies in Large Organizations," *Sloan Management Review* 26, no. 3 (Spring 1985): 19. Another excellent article is P. Shrivastava, "Integrating Strategy Formulation with Organizational Culture," *Journal of Business Strategy* 5, no. 3 (Winter 1985): 103–111.

9. James Brian Quinn, *Strategies for Changes: Logical Incrementalism* (Homewood, IL: Richard D. Irwin, 1980), 128–145. These political tactics are listed in A. Thompson and A. Strickland, *Strategic*

Management: Concepts and Cases (Plano, TX: Business Publications, 1984), 261.

10. William Guth and Ian MacMillan, "Strategy Implementation Versus Middle Management Self-Interest," *Strategic Management Journal* 7, no. 4 (July–August 1986): 321.

11. Joann Lublin, "Corporate Directors' Group Gives Repair Plan to Boards," *Wall Street Journal*, March 24, 2009, B4.

12. http://www.usatoday.com/money/companies/management/story/2012-05-14/ceo-firings/54964476/1.

13. Phred Dvorak, "Poor Year Doesn't Stop CEO Bonuses," *Wall Street Journal*, March 18, 2009, B1.

14. Louis Lavelle, "The Best and Worst Boards," *BusinessWeek*, October 7, 2002, 104–110.

15. Matt Murray, "Private Companies Also Feel Pressure to Clean Up Acts," *Wall Street Journal*, July 22, 2003, B1.

## PART 3

STRATEGY IMPLEMENTATION

## 7

Source: Yuri Arcurs/Shutterstock

MyManagementLab®

⭐ **Improve Your Grade!**

Over 10 million students improved their results using the Pearson MyLabs.
Visit **mymanagementlab.com** for simulations, tutorials, and end-of-chapter problems.

Implementing Strategies: Management and Operations Issues

CHAPTER OBJECTIVES

After studying this chapter, you should be able to do the following:

1. Construct an effective organizational chart.

2. Explain why corporate wellness has become so important in strategic planning.

3. Explain why strategy implementation is more difficult than strategy formulation.

4. Discuss the importance of annual objectives and policies in achieving organizational commitment for strategies to be implemented.

5. Explain why organizational structure is so important in strategy implementation.

6. Compare and contrast restructuring and reengineering.

7. Describe the relationship between production/operations and strategy implementation.

8. Explain how a firm can effectively link performance and pay to strategies.

9. Discuss employee stock ownership plans (ESOPs) as a strategic-management concept.

10. Describe how to modify an organizational culture to support new strategies.

ASSURANCE OF LEARNING **EXERCISES**

The following exercises are found at the end of this chapter.

The strategic-management process does not end on deciding what strategy or strategies to pursue. There must be a translation of strategic thought into strategic action. This translation is much easier if managers and employees of the firm understand the business, feel a part of the company, and through involvement in strategy-formulation activities have become committed to helping the organization succeed. Without understanding and commitment, strategy-implementation efforts face major problems. Vince Lombardi said: "The best game plan in the world never blocked or tackled anybody."

Implementing strategy affects an organization from top to bottom, including all the functional and divisional areas of a business. This chapter focuses on management issues most central to implementing strategies in 2014–2015 and Chapter 8 focuses on marketing, finance/accounting, R&D, and management information systems issues. TJX Companies is an example firm with excellent management practices.

Even the most technically perfect strategic plan will serve little purpose if it is not implemented. Many organizations tend to spend an inordinate amount of time, money, and effort on developing the strategic plan, treating the means and circumstances under which it will be implemented as afterthoughts! Change comes through implementation and evaluation, not through the plan. A technically imperfect plan that is implemented well will achieve more than the perfect plan that never gets off the paper on which it is typed.[1]

The Nature of Strategy Implementation

The strategy-implementation stage of strategic management is revealed in Figure 7-1, as illustrated with white shading. Successful strategy formulation does not guarantee successful strategy implementation. It is always more difficult to do something (strategy implementation) than to say you are going to do it (strategy formulation)! Although inextricably linked, strategy

EXCELLENT **STRATEGIC MANAGEMENT** SHOWCASED

The TJX Companies Inc.

Have you every shopped at the largest two discount clothing retailers in the USA, T. J. Maxx and Marshalls? The parent company of those clothing stores, TJX Companies, has formulated and is implementing excellent strategies. T. J. Maxx sells brand-name family apparel, accessories, women's shoes, domestics, giftware, and jewelry "at discount prices" at more than 1,010 stores nationwide. Marshalls offers a full line of shoes and a broader selection of menswear through about 900 stores. The company's HomeGoods chain of 399 stores in the USA focuses exclusively on home furnishings. T. K. Maxx is the company's European retail arm with more than 350 stores in the UK, Ireland, Germany, and now Poland, including 339 T. K. Maxx and 24 HomeSense stores. The company also operates about 310 stores in Canada, including 222 Winners, 87 HomeSense, and 13 Marshalls.

Same-store sales at TJX climbed 8.0 percent year-over-year in the 4-week period ended August 25, 2012. This rate of increase was in line with the year-ago period's growth. TJX's total sales climbed 10.0 percent for the aforementioned period to $1.9 billion from $1.7 billion in the year-ago period. As for the 30-week period ended August 25, 2012, comparable sales climbed 8 percent from the year-ago period.

Total sales for the same period went up 10.0 percent year over year to $12.4 billion. TJX's sales exceeded even management's expectations partly as a result of higher customer traffic in its USA, Canadian, and European divisions. At TJX's largest division, Marmaxx Group, comparable store sales growth of 9 percent during the 4-week period ended August 25, 2012.

TJX has reported increased comparable store sales and customer traffic for the past several quarters. TJX has an excellent, flexible off-price business model that allows the firm to react quickly and capitalize on market trends. TJX has a lower cost structure than many other traditional retailers.

Source: Based on a variety of sources.

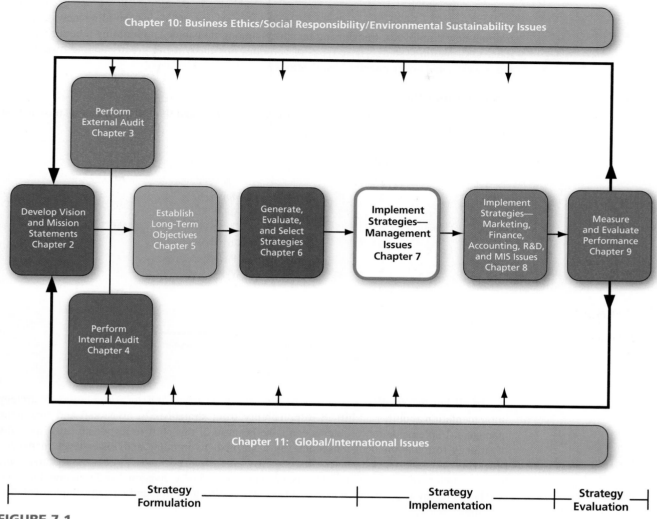

FIGURE 7-1

Comprehensive Strategic-Management Model

Source: Fred R. David, "How Companies Define Their Mission," *Long Range Planning* 22, no. 3 (June 1988): 40.

implementation is fundamentally different from strategy formulation. Strategy formulation and implementation can be contrasted in the following ways:

- Strategy formulation is positioning forces before the action.
- Strategy implementation is managing forces during the action.
- Strategy formulation focuses on effectiveness.
- Strategy implementation focuses on efficiency.
- Strategy formulation is primarily an intellectual process.
- Strategy implementation is primarily an operational process.
- Strategy formulation requires good intuitive and analytical skills.
- Strategy implementation requires special motivation and leadership skills.
- Strategy formulation requires coordination among a few individuals.
- Strategy implementation requires coordination among many individuals.

Strategy-formulation concepts and tools do not differ greatly for small, large, for-profit, or nonprofit organizations. However, strategy implementation varies substantially among different types and sizes of organizations. Implementing strategies requires such actions as altering sales territories, adding new departments, closing facilities, hiring new employees, changing an organization's pricing strategy, developing financial budgets, developing new employee benefits, establishing cost-control procedures, changing advertising strategies, building new facilities, training new employees, transferring managers among divisions, and building a better management information system. These types of activities obviously differ greatly among manufacturing, service, and governmental organizations.

Management Perspectives

In terms of "Quality of Management," *Fortune* recently ranked the following companies as best in the world:

Rank	Company
1	Koc Holding
2	McDonald's
3	Apple
4	Philip Morris International
5	Costco Wholesale
6	JP Morgan Chase
7	Wyndham Worldwide
8	Sysco
9	Walt Disney
10	TJX

Source: Based on: http://money.cnn.com/magazines/fortune/mostadmired/2012/best_worst/best5.html.

In all but the smallest organizations, the transition from strategy formulation to strategy implementation requires a shift in responsibility from strategists to divisional and functional managers. Implementation problems can arise because of this shift in responsibility, especially if strategy-formulation decisions come as a surprise to middle- and lower-level managers. Managers and employees are motivated more by perceived self-interests than by organizational interests, unless the two coincide. This is a primary reason why divisional and functional managers should be involved as much as possible in strategy-formulation and strategy-implementation activities.

As indicated in Table 7-1, management issues central to strategy implementation include establishing annual objectives, devising policies, allocating resources, altering an existing organizational structure, restructuring and reengineering, revising reward and incentive plans,

TABLE 7-1 Some Management Issues Central to Strategy Implementation

Establish annual objectives

Devise policies

Allocate resources

Alter an existing organizational structure

Restructure and reengineer

Revise reward and incentive plans

Minimize resistance to change

Match managers with strategy

Develop a strategy-supportive culture

Adapt production and operations processes

Develop an effective human resources function

Downsize and furlough as needed

Link performance and pay to strategies

minimizing resistance to change, matching managers with strategy, developing a strategy-supportive culture, adapting production and operations processes, developing an effective human resources function, and, if necessary, downsizing. Management changes are necessarily more extensive when strategies to be implemented move a firm in a major new direction.

Managers and employees throughout an organization should participate early and directly in strategy-implementation decisions. Their role in strategy implementation should build on prior involvement in strategy-formulation activities. Strategists' genuine personal commitment to implementation is a necessary and powerful motivational force for managers and employees. Too often, strategists are too busy to actively support strategy-implementation efforts, and their lack of interest can be detrimental to organizational success. The rationale for objectives and strategies should be understood and clearly communicated throughout an organization. Major competitors' accomplishments, products, plans, actions, and performance should be apparent to all organizational members. Major external opportunities and threats should be clear, and managers' and employees' questions should be answered. Top-down flow of communication is essential for developing bottom-up support.

Firms need to develop a competitor focus at all hierarchical levels by gathering and widely distributing competitive intelligence; every employee should be able to benchmark her or his efforts against best-in-class competitors so that the challenge becomes personal. For example, Starbucks Corp. recently instituted "lean production/operations" at its 11,000+ U.S. stores. This system eliminates idle employee time and unnecessary employee motions, such as walking, reaching, and bending. Starbucks says 30 percent of employees' time is motion and the company wants to reduce that. They say "motion and work are two different things."

Annual Objectives

Establishing annual objectives is a decentralized activity that directly involves all managers in an organization. Active participation in establishing annual objectives can lead to acceptance and commitment. **Annual objectives** are essential for strategy implementation because they (a) represent the basis for allocating resources; (b) are a primary mechanism for evaluating managers; (c) are the major instrument for monitoring progress toward achieving long-term objectives; and (d) establish organizational, divisional, and departmental priorities. Considerable time and effort should be devoted to ensuring that annual objectives are well conceived, consistent with long-term objectives, and supportive of strategies to be implemented. Approving, revising, or rejecting annual objectives is much more than a rubber-stamp activity. The purpose of annual objectives can be summarized as follows:

Annual objectives serve as guidelines for action, directing and channeling efforts and activities of organization members. They provide a source of legitimacy in an enterprise by justifying activities to stakeholders. They serve as standards of performance. They serve as an important source of employee motivation and identification. They give incentives for managers and employees to perform. They provide a basis for organizational design.[2]

Clearly stated and communicated objectives are critical to success in all types and sizes of firms. Annual objectives, stated in terms of profitability, growth, and market share by business segment, geographic area, customer groups, and product, are common in organizations. Figure 7-2 illustrates how the Stamus Company could establish annual objectives based on long-term objectives. Table 7-2 reveals associated revenue figures that correspond to the objectives outlined in Figure 7-2. Note that, according to plan, the Stamus Company will slightly exceed its long-term objective of doubling company revenues between 2012 and 2014.

Figure 7-2 also reflects how a hierarchy of annual objectives can be established based on an organization's structure. Objectives should be consistent across hierarchical levels and form a network of supportive aims. **Horizontal consistency of objectives** is as important as **vertical consistency of objectives**. For instance, it would not be effective for manufacturing to achieve more than its annual objective of units produced if marketing could not sell the additional units.

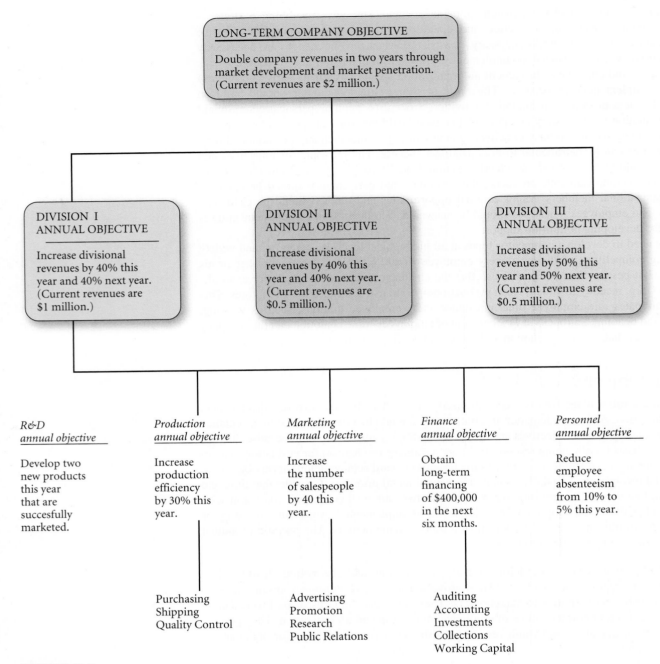

FIGURE 7-2

The Stamus Company's Hierarchy of Aims

Annual objectives should be measurable, consistent, reasonable, challenging, clear, communicated throughout the organization, characterized by an appropriate time dimension, and accompanied by commensurate rewards and sanctions. Too often, objectives are stated in generalities, with little operational usefulness. Annual objectives, such as "to improve communication" or "to improve performance," are not clear, specific, or measurable. Objectives should state quantity, quality, cost, and time—and also be verifiable. Terms and phrases such as *maximize*, *minimize*, *as soon as possible*, and *adequate* should be avoided.

Annual objectives should be compatible with employees' and managers' values and supported by clearly stated policies. More of something is not always better. Improved quality or

TABLE 7-2 The Stamus Company's Revenue Expectations (in $millions)

	2012	2013	2014
Division I Revenues	1.0	1.400	1.960
Division II Revenues	0.5	0.700	0.980
Division III Revenues	0.5	0.750	1.125
Total Company Revenues	**2.0**	**2.850**	**4.065**

reduced cost may, for example, be more important than quantity. It is important to tie rewards and sanctions to annual objectives so that employees and managers understand that achieving objectives is critical to successful strategy implementation. Clear annual objectives do not guarantee successful strategy implementation, but they do increase the likelihood that personal and organizational aims can be accomplished. Overemphasis on achieving objectives can result in undesirable conduct, such as faking the numbers, distorting the records, and letting objectives become ends in themselves. Managers must be alert to these potential problems.

Policies

Changes in a firm's strategic direction do not occur automatically. On a day-to-day basis, policies are needed to make a strategy work. Policies facilitate solving recurring problems and guide the implementation of strategy. Broadly defined, **policy** refers to specific guidelines, methods, procedures, rules, forms, and administrative practices established to support and encourage work toward stated goals. Policies are instruments for strategy implementation. Policies set boundaries, constraints, and limits on the kinds of administrative actions that can be taken to reward and sanction behavior; they clarify what can and cannot be done in pursuit of an organization's objectives. For example, Carnival's *Paradise* ship has a no smoking policy anywhere, anytime aboard ship. It was the first cruise ship to ban smoking comprehensively. Another example of corporate policy relates to surfing the Web while at work. About 40 percent of companies today do not have a formal policy preventing employees from surfing the Internet, but software is being marketed now that allows firms to monitor how, when, where, and how long various employees use the Internet at work.

Policies let both employees and managers know what is expected of them, thereby increasing the likelihood that strategies will be implemented successfully. They provide a basis for management control, allow coordination across organizational units, and reduce the amount of time managers spend making decisions. Policies also clarify what work is to be done and by whom. They promote delegation of decision making to appropriate managerial levels where various problems usually arise. Many organizations have a policy manual that serves to guide and direct behavior. Walmart has a policy that it calls the "10 Foot" Rule, whereby customers can find assistance within 10 feet of anywhere in the store. This is a welcomed policy in Japan, where Walmart is trying to gain a foothold; 58 percent of all retailers in Japan are mom-and-pop stores and consumers historically have had to pay "top yen" rather than "discounted prices" for merchandise.

Policies can apply to all divisions and departments (for example, "We are an equal opportunity employer"). Some policies apply to a single department ("Employees in this department must take at least one training and development course each year"). Whatever their scope and form, policies serve as a mechanism for implementing strategies and obtaining objectives. Policies should be stated in writing whenever possible. They represent the means for carrying out strategic decisions. Examples of policies that support a company strategy, a divisional objective, and a departmental objective are given in Table 7-3.

Some example issues that may require a management policy are provided in Table 7-4.

TABLE 7-3 A Hierarchy of Policies

Company Strategy
Acquire a chain of retail stores to meet our sales growth and profitability objectives.

Supporting Policies
1. "All stores will be open from 8 a.m. to 8 p.m. Monday through Saturday." (This policy could increase retail sales if stores currently are open only 40 hours a week.)
2. "All stores must submit a Monthly Control Data Report." (This policy could reduce expense-to-sales ratios.)
3. "All stores must support company advertising by contributing 5 percent of their total monthly revenues for this purpose." (This policy could allow the company to establish a national reputation.)
4. "All stores must adhere to the uniform pricing guidelines set forth in the Company Handbook." (This policy could help assure customers that the company offers a consistent product in terms of price and quality in all its stores.)

Divisional Objective
Increase the division's revenues from $10 million in 2014 to $15 million in 2015.

Supporting Policies
1. "Beginning in January 2014, each one of this division's salespersons must file a weekly activity report that includes the number of calls made, the number of miles traveled, the number of units sold, the dollar volume sold, and the number of new accounts opened." (This policy could ensure that salespersons do not place too great an emphasis in certain areas.)
2. "Beginning in January 2014, this division will return to its employees 5 percent of its gross revenues in the form of a Christmas bonus." (This policy could increase employee productivity.)
3. "Beginning in January 2014, inventory levels carried in warehouses will be decreased by 30 percent in accordance with a just-in-time (JIT) manufacturing approach." (This policy could reduce production expenses and thus free funds for increased marketing efforts.)

Production Department Objective
Increase production from 20,000 units in 2014 to 30,000 units in 2015.

Supporting Policies
1. "Beginning in January 2014, employees will have the option of working up to 20 hours of overtime per week." (This policy could minimize the need to hire additional employees.)
2. "Beginning in January 2014, perfect attendance awards in the amount of $100 will be given to all employees who do not miss a workday in a given year." (This policy could decrease absenteeism and increase productivity.)
3. "Beginning in January 2014, new equipment must be leased rather than purchased." (This policy could reduce tax liabilities and thus allow more funds to be invested in modernizing production processes.)

TABLE 7-4 Some Issues That May Require a Management Policy

- To offer extensive or limited management development workshops and seminars
- To centralize or decentralize employee-training activities
- To recruit through employment agencies, college campuses, or newspapers
- To promote from within or to hire from the outside
- To promote on the basis of merit or on the basis of seniority
- To tie executive compensation to long-term or annual objectives
- To offer numerous or few employee benefits
- To negotiate directly or indirectly with labor unions
- To delegate authority for large expenditures or to centrally retain this authority
- To allow much, some, or no overtime work
- To establish a high- or low-safety stock of inventory
- To use one or more suppliers
- To buy, lease, or rent new production equipment
- To greatly or somewhat stress quality control
- To establish many or only a few production standards
- To operate one, two, or three shifts
- To discourage using insider information for personal gain
- To discourage sexual harassment
- To discourage smoking at work
- To discourage insider trading
- To discourage moonlighting

Resource Allocation

Resource allocation is a central management activity that allows for strategy execution. In organizations that do not use a strategic-management approach to decision making, resource allocation is often based on political or personal factors. Strategic management enables resources to be allocated according to priorities established by annual objectives.

All organizations have at least four types of resources that can be used to achieve desired objectives: financial resources, physical resources, human resources, and technological resources. Allocating resources to particular divisions and departments does not mean that strategies will be successfully implemented. A number of factors commonly prohibit effective resource allocation, including an overprotection of resources, too great an emphasis on short-run financial criteria, organizational politics, vague strategy targets, a reluctance to take risks, and a lack of sufficient knowledge.

Below the corporate level, there often exists an absence of systematic thinking about resources allocated and strategies of the firm. Yavitz and Newman explain why:

> Managers normally have many more tasks than they can do. Managers must allocate time and resources among these tasks. Pressure builds up. Expenses are too high. The CEO wants a good financial report for the third quarter. Strategy formulation and implementation activities often get deferred. Today's problems soak up available energies and resources. Scrambled accounts and budgets fail to reveal the shift in allocation away from strategic needs to currently squeaking wheels.[3]

The real value of any resource allocation program lies in the resulting accomplishment of an organization's objectives. Effective resource allocation does not guarantee successful strategy implementation because programs, personnel, controls, and commitment must breathe life into the resources provided. Strategic management itself is sometimes referred to as a "resource allocation process."

Managing Conflict

Interdependency of objectives and competition for limited resources often leads to conflict. **Conflict** can be defined as a disagreement between two or more parties on one or more issues. Establishing annual objectives can lead to conflict because individuals have different expectations and perceptions, schedules create pressure, personalities are incompatible, and misunderstandings between line managers (such as production supervisors) and staff managers (such as human resource specialists) occur. For example, a collection manager's objective of reducing bad debts by 50 percent in a given year may conflict with a divisional objective to increase sales by 20 percent.

Establishing objectives can lead to conflict because managers and strategists must make trade-offs, such as whether to emphasize short-term profits or long-term growth, profit margin or market share, market penetration or market development, growth or stability, high risk or low risk, and social responsiveness or profit maximization. Trade-offs are necessary because no firm has sufficient resources to pursue all strategies that would benefit the firm. Table 7-5 reveals some important management trade-off decisions required in strategy implementation.

Conflict is unavoidable in organizations, so it is important that conflict be managed and resolved before dysfunctional consequences affect organizational performance. Conflict is not always bad. An absence of conflict can signal indifference and apathy. Conflict can serve to energize opposing groups into action and may help managers identify problems. General George Patton once said: "If everyone is thinking alike, then somebody isn't thinking."

Various approaches for managing and resolving conflict can be classified into three categories: avoidance, defusion, and confrontation. **Avoidance** includes such actions as ignoring the problem in hopes that the conflict will resolve itself or physically separating the conflicting individuals (or groups). **Defusion** can include playing down differences between conflicting parties while accentuating similarities and common interests, compromising so that there is neither a clear winner nor loser, resorting to majority rule, appealing to a higher authority, or redesigning present positions. **Confrontation** is exemplified by exchanging members of conflicting parties so that each can gain an appreciation of the other's point of view or holding a meeting at which conflicting parties present their views and work through their differences.

TABLE 7-5 Some Management Trade-Off Decisions Required in Strategy Implementation

To emphasize short-term profits or long-term growth

To emphasize profit margin or market share

To emphasize market development or market penetration

To lay off or furlough

To seek growth or stability

To take high risk or low risk

To be more socially responsible or more profitable

To outsource jobs or pay more to keep jobs at home

To acquire externally or to build internally

To restructure or reengineer

To use leverage or equity to raise funds

To use part-time or full-time employees

Matching Structure with Strategy

Changes in strategy often require changes in the way an organization is structured, for two major reasons. First, structure largely dictates how objectives and policies will be established. For example, objectives and policies established under a geographic organizational structure are couched in geographic terms. Objectives and policies are stated largely in terms of products in an organization whose structure is based on product groups. The structural format for developing objectives and policies can significantly impact all other strategy-implementation activities.

The second major reason why changes in strategy often require changes in structure is that structure dictates how resources will be allocated. If an organization's structure is based on customer groups, then resources will be allocated in that manner. Similarly, if an organization's structure is set up along functional business lines, then resources are allocated by functional areas. Unless new or revised strategies place emphasis in the same areas as old strategies, structural reorientation commonly becomes a part of strategy implementation.

Alfred Chandler promoted the notion that "changes in strategy lead to changes in organizational structure." Structure should be designed to facilitate the strategic pursuit of a firm and, therefore, follow strategy. Without a strategy or reasons for being (mission), companies find it difficult to design an effective structure. Chandler found a particular structure sequence to be repeated often as organizations grow and change strategy over time.

There is no one optimal organizational design or structure for a given strategy or type of organization. What is appropriate for one organization may not be appropriate for a similar firm, although successful firms in a given industry do tend to organize themselves in a similar way. For example, consumer goods companies tend to emulate the divisional structure-by-product form of organization. Small firms tend to be functionally structured (centralized). Medium-sized firms tend to be divisionally structured (decentralized). Large firms tend to use a **strategic business unit (SBU) structure** or matrix structure. As organizations grow, their structures generally change from simple to complex as a result of concatenation, or the linking together of several basic strategies.

Numerous external and internal forces affect an organization; no firm could change its structure in response to every one of these forces because to do so would lead to chaos. However, when a firm changes its strategy, the existing organizational structure may become ineffective. As indicated in Table 7-6, symptoms of an ineffective organizational structure include too many levels of management, too many meetings attended by too many people, too much attention being directed toward solving interdepartmental conflicts, too large a span of control, and too many unachieved objectives. Changes in structure can facilitate strategy-implementation efforts, but changes in structure should not be expected to make a bad strategy good, to make bad managers good, or to make bad products sell.

TABLE 7-6 Symptoms of an Ineffective Organizational Structure

1. Too many levels of management
2. Too many meetings attended by too many people
3. Too much attention being directed toward solving interdepartmental conflicts
4. Too large a span of control
5. Too many unachieved objectives
6. Declining corporate or business performance
7. Losing ground to rival firms
8. Revenue or earnings divided by number of employees or number of managers is low compared to rival firms

Structure undeniably can and does influence strategy. Strategies formulated must be workable, so if a certain new strategy required massive structural changes it would not be an attractive choice. In this way, structure can shape the choice of strategies. But a more important concern is determining what types of structural changes are needed to implement new strategies and how these changes can best be accomplished. There are seven basic types of organizational structure: functional, divisional by geographic area, divisional by product, divisional by customer, divisional process, strategic business unit (SBU), and matrix.

The Functional Structure

The most widely used structure is the functional or centralized type because this structure is the simplest and least expensive of the seven alternatives. A **functional structure** groups tasks and activities by business function, such as production and operations, marketing, finance and accounting, research and development, and management information systems. A university may structure its activities by major functions that include academic affairs, student services, alumni relations, athletics, maintenance, and accounting. Besides being simple and inexpensive, a functional structure also promotes specialization of labor, encourages efficient use of managerial and technical talent, minimizes the need for an elaborate control system, and allows rapid decision making.

Some disadvantages of a functional structure are that it forces accountability to the top, minimizes career development opportunities, and is sometimes characterized by low employee morale, line or staff conflicts, poor delegation of authority, and inadequate planning for products and markets.

A functional structure often leads to short-term and narrow thinking that may undermine what is best for the firm as a whole. For example, the research and development department may strive to overdesign products and components to achieve technical elegance, whereas manufacturing may argue for low-frills products that can be mass produced more easily. Thus, communication is often not as good in a functional structure. Schein gives an example of a communication problem in a functional structure:

The word "marketing" will mean product development to the engineer, studying customers through market research to the product manager, merchandising to the salesperson, and constant change in design to the manufacturing manager. Then when these managers try to work together, they often attribute disagreements to personalities and fail to notice the deeper, shared assumptions that vary and dictate how each function thinks.[4]

Most large companies have abandoned the functional structure in favor of decentralization and improved accountability. However, a large company that still operates from a functional type organizational design is Southwest Airlines, headquartered in Dallas, Texas. As illustrated in Figure 7-3, Southwest has only five top executives and no divisions, even though the firm operates 700 aircraft serving 72 cities in 37 states.

Table 7-7 summarizes the advantages and disadvantages of a functional organizational structure.

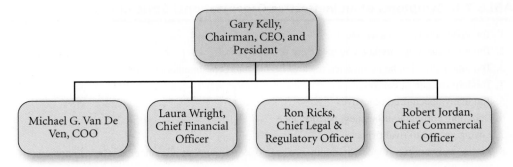

FIGURE 7-3

Southwest Airlines' Functional Organizational Chart

Source: Based on company documents.

The Divisional Structure

The **divisional structure** or **decentralized structure** is the second most common type used by U.S. businesses. As a small organization grows, it has more difficulty managing different products and services in different markets. Some form of divisional structure generally becomes necessary to motivate employees, control operations, and compete successfully in diverse locations. The divisional structure can be organized in one of four ways: *by geographic area*, *by product* or *service*, *by customer*, or *by process*. With a divisional structure, functional activities are performed both centrally and in each separate division.

Sun Microsystems recently reduced the number of its business units from seven to four. Kodak recently reduced its number of business units from seven by-customer divisions to five by-product divisions. As consumption patterns become increasingly similar worldwide, a by-product structure is becoming more effective than a by-customer or a by-geographic type divisional structure. In the restructuring, Kodak eliminated its global operations division and distributed those responsibilities across the new by-product divisions.

A divisional structure has some clear advantages. First and perhaps foremost, accountability is clear. That is, divisional managers can be held responsible for sales and profit levels. Because a divisional structure is based on extensive delegation of authority, managers and employees can easily see the results of their good or bad performances. As a result, employee morale is generally higher in a divisional structure than it is in a centralized structure. Other advantages of the divisional design are that it creates career development opportunities for managers, allows local control of situations, leads to a competitive climate within an organization, and allows new businesses and products to be added easily.

The divisional design is not without some limitations, however. Perhaps the most important limitation is that a divisional structure is costly, for a number of reasons. First, each division requires functional specialists who must be paid. Second, there exists some duplication of staff

TABLE 7-7 Advantages and Disadvantages of a Functional Organizational Structure

Advantages	Disadvantages
1. Simple and inexpensive	1. Accountability forced to the top
2. Capitalizes on specialization of business activities such as marketing and finance	2. Delegation of authority and responsibility not encouraged
3. Minimizes need for elaborate control system	3. Minimizes career development
4. Allows for rapid decision making	4. Low employee and manager morale
	5. Inadequate planning for products and markets
	6. Leads to short-term, narrow thinking
	7. Leads to communication problems

TABLE 7-8 Advantages and Disadvantages of a Divisional Organizational Structure

Advantages	Disadvantages
1. Accountability is clear	1. Can be costly
2. Allows local control of local situations	2. Duplication of functional activities
3. Creates career development chances	3. Requires a skilled management force
4. Promotes delegation of authority	4. Requires an elaborate control system
5. Leads to competitive climate internally	5. Competition among divisions can become so intense as to be dysfunctional
6. Allows easy adding of new products or regions	6. Can lead to limited sharing of ideas and resources
7. Allows strict control and attention to products, customers, or regions	7. Some regions, products, or customers may receive special treatment

services, facilities, and personnel; for instance, functional specialists are also needed centrally (at headquarters) to coordinate divisional activities. Third, managers must be well qualified because the divisional design forces delegation of authority; better-qualified individuals require higher salaries. A divisional structure can also be costly because it requires an elaborate, headquarters-driven control system. Fourth, competition between divisions may become so intense that it is dysfunctional and leads to limited sharing of ideas and resources for the common good of the firm. Table 7-8 summarizes the advantages and disadvantages of divisional organizational structure.

Ghoshal and Bartlett, two leading scholars in strategic management, note the following:

As their label clearly warns, divisions divide. The divisional model fragments companies' resources; it creates vertical communication channels that insulate business units and prevents them from sharing their strengths with one another. Consequently, the whole of the corporation is often less than the sum of its parts. A final limitation of the divisional design is that certain regions, products, or customers may sometimes receive special treatment, and it may be difficult to maintain consistent, companywide practices. Nonetheless, for most large organizations and many small firms, the advantages of a divisional structure more than offset the potential limitations.[5]

A *divisional structure by geographic area* is appropriate for organizations whose strategies need to be tailored to fit the particular needs and characteristics of customers in different geographic areas. This type of structure can be most appropriate for organizations that have similar branch facilities located in widely dispersed areas. A divisional structure by geographic area allows local participation in decision making and improved coordination within a region. Hershey Foods is an example company organized using the divisional-by-region type of structure, as illustrated in Figure 7-4. Analysts contend that this type of structure may not be best for Hershey because consumption patterns for candy are quite similar worldwide. An alternative—and perhaps better—type of structure for Hershey would be divisional by product because the company produces, and sells three types of products worldwide: (1) chocolate, (2) nonchocolate, and (3) grocery.

The *divisional structure by product (or services)* is most effective for implementing strategies when specific products or services need special emphasis. Also, this type of structure is widely used when an organization offers only a few products or services or when an organization's products or services differ substantially. The divisional structure allows strict control over and attention to product lines, but it may also require a more skilled management force and reduced top management control. General Motors, DuPont, Microsoft, and Procter & Gamble use a divisional structure by product to implement strategies. Microsoft introduced its new Surface Tablet for $499 in late 2012. The Surface is being sold online and in Microsoft retail stores, but not in stores such as Best Buy or Walmart, or even Amazon. Microsoft's divisional-by-product organizational structure is illustrated in Figure 7-5.

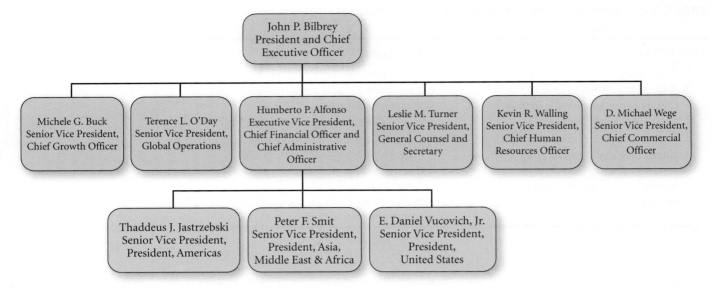

FIGURE 7-4

Hershey Foods' Divisional-by-Region Organizational Chart

Source: Based on company documents.

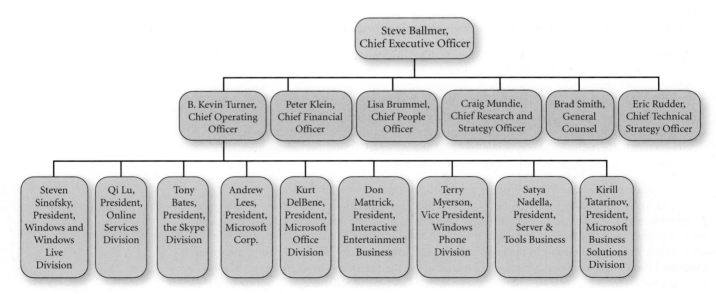

FIGURE 7-5

Microsoft's Divisional-by-Product Organizational Structure

Source: Based on company documents.

When a few major customers are of paramount importance and many different services are provided to these customers, then a *divisional structure by customer* can be the most effective way to implement strategies. This structure allows an organization to cater effectively to the requirements of clearly defined customer groups. For example, book publishing companies often organize their activities around customer groups, such as colleges, secondary schools, and private commercial schools. Some airline companies have two major customer divisions: passengers and freight or cargo services. Utility companies often use (1) commercial, (2) residential, and (3) industrial as their divisions by customer.

A *divisional structure by process* is similar to a functional structure, because activities are organized according to the way work is actually performed. However, a key difference between these two designs is that functional departments are not accountable for profits or revenues, whereas divisional process departments are evaluated on these criteria. An example of a divisional structure by process is a manufacturing business organized into six divisions: electrical work, glass cutting, welding, grinding, painting, and foundry work. In this case, all operations related to these specific processes would be grouped under the separate divisions. Each process (division) would be responsible for generating revenues and profits. The divisional structure by process can be particularly effective in achieving objectives when distinct production processes represent the thrust of competitiveness in an industry. Halliburton's organizational chart illustrated on the next page features aspects of the division-by-process design.

The Strategic Business Unit (SBU) Structure

As the number, size, and diversity of divisions in an organization increase, controlling and evaluating divisional operations become increasingly difficult for strategists. Increases in sales often are not accompanied by similar increases in profitability. The span of control becomes too large at top levels of the firm. For example, in a large conglomerate organization composed of 90 divisions, such as ConAgra, the chief executive officer could have difficulty even remembering the first names of divisional presidents. In multidivisional organizations, an SBU structure can greatly facilitate strategy-implementation efforts. ConAgra has put its many divisions into three primary SBUs: (1) food service (restaurants), (2) retail (grocery stores), and (3) agricultural products.

The SBU structure groups similar divisions into SBUs and delegates authority and responsibility for each unit to a senior executive who reports directly to the chief executive officer. This change in structure can facilitate strategy implementation by improving coordination between similar divisions and channeling accountability to distinct business units. In a 100-division conglomerate, the divisions could perhaps be regrouped into 10 SBUs according to certain common characteristics, such as competing in the same industry, being located in the same area, or having the same customers.

Two disadvantages of an SBU structure are that it requires an additional layer of management, which increases salary expenses. Also, the role of the group vice president is often ambiguous. However, these limitations often do not outweigh the advantages of improved coordination and accountability. Another advantage of the SBU structure is that it makes the tasks of planning and control by the corporate office more manageable.

News Corp. recently reorganized its operations into two SBUs: (1) Entertainment, which includes 20th Century Fox, Fox Broadcast News, and the Fox News Channel, and (2) Publishing, which includes The *Wall Street Journal*, *Times of London*, *The Sun* newspaper, *The Australian* newspaper, and HarperCollins book publishing. News Corp.'s Chairman and CEO, Rupert Murdoch, is retaining his family's 40 percent voting stake in what may result in two separate companies. Estimated 2014 revenue in billions of dollars by division within the Publishing SBU is as follows:

Australia newspapers (2.19)

Dow Jones (2.07)

U.K. newspapers (1.34)

Book publishing (1.25)

Marketing services (0.97)

Fox Sports (0.62)

REA Group (0.37)

NY Post, other (0.30)

Education business (0.12)

Apparently to groom a new CEO, Coca-Cola recently streamlined its organizational structure by converting to three SBUs: (1) The Americas Beverages headed by Cahillane, (2) Outside-The-Americas Beverages headed by Bozer, and (3) Outside-The-Americas Bottlers headed by Finan. Coke CEO Muhtar Kent said "Consolidating leadership under the three groups

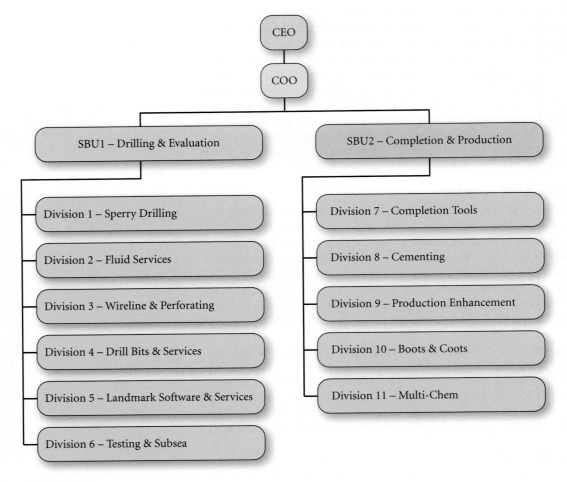

FIGURE 7-6

Halliburton Company's SBU Organizational Chart

Source: Based on http://www.halliburton.com/AboutUs/default.aspx?pageid=2458&navid=966.

will streamline reporting lines and intensify our focus on key markets." Either Mr. Cahillane and Mr. Bozer are expected to replace Mr. Kent as CEO sometime in the future, although Mr. Kent says: "As long as I'm having fun, my health allows me to continue and I'm generating good returns for our shareholders, and importantly as long as I'm smiling, which is important in anything you do, then I will continue."[6]

An excellent example of an SBU organizational chart is the one posted at the Halliburton Company website and shown in Figure 7-6. Note that six division executives report to the Drilling and Evaluation top executive, whereas five division heads report to the Completion and Production top executive. It is interesting and somewhat unusual that the 11 Halliburton divisions are organized by process rather than by geographic region or product.

The Matrix Structure

A **matrix structure** is the most complex of all designs because it depends on both vertical and horizontal flows of authority and communication (hence the term *matrix*). In contrast, functional and divisional structures depend primarily on vertical flows of authority and communication. A matrix structure can result in higher overhead because it creates more management positions. Other disadvantages of a matrix structure that contribute to overall complexity include dual lines of budget authority (a violation of the unity-of-command principle), dual sources of reward and punishment, shared authority, dual reporting channels, and a need for an extensive and effective communication system.

Despite its complexity, the matrix structure is widely used in many industries, including construction, health care, research, and defense. As indicated in Table 7-9, some advantages of a

TABLE 7-9 **Advantages and Disadvantages of a Matrix Structure**

Advantages	Disadvantages
1. Project objectives are clear	1. Requires excellent vertical and horizontal flows of communication
2. Employees can clearly see results of their work	2. Costly because creates more manager positions
3. Shutting down a project is easily accomplished	3. Violates unity of command principle
4. Facilitates uses of special equipment, personnel, and facilities	4. Creates dual lines of budget authority
5. Functional resources are shared instead of duplicated as in a divisional structure	5. Creates dual sources of reward and punishment
	6. Creates shared authority and reporting
	7. Requires mutual trust and understanding

matrix structure are that project objectives are clear, there are many channels of communication, workers can see the visible results of their work, and shutting down a project can be accomplished relatively easily. Another advantage of a matrix structure is that it facilitates the use of specialized personnel, equipment, and facilities. Functional resources are shared in a matrix structure, rather than duplicated as in a divisional structure. Individuals with a high degree of expertise can divide their time as needed among projects, and they in turn develop their own skills and competencies more than in other structures.

A typical matrix structure is illustrated in Figure 7-7. Note that the letters (A through Z4) refer to managers. For example, if you were manager A, you would be responsible for financial aspects of Project 1, and you would have two bosses: the Project 1 Manager on site and the CFO off site.

For a matrix structure to be effective, organizations need participative planning, training, clear mutual understanding of roles and responsibilities, excellent internal communication, and mutual trust and confidence. The matrix structure is being used more frequently by U.S. businesses because firms are pursuing strategies that add new products, customer groups, and technology to their range of activities. Out of these changes are coming product managers, functional managers, and geographic-area managers, all of whom have important strategic responsibilities. When several variables, such as product, customer, technology, geography, functional area, and line of business, have roughly equal strategic priorities, a matrix organization can be an effective structural form.

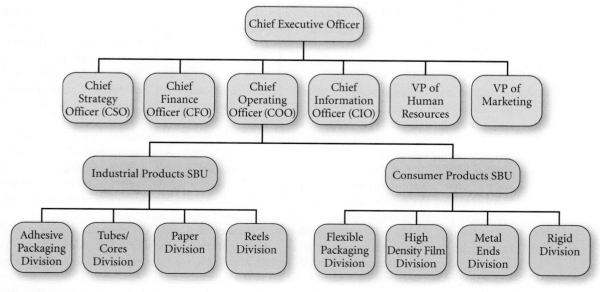

FIGURE 7-7

An Example Matrix Structure

Some Do's and Don'ts in Developing Organizational Charts

Students analyzing strategic-management cases are often asked to revise and develop a firm's organizational structure. This section provides some basic guidelines for this endeavor. There are some basic do's and don'ts in regard to devising or constructing organizational charts, especially for midsize to large firms. First of all, reserve the title CEO for the top executive of the firm. Don't use the title "president" for the top person; use it for the division top managers if there are divisions within the firm. Also, do not use the title "president" for functional business executives. They should have the title "chief," or "vice president," or "manager," or "officer," such as "Chief Information Officer," or "VP of Human Resources." Further, do not recommend a dual title (such as "CEO and president") for just one executive. Do not let a single individual be both chairman of the board, although Pfizer's CEO, Ian Read, is also chairman of the board. And Comverse Technology recently named Charles Burdick its president, chief executive officer, and chairman of the board. Actually, "chairperson" is much better than "chairman" for this title.

A significant movement among corporate America is to split the chairperson of the board and the CEO positions in publicly held companies.[7] The movement includes asking the New York Stock Exchange and Nasdaq to adopt listing rules that would require separate positions. About 50 percent of companies in the S&P 500 stock index have separate positions, up from 22 percent in 2002, but this still leaves plenty of room for improvement. Among European and Asian companies, the split in these two positions is much more common. For example, 79 percent of British companies split the positions, and all German and Dutch companies split the position. South Korea's Samsung Electronics in mid-2013 dissolved its COO position in favor of dual CEO's—but this practice in not common or popular in the USA.

Directly below the CEO, it is best to have a COO (chief operating officer) with any division presidents reporting directly to the COO. On the same level as the COO and also reporting to the CEO, draw in your functional business executives, such as a CFO (chief financial officer), VP of human resources, a CSO (chief strategy officer), a CIO (chief information officer), a CMO (chief marketing officer), a VP of R&D, a VP of legal affairs, an investment relations officer, maintenance officer, and so on. Note in Figure 7-8 that these positions are labeled and placed appropriately. Note that a controller or treasurer would normally report to the CFO.

In developing an organizational chart, avoid having a particular person reporting to more than one person in the chain of command. This would violate the unity-of-command principle of management that "every employee should have just one boss." Also, do not have the CFO, CIO, CSO, human resource officer, or other functional positions report to the COO. All these positions report directly to the CEO.

A key consideration in devising an organizational structure concerns the divisions. Note whether the divisions (if any) of a firm presently are established based on geography, customer, product, or process. If the firm's organizational chart is not available, you often can devise a chart based on the titles of executives. An important case analysis activity is for you to decide how the divisions of a firm should be organized for maximum effectiveness. Even if the firm presently has no divisions, determine whether the firm would operate better with divisions. In other words, which type of divisional breakdown do you (or your group or team) feel would be best for the firm in allocating resources, establishing objectives, and devising compensation incentives? This important strategic decision faces many midsize and large firms (and teams of students analyzing a strategic-management case).

As consumption patterns become more and more similar worldwide, the divisional-by-product form of structure is increasingly the most effective. Be mindful that all firms have functional staff below their top executive and often readily provide this information, so be wary of concluding prematurely that a particular firm uses a functional structure. If you see the word *president* in the titles of executives, coupled with financial-reporting segments, such as by product or geographic region, then the firm is divisionally structured.

If the firm is large with numerous divisions, decide whether an SBU type of structure would be more appropriate to reduce the span of control reporting to the COO. One never knows for sure if a proposed or actual structure is indeed most effective for a particular firm. Declining financial performance signals a need for altering the structure.

Some important guidelines to follow in devising organizational charts for companies are provided in Table 7-10.

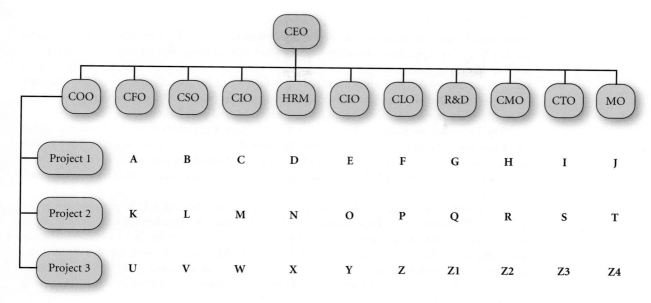

Note: Titles spelled out as follows.

Chief Executive Officer (CEO)
Chief Finance Officer (CFO)
Chief Strategy Officer (CSO)
Chief Information Officer (CIO)
Human Resources Manager (HRM)
Chief Operating Officer (COO)
Chief Legal Officer (CLO)
Research & Development Officer (R&D)
Chief Marketing Officer (CMO)
Chief Technology Officer (CTO)
Competitive Intelligence Officer (CIO)
Maintenance Officer (MO)

FIGURE 7-8

Typical Top Managers of a Large Firm

TABLE 7-10 Fifteen Guidelines for Developing an Organizational Chart

1. Instead of chairman of the board, make it chairperson of the board.
2. Make sure the board of directors reveals diversity in race, ethnicity, gender, and age.
3. Make sure the chair of the board is not also the CEO or president of the company.
4. Make sure the CEO of the firm does not also carry the title *president*.
5. Reserve the title *president* for the division heads of the firm.
6. Make sure the firm has a COO.
7. Make sure only presidents of divisions report to the COO.
8. Make sure functional executives such as CFO, CIO, CMO, CSO, R&D, CLO, CTO, and HRM report to the CEO, not the COO.
9. Make sure every executive has one boss, so lines in the chart should be drawn accordingly, assuring unity of command.
10. Make sure span of control is reasonable, probably no more than 10 persons reporting to any other person.
11. Make sure diversity in race, ethnicity, gender, and age is well represented among corporate executives.
12. Avoid a functional type structure for all but the smallest firms.
13. Decentralize, using some form of divisional structure, whenever possible.
14. Use an SBU type structure for large, multidivisional firms.
15. Make sure executive titles match product names as best possible in division-by-product and SBU-designated firms.

Restructuring

Restructuring and reengineering are becoming commonplace on the corporate landscape across the USA and Europe. **Restructuring**—also called **downsizing**, **rightsizing**, or **delayering**—involves reducing the size of the firm in terms of number of employees, number of divisions or units, and number of hierarchical levels in the firm's organizational structure. This reduction in size is intended to improve both efficiency and effectiveness. Restructuring is concerned primarily with shareholder well-being rather than employee well-being.

The lingering recession in Europe has forced many companies there to downsize, laying off managers and employees. This practice was historically rare in Europe because labor unions and laws required lengthy negotiations or huge severance checks before workers could be terminated. In contrast to the USA, labor union executives of large European firms sit on most boards of directors.

Job security in European companies is slowly moving toward a U.S. scenario, in which firms lay off almost at will. From banks in Milan to factories in Mannheim, European employers are starting to show people the door in an effort to streamline operations, increase efficiency, and compete against already slim and trim U.S. firms. Massive U.S.-style layoffs are still rare in Europe, but unemployment rates throughout the continent are rising quite rapidly. European firms still prefer to downsize by attrition and retirement rather than by blanket layoffs because of culture, laws, and unions.

In contrast, reengineering is concerned more with employee and customer well-being than shareholder well-being. **Reengineering**—also called *process management*, *process innovation*, or *process redesign*—involves reconfiguring or redesigning work, jobs, and processes for the purpose of improving cost, quality, service, and speed. Reengineering does not usually affect the organizational structure or chart, nor does it imply job loss or employee layoffs. Whereas restructuring is concerned with eliminating or establishing, shrinking or enlarging, and moving organizational departments and divisions, the focus of reengineering is changing the way work is actually carried out. Reengineering is characterized by many tactical (short-term, business-function-specific) decisions, whereas restructuring is characterized by strategic (long-term, affecting all business functions) decisions.

Developed by Motorola in 1986 and made famous by CEO Jack Welch at General Electric and more recently by Robert Nardelli, former CEO of Home Depot, **Six Sigma** is a quality-boosting process improvement technique that entails training several key persons in the firm in the techniques to monitor, measure, and improve processes and eliminate defects. Six Sigma has been widely applied across industries from retailing to financial services. CEO Dave Cote at Honeywell and CEO Jeff Immelt at General Electric spurred acceptance of Six Sigma, which aims to improve work processes and eliminate waste by training "select" employees who are given judo titles such as Master Black Belts, Black Belts, and Green Belts. Target Corp. claims more than $100 million in savings over the past six years resulting from its Six Sigma program.

Six Sigma was criticized in a *Wall Street Journal* article that cited many example firms whose stock price fell for a number of years after adoption of Six Sigma. The technique's reliance on the special group of trained employees is problematic and its use within retail firms such as Home Depot has not been as successful as in manufacturing firms.[8]

Restructuring

Firms often employ restructuring when various ratios appear out of line with competitors as determined through benchmarking exercises. Recall that **benchmarking** simply involves comparing a firm against the best firms in the industry on a wide variety of performance-related criteria. Some benchmarking ratios commonly used in rationalizing the need for restructuring are headcount-to-sales-volume, or corporate-staff-to-operating-employees, or span-of-control figures.

The primary benefit sought from restructuring is cost reduction. For some highly bureaucratic firms, restructuring can actually rescue the firm from global competition and demise. But the downside of restructuring can be reduced employee commitment, creativity, and innovation that accompanies the uncertainty and trauma associated with pending and actual employee layoffs. Avon Products recently restructured partly as a result of corruption investigations in its

Russia and Brazil operations. The company reduced its six commercial business units down to two—(1) Developed Markets and (2) Developing Markets—in essence going to a divisional by geographic region type structure. Avon has been reporting lower sales and profits amid missteps in key markets. Former CEO Andrea Jung installed five new regional heads and new presidents in Avon's U.S. and Russia markets.

Employers today are looking for people who can do things, not for people who make other people do things. Restructuring in many firms has made a manager's job an invisible, thankless role. More workers today are self-managed, entrepreneurs, interpreneurs, or team-managed. Managers today need to be counselors, motivators, financial advisors, and psychologists. They also run the risk of becoming technologically behind in their areas of expertise. "Dilbert" cartoons sometimes portray managers as enemies or as morons.

Linking Performance and Pay to Strategies

With so many people out of work and executive salaries so large, politicians are more and more giving shareholders greater control over executive pay. The Dodd-Frank Wall Street Reform and Consumer Protection Act grants shareholders advisory votes on compensation. A recent *Bloomberg Businessweek* article says companies should install five policies to improve their compensation practices:

1. Provide full transparency to all stakeholders. Novartis does an excellent job on this.
2. Reward long-term performance with long-term pay, rather than annual incentives. ExxonMobil does an excellent job on this.
3. Base executive compensation on actual company performance, rather than on stock price. Target, for example, bases executive pay on same-store sales growth rather than stock price.
4. Extend the time-horizon for bonuses. Replace short-term with long-term incentives. Goldman Sachs does an excellent job on this.
5. Increase equity between workers and executives. Delete many special perks and benefits for executives. Be more consistent across levels, although employees with greater responsibility must receive greater compensation.[10]

As firms acquire other firms in other countries, these pay differences can cause resentment and even turmoil. Larger pay packages of U.S. CEOs are socially less acceptable in many other countries. For example, in Japan, seniority rather than performance is the key factor in determining pay, and harmony among managers is emphasized over individual excellence.

How can an organization's reward system be more closely linked to strategic performance? How can decisions on salary increases, promotions, merit pay, and bonuses be more closely aligned to support the long-term strategic objectives of the organization? There are no widely accepted answers to these questions, but a dual bonus system based on both annual objectives and long-term objectives is becoming common. The percentage of a manager's annual bonus attributable to short-term versus long-term results should vary by hierarchical level in the organization. It is important that bonuses not be based solely on short-term results because such a system ignores long-term company strategies and objectives.

Many companies have recently instituted policies to allow their shareholders to vote on executive compensation policies. Aflac was the first U.S. corporation to voluntarily give shareholders an advisory vote on executive compensation. Aflac did this back in 2007. Apple did this in 2008, as did H&R Block. Several companies that instituted say-on-pay policies more recently were Ingersoll-Rand, Verizon, Motorola, Occidental Petroleum, and Hewlett-Packard. These new policies underscore how the financial crisis and shareholder outrage about top executive pay has affected compensation practice. None of the shareholder votes are binding on the companies, however, at least not so far. The U.S. House of Representatives recently passed a bill to formalize this shareholder tactic, which is gaining steam across the country as a means to combat exorbitant executive pay.

In an effort to cut costs and increase productivity, more and more Japanese companies are switching from seniority-based pay to performance-based approaches. Toyota has switched to a full merit system for 20,000 of its 70,000 white-collar workers. Fujitsu, Sony, Matsushita

Electric Industrial, and Kao also have switched to merit pay systems. This switching is hurting morale at some Japanese companies, which have trained workers for decades to cooperate rather than to compete and to work in groups rather than individually.

Richard Brown, CEO of Electronic Data Systems (EDS), once said,

> You have to start with an appraisal system that gives genuine feedback and differentiates performance. Some call it ranking people. That seems a little harsh. But you can't have a manager checking a box that says you're either stupendous, magnificent, very good, good, or average. Concise, constructive feedback is the fuel workers use to get better. A company that doesn't differentiate performance risks losing its best people.[11]

Profit sharing is another widely used form of incentive compensation. More than 30 percent of U.S. companies have profit-sharing plans, but critics emphasize that too many factors affect profits for this to be a good criterion. Taxes, pricing, or an acquisition would wipe out profits, for example. Also, firms try to minimize profits in a sense to reduce taxes.

For employee (rather than executive) bonuses and incentives, only 16 percent of U.S. companies are now using stock price, down from 29 percent in 2009.[12] Instead, companies are using profit in order to more closely link employees' incentives to spending and budget decisions. PepsiCo, for example, recently began using profit and cash flow instead of stock price to focus managers on profit and cash-flow targets. PepsiCo's CFO, Hugh Johnston, said: "The change allows our employees to make decisions about spending and profit trade-offs themselves, rather than simply being handed a budget to follow; it's something they can wrap their arms around and say, 'Now I understand how I can impact PepsiCo's stock price.'" PepsiCo's new compensation system based on profit enabled the company to lower its capital spending to 4.5 percent of sales in 2012, down from an historical average of about 5.5 percent. For upper-level executives, stock price is still the major variable used for compensation incentives, but for mid-and-lower level managers and employees, stock price is dependent on too many extraneous variables for it to be an effective compensation variable.

The good news for shareholders is that in 2013, over 50 percent of CEO compensation was directly associated with the performance of the firm, rather than salary—up from 35 percent in 2009 (*WSJ*, 3-21-13, p. B1). Note below that Indra Nooyi of PepsiCo was the third highest paid women CEO in 2012 in the USA:

1. Irene Rosenfeld at Kraft ($21.9M)
2. Debra Cafaro at Ventas ($18.5M)
3. Indra Nooyi at PepsiCo ($17.1M)
4. Meg Whitman at HP ($16.5M)
5. Ellen Kullman at DuPont ($15.9M)
6. Angela Braly at WellPoint ($13.3M)

Still another criterion widely used to link performance and pay to strategies is gain sharing. **Gain sharing** requires employees or departments to establish performance targets; if actual results exceed objectives, all members get bonuses. More than 26 percent of U.S. companies use some form of gain sharing; about 75 percent of gain-sharing plans have been adopted since 1980. Carrier, a subsidiary of United Technologies, has had excellent success with gain sharing in its six plants in Syracuse, New York; Firestone's tire plant in Wilson, North Carolina, has experienced similar success with gain sharing.

Criteria such as sales, profit, production efficiency, quality, and safety could also serve as bases for an effective **bonus system**. If an organization meets certain understood, agreed-on profit objectives, every member of the enterprise should share in the harvest. A bonus system can be an effective tool for motivating individuals to support strategy-implementation efforts. BankAmerica, for example, recently overhauled its incentive system to link pay to sales of the bank's most profitable products and services. Branch managers receive a base salary plus a bonus based both on the number of new customers and on sales of bank products. Every employee in each branch is also eligible for a bonus if the branch exceeds its goals. Thomas Peterson, a top BankAmerica executive, says, "We want to make people responsible for meeting their goals, so we pay incentives on sales, not on controlling costs or on being sure the parking lot is swept."

Five tests are often used to determine whether a performance-pay plan will benefit an organization:

1. *Does the plan capture attention?* Are people talking more about their activities and taking pride in early successes under the plan?
2. *Do employees understand the plan?* Can participants explain how it works and what they need to do to earn the incentive?
3. *Is the plan improving communication?* Do employees know more than they used to about the company's mission, plans, and objectives?
4. *Does the plan pay out when it should?* Are incentives being paid for desired results—and being withheld when objectives are not met?
5. *Is the company or unit performing better?* Are profits up? Has market share grown? Have gains resulted in part from the incentives?[13]

In addition to a dual bonus system, a combination of reward strategy incentives, such as salary raises, stock options, fringe benefits, promotions, praise, recognition, criticism, fear, increased job autonomy, and awards, can be used to encourage managers and employees to push hard for successful strategic implementation. The range of options for getting people, departments, and divisions to actively support strategy-implementation activities in a particular organization is almost limitless. Merck, for example, recently gave each of its 37,000 employees a 10-year option to buy 100 shares of Merck stock at a set price of $127. Steven Darien, Merck's vice president of human resources, says, "We needed to find ways to get everyone in the workforce on board in terms of our goals and objectives. Company executives will begin meeting with all Merck workers to explore ways in which employees can contribute more."

Managing Resistance to Change

No organization or individual can escape change. But the thought of change raises anxieties because people fear economic loss, inconvenience, uncertainty, and a break in normal social patterns. Almost any change in structure, technology, people, or strategies has the potential to disrupt comfortable interaction patterns. For this reason, people resist change. The strategic-management process itself can impose major changes on individuals and processes. Reorienting an organization to get people to think and act strategically is not an easy task.

Resistance to change can be considered the single greatest threat to successful strategy implementation. Resistance regularly occurs in organizations in the form of sabotaging production machines, absenteeism, filing unfounded grievances, and an unwillingness to cooperate. People often resist strategy implementation because they do not understand what is happening or why changes are taking place. In that case, employees may simply need accurate information. Successful strategy implementation hinges on managers' ability to develop an organizational climate conducive to change. Change must be viewed as an opportunity rather than as a threat by managers and employees.

Resistance to change can emerge at any stage or level of the strategy-implementation process. Although there are various approaches for implementing changes, three commonly used strategies are a force change strategy, an educative change strategy, and a rational or self-interest change strategy. A **force change strategy** involves giving orders and enforcing those orders; this strategy has the advantage of being fast, but it is plagued by low commitment and high resistance. The **educative change strategy** is one that presents information to convince people of the need for change; the disadvantage of an educative change strategy is that implementation becomes slow and difficult. However, this type of strategy evokes greater commitment and less resistance than does the force change strategy. Finally, a **rational change strategy** or **self-interest change strategy** is one that attempts to convince individuals that the change is to their personal advantage. When this appeal is successful, strategy implementation can be relatively easy. However, implementation changes are seldom to everyone's advantage.

The rational change strategy is the most desirable, so this approach is examined a bit further. Managers can improve the likelihood of successfully implementing change by carefully designing change efforts. Jack Duncan described a rational or self-interest change strategy as consisting of four steps. First, employees are invited to participate in the process of change and in the details of transition; participation allows everyone to give opinions, to feel a part of the change process, and to identify their own self-interests regarding the recommended change. Second, some motivation or incentive to change is required; self-interest can be the most important motivator. Third, communication is needed so that people can understand the purpose for the changes. Giving and receiving feedback is the fourth step: everyone enjoys knowing how things are going and how much progress is being made.[14]

Because of diverse external and internal forces, change is a fact of life in organizations. The rate, speed, magnitude, and direction of changes vary over time by industry and organization. Strategists should strive to create a work environment in which change is recognized as necessary and beneficial so that individuals can more easily adapt to change. Adopting a strategic-management approach to decision making can itself require major changes in the philosophy and operations of a firm.

Strategists can take a number of positive actions to minimize managers' and employees' resistance to change. For example, individuals who will be affected by a change should be involved in the decision to make the change and in decisions about how to implement the change. Strategists should anticipate changes and develop and offer training and development workshops so that managers and employees can adapt to those changes. They also need to effectively communicate the need for changes. The strategic-management process can be described as a process of managing change.

Organizational change should be viewed today as a continuous process rather than as a project or event. The most successful organizations today continuously adapt to changes in the competitive environment, which themselves continue to change at an accelerating rate. It is not sufficient today to simply react to change. Managers need to anticipate change and ideally be the creator of change. Viewing change as a continuous process is in stark contrast to an old management doctrine regarding change, which was to unfreeze behavior, change the behavior, and then refreeze the new behavior. The new "continuous organizational change" philosophy should mirror the popular "continuous quality improvement philosophy."

Creating a Strategy-Supportive Culture

Strategists should strive to preserve, emphasize, and build on aspects of an existing **culture** that support proposed new strategies. Aspects of an existing culture that are antagonistic to a proposed strategy should be identified and changed. Substantial research indicates that new strategies are often market-driven and dictated by competitive forces. For this reason, changing a firm's culture to fit a new strategy is usually more effective than changing a strategy to fit an existing culture. As indicated in Table 7-11, numerous techniques are available to alter

TABLE 7-11 Ways and Means for Altering an Organization's Culture

1. Recruitment
2. Training
3. Transfer
4. Promotion
5. Restructuring
6. Reengineering
7. Role modeling
8. Positive reinforcement
9. Mentoring
10. Revising vision and/or mission
11. Redesigning physical spaces/facades
12. Altering reward system
13. Altering organizational policies, procedures, and practices

an organization's culture, including recruitment, training, transfer, promotion, restructure of an organization's design, role modeling, positive reinforcement, and mentoring.

Schein indicated that the following elements are most useful in linking culture to strategy:

1. Formal statements of organizational philosophy, charters, creeds, materials used for recruitment and selection, and socialization
2. Designing of physical spaces, facades, and buildings
3. Deliberate role modeling, teaching, and coaching by leaders
4. Explicit reward and status system and promotion criteria
5. Stories, legends, myths, and parables about key people and events
6. What leaders pay attention to, measure, and control
7. Leader reactions to critical incidents and organizational crises
8. How the organization is designed and structured
9. Organizational systems and procedures
10. Criteria used for recruitment, selection, promotion, leveling off, retirement, and "excommunication" of people[15]

When Volkswagen AG acquired Porsche in late 2012, there was concern that the 75-year-old Volkswagen Chairman and patriarch, Ferdinand Piech's autocratic style would be at odds with Porsche's corporate culture. Porsche had for a long time placed a premium on individual effort among its engineers and designers, often encouraging competition among groups to come up with new design ideas and innovations. Time will tell if Volkswagen and Porsche can meld their cultures into a competitive advantage.

In the personal and religious side of life, the impact of loss and change is easy to see.[16] Memories of loss and change often haunt individuals and organizations for years. Ibsen wrote, "Rob the average man of his life illusion and you rob him of his happiness at the same stroke."[17] When attachments to a culture are severed in an organization's attempt to change direction, employees and managers often experience deep feelings of grief. This phenomenon commonly occurs when external conditions dictate the need for a new strategy. Managers and employees often struggle to find meaning in a situation that changed many years before. Some people find comfort in memories; others find solace in the present. Weak linkages between strategic management and organizational culture can jeopardize performance and success. Deal and Kennedy emphasized that making strategic changes in an organization always threatens a culture:

People form strong attachments to heroes, legends, the rituals of daily life, the hoopla of extravaganza and ceremonies, and all the symbols of the workplace. Change strips relationships and leaves employees confused, insecure, and often angry. Unless something can be done to provide support for transitions from old to new, the force of a culture can neutralize and emasculate strategy changes.[18]

Production and Operations Concerns When Implementing Strategies

Apple employs thousands of its own workers in China, but about 700,000 assembly workers at manufacturing contractors like Foxconn put together Apple products. It would be almost impossible to bring those jobs to the USA for at least three reasons. First of all, Foxconn—China's largest private employer and the manufacturer of an estimated 40 percent of the world's consumer electronic devices—pays its assembly workers far less than U.S. labor laws would allow. A typical salary is about $18 a day. Secondly, unlike U.S. plants, Foxconn and other Chinese manufacturing operations house employees in dormitories and can send hundreds of thousands of workers to the assembly lines at a moment's notice. On the lines, workers are subjected to what most Americans would consider unbearable long hours and tough working conditions. That system gives tech companies the efficiency needed to race products out the door, so speed is a bigger factor than pay. Finally, most of the component suppliers for Apple and other technology giants are also

TABLE 7-12 Production Management and Strategy Implementation

Type of Organization	Strategy Being Implemented	Production System Adjustments
Hospital	Adding a cancer center (Product Development)	Purchase specialized equipment and add specialized people.
Bank	Adding 10 new branches (Market Development)	Perform site location analysis.
Beer brewery	Purchasing a barley farm operation (Backward Integration)	Revise the inventory control system.
Steel manufacturer	Acquiring a fast-food chain (Unrelated Diversification)	Improve the quality control system.
Computer company	Purchasing a retail distribution chain (Forward Integration)	Alter the shipping, packaging, and transportation systems.

in China or other Asian countries. That geographic clustering gives companies the flexibility to change a product design at the last minute and still ship on time.

Production and operations capabilities, limitations, and policies can significantly enhance or inhibit the attainment of objectives. Production processes typically constitute more than 70 percent of a firm's total assets. A major part of the strategy-implementation process takes place at the production site. Production-related decisions on plant size, plant location, product design, choice of equipment, kind of tooling, size of inventory, inventory control, quality control, cost control, use of standards, job specialization, employee training, equipment and resource utilization, shipping and packaging, and technological innovation can have a dramatic impact on the success or failure of strategy-implementation efforts.

Examples of adjustments in production systems that could be required to implement various strategies are provided in Table 7-12 for both for-profit and nonprofit organizations. For instance, note that when a bank formulates and selects a strategy to add 10 new branches, a production-related implementation concern is site location. The largest bicycle company in the USA, Huffy, recently ended its own production of bikes and now contracts out those services to Asian and Mexican manufacturers. Huffy focuses instead on the design, marketing, and distribution of bikes, but it no longer produces bikes itself. The Dayton, Ohio, company closed its plants in Ohio, Missouri, and Mississippi.

Just-in-time (JIT) production approaches have withstood the test of time. JIT significantly reduces the costs of implementing strategies. With JIT, parts and materials are delivered to a production site just as they are needed, rather than being stockpiled as a hedge against later deliveries. Harley-Davidson reports that at one plant alone, JIT freed $22 million previously tied up in inventory and greatly reduced reorder lead time.

Factors that should be studied before locating production facilities include the availability of major resources, the prevailing wage rates in the area, transportation costs related to shipping and receiving, the location of major markets, political risks in the area or country, and the availability of trainable employees. Some of these factors explain why many manufacturing operations in China are moving back to Mexico, or to Vietnam, or even back to the USA.

Human Resource Concerns When Implementing Strategies

More and more companies are instituting furloughs to cut costs as an alternative to laying off employees. **Furloughs** are temporary layoffs and even white-collar managers are being given furloughs, once confined to blue-collar workers. A few organizations furloughing professional workers include Gulfstream Aerospace, Media General, Gannett, the University of Maryland, Clemson University, and Spansion. Most companies are still using temporary and part-time workers rather than hiring full-time employees, which suggests that high unemployment rates may be a long-term trend. More and more companies may follow Harley-Davidson's lead

TABLE 7-13 Labor Cost-Saving Tactics

Salary freeze

Hiring freeze

Salary reductions

Reduce employee benefits

Raise employee contribution to health-care premiums

Reduce employee 401(k)/403(b) match

Reduce employee workweek

Mandatory furlough

Voluntary furlough

Hire temporary instead of full-time employees

Hire contract employees instead of full-time employees

Volunteer buyouts (Walt Disney is doing this)

Halt production for three days a week (Toyota Motor is doing this)

Layoffs

Early retirement

Reducing or eliminating bonuses

Source: Based on Dana Mattioli, "Employers Make Cuts Despite Belief Upturn Is Near," *Wall Street Journal*, April 23, 2009, B4.

when that firm signed a new union contract recently that creates a tier of "casual workers" with no benefits and no minimum number of hours, allowing Harley to call up workers only as needed.[20] Table 7-13 lists ways that companies today are reducing labor costs to stay financially sound.

A well-designed strategic-management system can fail if insufficient attention is given to the human resource dimension. Human resource problems that arise when businesses implement strategies can usually be traced to one of three causes: (1) disruption of social and political structures, (2) failure to match individuals' aptitudes with implementation tasks, and (3) inadequate top management support for implementation activities.[21]

Strategy implementation poses a threat to many managers and employees in an organization. New power and status relationships are anticipated and realized. New formal and informal groups' values, beliefs, and priorities may be largely unknown. Managers and employees may become engaged in resistance behavior as their roles, prerogatives, and power in the firm change. Disruption of social and political structures that accompany strategy execution must be anticipated and considered during strategy formulation and managed during strategy implementation.

A concern in matching managers with strategy is that jobs have specific and relatively static responsibilities, although people are dynamic in their personal development. Commonly used methods that match managers with strategies to be implemented include transferring managers, developing leadership workshops, offering career development activities, promotions, job enlargement, and job enrichment.

A number of other guidelines can help ensure that human relationships facilitate rather than disrupt strategy-implementation efforts. Specifically, managers should do a lot of chatting and informal questioning to stay abreast of how things are progressing and to know when to intervene. Managers can build support for strategy-implementation efforts by giving few orders, announcing few decisions, depending heavily on informal questioning, and seeking to probe and clarify until a consensus emerges. Key thrusts that succeed should be rewarded generously and visibly.

Perhaps the best method for preventing and overcoming human resource problems in strategic management is to actively involve as many managers and employees as possible in the process. Although time consuming, this approach builds understanding, trust, commitment, and ownership and reduces resentment and hostility. The true potential of strategy formulation and implementation resides in people.

Employee Stock Ownership Plans (ESOPs)

An ESOP is a tax-qualified, defined-contribution, employee-benefit plan whereby employees purchase stock of the company through borrowed money or cash contributions. ESOPs empower employees to work as owners; this is a primary reason why the number of ESOPs have grown dramatically to more than 10,000 firms covering more than 14 million employees. ESOPs now control more than $600 billion in corporate stock in the USA.

Some ESOP companies include:

- W. L. Gore & Associates—maker of medical and industrial products as well as Gore-Tex
- Herman Miller—famous for making innovative office furniture
- KCI—a civil engineering firm
- HCSS—a software manufacturer for the heavy construction industry

Besides reducing worker alienation and stimulating productivity, ESOPs allow firms other benefits, such as substantial tax savings. Principal, interest, and dividend payments on ESOP-funded debt are tax deductible. Banks lend money to ESOPs at interest rates below prime. This money can be repaid in pretax dollars, lowering the debt service as much as 30 percent in some cases. "The ownership culture really makes a difference, when management is a facilitator, not a dictator," says Corey Rosen, executive director of the National Center for Employee Ownership. Fifteen employee-owned companies are listed in Table 7-14.

If an ESOP owns more than 50 percent of the firm, those who lend money to the ESOP are taxed on only 50 percent of the income received on the loans. ESOPs are not for every firm, however, because the initial legal, accounting, actuarial, and appraisal fees to set up an ESOP are about $50,000 for a small or midsized firm, with annual administration expenses of about $15,000. Analysts say ESOPs also do not work well in firms that have fluctuating payrolls and profits. Human resource managers in many firms conduct preliminary research to determine the desirability of an ESOP, and then they facilitate its establishment and administration if benefits outweigh the costs.

Wyatt Cafeterias, a southwestern U.S. operator of 120 cafeterias, also adopted the ESOP concept to prevent a hostile takeover. Employee productivity at Wyatt greatly increased since the ESOP began, as illustrated in the following quote:

The key employee in our entire organization is the person serving the customer on the cafeteria line. We now tell the tea cart server, "Don't wait for the manager to tell you how to do your job better or how to provide better service. You take care of it." Sure,

TABLE 7-14 Fourteen Example ESOP Firms

Firm	Headquarters Location
Publix Supermarkets	Florida
Tribune Company	Illinois
Lifetouch	Minnesota
John Lewis Partnership	United Kingdom
Mondragon Cooperative	Spain
Houchens Industries	Kentucky
Amsted Industries	Illinois
Mast General Store	North Carolina
HDR, Inc.	Nebraska
Yoke's Fresh Market	Washington
SPARTA, Inc.	California
Hy-Vee	Iowa
Bi-Mart	Washington
Ferrellgas Partners	Kansas

we're looking for productivity increases, but since we began pushing decisions down to the level of people who deal directly with customers, we've discovered an awesome side effect—suddenly the work crews have this "happy to be here" attitude that the customers really love.[22]

Balancing Work Life and Home Life

More women earn both undergraduate and graduate degrees in the USA than men, but a wage disparity still persists between men and women at all education levels.[23] Women on average make 25 percent less than men. The average age today for women to get married in the USA is 30 for those with a college degree, and 26 for those with just a high school degree. About 29 percent of both men and women in the USA today have a college degree, whereas in 1970 only 8 percent of women and 14 percent of men had college degrees.

A recent article in *Wall Street Journal* (12-5-12, A3) revealed that in the USA, women now hold 33.4 percent of legal jobs, including lawyers, judges, magistrates, and other judicial employees, up from 29.2 percent in 2000. Also, the percentage of women physicians and surgeons rose to 32.4 percent from 26.8 percent during that time. This is great news; however, the bad news is that the median salary for women lawyers is $90,000 versus $122,000 for men, and the median salary for female physicians is $112,128 versus $186,916 for men.

Globally, it is widely acknowledged that the best countries for working women are Norway, Sweden, Finland, and Denmark—that often rate above the USA. According to the World Economic Forum's 2012 report on the global gender gap overall, the USA ranked number 22 overall, and on wage equality, the USA ranked number 61 behind Madagascar, Cambodia, and Guyana. In that report, women in the USA make on average 67 percent of what men make, compared, for example, to 73 percent in Canada. Unmarried women in fact make more than men in many countries. Married women with children, however, usually make considerably lower than men.

Work and family strategies have become so popular among companies today that the strategies now represent a competitive advantage for those firms that offer such benefits as elder care assistance, flexible scheduling, job sharing, adoption benefits, an on-site summer camp, employee help lines, pet care, and even lawn service referrals. New corporate titles such as work and life coordinator and director of diversity are becoming common.

Working Mother magazine annually published its listing of "The 100 Best Companies for Working Mothers" (www.workingmother.com). Three especially important variables used in the ranking were availability of flextime, advancement opportunities, and equitable distribution of benefits among companies. Other important criteria are compressed weeks, telecommuting, job sharing, childcare facilities, maternity leave for both parents, mentoring, career development, and promotion for women. *Working Mother's* top 10 best companies for working women in 2012 are provided in Table 7-15. *Working Mother* also conducts extensive research to determine the best U.S. firms for women of color.

A corporate objective to become more lean and mean must today include consideration for the fact that a good home life contributes immensely to a good work life. The work and family issue is no longer just a women's issue. Some specific measures that firms are taking to address this issue are providing spouse relocation assistance as an employee benefit; providing company resources for family recreational and educational use; establishing employee country clubs, such as those at IBM and Bethlehem Steel; and creating family and work interaction opportunities. A study by Joseph Pleck of Wheaton College found that in companies that do not offer paternity leave for fathers as a benefit, most men take short, informal paternity leaves anyway by combining vacation time and sick days.

Some organizations have developed family days, when family members are invited into the workplace, taken on plant or office tours, dined by management, and given a chance to see exactly what other family members do each day. Family days are inexpensive and increase the employee's pride in working for the organization. Flexible working hours during the week are another human resource response to the need for individuals to balance work life and home life. The work and family topic is being made part of the agenda at meetings and thus is being discussed in many organizations.

TABLE 7-15 Top Ten Companies for Working Women

1. Bank of America—allows employees to define how they work.
2. Deloitte—grants employees four unpaid weeks off annually.
3. Ernst & Young (E&Y)—up to 75 percent of its employees work outside E&Y offices. Breastfeeding moms may rely on lactation rooms at most sites.
4. General Mills—women head five of the seven U.S. retail divisions.
5. Grant Thornton—offers 8 weeks of paid maternity leave and numerous flexible work options.
6. IBM—offers outstanding assistance to children of employees through its Special Care for Children program.
7. KPMG—employees may take 26 (job guaranteed, partially paid) weeks off following the birth or adoption of a child.
8. Procter & Gamble (P&G)—all P&G office employees may adjust the times that they start or finish work by two hours either way; 47 percent of all P&G hires in 2011 were women. Breastfeeding moms may rely on lactation rooms at most sites.
9. PricewaterhouseCoopers—many female partners go through the Breakthrough Leadership Development Program and achieve top executive positions.
10. WellStar Health System—has an in-house concierge service to help moms get things done.

Source: Based on 2012: http://www.workingmother.com/best-company-list/129110/7271.

There is great room for improvement in removing the glass ceiling domestically, especially considering that women make up 47 percent of the U.S. labor force. **Glass ceiling** refers to the invisible barrier in many firms that bars women and minorities from top-level management positions. The USA is a leader globally in promoting women and minorities into mid- and top-level managerial positions in business. Only 4.0 percent of Fortune 500 firms have a woman CEO. Table 7-16 gives the 21 Fortune 500 Women CEOs in 2013. These women are wonderful role models for women around the world.

TABLE 7-16 Fortune 500 Women CEOs in 2013

CEO	Company
Angela Braly	WellPoint
Patricia Woertz	Archer Daniels Midland
Marissa Mayer	Yahoo!
Indra Nooyi	PepsiCo
Irene Rosenfeld	Kraft Foods
Carol Meyrowitz	TJX
Virginia Rometty	IBM
Debra Reed	Sempra Energy
Deanna Mulligan	Guardian Life Insurance
Sherilyn McCoy	Avon Products
Denise Morrison	Campbell Soup
Maggie Wilderotter	Frontier Communications
Meg Whitman	Hewlett-Packard
Ilene Gordon	Corn Products
Heather Bresch	Mylan
Gracia Martore	Gannett
Ellen Kullman	DuPont
Ursula Burns	Xerox
Kathleen Mazzarella	Graybar Electric
Beth Mooney	Key Corp
Marillyn Hewson	Lockheed Martin Corp

Benefits of a Diverse Workforce

CEO Rosalind Brewer, the first African American and first woman to lead a Walmart business unit, is turning Walmart's SAM's Club into a $100 billion business. After taking over of SAM'S in 2012, Brewer says SAM's is raising membership fees, building stores in metropolitan areas instead of rural towns, adding brands like Eddie Bauer, Nautica, and Lucky Brand Jeans that differential SAM's from Walmart and other discount retailers. Brewer is also opening SAM's stores earlier to capture small businesspersons who buy the morning of their day's business. CEO Brewer is doing a great job trying to gain ground on Costco Wholesale, which logged nearly double the sales of SAM's Club in 2012.

In late 2012, when CEO Chris Kubasik at Lockheed Martin was fired for having an "improper" relationship with a fellow employee, a long-time Lockheed Martin female executive, Marillyn Hewson, was appointed as the company's new CEO. Three of the six largest Pentagon contractors now have female CEO's. Lockheed Martin is the world's largest defense contractor.

Advertising agencies are an example industry transitioning from being specialist Hispanic, African American, and Asian agencies to becoming multicultural, generalist agencies. Leading executives of culturally specialized agencies are defecting in large numbers to generalist agencies as companies increasingly embrace multicultural marketing using multicultural ad agencies. Companies such as Burger King are shifting their Hispanic and African American ad agencies to generalist firms such as Crispin. Church's Chicken says pooling everything at a generalist agency helps reinforce the multicultural component of its overall market strategy.[24]

In Latin and South America, the number of women in high office has increased dramatically in recent years. Brazil recently elected its first woman president, Dilma Rouseff. Both Argentina and Chile already have a woman president, Cristina Kirchner and Michelle Bachelet, respectively. Regarding the percent of national congressional seats held by women, Argentina has 38.3 percent followed by Honduras with 23.4 percent, as compared to Europe with 20.0 percent, Nordic countries at 41.6 percent, and Arab states at 11.1 percent.[25] Women now make up 53 percent of the work force in Latin and South America.

A recent study by McKinsey & Co. in Asia revealed that Asian companies' average return on equity improves from 15 percent to 22 percent when more and more women hold high-level positions.[26] Wang Jin at McKinsey says: "Women tend to be stronger in terms of collaboration and people development, while men tend to be stronger in individual decision making. By having more women at the senior level, companies are helping to improve organizational health as well as financial performance."[27] The percentage of women on corporate boards in Australia increased from 8.3 in 2010 to 14 percent in 2012.[28] Malaysia and South Korea are also making excellent progress integrating women into upper levels of management and subsidizing companies that build child-care facilities and help women juggle work and family life. In contrast, women in India still are expected to care for their family and extended family; also in India women often unfortunately have an abortion if they know their fetus is a girl. Overall in Asia, women comprise only 6 percent of corporate board seats, compared to 17 percent in Europe and 15 percent in the USA.

An organization can perhaps be most effective when its workforce mirrors the diversity of its customers. For global companies, this goal can be optimistic, but it is a worthwhile goal.

Corporate Wellness Programs

Recent articles detail how companies such as Johnson & Johnson (J&J), Lowe's Home-Improvement, the supermarket chain H-E-B, and Healthwise report impressive returns on investment of comprehensive, well-run employee wellness programs, sometimes as high as six to one.[29] A recent study by Fidelity Investments and the National Business Group on Health reports that nearly 90 percent of employers today offer some kind of wellness incentives or prizes to employees who "get healthier," up from 59 percent in 2009. For example, JetBlue Airways offers employees money—$25 for teeth cleanings and $400 for completing an Ironman triathlon, etc. Furniture company, KI, has all its employees divided into four groups based on "healthiness" with the most-healthy people paying $1,000 less on health insurance premiums than the least-healthy employees.

According to the 2013 National Survey of Employer-Sponsored Health Plans, the percentage of large employers (500+ employees) that offer lower health insurance premiums to nonsmokers increased from 9 percent in 2009 to 15 percent in 2012 (*WSJ*, 2-10-R5). In addition, 42 percent of large firms now offer onsite exercise or yoga classes, and 35 percent offer onsite Weight Watchers programs. J&J estimates that wellness programs have cumulatively saved the company $250 million on health-care costs over the past decade. All J&J facilities around the world are tobacco free. At the software firm SAS Institute headquartered in Cary, North Carolina, voluntary turnover of employees has dropped to just 4 percent, largely, the firm says, due to its effective wellness program. On the SAS main campus, 70 percent of employees use the recreation center at least twice a week. SAS is number 3 among *Fortune*'s "100 Best Companies to Work For." At Healthwise, CEO Don Kemper's personal commitment to wellness permeates the entire culture of the firm, from monthly staff meetings to an annual Wellness Day. Lowe's offers employees a monthly $50 discount on medical insurance if they pledge that they and covered dependents will not use any tobacco products.

Chevron is also a model corporate wellness company that sponsors many internal and external wellness activities. Chevron and other companies such as Biltmore that provide exemplary wellness programs think beyond diet and exercise and focus also on stress management by assisting employees with such issues as divorce, serious illness, death and grief recovery, child rearing, and care of aging parents. Biltmore's two-day health fairs twice a year focus on physical, financial, and spiritual wellness. At Lowe's headquarters, an impressive spiral staircase in the lobby makes climbing the stairs more appealing than riding the elevator. Such practices as "providing abundant bicycle racks," "conducting walking meetings," and "offering five minute stress breaks" are becoming common at companies to promote a corporate wellness culture.

Whole Foods Market headquartered in Austin, Texas, is another outstanding corporate wellness company with their employees receiving a 30 percent discount card on all products sold in their stores "if they maintain and document a healthy lifestyle." In addition, Wegman's Food Markets, headquartered in Rochester, New York, is another supermarket chain with an excellent corporate wellness program. More than 11,000 of Wegman's 39,000 employees recently took part in a challenge to eat five cups of fruit and vegetables and walk up to 10,000 steps a day for eight weeks. Wegman recently ranked number 4 among *Fortune*'s "100 Best Companies to Work For."

Firms are striving to lower the accelerating costs of employees' health-care insurance premiums. Many firms such as Scotts Miracle-Gro Company (based in Marysville, Ohio), IBM, and Microsoft are implementing wellness programs, requiring employees to get healthier or pay higher insurance premiums. Employees that do get healthier win bonuses, free trips, and pay lower premiums; nonconforming employees pay higher premiums and receive no "healthy" benefits. Wellness of employees has become a strategic issue for many firms. Most firms require a health examination as a part of an employment application, and healthiness is more and more becoming a hiring factor. Michael Porter, coauthor of *Redefining Health Care*, says, "We have this notion that you can gorge on hot dogs, be in a pie-eating contest, and drink every day, and society will take care of you. We can't afford to let individuals drive up company costs because they're not willing to address their own health problems."

Wellness programs provide counseling to employees and seek lifestyle changes to achieve healthier living. For example, trans fats are a major cause of heart disease. Near elimination of trans fats in one's diet will reduce one's risk for heart attack. Saturated fats are also bad, so one should avoid eating too much red meat and dairy products, which are high in saturated fats. Seven key lifestyle habits listed in Table 7-17 may significantly improve health and longevity. Boston Market recently removed all salt shakers off tables in its 476 restaurants. The company is also reducing salt by 20 percent in its rotisserie chicken, macaroni and cheese, and mashed potatoes. CEO George Michel says Boston Market will reduce salt levels by 15 percent menu-wide by the end of 2014. Pepper shakers remain on tables at Boston Market.

TABLE 7-17 The Key to Staying Healthy, Living to 100, and Being a "Well" Employee

1. Eat nutritiously—eat a variety of fruits and vegetables daily because they have ingredients that the body uses to repair and strengthen itself.
2. Stay hydrated—drink plenty of water to aid the body in eliminating toxins and to enable body organs to function efficiently; the body is mostly water.
3. Get plenty of rest—the body repairs itself during rest, so get at least seven hours of sleep nightly, preferably eight hours.
4. Get plenty of exercise—exercise vigorously at least 30 minutes daily so the body can release toxins and strengthen vital organs.
5. Reduce stress—the body's immune system is weakened when one is under stress, making the body vulnerable to many ailments, so keep stress to a minimum.
6. Do not smoke—smoking kills, no doubt about it anymore.
7. Take vitamin supplements—consult your physician, but because it is difficult for diet alone to supply all the nutrients and vitamins needed, supplements can be helpful in achieving good health and longevity.

Source: Based on Lauren Etter, "Trans Fats: Will They Get Shelved?" *Wall Street Journal*, December 8, 2006, A6; Joel Fuhrman, MD, *Eat to Live* (Boston: Little, Brown, 2003).

Special Note to Students

An integral part of managing a firm is continually and systematically seeking to gain and sustain competitive advantage through effective planning, organizing, motivating, staffing, and controlling. Rival firms engage in these same activities, so emphasize in your strategic-management case analysis how your firm implementing your recommendations will outperform rival firms. Remember to be prescriptive rather than descriptive on every page or slide in your project, meaning to be insightful, forward-looking, and analytical rather than just describing operations. It is easy to *describe* a company but is difficult to *analyze* a company. Strategic-management case analysis is about *analyzing* a company and its industry, uncovering ways and means for the firm to best gain and sustain competitive advantage. So communicate throughout your project how your firm, and especially your recommendations, will lead to improved growth and profitability versus rival firms. Avoid vagueness and generalities throughout your project, as your audience or reader seeks great ideas backed up by great analyses. Be analytical and prescriptive rather than vague and descriptive in highlighting every slide you show an audience.

Conclusion

Successful strategy formulation does not at all guarantee successful strategy implementation. Although inextricably interdependent, strategy formulation and strategy implementation are characteristically different. In a single word, strategy implementation means *change*. It is widely agreed that "the real work begins after strategies are formulated." Successful strategy implementation requires the support of, as well as discipline and hard work, from motivated managers and employees. It is sometimes frightening to think that a single individual can irreparably sabotage strategy-implementation efforts.

Formulating the right strategies is not enough because managers and employees must be motivated to implement those strategies. Management issues considered central to strategy implementation include matching organizational structure with strategy, linking performance and pay to strategies, creating an organizational climate conducive to change, managing political relationships, creating a strategy-supportive culture, adapting production and operations processes, and managing human resources. Establishing annual objectives, devising policies, and allocating resources are central strategy-implementation activities common to all organizations. Depending on the size and type of the organization, other management issues could be equally important to successful strategy implementation.

MyManagementLab®

Go to **mymanagementlab.com** to complete the problems marked with this icon ⭐.

Key Terms and Concepts

annual objectives (p. 209)

avoidance (p. 213)

benchmarking (p. 224)

bonus system (p. 226)

conflict (p. 213)

confrontation (p. 213)

culture (p. 228)

decentralized structure (p. 216)

defusion (p. 213)

delayering (p. 224)

divisional structure by geographic area, product, customer, or process (p. 216)

downsizing (p. 224)

educative change strategy (p. 227)

employee stock ownership plans (ESOP) (p. 232)

establishing annual objectives (p. 209)

force change strategy (p. 227)

functional structure (p. 215)

furloughs (p. 230)

gain sharing (p. 226)

glass ceiling (p. 234)

horizontal consistency of objectives (p. 209)

just-in-time (JIT) (p. 230)

matrix structure (p. 220)

policy (p. 211)

profit sharing (p. 226)

rational change strategy (p. 227)

reengineering (p. 224)

resistance to change (p. 227)

resource allocation (p. 213)

restructuring (p. 224)

rightsizing (p. 224)

self-interest change strategy (p. 227)

Six Sigma (p. 224)

strategic business unit (SBU) structure (p. 214)

vertical consistency of objectives (p. 209)

Issues for Review and Discussion

⭐ **7-1.** Discuss the glass ceiling in the United States, giving your ideas and suggestions.

7-2. Discuss three ways for linking performance and pay to strategies.

7-3. List the different types of organizational structure. Diagram what you think is the most complex of these structures and label your chart clearly.

7-4. List the advantages and disadvantages of a functional versus a divisional organizational structure.

⭐ **7-5.** Discuss recent trends in women and minorities becoming top executives in the United States.

⭐ **7-6.** Discuss recent trends in firms downsizing family-friendly programs.

7-7. List seven guidelines to follow in developing an organizational chart.

7-8. Women comprise only 6 percent of corporate board seats in Asia, compared to 17 percent in Europe and 15 percent in the United States. Why is this a problem globally for (1) companies with a low percent and (2) countries with a low percent?

7-9. College football coaches get paid millions, presumably because there is so much money involved in college football the need to win is paramount. However, head coaches are often fired when a season goes badly, such as Gene Chizik at Auburn University in late 2012. Coach Chizik's buyout provision (if fired before his contract ends, which happened) was $7 million, pretty typical for Division 1 top-tier head football coaches. In fact, the whole Auburn University football coaching staff, including Chizik, was bought out the same day (11-26-12) for $11.09 million. How could a head coach's compensation package be better structured to encourage winning, and at the same time not be so potentially costly to a university?

7-10. *Businessweek* says firms should "base executive compensation on actual company performance, rather than on the company's stock price." For example, Target Corp. bases executive pay on same-store sales growth rather than stock price. Discuss.

7-11. What do you especially like and dislike about Halliburton's organizational chart shown in the chapter? What would you change if anything? Why?

7-12. List four corporate wellness practices that could be especially effective for a company.

7-13. Women now make up 53 percent of the work force in Latin and South America. Do some research to determine how that percentage compares with other parts of the world. What are the implications for a business in doing business globally?

7-14. Advertising agencies are an example industry transitioning from specialist Hispanic, African American, and Asian firms to multicultural, generalist agencies. Why is this occurring? What other industries or institutions may follow suit? Why?

7-15. Describe three conflict situations in which to resolve the problems you would use (1) avoidance, (2) defusion, and (3) confrontation respectively.

7-16. List the five labor cost-saving activities that you believe would be most effective for Best Buy. Give a rationale for each activity.

7-17. The chapter says strategy formulation focuses on effectiveness, whereas strategy implementation focuses on efficiency. Which is more important, effectiveness or efficiency? Give an example of each concept.

7-18. In stating objectives, why should terms such as *increase, minimize, maximize, as soon as possible, adequate,* and *decrease* be avoided?

7-19. What are four types of resources that all organizations have? List them in order of importance for your university or business school.

7-20. Considering avoidance, defusion, and confrontation, which method of conflict resolution do you prefer most? Why? Which do you prefer least? Why?

7-21. Explain why Alfred Chandler's strategy-structure relationship commonly exists among firms.

7-22. If you owned and opened three restaurants after you graduated, would you operate from a functional or divisional structure? Why?

7-23. Explain how to choose between a divisional-by-product and a divisional-by-region organizational structure.

7-24. Think of a company that would operate best in your opinion by a division-by-services organizational structure. Explain your reasoning.

7-25. What are the two major disadvantages of an SBU-type organizational structure? What are the two major advantages? At what point in a firm's growth do you feel the advantages offset the disadvantages? Explain.

7-26. In order of importance in your opinion, list six advantages of a matrix organizational structure.

7-27. Why should division head persons have the title president rather than vice president?

7-28. Compare and contrast profit sharing with gain sharing as employee performance incentives.

7-29. List three resistance-to-change strategies. Give an example when you would use each method or approach.

7-30. In order of importance in your opinion, list six techniques or activities widely used to alter an organization's culture.

7-31. What are the benefits of establishing an ESOP in a company?

7-32. List reasons why is it important for an organization not to have a "glass ceiling."

7-33. Allocating resources can be a political and an ad hoc activity in firms that do not use strategic management. Why is this true? Does adopting strategic management ensure easy resource allocation? Why?

7-34. Describe the relationship between annual objectives and policies.

7-35. Identify a long-term objective and two supporting annual objectives for a familiar organization.

7-36. Identify and discuss three policies that apply to your present strategic-management class.

7-37. Explain the following statement: Horizontal consistency of goals is as important as vertical consistency.

7-38. Describe several reasons why conflict may occur during objective-setting activities.

7-39. In your opinion, what approaches to conflict resolution would be best for resolving a disagreement between a personnel manager and a sales manager over the firing of a particular salesperson? Why?

7-40. Describe the organizational culture of your college or university.

7-41. Explain why organizational structure is so important in strategy implementation.

7-42. In your opinion, how many separate divisions could an organization reasonably have without using an SBU-type organizational structure? Why?

7-43. Would you recommend a divisional structure by geographic area, product, customer, or process for a medium-sized bank in your local area? Why?

7-44. What are the advantages and disadvantages of decentralizing the wage and salary functions of an organization? How could this be accomplished?

7-45. Do you believe expenditures for child-care or fitness facilities are warranted from a cost-benefit perspective? Why or why not?

7-46. Explain why successful strategy implementation often hinges on whether the strategy-formulation process empowers managers and employees.

MyManagementLab®

Go to **mymanagementlab.com** for Auto-graded writing questions as well as the following Assisted-graded writing questions:

7-47. What are the two major disadvantages of an SBU-type organizational structure? What are the two major advantages? At what point in a firm's growth do you feel the advantages offset the disadvantages? Explain.

7-48. Would you recommend a divisional structure by geographic area, product, customer, or process for a medium-sized bank in your local area? Why?

7-49. Mymanagementlab Only—comprehensive writing assignment for this chapter.

Current Readings

Allio, Michael K. "Strategic Dashboards: Designing and Deploying Them to Improve Implementation." *Strategy and Leadership* 40, no. 5 (2012): 24–31.

Beeson, John, and Anna Marie Valerio. "The Executive Leadership Imperative: A New Perspective on How Companies and Executives Can Accelerate the Development of Women Leaders." *Business Horizons* 55, no. 5 (September 2012): 417–425.

Campbell, Benjamin A. Campbell, Russell Coff, and David Kryscynski. "Rethinking Sustained Competitive Advantage from Human Capital." *The Academy of Management Review* 37, no. 3 (July 2012): 376.

Csaszar, Felipe A. "Organizational Structure as a Determinant of Performance: Evidence from Mutual Funds." *Strategic Management Journal* 33, no. 6 (June 2012): 611–632.

Chng, Daniel Han Ming, Matthew S. Rodgers, Eric Shih, and Xiao-Bing Song. "When does incentive compensation motivate managerial behaviors? An experimental investigation of the fit between incentive compensation, executive core self-evaluation, and firm performance." *Strategic Management Journal* 33, no. 12 (December 2012): 1343–1362.

Davis, Paul J. "A Model for Strategy Implementation and Conflict Resolution in the Franchise Business." *Strategy and Leadership* 40, no. 5 (2012): 32–38.

Denning, Stephen. "Gary Hamel: Managing While Under the Influence of Innovation." *Strategy and Leadership* 40, no. 5 (2012): 12–18.

Dezsö, Cristian L., and David Gaddis Ross. "Does Female Representation in Top Management Improve Firm Performance? A Panel Data Investigation." *Strategic Management Journal* 33, no. 9 (September 2012): 1072–1089.

Fulmer, C. Ashley, and Michele J. Gelfand. "At What Level (and in Whom) We Trust: Trust Across Multiple Organization Levels." *Journal of Management* 38, no. 4 (July 2012): 1167.

Gulati, Ranjay, Phanish Puranam, and Michael Tushman. "Meta-Organization Design: Rethinking Design in Interorganizational and Community Contexts." *Strategic Management Journal* 33, no. 6 (June 2012): 571–586.

Karim, Samina, and Charles Williams. "Structural Knowledge: How Executive Experience with Structural Composition Affects Intrafirm Mobility and Unit Reconfiguration." *Strategic Management Journal* 33, no. 6 (June 2012): 681–709.

Katzenbach, Jon R., Ilona Steffen, and Caroline Kronley. "Cultural Change That Sticks." *Harvard Business Review* (July-August 2012): 110.

King, Eden B., Jeremy F. Dawson, Michael A. West, Veronica L. Gilrane, Chad I. Peddie, and Lucy Bastin. "Why Organizational and Community Diversity Matter: Representativeness and the Emergence of Incivility and Organizational Performance." *The Academy of Management Journal* 54, no. 6 (December 2011): 1103.

Larkin, Ian, Lamar Pierce, and Francesca Gino. "The Psychological Costs of Pay-for-Performance: Implications for the Strategic Compensation of Employees." *Strategic Management Journal* 33, no. 10 (October 2012): 1194–1214.

Lechner, Christoph, and Steven W. Floyd. "Group Influence Activities and the Performance of Strategic Initiatives." *Strategic Management Journal* 33, no. 5 (May 2012): 478–495.

Prats, Julia, Marc Sosna, and S. Ramakrishna Velamuri. "Managing in Different Growth Contexts." *California Management Review* 54, no. 4 (Summer 2012): 118–142.

Puranam, Phanish, Marlo Raveendran, and Thorbjorn Knudsen. "Organization Design: The Epistemic Interdependence Perspective." *The Academy of Management Review 37*, no. 3 (July 2012): 419.

Wulf, Julie. "The Flattened Firm: Not as Advertised." *Inside CMR* 55, no. 1 (Fall 2012): 5.

ASSURANCE OF LEARNING **EXERCISES**

EXERCISE 7A

Critique Corporate Organizational Charts

Purpose

There are tremendous benefits for a company (and an individual) to be well organized. Students generally know that being better organized usually yields higher grades. Competitiveness is so intense among companies in various industries that being well organized can make the difference between success and failure. This exercise gives you practice critiquing various organizational charts so that improved organizational designs for those companies can be devised.

Instructions

Step 1   In this chapter, refer back to three organizational charts that are illustrated: Southwest Airlines, Hershey Foods, and Microsoft. For each chart, identify four shortcomings based on the guidelines presented in this chapter.

Step 2   For one of those companies of your choosing, develop a new and improved organizational chart. Discuss why you believe that your new chart is better for the company.

EXERCISE 7B
Draw an Organizational Chart for PepsiCo Using a Free, Online Template

Purpose

Strategic management students and business executives are oftentimes asked to construct an organizational chart. This exercise will make you aware of various online websites that provide free software for developing an organizational chart. Some websites in particular are as follows:

> www.vertex42.com/ExcelTemplates/organizational-chart.html
> http://office.microsoft.com/en-us/templates/business-organizational-chart-
> TC006088976.aspx
> www.edrawsoft.com
> www.smartdraw.com/specials/orgchart.asp
> www.orgchart.net

Instructions

Do a Google search for "organizational charts" and examine various free templates for constructing a chart. Decide which template you think is most user friendly and effective. List some reasons why you decided on that particular template. Develop a sample organizational chart using the template you selected. Include 12 positions in your chart. Follow all guidelines provided in the chapter. In addition, use your template to develop an improved organizational chart for PepsiCo as illustrated in the Cohesion Case.

EXERCISE 7C
Do Organizations Really Establish Objectives?

Purpose

Objectives provide direction, allow synergy, aid in evaluation, establish priorities, reduce uncertainty, minimize conflicts, stimulate exertion, and aid in both the allocation of resources and the design of jobs. This exercise will enhance your understanding of how organizations use or misuse objectives.

Instructions

Step 1   Join with one other person in class to form a two-person team.

Step 2   Contact the owner or manager of an organization in your city or town. Request a 15-minute personal interview or meeting with that person for the purpose of discussing "business objectives." During your meeting, seek answers to the following questions:

    1. Do you believe it is important for a business to establish and clearly communicate long-term and annual objectives? Why or why not?

    2. Does your organization establish objectives? If yes, what type and how many? How are the objectives communicated to individuals? Are your firm's objectives in written form or simply communicated orally?

    3. To what extent are managers and employees involved in the process of establishing objectives?

    4. How often are your business objectives revised and by what process?

Step 3   Take good notes during the interview. Let one person be the note taker and one person do most of the talking. Have your notes typed up and ready to turn in to your professor.

Step 4   Prepare a five-minute oral presentation for the class, reporting the results of your interview. Turn in your typed report.

EXERCISE 7D
Understanding Your University's Culture

Purpose

It is something of an art to uncover the basic values and beliefs that are buried deeply in an organization's rich collection of stories, language, heroes, heroines, and rituals, yet culture can be the most important factor in implementing strategies.

Instructions

Step 1	On a separate sheet of paper, list the following terms: hero/heroine, belief, metaphor, language, value, symbol, story, legend, saga, folktale, myth, ceremony, rite, and ritual.
Step 2	For your college or university, give examples of each term. If necessary, speak with faculty, staff, alumni, administration, or fellow students of the institution to identify examples of each term.
Step 3	Report your findings to the class. Tell the class how you feel regarding cultural products being consciously used to help implement strategies.

Notes

1. Dale McConkey, "Planning in a Changing Environment," *Business Horizons*, September–October 1988, 66.
2. A. G. Bedeian, and W. F. Glueck, *Management,* 3rd ed. (Chicago: The Dryden Press, 1983), 212.
3. Boris Yavitz and William Newman, *Strategy in Action: The Execution, Politics, and Payoff of Business Planning* (New York: The Free Press, 1982), 195.
4. E. H. Schein, "Three Cultures of Management: The Key to Organizational Learning," *Sloan Management Review* 38, 1 (1996): 9–20.
5. S. Ghoshal, and C. A. Bartlett, "Changing the Role of Management: Beyond Structure to Processes." *Harvard Business Review* 73, 1 (1995): 88.
6. Mike Ester, "Coca-Cola Starts a Horse Race for Next CEO," *Wall Street Journal* (July 31, 2012): B1.
7. Joann Lublin, "Chairman-CEO Split Gains Allies," *Wall Street Journal*, March 30, 2009, B4.
8. Karen Richardson, "The 'Six Sigma' Factor for Home Depot," *Wall Street Journal*, January 4, 2007, C3.
9. "Want to Be a Manager? Many People Say No, Calling Job Miserable," *Wall Street Journal*, April 4, 1997, 1; Stephanie Armour, "Management Loses Its Allure," *USA Today*, October 10, 1997, 1B.
10. Bill George, "Executive Pay: Rebuilding Trust in an Era of Rage," *Bloomberg Businessweek*, September 13–19, 2010, 56.
11. Richard Brown, "Outsider CEO: Inspiring Change with Force and Grace," *USA Today* (July 19, 1999): 3B.
12. Emily Chasan, "Stock Loses Some Sway on Pay," *Wall Street Journal* (October 30, 2012): B4.
13. Yavitz and Newman, 58.
14. Jack Duncan, *Management* (New York: Random House, 1983): 381–390.
15. E. H. Schein, "The Role of the Founder in Creating Organizational Culture," *Organizational Dynamics* (Summer 1983): 13–28.
16. T. Deal and A. Kennedy, "Culture: A New Look Through Old Lenses," *Journal of Applied Behavioral Science* 19, no. 4 (1983): 498–504.
17. H. Ibsen, "The Wild Duck," in O. G. Brochett and L. Brochett (eds.), *Plays for the Theater* (New York: Holt, Rinehart & Winston, 1967); R. Pascale, "The Paradox of 'Corporate Culture': Reconciling Ourselves to Socialization," *California Management Review* 28, no. 2 (1985): 26, 37–40.
18. T. Deal and A. Kennedy, *Corporate Cultures: The Rites and Rituals of Corporate Life* (Reading, MA: Addison-Wesley, 1982): 256.
19. Robert Stobaugh, and Piero Telesio, "Match Manufacturing Policies and Product Strategy," *Harvard Business Review* 61, no. 2 (March–April 1983): 113.
20. Sudeep Reddy, "Employers Increasingly Rely on Temps, Part-Timers," *Wall Street Journal*, October 11, 2010, A4.
21. R. T. Lenz and Marjorie Lyles, "Managing Human Resource Problems in Strategy Planning Systems," *Journal of Business Strategy* 60, no. 4 (Spring 1986): 58.
22. J. Warren Henry, "ESOPs with Productivity Payoffs," *Journal of Business Strategy* (July–August 1989): 33.

23. Conor Dougherty, "Strides by Women, Still a Wage Gap," *Wall Street Journal*, March 1, 2011, A3. Also, David Jackson and Mimi Hall, "Women Gain in Education and Longevity," *USA Today*, March 2, 2011, 5A.

24. Suzanne Vranica, "Ad Firms Heed Diversity," *Wall Street Journal*, November 29, 2010, B7.

25. Paulo Prada, "Women Ascend in Latin America," *Wall Street Journal*, December 24, 2010, A10.

26. Kathy Chu, "Asian Women Fight Barriers," *Wall Street Journal* (July 2, 2012): B4.

27. Ibid.

28. Ibid.

29. Berry, Leonard L., Ann Mirabito, and William Baun, "What's The Hard Return On Employee Wellness Programs?" *Harvard Business Review*, December 2010, 104–112. Also, Jen Wieczner, "Your Company Wants to Make You Healthy." *Wall Street Journal*, April 9, 2013, R6.

## 8

Source: Demitrio Carrasco/Dorling Kindersley Ltd.

MyManagementLab®

⭐ **Improve Your Grade!**

More than 10 million students improved their results using the Pearson MyLabs.
Visit **mymanagementlab.com** for simulations, tutorials, and end-of-chapter problems.

Implementing Strategies: Marketing, Finance/Accounting, R&D, and MIS Issues

CHAPTER OBJECTIVES

After studying this chapter, you should be able to do the following:

1. Develop effective perceptual maps to position rival firms.

2. Develop effective perceptual maps to identify market segments and demand voids.

3. Determine the cash worth of any business.

4. Explain market segmentation and product positioning as strategy-implementation tools.

5. Discuss procedures for determining the worth of a business.

6. Develop projected financial statements to reveal the impact of strategy recommendations.

7. Perform EPS-EBIT analysis to evaluate the attractiveness of debt versus stock as a source of capital to implement strategies.

8. Discuss the nature and role of research and development in strategy implementation.

9. Explain how management information systems can determine the success of strategy-implementation efforts.

10. Explain business analytics and data mining.

ASSURANCE OF LEARNING EXERCISES

The following exercises are found at the end of this chapter.

Strategies have no chance of being implemented successfully in organizations that do not market goods and services well, in firms that cannot raise needed working capital, in firms that produce technologically inferior products, or in firms that have a weak information system. This chapter examines marketing, finance and accounting, research and development (R&D), and management information systems (MIS) issues that are central to effective strategy implementation. Special topics include market segmentation, market positioning, evaluating the worth of a business, determining to what extent debt or stock should be used as a source of capital, developing projected financial statements, contracting R&D outside the firm, and creating an information support system. Manager and employee involvement and participation are essential for success in marketing, finance and accounting, R&D, and MIS activities.

The Nature of Strategy Implementation

The quarterback can call the best play possible in the huddle, but that does not mean the play will go for a touchdown. The team may even lose yardage unless the play is executed (implemented) well. Less than 10 percent of strategies formulated are successfully implemented! There are many reasons for this low success rate, including failing to appropriately segment markets, paying too much for a new acquisition, and falling behind competitors in R&D. Panera Bread implements strategies especially well.

Strategy implementation directly affects the lives of plant managers, division managers, department managers, sales managers, product managers, project managers, personnel managers, staff managers, supervisors, and all employees. In some situations, individuals may not have participated in the strategy-formulation process at all and may not appreciate, understand, or even accept the work and thought that went into strategy formulation. There may even be foot dragging or resistance on their part. Managers and employees who do not understand the business and are not committed to the business may attempt to sabotage strategy-implementation efforts in hopes that the organization will return to its old ways. The strategy-implementation stage of the strategic-management process is highlighted in Figure 8-1 as illustrated with white shading.

EXCELLENT **STRATEGIC MANAGEMENT** SHOWCASED

Panera Bread Co.

Have you ever eaten at Panera Bread, a leader in the quick-casual restaurant business with 1,591 bakery-cafes in 40 states and Canada? Under the names Panera Bread, Saint Louis Bread Co., and Paradise Bakery & Café, Panera offers made-to-order sandwiches using a variety of artisan breads, including Asiago cheese bread, focaccia, and its classic sourdough bread. Panera's menu also features soups, salads, and gourmet coffees, as well as bread, bagels, and pastries to go. More than 660 of its locations are company-operated, whereas the rest are run by franchisees.

Panera Bread recently announced a new three-year share repurchase program to buy back up to $600 million worth of its own common stock (called *treasury stock* on balance sheets). The stock buyback aims to reduce the number of shares outstanding from 30 million and is expected to reinforce shareholders' confidence and boost the market value of the outstanding shares.

Panera remains well positioned to increase store sales and accelerate unit growth in the long run with the introduction of a new menu to compete more effectively with the likes of Chipotle Mexican Grill, Einstein Noah Restaurant Group, and Atlanta Bread Company. Based in Richmond Heights, Missouri, and founded in 1981, Panera Bread has 776 company owned bakery-cafes and the rest are franchised.

In July 2012, Panera Bread reported strong quarterly results with earnings of $1.50 per share and revenue increases of 18 percent year-over-year to $530.6 million. Panera's comparable net bakery-cafe sales expanded 5.9 percent. The company-owned comparable net bakery-cafe sales increased 7.1 percent whereas franchise-operated comparable net bakery-cafe sales grew 4.8 percent. Panera reported a 27 percent rise in earnings and an 18 percent sales increase in that quarter.

Source: A variety of sources.

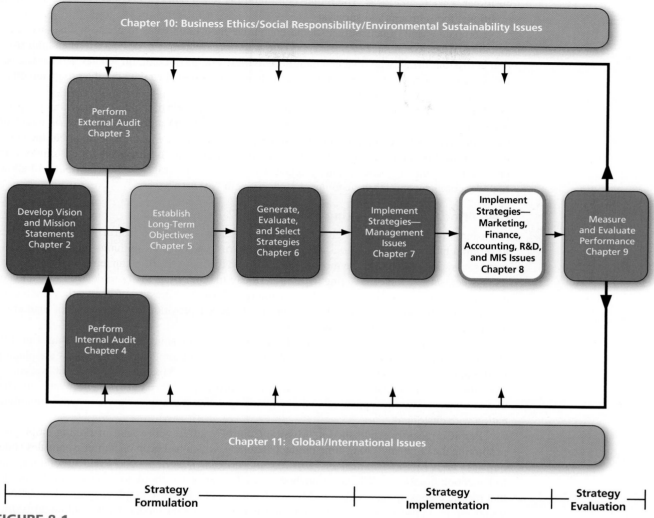

FIGURE 8-1

A Comprehensive Strategic-Management Model

Source: Fred R. David, "How Companies Define Their Mission," *Long Range Planning* 22, no. 3 (June 1988): 40.

Current Marketing Issues

Countless marketing variables affect the success or failure of strategy implementation efforts. Some example marketing decisions that may require policies are as follows:

1. How to make advertisements more interactive to be more effective
2. How to best take advantage of Facebook and Twitter conservations about the company and industry
3. To use exclusive dealerships or multiple channels of distribution
4. To use heavy, light, or no TV advertising versus online advertising
5. To limit (or not) the share of business done with a single customer
6. To be a price leader or a price follower
7. To offer a complete or limited warranty
8. To reward salespeople based on straight salary, straight commission, or a combination salary and commission

Marketing is more about building a two-way relationship with consumers than just informing consumers about a product or service. Marketers today must get their customers involved in their company website and solicit suggestions from customers in terms of product development, customer service, and ideas. The online community is much quicker, cheaper, and effective than traditional focus groups and surveys.

Companies and organizations should encourage their employees to create **wikis**—websites that allow users to add, delete, and edit content regarding frequently asked questions and information across the firm's whole value chain of activities. The most common wiki is Wikipedia, but wikis are user-generated content. Anyone can change the content in a wiki but the group and other editors can change the content submitted.

Firms should provide incentives to customers to share their thoughts, opinions, and experiences on the company website. Encourage customers to network among themselves on topics of their choosing on the company website. So the company website must not be all about the company—it must be all about the customer too. Perhaps offer points or discounts for customers who provide ideas and suggestions. This practice will not only encourage participation but will allow both the company and other customers to interact with "experts."

New Principles of Marketing

A business or organization's website must provide clear and simple instructions for customers to set up a blog or contribute to a wiki. Customers trust each others' opinions more than a company's marketing pitch, and the more they talk freely, the more the firm can learn how to improve its product, service, and marketing. Marketers today monitor blogs daily to determine, evaluate, and influence opinions being formed by customers. Customers must not feel like they are a captive audience for advertising at a firm's website. Table 8-1 provides new principles of marketing according to Parise, Guinan, and Weinberg.[1]

Wells Fargo and Bank of America **tweet** customers, meaning they post messages of 140 characters or less on Twitter.com to describe features of bank products. Some banks are placing marketing videos on YouTube. UMB Financial of Kansas City, Missouri, tweets about everything from the bank's financial stability to the industry's prospects. Steve Furman, Discover's director of e-commerce, says the appeal of social networking is that it provides "pure, instant" communication with customers.[2]

PepsiCo recently established a "Mission Control" staffed with social marketing employees promoting the company's long-time product Gatorade, which had been on a three-year sales slide. PepsiCo staffs Mission Control 24/7 to tweet encouragement to high-school athletes and respond to Facebook questions.[3] Whenever anybody uses Twitter or Facebook to comment on Gatorade, that message pops up on a screen in Mission Control and a PepsiCo employee joins that person's social circle. PepsiCo is a leading company that tracks social media, tracks online-ad traffic, heads off potential crises, builds support for products, and monitors consumer behavior in depth. Gatorade is under intense pressure from Coca-Cola's Powerade, whose sales are increasing in contrast to Gatorade's sales decreasing.

Although the exponential increase in social networking and business online has created huge opportunities for marketers, it also has produced some severe threats. Perhaps the greatest threat is that any kind of negative publicity travels fast online. For example, Taco Bell suffered from its ads that featured asking 50 Cent (aka Curtis Jackson) if he would change his name to 79 Cent or 89 Cent for a day in exchange for a $10,000 donation to charity. Seemingly minor ethical and

TABLE 8-1 The New Principles of Marketing

1. Do not just talk at consumers—work with them throughout the marketing process.
2. Give consumers a reason to participate.
3. Listen to—and join—the conversation outside your company's website.
4. Resist the temptation to sell, sell, sell. Instead attract, attract, attract.
5. Do not control online conversations; let it flow freely.
6. Find a "marketing technologist," a person who has three excellent skill sets (marketing, technology, and social interaction).
7. Embrace instant messaging and chatting.

Source: Based on Salvatore Parise, Patricia Guinan, and Bruce Weinberg, "The Secrets of Marketing in a Web 2.0 World," *Wall Street Journal*, December 15, 2008, R1.

questionable actions can catapult these days into huge public relations problems for companies as a result of the monumental online social and business communications.

In increasing numbers, people living in underdeveloped and poor nations around the world have smartphones but no computers. This is opening up even larger markets to online marketing. People in remote parts of Indonesia, Egypt, and Africa represent the fastest-growing customer base for Opera Software ASA, a Norwegian maker of Internet browsers for mobile devices. Cell phones are widely used now for data transfer, not just for phone calls.[4]

People ages 18 to 27 spend more time weekly on the Internet than watching television, listening to the radio, or watching DVDs or VHS tapes. Companies are rapidly coming to the realization that social networking sites and video sites are better means of reaching their customers than spending so many marketing dollars on traditional yellow pages or television, magazine, radio, or newspaper ads.

New companies such as Autonet Mobile based in San Francisco are selling new technology equipment for cars so that everyone in the vehicle can be online except, of course, the driver. This technology is accelerating the movement from hard media to web-based media. With this technology, when the vehicle drives into a new location, information on shows, museums, hotels, and other attractions in the location can be instantly downloaded.

Internet advertising is growing so rapidly that marketers are more and more allowed to create bigger, more intrusive ads that take up more space on the web page. Websites are allowing lengthier ads to run before short video clips play. And blogs are creating more content that doubles also as an ad. Companies are also waiving minimum ad purchases. Companies are redesigning their websites to be much more interactive and are building new sponsorship programs and other enticements on their sites. Editorial content and advertising content are increasingly being mixed on blogs.

A recent report by BIA/Kelsey reveals that social media ad spending should double in the USA between 2012 and 2016 from $4.8 billion to $9.6+ billion by 2016. BIA/Kelsey says about one-third of that ad spending will be from local advertisers, with their ad spending in the USA growing from $1.2 billion in 2012 to $3.1 billion in 2016.

According to the Interactive Advertising Bureau and Pricewaterhouse Coopers, mobile advertising grew 95 percent in the first half of 2012. The industry as a whole grew to an all-time high of $17 billion in revenues in the first half of 2012, up 14 percent over the prior year. Another marketing sector that grew rapidly in the first half of 2012 was digital video, a component of display advertising. Digital video grew 18 percent in 2012 from the prior year.

Google and Facebook are by far the dominant players in display advertising, together comprising 30 percent of the overall market in 2012. An eMarketer report predicts those two companies alone will sell 37 percent of all display ads by the end of 2014. Google had 15.4 percent of the market in 2012 ($2.31 billion) compared to Facebook's 14.4 percent ($2.16 billion). Yahoo! once dominated the display ad market but is on the decline with 9.3 percent of the market ($1.39 billion).

Market Segmentation

Two variables are of central importance to strategy implementation: **market segmentation** and **product positioning**. Market segmentation and product positioning rank as marketing's most important contributions to strategic management.

Market segmentation is widely used in implementing strategies, especially for small and specialized firms. Market segmentation can be defined as the subdividing of a market into distinct subsets of customers according to needs and buying habits.

EBay recently initiated a new market segmentation strategy to target consumers under 18 years old. "We're definitely looking at ways to legitimately bring younger people in," said Devin Wenig at eBay. "We won't allow a 15-year-old unfettered access to the site. We would want a parent, an adult as a ride-along." The under 18-age group are an increasingly savvy and desirable consumer segment for many businesses.

Market segmentation is an important variable in strategy implementation for at least three major reasons. First, strategies such as market development, product development, market penetration, and diversification require increased sales through new markets and products. To implement these strategies successfully, new or improved market-segmentation approaches are required. Second, market segmentation allows a firm to operate with limited resources because mass production, mass distribution, and mass advertising are not required. Market segmentation enables a small firm to compete successfully with a large firm by maximizing per-unit profits and per-segment sales. Finally, market segmentation decisions directly affect **marketing mix variables**: product, place, promotion, and price, as indicated in Table 8-2.

Perhaps the most dramatic new market-segmentation strategy is the targeting of regional tastes. Firms from Pizza Hut to Honda Motors are increasingly modifying their products to meet different regional preferences of customers around the world. Campbell's has a spicier version of its nacho cheese soup for the Southwest, and Burger King offers breakfast burritos in New Mexico but not in South Carolina. Geographic and demographic bases for segmenting markets are the most commonly employed, as illustrated in Table 8-3.

Evaluating potential market segments requires strategists to determine the characteristics and needs of consumers, to analyze consumer similarities and differences, and to develop consumer group profiles. Segmenting consumer markets is generally much simpler and easier than segmenting industrial markets, because industrial products, such as electronic circuits and forklifts, have multiple applications and appeal to diverse customer groups.

Segmentation is a key to matching supply and demand, which is one of the thorniest problems in customer service. Segmentation often reveals that large, random fluctuations in demand actually consist of several small, predictable, and manageable patterns. Matching supply and demand allows factories to produce desirable levels without extra shifts, overtime, and subcontracting. Matching supply and demand also minimizes the number and severity of stock-outs. The demand for hotel rooms, for example, can be dependent on foreign tourists, businesspersons, and vacationers. Focusing separately on these three market segments, however, can allow hotel firms to more effectively predict overall supply and demand.

Banks now are segmenting markets to increase effectiveness. "You're dead in the water if you aren't segmenting the market," says Anne Moore, president of a bank consulting firm in Atlanta. The Internet makes market segmentation easier today because consumers naturally form "communities" on the Web.

Retention-Based Segmentation

To aid in more effective and efficient deployment of marketing resources, companies commonly tag each of their active customers with three values:

Tag 1: Is this customer at high risk of canceling the company's service? One of the most common indicators of high-risk customers is a drop off in usage of the company's service. For example, in the credit card industry this could be signaled through a customer's decline in spending on his or her card.

Tag 2: Is this customer worth retaining? This determination boils down to whether the postretention profit generated from the customer is predicted to be greater than the cost incurred to retain the customer. Customers need to be managed as investments.

Tag 3: What retention tactics should be used to retain this customer? For customers who are deemed "save-worthy," it is essential for the company to know which save tactics are most likely

TABLE 8-2 The Marketing Mix Component Variables

Product	Place	Promotion	Price
Quality	Distribution channels	Advertising	Level
Features and options	Distribution coverage	Personal selling	Discounts and allowances
Style	Outlet location	Sales promotion	Payment terms
Brand name	Sales territories	Publicity	
Packaging	Inventory levels and		
Product line	locations		
Warranty	Transportation carriers		
Service level			
Other services			

Source: Based on E. Jerome McCarthy, *Basic Marketing: A Managerial Approach,* 9th ed. (Homewood, IL: Richard D. Irwin, Inc., 1987), 37–44. Used with permission.

TABLE 8-3 Alternative Bases for Market Segmentation

Variable	Typical Breakdowns
Geographic	
Region	Pacific, Mountain, West North Central, West South Central, East North Central, East South Central, South Atlantic, Middle Atlantic, New England
County Size	A, B, C, D
City Size	Under 5,000; 5,000–20,000; 20,001–50,000; 50,001–100,000; 100,001–250,000; 250,001–500,000; 500,001–1,000,000; 1,000,001–4,000,000; 4,000,001 or over
Density	Urban, suburban, rural
Climate	Northern, southern
Demographic	
Age	Under 6, 6–11, 12–19, 20–34, 35–49, 50–64, 65+
Gender	Male, female
Family Size	1–2, 3–4, 5+
Family Life Cycle	Young, single; young, married, no children; young, married, youngest child under 6; young, married, youngest child 6 or over; older, married, with children; older, married, no children under 18; older, single; other
Income	Under $10,000; $10,001–$15,000; $15,001–$20,000; $20,001–$30,000; $30,001–$50,000; $50,001–$70,000; $70,001–$100,000; over $100,000
Occupation	Professional and technical; managers, officials, and proprietors; clerical and sales; craftspeople; foremen; operatives; farmers; retirees; students; housewives; unemployed
Education	Grade school or less; some high school; high school graduate; some college; college graduate
Religion	Catholic, Protestant, Jewish, Islamic, other
Race	White, Asian, Hispanic, African American
Nationality	American, British, French, German, Scandinavian, Italian, Latin American, Middle Eastern, Japanese
Psychographic	
Social Class	Lower lowers, upper lowers, lower middles, upper middles, lower uppers, upper uppers
Personality	Compulsive, gregarious, authoritarian, ambitious
Behavioral	
Use Occasion	Regular occasion, special occasion
Benefits Sought	Quality, service, economy
User Status	Nonuser, ex-user, potential user, first-time user, regular user
Usage Rate	Light user, medium user, heavy user
Loyalty Status	None, medium, strong, absolute
Readiness Stage	Unaware, aware, informed, interested, desirous, intending to buy
Attitude Toward Product	Enthusiastic, positive, indifferent, negative, hostile

Source: Adapted from Philip Kotler, *Marketing Management: Analysis, Planning and Control,* © 1984: 256. Adapted by permission of Prentice-Hall, Inc., Upper Saddle River, New Jersey.

to be successful. Tactics commonly used range from providing "special" customer discounts to sending customers communications that reinforce the value proposition of the given service.[5]

The basic approach to tagging customers is to use historical retention data to make predictions about active customers regarding:

- Whether they are at high risk of canceling their service
- Whether they are profitable to retain
- What retention tactics are likely to be most effective

The idea with retention-based segmentation is to match up active customers with customers from historic retention data who share similar attributes. Using the theory that "birds of a feather flock together," the approach is based on the assumption that active customers will have similar retention outcomes as those of their comparable predecessor. This whole process is possible through business analytics or data mining (discussed later in this chapter).

Does the Internet Make Market Segmentation Easier?

Yes. The segments of people whom marketers want to reach online are much more precisely defined than the segments of people reached through traditional forms of media, such as television, radio, and magazines. People all over the world are congregating into virtual communities on the web by becoming members, customers, and visitors of websites that focus on an endless range of topics. People in essence segment themselves by nature of the websites that comprise their "favorite places," and many of these websites sell information regarding their "visitors." Businesses and groups of individuals all over the world pool their purchasing power in websites to get volume discounts.

Through its Connect feature, Facebook recently introduced a type of mobile advertising that targets consumers based on the apps they use from their phone. Connect lets users log into millions of websites and apps with their Facebook identity, so the company then targets ads based on that data. Facebook can also track what people do on their apps. Although Apple and Google also track users' mobile apps, those two firms disclose to users in their privacy policy that they can target ads based on apps the person has downloaded from its App Store and iTunes. Facebook charges advertisers every time an app is installed on a users' smartphone.[6] Privacy advocates contend that Facebook should provide ways for users to opt out of the mobile ad targeting.

Product Positioning/Perceptual Mapping

After markets have been segmented so that the firm can target particular customer groups, the next step is to find out what customers want and expect. This takes analysis and research. A severe mistake is to assume the firm knows what customers want and expect. Countless research studies reveal large differences between how customers define service and rank the importance of different service activities and how producers view services. Many firms have become successful by filling the gap between what customers and producers see as good service. What the customer believes is good service is paramount, not what the producer believes service should be.

Identifying target customers on which to focus marketing efforts sets the stage for deciding how to meet the needs and wants of particular consumer groups. Product positioning is widely used for this purpose. Positioning entails developing schematic representations that reflect how products or services compare to competitors' on dimensions most important to success in the industry. The following steps are required in product positioning (sometimes called perceptual mapping):

1. Select key criteria that effectively differentiate products or services in the industry.
2. Diagram a two-dimensional product-positioning map with specified criteria on each axis.
3. Plot major competitors' products or services in the resultant four-quadrant matrix.
4. Identify areas in the positioning map where the company's products or services could be most competitive in the given target market. Look for vacant areas (niches).
5. Develop a marketing plan to position the company's products or services appropriately.

Because just two criteria can be examined on a single product-positioning (perceptual) map, multiple maps are often developed to assess various approaches to strategy implementation. **Multidimensional scaling** could be used to examine three or more criteria simultaneously, but this technique requires computer assistance and is beyond the scope of this text.

Some rules for using product positioning as a strategy-implementation tool are the following:

1. Look for the hole or **vacant niche**. The best strategic opportunity might be an unserved segment.
2. Do not serve two segments with the same strategy. Usually, a strategy successful with one segment cannot be directly transferred to another segment.
3. Do not position yourself in the middle of the map. The middle usually means a strategy that is not clearly perceived to have any distinguishing characteristics. This rule can vary with the number of competitors. For example, when there are only two competitors, as in U.S. presidential elections, the middle becomes the preferred strategic position.[7]

An effective product-positioning strategy meets two criteria: (1) it uniquely distinguishes a company from the competition, and (2) it leads customers to expect slightly less service than a company can deliver. Network Equipment Technology is an example of a company that keeps customer expectations slightly below perceived performance. This is a constant challenge for marketers. Firms need to inform customers about what to expect and then exceed the promise. Underpromise and then overdeliver is the key!

The product positioning map, or **perceptual map**, in Figure 8-2, shows consumer perceptions of various automobiles on the two dimensions of sportiness and conservative and classy and affordable. This sample of consumers felt Porsche was the sportiest and classiest of the cars in the study (top right corner). They felt Plymouth was most practical and conservative (bottom left corner). Car manufacturers could focus their marketing efforts on various target groups, or even redesign features in their vehicles, based on research and survey information illustrated in perceptual maps. Perceptual maps can aid marketers in being more effective in spending money to promote products. Products, brands, or companies positioned close to one another are perceived as similar on the relevant dimensions. For example, in Figure 8-2, consumers see Buick, Chrysler, and Oldsmobile as similar. They are close competitors and form a competitive grouping. A company considering the introduction of a new or improved model may look for a vacant niche on a perceptual map. Some perceptual maps use different size circles to indicate the sales volume or market share of the various competing products.

Perceptual maps may also display consumers' ideal points. These points reflect ideal combinations of the two dimensions as seen by a consumer. Figure 8-3 reveals the results of a study of consumers' ideal points in the alcohol and spirits product space. Each dot represents one respondent's ideal combination of the two dimensions. Areas where there is a cluster of ideal points (such as A) indicates a **market segment**. Areas without ideal points are sometimes referred to as **demand voids**. A company considering introducing a new product will look for areas with a high density of ideal points. They will also look for areas without competitive rivals (a vacant niche), perhaps best done by placing both the (1) ideal points and (2) competing products on the same map.

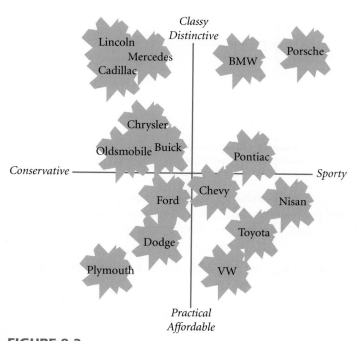

FIGURE 8-2

A Perceptual Map for the Automobile Industry

Source: Based on info at http://en.wikipedia.org/wiki/Perceptual_mapping.

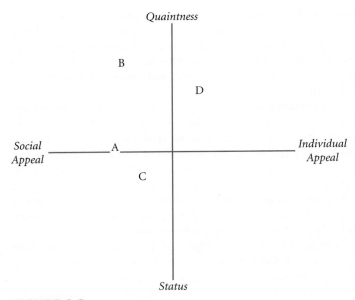

FIGURE 8-3

A Perceptual Map for the Alcohol and Spirits Industry

Source: Based on info at http://en.wikipedia.org/wiki/Perceptual_mapping.

Finance and Accounting Issues

In terms of "Financial Soundness," *Fortune* recently ranked the following companies as best in the world:

Rank	Company
1	Apple
2	McDonald's
3	Exxon Mobil
4	Philip Morris International
5	Intel
6	Google
7	GDF Suez
8	Procter & Gamble
9	Walmart Stores
10	Altria Group

Source: Based on http://money.cnn.com/magazines/
fortune/mostadmired/2012/best_worst/best6.html.

Several finance and accounting concepts central to strategy implementation are acquiring needed capital, developing projected financial statements, preparing financial budgets, and evaluating the worth of a business. Some examples of decisions that may require finance and accounting policies are these:

1. To raise capital with short-term debt, long-term debt, preferred stock, or common stock
2. To lease or buy fixed assets
3. To determine an appropriate dividend payout ratio
4. To use last-in, first-out (LIFO), first-in, first-out (FIFO), or a market-value accounting approach
5. To extend the time of accounts receivable
6. To establish a certain percentage discount on accounts within a specified period of time
7. To determine the amount of cash that should be kept on hand

Acquiring Capital to Implement Strategies

When students complete their recommendations page as part of a case analysis, or in actual company practice when a firm decides what strategies to pursue, it is necessary to address the questions: 1) Should the company obtain needed capital via stock or debt? 2) What would the firm's expected/projected EBIT values be given our recommendations?

Successful strategy implementation often requires additional capital. Besides net profit from operations and the sale of assets, two basic sources of capital for an organization are debt and equity. Determining an appropriate mix of debt and equity in a firm's capital structure can be vital to successful strategy implementation. An **earnings per share/earnings before interest and taxes (EPS/EBIT) analysis** is the most widely used technique for determining whether debt, stock, or a combination of debt and stock is the best alternative for raising capital to implement strategies. This technique involves an examination of the impact that debt versus stock financing has on earnings per share under various expectations for EBIT given specific recommendations (strategies to be implemented).

Theoretically, an enterprise should have enough debt in its capital structure to boost its return on investment by applying debt to products and projects earning more than the cost of the debt. In low-earning periods, too much debt in the capital structure of an organization can endanger stockholders' returns and jeopardize company survival. Fixed debt obligations generally must be met, regardless of circumstances. This does not mean that stock issuances are always better than debt for raising capital. When the cost of capital (interest rates) is low, such as in 2012/2013, debt may be better than stock to obtain capital, but the analysis still must be performed because high stock prices usually accompany low interest rates, making stock issuances attractive for obtaining capital. Some special concerns with stock issuances are dilution of ownership, effect on stock price, and the need to share future earnings with all new shareholders. Facebook's initial public offering in early 2012 was for $38 per share, but several months later the stock was selling for $21, so it is no guarantee even with an IPO that a firm's stock price will rise.

Another popular way for a company to raise capital is to issue corporate bonds, which is analogous to going to the bank and borrowing money, except that with bonds the company obtains the funds from investors rather than banks. Through the first seven months of 2012, companies sold almost $584 billion of bonds in the USA, according to Dealogic, up 6.5 percent from the same period in 2011.[8] For example, Bristol-Myers Squibb, a company with single-A investment credit ratings, sold $2 billion of bonds that paid 3.35 percent interest. Many foreign companies also issue bonds in the USA as a way to raise capital. Especially when a company's balance sheet is strong and its credit rating excellent, issuing bonds can be an effective, and certainly an alternative way to raise needed capital.

Before explaining EPS/EBIT analysis, it is important to know that EPS is earnings per share, which is net income divided by number of shares outstanding. Another term for shares outstanding is shares issued. Also know that EBIT is earnings before interest and taxes. Another name for EBIT is operating income. EBT is earnings before tax. EAT is earnings after tax

The purpose of EPS/EBIT analysis is to determine whether all debt, or all stock, or some combination of debt and stock yields the highest EPS values for the firm. EPS is perhaps the best measure of success of a company, so it is widely used in making the capital acquisition decision. EPS reflects the common "maximizing shareholders' wealth" overarching corporate objective. By chance if profit maximization is the company's goal, then in performing an EPS/EBIT analysis, you may focus more on the EAT row more than the EPS row. Large companies may have millions of shares outstanding, so even small differences in EPS across different financing options can equate to large sums of money saved by using that highest EPS value alternative. Any number of combination debt/stock (D/S) scenarios, such as 70/30 D/S or 30/70 D/S, may be examined in an EPS/EBIT analysis.

EPS/EBIT analysis may best be explained by working through an example for the XYZ Company, as provided in Table 8-4. Note that 100 percent stock is the best financing alternative as indicated by the EPS values of 0.0279 and 0.056. An EPS/EBIT chart can be constructed to determine the break-even point, where one financing alternative becomes more attractive than another. Figure 8-4 reveals that issuing common stock is the best financing alternative for the XYZ Company. As noted in Figure 8-4, the top row (EBIT) on the *x*-axis is graphed with the bottom row (EPS) on the *y*-axis, and the highest plotted line reveals the best method. Sometimes the

TABLE 8-4 EPS/EBIT Analysis for the XYZ Company

Input Data	The Number	How Determined
$Amount of Capital Needed	$100 million	Estimated $cost of recommendations
EBIT Range	$20 to $40 million	Estimate based on prior year EBIT and recommendations for the coming year(s)
Interest Rate	5 percent	Estimate based on cost of capital
Tax Rate	30 percent	Use prior year %: taxes divided by income before taxes, as given on income statement
Stock Price	$50	Use most recent stock price
#Shares Outstanding	500 million	For the debt columns, enter the existing #shares outstanding. For stock columns, use the existing #shares outstanding + the #new shares that must be issued to raise the needed capital, i.e., based on stock price. So divide the stock price into the $amount of capital needed.

	100% Debt		100% Stock		50/50 Debt/Stock Combo	
$ EBIT	20,000,000	40,000,000	20,000,000	40,000,000	20,000,000	40,000,000
$ Interest	5,000,000	5,000,000	0	0	2,500,000	2,500,000
$ EBT	15,000,000	35,000,000	20,000,000	40,000,000	17,500,000	37,500,000
$ Taxes	4,500,000	10,500,000	6,000,000	12,000,000	5,250,000	11,250,000
$ EAT	10,500,000	24,500,000	14,000,000	28,000,000	12,250,000	26,250,000
# Shares	500,000,000	500,000,000	502,000,000	502,000,000	501,000,000	501,000,000
$ EPS	0.0210	0.049	0.0279	0.056	0.0245	0.0523

Conclusion—the best financing alternative is 100% stock because the EPS values are largest; the worst financing alternative is 100% debt because the EPS values are lowest.

plotted lines will interact, so a graph is especially helpful in making the capital acquisition decision, rather than solely relying on a table of numbers.

It is important to note some limitations of EPS-EBIT analysis. First, flexibility is a limitation. As an organization's capital structure changes, so does its flexibility for considering future capital needs. Using all debt or all stock to raise capital in the present may impose fixed obligations, restrictive covenants, or other constraints that could severely reduce a firm's ability to raise additional capital in the future. Second, control is a limitation. When additional stock is issued to finance strategy implementation, ownership and control of the enterprise are diluted. This can be a serious concern in today's business environment of hostile takeovers, mergers, and acquisitions. Dilution of ownership could be a problem, and if so, debt could be better than stock regardless of determined EPS values in the analysis. Third, interest rates are a limitation. If rates are expected to rise, as they are doing in 2013/2014, then debt could be better than stock, regardless of the determined EPS values in the analysis. Fourth, if the firm is already too highly leveraged vs. industry average ratios, then stock may be best regardless of determined EPS values in the analysis. A fifth limitation is that the analysis assumes stock price, tax rate, and interest rates to be the same over all economic conditions. A sixth limitation is that the estimated EBIT low and high values are based on the prior year plus the impact of strategies to be implemented. But considering these six potential limitations, unless you have a compelling reason to overturn the highest last row EPS values dictating the EPS-EBIT analysis, then indeed those values should dictate the financing decision, because EPS is arguably the best measure of organizational performance.

IBM declared a third quarter 2012 cash dividend of $0.85 per common share, marking the third consecutive quarterly payout at that rate. IBM also authorized another $5 billion in additional funds to be used for its share repurchase program on top of the $6.7 billion remaining available for buybacks. That was $11.7 billion for its stock repurchase program in total or about 5.3 percent of its outstanding shares. IBM and thousands of other firms lately have significantly increased their share repurchases.

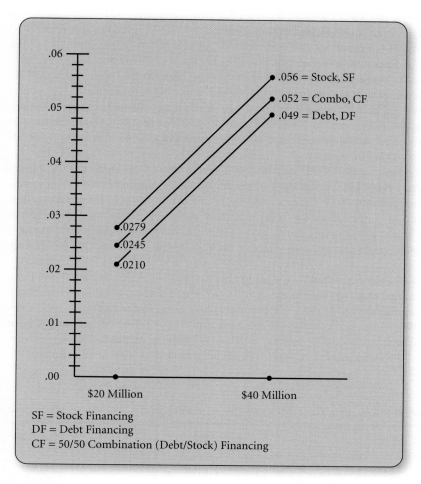

FIGURE 8-4

An EPS/EBIT Chart for the XYZ Company

Lowe's Companies is aggressively buying its own stock, increasing its **Treasury Stock** on its balance sheets. Many analysts say stock buybacks reflect optimism among companies and say it is a good sign. However, other analysts argue that buybacks eat cash that a firm could better use to grow the firm. Intel in late 2012 borrowed $6 billion to buy back more of its own stock. The low interest rate environment has spurred this activity. Even though Intel had the cash on its balance sheet to cover the transaction, the firm, like many large U.S. firms, have most of their cash in overseas accounts (that is, a large percentage of their revenues were derived in foreign countries). Many such firms prefer to leave their cash outside the USA because to use those funds to pay dividends or purchase treasury stock, for example, would trigger a big U.S. corporate income tax payment.

When using EPS/EBIT analysis, timing in relation to movements of stock prices, interest rates, and bond prices becomes important. In times of high stock prices, such as in 2013/2014, stock may prove to be the best alternative from both a cost and a demand standpoint. However, when cost of capital (interest rates) is low, debt is more attractive.

The USA has $9.7 trillion in outstanding debt, equal to 63 percent of gross domestic product (GDP). Based on that percentage, S&P lowered the U.S.'s AAA credit rating. It is interesting, however, that 147 of the S&P 500 companies have total debt that is 63 percent or greater than the company's revenue. For example, GE, Lennar, and Harley-Davidson have debt that is 300, 131, and 116 percent greater than their revenues, respectively. A key difference of course is that companies generate money whereas governments consume money. The U.S. government pays $210 billion in interest annually, about 10 percent of the $2.1 trillion it collects annually in taxes. Only 24 companies in the S&P 500 however incur interest payments that total at least 10 percent of their revenue.

Tables 8-5 and 8-6 provide EPS/EBIT analyses for two companies—Gateway Computers and Boeing. Notice in those analyses that the combination stock/debt options vary from 30/70 to 70/30. Any number of combinations could be explored. However, sometimes in preparing the EPS/EBIT graphs, the lines will intersect, thus revealing break-even points at which one financing alternative becomes more or less attractive than another. The slope of these lines will be determined by a combination of factors including stock price, interest rate, number of shares, and amount of capital needed. Also, it should be noted here that the best financing alternatives are indicated by the highest EPS values. In Tables 8-5 and 8-6, note that the tax rates for the companies vary considerably and should be computed from the respective income statements by dividing taxes paid by income before taxes.

In Table 8-5, the higher EPS values indicate that Gateway should use stock to raise capital in recession or normal economic conditions but should use debt financing under boom conditions. Stock is the best alternative for Gateway under all three conditions if EAT (profit maximization) were the decision criteria, but EPS (maximize shareholders' wealth) is the better ratio to make this decision. Firms can do many things in the short run to maximize profits, so investors and creditors consider maximizing shareholders' wealth to be the better criteria for making financing decisions.

In Table 8-6, note that Boeing should use stock to raise capital in recession (see 0.92) or normal (see 2.29) economic conditions but should use debt financing under boom conditions (see 5.07). Let us calculate here the number of shares figure of 1014.68 given under Boeing's stock alternative. Divide $10,000 M funds needed by the stock price of $53 = 188.68 M new shares to be issued + the 826 M shares outstanding already = 1014.68 M shares under the stock scenario. Along the final row, EPS is the number of shares outstanding divided by EAT in all columns.

TABLE 8-5 EPS/EBIT Analysis for Gateway (M = in millions)

Amount Needed: $1,000 M

EBIT Range: – $500 M to + $100 M to + $500 M

Interest Rate: 5%

Tax Rate: 0% (because the firm has been incurring a loss annually)

Stock Price: $6.00

# of Shares Outstanding: 371 M

	Common Stock Financing			Debt Financing		
	Recession	Normal	Boom	Recession	Normal	Boom
EBIT	(500.00)	100.00	500.00	(500.00)	100.00	500.00
Interest	0.00	0.00	0.00	50.00	50.00	50.00
EBT	(500.00)	100.00	500.00	(550.00)	50.00	450.00
Taxes	0.00	0.00	0.00	0.00	0.00	0.00
EAT	(500.00)	100.00	500.00	(550.00)	50.00	450.00
#Shares	537.67	537.67	537.67	371.00	371.00	371.00
EPS	**(0.93)**	**0.19**	**0.93**	**(1.48)**	**0.13**	**1.21**

	70 Percent Stock—30 Percent Debt			70 Percent Debt—30 Percent Stock		
	Recession	Normal	Boom	Recession	Normal	Boom
EBIT	(500.00)	100.00	500.00	(500.00)	100.00	500.00
Interest	15.00	15.00	15.00	35.00	35.00	35.00
EBT	(515.00)	85.00	485.00	(535.00)	65.00	465.00
Taxes	0.00	0.00	0.00	0.00	0.00	0.00
EAT	(515.00)	85.00	485.00	(535.00)	65.00	465.00
#Shares	487.67	487.67	487.67	421.00	421.00	421.00
EPS	**(1.06)**	**0.17**	**0.99**	**(1.27)**	**0.15**	**1.10**

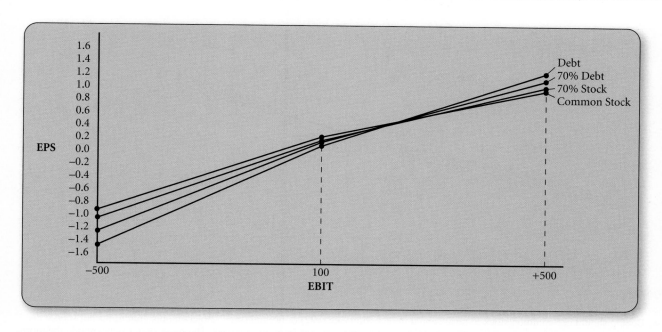

Conclusion: Gateway should use common stock to raise capital in recession or normal economic conditions but should use debt financing under boom conditions. Note that stock is the best alternative under all three conditions according to EAT (profit maximization), but EPS (maximize shareholders' wealth) is the better ratio to make this decision.

TABLE 8-6 EPS/EBIT Analysis for Boeing (M = in millions)

Amount Needed: $10,000 M

Interest Rate: 5%

Tax Rate: 7%

Stock Price: $53.00

# of Shares Outstanding: 826 M

	Common Stock Financing			Debt Financing		
	Recession	*Normal*	*Boom*	*Recession*	*Normal*	*Boom*
EBIT	1,000.00	2,500.00	5,000.00	1,000.00	2,500.00	5,000.00
Interest	0.00	0.00	0.00	500.00	500.00	500.00
EBT	1,000.00	2,500.00	5,000.00	500.00	2,000.00	4,500.00
Taxes	70.00	175.00	350.00	35.00	140.00	315.00
EAT	930.00	2,325.00	4,650.00	465.00	1,860.00	4,185.00
# Shares	1,014.68	1,014.68	1,014.68	826.00	826.00	826.00
EPS	**0.92**	**2.29**	4.58	**0.56**	**2.25**	**5.07**

	70% Stock—30% Debt			70% Debt—30% Stock		
	Recession	*Normal*	*Boom*	*Recession*	*Normal*	*Boom*
EBIT	1,000.00	2,500.00	5,000.00	1,000.00	2,500.00	5,000.00
Interest	150.00	150.00	150.00	350.00	350.00	350.00
EBT	850.00	2,350.00	4,850.00	650.00	2,150.00	4,650.00
Taxes	59.50	164.50	339.50	45.50	150.50	325.50
EAT	790.50	2,185.50	4,510.50	604.50	1,999.50	4,324.50
# Shares	958.08	958.08	958.08	882.60	882.60	882.60
EPS	**0.83**	**2.28**	**4.71**	**0.68**	**2.27**	**4.90**

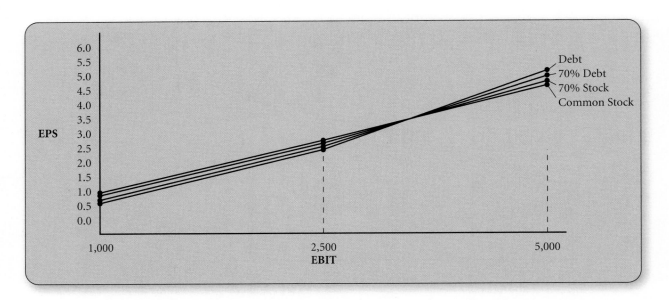

Conclusion: Boeing should use common stock to raise capital in recession (see 0.92) or normal (see 2.29) economic conditions but should use debt financing under boom conditions (see 5.07). Note that a dividends row is absent from this analysis. The more shares outstanding, the more dividends to be paid (if the firm pays dividends), which would lower the common stock EPS values.

Note in Table 8-5 and Table 8-6 that a dividends row is absent from both the Gateway and Boeing analyses. The more shares outstanding, the more dividends to be paid (if the firm indeed pays dividends). To consider dividends in an EPS/EBIT analysis, simply insert another row for "Dividends" right below the "EAT" row and then insert an "Earnings After Taxes and Dividends" row. Considering dividends would make the analysis more robust.

Note in both the Gateway and Boeing graphs, there is a breakeven point between the normal and boom range of EBIT where the debt option overtakes the 70/30 D/S option as the best financing alternative. A break-even point is where two lines cross each other. A break-even point is the EBIT level where various financing alternative represented by lines crossing are equally attractive in terms of EPS. Both the Gateway and Boeing graphs indicate that EPS values are highest for the 100 percent debt option at high EBIT levels. The two graphs also reveal that the EPS values for 100 percent debt increase faster than the other financing options as EBIT levels increase beyond the break-even point. At low levels of EBIT however, both the Gateway and Boeing graphs indicate that 100 percent stock is the best financing alternative because the EPS values are highest.

Projected Financial Statements

Projected financial statement analysis is a central strategy-implementation technique because it allows an organization to examine the expected results of various actions and approaches. This type of analysis can be used to forecast the impact of various implementation decisions (for example, to increase promotion expenditures by 50 percent to support a market-development strategy, to increase salaries by 25 percent to support a market-penetration strategy, to increase research and development expenditures by 70 percent to support product development, or to sell $1 million of common stock to raise capital for diversification). Nearly all financial institutions require at least three years of projected financial statements whenever a business seeks capital. A projected income statement and balance sheet allow an organization to compute projected financial ratios under various strategy-implementation scenarios. When compared to prior years and to industry averages, financial ratios provide valuable insights into the feasibility of various strategy-implementation approaches.

Primarily as a result of the Sarbanes-Oxley Act, companies today are being much more diligent in preparing projected financial statements to "reasonably rather than too optimistically" project future expenses and earnings. There is much more care not to mislead shareholders and other constituencies.

A 2015 projected income statement and a balance sheet for the Litten Company are provided in Table 8-7. The projected statements for Litten are based on five assumptions: (1) The company needs to raise $45 million to finance expansion into foreign markets; (2) $30 million of this total will be raised through increased debt and $15 million through common stock; (3) sales are expected to increase 50 percent; (4) three new facilities, costing a total of $30 million, will be constructed in foreign markets; and (5) land for the new facilities is already owned by the company. Note in Table 8-7 that Litten's strategies and their implementation are expected to result in a sales increase from $100 million to $150 million and in a net increase in income from $6 million to $9.75 million in the forecasted year.

TABLE 8-7 A Projected Income Statement and Balance Sheet for the Litten Company (in millions)

	Prior Year 2014	Projected Year 2015	Remarks
PROJECTED INCOME STATEMENT			
Sales	$100	$150.00	50% increase
Cost of Goods Sold	70	105.00	70% of sales
Gross Margin	30	45.00	
Selling Expense	10	15.00	10% of sales
Administrative Expense	5	7.50	5% of sales
Earnings Before Interest and Taxes	15	22.50	
Interest	3	3.00	
Earnings Before Taxes	12	19.50	
Taxes	6	9.75	50% rate
Net Income	**6**	**9.75**	
Dividends	2	5.00	
Retained Earnings	4	4.75	
PROJECTED BALANCE SHEET			
Assets			
Cash	5	7.75	Plug figure
Accounts Receivable	2	4.00	100% increase
Inventory	20	45.00	
Total Current Assets	27	56.75	
Land	15	15.00	
Plant and Equipment	50	80.00	Add three new plants at $10 million each
Less Depreciation	10	20.00	
Net Plant and Equipment	40	60.00	
Total Fixed Assets	55	75.00	
Total Assets	**82**	**131.75**	
Liabilities			
Accounts Payable	10	10.00	
Notes Payable	10	10.00	
Total Current Liabilities	20	20.00	
Long-term Debt	40	70.00	Borrowed $30 million
Additional Paid-in-Capital	20	35.00	Issued 100,000 shares at $150 each
Retained Earnings	2	6.75	$2 + $4.75
Total Liabilities and Net Worth	**82**	**131.75**	

There are six steps in performing projected financial analysis:

1. Prepare the projected income statement before the balance sheet. Start by forecasting sales as accurately as possible. Be careful not to blindly push historical percentages into the future with regard to revenue (sales) increases. Be mindful of what the firm did to achieve those past sales increases, which may not be appropriate for the future unless the firm takes similar or analogous actions (such as opening a similar number of stores, for example). If dealing with a manufacturing firm, also be mindful that if the firm is operating at 100 percent capacity running three eight-hour shifts per day, then probably new manufacturing facilities (land, plant, and equipment) will be needed to increase sales further.

2. Use the percentage-of-sales method to project cost of goods sold (CGS) and the expense items in the income statement. For example, if CGS is 70 percent of sales in the prior year (as it is in Table 8-7), then use that same percentage to calculate CGS in the future year—unless there is a reason to use a different percentage. Items such as interest, dividends, and taxes must be treated independently and cannot be forecasted using the percentage-of-sales method.

3. Calculate the projected net income.

4. Subtract from the net income any dividends to be paid for that year. This remaining net income is retained earnings (RE). Bring this retained earnings amount for that year (NI – DIV = RE) over to the balance sheet by adding it to the prior year's RE shown on the balance sheet. In other words, every year a firm adds its RE for that particular year (from the income statement) to its historical RE total on the balance sheet. Therefore, the RE amount on the balance sheet is a cumulative number rather than money available for strategy implementation! Note that RE is the first projected balance sheet item to be entered. As a result of this accounting procedure in developing projected financial statements, the RE amount on the balance sheet is usually a large number. However, it also can be a low or even negative number if the firm has been incurring losses. The only way for RE to decrease from one year to the next on the balance sheet is (1) if the firm incurred an earnings loss that year or (2) the firm had positive net income for the year but paid out dividends more than the net income. Be mindful that RE is the key link between a projected income statement and balance sheet, so be careful to make this calculation correctly.

5. Project the balance sheet items, beginning with retained earnings and then forecasting stockholders' equity, long-term liabilities, current liabilities, total liabilities, total assets, fixed assets, and current assets (in that order). Use the cash account as the plug figure—that is, use the cash account to make the assets total the liabilities and net worth. Then make appropriate adjustments. For example, if the cash needed to balance the statements is too small (or too large), make appropriate changes to borrow more (or less) money than planned.

6. List comments (remarks) on the projected statements. Any time a significant change is made in an item from a prior year to the projected year, an explanation (remark) should be provided. Remarks are essential because otherwise pro formas are meaningless.

Projected Financial Statement Analysis for Whole Foods Market

Because so many strategic management students have limited experience developing projected financial statements, let us apply the steps outlined on the previous pages to Whole Foods Market.

Whole Foods Market opened 16 stores in fiscal 2010. The projected statements given on the next page(s) are based on the following recommendations:

1. Whole Foods opens 40 new stores in 2011 and 60 new stores in 2012.
2. Whole Foods uses a 50/50 debt/stock combination to finance the 100 new stores.
3. After paying almost no dividends in 2010, Whole Foods starts paying dividends at $1.00 per share in 2011 and 2012.
4. Whole Foods boosts its advertising expenses by $20 million per year.
5. Whole Foods installs a new inventory control system that increases the company's low gross margin from 34.8 percent to 40.0 percent.
6. Whole Foods' per store revenues will increase 10 percent annually in 2011–2013 resulting from the new ad campaign and the improving economy.
7. Total cost of recommendations for two years are $800 million = $200 million per year to be raised through both debt and equity.

Whole Foods' actual consolidated income statements and balance sheets are provided in Table 8-8 and Table 8-9, respectively. The projected statements, based on the aforementioned recommendations, are provided in Table 8-10 and 8-11, respectively. Read carefully the notes (a through f), which reveal the rationale for various changes and exemplify the pro forma process. Note in Table 8-10 that Whole Foods' operating margin with the proposed strategic plan increases from 4.9 percent in 2010 to 16.9 percent in 2012. Note in Table 8-11 that Whole Foods' current ratio would be $3,580.3/$400 = 8.95, which is high. Thus, in 2012 the company could better use that money to perhaps pay down some of its $908 million in long-term debt.

The projected financial statements were prepared using the six steps outlined on prior pages and the above seven strategy statements. Note the cash account is used as the plug figure, and it is too high, so Whole Foods could reduce this number and concurrently reduce a liability or equity account the same amount to keep the statement in balance. Rarely is the cash account perfect on the first pass through, so adjustments are needed and made. However, these adjustments are *not* made on the projected statements given in Tables 8-10 and 8-11, so that the five strategy statements can be more readily seen on respective rows. Note the author's comments on Tables 8-10 and 8-11 that help explain changes in the numbers.

The U.S. Securities and Exchange Commission (SEC) conducts fraud investigations if projected numbers are misleading or if they omit information that's important to investors. Projected statements must conform with generally accepted accounting principles (GAAP) and must not be designed to hide poor expected results. The Sarbanes-Oxley Act requires CEOs and CFOs of corporations to personally sign their firms' financial statements attesting to their accuracy. These executives could thus be held personally liable for misleading or inaccurate statements. The collapse of the Arthur Andersen accounting firm, along with its client Enron, fostered a "zero-tolerance" policy among auditors and shareholders with regard to a firm's financial statements. But plenty of firms still "inflate" their financial projections and call them "pro formas," so investors, shareholders, and other stakeholders must still be wary of different companies' financial projections.[9]

On financial statements, different companies use different terms for various items, such as *revenues* or *sales* used for the same item by different companies. For net income, many firms use the term *earnings*, and many others use the term *profits*.

Financial Budgets

A **financial budget** is a document that details how funds will be obtained and spent for a specified period of time. Annual budgets are most common, although the period of time for a budget can range from one day to more than 10 years. Fundamentally, financial budgeting is a method

TABLE 8-8 Actual Whole Foods Market Income Statements (in millions)

	2010	2009
Revenue (a)	$9,005.8	$8,031.6
Cost of Goods Sold	5,870.4	5,277.3
Gross Profit	3,135.4	2,754.3
Gross Profit Margin	34.8%	34.3%
SG&A Expense	2,697.4	2,470.0
Depreciation & Amortization	275.6	266.7
Operating Income	438.0	284.3
Operating Margin	4.9%	3.5%
Nonoperating Income	6.9	3.4
Nonoperating Expenses	(33.0)	(36.9)
Income Before Taxes	411.8	250.9
Income Taxes (b)	165.9	104.1
Net Income After Taxes	245.8	146.8
Net Income	$245.8	$146.8

(a) Note that the 16 news stores in 2010 resulted in ($9,005.8 – 8,031.6 = 974.2 revenue increase = an average of $974.2 / 16 = $60.89) $60.89 million as the average revenue per new store.
(b) Note Whole Foods' effective tax rate is $165.9 / 411.8 = 40.3%.

TABLE 8-9 Actual Whole Foods Market Balance Sheets (in millions)

	2010	2009
Assets		
Current Assets		
Cash	$132.0	$430.1
Net Receivables	133.3	104.7
Inventories	323.5	310.6
Other Current Assets	572.7	209.9
Total Current Assets	1,161.5	1,055.4
Net Fixed Assets (a)	1,886.1	1,897.9
Other Noncurrent Assets	938.9	830.2
Total Assets	**3,986.5**	**3,783.4**
Liabilities		
Current Liabilities		
Accounts Payable	213.2	189.6
Short-Term Debt	0.4	0.4
Other Current Liabilities	534.3	494.0
Total Current Liabilities	747.9	684.0
Long-Term Debt	508.3	738.8
Other Noncurrent Liabilities	357.0	732.6
Total Liabilities	**1,613.2**	**2,155.5**
Shareholders' Equity		
Common Stock	500	400
Additional-paid-in-capital	1,274.7	869.7
Retained Earnings (b)	598.6	358.2
Total Shareholders' Equity	2,373.3	1,627.9
Total Liabilities and SE	**$3,986.5**	**$3,783.4**
Shares Outstanding (thou.)	172,033	140,542

(a) Since Whole Foods operated 300 stores in 2010, we can estimate cost per store = $1,886 / 300 = $6.3 million and use that cost # for each new store to be built.
(b) Note that Whole Foods reinvested back into the company $240.4 million of its total $245.8 million in net income, so in 2010 the company paid out only $5.4 million in dividends. We know that because $598.6 – $358.2 = $240.4.

for specifying what must be done to complete strategy implementation successfully. Financial budgeting should not be thought of as a tool for limiting expenditures but rather as a method for obtaining the most productive and profitable use of an organization's resources. Financial budgets can be viewed as the planned allocation of a firm's resources based on forecasts of the future.

There are almost as many different types of financial budgets as there are types of organizations. Some common types of budgets include cash budgets, operating budgets, sales budgets, profit budgets, factory budgets, capital budgets, expense budgets, divisional budgets, variable budgets, flexible budgets, and fixed budgets. When an organization is experiencing financial difficulties, budgets are especially important in guiding strategy implementation.

Perhaps the most common type of financial budget is the **cash budget**. The Financial Accounting Standards Board (FASB) has mandated that every publicly held company in the USA must issue an annual cash-flow statement in addition to the usual financial reports. The statement includes all receipts and disbursements of cash in operations, investments, and financing. It supplements the Statement on Changes in Financial Position formerly included in the annual reports of all publicly held companies. A cash budget for the year 2015 for the Toddler Toy Company is provided in Table 8-12. Note that Toddler is not expecting to have surplus cash until November 2015.

TABLE 8-10 Projected Whole Foods Market Income Statements (in millions)

	2010	2011	2012
Revenue (a)	$9,005.8	12,584.0	17,860.0
Cost of Goods Sold	5,870.4	7,550.0	10,716.0
Gross Profit	3,135.4	5,034.0	7,144.0
Gross Profit Margin (b)	34.8%	40%	40%
SG&A Expense (c)	2,697.4	3,782.0	4,109.0
Depreciation & Amortization	275.6	290	310.0
Operating Income	438.0	1,252.0	3,035.0
Operating Margin	4.9%	9.9%	16.9%
Nonoperating Income	6.9	0	0
Nonoperating Expenses	(33.0)	0	0
Income Before Taxes	411.8	1,252.0	3,035.0
Income Taxes (d)	165.9	504.0	1,223.0
Net Income After Taxes	245.8	748.0	1,812.0
Net Income	$245.8	748.0	1,812.0
Dividends	5.4	175.0	180.0
Retained Earnings	$240.4	573.0	1,632.0

(a) $60.89 million per new store + 10% increase for all stores, so in 2011 we have $60.89 × 40 = $2,435 + 9,005 = $11,440 + 10% = $12,584. In 2012 we have $60.89 × 60 = 3,653 + 12,584 = $16,237 + 10% = $17,860.

(b) increases to 40% due to better inventory control; note that 5,034/12,584 = 40% and 7,144/17,860 = 40%.

(c) same 29.9% of revenue + $20 million per year, new ad campaign; note that $12,584 × .299 + $20 = $3,782.

(d) same 40.3% rate as in 2010.

Financial budgets have some limitations. First, budgetary programs can become so detailed that they are cumbersome and overly expensive. Overbudgeting or underbudgeting can cause problems. Second, financial budgets can become a substitute for objectives. A budget is a tool and not an end in itself. Third, budgets can hide inefficiencies if based solely on precedent rather than on periodic evaluation of circumstances and standards. Finally, budgets are sometimes used as instruments of tyranny that result in frustration, resentment, absenteeism, and high turnover. To minimize the effect of this last concern, managers should increase the participation of subordinates in preparing budgets.

Company Valuation

Evaluating the worth of a business is central to strategy implementation because integrative, intensive, and diversification strategies are often implemented by acquiring other firms. Other strategies, such as retrenchment and divestiture, may result in the sale of a division of an organization or of the firm itself. Thousands of transactions occur each year in which businesses are bought or sold in the USA. In all these cases, it is necessary to establish the financial worth or cash value of a business to successfully implement strategies.

All the various methods for determining a business's worth can be grouped into three main approaches: what a firm owns, what a firm earns, or what a firm will bring in the market. But it is important to realize that valuation is not an exact science. The valuation of a firm's worth is based on financial facts, but common sense and intuitive judgment must enter into the process. It is difficult to assign a monetary value to some factors—such as a loyal customer base, a history of growth, legal suits pending, dedicated employees, a favorable lease, a bad credit rating, or good patents—that may not be reflected in a firm's financial statements. Also, different valuation methods will yield different totals for a firm's worth, and no prescribed approach is best for a certain situation. Evaluating the worth of a business truly requires both qualitative and quantitative skills.

TABLE 8-11 Projected Whole Foods Market Balance Sheets (in millions)

	2010	2011	2012
Assets			
Current Assets			
Cash	$132.0	$1,55.3	$3,260.3
Net Receivables	133.3	140.0	160.0
Inventories	323.5	330.0	360.0
Other Current Assets	572.7	0	0
Total Current Assets	1,161.5	2,020.3	3,580.3
Net Fixed Assets (a)	1,886.1	2,138.0	2,516.0
Other Noncurrent Assets	938.9	0	0
Total Assets	**$3,986.5**	**$4,159.3**	**$6,296.3**
Liabilities			
Current Liabilities			
Accounts Payable	213.2	300.0	400.0
Short-Term Debt	0.4	0	0
Other Current Liabilities	534.3	0	0
Total Current Liabilities	747.9	300.0	400.0
Long-Term Debt (b)	508.3	708.0	908.0
Other Noncurrent Liabilities	357.0	0	0
Total Liabilities	1,613.2	1,008.0	1,308.0
Shareholders' Equity			
Common Stock (c)	500.0	505.0	510.0
Additional-paid-in-capital (d)	1,247.7	1,474.7	1,674.7
Retained Earnings (e)	598.6	1,171.6	2,803.6
Total Shareholders' Equity	2,373.3	3151.3	4,988.3
Total Liabilities and SE	**$3,986.5**	**$4,159.3**	**$6,296.3**
Shares Outstanding (in thousands) (f)	172,033	177,033	182,033

(a) $6.3 M per store × 40 stores = 252 + 1,886 = 2,138; 6.3 × 60 = 378 + 2,139 = 2,516
(b) $200 M to be raised by debt annually
(c) add 5 M new shares annually since $40 per share and need $200 M to be raised by equity annually
(d) add $200 M annually thru stock issuance
(e) $ 598.6 + $ 573.0 = $1,171.6 + 1,632.0 = $2,803.6
(f) stock price = $40, $200 M needed per year thru equity, so 5 M new shares to be issued annually; thus
172,033 + 5 M = 177,033

The first approach in evaluating the worth of a business is determining its net worth or stockholders' equity. Net worth represents the sum of common stock, additional paid-in capital, and retained earnings. After calculating net worth, subtract an appropriate amount for goodwill and intangibles. Whereas intangibles include copyrights, patents, and trademarks, goodwill arises only if a firm acquires another firm and pays more than the book value for that firm.

It should be noted that FASB Rule 142 requires companies to admit once a year if the premiums they paid for acquisitions, called **goodwill**, were a waste of money. Goodwill is not a good thing to have on a balance sheet. Note in Table 8-13 that J.M. Smucker's $Goodwill to $Total Assets is a really high 33.5 percent, indicating that a third of the company's assets are "Goodwill," which is not good.

The second approach to measuring the value of a firm grows out of the belief that the worth of any business should be based largely on the future benefits its owners may derive through net profits. A conservative rule of thumb is to establish a business's worth as five times the firm's current annual profit. A five-year average profit level could also be used. When using this approach, remember that firms normally suppress earnings in their financial statements to minimize taxes.

TABLE 8-12 Six-Month Cash Budget for the Toddler Toy Company in 2015

Cash Budget (in thousands)	July	Aug.	Sept.	Oct.	Nov.	Dec.	Jan.
Receipts							
Collections	$12,000	$21,000	$31,000	$35,000	$22,000	$18,000	$11,000
Payments							
Purchases	14,000	21,000	28,000	14,000	14,000	7,000	
Wages and Salaries	1,500	2,000	2,500	1,500	1,500	1,000	
Rent	500	500	500	500	500	500	
Other Expenses	200	300	400	200	—	100	
Taxes	—	8,000	—	—	—	—	
Payment on Machine	—	—	10,000	—	—	—	
Total Payments	$16,200	$31,800	$41,400	$16,200	$16,000	$8,600	
Net Cash Gain (Loss) During Month	–4,200	–10,800	–10,400	18,800	6,000	9,400	
Cash at Start of Month if No Borrowing Is Done	6,000	1,800	–9,000	–19,400	-600	5,400	
Cumulative Cash (Cash at start plus gains or minus losses)	1,800	–9,000	–19,400	–600	5,400	14,800	
Less Desired Level of Cash	–5,000	–5,000	–5,000	–5,000	–5,000	–5,000	
Total Loans Outstanding to Maintain $5,000 Cash Balance	$3,200	$14,000	$24,400	$5,600	—	—	
Surplus Cash	—	—	—	—	400	9,800	

TABLE 8-13 Company Worth Analysis for J.M. Smucker, Microsoft Corp., and Zale Corp. (in millions, except stock price and EPS)

Input Data	J.M. Smucker	Microsoft Corp.	Zale Corp.
$ Shareholders' Equity (SE)	5,163	66,363	178
$ Net Income (NI)	460	17,000	–27
$ Stock Price (SP)	80	30	7
$ EPS	4.08	2.00	–.90
# of Shares Outstanding	109	8,330	32
$ Goodwill	3,050	13,542	100
$ Intangibles	3,190	3,170	0
$ Total Assets	9,115	121,271	1,171
Company Worth Analyses			
1. SE – Goodwill – Intangibles	$977	$49,741	$78
2. Net Income x 5	2,300	85,000	0
3. (SP / EPS) x NI	9,019	225,000	0
4. # of Shares Out x Stock Price	8,720	251,400	224
5. Four Method Average	$4,765	$161,285	$151
$ Goodwill / $ Total Assets	33.5%	11.1%	8.5%

The third approach is called the **price-earnings ratio method**. To use this method, divide the market price of the firm's common stock by the annual earnings per share and multiply this number by the firm's average net income for the past five years.

The fourth method can be called the **outstanding shares method**. To use this method, simply multiply the number of shares outstanding by the market price per share. If the purchase price is more than this amount, the additional dollars are called a **premium**. The outstanding shares method may be called the "**market value**" or "**market capitalization**" or "**book value**" of the firm. The premium is a per-share dollar amount that a person or firm is willing to pay beyond the book value of the firm to control (acquire) the other company. Bristol-Myers Squibb recently offered $31 a share to acquire Amylin Pharmaceuticals and that offer represented a 9.9 percent premium over Amylin's closing stock price the day of the offer. WellPoint, the second-largest insurer in the USA, recently acquired Amerigroup for $92 per share in cash, which was a whopping 43 percent premium to Amerigroup's closing stock price of $64.34. Amerigroup's stock soared 38 percent to $88.79 the day after the offer.

Table 8-13 provides the cash value analyses for three companies—J.M. Smucker, Microsoft Corp., and Zale Corp.—for fiscal year-end 2012. Notice that there is significant variation among the four methods used to determine cash value. For example, the worth of J.M. Smucker ranged from minus $1,077 to $9.019 billion. Obviously, if you were selling your company, you would seek the larger values, whereas if purchasing a company you would seek the lower values. In practice, substantial negotiation takes place in reaching a final compromise (or averaged) amount. Also recognize that if a firm's net income is negative, theoretically the approaches involving that figure would result in a negative number, implying that the firm would pay you to acquire them. Of course, you obtain all of the firm's debt and liabilities in an acquisition, so theoretically this would be possible.

Hewlett-Packard, Boston Scientific, Frontier Communications, and Republic Services (unfortunately for them) carry more goodwill on their balance sheet than their market (or book) value. This is a signal that their goodwill should be "written down," which means "reduced and recorded as an expense on the income statement." Nasdaq OMX Group's $5.1 billion in goodwill exceeds its $3.9 billion market capitalization by a precarious 31 percent. Jack Ciesielski, publisher of Analyst's Accounting Observer, says: "Writing down goodwill is an admission that the company screwed up when it budgeted what an acquired firm is worth." Sometimes it is OK to pay more for a company than its book value if the firm has technology or patents you need or economies of scale you desire or even to reduce competitive pricing pressure, but, like buying a house, paying a "premium" for a company is almost always not a good thing. Acquiring at a "discount" is far better for shareholders.

Because goodwill write-down accounting rules involve projections and judgments, companies have leeway for when to write down goodwill, and by how much. Microsoft for example in 2012 wrote down (reduced) their goodwill $6.2 billion, basically admitting that their previous acquisition of online-advertising firm aQuantive Inc. for $6.3 billion was ill advised—now recording that amount as an expense. Analysts expect Hewlett-Packard to soon write down some (or all) of the $6.6 billion in goodwill among the $10.1 billion total that they recently paid for British software maker Autonomy PLC.[10]

If the purchase price is less than the stock price times number of shares outstanding, rather than more, that difference is called a **discount**. For example, when Clayton Doubilier & Rice LLC recently acquired Emergency Medical Services (EMS) Corp. for $2.9 billion, a 9.4 percent discount below EMS's stock price of $64.00.

Business evaluations are becoming routine in many situations. Businesses have many strategy-implementation reasons for determining their worth in addition to preparing to be sold or to buy other companies. Employee plans, taxes, retirement packages, mergers, acquisitions, expansion plans, banking relationships, death of a principal, divorce, partnership agreements, and IRS audits are other reasons for a periodic valuation. It is just good business to have a reasonable understanding of what a firm is worth. This knowledge protects the interests of all parties involved.

Ryan Brewer, an assistant professor of finance at Indiana University-Purdue University Columbus, recently calculated the monetary value of top college football teams. Brewer examined each program's revenues and expenses and made cash-flow adjustments, risk assessments and growth projections for each school. Brewer's results for 69 college programs are provided in Table 8-14. Note that Texas was the most valuable college football program in 2012, followed by Michigan. Interestingly, all of these programs are "non-profit." As a point of reference, the NFL's Jacksonville Jaguars sold in late 2011 for about $760 million.

TABLE 8-14 The Monetary Value of Various College Football Programs

Sticker Shock The value, in millions, of major-conference college-football programs, plus Notre Dame and BYU:

Rank	SCHOOL	VALUE	Rank	SCHOOL	VALUE	Rank	SCHOOL	VALUE	Rank	SCHOOL	VALUE
1	Texas	$761.7	19	Oregon	$264.6	37	Virginia	$146.3	55	Mississippi St.	$99.3
2	Michigan	$731.9	20	Washington	$259.9	38	Purdue	$145.1	56	Maryland	$96.0
3	Florida	$599.7	21	Michigan St.	$224.8	39	N.C. State	$143.0	57	California	$92.6
4	Notre Dame	$597.4	22	Texas Tech	$211.0	40	Indiana	$142.7	58	Syracuse	$91.4
5	Ohio St.	$586.6	23	Oklahoma St.	$209.1	41	Iowa St.	$140.3	59	Texas Christian	$76.6
6	Auburn	$508.1	24	Kansas St.	$207.1	42	Minnesota	$139.7	60	Louisville	$75.4
7	Georgia	$481.8	25	Colorado	$202.9	43	BYU	$136.1	61	Washington St.	$73.4
8	Alabama	$476.0	26	Kentucky	$202.7	44	Arizona	$126.8	62	Baylor	$71.3
9	LSU	$471.7	27	Clemson	$201.8	45	UCLA	$125.8	63	Rutgers	$64.1
10	Oklahoma	$454.7	28	USC	$197.8	46	Utah	$119.7	64	Duke	$62.0
11	Iowa	$384.4	29	Georgia Tech	$188.4	47	Oregon St.	$118.8	65	Pittsburgh	$59.6
12	Tennessee	$364.6	30	Virginia Tech	$171.5	48	Illinois	$117.3	66	Vanderbilt	$57.3
13	Nebraska	$360.1	31	Arizona St.	$164.6	49	Mississippi	$111.7	67	Missouri	$56.4
14	Arkansas	$332.0	32	West Virginia	$159.4	50	Boston College	$110.2	68	Cincinnati	$48.9
15	S.Carolina	$311.9	33	Florida St.	$159.0	51	Kansas	$103.4	69	Temple	$46.9
16	Penn St.	$300.8	34	Miami(Fla.)	$157.7	52	Connecticut	$101.8			
17	Wisconsin	$296.1	35	Northwestern	$148.8	53	South Florida	$101.2			
18	Texas A&M	$278.5	36	Stanford	$148.7	54	North Carolina	$99.8			

Source: Ryan Brewer, Indiana University-Purdue University Columbus.
Note: Excludes Wake Forest; based on information at http://online.wsj.com/article/SB10001424127887324391104578225802183417888.html.

Deciding Whether to Go Public

Hundreds of companies in 2012 held **initial public offerings (IPOs)** to move from being private to being public. These firms took advantage of high stock market prices. For example, some recent IPOs include computer-network-security firm Palo Alto Networks Inc., search engine Kayak Software Corp., guitar maker Fender Musical Instruments, discount retailer Five Below, and pharmaceutical developer Durata Therapeutics, health-food retailer Natural Grocers by vitamin Cottage, software firm E2open, and Chuy's Holdings, a U.S.-based operator of Mexican restaurants. MGM Holdings, parent of the film studio Metro-Goldwyn-Mayer, just hired Goldman Sachs Group to develop a public stock offering for the company. MGM hopes its new "Hobbit" and "Skyfall" movies will help its pending IPO.

Groupon, the firm that offers daily deals on services, went public in November 2011 at $20 per share or $13 billion in market capitalization, but less than a year later Groupon stock was selling for $6.00 per share and the company's market capitalization had dropped to less than $5 billion. Zynga and Facebook's recent IPO's also turned sour quite quickly.

Going public means selling off a percentage of a company to others to raise capital; consequently, it dilutes the owners' control of the firm. Going public is not recommended for companies with less than $10 million in sales because the initial costs can be too high for the firm to generate sufficient cash flow to make going public worthwhile. One dollar in four is the average total cost paid to lawyers, accountants, and underwriters when an initial stock issuance is under $1 million; $1 in $20 will go to cover these costs for issuances over $20 million.

In addition to initial costs involved with a stock offering, there are costs and obligations associated with reporting and management in a publicly held firm. For firms with more than $10 million in sales, going public can provide major advantages. It can allow the firm to raise capital to develop new products, build plants, expand, grow, and market products and services more effectively.

Research and Development (R&D) Issues

In terms of "Innovation," *Fortune* recently ranked the following companies as best in the world. Note that Apple retained its number-1 ranking from the prior year.

Rank	Company
1	Apple
2	Sistema
3	GDF Suez
4	Limited Brands
5	Qualcomm
6*	Enterprise Products Partners
6*	Koc Holding
8	Amazon.com
9	Sealed Air
10	Nike

Source: Based on http://money.cnn.com/magazines/fortune/most-admired/2012/best_worst/best1.html.

Research and development (R&D) personnel can play an integral part in strategy implementation. These individuals are generally charged with developing new products and improving old products in a way that will allow effective strategy implementation. R&D employees and managers perform tasks that include transferring complex technology, adjusting processes to local raw materials, adapting processes to local markets, and altering products to particular tastes and specifications. Strategies such as product development, market penetration, and related diversification require that new products be successfully developed and that old products be significantly improved.

Technological improvements that affect consumer and industrial products and services shorten product life cycles. Companies in virtually every industry are relying on the development of new products and services to fuel profitability and growth.[11] Surveys suggest that the most successful organizations use an R&D strategy that ties external opportunities to internal strengths and is linked with objectives. Well-formulated R&D policies match market opportunities with internal capabilities. R&D policies can enhance strategy implementation efforts to:

1. Emphasize product or process improvements.
2. Stress basic or applied research.
3. Be leaders or followers in R&D.
4. Develop robotics or manual-type processes.
5. Spend a high, average, or low amount of money on R&D.
6. Perform R&D within the firm or to contract R&D to outside firms.
7. Use university researchers or private-sector researchers.

R&D policy among rival firms often varies dramatically. For example, Pfizer spends only about $5 billion annually on R&D even though the firm has about $70 billion in annual revenues, whereas rival Merck spends about $10 billion annually on R&D with annual revenue of about $50 billion. Underlying this difference in strategy between the two pharmaceutical giants is a philosophical disagreement over the merits of heavy investment to discover new drugs versus waiting for others to spend the money and discover and then follow up with similar products. Pfizer and Merck "are going in different directions," said Les Funtleyder, portfolio manager of the Miller Tabak Health Care Transformation mutual fund.

There must be effective interactions between R&D departments and other functional departments in implementing different types of generic business strategies. Conflicts between marketing, finance and accounting, R&D, and information systems departments can be minimized with clear policies and objectives. Table 8-15 gives some examples of R&D activities that could be required for successful implementation of various strategies. Many U.S. utility, energy, and automotive companies are employing their R&D departments to determine how the firm can effectively reduce its gas emissions.

TABLE 8-15 Research and Development Involvement in Selected Strategy-Implementation Situations

Type of Organization	Strategy Being Implemented	R&D Activity
Pharmaceutical company	Product development	Test the effects of a new drug on different subgroups.
Boat manufacturer	Related diversification	Test the performance of various keel designs under various conditions.
Plastic container manufacturer	Market penetration	Develop a biodegradable container.
Electronics company	Market development	Develop a telecommunications system in a foreign country.

Many firms wrestle with the decision to acquire R&D expertise from external firms or to develop R&D expertise internally. The following guidelines can be used to help make this decision:

1. If the rate of technical progress is slow, the rate of market growth is moderate, and there are significant barriers to possible new entrants, then in-house R&D is the preferred solution. The reason is that R&D, if successful, will result in a temporary product or process monopoly that the company can exploit.
2. If technology is changing rapidly and the market is growing slowly, then a major effort in R&D may be risky because it may lead to the development of an ultimately obsolete technology or one for which there is no market.
3. If technology is changing slowly but the market is growing quickly, there generally is not enough time for in-house development. The prescribed approach is to obtain R&D expertise on an exclusive or nonexclusive basis from an outside firm.
4. If both technical progress and market growth are fast, R&D expertise should be obtained through acquisition of a well-established firm in the industry.[12]

There are at least three major R&D approaches for implementing strategies. The first strategy is to be the first firm to market new technological products. This is a glamorous and exciting strategy but also a dangerous one. Even Apple found this to be dangerous as per Samsung. Firms such as 3M and General Electric have been successful with this approach, but many other pioneering firms have fallen, with rival firms seizing the initiative.

A second R&D approach is to be an innovative imitator of successful products, thus minimizing the risks and costs of start-up. This approach entails allowing a pioneer firm to develop the first version of the new product and to demonstrate that a market exists. Then, laggard firms develop a similar product. This strategy requires excellent R&D and marketing personnel.

A third R&D strategy is to be a low-cost producer by mass-producing products similar to but less expensive than products recently introduced. As a new product is accepted by customers, price becomes increasingly important in the buying decision. Also, mass marketing replaces personal selling as the dominant selling strategy. This R&D strategy requires substantial investment in plant and equipment but fewer expenditures in R&D than the two approaches described previously. Dell and Lenovo have utilized this third approach to gain competitive advantage.

R&D activities among U.S. firms need to be more closely aligned to business objectives. There needs to be expanded communication between R&D managers and strategists. Corporations are experimenting with various methods to achieve this improved communication climate, including different roles and reporting arrangements for managers and new methods to reduce the time it takes research ideas to become reality.

Perhaps the most current trend in R&D management has been lifting the veil of secrecy whereby firms, even major competitors, are joining forces to develop new products. Collaboration is on the rise as a result of new competitive pressures, rising research costs, increasing regulatory issues, and accelerated product development schedules. Companies not only are working more closely with each other on R&D, but they are also turning to consortia at universities for their R&D needs. More than 600 research consortia are now in operation in the USA.

Management Information Systems (MIS) Issues

Firms that gather, assimilate, and evaluate external and internal information most effectively are gaining competitive advantages over other firms. Having an effective **management information system (MIS)** may be the most important factor in differentiating successful from unsuccessful firms. The process of strategic management is facilitated immensely in firms that have an effective information system.

Information collection, retrieval, and storage can be used to create competitive advantages in ways such as cross-selling to customers, monitoring suppliers, keeping managers and employees informed, coordinating activities among divisions, and managing funds. Like inventory and human resources, information is now recognized as a valuable organizational asset that can be controlled and managed. Firms that implement strategies using the best information will reap competitive advantages in the twenty-first century.

A good information system can allow a firm to reduce costs. For example, online orders from salespersons to production facilities can shorten materials ordering time and reduce inventory costs. Direct communications between suppliers, manufacturers, marketers, and customers can link together elements of the value chain as though they were one organization. Improved quality and service often result from an improved information system.

Firms must increasingly be concerned about computer hackers and take specific measures to secure and safeguard corporate communications, files, orders, and business conducted over the Internet. Thousands of companies today are plagued by computer hackers who include disgruntled employees, competitors, bored teens, sociopaths, thieves, spies, and hired agents. Computer vulnerability is a giant, expensive headache.

Headquartered in Short Hills, New Jersey, Dun & Bradstreet is an example company that has an excellent information system. Every D&B customer and client in the world has a separate nine-digit number. The database of more than 200 million businesses worldwide contains of information associated with each number. The D-U-N-S # has become so widely used that it is like a business Social Security number. D&B reaps great competitive advantages from its information system.

In many firms, information technology is doing away with the workplace and allowing employees to work at home or anywhere, anytime. The mobile concept of work allows employees to work the traditional 9-to-5 workday across any of the 24 time zones around the globe. Affordable desktop videoconferencing software allows employees to "beam in" whenever needed. Any manager or employee who travels a lot away from the office is a good candidate for working at home rather than in an office provided by the firm. Salespersons or consultants are good examples, but any person whose job largely involves talking to others or handling information could easily operate at home with the proper MIS.[13]

Business Analytics

Business analytics is a MIS technique that involves using software to mine huge volumes of data to help executives make decisions. Sometimes called predictive analytics, machine learning, or data mining, this software enables a researcher to assess and use the aggregate experience of an organization, a priceless strategic asset for a firm. The history of a firm's interaction with its customers, suppliers, distributors, employees, rival firms, and more can all be tapped with **data mining** to generate predictive models. Business analytics is similar to the actuarial methods used by insurance companies to rate customers by the chance of positive or negative outcomes. Every business is basically a risk management endeavor! Therefore, like insurance companies, all businesses can benefit from measuring, tracking, and computing the risk associated with hundreds of strategic and tactical decisions made everyday. Business analytics enables a company to benefit from measuring and managing risk.

As more and more products become commoditized (so similar as to be indistinguishable), competitive advantage more and more hinges on improvements to business processes. Business analytics can provide a firm with proprietary business intelligence regarding, for example, which segment(s) of customers choose your firm versus those who defer, delay, or defect to a competitor and why. Business analytics can reveal where competitors are weak so that marketing and sales activities can be directly targeted to take advantage of resultant opportunities (knowledge).

In addition to understanding consumer behavior better, which yields more effective and efficient marketing, business analytics also is being used to slash expenses by, for example, withholding retention offers from customers who are going to stay with the firm anyway, or managing fraudulent transactions involving invoices, credit care purchases, tax returns insurance claims, mobile phone calls, online ad clicks, and more.

A key distinguishing feature of business analytics is that it is predictive rather than retrospective, in that it enables a firm to learn from experience and to make current and future decisions based on prior information. Deriving robust predictive models from data mining to support hundreds of commonly occurring business decisions is the essence of learning from experience. The mathematical models associated with business analytics can dramatically enhance decision making at all organizational levels and all stages of strategic management. In a sense, art becomes science with business analytics resulting from the mathematical generalization of thousands, millions, or even billions of prior data points to discover patterns of behavior for optimizing the deployment of resources.

IBM's former CEO Samuel Palmisano announced that IBM is moving aggressively into business analytics, trying to overtake Oracle's market share lead.[14] IBM's annual business analytics revenues of about $40 billion are growing about 15 percent every quarter compared to the industry growing about 15 percent annually. IBM's acquisition of SPSS for $1.2 billion, among other recent acquisitions, launched the firm heavily into the business analytics consulting business. Microsoft currently has a software program called PowerPivot that offers data-mining capability in a spreadsheet-like way, but this is not nearly as powerful as business analytics software. IBM recently completed a business analytics project for the New York City Fire Department whereby buildings in the city were assessed for risk.

Special Note to Students

Regardless of your business major, be sure to capitalize on that special knowledge in delivering your strategic management case analysis. Whenever the opportunity arises in your oral or written project, reveal how your firm can gain and sustain competitive advantage using your marketing, finance and accounting, or MIS recommendations. Continuously compare your firm to rivals and draw insights and conclusions so that your recommendations come across as well conceived. Never shy away from the EPS/EBIT or projected financial statement analyses because your audience must be convinced that what you recommend is financially feasible and worth the dollars to be spent. Spend sufficient time on the nuts-and-bolts of those analyses, so fellow students (and your professor) will be assured that you did them correctly and reasonably. Too often, when students rush at the end, it means their financial statements are overly optimistic or incorrectly developed—so avoid that issue. The marketing, finance and accounting, and MIS aspects of your recommended strategies must ultimately work together to gain and sustain competitive advantage for the firm—so point that out frequently. By the way, the free student excel template at www.strategyclub.com can help immensely in performing EPS-EBIT analysis.

Conclusion

Successful strategy implementation depends on cooperation among all functional and divisional managers in an organization. Marketing departments are commonly charged with implementing strategies that require significant increases in sales revenues in new areas and with new or improved products. Finance and accounting managers must devise effective strategy-implementation approaches at low cost and minimum risk to that firm. R&D managers have to transfer complex technologies or develop new technologies to successfully implement strategies. Information systems managers are being called upon more and more to provide leadership and training for all individuals in the firm. The nature and role of marketing, finance and accounting, R&D, and MIS activities, coupled with the management activities described in Chapter 7, largely determine organizational success.

MyManagementLab®

Go to **mymanagementlab.com** to complete the problems marked with this icon ⭐.

Key Terms and Concepts

book value (p. 268)
business analytics (p. 272)
cash budget (p. 264)
data mining (p. 272)
demand void (p. 253)
discount (p. 268)
EPS/EBIT analysis (p. 255)
financial budget (p. 263)
goodwill (p. 266)
initial public offering (IPO) (p. 269)
management information system (MIS) (p. 272)
market capitalization (p. 268)
market segment (p. 253)
market segmentation (p. 249)

market value (p. 268)
marketing mix variables (p. 250)
multidimensional scaling (p. 252)
outstanding shares method (p. 267)
perceptual mapping (p. 253)
premium (p. 268)
price-earnings ratio method (p. 267)
product positioning (p. 249)
projected financial statement analysis (p. 260)
research and development (R&D) (p. 270)
treasury stock (p. 257)
tweet (p. 248)
vacant niche (p. 252)
wikis (p. 248)

Issues for Review and Discussion

⭐ **8-1.** Do you agree with privacy advocates who contend that Facebook should provide ways for users to opt out of the mobile ad targeting? Why or why not?

8-2. Develop a perceptual map for the six colleges and universities closest to your institution. Illustrate a *market segment* and a *demand void* in your map. What are the strategic implications of your map?

8-3. Bristol-Myers Squibb, a company with single-A investment credit ratings, recently sold $2 billion of bonds that paid 3.35 percent interest. What are the pros and cons of this activity compared to issuing stock or borrowing money from a bank in terms of raising capital?

8-4. Lowe's Companies is aggressively buying its own stock. What are situations when this practice is recommended or especially beneficial?

8-5. The chapter says Hewlett-Packard has more $goodwill than the $book value of the firm. Explain what this means, how it could occur, and what can be done about this situation?

8-6. Define and give an example of *business analytics*. Why is this technique becoming so widely used in organizations today?

8-7. Give a hypothetical example where Company A buys Company B for a 15.0 percent premium.

8-8. Give a hypothetical example where Company A buys Company B for a 15.0 percent discount.

8-9. What is treasury stock? When should a company purchase treasury stock?

8-10. What is an IPO? When is an IPO good for a company? Why did Facebook use an IPO? Was that a wise strategic move? Why?

8-11. Discuss the new principles of marketing according to Parise, Guinan, and Weinberg.

⭐ **8-12.** For companies in general, identify and discuss three opportunities and three threats associated with social networking activities on the Internet.

8-13. Do you agree or disagree with the following statement? "Television viewers are passive viewers of ads, whereas Internet users take an active role in choosing what to look at—so customers on the Internet are tougher for marketers to reach." Explain your reasoning.

8-14. How important or relevant do you believe "purpose-based marketing" is for organizations today?

8-15. Why is it essential for organizations to segment markets and target particular groups of consumers?

8-16. Explain how and why the Internet makes market segmentation easier.

8-17. A product-positioning rule given in the chapter is that "When there are only two competitors, the middle becomes the preferred strategic position." Illustrate this for the cruise ship industry, where two firms, Carnival and Royal Caribbean, dominate. Illustrate this for the commercial airliner building industry, where Boeing and Airbus dominate.

8-18. How could or would dividends affect an EPS/EBIT analysis? Would it be correct to refer to "earnings after taxes, interest, and dividends" as retained earnings for a given year?

8-19. In performing an EPS/EBIT analysis, where do the first-row (EBIT) numbers come from?

8-20. In performing an EPS/EBIT analysis, where does the tax rate percentage come from?

8-21. For the Litten Company in Table 8-7, what would the Retained Earnings value have to have been in 2013 on the balance sheet, given that the 2014 NI-DIV value was $4?

8-22. Show algebraically that the price earnings ratio formula is identical to the number of shares outstanding times stock price formula. Why are the values obtained from these two methods sometimes different?

8-23. In accounting terms, distinguish between intangibles and goodwill on a balance sheet. Why do these two items generally stay the same on projected financial statements?

8-24. Explain how you would estimate the total worth of a business.

8-25. Diagram and label clearly a product-positioning map that includes six fast-food restaurant chains.

8-26. Explain why EPS/EBIT analysis is a central strategy-implementation technique.

✪ **8-27.** Discuss the limitations of EPS/EBIT analysis.

8-28. Explain how marketing, finance and accounting, R&D, and MIS managers' involvement in strategy formulation can enhance strategy implementation.

8-29. Consider the following statement: "Retained earnings on the balance sheet are not monies available to finance strategy implementation." Is it true or false? Explain.

8-30. Explain why projected financial statement analysis is considered both a strategy-formulation and a strategy-implementation tool.

8-31. Describe some marketing, finance and accounting, R&D, and MIS activities that a small restaurant chain might undertake to expand into a neighboring state.

8-32. What effect is e-commerce having on firms' efforts to segment markets?

8-33. Complete the following EPS/EBIT analysis for a company whose stock price is $20, interest rate on funds is 5 percent, tax rate is 20 percent, number of shares outstanding is 500 million, and EBIT range is $100 million to $300 million. The firm needs to raise

$200 million in capital. Use the accompanying table (to the right) to complete the work.

8-34. Under what conditions would retained earnings on the balance sheet decrease from one year to the next?

8-35. In your own words, list all the steps in developing projected financial statements.

8-36. Based on the financial statements provided for PepsiCo (p. 29), how much dividends in dollars did PepsiCo pay in 2011? In 2012?

8-37. Based on the financial statements provided in this chapter for the Litten Company, calculate the value of this company if you know that its stock price is $20 and it has 1 million shares outstanding. Calculate four different ways and average.

8-38. Why should you be careful not to use historical percentages blindly in developing projected financial statements?

8-39. In developing projected financial statements, what should you do if the dollar amount you must put in the cash account (to make the statement balance) is far more (or less) than desired?

8-40. Why is it both important and necessary to segment markets and target groups of customers, rather than market to all possible consumers?

8-41. In full detail, explain the following EPS/EBIT chart.

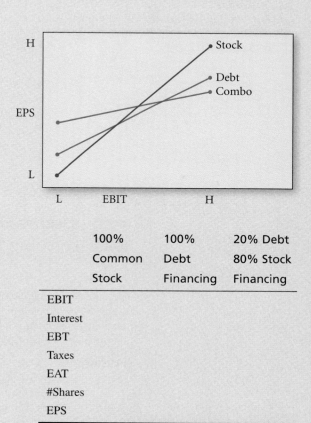

	100% Common Stock	100% Debt Financing	20% Debt 80% Stock Financing
EBIT			
Interest			
EBT			
Taxes			
EAT			
#Shares			
EPS			

MyManagementLab®

Go to **mymanagementlab.com** for Auto-graded writing questions as well as the following Assisted-graded writing questions:

8-42. Why is it essential for organizations to segment markets and target particular groups of consumers?

8-43. Explain how you would estimate the total worth of a business.

8-44. Mymanagementlab Only—comprehensive writing assignment for this chapter.

Current Readings

Aaker, David A. "Win the Brand Relevance Battle and then Build Competitor Barriers." *California Management Review* 54, no. 2 (Winter 2012): 43–57.

Balmer, John M. T. "Corporate Brand Management Imperatives: Custodianship, Credibility, and Calibration." *California Management Review* 54, no. 3 (Spring 2012): 6–33.

Crittenden, Victoria L., William F. Crittenden. "Strategic Marketing in a Changing World." *Business Horizons* 55, no. 3 (May 2012): 215–217.

Denning, Stephen. "From Maximizing Shareholder Value to Delighting the Customer." *Strategy and Leadership* 40, no. 4 (2012): 12–16.

Fox, Justin, and Jay W. Lorsch. "What Good Are Shareholders?" *Harvard Business Review* (July-August 2012): 48.

Guillén, Mauro F., and Esteban Garcia-Canal. "Execution as Strategy." *Harvard Business Review* (October 2012): 103.

Kumar, V., and Rohan Mirchandani. "Increasing the ROI of Social Media Marketing." *MIT Sloan Management Review* 54, no. 1 (Fall 2012): 55.

Muller, Amy, Nate Hutchins, and Miguel Cardoso Pinto. "Applying Open Innovation Where Your Company Needs It Most." *Strategy and Leadership* 40, no. 3 (2012): 35–42.

Quigley, Timothy J., and Donald C. Hambrick. "When the Former CEO Stays on as Board Chair: Effects on Successor Discretion, Strategic Change, and Performance." *Strategic Management Journal* 33, no. 7 (July 2012): 834–859.

ASSURANCE OF LEARNING **EXERCISES**

EXERCISE 8A
Develop Product Positioning Maps for PepsiCo

Purpose

Organizations continually monitor how their products and services are positioned relative to competitors. Product positioning maps, often called perceptual maps, provide useful strategic information for marketing managers as well as corporate executives responsible for strategic planning. PepsiCo uses perceptual maps in strategic planning.

Instructions

Step 1	Review the competitors section in the Cohesion Case on PepsiCo. Review both PepsiCo and Coca-Cola Company's corporate websites especially in terms of brands and products.
Step 2	PepsiCo needs six product positioning (perceptual) maps that reveal the company's competitive position vs Coca-Cola in (1) sports/energy drinks, (2) bottled water, (3) juices, (4) carbonated beverages, (5) sparkling beverages, and (6) teas and coffees.
Step 3	Select one area (brand category) and prepare an excellent perceptual map for PepsiCo's chief marketing officer (CMO).

EXERCISE 8B
Gain Practice Developing Perceptual Maps

Purpose

In product (or market) positioning, a key is to use what dimensions of a product are most important to consumers. A positioning map with price and quality is obvious, but other dimensions may be more important. Think strategically. Some possible positioning dimensions for beer and shampoo are given below:

> **Beer**—high or low calorie, dark or light, domestic or imported, brand name or store brand
> **Shampoo**—dandruff control, harsh or light, perfume level, conditioner included or not

Instructions

For (1) beer and (2) shampoo products that you are familiar with, develop positioning (perceptual) maps that reflect your knowledge of particular products in these categories. Include four products in both your beer map and your shampoo map. Below each map give a rationale as per your favorite brand.

EXERCISE 8C
Perform an EPS/EBIT Analysis for PepsiCo

Purpose

An EPS/EBIT analysis is one of the most widely used techniques for determining the extent that debt or stock should be used to finance strategies to be implemented. This exercise can give you practice performing EPS/EBIT analysis.

Instructions

> Amount PepsiCo needs: $1B = to acquire Monster Beverage
> Interest rate: 3%
> Tax rate: 2,090/8,304 = 25.2% is PepsiCo's tax rate in 2012
> Stock price: $83 in May 2013
> Number of shares outstanding: 1.544B
> Prepare an EPS-EBIT analysis for PepsiCo. Determine whether PepsiCo should use all debt, all stock, or a 50-50 combination of debt and stock to finance this market-development strategy.
> Develop an EPS-EBIT chart after completing the EPS-EBIT table.
> Give a three sentence recommendation for PepsiCo's CFO.

EXERCISE 8D
Prepare Projected Financial Statements for PepsiCo

Purpose

This exercise is designed to give you experience preparing projected financial statements. Pro forma analysis is a central strategy-implementation technique because it allows managers to anticipate and evaluate the expected results of various strategy-implementation approaches.

Instructions

Step 1   Work with a classmate. Develop a 2014 projected income statement and balance sheet for PepsiCo. Assume that PepsiCo plans to raise $900 million in 2014 to increase its market share, and plans to obtain 50 percent financing from a bank and 50 percent financing from a stock issuance. Make other assumptions as needed, and state them clearly in written form.

Step 2   Compute PepsiCo's current ratio, debt-to-equity ratio, and return-on-investment ratio for 2014. How do your 2014 ratios compare to the 2012 and 2013 ratios? Why is it important to make this comparison? Use http://finance.yahoo.com to obtain actual 2013 financial statements.

Step 3   Bring your projected statements to class, and discuss any problems or questions you encountered.

Step 4   Compare your projected statements to the statements of other students. What major differences exist between your analysis and the work of other students?

EXERCISE 8E
Determine the Cash Value of PepsiCo

Purpose

It is simply good business to periodically determine the financial worth or cash value of your company. This exercise gives you practice determining the total worth of a company using several methods. Use year-end 2012 data as given in the Cohesion Case.

Instructions

Step 1   Calculate the financial worth of PepsiCo based on four methods: (1) the net worth or stockholders' equity, (2) the future value of PepsiCo's earnings, (3) the price-earnings ratio, and (4) the outstanding shares method.

Step 2   In a dollar amount, how much is PepsiCo worth?

Step 3   Compare your analyses and conclusions with those of other students.

EXERCISE 8F
Develop a Product-Positioning Map for Your University

Purpose

The purpose of this exercise is to give you practice developing product-positioning maps. Nonprofit organizations, such as universities, are increasingly using product-positioning maps to determine effective ways to implement strategies.

Instructions

Step 1   Join with two other people in class to form a group of three.

Step 2   Jointly prepare a product-positioning map that includes your institution and four other colleges or universities in your state.

Step 3   At the chalkboard, diagram your product-positioning map.

Step 4   Discuss differences among the maps diagrammed on the board.

EXERCISE 8G
Do Banks Require Projected Financial Statements?

Purpose

The purpose of this exercise is to explore the practical importance and use of projected financial statements in the banking business.

Instructions

Contact two local bankers by phone and seek answers to the questions that follow. Record the answers you receive, and report your findings to the class.

1. Does your bank require projected financial statements as part of a business loan application?
2. How does your bank use projected financial statements when they are part of a business loan application?
3. What special advice do you give potential business borrowers in preparing projected financial statements?

Notes

1. Salvatore Parise, Patricia Guinan, and Bruce Weinberg, "The Secrets of Marketing in a Web 2.0 World," *Wall Street Journal*, December 15, 2008, R1.
2. Kathy Chu and Kim Thai, "Banks Jump on Twitter Wagon," *USA Today*, May 12, 2009, B1.
3. Valerie Bauerlein, "Gatorade's Mission: Sell More Drinks," *Wall Street Journal*, September 14, 2010, B6.
4. Susanne Vranica, "Veteran Marketer Promotes a New Kind of Selling," *Wall Street Journal*, October 31, 2008, B4.
5. Gupta, Sunil, and Donald R. Lehmann, *Managing Customers as Investments: The Strategic Value of Customers in the Long Run* ("Customer Retention" section) (Upper Saddle River, NJ: Pearson Education/ Wharton School Publishing, 2005).
6. Shayndi Raice, "Facebook to Target Ads Based on App Usage," *Wall Street Journal* (July 7, 2012): B3.
7. Ralph Biggadike, "The Contributions of Marketing to Strategic Management," *Academy of Management Review* 6, no. 4 (October 1981): 627.
8. Patrick McGee, "Corporate Debt Has Allure," *Wall Street Journal* (August 3, 2012): C1.
9. Michael Rapoport, "Pro Forma Is a Hard Habit to Break," *Wall Street Journal*, September 18, 2003, B3A.
10. Scott Thurm, "Buyers Beware: The Goodwill Games," *Wall Street Journal* (August 14, 2012): B1.
11. Amy Merrick, "U.S. Research Spending to Rise Only 3.2 Percent," *Wall Street Journal*, December 28, 2001, A2.
12. Pier Abetti, "Technology: A Key Strategic Resource," *Management Review* 78, no. 2 (February 1989): 38.
13. Adapted from Edward Baig, "Welcome to the Officeless Office," *Businessweek*, June 26, 1995.
14. Spencer Ante, "IBM Ready for Close-Up," *Wall Street Journal*, January 18, 2011, B4.

STRATEGY EVALUATION

Source: auremar/Shutterstock

MyManagementLab®
⭐ Improve Your Grade!
More than 10 million students improved their results using the Pearson MyLabs.
Visit **mymanagementlab.com** for simulations, tutorials, and end-of-chapter problems.

Strategy Review, Evaluation, and Control

CHAPTER OBJECTIVES

After studying this chapter, you should be able to do the following:

1. Describe a practical framework for evaluating strategies.

2. Explain why strategy evaluation is complex, sensitive, and yet essential for organizational success.

3. Discuss the importance of contingency planning in strategy evaluation.

4. Explain the role of auditing in strategy evaluation.

5. Describe and develop a Balanced Scorecard.

6. Discuss three 21st-century challenges in strategic management.

ASSURANCE OF LEARNING EXERCISES

The following exercises are found at the end of this chapter.

The best formulated and best implemented strategies become obsolete as a firm's external and internal environments change. It is essential, therefore, that strategists systematically review, evaluate, and control the execution of strategies. This chapter presents a framework that can guide managers' efforts to evaluate strategic-management activities, to make sure they are working, and to make timely changes. Guidelines are presented for formulating, implementing, and evaluating strategies. IBM is an example company that historically has reinvented itself a number of times by continually evaluating its strategies and taking bold corrective actions promptly as needed.

The Nature of Strategy Evaluation

The strategic-management process results in decisions that can have significant, long-lasting consequences. Erroneous strategic decisions can inflict severe penalties and can be exceedingly difficult, if not impossible, to reverse. Most strategists agree, therefore, that strategy evaluation is vital to an organization's well-being; timely evaluations can alert management to problems or potential problems before a situation becomes critical. Strategy evaluation includes three basic activities: (1) examining the underlying bases of a firm's strategy, (2) comparing expected results with actual results, and (3) taking corrective actions to ensure that performance conforms to plans. The strategy-evaluation stage of the strategic-management process is illustrated in Figure 9-1 with white shading.

Adequate and timely feedback is the cornerstone of effective strategy evaluation. Strategy evaluation can be no better than the information on which it is based. Too much pressure from top managers may result in lower managers contriving numbers they think will be satisfactory.

Strategy evaluation can be a complex and sensitive undertaking. Too much emphasis on evaluating strategies may be expensive and counterproductive. No one likes to be evaluated too closely! The more managers attempt to evaluate the behavior of others, the less control they have. Yet too little or no evaluation can create even worse problems. Strategy evaluation is essential to ensure that stated objectives are being achieved.

EXCELLENT STRATEGIC MANAGEMENT SHOWCASED

International Business Machines (IBM)

Headquartered in Armonk, New York, and known as "Big Blue," IBM is a multinational technology and consulting firm that manufactures and sells computer hardware, software, infrastructure, as well as hosting and consulting products and services ranging from mainframe computers to nanotechnology and business analytics. In 2012, *Fortune* ranked IBM the number-2 largest U.S. firm in terms of number of employees (433,362), the number-4 largest in terms of market capitalization, the number-9 most profitable, and the number-19 largest firm in terms of revenue. Other IBM rankings for 2011–2012 include number-1 company for leaders (*Fortune*), number-1 green company worldwide (*Newsweek*), number-2 best global brand (*Interbrand*), number-2 most respected company (*Barron's*), number-5 most admired company (*Fortune*), and number-18 most innovative company (*Fast Company*).

IBM holds more patents than any other U.S.-based technology company and has nine research laboratories worldwide. Its employees have earned five Nobel Prizes, six Turing Awards, nine National Medals of Technology, and five National Medals of Science. Famous inventions by IBM include the automated teller machine (ATM), the floppy disk, the hard disk drive, the magnetic stripe card, the relational database, the Universal Product Code (UPC), the financial swap, SABRE airline reservation system, DRAM, and Watson artificial intelligence.

IBM owns statistical package for the social sciences (SPSS). For 2012, *Vault* ranked IBM Global Technology Services number 1 in tech consulting for cyber security, operations and implementation, and public sector and number 2 in outsourcing.

In January 2012, IBM hired its first female CEO, Virginia M. Rometty. For Q2 of 2013, IBM's software revenues were up 4 percent, while the company's mainframe revenue increased 10 percent, and its revenue from business analytics grew 11 percent. The company's cloud revenue in the first half of 2013 was up more than 70 percent from the prior year period. IBM, in 2012, acquired Texas Memory Systems and Kenexa, the latter for $1.3 billion. IBM has successfully transitioned from computer hardware to information technology, business services, consulting, and software units that are among the largest in the world. IBM is also one of the largest providers of semiconductors, and it has industry-leading enterprise server and data-storage products lines. IBM serves customers globally across almost all industries.

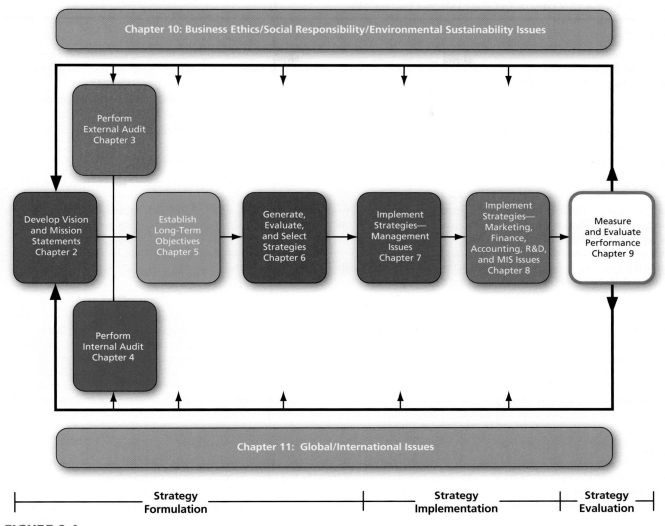

FIGURE 9-1

A Comprehensive Strategic-Management Model

Source: Fred R. David, "How Companies Define Their Mission," *Long Range Planning* 22, no. 3 (June 1988): 40.

In many organizations, strategy evaluation is simply an appraisal of how well an organization has performed. Have the firm's assets increased? Has there been an increase in profitability? Have sales increased? Have productivity levels increased? Have profit margin, return on investment, and earnings-per-share ratios increased? Some firms argue that their strategy must have been correct if the answers to these types of questions are affirmative. Well, the strategy or strategies may have been correct, but this type of reasoning can be misleading because strategy evaluation must have both a long-run and short-run focus. Strategies often do not affect short-term operating results until it is too late to make needed changes.

It is impossible to demonstrate conclusively that a particular strategy is optimal or even to guarantee that it will work. One can, however, evaluate it for critical flaws. Richard Rumelt offered four criteria that could be used to evaluate a strategy: consistency, consonance, feasibility, and advantage. Described in Table 9-1, **consonance** and **advantage** are mostly based on a firm's external assessment, whereas **consistency** and **feasibility** are largely based on an internal assessment.

Strategy evaluation is important because organizations face dynamic environments in which key external and internal factors often change quickly and dramatically. Success today is no guarantee of success tomorrow! Joseph Stalin was a ruthless leader (from 1928 on) and premier

TABLE 9-1 Rumelt's Criteria for Evaluating Strategies

Consistency

A strategy should not present inconsistent goals and policies. Organizational conflict and interdepartmental bickering are often symptoms of managerial disorder, but these problems may also be a sign of strategic inconsistency. Three guidelines help determine if organizational problems are the result of inconsistencies in strategy:

- If managerial problems continue despite changes in personnel and if they tend to be issue-based rather than people-based, then strategies may be inconsistent.
- If success for one organizational department means, or is interpreted to mean, failure for another department, then strategies may be inconsistent.
- If policy problems and issues continue to be brought to the top for resolution, then strategies may be inconsistent.

Consonance

Consonance refers to the need for strategists to examine *sets of trends*, as well as individual trends, in evaluating strategies. A strategy must represent an adaptive response to the external environment and to the critical changes occurring within it. One difficulty in matching a firm's key internal and external factors in the formulation of strategy is that most trends are the result of interactions among other trends. For example, the daycare explosion came about as a combined result of many trends that included a rise in the average level of education, increased inflation, and an increase in women in the workforce. Although single economic or demographic trends might appear steady for many years, there are waves of change going on at the interaction level.

Feasibility

A strategy must neither overtax available resources nor create unsolvable subproblems. The final broad test of strategy is its feasibility; that is, can the strategy be attempted within the physical, human, and financial resources of the enterprise? The financial resources of a business are the easiest to quantify and are normally the first limitation against which strategy is evaluated. It is sometimes forgotten, however, that innovative approaches to financing are often possible. Devices, such as captive subsidiaries, sale-leaseback arrangements, and tying plant mortgages to long-term contracts, have all been used effectively to help win key positions in suddenly expanding industries. A less quantifiable, but actually more rigid, limitation on strategic choice is that imposed by individual and organizational capabilities. In evaluating a strategy, it is important to examine whether an organization has demonstrated in the past that it possesses the abilities, competencies, skills, and talents needed to carry out a given strategy.

Advantage

A strategy must provide for the creation or maintenance of a competitive advantage in a selected area of activity. Competitive advantages normally are the result of superiority in one of three areas: (1) resources, (2) skills, or (3) position. The idea that the positioning of one's resources can enhance their combined effectiveness is familiar to military theorists, chess players, and diplomats. Position can also play a crucial role in an organization's strategy. Once gained, a good position is defensible—meaning that it is so costly to capture that rivals are deterred from full-scale attacks. Positional advantage tends to be self-sustaining as long as the key internal and environmental factors that underlie it remain stable. This is why entrenched firms can be almost impossible to unseat, even if their raw skill levels are only average. Although not all positional advantages are associated with size, it is true that larger organizations tend to operate in markets and use procedures that turn their size into advantage, whereas smaller firms seek product or market positions that exploit other types of advantage. The principal characteristic of good position is that it permits the firm to obtain advantage from policies that would not similarly benefit rivals without the same position. Therefore, in evaluating strategy, organizations should examine the nature of positional advantages associated with a given strategy.

Source: Adapted from Richard Rumelt, "The Evaluation of Business Strategy," in W. F. Glueck (ed.), *Business Policy and Strategic Management* (New York: McGraw-Hill, 1980), 359–367. Used with permission.

(from 1941 on) of the Soviet Union until his death in 1953. A famous quote from Stalin was: *History shows that there are no invincible armies.* This quote reveals that even the mightiest, most successful firms must continually evaluate their strategies and be wary of rival firms. An organization should never be lulled into complacency with success. Countless firms have thrived one year only to struggle for survival the following year. Peter Drucker said: Unless strategy evaluation is performed seriously and systematically, and unless strategists are willing to act on the results, energy will be used up defending yesterday."

Demise can come quickly. For example, the large clothing retailer J.C. Penney, based in Plano, Texas, was profitable and fine, until they hired CEO Ron Johnson in November 2011. Johnson implemented a new strategic plan at Penney's that included doing away with coupons, promotions, and discounting in favor of his "fair and square pricing" policy, building branded boutiques stores-within stores, replacing their chief marketing officer, Michael Francis, with himself, adding more celebrity brands and high-tech features to attract younger customers, exiting from the outlet business, and extensive, expensive remodeling. Johnson envisioned all Penney stores to have tables with iPads for customers to use, and activities for kids such as making greeting cards, and even Pilates and yoga classes within stores.[1] Moody's Investors Service downgraded Penney's long-term debt two notches to Ba3 from Ba1 in August 2012; Penney's is still unprofitable in late 2013.

Another example of quick demise is Hewlett-Packard, which delivered an $8.9 billion loss in its fiscal third quarter of 2012 as the firm's revenue dropped to $29.7 billion. Consumers are flocking in the millions to tablets and away from desktop and laptop computers, crushing HP who had not anticipated such as swift switch in consumer preferences. This consumer trend is also crushing another U.S. icon company, Intel, which reported a 14-percent drop in third-quarter 2012 profits.

Strategy evaluation is becoming increasingly difficult with the passage of time, for many reasons. Domestic and world economies were more stable in years past, product life cycles were longer, product development cycles were longer, technological advancement was slower, change occurred less frequently, there were fewer competitors, foreign companies were weak, and there were more regulated industries. Other reasons why strategy evaluation is more difficult today include the following trends:

1. A dramatic increase in the environment's complexity
2. The increasing difficulty of predicting the future with accuracy
3. The increasing number of variables
4. The rapid rate of obsolescence of even the best plans
5. The increase in the number of both domestic and world events affecting organizations
6. The decreasing time span for which planning can be done with any degree of certainty[2]

A fundamental problem facing managers today is how to control employees effectively in light of modern organizational demands for greater flexibility, innovation, creativity, and initiative from employees.[3] How can managers today ensure that empowered employees acting in an entrepreneurial manner do not put the well-being of the business at risk? The potential costs to companies in terms of damaged reputations, fines, missed opportunities, and diversion of management's attention are enormous.

When empowered employees are held accountable for and pressured to achieve specific goals and are given wide latitude in their actions to achieve them, there can be dysfunctional behavior. For example, Nordstrom, the upscale fashion retailer known for outstanding customer service, was subjected to lawsuits and fines when employees underreported hours worked to increase their sales per hour—the company's primary performance criterion.

The Process of Evaluating Strategies

Strategy evaluation is necessary for all sizes and kinds of organizations. Strategy evaluation should initiate managerial questioning of expectations and assumptions, should trigger a review of objectives and values, and should stimulate creativity in generating alternatives and formulating criteria of evaluation.[4] Regardless of the size of the organization, a certain amount of **management by wandering around** at all levels is essential to effective strategy evaluation. Strategy-evaluation activities should be performed on a continuing basis, rather than at the end of specified periods of time or just after problems occur. Waiting until the end of the year, for example, could result in a firm *closing the barn door after the horses have already escaped.*

Evaluating strategies on a continuous rather than on a periodic basis allows benchmarks of progress to be established and more effectively monitored. Some strategies take years to implement; consequently, associated results may not become apparent for years. Successful strategies combine patience with a willingness to promptly take corrective actions when necessary. There always comes a time when corrective actions are needed in an organization! Centuries ago, a writer (perhaps Solomon) made the following observations about change:

There is a time for everything,

A time to be born and a time to die,

A time to plant and a time to uproot,

A time to kill and a time to heal,

A time to tear down and a time to build,

A time to weep and a time to laugh,

A time to mourn and a time to dance,

A time to scatter stones and a time to gather them,

A time to embrace and a time to refrain,

A time to search and a time to give up,

A time to keep and a time to throw away,

A time to tear and a time to mend,

A time to be silent and a time to speak,

A time to love and a time to hate,

A time for war and a time for peace.[5]

Managers and employees of the firm should be continually aware of progress being made toward achieving the firm's objectives. As key success factors change, organizational members should be involved in determining appropriate corrective actions. If assumptions and expectations deviate significantly from forecasts, then the firm should renew strategy-formulation activities, perhaps sooner than planned. In strategy evaluation, like strategy formulation and strategy implementation, people make the difference. Through involvement in the process of evaluating strategies, managers and employees become committed to keeping the firm moving steadily toward achieving objectives.

A Strategy-Evaluation Framework

Table 9-2 summarizes strategy-evaluation activities in terms of key questions that should be addressed, alternative answers to those questions, and appropriate actions for an organization to take. Notice that corrective actions are almost always needed except when (1) external and internal factors have not significantly changed and (2) the firm is progressing satisfactorily toward achieving stated objectives. Relationships among strategy-evaluation activities are illustrated in Figure 9-2.

Reviewing Bases of Strategy

As shown in Figure 9-2, **reviewing the underlying bases of an organization's strategy** could be approached by developing a revised EFE Matrix and IFE Matrix. A **revised IFE Matrix** should focus on changes in the organization's management, marketing, finance and accounting, production and operations, research and development (R&D), and management information systems (MIS) strengths and weaknesses. A **revised EFE Matrix** should indicate how effective

TABLE 9-2 A Strategy-Evaluation Assessment Matrix

Have Major Changes Occurred in the Firm's Internal Strategic Position?	Have Major Changes Occurred in the Firm's External Strategic Position?	Has the Firm Progressed Satisfactorily Toward Achieving Its Stated Objectives?	Result
No	No	No	Take corrective actions
Yes	Yes	Yes	Take corrective actions
Yes	Yes	No	Take corrective actions
Yes	No	Yes	Take corrective actions
Yes	No	No	Take corrective actions
No	Yes	Yes	Take corrective actions
No	Yes	No	Take corrective actions
No	No	Yes	Continue present strategic course

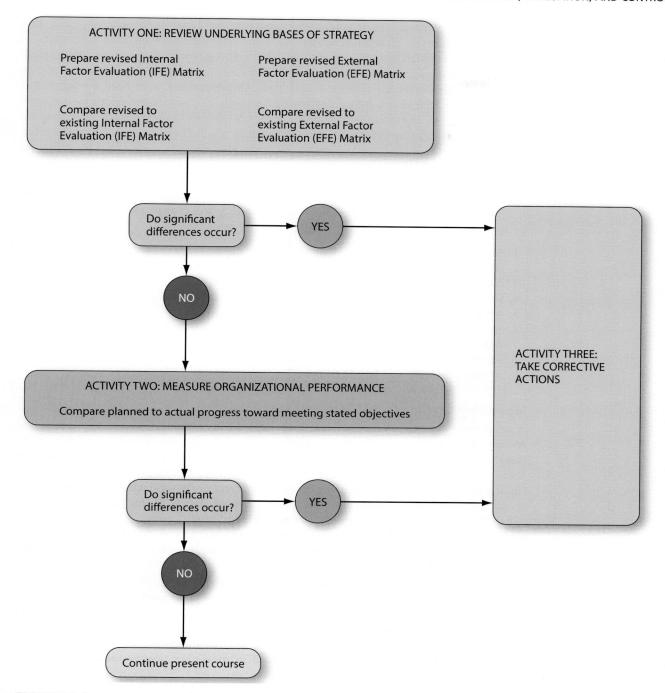

FIGURE 9-2

A Strategy-Evaluation Framework

a firm's strategies have been in response to key opportunities and threats. This analysis could also address such questions as the following:

1. How have competitors reacted to our strategies?
2. How have competitors' strategies changed?
3. Have major competitors' strengths and weaknesses changed?
4. Why are competitors making certain strategic changes?
5. Why are some competitors' strategies more successful than others?
6. How satisfied are our competitors with their present market positions and profitability?
7. How far can our major competitors be pushed before retaliating?
8. How could we more effectively cooperate with our competitors?

Numerous external and internal factors can prevent firms from achieving long-term and annual objectives. Externally, actions by competitors, changes in demand, changes in technology, economic changes, demographic shifts, and governmental actions may prevent objectives from being accomplished. Internally, ineffective strategies may have been chosen or implementation activities may have been poor. Objectives may have been too optimistic. Thus, failure to achieve objectives may not be the result of unsatisfactory work by managers and employees. All organizational members need to know this to encourage their support for strategy-evaluation activities. Organizations desperately need to know as soon as possible when their strategies are not effective. Sometimes managers and employees on the front lines discover this well before strategists.

External opportunities and threats and internal strengths and weaknesses that represent the bases of current strategies should continually be monitored for change. It is not really a question of *whether* these factors will change but rather *when* they will change and in what ways. Here are some key questions to address in evaluating strategies:

1. Are our internal strengths still strengths?
2. Have we added other internal strengths? If so, what are they?
3. Are our internal weaknesses still weaknesses?
4. Do we now have other internal weaknesses? If so, what are they?
5. Are our external opportunities still opportunities?
6. Are there now other external opportunities? If so, what are they?
7. Are our external threats still threats?
8. Are there now other external threats? If so, what are they?
9. Are we vulnerable to a hostile takeover?

Measuring Organizational Performance

Another important strategy-evaluation activity is **measuring organizational performance**. This activity includes comparing expected results to actual results, investigating deviations from plans, evaluating individual performance, and examining progress being made toward meeting stated objectives. Both long-term and annual objectives are commonly used in this process. Criteria for evaluating strategies should be measurable and easily verifiable. Criteria that predict results may be more important than those that reveal what already has happened. For example, rather than simply being informed that sales in the last quarter were 20 percent under what was expected, strategists need to know that sales in the next quarter may be 20 percent below standard unless some action is taken to counter the trend. Really effective control requires accurate forecasting.

Failure to make satisfactory progress toward accomplishing long-term or annual objectives signals a need for corrective actions. Many factors, such as unreasonable policies, unexpected turns in the economy, unreliable suppliers or distributors, or ineffective strategies, can result in unsatisfactory progress toward meeting objectives. Problems can result from ineffectiveness (not doing the right things) or inefficiency (poorly doing the right things).

Many variables can and should be included in measuring organizational performance. As indicated in Table 9-3, typically a favorable or unfavorable variance is recorded monthly, quarterly, and annually, and resultant actions needed are then determined.

Determining which objectives are most important in the evaluation of strategies can be difficult. Strategy evaluation is based on both quantitative and qualitative criteria. Selecting the exact set of criteria for evaluating strategies depends on a particular organization's size, industry, strategies, and management philosophy. An organization pursuing a retrenchment strategy, for example, could have an entirely different set of evaluative criteria from an organization pursuing a market-development strategy. Quantitative criteria commonly used to evaluate strategies are financial ratios, often monitored for each segment of the firm. Strategists use ratios to make three critical comparisons: (1) comparing the firm's performance over different time periods, (2) comparing the firm's performance to competitors', and (3) comparing the firm's performance to industry averages.

Some potential problems are associated with using only quantitative criteria for evaluating strategies. First, most quantitative criteria are geared to annual objectives rather than long-term objectives. Also, different accounting methods can provide different results on

TABLE 9-3 A Sample Framework for Measuring Organizational Performance

Factor	Actual Result	Expected Result	Variance	Action Needed
Corporate Revenues				
Corporate Profits				
Corporate ROI				
Region 1 Revenues				
Region 1 Profits				
Region 1 ROI				
Region 2 Revenues				
Region 2 Profits				
Region 2 ROI				
Product 1 Revenues				
Product 1 Profits				
Product 1 ROI				
Product 2 Revenues				
Product 2 Profits				
Product 2 ROI				

ROI, return on investment.

many quantitative criteria. Third, intuitive judgments are almost always involved in deriving quantitative criteria. Thus, qualitative criteria are also important in evaluating strategies. Human factors such as high absenteeism and turnover rates, poor production quality and quantity rates, or low employee satisfaction can be underlying causes of declining performance. Marketing, finance and accounting, R&D, or MIS factors can also cause financial problems.

Some additional key questions that reveal the need for qualitative or intuitive judgments in strategy evaluation are as follows:

1. How good is the firm's balance of investments between high-risk and low-risk projects?
2. How good is the firm's balance of investments between long-term and short-term projects?
3. How good is the firm's balance of investments between slow-growing markets and fast-growing markets?
4. How good is the firm's balance of investments among different divisions?
5. To what extent are the firm's alternative strategies socially responsible?
6. What are the relationships among the firm's key internal and external strategic factors?
7. How are major competitors likely to respond to particular strategies?

Taking Corrective Actions

The final strategy-evaluation activity, **taking corrective actions**, requires making changes to competitively reposition a firm for the future. As indicated in Table 9-4, examples of changes that may be needed are altering an organization's structure, replacing one or more key individuals, selling a division, or revising a business mission. Other changes could include establishing or revising objectives, devising new policies, issuing stock to raise capital, adding additional salespersons, differently allocating resources, or developing new performance incentives. Taking corrective actions does not necessarily mean that existing strategies will be abandoned or even that new strategies must be formulated.

The probabilities and possibilities for incorrect or inappropriate actions increase geometrically with an arithmetic increase in personnel. Any person directing an overall undertaking must check on the actions of the participants as well as the results that they have achieved. If either the actions or results do not comply with preconceived or planned achievements, then corrective actions are needed.[6]

TABLE 9-4 Corrective Actions Possibly Needed to Correct Unfavorable Variances

1. Alter the firm's structure
2. Replace one or more key individuals
3. Divest a division
4. Alter the firm's vision or mission
5. Revise objectives
6. Alter strategies
7. Devise new policies
8. Install new performance incentives
9. Raise capital with stock or debt
10. Add or terminate salespersons, employees, or managers
11. Allocate resources differently
12. Outsource (or rein in) business functions

The largest office-supplies chain in the USA with 2,295 stores globally and 1,500 in the USA, Staples, is taking corrective actions to try to survive in the big-box office-supply store business. Many analysts say it is too little too late, but Staples is reducing its U.S. store space by 15 percent between 2013 and 2015 and is opening smaller stores more focused on mobile applications. Especially hurting Staples (and OfficeMax and Office Depot) are trends such as: (a) consumers prefer to purchase office supplies online (cheaper) from rivals such as Amazon, and (b) there is falling demand for office supplies since handheld devices such as the iPad have reduced demand for personal computers, printers, and even paper. Staples does own a fleet of vehicles that can deliver orders for free the next day, as compared to Amazon that only offers free two-day deliveries to members paying $79 a year to be part of Amazon Prime.

No organization can survive as an island; no organization can escape change. Taking corrective actions is necessary to keep an organization on track toward achieving stated objectives. In his thought-provoking books *Future Shock* and *The Third Wave*, Alvin Toffler argued that business environments are becoming so dynamic and complex that they threaten people and organizations with **future shock**, which occurs when the nature, types, and speed of changes overpower an individual's or organization's ability and capacity to adapt. Strategy evaluation enhances an organization's ability to adapt successfully to changing circumstances.

Taking corrective actions raises employees' and managers' anxieties. Research suggests that participation in strategy-evaluation activities is one of the best ways to overcome individuals' resistance to change. According to Erez and Kanfer, individuals accept change best when they have a cognitive understanding of the changes, a sense of control over the situation, and an awareness that necessary actions are going to be taken to implement the changes.[7]

Strategy evaluation can lead to strategy-formulation changes, strategy-implementation changes, both formulation and implementation changes, or no changes at all. Strategists cannot escape having to revise strategies and implementation approaches sooner or later. Hussey and Langham offered the following insight on taking corrective actions:

> Resistance to change is often emotionally based and not easily overcome by rational argument. Resistance may be based on such feelings as loss of status, implied criticism of present competence, fear of failure in the new situation, annoyance at not being consulted, lack of understanding of the need for change, or insecurity in changing from well-known and fixed methods. It is necessary, therefore, to overcome such resistance by creating situations of participation and full explanation when changes are envisaged.[8]

Corrective actions should place an organization in a better position to capitalize on internal strengths; to take advantage of key external opportunities; to avoid, reduce, or mitigate external threats; and to improve internal weaknesses. Corrective actions should have a proper time horizon and an appropriate amount of risk. They should be internally consistent and socially responsible. Perhaps most important, corrective actions strengthen an organization's competitive position in its basic industry. Continuous strategy evaluation keeps strategists close to the pulse of an organization and provides information needed for an effective strategic-management system. Carter Bayles described the benefits of strategy evaluation as follows:

> Evaluation activities may renew confidence in the current business strategy or point to the need for actions to correct some weaknesses, such as erosion of product superiority or technological edge. In many cases, the benefits of strategy evaluation are much more far-reaching, for the outcome of the process may be a fundamentally new strategy that will lead, even in a business that is already turning a respectable profit, to substantially increased earnings. It is this possibility that justifies strategy evaluation, for the payoff can be very large.[9]

The Balanced Scorecard

Developed in 1993 by Harvard Business School professors Robert Kaplan and David Norton, and refined continually through today, the Balanced Scorecard is a strategy evaluation and control technique. **Balanced Scorecard** derives its name from the perceived need of firms to "balance" financial measures that are oftentimes used exclusively in strategy evaluation and control with nonfinancial measures such as product quality and customer service. An effective Balanced Scorecard contains a carefully chosen combination of strategic and financial objectives tailored to the company's business.

As a tool to manage and evaluate strategy, the Balanced Scorecard is currently in use at Sears, United Parcel Service, 3M Corporation, Heinz, and hundreds of other firms. For example, 3M Corporation has a financial objective to achieve annual growth in earnings per share of 10 percent or better, as well as a strategic objective to have at least 30 percent of sales come from products introduced in the past four years. The overall aim of the Balanced Scorecard is to "balance" shareholder objectives with customer and operational objectives. Obviously, these sets of objectives interrelate and many even conflict. For example, customers want low price and high service, which may conflict with shareholders' desire for a high return on their investment. The Balanced Scorecard concept is consistent with the notions of continuous improvement in management (CIM) and total quality management (TQM).

The Balanced Scorecard basic premise is that firms should establish objectives and evaluate strategies on criteria other than financial measures. Financial measures and ratios are vitally important in strategic planning, but of equal importance are factors such as customer service, employee morale, product quality, pollution abatement, business ethics, social responsibility, community involvement, and other such items. In conjunction with financial measures, these "softer" factors comprise an integral part of both the objective-setting process and the strategy-evaluation process. A Balanced Scorecard for a firm is simply a listing of all key objectives to work toward, along with an associated time dimension of when each objective is to be accomplished, as well as a primary responsibility or contact person, department, or division for each objective.

The Balanced Scorecard is an important strategy-evaluation tool. It is a process that allows firms to evaluate strategies from four perspectives: financial performance, customer knowledge, internal business processes, and learning and growth. The *Balanced Scorecard* analysis requires that firms seek answers to the following questions and use that information, in conjunction with financial measures, to adequately and more effectively evaluate strategies being implemented:

1. How well is the firm continually improving and creating value along measures such as innovation, technological leadership, product quality, operational process efficiencies, and so on?
2. How well is the firm sustaining and even improving on its core competencies and competitive advantages?
3. How satisfied are the firm's customers?

A sample Balanced Scorecard is provided in Table 9-5. Notice that the firm examines six key issues in evaluating its strategies: (1) Customers, (2) Managers/Employees, (3) Operations/Processes, (4) Community/Social Responsibility, (5) Business Ethics/Natural Environment, and (6) Financial. The basic form of a Balanced Scorecard may differ for different organizations. The Balanced Scorecard approach to strategy evaluation aims to balance long-term with short-term concerns, to balance financial with nonfinancial concerns, and to balance internal

TABLE 9-5 An Example Balanced Scorecard

Area of Objectives	Measure or Target	Time Expectation	Primary Responsibility
Customers			
1.			
2.			
3.			
4.			
Managers/Employees			
1.			
2.			
3.			
4.			
Operations/Processes			
1.			
2.			
3.			
4.			
Community/Social Responsibility			
1.			
2.			
3.			
4.			
Business Ethics/Natural Environment			
1.			
2.			
3.			
4.			
Financial			
1.			
2.			
3.			
4.			

with external concerns. The Balanced Scorecard would be constructed differently, that is, adapted to particular firms in various industries with the underlying theme or thrust being the same, which is to evaluate the firm's strategies based on both key quantitative and qualitative measures.

The Balanced Scorecard Institute has a Certification Program that includes two levels of certification: Balanced Scorecard Master Professional (BSMP) and Balanced Scorecard Professional (BSP), both of which are offered in association with George Washington University and are achievable through public workshop participation. The website for this program is http://www.balancedscorecard.org/.

Published Sources of Strategy-Evaluation Information

A number of publications are helpful in evaluating a firm's strategies. For example, *Fortune* annually identifies and evaluates the Fortune 1,000 (the largest manufacturers) and the Fortune 50 (the largest retailers, transportation companies, utilities, banks, insurance companies, and diversified financial corporations in the USA). *Fortune* ranks the best and worst

TABLE 9-6 The Most and Least Admired Companies in Management Quality in Various Industries in 2012

Most Admired	Least Admired
Koc Holding	Sears Holdings
McDonald's	China South Industries Group
Apple	MF Global Holdings
Philip Morris International	NewPage Holding
Costco Wholesale	Gas Natural Fenosa
J.P. Morgan Chase	Yahoo!
Wyndham Worldwide	AMR
Sysco	GDF Suez
Walt Disney	Dongfeng MG
	China FAW Group

Source: Based on information accessed November 1, 2012 at http://money.cnn.com/magazines/fortune/most-admired/2012/best_worst/best5.html.

performers on various factors, such as return on investment, sales volume, and profitability. *Fortune* annually publishes its strategy-evaluation research in an article titled "World's Most Admired Companies." Nine key attributes serve as evaluative criteria: people management; innovativeness; products quality; financial soundness; social responsibility; use of assets; long-term investment; global competitiveness; and quality of management. *Fortune's* 2012 evaluation in Table 9-6 reveals the firms most admired (best managed) in their industry.

Businessweek, Industry Week, and *Dun's Business Month* periodically publish detailed evaluations of U.S. businesses and industries. Although published sources of strategy-evaluation information focus primarily on large, publicly held businesses, the comparative ratios and related information are widely used to evaluate small businesses and privately owned firms as well.

Characteristics of an Effective Evaluation System

Strategy evaluation must meet several basic requirements to be effective. First, strategy-evaluation activities must be economical; too much information can be just as bad as too little information, and too many controls can do more harm than good. Strategy-evaluation activities also should be meaningful; they should specifically relate to a firm's objectives. They should provide managers with useful information about tasks over which they have control and influence. Strategy-evaluation activities should provide timely information; on occasion and in some areas, managers may daily need information. For example, when a firm has diversified by acquiring another firm, evaluative information may be needed frequently. However, in an R&D department, daily or even weekly evaluative information could be dysfunctional. Approximate information that is timely is generally more desirable as a basis for strategy evaluation than accurate information that does not depict the present. Frequent measurement and rapid reporting may frustrate control rather than give better control. The time dimension of control must coincide with the time span of the event being measured.

Strategy evaluation should be designed to provide a true picture of what is happening. For example, in a severe economic downturn, productivity and profitability ratios may drop alarmingly, although employees and managers are actually working harder. Strategy evaluations should fairly portray this type of situation. Information derived from the strategy-evaluation process should facilitate action and should be directed to those individuals in the organization who need to take action based on it. Managers commonly ignore evaluative reports that are provided only for informational purposes; not all managers need to receive all reports. Controls need to be action-oriented rather than information-oriented.

The strategy-evaluation process should not dominate decisions; it should foster mutual understanding, trust, and common sense. No department should fail to cooperate with another in evaluating strategies. Strategy evaluations should be simple, not too cumbersome, and not too restrictive. Complex strategy-evaluation systems often confuse people and accomplish little. The test of an effective evaluation system is its usefulness, not its complexity.

Large organizations require a more elaborate and detailed strategy-evaluation system because it is more difficult to coordinate efforts among different divisions and functional areas. Managers in small companies often communicate daily with each other and their employees and do not need extensive evaluative reporting systems. Familiarity with local environments usually makes gathering and evaluating information much easier for small organizations than for large businesses. But the key to an effective strategy-evaluation system may be the ability to convince participants that failure to accomplish certain objectives within a prescribed time is not necessarily a reflection of their performance.

There is no one ideal strategy-evaluation system. The unique characteristics of an organization, including its size, management style, purpose, problems, and strengths, can determine a strategy-evaluation and control system's final design. Robert Waterman offered the following observation about successful organizations' strategy-evaluation and control systems:

> Successful companies treat facts as friends and controls as liberating. Morgan Guaranty and Wells Fargo not only survive but thrive in the troubled waters of bank deregulation, because their strategy evaluation and control systems are sound, their risk is contained, and they know themselves and the competitive situation so well. Successful companies have a voracious hunger for facts. They see information where others see only data. Successful companies maintain tight, accurate financial controls. Their people don't regard controls as an imposition of autocracy but as the benign checks and balances that allow them to be creative and free.[10]

Contingency Planning

A basic premise of good strategic management is that firms plan ways to deal with unfavorable and favorable events before they occur. Too many organizations prepare contingency plans just for unfavorable events; this is a mistake, because both minimizing threats and capitalizing on opportunities can improve a firm's competitive position.

Regardless of how carefully strategies are formulated, implemented, and evaluated, unforeseen events, such as strikes, boycotts, natural disasters, arrival of foreign competitors, and government actions, can make a strategy obsolete. To minimize the impact of potential threats, organizations should develop contingency plans as part of their strategy-evaluation process. **Contingency plans** can be defined as alternative plans that can be put into effect if certain key events do not occur as expected. Only high-priority areas require the insurance of contingency plans. Strategists cannot and should not try to cover all bases by planning for all possible contingencies. But in any case, contingency plans should be as simple as possible.

Some contingency plans commonly established by firms include the following:

1. If a major competitor withdraws from particular markets as intelligence reports indicate, what actions should our firm take?
2. If our sales objectives are not reached, what actions should our firm take to avoid profit losses?
3. If demand for our new product exceeds plans, what actions should our firm take to meet the higher demand?
4. If certain disasters occur—such as loss of computer capabilities; a hostile takeover attempt; loss of patent protection; or destruction of manufacturing facilities because of earthquakes, tornadoes, or hurricanes—what actions should our firm take?
5. If a new technological advancement makes our new product obsolete sooner than expected, what actions should our firm take?

Too many organizations discard alternative strategies not selected for implementation although the work devoted to analyzing these options would render valuable information. Alternative strategies not selected for implementation can serve as contingency plans in case the strategy or strategies selected do not work. U.S. companies and governments are increasingly considering nuclear-generated electricity as the most efficient means of power generation. Many contingency plans certainly call for nuclear power rather than for coal- and gas-derived electricity.

When strategy-evaluation activities reveal the need for a major change quickly, an appropriate contingency plan can be executed in a timely way. Contingency plans can promote a strategist's ability to respond quickly to key changes in the internal and external bases of an organization's current strategy. For example, if underlying assumptions about the economy turn out to be wrong and contingency plans are ready, then managers can make appropriate changes promptly.

In some cases, external or internal conditions present unexpected opportunities. When such opportunities occur, contingency plans could allow an organization to quickly capitalize on them. Linneman and Chandran reported that contingency planning gave users, such as DuPont, Dow Chemical, Consolidated Foods, and Emerson Electric, three major benefits: (1) It permitted quick response to change, (2) it prevented panic in crisis situations, and (3) it made managers more adaptable by encouraging them to appreciate just how variable the future can be. They suggested that effective contingency planning involves a five-step process:

1. Identify both good and bad events that could jeopardize strategies.
2. Determine when the good and bad events are likely to occur.
3. Determine the expected pros and cons of each contingency event.
4. Develop contingency plans for key contingency events.
5. Determine early warning trigger points key contingency events.[11]

Auditing

A frequently used tool in strategy evaluation is the audit. **Auditing** is defined by the American Accounting Association (AAA) as "a systematic process of objectively obtaining and evaluating evidence regarding assertions about economic actions and events to ascertain the degree of correspondence between these assertions and established criteria, and communicating the results to interested users."[12]

Auditors examine the financial statement of firms to determine whether they have been prepared according to *generally accepted accounting principles* (**GAAP**) and whether they fairly represent the activities of the firm. Independent auditors use a set of standards called *generally accepted auditing standards (***GAAS***)*. Public accounting firms often have a consulting arm that provides strategy-evaluation services.

The new era of *international financial reporting standards (***IFRS***)* appears unstoppable, and businesses need to go ahead and get ready to use IFRS. Many U.S. companies now report their finances using both the old GAAP and the new IFRS. "If companies don't prepare, if they don't start three years in advance," warns business professor Donna Street at the University of Dayton, "they're going to be in big trouble." GAAP standards comprised 25,000 pages, whereas IFRS comprises only 5,000 pages, so in that sense IFRS is less cumbersome.

This accounting switch from GAAP to IFRS in the United States is going to cost businesses millions of dollars in fees and upgraded software systems and training. U.S. CPAs need to study global accounting principles intensely, and business schools should go ahead and begin teaching students the new accounting standards. Most large accounting firms and multinational firms favor the switch to IFRS saying it will simplify accounting, make it easier for investors to compare firms across countries, and make it easier to raise capital globally. But many smaller firms oppose the upcoming change say it will be too costly; some firms are uneasy about the idea of giving an international body the authority to write accounting rules for the USA. Some firms also would pay higher taxes because last in, first out (LIFO) inventory methods are not allowed under IFRS.[13] The International Accounting Standards Board (IASB) has publicly expressed "regret" over the USA's slowness in adopting IFRS.

The U.S. Chamber of Commerce supports a change, saying it will lead to much more cross-border commerce and will help the USA compete in the world economy. Already the European Union and 113 nations have adopted or soon plan to use international rules, including Australia, China, India, Mexico, and Canada. So the USA likely will also adopt IFRS rules, but this switch could unleash a legal and regulatory nightmare. A few U.S. multinational firms already use IFRS for their foreign subsidiaries, such as United Technologies (UT). UT derives more than 60 percent of its revenues from abroad and is already training its entire staff to use IFRS.

Movement to IFRS from GAAP encompasses a company's entire operations, including auditing, oversight, cash management, taxes, technology, software, investing, acquiring, merging, importing, exporting, pension planning, and partnering. Switching from GAAP to IFRS is also likely to be plagued by gaping differences in business customs, financial regulations, tax laws, politics, and other factors. One critic of the upcoming switch is Charles Niemeier of the Public Company Accounting Oversight Board, who says the switch "has the potential to be a Tower of Babel," costing firms millions when they do not even have thousands to spend.

Others say the switch will help U.S. companies raise capital abroad and do business with firms abroad. Perhaps the biggest upside of the switch is that IFRS rules are more streamlined and less complex than GAAP. Lenovo is a big advocate of IFRS as they desire to be a world company rather than a U.S. or Chinese company, so the faster the switch to IFRS, the better for them. The bottom line is that IFRS is coming to the United States, sooner rather than later, so we all need to gear up for this switch as soon as possible.

21st-Century Challenges in Strategic Management

Three particular challenges or decisions that face all strategists today are (1) deciding whether the process should be more an art or a science, (2) deciding whether strategies should be visible or hidden from stakeholders, and (3) deciding whether the process should be more top-down or bottom-up in their firm.[14]

The Art or Science Issue

This textbook is consistent with most of the strategy literature in advocating that strategic management be viewed more as a science than an art. This perspective contends that firms need to systematically assess their external and internal environments, conduct research, carefully evaluate the pros and cons of various alternatives, perform analyses, and then decide on a particular course of action. In contrast, Mintzberg's notion of "crafting" strategies embodies the artistic model, which suggests that strategic decision making be based primarily on holistic thinking, intuition, creativity, and imagination.[15] Mintzberg and his followers reject strategies that result from objective analysis, preferring instead subjective imagination. "Strategy scientists" reject strategies that emerge from emotion, hunch, creativity, and politics. Proponents of the artistic view often consider strategic planning exercises to be time poorly spent. The Mintzberg philosophy insists on informality, whereas strategy scientists (and this text) insist on more formality. Mintzberg refers to strategic planning as an "emergent" process whereas strategy scientists use the term *deliberate* process.[16]

The answer to the art-versus-science question is one that strategists must decide for themselves, and certainly the two approaches are not mutually exclusive. In deciding which approach is more effective, however, consider that the business world today has become increasingly complex and more intensely competitive. There is less room for error in strategic planning. Recall that Chapter 1 discussed the importance of intuition, experience, and subjectivity in strategic planning, and even the weights and ratings discussed in Chapters 3, 4, and 6 certainly require good judgment. But the idea of deciding on strategies for any firm without thorough research and analysis, at least in the mind of these authors, is unwise. Certainly, in smaller firms there can be more informality in the process compared to larger firms, but even for smaller firms, a wealth of competitive information is available on the Internet and elsewhere and should be collected, assimilated, and evaluated before deciding on a course of action on which survival of the firm may hinge. The livelihood of countless employees and shareholders may hinge on the effectiveness of strategies selected. Too much is at stake to be less than thorough in formulating strategies. It is not wise for a strategist to rely too heavily on gut feeling and opinion instead of research data, competitive intelligence, and analysis in formulating strategies.

The Visible or Hidden Issue

An interesting aspect of any competitive analysis discussion is whether strategies themselves should be secret or open within firms. The Chinese warrior Sun Tzu and military leaders today strive to keep strategies secret because war is based on deception. However, for a business organization, secrecy may not be best. Keeping strategies secret from employees and stakeholders at large could severely inhibit employee and stakeholder communication, understanding, and commitment and also forgo valuable input that these persons could have regarding formulation or implementation of that strategy. Thus, strategists in a particular firm must decide for themselves whether the risk of rival firms easily knowing and exploiting a firm's strategies is worth the benefit of improved employee and stakeholder motivation and input. Most executives agree that some strategic information should remain confidential to top managers, and that steps should be taken to ensure that such information is not disseminated beyond the inner circle. For a firm that you may own or manage, would you advocate openness or secrecy in regard to strategies being formulated and implemented?

There are certainly good reasons to keep the strategy process and strategies themselves visible and open rather than hidden and secret. There are also good reasons to keep strategies hidden from all but top-level executives. Strategists must decide for themselves what is best for their firms. This text comes down largely on the side of being visible and open, but certainly this may not be best for all strategists and all firms. As pointed out in Chapter 1, Sun Tzu argued that all war is based on deception and that the best maneuvers are those not easily predicted by rivals. Business and war are analogous.

Some reasons to be completely open with the strategy process and resultant decisions are these:

1. Managers, employees, and other stakeholders can readily contribute to the process. They often have excellent ideas. Secrecy would forgo many excellent ideas.
2. Investors, creditors, and other stakeholders have greater basis for supporting a firm when they know what the firm is doing and where the firm is going.
3. Visibility promotes democracy, whereas secrecy promotes autocracy. Domestic firms and most foreign firms prefer democracy over autocracy as a management style.
4. Participation and openness enhance understanding, commitment, and communication within the firm.

Reasons why some firms prefer to conduct strategic planning in secret and keep strategies hidden from all but the highest-level executives are as follows:

1. Free dissemination of a firm's strategies may easily translate into competitive intelligence for rival firms who could exploit the firm given that information.
2. Secrecy limits criticism, second guessing, and hindsight.
3. Participants in a visible strategy process become more attractive to rival firms who may lure them away.
4. Secrecy limits rival firms from imitating or duplicating the firm's strategies and undermining the firm.

The obvious benefits of the visible versus hidden extremes suggest that a working balance must be sought between the apparent contradictions. Parnell says that in a perfect world all key individuals both inside and outside the firm should be involved in strategic planning, but in practice particularly sensitive and confidential information should always remain strictly confidential to top managers.[17] This balancing act is difficult but essential for survival of the firm.

The Top-Down or Bottom-Up Approach

Proponents of the top-down approach contend that top executives are the only persons in the firm with the collective experience, acumen, and fiduciary responsibility to make key strategy decisions. In contrast, bottom-up advocates argue that lower- and middle-level managers and employees who will be implementing the strategies need to be actively involved in the process of formulating the strategies to ensure their support and commitment. Recent strategy research and this textbook emphasize the bottom-up approach, but earlier work by Schendel and Hofer stressed the need for firms to rely on perceptions of their top managers in strategic planning.[18] Strategists must reach a working balance of the two approaches in a manner deemed best for their firms at a particular time, while cognizant of the fact that current research supports the bottom-up approach, at least among U.S. firms. Increased education and diversity of the workforce at all levels are reasons why middle- and lower-level managers—and even nonmanagers—should be invited to participate in the firm's strategic planning process, at least to the extent that they are willing and able to contribute.

Special Note to Students

Just Google the words *balanced scorecard images* and you will see more than 100 actual Balanced Scorecards being used as a tool by various organizations to gain and sustain competitive advantage. Note the variation in format. In performing your case analysis, develop and present a Balanced Scorecard that you recommend to help your firm monitor and evaluate progress toward stated objectives. Effective, timely evaluation of strategies can enable a firm to adapt quickly to changing conditions, and a Balanced Scorecard can assist in this endeavor. Couch your discussion of the Balanced Scorecard in terms of competitive advantage versus rival firms.

Conclusion

This chapter presents a strategy-evaluation framework that can facilitate accomplishment of annual and long-term objectives. Effective strategy evaluation allows an organization to capitalize on internal strengths as they develop, to exploit external opportunities as they emerge, to recognize and defend against threats, and to mitigate internal weaknesses before they become detrimental.

Strategists in successful organizations take the time to formulate, implement, and then evaluate strategies deliberately and systematically. Good strategists move their organization forward with purpose and direction, continually evaluating and improving the firm's external and internal strategic positions. Strategy evaluation allows an organization to shape its own future rather than allowing it to be constantly shaped by remote forces that have little or no vested interest in the well-being of the enterprise.

Although not a guarantee for success, strategic management allows organizations to make effective long-term decisions, to execute those decisions efficiently, and to take corrective actions as needed to ensure success. Computer networks and the Internet help to coordinate strategic-management activities and to ensure that decisions are based on good information. A key to effective strategy evaluation and to successful strategic management is an integration of intuition and analysis:

> A potentially fatal problem is the tendency for analytical and intuitive issues to polarize. This polarization leads to strategy evaluation that is dominated by either analysis or intuition, or to strategy evaluation that is discontinuous, with a lack of coordination among analytical and intuitive issues.[19]

Strategists in successful organizations realize that strategic management is first and foremost a people process. It is an excellent vehicle for fostering organizational communication. People are what make the difference in organizations.

The real key to effective strategic management is to accept the premise that the planning process is more important than the written plan, that the manager is continuously planning and does not stop planning when the written plan is finished. The written plan is only a snapshot as of the moment it is approved. If the manager is not planning on a continuous basis—planning, measuring, and revising—the written plan can become obsolete the day it is finished. This obsolescence becomes more of a certainty as the increasingly rapid rate of change makes the business environment more uncertain.[20]

MyManagementLab®

Go to **mymanagementlab.com** to complete the problems marked with this icon .

Key Terms and Concepts

advantage (p. 283)
auditing (p. 295)
Balanced Scorecard (p. 291)
consistency (p. 283)
consonance (p. 283)
contingency plans (p. 294)
feasibility (p. 283)
future shock (p. 290)

GAAS, GAAP, and IFRS (p. 295)
management by wandering around (p. 285)
measuring organizational performance (p. 288)
reviewing the underlying bases of an organization's
  strategy (p. 286)
revised EFE Matrix (p. 286)
revised IFE Matrix (p. 286)
taking corrective actions (p. 289)

Issues for Review and Discussion

9-1. If a firm has two regions and two products, develop a sample framework for measuring organizational performance.

9-2. Compare strategy formulation with strategy implementation in terms of each being an art or a science.

9-3. Do an Internet search using the keywords *Balanced Scorecard Images*. Pick out two images among the hundred available. Compare and contrast the two images and processes as to effectiveness.

9-4. Do an Internet search using the keywords *GAAP to IFRS* to update yourself on this important transition coming soon in the United States.

9-5. How does an organization know if it is pursuing "optimal" strategies?

9-6. Discuss the nature and implications of the upcoming accounting switch from GAAP to IFRS in the USA.

9-7. Ask an accounting professor at your college or university the following question and report back to the class: "To what extent would my learning the IFRS standards on my own give me competitive advantage in the job market?"

9-8. Give an example of "consonance" other than the one provided by Rumelt in the chapter.

9-9. Evaluating strategies on a continuous rather than a periodic basis is desired. Discuss the pros and cons of this statement.

9-10. How often should an organization's vision or mission be changed in light of strategy evaluation activities?

9-11. Compare Mintzberg's notion of "crafting" strategies with this textbook's notion of "gathering and assimilating information" to formulate strategies.

9-12. Why has strategy evaluation become so important in business today?

9-13. BellSouth Services is considering putting divisional EFE and IFE matrices online for continual updating. How would this affect strategy evaluation?

9-14. What types of quantitative and qualitative criteria should be used to evaluate a company's strategy?

9-15. As owner of a local, independent supermarket, explain how you would evaluate the firm's strategy.

9-16. Under what conditions are corrective actions not required in the strategy-evaluation process?

9-17. Identify types of organizations that may need to evaluate strategy more frequently than others. Justify your choices.

9-18. As executive director of the state forestry commission, in what way and how frequently would you evaluate the organization's strategies?

9-19. Identify some key financial ratios that would be important in evaluating a bank's strategy.

9-20. Strategy evaluation allows an organization to take a proactive stance toward shaping its own future. Discuss the meaning of this statement.

9-21. Explain and discuss the Balanced Scorecard.

9-22. Why is the Balanced Scorecard an important topic both in devising objectives and in evaluating strategies?

9-23. Develop a Balanced Scorecard for a local fast-food restaurant.

9-24. Do you believe strategic management should be more visible or hidden as a process in a firm? Explain.

9-25. Do you feel strategic management should be more a top-down or bottom-up process in a firm? Explain.

9-26. Do you believe strategic management is more an art or a science? Explain.

MyManagementLab®

Go to **mymanagementlab.com** for Auto-graded writing questions as well as the following Assisted-graded writing questions:

9-27. Why is the Balanced Scorecard an important topic both in devising objectives and in evaluating strategies?

9-28. Do you believe strategic management should be more visible or hidden as a process in a firm? Explain.

9-29. Mymanagementlab Only—comprehensive writing assignment for this chapter.

Current Readings

Aguinis, Herman, Ryan K. Gottfredson, and Harry Joo. "Delivering Effective Performance Feedback: The Strengths-Based Approach." *Business Horizons* 55, no. 2 (March 2012): 105–111.

Lafley, A.G., Roger L. Martin, Jan W. Rivkin, and Nicolaj Siggelkow. "Bringing Science to the Art of Strategy." *Harvard Business Review* (September 2012): 56.

Lux, Sean, T. Russell Crook, and Terry Leap. "Corporate Political Activity: The Good, the Bad, and the Ugly." *Business Horizons* 55, no. 3 (May 2012): 307–312.

Kahane, Adam. "Transformative Scenario Planning: Changing the Future by Exploring Alternatives."

Strategy and Leadership 40, no. 5 (2012): 19–23.

Mauboussin, Michael J. "The True Measures of Success." *Harvard Business Review* (October 2012): 46.

Peltola, Soili. "Can an Old Firm Learn New Tricks? A Corporate Entrepreneurship Approach to Organizational Renewal." *Business Horizons* 55, no. 1 (January 2012): 43–51.

Stieger, Daniel, Kurt Matzler, Sayan Chatterjee, and Florian Ladstaetter-Fussenegger. "Democratizing Strategy: How Crowdsourcing Can Be Used For Strategy Dialogues." *California Management Review* 54, no. 4 (Summer 2012): 44–68.

ASSURANCE OF LEARNING **EXERCISES**

EXERCISE 9A
Examine 100 Balanced Scorecards

Purpose
The Army Surgeon General and Commander of the U.S. Army Medical Command use the Balanced Scorecard as "the principal tool by which they improve operational and fiscal effectiveness and better meet the needs of patients and stakeholders." This exercise will give your experience evaluating many different formats for the Balanced Scorecard. It will also give you exposure to many different organizations that currently use the Balanced Scorecard as part of their strategic planning.

Instructions
Step 1   Do a Google search using the terms *balanced scorecard images*. Review the many different formats of the Balanced Scorecard currently being used by organizations. Decide on three formats that you believe are particularly effective.

Step 2   Do a Google search using the terms *balanced scorecard adopters*. Review the many different organizations currently using the Balanced Scorecard as part of their strategic planning. Select three different companies or organizations. Compare and contrast their use of the Balanced Scorecard technique.

Step 3   Prepare a three-page Executive Summary of your Balanced Scorecard analysis and recommendations.

EXERCISE 9B
Prepare a Strategy-Evaluation Report for PepsiCo

Purpose
This exercise can give you experience locating strategy-evaluation information. Use of the Internet coupled with published sources of information can significantly enhance the strategy-evaluation process. Performance information on competitors, for example, can help put into perspective a firm's own performance.

Instructions
Step 1   Locate strategy-evaluation information regarding PepsiCo's performance last quarter and analysts' thoughts on PepsiCo's overall strategy going forward.

Step 2   Summarize your research findings by preparing a strategy-evaluation report for your instructor. Include in your report a summary of PepsiCo's strategies and performance in 2012 and a summary of your conclusions regarding the effectiveness of PepsiCo's strategies.

Step 3   Based on your analysis, do you feel that PepsiCo is pursuing effective strategies? What recommendations would you offer to PepsiCo's chief executive officer?

EXERCISE 9C
Evaluate Your University's Strategies

Purpose
An important part of evaluating strategies is determining the nature and extent of changes in an organization's external opportunities and threats and internal strengths and weaknesses. Changes in these underlying key factors can indicate a need to change or modify the firm's strategies.

Instructions
As a class, discuss positive and negative changes in your university's external and internal factors during your college career. Begin by listing on the board new or emerging opportunities and threats. Then identify strengths and weaknesses that have changed significantly during your college career. In light of the external and internal changes that were identified, discuss whether your university's strategies need modifying. Are there any new strategies that you would recommend? Make a list to recommend to your department chair, dean, president, or chancellor.

Notes

1. Karen Talley, "Sales Plunge Another 23% at Penney," *Wall Street Journal* (August 11–12): B3.
2. Dale McConkey, "Planning in a Changing Environment," *Business Horizons*, September–October 1988, 64.
3. Robert Simons, "Control in an Age of Empowerment," *Harvard Business Review*, March–April 1995, 80.
4. Dale Zand, "Reviewing the Policy Process," *California Management Review* 21, no. 1 (Fall 1978): 37.
5. Eccles. 3:1–8.
6. Claude George Jr., *The History of Management Thought* (Upper Saddle River, New Jersey: Prentice Hall, 1968), 165–166.
7. M. Erez and F. Kanfer, "The Role of Goal Acceptance in Goal Setting and Task Performance," *Academy of Management Review* 8, no. 3 (July 1983): 457.
8. D. Hussey and M. Langham, *Corporate Planning: The Human Factor* (Oxford, England: Pergamon Press, 1979), 138.
9. Carter Bayles, "Strategic Control: The President's Paradox," *Business Horizons* 20, no. 4 (August 1977): 18.
10. Robert Waterman, Jr., "How the Best Get Better," *BusinessWeek*, September 14, 1987, 105.
11. Robert Linneman and Rajan Chandran, "Contingency Planning: A Key to Swift Managerial Action in the Uncertain Tomorrow," *Managerial Planning* 29, no. 4 (January–February 1981): 23–27.
12. American Accounting Association, *Report of Committee on Basic Auditing Concepts*, 1971, 15–74.
13. Michael Rapoport, "Delay Seen (Again) For New Rules on Accounting," *Wall Street Journal* (July 6, 2012): C1; Michael Rapoport, "Accounting Panel Expresses 'Regret' Over U.S. Stance," *Wall Street Journal* (July 16, 2012): C5.
14. John Parnell, "Five Critical Challenges in Strategy Making," *SAM Advanced Management Journal* 68, no. 2 (Spring 2003): 15–22.
15. Henry Mintzberg, "Crafting Strategy," *Harvard Business Review*, July–August 1987, 66–75.
16. Henry Mintzberg and J. Waters, "Of Strategies, Deliberate and Emergent," *Strategic Management Journal* 6, no. 2: 257–272.
17. Parnell, 15–22.
18. D. E. Schendel and C. W. Hofer (Eds.), *Strategic Management* (Boston: Little, Brown, 1979).
19. Michael McGinnis, "The Key to Strategic Planning: Integrating Analysis and Intuition," *Sloan Management Review* 26, no. 1 (Fall 1984): 49.
20. McConkey, 72.

## PART 5

KEY STRATEGIC-MANAGEMENT TOPICS

Source: Petro Feketa/Fotolia

MyManagementLab®

⭐ **Improve Your Grade!**

Over 10 million students improved their results using the Pearson MyLabs.
Visit **mymanagementlab.com** for simulations, tutorials, and end-of-chapter problems.

Business Ethics, Social Responsibility, and Environmental Sustainability

CHAPTER OBJECTIVES

After studying this chapter, you should be able to do the following:

1. Discuss the ethics of workplace romance.

2. Explain why concern for wildlife is a strategic issue for firms.

3. Explain why good ethics is good business in strategic management.

4. Explain how firms can best ensure that their code of business ethics guides decision making instead of being ignored.

5. Explain why whistle-blowing is important to encourage in a firm.

6. Discuss the nature and role of corporate sustainability reports.

7. Discuss specific ways that firms can be good stewards of the natural environment.

8. Explain ISO 14000 and 14001.

9. Discuss recent trends in bribery law.

ASSURANCE OF LEARNING **EXERCISES**

The following exercises are found at the end of this chapter.

EXERCISE 10A How Does Your Municipality Compare to Others on Being Pollution-Safe?

EXERCISE 10B Evaluate PepsiCo's Global Code of Conduct

EXERCISE 10C Compare and Evaluate Sustainability Reports

EXERCISE 10D The Ethics of Spying on Competitors

EXERCISE 10E Who Prepares a Sustainability Report?

Although the three sections of this chapter (business ethics, social responsibility, and sustainability) are distinct, the topics are quite related. Many people, for example, consider it unethical for a firm to be socially irresponsible. **Social responsibility** refers to actions an organization takes beyond what is legally required to protect or enhance the well-being of living things. **Sustainability** refers to the extent that an organization's operations and actions protect, mend, and preserve rather than harm or destroy the natural environment. Polluting the environment, for example, is unethical, irresponsible, and in many cases illegal. Business ethics, social responsibility, and sustainability issues therefore are interrelated and impact all areas of the comprehensive strategic-management model, as illustrated in Figure 10-1 with white shading.

A sample company that adheres to the highest ethical standards and that uses excellent strategic planning and has an outstanding commitment to corporate sustainability is Apple.

Business Ethics

The Institute of Business Ethics (IBE) recently did a study titled "Does Business Ethics Pay?" and concluded that companies displaying a "clear commitment to ethical conduct" consistently outperform companies that do not display ethical conduct. Philippa Foster Black of the IBE stated: "Not only is ethical behavior in business life the right thing to do in principle, it pays off in financial returns." Alan Simpson said: "If you have integrity, nothing else matters. If you don't have integrity, nothing else matters." Table 10-1 provides some results of the IBE study.

EXCELLENT STRATEGIC MANAGEMENT SHOWCASED

Apple Inc.

Apple's stock has dropped lately, but the company was still the most profitable company in the world last quarter, posting $13.6 billion in net income. In Q4 of 2012, Apple's iPhone 5 was the world's best selling smartphone, followed in second place by the iPhone 4S.

Apple recently re-registered all its products with the U.S. government-backed voluntary registry of green electronics. Called Epeat, the registry was created in collaboration among government agencies, activist groups, and manufacturers. Epeat-certified computers and devices are designed with higher energy efficiency and for ease of use in recycling. San Francisco had released a letter informing all of the city's 50 agencies that Apple's laptops and desktops would "no longer qualify" for purchase unless Apple registered its products with Epeat. The federal government requires that its laptops and desktops be Epeat-certified.

Apple has its own recycling program that reportedly recycles about 70 percent of its iPhones. The iPhone5 has raised consumer awareness of sustainability issues when it comes to electronic devices because the person's old device may be worth some good money and throwing a phone away is not the best option. "There's a market for all models of iPhones," said Andy Bates, Vice-President of the Colorado-based Wireless Alliance, a cell phone recycling company that has about 14,000 collection points nationwide and brings in up to 80,000 cell phones a month. "Your iPhone should be reused 99 percent of the time so that it doesn't have a major impact on e-waste. It should be recycled at some point." Verizon has an excellent wireless trade-in program in which customers can get their iPhone appraised and then valued via an electronic gift card. Verizon's program has diverted more than 75 tons of e-waste from landfills.

Apple is engaged in a fierce competitive battle with Samsung and Amazon as the three technology giants go head to head in more digital areas. Amazon is now testing its own smartphone and is expected to soon launch a vastly new and improved Kindle Fire tablet aimed at taking over Apple's iPad business. And Amazon recently purchased Yap and UpNext, two software companies that focus on mobile maps and voice recognition, both areas in which Apple wants to offer unique features for iPhone users. While Amazon tries to out-execute Apple, Apple at the same time is moving aggressively into Amazon areas. For example, Apple has developed new technology to build interactive e-books, called iBooks Author. Amazon's Kindle App was recently the fifth-most downloaded free iPad app of all time, and Amazon sells thousands of iPods and iPhones on its website. For now, Apple still has 60 percent of the tablet business globally and Amazon has 60 percent of the digital-book business globally, but those numbers too are changing daily. Both Apple and Amazon have excellent strategic plans and are basically crushing thousands of other retailers from Best Buy and RadioShack to small mom-and-pops.

Source: Based on Ian Sherr, "Apple Goes Back to Green Registry," *Wall Street Journal* (July 16, 2012): B3. Also, Jessica Vascellaro and Greg Bensinger, "Apple-Amazon War Heats Up," *Wall Street Journal* (July 26, 2012): B3. Also, Lorraine Luk and Jessica Lessin, "Apple Tests Designs for New Television," *Wall Street Journal* (December 13, 2012): B1.

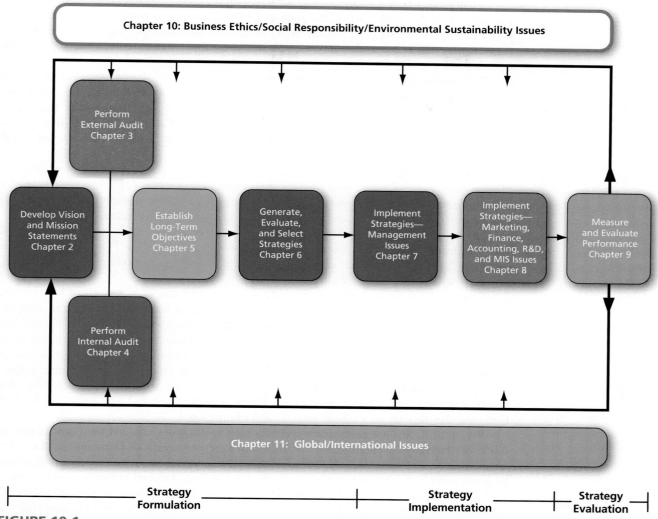

FIGURE 10-1

A Comprehensive Strategic-Management Model

Source: Fred R. David, "How Companies Define Their Mission," *Long Range Planning* 22, no. 3 (June 1988): 40.

Good ethics is good business. Bad ethics can derail even the best strategic plans. This chapter provides an overview of the importance of business ethics in strategic management. **Business ethics** can be defined as principles of conduct within organizations that guide decision making and behavior. Good business ethics is a prerequisite for good strategic management; good ethics is just good business!

TABLE 10-1   Seven Principles of Admirable Business Ethics

1. Be trustworthy, because no individual or business wants to do business with an entity they do not trust.
2. Be openminded, continually asking for "ethics-related feedback" from all internal and external stakeholders.
3. Honor all commitments and obligations.
4. Do not misrepresent, exaggerate, or mislead with any print materials.
5. Be visibly a responsible community citizen.
6. Utilize your accounting practices to identify and eliminate questionable activities.
7. Follow the motto: Do unto others as you would have them do unto you.

Source: Based on http://sbinformation.about.com/od/bestpractices/a/businessethics.htm.

A rising tide of consciousness about the importance of business ethics is sweeping the USA and the rest of the world. Strategists such as CEOs and business owners are the individuals primarily responsible for ensuring that high ethical principles are espoused and practiced in an organization. All strategy formulation, implementation, and evaluation decisions have ethical ramifications.

Newspapers and business magazines daily report legal and moral breaches of ethical conduct by both public and private organizations. Being unethical can be expensive. For example, some of the largest payouts for class-action legal fraud suits ever were against Enron ($7.16 billion), WorldCom ($6.16 billion), Cendant ($3.53 billion), Tyco ($2.98 billion), AOL Time Warner ($2.5 billion), Nortel Networks ($2.47 billion), and Royal Ahold ($1.09 billion).

Other business actions considered to be unethical include misleading advertising or labeling, causing environmental harm, poor product or service safety, padding expense accounts, insider trading, dumping banned or flawed products in foreign markets, not providing equal opportunities for women and minorities, overpricing, moving jobs overseas, and sexual harassment.

The Food and Drug Administration (FDA) recently warned both Avon Products and L'Oreal about misleading marketing of certain of its antiwrinkle products. The FDA's position is that Avon and L'Oreal's claims that discuss things like the stimulation of skin cells or reactivating the skin's repair process are not true.

Yahoo!'s CEO Scott Thompson recently was forced to resign as a result of his "resume padding or inflating." J.P. Morgan Chase CEO Jamie Dimon is currently under fire after the investment bank's $2.3 billion trading blunder that has already cost a key deputy her job. Increasingly, executives' and managers' personal and professional decisions are placing them in the cross hairs of angry shareholders, disgruntled employees, and even their own boards of directors—making even the imperious CEO far more vulnerable to personal, public, and corporate missteps than ever before. "Certainly, anybody who is doing something that can be construed as unethical, immoral or greedy is being taken to task," says Paul Dorf of Compensation Resources, a consultant to boards of directors.[1]

Social media and business-centric websites such as glassdoor.com and vault.com as well as disclosure mandates required under Sarbanes-Oxley are just several of many outlets that today quickly spread fact and rumor about the inside dealings of Corporate America, revealing ethical breaches and internal business practices that may never have surfaced before the Internet and a 24/7 media culture. "God forbid anyone who isn't squeaky-clean these days or misrepresents their credentials at the top of the company," says Wendy Patrick, who teaches business ethics at San Diego State University. "Anything embarrassing and you begin to question everything. If they aren't making good decisions in their personal lives, it can bleed over to the way they run their companies."

"The pressure and scrutiny on performance has shortened the tenure of the average CEO from about 10 years to about 5½ years since the 1990s," says John Challenger of consultants Challenger Gray and Christmas. Challenger notes that 42 CEOs were forced out of their jobs in 2011 and that pace is up 5 percent in 2012.[2]

Code of Business Ethics

A new wave of ethics issues related to product safety, employee health, sexual harassment, AIDS in the workplace, smoking, acid rain, affirmative action, waste disposal, foreign business practices, cover-ups, takeover tactics, conflicts of interest, employee privacy, inappropriate gifts, and security of company records has accentuated the need for strategists to develop a clear **code of business ethics**. Internet fraud, hacking into company computers, spreading viruses, and identity theft are other unethical activities that plague every sector of online commerce.

Merely having a code of ethics, however, is not sufficient to ensure ethical business behavior. A code of ethics can be viewed as a public relations gimmick, a set of platitudes, or window dressing. To ensure that the code is read, understood, believed, and remembered, periodic ethics workshops are needed to sensitize people to workplace circumstances in which ethics issues may arise.[3] If employees see examples of punishment for violating the code as well as rewards for upholding the code, this reinforces the importance of a firm's code of ethics. The website www.ethicsweb.ca/codes provides guidelines on how to write an effective code of ethics.

An Ethics Culture

Reverend Billy Graham once said: "When wealth is lost, nothing is lost; when health is lost, something is lost; when character is lost, all is lost." An ethics "culture" needs to permeate organizations! To help create an ethics culture, Citicorp developed a business ethics board game that is played by thousands of employees worldwide. Called "The Word Ethic," this game asks players business ethics questions, such as how do you deal with a customer who offers you football tickets in exchange for a new, backdated IRA? Diana Robertson at the Wharton School of Business believes the game is effective because it is interactive. Many organizations have developed a code-of-conduct manual outlining ethical expectations and giving examples of situations that commonly arise in their businesses.

One reason strategists' salaries are high is that they must take the moral risks of the firm. Strategists are responsible for developing, communicating, and enforcing the code of business ethics for their organizations. Although primary responsibility for ensuring ethical behavior rests with a firm's strategists, an integral part of the responsibility of all managers is to provide ethics leadership by constant example and demonstration. Managers hold positions that enable them to influence and educate many people. This makes managers responsible for developing and implementing ethical decision making. Gellerman and Drucker, respectively, offer some good advice for managers:

All managers risk giving too much because of what their companies demand from them. But the same superiors, who keep pressing you to do more, or to do it better, or faster, or less expensively, will turn on you should you cross that fuzzy line between right and wrong. They will blame you for exceeding instructions or for ignoring their warnings. The smartest managers already know that the best answer to the question "How far is too far?" is don't try to find out.[4]

A man (or woman) might know too little, perform poorly, lack judgment and ability, and yet not do too much damage as a manager. But if that person lacks character and integrity—no matter how knowledgeable, how brilliant, how successful—he destroys. He destroys people, the most valuable resource of the enterprise. He destroys spirit. And he destroys performance. This is particularly true of the people at the head of an enterprise because the spirit of an organization is created from the top. If an organization is great in spirit, it is because the spirit of its top people is great. If it decays, it does so because the top rots. As the proverb has it, "Trees die from the top." No one should ever become a strategist unless he or she is willing to have his or her character serve as the model for subordinates.[5]

No society anywhere in the world can compete long or successfully with people stealing from one another or not trusting one another, with every bit of information requiring notarized confirmation, with every disagreement ending up in litigation, or with government having to regulate businesses to keep them honest. Being unethical is a recipe for headaches, inefficiency, and waste. History has proven that the greater the trust and confidence of people in the ethics of an institution or society, the greater its economic strength. Business relationships are built mostly on mutual trust and reputation. Short-term decisions based on greed and questionable ethics will preclude the necessary self-respect to gain the trust of others. More and more firms believe that ethics training and an ethics culture create strategic advantage. Max Killan said: "If business is not based on ethical grounds, it is of no benefit to society, and will, like all other unethical combinations, pass into oblivion."

Whistle-Blowing

Harris Corporation and other firms warn managers and employees that failing to report an ethical violation by others could bring discharge. The Securities and Exchange Commission (SEC) recently strengthened its whistle-blowing policies, virtually mandating that anyone seeing unethical activity report such behavior. **Whistle-blowing** refers to policies that require employees to report any unethical violations they discover or see in the firm.

Whistle-blowers in the corporate world receive up to 25 percent of the proceeds of legal proceedings against firms for wrongdoing. Whistle-blower payouts are becoming more and more common. In late 2012, Brad Birkenfeld, the former Zurich-based UBS AG banker who told the Internal Revenue Service (IRS) how the bank helped thousands of Americans evade taxes, received an IRS award of $104 million, perhaps the largest payout ever for an individual U.S. whistle-blower. The largest bank in Switzerland, UBS's Birkenfeld told IRS agents how UBS bankers came to the USA to woo rich Americans, managed $20 billion of their assets, and helped them cheat the IRS. He pleaded guilty to conspiracy in 2008, a year after reporting the bank's conduct to the Justice Department, U.S. Senate, IRS, and Securities and Exchange Commission. Birkenfeld went briefly to prison for his involvement in the bank scheme, but UBS avoided prosecution in the USA by agreeing to pay $780 million, disclosing data on more than 250 Swiss accounts, and admitting it helped foster tax evasion. It later agreed to hand over data on another 4,450 accounts. Since Birkenfeld came forward, at least 33,000 Americans have voluntarily disclosed offshore accounts to the IRS, generating more than $5 billion.

In October 2012, the IRS in a separate case paid another whistle-blower $38 million which was between 15 and 30 percent of the taxes recovered from another large corporation. The name of this company and the whistle-blower remain completely confidential, proving that the IRS can reward corporate whistle-blowers without ever revealing their identity. Pfizer paid out $2.3 billion in a whistle-blower settlement case and Eli Lilly paid out $1.4 billion. Most firms have internal whistle-blowing incentives and policies and try to keep such matters internal, but recent laws and court cases are shifting disclosure and settlements outside the firm.[6]

An accountant recently tipped off the IRS that his employer was skimping on taxes and received $4.5 million in the first IRS whistle-blower award. The accountant's tip netted the IRS $20 million in taxes and interest from the errant financial-services firm. The award represented a 22 percent cut of the taxes recovered. The IRS program, designed to encourage tips in large-scale cases, mandates awards of 15 to 30 percent of the amount recouped. "It's a win-win for both the government and taxpayers. These are dollars that are being returned to the Treasury that otherwise wouldn't be," said lawyer Eric Young.

Ethics training programs should include messages from the CEO or owner of the business emphasizing ethical business practices, the development and discussion of codes of ethics, and procedures for discussing and reporting unethical behavior. Firms can align ethical and strategic decision making by incorporating ethical considerations into long-term planning, by integrating ethical decision making into the performance appraisal process, by encouraging whistle-blowing or the reporting of unethical practices, and by monitoring departmental and corporate performance regarding ethical issues.

Bribes

Bribery is defined by *Black's Law Dictionary* as the offering, giving, receiving, or soliciting of any item of value to influence the actions of an official or other person in discharge of a public or legal duty. A **bribe** is a gift bestowed to influence a recipient's conduct. The gift may be any money, good, right in action, property, preferment, privilege, emolument, object of value, advantage, or merely a promise or undertaking to induce or influence the action, vote, or influence of a person in an official or public capacity. Bribery is a crime in most countries of the world, including the United States.[7]

The U.S. Foreign Corrupt Practices Act (FCPA) that governs bribery is being enforced more strictly. This act and a new provision in the Dodd-Frank financial-regulation law allows company employees or others who bring cases of financial fraud, such as bribery, to the government's attention to receive up to 30 percent of any sum recovered. Bribery suits against a company also expose the firm to shareholder lawsuits.

In 2012, Pfizer paid $60.2 million to settle a federal investigation into bribery overseas whereby the firm was accused of bribing doctors, hospitals administrators, and regulators in several countries in Europe and Asia to prescribe their medicines. Pfizer allegedly gave doctors in China cellphones and tea sets, while plying Croatian doctors with cash and international trips, and then sought to hide the bribery by recording the payments in accounting records as legitimate expenses.

Avon Products is currently being investigated for bribery charges related to their winning the first direct-sales license awarded by China to a foreign company. Even former Avon CEO Andrea Jung is being interrogated through her attorney Theodore Wells Jr. Avon is also being examined for spending millions of dollars in Brazil and France to consultants hired to assist the company with tax bills in those countries.

A recent (11-15-12) *Wall Street Journal* article titled "Bribery Law Dos and Don'ts" provides a synopsis of the recent 130-page document released by the U.S. Justice Department and the SEC to respond to complaints from companies that ambiguity in the FCPA has forced them to abandon business in high-risk countries and spend millions of dollars investigating themselves.[8] Numerous examples of bribery are given, such as "1) providing a $12,000 birthday trip for a government official from Mexico that incudes visits to wineries and museums" or 2) $10,000 spent on a government official for drinks, dinners, and entertainment."

In mid-2013, the SEC began investigating electronics giant Panasonic for bribery within its subsidiary, Avionics, based in Lake Forest, California. From 2009 to mid-2013, the U.S. Justice Department filed 110 bribery cases and the SEC filed 80 bribery cases.

The United Kingdom's new Bribery Law forbids any company doing any business in the United Kingdom from bribing foreign or domestic officials to gain competitive advantage. The British law is more stringent even than the similar U.S. FCPA. The British Bribery Law carries a maximum 10-year prison sentence for those convicted of bribery. The law stipulates that "failure to prevent bribery" is an offense and stipulates that facilitation payments, or payments to gain access, are not a valid defense to prevent bribery.

Great Britain's Bribery Act applies even to bribes between private businesspersons, and if the individual who makes the payment does not realize the transaction was a bribe, he or she is still liable. The new bribery law is being enforced by Britain's Serious Fraud Office (SFO) and boosts the maximum penalty for bribery to 10 years in prison from 7, and sets no limits on fines. More and more nations are taking a tougher stance against corruption, and companies worldwide are installing elaborate programs to avoid running afoul of the FCPA or the SFO.

Paying bribes is considered both illegal and unethical in the USA, but in some foreign countries, paying bribes and kickbacks is acceptable. Tipping is even considered bribery in some countries. Important antibribery and extortion initiatives are advocated by many organizations, including the World Bank, the International Monetary Fund, the European Union (EU), the Council of Europe, the Organization of American States, the Pacific Basin Economic Council, the Global Coalition for Africa, and the United Nations.

The U.S. Justice Department recently increased its prosecutions of alleged acts of foreign bribery. Businesses have to be much more careful these days. For years, taking business associates to lavish dinners and giving them expensive holiday gifts and even outright cash may have been expected in many countries, such as South Korea and China, but there is now stepped-up enforcement of bribery laws.

The SEC and Justice Department are investigating several pharmaceutical companies, including Merck, AstraZeneca PLC, Bristol-Myers Squibb, and GlaxoSmithKline PLC, for allegedly paying bribes in certain foreign countries to boost sales and speed approvals. Four types of violations are being reviewed: bribing government-employed doctors to purchase drugs; paying company sales agents commissions that are passed along to government doctors; paying hospital committees to approve drug purchases; and paying regulators to win drug approvals. Johnson & Johnson recently paid $70 million to settle allegations that it paid bribes to doctors in Greece, Poland, and Romania to use their surgical implants and to prescribe its drugs. Pfizer paid $60 million to resolve similar probes to win business overseas.

The SEC and the Justice Department are also investigating Hewlett-Packard for allegedly paying Russian government officials bribes to secure a $44.5 million information technology network. Similarly, the engineering giant Siemens AG is being investigated on bribery charges related to a $27 million traffic-control system installed in Moscow, Russia.

The U.S. FCPA prohibits U.S. companies from paying or offering to pay foreign government officials or employees of state companies to gain a business advantage. Under the U.S. Dodd-Frank Act, passed in 2010, employees are encouraged to report possible acts of bribery and whistle-blowers are rewarded between 10 percent and 30 percent of any financial sanctions against companies.

Workplace Romance

Director of the U.S. Central Intelligence Agency (CIA), Gen. David Petraeus abruptly resigned in November 2012, citing workplace romance as the reason. Petraeus wrote in the letter to his staff that he was going to the White House to ask President Obama "for personal reasons" to resign. "After being married for more than 37 years, I showed extremely poor judgment by engaging in an extramarital affair," Petraeus wrote in his letter. "Such behavior is unacceptable, both as a husband and as a leader of an organization such as ours." Petraeus's wife is Holly Petraeus whom he met when he was a cadet at the U.S. Military Academy at West Point.

Just hours after Petraeus resigned, the CEO of Lockheed Martin Corp., Chris Kubasik, was fired for having a "close personal relationship" with a subordinate. The company said the CEO's "improper conduct" violated the company's code of ethics. Kubasik, who is married, had his relationship revealed by a whistle-blower, at which point Lockheed hired external investigators to examine the allegation. Lockheed manufactures numerous military products, so the firm is perhaps more prudent than most in monitoring relationships because spying is a concern within defense firms.

Workplace romance is an intimate relationship between two truly consenting employees, as opposed to *sexual harassment,* which the Equal Employment Opportunity Commission (EEOC) defines broadly as unwelcome sexual advances, requests for sexual favors, and other verbal or physical conduct of a sexual nature. Sexual harassment (and discrimination) is illegal, unethical, and detrimental to any organization and can result in expensive lawsuits, lower morale, and reduced productivity.

Workplace romance between two consenting employees simply happens, so the question is generally not whether to allow the practice, and or even how to prevent it, but rather how best to manage the phenomena. An organization probably should not strictly forbid workplace romance because such a policy could be construed as an invasion of privacy, overbearing, or unnecessary. Some romances actually improve work performance, adding a dynamism and energy that translates into enhanced morale, communication, creativity, and productivity.[9]

However, it is important to note that workplace romance can be detrimental to workplace morale and productivity, for a number of reasons that include:

1. Favoritism complaints can arise.
2. Confidentiality of records can be breached.
3. Reduced quality and quantity of work can become a problem.
4. Personal arguments can lead to work arguments.
5. Whispering secrets can lead to tensions and hostilities among coworkers.
6. Sexual harassment (or discrimination) charges may ensue, either by the involved female or a third party.
7. Conflicts of interest can arise, especially when well being of the partner trumps well-being of the company.

In some states, such as California, managers can be held personally liable for damages that arise from workplace romance. Organizations should establish guidelines or policies that address workplace romance, for at least six reasons:

1. Guidelines can enable the firm to better defend itself against and avoid sexual harassment or discrimination charges.
2. Guidelines can specify reasons (such as the seven listed previously) why workplace romance may not be a good idea.
3. Guidelines can specify resultant penalties for romancing partners if problems arise.
4. Guidelines can promote a professional and fair work atmosphere.
5. Guidelines can help assure compliance with federal, state, and local laws and recent court cases.
6. Lack of any guidelines sends a lackadaisical message throughout the firm.

Workplace romance guidelines should apply to all employees at all levels of the firm and should specify certain situations in which affairs are especially discouraged, such as supervisor and subordinate. Company guidelines or policies in general should discourage workplace romance because "the downside risks generally exceed the upside benefits" for the firm. Best Buy CEO Brian Dunn recently resigned when directors learned of his inappropriate relationship with a young subordinate, a violation of that company's code of ethics. Based in Fremont, California, IGate Corp., fired its CEO, Phaneesh Murthy, in May 2013 for allegedly failing to report a workplace romance relationship that turned into a sexual harassment issue with a subordinate.

Flirting is a step down from workplace romance, but a new full-page *Wall Street Journal* article titled "The New Rules of Flirting" reveal the do's and don'ts of flirting.[10] Flirting is defined by researchers as "romantic behavior that is ambiguous and goal oriented," or said differently, "ambiguous behavior with potential sexual or romantic overtones that is goal-oriented." A few flirting rules given in the article are:

1. Do not flirt with someone you know is looking for a relationship if you are not interested in a new relationship.
2. Do flirt within a relationship that you want to strengthen.
3. Do not flirt to make your partner jealous because this is manipulative behavior.
4. Flirting between power differences, such as boss and employee or professor and student, usually leads to trouble, as many defendants in sexual-harassment complaints know.
5. Do not make physical contact with the person you are flirting with, unless it is within a desired relationship.

Among colleges and universities, the federal Office of Civil Rights (OCR) has stepped up its investigation of sexual harassment cases brought forward by female students against professors. Yale University has been in the news in this regard as well as numerous other institutions currently being investigated. At no charge to the student, the OCR will investigate a female student's claim if evidence is compelling.

A *Wall Street Journal* article recapped U.S. standards regarding boss and subordinate love affairs at work.[11] Only 5 percent of all firms sampled had no restrictions on such relationships; 80 percent of firms have policies that prohibit relationships between a supervisor and a subordinate. Only 4 percent of firms strictly prohibited such relationships, but 39 percent of firms had policies that required individuals to inform their supervisors whenever a romantic relationship begins with a coworker. Only 24 percent of firms required the two persons to be in different departments.

In Europe, romantic relationships at work are largely viewed as private matters and most firms have no policies on the practice. However, European firms are increasingly adopting explicit, U.S.-style sexual harassment laws. The U.S. military strictly bans officers from dating or having sexual relationships with enlistees. At the World Bank, sexual relations between a supervisor and an employee are considered "a de facto conflict of interest which must be resolved to avoid favoritism." World Bank president Paul Wolfowitz recently was forced to resign as a result of a relationship he had with a bank staff person.

A recent *Bloomberg Businessweek* article reports that in the sluggish job market, employees are filing sexual harassment complaints as a way to further their own job security. Many of these filings are increasingly third-party individuals not even directly involved in the relationship but alleging their own job was impacted. Largely the result of the rise of third-party discrimination claims, the EEOC recovers about $500 million on behalf of office romance victims.[12]

Social Responsibility

Fortune annually lists the most admired and least admired companies globally on social responsibility. *Fortune*'s 2012 top three most admired socially responsible companies are GDF Suez, Marquard & Bahls, and RWE. The top three least admired companies are China Railway Group, China Railway Construction, and China State Construction Engineering.[13] Chinese firms dominate the least admired list.

Walmart was socially responsible in the wake of the earthquake and tsunami that devastated Japan in 2011. Following the catastrophe, Walmart quickly mobilized a local relief effort to deliver supplies such as water and flashlights to survivors. Walmart has a history of helping immensely in times of crisis—the retailer was also able to get supplies to people who needed them following Hurricane Katrina.

Some strategists agree with Ralph Nader, who proclaims that organizations have tremendous social obligations. Nader points out, for example, that ExxonMobil has more assets than most countries, and because of this, such firms have an obligation to help society cure its many ills. Other people, however, agree with the economist Milton Friedman, who asserts that organizations have no obligation to do any more for society than is legally required. Friedman may contend that it is irresponsible for a firm to give monies to charity.

Do you agree more with Nader or Friedman? Surely we can all agree that the first social responsibility of any business must be to make enough profit to cover the costs of the future because if this is not achieved, no other social responsibility can be met. Indeed, no social need can be met by the firm if the firm fails.

Strategists should examine social problems in terms of potential costs and benefits to the firm and focus on social issues that could benefit the firm most. For example, should a firm avoid laying off employees so as to protect the employees' livelihood, when that decision may force the firm to liquidate?

Social Policy

The term **social policy** embraces managerial philosophy and thinking at the highest level of the firm, which is why the topic is covered in this textbook. Social policy concerns what responsibilities the firm has to employees, consumers, environmentalists, minorities, communities, shareholders, and other groups. After decades of debate, many firms still struggle to determine appropriate social policies.

The impact of society on business and vice versa is becoming more pronounced each year. Corporate social policy should be designed and articulated during strategy formulation, set and administered during strategy implementation, and reaffirmed or changed during strategy evaluation.[14]

Firms should strive to engage in social activities that have economic benefits. Merck & Co. once developed the drug ivermectin for treating river blindness, a disease caused by a fly-borne parasitic worm endemic in poor tropical areas of Africa, the Middle East, and Latin America. In an unprecedented gesture that reflected its corporate commitment to social responsibility, Merck then made ivermectin available at no cost to medical personnel throughout the world. Merck's action highlights the dilemma of orphan drugs, which offer pharmaceutical companies no economic incentive for profitable development and distribution. Merck did however garner substantial goodwill among its stakeholders for its actions.

Social Policies on Retirement

Some countries around the world are facing severe workforce shortages associated with their aging populations. The percentage of persons age 65 or older exceeds 20 percent in Japan, Italy, and Germany—and will reach 20 percent in 2018 in France. In 2036, the percentage of persons age 65 or older will reach 20 percent in the USA and China. Unlike the USA, Japan is reluctant to rely on large-scale immigration to bolster its workforce. Instead, Japan provides incentives for its elderly to work until ages 65 to 75. Western European countries are doing the opposite, providing incentives for its elderly to retire at ages 55 to 60. The International Labor Organization says 71 percent of Japanese men ages 60 to 64 work, compared to 57 percent of American men and just 17 percent of French men in the same age group.

Sachiko Ichioka, a typical 67-year-old man in Japan, says, "I want to work as long as I'm healthy. The extra money means I can go on trips, and I'm not a burden on my children." Better diet and health care have raised Japan's life expectancy now to 82, the highest in the world. Japanese women are having on average only 1.28 children compared to 2.04 in the USA. Keeping the elderly at work, coupled with reversing the old-fashioned trend of keeping women at home, are Japan's two key remedies for sustaining its workforce in factories and businesses. This prescription for dealing with problems associated with an aging society should be considered by many countries around the world. The Japanese government is phasing in a shift from age 60 to age 65 as the date when a person may begin receiving a pension, and premiums paid by Japanese employees are rising while payouts are falling. Unlike the USA, Japan has no law against discrimination based on age.

Worker productivity increases in Japan are not able to offset declines in number of workers, thus resulting in a decline in overall economic production. Like many countries, Japan does not view immigration as a good way to solve this problem. Japan's shrinking workforce has become such a concern that the government just recently allowed an unspecified number of Indonesian and Filipino nurses and caregivers to work in Japan for two years. The number of working-age

TABLE 10-2 The Best and Worst Companies Globally in Regard to Being Socially Responsible

The Best	The Worst
1. GDF Suez	1. China Railway Group
2. Marquard & Bahls	2. China Railway Construction
3. RWE	3. China State Construction Engineering
4. Altria Group	4. China South Industries Group
5. Starbucks	5. China FAW Group
6. Walt Disney	6. Aviation Industry Corporation of China
7. United Natural Foods	7. Dongfeng Motor
8. Sealed Air	8. MF Global Holdings
9. Chevron	9. China North Industries
10. Whole Foods Market	10. Hon Hai Precision Industry

Sources: Based on http://money.cnn.com/magazines/fortune/most-admired/2012/best_worst/best4.html and http://money.cnn.com/magazines/fortune/most-admired/2012/best_worst/worst4.html.

Japanese—those between ages 15 and 64—is projected to shrink to 70 million by 2030. Using foreign workers is known as *gaikokujin roudousha* in Japanese. Many Filipinos have recently been hired now to work in agriculture and factories throughout Japan.

Fortune's best and worst companies globally in regard to being socially responsible in 2012 are listed in Table 10-2. Note that the 10 worst companies are all based in China.

Environmental Sustainability

In October of every year, three world renowned corporate sustainability rankings are published: (1) the Dow Jones Sustainability Index (DJSI), (2) the Carbon Disclosure Project, and (3) *Newsweek's* "Green" rankings. Regarding the DJSI, some notable companies that were added to the DJSI 2012 Index for being especially sustainable were Microsoft, Target, Hewlett-Packard, and the Canadian National Railway Company. Some notable companies that were kicked out of the 2012 DJSI sustainability rankings were GlaxoSmithKline PLC, Duke Energy, IBM, United Technologies, and Dell.

Launched in 1999, DJSI annually reveals the best corporations in the world in various industries in terms of sustainability. A few of the number-1 (best) companies in the world on sustainability in the DJSI 2012 in their respective industries were: BMW, Unilever NV, Roche Holding AG, Siemens AG, Alcatel-Lucent SA, and Air France-KLM.

The strategies of both companies and countries are increasingly scrutinized and evaluated from a natural environment perspective. Companies such as Walmart now monitor not only the price its vendors offer for products, but also how those products are made in terms of environmental practices, as well as safety and infrastructure soundness particularly of Southeast Asia factories. A growing number of business schools offer separate courses and even a concentration in environmental management.

Businesses must not exploit and decimate the natural environment. Mark Starik at George Washington University says, "Halting and reversing worldwide ecological destruction and deterioration is a strategic issue that needs immediate and substantive attention by all businesses and managers. According to the International Standards Organization (ISO), the word **environment** is defined as "surroundings in which an organization operates, including air, water, land, natural resources, flora, fauna, humans, and their interrelation." This chapter illustrates how many firms are gaining competitive advantage by being good stewards of the natural environment.

Employees, consumers, governments, and society are especially resentful of firms that harm rather than protect the natural environment. Conversely people today are especially appreciative of firms that conduct operations in a way that mends, conserves, and preserves the natural environment. Consumer interest in businesses preserving nature's ecological balance and fostering a clean, healthy environment is high.

No business wants a reputation as being a polluter. A bad sustainability record will hurt the firm in the market, jeopardize its standing in the community, and invite scrutiny by regulators, investors, and environmentalists. Governments increasingly require businesses to behave responsibly and require, for example, that businesses publicly report the pollutants and wastes their facilities produce.

In terms of megawatts of wind power generated by various states in the United States, Iowa's 2,791 recently overtook California's 2,517, but Texas's 7,118 megawatts dwarfs all other states. Minnesota also is making substantial progress in wind power generation. New Jersey recently outfitted 200,000 utility poles with solar panels, which made it the nation's second-largest producer of solar energy behind California. New Jersey is also adding solar panels to corporate rooftops. The state's $514 million solar program doubled its solar capacity to 160 megawatts in 2013. The state's goal is to obtain 3 percent of its electricity from the sun and 12 percent from offshore wind by 2020.

What Is a Sustainability Report?

A sustainability report reveals a firm's operations impact the natural environment. This document discloses to shareholders information about the firm's labor practices, product sourcing, energy efficiency, environmental impact, and business ethics practices.

It is good business for a company to provide a sustainability report annually to the public. With 60,000 suppliers and more than $350 billion in annual sales, Walmart works with its suppliers to make sure they provide such reports. Many firms use the Walmart sustainability report as a benchmark, guideline, and model to follow in preparing their own report.

The Global Reporting Initiative recently issued a set of detailed reporting guidelines specifying what information should go into sustainability reports. The proxy advisory firm Institutional Shareholder Services reports that an increasing number of shareholder groups are pushing firms to provide sustainability information annually. Two companies that released sustainability reports for the first time in 2012 were Hyatt Hotels & Resorts and Las Vegas Sands Corporation. Rival firm Hilton Worldwide does not have a stand-alone sustainability report, but Marriott and Wyndham Worldwide do release annual sustainability reports and of late revealed excellent reductions in energy, water, waste, and carbon dioxide emissions.

Walmart encourages and expects its 1.35 million U.S. employees to adopt what it calls Personal Sustainability Projects, which include such measures as organizing weight-loss or smoking-cessation support groups, biking to work, or starting recycling programs. Employee wellness can be a part of sustainability.

Walmart is installing solar panels on its stores in California and Hawaii, providing as much as 30 percent of the power in some stores. It may go national with solar power if this test works well. Also moving to solar energy is department-store chain Kohl's Corp., which is converting 64 of its 80 California stores to use solar power. There are big subsidies for solar installations in some states.

Home Depot, the world's second largest retailer behind Walmart, recently more than doubled its offering of environmentally friendly products such as all-natural insect repellent. Home Depot has made it much easier for consumers to find its organic products by using special labels similar to Timberland's (the outdoor company) Green Index tags.

Managers and employees of firms must be careful not to become scapegoats blamed for company environmental wrongdoings. Harming the natural environment can be unethical, illegal, and costly. When organizations today face criminal charges for polluting the environment, they increasingly turn on their managers and employees to win leniency. Employee firings and demotions are becoming common in pollution-related legal suits. Managers were fired at Darling International, Inc., and Niagara Mohawk Power Corporation for being indirectly responsible for their firms polluting water. Managers and employees today must be careful not to ignore, conceal, or disregard a pollution problem, or they may find themselves personally liable.

Lack of Standards Changing

A few years ago, firms could get away with placing "green" terminology on their products and labels using such terms as *organic*, *green*, *safe*, *earth-friendly*, *nontoxic*, or *natural* because there were no legal or generally accepted definitions. Today, however, these terms carry much more specific connotations and expectations. Uniform standards defining environmentally responsible company actions are rapidly being incorporated into the legal landscape. It has become more and more difficult for firms to make "green" claims when their actions are not substantive, comprehensive, or even true. Lack of standards once made consumers cynical about corporate environmental claims, but those claims today are increasingly being challenged in courts. Joel Makower says, "One of the main reasons to truly become a green firm is for your employees. They're the first group that needs assurance than any claims you make hold water."[15]

Around the world, political and corporate leaders now realize that the "business green" topic will not go away and in fact is gaining ground rapidly. Strategically, companies more than ever must demonstrate to their customers and stakeholders that their green efforts are substantive and set the firm apart from competitors. A firm's performance facts and figures must back up their rhetoric and be consistent with sustainability standards.

Managing Environmental Affairs in the Firm

The ecological challenge facing all organizations requires managers to formulate strategies that preserve and conserve natural resources and control pollution. Special natural environment issues include ozone depletion, global warming, depletion of rain forests, destruction of animal habitats, protecting endangered species, developing biodegradable products and packages, waste management, clean air, clean water, erosion, destruction of natural resources, and pollution control. Firms increasingly are developing green product lines that are biodegradable or are made from recycled products. Green products sell well.

Managing as if "health of the planet" matters requires an understanding of how international trade, competitiveness, and global resources are connected. Managing environmental affairs can no longer be simply a technical function performed by specialists in a firm; more emphasis must be placed on developing an environmental perspective among all employees and managers of the firm. Many companies are moving environmental affairs from the staff side of the organization to the line side, thus making the corporate environmental group report directly to the chief operating officer. Firms that manage environmental affairs will enhance relations with consumers, regulators, vendors, and other industry players, substantially improving their prospects of success.

Environmental strategies could include developing or acquiring green businesses, divesting or altering environment-damaging businesses, striving to become a low-cost producer through waste minimization and energy conservation, and pursuing a differentiation strategy through green-product features. In addition, firms could include an environmental representative on their board of directors, conduct regular environmental audits, implement bonuses for favorable environmental results, become involved in environmental issues and programs, incorporate environmental values in mission statements, establish environmentally oriented objectives, acquire environmental skills, and provide environmental training programs for company employees and managers.

Preserving the environment should be a permanent part of doing business for the following reasons:

1. Consumer demand for environmentally safe products and packages is high.
2. Public opinion demanding that firms conduct business in ways that preserve the natural environment is strong.
3. Environmental advocacy groups now have more than 20 million Americans as members.
4. Federal and state environmental regulations are changing rapidly and becoming more complex.
5. More lenders are examining the environmental liabilities of businesses seeking loans.
6. Many consumers, suppliers, distributors, and investors shun doing business with environmentally weak firms.
7. Liability suits and fines against firms having environmental problems are on the rise.

More firms are becoming environmentally proactive—doing more than the bare minimum to develop and implement strategies that preserve the environment. The old undesirable alternative of being environmentally reactive—changing practices only when forced to do so by law or consumer pressure—more often today leads to high cleanup costs, liability suits, reduced market share, reduced customer loyalty, and higher medical costs. In contrast, a proactive policy views environmental pressures as opportunities and includes such actions as developing green products and packages, conserving energy, reducing waste, recycling, and creating a corporate culture that is environmentally sensitive.

ISO 14000/14001 Certification

Based in Geneva, Switzerland, the International Organization for Standardization (ISO) is a network of the national standards institutes of 147 countries, with one member per country. ISO is the world's largest developer of sustainability standards. Widely accepted all over the world, ISO standards are voluntary because ISO has no legal authority to enforce their implementation. ISO itself does not regulate or legislate.

Governmental agencies in various countries, such as the Environmental Protection Agency (EPA) in the USA, have adopted ISO standards as part of their regulatory framework, and the standards are the basis of much legislation. Adoptions are sovereign decisions by the regulatory authorities, governments, or companies concerned.

ISO 14000 refers to a series of voluntary standards in the environmental field. The ISO 14000 family of standards concerns the extent to which a firm minimizes harmful effects on the environment caused by its activities and continually monitors and improves its own environmental performance. Included in the ISO 14000 series are the ISO 14001 standards in fields such as environmental auditing, environmental performance evaluation, environmental labeling, and life-cycle assessment.

ISO 14001 is a set of standards adopted by thousands of firms worldwide to certify to their constituencies that they are conducting business in an environmentally friendly manner. ISO 14001 standards offer a universal technical standard for environmental compliance that more and more firms are requiring not only of themselves but also of their suppliers and distributors.

The ISO 14001 standard requires that a community or organization put in place and implement a series of practices and procedures that, when taken together, result in an **environmental management system (EMS)**. ISO 14001 is not a technical standard and as such does not in any way replace technical requirements embodied in statutes or regulations. It also does not set prescribed standards of performance for organizations. Not being certified with ISO 14001 can be a strategic disadvantage for towns, counties, and companies because people today expect organizations to minimize or, even better, to eliminate environmental harm they cause.[16] The major requirements of an EMS under ISO 14001 include the following:

- Show commitments to prevention of pollution, continual improvement in overall environmental performance, and compliance with all applicable statutory and regulatory requirements.
- Identify all aspects of the organization's activities, products, and services that could have a significant impact on the environment, including those that are not regulated.
- Set performance objectives and targets for the management system that link back to three policies: (1) prevention of pollution, (2) continual improvement, and (3) compliance.
- Meet environmental objectives that include training employees, establishing work instructions and practices, and establishing the actual metrics by which the objectives and targets will be measured.
- Conduct an audit operation of the EMS.
- Take corrective actions when deviations from the EMS occur.

Wildlife

In mid-2012, South Korea announced plans to resume whaling despite a 1986 moratorium on commercial whaling. Many countries are upset at these plans, including Australia where the Prime Minister Julia Gillard said: "We are completely opposed to whaling; there's no excuse for scientific whaling." Only a few countries, such as Norway, Japan, and Russia, favor and engage in commercial whaling.

Fairmont Hotels & Resorts in 2012 instituted a policy removing shark fin soup from its menu, following the lead of Shangri-La Hotels & Resorts. Even the Chinese government has recently stopped serving shark fin soup at most official banquets. Studies reveal that many shark species have been reduced 90 percent in recent decades, largely by overfishing for shark fins. The demand for shark fin soup in Asia is arguably the major cause of the alarming decline of blue sharks off the British coast and much of the Atlantic. Scientists from the United Kingdom and Portugal recently tracked sharks and confirm that sharks are being deliberately targeted by fishermen with long-line fishing that can stretch as long as 100 km. The fins are cut off and the bodies discarded onsite. Blue sharks are the most frequently caught shark species, with drastic population declines. Many shark species are now classified as "near-threatened" on the International Union for Conservation of Nature (IUCN) Red List.[17]

The European Parliament in late 2012 voted with an overwhelming 566–47 margin to force all boats in EU waters and EU-registered boats around the world to land sharks with their fins attached and prove the animal had not been thrown back. Uta Bellion of the Pew Environment Group said: "the parliament's vote is a major milestone in ending the wasteful practice of shark finning." EU fisheries chief Maria Damanaki said the law would "ease control and help us eradicate shark finning," which she called cruel to the animals and a vast waste of resources. Sharks are vulnerable to over-exploitation because they mature late and give birth to small numbers of young at a time. Shark fins are in high demand in Asia for soup and alleged cures. Damanaki said some 75 million sharks a year are killed for the use of their fins only, with the EU being the biggest exporter. As a result, the hammerhead shark is as good as extinct in the Mediterranean Sea. Damanaki has compared shark finning to killing elephants only for their tusks.

Arctic sea ice shrank to a record low of 1.32 million square miles (3.41 million square km) in late 2012 according to the National Oceanic and Atmospheric Agency. However, polar bears' designation as a threatened species is being challenged in a U.S. appeals court. A decision is expected in 2013. Alaska and oil companies have argued that Endangered Species Act protections for polar bears diminish opportunities for Alaska energy development. The state has said in its appeals court filing that bears have survived previous warming periods and most populations have grown or remained stable despite shrinkage of ice. The case is *Safari Club International et al v. Ken Salazar et al and Center for Biological Diversity et al*, No. 11-5219.

According to the Convention on the International Trade in Endangered Species (CITES), more than 25,000 elephants are killed each year for their ivory—even though international trade in ivory has been outlawed since 1989.

A recent *Wall Street Journal* article titled "America Gone Wild" talks about how wildlife populations in the USA have experienced an "astonishing resurgence."[18] A drawback of the resurgence is that the total cost of wildlife damage to U.S. crops, landscaping, and infrastructure now exceeds $28 billion a year, including $1.5 billion from deer-vehicle crashes alone.

Solar Power

The Solar Energy Industries Association reported in late 2012 that the USA is on pace to install as much solar power in 2012 as it did in the prior eleven put together, at least 2,500 megawatts, the equivalent of more than two nuclear-power plants. GTM Research says the U.S. solar-power industry grew 71 percent in 2012 and will grow 20 to 40 percent annually through 2016. To cut greenhouse-gas emissions and fight climate change, states such as California have created subsidies for solar power developers and requirements for utilities to buy solar power. China supplies nearly half of the solar panels used globally but two leading U.S. suppliers of solar panels are Solarcity, which has more than 2,000 employees, and Sunrun Inc. Thousands of companies are looking into install solar panels as part of their sustainability efforts.

Table 10-3 reveals the impact that bad environmental policies have on two of nature's many ecosystems.

TABLE 10-3   Songbirds and Coral Reefs Need Help

Songbirds

Be a good steward of the natural environment to save our songbirds. Bluebirds are one of 76 songbird species in the USA that have dramatically declined in numbers in the last two decades. Not all birds are considered songbirds, and why birds sing is not clear. Some scientists say they sing when calling for mates or warning of danger, but many scientists now contend that birds sing for sheer pleasure. Songbirds include chickadees, orioles, swallows, mockingbirds, warblers, sparrows, vireos, and the wood thrush. "These birds are telling us there's a problem, something's out of balance in our environment," says Jeff Wells, bird conservation director for the National Audubon Society. Songbirds may be telling us that their air or water is too dirty or that we are destroying too much of their habitat. People collect Picasso paintings and save historic buildings. "Songbirds are part of our natural heritage. Why should we be willing to watch songbirds destroyed any more than allowing a great work of art to be destroyed?" asks Wells. Whatever message songbirds are singing to us today about their natural environment, the message is becoming less and less heard nationwide. Listen when you go outside today. Each of us as individuals, companies, states, and countries should do what we reasonably can to help improve the natural environment for songbirds.[19] A recent study concludes that 67 of the 800 bird species in the USA are endangered, and another 184 species are designated of "conservation concern." The birds of Hawaii are in the greatest peril.

Coral Reefs

Be a good steward of the natural environment to save our coral reefs. The ocean covers more than 71 percent of the earth. The destructive effect of commercial fishing on ocean habitats coupled with increasing pollution runoff into the ocean and global warming of the ocean have decimated fisheries, marine life, and coral reefs around the world. The unfortunate consequence of fishing over the last century has been overfishing, with the principal reasons being politics and greed. Trawl fishing with nets destroys coral reefs and has been compared to catching squirrels by cutting down forests because bottom nets scour and destroy vast areas of the ocean. The great proportion of marine life caught in a trawl is "by-catch" juvenile fish and other life that are killed and discarded. Warming of the ocean as a result of carbon dioxide emissions also kills thousands of acres of coral reefs annually. The total area of fully protected marine habitats in the USA is only about 50 square miles, compared to some 93 million acres of national wildlife refuges and national parks on the nation's land. A healthy ocean is vital to the economic and social future of the nation—and, indeed, all countries of the world. Everything we do on land ends up in the ocean, so we all must become better stewards of this last frontier on earth to sustain human survival and the quality of life.[20]

Special Note to Students

No company or individual wants to do business with someone who is unethical or is insensitive to natural environment concerns. It is no longer just cool to be environmentally proactive, it is expected, and in many respects is the law. Firms are being compared to rival firms every day on sustainability and ethics behavior, actually every minute on Facebook, Twitter, Myspace, LinkedIn, and YouTube. Issues presented in this chapter therefore comprise a competitive advantage or disadvantage for all organizations. Thus, you should include in your case analysis recommendations for your firm to exceed stakeholder expectations on ethics, sustainability, and social responsibility. Make comparisons to rival firms to show how your firm can gain or sustain competitive advantage on these issues. Reveal suggestions for the firm to be a good corporate citizen and promote that for competitive advantage. Be mindful that the first responsibility of any business is to stay in business, so use cost/benefit analysis as needed to present your recommendations effectively.

Conclusion

In a final analysis, ethical standards come out of history and heritage. Our predecessors have left us with an ethical foundation to build on. Even the legendary football coach Vince Lombardi knew that some things were worth more than winning, and he required his players to have three kinds of loyalty: to God, to their families, and to the Green Bay Packers, "in that order." Employees, customers, and shareholders have become less and less tolerant of business ethics violations in firms, and more and more appreciative of model ethical firms. Information-sharing across the Internet increasingly reveals such model firms versus irresponsible firms.

Consumers across the country and around the world appreciate firms that do more than is legally required to be socially responsible. But staying in business while adhering to all laws and regulations must be a primary objective of any business. One of the best ways to be socially responsible is for the firm to proactively conserve and preserve the natural environment. For example, to develop a corporate sustainability report annually is not legally required, but such a report, based on concrete actions, goes a long way toward assuring stakeholders that the firm is worthy of their support. Business ethics, social responsibility, and environmental sustainability are interrelated and key strategic issues facing all organizations.

MyManagementLab®

Go to **mymanagementlab.com** to complete the problems marked with this icon ⭐.

Key Terms and Concepts

bribe (p. 308)
bribery (p. 308)
business ethics (p. 305)
code of business ethics (p. 306)
environment (p. 313)
environmental management system (EMS) (p. 316)
ISO 14000 (p. 316)

ISO 14001 (p. 316)
sexual harrassment (p. 310)
social policy (p. 312)
social responsibility (p. 304)
sustainability (p. 304)
whistle-blowing (p. 307)
workplace romance (p. 310)

Issues for Review and Discussion

⭐ **10-1.** Discuss the ethics of workplace romance.

10-2. Explain why concern for wildlife is a strategic issue for firms.

10-3. Explain why whistle-blower payouts by the federal government to informants are becoming more and more common.

10-4. Compare and contrast the British Bribery Law with the U.S. bribery law.

10-5. Compare procedures in the corporate world versus a university setting in terms of how sexual harassment complaints are investigated outside the organization.

10-6. Compare the EEOC with the OCR in terms of mission and scope of operations.

10-7. AOL has 100 lobbyists on its payroll and spent about $20 million on lobbying in Washington, DC in 2013. Is this ethical?

10-8. If you owned a small business, would you develop a code of business conduct? If yes, what variables would you include? If no, how would you ensure that ethical business standards were being followed by your employees?

⭐ **10-9.** What do you feel is the relationship between personal ethics and business ethics? Are they or should they be the same?

10-10. How can firms best ensure that their code of business ethics is read, understood, believed, remembered, and acted on, rather than ignored?

10-11. Why is it important *not* to view the concept of whistle-blowing as "tattle-telling" or "ratting" on another employee?

10-12. List six desired results of "ethics training programs" in terms of recommended business ethics policies and procedures in the firm.

⭐ **10-13.** Discuss bribery. Would actions such as politicians adding earmarks in legislation or pharmaceutical salespersons giving away drugs to physicians constitute bribery? Identify three business activities that would constitute bribery and three actions that would not.

10-14. How could a strategist's attitude toward social responsibility affect a firm's strategy? On a 1-to-10 scale ranging from Nader's view to Friedman's view, what is your attitude toward social responsibility?

10-15. How do social policies on retirement differ in various countries around the world?

10-16. Firms should formulate and implement strategies from an environmental perspective. List eight ways firms can do this.

10-17. Discuss the major requirements of an EMS under ISO 14001.

MyManagementLab®

Go to **mymanagementlab.com** for Auto-graded writing questions as well as the following Assisted-graded writing questions:

10-18. Firms should formulate and implement strategies from an environmental perspective. List eight ways firms can do this.

10-19. Discuss the major requirements of an EMS under ISO 14001.

10-20. Mymanagementlab Only—comprehensive writing assignment for this chapter.

Current Readings

Aguinis, Herman and Ante Glavas. "What We Know and Don't Know About Corporate Social Responsibility: A Review and Research Agenda." *Journal of Management* 38, no. 4 (July 2012): 932.

Barnett, Michael L., and Robert M. Salomon. "Does it pay to be really good? Addressing the shape of the relationship between social and financial performance." *Strategic Management Journal* 33, no. 11 (November 2012): 1304–1320.

Fremeth, Adam R., and Brian K. Richter. "Profiting from Environmental Regulatory Uncertainty: Integrated Strategies for Competitive Advantage." *California Management Review* 54, no. 1 (Fall 2011): 145–165.

Lange, Donald, and Nathan T. Washburn. "Understanding Attributions of Corporate Social Irresponsibility." *The Academy of Management Review 37*, no. 2 (April 2012): 300.

Langvardt, Arlen W. "Business Ethics and Intellectual Property in the Global Marketplace." *Business Horizons* 55, no. 4 (July 2012): 325–327.

Karnani, Aneel. "Doing Well by Doing Good: The Grand Allusion." *California Management Review* 53, no. 2 (Winter 2011): 69–86.

Kleyn, Nicola, Russell Abratt, Kerry Chipp, and Michael Goldman. "Building a Strong Corporate Ethical Identify: Key Findings From Suppliers." *California Management Review* 54, no. 3 (Spring 2012): 61–76.

Langvardt, Arlen W. "Ethical Leadership and the Dual Roles of Examples." *Business Horizons* 55, no. 4 (July 2012): 373–384.

Mayer, David M., Karl Aquino, Rebecca L. Greenbaum, and Maribeth Kuenzi. "Who Displays Ethical Leadership, and Why Does It Matter? An Examination of Antecedents and Consequences of Ethical Leadership." *The Academy of Management Journal 55*, no. 1, February 2012): 151.

Peloza, John, Moritz Loock, James Cerruti, and Micahel Muyot. "Sustainability: How Stakeholder Perceptions Differ from Corporate Reality." *Inside CMR* 55, no. 1 (Fall 2012): 74.

Ramchander, Sanjay, Robert G. Schwebach, and KIM Staking. "The Informational Relevance of Corporate Social Responsibility: Evidence from DS400 Index Reconstitutions." *Strategic Management Journal* 33, no. 3 (March 2012): 303–314.

Rubin, Joel D. "Fairness in Business: Does it Matter, and What Does it Mean?" *Business Horizons* 55, no. 1 (January 2012): 11–15.

Schaubroeck, John M., Sean T. Hannah, Bruce J. Avolio, Steve W. J. Kozlowski, Robert G. Lord, Linda K. Treviño, Nikolaos Dimotakis, and Ann C. Peng. "Embedding Ethical Leadership within and across Organization Levels." *Academy of Management Journal* 55, no. 5 (October 2012): 1053.

Vallaster, Christine, Adam Lindgreen, and François Maon. "Strategically Leveraging Corporate Social Responsibility: A Corporate Branding Perspective." *California Management Review* 54, no. 3 (Spring 2012): 34–60.

Wang, Taiyuan, and Pratima Bansal. "Social Responsibility in New Ventures: Profiting from a Long-term Orientation." *Strategic Management Journal* 33, no. 10 (October 2012): 1135–1153.

Wong, Elaine M., Margaret E. Ormiston, and Philip E. Tetlock. "The Effects of Top Management Team Integrative Complexity and Decentralized Decision Making on Corporate Social Performance." *The Academy of Management Journal 54*, no. 6 (December 2011): 1207.

ASSURANCE OF LEARNING EXERCISES

EXERCISE 10A
How Does Your Municipality Compare to Others on Being Pollution-Safe?

Purpose

Sometimes it is difficult to know how safe a particular municipality or county is regarding industrial and agricultural pollutants. A website that provides consumers and businesses excellent information in this regard is http://scorecard.goodguide.com/. This type of information is often used in assessing where to locate new business operations.

Instructions

Go to http://scorecard.goodguide.com/. Put in your zip code. Print off the information available for your city or county regarding pollutants. Prepare a comparative analysis of your municipality versus state and national norms on pollution issues. Does your locale receive an A, B, C, D, or F?

EXERCISE 10B
Evaluate PepsiCo's Global Code of Conduct

Purpose

Different companies have different standards of business conduct. One way to evaluate a firm's standards is to compare company documents to a leading rival firm. A major rival firm for PepsiCo is Coca-Cola Company. PepsiCo has a 38-page Global Code of Conduct document posted on their corporate website. This exercise gives you practice comparing and evaluating standards of business conduct.

Instructions

Step 1   On a separate sheet of paper, list three aspects that you like most and three aspects that you like least about the PepsiCo statement.

Step 2   Explain why having a code of business ethics is not sufficient for ensuring ethical behavior in an organization. What other means are necessary to help ensure ethical behavior? Give the class an example of a breach of ethical conduct that you recall in your work experience.

EXERCISE 10C
Compare and Evaluate Sustainability Reports

Purpose

Sustainability reports are increasingly becoming expected or even required by business organizations. This exercise will give you practice comparing and evaluating sustainability reports. Coca-Cola's most recent sustainability report is found at http://www.thecoca-colacompany.com/sustainability-report/index.html. PepsiCo, at the http://www.pepsico.com/Purpose/Sustainability-Reporting.html website, prompts everyone to build their own sustainability report for their operations by clicking on various areas of sustainability. It appears that PepsiCo does not actually have an annual, single, published sustainability report. For purposes of this exercise however, focus on PepsiCo's Environmental Sustainability document.

Instructions

Step 1   Go to the two respective company websites and print off the two documents cited. Compare and contrast the documents. List three aspects of each document that you like most and three aspects that you like least about each company's sustainability report. Which company's document do you like best? Why do you think it is best?

Step 2   Explain why having a sustainability report is not sufficient for ensuring excellent natural environment behavior. What other means besides the document itself are needed to assure ethical behavior in regard to preserving the natural environment?

Step 3   Prepare a two-page executive summary that provides an overview of the PepsiCo document versus the Coca-Cola Company document as well as your assessment of the strengths and weaknesses of each document.

EXERCISE 10D
The Ethics of Spying on Competitors

Purpose

This exercise gives you an opportunity to discuss in class ethical and legal issues related to methods being used by many companies to spy on competing firms. Gathering and using information about competitors is an area of strategic management that Japanese firms do more proficiently than U.S. firms.

Instructions

On a separate sheet of paper, number from 1 to 18. For the 18 spying activities listed as follows, indicate whether or not you believe the activity is ethical or unethical and legal or illegal. Place either an *E* for ethical or *U* for unethical, and either an *L* for legal or an *I* for illegal for each activity. Compare your answers to those of your classmates and discuss any differences.

1. Buying competitors' garbage
2. Dissecting competitors' products
3. Taking competitors' plant tours anonymously
4. Counting tractor-trailer trucks leaving competitors' loading bays
5. Studying aerial photographs of competitors' facilities
6. Analyzing competitors' labor contracts
7. Analyzing competitors' help-wanted ads
8. Quizzing customers and buyers about the sales of competitors' products
9. Infiltrating customers' and competitors' business operations
10. Quizzing suppliers about competitors' level of manufacturing
11. Using customers to buy out phony bids
12. Encouraging key customers to reveal competitive information
13. Quizzing competitors' former employees
14. Interviewing consultants who may have worked with competitors
15. Hiring key managers away from competitors
16. Conducting phony job interviews to get competitors' employees to reveal information
17. Sending engineers to trade meetings to quiz competitors' technical employees
18. Quizzing potential employees who worked for or with competitors

 EXERCISE 10E
Who Prepares a Sustainability Report?

Purpose

The purpose of this activity is to determine the nature and prevalence of Sustainability Reports among companies in your state.

Instructions

Visit the websites of at least five different large businesses in your area. Seek answers to the following questions. Follow up with a phone call(s) or actually visit the business if needed. Present your findings in a written report to your instructor.

1. Does your company prepare a sustainability report? If yes, please describe the nature and scope of the report.
2. Are environmental criteria included in the performance evaluation of managers? If yes, please specify the criteria.
3. Are environmental affairs more a technical function or a management function in your company?
4. Does your firm offer any environmental workshops for employees? If yes, please describe them.

Notes

1. http://www.usatoday.com/money/companies/management/story/2012-05-14/ceo-firings/54964476/1
2. Ibid.
3. Joann Greco, "Privacy—Whose Right Is It Anyhow?" *Journal of Business Strategy*, January–February 2001, 32.
4. Ashby Jones and JoAnn Lublin, "New Law Prompts Blowing Whistle," *Wall Street Journal*, November 1, 2010, B1.
5. Saul Gellerman, "Why 'Good' Managers Make Bad Ethical Choices," *Harvard Business Review* 64, no. 4 (July–August 1986): 88.
6. Peter Drucker, *Management: Tasks, Responsibilities, and Practices* (New York: Harper & Row, 1974), 462, 463.
7. www.wikipedia.org.

8. Joe Palazzolo and Christopher Matthews, "Bribery Law Do's and Don'ts," *Wall Street Journal* (November 15, 2012): B1.
9. http://www.businessknowhow.com/manage/romance.htm
10. Elizabeth Bernstein "The New Rules of Flirting," *Wall Street Journal* (11-13-12): D1.
11. Phred Dvorak, Bob Davis, and Louise Radnofsky, "Firms Confront Boss-Subordinate Love Affairs," *Wall Street Journal*, October 27, 2008, B5.
12. Spencer Morgan, "The End of the Office Affair," *Bloomberg Businessweek*, September 20–26, 2010, 74.
13. http://money.cnn.com/magazines/fortune/most-admired/2012/best_worst/best4.html and http://money.cnn.com/

magazines/fortune/most-admired/2012/best_worst/
worst4.html.

14. Archie Carroll and Frank Hoy, "Integrating Corporate
    Social Policy into Strategic Management," *Journal of
    Business Strategy* 4, no. 3 (Winter 1984): 57.

15. Kerry Hannon, "Businesses' Green Opportunities Are
    Wide, But Complex," *USA Today*, January 2, 2009, 5B.

16. Adapted from the www.iso14000.com website and the
    www.epa.gov website.

17. http://www.guardian.co.uk/environment/2012/mar/09/
    shark-fin-soup-blue-sharks-uk

18. Jim Sterba, "America Gone Wild," *Wall Street Journal*
    (11-8-12): p. C1.

19. Tom Brook, "Declining Numbers Mute Many Birds'
    Songs," *USA Today*, September 11, 2001, 4A.

20. John Ogden, "Maintaining Diversity in the Oceans,"
    Environment, April 2001, 29–36.

Source: wavebreakmedia/Shutterstock

MyManagementLab®

⭐ Improve Your Grade!

Over 10 million students improved their results using the Pearson MyLabs.
Visit **mymanagementlab.com** for simulations, tutorials, and end-of-chapter problems.

Global and International Issues

CHAPTER OBJECTIVES

After studying this chapter, you should be able to do the following:

1. Discuss the nature and implications of labor union membership across Europe.

2. Discuss income tax rates and practices across countries.

3. Explain the advantages and disadvantages of entering global markets.

4. Discuss protectionism as it impacts the world economy.

5. Explain when and why a firm (or industry) may need to become more or less global in nature to compete.

6. Discuss the global challenge facing U.S. firms.

7. Compare and contrast business culture in the United States with many other countries.

8. Describe how management style varies globally.

9. Discuss communication differences across countries.

10. Discuss Africa as the newest hotspot for business entry.

ASSURANCE OF LEARNING **EXERCISES**

The following exercises are found at the end of this chapter.

As illustrated in Figure 11-1 with white shading, global considerations impact virtually all strategic decisions. The boundaries of countries no longer can define the limits of our imaginations. To see and appreciate the world from the perspective of others has become a matter of survival for businesses. The underpinnings of strategic management hinge on managers gaining an understanding of competitors, markets, prices, suppliers, distributors, governments, creditors, shareholders, and customers worldwide. The price and quality of a firm's products and services must be competitive on a worldwide basis, not just on a local basis. Shareholders expect substantial revenue growth, so doing business globally is one of the best ways to achieve this end. As indicated in the boxed insert, Domino's is an example business that has grown dramatically with a well-conceived rollout of stores across the world.

The consulting firm A.T. Kearney reported in mid-2013 that the USA for the first time since 2001 has replaced China as the country with the highest prospects for foreign direct investment (FDI). Brazil is number 3, followed by Canada, India, Australia, Germany, United Kingdom (UK), Mexico, and Singapore. China's allure has dimmed lately due to rising wages, whereas the USA's surge in oil and gas production promises lower energy costs, coupled with high respect for human rights and freedom, and has led to renewed interest in the USA for FDI.

Exports of goods and services from the USA account for only 11 percent of U.S. gross domestic product, so the USA is still largely a domestic, continental economy. What happens inside the USA largely determines the strength of the economic recovery. In contrast, as a percent of gross domestic product (GDP), exports comprise 35.3 percent of the German economy, 24.5 percent of the Chinese economy, and 156 percent of the Singapore economy. Singapore's number is so high because they import oil and other products and then re-export them globally. A point here also is that the USA has substantial room for improvement in doing business globally based on the 11 percent exports to GDP number.

EXCELLENT **STRATEGIC MANAGEMENT** SHOWCASED

Domino's Pizza

The recognized world leader in pizza delivery, Domino's Pizza opened its first store in Nigeria in 2012. Eat 'N' Go Restaurant Group, the master franchisee for Domino's Pizza Nigeria, plans to become the premier food operator in Africa by bringing affordable food and drink and social responsibility to every market in which they open stores. "We are eager to deliver Domino's Pizza to the people of Nigeria, so that they can experience the delicious, quality pizza that is loved around the world," said Eric Andre, Eat 'N' Go Restaurant Group managing director.

Exceptionally well managed strategically, Domino's makes and sells pizza in more than 70 markets worldwide, with more than half of its global retail sales coming from international stores, making up more than a third of its adjusted operating income. India is the third largest market for Domino's Pizza after the USA and the UK and has a sales growth of more than 22 percent, hence it's no surprise that the pizza chain intends to establish a 100 new restaurants in India in the near future.

Founded in 1960, Domino's Pizza is the recognized world leader in pizza delivery. As of the second quarter of 2012, through its locally owned and operated franchises globally, Domino's operated a network of 9,924 franchised and company-owned stores in the USA and more than 70 countries. During the second quarter of 2012, Domino's had global retail sales of nearly $1.7 billion, comprised of more than $808 million domestically and nearly $865 million internationally. Domino's had global retail sales of more than $6.9 billion in 2011, comprised of more than $3.4 billion domestically and more than $3.5 billion internationally.

Domino's Pizza opened its 10,000th store somewhere in the world in late 2012 after opening its 9,999th store in Carlsbad, California, that featured a new-image "Pizza Theater" and a new product, Handmade Pan Pizza. The Pizza Theater design puts the art and skill of pizza-making at the front of the store, which also features a comfortable lobby, open area for viewing the pizza-making process, seating for in-store dining, the ability to order from an in-store kiosk, and track a carryout order electronically. "There is a standard out there for pan pizza that we realized could be better," said Patrick Doyle, Domino's Pizza president and CEO. "The reason most people buy a pan pizza is for the crust, and that key component should be fresh, never frozen. But what we think ultimately doesn't matter; I'd encourage customers to taste for themselves." Pan pizza makes up one in every five pizzas sold in the USA. In addition to launching its pan pizza in all of its nearly 5,000 stores in the USA, Domino's began a national television campaign offering medium two-topping Handmade Pan Pizzas for $7.99 each.

Source: Based on Bruce Horovitz, "Domino's to roll out pan pizza today," *USA Today* (September 24, 2012): 2B.

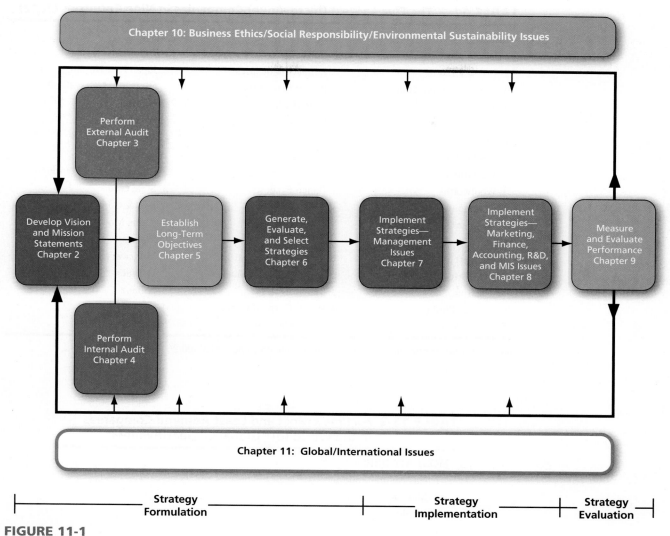

FIGURE 11-1

A Comprehensive Strategic-Management Model

Source: Fred R. David, "How Companies Define Their Mission," *Long Range Planning* 22, no. 3 (June 1988): 40.

A world market has emerged from what previously was a multitude of distinct national markets, and the climate for international business today is more favorable than in years past. Mass communication and high technology have created similar patterns of consumption in diverse cultures worldwide. This means that many companies may find it difficult to survive by relying solely on domestic markets.

It is no exaggeration that in an industry that is, or is rapidly becoming, global, the riskiest possible posture is to remain a domestic competitor. The domestic competitor will watch as more aggressive companies use this growth to capture economies of scale and learning. The domestic competitor will then be faced with an attack on domestic markets using different (and possibly superior) technology, product design, manufacturing, marketing approaches, and economies of scale.[1]

As a point of global reference, the 5 largest companies in nine different countries are listed in Table 11-1. The largest of all 45 companies listed is Walmart, headquartered in Bentonville, Arkansas, and employing 2.1 million people worldwide. *Fortune* annually determines the most admired and least admired companies in the world in terms of "global competitiveness." Table 11-2 reveals the rankings in early 2012.

TABLE 11-1 The Five Largest (by revenue) Companies in Nine Countries (2012)

Britain	India	Japan
1. BP	1. Indian Oil	1. Toyota Motor
2. HSBC Holdings	2. Reliance Industries	2. Japan Post Holdings
3. Lloyds Banking Group	3. Bharat Petroleum	3. Nippon TeleG & TeleP
4. Tesco	4. State Bank of India	4. Hitachi
5. Aviva	5. Hindustan Petroleum	5. Honda Motor
Australia	Brazil	China
1. BHP Billiton	1. Petrobras	1. Sinopec Group
2. Wesfarmers	2. Banco do Brasil	2. China National Petroleum
3. Woolworths	3. Banco Bradesco	3. State Grid
4. Commonwealth Bank	4. Vale	4. Ind. & Com. Bank of China
5. Westpac Banking	5. JBS	5. China Mobile Communi.
USA	Canada	Germany
1. Walmart Stores	1. Manulife Financial	1. Volkswagen
2. ExxonMobil	2. Royal Bank of Canada	2. Daimier
3. Chevron	3. Suncor Energy	3. Allianz
4. Conoco Phillips	4. Power Corp. of Canada	4. E. ON
5. Fannie Mae	5. George Weston	5. Siemens

Source: Based on http://money.cnn.com/magazines/fortune/global500/2011/countries/US.html.

TABLE 11-2 *Fortune's* Most and Least Admired Companies in the World for "Global Competitiveness"

MOST ADMIRED
1. Gas Natural Fenosa
2. McDonald's
3. Nestle
4. Apple
5. IBM
6. Procter & Gamble
7. Philip Morris International
8. Yum Brands
9. Caterpillar
10. RWE

LEAST ADMIRED
1. WellCare Health Plans
2. Universal American
3. Coventry Health Care
4. Amerigroup
5. China South Industries Group
6. Health Net
7. Cracker Barrel Old Country Store
8. Jack in the Box
9. China FAW Group
10. Dongfeng Motor

Source: Based on http://money.cnn.com/magazines/fortune/most-admired/2012/best_worst/best9.html and http://money.cnn.com/magazines/fortune/most-admired/2012/best_worst/worst9.html.

Multinational Organizations

Organizations that conduct business operations across national borders are called **international firms** or **multinational corporations.** The strategic-management process is conceptually the same for multinational firms as for purely domestic firms; however, the process is more complex for international firms as a result of more variables and relationships. The social, cultural, demographic, environmental, political, governmental, legal, technological, and competitive opportunities and threats that face a multinational corporation are almost limitless, and the number and complexity of these factors increase dramatically with the number of products produced and the number of geographic areas served.

More time and effort are required to identify and evaluate external trends and events in multinational corporations than in domestic corporations. Geographic distance, cultural and national differences, and variations in business practices often make communication between domestic headquarters and overseas operations difficult. Strategy implementation can be more difficult because different cultures have different norms, values, and work ethics.

For example, in 2013 Home Depot closed all seven of its remaining big-box stores in China after years of losses. That firm joins a growing list of retailers who stumbled in China by failing to consider local culture and customs. Historically cheap labor, coupled with apartment-based living in China, were two reasons why Home Depot, which entered China in 2006, never gained traction in that country. Mattel and Best Buy are other firms that faltered in China. Yum Brands, which owns Kentucky Fried Chicken and Pizza Hut, obtains almost 50 percent of its revenues from China, but the company's same-store sales in China dropped 4 percent in the fourth quarter of 2012, resulting primarily from thousands of new fast-food restaurants opening in China every year.

Even variables such as unemployment rates vary greatly across countries as indicated in Table 11.3. Note that Spain has the highest and Austria the lowest unemployment rate among the European countries listed. Unemployment rates are a good indicator of consumers' disposable income for purchasing all kinds of things, and the rates are a good indicator of a country's overall financial soundness and attractiveness for doing business.

In late 2012, France lost its triple-A rating by Moody's Investors Service after the S&P Ratings Services delivered a stinging critique of President Francois Hollande's attempts to turn the French economy around. Hollande is trying to shift 20 billion euros from payroll taxes to taxes on consumers, and he is pushing for 25 billion of new taxes to cut the country's deficit to 3 percent of GDP in 2013 from the expected 4.5 percent.

TABLE 11.3 Variations in Unemployment Rates Across Europe (2012)

Country	Unemployment Rate (%)
Spain	25.1
Greece	23.1
Portugal	15.7
Ireland	14.9
Euro-zone average	11.3
Italy	10.7
France	10.3
Finland	7.6
Belgium	7.2
Germany	5.5
Austria	4.5

Source: Based on Eurostat and Gabriele Steinhauser, "Euro Zone Considers Central Budget to Fix Cracks," *Wall Street Journal* (September 26, 2012): A12.

Multinational corporations (MNCs) face unique and diverse risks, such as expropriation of assets, currency losses through exchange rate fluctuations, unfavorable foreign court interpretations of contracts and agreements, social/political disturbances, import/export restrictions, tariffs, and trade barriers. Strategists in MNCs are often confronted with the need to be globally competitive and nationally responsive at the same time. With the rise in world commerce, government and regulatory bodies are more closely monitoring foreign business practices. The U.S. Foreign Corrupt Practices Act, for example, monitors business practices in many areas.

Before entering international markets, firms should scan relevant journals and patent reports, seek the advice of academic and research organizations, participate in international trade fairs, form partnerships, and conduct extensive research to broaden their contacts and diminish the risk of doing business in new markets. Firms can also offset some risks of doing business internationally by obtaining insurance from the U.S. government's Overseas Private Investment Corporation (OPIC).

Advantages and Disadvantages of International Operations

Firms have numerous reasons for formulating and implementing strategies that initiate, continue, or expand involvement in business operations across national borders. Perhaps the greatest advantage is that firms can gain new customers for their products and services, thus increasing revenues. Growth in revenues and profits is a common organizational objective and often an expectation of shareholders because it is a measure of organizational success.

Potential advantages to initiating, continuing, or expanding international operations are as follows:

1. Firms can gain new customers for their products.
2. Foreign operations can absorb excess capacity, reduce unit costs, and spread economic risks over a wider number of markets.
3. Foreign operations can allow firms to establish low-cost production facilities in locations close to raw materials or cheap labor.
4. Competitors in foreign markets may not exist, or competition may be less intense than in domestic markets.
5. Foreign operations may result in reduced tariffs, lower taxes, and favorable political treatment.
6. Joint ventures can enable firms to learn the technology, culture, and business practices of other people and to make contacts with potential customers, suppliers, creditors, and distributors in foreign countries.
7. Economies of scale can be achieved from operation in global rather than solely domestic markets. Larger-scale production and better efficiencies allow higher sales volumes and lower-price offerings.
8. A firm's power and prestige in domestic markets may be significantly enhanced if the firm competes globally. Enhanced prestige can translate into improved negotiating power among creditors, suppliers, distributors, and other important groups.

The availability, depth, and reliability of economic and marketing information in different countries vary extensively, as do industrial structures, business practices, and the number and nature of regional organizations. There are also numerous potential disadvantages of initiating, continuing, or expanding business across national borders, such as the following:

1. Foreign operations could be seized by nationalistic factions.
2. Firms confront different and often little-understood social, cultural, demographic, environmental, political, governmental, legal, technological, economic, and competitive forces when doing business internationally. These forces can make communication difficult in the firm.
3. Weaknesses of competitors in foreign lands are often overestimated, and strengths are often underestimated. Keeping informed about the number and nature of competitors is more difficult when doing business internationally.

4. Language, culture, and value systems differ among countries, which can create barriers to communication and problems managing people.
5. Gaining an understanding of regional organizations such as the European Economic Community, the Latin American Free Trade Area, the International Bank for Reconstruction and Development, and the International Finance Corporation is difficult but is often required in doing business internationally.
6. Dealing with two or more monetary systems can complicate international business operations.

The Global Challenge

Few companies can afford to ignore the presence of international competition. Firms that seem insulated and comfortable today may be vulnerable tomorrow; for example, foreign banks do not yet compete or operate in most of the USA, but this too is changing.

The U.S. economy is becoming much less American. A world economy and monetary system are emerging. Corporations in every corner of the globe are taking advantage of the opportunity to obtain customers globally. Markets are shifting rapidly and in many cases converging in tastes, trends, and prices. Innovative transport systems are accelerating the transfer of technology. Shifts in the nature and location of production systems, especially to China and India, are reducing the response time to changing market conditions. China has more than 1.3 billion residents and a dramatically growing middle class anxious to buy goods and services.

Business in Brazil is booming, with that country having more than a 7 percent annual growth in GDP. The capital of Brazil, Rio de Janeiro, is making massive preparations for the 2016 Summer Olympics, including a $5 billion investment program to extend the subway system, improve railroads, and construct new highways. Two firms in Rio that are growing exponentially are Petrobras, the world's fourth-largest oil producer, and Vale, the world's largest iron-ore mining company. Rio de Janeiro is Brazil's second largest manufacturing center in the country, but its scenic beauty and elaborate port facilities are world renowned.

More and more countries around the world are welcoming foreign investment and capital. As a result, labor markets have steadily become more international. East Asian countries are market leaders in labor-intensive industries, Brazil offers abundant natural resources and rapidly developing markets, and Germany offers skilled labor and technology. The drive to improve the efficiency of global business operations is leading to greater functional specialization. This is not limited to a search for the familiar low-cost labor in Latin America or Asia. Other considerations include the cost of energy, availability of resources, inflation rates, tax rates, and the nature of trade regulations.

Many countries became more protectionist during the recent global economic recession. **Protectionism** refers to countries imposing tariffs, taxes, and regulations on firms outside the country to favor their own companies and people. Most economists argue that protectionism harms the world economy because it inhibits trade among countries and invites retaliation.

Advancements in telecommunications are drawing countries, cultures, and organizations worldwide closer together. Foreign revenue as a percentage of total company revenues already exceeds 50 percent in hundreds of U.S. firms, including ExxonMobil, Gillette, Dow Chemical, Citicorp, Colgate-Palmolive, and Texaco.

A primary reason why most domestic firms do business globally is that growth in demand for goods and services outside the USA is considerably higher than inside. For example, the domestic food industry is growing just 3 percent per year, so Kraft Foods, the second largest food company in the world behind Nestlé, is focusing on foreign acquisitions.

Shareholders and investors expect sustained growth in revenues from firms; satisfactory growth for many firms can only be achieved by capitalizing on demand outside the USA. Joint ventures and partnerships between domestic and foreign firms are becoming the rule rather than the exception!

Fully 95 percent of the world's population lives outside the USA, and this group is growing 70 percent faster than the U.S. population. The lineup of competitors in virtually all industries is global. General Motors, Ford, and Chrysler compete with Toyota and Hyundai.

General Electric and Westinghouse battle Siemens and Mitsubishi. Caterpillar and John Deere compete with Komatsu. Goodyear battles Michelin, Bridgestone/Firestone, and Pirelli. Boeing competes with Airbus. Only a few U.S. industries—such as furniture, printing, retailing, consumer packaged goods, and retail banking—are not yet greatly challenged by foreign competitors. But many products and components in these industries too are now manufactured in foreign countries. International operations can be as simple as exporting a product to a single foreign country or as complex as operating manufacturing, distribution, and marketing facilities in many countries.

Globalization

Based in Wayne, New Jersey, Toys "R" Us is adding 30 new stores in China in 2013–2014 and launching heavy online selling efforts in China. The company knows that a growing middle class in China see playtime as increasingly essential. The firm's focus in China is on "educational toys," such as microscopes and building blocks. Sales of toys in China is growing about 20 percent annually, as increasingly affluent consumers make sure their children have plenty to play with, especially educational toys rather than Barbie Dolls.

Companies growing perhaps even faster than in China or India are those located in Thailand, Vietnam, Philippines, Indonesia, and Singapore in Southeast Asia. A *Wall Street Journal* article (12-4-12, C4) detailed how the growing middle class in these countries are hungry to consume products and services from around the world. The governments of these countries have become stable and are spending heavily on infrastructure projects. African countries too are rapidly becoming attractive for business. GE in mid-2013 began building a huge power plant in Tanzania in East Africa. The International Monetary Fund (IMF) reported in mid-2013 that by 2018, five of the world's fastest growing economies will be in sub-Saharan Africa. The IMF says Africa's economy will grow 5.6 percent in 2013 compared to 3.6 percent worldwide. Shareholders of all companies want high growth; Africa offers high growth.

Globalization is a process of doing business worldwide, so strategic decisions are made based on global profitability of the firm rather than just domestic considerations. A global strategy seeks to meet the needs of customers worldwide, with the highest value at the lowest cost. This may mean locating production in countries with the lowest labor costs or abundant natural resources, locating research and complex engineering centers where skilled scientists and engineers can be found, and locating marketing activities close to the markets to be served.

A **global strategy** includes designing, producing, and marketing products with global needs in mind, instead of considering individual countries alone. A global strategy integrates actions against competitors into a worldwide plan. Today, there are global buyers and sellers and the instant transmission of money and information across continents.

It is clear that different industries become global for different reasons. The need to amortize massive research and development (R&D) investments over many markets is a major reason why the aircraft manufacturing industry became global. Monitoring globalization in one's industry is an important strategic-management activity. Knowing how to use that information for one's competitive advantage is even more important. For example, firms may look around the world for the best technology and select one that has the most promise for the largest number of markets. When firms design a product, they design it to be marketable in as many countries as possible. When firms manufacture a product, they select the lowest-cost source, which may be Japan for semiconductors, Sri Lanka for textiles, Malaysia for simple electronics, and Europe for precision machinery.

Corporate Tax Rates Globally

Corporate tax rates vary considerably across countries and companies. Bermuda has a zero corporate income tax rate. Ireland has a 12.5 corporate tax rate. Many Internet companies have established headquarters and get the bulk of their European revenue in Ireland. For example, although Google has more than 300 employees in France, Google's customers in

France buy ads from Google Ireland Ltd., so Google pays France fees through a marketing agreement, rather than paying the 34 percent corporate tax rate in France. Microsoft has a similar arrangement in France as Google. Tax rates in countries are important in strategic decisions regarding where to build manufacturing facilities or retail stores or even where to acquire other firms. Japan recently cut its corporate tax rate by five percentage points, leaving the USA with the highest corporate tax rate among all nations in the world. Having the highest corporate tax rates is not a good position for the USA because it competes with other nations as a location for investment. High corporate tax rates deter investment in new factories and also provide strong incentives for corporations to avoid and evade taxes. However, it should be pointed out here that a recent *Wall Street Journal* article (7-2-13, p. A4) reported that on average, large, profitable U.S. companies pay a U.S. federal income tax rate of 12.6 percent of their worldwide income, compared to the average individual federal income-tax rate of 7.2 percent.

Since the 1980s, most countries have been steadily lowering their tax rates, but the United States has not cut its top statutory corporate tax rate since 1993. Top combined statutory rates among developed countries, excluding the USA, fell from an average of about 48 percent in the early 1980s to less than 25 percent in 2013.

Even within countries there is significant variation in federal taxes paid. For example, Carnival, the world's largest cruise line company, is incorporated in Panama and pays an effective tax rate of less than 1 percent even though the company is headquartered in Miami, Florida.

To avoid paying U.S. taxes on income made in other countries, many U.S. companies are cash-rich outside the USA but cash-poor inside the USA, and they bring cash back to the USA only as needed. For example in late 2012, Microsoft had $66.6 billion in total cash, but only $8.6 billion in the USA. General Electric had $85.5 billion in total cash, but only $30.7 billion in the USA. Emerson Electric has $2 billion in total cash with almost all of it in Europe and Asia so the firm had to borrow money in the USA rather than bring its cash back and pay a 35 percent corporate USA tax on corporate profits minus whatever ax it has already paid overseas. A *Wall Street Journal* article (12-4-12, p. B1) details this repercussion of the USA having the highest tax rate in the world. The article reveals that Johnson & Johnson keeps virtually all of its $24.5 billion in cash outside the USA, as does Illinois Tool Works Inc. Whirlpool has 85 percent of its cash offshore. Bruce Nolop, former CFO of Pitney Bowes explains it this way: "You end up with the really peculiar result where you are borrowing money in the USA, while you show cash on the balance sheet that is trapped overseas. It is a totally inefficient capital structure." The U.S. tax system, unfortunately for Americans, is structured so that companies can cut their tax bill by shifting income offshore to lower-tax countries.

An increasing number of U.S. companies are reincorporating in foreign countries to reduce their tax burden, and doing this typically by acquiring a foreign firm. Some U.S. firms that recently relocated are Aon Corp., Eaton Corp, Ensco International, D.E. Master Blenders, Transocean Ltd., Noble Corp, Weatherford International Ltd., and Rowan Companies. The 102-year old Eaton Corp. moved its headquarters from Cleveland, Ohio, to downtown Dublin, Ireland, and expects to save about $160 million in taxes annually solely as a result of the move. Critics of the USA tax code also point out that most developed countries tax only domestic earnings, whereas the USA taxes company profits earned abroad.

As indicated in Table 11-4, the top national statutory corporate tax rates in 2012 among sample countries ranged from 10 percent in Serbia to 35 percent in the USA. Note the countries that have a flat tax, which often, on adoption, triggers a surge in foreign direct investment.

Other factors besides the corporate tax rate obviously affect companies' decisions of where to locate plants and facilities and whether to acquire other firms. For example, the large, affluent market and efficient infrastructure in both Germany and Britain attract companies, but the high labor costs and strict labor laws there keep other companies away. The rapidly growing GDP in Brazil and India attracts companies, but violence and political unrest in Middle East countries deter investment. The USA perhaps should lower its rate to reward companies that invest in jobs domestically. Lowering the U.S. corporate tax rate should also reduce unemployment and spur growth domestically.

TABLE 11-4 Corporate Tax Rates Across Countries in 2012 (from high to low)

Country	Corporate Tax Rate (%)
USA	35
Brazil	34
France	33.33
Germany	33
India	30
Mexico	30
Italy	27.5
Japan	25.5
Israel	25
Austria	25
China	25.
Portugal	25
Finland	24.5
U.K.	24
Ukraine	21
Estonia	21
Russia	20
Greece	20
Croatia	20
Libya	20
Netherlands	20
Turkey	20
Poland	19
Czech Republic	19
Hungary	19
Singapore	17
Canada	16.5
Hong Kong	16.5
Romania	16
Latvi	15
Lithuani	15
Ireland	12.5
Serbi	10
Bulgaria	10
Cyprus	10

Source: Based on 11-1-12 information at http://www.worldwide-tax.com/#partthree.

United States versus Foreign Business Cultures

An excellent website to visit on this topic is www.worldbusinessculture.com. There you may select any country in the world and check out how business culture varies in that country vs. other lands. To compete successfully in world markets, U.S. managers must obtain a better knowledge of historical, cultural, and religious forces that motivate and drive people in other countries. In Japan, for example, business relations operate within the context of **Wa**, which stresses group harmony and social cohesion. In China, business behavior revolves around **guanxi**, or personal relations. In South Korea, activities involve concern for **inhwa**, or harmony based on respect of hierarchical relationships, including obedience to authority.[2]

In Europe, it is generally true that the farther north on the continent, the more participatory the management style. Most European workers are unionized and enjoy more frequent vacations and holidays than U.S. workers. A 90-minute lunch break plus 20-minute morning and afternoon breaks are common in European firms. Guaranteed permanent employment is typically a part of employment contracts in Europe. In socialist countries such as France, Belgium, and the United Kingdom, the only grounds for immediate dismissal from work is a criminal offense. A six-month trial period at the beginning of employment is usually part of the contract with a European firm. Many Europeans resent pay-for-performance, commission salaries, and objective measurement and reward systems. This is true especially of workers in southern Europe. Many Europeans also find the notion of team spirit difficult to grasp because the unionized environment has dichotomized worker–management relations throughout Europe.

A weakness of some U.S. firms in competing with Pacific Rim firms is a lack of understanding of Asian cultures, including how Asians think and behave. Spoken Chinese, for example, has more in common with spoken English than with spoken Japanese or Korean. U.S. managers consistently put more weight on being friendly and liked, whereas Asian and European managers often exercise authority without this concern. Americans tend to use first names instantly in business dealings with foreigners, but foreigners find this presumptuous. In Japan, for example, first names are used only among family members and intimate friends; even longtime business associates and coworkers shy away from the use of first names. Table 11-5 lists other cultural differences or pitfalls that U.S. managers need to know about.

U.S. managers have a low tolerance for silence, whereas Asian managers view extended periods of silence as important for organizing and evaluating one's thoughts. U.S. managers are much more action-oriented than their counterparts around the world; they rush to appointments, conferences, and meetings—and then feel the day has been productive. But for many foreign managers, resting, listening, meditating, and thinking is considered productive. Sitting through a conference without talking is unproductive in the United States, but it is viewed as positive in Japan if one's silence helps preserve unity.

U.S. managers place greater emphasis on short-term results than foreign managers. In marketing, for example, Japanese managers strive to achieve "everlasting customers," whereas many Americans strive to make a onetime sale. Marketing managers in Japan see making a sale

TABLE 11-5 Cultural Pitfalls That May Help You Be a Better Manager

- Waving is a serious insult in Greece and Nigeria, particularly if the hand is near someone's face.
- Making a "good-bye" wave in Europe can mean "No," but it means "Come here" in Peru.
- In China, last names are written first.
- A man named Carlos Lopez-Garcia should be addressed as Mr. Lopez in Latin America but as Mr. Garcia in Brazil.
- Breakfast meetings are considered uncivilized in most foreign countries.
- Latin Americans are on average 20 minutes late to business appointments.
- Direct eye contact is impolite in Japan.
- Do not cross your legs in any Arab or many Asian countries—it is rude to show the sole of your shoe.
- In Brazil, touching your thumb and first finger—an American "Okay" sign—is the equivalent of raising your middle finger.
- Nodding or tossing your head back in southern Italy, Malta, Greece, and Tunisia means "No." In India, this body motion means "Yes."
- Snapping your fingers is vulgar in France and Belgium.
- Folding your arms across your chest is a sign of annoyance in Finland.
- In China, leave some food on your plate to show that your host was so generous that you could not finish.
- Do not eat with your left hand when dining with clients from Malaysia or India.
- One form of communication works the same worldwide. It is the smile—so take that along wherever you go.

as the beginning, not the end, of the selling process. This is an important distinction. Japanese managers often criticize U.S. managers for worrying more about shareholders, whom they do not know, than employees, whom they do know. Americans refer to "hourly employees," whereas many Japanese companies still refer to "lifetime employees."

Rose Knotts recently summarized some important cultural differences between U.S. and foreign managers.[3] Awareness and consideration of these differences can enable a manager to be more effective, regardless of his or her own nationality.

1. Americans place an exceptionally high priority on time, viewing time as an asset. Many foreigners place more worth on relationships. This difference results in foreign managers often viewing U.S. managers as "more interested in business than people."
2. Personal touching and distance norms differ around the world. Americans generally stand about three feet from each other when carrying on business conversations, but Arabs and Africans stand about one foot apart. Touching another person with the left hand in business dealings is taboo in some countries.
3. Family roles and relationships vary in different countries. For example, males are valued more than females in some cultures, and peer pressure, work situations, and business interactions reinforce this phenomenon.
4. Business and daily life in some societies are governed by religious factors. Prayer times, holidays, daily events, and dietary restrictions, for example, need to be respected by managers not familiar with these practices in some countries.
5. Time spent with the family and the quality of relationships are more important in some cultures than the personal achievement and accomplishments espoused by the traditional U.S. manager.
6. Many cultures around the world value modesty, team spirit, collectivity, and patience much more than competitiveness and individualism, which are so important in the United States.
7. Punctuality is a valued personal trait when conducting business in the USA, but it is not revered in many of the world's societies. Eating habits also differ dramatically across cultures. For example, belching is acceptable in some countries as evidence of satisfaction with the food that has been prepared. Chinese culture considers it good manners to sample a portion of each food served.
8. To prevent social blunders when meeting with managers from other lands, one must learn and respect the rules of etiquette of others. Sitting on a toilet seat is viewed as unsanitary in most countries, but not in the USA. Leaving food or drink after dining is considered impolite in some countries, but not in China. Bowing instead of shaking hands is customary in many countries. Some cultures view Americans as unsanitary for locating toilet and bathing facilities in the same area, whereas Americans view people of some cultures as unsanitary for not taking a bath or shower every day.
9. Americans often do business with individuals they do not know, unlike businesspersons in many other cultures. In Mexico and Japan, for example, an amicable relationship is often mandatory before conducting business.

In many countries, effective managers are those who are best at negotiating with government bureaucrats rather than those who inspire workers. Many U.S. managers are uncomfortable with nepotism, which are practiced in some countries. The USA defends women from sexual harassment, and defends minorities from discrimination, but not all countries embrace the same values. For example, in Indonesia, in mid-2013, legislators were considering making sex among singles a crime with up to a 5-year prison sentence, and cohabitation a crime with up to 1 year in prison.

U.S. managers in China have to be careful about how they arrange office furniture because Chinese workers believe in **feng shui**, the practice of harnessing natural forces. U.S. managers in Japan have to be careful about **nemaswashio**, whereby Japanese workers expect supervisors to alert them privately of changes rather than informing them in a meeting. Japanese managers have little appreciation for versatility, expecting all managers to be the same. In Japan, "If a nail sticks out, you hit it into the wall," says Brad Lashbrook, an international consultant for Wilson Learning.

Probably the biggest obstacle to the effectiveness of U.S. managers—or managers from any country working in another—is the fact that it is almost impossible to change the attitude of a foreign workforce. "The system drives you; you cannot fight the system or culture," says Bill Parker, president of Phillips Petroleum in Norway.

Communication Differences Across Countries

Americans increasingly interact with managers in other countries, so it is important to understand foreign business cultures. Americans often come across as intrusive, manipulative, and garrulous; this impression may reduce their effectiveness in communication. *Forbes* provided the following cultural hints from Charis Intercultural Training:

1. Italians, Germans, and French generally do not soften up executives with praise before they criticize. Americans do soften up folks, and this practice seems manipulative to Europeans.
2. Israelis are accustomed to fast-paced meetings and have little patience for U.S. informality and small talk.
3. British executives often complain that U.S. executives chatter too much. Informality, egalitarianism, and spontaneity from Americans in business settings jolt many foreigners.
4. Europeans feel they are being treated like children when asked to wear name tags by Americans.
5. Executives in India are used to interrupting one another. Thus, when U.S. executives listen without asking for clarification or posing questions, they are viewed by Indians as not paying attention.
6. When negotiating orally with Malaysian or Japanese executives, it is appropriate to allow periodically for a time of silence. However, no pause is needed when negotiating in Israel.
7. Refrain from asking foreign managers questions such as "How was your weekend?" That is intrusive to foreigners, who tend to regard their business and private lives as totally separate.[4]

Business Culture Across Countries[5]

A recent *USA Today* article (9-24-12, p. 8A) titled "Arab Spring Leaving Women Out in Cold" reveals that the recent changeover of regimes in Middle Eastern countries has unfortunately resulted in arguably less rights for women. Nawal Al Saadawi says for example in Egypt "Things didn't improve for women, and we are going backward." Even in a relatively progressive Middle Eastern country such as Morocco, there is legislation that allows men who rape or have sex with minors to avoid prosecution by wedding their victims. Sexual harassment of women in the streets, according to the article, especially spikes during Muslim holidays. Perhaps the worst country for women's rights is Afghanistan, although Saudi Arabia is quite restrictive. In contrast, South Korea elected its first female president late in 2012. She is Park Geun-hye, the daughter of the general who ruled the country in the 1960s and 1970s. Park joins the following other current female presidents of countries:

Australia, Julia Gillard

Denmark, Helle Thorning-Schmidt

Germany, Angela Merkel

Iceland, Johanna Sigurdardottir

Switzerland, Eveline Widmer-Schlumpf

Many countries have in the past have had female presidents, including Canada, Chile, Israel, New Zealand, Norway, Slovak Republic, Turkey, and the United Kingdom.

Another recent *USA Today* article (12-4-12, 6B) titled "Europe Tries to Put Women on Boards" reveals that in the UK, 20 percent of senior management is female, but this is higher than in the Netherlands where the percentage is 18, Denmark at 15, or Germany at 13. Germany's upper house of parliament recently approved a bill to guarantee that women make up 20 percent of boards at publicly traded companies by 2018, and 40 percent by 2023. Chancellor Angela Merkel of Germany, however, has said that she prefers voluntary measures over mandatory quotas. In Norway, 40 percent of nonexecutive board members of publicly listed companies are women, which is perhaps best of all countries on the planet.

Mexico—Business Culture

Mexico is an authoritarian society in terms of schools, churches, businesses, and families. Employers seek workers who are agreeable, respectful, and obedient, rather than innovative, creative, and independent. Mexican workers tend to be activity oriented rather than problem solvers. When visitors walk into a Mexican business, they are impressed by the cordial, friendly atmosphere. This is almost always true because Mexicans desire harmony rather than conflict; desire for harmony is part of the social fabric in worker–manager relations. There is a much lower tolerance for adversarial relations or friction at work in Mexico as compared to the USA.

Mexican employers are paternalistic, providing workers with more than a paycheck, but in return they expect allegiance. Weekly food baskets, free meals, free bus service, and free day care are often part of compensation. The ideal working condition for a Mexican worker is the family model, with people all working together, doing their share, according to their designated roles. Mexican workers do not expect or desire a work environment in which self-expression and initiative are encouraged. Whereas U.S. business embodies individualism, achievement, competition, curiosity, pragmatism, informality, spontaneity, and doing more than expected on the job, Mexican businesses stress collectivism, continuity, cooperation, belongingness, formality, and doing exactly what is told.

In Mexico, business associates rarely entertain each other at their homes, which are places reserved exclusively for close friends and family. Business meetings and entertaining are nearly always done at a restaurant. Preserving one's honor, saving face, and looking important are also exceptionally important in Mexico. This is why Mexicans do not accept criticism and change easily; many find it humiliating to acknowledge having made a mistake. A meeting among employees and managers in a business located in Mexico is a forum for giving orders and directions rather than for discussing problems or participating in decision making. Mexican workers want to be closely supervised, cared for, and corrected in a civil manner. Opinions expressed by employees are often regarded as back talk in Mexico. Mexican supervisors are viewed as weak if they explain the rationale for their orders to workers.

Mexicans do not feel compelled to follow rules that are not associated with a particular person in authority they work for or know well. Thus, signs to wear earplugs or safety glasses, or attendance or seniority policies, and even one-way street signs are often ignored. Whereas Americans follow the rules, Mexicans often do not.

Life is slower in Mexico than in the USA. The first priority is often assigned to the last request, rather than to the first. Telephone systems break down. Banks may suddenly not have pesos. Phone repair can take a month. Electricity for an entire plant or town can be down for hours or even days. Business and government offices may open and close at odd hours. Buses and taxis may be hours off schedule. Meeting times for appointments are not rigid. Tardiness is common everywhere. Effectively doing business in Mexico requires knowledge of the Mexican way of life, culture, beliefs, and customs.

In Mexico, when greeting others, it is customary for women to pat each other on the right forearm or shoulder, rather than shaking hands. Men shake hands or, if close friends, use the traditional hug and back slapping upon greeting. If visiting a Mexican home, bring a gift such as flowers or sweets. Avoid marigolds because they symbolize death. Arrive up to 30 minutes late, but definitely not early. Avoid red flowers which have a negative connotation. White flowers are an excellent choice. If you receive a gift, open it immediately and react enthusiastically. At dinner, do not sit until you are invited to and wait to be told where to sit. This is true in most foreign countries and in the USA. Do not begin eating until the hostess starts. Only men give toasts in Mexico. It is also polite to leave some food on your plate after a meal. For business appointments, as opposed to home visits, it is best to arrive on time, although your Mexican counterparts may be up to 30 minutes late. Do not get irritated at their lack of punctuality.

Mexicans often judge or stereotype a person by who introduces them and changing that first impression is difficult in business. Expect to answer questions about personal background, family, and life interests—because Mexicans consider trustworthiness and character to be of upmost importance. Mexicans are status conscious, so business titles and rank are important. Face-to-face meetings are preferred over telephone calls, letters, or e-mail. Negotiations in Mexico include a fair amount of haggling, so do not give a best offer first.

Japan—Business Culture

Japan elected a new prime minister, Shinzo Abe, in December 2012. Abe promises aggressive new monetary policy, big public works spending, and full economic recovery. Walmart believes in Abe because it, under the name Seiyu Ltd., is adding 22 stores in Japan in 2013–2014, to go along with its already 368 stores in Japan. Two trends in Japan driving the Walmart expansion are (1) single-person households, especially among the elderly, are continuing to grow and (2) people have less money to spend. Japanese consumers have traditionally equated discounts with poor quality, but that is changing. Also, Walmart gained much support throughout Japan with its quick response flying in water and food immediately after the earthquake and tsunami hit Japan in 2011.

The Japanese place great importance on group loyalty and consensus, a concept called *Wa*. Nearly all corporate activities in Japan encourage Wa among managers and employees. Wa requires that all members of a group agree and cooperate; this results in constant discussion and compromise. Japanese managers evaluate the potential attractiveness of alternative business decisions in terms of the long-term effect on the group's Wa. This is why silence, used for pondering alternatives, can be a plus in a formal Japanese meeting. Discussions potentially disruptive to Wa are generally conducted in informal settings, such as at a bar, so as to minimize harm to the group's Wa. Entertaining is an important business activity in Japan because it strengthens Wa. Formal meetings are often conducted in informal settings. When confronted with disturbing questions or opinions, Japanese managers tend to remain silent, whereas Americans tend to respond directly, defending themselves through explanation and argument.

Americans have more freedom to control their own fates than do the Japanese. The USA offers more upward mobility to its people, as indicated below:

America is not like Japan and can never be. America's strength is the opposite: It opens its doors and brings the world's disorder in. It tolerates social change that would tear most other societies apart. This openness encourages Americans to adapt as individuals rather than as a group. Americans go west to California to get a new start; they move east to Manhattan to try to make the big time; they move to Vermont or to a farm to get close to the soil. They break away from their parents' religions or values or class; they rediscover their ethnicity. They go to night school; they change their names.[6]

Most Japanese managers are reserved, quiet, distant, introspective, and other oriented, whereas most U.S. managers are talkative, insensitive, impulsive, direct, and individual oriented. Americans often perceive Japanese managers as wasting time and carrying on pointless conversations, whereas U.S. managers often use blunt criticism, ask prying questions, and make quick decisions. These kinds of cultural differences have disrupted many potentially productive Japanese–American business endeavors. Viewing the Japanese communication style as a prototype for all Asian cultures is a stereotype that must be avoided.

In Japan, a person's age and status are of paramount importance, whether in the family unit, the extended family, or a social or business situation. Schoolchildren learn early that the oldest person in the group is to be honored. Older folks are served first and their drinks are poured for them. Greetings in Japan are formal and ritualized. Wait to be introduced because it may be viewed as impolite to introduce yourself, even in a large gathering. Foreigners may shake hands, but the traditional form of greeting is to bow. The deeper you bow, the more respect you show, but at least bow the head slightly in greetings.

In gift giving in Japan, chocolates or small cakes are excellent choices, but do not give lilies, camellias, lotus blossoms, or white flowers because they all are associated with funerals. Do not give potted plants because they encourage sickness, although a bonsai tree is always acceptable. Give items in odd numbers, but avoid the number 9. Gifts are not opened when received. If going to a Japanese home, remove your shoes before entering and put on the slippers left at the doorway. Leave shoes pointing away from the doorway you are about to walk through. If going to the toilet in a Japanese home, put on the toilet slippers and remove them when you exit.

In Japan, when finally seated for dinner, never point the chopsticks. Learn how to use chopsticks before visiting Japan and do not pierce food with chopsticks. Japanese oftentimes slurp their noodles and soup, but mixing other food with rice is inappropriate. Instead of mixing, eat a bit of rice and then a bit of food. To signify that you do not want more rice or drink, leave some in the bowl or glass. Conversation over dinner is generally subdued in Japan because they prefer to savor their food.

Unlike Americans, Japanese prefer to do business on the basis of personal relationships rather than impersonally speaking over the phone or by written correspondence. Therefore, build and maintain relationships by sending greeting, thank you, birthday, and seasonal cards. You need to be a good "correspondent" to effectively do business with the Japanese. Punctuality is important so arrive on time for meetings and be mindful that it may take several meetings to establish a good relationship. The Japanese are looking for a long-term relationship. Always give a small gift as a token of your appreciation, and present it to the most senior person at the end of any meeting.

Like many Asian and African cultures, the Japanese are non-confrontational. They have a difficult time saying "no," so you must be vigilant at observing their nonverbal communication. Rarely refuse a request, no matter how difficult or non-profitable it may appear at the time. In communicating with Japanese, phrase questions so that they can answer *yes*. For example, do you disagree with this? Group decision making and consensus are vitally important. The Japanese often remain silent in meetings for long periods of time and may even close their eyes when they want to listen intently.

Business cards are exchanged in Japan constantly and with excitement. Invest in quality business cards and keep them in pristine condition. Do not write on them. Have one side of your card translated in Japanese and give it to the person with the Japanese side facing the recipient. Business cards are generally given and received with two hands and a slight bow. Examine any business card you receive carefully.

Brazil—Business Culture

In both Brazil and the USA, men greet each other by shaking hands while maintaining steady eye contact. Women greet each other with kisses in Brazil, starting with the left and alternating cheeks. Hugging and backslapping are also common greetings among Brazilian close friends. If a woman wishes to shake hands with a man, she should extend her hand first. Brazilians speak Portuguese. If going to someone's house in Brazil, bring the hostess flowers or a small gift. Orchids are nice, but avoid purple or black, because these are mourning colors. Arrive at least 30 minutes late if your invitation is for dinner and arrive up to an hour late for a party or large gathering. Never arrive early. Brazilians dress with a flair and judge others on their appearance, so even casual dress is more formal than in many other countries. Always err on the side of over-dressing in Brazil rather than under-dressing.

Avoid embarrassing a Brazilian by criticizing an individual publically; that causes that person to lose face with all others at a business meeting, and the person making the criticism also loses face because they have disobeyed the unwritten Brazilian rule. It is considered acceptable, however, to interrupt someone who is speaking. Face-to-face, oral communication is preferred over written communication. As for business agreements, Brazilians insist on drawing up detailed legal contracts. They are more comfortable doing business with and negotiating with people than companies. Therefore, wait for a Brazilian colleagues to raise the business subject. Never rush the prebusiness relationship-building time. Brazilians take their time when negotiating. Use local lawyers and accountants for negotiations because Brazilians resent an outside legal presence.

Appointments are commonly cancelled or changed at the last minute in Brazil, so do not be surprised or get upset. In the cities of Sao Paulo and Brasilia, arrive on time for meetings, but in Rio de Janeiro arrive a few minutes late for a meeting. Do not appear impatient if kept waiting, because relationship building always takes precedence over adhering to a strict schedule. Brazilians pride themselves on dressing well, so men should wear conservative, dark-colored business suits or even three-piece suits for executives. Women should wear suits or dresses that are elegant and feminine with good, quality accessories. And ladies, manicures are expected.

Germany—Business Culture

Business communication in Germany is formal, so the home is a welcome, informal place. Germans take great pride in their home, which is generally neat and tidy inside and out. Only close friends and relatives are invited into the sanctity of a person's house, so consider that an honor if you get that invitation, and bring a gift, such as chocolates or yellow roses or tea roses—but not red roses, which symbolize romantic intentions. Also do not bring carnations, lilies, or chrysanthemums, which in Germany symbolize mourning. If you bring wine to a

German's home, it should be imported, French or Italian. Always arrive on time but never early, and always send a handwritten note the following day to thank your hostess for her hospitality.

When it is time to have dinner, remain standing until invited to sit down. As is custom in many countries, you may be shown to a particular seat. Table manners in Germany are strictly Continental with the fork being held in the left hand and the knife in the right while eating. Do not begin eating until the hostess starts or someone says *guten appetit* ("good appetite"). Wait for the hostess to place her napkin in her lap before doing so yourself and do not rest your elbows on the table. Cut as much of your food with your fork as possible because this compliments the cook by indicating the food is tender. Break bread or rolls apart by hand, but if a loaf is in the middle for all, then touch only what you extract to eat. This sanitary practice is a must in all countries including the USA. Finish everything on your plate and indicate you have finished eating by laying your knife and fork parallel across the right side of your plate, with the fork over the knife.

Germans are like Americans in that they do not need a personal relationship to do business. They are more interested in a businessperson's academic credentials and their company's credentials. A quick, firm handshake is the traditional greeting, even with children. At the office, Germans do not have an open-door policy and often work with their office door closed, so knock and wait to be invited to enter. Appointments are mandatory and should be made one to two weeks in advance. Germans are often direct to the point of bluntness. Punctuality is extremely important in Germany, so if you are going to be delayed, telephone immediately and offer an explanation. It is rude to cancel a meeting at the last minute and this could jeopardize the whole business relationship. German meetings adhere to strict agendas, including starting and ending times. Germans maintain direct eye contact while speaking.

There is a strict protocol to follow in Germany when entering a room—the eldest or highest-ranking person enters first and men enter before women if their age and status are roughly equivalent. Germans are detail oriented and want to understand every innuendo before coming to an agreement. Business decision making is autocratic and held at the top of the company. Final decisions will not be changed and are expected to be implemented by lower-level managers and employees with no questions asked. Americans are more flexible in many respects than Germans.

Egypt—Business Culture

In Egypt, greetings are based on both social class and religion, so follow the lead of others. Handshakes, although limp and prolonged, are the customary greeting among Egyptians of the same sex. Handshakes are always given with a hearty smile and direct eye contact. Once a relationship has developed, it is common to greet with a kiss on one cheek and then the other, while shaking hands, men with men and women with women. In greetings between men and women, the woman will extend her hand first. Otherwise, a man should bow his head in greeting.

If you are invited to an Egyptian's home, remove your shoes before entering, just as you would do in China and Japan. As a gift, bring chocolates, sweets, or pastries to the hostess. Do not give flowers, which are usually reserved for weddings or the ill, unless you know that the host will appreciate them. Always give gifts with the right hand or both hands if the gift is heavy. Gifts are not opened when received. Never sit at a dinner table until the host or hostess tells you where to sit. Eat with the right hand only and compliment the host by taking second helpings. Always show appreciation for the meal. Putting salt or pepper on your food is considered an insult to a cook. This is true to a lesser extent even in the USA. Leave a small amount of food on your plate when you have finished eating. Otherwise your Egyptian host may keep bringing you more food.

Egyptians prefer to do business with those they know and respect, so expect to spend time cultivating a personal relationship before business is conducted. Who you know is more important than what you know in Egypt, so network and cultivate a number of contracts. You should expect to be offered coffee or tea whenever you meet someone in Egypt because this demonstrates hospitality. Even if you do not want the drink, always accept the beverage because declining the offer is viewed as rejecting the person.

In Egypt, appearance is important, so wear, conservative clothes and present yourself well at all times. For Egyptians, direct eye contact is a sign of honesty, so be prepared for overly intense stares. Hierarchy and rank are important. Unlike in Germany, Egyptian business people do have an open-door policy, even when they are in a meeting, so you may experience frequent interruptions as others wander into the room and start a different discussion. It is best that you not try to bring the topic back to the original discussion until the new person leaves. Business meetings generally start after prolonged inquiries about health, family, and such.

Egyptians must know and like you to conduct business. Personal relationships are necessary for long-term business. The highest-ranking person makes decisions, after obtaining group consensus. Decisions are reached after great deliberation. In Egypt, business moves at a slow pace and society is extremely bureaucratic—even in the post-Hosni Mubarak era. Egyptians respect age and experience and engage in a fair amount of haggling. They are tough negotiators and do not like confrontation or having to say *no*. Egyptian women must be careful to cover themselves appropriately. Skirts and dresses should cover the knee and sleeves should cover most of the arm. Women are daily gaining more rights, however, throughout the Middle East, and that is a good thing. In late 2011, women in Saudi Arabia were finally granted the right to vote, but women still are not allowed to drive cars in that country.

China—Business Culture

In China, greetings are formal and the oldest person is always greeted first. Like in the United States, handshakes are the most common form of greeting. Many Chinese will look toward the ground when greeting someone. The Chinese have an excellent sense of humor. They can easily laugh at themselves if they have a comfortable relationship with the other person. In terms of gifts, a food basket makes an excellent gift, but do not give scissors, knives, or other cutting utensils because these objects indicate severing of the relationship. Never give clocks, handkerchiefs, flowers, or straw sandals because they are associated with funerals. Do not wrap gifts in white, blue, or black paper. In China, the number 4 is unlucky, so do not give four of anything. Eight is the luckiest number, so giving eight of something is a great idea.

If invited to a Chinese person's home, consider this a great honor and arrive on time. Remove your shoes before entering the house and bring a small gift to the hostess. Eat heartily to demonstrate that you are enjoying the food. Use chopsticks and wait to be told where to sit. You should try everything that is offered and never eat the last piece from the serving tray. Hold the rice bowl close to your mouth while eating. Do not be offended if a Chinese person makes slurping or belching sounds; it merely indicates that they are enjoying their food.

The Chinese rarely do business with companies or people they do not know. Your position on an organizational chart is extremely important in business relationships. Gender bias is generally not an issue. Meals and social events are not the place for business discussions. There is a demarcation between business and socializing in China, so try to be careful not to intertwine the two.

Like in the USA and Germany, punctuality is important in China. Arriving late to a meeting is an insult and could negatively affect your relationship. Meetings require patience because mobile phones ring frequently and conversations tend to be boisterous. Never ask the Chinese to turn off their mobile phones because this causes you both to lose face. The Chinese are non-confrontational and virtually never overtly say *no*. Rather, they will say "they will think about it" or "they will see." The Chinese are shrewd negotiators, so an initial offer or price should leave room for negotiation.

India—Business Culture

According to United Nations' statistics, India's rate of female participation in the labor force is 34.2 percent, which is quite low, especially because women make up 42 percent of college graduates in India. But Indian women with a college degree are expected to let their careers take a back seat to caring for their husband, children, and elderly parents. "The measures of daughterly guilt are much higher in Indian women than in other countries," says Sylvia Ann Hewlett, president of the Center for Work-Life Policy, a Manhattan think tank, who headed a recent study on the challenges Indian women face in the workplace.[8] Sylvia says, "Since taking care of elderly parents usually becomes a reality later in a woman's career, it takes them out of the workplace just when they should be entering top management roles." That is why gender disparities at Indian companies unfortunately grow more pronounced at higher levels of management.

Like in many Asian cultures, people in India do not like to say *no*, verbally or nonverbally. Rather than disappoint you, they often will say something is not available, will offer you the response that they think you want to hear, or will be vague with you. This behavior should not be considered dishonest. Shaking hands is common in India, especially in the large cities among the more educated who are accustomed to dealing with westerners. Men may shake hands with other men and women may shake hands with other women; however, there are seldom handshakes between men and women because of religious beliefs.

Indians believe that giving gifts eases the transition into the next life. Gifts of cash are common, but do not give frangipani or white flowers because they represent mourning. Yellow, green, and red are lucky colors, so use them to wrap gifts. Because Hindus consider cows to be sacred, do not give gifts made of leather to Hindus. Muslims should not be given gifts made of pigskin or alcoholic products. Gifts are usually not opened when received.

Before entering an Indian's house, take off shoes just as you would in China or Japan. Politely turn down the host's first offer of tea, coffee, or snacks. You will be asked again and again. Saying no to the first invitation is part of the protocol. Be mindful that neither Hindus nor Sikhs eat beef, and many are vegetarians. Muslims do not eat pork or drink alcohol. Lamb, chicken, and fish are the most commonly served main courses. Table manners are somewhat formal, but much Indian food is eaten with the fingers. Like most places in the world, wait to be told where and when to sit at dinner. Women in India typically serve the men and eat later. You may be asked to wash your hands before and after sitting down to a meal. Always use your right hand to eat, whether using utensils or your fingers. Leave a small amount of food on your plate to indicate that you are satisfied. Finishing all your food means that you are still hungry, which as true in Egypt, China, Mexico, and many countries.

Indians prefer to do business with those with whom they have established a relationship built on mutual trust and respect. Punctuality is important. Indians generally do not trust the legal system, and someone's word is often sufficient to reach an agreement. Do not disagree publicly with anyone in India.

Titles such as professor, doctor, or engineer are important in India, as is a person's age, university degree, caste, and profession. Use the right hand to give and receive business cards. Business cards need not be translated into Hindi but always present your business card so the recipient may read the card as it is handed to them. This is a nice, expected gesture in most countries around the world.

Nigeria—Business Culture

With the largest population of any country in Africa and the largest city in Africa (Lagos), Nigeria on the west coast bordering the Gulf of Guinea, is a democratic country with English as its official language. Half of Nigeria's population is under age 18. With a growing economy, Nigeria's constitution guarantees religious freedom. Christians in Nigeria live mostly in the south, whereas Muslims live mostly in the north. Native religions in which people believe in deities, spirits, and ancestor worship are spread throughout Nigeria, as are different languages. Christmas and Easter are national holidays. Muslims observe Ramadan, the Islamic month of fasting, and the two Eids. Working hours in the north often vary from the south, primarily because Muslims do not work on their holy day—Friday.

Endowed with vast quantities of natural resources and being the sixth largest oil-producing nation on the planet, Nigeria has a well-educated and industrious people who are proud of their country. Nigerians are fond of the expression, "When Nigeria sneezes, the rest of Africa catches a cold (except South Africa)." Nigeria re-elected its president in 2011, a zoology professor-turned-president, Goodluck Jonathan.

In Nigeria, extended families are still the backbone of social and business systems. Grandparents, cousins, aunts, uncles, sisters, brothers, and in-laws all work as a unit through life. Hierarchy and seniority within extended families are important; the oldest person in a group is revered and honored, and is greeted and served first. In return, however, the most senior person has the responsibility to make good decisions for the extended family.

The most common greeting in Nigeria is a handshake with a warm, welcoming smile. Muslims will not generally shake hands with members of the opposite sex. Nigerians do not use first names readily, so wait to be invited to do this before engaging. Gift giving is common and even expected, but gifts from a man to a woman must be said to come from the man's mother, wife, sister, or other female relative, never from the man himself. Never rush a greeting because that is extremely rude; rather, spend time inquiring about the other person's general well-being.

Foreigners who take the time to get to know a Nigerian as a person are often welcomed into the Nigerian's inner circle of family and close friends. Nigerians are generally outgoing and friendly, especially in the southwest, where the Yoruba often use humor even during business meetings and serious discussions.

To combat the AIDS epidemic in sub-Saharan Africa, the World Bank is now paying young girls cash to stop accepting gifts and cash from older men in exchange for sex. This "sugar daddy" relationship is common in many African countries and is fueling the AIDS problem because the percent of men aged 30–34 that test positive for HIV is upward of 30 percent in countries such as Zimbabwe. The World Bank has a billboard in the Mbare vegetable market in Harare, Zimbabwe, that reads, "Your future is brighter without a sugar daddy."

Business Climate Across Countries/Continents

The World Bank and the International Finance Corporation annually rank 183 countries in terms of their respective ease of doing business (http://www.doingbusiness.org/rankings). The index ranks nations from 1 (best) to 183 (worst). For each nation, the ranking is calculated as the simple average of the percentile rankings on how easy is it to: (1) start a business, (2) deal with construction permits, (3) register property, (4) get credit, (5) protect investors, (6) pay taxes, (7) trade across borders, (8) enforce contracts, (9) resolving insolvency, and (10) get electricity.

Among all countries on the planet, Morocco improved its ranking most in 2012, climbing 21 places to 94, by simplifying the construction permitting process, easing the administrative burden of tax compliance, and providing greater protections to minority shareholders. Table 11-6 reveals the 2012 Ease of Doing Business rankings for the top 10 nations in various regions of the world. Note for example that Norway is rated the sixth best country on the planet for ease of doing business and Chile is the best country in South America.

Union Membership Across Europe

There is great variation in Europe as per levels of union membership, ranging from 74 percent of employees in Finland and 71 percent in Sweden to 9 percent in Lithuania and 8 percent in France. However, percentage of union membership is not the only indicator of strength because in France for example, unions have repeatedly shown that despite low levels of membership they are able to mobilize workers in mass strikes and demonstrations to great effect.

The average level of union membership across the whole of the European Union (EU), weighted by the numbers employed in the different member states, is 23 percent compared to about 11 percent in the USA. The European average is held down by relatively low levels of membership in some of the larger EU states, Germany with 19 percent, France with 8 percent, Spain with 16 percent, and Poland with 15 percent. The three smallest states, Cyprus, Luxembourg, and Malta, have levels well above the average.

TABLE 11-6 The Top 10 Nations to Do Business With Across Continents

Overall Best	East Asia Pacific	East Europe Central Asia	Latin America Caribbean	Mid-East Africa	South Africa
1. Singapore	Singapore	Georgia	Chile	Saudi Arabia	Mauritius
2. Hong Kong	Hone Kong	Latvia	Peru	UAE	S. Africa
3. New Zealand	Thailand	Macedonia	Colombia	Qatar	Rwanda
4. USA	Malaysia	Lithuania	Puerto Rico	Bahrain	Botswana
5. Denmark	Taiwan	Cyprus	St. Lucia	Tunisia	Ghana
6. Norway	Tonga	Kazakhstan	Mexico	Oman	Nambia
7. United Kingdom	Samoa	Armenia	Antiqua	Kuwait	Zambia
8. South Korea	Solomon Isls.	Montenegro	Panama	Morocco	Seychelles
9. Iceland	Vanuatu	Bulgaria	Dominica	Jordan	Kenya
10. Ireland	Fiji	Azerbajan	Trinidad	Yemen	Ethiopia

Source: Based on information at http://www.doingbusiness.org/rankings in November 2012.

The three Nordic countries of Denmark, Sweden, and Finland are at the top of the table with around 70 percent of all employees in unions. In part this is because, as in Belgium, which also has above average levels of union density, unemployment and other social benefits are normally paid out through the union. High union density in the Nordic countries also reflects an approach that sees union membership as a natural part of employment, as shown by the relatively high proportion of employees (around 53 percent) who are union members in Norway, where unemployment benefits are not paid through the unions.

Central and Eastern Europe nations generally have below average levels of union membership. In Poland for example 16 percent of employees are estimated to be union members. Level of union membership is clearly trending downward all over Europe. Only 8 out of the 27 EU states plus Norway—Belgium, Cyprus, Ireland, Italy, Luxembourg, Malta, Norway and Spain—have seen a gain in union members among the employed in recent years, and in most of these countries. This growth has not kept pace with the overall growth in employment, meaning that union density has drifted downward. The two exceptions appear to be Ireland and Italy where union membership is slowly growing.

African Countries

In 2012, 23 African countries held democratic elections, whereas in 1989 only 3 African countries were considered democracies. Currencies in Africa are stabilizing and many countries are fund-raising to build modern highways, ports, and power grids. African countries are winning over investors as indicated by Zambia raising $750 million in bonds recently, followed by Rwanda, Nigeria, and Kenya doing the same. Yields on some African bonds are only slightly higher than the yield on the debt of some troubled European economies, such as Spain. Investors are looking closely at Africa now in the wake of low interest rates and slow growth elsewhere on the planet.[7]

Many African companies are expanding in Africa, such as South Africa's Shoprite Group in 2013 adding 223 stores in 16 African countries other than South Africa. Shoprite is especially targeting Nigeria and the Congo. Dangote Group, based in Nigeria, is building a cement factory in Zambia, and Togo-based Ecobank Transnational now operates in 32 African countries. Domino's recently opened stores in Nigeria, Egypt, Morocco, and Kenya. Reasons companies are opening outlets in Africa is the rapidly growing middle class and an average GDP growth of 5 percent for the continent through 2017 according to the IMF. Also, the World Bank saying food demand across Africa will double between 2012 and 2020.

Financial troubles in Europe, as well as rioting in the Muslim world, are problems for African currencies, such as the Ghana cedi and the Kenya shilling, which depreciated rapidly in 2012. Perennial challenges remain in Africa, such as lack of reliable roads, phone lines, and power grids, but consumer spending in Africa is expected to double from $500 billion in 2012 to $1 trillion in 2020, creating great opportunities for thousands of firms.[8]

Marriott added its first sub-Saharan Africa hotel in 2013, in the capital of Rwanda, which is Kigali. Rwanda's GDP has grown 8 percent annually since 2004 as their president, Paul Kagame, wants to turn the tiny, landlocked equatorial country into an African Singapore. Marriott previously had 7 hotels in northern Africa (Morocco, Algiers, and Egypt), but none below the Sahara desert. Marriott now plans to build 2 hotels in Ghana, 2 in Nigeria, and 2 in Ethiopia between 2013 and 2015. "Most of Africa is a bit of a blank piece of paper for the hospitality industry," says Alex Kyriakidis, chief of Marriott's Middle East and Africa division. South Africa's Protea Hospitality Group plans to add 9 hotels in 2013–2014 to its 36 African properties outside its home country. All total, 208 new, large hotels were added across Africa in 2012 compared to 159 the prior year. Many firms are globally acquiring firms in Africa, such as India's number-2 tire maker, Apollo Tyres, recently buying South Africa's Dunlop Tyres for $62 million. Apollo plans to triple sales to $6 billion by 2015, with 60 percent of that revenue coming from outside India.

Airlines are beginning to really serve Africa, led by Delta in the USA and Persian Gulf carriers such as Qatar Airways, Emirates, and Etihad Airways. The five largest airports in sub-Saharan Africa ranked by available seats in June 2013 were:

Johannesburg, South Africa (278,392)

Addis Ababa, Ethiopia (167,408)

Khartoum, Sudan (142,408)

Nairobi, Kenya (126,729)

Lagos, Nigeria (120,034)

The McKinsey Global Institute reports that approximately 40 percent of Africans now live in urban areas and the number of households with discretionary income should increase 50 percent by the end of this decade.[9] Graham Allan, CEO of Yum Restaurants International, recently said, "A lot of companies, especially Chinese ones, have invested in Africa; we share the general view that Africa over the next 10 to 20 years will have massive potential." McKinsey & Co. says the number of consumers who can spend beyond bare necessities is greater now in Africa than India. From 2000 to 2009, foreign direct investment in Africa increased 600 percent to $58.56 billion.

Walmart recently acquired South African retailer Massmart Holdings for $4.6 billion, providing the company with 290 stores in 13 African countries: Ghana, Nigeria, Zambia, Botswana, Namibia, South Africa, Lesotho, Mozambique, Zimbabwe, Mauritius, Malawi, Tanzania, and Uganda. The Walmart acquisition paves the way for many firms now viewing Africa as a deal-making destination. For example, HSBC Holdings is trying to acquire a majority stake in Nedbank Group, South Africa's fourth-largest bank, and Nippon Telegraph and Telephone in Japan is buying Africa's largest technology company, Dimension Data. Huge purchases such as these have been a wake-up call to the rest of the world, which now views Africa as a growing, attractive new market.

Table 11-7 provides a summary of the economic situation in 12 African countries. Note that Angola is rated lowest in terms of doing business, whereas South Africa is rated highest. Recent regime changes in Egypt, Tunisia, Libya, and Algeria may spur further investment in Africa as democracy and capitalism strengthens. Many multinational companies are now gaining first mover advantages by engaging Africa at all levels. For example, Nokia and Coca-Cola have distribution networks in nearly every African country. Unilever has a presence in 20 of Africa's 50 countries. Nestlé is in 19 African countries, Barclays is in 12, Societe Generale is in 15, and Standard Chartered Bank is in 14. Africa has about 10 percent of the world's oil reserves, 40 percent of its gold ore, and 85 percent of the world's deposits of chromium and platinum. Africa's population is young, growing, and moving into jobs in the cities. Forty percent of Africans today live in the cities, a proportion close to China and India. *The general stereotype*

TABLE 11-7 Sampling of African Countries— Ease-of-Doing-Business Rankings

	Population in Millions	Ease of Doing Business Among all Countries	Capital City
South Africa	49	35 out of 183	Pretoria
Tunisia	11	46 out of 183	Tunis
Ghana	24	63 out of 183	Accra
Morocco	32	94 out of 183	Rabat
Kenya	39	109 out of 183	Nairobi
Egypt	79	110 out of 183	Cairo
Ethiopia	86	111 out of 183	Addis Ababa
Uganda	33	123 out of 183	Kampala
Nigeria	150	133 out of 183	Abuja
Sudan	41	135 out of 183	Khartoum
Mozambique	22	139 out of 183	Maputo
Angola	13	172 out of 183	Luanda

Source: Based on information at http://www.doingbusiness. org/rankings on November 1, 2012.

of Africa is rapidly changing from subsistence farmers avoiding lions, to millions of smartphone carrying consumers in cities purchasing products.

Africa has the world's largest deposits of platinum, chrome, and diamonds—and many Chinese companies in particular are investing there. Africa's largest food retailer, Shoprite Holdings, has more than 1,000 stores in 17 countries. Shoprite is a potential acquisition target being considered by European retailers Carrefour and Tesco. Diageo PLC sells Guinness beer, Smirnoff vodka, Baileys liqueur, and Johnnie Walker whiskey in more than 40 countries across Africa. Nestlé SA now has more than 25 factories in Africa.

Yum Brands recently doubled the number of Kentucky Fried Chicken (KFC) outlets in Africa to 1,200 and increased its revenue from the continent to almost $2 billion. "Africa wasn't even on our radar screen 10 years ago, but now we see it exploding with opportunity" says David Novak, Yum's chairman and CEO. Yum Brands is excited about Africa's growing middle class, vast population, and improving political stability of most African governments. Yum Brands is especially targeting Nigeria, Namibia, Mozambique, Ghana, Zambia, and South Africa. The company says it wants to reach more of Africa's one billion people than its current customer base of 180 million. But KFC currently has about 45 percent of South Africa's fast-food market, followed by Nando's with 6 percent and McDonald's with 5 percent. KFC is opening 25 new outlets in Ghana in 2013-2014, part of the company's 1,200 KFCs in Africa by year-end 2014.

Ghana recently became Africa's newest oil-producing nation when the 1.5-billion-barrel Jubilee field began pumping oil. Although Ghana's estimated 4 billion barrels of reserves are about a third those of Nigeria, Ghana has a stable political and economic situation. Ethiopia is also doing well economically. SABMiller PLC recently invested $20 million in a manufacturing plant in Ethiopia's large city, Ambo. That factory today produces 40,000 glass bottles of mineral water per hour. Ambo sells for about $6 a bottle in New York restaurants. Ambo water is part of the SABMiller portfolio that includes 45 African beers.[10]

Nairobi, Kenya, is the center of several major telecom companies trying to gain market share in the rapidly growing African cellphone business. Vodafone Safaricom Ltd. dominates the Kenyan telecommunications sector with 77 percent market share, but India's Bharti Airtel Ltd. boosted its market share in the last year to almost 20 percent. There are currently more than 440 million mobile subscribers in Africa generating more than $15 billion in telecom revenue annually. All of Africa is coming online, representing huge opportunities for countless companies. McKinsey & Co. estimates that within five years another 220 million Africans that today can meet only basic needs will join the middle class as consumers.[11] There are more than 950 million people who live in Africa.

China

In late 2012, China's economy began to accelerate after nearly two years of slowing growth. China's industrial production grew 9.6 percent in October 2012, up from a 9.2 percent gain in September. China's GDP grew at 7.4 percent in the third quarter of 2012 year-over-year. Analysts expect continued increasing growth, giving a lift to global economic prospects. Although the USA is the world's largest economy with a GDP of over $15 trillion annually, China recently passed Japan to become the world's second-largest economy with a GDP of about $5.75 trillion annually, compared to Japan's $6 trillion. China, however, is still an emerging economy, as indicated by a per-capita GDP of $10,000, compared to the USA and Japan per-capita GDPs of $48,000 and $47,000, respectively. China's economic (GDP) growth of over 9 percent annually for several decades is, however, much faster than either the USA or Japan. Premier Wen Jiabao recently proclaimed that China's annual GDP growth will be held to 7.0 percent if possible to constrain inflation. Goldman Sachs predicts that China will overtake the USA as the world's largest economy by 2027.

China's rapid growth has created substantial pollution, extensive inequality, and deeply embedded corruption. In fact, China's communist government is concerned that political unrest in the Middle East may spread to China in a "Jasmine Revolution" because the masses in China barely make enough to survive. The World Bank estimates that more than 100 million Chinese citizens, nearly the size of Japan's entire population, live on less than $2 a day—but China's middle class is growing rapidly.

For many decades, low wage rates in China helped keep world prices low on hundreds of products—but that is changing, because all 31 Chinese provinces and regions recently boosted their minimum wage for the second consecutive year. Analysts expect demand for workers in China to outstrip supply by 2014, and this is contributing to rapidly rising wage rates and worldwide inflation. Commercial and industrial development in China's west has turned interior cities such as Chongqing into production centers that compete for labor with coastal factories. According to Credit Suisse in Hong Kong, pay to migrant laborers who fuel China's export industry rose 40 percent in 2010 and 30 percent in 2011, and similar increases are expected in 2012. Average monthly pay in 2009 in Shenzhen on the southern China coast was $235, compared to Seoul's $1,220, Taipei's $888, Ho Chi Minh City's $100, Jakarta's $148, and $47 in Dhaka, Bangladesh.[12]

China has become the biggest trading partner for Australia, Japan, Korea, India, Russia, and South Africa and has replaced the USA as the top export market for Brazil. The world's two fastest-growing major economies, China and India, recently announced that the two countries will more than double their bilateral trade between 2010 and 2015 to $100 billion.[13] China is opening its large consumer markets more to Indian goods. China may soon support India having a permanent seat on the United Nations Security Council. China has long opposed a permanent seat for India. The increased cooperation between China and India is good news for companies worldwide doing business in that part of Asia.

As indicated in Table 11-7, China ranks 91st out of 183 countries in terms of doing business, for a variety of reasons ranging from human rights issues to substantial disregard for copyright, patent, and trademark rules of law. Best Buy and Home Depot are example companies that are closing stores in China. Both firms have not competed well in China as a result of being too "high priced" compared to home-grown, similar businesses. The Chinese are price conscious. In contrast, luxury handbag maker, Coach Inc. has made China the cornerstone of its international strategy as the firm's sales and profits are rising sharply in China. Interestingly, Coach is adding more products for men and opening men's stores in China.

China is gaining a stronger and stronger foothold into Japanese businesses. The five largest recent Chinese investments in Japan are Mitsubishi UFJ Financial (92 billion yen), Canon (74.5 billion yen), Sumitomo Mitsui (57.9 billion yen), Nippon T&T (49.2 billion yen), Mitsubishi (47.8 billion yen), Takeda Pharm (45.4 billion yen), and Sony (41.6 billion yen). The Japanese investment adviser Chibagin Asset Management says China state funds have recently more than doubled their investment in Japan to 1.62 trillion yen in 90 companies.

Note also in Table 11-8 that Singapore is rated the best country on the planet for doing business.

TABLE 11-8 Sampling of Asian Countries— Ease-of-Doing-Business Rankings

	Population in Millions	Ease of Doing Business Among all Countries	Capital City
Singapore	5	1 out of 183	Singapore
South Korea	49	8 out of 183	Seoul
Malaysia	26	18 out of 183	Kuala Lumpur
Thailand	66	19 out of 183	Bangkok
Japan	127	20 out of 183	Tokyo
Taiwan	23	25 out of 183	Taipei
China	1,500	91 out of 183	Beijing
Pakistan	175	105 out of 183	Islamabad
Russia	140	120 out of 183	Moscow
Indonesia	241	129 out of 183	Jakarta
India	1,160	132 out of 183	New Delhi
Philippines	98	136 out of 183	Manila

Source: Based on information at http://www.doingbusiness. org/rankings on November 1, 2012.

Philippines

A highly educated, English speaking country, the Philippines overtook India in early 2011 in call-center jobs, employing 350,000 compared with India's 330,000.[14] Call centers in the Philippines produced $7.4 billion in revenue in 2011, and that figure is growing about 15 percent annually. The Philippines recently also overtook Indonesia as the world's biggest supplier of voice-based call-center services.[15] Citigroup and Chase are just two companies outsourcing customer calls, back-office work, and other operations to the Philippines. A major reason why the Philippines is an attractive place for call centers is the country's overall business culture to "deliver absolutely fantastic service." An associate professor at the City University of Hong Kong, Jane Lockwood, says "Filipinos go out of their way, not just in call centers, but in tourism and events management, to ensure people are well looked after."[16]

As indicated in Table 11-8, the Philippines has about 98 million people, making the country the world's 12th largest in population. Located in Southeast Asia, the Philippines was a founding member of the United Nations and is active in that organization. Filipinos love Americans who rescued them in World War II. Thousands of Filipinos today work all-night shifts to accommodate the normal 8 am-to-5 pm business time zone in the USA. Philippines president Benigno Aquino recently indicated that services outsourced to the Philippines from around the world will generate up to $100 billion in 2020, representing 20 percent of the global offshoring market share.

Unemployment is at 6.9 percent in the Philippines, but under-employment—defined as people who work only part-time or with minimal incomes—is 18 percent. The average per capita income of Filipinos is about $1,790 a year, so hundreds of thousands of Filipinos work outside the country. In fact, the Philippines' economy depends greatly on outside workers sending monies back to the country and also traveling to and from the country.

The television advertising market in the Philippines is nearly $4 billion annually, larger than India's and on par with Indonesia's.[17] Television is the most enjoyed media among the Philippines' 7,100 island people, whereas newspapers are the most important media outlet in India. Television ads comprise 75 percent of advertising spending in the Philippines.

Among major emerging economies, the Philippines has only a 9 percent Internet penetration rate among its population, which is low compared to China (28.9%), Nigeria (28.4%), Mexico (28.3%), and Russia (29.0%). But the Philippines' 9 percent rate is above the Internet penetration rate among Indonesia's population (8.7%) and India's population (5.1%).[18] These percentages reveal the percentage of the country's people that could shop online.

Taiwan

Located off the southeast coast of mainland China, Taiwan has a dynamic, capitalist, export-driven economy with gradually decreasing state involvement in investment and foreign trade. Many large, government-owned banks and industrial firms are being privatized in Taiwan. Real annual growth in GDP has averaged about 8 percent during the past three decades. Exports have provided the primary impetus for industrialization. The trade surplus is substantial, and foreign reserves are the world's fifth largest. As indicated in Table 11-8, Taiwan is rated 25th among all countries in the world for doing business.

Both exports and imports for the year reached record levels, totaling U.S. $274 billion and $251 billion, respectively. Agriculture constitutes only 2 percent of Taiwan's GDP, down from 35 percent in 1952. Some brands from Taiwan that are leaders globally include: Acer, HTC, ASUS, TrendMicro, MasterKong, Want-Want, Maxxis, Giant, Synnex, Transcend, Uni-President, Advantech, D-Link, ZyXel, Merida, Johnson, Gigabyte, CyberLink, Genius, and Depo.

India

India passed a law in late 2011 that for the first time allows foreign firms to own 100 percent of some Indian retail ventures, up from a previous 51 percent. One company taking advantage of this change in the law is IKEA that is opening up 25 new stores in India between 2012 and 2015. Since India's growth in GDP has fallen to below 6 percent, the Indian government began to allow much greater foreign investment especially in Indian retail, airlines, and broadcasting in 2012.[19] The country also greatly reduced the expensive government subsidies on diesel fuel and Indian banks are lowering interest rates also to spur growth.

In late 2012, India instituted a five-year road map to improve it finances, aiming to narrow its budget deficit to 5.3 percent of gross domestic product to 3 percent by 2017. A slowdown in growth to 5 percent in 2012, coupled with massive welfare spending, has led to an unmanageable budget deficit in India. Complicating matters in India are high interest rates and some corruption scandals. The Indian Parliament recently approved higher overseas ownership in their insurance and pension investments sectors of the economy.

The Indian government is slowly improving the country's education system, but an enormous amount of work remains. Only 74 percent of Indian men and 48 percent of Indian women are literate, compared to 96 percent of men and 88 percent of women in China. India's "knowledge economy" employs only about 2.23 million people out of 750 million available.

Prime Minister Manmohan Singh's government has instituted education reforms, so the number of Indian children out of school has dropped greatly from 18 million in 2000. Dropout ratios in primary schools have improved as well. However, at present only 12 percent of India's citizens enter higher education, and the government hopes to increase this to 21 percent by 2017. The Indian Institutes of Technology—a group of universities focused on engineering and technology—are world renowned but offer only a miniscule 7,000 places to students each year. There is elaborate red tape required to establish and operate any business in India. Also, India's tax code is archaic and many new sectors are not even open to foreign direct investment.

India will surpass China as the most populated country in 2030. India's highest density growth and population is in the northwest and east-central areas of the country. India has a literacy rate now of 74 percent, up from 65 percent a decade ago.

Germany

Germany's cars, machinery, and other products are in high demand in Asia, especially China. As Europe's debt crisis has pushed the euro lower, German goods are more competitive abroad. The economic and fiscal crises in Greece, Ireland, Portugal, and Spain have only limited direct impact on Germany's $3.24 trillion economy. There is a growing north-south divide in Europe, with the north doing much better economically than the south. Germany's budget deficit was 3.5 percent in 2010, the first time in years that the country has exceeded the 3 percent limit set by EU budget rules, but that percent is well below the deficit in the USA, the UK, and Japan— so overall the German economy is healthy. Note in Table 11-9 that Germany ranks 22nd out of 183 countries in ease of doing business.

German automobile producers such as Daimler AG, BMW AG, and Volkswagen AG have fallen behind rivals such as GM, Renault SA, and Nissan Motor in mass-producing electric cars. The German companies are playing catch up in this key area of industrial growth, partly because the German government has committed just $688 million in state support for electric battery research and infrastructure projects, such as car-charging stations. That amount is only a small fraction of the U.S. (and Chinese) government support for electric cars. Because one

TABLE 11-9 Sampling of European Countries— Ease-of-Doing-Business Rankings

	Population in Millions	Ease of Doing Business Among All Countries	Capital City
UK	62	7 out of 183	London
Sweden	9	14 out of 183	Stockholm
Germany	83	19 out of 183	Berlin
France	64	29 out of 183	Paris
Czech Republic	11	64 out of 183	Prague
Turkey	77	71 out of 183	Ankara
Italy	59	87 out of 183	Rome
Ukraine	46	152 out of 183	Kiev

Source: Based on information at http://www.doingbusiness.org/rankings on November 1, 2012.

out of seven German jobs is connected to the country's car markers and domestic suppliers, this issue is important. More than 15 percent of German exports stem from the automobile industry. Germany also fallen way behind in electric car lithium-ion battery development and production.

The EU is a single economic bloc with free movement of people, goods, and services among its 27 nations, but in matters such as taxes and labor costs, each country sets its own rules. Businesses entering Europe for the first time need to carefully research the various countries. Belgium, for example, has the highest labor costs in Europe with 53 percent of workers there being unionized, but that percent is only the fifth highest in Europe.

Germany has one of Europe's fastest aging and shrinking populations. Germany now faces shortages of skilled labor and aggressive recruiting from abroad for the country's top engineering and scientific talent.[20] More people emigrate from Germany than relocate to Germany, especially highly educated professionals—partly because Germany has a restrictive labor code and inward-looking hiring practices. Germany might need to follow the lead of Italy, which has the same, albeit more severe, problem but has enacted excellent new laws and incentives to both keep and attract young, highly educated professionals.

Mexico

In late 2012, Mexico elected a new president, Enrique Pena Nieto, who inherits a country with a homicide rate of 24 per 100,000 residents up from 10 per 100,000 in 2006. But homicides in Mexico fell 7 percent in the first nine months of 2012, and Nieto plans to continue his predecessor's war on drug cartels and war on corruption. For example, all 600 municipal policemen in Mexico's business-leading city of Monterrey were fired recently and replaced with Mexican military personnel because of suspected corruption.

Mexico has recently reenergized its automobile manufacturing industry and now is the fourth largest automobile exporter on the planet, behind Germany, Japan, and South Korea. One in 10 cars sold in 2011 in the USA was made in Mexico.[21] Every new taxi in New York City's fleet is made in Mexico. Almost all major automobile producers globally have recently announced plans to build new plants in Mexico, including the upcoming new $1.3 billion Volkswagen plant. An already existing Volkswagen plant in Puebla, Mexico, is the company's largest in North America, with a capacity to produce 2,500 cars a day. "Mexico is extremely competitive," says Carlos Ghosn, Nissan's CEO. Ghosn cites the high productivity of Mexican employees, currency advantages, and the typical $40 per day wage rate for Mexican assembly-line workers, which is approaching the average manufacturing wage in China of $3 per hour. Honda is opening a 3,200-employee factory in 2014 in Mexico to produce its subcompact model Fit. Another key advantage for producing vehicles in Mexico over Europe and Asia is that shipment to the USA takes only a day or two, instead of a few weeks by ship.

No country was hurt more in the last decade by the rise of China than Mexico, but Chinese policy today is to boost wages to boost consumer spending. The Boston Consulting Group estimates that "China's average manufacturing wage exceeded Mexico's in 2012 for the first time, when accounting for differences in productivity; Mexican workers typically produce more per hour than Chinese workers."[22] The average wage plus benefits across Mexico is $3.50 an hour. This fact, coupled with China's rising wages and slowing growth and Mexico's close proximity to the USA, represents a great opportunity for Mexico to recoup some of a lot of the manufacturing prowess it lost in the last decade to China. Viaststems Group, based in St. Louis, recently shifted some of its manufacturing back to Mexico from China. Although Dell Inc. computers are produced by Foxconn in China, U.S. customers can order a customized Dell computer online that is assembled and delivered from a 1,200-acre Foxconn plant near Ciudad Juarez.

Foreign direct investment (FDI) in Mexico in 2013 surged to almost $30 billion, led by automobile manufacturers such as Volkswagen AG building new factories, and auto-parts suppliers such as Delphi Automotive PLC following. Home Depot will soon have 125 stores in Mexico. The FDI surge is expected to last at least through 2018, spurred by low wages, and government policies that allow foreign companies to import raw materials without paying duties or tariffs, a 30 percent corporate tax rate, and rising wages in China. However, note in Table 11-10 that Mexico fell from 35th place to 53rd place in the last two years among all nations in terms of ease of doing business.

TABLE 11-10   Sampling of North and South American Countries—Ease-of-Doing-Business Rankings

	Population in Millions	Ease of Doing Business Among all Countries	Capital City
USA	308	4 out of 183	Washington, DC
Canada	34	13 out of 183	Ottawa
Chile	17	39 out of 183	Santiago
Peru	30	41 out of 183	Lima
Mexico	112	53 out of 183	Mexico City
Argentina	41	113 out of 183	Buenos Aires
Brazil	199	126 out of 183	Brasilia
Ecuador	15	130 out of 183	Quito
Bolivia	10	153 out of 183	La Paz
Venezuela	27	177 out of 183	Caracus

Source: Based on information at http://www.doingbusiness.org/rankings on November 1, 2012.

Mexico is especially attractive for manufacturing products that are bulky or costly to transport, so for example, Nissan Motor and Volkswagen AG are planning to build factories in Mexico. The key variable hurting Mexico is drug-related violence since a 2011 United National report says Mexico's homicide rate was 18.1 people per 100,000 compared with a per capita rate of about 5.0 in the USA and 1.1 in China. If Mexico can improve its security situation as it intends, then hundreds of firms may consider moving back there from China (and India).

Special Note to Students

Even the smallest businesses today regularly serve customers globally and gain competitive advantages and economies of scale doing so. Many iconic U.S. businesses, such as Tupperware, obtain more than 80 percent of their revenue from outside the USA. Therefore, in performing a strategic-management case analysis, you must evaluate the scope, magnitude, and nature of what your company is doing globally compared to rival firms. Then, determine what your company should be doing to garner global business. Continuously throughout your presentation or written report, compare your firm to rivals in terms of global business and make recommendations based on careful analysis. Be "prescriptive and insightful" rather than "descriptive and mundane" with every slide presented to pave the way for your specific recommendations with costs regarding global reach of your firm.

Conclusion

The population of the world has surpassed 7 billion. Just as they did for centuries before Columbus reached America, businesses search for new opportunities beyond their national boundaries for centuries to come. There has never been a more internationalized and economically competitive society than today's model. Some U.S. industries, such as textiles, steel, and consumer electronics, are in disarray as a result of the international challenge.

Success in business increasingly depends on offering products and services that are competitive on a world basis, not just on a local basis. If the price and quality of a firm's products and services are not competitive with those available elsewhere in the world, the firm may soon face extinction. Global markets have become a reality in all but the most remote areas of the world. Certainly throughout the USA, even in small towns, firms feel the pressure of world competitors.

This chapter has provided some basic global information that can be essential to consider in developing a strategic plan for any organization. The advantages of engaging in international business may well offset the drawbacks for most firms. It is important in strategic planning to be effective, and the nature of global operations may be the key component in a plan's overall effectiveness.

MyManagementLab®

Go to **mymanagementlab.com** to complete the problems marked with this icon ⭐.

Key Terms and Concepts

feng shui (p. 336)
global strategy (p. 332)
globalization (p. 332)
guanxi (p. 334)
international firms (p. 329)

inhwa (p. 334)
multinational corporations (p. 329)
nemaswashio (p. 336)
protectionism (p. 331)
Wa (p. 334)

Issues for Review and Discussion

11-1. Why are some U.S. companies, such as Eaton, reincorporating in foreign countries, such as to Dublin, Ireland, as did Eaton? What are the pros and cons of that strategy?

11-2. Give specifics regarding the nature and role of "Union Membership across Europe." What are the strategic implications of these facts and figures?

11-3. Give specifics regarding income tax rates and practices across countries, and associated strategic implications.

11-4. Exports from the USA comprise about 11 percent of GDP, compared to about 35 percent of Germany's GDP. What are implications of this for U.S. firms doing business globally?

11-5. Make a good argument for keeping the statutory corporate tax rate in the United States the highest in the world. Make the counterargument.

11-6. A company is planning to begin operations in Switzerland. That company's EFE Matrix includes 20 factors. How much weight (1.0 to 0.01) would you place on the corporate tax rate factor? Discuss.

⭐ **11-7.** Explain how awareness of business culture across countries can enhance strategy implementation.

11-8. Describe the business culture in Brazil.

11-9. Describe the business culture in Germany.

11-10. Describe the business culture in Egypt.

11-11. Describe the business culture in China.

11-12. Describe the business culture in India.

11-13. Describe the business culture in Mexico.

11-14. Describe the business culture in Japan.

11-15. List in prioritized order the top four countries in Africa that are safe, worthwhile, and potentially lucrative for opening new business operations. Give a rationale for each.

11-16. What are several especially attractive aspects of the Philippines for beginning business operations in that country? What are some drawbacks?

11-17. Do some research on Singapore to determine whether you agree that the country merits its number-1 ranking globally in attractiveness for doing business.

⭐ **11-18.** To what extent do you feel political unrest in the Middle East will spread outside the region? Would that be a good or bad thing for global business? What countries do you feel may experience political unrest? Why?

11-19. About 53 percent of people in Belgium are members of a labor union. Compare and contrast the labor union situation across European countries and comment on the positive or negative impact this factor has on attracting business investment into those countries.

11-20. Explain why consumption patterns are becoming similar worldwide. What are the strategic implications of this trend?

11-21. What are the advantages and disadvantages of beginning export operations in a foreign country?

11-22. What are the major differences between U.S. and multinational operations that affect strategic management?

11-23. Why is globalization of industries a common factor today?

11-24. Compare and contrast U.S. versus foreign cultures in terms of doing business.

11-25. List six reasons that strategic management is more complex in a multinational firm.

⭐ **11-26.** Do you feel that protectionism is good or bad for the world economy? Why?

⭐ **11-27.** Why are some industries more "global" than others? Discuss.

11-28. *Wa, guanxi,* and *inhwa* are important management terms in Japan, China, and South Korea, respectively. What would be analogous terms to describe U.S. management practices?

11-29. Why do many Europeans find the notion of "team spirit" in a work environment difficult to grasp?

11-30. In China, *feng shui* is important in business, whereas in Japan, *nemaswashio* is important. What are analogous U.S. terms and practices?

11-31. Compare tax rates in the USA versus other countries. What impact could these differences have on "keeping jobs at home"?

11-32. Discuss requirements for doing business in India.

MyManagementLab®

Go to **mymanagementlab.com** for Auto-graded writing questions as well as the following Assisted-graded writing questions:

11-33. Make a good argument for keeping the statutory corporate tax rate in the United States the highest in the world. Make the counterargument.

11-34. What are the advantages and disadvantages of

beginning export operations in a foreign country?

11-35. Mymanagementlab Only—comprehensive writing assignment for this chapter.

Current Readings

Aguinis, Herman, Harry Joo, Ryan K. Gottfredson. "Performance Management Universals: Think Globally and Act Locally." *Business Horizons* 55, no. 4 (July 2012): 385–392.

Berthon, Pierre R., Leyland F. Pitt, Kirk Plangger, and Daniel Shapiro. "Marketing Meets Web 2.0, Social Media, and Creative Consumers: Implications for International Marketing Strategy." *Business Horizons* 55, no. 3 (May 2012): 261–271.

Bloom, Nicholas, Christos Genakos, Raffaella Sadun, and John Van Reenen. "Management Practices Across Firms and Countries." *The Academy of Management Perspectives 26*, no. 1 (February 2012): 12.

Govindarajan, Vijay and Chris Trimble. "Reverse Innovation: A Global Growth Strategy That Could Pre-empt Disruption at Home." *Strategy and Leadership* 40, no. 5 (2012): 5–11.

Honeycutt, Earl D., Vincent P. Magnini, and Shawn T. Thelen. "Solutions for Customer Complaints About Offshoring and Outsourcing Services." *Business Horizons* 55, no. 1 (January 2012): 33–42.

Ichii, Shigeki, Susumu Hattori, and David Michael. "How to Win in Emerging Markets: Lessons from Japan." *Harvard Business Review* (May 2012): 126.

Ignatius, Adi. "Captain Planet." *Harvard Business Review* (June 2012): 112.

Pagnattaro, Marisa Anne. "Preventing Know-How From Walking Out the Door in China: Protection of Trade Secrets." *Business Horizons* 55, no. 4 (July 2012): 329–337.

Porter, Michael E., and Jan W. Rivkin. "Choosing the USA." *Harvard Business Review* (March 2012): 80.

Ramamurti, Ravi. "Competing with Emerging Market Multinationals." *Business Horizons* 55, no. 3 (May 2012): 241–249.

Thomas, Robert J., Joshua Bellin, Claudy Jules, and Nandani Lynton. "Global Leadership Teams: Diagnosing Three Essential Qualities." *Strategy and Leadership* 40, no. 4 (2012): 25–29.

Underwood, Robert L. "Automotive Foreign Direct Investment in the USA: Economic and Market Consequences of Globalization." *Business Horizons* 55, no. 5 (September 2012): 463–474.

Waldman, David A., Mary Sully de Luque, and Danni Wang. "What Can We Really Learn About Management Practices Across Firms and Countries?" *The Academy of Management Perspectives 26*, no. 1 (February 2012): 34.

ASSURANCE OF LEARNING EXERCISES

EXERCISE 11A
Compare Business Cultures Across Countries

Purpose

PepsiCo does business in more than 100 countries. Various websites give excellent detail that compare and contrast business culture across countries. One excellent website is http://www.kwintessential. co.uk/resources/country-profiles.html, where you can click on more than 100 countries and obtain a synopsis of a country's business culture. (*Note:* The culture part of this chapter is partly based on information at this website.) After clicking on a country at that website, you may scroll down to reach the section titled "Business Etiquette and Protocol." This exercise gives you experience gaining information about business culture in virtually any country. Being knowledgeable of various countries' business culture can make you a more effective manager or communicator with people or organizations in that country. This information is especially critical to firms such as PepsiCo that do business globally.

Step 1 Go to the website named. Click on any two countries located on different continents. Scroll down to the "Business Etiquette and Protocol" section of each country. Print this material.

Step 2 Come to class prepared to give an oral presentation that compares the business culture in the two countries you selected.

EXERCISE 11B

Staples Wants to Enter Africa to Help Them

Purpose

Staples, Inc. is the largest office supply company in the world. Staples has found ways to survive and actually thrive in the face of online competitors such as Amazon, Walmart, and Costco that also sell a wide array of office supplies. Staples' retail, online, and mail order delivery presence gives it a competitive edge and now, having just increased its dividend payout, Staples wants Africa.

More and more companies every day decide to begin doing business in Africa. Research is necessary to determine the best strategy for being the first mover in many African countries (that is, being the first competitor doing business in various countries).

Instructions

Step 1   Print off a map of Africa.
Step 2   Print off demographic data on 10 African countries.
Step 3   Gather competitive information regarding the presence of office-supply firms doing business in Africa.
Step 4   List in prioritized order eight countries in which you would recommend Staples to build stores. Country 1 is your best, and country 2 is your next best. Based on your research, indicate how many Staples stores you would recommend building over the next three years in each country. List in prioritized order three cities in each of your eight African countries where you believe Staples should build most of its stores.

EXERCISE 11C

Does Your University Recruit in Foreign Countries?

Purpose

A competitive climate is emerging among colleges and universities around the world. Colleges and universities in Europe and Japan are increasingly recruiting U.S. students to offset declining enrollments. Foreign students already make up more than a third of the student body at many U.S. universities. The purpose of this exercise is to identify particular colleges and universities in foreign countries that recruit U.S. students.

Instructions

Step 1   Select a foreign country. Conduct research to determine the number and nature of colleges and universities in that country. What are the major educational institutions in that country? What programs are those institutions recognized for offering? What percentage of undergraduate and graduate students attending those institutions are U.S. citizens? Do these institutions actively recruit U.S. students? Are any of the schools of business at the various universities AACSB-International accredited?
Step 2   Prepare a report that summarizes your research findings. Present your report to the class.

EXERCISE 11D

Assess Differences in Culture Across Countries

Purpose

Americans can be more effective in dealing with businesspeople from other countries if they have some awareness and understanding of differences in culture across countries. This is a fun exercise that provides information for your class regarding some of these key differences.

Instructions

Step 1   Identify four individuals who either grew up in a foreign country or who have lived in a foreign country for more than one year. Interview those four persons. Try to have four different countries represented. During each interview, develop a list of eight key differences between U.S. style and custom and that particular country's style and custom in terms of various aspects of speaking, meetings, meals, relationships, friendships, and communication that could impact business dealings.

Step 2   Develop a 15-minute PowerPoint presentation for your class and give a talk summarizing your findings. Identify in your talk the persons you interviewed as well as the length of time those persons lived in the respective countries. Give your professor a hard copy of your PowerPoint presentation.

 EXERCISE 11E
How Well Traveled Are Business Students at Your University?

Purpose

It would be interesting to know how traveled students are at your university and also how those students consider their travels to be helpful in becoming an effective businessperson. Generally speaking, the more one has traveled, especially outside the USA, the more tolerant, understanding, and appreciative one is for diversity. Many students even state on their resume the extent to which they have traveled, both across the USA and perhaps around the world.

Instructions

Administer the following survey to at least 30 business students, including your classmates in the strategic management course. Analyze the results. Give a 15-minute presentation to your class regarding your findings. Turn in a written report of your findings to your professor.

The Survey

1. How many states in the USA have you visited?
2. How many states in the USA have you lived in for at least three months?
3. How many countries outside the USA have you visited?
4. List the countries outside the USA that you have visited.
5. How many countries outside the USA have you lived in for at least three months?
6. List the countries outside the USA that you have lived in for at least three months.
7. To what extent do you feel that traveling across the USA can make a person a more effective businessperson? Use a 1-to-10 scale, where 1 is "Cannot Make a Difference" and 10 is "Can Make a Tremendous Difference."
8. To what extent do you feel that visiting countries outside the USA can make a person a more effective business person? Use a 1-to-10 scale, where 1 is "Cannot Make a Difference" and 10 is "Can Make a Tremendous Difference."
9. To what extent do you feel that living in another country can make a person a more effective businessperson? Use a 1-to-10 scale, where 1 is "Cannot Make a Difference" and 10 is "Can Make a Tremendous Difference."
10. What three important ways so you feel that traveling or living outside the USA would be helpful to a person in being a more effective businessperson?

Notes

1. Frederick Gluck, "Global Competition in the 1990s," *Journal of Business Strategy* (Spring 1983): 22–24.
2. Jon Alston, "Wa, Guanxi, and Inhwa: Managerial Principles in Japan, China and Korea," *Business Horizons* 32, no. 2 (March–April 1989): 26.
3. Rose Knotts, "Cross-Cultural Management: Transformations and Adaptations," *Business Horizons*, January–February 1989, 29–33.
4. Lalita Khosla, "You Say Tomato," *Forbes*, May 21, 2001, 36.
5. Some of the narrative in this section is based on information at: http://www.kwintessential.co.uk/resources/country-profiles.html and http://www.kwintessential.co.uk/resources/global-etiquette/.
6. Mehul Srivastava, "Keeping Women on the Job in India," *Bloomberg Businessweek*, March 7–13, 2011, 11–12; Stratford Sherman, "How to Beat the Japanese? *Fortune*, April 10, 1989, 145.
7. Patrick McGroarty, "Debt Investors Put Faith in a More Stable Africa," *Wall Street Journal* (October 24, 2012): C1.
8. Ibid.

9. Julie Jargon, "KFC Savors Potential in Africa," *Wall Street Journal*, December 8, 2010, B1. Peter Wonacott, "A Continent of New Consumers Beckons," *Wall Street Journal*, January 13, 2011, B1.

10. Peter Wonacott, "SABMiller Taps Ethiopia's Holy Water," *Wall Street Journal*, January 13, 2011, B1.

11. Sarah Childress, "Telecom Giants Battle for Kenya," *Wall Street Journal*, January14, 2011, B1.

12. Sophie Leung and Simon Kennedy with Cotton Timberlake and Chris Burritt, "Global Inflation Starts With Chinese Workers," *Bloomberg Businessweek*, March 7–13, 2011, 9–10.

13. Arpan Mukherjee and Abhrajit Gangopadhyay, "India, China Aim to Double Trade," *Wall Street Journal*, December 17, 2010, A15.

14. Michelle Yun and Kathy Chu, "Philippines May Answer Call," *USA Today*, January 10. 2011, 1–2B.

15. Ibid.

16. James Hookway, "Dollar's Fall Rocks Far-Flung Families," *Wall Street Journal*, February 25, 2011, A12.

17. James Hookway, "High Drama for Philippine TV," *Wall Street Journal*, March 3, 2011, B10.

18. Amol Sharma, "Dot-Coms Begin to Blossom in India," *Wall Street Journal*, April 12, 2011, B1.

19. Rumman Ahmed and Romit Guha, "India Faces Fight Over Foreign Firms," *Wall Street Journal (September* 17, 2012): A12.

20. Vanessa Fuhrmans, "Exodus of Skilled Labor Saps Germany," *Wall Street Journal*, March 11, 2011, A12.

21. Nicholas Casey, "In Mexico, Auto Plants Hit the Gas," *Wall Street Journal* (11-20-12): A1.

22. Luhnow, David and Bob Davis, "For Mexico, an Edge on China," *Wall Street Journal* (September 17, 2012): A12.

## PART 6

STRATEGIC-MANAGEMENT CASE ANALYSIS

Source: Africa Studio/Fotolia

MyManagementLab®

⭐ Improve Your Grade!

Over 10 million students improved their results using the Pearson MyLabs.
Visit **mymanagementlab.com** for simulations, tutorials, and end-of-chapter problems.

How to Prepare and Present a Case Analysis

CHAPTER OBJECTIVES

After studying this chapter, you should be able to do the following:

1. Describe the case method for learning strategic-management concepts.

2. Identify the steps in preparing a comprehensive written case analysis.

3. Describe how to give an effective oral case analysis presentation.

4. Discuss special tips for doing a case analysis.

ASSURANCE OF LEARNING EXERCISES

The following exercises are found at the end of this chapter.

Oral Presentation—Step 1 Introduction (2 minutes)

Oral Presentation—Step 2 Mission and Vision (4 minutes)

Oral Presentation—Step 3 Internal Assessment (8 minutes)

Oral Presentation—Step 4 External Assessment (8 minutes)

Oral Presentation—Step 5 Strategy Formulation (14 minutes)

Oral Presentation—Step 6 Strategy Implementation (8 minutes)

Oral Presentation—Step 7 Strategy Evaluation (2 minutes)

Oral Presentation—Step 8 Conclusion (4 minutes)

The purpose of this section is to help you analyze strategic-management cases. Guidelines for preparing written and oral case analyses are given, and suggestions for preparing cases for class discussion are presented. Steps to follow in preparing case analyses are provided. Guidelines for making an oral presentation are described.

What Is a Strategic-Management Case?

A *strategic-management case* describes an organization's external and internal conditions and raises issues concerning the firm's mission, strategies, objectives, and policies. Most of the information in a strategic-management case is established fact, but some information may be opinions, judgments, and beliefs. Strategic-management cases are more comprehensive than those you may have studied in other courses. They generally include a description of related management, marketing, finance and accounting, production and operations, research and development (R&D), management information systems (MIS), and natural environment issues. A strategic-management case puts the reader at the scene of the action by describing a firm's situation at some point in time. Strategic-management cases are written to give you practice applying strategic-management concepts. The case method for studying strategic management is often called *learning by doing*.

Guidelines for Preparing Case Analyses

The Need for Practicality

There is no such thing as a complete case, and no case ever gives you all the information you need to conduct analyses and make recommendations. Likewise, in the business world, strategists never have all the information they need to make decisions: information may be unavailable or too costly to obtain, or it may take too much time to obtain. So in analyzing strategic-management cases, do what strategists do every day—make reasonable assumptions about unknowns, clearly state assumptions, perform appropriate analyses, and make decisions. *Be practical.* For example, in performing a projected financial analysis, make reasonable assumptions, appropriately state them, and proceed to show what impact your recommendations are expected to have on the organization's financial position. Avoid saying, "I don't have enough information." Always supplement the information provided in a case with Internet and library research.

The Need for Justification

The most important part of analyzing cases is not what strategies you recommend but rather how you support your decisions and how you propose that they be implemented. There is no single best solution or one right answer to a case, so give ample justification for your recommendations. This is important. In the business world, strategists usually do not know if their decisions are right until resources have been allocated and consumed. Then it is often too late to reverse a decision. This cold fact accents the need for careful integration of intuition and analysis in preparing strategic management case analyses.

The Need for Realism

Avoid recommending a course of action beyond an organization's means. *Be realistic.* No organization can possibly pursue all the strategies that could potentially benefit the firm. Estimate how much capital will be required to implement what you recommended. Determine whether debt, stock, or a combination of debt and stock could be used to obtain the capital. Make sure your recommendations are feasible. Do not prepare a case analysis that omits all arguments and information not supportive of your recommendations. Rather, present the major advantages and disadvantages of several feasible alternatives. Try not to exaggerate, stereotype, prejudge, or overdramatize. Strive to demonstrate that your interpretation of the evidence is reasonable and objective.

The Need for Specificity

Do not make broad generalizations such as "The company should pursue a market penetration strategy." Be specific by telling *what, why, when, how, where,* and *who.* Failure to use specifics is the single major shortcoming of most oral and written case analyses. For example, in an internal audit say, "The firm's current ratio fell from 2.2 in 2013 to 1.3 in 2014, and this is considered to be a major weakness," instead of "The firm's financial condition is bad." But recall from the chapters that selected external and internal factors need to be "*actionable*" to the extent possible, and financial ratios in general are not actionable. Rather than concluding from a Strategic Position and Action Evaluation (SPACE) Matrix that a firm should be defensive, be more specific, saying, "The firm should consider closing three plants, laying off 280 employees, and divesting itself of its chemical division, for a net savings of $20.2 million in 2014." Use ratios, percentages, numbers, and dollar estimates. Businesspeople dislike generalities and vagueness.

The Need for Originality

Do not necessarily recommend the course of action that the firm plans to take or actually undertook, even if those actions resulted in improved revenues and earnings. The aim of case analysis is for you to consider all the facts and information relevant to the organization at the time, to generate feasible alternative strategies, to choose among those alternatives, and to defend your recommendations. Put yourself back in time to the point when strategic decisions were being made by the firm's strategists. Based on the information available then, what would you have done? Support your position with charts, graphs, ratios, analyses, and the like—not a revelation from the library. You can become a good strategist by thinking through situations, making management assessments, and proposing plans yourself. *Be original.* Compare and contrast what you recommend versus what the company plans to do or did.

The Need to Contribute

Strategy formulation, implementation, and evaluation decisions are commonly made by a group of individuals rather than by a single person. Therefore, your professor may divide the class into three- or four-person teams and ask you to prepare written or oral case analyses. Members of a strategic-management team, in class or in the business world, differ on their aversion to risk, their concern for short-run versus long-run benefits, their attitudes toward social responsibility, and their views concerning globalization. There are no perfect people, so there are no perfect strategies. Be open-minded to others' views. *Be a good listener and a good contributor.*

Preparing a Case for Class Discussion

Your professor may ask you to prepare a case for class discussion. Preparing a case for class discussion means that you need to read the case before class, make notes regarding the organization's external opportunities and threats and internal strengths and weaknesses, perform appropriate analyses, and come to class prepared to offer and defend some specific recommendations.

The Case Method versus Lecture Approach

The case method of teaching is radically different from the traditional lecture approach, in which little or no preparation is needed by students before class. The *case method* involves a classroom situation in which students do most of the talking; your professor facilitates discussion by asking questions and encouraging student interaction regarding ideas, analyses, and recommendations. Be prepared for a discussion along the lines of "What would you do, why would you do it, when would you do it, and how would you do it?" Prepare answers to the following types of questions:

- What are the firm's most important external opportunities and threats?
- What are the organization's major strengths and weaknesses?
- How would you describe the organization's financial condition?
- What are the firm's existing strategies and objectives?
- Who are the firm's competitors, and what are their strategies?
- What objectives and strategies do you recommend for this organization? Explain your reasoning. How does what you recommend compare to what the company plans?
- How could the organization best implement what you recommend? What implementation problems do you envision? How could the firm avoid or solve those problems?

The Cross-Examination

Do not hesitate to take a stand on the issues and to support your position with objective analyses and outside research. Strive to apply strategic-management concepts and tools in preparing your case for class discussion. Seek defensible arguments and positions. Support opinions and judgments with facts, reasons, and evidence. Crunch the numbers before class! Be willing to describe your recommendations to the class without fear of disapproval. Respect the ideas of others, but be willing to go against the majority opinion when you can justify a better position.

Strategic-management case analysis gives you the opportunity to learn more about yourself, your colleagues, strategic management, and the decision-making process in organizations. The rewards of this experience will depend on the effort you put forth, so do a good job. Discussing business policy cases in class is exciting and challenging. Expect views counter to those you present. Different students will place emphasis on different aspects of an organization's situation and submit different recommendations for scrutiny and rebuttal. Cross-examination discussions commonly arise, just as they occur in a real business organization. Avoid being a silent observer.

Preparing a Written Case Analysis

In addition to asking you to prepare a case for class discussion, your professor may ask you to prepare a written case analysis. Preparing a written case analysis is similar to preparing a case for class discussion, except written reports are generally more structured and more detailed. There is no ironclad procedure for preparing a written case analysis because cases differ in focus; the type, size, and complexity of the organizations being analyzed also vary.

When writing a strategic-management report or case analysis, avoid using jargon, vague or redundant words, acronyms, abbreviations, sexist language, and ethnic or racial slurs. And watch your spelling! Use short sentences and paragraphs and simple words and phrases. Use quite a few subheadings. Arrange issues and ideas from the most important to the least important. Arrange recommendations from the least controversial to the most controversial. Use the active voice rather than the passive voice for all verbs; for example, say "Our team recommends that the company diversify" rather than "It is recommended by our team to diversify." Use many examples to add specificity and clarity. Tables, figures, pie charts, bar charts, timelines, and other kinds of exhibits help communicate important points and ideas. Sometimes a picture *is* worth a thousand words.

The Executive Summary

Your professor may ask you to focus the written case analysis on a particular aspect of the strategic-management process, such as (1) to identify and evaluate the organization's existing vision, mission, objectives, and strategies; or (2) to propose and defend specific recommendations for the company; or (3) to develop an industry analysis by describing the competitors, products, selling techniques, and market conditions in a given industry. These types of written reports are sometimes called *executive summaries*. An executive summary usually ranges from three to five pages of text in length, plus exhibits.

The Comprehensive Written Analysis

Your professor may ask you to prepare a *comprehensive written analysis*. This assignment requires you to apply the entire strategic-management process to the particular organization. When preparing a comprehensive written analysis, picture yourself as a consultant who has been asked by a company to conduct a study of its external and internal environment and to make specific recommendations for its future. Prepare exhibits to support your recommendations. Highlight exhibits with some discussion in the paper. Comprehensive written analyses are usually about 10 pages in length, plus exhibits. Throughout your written analysis, emphasize how your proposed strategies will enable the firm to gain and sustain competitive advantage. Visit www.strategyclub.com for examples.

Steps in Preparing a Comprehensive Written Analysis

In preparing a *written* case analysis, you could follow the steps outlined here, which correlate to the stages in the strategic-management process and the chapters in this text. (Note—The steps in presenting an *oral* case analysis are given on pages 367–369, are more detailed, and could be used here).

Step 1   Identify the firm's existing vision, mission, objectives, and strategies.

Step 2   Develop vision and mission statements for the organization.

Step 3   Identify the organization's external opportunities and threats.

Step 4   Construct a Competitive Profile Matrix (CPM).

Step 5   Construct an External Factor Evaluation (EFE) Matrix.

Step 6   Identify the organization's internal strengths and weaknesses.

Step 7   Construct an Internal Factor Evaluation (IFE) Matrix.

Step 8   Prepare a Strengths-Weaknesses-Opportunities-Threats (SWOT) Matrix, Strategic Position and Action Evaluation (SPACE) Matrix, Boston Consulting Group (BCG) Matrix, Internal-External (IE) Matrix, Grand Strategy Matrix, and Quantitative Strategic Planning Matrix (QSPM) as appropriate. Give advantages and disadvantages of alternative strategies.

Step 9   Recommend specific strategies and long-term objectives. Show how much your recommendations will cost. Clearly itemize these costs for each projected year. Compare your recommendations to actual strategies planned by the company.

Step 10   Specify how your recommendations can be implemented and what results you can expect. Prepare forecasted ratios and projected financial statements. Present a timetable or agenda for action.

Step 11   Recommend specific annual objectives and policies.

Step 12   Recommend procedures for strategy review and evaluation.

Making an Oral Presentation

Your professor may ask you to prepare a strategic-management case analysis, individually or as a group, and present your analysis to the class. Oral presentations are usually graded on two parts: content and delivery. *Content* refers to the quality, quantity, correctness, and appropriateness of analyses presented, including such dimensions as logical flow through the presentation, coverage of major issues, use of specifics, avoidance of generalities, absence of mistakes, and feasibility of recommendations. *Delivery* includes such dimensions as audience attentiveness, clarity of visual aids, appropriate dress, persuasiveness of arguments, tone of voice, eye contact, and posture. Great ideas are of no value unless others can be convinced of their merit through clear communication. The guidelines presented here can help you make an effective oral presentation.

Organizing the Presentation

Begin your presentation by introducing yourself and giving a clear outline of topics to be covered. If a team is presenting, specify the sequence of speakers and the areas each person will address. At the beginning of an oral presentation, try to capture your audience's interest and attention. You could do this by displaying some products made by the company, telling an interesting short story about the company, or sharing an experience you had that is related to the company, its products, or its services. You could develop or obtain a video to show at the beginning of class; you could visit a local distributor of the firm's products and tape a personal interview with the business owner or manager. A light or humorous introduction can be effective at the beginning of a presentation.

Be sure the setting of your presentation is well organized, with seats for attendees, flip charts, a transparency projector, and whatever else you plan to use. Arrive at the classroom at least 15 minutes early to organize the setting, and be sure your materials are ready to go. Make sure everyone can see your visual aids well.

Controlling Your Voice

An effective rate of speaking ranges from 100 to 125 words per minute. Practice your presentation aloud to determine if you are going too fast. Individuals commonly speak too fast when nervous. Breathe deeply before and during the presentation to help yourself slow down. Have a cup of water available; pausing to take a drink will wet your throat, give you time to collect your thoughts, control your nervousness, slow you down, and signal to the audience a change in topic.

Avoid a monotone voice by placing emphasis on different words or sentences. Speak loudly and clearly, but do not shout. Silence can be used effectively to break a monotone voice. Stop at the end of each sentence, rather than running sentences together with *and* or *uh*.

Managing Body Language

Be sure not to fold your arms, lean on the podium, put your hands in your pockets, or put your hands behind you. Keep a straight posture, with one foot slightly in front of the other. Do not turn your back to the audience; doing so is not only rude, but it also prevents your voice from projecting well. Avoid using too many hand gestures. On occasion, leave the podium or table and walk toward your audience, but do not walk around too much. Never block the audience's view of your visual aids.

Maintain good eye contact throughout the presentation. This is the best way to persuade your audience. There is nothing more reassuring to a speaker than to see members of the audience nod in agreement or smile. Try to look everyone in the eye at least once during your presentation, but focus more on individuals who look interested than on those who seem bored. To stay in touch with your audience, use humor and smiles as appropriate throughout your presentation. A presentation should never be dull!

Speaking from Notes

Be sure not to read to your audience because reading puts people to sleep. Perhaps worse than reading is merely reciting what you have memorized. Do not try to memorize anything. Rather, practice unobtrusively using notes. Make sure your notes are written clearly so you will not flounder when trying to read your own writing. Include only main ideas on your note cards. Keep note cards on a podium or table if possible so that you will not drop them or get them out of order; walking with note cards tends to be distracting.

Constructing Visual Aids

Make sure your visual aids are legible to individuals in the back of the room. Use color to highlight special items. Avoid putting complete sentences on visual aids; rather, use short phrases and then orally elaborate on issues as you make your presentation. Generally, there should be no more than four to six lines of text on each visual aid. Use clear headings and subheadings. Be careful about spelling and grammar; use a consistent style of lettering. Use masking tape or an easel for posters—do not hold posters in your hand. Transparencies and handouts are excellent aids; however, be careful not to use too many handouts or your audience may concentrate on them instead of you during the presentation.

Answering Questions

It is best to field questions at the end of your presentation, rather than during the presentation itself. Encourage questions, and take your time to respond to each one. Answering questions can be persuasive because it involves you with the audience. If a team is giving the presentation, the audience should direct questions to a specific person. During the question-and-answer period, be polite, confident, and courteous. Avoid verbose responses. Do not get defensive with your answers, even if a hostile or confrontational question is asked. Staying calm during potentially disruptive situations, such as a cross-examination, reflects self-confidence, maturity, poise, and command of the particular company and its industry. Stand up throughout the question-and-answer period.

Tips for Success in Case Analysis

Strategic-management students who have used this text over 14 editions offer you the following tips for success in doing case analysis. The tips are grouped into two basic sections: (1) Content Tips and (2) Process Tips. Content tips relate especially to the content of your case analysis, whereas the Process tips relate mostly to the process that you and your group mates undergo in preparing and delivering your case analysis/presentation.

Content Tips

1. Use the www.strategyclub.com website resources. The free excel student template provided there is especially useful as are the sample PowerPoint case analyses on a couple of companies.
2. In preparing your external assessment, use the S&P *Industry Survey* material in your college library.
3. Go to http://finance.yahoo.com or http://money.msn.com and enter your company's stock symbol.
4. View your case analysis and presentation as a product that must have some competitive factor to favorably differentiate it from the case analyses of other students.
5. Develop a mind-set of *why*, continually questioning your own and others' assumptions and assertions.
6. Because strategic management is a capstone course, seek the help of professors in other specialty areas when necessary.
7. Read your case frequently as work progresses so you do not overlook details.
8. At the end of each group session, assign each member of the group a task to be completed for the next meeting.
9. Become friends with the library and the Internet.
10. Be creative and innovative throughout the case analysis process.
11. A goal of case analysis is to improve your ability to think clearly in ambiguous and confusing situations; do not get frustrated that there is no single best answer.
12. Do not confuse symptoms with causes; do not develop conclusions and solutions prematurely; recognize that information may be misleading, conflicting, or wrong.
13. Work hard to develop the ability to formulate reasonable, consistent, and creative plans; put yourself in the strategist's position.
14. Develop confidence in using quantitative tools for analysis. They are not inherently difficult; it is just practice and familiarity you need.
15. Strive for excellence in writing and in the technical preparation of your case. Prepare nice charts, tables, diagrams, and graphs. Use color and unique pictures. No messy exhibits! Use PowerPoint.
16. Do not forget that the objective is to learn; explore areas with which you are not familiar.
17. Pay attention to detail.
18. Think through alternative implications fully and realistically. The consequences of decisions are not always apparent. They often affect many different aspects of a firm's operations.
19. Provide answers to such fundamental questions as *what*, *when*, *where*, *why*, *who*, and *how*.
20. Do not merely recite ratios or present figures. Rather, develop ideas and conclusions concerning the possible trends. Show the importance of these figures to the corporation.
21. Support reasoning and judgment with factual data whenever possible.
22. Your analysis should be as detailed and specific as possible.
23. A picture speaks a thousand words, and a creative picture gets you an A in many classes.
24. Emphasize the Recommendations and Strategy Implementation sections. A common mistake is to spend too much time on the external or internal analysis parts of your paper or presentation. The recommendations and implementation sections are the most important part.
25. Throughout your case analysis, emphasize how your proposed strategic plan will enable the firm to gain and sustain competitive advantage.

Process Tips

1. When working as a team, encourage most of the work to be done individually. Use team meetings mostly to assimilate work. This approach is most efficient.
2. If allowed to do so, invite questions throughout your presentation.
3. During the presentation, keep good posture, eye contact, and voice tone, and project confidence. Do not get defensive under any conditions or with any questions.
4. Prepare your case analysis in advance of the due date to allow time for reflection and practice. Do not procrastinate.
5. Maintain a positive attitude about the class, working *with* problems rather than against them.
6. Keep in tune with your professor, and understand his or her values and expectations.
7. Other students will have strengths in functional areas that will complement your weaknesses, so develop a cooperative spirit that moderates competitiveness in group work.
8. When preparing a case analysis as a group, divide into separate teams to work on the external analysis and internal analysis.
9. Have a good sense of humor.
10. Capitalize on the strengths of each member of the group; volunteer your services in your areas of strength.
11. Set goals for yourself and your team; budget your time to attain them.
12. Foster attitudes that encourage group participation and interaction. Do not be hasty to judge group members.
13. Be prepared to work. There will be times when you will have to do more than your share. Accept it, and do what you have to do to move the team forward.
14. Think of your case analysis as if it were really happening; do not reduce case analysis to a mechanical process.
15. To uncover flaws in your analysis and to prepare the group for questions during an oral presentation, assign one person in the group to actively play the devil's advocate.
16. Do not schedule excessively long group meetings; two-hour sessions are about right.
17. Push your ideas hard enough to get them listened to, but then let up; listen to others and try to follow their lines of thinking; follow the flow of group discussion, recognizing when you need to get back on track; do not repeat yourself or others unless clarity or progress demands repetition.
18. Develop a case-presentation style that is direct, assertive, and convincing; be concise, precise, fluent, and correct.
19. Have fun when at all possible. Preparing a case is frustrating at times, but enjoy it while you can; it may be several years before you are playing CEO again.
20. In group cases, do not allow personality differences to interfere. When they occur, they must be understood for what they are—and then put aside.
21. Get things written down (drafts) as soon as possible.
22. Read everything that other group members write, and comment on it in writing. This allows group input into all aspects of case preparation.
23. Adaptation and flexibility are keys to success; be creative and innovative.
24. Neatness is a real plus; your case analysis should look professional.
25. Let someone else read and critique your presentation several days before you present it.
26. Make special efforts to get to know your group members. This leads to more openness in the group and allows for more interchange of ideas. Put in the time and effort necessary to develop these relationships.
27. Be constructively critical of your group members' work. Do not dominate group discussions. Be a good listener and contributor.
28. Learn from past mistakes and deficiencies. Improve on weak aspects of other case presentations.
29. Learn from the positive approaches and accomplishments of classmates.

Sample Case Analysis Outline

There are musicians who play wonderfully without notes and there are chefs who cook wonderfully without recipes, but most of us prefer a more orderly cookbook approach, at least in the first attempt at doing something new. Therefore the following eight steps may serve as a basic outline for you in presenting a strategic plan for your firm's future. This outline is not the only approach used in business and industry for communicating a strategic plan, but this approach is time-tested, it does work, and it does cover all of the basics. You may amend the content, tools, and concepts given to suit your own company, audience, assignment, and circumstances, but it helps to know and understand the rules before you start breaking them.

Depending on whether your class is 50 minutes or 75 minutes and how much time your professor allows for your case presentation, the following outlines what generally needs to be covered. A recommended time (in minutes) as part of the presentation is given for an overall 50-minute event. Even if you do not have time to cover all areas in your oral presentation, you may be asked to prepare these areas and give them to your professor as a written case analysis. Be sure in an oral presentation to manage time knowing that your recommendations and associated costs are the most important part. You should go to www.strategyclub.com and use that information and software in preparing your case analysis. Good luck.

Current Readings

Kearney, Eric, Diether Gebert, and Sven Voelpel. "When Diversity Benefits Teams: The Importance of Team Members' Need for Cognition." *Academy of Management Journal*, June 2009, 581–598.

STEPS IN PRESENTING AN ORAL CASE ANALYSIS

ORAL PRESENTATION—STEP 1
Introduction (2 minutes)

a. Introduce yourselves by name and major. Establish the time setting of your case and analysis. Prepare your strategic plan for the three years 2014–2016.
b. Introduce your company and its products or services; capture interest.
c. Show the outline of your presentation and tell who is doing what parts.
d. Let your audience know that the primary motivation, rationale, or intent of every slide is to reveal how the firm can best gain and sustain competitive advantage.

ORAL PRESENTATION—STEP 2
Mission and Vision (4 minutes)

a. Show existing mission and vision statements if available from the firm's website, annual report, or elsewhere.
b. Show your "improved" mission and vision and tell why it is improved.
c. Compare your mission and vision to a leading competitor's statements.
d. Comment on your vision and mission in terms of how they support the strategies you envision for your firm.

ORAL PRESENTATION—STEP 3
Internal Assessment (8 minutes)

a. Give your financial ratio analysis. Highlight especially good and bad ratios. Do not give definitions of the ratios and do not highlight all the ratios.
b. Show the firm's organizational chart found or "created based on executive titles." Identify the type of chart as well as good and bad aspects. Unless all white males comprise the chart, peoples' names are generally not important because positions reveal structure as people come and go.
c. Present your improved or recommended organizational chart. Tell why you feel it is improved over the existing chart.
d. Show a market positioning map with firm and competitors. Discuss the map in light of strategies you envision for firm versus competitors' strategies.
e. Identify the marketing strategy of the firm in terms of good and bad points versus competitors and in light of strategies you envision for the firm.

    f. Show a map locating the firm's operations. Discuss in light of strategies you envision. Also, perhaps show a value chain analysis chart.

    g. Discuss (and perhaps show) the firm's website and Facebook page in terms of good and bad points compared to rival firms.

    h. Show your "value of the firm" analysis.

    i. List 20 of the firm's strengths and weaknesses. Go over each one listed without "reading" them verbatim.

    j. Show and explain your Internal Factor Evaluation (IFE) Matrix.

ORAL PRESENTATION—STEP 4
External Assessment (8 minutes)

    a. Identify and discuss major competitors. Use pie charts, maps, tables, or figures to show the intensity of competition in the industry.

    b. Show your Competitive Profile Matrix. Include at least 12 factors and two competitors.

    c. Summarize key industry trends citing Standard & Poor's *Industry Survey* or Chamber of Commerce statistics, and so on. Highlight key external trends as they impact the firm, including trends that are economic, social, cultural, demographic, geographic, technological, political, legal, governmental, and to do with the natural environment.

    d. List 20 of the firm's opportunities and threats. Make sure your opportunities are not stated as strategies. Go over each one listed without "reading" them verbatim.

    e. Show and explain your External Factor Evaluation (EFE) Matrix.

ORAL PRESENTATION—STEP 5
Strategy Formulation (14 minutes)

    a. Show and explain your SWOT Matrix, highlighting each of your strategies listed.

    b. Show and explain your SPACE Matrix, using half of your "space time" on calculations and the other half on implications of those numbers. Strategy implications must be specific rather than generic. In other words, use of a term such as *market penetration* is not satisfactory alone as a strategy implication.

    c. Show your Boston Consulting Group (BCG) Matrix. Again focus on both the numbers and the strategy implications. Do multiple BCG Matrices if possible, including domestic versus global, or another geographic breakdown. Develop a product BCG if at all possible. Comment on changes to this matrix as per strategies you envision. Develop this matrix even if you do not know the profits per division and even if you have to estimate the axes information. However, make no wild guesses on axes or revenue/profit information.

    d. Show your Internal-External (IE) Matrix. Because this analysis is similar to the BCG, see the preceding comments.

    e. Show your Grand Strategy Matrix. Again focus on implications after giving the quadrant selection. Reminder: Use of a term such as *market penetration* is not satisfactory alone as a strategy implication. Be more specific. Elaborate.

    f. Show your Quantitative Strategic Planning Matrix (QSPM). Be sure to explain your strategies to start with here. Do not go back over the internal and external factors. Avoid having more than one 4, 3, 2, or 1 in a row. If you rate one strategy, you need to rate the other because that particular factor is affecting the choice. Work row by row rather than column by column on preparing the QSPM.

    g. Present your recommendations page. This is the most important page in your presentation. Be specific in terms of both strategies and estimated costs of those strategies. *Total your estimated costs.* You should have 10 or more strategies. Divide your strategies into two groups: (1) Existing Strategies to Be Continued and (2) New Strategies to Be Started.

ORAL PRESENTATION—STEP 6
Strategy Implementation (8 minutes)

    a. Show and explain your earnings per share/earnings before interest and taxes (EPS/ EBIT) analysis to reveal whether stock, debt, or a combination is best to finance your recommendations. Graph the analysis. Decide which approach to use if there are any given limitations of the analysis.

b. Show your projected income statement. Relate changes in the items to your recommendations rather than blindly going with historical percentage changes.

c. Show your projected balance sheet. Relate changes in your items to your recommendations. Be sure to show the retained earnings calculation and the results of your EPS/EBIT decision.

d. Show your projected financial ratios and highlight several key ratios to show the benefits of your strategic plan.

ORAL PRESENTATION—STEP 7
Strategy Evaluation (2 minutes)

a. Prepare a Balanced Scorecard to show your expected financial and nonfinancial objectives recommended for the firm.

ORAL PRESENTATION—STEP 8
Conclusion (4 minutes)

a. Compare and contrast your strategic plan versus the company's own plans for the future.

b. Thank audience members for their attention. Genuinely seek and gladly answer questions.

Strategic Management Cases

Domino's Pizza, Inc., 2013

www.dominos.com, DPZ

Based in Ann Arbor, Michigan, Domino's is the largest pizza delivery company in the USA having a 22.5 percent share of the pizza delivery market. Domino's digital ordering channels include online ordering at www.dominos.com, mobile ordering at http://mobile.dominos.com, and ordering on iPhone, Kindle Fire, and Android apps. More than $2 billion of Domino's pizza is ordered online annually. There are more than 10,300 Domino's stores in over 70 countries. Domino's had sales of over $7.4 billion in 2012, with $3.6 billion of that coming from the USA.

Copyright by Fred David Books LLC. (Written by Forest R. David)

History

Growing up in foster homes most of their childhood, Tom Monaghan and his brother James borrowed $900 in 1960 to purchase a mom-and-pop pizza store in Ypsilanti, Michigan, named Domi-Nick's. After trading his brother James a Volkswagen Beetle for his half of the business in 1961, Tom changed the store name in 1965 from Domi-Nick's to Domino's Pizza Inc. The company experienced steady growth during the 1960s, and by 1978, there were 200 Domino's stores in the USA. During the 1980s, the company expanded rapidly both in the USA and internationally. By the end of the decade, Domino's had more than 5,000 stores in the USA, Canada, United Kingdom, Japan, Australia, and Colombia. By 1998, there were more than 6,000 Dominos, with 1,500 located outside the USA. Tom Monaghan retired in 1998 and sold 93 percent of the company (worth $1 billion) to Bain Capital Inc. In the six years following the sale, Domino's enjoyed great success under Bain Capital and in 2004 Domino's became a publically traded company on the New York Stock Exchange under the ticker symbol DPZ. The initial stock price was $16 per share and placed a value on the company at more than $2 billion (double the price Bain paid).

Domino's changed its 49-year-old recipe at year end 2009 and started a heavily advertised marketing campaign called "new inspired pizza." Domino's stock price appreciated from around $8 a share at the start of 2010 to $60 in mid-2003. Fueled by the new recipe and new products, Domino's celebrated its 50th anniversary in 2010 and was awarded best pizza chain in 2010 and 2011 by *Pizza Today* magazine, marking the first time ever that the same pizza chain had received the award in consecutive years. Domino's CEO Patrick Doyle was named the best CEO of 2011 by CNBC. Domino's was recently ranked number 1 in *Forbes* magazine's "Top 20 Franchises for the Money" list.

About 96 percent of Domino's stores are owned by franchisees. There are very few company-owned Domino's stores.

Corporate Philosophy and Mission Statement

Domino's does not have a stated vision statement, but the company mission statement is as follows: "Exceptional franchisees and team members on a mission to be the best pizza delivery company in the world." Domino's "guiding principles" are based on the concept of one united brand, system and team:

- putting people first;
- striving to make every customer a loyal customer;
- delivering with smart hustle and positive energy; and
- winning by improving results every day. (2012 *Annual Report*)

Organizational Structure

As indicated in Exhibit 1, Domino's has 11 top executives, mostly executive vice-presidents (EVPs). It appears that Domino's operates from a functional organizational structure with Doyle being "where the buck stops," although for a firm of this size, a divisional or strategic business

EXHIBIT 1 Domino's Organizational Chart

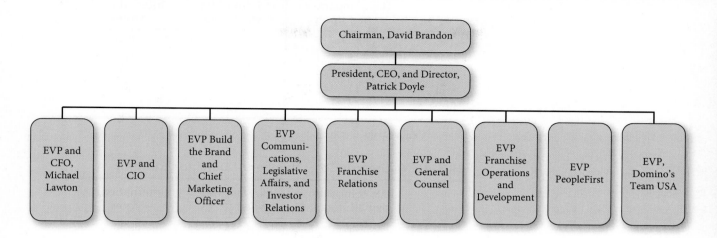

unit type structure by region (or by franchised versus company owned) may be more effective in promoting delegation of authority, responsibility, and accountability.

Business Segments

Domino's provides financial information for four key business segments: (1) domestic company-owned stores, (2) domestic franchise stores, (3) domestic supply chain, and (4) international. Note in Exhibit 2 that the largest revenue-generating segment is the domestic supply chain with more than 50 percent of all revenue. Note also the large revenue numbers for the relatively few company owned stores, because each Domino's domestic franchisee owns his or her own store(s) and reports their revenues on their own personal financial statements rather than Domino's. From franchisees, Domino's reports only the royalties and advertising fees it receives from franchisees as revenue. The financial data for the international supply chain centers are included in the international division, not under the domestic supply chain division. Also note in Exhibit 2 the slight revenue decline in 2012 for domestic company-owned stores.

Exhibit 3 reveals that for 2012, Domino's international stores had the highest growth in revenue, followed by U.S. company-owned stores. However the sales growth among all three segments slowed in 2012.

Exhibit 4 reveals that Domino's growth in number of stores is highest outside the USA, with the actual number of company-owned stores in the USA falling to 388. About 10,000 employees work for Domino's, but counting all workers for all franchisees, this number is closer to 205,000.

EXHIBIT 2 Finances by Segment (in millions)

Business Segment	Revenue, 2012	Revenue, 2011	Revenue, 2010	Revenue Increase (%)
Domestic company-owned stores	$324	$336	$345	(3.6)
Domestic franchise	195	187	173	4.3
Domestic supply chain	942	928	876	1.5
International	217	201	176	8.0
TOTAL	$1,678	$1,652	$1,571	1.6

Source: Company documents.
Note: Domino's 2012 year ended 1-31-13.

EXHIBIT 3 Same Store Sales Growth (Percent)

	U.S. company-owned stores	U.S. franchise-owned stores	International stores
2008	−2.2	−5.2	6.2
2009	−0.9	0.6	4.3
2010	9.7	10.0	6.9
2011	4.1	3.4	6.8
2012	1.3	3.2	5.2

Source: Company documents.

EXHIBIT 4 Growth: Total Number of Domino's Stores

	U.S. company-owned stores	U.S. franchise-owned stores	International stores
2008	489	4,558	3,736
2009	466	4,461	4,072
2010	454	4,475	4,422
2011	394	4,513	4,835
2012	388	4,540	5,327

Source: Company documents.

Domestic Supply Chain

Domino's domestic supply chain supplies franchisees with dough, vegetables, ovens, uniforms, and much more, enabling better control, pizza consistency, and timely delivery of products. This backward integration strategy enables Domino's to offer pizza at lower prices and allows store managers to focus on store operations rather than mixing dough on site, prepping vegetables, and bargaining with independent suppliers for ingredients. Domino's has 16 regional dough-manufacturing and supply chain centers and leases a fleet of more than 400 trucks to aid in delivering products to stores twice a week. However, Dominos' franchisees are not required to purchase supplies from Domino's, but interestingly more than 99 percent do purchase all its supplies from the company's domestic supply chain segment. To ensure this division remains viable, Domino's provides profit-sharing incentives to franchisees to buy its products from Domino's. In addition to the 16 domestic supply chain centers, Domino's also operates 6 supply chain centers outside the USA.

Domestic Stores

The company's domestic stores division includes a network of 4,540 stores operated by 1,026 franchisees and 388 company-owned stores in the USA. Domino's desires to have all of its stores owned and operated by franchisees, but if certain stores are underperforming, Domino's often will purchase these stores in hopes of turning them around and then refranchising them at a later date. Domino's uses company-owned stores as test sites for new products, promotions, new potential store layout improvements, and as test sites for prospective new franchisees.

Although the typical franchisee of Domino's operates 4 stores, the nine largest franchisees operate more than 50 stores, including the largest domestic franchisee that operates 135 stores. Currently, Domino's has 1,077 different domestic franchisees with the average franchisee being in Domino's system for an impressive 14 years. Much of this longevity can be attributed to Domino's requiring prospective franchisees to manage a store for 1 year before entering into a long-term contract with Domino's. Domino's feels this system is unique to the pizza industry and provides a competitive advantage over rival pizza firms.

International Division

Domino's has 5,327 franchise stores outside the USA. The company's international revenues as a percent of total revenues increased to 13.0 percent in 2012, up from 11.2 percent in 2010. Exhibit 5 provides is a breakdown of Domino's stores in the top 10 markets, which account for

EXHIBIT 5 Top 10 Countries Where Domino's Are Located

Country	Number of Stores, 2011	Number of Stores, 2012	% Change
United Kingdom	670	720	7.5
Mexico	577	581	0.7
Australia	450	464	3.1
India	439	522	25.7
South Korea	358	372	3.9
Canada	354	368	3.9
Turkey	220	284	29.0
Japan	205	245	19.5
France	195	215	10.3
Taiwan	141	140	–

Source: Company documents.

more than 75 percent of all Domino's international stores. Note that the United Kingdom has the most Domino's of all countries, followed by Mexico. Among the company's six "international" supply chain centers, four of these are in Canada, one is in Alaska, and one is in Hawaii. (It is unclear why Domino's categorizes Alaska and Hawaii as international). As with Domestic franchisee stores, most of the company's revenue in the international division comes from royalty payments and advertising, as well as the sales of food and supplies to certain markets (predominantly Canada, Alaska, and Hawaii). Note in Exhibit 5 the rapid growth in Domino's stores in India, Turkey, and Japan. The largest Domino's franchisee outside the USA operates 911 stores.

Internal Issues

Domino's has a vertically integrated supply chain where they have backward control to some extent over many of its supplies such as dough, veggies, equipment, and uniforms and forward control over around 400 retail stores that are company owned. Domino's offers little to nothing in terms of healthy food options on the menu, such as salads or fruit. Although this approach enables Domino's to focus exclusively on pizza, this practice also increases the firm's vulnerability to the increasingly health-minded customer and possible government mandates for fast-food restaurants to stop using certain ingredients and preservatives, and potentially forcing all restaurants to label all nutrition information on the menu at the point of sale. Such a law would not be favorable to Domino's.

Domino's attributes much of its success to an incentive-based system for franchisees in which it actively shares in profits through increasing demand for new stores and through purchasing supplies from the Domino's supply chain. Domino's individual franchisee stores and company-owned stores also enjoy a simple and effective store layout enabling pizza delivery and carryout orders to be processed and executed efficiently as compared to many competitors. Unlike Domino's, many rival pizza firms use a dine-in business model, which is much more costly than Domino's strategy. Competitive advantages such as these make Domino's an attractive franchisee option in the quick-service restaurant (QSR) market because overhead and investment is generally cheaper than competing firms.

Sustainability

Sustainability refers to the extent that an organization's operations and actions protect, mend, and preserve rather than harm or destroy the natural environment. Many firms today develop an annual sustainability report, similar to an annual report, to reveal to stakeholders its actions and commitment to sustainability. However, Domino's does not produce an annual sustainability report nor does the company have a sustainability statement on its website.

Advertising and Sales Force

Dominos domestic stores contributed 5.5 percent of all retail sales to support national and local advertising campaigns. Domino's expects this rate to remain unchanged for the foreseeable future. Much of those monies are devoted to mass-mail flyers promoting specials at the local Domino's.

Domino's Pulse Point-of-Sale System

To maximize efficiencies and provide timely financial and marketing data, Domino's requires all stores to install and use its PULSE system that now exists in all company-owned stores and 98 percent of franchisee-owned stores. The system enables touch-screen ordering that improves order accuracy and efficiency and provides the driver with directions and the best route to take for multiple deliveries, saving time and money. In addition, the PULSE system better enables Domino's to ensure it receives full royalties from all transactions in what is often a cash business, assuming the franchisees are honest and always use the PULSE system when receiving orders.

Finance

Domino's recent income statements and balance sheets are provided in Exhibits 6 and 7, respectively. Note that Domino's revenues increased 2.6 percent in 2012 and the firm's long-term debt rose slightly to $1.53 billion. Note the company has zero goodwill on its balance sheet.

EXHIBIT 6 Domino's Pizza, Statements of Income (In thousands, except per share amounts)

	2010	2011	2012
REVENUES:			
Domestic company-owned stores	$ 345,636	$ 336,349	$ 323,652
Domestic franchise	173,345	187,007	195,000
Domestic supply chain	875,517	927,904	942,219
International	176,396	200,933	217,568
Total revenues	1,570,894	1,652,193	1,678,439
COST OF SALES:			
Domestic company-owned stores	278,297	267,066	247,391
Domestic supply chain	778,510	831,665	843,329
International	75,498	82,946	86,381
Total cost of sales	1,132,305	1,181,677	1,177,101
OPERATING MARGIN	438,589	470,516	501,338
GENERAL AND ADMINISTRATIVE	210,887	211,371	219,007
INCOME FROM OPERATIONS	227,702	259,145	282,331
INTEREST INCOME	244	296	304
INTEREST EXPENSE	(96,810)	(91,635)	(101,448)
OTHER	7,809	–	–
INCOME BEFORE PROVISION FOR INCOME TAXES	138,945	167,806	181,187
PROVISION FOR INCOME TAXES	51,028	62,445	68,795
NET INCOME	$ 87,917	$ 105,361	$ 112,392
EARNINGS PER SHARE:			
Common Stock—basic	$ 1.50	$ 1.79	$ 1.99
Common Stock—diluted	$ 1.45	$ 1.71	$ 1.91

Source: 2012 *Form 10K*, p. 50.

EXHIBIT 7 Domino's Pizza, Balance Sheets (In thousands except share and per share amounts)

	2011	2012
ASSETS		
CURRENT ASSETS:		
Cash and cash equivalents	$ 50,292	$ 54,813
Restricted cash and cash equivalents	92,612	60,015
Accounts receivable, net of reserves of $5,446 in 2011 and $5,906 in 2012	87,200	94,103
Inventories	30,702	31,061
Notes receivable, net of reserves of $324 in 2011 and $630 in 2012	945	1,858
Prepaid expenses and other	12,232	11,210
Advertising fund assets, restricted	36,281	37,917
Deferred income taxes	16,579	15,290
Total current assets	326,843	306,267
PROPERTY, PLANT AND EQUIPMENT:		
Land and buildings	23,714	24,460
Leasehold and other improvements	79,518	80,279
Equipment	171,726	168,452
Construction in Process	6,052	9,967
	281,010	283,158
Accumulated depreciation and amortization	(188,610)	(191,713)
Property, plant and equipment, net	92,400	91,445
OTHER ASSETS:		
Investments in marketable securities, restricted	1,538	2,097
Notes receivable, less current portion, net of reserves of $1,735 in 2011 and $814 in 2012	5,070	3,028
Deferred financing costs, net of accumulated amortization of $25,590 in 2011 and $5,201 in 2012	16,051	34,787
Goodwill	16,649	16,598
Capitalized software, net of accumulated amortization of $51,274 in 2011 and $48,381 in 2012	8,176	11,387
Other assets, net of accumulated amortization of $4,070 in 2011 and $4,404 in 2012	8,958	8,635
Deferred income taxes	4,858	3,953
Total other assets	61,300	80,485
Total assets	$ 480,543	$ 478,197
LIABILITIES AND STOCKHOLDERS' DEFICIT	**2011**	**2012**
CURRENT LIABILITIES:		
Current portion of long-term debt	$ 904	$ 24,349
Accounts payable	69,714	77,414
Accrued compensation	21,691	21,843
Accrued interest	15,775	15,035
Insurance reserves	13,023	12,964
Legal reserves	10,069	5,025
Advertising fund liabilities	36,281	37,917
Other accrued liabilities	29,718	34,951
Total current liabilities	$ 197,175	$ 229,498

(Continued)

EXHIBIT 7 Continued

	2011	2012
LONG-TERM LIABILITIES:		
Long-term debt, less current portion	$ 1,450,369	$ 1,536,443
Insurance Reserves	21,334	24,195
Deferred income taxes	5,021	7,001
Other accrued liabilities	16,383	16,583
Total long-term liabilities	1,493,107	1,584,222
Total liabilities	1,690,282	1,813,720
COMMITMENTS AND CONTINGENCIES		
STOCKHOLDERS' DEFICIT:		
Common stock, par value $0.01 per share; 170,000,000 shares authorized; 57,741,208 in 2011 and 56,313,249 in 2012 issued and outstanding	577	563
Preferred stock, par value $0.01 per share; 5,000,000 shares authorized, none issued	–	–
Additional paid-in capital	–	1,664
Retained deficit	(1,207,915)	(1,335,364)
Accumulated other comprehensive loss	(2,401)	(2,386)
Total stockholders' deficit	(1,209,739)	(1,335,523)
Total liabilities and stockholders' deficit	$ 480,543	$ 478,197

Source: 2012 *Form 10K,* pp 48-49.

Competitors

Competition in both the USA and international pizza-delivery and carry-out business is extremely intense, with Pizza Hut (owned by Yum Brands) being the largest competitor in the industry. Pizza Hut's revenues are more than 60 percent greater than Domino's. Papa John's and Little Caesars are also fierce rivals in the industry. In fact, Little Caesars was listed as the fastest-growing pizza chain in 2010, with revenues up 13.6 percent over 2009, followed by Pizza Hut's 8 percent increase and Domino's 7.2 percent increase. In addition to the three main rivals, Domino's faces intense competition from many local mom-and-pop pizza stores, frozen pizzas from the grocery store, as well as hundreds of non-pizza fast-food options. Pizza Hut, Domino's, and Papa John's account for 51 percent of all consumer spending on pizza delivery stores in the USA, with the other 49 percent coming from regional or mom-and-pop establishments.

Internationally, Pizza Hut and Domino's are the main players in the industry, but various countries have numerous national companies and thousands of mom-and-pop pizza and Italian restaurants vie for business as well. As with the domestic market, some customers consider local pizza stores to offer better quality products than large chains and are willing to pay marginally higher prices for this perceived quality.

Another competitor is Pizza Inn Holdings, Inc., based in The Colony, Texas. Pizza Inn owns 10 stores and franchises out 300 more stores.

Pizza Hut

A division of Yum Brands, Pizza Hut is based in Plano, Texas, and operates more than 7,200 restaurants in the USA and more than 5,600 restaurants internationally in more than 90 countries. In contrast to Domino's, almost all Pizza Huts are dine-in restaurants. Pizza Huts serve pan pizza, as well as its thin n' crispy, stuffed crust, hand tossed, and sicilian. Other menu items include pasta, salads, and sandwiches. Pizza Huts offer dine-in service at its famous red-roofed restaurants, as well as carryout and delivery service. About 15 percent of all Pizza Huts are company-operated, whereas the remaining stores are franchised. The world's largest fast food company, YUM Brands also owns and operates Kentucky Fried Chicken (KFC), Long John Silvers, and Taco Bell. Pizza Hut is Domino's major pizza rival outside of the USA.

Papa John's International, Inc.

Headquartered in Louisville, Kentucky, and founded in 1985, Papa John's operates 3,883 pizza restaurants with 3,255 of these being franchisee-owned and 628 being company-owned stores. Papa John's has restaurants in all 50 U.S. states and 32 foreign markets. The company currently has 16,500 full-time employees and markets its pizza under the slogan "better ingredients, better pizza." Between 2001 and 2012, Papa John's was ranked number one (by the American Customer Satisfaction Index) among national pizza chains for 10 of the 11 years during this period. The company reported revenue of more than $1.2 billion for year-end 2011, and consistent with the industry, it shows no revenue allocated to research and development. Papa John's carries $75 million in goodwill on its balance sheet; founder and CEO John Schnatter owns more than 20 percent of the chain. Papa John's offers several different pizza styles and topping choices, as well as a few specialty pies such as The Works and The Meats. Papa John's stores typically offer delivery and carryout service only.

Exhibit 8 provides a comparison between Domino's and Papa John's. Note that Domino's appears to generate more revenue with less employees, but that is not true because employees at franchised stores are not Domino's employees. Pizza Inn's 57 employees work at company-owned restaurants, not franchised stores.

Pizza Inn Holdings, Inc.

Pizza Inn is a relatively small chain of franchised quick-service pizza restaurants, with more than 300 locations in the USA and the Middle East. Pizza Inns offer pizzas, pastas, and sandwiches, along with salads and desserts. Most locations offer buffet-style and table service, whereas other units are strictly delivery and carryout units. The chain also has limited-menu express carryout units in convenience stores and airport terminals, and on college campuses. Pizza Inn's domestic locations are concentrated in more than 15 southern states, with about half located in Texas and North Carolina.

Little Caesars

Headquartered in Detroit, Michigan, and privately held, Little Caesars is famous for its advertising slogan, "Pizza! Pizza!" which was introduced in 1979. The phrase refers to two pizzas being offered for the comparable price of a single pizza from competitors. In November 2010, Little Caesars introduced Pizza! Pizza! Pantastic, denying that the return of "Pizza! Pizza!" had any relationship to the recent success of Domino's. Little Caesars operates under its parent Little Caesars Enterprises and is estimated to be the fourth largest pizza chain in the USA. Little Caesars operates in 30 foreign countries.

External Issues

Domino's competes in the Quick Service Restaurant (QSR) pizza category, which consists of two categories: 1) delivery and 2) carry-out. Delivery revenues for the industry in 2012 were $9.6 billion, up only slightly the last few years. The delivery portion accounts for 30 percent

EXHIBIT 8 A Comparison Between Domino's and Papa John's

	Domino's	Papa John's	Pizza Inn Holdings
Revenue	1.65B	1.24B	43.5M
Market Capitalization	1.76B	1.16B	20.1M
Gross Margin	0.29	0.31	0.12
Net Income	98.99M	55.97M	888K
EPS	1.63	2.24	0.10
Price/Earnings Ratio	18.67	21.69	24.51
Number of Employees	10K	16.5K	57

EPS, earnings per share.
Source: Company documents.

of the total QSP pizza revenues. However, the carry-out portion of the industry grew revenues from $14.1 billion in 2011 to $14.6 billion in 2012. Domino's is the market leader in delivery and second largest in carry-out. Outside of the USA, pizza delivery is underdeveloped, with Domino's and one rival being the only firms.

Nutrition Concerns

An area of concern for all fast-food establishments, including pizza stores, is the growing health-minded customer, as well as the growing pressure from government agencies to label all products with nutrition information. There have been battles between the restaurant industry and government agencies for many years, but much like the tobacco industry (in respect to labeling its products). It appears the war is close to being lost for the restaurant industry. Domino's item-izes nutrition information on its website, but forces the customer to add the calories for crust, sauce, cheese, and topping, and then divide by the number of slices to derive the total calorie count per slice. After doing the calculations, one large slice of hand-tossed pepperoni pizza for example has 300 calories and 12 grams of fat, and there are 8 slices in a pizza. To complicate matters for restaurants such as Domino's, it is difficult to provide accurate nutrition labels when there can be an almost endless combination of ingredients on a pizza. For example, someone may order a large sausage pizza with onions and olives whereas someone else might order extra cheese and tomatoes. Having to print out nutrition labels for all these combinations would be quite costly as opposed to a restaurant like McDonald's where it can print the nutrition label on the Big Mac because there is uniformity in ingredients and the label is understood to be for the base item. However, Domino's PULSE system could possibly be adjusted to resolve this potential issue.

Chipotle Mexican Grill claims to only use meat and dairy products from free-ranging cattle, as opposed to cattle injected with growth hormones. Domino's Pizza markets its pizzas as having gluten-free crust. This is an attempt to win over health-conscious customers, comply with government regulations, and make current customers feel a little less guilty about eating pizza. The tug of war between customers, governments, lawyers, and the restaurant industry on health issues is likely to continue for some time.

In response to these challenges, many restaurants have opted for healthy menu options. Wendy's, for example, has promoted several meal combinations that contain less than 10 grams of fat. All of these items were originally on its menu, just not marketed in that manner. Wendy's has added side salads and fruit to help cut down on calories, fat, and sodium. Subway is also famous for marketing its products as healthy alternatives to other fast-food options. Domino's, and many pizza competitors, offer few to no menu options for the health-conscious consumer.

Barriers to Entry

Barriers to entry are relatively low for the restaurant industry, but rivalry (competitiveness) among firms is exceptionally high. One large contributing factor for the low barriers to entry is many small entrepreneurs can open mom-and-pop establishments and bypass the franchise fees, royalties, selection process, and so on of owning a franchised restaurant and lease an existing building relatively cheap. However, even avoiding high fixed costs, variable costs are often high and small-scale entrepreneurs are not able to compete with larger franchise stores, who can better negotiate pricing on food, packaging, and other supplies. In the QSR industry, the bargaining power of consumers is quite powerful, availability of restaurant options in most places is abundant, and consequently there is intense price competitiveness among rival firms. Even if you are sure you want pizza for lunch or dinner, you likely have many options.

Economic Factors

The current landscape in the QSR business is a bimodal population distribution with a large population of bargain-minded customers seeking deals on cheaper end fast food options, and another population of more affluent consumers targeting middle to higher-end restaurants. Domino's is well positioned strategically to target the first group of consumers because there are many more of them; Domino's often has excellent sales and discounts to target this group.

Among the subset of customers who are value shoppers, many of these are also shoppers of quality and are willing to wait in line a little longer or pay a little more for better quality food products. Domino's has recently capitalized on this well with the introduction of its artisan pizzas and new recipes (or higher quality products) for its crust, sauce, and cheeses. In addition, Domino's offers many pick up specials. Although an inconvenience over delivery, many customers in today's climate are willing to tolerate a degree of inconvenience that they historically were not if they can get a better deal.

Similar to Domino's, many restaurant owners in the fast-food industry have experienced stronger growth in international markets than domestic markets. This trend is expected to continue, especially in China and other developing nations because many U.S. fast-food options are still novel, even in Europe. According to the S&P Industry Surveys, QSRs are expected to see a sales increase of 3 percent in 2012 and orders to increase 1.5 percent as a result in large part of consumers trading down to cheaper restaurant alternatives. There also is a steadily growing international appetite for U.S. fast food and an improving global economy. These positive trends are expected to continue into 2013 and should bode well for Domino's with its strong international presence.

Ethics and Corporate Citizenship

Domino's has two extensive "Code of Ethics" documents on its website: one statement for its employees and one statement for its executives. The documents outline matters such as: conflicts of interest, how to report unethical conduct, fair dealing with all employees, compliance with laws, proper way to use company assets, and much more.

In addition to Domino's Code of Ethics statements, the company is noted for its corporate citizenship record in particular with St. Jude Children's Research Hospital. Since 2006, Domino's has donated more than $12 million to St. Jude and has hosted pizza parties for patients and its families on St. Jude properties.

In 1986, Domino's launched its Pizza Partners Foundation with a mission of "team members helping team members." The foundation is 100-percent funded by team member and franchise contributions and has disbursed nearly $12 million to aid team members facing crisis situations such as fire, illness, or other personal tragedies.

The Future

As CEO Doyle and his management team contemplate the future direction of Domino's, it has much to consider. Should the firm continue its aggressive market development strategies and accept the risk associated with expanding into markets it has little expertise operating within? What new geographic locations or regions should Domino's focus? Should Domino's simply follow Pizza Hut's international rollout of stores? How would this expansion affect the corporate structure of Domino's? Would restructuring by geographic division and thus establishing offices in Asia, the Middle East, and South America better enable them to manage these more risky environments? Can Domino's afford this financially? Should Domino's consider offering salads or a line of healthy menu options? Should Domino's purchase trucks to deliver its products rather than incurring such heavy leasing expenses?

Domino's needs a clear three-year strategic plan. Prepare this document for the company.

Spirit Airlines, Inc., 2013

www.spirit.com, SAVE

Headquartered in Miramar, Florida, Spirit Airlines competes in the ultra-low cost carrier (ULCC) airline industry in the USA, Caribbean, and Latin America. Spirit offers some of the lowest fares in the industry, usually up to $100 less than competitors and sometimes as cheap as $9 plus taxes and fees. Spirit targets customers who are paying for their own travel rather than business-class customers. Spirit charges passengers fees of up to $45 for a carry-on and checked bags. Everything on a Spirit flight costs, including water and snacks, selecting a seat, and maybe soon even to get off the plane before others. Spirit charges a fee of $5 to passengers who have their boarding passes printed by the check-in agent. Spirit's weight limit for checked luggage is 40 pounds per bag, charging $25 for the first 9 extra pounds, and up to $100 for bags approaching 100 pounds. Despite the fees, thousands of customers are loyal to Spirit because of its low-priced tickets. Spirit has reconfigured all its planes for high-density seating. For example, their A319 planes seat 145 passengers, 25 more than the same plane being used by United.

Spirit currently has more than 200 flights a day and serves 52 airports with 4 focused airports consisting of Chicago, Dallas Ft. Worth, Detroit, and Las Vegas. Other Spirit hubs are Ft. Lauderdale, Myrtle Beach, and Atlantic City. Spirit has a fleet of 43 Airbus aircraft and employs more than 3,033 full-time employees, but is rapidly adding flights, planes, employees, and customers. Spirit leases planes rather than buys planes.

Copyright by Fred David Books LLC. (Written by Forest R. David)

History

Spirit Airlines was founded in Michigan as Clipper Trucking Company in 1964, and in 1974, the company changed its name to Ground Air Transfer, Inc. The company operated this way for nine years until 1983 when it became a passenger airline called Charter One. Charter One specialized as a tour operator taking customers to such locations as Atlantic City, Las Vegas, and the Bahamas. In 1990, Charter One received its Air Carrier Certificate from the Federal Aviation Administration allowing air charter operations. In 1992, Charter One changed its name to Spirit Airlines, Inc. and increased its destinations to include such cities as Fort Lauderdale, Detroit, Myrtle Beach, Los Angeles, New York, and many more.

Spirit's average fleet age is 4.5 years old, the third youngest airline, fleet in the Americas after Virgin America and the Mexican airline, Volaris. Big front seats are available on all Spirit aircraft, although they are sold as an upgrade and not as a distinct class of service. These seats are wider because of its two-by-two configuration, whereas the standard economy seats feature a three-by-three configuration.

Spirit added about 50 new destinations in 2012, all at rock-bottom fares. Spirit packs 178 seats on its A320 aircraft jets that usually have 150 seats. Most airlines offer at least three more inches of legroom in the aisles of their planes as compared to Spirit. Spirit is financially doing great, but it does have critics, such as Jami Counter, senior director of SeatGuru, which informs travelers about airline cabin features. Jami says "Spirit is as bare-bones as bare-bones can be, basically stripping everything from the flight experience and charging for anything they view as an add-on. And part of that is cramming as many seats in the plane as possible. The flight experience is probably the worst in the USA."

Vision and Mission

Spirit's president and CEO, Ben Baldanza, says: "Our vision is to make sure the customer who can't afford to pay current airline prices has an option to still travel." The CEO goes on to say that "Whenever we add a new market or a new service, we always try to price that market at lower than the prevailing fares in that market to bring back some people who've been priced out."

Spirit does not have a mission statement, but its company slogan is: "The Ultra Low Cost Airline for the Americas."

EXHIBIT 1 Spirit Airlines' Organizational Chart

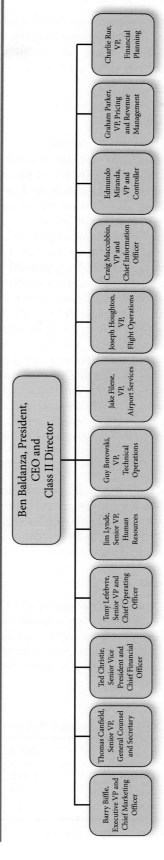

Source: Based on company documents.

Organizational Structure

Spirit appears to operate from a functional organizational structure as illustrated in Exhibit 1. Note the absence of any women among top management and the absence of any divisions (segments), although the company does provide a revenue breakdown by United States versus Latin America. Perhaps executives not listed in Exhibit 1 report to the chief operations officer (COO) as division heads.

Internal Issues

Statement of Ethics and Governance

Spirit has a detailed Code of Ethics provided on its website that pertains to all directors, officers, and employees. The code provides all the standards expected of Spirit employees and reveals how to report violations and what to do if an employee is not sure of how to address a particular problem. The code also clearly outlines acceptable conduct with employees, customers, and business suppliers, conflicts of interest, dealings with the government, and considerably more. In addition to the Code of Ethics, Spirit also provides detailed corporate governance guidelines. Issues such as the size of the board, level of independence the board should have, director-selection processes, term limits, responsibilities, compensation, access to senior management, and much more is included in the document. Spirit has standing committees to address issues such as audits, finance, violations of ethics, and compensation.

In April 2012, citing the airline's strict refund policy, Spirit Airlines would not issue a refund to dying veteran, Jerry Meekins, who chose to purchase a nonrefundable ticket though other options were available. The 76-year-old Vietnam veteran and former Marine tried to get his $197 back after learning his esophageal cancer was terminal and being told by his doctor not to fly from Florida to Atlantic City. The decision caused outrage among veterans' groups and the general public, some of whom threatened to boycott Spirit unless a refund and apology were issued. On May 4, Spirit CEO Ben Baldanza apologized for how the situation was handled and announced that he would personally refund Meekins' ticket and that the airline would make a $5,000 donation to the Wounded Warrior Project in Meekins's name.

Segment Data

As indicated in Exhibit 2, Spirit provides revenue data in two categories: Domestic and Latin America. Note the 103 percent growth in the domestic segment from 2009 to 2012 compared to 29 percent growth in the Latin American segment. Spirit's domestic revenues were 86 percent of all revenue in 2012, up from 80 percent in 2009. No single international market accounted for more than 4 percent of total revenue.

Current Strategies

Spirit's low cost leadership strategy, or ULCC as it is referred to in the industry, allows customers to purchase only what items they deem necessary. Spirit markets themselves as offering transparent pricing and does not consider themselves a no frills airline, but rather a frills-for-fee airline. Spirit offers the same amenities as higher cost airlines if the customer wishes to purchase the amenities. Spirit's strategy is analogous somewhat to discount carrier Ryanair's strategy in Europe.

EXHIBIT 2 Spirit's Revenues by Category (in thousands)

	2012	2011	2010	2009
Domestic	$1,135	$900	$635	$558
Latin America	$183	171	156	142
Total	$1,318	$1,071	$791	$700

Source: Company documents.

By charging for bags, drinks, and food, Spirit is able to keep costs low, generate extra revenue for these items, and reduce weight, which reduces fuel consumption. Charging for bags encourages customers to pack lighter and perhaps get by with less expensive carry-on bags as opposed to checked bags. This allows quicker turnaround times at airport gates. In addition to the cost savings, nonticket revenue is an important component of Spirit's business model because customers, according to Spirit's research, seem less price-sensitive to drinks, pillows, and even bags than ticket prices. Since 2006, Spirit's nonticket revenue has increased 800 percent as a result in part to bag and drink fees, but also through the $9 fare club subscription service, Spirit credit card, and the sale of advertising to third parties on Spirit's website and on-board aircraft.

Spirit's strategic plan is to aggressively expand geographically (market development) and gain more market share (market penetration) in the United States, Caribbean, and Latin America. Many travel destinations in the Caribbean and Latin America have historically only been served by large carriers charging relatively higher prices. But many cost-minded flyers visit these areas, so there is substantial room for growth in these markets.

To support Spirit's expansion strategy, the company has on order 106 Airbus 320 aircraft with delivery ranging from 2012 through 2021 as well as spare and replacement engines that are on order between 2012 through 2018. Spirit expects to take delivery of seven aircraft in each of 2013, and 2014, and then 10 airplanes in 2015, and an additional 75 planes between 2016 and 2021. Spirit's use of the A320 over the A319 enables the carrier to configure the planes to hold 178 passengers as opposed to 150 on the smaller A319 that rival carrier Jet Blue primarily uses.

Locations

Spirit currently operates more than 200 flights a day to 50 different airports throughout North America, the Caribbean, and Latin America. Approximately 54 percent of all flights are to or from the home base in Fort Lauderdale, and a large percentage of the balance originate from Detroit, Las Vegas, Atlantic City, Chicago, Orlando, and Myrtle Beach. Global operations include service to Canada, Mexico, all of Central America, Colombia, Peru, and much of the Caribbean. However, many of the global flights are seasonal, and even the flights that are year round, many only fly once or twice a week to these locations. Spirit's single largest airport is Ft. Lauderdale/Hollywood, with over 20 percent of all Spirit flights operating to or from Ft. Lauderdale.

Marketing

Spirit focuses on direct marketing to price-sensitive consumers rather than focusing on higher end business travelers. Spirit actively promotes its lowest fares in the industry business model. Sprit spends a paltry 0.2 to 0.5 percent of total revenues on advertising for customers who pay their own way and spends nothing on corporations, government agencies, or other business-class travelers. Spirit relies heavily on repeat customers, word-of-mouth, and its email distribution systems that consist of more than five million e-mail addresses. In addition, Spirit also heavily markets its $9 club online, in radio and TV advertisements, in airport kiosks, and in flight promotions.

A striking weakness for Spirit is its lack of a marketing alliance within the airline industry. Competitors such as Delta, American, and US Airways all have alliances with other airlines enabling them to share codes, combine frequent-flier programs, aid in connections, and much more. Lack of affiliation with an alliance puts Spirit in a competitive disadvantage, particularly on international routes, and may partially explain why this area of the business is not growing as fast as the domestic segment.

Finance

Spirit's recent income statements and balance sheets are provided in Exhibits 3 and 4 respectively. Note the 13.2 percent operating profit margin in 2012. Note that Spirit's non-ticket revenue increased to 41 percent of revenues in 2012 from 36 percent the prior year.

EXHIBIT 3

Spirit Airlines, Inc.
Statements of Operations
(*In thousands, except per share data*)

	Year Ended December 31		
	2012	2011	2010
Operating revenues:			
Passenger	$ 782,792	$ 689,650	$ 537,969
Non-ticket	535,596	381,536	243,296
Total operating revenue	**1318,388**	**1,071,186**	**781,265**
Operating expenses:			
Aircraft fuel	471,763	388,046	248,206
Salaries, wages and benefits	218,919	181,742	156,443
Aircraft rent	143,572	116,485	101,345
Landing fees and other rents	68,368	52,794	48,118
Distribution	56,668	51,349	41,179
Maintenance, materials and repairs	49,460	34,017	27,035
Depreciation and amortization	15,256	7,760	5,620
Other operating	127,886	91,172	83,748
Loss on disposal of assets	956	255	77
Special charges (credits)	(8,450)	3,184	621
Total operating expenses	**1,144,398**	**926,804**	**712,392**
Operating income	**173,990**	**144,382**	**68,873**
Other (income) expense:			
Interest expense	1,350	24,781	50,313
Capitalized interest	(1,350)	(2,890)	(1,491)
Interest income	(925)	(575)	(328)
Other expense	331	235	194
Total other (income) expense	**(594)**	**21,551**	**48,688**
Income before income taxes	174,584	122,831	20,185
Provision for income taxes	66,124	46,383	(52,296)
Net income	**$ 108,460**	**$ 76,448**	**$ 72,481**
Net income per share, basic	**$ 1.50**	**$ 1.44**	**$ 2.77**
Net income per share, diluted	**$ 1.49**	**$ 1.43**	**$ 2.72**

Source: 2012 *Form 10K*, p. 60.

Competitors

The airline industry is highly competitive on price, flight schedules, newness and roominess of aircraft, amenities, and frequent-flier programs just to name a few. In recent years, many airlines have participated in alliances and mergers; Southwest and AirTran merged in 2011 and United and Continental merged in 2010, allowing them greater liquidity and access to capital that smaller airlines such as Spirit and Jet Blue do not have. Alliances such as OneWorld, SkyTeam, and Star Alliance allow larger and regional airlines to share marketing relationships, increase destinations, access to restrictive markets, and provide the ability to use cheaper air craft to service small markets. Currently, Spirit does not engage any type of alliance, which gives Spirit much more flexibility in pricing, policies, and procedures. Spirit's single largest overlap in routes is with American Airlines at 60 percent.

Southwest and JetBlue no longer have the lowest airline prices. Spirit, along with Allegiant Air and Frontier, now has the legitimate claim as the industry's lowest-cost flyers.

EXHIBIT 4 Spirit's Balance Sheets

Spirit Airlines, Inc.
Balance Sheets
(In thousands, except share data)

	December 31, 2012	December 31, 2011
Assets		
Current assets:		
Cash and cash equivalents	$ 416,816	$ 343,328
Accounts receivable, net	22,740	15,425
Deferred income taxes	12,591	20,738
Other current assets	95,210	63,217
Total current assets	**547,357**	**442,708**
Property and equipment:		
Flight equipment	2,648	4,182
Ground and other equipment	43,580	46,608
Less accumulated depreciation	(17,825)	(27,580)
	28,403	23,210
Deposits on flight equipment purchase contracts	96,692	91,450
Aircraft maintenance deposits	122,379	120,615
Deferred heavy maintenance and other long-term assets	125,053	67,830
Total assets	**$ 919,884**	**$ 745,813**
Liabilities and shareholders' equity		
Current liabilities:		
Accounts payable	$ 24,166	$ 15,928
Air traffic liability	131,414	112,280
Other current liabilities	121,314	98,856
Total current liabilities	**276,894**	**227,064**
Long-term deferred income taxes	33,216	12,108
Deferred credits and other long-term liabilities	27,239	39,935
Shareholders' equity:		
Common stock: Common stock, $.0001 par value, 240,000,000 shares authorized at December 31, 2012 and 2011, respectively; 70,861,822 and 61,954,576 issued and 70,801,782 and 61,946,361 outstanding as of December 31,2012 and 2011, respectively	6	6
Common stock: Non-Voting common stock: $.0001 par value, 50,000,000 shares authorized at December 31, 2012 and 2011, respectively; 1,669,205 and 10,576,180 issued and outstanding as of December 31, 2012 and 2011, respectively	1	1
Additional paid-in-capital	504,527	496,136
Treasury stock, at cost: 60,040 and 8,215 as of December 31, 2012 and 2011, respectively	(1,151)	(129)
Retained earnings (deficit)	79,152	(29,308)
Total shareholders' equity	**582,535**	**466,706**
Total liabilities and shareholders' equity	**$ 919,884**	**$ 745,813**

Source: 2012 Form 10K, p. 61.

Spirit spokeswoman Misty Pinson says that her airline aims to have a total fare that is at least 25-percent lower than any other available ticket price for any route that Spirit serves. Not even a glass of water is free on Spirit, but no carrier in the USA beats Spirit on ticket price.

The airline industry is somewhat easy to enter as airlines such as Spirit lease some or all of its aircraft. Even a restaurant company such as Hooters was able to lease planes, hire pilots, staff, and make a go at the industry. Of course, in the end, Hooters was forced to divest its airline business and stick to its niche of serving chicken wings, beer and sports.

EXHIBIT 5 A Financial Comparison of Spirit with American and JetBlue

	Spirit	American	JetBlue
Market Capitalization ($)	1.61B	174M	1.6B
Number of Employees	3.1K	80.1K	11.9K
Revenue	1.14B	25.5B	4.7B
Gross Margin	0.28	0.20	0.28
Net Income	92.0M	(3.2B)	113M
EPS Ratio	1.41	(9.55)	0.35
P/E Ratio	15.71	N/A	16.15

Note: EPS is earnings per share; P/E, price-to-earnings ratio.

Perhaps the most competitive aspect in the airline industry is ticket price because many carriers use the same airports and customers generally have options regarding which carrier to fly with. Anyone can search various travel sites such as Orbitz and Priceline.com to easily determine the most attractive prices and routes. Despite airlines' efforts to conserve fuel by charging for bags, thus reducing weight, airlines readily admit, albeit two-faced, that carrying extra passengers as opposed to having an empty seat does little to impact the overall fuel cost of the trip. The incremental extra cost of selling unused seats can be drastically offset by selling the seats even at a perceived steal for the customer. Spirit has its "red light sales" in which the company provides many flights for as cheap as $9 and many others for less than $50 one-way. Selling the seats even at these discounted fares can add tremendously to net profit at the end of the year as opposed to letting the seat remain vacant.

The three principle competitors for Spirit on domestic routes are American Airlines, Delta Airlines, and JetBlue Airways. Approximately 60 percent of Spirit destinations also are serviced by American and Delta; American and JetBlue are the main competitors in the Caribbean and Latin America. Note in Exhibit 5 that Spirit has fewer employees and revenue than either American or JetBlue, but Spirit has the highest earnings per share (EPS).

American

AMR Corporation, headquartered in Fort Worth, Texas, in conjunction with AMR Eagle Holding Corporation, operates about 3,400 daily flights to more than 250 cities and 50 different countries around the world. Once the largest airline in the world, AMR now trails both Delta and United Continental in total U.S. market share. As a result of declining market share from lack of an effective strategic response to changing market conditions, AMR entered a voluntary reorganization under Chapter 11 bankruptcy in November of 2011. Interestingly enough, US Airways stock tripled the same day AMR formally declared Chapter 11, signaling that investors thought US Airways may now acquire AMR cheaply. As of July 2013, AMR and US Airways were still two separate companies, but a pending merger is still expected by many investors and analysts. If a successful merger takes place as expected in late 2013, the new company, American Airlines Group, will be the largest airline in the world, even larger than Delta and United Continental in U.S. market share.

JetBlue Airways

Headquartered in Long Island City, New York, JetBlue operates approximately 700 daily flights to 22 different states, Mexico, the Caribbean, and Latin America. Starting in November 2012, the airline also began serving Grand Cayman Island, bringing the total different Caribbean destinations served to 23. The company operates several aircraft including 120 of the same Airbus A320s that Spirit operates, but in addition JetBlue also uses 49 Brazilian-made Embraer 190 aircraft. In addition to providing some of the best rates in the industry, JetBlue also provides some of the best in-flight entertainment in the industry with its voice communication, satellite television and radio, wireless data links, and more.

As part of its environmentally friendly policies, JetBlue discontinued disposable headphones in 2008 and encourages customers to bring their own. Furthering its sustainability strategy, JetBlue also markets the following: (a) using only one engine to taxi, (b) using ground power instead of engines at the gate for air-conditioning, (c) using the latest GPS technology to develop more efficient routes, (d) using lighter seats and LED lighting, (e) not offering in-flight magazines to save paper, and many more ecofriendly options. Critics suggest the true intent of these moves by JetBlue is to cut costs similar to other airlines.

Delta Airlines

Headquartered and founded in 1924 in Atlanta, Georgia, Delta provides service to 342 destinations in 61 different countries via a mainline fleet of approximately 700 aircraft. In addition to its Atlanta hub, Delta also operates hubs in Amsterdam, Cincinnati, Detroit, Memphis, New York–JFK, Paris, and Tokyo.

In 2011, Delta was named the world's most admired airline company by *Fortune* magazine and the "Top Tech-Friendly USA Airline" by *PCWorld* magazine. In addition to these accolades, Delta has an industry-leading global network with the markets it serves. As the founding member of SkyTeam global alliance, Delta furthers is presence around the globe and has joint ventures with Air France–KLM and Alitalia Airlines in Italy. Delta's SkyMiles program is the largest frequent-flier program in the world and is supplemented with BusinessElite and more than 50 Sky Clubs in airports worldwide.

External Issues

Oil Prices

One of the largest absorbers of revenue in the airline industry is the cost of fuel. About 26 percent of all air-carrier revenue is used to pay the fuel bill. Back in 2008, a whopping 36 percent of revenues went toward fuel when oil hit an all time high of $147 a barrel and jet fuel was $4.32 gallon. Jet fuel today is much lower as oil prices have dropped significantly from its highs a few years ago.

One possible way to counter volatile fuel prices is to purchase futures contracts to hedge against rising prices by accepting a price at what the firm hopes is lower than the price will be at the time the fuel is needed. During the economic downturn, many airlines stopped hedging because it expected fuel prices to decline, and most benefited tremendously from this strategy. However, as the market rebounded and oil again resumed its uptrend, many airlines started to participate in hedging once again and for most the results were disastrous.

Labor

Labor is either the largest or second-largest expense for the airlines depending on the current price of oil. Labor accounts for a fairly consistent 20 to 25 percent of total revenue each year and is divided into several areas: flight crews (pilots and engineers), flight attendants, ground service, maintenance, customer service, and dispatchers. Most employees belong to one of a dozen major unions that plague the airline industry. A few examples are the Association of Flight Attendants, Air Line Pilots Association, and the Association of Machinists and Aerospace Workers. It is not uncommon for the airline to be in discussion with several unions at one particular time and negotiations can extend upward of two years. However, strikes are not that common because the law in the USA requires labor disputes to be submitted to the National Mediation Board and a "cooling off period" must pass before the strike can be enacted.

Spirit currently has 54 percent of its total workforce represented by labor unions, up from 52 percent the prior year. This is problematic for Spirit because the cost of labor could increase drastically based on labor decisions with other airlines, and there is also the risk a large percent of the 46 percent of employees not represented by unions may join a union. Spirit has reduced its labor costs as a percent of total operating costs to 19.1 in 2012, down from 19.6 and 22.0 the prior years. Spirit now has 3,033 employees, including 680 pilots.

Ancillary Fees

Although Spirit views its frills-for-fee strategy as customer friendly, many customers disagree and get irate. However, Spirit is by no means the only airline to implement these ancillary fees and it appears these fees are here to stay. In 2010 the U.S. airline industry collected $8 billion in baggage, drink, food, and other fees not associated with the price of a ticket, up 47 percent from 2008. Although many customers are not happy with the fees, most are willing to pay the extra and airlines who have attempted to differentiate as a high-end, high frills airline have experienced little growth in customer loyalty from this approach. The only exception is for business class travelers who purchase higher priced seats and are more profitable on balance for the airline. But the number of business-class travelers is declining. Some airlines wave all extra fees for business-class travelers.

Increased Taxes

As governments look to increase their own revenues, airlines have been targeted as potential revenue streams. The USA has put new taxes into place that are embedded into all airplane ticket prices at the time of purchase. Spirit and others airlines have fought for disclosure of these taxes and are now able to separate the taxes and fare prices, but the tax often exceeds the actual ticket price at Spirit.

The Barack Obama administration has recently proposed two new taxes on the airline industry. The first addition would be a $100 departure tax to all flights leaving a U.S.-based airport. The second proposed tax is to increase the "passenger security tax" from $2.50 per passenger to $5 and then triple the current tax to $7.50 by 2017. The taxes are expected to impose a $36 billion burden on flights in the USA over the next 10 years. Interestingly, in the previous 10 years, the best year ever for domestic airlines, the airlines posted a profit of $3.6 billion, which is the exact amount of the annual tax burden purposed by the Obama administration.

Environmental Issues

Airlines face increasing pressure to be more proactive in combating greenhouse gasses and noise pollution. Some organizations such as the European Union have even imposed further penalties and restrictions on carbon emissions. To combat this concern, airlines to their credit have invested in more fuel-efficient designs of planes and engines and have marketed these changes to their customers. Critics suggest airlines are only undertaking these measures as a means to cut their own fuel burden and have little regard for the environment as a whole.

One interesting aspect on this front is the increased usage of biofuels (cooking oil) in conjunction with jet fuel. United Airlines has experimented using 40 percent biofuel and many other airlines have experimented using 20-percent biofuel blended with jet fuel. Biofuel can perform as good or better than 100-percent jet fuel and can drastically reduce emissions and possibly increase fuel economy. However, biofuels remain much more expensive and full implementation of supplementing with biofuels is still several years away.

Stranded Passengers

The Department of Transportation (DOT) in the USA has a rule that provides protection for passengers stuck on the tarmac for domestic flights. The rule is that airlines must not force passengers to remain on the aircraft for more than three hours. Exceptions are when it would be too disruptive to return to the gate or for security or safety reasons. The rule was established after several flights forced passengers to endure sitting on the tarmac with no toilets, food, or drink for extended periods of time. In 2011, American Eagle was fined $900,000 ($27,500 per passenger) for several lengthy tarmac delays. The rules have had one apparently unintended but yet easily foreseeable consequence of increased flight cancelations if there is a risk of a three-hour delay. In 2012, a domestic flight from the east to the west coast could expect to generate revenues upward of $100,000, assuming 250 passengers. However a $27,500 fine per customer for a delay would impose a penalty of $6.9 million. It is this risk-to-reward ratio being out of balance that sometimes causes airlines to cancel fights (which there is no penalty for) and ultimately force what would be a three-hour delay into a much longer delay for the passengers.

Future

Spirit has committed to ordering many new planes so the primary strategic decision for the company is what cities and countries to add to its destination list. How many flights per day should be offered to various cities from various other cities? Should Spirit expand to more Latin American and South American countries and which ones would be best when? To go along with expansion, the company needs both a marketing plan and a human resources plan to support growth. Spirit is actually doing so well financially that the firm could, if desired, seek to acquire another airline, perhaps an airline based in Mexico or Brazil. And there is no reason why Spirit could not penetrate Canada and even the USA with more flights to more cities.

Prepare a three-year strategic plan for Spirit given its existing commitments to purchase or lease additional planes annually for the next five years.

Buffalo Wild Wings, Inc., 2013

www.buffalowildwings.com, BWLD

Headquartered in Minneapolis, Minnesota, Buffalo Wild Wings (BWW) is the largest chicken wing–based sports bar in the USA. BWW offers a welcoming atmosphere, open layout catering to families, sports enthusiasts, and chicken wing lovers. The typical store offers 20 to 30 different beers on draft and tap, up to 10 projection TV screens, and up to 50 smaller TVs for people to watch sporting events.

BWW specializes in traditional bone-in chicken wings and boneless chicken wings complimented by its 16 different wing sauces. BWW also sells burgers, other finger foods, and alcoholic beverages. The typical restaurant offers a diverse selection of beers, wines, and liquor options. As of year end 2012, BWW operated 891 stores of which 381 were company-owned and 510 were franchisee-owned. The company expects to increase its total number of restaurants by 105 in 2013 and approximately by the same amount in 2014. The typical restaurant is between 4,000 and 10,000 square feet and costs around $2 million to build, including the land, building, appliances, etc. Each has 50 high-definition flat-screen TV's and 10 large projection screen TV's. Takeout orders comprise 14 percent of BWW sales.

In their company-owned restaurants, BWW employs 25,500 people, 2,800 full-time and 22,300 part-time, which it calls team members. Five of the top nine executives are females including the CEO, Sally J. Smith. BWW operates its 817 stores in 48 U.S. states and Canada. BWW opened five new restaurants in 2012 on the parking lots of big-box retail stores such as Home Depot. BWW expects to have 1,500 restaurants in the USA and Canada by 2016, and many of them will be in vacant space of Sears stores, parking lots, and malls.

Copyright by Fred David Books LLC. (Written by Forest R. David)

History

In 1981, James Disbrow, from Buffalo, New York, along with friend, Scott Lowery, went looking for a Buffalo-style chicken wing restaurant around the campus of Kent State University in Ohio while judging a figure skating competition. Unable to find a satisfactory restaurant in the area similar to what they knew was good from back home, the concept of opening Buffalo Wild Wings and expanding this tradition of Buffalo, New York, to other areas of the country was born. The first restaurant named Buffalo Wild Wings & Weck or BW3, was opened in Columbus, Ohio, in 1982 near the campus of Ohio State University. In 1991, BWW began its franchising program and in 2003 the company completed its initial public offering.

Vision and Mission

BWW refers to its mission statement in its code of ethics, but the firm does not provide an explicit mission or vision statement on its website or its annual report. However, BWW does provide its "concept and business strategy" as follows:

> Continue to strengthen the Buffalo Wild Wings brand
> Deliver a unique guest experience
> Offer boldly-flavored menu items with broad appeal
> Create an inviting, neighborhood atmosphere,
> Focus on operational excellence,
> Open restaurants in new and exciting domestic markets and new countries and
> Increase same-store sales, average unit volumes and profitability.

EXHIBIT 1 BWW's Organizational Design

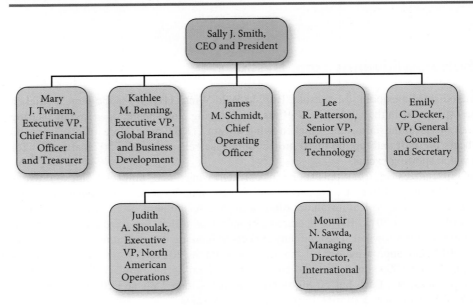

Source: Company documents.

Organizational Chart

As indicated in Exhibit 1, BWW appears to operate from a divisional by geographic region structure.

Internal Issues

Statement of Ethics and Governance

BWW has two statements of ethics: one for regular employees and one for executives. For employees, the Code of Ethics provides an overall standard for ethical conduct in conjunction with what is viewed today as ethical business behavior. The statement also provides the following: (a) how to report violations of conduct, (b) extensive personal conduct policies, (c) conflicts of interests, (d) protecting trade secrets, (e) disclosure of financial data, (f) environmental impact, and much more. The executive code of ethics is similar to the document for employees. Both codes of ethics stress doing the job to the best of one's ability and seeking help before making a decision on any matters of which the employee is not sure of.

BWW provides a well-detailed corporate governance document for view on its website. This document stresses all key issues related to the governance of BWW, including but not limited to: board size, board leadership policies, selection of new directors, retirement, compensation, and stock ownership policies.

Business Segments

As indicated in Exhibit 2, 22 percent of BWW's revenues come from alcoholic beverages. Not included in the chart but important to note is that 13 percent of BWW's sales come from takeout orders, an area in which BWW states it does not try to compete on and do not consider takeout wing establishments its primary competitors. But 13 percent is quite large and may be a growth area for the company in the future.

Exhibit 3 reveals strong revenue growth for BWW's company-owned and franchised stores over the last three years. Revenue from company-owned stores increased 34 percent in 2012. Exhibit 4 reveals average revenue per store. Note that franchised stores are outperforming company-owned stores on average, but this is partly the result of BWW repurchasing underperforming franchised stores.

EXHIBIT 2 A BWW Revenue-by-Product Percentage Analysis

Traditional Wings	Boneless Wings	Alcoholic Beverages	Other Food/ Beverages	Years
20%	19%	24%	37%	2011
20%	19%	22%	39%	2012

Source: Company documents.

EXHIBIT 3 BWW Revenue Analysis: Company Owned versus Franchised Restaurants

	2012	2011	2010	2009
Company Owned	$964M	$717M	555M	489M
Franchised	$1,510M	$1,326M	1,148M	992M

Source: Company documents.

EXHIBIT 4 BWW's Average Revenue per Restaurant

	2011	2010	2009
Company Owned	$2.25M	2.14M	2.11M
Franchised	$2.66M	2.43M	2.36M

Source: Company documents.

Strategies

BWW is currently employing both market penetration and market development strategies and plans to have around 1,500 restaurants within the next several years, nearly double what they currently own. BWW is considering adding locations outside its current two countries: USA and Canada. The company also expects to maintain its 60–40 split of franchised-owned to company-owned stores. Opening new stores especially in new countries would create additional risks, such as limited brand awareness, supply chain issues, unknown competitors, and much more. BWW is considering expanding into international markets via joint ventures with an established global brand.

Exhibit 5 reveals BWW growth over recent years. Note in 2012 the 19 percent growth in company-owned stores and 2.4 percent for franchised stores.

Marketing and Advertising

Since its inception in 1982, BWW has specialized in offering a unique brand experience for guests with the wide array of 6 award-winning sauces, beer variety, conveniently located TVs, a great social and sporting atmosphere, and though not acknowledged by the company, sex appeal with young attractive female waitresses. BWW instituted Tablegating at its

EXHIBIT 5 BWW's Growth: Number of Restaurants

	2012	2011	2010	2009
Company-Owned	381	319	259	232
Franchised	510	498	473	420

Source: Company documents.

restaurants in 2011 to promote sporting events, good food, beverages, and fellowship among fans. BWW maintains a year-round advertising presence but increases this advertising around its peak seasons, generally NCAA football in the fall and NCAA basketball in the spring. Each BWW franchise pays a royalty fee of 5.0 percent and an advertising fee of 3.5 percent of restaurant sales.

Finance

In 2011 alone, BWW built 50 new company-owned stores and repurchased 18 franchised stores. Exhibits 6 and 7 are the financial statements for BWW. Note net income increased 13.6 percent from 2011 to 2012. Note on the balance sheet that BWW currently has $32 million in goodwill, up from $17 million in 2011.

EXHIBIT 6 BWW's Income Statements

(Amounts in thousands except per share data)

	Fiscal years ended		
	December 30, 2012	December 25, 2011	December 26, 2010
Revenue:			
Restaurant sales	$ 963,963	717,395	555,184
Franchise royalties and fees	76,567	67,083	58,072
Total revenue	**1,040,530**	**784,478**	**613,256**
Costs and expenses:			
Restaurant operating costs:			
Cost of sales	303,653	203,291	160,877
Labor	289,167	215,649	167,193
Operating	141,417	109,654	88,694
Occupancy	54,147	44,005	36,501
Depreciation and amortization	67,462	49,913	39,205
General and administrative	84,149	72,689	53,996
Preopening	14,630	14,564	8,398
Loss on asset disposals and store closures	3,291	1,929	2,051
Total costs and expenses	957,916	711,694	556,915
Income from operations	82,614	72,784	56,341
Investment income	754	118	684
Earnings before income taxes	83,368	72,902	57,025
Income tax expense	26,093	22,476	18,625
Net earnings	**$ 57,275**	**50,426**	**38,400**
Earnings per common share – basic	$ 3.08	2.75	2.11
Earnings per common share – diluted	$ 3.06	2.73	2.10
Weighted average shares outstanding – basic	18,582	18,337	18,175
Weighted average shares outstanding – diluted	18,705	18,483	18,270

Source: 2012 Form 10K, p. 38.

EXHIBIT 7 BWW's Balance Sheets

(Dollar amounts in thousands)

	December 30, 2012	December 25, 2011
ASSETS		
Current assets:		
Cash and cash equivalents	$ 21,340	$ 20,530
Marketable securities	9,579	39,956
Accounts receivable, net of allowance of $25	20,203	12,165
Inventory	7,820	6,311
Prepaid expenses	3,869	3,707
Refundable income taxes	4,122	7,561
Deferred income taxes	5,774	6,323
Restricted assets	52,829	42,692
Total current assets	125,536	139,245
Property and equipment, net	386,570	310,170
Reacquired franchise rights, net	37,370	21,028
Goodwill	32,365	17,770
Other assets	9,246	7,146
Total assets	**$ 591,087**	**$ 495,359**
LIABILITIES AND STOCKHOLDERS' EQUITY		
Current liabilities:		
Unearned franchise fees	$ 1,763	$ 1,852
Accounts payable	36,418	30,089
Accrued compensation and benefits	39,637	30,499
Accrued expenses	11,461	7,580
System-wide payables	51,564	44,250
Total current liabilities	140,843	114,270
Long-term liabilities:		
Other liabilities	1,752	1,544
Deferred income taxes	37,128	38,512
Deferred lease credits	27,992	23,047
Total liabilities	207,715	177,373
Commitments and contingencies		
Stockholders' equity:		
Undesignated stock, 1,000,000 shares authorized, none issued	—	—
Common stock, no par value. Authorized 44,000,000 shares; issued and outstanding 18,623,370 and 18,377,920, respectively	121,450	113,509
Retained earnings	262,047	204,772
Accumulated other comprehensive loss	(125)	(295)
Total stockholders' equity	383,372	317,986
Total liabilities and stockholders' equity	**$ 591,087**	**$ 495,359**

Source: 2012 *Form 10K,* p. 37.

Locations

BWW's home office in Minneapolis consists of 48,000 square feet and is under a lease that terminates in 2017 with an option to renew for another five-year term. BWW has 891 restaurants in 49 different U.S. states and 7 additional restaurants in Ontario, Canada. Exhibit 8 provides the top 10 U.S. markets ranked by total number of BWW restaurants. Note that Texas has the most BWWs, followed by Ohio. Exhibit 9 reveals that approximately 43 percent of all BWW restaurants are located in Midwestern states. The Northeast, West, Canada, and other world locations are still relatively untapped by BWW.

Restaurant Franchise Operations

Approximately 59 percent of all BWWs are franchised and owned and operated by the franchisee. Franchises fees range from $25,000 to $42,500 depending on the owner's restaurant experience and the number of stores he or she currently operates. The general lease is typically for a 20-year initial term with the possibly to renew subject on certain conditions that the company does not specify.

In addition to the initial start-up costs, franchisees also pay royalty fees of 5 percent on all restaurant sales, with an additional 3.5 percent of sales revenue being attributed to advertising. There is a provision in all contracts whereby BWW can increase the fees by 0.5 percent once every three years. It is unclear from company documents whether this would amount to a 5.5 percent fee or a 5.025 percent fee. BWW does not expect to enact this provision in the next two years.

EXHIBIT 8 BWW's Top 10 U.S. States (Number of Stores)

	2011	2012	2011	2012	2011	2012
USA	Company-Owned		Franchised		Total	
Texas	37	43	51	45	88	88
Ohio	32	32	53	53	85	85
Illinois	13	18	46	43	59	61
Indiana	7	7	42	42	49	49
Michigan	0	0	43	47	43	47
California	11	18	24	28	35	46
Virginia	15	16	20	20	35	36
Florida	4	5	26	27	30	32
Minnesota	23	23	5	5	28	28
Missouri	7	6	20	21	27	27

Source: Company documents.

EXHIBIT 9 BWWs' by U.S. Region (2011)

Region	Total Stores	Percent
Midwest	353	43
Southeast	282	35
West	107	13
Northeast	71	9
Canada	4	-
Total	817	100%

Source: Company documents.

Competitors

In the competitive restaurant industry, BWW is attracting customers based on taste, quality, service, and ambience. Primary competitors include Hooters, T.G.I Friday's, Chili's, Applebees, and many regional and mom-and-pop sports bars across the USA and Canada. In addition to sports bars and chicken wing-themed establishments, BWW does not consider quick-service restaurants (QSR), such as McDonald's and Kentucky Fried Chicken, as competitors, nor surprisingly quick takeout chicken wing establishments. This corporate view is surprising because many quick-service chicken wing stores can offer much lower prices than BWW because its overhead is significantly less. Recall that 13 percent of all BWW sales are derived from takeout customers. This 13 percent can somewhat be considered a gift because BWW does not promote its takeout business with volume discounts, "tailgate specials," or any other marketing strategy.

Exhibit 10 provides a financial comparison of BWW with DineEquity (owner of Applebees's) and Brinker International (owner of Chili's). Note that BWW has the highest price-earnings ratio but has the lowest revenues among the three.

T.G.I. Friday's

With about 1,000 locations worldwide, T.G.I. Friday's (often shortened to "Friday's" in most countries, and stylized "FRiDAY'S", or "T.G.I.s" in the United Kingdom and the Republic of Ireland) is a U.S. restaurant chain focusing on casual dining, similar to BWW. T.G.I is owned by the Carlson Companies, a privately-held firm, so financial information is difficult to obtain about T.G.I Friday's. The company name, however, is taken from the expression TGIF, which stands for "Thank Goodness It's Friday," although some recent television commercials for the chain have also made use of the alternative phrase, "Thank God It's Friday." The company is known for its red-striped canopies, brass railings, Tiffany lamps, and frequent use of antiques as décor.

Hooters

HOA Restaurant Group (Hooters), based in Atlanta, Georgia, was founded in 1983 in Clearwater, Florida, and currently operates more than 430 franchise restaurants in more than 27 different countries, and additionally, the company operates 160 stores. The theme and concept of Hooters has changed little over the last 30 years and chicken wings is a main product served. The typical Hooters restaurant experience includes the sex appeal of female waitresses, jukebox-style music, sports on television, and a menu that focuses around chicken wings, but also includes seafood, salads, and sandwiches. Around 68 percent of all Hooters sales are derived from food and nonalcoholic beverages, 28 percent from beer or other alcoholic beverages, and 4 percent from merchandise, such as Hooters calendars and appeal.

EXHIBIT 10 **A Financial Comparison of BWW with Brinker International and DineEquity**

	BWW	DineEquity	Brinker Int.
Market Capitalization	1.61B	804M	2.4B
Number of Employees	2.8K	640	60.3K
Revenue	1.04B	1.02B	2.81B
Gross Margin	0.26	0.40	0.18
Net Income	57.2M	72.6M	146M
EPS Ratio	2.90	4.00	1.77
P/E Ratio	29.91	10.99	18.00

EPS, earnings per share; P/E, price-to-earnings.

Source: Company documents.

Applebee's

Founded in 1976 as the International House of Pancakes (IHOP) and based in Glendale, California, with 640 full-time employees, DineEquity today operates both Applebee's Neighborhood Grill and Bar and IHOP. As of year-end 2011, the company operated 1,842 Applebee's franchise restaurants in the USA and 16 different foreign markets and 177 additional company-owned restaurants. There were 1,535 IHOP-franchised restaurants in the USA and 5 in foreign markets and 10 company-owned IHOP restaurants. DineEquity has experienced a 40-percent decline in revenues from $1.4 billion in 2009 to $1.0 billion in 2011.

The Applebee's segment of DineEquity competes with BWW by serving chicken wings, burgers, and other bar finger foods along with alcoholic and nonalcoholic beverage items. Applebee's also sells steaks, its most popular item, and have begun a new fresh menu offering new chicken, seafood, and salads in an attempted to capitalize on a healthier-minded consumer. In addition to the historical similarity in food times with BWW, Applebee's also markets itself as a neighborhood bar and grill and provides a limited sports bar atmosphere around the bar area during times of significant sporting events. New CEO Mike Archer of Applebee's is currently reducing the pop culture feel of Applebee's decor, adding healthier items such as its less-than 500-calorie menu, so it has yet to be determined how close of a competitor of BWW Applebee's will remain.

Chili's

Founded in 1975 as Chili's in Dallas, Texas, Brinker International operates both Chili's Grill & Bar and Maggianos's Little Italy. As of year-end 2011, Brinker operated 1,534 Chili's and 45 Maggiano's. The company has restaurants in all 50 states and in more than 30 countries. The company experienced an 18-percent decline in revenues from $3.2 billion in 2009 to $2.7 billion in 2011. The Chili's segment most closely competes with BWW offering many similar food items, alcoholic beverages, and a care-free atmosphere. However, Chili's does not incorporate a sports bar aspect into its stores.

External Issues

Chicken wing prices in 2012 increased 62.8 percent over the prior year to an average price per pound of $1.97. Chicken wings accounted for 27 percent of BWW's cost of sales in 2012, up from 19 percent the prior year.

Domestic Economy

Unemployment is hovering just above 8 percent and interest rates are low but banks are not readily lending. Consumers continue to pinch pennies. "Dining out easily can be postponed, so many restaurants are a "very visible indicator" of what's happening in the economy," says Malcolm Knapp, a New York-based consultant who created the Knapp-Track Index and has monitored the industry since 1970. "Amid declining confidence, consumers don't have the appetite to eat away from home as frequently," he said. The USA is facing more than $600 billion in higher taxes and reductions in defense and other government programs in 2013. U.S. retail sales are weakening, and consumer sentiment, measured by the Bloomberg Comfort Index, is declining. "It doesn't feel like we're out of a recession for many middle-class American households," Knapp said. In what's become an "allocation nation," consumers must choose between different categories of discretionary spending, and dining out is "very sensitive" to changing habits.

Commodity Prices

BWW does not engage in any form of futures contracts for purchasing wings, instead purchasing at market prices and accepting the volatility that comes with that strategy. BWW acknowledges this problem and is actively looking for a long-term pricing agreement but has yet to come to agreement with any provider of chicken wings. Also, most BWW supplies are provided by third parties, leaving BWW with limited little control over its supply chain. Failure to deliver chicken wings, sauce, paper products, beverages, and such on time could severely impact its business.

Future

BWW is one of the fastest-growing restaurant chains in the USA and also one of the hottest stocks for investors. The company's strategy to focus on chicken wings, beer, sports, and attractive waitresses continues to be a winning business model. Perhaps the most important challenge facing BWW is with its expansion policy. The company expects to double its total stores in the next three to four years. CEO Sally Smith is currently faced with continuing expansion in stronghold markets in the Midwest and Southeast or exploring markets in the Northeast, West, Canada, and other international markets. BWW has two franchise development agreements for restaurants in the Middle East and Puerto Rico.

BWW lacks control over its supply chain and has no real futures contracts in place to hedge against volatile chicken wing prices. Should CEO Smith actively establish contracts with chicken producers to buy chicken wings on a futures contract? Are there other backward integration strategies CEO Smith could pursue to help protect against untimely delivery, poor quality, or volatile pricing of supply chain products?

Another strategic issue facing BWW is its neglect of the takeout business. Although the company focuses on selling a casual sporty dining environment, many sports fans enjoy watching games at home, tailgating at the event, or even just enjoying a day at the lake or beach. Currently BWW does not offer any type of marketing package or takeout options for this customer group, rather it expects the customer to pay full menu dine-in prices with little price discount for volume purchases. However, with 13 percent of sales, and a much larger percent of food sales because takeout typically does not include alcohol, there is an opportunity to grow this business.

Develop a three-year strategic plan for CEO Sally Smith at BWW.

Rite Aid Corporation, 2013

www.riteaid.com, RAD

Headquartered in Camp Hill, Pennsylvania, and incorporated in Delaware, Rite Aid is the third-largest retail drugstore chain in the USA based on both revenue and number of stores. Rite Aid operates 4,623 stores in 31 states and the District of Columbia and has 89,000 associates, of which 13 percent were pharmacists, 43 percent were part-time, and 26 percent were members of a union. Rite Aid's fiscal 2013 year ended on March 2, 2013.

Rite Aid stores sell prescription drugs and other merchandise, dubbed "front-end products" such as over-the-counter medications, beauty products, cosmetics, household items, beverages, snack foods, greeting cards, seasonal merchandise, and much more. Currently prescription drugs account for 67.6 percent of revenue, whereas front-end products account for 32.4 percent of revenue. The average size Rite Aid store is 12,600 square feet with 61 percent of the stores free standing and 40 percent built into another building such as a strip mall. Approximately 52 percent of stores include a drive through, 24 percent include a one-hour photo and 47 percent include a General Nutrition Corporation (GNC) store inside.

Although performing poorly and in financial trouble, Rite Aid tries to distinguish itself from other drugstores with its wellness + loyalty program, plus their private brands that account for 18.3 percent of front-end sales, and a strategic alliance with GNC, the leading retailer of vitamin and mineral supplements. In the prior fiscal year that ended March 1, 2012, Rite Aid private brands comprised 17 percent of sales. However, CVS and Walgreens, as well as pharmacies in mass discounters such as Walmart and Target, are crushing Rite Aid, which needs a clear strategic plan and turnaround strategy to survive the next few years.

Copyright by Fred David Books LLC. (Written by Forest R. David)

History

Rite Aid opened its first store in 1962 as Thrift D Discount Center in Scranton, Pennsylvania. Thrift D Discount Center grew rapidly and in 1968 changed its name to Rite Aid Corporation and was listed on the American Stock Exchange only to switch to the New York Stock Exchange in 1970. The company grew rapidly and by 1972 operated 267 stores in 10 different states, and by 1981, was, and remains to this day, the third-largest drugstore chain in the USA. When Rite Aid celebrated its twenty-fifth year in operation in 1987, the company continued its acquisition and market penetration strategy by acquiring 420 stores in 10 different states plus the District of Columbia, bringing the total number of Rite Aid stores to 2,000, at that time the nation's largest drugstore chain based on total stores.

In 1995, Rite Aid acquired Perry Drug Stores in Michigan and a year later acquired Thrifty PayLess Holdings, the largest drugstore chain in the western USA. Also in 1996, Rite Aid entered the Gulf Coast market with the acquisition of Harco, based in Alabama and then acquired K&B Inc. based in New Orleans. Rite Aid formed a strategic partnership with GNC whereby the two companies have cobranded a line of vitamins and nutritional supplements called PharmAssure that are sold in both Rite Aid and GNC stores nationwide.

In 2007, Rite Aid acquired (for more than $4 billion from Canadian drugstore chain Jean Coutu), the U.S. drugstore chain named Brooks and Eckerd. This acquisition established Rite Aid as the largest drugstore chain on the East coast, and all 1,850 Brooks and Eckerd stores were renamed and rebranded as Rite Aid; but the acquisition left Rite Aid heavily in debt and with redundant stores in some areas.

Today, Rite Aid is clinging to its position as a distant third (behind CVS and Walgreens) in the U.S. retail drugstore business. Unprofitable and operating more than 4,700 drugstores in about 30 states and the District of Columbia, Rite Aids fills prescriptions (about two-thirds of sales) and sells health and beauty aids, convenience foods, greeting cards, and other items, including some 3,000 Rite Aid brand private-label products.

Vision and Mission

According to its website, Rite Aid's mission statement is:

"To be a successful chain of friendly, neighborhood drugstores. Our knowledgeable, caring associates work together to provide a superior pharmacy experience, and offer everyday products and services that help our valued customers lead healthier, happier lives."

The company has no stated vision statement.

Organizational Structure

Rite Aid appears to use a divisional-by-geographic region organizational structure as portrayed in Exhibit 1. Doing business only in the USA, Rite Aid has five divisions: Southern, Northeast, Mid-Atlantic, Western, and New York City Metro. Note in Exhibit 1 that the division heads are lower levels of top management, which may be a problem. For example, do the executive vice-president's noted in the chart have authority and responsibility over the division senior vice-president head persons. Note also that there are only three women among the top 31 executives.

Internal Issues

Statement of Ethics

Rite Aid has two separate Codes of Ethic posted on its website. One code reinforces the overall commitment of Rite Aid and its associates, board of directors, and the companies that do business with Rite Aid, whereas the second code is principally targeted for the chief executive officer (CEO) and senior officers within the company. Rite Aid's Codes of Ethics provide guidelines for many workplace issues including but not limited to: associate privacy, equal employment and discrimination, sexual and other forms of harassment, environmental policies, safety in the work place, drugs and alcohol, weapons in the work place, and much more. The Code of Ethics also establishes conditions of ethical behavior for the company as a whole. Some examples discussed in the code are: dealing with suppliers, dealing with conflicts of interest, receiving and giving gifts, confidential information and trade secrets, document records, and insider trading. The code also describes in detail how to function with integrity in respect to honest advertising, fair billing of prescription drugs, and product safety. Finally the Code of Ethics discusses interaction with local, state, and the national government, mainly focusing on gifts to politicians, political contributions, and lobbying activities.

Segment Data

Rite Aid provides data for four unique business segments. As indicated in Exhibit 2, prescription drugs account for approximately 68 percent of sales. It is interesting that titles of the company executives do not indicate a divisional-by-product structure so apparently there is none. Front-end products (all products that are not prescription drugs) account for the balance of 32 percent of revenue. Approximately 17 percent of the company's front-end sales can be attributed to private branded products; Rite Aid plans to increase the offerings of Rite Aid branded products in 2013–2015.

Properties

Rite Aid does no business outside the USA. Rite Aid's store size varies depending on location with stores in the East averaging 11,100 square feet per store and stores in the West averaging 19,500 square feet for an overall average of 12,600 square feet. Exhibit 3 provides a breakdown of the store count for the top 10 states in which Rite Aid operates. Note that the only western state in the top 10 in store count is California. Note also that no state added stores in fiscal 2013. Exhibit 4 reveals further attributes about Rite Aid stores.

More than 4,400 of Rite Aid stores, or approximately 94 percent are under noncancelable leases with terms of 10 to 22 years. Rental payments are set at comparable fair market rates and certain leases also require additional payments based on sales volumes, reimbursement for

EXHIBIT 1 Rite Aid's Organizational Structure

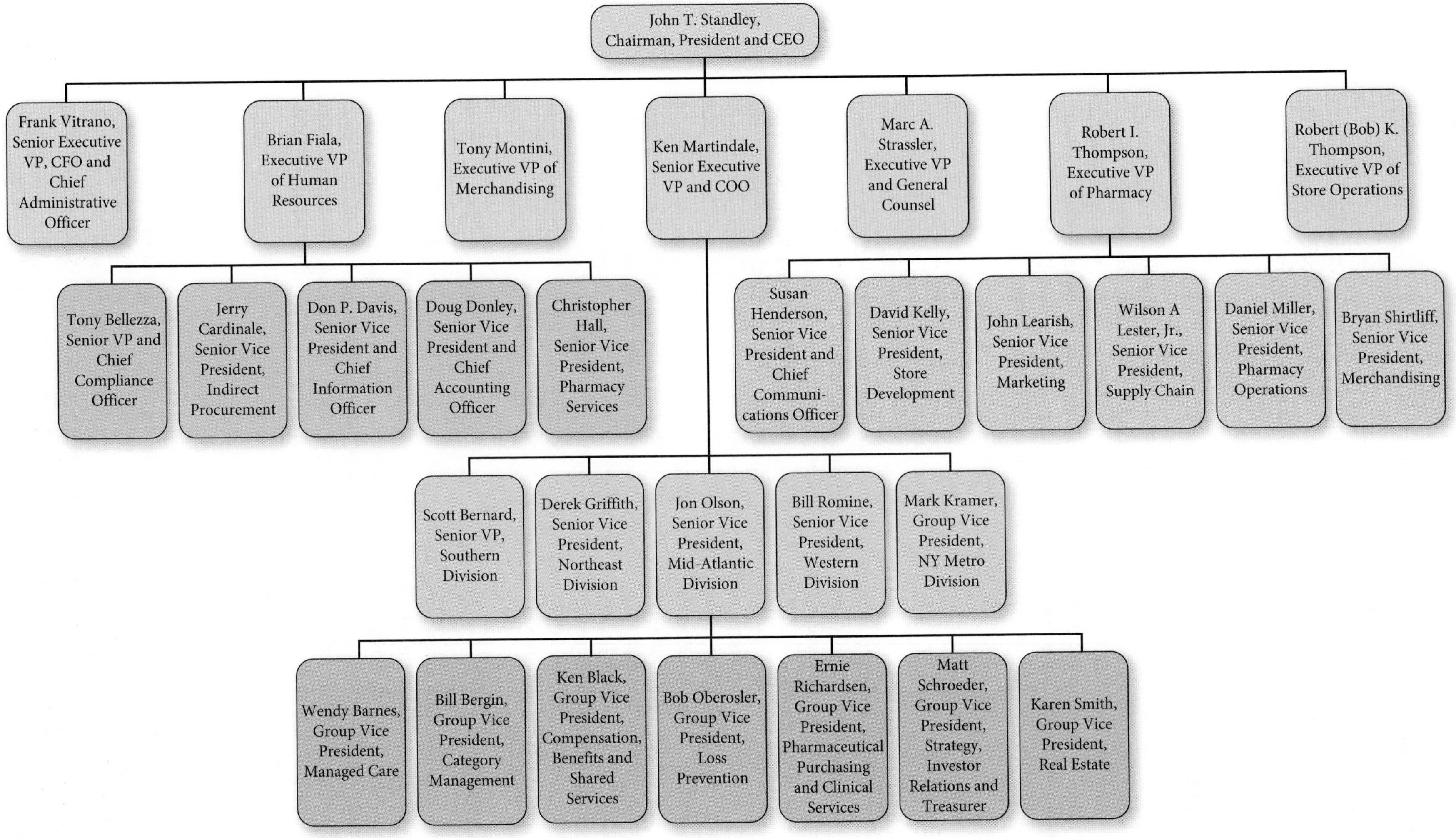

John T. Standley, Chairman, President and CEO

Frank Vitrano, Senior Executive VP, CFO and Chief Administrative Officer

Brian Fiala, Executive VP of Human Resources

Tony Montini, Executive VP of Merchandising

Ken Martindale, Senior Executive VP and COO

Marc A. Strassler, Executive VP and General Counsel

Robert I. Thompson, Executive VP of Pharmacy

Robert (Bob) K. Thompson, Executive VP of Store Operations

Tony Bellezza, Senior VP and Chief Compliance Officer

Jerry Cardinale, Senior Vice President, Indirect Procurement

Don P. Davis, Senior Vice President and Chief Information Officer

Doug Donley, Senior Vice President and Chief Accounting Officer

Christopher Hall, Senior Vice President, Pharmacy Services

Susan Henderson, Senior Vice President and Chief Communications Officer

David Kelly, Senior Vice President, Store Development

John Learish, Senior Vice President, Marketing

Wilson A Lester, Jr., Senior Vice President, Supply Chain

Daniel Miller, Senior Vice President, Pharmacy Operations

Bryan Shirtliff, Senior Vice President, Merchandising

Scott Bernard, Senior VP, Southern Division

Derek Griffith, Senior Vice President, Northeast Division

Jon Olson, Senior Vice President, Mid-Atlantic Division

Bill Romine, Senior Vice President, Western Division

Mark Kramer, Group Vice President, NY Metro Division

Wendy Barnes, Group Vice President, Managed Care

Bill Bergin, Group Vice President, Category Management

Ken Black, Group Vice President, Compensation, Benefits and Shared Services

Bob Oberosler, Group Vice President, Loss Prevention

Ernie Richardsen, Group Vice President, Pharmaceutical Purchasing and Clinical Services

Matt Schroeder, Group Vice President, Strategy, Investor Relations and Treasurer

Karen Smith, Group Vice President, Real Estate

Source: Chart constructed based on company documents.

EXHIBIT 2 Rite Aid's Revenue Breakdown

Product Class	Sales (%)
Prescription drugs	67.6
Over-the-counter medications and personal care	9.9
Health and beauty aids	5.2
General merchandise and other	17.3

Source: Company documents.

EXHIBIT 3 Rite Aid Locations

	Fiscal 2012	Fiscal 2013
State	Store Count	Store Count
New York	630	620
California	588	583
Pennsylvania	548	540
Michigan	282	279
New Jersey	264	262
North Carolina	228	226
Ohio	227	224
Virginia	192	192
Georgia	191	189
Massachusetts	155	153

Source: Company documents.

EXHIBIT 4 A Profile of Rite Aid Stores (March 2012)

	Fiscal 2012	Fiscal 2013	2012	2013
Attribute	Number		Percentage (%)	
Freestanding Store	2,803	2,800	60.1	60.6
Drive-Through Pharmacy	2,400	2,400	51.4	51.9
GNC Stores Inside Rite Aid	2,138	2,186	45.8	47.3

Source: Company documents.

taxes, maintenance, and building insurance. Rite Aid outright owns 259 stores and also owns its corporate headquarters a 205,000-square-foot building in Camp Hill, Pennsylvania, and leases another building more than 366,000 square feet in neighboring Harrisburg. Rite Aid in addition owns or leases 17 distribution centers across the USA that average approximately 425,000 square feet, and, for some reason, owns a 55,800-square-foot ice cream manufacturing facility in California.

Current Strategies

Rite Aid's strategy is to become the neighborhood destination for health and wellness for all Americans. The company in fiscal 2013 converted 500 more stores to their wellness format. Rite Aid's Wellness and Loyalty Program, established in April 2010, allows customers to accumulate points on purchases in both front-end products and prescription drugs by achieving Bronze, Silver, and Gold levels. Rite Aid has more than 25 million members enrolled in the program. Currently 74 percent of front-end sales and 68 percent of prescriptions are filled by members of the program. Members also tend to do more business with Rite Aid on both front-end items and prescription drugs.

In addition to the new Wellness and Loyalty Program, Rite Aid has increased the number of immunizing pharmacists to 11,000 to cover all Rite Aid stores and in fiscal 2013 administered 2.4 million flu shots. The 2.4 million was up 60 percent from 1.5 million the prior year. Rite Aid also actively promotes its private brands and currently has more than 3,000 different Rite Aid brands, many that Rite Aid considers its "price fighter" or best value for the money.

Also helping to increase same-store sales is Rite Aid's partnership with GNC. Rite Aid has more than 2,100 GNC stores located within Rite Aid stores and a commitment to open additional stores by December 2014.

Technology

Rite Aid's information system allows customers to fill or refill prescriptions at any Rite Aid in the country. The system provides pharmacists with warnings of possible drug interactions. Customers can order its prescriptions over the Internet or telephone through Rite Aid's automated-response system. Efficiency derived from the use of technology allows Rite Aid's pharmacists to spend more time consulting and advising customers on supplementary products that the customers may find useful and creating a friendly atmosphere leading to more customer loyalty. Customers may also place orders on both the iPhone and Android platforms.

Suppliers

Rite Aid is currently under a contract with McKesson Corporation to deliver both brand-name and generic pharmaceuticals. About 91 percent of all prescription drugs are purchased through McKesson, leaving Rite Aid dependent on McKesson for timely supplying drugs. Rite Aid's contract with McKesson expires in March 2016. About 80 percent of all generic drugs are purchased directly from the manufacturer. Front-end products are purchased through numerous other manufacturers.

Marketing

In fiscal 2013, Rite Aid's marketing and advertising expense was $336 million, down from $369 million the prior year, mostly as a result of weekly circular advertising flyers focusing on price promotions to drive customers to stores. The ads also promote the firm's Wellness and Loyalty Program, market the Rite Aid private-branded products, and try to convince consumers that Rite Aid should be its first choice for health and wellness products.

Finance

Rite Aid is highly leveraged with more than $5.9 billion in long-term debt, so debt financing is not a good option for the company going forward. A large portion of the company's cash flow is dedicated to servicing debt. Even with all of its acquisitions over the years, Rite Aid's goodwill remains $0 so that is good, but Rite Aid's stock price has been less than $3 per share for five years and is still $3 as of 8-15-13, so equity financing is also not an attractive financing option. The low stock price could also make the company vulnerable to a hostile takeover, but the large debt and negative stockholders' equity may reduce this concern. If a firm's stock value drops below the minimum New York Stock Exchange listing price, then the security could be delisted from the exchange.

Rite Aid's relationship with Canadian pharmacy chain Jean Coutu Group (through the acquisition of Brooks Eckerd), which controls 25 percent of the voting power, also hinders Rite Aid's financial position. Based in Longueuil, Quebec, Canada, Jean Coutu owned Eckerd when Rite Aid made that acquisition. Jean Coutu today operates about 400 franchised stores in Quebec, New Brunswick, and Ontario. In April 2012, Jean Coutu sold on the open market 56 million shares of Rite Aid. That sell was part of Jean Coutu's initial $234.4 million stake in Rite Aid. Jean Coutu would be a rival if Rite Aid expanded to Canada. What is there to prevent even a firm such as CVS from buying Jean Coutu's bulk amount of Rite Aid common stock?

Rite Aid's current income statements and balance sheets are provided in Exhibits 5 and 6, respectively. Note the $118 million earnings in fiscal 2013, coming off bad losing years.

Competitors

There are more than 44,000 drugstores in the USA with slightly more than half of these stores belonging to chains and the rest being independent mom-and-pop operations. Mail-order drug companies such as www.drugstore.com, as well as large discount firms such as Walmart, significantly erode potential sales for Rite Aid. Prescription drug sales, where around 60 percent of drugstore sales originate from, total about $150 billion annually and are expected to increase as the economy improves, baby boomers age, a strong drug pipeline, and the introduction of healthcare reform.

Walgreens, CVS Caremark, and Rite Aid are the three-largest drugstore chains in the USA by store number and revenues, respectively. These top three chains represent 47 percent of total retail drugstore sales and 63 percent of the retail chain drugstore sales. With 37 percent of the retail chain drugstore sales not coming from the big three, there remains room for acquisitions for the big players if they chose that strategy. Historically, Rite Aid has been the acquirer, but its weak financial condition now makes it more likely that they would be acquired.

Note in Exhibit 7 that Rite Aid generates more revenue per employee than Walgreens but less than CVS. The key statistic in Exhibit 7 however is that Rite Aid's two major rivals are financially stable.

EXHIBIT 5 Rite Aid's Income Statement (All amounts in thousands except per share amounts)

| | Year Ended | | |
	March 2, 2013 (52 Weeks)	March 3, 2012 (53 Weeks)	February 26, 2011 (52 Weeks)
Revenues	$ 25,392,263	$ 26,121,222	$ 25,214,907
Costs and expenses:			
Cost of goods sold	18,073,987	19,327,887	18,522,403
Selling, general and administrative expenses	6,600,765	6,531,411	6,457,833
Lease termination and impairment charges	70,859	100,053	210,893
Interest expense	515,421	529,255	547,581
Loss on debt retirements, net	140,502	33,576	44,003
Gain on sale of assets, net	(16,776)	(8,703)	(22,224)
	25,384,758	26,513,479	25,760,489
Income (loss) before income taxes	7,505	(392,257)	(545,582)
Income tax (benefit) expense	(110,600)	(23,686)	9,842
Net income (loss)	**$ 118,105**	**$ (368,571)**	**$ (555,424)**
Computation of income (loss) applicable to common stockholders:			
Net income (loss)	**$ 118,105**	**$ (368,571)**	**$ (555,424)**
Accretion of redeemable preferred stock	(102)	(102)	(102)
Cumulative preferred stock dividends	(10,528)	(9,919)	(9,346)
Income (loss) attributable to common stockholders—basic and diluted	$ 107,475	$ (378,592)	$ (564,872)
Basic and diluted income (loss) per share	$ 0.12	$ (0.43)	$ (0.64)

EPS, earnings per share.

Source: 2013 *Form 10K,* page 63.

EXHIBIT 6 Rite Aid's Balance Sheet (All amounts in thousands except per share amounts)

	March 2, 2013	March 3, 2012
ASSETS		
Current assets:		
Cash and cash equivalents	$ 129,452	$ 162,285
Accounts receivable, net	929,476	1,013,233
Inventories, net	3,154,742	3,138,455
Prepaid expenses and other current assets	195,377	190,613
Total current assets	4,409,047	4,504,586
Property, plant and equipment, net	1,895,650	1,902,021
Other intangibles, net	464,404	528,775
Other assets	309,618	428,909
Total assets	$ 7,078,719	$ 7,364,291
LIABILITIES AND STOCKHOLDERS' DEFICIT		
Current liabilities:		
Current maturities of long-term debt and lease financing obligations	$ 37,311	$ 79,421
Accounts payable	1,384,644	1,426,391
Accrued salaries, wages and other current liabilities	1,156,315	1,064,507
Total current liabilities	2,578,270	2,570,319
Long-term debt, less current maturities	5,904,370	6,141,773
Lease financing obligations, less current maturities	91,850	107,007
Other noncurrent liabilities	963,663	1,131,948
Total liabilities	9,538,153	9,951,047
Commitments and contingencies	—	—
Stockholders' deficit:		
Preferred stock—series G, par value $1 per share; liquidation value $100 per share; 2,000 shares authorized; shares issued .007 and .006	1	1
Preferred stock—series H, par value $1 per share; liquidation value $100 per share; 2,000 shares authorized; shares issued 1,821 and 1,715	182,097	171,569
Common stock, par value $1 per share; 1,500,000 shares authorized; shares issued and outstanding 904,268 and 898,687	904,268	898,687
Additional paid-in capital	4,280,831	4,278,988
Accumulated deficit	(7,765,262)	(7,883,367)
Accumulated other comprehensive loss	(61,369)	(52,634)
Total stockholders' deficit	(2,459,434)	(2,586,756)
Total liabilities and stockholders' deficit	$ 7,078,719	$ 7,364,291

Source: 2013 *Form 10K*, p. 62.

EXHIBIT 7 A Financial Comparison of Rite Aid, Walgreens, and CVS

	Rite Aid	Walgreens	CVS
Number of Employees	89,000	176,000	202,000
Net Income ($)	118M	2.57B	3.56B
Revenue ($)	25.3B	72.5B	112.2B
Revenue ($)/Employee	284K	411K	555K
EPS Ratio ($)	0.12	2.91	2.64
Market Capitalization	2.71B	25.85B	61.01B

EPS, earnings per share.

Walgreens

Founded in 1901 and based in Deerfield, Illinois, Walgreens operates 7,900 drugstores in all 50 states, the District of Columbia, and Puerto Rico. With more than 176,000 full-time employees and sales of more than $72 billion, Walgreens is the largest drugstore in both sales and number of stores in the USA. The company is a full-fledge brick-and-mortar drugstore offering a full pharmacy and front-end products as well as one-hour photo services.

In 2011, Walgreens was involved in an ongoing dispute with Express Scripts, its pharmacy benefit manager (PBM), over contractual renewal terms. Walgreens had informed its customers that it is no longer part of the Express Scripts network. However in July 2012, the companies resolved their dispute, so Express Scripts now continues to supply Walgreens with the necessary prescriptions. During the lag though, Walgreens was not able to service customers whose prescription plans are managed by Express, thus costing Walgreens many of its Express-reliant customers and losing not only prescription sales to these customers but also front-end sales. Despite the July agreement, Walgreens still fears Express possibly merging with Express' largest competitor, Medco Health Solutions, which could severely hurt Walgreens' position in obtaining the necessary prescriptions depending on the terms of the new agreement, which are not made public.

Walgreens recently expanded into Europe through its $6.7 billion acquisition of 45 percent of Alliance Boots GmbH in Germany. This acquisition could have large potential benefits for Walgreens in the months ahead. Some analysts, however, contend that Walgreens paid too much for Alliance and should not move to acquire the remaining 55 percent of that company. The acquisition supposedly brings cross benefits to both companies whereby Walgreens gains exposure to an international market, helping it create a network of stores globally, and the deal allows Alliance Boots to enter the U.S. market, which it was eying for the past 10 years. The combined entity is supposed to be one of the biggest drugstore businesses with about 11,600 stores across 12 countries with more than 170,000 pharmacies, hospitals, and health centers.

CVS Caremark

Founded in 1892 in Woonsocket, Rhode Island, CVS operates 7,352 retail drugstores, 570 MinuteClinics, 31 retail specialty pharmacy stores, 12 specialty mail-order pharmacies, and 4 mail-order pharmacies. CVS offers many of the same products chief competitors Walgreens and Rite Aid offers, including prescription drugs, over-the-counter drugs, food, snacks, beauty products, and one-hour photo services.

In 2007, CVS acquired Caremark RX, (a PBM), in a backward integration strategy, although many experts questioned the synergy and benefits of such an alliance. One of the main concerns was that PMBs aim is to reduce costs for the consumers whereas a retail store aim is to maximize sales. Within the first two years of the merger, CVS experienced a loss of more than $4 billion in PBM business to competitors. However, starting in 2010, CVS began to experience a profit from the merger, picking up a $575 million contract with a retirement system in California, a $9 billion annual contract with Aetna Inc., and a $3 billion in sales from federal employees' plans.

Mail-Order Drugstores

Mail-order drugstores and pharmacies are the fastest-growing format in the drugstore industry. They vary from simply providing vitamins and supplements to providing over-the-counter drugs cheaper, to providing full prescription needs. Its main customer is people with an ongoing condition such as diabetes that have ongoing treatment needs. Typically, mail-order stores will fill prescriptions in up to a 90-day supply instead of the typical 30- to 60-day supply drugstores use. Brick-and-mortar drugstores offer lower duration supplies hoping to entice customers to purchase other front-end products while in its stores, but the convenience of online shopping with products mailed to the customer's house, the reduction of copays from receiving fewer prescriptions per year, and often overall lower prices because overhead of mail-order stores is considerably less, is expected on balance to hurt brick-and-mortar stores. Some stores such as CVS have expanded into the mail-order business, but CVS maintains more than 7,000 retail stores.

External Issues

People globally are getting older, so the consumption of prescription and nonprescription drugs is expected to increase quite dramatically in the years ahead, benefiting drugstore companies such as Rite Aid. The Affordable Care Act was recently upheld in the USA, benefiting drugstores. Although Rite Aid competes only in the USA, emerging economies globally are also purchasing more and more prescription and nonprescription drugs because those societies strive to become healthier. As Rite Aid's rivals such as Walgreens gain economies of scale doing business outside the USA, that trend hurts Rite Aid. Increasing penetration of cell phones and wireless devices globally also is spurring consumers to purchase more medicines and vitamins.

There is a general trend in the USA and elsewhere toward greater awareness of healthiness as well as information on how to stay healthy. This trend helps drugstores. Corporate wellness programs are gaining widespread acceptance in the business world and this too helps drugstores. But competition is exceptionally intense, so a clear strategic plan is essential to gain and sustain competitive advantage in a growing industry with growing numbers of consumers.

Generic Drugs

Hundreds of prescription drugs have recently become generic or even over-the-counter after their patents have expired. The Food and Drug Administration provides patent protection to drug companies so those firms can recover research and development costs and eventually make a profit without the risk of competition. However, when the patents expire, generic companies can market the same chemical drug at fractions of the cost to the consumer. Despite their lower sales prices, generics now account for about 78 percent of all prescriptions filled and yield a much higher gross margin for pharmacies than brand-named drugs. The average generic drug price is less than $40 whereas the average brand-name drug is about $155. About $98 billion in prescription sales will lose patent protection by 2015, resulting in an estimated $26 billion in sales from generic drugs and greatly benefiting drugstores such as Rite Aid, but of course the task is to best attract and keep customers who have many choices and thus great bargaining power.

Greater Convenience

To compete with mail-order stores, traditional drugstores are increasing the number of free-standing stores with drive-through pharmacies and investing in technology that fills prescriptions. Many drugstores are now open 24 hours a day, but the pharmacy and 1-hour photo aspects are generally only open during normal business hours.

To provide customers greater convenience, Walgreens recently added a line of grocery items. This strategy appears to be working well for Walgreens, so analysts expect Rite Aid and CVS to follow suit in the coming months or years, perhaps sooner than later.

Store Brands

Focusing on low cost-minded customers, many drugstores now have developed their own store-branded products and even offer deep discounts through their rewards programs for customers who purchase their respective brands. CVS for example has recently launched "Just the Basics" brand with more than 100 items targeted at value-minded customers. This product line currently makes up more than 17 percent of CVS front-end sales. CVS plans to further increase its private-branded products. In addition to CVS, Rite Aid has its "price fighter" store brands that total to more than 3,000 individual products. Much like generic drugs, these products are cheaper for the consumer but offer larger margins for the corporation. Store branding is expected to be a main strategy of all players in the drugstore industry.

New Healthcare Laws

In 2008, approximately 46 million Americans lacked health insurance. With the passage of the Affordable Care Act, an additional 32 million formally uninsured Americans will now be covered. It is estimated that the Affordable Care Act will cost more than $938 billion over the next 10 years, leaving many opportunities for retail drugstore operations. By 2019, it is expected that health insurance will be available for 95 percent of all Americans, up from 85 percent in 2012.

The Future

Rite Aid's big problem is high indebtedness, which stifles the firm's ability to make strategic moves and creates high interest expenses. Rumors are beginning to surface that Walgreens may be interested in acquiring Rite Aid to compete better against CVS. Although a deal would help Walgreens grow, it would also saddle the company with Rite Aid's debt.

Even if Rite Aid would consider a friendly takeover by Walgreens, a clear strategic plan would be essential for Rite Aid's shareholders to recoup its investment in the firm. Even in a hostile takeover attempt, a clear strategic plan would be vital for Rite Aid shareholders.

Best Buy Co., Inc., 2014

www.bby.com, BBY

Headquartered in Richfield, Minnesota, Best Buy Co., Inc. is the world's largest consumer electronics retailer with 1,400 stores that carry phone products, computers, televisions, appliances, cameras, and much more. In addition to its product line, Best Buy also offers service contracts, extended warranty, and product repair. Best Buy Co., Inc. is the parent company of Best Buy, Five Star, Future Shop, Pacific Sales, Geek Squad, CinemaNow, Magnolia Audio, and The Phone House stores. With 165,000 full-time employees, Best Buy is struggling to reinvent itself amid fierce competition from Apple and Amazon. A huge problem for Best Buy is that people shop there to get educated and then buy online at cheaper prices.

The brick-and-mortar business model is in severe trouble, especially for retailers that do not sell perishable goods (such as Best Buy and RadioShack). With the popularity and cost effectiveness of online shopping, coupled with a lack of sales taxes and not having the expense of operating large stores, online retailers have a huge competitive advantage. Best Buy stores serve as showrooms for online retailers. Best Buy has expensive long-term leases on its buildings and those leases must be honored, unless the firm goes into bankruptcy, which some analysts say is inevitable, especially without a clear strategic plan going forward. Best Buy's fiscal 2013 ended on February 1, 2013.

Copyright by Fred David Books LLC. (Written by Forest R. David)

History

Founded in Saint Paul, Minnesota, in 1966, Best Buy (then named Sound of Music) was started by Richard Schulze and Gary Smoliak. After acquiring two small stores in 1967, the Sound of Music went public in 1969, and enacted an employee stock option plan. By 1970, the Sound of Music hit $1 million in annual revenues.

The name Best Buy first originated in 1981 after a tornado hit a store in Roseville, Minnesota, resulting in a major sale dubbed as "Best Buy," which subsequently became an annual event, and in 1983 Sound of Music officially changed its name to Best Buy Co., Inc. After the name change, Best Buy increased average store selling space and began offering a wider range of products, many of them at discounted prices.

During the 1990s, Best Buy continued to grow, hitting the $1 billion mark in annual revenues. Best Buy launched bestbuy.com in 2000 and acquired the Canada-based electronics chain Future Shop in 2001. Future Shop still operates under its original name and still operates independently from Best Buy. Best Buy acquired Geek Squad, the 24-hour computer support taskforce in 2002 and opened its first Canadian Best Buy store in Ontario in the same year.

In 2006, Best Buy's common stock closed at an all-time high of $59.50 and in 2008 the chain opened its 1,000th physical store in the Mall of America, one of the largest malls in the world, located in Bloomington, Minnesota. Best Buy continued international expansion in 2008 by opening stores in Puerto Rico, Mexico, and Shanghai, China. In 2009, the company opened stores in Turkey and the United Kingdom. Best Buy planned to expand heavily into the United Kingdom (UK) when the company hired Brian Dunn as its CEO. Dunn had started at Best Buy 25 years previously as a salesperson and was widely liked by all rank-and-file workers at the time of the appointment because they viewed Dunn as "one of their own." Sluggish growth of sales in the United Kingdom led to Best Buy closing 11 Best Buy Europe stores in 2011.

Best Buy CEO Brian Dunn resigned in 2012. Less than a month later, founder and chairman Schulze was forced to resign, partly because he did not reveal that CEO Dunn, who is married, had an inappropriate relationship with a 29-year old subordinate female employee, which is violation of the company's Code of Ethics. Dunn allegedly misused company funds in conjunction with the relationship. Schulze was replaced by Hatim Tyabi in mid-2012. George Mikan III became Best Buy's CEO in late 2012. Schulze, age 71, offered about $10 billion or $25 per share to buy Best Buy and take the company private. He already owns 20 percent of the company's stock. Shareholders and analysts are skeptical of Schulze's offer. In August 2012, Hubert Joly was hired as CEO, but the company's stock was down another 10 percent in response to the announcement.

Vision and Mission

Best Buy does not have a written vision statement. The company's mission statement is as follows:

> Our formula is simple: we're a growth company focused on better solving the unmet needs of our customers—and we rely on our employees to solve those puzzles. Thanks for stopping.

Organizational Structure

Best Buy currently uses a divisional-by-geographic region organizational structure. As noted in Exhibit 1, the company has a chief administrative officer rather than a chief operating officer for the divisional heads to report.

Segments

Best Buy operates under two distinct business segments: domestic and international. The domestic segment includes all states, districts and territories of the USA, including Puerto Rico. The international segment includes all of Canada, China, Mexico, and Europe. Best Buy reports domestic revenues of $33.3 and $37.6 billion in fiscal 2013 and 2012, respectively, and international revenues of $11.7 and $11.9 billion in 2013 and 2012, respectively. For 2013, approximately 26 percent of total revenue was from domestic operations.

Despite Best Buy claiming and presenting data based on geographic region, it is possible that Best Buy is in fact a strategic business unit (SBU) structure with the two geographic regions serving as the two distinct SBUs. However, the executive titles provided in Exhibit 1 suggest a purely divisional-by-geographic structure rather than an SBU.

Domestic

There were 1,056 U.S. Best Buy stores at fiscal year-end 2013, and 409 U.S. Best Buy Mobile Stand-Alone stores. During fiscal 2013, Best Buy closed 47 U.S. Best Buy stores while opening 105 U.S. Best Buy mobile stand-alone stores.

Within the domestic segment, Best Buy further breaks down the SBU by products and services and assigns employees to distinct leadership teams for each respective product and service. Teams are empowered to determine the most effective ways to market products and services through Best Buy's channels, retail stores and online, and call centers. Further, Best Buy breaks down its domestic SBU into six different revenue categories: consumer electronics, computing and mobile phones, entertainment, appliances, services, and other.

Consumer electronics includes items such as TVs, e-Readers, navigation products, cameras, mp3 players, musical instruments, home theater systems, and much more. Computing and mobile phone segment includes items such as: notebook and desktop computers, tablets, monitors, phones, phone subscription plans, storage devices, printers, and random office supplies. Entertainment segment includes video gaming hardware and software, DVDs, CDs, and computer software. Best Buy's appliances category includes both large and small household appliances. The service category includes: service contracts, extended warranties, product repair, installation of home theater systems, and much more. Exhibit 2 reveals the percentage of revenue in each domestic product arena. Note all the negative numbers.

Exhibit 2 reveals that consumer electronics has been in a steady decline for each of the last two years. Much of the decline can be attributed to soft market for TVs and the overall declining prices of TVs. The overall TV market is much weaker than the most recent 5.4 percent decline indicates because this number would have been much worse if not for the high customer interest in e-Readers.

At fiscal year-end 2013 (March 1, 2013), there were 872 Carphone Warehouse stores and 1,517 Phone House stores in Europe, while in Canada there were 140 Future Shop stores,

EXHIBIT 1 Best Buy's Organizational Structure

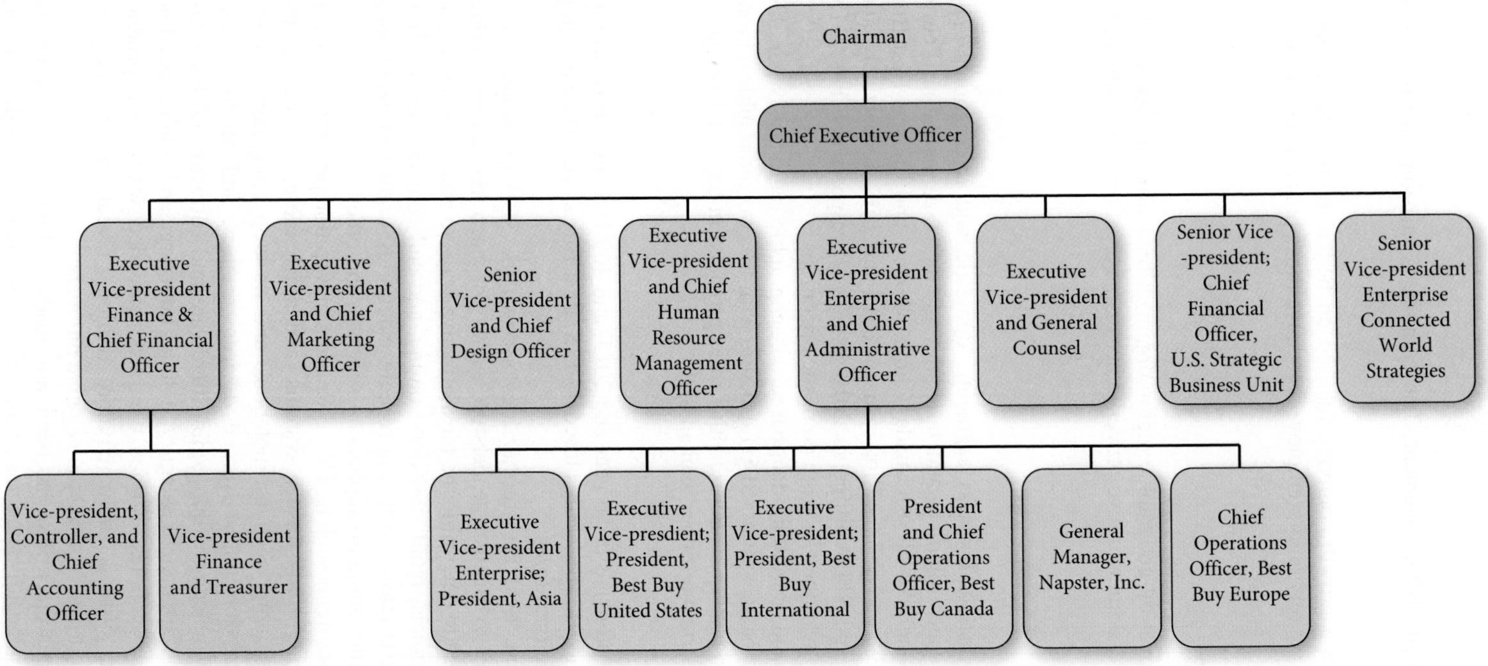

```
                    ┌──────────────┐
                    │   Chairman   │
                    └──────┬───────┘
                    ┌──────┴───────────┐
                    │ Chief Executive  │
                    │     Officer      │
                    └──────────────────┘
```

- Chairman
- Chief Executive Officer
  - Executive Vice-president Finance & Chief Financial Officer
    - Vice-president, Controller, and Chief Accounting Officer
    - Vice-president Finance and Treasurer
  - Executive Vice-president and Chief Marketing Officer
  - Senior Vice-president and Chief Design Officer
  - Executive Vice-president and Chief Human Resource Management Officer
  - Executive Vice-president Enterprise and Chief Administrative Officer
    - Executive Vice-president Enterprise; President, Asia
    - Executive Vice-president; President, Best Buy United States
    - Executive Vice-president; President, Best Buy International
    - President and Chief Operations Officer, Best Buy Canada
    - General Manager, Napster, Inc.
    - Chief Operations Officer, Best Buy Europe
  - Executive Vice-president and General Counsel
  - Senior Vice-president; Chief Financial Officer, U.S. Strategic Business Unit
  - Senior Vice-president Enterprise Connected World Strategies

EXHIBIT 2 Best Buy's Revenue by Product

	Revenue Mix by Product (%)			Same-Store Sales (%)		
	Fiscal Year End			Fiscal Year End		
	February 2011	March 2012	March 2013	February 2011	March 2012	March 2013
Consumer electronics	37	36	18	(6.3)	(5.4)	(7.0)
Computing and mobile phones	37	40	61	3.6	6.0	(0.3)
Entertainment	14	12	4	(13.3)	(16.3)	(13.4)
Appliances	5	5	10	7.0	10.6	2.9
Services	6	6	7	0.5	(0.6)	(1.3)
Other	1	1	(-)	—	—	—
Total	100	100		(3.0)	(1.6)	(2.5)

Source: Company documents.

72 Best Buy stores, and 49 Best Buy Mobile stores. In China there were 211 Five Star stores, and in Mexico there were 14 Best Buy stores. Computing and mobile phones experienced a 6-percent increase in same-store sales from fiscal 2011, primarily from tablets and mobile phones.

The entertainment segment continues to experience significant same-store declines as a result primarily of the decline in the video gaming industry and decline in sales of music and movies because many more people are downloading music offline and watching movies through outlets such as Red Box, Netflix, and Time Warner Cable's movies on demand.

Best Buy attributes the increase in appliances to promotional sales, but the slowly improving housing market in some parts of the country could explain this increase.

International

The United Kingdom and Ireland only have Carphone Warehouse stores, whereas mainland Europe only has the Phone House Stores. Canada is home to Future Shop, Best Buy, and Best Buy Mobile stand-alone stores. China is the exclusive home to only Five Star stores. In fiscal 2013, Best Buy introduced its Best Buy Express concept in Mexico. Best Buy Europe opened 122 new stores in fiscal 2013 while closing 126 other stores. Outside the USA and Europe, Best Buy opened 40 new stores and closed 21 in 2013.

Internal Issues

Statement of Ethics and Governance

Best Buy has a detailed Code of Ethics on its website, addressing the culture at Best Buy, outlining ethical behavior expected of all constituents of Best Buy, and detailing how to report violations of ethical behavior. In the wake of the embarrassing resignation of Dunn and Schulze's dismissal, the current Code of Ethics provided on Best Buy's website (several months after the dismissals) begins with a letter from former Dunn addressing the code and thanking all employees and constituents of Best Buy for their ethical behavior.

In 2010, two years before the ethical fiasco with Dunn and Schulze, research company Management CV Inc., disclosed several questionable issues, which as of 2012 are still an ongoing problem according to Management CV Inc. For example, Best Buy paid Schulze $1 million in 2011 to rent two stores he owned with one of these leases running through 2018. Schulze's daughter, the founder of Best Buy Children's Foundation, currently works as both the chairwoman and CEO of this foundation with a base salary of $242,000 and bonuses of approximately $120,000 annually. Her husband also has worked with Best Buy. A contract with Phoenix Fixtures, Schulze brother's business, has led to spending more than $70 million in fixtures for stores from 2008 to 2012. In addition, Best Buy has paid close to $4 million for chartered aircraft owned by Schulze Trust. The questionable ethics is not limited to the Schulze family either because there have been many contracts between Best Buy and businesses that have connections with Best Buy board members.

EXHIBIT 3 A Breakdown of Best Buy Stores

	Total Stores at Year End			
	March 2010	February 2011	March 2012	March 2013
Best Buy	1,069	1,099	1,103	1,099
Best Buy Mobile stand alone	74	177	305	177
Pacific Sales	35	35	34	35
Magnolia Audio Video	6	6	5	6
Geek Squad	6	—	—	—
Total Domestic Segment Stores	1,190	1,317	1,447	1,317

Source: Company documents.

Properties

Exhibit 3 below reveals a three-year trend for domestic stores in each of Best Buy's various segments. Many customers do not even know Best Buy's traditional stores offer mobile devices and service plans.

At fiscal year-end 2013, Best Buy had 1,503 domestic stores, up from 1,447 the prior year—and had 2,876 international stores, up from 2,861 the prior year. Exhibit 4 reveals the top-five markets based on store count in the domestic segment, and Exhibit 5 reveals the total number of stores in the international segment.

Suppliers

Best Buy's largest supplier is Apple, followed by Samsung, Hewlett-Packard, Sony, and LG Electronics, which together represent 45 percent of total merchandise purchased. Best Buy could possibly be subject to significant revenue reductions if any one of these top five suppliers

EXHIBIT 4 Number of Best Buy Stores in the Five Top U.S. States (Fiscal 2012)

State	Best Buy Stores	Best Buy Mobile Stand-alone Stores	Pacific Sales Stores	Magnolia Audio Video Stores
California	126	29	31	3
Texas	110	25	—	—
Florida	67	30	—	—
Illinois	58	14	—	—
New York	55	13	—	—

Source: Company documents.

EXHIBIT 5 Number of Best Buy Stores Outside the USA

	Total Stores at Year End			
	March 2010	February 2011	March 2012	2013
Best Buy Europe	2,371	2,357	2,393	2,357
Canada				
Future Shop	144	146	149	146
Best Buy	64	71	77	71
Best Buy Mobile stand-alone	4	10	30	10
China (Five Star Only)	158	166	204	166
Mexico (Best Buy Only)	5	6	8	6
Total	2,746	2,876	2,861	2,756

Source: Company documents.

were unable to or chose not to continue to provide products to Best Buy. Best Buy does not have long-term contracts with suppliers, but the company does not foresee any problems in the future with suppliers not being able to meet the demands of Best Buy. Without long-term contracts, Best Buy is more flexible regarding which suppliers to do business with, but the fact is a supplier such as Apple is also a competitor and could potentially crush Best Buy if desired.

Finance

EXHIBIT 6 Best Buy's Income Statements

	11 Months Ended		12 Months Ended	
Fiscal Years Ended	February 2, 2013	January 28, 2012	March 3, 2012	February 26, 2011
	(Unaudited recast)			
Revenue	**$ 45,085**	**$ 46,064**	**$ 50,705**	**$ 49,747**
Cost of goods sold	34,435	34,693	38,113	37,197
Restructuring charges—cost of goods sold	1	19	19	9
Gross profit	10,649	11,352	12,573	12,541
Selling, general and administrative expenses	9,502	9,339	10,242	10,029
Restructuring charges	450	34	39	138
Goodwill impairments	822	1,207	1,207	—
Operating income (loss)	(125)	772	1,085	2,374
Other income (expense)				
Gain on sale of investments	18	55	55	—
Investment income and other	33	37	37	43
Interest expense	(112)	(121)	(134)	(86)
Earnings (loss) from continuing operations before income tax expense and equity in income (loss) of affiliates	(186)	743	1,043	2,331
Income tax expense	231	622	709	779
Equity in income (loss) of affiliates	(4)	(3)	(4)	2
Net earnings (loss) from continuing operations	**(421)**	**118**	**330**	**1,554**
Gain (loss) from discontinued operations (Note 4), net of tax of $(2), $83, $89 and $65	1	(295)	(308)	(188)
Net earnings (loss) including noncontrolling interests	**(420)**	**(177)**	**22**	**1,366**
Net earnings from continuing operations attributable to noncontrolling interests	(22)	(1,378)	(1,387)	(127)
Net loss from discontinued operations attributable to noncontrolling interests	1	130	134	38
Net earnings (loss) attributable to Best Buy Co., Inc. shareholders	**$ (441)**	**$ (1,425)**	**$ (1,231)**	**$ 1,277**
Basic earnings (loss) per share attributable to Best Buy Co., Inc. shareholders				
Continuing operations	$ (1.31)	$ (3.38)	$ (2.89)	$ 3.51
Discontinued operations	0.01	(0.45)	(0.47)	(0.37)
Basic earnings (loss) per share	$ (1.30)	$ (3.83)	$ (3.36)	$ 3.14
Weighted-average common shares outstanding (in millions)				
Basic	338.6	372.5	366.3	406.1
Diluted	338.6	372.5	366.3	416.5

Source: 2013 *Form 10K,* p. 60.
All amounts in millions of U.S. dollars except per share amounts.
EPS, earnings per share.

EXHIBIT 7 Best Buy's Balance Sheets

	February 2, 2013	March 3, 2012
Assets		
Current Assets		
Cash and cash equivalents	$ 1,826	$ 1,199
Receivables	2,704	2,288
Merchandise inventories	6,571	5,731
Other current assets	946	1,079
Total current assets	12,047	10,297
Property and Equipment		
Land and buildings	756	775
Leasehold improvements	2,386	2,367
Fixtures and equipment	5,120	4,981
Property under capital lease	113	129
	8,375	8,252
Less accumulated depreciation	5,105	4,781
Net property and equipment	3,270	3,471
Goodwill	528	1,335
Tradenames, Net	131	130
Customer Relationships, Net	203	229
Equity and Other Investments	86	140
Other Assets	522	403
Total Assets	$ 16,787	$ 16,005
Liabilities and Equity		
Current Liabilities		
Accounts payable	$ 6,951	$ 5,364
Unredeemed gift card liabilities	428	456
Accrued compensation and related expenses	520	539
Accrued liabilities	1,639	1,685
Accrued income taxes	129	288
Short-term debt	596	480
Current portion of long-term debt	547	43
Total current liabilities	10,810	8,855
Long-Term Liabilities	1,109	1,099
Long-Term Debt	1,153	1,685
Contingencies and Commitments		
Equity		
Best Buy Co., Inc. Shareholders' Equity		
Preferred stock, $1.00 par value: Authorized—400,000 shares; Issued and outstanding—none	—	—
Common stock, $0.10 par value: Authorized—1.0 billion shares; Issued and outstanding—338,276,000 and 341,400,000 shares, respectively	34	34
Additional paid-in capital	54	—
Retained earnings	2,861	3,621
Accumulated other comprehensive income	112	90
Total Best Buy Co., Inc. shareholders' equity	3,061	3,745
Noncontrolling interests	654	621
Total equity	3,715	4,366
Total Liabilities and Equity	$ 16,787	$ 16,005

Source: 2013 *Form 10K*, p. 61.
All amounts in millions of U.S. dollars except per share amounts.

EXHIBIT 8 Best Buy Operating Statistics

	2013	2012	2011
Comparable stores sales gain (decline)	(2.9%)	(1.7%)	(1.8%)
Operating income (loss) rate	(0.3%)	2.1%	4.8%

Source: Company documents.

Current Performance

Exhibit 8 reveals recent operating statistics for Best Buy. Note the fiscal 2013 comparable store sales decline of 2.9 percent.

Competition

Stores such as Walmart, the world's largest retailer, and Costco are expanding their selection of TVs, notebook computers, cameras, mp3 players, and other electronic devices at prices typically lower than traditional merchants in the industry such as Best Buy. Online shopping at Amazon. com, overstock.com, eBay, and other online merchants creates a rough ocean for firms such as Best Buy to navigate.

Many retailers are entering overseas markets especially in Asia. For example, Office Depot generates close to 30 percent of their sales overseas, whereas Best Buy generates 27 percent and Staples generates 22 percent of sales. Amazon.com generated 44 percent of 2012 sales from outside the USA. Many brick-and-mortar retailers are adding services such as in-home installation as a way to differentiate themselves from online merchants and Walmart. Also, many retailers are focusing on sustainability as a means of differentiating their business as many of the products and services are the same. Best Buy was recently named one of the greenest companies in the USA. Many retailers are expanding their marketing of gift cards. Research reveals that many customers who enter the store with a gift card often spend more than the card amount. In addition, after several years of a gift card full amount not being used, companies are allowed to assume the card's unused credit as assets on their financial statements.

Exhibit 9 gives a quick synopsis of Best Buy and two of its many rival companies. Note that Amazon has one-third the number of Best Buy employees yet generates roughly the same revenue. Amazon's revenue-to-employee ratio reveals how they dominate in terms of cost efficiencies, price, and convenience. Best Buy's market capitalization is a fraction of both Walmart and Amazon's. RadioShack is a huge competitor to Best Buy and both companies are arguably on the brink of financial disaster.

Amazon

Amazon.com, an online retailer, operates worldwide focusing on price, convenience, selection, and timely delivery. Founded in 1994 as an online bookseller, Amazon has expanded its product line over the last decade and formed agreements with other retailers to sell their products under the Amazon.com name. Amazon is also the manufacturer and seller of the Kindle e-reader that allows customers to instantly order many books for $9.99. In 2011, Amazon experienced a 56-percent increase in electronic sales following an electronic merchandise growth rate of 66 percent in 2010.

EXHIBIT 9 A Synopsis of Best Buy and Two Rival Firms

	Best Buy	Walmart	Amazon
Number of Employees	165,000	2.2M	56,200
Net Income ($)	(441M)	16.08B	560M
Revenue ($)	45.1B	455.7B	51.4B
Revenue/Employee ($)	273K	207K	914K
EPS Ratio ($)	−1.31	4.64	1.21
Market Capitalization	9.29B	244.7B	97.0B

Historically, Amazon reinvested most of profits, and even took on extra debt, to further expand the Amazon footprint. In recent years Amazon has begun to pay down debt and even hoard cash. For example, at year-end 2009, Amazon had $3.2 billion in cash on their balance sheet, and by year-end 2011, the company had $5.3 billion. Amazon reports $0 long-term debt over the three-year period of 2009 to 2011. Retained earnings have increased from $172 million in 2009 to a staggering $1.9 billion by year-end 2011.

One potential area of concern for Amazon is the large amount of goodwill on their balance sheet. As of 2011, Amazon had $1.9 billion in goodwill up from $1.2 billion in 2009. Some of Amazon's recent purchases include Zappos.com, an online shoe store, and Quidsi, the parent company of diapers.com and soap.com. Amazon also acquired LoveFilm a European-based company similar to Netflix. As Amazon continues to purchase firms to further diversify its business, it needs to be mindful of potentially paying too much as indicated by the nearly $2 billion in goodwill on its balance sheet.

Amazon is pursuing forward integration by quietly installing large metal cabinets, called Amazon Lockers, in hundreds of grocery, 7-Eleven, and drugstores that accept the packages for customers for later pickup. This strategy especially dispels the concern of urban apartment dwellers, who fear they will miss an Amazon delivery or have their item stolen. This strategy also combats a growing problem of thieves following UPS and FedEx trucks and stealing packages at doorsteps. Amazon has lockers in the USA and United Kingdom. This strategy entails Amazon emailing customers a code to open the locker holding their merchandise. Curtailing failed deliveries is essential for Amazon because otherwise consumers might actually make their purchase in a Best Buy brick-and-mortar store. Amazon pays a small fee each month to store owners where it has lockers.

RadioShack Corp.

Although struggling to survive, RadioShack, like Best Buy, is a huge consumer electronics goods and services retailer with about 4,475 stores in the USA, Mexico, Puerto Rico, and the U.S. Virgin Islands. RadioShack's operations include Target Mobile, dealer outlets, RadioShack de Mexico, and RadioShack.com. RadioShack operates 1,496 Target Mobile centers and has a network of 1,091 RadioShack dealer outlets, including 33 located outside of North America. The company recently discontinued its kiosks segment.

RadioShack's stock price has continuously dropped of late to about $3.00 per share in October 2013 as company revenues and profits have plummeted. The company suspended its dividend payment in 2012. People want RadioShack (and Best Buy's) products, but they simply make their purchase at Amazon, eBay, Target, Costco Wholesale, or Walmart.

RadioShack is another electronics brick-and-mortar retailer on a fast decline in the face of online shopping. The company has more than $500 million in cash and equivalents, and its next debt repayment of $375 million is due in August 2013. By suspending its dividend, the company will save $50 million per year to help cover its interest expenses, which only totals $31 million within the next year. Beyond interest and debt, and like Best Buy, RadioShack is contractually obligated to pay its leases and product and marketing agreements, which within the next year total $195 million and $316 million, respectively. Also like Best Buy, RadioShack's credit has recently been downgraded to junk status. It still has $390 million available of a $450 million revolving credit facility through early 2016 to help it survive. The company's CEO, Jim Gooch, says RadioShack "will focus on cellphones and tying together its brick-and-mortar stores with its website." Analysts say that is way too vague of a strategic plan and is way too little too late for the company to survive.

Walmart

Walmart, founded in 1945 in Bentonville, Arkansas, has more than 2.2 million full-time employees and operates retail stores, restaurants, supermarkets, supercenters, warehouse clubs, apparel stores, and much more. If there is any product someone wants, Walmart likely offers the product at an attractive price point. The company emphasizes low prices and provides flat screen TVs, phones, mp3 players, cameras, notebook computers, and many other electronics at prices typically lower than Best Buy. In addition to electronics, Walmart is so diversified, especially with its grocery business, that it is able to withstand downturns in the economy better than most retailers. Currently, Walmart operates more than 10,000 retail stores under 69 different brand names in 27 different countries.

External Issues

Internet Shopping

With tax-free benefits still present for online sales, coupled with convenience, lower prices, and more variety, online sales are increasing at a much rate faster than traditional retail sales. Online sales could reach 15 percent of total retail sales by 2015. These numbers still leave the majority of retail sales to brick-and-mortar establishments.

Currently there is no state sales tax on many Internet purchases in the USA. This savings can provide consumers who buy and sell products online from a central location up to a 10-percent price advantage over rival firms who have brick-and-mortar locations in the respective state of the transaction. However, there is growing sentiment among U.S. politicians to even this playing field, and it is expected that states could receive a $23 billion windfall from taxed sales on the Internet. Many states financially need the money badly. Taxing Internet sales would make it more likely consumers would patronize local stores rather than buying off the Internet. This would be especially true for firms such as Best Buy who sell many higher ticket priced items. For example, a $500 notebook computer purchased in state and local township with 8 percent combined sales taxes would cost a consumer an extra $40 in tax, so removing this potential $40 savings from online sales should benefit stores such as Best Buy.

Even if the tax-free environment on most Internet transactions is removed, firms such Best Buy still face an uphill battle with online merchants. Amazon.com for example offers free shipping on many orders more than $25 and in addition offers the same product from many different merchants allowing customers to price check easily and conveniently. In addition, customers can view product reviews and comments from users of the products as part of their research. Furthering the online threat for brick-and-mortar establishments such as Best Buy is the increased use of smartphones for price checking while shopping in brick-and-mortar stores. Forrester Research reports there were 82 million smartphones in the USA in 2010 and this number is expected to increase to 159 million by 2015. Ironically, the mobile phone that Best Buy is betting so heavily on in the future is also the device that allows customers to price shop competing firms for other products while shopping in Best Buy.

Customers often will visit a store such as Best Buy to talk to experienced sales people and to view the products before purchasing elsewhere. This was one of the contributing reasons why Best Buy did not work in China. Chinese customers simply used Best Buy as an information agent and purchased elsewhere.

Social Media

A 2011 *Social Media's Impact on Customer Engagement* report revealed that more than 70 percent of firms say they are no longer are able to avoid using social media in its marketing and communications with customers. Forrester Research reports that Best Buy and Amazon. com are two of the most proactive companies when using and implementing social media into their business operations. For example, Best Buy aids consumers through Twelpforece, where customers can send a tweet about consumer electronics problems to an account that is shared by 2,500 Best Buy employees. Amazon's success with social media is based largely on its ratings and reviews from customers, providing both Amazon and potential customers meaningful information in pricing, quality, and features of the products offered. Although social media may seem as burdensome to some corporations, failure to take full advantage of this technology will likely leave corporations at a distinct disadvantage with rival firms.

Future

Regardless if Schulze or someone else acquires Best Buy or the firm continues to operate on its own, a clear, detailed strategic plan will be essential for the firm to navigate such turbulent water ahead. Walmart and Amazon especially continue to take market share from Best Buy, and many other firms too are joining in the fray. If the company is not real careful, it will go the way of its former rival Circuit City and be forced to eventually liquidate. Some analysts ponder who will declare bankruptcy first, Best Buy or RadioShack, arguing that the writing is on the wall for both firms, unless an effective strategic plan can be formulated and implemented pronto.

Assist new CEO Hubert Joly in developing a strategic plan for Best Buy.

Publix Super Markets, Inc., 2013

www.publix.com

Headquartered in Lakeland, Florida, Publix operates grocery stores in Florida, Tennessee, Georgia, and South Carolina. More than two-thirds of Publix's 1,069 stores are in Florida. With 158,000 employees, Publix is the largest employee owned supermarket in the USA. Publix's employees today own about 31 percent of the company, which is still run by the George Jenkins family as an employee stock ownership plan (ESOP) company. Free Wi-Fi is available in all Publix grocery stores, both for customers and employees. Publix emphasizes service and a family-friendly image rather than low price. Publix's slogan is "Where Shopping Is a Pleasure."

Publix's sales for the second quarter of 2013 were $7 billion, a 3.8 percent increase from last year's $6.8 billion. Comparable-store sales for Q2 of 2013 increased 2.1 percent, while net earnings were $400.9 million, compared to $381.6 million in 2012, an increase of 5 percent. On August 1, 2013, Publix's board of directors increased the company's stock price from $26.90 per share to $27.55 per share. Publix stock is not publicly traded and is made available for sale only to current Publix associates (employees), members of its board of directors, and founders of the company.

Like its rivals, Publix stores sell dairy, produce, deli, bakery, traditional food items, meats as well as typical health, beauty products that can be found in a grocery store. Many Publix stores also have pharmacy, sushi bars, cafes, a bank, and floral segments. Currently ranked number 67 on *Fortune* magazine's list of 100 Best Companies to Work For and is ranked number 6 on *Forbes'* list of America's Largest Private Companies, Publix is the largest private company in Florida ranks number 106 among all *Fortune* 500 companies. Publix is the fourteenth-largest U.S. retailer.

Publix rival Supervalu reported sales down 4.3 percent in the third quarter of 2012, and rival Safeway also reported falling sales, as those companies (and Publix) struggle to compete with dollar stores, drugstores, and mass-market retailers, such as Walmart, all of whom are expanding their grocery departments and offering lower prices than conventional supermarkets. Supervalu, with its network of 4,400 supermarkets, reported a third-quarter 2012 loss of $111 million compared to a year-earlier profit of $60 million.

Copyright by Fred David Books LLC. (Written by Forest R. David)

History

In 1930, George Jenkins left a secure job in the middle of the Great Depression to open the first Publix Foods grocery store in Winter Haven, Florida. Mr. George, as everyone called him, understood the need for high morale in the workplace and initiated a profit-sharing plan and ESOP that is still present in Publix today. Chairman and founder, Mr. George began offering stock to Publix employees the same year he opened the first store.

By 1940, Publix stores were revolutionary in the sense they had air-conditioning, florescent lights, eight-foot wide isles, pumped in music, cold cases for frozen foods, donut and flower shops, and even electric doors. Other décor included glass, marble, and stucco. People would travel for many miles to shop at the Publix "food palace." In 1945, Publix purchased 19 All American food stores and subsequently converted them into Publix stores to meet rising demand. In the 1950s, Publix moved their headquarters to Lakeland, Florida, and built a large distribution warehouse there as well.

Throughout the 1960s, Publix expanded over the entire state of Florida and by 1974 had reached $1 billion in sales and then $5 billion by 1989. In 1991, Publix opened a supermarket in Savannah, Georgia, and a distribution center in Lawrenceville, Georgia. Publix soon expanded into South Carolina and Alabama, and in 2002 opened the first Publix grocery store in Tennessee. In 2009, Publix opened its 1,000th store becoming only one of five U.S. grocery retailers to operate more than 1,000 stores.

In its history, Publix has never had a layoff of employees. The company has a tuition employee reimbursement program originally designed for degree-seeking students. This benefit has recently become available to Publix employees taking individual courses or technical training, including online courses. The program is available to all Publix employees who work an average of 10 hours per week for six months.

Internal Issues

Vision and Mission

Publix's vision is "to become the premier provider of quality grocery items for American families." The company's mission statement is:

> Our Mission at Publix is to be the premier quality food retailer in the world. To that end we commit to be:
>
> - Passionately focused on Customer Value,
> - Intolerant of Waste,
> - Dedicated to the Dignity, Value and Employment Security of our Associates,
> - Devoted to the highest standards of stewardship for our Stockholders, and
> - Involved as Responsible Citizens in our Communities.

In contrast, Kroger's mission is as follows:

> Our mission is to be a leader in the distribution and merchandising of food, pharmacy, health and personal care items, seasonal merchandise, and related products and services.

Supervalu is a major competitor to Publix. Supervalu's mission is:

> We will provide America's Neighborhoods with a superior grocery shopping experience enhanced by local expertise, national strength and a passion for our customers.

Organizational Structure

As illustrated in Exhibit 1, it appears that Publix operates from a functional organizational structure. Note there are no regional presidents by state or region or type of store. Some analysts contend that Publix is too large an organization to still be operating from a centralized, functional design. Although executive titles in Exhibit 1 do not reflect a divisional structure, some researchers say Publix is organized into four divisions: Miami, Atlanta, Lakeland, and Jacksonville.

EXHIBIT 1 Publix's Organizational Chart

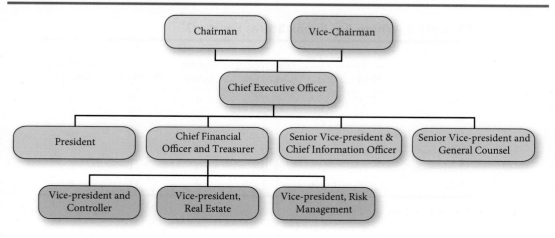

Facilities Location

Publix has leases to open new supermarkets in North Carolina in 2014. Exhibit 2 reveals where Publix's facilities and stores are located. In total, Publix operates more than 48-million square feet of supermarket space with supermarkets varying in size from 28,000 to 61,000 square feet. Typically Publix supermarkets are located in strip shopping areas, and most of these stores are leased but the company has some standalone stores. Publix operates 1,069 supermarkets, eight distribution centers, and six manufacturing facilities. Almost all their distribution and manufacturing facilities are located in Florida and a few in Georgia. Among the six manufacturing plants are three dairy plants, two bakeries, and one deli plant. To aid in control and cost reduction, Publix is backward integrated with more than 72 percent of all products (based on cost) being delivered through Publix distribution centers. Publix is not dependent on any one or few suppliers for any meaningful amount of total sales. Publix is more backward integrated than most grocery chains with their private label items such as dairy and bakery being manufactured solely by and for Publix.

Sustainability

Publix is building more energy-efficient stores, minimizing water use, offering reusable shopping bags, and working with suppliers on more environmentally friendly packaging options. Publix emphasizes for employees to pack more items per bag and this program has helped reduce the total bags used per day by one million. Publix sold more than 21 million reusable bags priced at $0.99 each between 2007 and 2012. Publix offers customers options for bagging groceries: choosing paper, plastic, or reusable bags. Publix's annual total recycling rate is about 50 percent with 221,900 tons of cardboard, 8,800 tons of plastic, and 3,200 tons of mixed paper being recycled annually. Publix Pharmacy customers return more than 2.8 million vials for recycling annually.

Awards

Publix has won many local, regional, and national industry and philanthropic awards. Some recent awards are:

- One of the "100 Best Companies to Work For" (1998–2012), *Fortune*
- One of the "Best Places to Work in IT"(2005–2010), *Computerworld*
- One of the "Best Companies to Work for in Florida" (2009), *Florida Trend*
- Sustainability Excellence Award (2009), *Supermarket News*
- One of the "Most Admired Companies" (1994–2009), *Fortune*
- "Green Grocer" Award (2008), *Progressive Grocer* magazine

Advertising

In 2012, 2011, and 2010, Publix spent $208 million, $202 million, and $192 million respectively on advertising.

EXHIBIT 2 Where Are Publix Stores Located?

	Super Markets		GreenWise Markets	Publix Sabor	Publix Pix	Cooking Schools
	2011	2012				
Florida	751	757	3	4	8	8
Georgia	179	180	0	0	2	1
South Carolina	45	47	0	0	0	0
Alabama	51	52	0	0	0	0
Tennessee	32	33	0	0	1	0
Total	1,058	1,069	3	4	11	9

Source: Company documents.

Segments

Publix's *Form 10K* does not provide a by-segment breakdown of revenues or profits by any division or region, except to say that their (a) grocery segment contributes 85 percent of revenue and its (b) other segment provides 15 percent, and those percentages have not changed much in recent years. Although not disclosed in the *Form 10K*, Publix actually has segments and regions as described in this section.

Apron's Cooking School

Publix operates seven Apron's cooking schools, located in Boca Raton, Jacksonville, Plantation, Sarasota, Tampa, Tallahassee, Florida, and Alpharetta, Georgia. Classes are geared toward all cooks wanting to expand their repertoire and feature renowned chefs, authors, and cooking celebrities, as well as experienced cooking instructors. The classes are designed to teach skills including basic techniques and wine pairing. Publix also offers classes for children ages 8 to 12, with separate classes for 13- to 18-year olds and adults.

Publix GreenWise Markets

Publix GreenWise Markets is a concept the company introduced in response to the increase in the number and profitability of health food stores. GreenWise Markets were created to increase awareness of nutrition and focus on organic and natural items. These stores are similar to the Whole Food Market chain. Most regular Publix stores have a GreenWise section, but the first standalone GreenWise Market grocery store opened in 2007 in Palm Beach Gardens. These stores include salad and hot bars.

Publix Sabor

Publix operates six stores, branded "Publix Sabor" (*sabor* is Spanish for "flavor"), which cater to Hispanic Americans living in Florida and offer products for Hispanics. Four Publix Sabor locations are in the Miami area, one is in Orlando, and a sixth in Palm Beach opened in the summer of 2012. Publix Sabor locations have bilingual English-Spanish employees, open seating cafés, and a wide selection of hot foods. Publix offers cafés and hot foods because many Hispanic Americans grew up in foreign cities, which had open public squares where people socialize and eat.

Pharmacy

Publix's first in-store pharmacy was opened in 1986 in Altamonte Springs, Florida. By 1995, one-third of Publix stores had a pharmacy and today, approximately 81 percent of Publix stores include a pharmacy. Publix Pharmacies consistently ranked number one for customer satisfaction among supermarket pharmacies in several surveys conducted by independent research companies.

Publix offers several types of free antibiotics to its customers. Customers must have a prescription; they are given a maximum of a two-week supply. These medications include amoxicillin and ampicillin and even penicillin. Publix also offers another free prescription, metformin, for Type II Diabetes, the generic of Glucophage. In August 2011, Publix began offering Lisinopril, a angiotensin-converting enzyme inhibitor that is used to prevent, treat, or improve symptoms of high blood pressure, certain heart conditions, diabetes, and certain chronic kidney conditions, as another free prescription. Customers can get a 30-day supply of this vital prescription for free at any Publix Pharmacy. Publix also offers free flu shots to associates (employees) and shots for $20 for their family member(s).

DVD Kiosks

In September 2009, Publix reported it started adding Blockbuster DVD rental kiosks to its stores, with the movie rentals starting at $1 per day. In 2010, Publix completed its rollout of Blockbuster Express kiosks to its stores.

Publix Pix and Publix Liquors

Publix operates 11 Publix Pix gasoline-convenience stores. Locations are limited during the trial basis of the concept. In addition is Publix Liquors, a stand-alone liquor store. The liquor sales will be in an area accessed via an entrance separated from the supermarket, as required by local laws. The company is modeling this after many other grocery chains. Currently, all Publix Pix locations are adjacent to a Publix Super Market. Publix opened its first stand-alone liquor store in 2009 in Orlando.

Finance

Publix's Stock

As an ESOP, Publix's common stock is not traded on any of the established securities exchange markets. As of February 5, 2013, there were 7.7 million shares of Publix stock outstanding. With no open market providing daily stock transactions there is no clear market value for the stock so the board sets the stock price based on several factors including (a) state of the economy, (b) comparisons of similarly publically traded companies, and (c) after an analysis of Publix's own financial statements. Publix paid a cash dividend on common stock of $0.89 in 2012, $0.53 in 2011, and $0.46 in 2010. Although not obligated to pay dividends, the board foresees paying comparable cash dividends in the future, on June 1 of each year.

Publix offers stock to its associates through three programs: Profit plan (ESOP), purchase plan, and 401(k) plan. The profit plan generally gives an associate who has worked 1,000 hours in an anniversary 7 to 10 percent of the regularly pay earned in the form of free stock the following March 1. An associate must work three years to be vested in the plan. The plan is at no cost to the associate. Publix associates may buy the stock outright in the purchase plan, however there is a six-month restriction on buying stock once it is sold. Publix matches 50 percent of 3 percent of eligible wages through the 401(k) plan, up to $750 per year in matched contributions. Publix offers stock to its board of directors through a separate plan.

Income Statements

Publix's recent income statements are provided in Exhibit 3. Note that the company's revenues increased 1.9 percent in 2012 to $27.5 billion whereas net income increased 4.0 percent to $1.55 billion.

Balance Sheets

Publix's recent balance sheets are provided in Exhibit 4. Note that the company has zero goodwill, which is good, and overall is in excellent financial condition.

EXHIBIT 3

PUBLIX SUPER MARKETS, INC.
Consolidated Statements of Earnings Years ended December 29, 2012,
December 31, 2011 and December 25, 2010

	2012	2011	2010
	(Amounts are in thousands, except per share amounts)		
Revenues:			
Sales	$27,484,766	$26,967,389	$25,134,054
Other operating income	222,006	211,375	194,000
Total revenues	**27,706,772**	**27,178,764**	**25,328,054**
Costs and expenses:			
Cost of merchandise sold	19,910,984	19,520,370	18,111,443
Operating and administrative expenses	5,630,537	5,523,469	5,295,287
Total costs and expenses	25,541,521	25,043,839	23,406,730
Operating profit	2,165,251	2,134,925	1,921,324
Investment income	88,449	99,039	91,835
Other-than-temporary impairment losses	—	(6,082)	—
Investment income, net	88,449	92,957	91,835
Other income, net	48,894	33,891	26,259
Earnings before income tax expense	2,302,594	2,261,773	2,039,418
Income tax expense	750,339	769,807	701,271
Net earnings	**$1,552,255**	**1,491,966**	**1,338,147**
Weighted average shares outstanding	782,553	784,815	786,378
Basic and diluted earnings per share	$1.98	$1.90	$1.70

Source: 2012 *Form 10K*, p. 24.

EXHIBIT 4 Publix's Balance Sheets (000 Omitted)

PUBLIX SUPER MARKETS, INC.
Consolidated Balance Sheets

	2012	2011
	(Amounts are in thousands)	
Assets		
Current assets:		
Cash and cash equivalents	$ 337,400	366,853
Short-term investments	797,260	447,972
Trade receivables	519,137	542,990
Merchandise inventories	1,409,367	1,361,709
Deferred tax assets	57,834	59,400
Prepaid expenses	28,124	24,316
Total current assets	3,149,122	2,803,240
Long-term investments	4,235,846	3,805,283
Other noncurrent assets	202,636	171,179
Property, plant and equipment:		
Land	688,812	592,843
Buildings and improvements	2,249,176	2,062,833
Furniture, fixtures and equipment	4,587,883	4,540,988
Leasehold improvements	1,385,823	1,321,646
Construction in progress	67,775	103,006
	8,979,469	8,621,316
Accumulated depreciation	(4,288,753)	(4,132,786)
Net property, plant and equipment	4,690,716	4,488,530
Total Assets	$ 12,278,320	11,268,232
Liabilities and Equity		
Current liabilities:		
Accounts payable	$ 1,306,996	$ 1,133,120
Accrued expenses:		
Contribution to retirement plans	430,395	405,818
Self-insurance reserves	138,998	125,569
Salaries and wages	109,091	110,207
Other	230,486	221,713
Current portion of long-term debt	5,018	15,124
Federal and state income taxes	—	39,225
Total current liabilities	2,220,984	2,050,776
Deferred tax liabilities	327,294	316,802
Self-insurance reserves	212,728	219,660
Accrued postretirement benefit cost	116,721	103,595
Long-term debt	153,454	119,460
Other noncurrent liabilities	118,321	116,482
Total liabilities	3,149,502	2,926,775
Stockholders' Equity:		
Common stock of $1 par value. Authorized 1,000,000 shares; issued and outstanding 776,094 shares in 2012 and 779,675 shares in 2011	776,094	779,675
Additional paid-in capital	1,627,258	1,354,881
Retained earnings	6,640,538	6,131,193
Accumulated other comprehensive earnings	38,289	30,261
Common stock related to ESOP	(2,272,963)	(2,137,217)
Total stockholders' equity	6,809,216	6,158,793
Noncontrolling interests	46,639	45,447
Total equity	9,128,818	8,341,457
Commitments and contingencies	—	—
Total Liabilities and SE equity	$12,278,320	11,268,232

Source: 2012 *Form 10K*, p. 23.

Competition

Amazon is getting more and more into the online grocery business, initially in California but now moving east rapidly towards Publix's territory. The grocery store business has low margins given the intense price competition, high food inflation, and high spoilage of inventory. Competitors include national and regional grocery stores, super centers, drugstores, specialty stores, convenience stores, and even restaurants. Most firms attempt to compete on either price, or selection of high-end goods. Location also is a driving factor in competition but usually after price for most customers. Publix competes with national chains Kroger, Supervalu, Safeway, Costco, and Walmart. In addition, regional competitors include BI-LO, Winn-Dixie, Ingles, Piggy Wiggly, and Fresh Market. Food Lion recently closed 113 underperforming stores, including all its Florida and Kentucky stores, and rebranding some others as part of their new market strategy.

Publix has grown faster and been more profitable than Winn-Dixie Stores and BI-LO, two major rival grocery store chains that are also headquartered in Florida. In March 2012, Winn-Dixie became a wholly owned subsidiary of BI-LO Holdings. At that time, BI-LO moved its headquarters from Greenville, South Carolina, to Winn-Dixie's headquarters site in Jacksonville, Florida. Together, Winn-Dixie and BI-LO operate 690 grocery stores in eight southeastern states, with heavy emphasis in Florida.

Exhibit 5 reveals comparative competitive information for Publix versus several rival grocery chains. Note that Publix trails the three rivals in revenue per employee, which is not good, but Publix's earnings per share leads all rivals, which is good.

Kroger

Kroger is a major competitor to Publix and is doing great. The company increased its dividend payout by 30 percent in late 2012. Kroger operates 2,435 grocery stores in 31 states, with half of these having fuel centers. Founded in 1883 and headquartered in Cincinnati, Ohio, Kroger has more than 330,000 employees. Kroger also operates department stores, drugstores, jewelry stores, convenience stores, and service stores. Kroger manufactures certain food items for their grocery store business. Kroger is a well-diversified company, offering 15 different branded grocery stores, two "price-impact warehouse" food stores, Fred Meyer department stores, four market place stores, six convenience stores, four jewelry stores, and three service stores that include Kroger finance, and The Little Clinic.

One of the world's largest retailers, Kroger's banner name businesses include City Market, Dillons, Jay C, Food 4 Less, Fry's, King Soopers, QFC, Ralphs, and Smith's. Kroger owns and operates 789 convenience stores, 337 fine jewelry stores, 1,109 supermarket fuel centers, and 38 food-processing plants in the USA. Recognized by *Forbes* as the most generous company in the USA, Kroger supports hunger relief, breast cancer awareness, the military and their families, and more than 30,000 schools and grassroots organizations in the communities it serves. Kroger contributes food and funds equal to 160 million meals a year through more than 80 Feeding America food bank partners.

EXHIBIT 5 Comparative Information Among Grocery Chain Firms

	Publix	Kroger	Supervalu	Safeway
Number of Employees	158K	339K	130K	178K
Net Income ($)	1.55B	605M	−1.04B	568M
Revenue ($)	27.53B	91.9B	36.1B	43.8B
Revenue ($)/Employee	174K	271K	277K	246K
EPS Ratio ($)	1.90	1.05	−4.91	1.75
Market Capitalization	19.3B	11.96B	570M	3.78B

EPS, earnings per share.
Source: Company documents.

Kroger has self-use health screening kiosks in almost all locations nationwide. Assessments include blood pressure, weight, body composition, BMI, color vision, and the ability to upload blood glucose numbers and other biometric results. "Our customers tell us they want to make healthy choices but don't always know where to start," said Matthew Feltman, Kroger's health strategy coordinator. "We're pleased to expand the availability of Kroger HealthCENTERs to help customers take their first steps toward overall health and wellness." Kroger customers will be able to create personal health record accounts, which they can access at any time at Kroger. com, to chart their progress. They will also have access to health information and solutions designed to help them in their personal health and fitness goals.

Supervalu

Supervalu is a major rival to Publix, but it is not doing so well. In late 2012, Supervalu initiated a cost-reduction program, reduction of capital expenditures, and also suspended its quarterly dividend. In addition, Supervalu closed 60 underperforming stores, including 38 in its retail food reporting segment and 22 Save-A-Lot locations. The largest cuts will come from the Albertsons chain, which will shut 27 locations. Supervalu had revenue of $36.1 billion in its fiscal 2012, but it has endured three consecutive years of declining revenues.

Supervalu operates under the brand names Acme, Albertsons, Farm Fresh, Save-A-Lot, and several others. Supervalu has more than 4,000 stores with more than 1,300 being hard discount stores. Approximately 1,900 stores were independently owned and 798 had an in-store pharmacy. Supervalu's footprint stretches across the USA including Alaska, but the bulk of all stores are in the Eastern USA. Founded in 1871 and headquartered in Eden Prairie, Minnesota, Supervalu has 130,000 employees.

Supervalu has been struggling since 2007 when their stock price was an all-time high of just under $50. In the fall 2012, the stock price was near $2. Much of the decline can be attributed to a failed acquisition strategy when the firm acquired Albertsons grocery store and a logistics company during the height of the stock market run-up in 2005 and 2007. Goodwill for Supervalu totaled $6.9 billion in 2008 and $3.7 billion in 2010 but dropped to $800M in 2012. However, Supervalu paid way over fair value for their acquisitions and today is a highly leveraged company with debt to equity ratio of 98 compared to 1 for the industry average. Also, inventory turnover, an extremely important ratio when dealing with perishable goods, is 12 for Supervalu compared to 18 for the industry and 19.8 for Publix.

Safeway

Safeway is a major rival to Publix. Safeway operates more than 2,000 food and drugstores across North America under the brand names Safeway, Vons, Randalls, Tom Thumb, Genuardi's, and Carrs. Safeway also operates floral, pharmacy, coffee shops, and fuel centers within their grocery and drugstores. The company also operates 156 food stores in Mexico with a 49-percent interest in Casa Ley, S.A. de C.V. Headquartered in Pleasanton, California, Safeway was founded in 1915 and has 178,000 employees.

Safeway recently divested its gift card business, Blackhawk Network Holdings, in a planned initial public offering (IPO). Spin-offs generally benefit a firm's stock price because the parts of the original firm are usually valued more than the whole. Safeway's stock price to earnings ratio of 8.6 in September 2012 is below Kroger's 21.5, Whole Foods Market's 41.3, Harris Teeter Supermarkets' 19.4, and The Fresh Market's 47.7.

External Issues

Food Inflation

Unlike most retailers, food retailers measure financial performance based on gross profit margin as opposed to gross profit dollars. The difference can be attributed to the volatile price of foods, which are subject to droughts, insect plagues, and high or low inflation. For example, food inflation only rose 0.3 and 0.5 percent in 2010 and 2009, respectively, but rose 6.4 and 4.2 percent in 2008 and 2007, respectively. However, in 2011, food prices rose 6.2 percent with partly the result of an 11-percent rise in fats and oils, 9 percent in dairy, and 7.4 percent in meats and eggs. Inflation or even deflationary constraints are a common battle among food retailers. Excessive heat or cold or severe droughts can lead to rapid rise in food prices.

Consumers are cutting back on discretionary purchases even among grocery items. Customers are visiting grocery stores more often but are buying less at each visit because their visits are targeted at finding items on sale or promotions. A related trend that may benefit Publix is that customers are increasingly buying store-branded products instead of the more expensive brand names. However, customers are also increasingly trading down to lower-priced dollar stores for food items. Well-off customers still have money, however, and have not altered their shopping habits as much as the average customer.

Natural and Organic Foods

Focusing more on natural and organic food is one viable strategy to counter higher food inflation and less disposable income among customers. Typically, customers who purchase natural and organic foods are loyal customers who believe in the perceived benefits of such a diet and are less willing to accept adequate substitute products. Most customers of natural and organic foods belong to a higher income bracket, and in 2010, foods in this category rose 7.7 percent whereas overall grocery items only rose 1.0 percent. Currently, however, organic foods only account for around 2 percent of total food sales worldwide, but the market is growing at a much faster rate than the overall grocery market both in both developed and undeveloped nations. This is somewhat surprising considering organic foods typically range between 10 to 40 percent more than their respective nonorganic products.

Interestingly, the United Kingdom's Food Standards Agency recently stated that although consumers may elect to purchase organic fruits, vegetables, and meats for their perceived health benefits, research so far does not support in any way that these foods are more nutritious than nonorganic counterparts. Nevertheless, with the growing health-minded public, increasing offerings of organic and natural foods should remain a viable strategy and component to any food-related business.

Labor Costs

Labor costs are one of the greatest operating costs for supermarkets, accounting for more than 50 percent of total operating expenses. Part of the expense can be attributed to the unionization of many supermarket chains but even without a union, supermarkets must strive to keep labor costs low just to breakeven.

In-Store Dietitian

Hy-Vee is the only grocery chain in the country that posts a registered dietitian in almost every one of its 235 stores. In rural areas, some of its more than 190 dietitians serve a cluster of stores. A phenomenon sweeping the grocery business is to capitalize on growing consumer awareness of the role food plays in health and wellness and to find new ways to fend off competition from specialty markets like Whole Foods, and even big-box stores such as Walmart. "There's been an explosion of interest in having a dietitian among grocery store retailers in the last three or four years," said Annette Maggi, chairwoman of the supermarket subgroup of the food and culinary professionals practice group at the Academy of Nutrition and Dietetics and a consultant to the retail and food manufacturing industries. Jane Andrews at the grocery chain Wegmans is the most renown of supermarket dietitians, becoming the first dietitian on its staff in 1988 and now supervising a team of six. Other regional chains like Meijer, Giant Eagle, Bashas', and H-E-B also have dieticians. Kroger, which already has dietitians on staff, is adding more of them to its King Soopers chain in the west. Publix might should consider this new feature.

A reasonable question is how can a grocery store calculate the financial return on its investment in dietitians. Grocers increasingly find that dietitians bring customers into stores, offering in-store consultations and store tours with customers, holding cooking classes, assembling take-home meals, taking biometric screenings, doing presentations in schools, businesses, and civic events, working with merchandisers, helping set up community gardens, assessing products for nutritional value, and a variety of other things. The dietitian's role is expanding, said Phil Lempert, a grocery industry expert and author of the blog Supermarket Guru. "The field of nutrition is getting more and more complicated," Mr. Lempert said. "Merchants used to buy on price and promotion, but you can't buy that way any more with all the product claims. You need someone around who understands whether products can really deliver, whether they're safe."

The Future

Publix plans to open 24 new supermarkets in 2013. Many analysts contend that traditional grocery retailers such as Publix may not survive long term because big-box grocery stores such as Walmart are offering groceries at significantly lower prices, largely to drive traditional grocery chains out of business. Also, pharmacies such as Walgreens, CVS, and Rite Aid are increasingly selling groceries at cost to drive traffic into the stores. Furthermore, discount chains such as Family Dollar, Dollar General, and Dollar Tree are taking more and more business from traditional grocery store chains. For these and other reasons, the grocery chains that are most diversified, such as Kroger, are doing best.

Publix is trying to diversify further, conducting trials of various boutiques, including a cologne and perfume fragrance department, in conjunction with Camrose Trading. Publix is experimenting with a gourmet deli at its Lake Mary Collection store in Lake Mary, Florida. Publix has grown rapidly for much of their existence but the world is changing more rapidly now. Should Publix continue to expand across the Southeast, entering new markets where customers may have never heard of Publix and have no brand association with the company? Or would it be better for Publix to focus on increasing store locations and attracting customers in their current markets? Which of Publix's segment businesses, if any, should the firm add more of in the future, and why?

Publix is a well-known ESOP company with only employees having the opportunity to purchase stock. Is it time for Publix to list their stock for public sale on an exchange? With the low margins in the industry, would this enable Publix to more effectively finance operations? With the growing trend in heath conscious customers, should Publix increase their organic and natural food offerings and attempt to attract this style of customer and build more GreenWise Market stores? How rapidly and where (if anywhere) should Publix add new stores?

JPMorgan Chase & Co., 2013

www.jpmorganchase.com, JPM

Headquartered in New York City, JPMorgan & Chase (JPM) is a financial holding company that competes worldwide, serving customers for more than 200 years, making it one of the oldest financial intuitions in the USA. Considered to be the largest bank in the USA, JPM has total assets of more than $2.3 trillion and employs more than 240,000 people in more than 60 countries around the globe. JPM's stock is one of the 30 components of the Dow Jones Industrial Average. The hedge fund unit of JPM is one of the largest in the USA.

JPM in mid-2013 announced plans to stop trading in physical commodities, but in August 2013, JPM purchased the over-the-counter business in commodity derivatives of Switzerland's UBS AG. The deal excluded precious metals and index-based trades, but included hedge positions on financial exchanges. Zurich-based UBS is closing the majority of its commodities "flow" trading business involving raw materials and financial derivatives as part of its slimming down and laying off 10,000 employees.

JPM operates under two principle brands, (1) JPMorgan and (2) Chase. The JPMorgan brand focuses on large multinational corporations, governments, wealthy individuals, and institutional investors. The Chase brand is further divided into two distinct segments: (1) consumer business and (2) commercial banking business. The Chase consumer business includes such businesses as traditional bank branches, ATMs, credit cards, home finance, retirement and investing, and merchant services among others. The Chase commercial banking business includes such areas as business credit, corporate client banking, commercial term lending, and community development. The two JPM brands overlap so much in terms of regions and products that the company does not report revenues or income by the two brands.

Copyright by Fred David Books LLC. (Written by Forest R. David)

History

Dating back to 1799, JPM is one of the oldest financial institutions in the world. The heritage of the House of Morgan traces its roots to the partnership of Drexel, Morgan & Co., which in 1895 was renamed J.P. Morgan & Co. Arguably the most influential financial institution of its era, J.P. Morgan & Co. financed the formation of the United States Steel Corporation, which took over the business of Andrew Carnegie and others and was the world's first billion-dollar corporation. In 1895, J.P. Morgan & Co. supplied the United States government with $62 million in gold to float a bond issue and restore the treasury surplus of $100 million. In 1892, the company began to finance the New York, New Haven, and Hartford Railroad and led it through a series of acquisitions that made it the dominant railroad transporter in New England. Although his name was big, Morgan owned only 19 percent of Morgan assets. The rest was owned by the Rothschild family following a series of bailouts and rescues attributed by some to Morgan's stubborn will and seemingly "nonexistent" investment savvy.

In 2004, JPM merged with Chicago-based Bank One Corp., bringing on board current chairman and Chief Executive Officer (CEO) Jamie Dimon as president and Chief Operating Officer and designating him as CEO William Harrison, Jr.'s successor. Dimon's pay was pegged at 90 percent of Harrison's. Dimon quickly made his influence felt by embarking on a cost-cutting strategy, and replaced former JPMorgan Chase executives in key positions with Bank One executives—many of whom were with Dimon at Citigroup. Dimon became CEO and chairman of JPM in 2006.

JPM has acquired more than 1,200 financial institutions over its life. Several key acquisitions during the last 20 years include in 1991 Chemical Banking Corp., the second largest bank in the USA and in 1995, First Chicago Corp., the largest bank in the Midwest. The acquisition responsible for the current name of the company was in 2000 when J.P. Morgan & Co. merged with The Chase Manhattan Corp. In 2010, JPM acquired Cazenove, an advisory and underwriting joint venture established in 2004 in the United Kingdom. Since 2010, JPM has refrained from making acquisitions that had historically been its trademark.

Internal Issues

Vision and Mission

JPM does not list a formal mission statement, but the company vision statement is:

> At JPMorgan Chase, we want to be the best financial services company in the world. Because of our great heritage and excellent platform, we believe this is within our reach.

Organizational Structure

Some analysts contend that JPM has organizational design problems because there are numerous CEOs, no presidents, dual-title individuals, lack of a clear JP Morgan-versus-Chase dichotomy, and overall, too many top-level executives. As best as can be determined, the existing organizational chart for JPM is given in Exhibit 1. Note that Jamie Dimon is both chairman of the board and CEO, a practice being shunned by more and more by corporations.

In 2013, the company replaced its Chief Financial Officer, Doug Braunstein, with Marianne Lake, who is now one of the most powerful women on Wall Street. Lake joins asset-management chief Mary Erdoes as the only two women on the bank's elite 14-member operating committee.

Ethics Issues

JPM has an extensive Code of Conduct and Code of Ethics posted on its website. Part of the company's code of conduct says in part: "The Code is based on our fundamental understanding that no one at JPMorgan Chase should ever sacrifice integrity—or give the impression that they have—even if they think it would help the firm's business." The company's code of ethics is more lengthy, and says in part: "The purpose of this Code of Ethics is to promote honest and ethical conduct and compliance with the law, particularly as related to the maintenance of the firm's financial books and records and the preparation of its financial statements."

Despite having extensive ethical-based statements, JPM has had its fair share of ethical issues over the years. In January 2011, JPM admitted that it wrongly overcharged several thousand military families for their mortgages, including active-duty personnel in Afghanistan. The bank also admitted it improperly foreclosed on more than a dozen military families; both actions were in clear violation of the Service Members Civil Relief Act, which automatically lowers mortgage rates to 6 percent and bars foreclosure proceedings of active-duty personnel. The overcharges may have never come to light were it not for legal action taken by Marine Capt. Jonathan Rowles, a fighter pilot. Both Captain Rowles and his spouse Julia accused Chase of violating the law and harassing the couple for nonpayment.

In April 2012, hedge fund insiders became aware that the market in credit default swaps was possibly being affected by the activities of Bruno Iksil, a trader for JPM, referred to as "the London whale" in reference to the huge positions he was taking. Heavy opposing bets to his positions are known to have been made by traders, including another branch of JPM that purchased the derivatives offered by JPM in such high volume. Early reports were denied and minimized by the firm in an attempt to minimize exposure. Major losses of $2 billion were reported by the firm in May 2012 in relationship to these trades and updated to $4.4 billion on July 13, 2012. The disclosure, which resulted in headlines in the media, did not disclose the exact nature of the trading involved, which remains in progress and as of June 28, 2012, was continuing to produce losses that could total as much as $9 billion under worst case scenarios. The item traded, possibly related to CDX IG 9, an index based on the default risk of major U.S. corporations, has been described as a "derivative of a derivative." On the company's emergency conference call, JPM CEO Jamie Dimon said the strategy was "flawed, complex, poorly reviewed, poorly executed, and poorly monitored." The episode is being investigated by the Federal Reserve, the Securities and Exchange Commission (SEC), and the FBI.

Strategy

JPM strategies revolve around the areas of (a) international expansion of its wholesale business and global corporate bank, (b) small business growth, (c) commodities, (d) growth in branch network, and (e) growth in private client business.

EXHIBIT 1 JPM's Organizational Chart

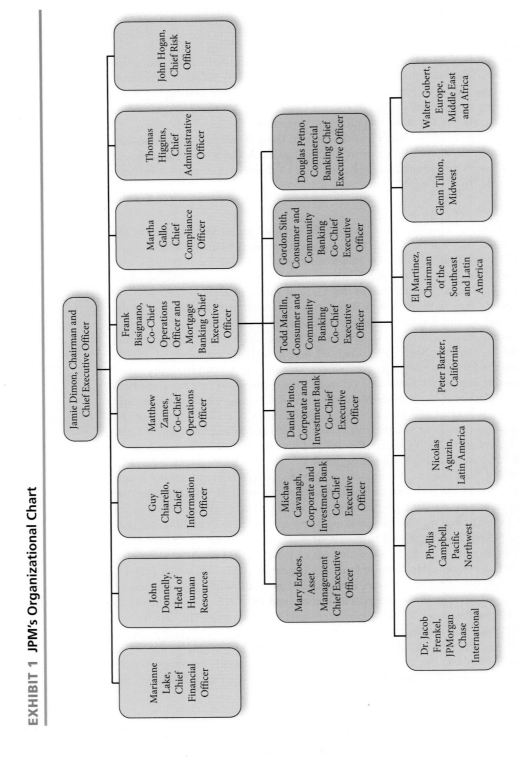

Source: Extrapolated based on executive titles given on the corporate website.

JPM's international expansion strategy aims to increase the firm's global presence through an aggressive international expansion plan. JPM is focused on expanding its asset management, investment bank, and treasury and securities services segments in Asia, Latin America, Africa, and the Middle East. Additionally, slowly expanding into newly emerging or even frontier markets, JPM's clients in this expansion plan include multinational corporations, sovereign wealth funds, and public entities. In 2008, JPM had approximately 200 clients in Brazil, China, and India combined, but by 2012, the number of clients in these nations had expanded to 800. By 2017, JPM is expected to have more than 2,000 clients in these nations.

U.S. small businesses remain a central focus of the Chase arm of JPM. In 2011 alone, Chase provided more than $17 billion of credit to domestic small businesses, up 52 percent from 2010, indicating Chase believes the economic recovery is robust enough to tolerate any short-term downward pressures. The $17 billion of credit in 2011 makes Chase the number-1 Small Business Administration (SBA) leader nationwide for the second straight year. In addition, JPM is also the number-1 SBA lender to women- and minority-owned businesses. To help facilitate growth in the small business arm, JPM has added more than 1,200 relationship managers and business bankers since 2009 and anticipates an aggressive hiring of bankers for the foreseeable future.

With the 2011 acquisition of Sempra, JPM is currently one of the top-three firms in the world in commodity dealings. Growth from 2011 to 2012 grew by 10 percent to bring total commodity clients to more than 2,200, as well as increased commodity packaging and selling to existing clients. JPM expects commodity demand to increase with the growth of emerging markets and anticipates increased business in the various commodity asset classes the firm currently offers.

Surprising to some, JPM is actively growing its physical branches despite many predictions from outside pundits who suggest that brick-and-mortar branches are a relic of the past. JPM's own research suggests however that although 17 million JPM customers do much of their banking business online, they still value a face-to-face conversation when it comes to taking out a mortgage, applying for a credit card, or seeking general financial advice in a physical branch location. Currently 45 percent of Chase credit cards and 50 percent of retail mortgages are sold on site at branch locations.

Segments

Within its two brands, JPM operates under seven major business segments as indicated in Exhibit 2, with respective revenues given. Note that JPM's revenues have been declining in three of the seven segments.

Exhibit 3 provides a breakdown of JPM revenues and net income over the geographic regions where the bank does business. Note that North America accounts for 81 percent of revenues and 86 percent of net income. Note also the dramatic drop in North American revenues in 2011 associated with a dramatic increase in associated net income.

Investment Bank

Within JPM's investment bank segment, $8,303 million of the $26,274 million was derived from noninterest sources, with the balance of $17,971 derived from interest sources. Clients of the investment bank division include corporations, financial institutions, and government and institutional investors. Investment bank activities include advising on business strategy and structure, raising capital though debt or equity, derivative instruments, prime brokerage, and research.

Exhibit 4 provides a geographic breakdown of JPM's investment bank segment. Note the decline in revenue from North America and Asia and Pacific, but the increase in revenue from other areas globally. Total 2011 net income from this division totaled $1,678 million.

Bonds trading is an important part of JPM's Investment Bank. A *Wall Street Journal* article (11-2-12, p. C3) reported that JPM's 12.3 percent market share in the USA in bonds trading was the largest among all banks, followed by Deutsche Bank (10.5 percent), Barclays (9.9 percent), Bank of America (9.6 percent), and Goldman Sachs (8.3 percent). A part of fixed-income operations, bond-trading is risky business. That is why UBS AG recently exited the bond-trading business to focus its investment bank on less-risky businesses such as advising on mergers and stock underwriting.

EXHIBIT 2 JPM's Financial Results by Segment (in millions $)

Revenue by Product	2012	%Change	2011	2010
Consumer & Community Banking	49,945	+9	45,687	48,927
Corporate & Investment Bank	34,326	+1	33,984	33,477
Commercial Banking	6,825	+6	6,418	6,040
Asset Management	9,946	+4	9,543	8,984
Corporate/Private Equity	(1,152)	−128	4,135	7,414
Total	99,890	0	99,767	104,842

Net Income by Product	2012		2011	2010
Consumer & Community Banking	10,611	+71	6,202	4,578
Corporate & Investment Bank	8,406	+05	7,993	7,718
Commercial Banking	2,646	+12	2,367	2,084
Asset Management	1,703	+07	1,592	1,710
Corporate/Private Equity	(2,082)	−353	822	1,280
Total	21,284	+12	18,976	17,370

Return on Equity (%) by Product	2012		2011	2010
Consumer & Community Banking	25		15	11
Corporate & Investment Bank	18		17	17
Commercial Banking	28		30	26
Asset Management	24		25	26
Corporate/Private Equity	NM		NM	NM
Total				

EXHIBIT 3 JPM's Revenues and Net Income by Region Globally (in millions)

	Revenue				Net Income			
	2012	2011	2010	2009	2012	2011	2010	2009
Europe, Middle East. and Africa	$10,522	$16,212	$14,135	$16,294	$1,508	$4,844	$3,635	$5,212
Asia and Pacific	5,605	5,992	6,073	5,429	$1,048	1,380	1,614	1,286
Latin America and Caribbean	2,328	2,273	1,750	1,867	$454	340	362	463
Total International	18,455	24,477	21,958	23,590	$3,010	6,564	5,611	6,961
North America	78,576	72,757	80,736	76,844	$18,274	12,412	11,759	4,767
Total JPM	$97,031	$97,234	$102,694	$100,434	$21,284	$18,976	$17,370	$11,728

Source: Annual Report, page 300.

EXHIBIT 4 JPM's Investment Bank Revenue Breakdown by Region (in millions)

	2011	2010	2009
Europe, Middle East, and Africa	8,418	7,380	9,164
Asia and Pacific	3,334	3,809	3,470
Latin America and Caribbean	1,079	897	1,157
North America	13,443	14,131	14,318
Net Revenue	$26,724	$26,212	$28,109
Net Income	$6,789	$6,639	$6,899

Source: 2011 Annual Report, page 84.

Retail Financial Services

JPM's retail financial services segment accounts for about 27 percent of 2011 net revenues with $10,405 million of the segments, $26,538 million being derived from noninterest sources, with the balance of $16,133 derived from interest sources. The retail financial services segment includes: bank branches, ATMs, mortgages, real estate, among others. JPM customers have access to more than 17,200 ATMs and 5,500 bank branches. The Chase business segment currently services more than 8 million loans in 23 states and services more than $150 billion of mortgage originations each year.

Exhibit 5 provides a breakdown of businesses within JPM's financial services segment. Note the decreases in both revenue and net income in 2011.

Card Services and Auto

JPM's credit card services and auto segment accounted for about 19 percent of 2011 net revenues with $4,892 million of the segments, $19,141 million being derived from noninterest sources with the balance of $14,249 derived from interest sources. The segment accounts for more than $132 billion in credit card loans with over 65 million open credit card accounts, making JPM one of the largest credit card issuers in the USA. JPM customers can also obtain financing through 17,200 auto dealerships and 2,000 schools and universities. Exhibit 6 provides a breakdown of businesses within JPM's credit card and auto segment. Note the reduction in revenues but increase in net income over the last three years.

Finance

JPM earned an all-time record of $19 billion in net income in 2011, up 9 percent from the previous record of $17.4 billion the prior year. The company's net income would have been considerably more, except for losses from the JPM mortgage business. Mortgage losses are expected to continue for a while longer, but the bulk of JPM bad mortgages have already been absorbed.

JPM's recent income statements are provided in Exhibit 7. Note the unusual decline in revenue associated with the increase in net income.

JPM reinstated its annual dividend of $1.00 per share in April of 2011 and increased it to $1.20 a share in April of 2012. Although JPM's goodwill has remained the same over the last

EXHIBIT 5 JPM's Retail Financial Services Revenue Breakdown by Product (in millions)

	2011	2010	2009
Lending- and deposit-related fees	$3,190	$3,061	$3,897
Asset management, administration, and commissions	1,991	1,776	1,665
Mortgage fees and related income	2,714	3,855	3,794
Credit card income	2,025	1,955	1,634
Other income	485	580	424
Net Revenue	$26,538	$28,447	$29,797
Net Income	$1,678	$1,728	$(335)

Source: 2011 *Annual Report*, page 85.

EXHIBIT 6 A Breakdown of JPM's Credit Card Business (in millions)

	2011	2010	2009
Credit card revenue	$4,127	$3,514	$3,613
Other income	765	764	93
Total revenue	$19,141	$20,472	$23,199
Net income/(loss)	$4,544	$2,872	$(1,793)

Source: 2011 *Annual Report,* page 94.

EXHIBIT 7 JPM's Income Statement (in millions)

	2012	2011	2010
Interest Income, Bank	56,063.0	61,293.0	63,782.0
Total Interest Expense	11,153.0	13,604.0	12,781.0
Non-Interest Income, Bank	52,121.0	49,545.0	51,693.0
Total Revenue	**97,031.0**	**97,234.0**	**102,694.0**
Loan Loss Provision	3,385.0	7,574.0	16,639.0
Non-Interest Expense, Bank	64,729.0	62,911.0	61,196.0
Income Before Tax	**28,917.0**	**26,749.0**	**24,859.0**
Income Tax Total	7,633.0	7,773.0	7,489.0
Income After Tax	**21,284.0**	**18,976.0**	**17,370.0**
Minority Interest	0.0	0.0	0.0
Equity In Affiliates	0.0	0.0	0.0
U.S. GAAP Adjustment	0.0	0.0	0.0
Net Income Before Extra Items	**21,284.0**	**18,976.0**	**17,370.0**
Total Extraordinary Items	0.0	0.0	0.0
Net Income	**21,284.0**	**18,976.0**	**17,370.0**

Source: Company documents.

three years, total goodwill of $48 billion indicates a history of paying more than fair market value for many acquisitions. JPM's long-term debt is declining as shown in Exhibit 8.

Competition

Banks are seemingly everywhere on every corner and online. Some analysts say bank products and services are becoming more and more like commodities, all being similar. An interesting note is that foreign banks have not yet penetrated into the U.S. marketplace. But online banks are proliferating.

JPM competes with literally hundreds of banks but a few key rivals are showcased in Exhibit 9. Note that JPM has higher revenue per employee and earnings per share (EPS) than Bank of America or Citigroup.

Bank of America

Headquartered today in Charlotte, North Carolina, and having total assets exceeding $2.5 billion, Bank of America is the second largest U.S. bank, trailing only JPM, and is the largest bank according to number of employees. Bank of America has a relationship with 99 percent of the *Fortune* 500 companies and 83 percent of the *Fortune Global* 500. The 2008 acquisition of Merrill Lynch made Bank of America the world's largest wealth management corporation and a major player in the investment banking market.

As of May 2012, Bank of America served more than 5,700 banking centers and had more than 17,000 ATMs serving customers in more than 150 countries and had branches in more than 40 countries. During 2011, Bank of America began laying off an estimated 36,000 people, contributing to intended savings of $5 billion per year by 2014. In December 2011, *Forbes* ranked Bank of America's financial health 91st out of the nation's largest 100 banks and thrift institutions. Bank of America will cut around 16,000 jobs in a quicker fashion by the end of 2012 as revenue continues to decline because of new regulations and a slow economy. This will put a plan one year ahead of time to eliminate 30,000 jobs under a cost-cutting program called Project New BAC. Bank of America generates 90 percent of its revenues in its domestic market and continues to buy businesses in the USA. The core of Bank of America's strategy is to be the number-one bank in its domestic market. It has achieved this through key acquisitions.

EXHIBIT 8 JPM's Balance Sheets (in millions)

	2012	2011	2010
Assets			
Cash & Due From Banks	53,723	59,602	27,567
Other Earning Assets, Total	1,358,307	1,271,811	1,174,042
Net Loans	711,860	696,111	660,661
Property/Plant/Equipment, Total - Net	14,519	14,041	13,355
Goodwill, Net	48,175	48,188	48,854
Intangibles, Net	9,849	10,430	17,688
Long Term Investments	0	0	0
Other Long Term Assets, Total	0	0	0
Other Assets, Total	162,708	165,609	175,438
Total Assets	**2,359,141**	**2,265,792**	**2,117,605**
Liabilities and Shareholders' Equity			
Accounts Payable	195,240	202,895	170,330
Payable/Accrued	0	0	0
Accrued Expenses	0	0	0
Total Deposits	1,193,593	1,127,806	930,369
Other Bearing Liabilities, Total	0	0	0
Total Short Term Borrowings	392,762	362,048	415,551
Policy Liabilities	0	0	0
Notes Payable/Short Term Debt	0	0	0
Current Port. of LT Debt/Capital Leases	0	0	0
Other Current Liabilities, Total	0	0	0
	312,215	322,752	348,302
Total Long Term Debt			
Deferred Income Tax	0	0	0
Minority Interest	0	0	0
Other Liabilities, Total	61,262	66,718	76,947
Total Liabilities	**2,155,072**	**2,082,219**	**1,941,499**
Redeemable Preferred Stock	0	0	0
Preferred Stock - Non Redeemable, Net	9,058	7,800	7,800
Common Stock	4,105	4,105	4,105
Additional Paid-In Capital	94,604	95,602	97,415
Retained Earnings (Accumulated Deficit)	104,223	88,315	73,998
Treasury Stock—Common	−12,002	−13,155	−8,160
ESOP Debt Guarantee	0	0	0
Unrealized Gain (Loss)	0	0	0
Other Equity, Total	4,081	906	948
Total Equity	**204,069**	**183,573**	**176,106**
Total Liabilities & Shareholders' Equity	**2,359,140**	**2,265,792**	**2,117,605**
Total Common Shares Outstanding	3,803.95	3,772.7	3,910.3

Source: Company documents.

Citigroup

Citigroup was formed on October 9, 1998, following the $140 billion merger of Citicorp and Travelers Group to create the world's largest financial services organization. The history of the company is comprised of many acquired firms such as the City Bank of New York (later named

EXHIBIT 9 A Synopsis of Large Banks

	JPM	Bank of America	Citigroup
Number of Employees	261K	279K	263K
Net Income ($)	17.5B	−1.31B	10.7B
Revenue ($)	90.5B	76.8B	66.3B
Revenue ($)/Employee	346K	275K	252K
EPS Ratio ($)	4.5	−0.13	3.59
Market Capitalization	129B	80.6B	74.1B

Source: Company documents.

Citibank) in 1812; Bank Handlowy in 1870; Smith Barney in 1873, Banamex in 1884; and Salomon Brothers in 1910.

Based today in New York City, Citigroup is a diversified financial services holding company broken down into two segments, Citicorp and Citi Holdings, providing global banking, advisory services, derivative services, brokerage, and much more. Citigroup today is the largest banking enterprise in the world based on geographic coverage with operations in 140 nations and more than 16,000 offices worldwide.

On Tuesday, March 13, 2012, the Federal Reserve reported Citigroup as one of the 4 financial institutions, out of 19, that have failed its stress tests. The tests make sure banks have enough capital to withstand huge losses in a financial crisis like one Citigroup faced in 2008 and early 2009 when it almost collapsed. The 2012 stress tests determine whether banks could withstand a financial crisis with unemployment at 13 percent, stock prices cut in half, and home prices decreased by 21 percent from current levels. According to Citi and the Federal Reserve stress test report, Citi failed the stress tests because of Citi's high capital return plan and its international loans rated by the Federal Reserve to be at higher risk than its domestic U.S. loans. Citi gets half their revenues from its international businesses. In comparison, Bank of America, which passed the stress test and did not ask for a capital return to investors, gets 78 percent of its revenue in the USA.

Wells Fargo & Co.

Founded in 1852 and headquartered in San Francisco, Wells Fargo is a nationwide, diversified, community-based financial services company with $1.4 trillion in assets. Wells Fargo provides banking, insurance, investments, mortgage, and consumer and commercial finance through more than 9,000 stores, 12,000 ATMs, the Internet, and has offices in more than 35 countries to support the bank's customers who conduct business in the global economy. With more than 265,000 employees, Wells Fargo serves one in three households in the USA. Wells Fargo was ranked number 26 on *Fortune's* 2012 rankings of the largest corporations in the USA. Wells Fargo's vision is to satisfy all our customers' financial needs and help them succeed financially.

As most large banks retreat from the trading business, Wells Fargo is expanding. The fourth-largest U.S. bank says it can earn solid returns in investment banking while taking little risk for itself. It is focusing on services that its corporate lending customers need, such as stock and bond underwriting and merger advice. For investors, it is looking at areas such as processing futures and swaps trades.

The Wells Fargo Securities unit is relatively small now, but in a few years, the unit could account for twice as much of the firm's revenue, an estimated 10 percent compared to its current 5 percent, Deutsche Bank analyst Matt O'Connor wrote in a report in May 2012. For JPM, Bank of America, and Citigroup, that percentage is closer to 20 to 25 percent. A much bigger proportion of Wells Fargo's revenue comes from traditional commercial and retail banking businesses: residential mortgages, lines of credit for corporations, and so on.

Online Banks

Online banks are growing rapidly in number and taking market share from large banks. The website http://www.mybanktracker.com/best-online-banks rates more than 30 online banks in

EXHIBIT 10 The Best Online U.S. Banks
(1= best, 18 = least best)

1. Ally	10. Discover Bank
2. Bank of Internet	11. UFB Bank
3. ING Direct	12. Simple
4. Charles Schwab Bank	13. Incredible Bank
5. Sallie Mae Bank	14. Nationwide Bank
6. USAA	15. First Internet Bank
7. TIAA Direct	16. One United Bank
8. Barclays Bank	17. Presidential Online Bank
9. State Farm Bank	18. E*TRADE

Source: Based on info at http://www.mybanktracker.com/best-online-banks.

the USA in terms of having low fees, low interest rates, excellent technology, and great customer service. Exhibit 10 reveals in rank order the top 18 Internet Banks in the USA. Note that Ally is number 1 and E*TRADE is number 18.

External Issues

Regulatory Reform

Following the 2007 to 2009 financial crisis, President Barack Obama signed the Dodd-Frank Wall Street Reform and Consumer Protection Act in 2010 that affects all aspects of the financial industry. Provisions include: prohibition of proprietary trading, restrictions on who can own hedge funds, establishing the Financial Stability Oversight Council, elimination of the Office of Thrift Supervision, and much more. The new regulations are expected to greatly increase the fees all financial institutions must pay. Provisions of Dodd-Frank aim to avoid situations in which large banks (such as AIG and Citigroup) are bailed out by the government because they are "too big to fail." Dodd-Frank did ease public perception and opinion of the financial crisis and may in fact apply to middle-size firms. However, recent research reveals that the largest institutions are so interconnected worldwide that, should a similar financial situation arise again, world governments again would be forced to save these behemoths. It is expected that there will be more than 14,000 new regulatory requirements enacted by 2015.

Mobile Payments

One of the hottest topics and business challenges facing banks today is the advent of mobile payment systems and the new competitors that enter the market associated with these payment systems. *Bank Technology News* even stated in 2012 that credit and debit cards used today are soon headed to the museum to be replaced by a linkage of mobile, Web, and point of sale options. As of 2012, there were more than five billion mobile phone users in the world, with more than 70 percent of the world's population having a mobile phone, yet only half the world's population having a bank account. Juniper Research reports that the market for global payments should exceed $600 billion by 2013. Businesses such as Intuit's GoPayment are already available for the Apple iPhones and Android platforms.

Near Field Communications (NFC) is allowing customers to pay for products using their mobile phones at retail stores. Big players such as MasterCard, American Express, Visa, eBay, and Google are also establishing mobile payment systems. Traditional banks such as JPM perhaps need to form strategic alliances to participate in this new arena because less people will be using cash, checks, and plastic cards to perform their business transactions.

Mortgage Business

As of 2012 there were 76 million homes in the USA with 52 million of these homes having a mortgage, and 4.7 million of these homes in a delinquent state. Around 2.5 million of the delinquent homes are worth less than their mortgage and around 10 million homeowners who are not delinquent are paying mortgage notes that are worth less than their home. About

25 percent of these homes are expected to go into default because homeowners either cannot afford to continue paying or are simply unwilling to pay more for a home than it is worth.

Future

Going up and up on fees much like the U.S. Postal Service Office, are large banks on permanent decline? The *Wall Street Journal* (9-12-12, p. A1) reported that the percentage of Americans who own checking accounts dropped from 92 to 88 percent between 2010 and 2011, whereas the number of Americans who own a major credit card dropped from 74 to 67 percent, and those who own a major debit or check card dropped from 78 to 66 percent. In other words, Americans are using traditional banks less and less. In fact, the article reports that 8.2 percent of the nation's households, nearly 12 million, are managing their finances without a bank. Bank overdraft fees, according to the article, cost Americans $31.6 billion in 2011. Consumer behavior is definitely shifting from bank credit and debit cards to prepaid debit cards offered by both NetSpend and Green Dot. Pew Charitable Trusts estimates the total dollars that flow through prepaid debit cards will reach $201.9 billion in 2013, up from $28.6 billion in 2009.

A movement called "Bank Transfer Day" emerged in November 2011. In February 2012, J.D. Power & Associates reported that customers of large, regional, and mid-sized banks were defecting at a higher rate because of frustration over factors such as fees and poor customer service. According to their survey, 9.6 percent of customers said they had switched to a new banking provider within the last year, compared to 8.7 and 7.7 percent in the previous two years. The main beneficiaries of the defections are credit unions and smaller banks, which experienced an average increase of 10.3 percent in the acquisition of new customers, versus 8.1 percent a year previously. In March 2012, the National Credit Union Administration reported that credit unions added 1.3 million members in 2011, hitting a record 91.8 million. Online banks are also gaining and increasingly sustaining competitive advantage over large banks.

Cash Advance Centers Inc. is the largest payday lending company in the USA and is widely being used now in lieu of doing business with a bank. That company reports that 22 percent of its customers earn more than $75,000, so the point here is that avoiding bank fees and such is becoming popular not only with individuals of lower incomes but also with people of medium incomes.

JPM needs a clear strategic plan for the future. Help JPM's top managers by preparing a recommended strategic plan for the company.

Walt Disney Company, 2013

www.disney.com, DIS

Headquartered in Burbank, California, Walt Disney Company (Disney) and its subsidiaries compete in the entertainment and media broadcasting industry worldwide. Serving customers for nearly 100 years, Disney is a diversified conglomerate, owning ABC, ESPN, theme parks, cruise lines, and more. As a member of the DOW 30 and the world's largest media conglomerate, Disney owns ABC television and cable networks such as ABC Family, Disney Channel, and ESPN (80 percent). Disney owns 8 television stations and 35 radio stations as well as Walt Disney Studios that produces films through Walt Disney Pictures, Disney Animation, and Pixar. Disney's Marvel Entertainment is a top comic book publisher and film producer. Disney owns and operates huge cruise boats, as well as 14 popular theme parks around the world.

Disney's earnings in Q3 of 2013 equaled the prior year's number, while revenue increased 4 percent, led by Disney's theme parks, resorts, and cable networks such as ESPN. For Q3 of 2013, Disney earned $1.85 billion, on revenue of $11.6 billion, up from $11.1 billion. Revenue at Disney's parks and resorts grew 7 percent to $3.7 billion. Cable networks revenue grew 8 percent to $3.9 billion, led by ESPN, A&E and U.S. Disney channels. A laggard, Disney's broadcast revenue was unchanged at nearly $1.5 billion. Overall, Disney's media networks business grew 5 percent to $5.4 billion. For Q3 of 2013, Disney's movie studio revenue fell 2 percent to $1.6 billion, due to poor results from the movies "The Lone Ranger" and "Iron Man 3."

Copyright by Fred David Books LLC. (Written by Forest R. David)

History

Walt Disney and his brother Roy arrived in California in the summer of 1923 to sell a cartoon called *Alice's Wonderland*. A distributor named M. J. Winkler contracted to distribute the *Alice Comedies* on October 16, 1923, and the Disney Brothers Cartoon Studio was founded. Over the years, the company produced many cartoons, from *Oswald the Lucky Rabbit* (1927) to *Silly Symphonies* (1932), *Snow White and the Seven Dwarfs* (1937), and *Pinocchio* and *Fantasia* (1940). The company name was changed to Walt Disney Studio in 1925. Mickey Mouse emerged in 1928 with the first cartoon in sound. In 1950, Disney completed its first live action film, *Treasure Island*, and in 1954, the company began television with the Disneyland anthology series. In 1955, Disney's most successful series, *The Mickey Mouse Club*, began, and the new Disneyland Park opened in Anaheim, California.

Disney created a series of releases from 1950s through 1970s, including *The Shaggy Dog*, *Zorro*, *Mary Poppins*, and *The Love Bug*. Walt Disney died in 1966. In 1969, Disney started its educational films and materials. Another important time of Disney's history was opening Walt Disney World in Orlando, Florida, in 1971. In 1982, the Epcot Center opened as part of Walt Disney World. The following year, Tokyo Disneyland opened.

After leaving network television in 1983, Disney introduced its cable network, The Disney Channel. In 1985, Disney's Touchstone division began the successful *Golden Girls* and Disney Sunday Movie. In 1988, Disney opened Grand Floridian Beach and Caribbean Beach Resorts at Walt Disney World along with three new gated attractions: the Disney/MGM Studios Theme Park, Pleasure Island, and Typhoon Lagoon. Filmmaking soon hit new heights as Disney led Hollywood studios in box-office gross for the first time. Some of the successful films were: *Who Framed Roger Rabbit*, *Good Morning Vietnam*, *Three Men and a Baby*, and later, *Honey, I Shrunk the Kids*, *Dick Tracy*, *Pretty Woman*, and *Sister Act*. Disney moved into new areas by starting Hollywood Pictures and acquiring the Wrather Corp. (owner of the Disneyland Hotel) and television station KHJ (Los Angeles), which was renamed KCAL. In merchandising, Disney purchased Childcraft and opened numerous highly successful and profitable Disney Stores.

By 1992, Disney's animation reached new heights with *The Little Mermaid*, *Beauty and the Beast*, and *Aladdin*. Also that year, Disneyland Paris opened. During the 1990s, Disney introduced Broadway shows, opened 725 Disney Stores, acquired the California Angels baseball team to add to its hockey team, opened Disney's Wide World of Sports in Walt Disney World, and acquired Capital Cities/ABC.

From 2000 to 2007, Disney created new attractions in its theme parks, produced many successful films, opened new hotels, and built Hong Kong Disneyland. Disney acquired Pixar in 2006, Marvel in 2009, and launched *Disney Dream*, a new cruise liner in 2011. Newer Disney initiatives include the April 2011 groundbreaking of Shanghai Disney Resort at a price tag of $4.4 billion and expected opening day slated for sometime in 2015. In February 2012, Disney finalized acquisition of UTV Software Communications, an Indian entertainment company. In October of 2012, Disney announced plans to acquire Lucasfilm, producers of the popular *Star Wars* movies. The acquisition is expected to cost $4.05 billion. Disney plans to release *Star Wars Episode VII* in 2015.

Internal Issues

Vision and Mission
Disney's vision is "to make people happy."

Organizational Structure
As indicated in Exhibit 1, Disney operates using a strategic business unit (SBU) organizational structure that consists of five diverse, but all family entertainment segments: (1) media networks, (2) parks and resorts, (3) studio entertainment, (4) consumer products, and (5) interactive media. The president, chief executive officer, and director of Walt Disney is Robert Iger. There is no chief operations officer (COO) in the Disney hierarchy, but Andy Bird, Chairman of Walt Disney International, functions like a COO.

Segments

Disney provides segment revenue and operating income for each of their five SBUs. Exhibit 2 displays the three most recent years of revenue and operating income per Disney SBU, along with a percentage change for each of the last two years. Note that total consolidated revenues and operating income increased in 2012 and 2011, albeit at a decreasing rate during the most recent period. Note that the consumer products and the interactive media segments are small compared to media networks and parks and resorts.

Media Networks
Media networks is the largest Disney SBU in both revenues and operating income, accounting for 45 percent of all revenues in 2012. Revenue growth in 2012 came from increased affiliate fees, higher advertising rates, increased viewership of ESPN programs and the shows *Castle*, *Once Upon a Time*, and *Revenge*. The positive growth was limited by lower home entertainment revenues from programs such as *Lost* and lower Disney Channel viewership. Production costs increased as college sports, as well as NFL, MLB, NBA, and Wimbledon were able to negotiate more lucrative contracts. For example, the Southeastern Conference (SEC) signed a deal with ESPN in 2008 for $2 billion for 15-year rights to broadcast football and men's and women's basketball games. However, with the 2012 additions of Texas A&M and Missouri to the SEC, the previous contract is contractually renegotiable and a new, much more expensive, contract is expected in the near future.

With media networks, Disney owns and operates the ABC Television Network that reaches 99 percent of all U.S. households. This segment also includes ABC-owned Television Stations Group, ABC Studios, Disney Channels Worldwide, ABC Family, SOAPnet, Disney ABC Domestic Television, Disney Media Distribution, Hyperion, and Radio Disney network. The ABC Television Network operates more than 220 affiliated stations across the USA. Disney channels worldwide consists of 94 kids and family entertainment channels available in 169 countries and 33 languages. ABC Family is a mixture of series and movies. SOAPnet owns character-driven

EXHIBIT 1 Disney's Organizational Chart

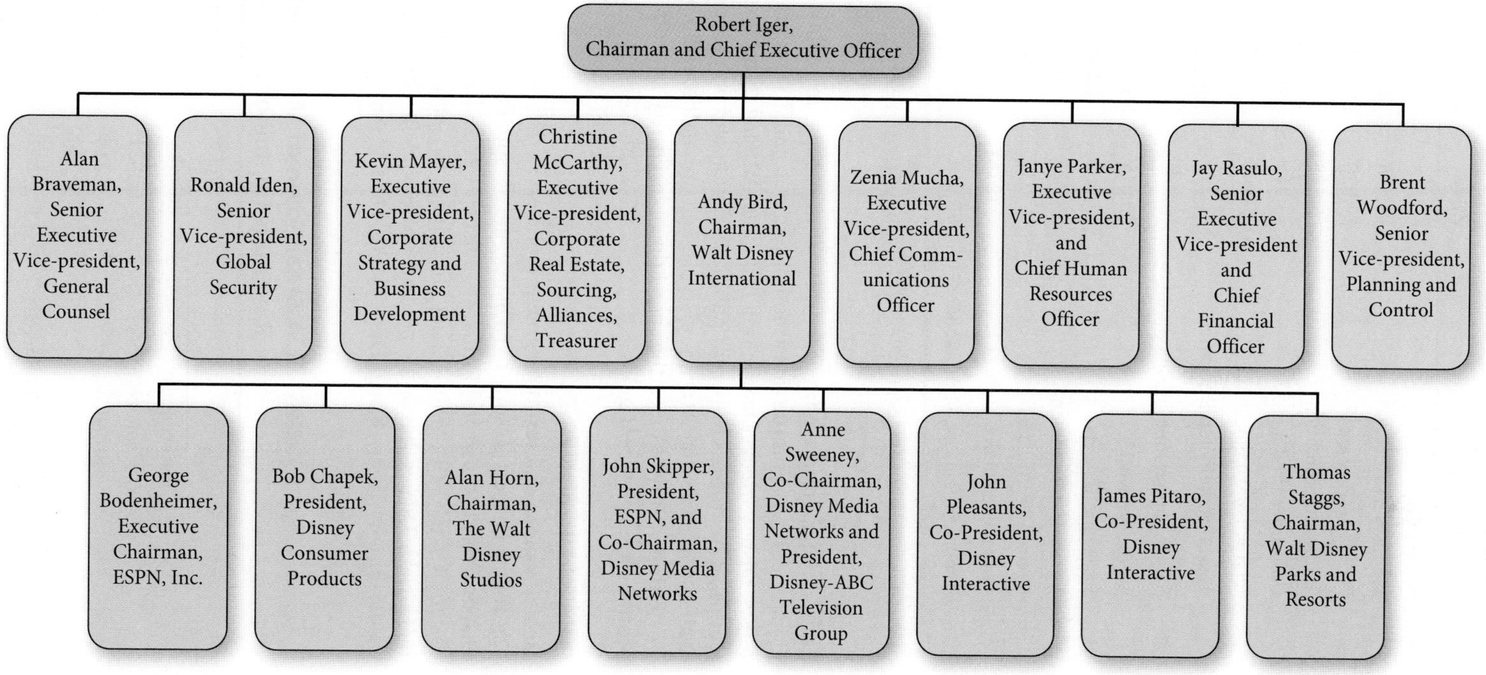

Robert Iger, Chairman and Chief Executive Officer

- Alan Braveman, Senior Executive Vice-president, General Counsel
- Ronald Iden, Senior Vice-president, Global Security
- Kevin Mayer, Executive Vice-president, Corporate Strategy and Business Development
- Christine McCarthy, Executive Vice-president, Corporate Real Estate, Sourcing, Alliances, Treasurer
- Andy Bird, Chairman, Walt Disney International
- Zenia Mucha, Executive Vice-president, Chief Communications Officer
- Janye Parker, Executive Vice-president, and Chief Human Resources Officer
- Jay Rasulo, Senior Executive Vice-president and Chief Financial Officer
- Brent Woodford, Senior Vice-president, Planning and Control

Under Andy Bird, Chairman, Walt Disney International:

- George Bodenheimer, Executive Chairman, ESPN, Inc.
- Bob Chapek, President, Disney Consumer Products
- Alan Horn, Chairman, The Walt Disney Studios
- John Skipper, President, ESPN, and Co-Chairman, Disney Media Networks
- Anne Sweeney, Co-Chairman, Disney Media Networks and President, Disney-ABC Television Group
- John Pleasants, Co-President, Disney Interactive
- James Pitaro, Co-President, Disney Interactive
- Thomas Staggs, Chairman, Walt Disney Parks and Resorts

Source: Based on information in company documents.

443

EXHIBIT 2 A Breakdown of Disney Revenues by SBU

(in millions)	2012	2011	2010	2012 vs. 2011	2011 vs. 2010
				Change (%)	
Revenues:					
Media Networks	$19,436	$18,714	$17,162	4%	9%
Parks and Resorts	12,920	11,797	10,761	10%	10%
Studio Entertainment	5,825	6,351	6,701	(8)%	(5)%
Consumer Products	3,252	3,049	2,678	7%	14%
Interactive Media	845	982	761	(14)%	29%
Total Consolidated Revenues	$42,278	$40,893	$38,063	3%	7%
Segment operating income:					
Media Networks	$6,619	$6,146	$5,132	8%	20%
Parks and Resorts	1,902	1,553	1,318	22%	18%
Studio Entertainment	722	618	693	17%	(11)%
Consumer Products	937	816	677	15%	21%
Interactive Media	(216)	(308)	(234)	30%	(32)%
Total segment operating income	$9,964	$8,825	$7,586	13%	16%

Source: Company documents. 2012 *Annual Report,* p. 31.

soapy drama, from daytime and primetime soaps, to reality shows and movies. Disney ABC Domestic Television provides motion pictures and TV programming to U.S.-based media platforms. Disney Media Distribution is an international distributor of branded and nonbranded content to all platforms. Hyperion publishes fiction and nonfiction titles for adults. Radio Disney is available in more than 40 U.S. markets, and on satellite radio, mobile apps, and the Web.

Exhibit 3 reveals a further breakdown of Disney's media networks' revenues and operating profits. Note the recent gains.

Parks and Resorts

Disney's parks and resorts segment includes 10 divisions: (1) Disneyland Resorts in California, (2) Tokyo Disney Resort, (3) Disneyland Resort Paris, (4) Hong Kong Disneyland, (5) Walt Disney World Resort in Florida, (6) Disney Cruise Line, (7) Adventures by Disney, (8) Disney Vacation Club, (9) Walt Disney Imagineering, and (10) Aluani, a Disney Resort and Spa in Hawaii. Disney has a 51 percent ownership in Disneyland Resort Paris and a 47 percent ownership in Hong Kong Disneyland. Disney's newest theme park will be in the Pudong

EXHIBIT 3 A Breakdown of Media Networks Revenues (in millions)

	2012	2011	Change (%)
Revenues:			
Cable Networks	13,621	12,877	6
Broadcasting	5,815	5,837	—
	19,436	18,714	4
Operating Income:			
Cable Networks	5,704	5,233	9
Broadcasting	915	913	—
	6,619	6,146	8

Source: 2012 *Annual Report,* p. 33.

EXHIBIT 4

	Domestic			International			Total		
	2012	2011	2010	2012	2011	2010	2012	2011	2010
Parks									
Increase in attendance	3%	1%	(1)%	6%	6%	1%	4%	2%	(1)%
Increase in Per Capital Guest Spending	7%	8%	3%	1%	2%	3%	5%	6%	3%
Hotels									
Occupancy	81%	82%	82%	85%	88%	85%	——	83%	82%
Available Room Nights (in thousands)	9,850	9,625	9,629	2,468	$2,466	2,466	12,318	12,091	12,095
Per Room Guest Spending	$257	$241	$224	$317	$294	$273	$270	$251	$234

[a]Per capita guest spending and per room guest spending include the impact of foreign currency translation. Guest spending statistics for Disneyland Paris were converted from euros into U.S. dollars at weighted average exchange rates of 1.36 and 1.35 for fiscal 2010 and 2009, respectively.
[b]Per room guest spending consists of the average daily hotel room rate as well as guest spending on food, beverages, and merchandise at the hotels. Hotel statistics include rentals of Disney Vacation Club units.

Source: Walt Disney Company, *Annual Report,* page 34 (2012).

district of Shanghai opening in 2015. Exhibit 2 revealed that Disney's parks and resorts revenue for 2012 increased 10 percent to $12.9 billion, and operating income increased 22 percent to $1.9 billion. Results for 2012 reflected increases at nearly all theme parks, except a decrease at Disneyland Paris.

The new 4,000-passenger ship, *Disney Dream*, was christened at Port Canaveral in 2011 and was designed especially for families. *Disney Dream* joins *Disney Magic* and *Disney Wonder*. Another new ship, *Disney Fantasy*, joined the Disney fleet in 2012. *Disney Dream* will sail to Disney's private island, Castaway Cay.

Revenue in this segment is generated primarily from the sale of admissions tickets to the theme parks, as well as hotel room charges per night and sales from merchandise, food, and beverages. Revenue also comes from rentals and sales from vacation club properties and sales of cruise vacations.

Exhibits 4 and 5 reveal that Disney domestic revenues from its parks and resorts division increased 11 percent in 2011, to $12.9 billion, resulting from customers spending 6 percent more, mainly from higher ticket and hotel prices. Revenue growth was 6 percent in international operations stemming from 4 percent in higher spending, a 3-percent volume increase, and a 3-percent gain on foreign currency appreciation.

Studio Entertainment

Disney produces live-action and animated motion pictures, direct-to-video programming, musical recordings, and live-stage plays. Disney motion pictures are distributed under the names: Theatrical Market, Home Entertainment Market, Television Market, Disney Music Group, and

EXHIBIT 5 Parks and Resorts: Revenue and Operating Income

(in millions)	2012	2011	2010	Change (%)
Revenues:				
Domestic	$10,339	$9,302	$8,404	11%
International	$2,581	2,495	2,357	3%
	$12,920	$11,797	$10,761	10%
Segment operating income:				
	$1,902	$1,553	$1,318	22%

Source: Walt Disney Company, *Annual Report,* page 33 (2012).

EXHIBIT 6 Studio Entertainment: Revenue and Operating Income

(in millions)	2012	2011	2010	Change (%)
Revenues:				
Theatrical Distribution	$1,470	$1,733	$2,050	(15)%
Home Entertainment	$2,221	2,435	2,666	(9)%
Television Distribution and Other	$2,134	2,183	1,985	(2)%
Total Revenues	$5,825	$6,351	$6,701	(8)%
Segment operating income:				
	$722	$618	$693	+17%

Source: Walt Disney Company, *Annual Report,* page 34 (2012).

Disney Theatrical Productions. Disney has also licensed the rights to produce and distribute features films such as *Spider-man*, *The Fantastic Four*, and *X-Men* to third-party studios. Disney earns a licensing fee on these films, whereas the third-party studio incurs the cost to produce and distribute the films. Currently Disney has a diverse business line in the studio entertainment SBU consisting of: Marvel, Touchstone, Pixar, Disneynature, Disney Studios Motion Pictures, and more Disney-branded services. Disney's studio entertainment revenues for 2012 decreased 8 percent to $5.8 billion and segment operating income increased 17 percent to $722 million. Exhibit 6 reveals a revenue breakdown for this segment.

Consumer Products

Disney's consumer products segment partners with licenses, manufacturers, publishers, and retailers worldwide who design, promote, and sell a wide variety of products based on new and existing Disney characters. Product offerings are: (a) character merchandise and publications licensing, (b) books and magazines, and (c) The Disney Store. Disney released in mid-2011 a new toy line that captured the fantasy, action, and adventure of *Pirates of the Caribbean: On Stranger Tides*. Disney is perhaps the largest worldwide licensor of character-based merchandise and producer and distributor of children's film-related products based on retail sales. Disney's consumer products revenues for 2012 increased 7 percent to $3.25 billion; operating income increased 15 percent to $937 million.

Interactive Media

Disney's interactive media segment creates and delivers games and media for smartphones and tablets. Interactive media revenues for 2012 decreased 14 percent to $845 million and operating income incurred a loss of $216 million. As indicated in Exhibit 8, games and subscription revenue increased 36 percent in 2011, but the segment has incurred losses for several years, as revealed in Exhibit 2.

EXHIBIT 7 Consumer Products: Revenue and operating income

(in millions)	2012	2011	2010	Change (%)
Revenues:				
Licensing and Publishing	$2,056	$1,933	$1,725	6%
Retail and Other	1,196	1,116	953	7%
Total Revenues	$3,252	$3,049	$2,678	7%
Segment operating income:				
	$937	$816	$677	15%

Source: Walt Disney Company, *Annual Report,* page 35.

EXHIBIT 8 Interactive: Revenue and Operating Income

(in millions)	2012	2011	2010	Change (%)
Revenues:				
Games Sales and Subscriptions	$613	$768	$563	(20)%
Advertising and Other	232	214	198	8%
Total Revenues	845	982	$761	(14)%
Segment operating income:				
	$(216)	$(308)	$(234)	(30)%

Finance

Income Statement

Disney's 2012 income statement is provided in Exhibit 9. Note the 17.4 percent increase in net income.

Balance Sheets

Disney's 2012 balance sheets are provided in Exhibit 10. Note that Disney has $2.45 billion of "projects in progress." Also, note the $25 billion in goodwill, fully one-third of total assets, which is not a good thing. Long-term debt is staying about the same at $10 billion, which is a lot of debt to service.

Competition

Disney competes directly with NBC Universal, Paramount Pictures, Time Warner, CBS Corp., News Corp., Carnival Corp., and Royal Caribbean and indirectly with all family entertainment oriented businesses globally. In essence, all hotels, restaurants, water parks, and attractions anywhere near Disney's 14 theme parks, are rival businesses, such as Sea World, Marineland, and Silver Springs in Florida. There is a large, new (China state run) theme park scheduled to open in 2014 right beside the Disney theme park (also slated for opening in 2014) in Shanghai, China, so that will be a major competitor.

EXHIBIT 9 Disney's Recent Income Statements
(in millions of dollars, except EPS)

Income Statement	2012	2011
Revenues	42,278	40,893
Costs and expenses	(33,415)	(33,112)
Restructuring	(100)	(55)
Other revenue	239	75
Net interest expense	(369)	(343)
Equity in the income	627	585
Income before taxes	9,260	8,043
Income taxes	(3,087)	(2,785)
Net income	6,173	5,258
Noncontrolling interests	(491)	(451)
Net income	$5,682	$4,807
EPS	3.13	2.52
Shares outstanding (in thousands)	1,818	1,909

EPS, earnings per share.
Source: Company documents.

EXHIBIT 10 Disney's Unaudited Balance Sheets (in millions)

	2012	2011
Assets		
Current Assets		
Cash and cash equivalents	3,387	3,185
Receivables	6,540	6,182
Inventories	1,537	1,595
Television costs	676	674
Deferred income taxes	765	1,487
Other current assets	804	634
Total current assets	13,709	13,757
Film and television costs	4,541	4,357
Investments	2,723	2,435
Parks, resorts and other property	38,582	35,515
Accumulated depreciation	(20,687)	(19,572)
	17,895	15,943
Projects in progress	2,453	2,625
Land	1,164	1,127
	21,512	19,695
Intangible assets	5,015	5,121
Goodwill	25,110	24,145
Other assets	2,288	2,614
Total Assets	**74,898**	**72,124**
Liabilities and Equity		
Current Liabilities		
Accounts payable	6,393	6,362
Current portion of borrowings	3,614	3,055
Unearned royalties	2,806	2,671
Total current liabilities	12,813	12,088
Borrowings	10,697	10,922
Deferred income taxes	2,251	2,866
Other long-term liabilities	7,179	6,795
Preferred Stock, $.01 par value, 100 million shares authorized but none issued		
Common Stock, 4.6 billion shares, 2.8 and 2.7 billion shares issues respectively	31,731	30,296
Retained earnings	42,965	38,375
Accumulated other loss	(3,266)	(2,630)
	71,430	66,041
Treasury Stock, 1.0 billion shares	(31,671)	(28,656)
Total Equity	39,759	37,385
Noncontrolling interests	2,199	2,068
Total Equity	41,958	39,453
Total Liabilities and Shareholders' Equity	**74,898**	**72,124**

Source: Company documents.

CBS Corp.

Headquartered in New York City, CBS is a large media conglomerate with operations in television, radio, online content, and publishing. CBS Broadcasting operates the number-1 rated CBS television network, along with a group of local TV stations. CBS also owns cable network Showtime and produces and distributes TV programming through CBS Television Studios and CBS Television Distribution. Also competing with Disney, other operations include CBS Radio, CBS Interactive, and book publisher Simon & Schuster. In addition, CBS Outdoor is a leading operator of billboards and outdoor advertising. Chairman Sumner Redstone controls CBS through National Amusements.

Time Warner, Inc.

Headquartered in New York City, Time Warner is the world's third-largest media conglomerate behind Walt Disney and News Corp., with operations spanning television, film, and publishing. Time Warner owns Turner Broadcasting that runs a portfolio of popular cable TV networks including CNN, TBS, and TNT. Time Warner also operates pay-TV channels HBO and Cinemax, all of which compete with Disney. Time Warner owns Warner Bros. Entertainment that includes films studios (Warner Bros. Pictures, New Line Cinema), TV production units (Warner Bros. Television Group), and comic book publisher DC Entertainment.

News Corp.

Headquartered in New York City, News Corp. is the second largest media conglomerate in the world, trailing only Walt Disney. News Corp. owns film, TV, and publishing businesses that make and distribute movies through Fox Filmed Entertainment. Owned by News Corp., FOX Broadcasting has more than 200 affiliate stations in the USA and owns and operates about 25 TV stations, as well as a portfolio of cable networks. Publishing assets of News Corp. include newspaper publishers Dow Jones (*The Wall Street Journal*) and News International (*The Times*, *The Sun*), and book publisher HarperCollins. News Corp. has stakes in British Sky Broadcasting (BSkyB) and Sky Deutschland. The company has recently split into two parts.

Carnival Corp.

Headquartered in Miami, Florida, Carnival is the world's number-1 cruise operator, owning and operating a dozen cruise lines and about 100 ships with a total passenger capacity of more than 190,000. Carnival operates in North America primarily through its Princess Cruise Line, Holland America, and Seabourn luxury cruise brand, as well as its flagship Carnival Cruise Lines unit. Brands such as AIDA, P&O Cruises, and Costa Cruises offer services to passengers in Europe, and the Cunard Line runs luxury trans-Atlantic liners. Carnival's cruise boats compete with the Disney cruise boats wherever Disney sails. Another large cruise line company, Royal Caribbean, also competes with Disney ships wherever they sail.

Paramount Pictures Corp.

Headquartered in Hollywood, California, and a subsidiary of Viacom, Paramount produces and distributes films through Paramount Pictures (*Tranformers: Dark of the Moon*) and Paramount Vantage (*Capitalism: A Love Story*). The Paramount Pictures library consists of some 3,500 films, including classic hits from the *Star Trek*, *Godfather*, and *Indiana Jones* series, and releases about a dozen new titles annually. Competing with Disney, Paramount Pictures distributes movies on video and DVD through Paramount Home Entertainment.

Lucasfilm

In October 2012, Disney acquired Lucasfilm for a whopping $4.05 billion, with Disney paying approximately half of that money in cash and issuing approximately 40 million shares at closing. Headquartered in San Francisco, California, and founded by George Lucas in 1971, Lucasfilm is a large, privately held, entertainment company that has motion-picture and television production operations. Lucasfilm's global activities include (a) Industrial Light & Magic and Skywalker Sound that serves the digital needs of the entertainment industry for visual-effects and audio post-production, (b) LucasArts, a leading developer and publisher of interactive entertainment software worldwide, (c) Lucas Licensing that manages the global merchandising activities for Lucasfilm's entertainment properties, (d) Lucasfilm Animation, (e) Lucas Online that creates Internet-based content for Lucasfilm's entertainment properties and businesses, and

(f) Lucasfilm Singapore that produces digital animated content for film and television, as well as visual effects for feature films and multi-platform games.

With the Lucasfilm acquisition, Disney obtains a substantial portfolio of cutting-edge entertainment technologies that have kept audiences enthralled for many years. Kathleen Kennedy, current co-chairman of Lucasfilm, will become President of Lucasfilm, reporting to Walt Disney Studios Chairman Alan Horn. Additionally she will serve as the brand manager for *Star Wars*, working directly with Disney's global lines of business to build, further integrate, and maximize the value of this global franchise. Kennedy will serve as executive producer on new *Star Wars* feature films, with George Lucas serving as creative consultant. *Star Wars Episode 7* is targeted for release in 2015, with more feature films expected to continue the *Star Wars* saga and grow the franchise well into the future.

The Future

Disney is busy completing its Shanghai theme park while at the same time integrating the Lucasfilm acquisition into its operations. Analysts ponder whether the Lucasfilm acquisition added more goodwill to the Disney balance sheet that already is too laden with that burden. As the world comes online, the opportunities, as well as the threats, abound for Disney. Strategic decisions have to be made in terms of what segments to bolster and what segments to focus on improving. The interactive media segment has not turned a profit in a number of years.

Kevin Mayer is Disney's Executive Vice-president for Corporate Strategy and Business Development. Help Mr. Mayer by preparing a draft three-year strategic plan for Disney.

Lowe's Companies, Inc., 2013

www.lowes.com, LOW

Headquartered in Mooresville, North Carolina, Lowe's is among *Fortune*'s top 50 companies and is the second-largest home improvement store in the world, trailing only Atlanta, Georgia-based Home Depot. Lowe's operates 1,745 stores totaling 197 million square feet of retail selling space with all Lowe's stores being located in the USA, Canada, and Mexico. Lowe's has an agreement, as a one-third owner, with Australian Woolworths Limited to develop a Lowe's-themed store in Australia.

Lowe's in late 2013 acquired Orchard Supply Hardware for approximately $205 million in cash, plus the assumption of payables owed to nearly all of Orchard's suppliers. The acquisition gave Lowe's a new customer base in California. Lowe's plans to have Orchard operate as a separate, standalone business, retaining its brand under the leadership of Orchard's current management team. Based in San Jose, California, and with fiscal 2012 annual revenue of $657 million, Orchard operates 91 neighborhood hardware and garden stores primarily located in densely populated markets in California. Under the terms of the transaction, Lowe's acquired at least 60 of these stores. On average, Orchard stores have about 36,000 square feet of selling space, compared to 113,000 square feet for an average Lowe's home improvement store. Lowe's currently operates 110 stores in California.

Lowe's stores offer appliances, lawn and garden, lumber, plumbing, electrical, power tools, flooring, and much more for home repair and construction. Lowe's principle goal is "to execute better than our competitors, and make the process of home improvement as seamless and simple as possible for customers." Lowe's customers are primarily homeowners, renters, homebuilders, and commercial construction firms. Lowe's has 160,000 full-time employees and 85,000 part-time employees, all of whom are led by CEO Robert Niblock. Lowe's has a chief rival, Home Depot, which reported a profit of $4.5 billion in 2012 on sales of $74.75 billion.

Lowe's fiscal 2012 sales increased 0.6 percent to $50.5 billion, while earnings increased 6.5 percent to $2.0 billion. But Lowe's total customer transactions in 2012 declined to 804 million from 810 million the prior year. Lowe's fiscal year 2012 ended January 31, 2013.

Copyright by Fred David Books LLC. (Written by Forest R. David)

History

The first Lowe's was opened in North Wilkesboro, North Carolina, in 1921 by Lucius Lowe as "Lowe's North Wilkesboro Hardware." However, from the start, in addition to hardware, the store also offered produce, groceries, tobacco products, and dry goods. Lowe died in 1940 and his daughter Ruth Buchan inherited the business and sold it the same year to her brother Jim Lowe. In 1946, Lowe's was officially founded. Jim Lowe hired Ruth's husband, Carl Buchan, after World War II and the two men ran the store together until 1952 when they split, with Buchan taking control of the hardware business and Jim Lowe opening up Lowes Foods in 1954, which is still operational today.

After the split, Buchan began expanding Lowe's throughout the 1950s opening stores in several North Carolina markets. However, Buchan died from a heart attack in 1960 at age 44, and Lowe's five-man executive team took the company public in 1961. The following year, Lowe's totaled 21 stores and had annual revenues of over $32 million.

During the 1960s and 1970s, the U.S. housing market expanded rapidly with professional builders becoming Lowe's primary customer. In 1982, Lowe's reported its first billion-dollar revenue year with a record profit of $25 million. Starting in the 1980s, however, Lowe's, in addition to builders, started focusing on the home do-it-yourself (DIY), whose aim was for weekend projects to add value to their homes.

In 1994, the "modern" Lowe's began with all new store expansion, having stores greater than 85,000 square feet of retail space. As of 2012, Lowe's opens two styles of stores: 117,000-square foot stores in large markets and relatively smaller 94,000-square foot stores in smaller markets. In 2007, Lowe's opened its first stores in Canada, where it currently operates

20 stores and in 2010 the first store opened in Mexico. Lowe's plans to open 150 stores in Australia in the next five years.

Internal Issues

Vision and Mission

The Lowe's mission statement is:

Lowe's Promise: We are committed to delivering better customer experiences across the entire home improvement spectrum, by pulling together the best combination of possibilities, support and value for customers wherever and whenever they choose to engage.

Lowe's vision statement is as follows:

We will provide customer-valued solutions with the best prices, products and services to make Lowe's the first choice for home improvement.

Lowe's focuses its employees on the following core values:

- Customer Focused
- Teamwork
- Ownership
- Passion for Execution
- Respect
- Integrity

Lowe's markets the slogan:

Never stop improving.

Organizational Structure

As illustrated in Exhibit 1, Lowe's operates from a divisional-by-region organizational structure. Some analysts suggest that Lowe's may have too many top executives.

Lowe's Locations

Exhibit 2 reveals where all the Lowe's stores are located. The company plans to open 10 new stores in 2013.

Supply Chain

Lowe's receives products from more than 7,000 venders with the largest single vender only supplying around 7 percent of total purchases. To facilitate product movement, Lowe's operates 14 highly automated regional distribution centers in the USA with each distribution center serving around 120 stores. In addition, Lowe's operates 15 flatbed distribution centers for items such as vinyl siding, ladders, lumber, and other products that require special handing.

Lowe's considers its supply chain finance (SCF) to be one of its top means for gaining competitive advantage over rival firms such as Home Depot, Ace, and True Value. Because most rival firms offer the same or similar products, maximizing SCF efficiencies can be critically important. Lowe's considers three key areas of its SCF strategy to be (1) standardization of payment terms, (2) incentives for buying organization, and (3) break even for the suppliers.

Sustainability

Lowe's emphasizes sustainability and in 2012 was awarded the ENERGY STAR Sustained Excellence Award for the third straight year and also was awarded the WaterSense award from the EPA for the fourth straight year. The awards can be attributed to Lowe's overall mission to protect the natural environment by continually expanding product offerings that are Energy Star and WaterSense qualified as well as offering numerous solar-powered alternatives.

EXHIBIT 1 Lowe's Organizational Structure

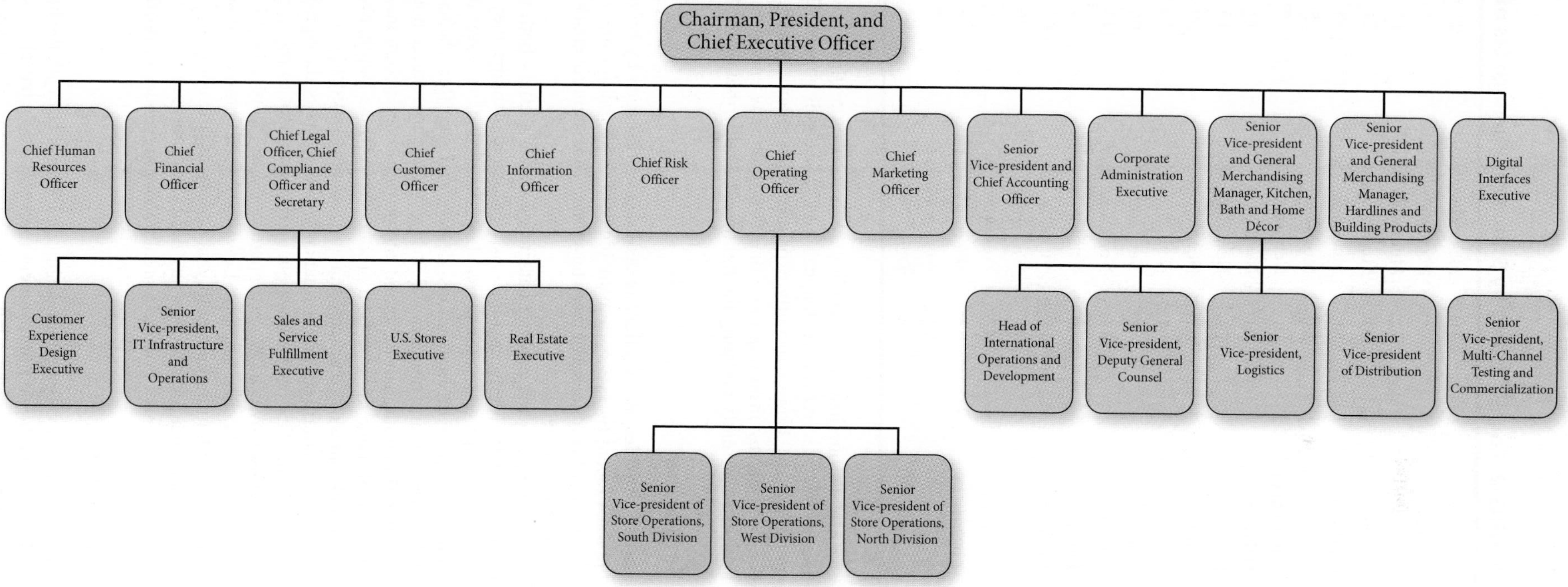

Source: Based on company documents.

EXHIBIT 2 Lowe's Stores by State and Province (as of February 3, 2013)

Alabama	39	Massachusetts	27	Oklahoma	29
Alaska	5	Michigan	47	Oregon	13
Arizona	32	Minnesota	11	Pennsylvania	81
Arkansas	20	Mississippi	24	Rhode Island	5
California	110	Missouri	48	Wyoming	1
Colorado	28	Montana	5	South Carolina	49
Connecticut	16	Nebraska	5	South Dakota	3
Delaware	10	Nevada	17	Tennessee	60
Florida	120	New Hampshire	13	Texas	141
Georgia	63	New Jersey	39	Utah	16
Hawaii	4	New Mexico	14	*Total U.S. Stores*	*1,715*
Idaho	8	New York	66	Alberta	6
Illinois	37	North Carolina	111	British Columbia	2
Indiana	44	Vermont	2	Ontario	26
Iowa	11	Virginia	67	Saskatchewan	1
Kansas	11	Washington	36	*Total Canadian Stores*	*34*
Kentucky	42	West Virginia	18	Nuevo Leon, Mexico	5
Louisiana	31	Wisconsin	8	*Total Stores*	*1,745*
Maine	11	North Dakota	3		
Maryland	28	Ohio	83		

Lowe's has installed recycling centers in more than 1,700 stores across the USA, helping customers to recycle rechargeable batteries, cell phones, fluorescent light bulbs and plastic shopping bags. Lowe's recently expanded its appliance recycling programs and reduced its carbon footprint by installing more than 3 million new energy-efficient fluorescent laps in stores. Lowe's is currently updating the lighting at 34 distribution facilities.

Segments

Lowe's provides an excellent breakdown of revenues by product category. Exhibit 3 provides the most recent two years of available data. Note that no single category accounts for more than 11 percent of revenues and there have been consistent revenues across all categories over the two most recent years.

Within the wide product categories, Lowe's offers both national brand-name and private-brand products. Many customers shop for brand name they know and trust to be the same regardless of the store they are sold. Private brands however do provide product differentiation from competitors in innovations, design, and are often cheaper as well. Lowe's private brands include tools, paint, plumbing, flooring, lumber, and much more. Virtually all product categories are offered in both national brand and private-branded options. Lowe's also offers a much larger selection of home improvement products than Home Depot, even offering designer towels, towel racks, and many more upscale home-decorating options.

Lowes also offers credit financing to customers through its consumer credit card with GE Money Bank. The card allows qualified customers to receive 5 percent off all purchases, and with purchases over $299, customers can select to receive no interest financing or 5 percent off the purchase price. In addition, Lowe's offers a commercial account for small- to medium-size businesses with minimal monthly payments and the company also provides accounts receivables for commercial customers that pay in full each month.

Lowe's does not provide a breakdown of revenues or profits by geographic region.

Strategies

Lowe's initial strategy was focusing on builders but with the housing boom in the 1960s, Lowe's added the DIY home improvement market. Lowe's has always engaged in both market development and market penetration, adding stores across the USA and now in Canada, Mexico, and

EXHIBIT 3 Lowe's Sales by Product Category

	2012		2011[1]		2010[1]	
	Total Sales	%	Total Sales	%	Total Sales	%
Plumbing	$ 5,448	11%	$ 5,400	11%	$ 5,146	11%
Appliances	5,210	10	5,341	11	5,392	11
Tools & Outdoor Power Equipment	4,967	10	4,749	9	4,563	9
Lawn & Garden	4,390	9	4,411	9	4,363	9
Fashion Electrical	4,049	8	4,034	8	3,744	8
Lumber	3,448	7	3,256	6	3,205	6
Seasonal Living	3,332	7	3,239	6	3,137	6
Paint	3,306	6	3,219	6	3,068	6
Home Fashions, Storage & Cleaning	3,026	6	2,997	6	2,891	6
Flooring	2,857	6	2,857	6	2,771	6
Millwork	2,791	5	2,897	6	3,067	6
Building Materials	2,790	5	3,040	6	2,760	6
Hardware	2,702	5	2,691	5	2,561	5
Cabinets & Countertops	1,817	4	1,810	4	1,810	4
Other	388	1	267	1	337	1
Totals	$ 50,521	100%	$ 50,208	100%	$ 48,815	100%

(Dollars in millions)

[1]*Certain prior period amounts have been reclassified to conform to current product category classifications.*
Source: 2012 *Annual Report,* p. 65.

Australia. Having two store sizes is an advantage because Lowe's tailors the respective store size market to particular markets. Lowe's does, however, experiment with various layouts at various locations; nevertheless, having the same principle layout at most stores provides customers familiar in their shopping experience. Also, Lowe's has slightly larger stores than rival Home Depot with an average store size of 113,000 to 105,000 square feet. Both Lowe's and Home Depot have on average 32,000 square feet of garden space. Lowe's also stocks 40,000 items, up to 10,000 more than certain Home Depot stores. Having wider isles, more signs, and better store lighting are also competitive advantages of Lowe's. In addition, Lowe's has around 69 to 89 percent full-time employees to Home Depot's 59 percent. Despite these "competitive advantages," Home Depot is outperforming Lowe's, and by what some analysts say is by alarming margins.

Lowe's is continuing its expansion and is attempting to better attract customers who normally would not visit home improvement stores. In addition, Lowe's has implemented a new strategy to attract an increasing number of female customers.

Lowe's has over 190,000 products online and recently started shipping items to customers from service stores and regional distribution centers. Historically, Lowe's only shipped online purchased items from its dedicated Internet warehouse. This new strategy enables Lowe's to provide faster deliveries, reduce order filling costs, and improve profitability overall. Building on the increased online presence, Lowe's plans to reduce its brick-and-mortar expansion plans by 15 stores annually thereafter, or around a 50 percent reduction in planned new stores.

Finance

Lowe's recent balance sheets are provided in Exhibit 5.

The Economy

Home prices are slowly rising in the USA and home construction too is rising, both good news for Lowe's. June 2012 new home sales in the USA were up 15.1 percent over the prior year.

EXHIBIT 4 Lowe's Companies, Inc. Income Statement

	(In millions, except per share and percentage data) Fiscal years ended on		
	February 1, 2013	February 3, 2012	January 28, 2011
Net sales	$ 50,521	$ 50,208	$ 48,815
Cost of sales	33,194	32,858	31,663
Gross margin	17,327	17,350	17,152
Expenses:			
Selling, general and administrative	12,244	12,593	12,006
Depreciation	1,523	1,480	1,586
Interest—net	423	371	332
Total expenses	**14,190**	**14,444**	**13,924**
Pre-tax earnings	**3,137**	**2,906**	**3,228**
Income tax provision	1,178	1,067	1,218
Net earnings	$ 1,959	$ 1,839	$ 2,010
Basic earnings per common share	**$ 1.69**	**$ 1.43**	**$ 1.42**
Diluted earnings per common share	**$ 1.69**	**$ 1.43**	**$ 1.42**
Cash dividends per share	**$ 0.62**	**$ 0.53**	**$ 0.42**

Source: 2012 *Annual Report,* p. 38.

Sales of existing homes are increasing, up to 4.37 million units in June 2012 from 4.18 units in June 2011 or a 4.5-percent increase. Unemployment rates have fallen to just below 8 percent in the USA, and are trending downward, good news for Lowe's. More and more people are remodeling their homes, also good news for Lowe's. The top four homebuilders in the USA are: D.R. Horton Inc., KB Homes, PulteGroup Inc., and Lennar Corp.; all four companies are growing and this is good news for Lowe's.

The 30-year fixed mortgage rate is over 3 percent and rising. Despite low rates however, banks are still reluctant to lend. Throughout much of the previous decade, banks would allow someone to purchase a home with as little as 5 percent down, but now banks are commonly requiring 20 percent cash down. In addition, banks are also requiring higher credit scores to qualify for a mortgage. Scores as high as 720 would historically be automatic for a loan, but scores as high as 755 are now *not* automatic for approval. Low interest rates are allowing many people to refinance their homes, thus providing them with additional cash to potentially spend on home improvement projects.

CEO Frank Blake of Home Depot in October 2012 said: "This housing market has been very very bad and it's going to take some time to recover." Blake's comments were on the heels of the Federal Reserve blaming the U.S. housing situation for the country's overall slow economic recovery. In Blake's opinion, when customers start to consider home improvement projects, such as installing a new granite countertop as a home investment rather than a cost, then the housing market is likely heading for a more sustainable recovery.

Competition

Largely dependent on the state of the economy and especially the state of the housing market, competition is intense in the home improvement industry. Major players Lowe's and Home Depot have the greatest market share, but many other firms such as True Value Hardware, Ace Hardware, and even Walmart all facilitate increased competition. For example, Ace markets its business as a one-stop place where a customer can receive friendly help with an appropriated size store that enables customers to find everything they need "without the use of a gps." This marketing strategy is clearly aimed at behemoths Lowe's and Home Depot and suggests that by being large warehouse stores, customers do not receive the personal attention Ace can deliver. True Value positions its business model around each store being independently owned and operated, providing customers with a store that offers products more tailored to local needs.

EXHIBIT 5 Lowe's Companies, Inc. Balance Sheet

	(In millions, except par value and percentage data)	
	February 1, 2013	February 3, 2012
Assets		
Current assets:		
Cash and cash equivalents	$ 541	$ 1,014
Short-term investments	125	286
Merchandise inventory—net	8,600	8,355
Deferred income taxes—net	217	183
Other current assets	301	234
Total current assets	**9,784**	**10,072**
Property, less accumulated depreciation	21,477	21,970
Long-term investments	271	504
Other assets	1,134	1,013
Total assets	**$ 32,666**	**$ 33,559**
Liabilities and shareholders' equity		
Current liabilities:		
Current maturities of long-term debt	$ 47	$ 592
Accounts payable	4,657	4,352
Accrued compensation and employee benefits	670	613
Deferred revenue	824	801
Other current liabilities	1,510	1,533
Total current liabilities	**7,708**	**7,891**
Long-term debt, excluding current maturities	9,030	7,035
Deferred income taxes—net	455	531
Deferred revenue—extended protection plans	715	704
Other liabilities	901	865
Total liabilities	**18,809**	**17,026**
Commitments and contingencies		
Shareholders' equity:		
Preferred stock—$5 par value, none issued	—	—
Common stock—$.50 par value;		
Shares issued and outstanding		
February 1, 2013 1,110		
February 3, 2012 1,241	555	621
Capital in excess of par value	26	14
Retained earnings	13,224	15,852
Accumulated other comprehensive income	52	46
Total shareholders' equity	**13,857**	**16,533**
Total liabilities and shareholders' equity	**$ 32,666**	**$ 33,559**

Source: 2012 *Annual Report*, p. 39.

In addition to brand-name stores, there are thousands of local mom-and-pop hardware stores that customers trust and frequent.

Lowe's and Home Depot compete with many stores offering similar products. Walmart offers many of the same lawn and garden options, as well as lights, paint, tools, and many other

EXHIBIT 6 A Comparison of Lowe's with Home Depot

	Lowe's	Home Depot
Number of Employees	161K	331K
Net Income ($)	1.9B	4.1B
Revenue ($)	51.1B	71.4B
Revenue ($)/Employee	317K	216K
EPS Ratio ($)	1.52	2.65
Market Capitalization	31.3B	78.9B

home improvement items. Sears, Big Lots, SAMs, Costco, and thousands of specialty stores that focus exclusively on lighting or flooring for example are also fierce competitors. Although many building contractors use Lowe's or Home Depot's programs for purchasing materials, many are loyal to other local businesses. The Internet is also becoming more and more of a competitor for firms in the home improvement industry.

Lowe's has not been performing as well as Home Depot. Note in Exhibit 6 that Home Depot has more than double the earnings of Lowe's and has a significantly higher earnings per share (EPS).

Home Depot

Founded in 1978 in Atlanta, Georgia, Home Depot is the largest home improvement chain in the world with over 2,250 retail stores in all 50 U.S. states, Puerto Rico, Guam, Canada, and Mexico. Home Depot is the fourth-largest retailer in the USA and fifth largest in the world. Home Depot offers a large assortment of home improvement products at fair prices. At a Home Depot, customers can find experienced sales associates in flooring, plumbing, electrical, gardening, and many other areas. Home Depot offers in-home installation to any customers who do not wish to install their own flooring, sinks, and other products. Major brands that are sold exclusively at the Home Depot include: BEHR Paint, Chem-Dry, Homelite, Martha Steward Living, Thomasville, among others. Home Depot recently replaced its old slogan: "You can do it. We can help" with: "More saving. More doing."

Home Depot is expanding its Internet business rather than expanding overseas, according to its CEO Frank Blake. Blake's comments came on the heels of Home Depot closing all seven of its China-based stores in October of 2012, after a failed expansion attempt there. Blake also offered the comment that Home Depot can live without having a brick-and-mortar presence in Brazil or any other country. But what they cannot afford to do is *not* be the best home improvement company in the world. Home Depot still sells products to Chinese customers on its website, 360buy.com, and is continually looking to partner with other e-commerce sites. The trend toward shopping from the Internet, in particular mobile applications on smartphones, is a trend Home Depot plans to capitalize on.

True Value

Headquartered in Chicago, Illinois, True Value has more than 5,000 independent retail hardware store locations worldwide. All of the stores are independently owned and operated by regular people. True Value has 12 regional distribution centers and more than 3,000 associates. True Value supports True Value Hardware and Home Center Stores as well as Grand Rental Station, Party Central, Taylor Rental, Induserve Supply, and Home & Garden Showplace.

Home & Garden Showplace acts as the garden center identity of True Value. There are more than 260 Home & Garden Showplace stores across the USA. Like all True Value stores, each store is independently owned and purchases retail merchandise through True Value's distribution centers and various True Value buying programs. The other divisions of True Value total more than 400 stores across the USA and are also all independently owned and operated.

All True Value store locations vary from small towns to large cities and stores reflect various sizes. Each respective independent retailer offers product categories and assortments tailored to local customer needs allowing customers across the country to shop a business that is uniquely focused on local needs. According to True Value, all its well-stocked stores offer superior customer service and a compelling shopping experience.

From 2009 to 2011, True Value reported net revenues of $1.8 billion in each of the three years, and long-term debt of $121, $137, and $143 million, respectively. In 2012, True Value's stated goals were to grow retail sales by 2 percent, expand by adding another 100 stores with more than 1.1 million square feet of selling space, investing in a new Farm and Ranch category, and providing shareholders with a dividend for the sixth consecutive year.

Ace Hardware

Founded in 1924 in Oak Brook, Illinois, Ace Hardware was named after Ace fighter pilots of World War I who overcame all odds in fighting for the Allied Forces. Ace has more than 4,400 locations across the USA and operates locations in 60 different countries. Ace competes much like True Value with all stores being independently owned and operated. Ace, like True Value, markets this strategy as enabling business owners to tailor their products to meet local customers' needs more effectively. Also, it places more of the initial capital risk on the franchisee and offers many products under the Ace brand. This store branding generally produces higher margins than selling brand-name items.

According to *Franchise Times*, Ace is the sixth largest franchise operation in the world trailing only McDonald's, 7-Eleven, KFC, Subway, and Burger King. Ace has received numerous awards in customer satisfaction. J.D. Power and Associates ranked Ace the highest in customer satisfaction among home improvement stores for five years in a row from 2007 to 2011; Ace was ranked the same by *Business Week* from 2008 to 2010.

Future

Lowe's opened its first store in Canada in 2007 and currently has 34 stores across the country. Lowe's has recently shown interest in acquiring Rona, a Canadian-based chain that has 79 big box locations and more than 700 smaller stores. A takeover by Lowe's would provide a substantial footprint in Canada, but in September 2012, Lowe's withdrew its friendly offer for Rona and some analysts believe that the move is a precursor to a hostile takeover. Lowe's activity in Canada is a stark contrast to announced store closings in its U.S. operations. Lowe's is closing 20 underperforming U.S. stores in 2012 and reducing its pace of growth.

U.S. big box stores such as Target are popping up all over Canada, and these retailers are basking in the benefits of pent-up Canadian consumer demand. However, setting up and operating a retail store in Canada poses some unique challenges because all packaging and labeling must follow Canadian rules, including using both English and using metric weights and measurements. Stores operating in Quebec must also be able to serve customers in French, have French on all signage and advertising material, and produce French versions of web pages. With the Canadian population approximately one-tenth of that of the USA, the added administrative and legal expenses have often been deemed by large retailers to not be worth the effort. Should Lowe's expand into Canada, or renew efforts to acquire Rona?

Would you recommend Lowe's enter the Australian market with 150 new stores as currently planned in an attempt to match Ace's international presence. Lowe's currently operates two different size stores to better serve local markets. However both of these store fronts are similar in size. Would you recommend Lowe's reduce the size of its stores to match Home Depot, and even smaller stores such as Ace and True Value?

Analysts believe Lowe's will hold steady in coming years in terms of revenues and profitability, primarily because the housing market and general economy are improving. But shareholders and investors expect more than flat earnings.

What do you think are the best strategies for Lowe's to outperform Home Depot as the housing market and world economy continue to improve? Design a three-year plan for CEO Niblock with specifics outlying the appropriate course of action.

United Parcel Service, Inc., 2013

www.ups.com, UPS

Headquartered in Atlanta, Georgia, United Parcel Service (UPS) is the largest logistics company in the world based on revenue and package volume. Operating in the air delivery and freight services industry, UPS delivers packages up to 150 pounds across the USA and to 220 countries worldwide. Serving customers since 1907, UPS operates a fleet of more than 100,000 cars, vans, trucks, tractors, and motorcycles and more than 530 aircraft and uses 35,000 transport cargo containers. In addition, UPS has 39,100 drop boxes, 2,100 customer centers, 4,700 independently owned UPS stores, and perhaps most importantly, 83,900 drivers.

UPS's Q2 of 2013 revenue increased 1.2 percent as the company's daily international package volume improved 5 percent and domestic volume grew 1.9 percent from the prior year. For Q2, UPS delivered 15.7 million packages per day, an increase of 2.3 percent over the prior-year period. The company's domestic Q2 revenue improved to $8.24 billion, up 2.3 percent; domestic revenue per piece was up 0.3 percent. The company's daily package volume improved 1.9 percent, compared to the same period last year, driven by residential shipments from e-commerce customers. Declining letter volume led to a 1.5 percent drop in Next Day Air. For Q2 of 2013, UPS's international daily package volume grew 5.0 percent and revenue increased 1.6 percent to $3.06 billion. Daily Export shipments increased 5.0 percent, led by Europe and Asia. Customers globally continue to trade down to slower moving solutions, resulting in a 3.4 percent decline in UPS's export revenue per piece.

UPS global air network is headquartered in Louisville, Kentucky, where the company can process 416,000 packages per hour! UPS has numerous other airport hubs across the USA and in Germany, Canada, Hong Kong, Singapore, Taiwan, and China. A member of both the Dow Jones 30 Composite and Dow Transportation indexes, UPS employs 399,000 full-time employees (323,000 in the USA and 76,000 outside of the USA). A total of 349,000 of these employees were members of a union. UPS operates under three principle segments: (1) U.S. Domestic Package, (2) International Package, and the newer and much smaller (3) Supply Chain and Freight segment. UPS's major competitors are FedEx and the United States Postal Service.

Although UPS's primary business is the timely delivery of packages and documents, the company has extended its capabilities in recent years to encompass the broader spectrum of services known as supply chain solutions, such as freight forwarding, customs brokerage, fulfillment, returns, financial transaction, and even repairs. UPS is also a leading provider of less-than-truckload transportation services.

Copyright by Fred David Books LLC. (Written by Forest R. David)

History

UPS was founded in 1907 by teenagers Claude Ryan and Jim Casey as the American Messenger Company in Seattle, Washington. The teenagers saw an opportunity with the limited telephone and automobile options to run errands, carry notes, and make home deliveries for drugstores. The early strategy of UPS was to compete on cost by offering the best prices while maintaining dependable and courtesy service.

By 1913, the telephone was more common, reducing the need for messenger services, so the American Messenger Company changed its name to Merchant's Parcel Delivery and merged with Evert McCabe's to focus almost exclusively on package delivery of drugstore and grocery store packages to people's homes. The acquisition of Evert McCabe's added motorcycles and a single Ford Motel T to the business, so by 1916 "UPS" had an expanding fleet of delivery vehicles. Soon the company expanded its business to also deliver department store packages to homes in the Seattle area.

Geographic expansion continued throughout the 1920s, including air service, and the company expanded into cities along the entire Pacific coast. The company changed its name to United Parcel Service and moved its headquarters to New York. UPS continued to grow over the years, and in 1975 the company began serving Toronto, Canada, marking the first time UPS served customers outside the USA. The following year, UPS began operations in Germany, and then in 1989, with the purchase of a British document company, UPS was serving customers virtually worldwide.

The 1990s saw UPS adapt well to the growing presence of electronic data and package tracking. The company moved its headquarters to Atlanta, Georgia, in 1994. Operating as a private company for the first 90 years, UPS offered 10 percent of its stock to the public in 1999, giving the company the ability to raise capital through equity and make acquisitions more easily.

UPS's 1999 acquisitions of Challenge Air resulted in UPS becoming the largest air cargo carrier in Latin America. Other acquisitions in the United Kingdom and Poland expanded UPS's global reach throughout Europe. UPS has to date acquired more than 40 companies ranging from shipping and trucking to finance and international trade services.

UPS's supply chain solutions capabilities are available to clients in over 220 countries and territories. UPS's 2012 revenues increased 1.9 percent to $54.1 billion, but net income decreased 78.8 percent to $807 million. The company's 2012 return on assets (ROA) dropped to 2.2 percent, from 11.1 percent the prior year. In 2013, UPS is trying to close on its acquisition of the European firm, TNT Express, for $6.8 billion, which will expand its presence in the European and Asian markets.

Internal Issues

Vision and Mission

The UPS vision is provided on the company website, as follows:

> Our goal is to synchronize the world of commerce by developing business solutions that create value and competitive advantages for our customers.

> The company provides the following mission statement on its website:

> Mission: What We Seek to Achieve

- Grow our global business by serving the logistics needs of customers, offering excellence and value in all that we do.

- Maintain a financially strong company—with broad employee ownership—that provides a long-term competitive return to our shareowners.

- Inspire our people and business partners to do their best, offering opportunities for personal development and success.

- Lead by example as a responsible, caring, and sustainable company making a difference in the communities we serve.

> UPS describes the nature of its business in the following way:

> As the world's largest package delivery company and a leading global provider of specialized transportation and logistics services, UPS continues to develop the frontiers of logistics, supply chain management, and e-Commerce … combining the flows of goods, information, and funds.

Sustainability

UPS provides an elaborate Sustainability Report on its website, after giving the following sustainability statement:

> UPS is committed to operating our business in a socially, environmentally and economically responsible manner. We publish annual programs on goal attainment.

UPS was recently recognized as one of only 10 U.S. corporations to receive an A+ for superior transparency from companies registered with the Global Reporting Initiative (GRI). "One of the guiding principles to UPS's sustainability strategy is our commitment to transparency," UPS Chairman and CEO Scott Davis wrote in the organization's 2011 Sustainability Report. "We are disclosing more information than ever.... We have reported our five-year progress, successes and challenges. Now, we are focused ahead." Chief Sustainability Officer Scott Wicker reported that UPS now uses a "materiality matrix" to track how the company's interests match or differ from those of other stakeholders. A recent GRI report recognized UPS for (a) driving 85 million fewer miles, saving 8.4 million gallons of fuel and 83,000 metric tons of carbon dioxide emissions using advanced route-planning technology, (b) expanding telematics technology to eliminate more than 98 million minutes of engine idling time, saving 653,000 gallons of fuel, and (c) earning the highest Carbon Disclosure Project score among all U.S. companies, and tying with three others for the top score in the world.

Speaking at *Fortune's* Brainstorm Green 2012, UPS Chief Operations Officer (COO) David Abney said: "Sustainability is a way of life. It's always high on our radar screen." The UPS Foundation, the charitable arm of the firm, recently started a long-term effort to support employee volunteer activities to plant more than 1 million trees around the world, beginning with tree-planting initiatives in China, Canada, Haiti, the Netherlands, Norway, Russia, Uganda, and the United States by the end of 2013. UPS was rated #1 in *Fortune* Magazine's 2012 "World's Most Admired" for the Delivery Industry.

Culture and Ethics

The company code of ethics is provided at on the UPS website under Governance Documents (http://www.investors.ups.com/phoenix.zhtml?c=62900&p=irol-govhighlights).

Additionally, UPS has what it refers to on its website as a "distinctive culture." The statement reads as follows:

> We believe that the dedication of our employees results in large part from our distinctive "employee-owner" concept. Our employee stock ownership tradition dates from 1927, when our founders, who believed that employee stock ownership was a vital foundation for successful business, first offered stock to employees. To facilitate employee stock ownership, we maintain several stock-based compensation programs.

The company's brown-clothed drivers and employees and brown trucks symbolize the firm's commitment to a distinctive culture, anchored by employee ownership of a large part of the firm. UPS is highly unionized.

After donating $150,000 to the Irving-based Boy Scouts of America, UPS announced recently that the company will no longer fund them, until gay scouts and leaders are allowed to be members. The *Atlanta Business Chronicle* reported that the Gay & Lesbian Alliance Against Defamation (GLADD) said it was told by UPS that under revised guidelines of The UPS Foundation, it will not support organizations that are unable to attest to having a policy that aligns with the foundation's nondiscrimination policy.

Organizational Structure

Among UPS's top eight corporate executives, there are two women and one African American. Exhibit 1 reveals UPS's current organizational chart. Note the company uses a divisional-by-geographic region structure.

Strategy

During calendar 2012, UPS opened 12 new dedicated health care facilities on four continents, bringing the company total to 37. UPS strives daily to provide customers competitive prices and excellent services worldwide. UPS benefits from several key trends in the marketplace, including (a) expansion of global trade, (b) growth in emerging markets,

EXHIBIT 1 UPS's Organizational Structure

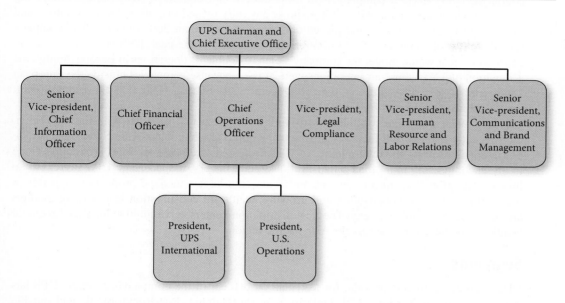

Source: Based on information on the company's website.

(c) outsourcing, (d) retail commercial growth, and (e) increasing trade across borders. These are reasons why UPS recently acquired Italy-based Pieffe Group, a pharmaceutical logistics company that helps enhance the trust that European-based pharmaceutical and biotech companies have for UPS to handle the delivery of its products and services. UPS's principle strategy is to identify successful businesses outside the USA and form alliances with them in the hope of eventually acquiring them. China remains the key emerging market with air hubs in Shanghai and Shenzhen. Recent UPS Chinese investments include adding intra-Asia and around-the-world flight frequencies, striving to serve customers more efficiently in Asia, Europe, and around the world. UPS already services more than 40 Asian nations through more than 20 alliances. In Vietnam alone, since a 2010 alliance, UPS's volume in that country has doubled.

UPS plans to increase its market share in Europe, where half of all its international revenue derives from; strong growth is expected to continue in Germany, the United Kingdom, France, Italy, Spain, and the Netherlands. Despite lingering economic troubles in Europe, UPS is expanding its European Air hub in Cologne, Germany, by 70 percent to a total capacity of 190,000 packages per hour. For reference, this is still well short of the hub in Louisville, Kentucky, that processes more than 400,000 packages per hour. The expansion of the Cologne hub was completed in 2013. In addition, the 2012 acquisition of Belgium-based Kiala S.A. enables e-commerce retailers to offer its customers timely delivery to retail locations or people's homes.

UPS's 2009 acquisition of Turkey-based Unsped Paket Servisi has led to double-digit growth to and from that country. South and Central America economies are growing along with Mexico, and UPS is currently well positioned in those countries as well.

Effective December 31, 2012, UPS instituted a 4.5 percent rate increase for UPS Air and U.S.-originating International Services shipments. UPS breaks the rate increase into two parts: a 6.5 percent base rate on UPS Air and International Services minus a two percentage point reduction in fuel surcharges on such shipments. UPS Ground base rates also increased on that date, by 5.9 percent, mitigated by a single percentage point reduction in the fuel surcharge, resulting in an average 4.9 percent price hike. UPS Next Day Air Freight, Second Day Air Freight, and Three-Day Freight rates for shipments among U.S., Canadian, and Puerto Rican locations also rose by 4.9 percent.

UPS recently closed on its $6.58 billion deal to acquire TNT Express N.V., an international courier delivery-services company with headquarters in Hoofddorp, Netherlands. Competing primarily with FedEx and DHL, TNT Express has fully owned operations in 65 countries and delivers documents, parcels, and pieces of freight to more than 200 countries. The company recorded sales of more than €7.2 billion in 2011. As part of the deal, UPS is seeking to avoid concessions that would hinder the company's plan to double its operations in Europe through the acquisition of TNT whose air operations were at issue because companies outside the European Union cannot hold stakes of more than 49 percent in airlines. The TNT Express deal will mark the largest acquisition ever for UPS.

To expand its global healthcare distribution facility network in the Asia Pacific region, UPS recently opened new facilities in Hangzhou and Shanghai, China, and Sydney, Australia. These openings bring the total number of UPS dedicated healthcare facilities around the globe to 36, encompassing more than a half-million square meters of space. The UPS strategy is to invest in its global healthcare network to become the largest medical products transporter in the world. Increased globalization and growing healthcare consumption in emerging markets are the impetus for this strategy. The new distribution centers serve multinational and regional healthcare manufacturers across the Asia Pacific region.

Segments

UPS's top 20 customers account for less than 10 percent of the company's revenue. UPS has major air hubs in Hartford, CN; Ontario, CA; Philidalphia, PA; Rockford, IL and outside of the United States in Hamilton, Ontario; Cologne, Germany; Shanghai China; Shenzhen, China; Raipei, Taiwan; Incheon, South Korea; Hong Kong, and Singapore. UPS reports revenues and operating profits in three different segments: (1) U.S. Domestic Package, (2) International Package, and (3) Supply Chain and Freight. Exhibit 2 reveals that UPS's Supply Chain and Freight division accounts for about 17 percent of all revenue and 10 percent of all operating profits. Also note that more than half of UPS's profits come from its U.S. operations, so there is a lot of room for growth globally, which is another reason for the TNT Express acquisition. But South America, Australia, and to a lesser degree, Asia, are not UPS strongholds to say the least.

EXHIBIT 2 Selected Income Statement Data

	Years Ended December 31,				
	2012	2011	2010	2009	2008
Revenue:					
U.S. Domestic Package	$ 32,856	$ 31,717	$ 29,742	$ 28,158	$ 31,278
International Package	12,124	12,249	11,133	9,699	11,293
Supply Chain & Freight	9,147	9,139	8,670	7,440	8,915
Total revenue	**54,127**	**53,105**	**49,545**	**45,297**	**51,486**
Operating expenses:					
Compensation and benefits	33,102	27,575	26,557	25,933	29,826
Other	19,682	19,450	17,347	15,856	20,041
Total operating expenses	52,784	47,025	43,904	41,789	49,867
Operating profit (loss):					
U.S. Domestic Package	459	3,764	3,238	1,919	823
International Package	869	1,709	1,831	1,279	1,246
Supply Chain and Freight	15	607	572	310	(450)
Total operating profit	1,343	6,080	5,641	3,508	1,619

Source: 2012 Form 10K, p. 21.

EXHIBIT 3 U.S. Domestic Package Operations

	Year Ended December 31,			% Change
	2012	2011	2010	2012/2011
Average Daily Package Volume (in thousands):				
Next Day Air	1,277	1,206	1,205	5.9%
Deferred	1,031	975	941	5.7%
Ground	11,588	11,230	11,140	3.2%
Total Avg. Daily Package Volume	13,896	13,411	13,286	3.6%
Average Revenue Per Piece:				
Next Day Air	$ 19.93	$ 20.33	$ 19.14	(2.0)%
Deferred	13.06	13.32	12.50	(2.0)%
Ground	7.89	7.78	7.43	1.4%
Total Avg. Revenue Per Piece	$ 9.38	$ 9.31	$ 8.85	0.8%
Operating Days in Period	252	254	253	
Revenue (in millions):				
Next Day Air	$ 6,412	$ 6,229	$ 5,835	2.9%
Deferred	3,392	3,299	2,975	2.8%
Ground	23,052	22,189	20,932	3.9%
Total Revenue	$ 32,856	$ 31,717	$ 29,742	3.6%

Source: UPS 2012 *Form 10K,* p. 24.

U.S. Domestic Package Segment

UPS's U.S. Domestic Package division reported revenues of $32.8 billion in 2012, up from $31.7 billion in 2011, a 3.6 percent increase. Operating profits decreased around 87.8 percent during this same time period. This division of UPS focuses on timely delivery of small packages across the USA offers customers same-, next-, two-, and three-day alternatives or standard shipping depending on how fast the delivery is needed. UPS delivers more than 11 million packages daily in the USA with most being delivered between one to three business days. Within this segment, UPS has an alliance with the United States Postal Service (USPS) called SurePost, a service for customers who are sending or receiving nonurgent lightweight shipments in which UPS handles the long haul ground transportation and USPS makes the final home delivery. Note in Exhibit 3, UPS's "Next Day Air" and their "Deferred" business reported declines in business in 2012 versus 2011. Note in Exhibit 2 the 88 percent drop in UPS's 2012 operating profit in their domestic segment.

International Package Segment

UPS's International Package Reporting Segment includes all package operations outside the USA. This segment offers a wide selection of price and delivery options, such as Express Plus, Express, and Express Saver for urgent shipments. More traditional shipments that do not require express service can use UPS Worldwide. In addition, customers in the USA, Mexico, Canada, and Europe can use UPS Transborder Standard delivery services for its shipments.

Among the international regions served, Europe is the largest UPS customer and accounts for around half of the company's international revenue. UPS expects Europe to continue being a large revenue source in the future because of the fragmented nature of the market in Europe and the fact that exports make up a large part of Europe's gross domestic product (GDP). Additionally, UPS's TNT Express acquisition will nearly double UPS's business in Europe.

Asia is somewhat of a new frontier for UPS, but that continent offers the fastest growth opportunities. Note in Exhibit 4 that UPS's international segment reported quite a few negative numbers in 2012 versus 2011.

EXHIBIT 4 **International Package Operations**

	Year Ended December 31,			% Change
	2012	2011	2010	2012/2011
Average Daily Package Volume (In Thousands):				
Domestic	1,427	1,444	1,403	(1.2)%
Export	972	942	885	3.2%
Total Avg. Daily Package Volume	2,399	2,386	2,288	0.5%
Average Revenue Per Piece:				
Domestic	$ 7.04	$ 7.17	$ 6.66	(1.8)%
Export	36.88	37.85	36.77	(2.6)%
Total Avg. Revenue Per Piece	$ 19.13	$ 19.28	$ 18.31	(0.8)%
Operating Days in Period	252	254	253	
Revenue (In Millions):				
Domestic	$ 2,531	$ 2,628	$ 2,365	(3.7)%
Export	9,033	9,056	8,234	(0.3)%
Cargo	560	565	534	(0.9)%
Total Revenue	$12,124	$12,249	$11,133	(1.0)%
Operating Expenses (In Millions):				
Operating Expenses	$11,255	$10,540	$ 9,302	6.8%
Defined Benefit Plan Mark-to-Market Charge	(941)	(171)	(42)	
Adjusted Operating Expenses	$10,314	$10,369	$ 9,260	(0.5)%
Operating Profit (In Millions) and Operating Margin:				
Operating Profit	$ 869	$ 1,709	$ 1,831	(49.2)%

Source: UPS's 2012 *Form 10K*, p. 28.

Supply Chain and Freight

UPS's Supply Chain and Freight segment includes logistics services, UPS freight business, and financial offerings through UPS Capital. As of December 2012, UPS managed supply chains in more than 195 countries and territories with more than 35 million square feet of distribution space. Because of the complex nature of supply chains, UPS offers the following services: freight forwarding, customs brokerage, logistics and distribution, UPS freight, and UPS capital.

UPS is the second-largest freight forwarding company in the USA and is among the top six internationally. A freight forwarder or forwarding agent is a person or company that organizes shipments for individuals or companies to get large orders from the manufacturer to market or final point of distribution. A forwarder is not typically a carrier but is an expert in supply chain management. In other words, a freight forwarder is a "travel agent" for the cargo industry, or a third-party logistics provider. Thus, instead of transporting cargo, UPS oftentimes just facilitates the movement of cargo ranging from raw agricultural products to manufactured goods. Cargo can travel on a variety of carrier types, including ships, airplanes, trucks, railroads, or all of these modes, and oftentimes not on UPS-owned assets.

UPS Freight is the long-haul segment of UPS providing long distance transportation of packages in all 50 states, several U.S. territories, and Mexico. UPS Capital aids customers in export and import financing, as well as protecting goods and payment solutions.

Finance

For calendar 2012, UPS's overall volume grew 2.8 percent. The company's business-to-business volume showed no growth, partly due to the increasing migration of traditional retail to on-line retail. UPS's income statements are provided in Exhibit 5. Balance sheets are provided in Exhibit 6.

EXHIBIT 5 UPS's Income Statements (in millions, except per share amounts)

	Years Ended December 31,		
	2012	2011	2010
Revenue	$ 54,127	$ 53,105	$ 49,545
Operating Expenses:			
Compensation and benefits	33,102	27,575	26,557
Repairs and maintenance	1,228	1,286	1,131
Depreciation and amortization	1,858	1,782	1,792
Purchased transportation	7,354	7,232	6,640
Fuel	4,090	4,046	2,972
Other occupancy	902	943	939
Other expenses	4,250	4,161	3,873
Total Operating Expenses	52,784	47,025	43,904
Operating Profit	1,343	6,080	5,641
Other Income and (Expense):			
Investment income	24	44	3
Interest expense	(393)	(348)	(354)
Total Other Income and (Expense)	(369)	(304)	(351)
Income Before Income Taxes	974	5,776	5,290
Income Tax Expense	167	1,972	1,952
Net Income	$ 807	$ 3,804	$ 3,338
Basic Earnings Per Share	$ 0.84	$ 3.88	$ 3.36
Diluted Earnings Per Share	$ 0.83	$ 3.84	$ 3.33

Source: UPS's 2012 *Form 10K*, p. 58.

EXHIBIT 6 UPS's Balance Sheets (in millions)

	December 31,	
	2012	2011
ASSETS		
Current Assets:		
Cash and cash equivalents	$ 7,327	$ 3,034
Marketable securities	597	1,241
Accounts receivable, net	6,111	6,246
Deferred income tax assets	583	611
Other current assets	973	1,152
Total Current Assets	15,591	12,284
Property, Plant and Equipment, Net	17,894	17,621
Goodwill	2,173	2,101
Intangible Assets, Net	603	585
Investments and Restricted Cash	307	303
Derivative Assets	535	483
Deferred Income Tax Assets	684	118
Other Non-Current Assets	1,076	1,206
Total Assets	$ 38,863	$ 34,701

(*continued*)

EXHIBIT 6 Continued

	December 31,	
	2012	2011
LIABILITIES AND SHAREOWNERS' EQUITY		
Current Liabilities:		
Current maturities of long-term debt and commercial paper	$ 1,781	$ 33
Accounts payable	2,278	2,300
Accrued wages and withholdings	1,927	1,843
Self-insurance reserves	763	781
Other current liabilities	1,641	1,557
Total Current Liabilities	8,390	6,514
Long-Term Debt	11,089	11,095
Pension and Postretirement Benefit Obligations	11,068	5,505
Deferred Income Tax Liabilities	48	1,900
Self-Insurance Reserves	1,980	1,806
Other Non-Current Liabilities	1,555	773
Shareowners' Equity:		
Class A common stock (225 and 240 shares issued in 2012 and 2011)	3	3
Class B common stock (729 and 725 shares issued in 2012 and 2011)	7	7
Additional paid-in capital	—	—
Retained earnings	7,997	10,128
Accumulated other comprehensive loss	(3,354)	(3,103)
Deferred compensation obligations	78	88
Less: Treasury stock (1 and 2 shares in 2012 and 2011)	(78)	(88)
Total Equity for Controlling Interests	4,653	7,035
Noncontrolling Interests	80	73
Total Shareowners' Equity	4,733	7,108
Total Liabilities and Shareowners' Equity	$ 38,863	$ 34,701

Source: UPS's 2012 *Form 10K,* p. 57.

External Issues

Changing Consumer Behavior

More and more people are no longer willing to pay more for an overnight delivery service. They would rather wait another day for the goods to be delivered, instead of paying a premium for quicker delivery. This change in customer preferences and attitude appears to be permanent, regardless of the economy.

Companies Exporting More

UPS anticipates that most high-tech companies expect to export more cell phones, tablets, and other electronics over the next several years to growing middle-class populations in developing nations. The Barack Obama administration has a goal to double exports by 2015. Scott Davis, UPS chief executive officer, is on the President's Export Council and has touted free trade agreements as critical for boosting U.S. exports and the economy. A free trade agreement between the USA and Panama will soon go into effect, following on the heels of such agreements with Colombia and South Korea. Some analysts expect that high-tech product sales and shipments are expected to grow by 22 percent in India, the Middle East, and Africa over the next three to five years. Those same analysts expect such sales increases to range from 18 percent in Brazil and 19 percent in the rest of South America to 15 percent in Eastern Europe, 13 percent in Korea, and 8 percent in China and in other Asian nations.

Many executives are planning to modify its distribution networks to handle more volume at East Coast ports once a wider Panama Canal is opened to bigger ships around 2015. Quite a few companies plan to shift from air to ocean freight when that happens, so many East Coast ports are heavily investing in dredging and other projects to be able to accept bigger ships. Both FedEx and UPS have already seen a shift in demand for shipping products cheaper, such as by sea, rather than premium-priced express air services, because of the weakening global economy.

Internet and Catalog Purchasing

About 40 percent of total UPS shipments are from businesses-to-consumers, compared with about one-third from a few years ago. It expects these shipments, typically from large catalog or Internet retailers, to grow to half of all packages during the holiday season. Consumers are expected to do more and more online shopping. UPS and its smaller rival FedEx can benefit twice when consumers shop online: UPS ships the gift to the receiver, and it also ships the unwanted presents that are later returned. Online sales are expected to grow at four times the pace of traditional retail sales in 2012. This trend is helping UPS's earnings despite weakness in trade between businesses. Business-to-business shipments are typically between a manufacturer and a retailer, and are closely tied to industrial production.

Competitors

As indicated in Exhibit 7, UPS competes with USPS and FedEx. Another large competitor is DHL International. Exhibit 6 reveals that UPS generates more revenue per employee than either the USPS or FedEx. Note how low the USPS is on revenue per employee.

USPS

USPS incurred a record loss of $15.9 billion for its fiscal year 2012, which it blamed primarily on a mandate to set aside billions of dollars for a retirement heath fund. The USPS loss included $11.1 billion in defaulted payments it owes to "prefund" health benefits for future retirees. Postal officials have complained for years about these prepayments, which are required by Congress, to pay for future retirees. The USPS points out that other federal agencies do not have similar mandates for prefunding.

The $15.9 billion loss was more than triple the $5.1 billion in loss the USPS posted in the prior year. Fredric Rolando, president of the National Association of Letter Carriers, recently blamed the congressionally mandated prefunding for the bulk of USPS's financial woes. The USPS is highly unionized.

USPS has been struggling with declines in mail revenue for a variety of reasons, including everyone's transition to e-mail. To combat massive losses, USPS plans to cut 150,000 workers through 2015, reduce existing staffers' work hours and hike the price on first-class stamps by 3 cents to 49 cents. USPS officials are considering a scale back of delivery service to five days, ceasing its low-volume, low-revenue, Saturday service. The notion of five-day service however is intensely unpopular in Congress and unlikely to prevail.

EXHIBIT 7 Comparing UPS to Rivals

	USPS	UPS	FedEx
Number of Employees	551K	222K	230K
Net Income ($)	—	3.26B	2.02B
Revenue ($)	65.7B	53.66B	42.95B
Revenue ($)/Employee	119K	241K	187K
EPS Ratio ($)	—	3.38	6.40
Market Capitalization	—	66.8B	27.1B

EPS, earnings per share.

Unlike other federal agencies, the USPS does not technically receive taxpayer support, though it has borrowed $15 billion from the U.S. Treasury.

FedEx

Headquartered in Memphis, Tennessee, FedEx is the world's number-1 express transportation provider, delivering about 3.5 million packages daily to more than 220 countries and territories from about 2,000 FedEx Office shops. FedEx owns and operates a fleet of about 690 aircraft and more than 50,000 motor vehicles and trailers. To complement its express delivery business, FedEx Ground provides small-package ground delivery in North America, and less-than-truckload (LTL) carrier FedEx Freight hauls larger shipments. FedEx Office Stores offer a variety of document-related and other business services and serve as retail hubs for other FedEx units.

FedEx is spending $100 million to build a new 134,000-square-meter international express and cargo hub, to be up and running at the airport in Pudong, China, by 2017. FedEx said it will be capable of handling 36,000 parcels and documents per hour. The new facility's annual sorting capacity may reach more than 90 million items, meeting the demand in the next 20 years.

Shanghai is forecast to become the world's top air cargo hub by 2015, with a throughput of more than more than 5 million tons. Major domestic airlines have based 80 percent of its freight capacities at the Pudong airport, which now ranks number 3 by cargo turnover, after Hong Kong and Memphis.

FedEx is expanding its services across the USA, Canada, and Mexico. The company is expanding its Priority next-day services in its FedEx Freight segment by opening a new service center in Rochester, New York, that will cater to 13 U.S. and Canadian markets dealing in cross-border shipments to and from Toronto and Montreal. In Mexico, FedEx recently added two new service centers—one each in Culiacán and Silao—to strengthen its freight network in northwestern and north central part of Mexico. FedEx is building a new hub in Guangzhou, China, for catering to 100 new Chinese cities within the next five years.

As for acquisitions, FedEx completed the take over of Polish courier company, Opek Sp. z o.o., and French B2B Express transportation company, TATEX, both in mid-2012. Then FedEx acquired Rapidão Cometa, a Brazilian transportation and logistics company. These acquisitions should provide FedEx greater operational efficiencies, provide a competitive edge, generate significant long-term synergies, support international business growth, and drive higher profitability.

DHL

Headquartered in Germany and privately held, DHL is a gigantic package delivery company that constitutes the express delivery and logistics business segments of its parent, Deutsche Post. DHL is a leader in the worldwide market for express delivery services, operating through four divisions: Express, Global Forwarding and Freight Forwarding, Mail, and Supply Chain. (Mail service in Germany is handled by the Deutsche Post brand; DHL handles all of the Global Mail business). DHL's Express courier service network spans more than 220 countries and territories using a fleet of 32,000 vehicles and about 250 aircraft. DHL's supply chain division maintains some 23 million square meters (almost 250 million square feet) of warehouse space.

The Future

UPS is on the hunt for businesses similar to TNT Express in Europe that it recently acquired. Similar businesses in Asia, Australia, South America, and Africa would enable UPS to extend its services globally. More than half of UPS's revenues still comes from the USA, yet 95 percent of the world's population lives outside the USA. More and more people are buying and selling online, which is a key positive trend for UPS in the future. A key threat however is that rival FedEx is aggressive and savvy and also on the hunt to make acquisitions. FedEx does not like being number 2 in the global packaging business. UPS needs a clear strategic plan going forward.

United States Postal Service, 2013

www.usps.com

An agency of the federal government, the United States Postal Service (USPS) is responsible for providing postal service to citizens at a uniform cost regardless of geography. Founded in 1775 in Philadelphia during the Second Continental Congress, the USPS appointed Benjamin Franklin as the first Postmaster General. USPS has not received any taxpayer funds since the early 1980s, with the exception of minor subsidies for costs associated with overseas voters. USPS hit an all-time high in mail volume in 2006. As of 2012, the USPS employs more than 574,000 workers and operates more than 218,000 vehicles, which makes USPS the largest operator of a single vehicle fleet in the world. The USPS fiscal year ends on September 30.

USPS is the only delivery service that reaches every address in the nation, 151 million residences, businesses, and post office boxes. USPS receives no tax dollars for operating expenses and relies on the sale of postage, products, and services to fund its operations. With 32,000 retail locations and the most frequently visited website in the federal government (usps.com), USPS has an annual revenue of more than $65 billion and delivers nearly 40 percent of the world's mail.

USPS is the third-largest civilian employer in the USA, trailing only the federal government and Walmart. USPS delivers around 660 million pieces of mail to 142 million delivery points each day. USPS operates 31,000 post offices and has more than 218,000 vehicles currently in operation. However, USPS recorded a loss of $15.9 billion in its fiscal year 2012 that ended September 2012. Of that amount, the accrual for mandated retiree health benefits payments accounted for a whopping $11.1 billion. USPS has defaulted on these obligations to conserve cash to fund operations, demonstrating the depth and urgency of its current financial predicament.

In August 2013, the USPS launched major changes to its Priority Mail services, with improved features including free insurance, improved USPS Tracking™ and 1-, 2-, or 3-day-specific delivery. These new services are expected to generate more than a half a billion dollars in new revenue over the next year.

Copyright by Fred David Books LLC. (Written by Forest R. David)

History

After being founded in 1775, the USPS grew steadily, mainly distributing mail by horseback, stagecoach, and steam engine in the early years. Steamboats were used as early as 1813 to carry mail between locations where roads did not exist. With the growing railroad industry, USPS began using the Pennsylvania Line in 1832, and by 1838, rail became the primary means of long distance travel of mail.

The first stamps were issued in 1847, and the 5-cent stamp paid for a letter with a weight of 1 ounce or less and traveling less than 300 miles. The 10-cent postage stamp would mail a letter greater than 300 miles or up to two ounces. Also in 1847, the U.S. Mail Steamship Company acquired the rights to deliver mail from New York City to New Orleans and Havana. In the following years, other steamship companies obtained rights to deliver mail along with several railroads.

In 1896, USPS started rural free delivery and with the inauguration of parcel post in 1913, significantly increased the volume of mail shipped nationwide and also increased the efficiency of mail shipments. The new developments led to mail-order business increasing and allowed customers in rural areas access to many products they otherwise would have had to travel to a city to obtain. In 1918, USPS started air-mail service, which previously was handled by the U.S. Army Air Service. This service started with 4 pilots and expanded to 36 pilots within the first year of operation. Domestic air mail was abandoned in 1975 and international air mail in 1995 because air mail became standard for most all long-distance mail.

A few key USPS dates:

1775—Benjamin Franklin appointed first Postmaster General by the Continental Congress

1847—U.S. postage stamps issued

1860—Pony Express began

1963—ZIP code inaugurated

1970—Express Mail® began experimentally

1971—United States Postal Service® began operations

1983—ZIP+4® code began

1992—Self-adhesive stamps introduced nationwide

1994—USPS launched public Internet site

2006—Postal Accountability and Enhancement Act signed

2007—"Forever" stamp issued

2008—Competitive pricing for expedited mail began

Internal Issues

Vision and Mission

USPS has a mission statement posted on its website:

> The Postal Service shall have as its basic function the obligation to provide postal services to bind the Nation together through the personal, educational, literary, and business correspondence of the people. It shall provide prompt, reliable, and efficient services to patrons in all areas and shall render postal services to all communities.

The organization has no vision statement.

Organizational Structure

USPS uses a divisional-by-geographic organizational structure, as illustrated in Exhibit 1. Note there are seven regions that report to the USPS Chief Operations Officer.

Governance

The USPS has an 11-member Board of Governors that functions as its governing body. The Board has responsibilities comparable to the board of directors of a publicly held corporation. The USPS Board is made up of nine Governors appointed by the President of the USA with the advice and consent of the Senate. No more than five Governors can be members of the same political party. The Board currently has three seats vacant. The other two members of the Board are the Postmaster General and the Deputy Postmaster General. The Governors appoint the Postmaster General, who serves at their pleasure without a specific term of office. The Governors, together with the Postmaster General, appoint the Deputy Postmaster General.

Segments

By law, USPS is divided into two categories termed *market-dominate* and *competitive*. However, in practice, USPS operates as one integrated network throughout the USA, accounting for 95 percent of all revenue with only 5 percent being generated internationally. In analyzing revenue sources, it is best to compare the different services USPS offers. The bulk of all revenue is generated from three different services: (1) First Class Mail, (2) Standard Mail, and (3) Packages. Minority revenue sources are international, periodicals, mailboxes, money orders, insurance on packages, delivery confirmation, and other add-on fees for shipping letters and parcels.

Exhibit 2 reveals revenues based on product categories. The largest generator of revenue for USPS comes from First Class Mail, generating around 45 percent. Like most product categories, First Class Mail has experienced declining revenues for the last several years, falling

EXHIBIT 1 USPS's Organizational Structure

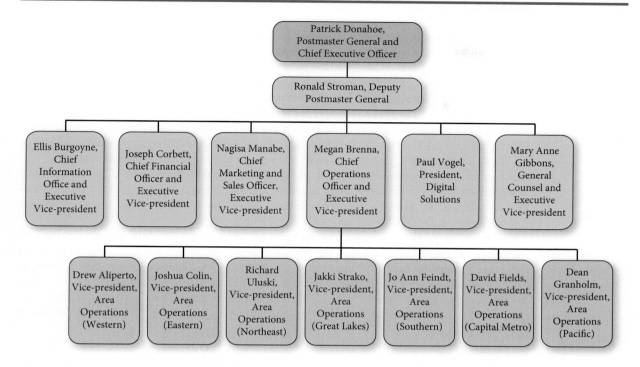

Source: Based on information at www.usps.com.

another 4 percent in 2012. First Class Mail is an option for customers wishing to send letters, bill payments, postcards, or any other flat-letter object up to 13 ounces for both domestic and international delivery.

Standard Mail accounts for around 25 percent of total revenue for the USPS and is the second-largest source of sales. Unlike First Class Mail, Standard Mail has not experienced volume declines in each of the last several years. In fact, Standard Mail actually saw a marginal increase in revenue from 2010 to 2011 but experienced a small decrease from 2011 to 2012 as

EXHIBIT 2 A Product Breakdown of USPS Revenues

Operating Revenue by Service Line[*] (Dollars in millions)	2012	2011	2010
First-Class Mail[1]	$ 28,867	$ 30,030	$ 32,111
Standard Mail[2]	16,428	17,175	16,728
Shipping & Packages[3]	11,596	10,670	10,156
International	2,816	2,585	2,388
Periodicals	1,731	1,821	1,879
Other[4]	3,785	3,430	3,790
Total Operating Revenue by Service Line	**$ 65,223**	**$ 65,711**	**$ 67,052**

[*]Note: The totals for certain mail categories for the prior year have been reclassified to better reflect classifications used in the current year. These reclassifications did not impact total operating revenue for the prior year.
[1]Excludes First-Class Mail Parcels.
[2]Excludes Standard Mail Parcels.
[3]Includes Priority Mail, Parcel Select Mail, Parcel Return Service Mail, Standard Parcels, Package Service Mail, First-Class Mail Parcels, First-Class Package Service, and Express Mail.
[4]Includes P.O. Box Services, Certified Mail, Return Receipts, Insurance, Other Ancillary Fees, Shipping and Mailing Supplies, and other operating revenue.

Source: Annual Report, page 26.

revealed in Exhibit 2. Standard Mail includes all mail weighing less than 16 ounces that is not required to be sent first class. Generally Standard Mail (sometimes called bulk) is limited to advertising and is considered by many to be junk mail. Interestingly enough, even though this category of mail has held constant revenues, the USPS often will delay delivery of such mailings to better manage overtime for postal employees.

Lastly, shipping and packages make up approximately 18 percent of total revenue and has experienced marginal sales growth in each of the last three years. Competing in the parcel business is one of the USPS strategic objectives and an area it is actively trying to increase its market share in respect to three primary competitors: (1) United Parcel Service (UPS), (2) FedEx, and (3) DHL. The parcel business is broken down into several subcategories: First Class Packages, Priority Mail, and Express Mail. First Class Packages, sometimes simply called "Package Services" are available for parcels up to 70 pounds and include library mail and media mail that are shipped at a discounted rate. Priority Mail is offered for both domestic and 190 international destinations. Domestic Priority Mail is marketed to have packages delivered in two to three business days and is also available for packages up to 70 pounds. Customers may also select several flat rate boxes under the USPS's policy "if it fits, it ships."

The USPS international category includes all services that are shipped to destinations outside the USA, and its revenues are recorded under this single category, instead of under the other categories to avoid duplication of revenues. As indicated in Exhibit 2, international services account for around 4 percent of all revenue in 2012. Periodicals accounted for 2.5 percent of all revenues in 2012 and miscellaneous services such as post office boxes, insurance, delivery confirmation, money orders, and others accounted for close to 6 percent of total revenues in 2012.

Exhibit 3 reveals total volume of each of the respective service categories. Note that Standard Mail, or junk mail, accounts for around 50 percent of all volume done by the USPS. This mail ships at a reduced rate and increases stops at residential homes who may not be receiving any First Class Mail or packages on the particular day they receive Standard Mail. Compounding this problem, First Class Mail volume is expected to continue to decline as people increasingly use e-mail, text messages, and pay bills online. First Class Mail still remains the most profitable category for the USPS, but for each unit drop in First Class Mail it is expected Standard Mail volume will have to increase by three units to breakeven. One area that the USPS is actively attempting to expand on is that of packages, which currently only account for 2 percent of all volume done yet make up 18 percent of revenue.

EXHIBIT 3 A Product Breakdown of USPS Volume (pieces in millions)

Volume by Service Line[*] (pieces in millions)	2012	2011	2010
First-Class Mail[1]	68,696	72,522	77,592
Standard Mail[2]	79,496	83,957	81,841
Shipping & Packages[3]	3,502	3,258	3,057
International	926	987	594
Periodicals	6,741	7,077	7,269
Other[4]	498	496	506
Total Volume by Service Line	**159,859**	**168,297**	**170,859**

[*]Note: The totals for certain mail categories for the prior year have been reclassified to better reflect classifications used in the current year. These reclassifications did not impact total mail volume for the prior year.
[1]Excludes First-Class Mail Parcels.
[2]Excludes Standard Mail Parcels.
[3]Includes Priority Mail, Parcel Select Mail, Parcel Return Service Mail, Standard Parcels, Package Service Mail, First-Class Mail Parcels, First-Class Package Service, and Express Mail.
[4]Includes the U.S. Postal Service's Mail and Free Mail provided to certain groups.
Source: Annual Report, page 27.

Employment

USPS employees are grouped into three major categories: (1) mail carriers, (2) mail handlers, and (3) clerks. Mail carriers, broken down into city and rural carriers, often called *mailmen*; they prepare and deliver mail to city and rural areas alike. City carriers work 40 hours a week and are paid automatic overtime for any hours more than 40. At times, they are required to work "under time" when mail demand is not as high and supervisors predict the carriers designated route will take less than 8 hours. In avoiding overtime fees, it is common for supervisors to use a technique called "pivoting" in which bulk mail and advertisements are set aside for a day or two if mail loads are expected to be below the normal 8-hour work day those days.

Rural carriers do not operate under a 40-hour work week because their mail demand is more difficult to predict. Instead, they are evaluated on a period of two to four weeks, and overtime assessments are made after completion of the period. Both city and rural carriers are required to work during daylight and darkness in any kind of weather and be able to carry parcels up to 80 pounds, although the maximum shipment weight the USPS allows is 70 pounds.

The other two principle jobs employed by the USPS are mail handlers and clerks. Mail handlers are the people behind the scenes who separate, load, and unload mail and parcels based on ZIP code and station. They generally work at the plants or larger mail facilities. Clerks are the individuals one will encounter on a trip to the post office. They handle customer service and sort mail at the local post office for the carriers.

The USPS workforce is heavily unionized and is represented by four labor unions: (1) American Postal Workers Union (APWU), (2) National Association of Letter Carriers (NALC), (3) National Rural Letter Carriers Association (NRLCA) and (4) National Postal Mail Handlers Union (NPMHU). All jobs at USPS that do not fall in one of the three main categories of employment are covered with the clerks by the APWU. Some union policies are quite restrictive on the postal service. For example it is standard policy after a letter carrier has served 360 days, they can be represented by the NALC for reduced working hours, or for "just cause" any issue determined to be unfavorable by the union member. As mail volume continues to decrease to the increased use of e-mail, bank draft billing, and the transition from junk mail advertising to Internet, USPS is constantly downsizing operations, replacing many positions with machines and consolidating mail routes.

The number of career USPS full-time employees dropped from 583,908 in 2010, to 557,251 in 2011, and then to 528,458 in 2012. That is a 4.6- and 5.2-percent drop in the number of employees annually.

Finance

Chief Financial Officer Joseph Corbett said: "Our recent work hour reductions reflect our efforts to improve productivity and to respond to the decline in mail volume. Since 2000, we have reduced work hours by a cumulative total of 504 million work hours, equivalent to 286,000 employees, or $21 billion in expense savings each year. At the end of 2012 fiscal year, we (USPS) have reached our statutory debt ceiling of $15 billion for the first time. "Our liquidity continues to be a major concern and underscores the need for passage of legislation that gives the Postal Service a more flexible business model to improve its cash flow," said Corbett. "Despite reaching the debt limit, the Postal Service mail operations and delivery continue as usual and employees and suppliers continue to be paid on-time."

The USPS 2012 *Annual Report* states: "In the absence of legislative reform that enables meaningful operational changes and cost reductions, the Postal Service could incur annual losses as great as $18.2 billion by 2015. Fortunately, such an undesirable outcome is avoidable."

As revealed in Exhibit 4, USPS reported a record net loss of $15.9 billion in its fiscal year ending September 2012, but $11.1 billion were payments to prefund retiree healthcare benefits, a policy that USPS—but no other government agency—is required to do. Setting aside the $11.1 billion in prefunded retiree healthcare benefits, the $15.9 billion loss would have totaled a $4.8 billion loss, which came on the heels of a $5.1 billion loss in fiscal 2011. Note in Exhibit 5 that USPS owns about $44 billion in buildings and equipment.

In line with the five-year plan, the USPS was able to grow its package services business by $926 million or 8.7 percent. Despite the gains the package business, revenues derived from first

EXHIBIT 4 **The USPS Income Statements**

(Dollars in millions)	Years Ended September 30,		
	2012	2011	2010
Operating revenue	$ 65,223	$ 65,711	$ 67,052
Operating expenses			
Compensation and benefits	47,689	48,310	48,909
Retiree health benefits	13,729	2,441	7,747
Workers' compensation	3,729	3,672	3,566
Transportation	6,630	6,389	5,878
Other	9,187	9,822	9,326
Total operating expenses	80,964	70,634	75,426
Loss from operations	**(15,741)**	**(4,923)**	**(8,374)**
Interest and investment income	25	28	25
Interest expense	(190)	(172)	(156)
Net loss	**$ (15,906)**	**$ (5,067)**	**$ (8,505)**

Source: 2012 *Annual Report*, page 78.

EXHIBIT 5 **The USPS Balance Sheets**

(Dollars in millions)	September 30,	
	2012	2011
Current Assets		
Cash and cash equivalents	$ 2,319	$ 1,488
Receivables:		
Foreign countries	509	669
U.S. Government	142	154
Other	308	255
Receivables before allowances	959	1,078
Less: Allowance for doubtful accounts	41	37
Total receivables, net	918	1,041
Supplies, advances and prepayments	126	120
Total Current Assets	**3,363**	**2,649**
Noncurrent Assets		
Property and Equipment, at Cost		
Buildings	24,452	24,263
Equipment	20,143	20,409
Land	2,919	2,952
Leasehold improvements	1,208	1,112
	48,722	48,736
Less: Allowances for depreciation and amortization	30,187	29,023
	18,535	19,713
Construction in progress	328	624
Total Property and Equipment, Net	**18,863**	**20,337**
Other Assets—Principally Revenue Forgone Receivable	385	427
Total Noncurrent Assets	**19,248**	**20,764**
Total Assets	**$ 22,611**	**$ 23,413**

EXHIBIT 5 Continued

	September 30,	
(Dollars in millions)	2012	2011
Current Liabilities		
Compensation and benefits	$ 1,856	$ 2,390
Retiree health benefits	11,205	7
Workers' compensation	1,337	1,255
Payables and accrued expenses:		
Trade payables and accrued expenses	1,159	1,041
Foreign countries	583	652
U.S. Government	93	119
Total payables and accrued expenses	1,835	1,812
Deferred revenue-prepaid postage	4,014	3,497
Customer deposit accounts	1,210	1,386
Outstanding postal money orders	677	688
Prepaid box rent and other deferred revenue	475	502
Debt	9,500	7,500
Total Current Liabilities	**32,109**	**19,037**
Noncurrent Liabilities		
Workers' compensation costs	16,230	13,887
Employees' accumulated leave	1,855	2,030
Deferred appropriation and other revenue	194	326
Long-term portion capital lease obligations	410	460
Deferred gains on sales of property	313	345
Contingent liabilities and other	846	768
Debt	5,500	5,500
Total Noncurrent Liabilities	**25,348**	**23,316**
Total Liabilities	**57,457**	**42,353**
Net Deficiency		
Capital contributions of the U.S. government	3,132	3,132
Deficit since 1971 reorganization	(37,978)	(22,072)
Total Net Deficiency	**(34,846)**	**(18,940)**
Total Liabilities and Net Deficiency	**$ 22,611**	**$ 23,413**

Source: 2012 *Annual Report*, page 79.

class mail and standard mail dropped 3.9 and 4.3 percent, respectively. USPS did mention that the rate of the decline in First Class Mail did slow in 2012 possibly as a result of the strategy to encourage increased First Class postal usage. In total, operating revenue change over the two most recent years was relatively stable, totaling $65.2 billion in 2012 compared to $65.7 billion in 2011.

Exhibit 6 provides a breakdown of operating expenses for the USPS over the three most recent years. Compensation and benefits alone accounted for 73 percent of 2012 revenues. Of the $47.7 billon in compensation and benefits expense, around 12.3 percent or $5.9 billion were paid to USPS retirees. Also note, the $11.1 billion prefunding for workers' health benefits accounted for 17 percent of total revenue in 2012; however no payments were made to this category in 2011. In total, the $15.9 billion loss in 2012 accounted for 125 percent of total revenues.

Strategy

In 2011, the Postmaster General outlined the following key objectives to improve the financial position of USPS: "1) become a leaner, smarter, faster organization, 2) compete for the package business, 3) strengthen our business-to-customer channel, and 4) improve our customers

EXHIBIT 6 USPS Breakdown of Expenses

Operating Expenses (dollars in millions)	2012	2011	2010
Compensation and Benefits	$ 47,689	$ 48,310	$ 48,909
Retiree Health Benefit Premiums	2,629	2,441	2,247
PSRHBF Prefunding	11,100	-	5,500
Workers' Compensation	3,729	3,672	3,566
Transportation	6,630	6,389	5,878
Other Expenses	9,187	9,822	9,326
Total Operating Expenses	**$ 80,964**	**$ 70,634**	**$ 75,426**

Source: 2012 *Annual Report*, page 31.

experience." To better execute on the objectives, in 2012 USPS released a five-year plan on how to achieve the stated objectives.

Become Leaner, Smarter, and Faster
In an attempt to become leaner, smarter, and faster, USPS plans to redesign its operating network by closing many of its mail-processing facilities and distribution plants as well as rescheduling of transportation routes. Currently there are 461 mail-processing locations considered for consolidation. The first phase of 140 consolidations through 2013 and a second phase expected to begin in 2014 of 89 additional consolidations is expected to save $2.1 billion annually. Also, USPS plans to reduce retail window hours at local post offices but currently it does not plan on eliminating any post office locations. This strategy is aimed mostly at smaller post offices in rural areas. Around 13,000 such rural post offices are expected to become part-time post offices, operating with the reduced hours. Once the plan of reducing operating hours in rural post offices is fully implemented in 2014, savings are expected to total $500 million annually. In addition, USPS plans to increase private sector partnerships such as its current partnership with UPS and use tools such as Six Sigma to help better train employees on methods of reducing waste and improving customer service. In total, direct savings of $2.6 billion annual are expected under the strategies in this category.

Compete for the Package Business
USPS is increasing its efforts to compete for the more profitable package business by improving its tracking of packages and scanning of barcodes, so that every package has 100 percent visibility. Currently, customers can track UPS and FedEx packages in close to real time. However, USPS customers experience long delays, and it is not uncommon for a package to show it left the facility and the next update not be available until it arrives at its final destination. In addition to tracking, USPS plans to fully implement package intercept technologies in which commercial customers can request packages be redirected or returned before the final day of delivery is made. USPS also plans to better market its flat-rate package options to customers and introduce MetroPost, which will offer same-day delivery in select metro areas.

Strengthen the Business-to-Customer Channel
USPS plans to strengthen its business-to-customer channels, but no specifics are available other than "to develop new platforms" that will help small businesses more effectively manage its direct-mail campaigns, but USPS does not state what these programs are, what they cost, or any time table. Other ideas include the continuation of marketing of the Every Door Direct Mail campaign and a continuation of encouraging businesses to use the mail as a means of communication.

Improve Customers' Experience
To improve customer service, USPS plans to offer better mobile applications to facilitate online shopping through usps.com. In addition, USPS hopes to implement what it calls Village Post Offices, which are partnerships with retailers in which customers can pick up their packages there, reducing the dependence on the traditional post office.

External Issues

Besides the movement away from mail to e-mail, other external issues harming the USPS bottom line include the economic recession, increased number of delivery points, increasing fuel prices, increasing healthcare premiums, and the increasing use of other electronic communications reducing the volume of First Class Mail. Union relations and obligations are severely hurting USPS, as is increasing competition from traditional competitors such as DHL, UPS, and FedEx. Competition also is coming from growing wireless communication networks around the world including e-mail, text messages, television, radio, electronic funds transfers, and much more. It is expected that First Class and Standard Mail volumes will continue to decreases in the presence of growing wireless communication networks, and the package business is expected to remain highly competitive.

Congressional Oversight

With USPS being a government agency, it faces heavy regulatory requirements. Often the variety of stakeholders USPS serves has interests that are in conflict with one other. However, in the latest review of the Oxford Strategic Consulting ranking of best post offices in the world, USPS ranked number one overall for providing ease of access to service, efficiency, and public trust.

USPS faces many challenges in respect to governmental oversight. Laws such as the Postal Accountability and Enhancement Act, which became law in 2006, dictate and limit USPS's ability to institute new services or products, develop new revenue streams, and manage its cost structure. One of the key price limit issues is based on the rate of inflation measured by the consumer price index (CPI). Many of the USPS higher costs such as wages, health benefit programs, and retirement benefits tend to rise more quickly than the CPI and thus place tremendous pressure on USPS because it is unable to effectively keep pace with increased costs. Further limiting management in its development of new services or products also cuts into the bottom line.

USPS's business plan includes the following actions that require legislative action:

- Allowing the Postal Service to determine delivery frequency
- Allowing the Postal Service to offer non-postal products and services
- Developing a more streamlined governance model for the Postal Service that would allow for quicker pricing and product decisions
- Instructing arbitrators that, during labor negotiations, they must take into account the financial condition of the Postal Service when rendering decisions
- Resolving the overfunding of the Postal Service's obligation to the Federal Employees' Retirement System (FERS).

Unions

Virtually all employees of the USPS are represented by labor unions, which represent employees heavily on cost of living adjustments. Unions also limit the ability of the USPS to reduce the size of the labor force despite declining volumes and less workers being needed. The USPS is thus forced to offer early retirement or reduce time worked and avoid paying overtime at all costs. USPS is under constant threat of union strikes and has no assurances that contracts will be able to be negotiated even though arbitration.

Competitors

As indicated in Exhibit 7, USPS competes with UPS and FedEx. Note that Exhibit 7 reveals that UPS generates more revenue per employee than either the USPS or FedEx. Note how low the USPS ratio is regarding revenue per employee, suggesting high inefficiency.

UPS

Headquartered in Atlanta, Georgia, UPS is the largest logistics company in the world based on revenue and package volume. Operating in the air delivery and freight services industry, UPS delivers packages up to 150 pounds across the USA and to 220 countries worldwide. Serving customers since 1907, UPS operates a fleet of more than 100,000 cars, vans, trucks, tractors, and

EXHIBIT 7 A Financial Synopsis of USPS, UPS, and FedEx

	USPS	UPS	FedEx
Number of Employees	551K	222K	230K
Net Income ($)	—	3.26B	2.02B
Revenue ($)	65.7B	53.66B	42.95B
Revenue ($)/Employee	119K	241K	187K
EPS Ratio ($)	—	3.38	6.40
Market Cap.	—	66.8B	27.1B

EPS, earnings per share.

motorcycles and more than 530 aircraft and uses 35,000 transport cargo containers. In addition, UPS has 40,000 drop boxes, 1,000 customer centers, 4,700 independently owned UPS stores, and perhaps most importantly, 86,300 drivers.

UPS global air network is headquartered in Louisville, Kentucky, where the company can process 416,000 packages per hour! UPS has numerous other airport hubs across the USA and in Germany, Canada, Hong Kong, Singapore, Taiwan, and China. A member of both the Dow Jones 30 Composite and Dow Transportation indexes, UPS employs more than 220,000 full-time employees. UPS operates under three principle segments: (1) U.S. Domestic Package, (2) International Package, and the newer and much smaller (3) Supply Chain and Freight segment. UPS's major competitors are FedEx and the USPS.

FedEx

Headquartered in Memphis, Tennessee, FedEx is the world's number-1 express transportation provider, delivering about 3.5 million packages daily to more than 220 countries and territories from about 2,000 FedEx Office shops. FedEx owns and operates a fleet of about 690 aircraft and more than 50,000 motor vehicles and trailers. To complement its express delivery business, FedEx Ground provides small-package ground delivery in North America, and less-than-truckload (LTL) carrier FedEx Freight hauls larger shipments. FedEx Office stores offer a variety of document-related and other business services and serve as retail hubs for other FedEx units.

FedEx is expanding its services across the USA, Canada, and Mexico. The company is expanding its Priority next-day services in its FedEx Freight segment by opening a new service center in Rochester, New York, that will cater to 13 U.S. and Canadian markets dealing in cross-border shipments to and from Toronto and Montreal. In Mexico, FedEx recently added two new service centers—one each in Culiacán and Silao—to strengthen its freight network in northwestern and north central part of Mexico. FedEx is building a new hub in Guangzhou, China, for catering to 100 new Chinese cities within the next five years.

DHL

Although headquartered in Germany and privately held, DHL is a gigantic package delivery company that constitutes the express delivery and logistics business segments of its parent, Deutsche Post. DHL is a leader in the worldwide market for express delivery services, operating through four divisions: Express, Global Forwarding and Freight Forwarding, Mail, and Supply Chain. (Mail service in Germany is handled by the Deutsche Post brand; DHL handles all of the Global Mail business). DHL's Express courier service network spans more than 220 countries and territories using a fleet of 32,000 vehicles and about 250 aircraft. DHL's supply chain division maintains some 23 million square meters (almost 250 million square feet) of warehouse space.

The Future

To combat massive losses, the USPS desires to cut 150,000 workers through 2015, reduce existing staffers' work hours, and hike the price on first-class stamps by three cents to 49 cents. USPS officials are also considering a scale back of delivery service to five days, ceasing its low-volume, low-revenue, Saturday service, saving $3 billion annually. The notion of five-day service however is unpopular in Congress and unlikely to prevail. Various USPS unions also oppose that and other similar moves.

Some analysts suggest that USPS needs a strategy to eventually require Americans to go to the local post office to obtain their mail, rather than USPS bringing mail to everybody everywhere, and to require many of those persons to also have post office boxes. Delivering mail to everyone's home at the top of every mountain and the end of every river perhaps is just not necessary in this day and time of e-mail and wireless communication. Some analysts believe a transition to phasing out USPS drivers and requiring everyone to have their own post office box could enable a drop in first class stamps to 17 cents, in contrast to USPS's current strategy of seemingly going up annually on postage rates. Analysis is needed to determine the feasibility of such as strategy. The actual number of post offices in the USA has dropped minutely from 27,077 in 2010 to 26,755 at fiscal year end 2012.

A recent bill introduced in Congress by Rep. Darrell Issa (R-Calif.) proposes a USPS centralized delivery system to transition away from traditional curbside or door-to-door delivery to mandate that Americans pick up their mail in personal boxes at their residences. USPS has already begun offering centralized mail delivery for new community developments, industrial parks, and shopping malls. Some of the following facts are prompting this transition:

- Currently 35 million residences and businesses get mail delivered to their doorstep.
- It costs $353 per stop for a delivery in most American cities, taking into account such things as salaries and cost of transport. In contrast, curbside mail box delivery costs $224, while cluster boxes cost $160.
- Delivering mail is the agency's largest fixed cost — $30 billion. Ending such door deliveries would save $4.5 billion a year.

A bill may eventually be passed because the USPS continues to bleed. The agency lost $1.9 billion in Q2 of 2013, and $1.3 billion the previous quarter, compounding the problem of its considerable existing debt obligations.

USPS needs a clear strategic plan for the next three to six years to reverse monumental losses being incurred every quarter.

Crocs, Inc., 2013

www.crocs.com, CROX

Headquartered in Niwot, Colorado, Crocs, Inc. produces Crocs shoes, one of the most comfortable shoes ever designed. The awkward, even clumsy look of the Crocs shoe is offset by unbelievable comfort. One of the world leaders in casual footwear and apparel for men, women, and children, Crocs' shoes offer unmatched comfort derived from Croslite, a proprietary material that gives Crocs its soft, lightweight, waterproof, and odor-resistant qualities. Crocs are produced in many different styles, including boots, sandals, sneakers, flats, golf shoes, mules, and the popular original clog style, which is offered in more than 20 colors. Most of the other styles are limited to six colors or two-color combinations.

Crocs makes shoes specifically for companies in the healthcare and airline industries as well as for diabetic needs markets. Crocs has an alliance with the American Nurses Association, providing nurses with a 25 percent discount on shoes. Croc "Fuzz Collection" is designed with removable woolly liners that enable the shoe to be worn in winter or summer and the Jibbitz line, marketed primarily at children, manufactures declarative clip on items, often of Disney characters, for use in the ventilation holes of the shoes.

For the first time in its history, Crocs reported revenues of more than $1 billion at year-end 2011 and in 2012 celebrated its 10th birthday. To date, Crocs has sold more than 200 million pairs of shoes to customers in more than 90 countries through its retail stores, outlets, kiosks, and Web stores. Crocs Web stores operate under the brand names Crocs Work, Crocs Rx, Ocean Minded, and Jibbitz. As of year-end 2012, Crocs operated 121 kiosks, mostly in malls, 287 retail stores, 129 outlet stores, and 43 Web stores around the world. With more than 4,100 employees, Crocs manufactures its shoes mainly in Mexico, but it has other manufacturers in Italy, Romania, Bosnia and Herzegovina, and China.

Crocs' major rival, Columbia Sportswear Company (COLM), in late 2013 strengthened its presence in India by forming a distribution agreement with the New Delhi-based Chogori India Retail Ltd. As per the agreement, Chogori will serve as the sole distributor of Columbia's brands in India. Chogori owns 32 stores in 14 cities in India and is the exclusive retailer of Hi-Tec, the British footwear brand and American footwear brand, Crocs.

Copyright by Fred David Books LLC. (Written by Forest R. David)

History

Crocs was founded by friends Scott Seamans, Lyndon "Duke" Hanson, and George Boedecker Jr. in 2002 who desired to manufacture and distribute a foam clog style shoe they purchased from a company in Quebec, Canada, called Foam Creations. Foam Creations was marketing the shoe solely for use as a spa shoe, however, Boedecker, former Chief Operations Officer of International Sales at Quiznos Corp. in Canada, envisioned a brighter future for the product than limiting the marketing only to spas. Soon after securing rights to the shoe, Crocs unveiled its first official shoe under the Crocs brand named, called the *Beach*, at the 2002 Fort Lauderdale, Florida Boat Show. All 200 pairs available at the show were sold almost instantaneously. In 2004, Crocs officially purchased Foam Creations and with it rights to Croslite, the principle material that provides Crocs their comfort and medically beneficial properties. In 2006, Crocs expanded their brand by acquiring Jibbitz, from a stay-at-home mom, for $10 million, and acquired Bite Footware and Ocean Minded in 2007. In 2008, Crocs acquired two European based companies, Tidal Trade and Tagger.

In 2006, Crocs had an initial public offering (IPO), selling stock and raising funds through equity financing for the first time. Fortunately for Crocs, the 2006 IPO corresponded with the rapid advancement of sales in what *Salon* described as "somehow just caught fire" in reference to demand for the product. Crocs' stock price subsequently jumped from around $15 in 2006 to more than $75 by 2007, amounting to a 400-percent return for IPO investors in a little more than a year. However, along with increasing sales, critics of Crocs were coming equally as fast. In 2007, fashion consultant Tim Gunn was quoted in *Time Magazine* as saying "the Croc looks like a plastic hoof. How can you take that seriously?" In addition to *Time*, the *Washington Post* and *New York Times* printed critical reviews of the shoes. The ongoing negative press coincided with a weakening global economy and resulted in Crocs' stock price falling from $75 per share in late 2007 to under $0.80 per share by year-end 2008. Fortunately for Crocs, the stock and company rebounded an amazing 4,000 percent to $32 per share in 2011. Revenues also hit an all-time high of $1 billion at year-end 2011.

Along with Crocs robust rise as a powerful player in the shoe industry in 2006, the year witnessed other firms manufacturing or distributing products deemed "croc-offs" a unique play on words indicating Crocs patents were being infringed. In 2007, many of these "croc-offs" were seized in the Philippines and Denmark. However today, there are still competitors offering similar looking shoes under various brand names such as Airwalk, Poliwalks, and NothingZ. Unfortunately for Crocs, Inc., croc-offs can be purchased today at discount stores, beach stores, superstores, and similar shopping outlets.

Internal Issues

Mission Statement

According to the company website, Crocs provides two separate mission statements, one for Crocs, Inc. and one for Ocean Minded. Crocs' mission is: "To bring profound comfort, fun and innovation to the world's feet." Ocean Minded's mission is: "To become the global leader in sustainable lifestyle footwear, apparel and accessories whilst ensuring that the four pillars of the Ocean Minded brand—Quality, Authenticity, Responsibility and Community—resonate throughout our company, products, associates and actions."

Organizational Structure

Crocs' organizational structure consists of all white males, as indicated in Exhibit 1. Notice the firm operates using a division-by-region organizational design. Shares of Crocs' stock dropped 5.1 percent on 8-8-13 after Sterne Agee analysts downgraded the company to underperform, due to a perceived lack of talented top executives. The analysts also have concerns about Crocs' relationship with backjoy.com—which includes several former Crocs executives—calling it "too close for comfort."

EXHIBIT 1 Organizational Structure

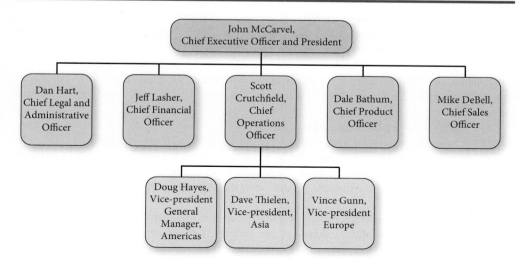

Source: Based on company documents.

Segments

In 2012, Crocs operated 43 company-owned Internet web stores, up from 42 and 37 the prior two years respectively. But the company's Internet sales dropped to 9.1 percent of total revenue in 2012 from 9.6 percent the prior year. For 2012, 57.5 percent of Crocs' revenues were derived from sales to wholesale distributors, down from 59.8 and 60.8 percent the prior two years, respectively. Distributors include Dick's Sporting Goods, Famous Footwear, Kohl's, and Nordstrom, but no single customer accounts for 10 percent or more of revenues.

By Product

Crocs footwear accounts for about 96 percent of total revenues, with accessories, primarily from Jibbitz, producing the remaining revenues. Footwear products are divided into four main categories: (1) Core-Comfort, (2) Active, (3) Casual, and (4) Style. Core-Comfort category includes the classic Crocs and all close derivatives from the original design. The Active product offerings are designed for activities such as boating, walking, and hiking. The remaining two categories of shoes are designed with style in mind, taking more of an equal role with comfort, and Crocs hopes this line of shoes will expand the pool of "wearing occasions" for customers.

Crocs also operates under three different brands: (1) Crocs, (2) Ocean Minded, and (3) Jibbitz. Although Crocs does not report revenues or operating incomes by brand, the three brands are quite distinct and even have their own mission statements. The Crocs brand is the traditional clog-looking shoe and in line with the Core-Comfort category. Crocs describes the Crocs brand shoe as being: innovative, fun, comfortable, and simple. Even going as far to state "in a world full of bells and whistles, less is more." Crocs' Ocean Minded brand, which was acquired in 2007 keeping the name Ocean Minded, includes the Active, Casual, and Style categories of shoes. The Ocean Minded brand specializes in ocean or water sports themed items. Flip flops, boat shoes, and shoes for surfing are all possible options. In addition, shoes with wooly liners, high-quality leather, hiking shoes, and more everyday shoes are also produced by Ocean Minded. Ocean Minded brand shoes have their own website at www.oceanminded.com. Finally, the Jibbitz brand produces accessories designed for use with Crocs brand shoes as well as a means to personalize purses, cell phone cases, beach bags, backpacks, and more. Jibbitz has contracts with Disney, Marvel, and Lego, among others to produce trademarked items.

By Region

Crocs' organizational structure is set up by geographic region, and so are the reporting business segments. As indicated in Exhibit 2, Crocs' revenues and operating incomes are reported under three segments: Americas, Europe, and Asia. Exhibit 2 provides a breakdown of the most recent financial information for Crocs. Note the company is doing well in all three geographic regions.

The Crocs' Americas segment includes all revenues in North and South America. Products are sold wholesale to sporting goods, department, and specialty retail stores as well as direct to the consumer through about 200 company-operated stores and Web stores. About 45 percent of all revenues are derived from the Americas segment, making it the largest of the three reporting segments. The bulk of business for Crocs is located outside the USA. Despite 45 percent of revenues being derived from the Americas, only 32 percent of operating income came from this segment.

Crocs' Asia segment has experienced stable total revenues each of the last three years, culminating with 38 percent of total revenues being derived from this segment in 2011. The Asian segment accounted for an impressive 51 percent of operating income in 2011. Locations included are Asia, Australia, New Zeeland, the Middle East, and South Africa. Products are sold in a similar manner as in the Americas. Crocs operated 198 company stores in Asia based on year-end 2010 data.

The European segment, which includes Russia, is the smallest Crocs segment based on revenues, operating income, and number of stores. In 2011, total revenues and operating income each accounted for around 17 percent of their respective measures. Like the Americas and Asia, products are sold to wholesale distributers in Europe. Crocs operated 35 direct-to-consumer stores as of year-end 2010 in European markets.

EXHIBIT 2 Crocs' Revenues by Channel

($ thousands)	Year Ended December 31, 2012	2011	Change %
Channel revenues:			
Wholesale:			
Americas	$ 235,988	$ 214,062	10.2%
Asia	298,350	259,104	15.1
Europe	110,947	124,995	(11.2)
Other businesses	574	191	200.5
Total Wholesale	645,859	598,352	7.9
Consumer-direct:			
Retail:			
Americas	196,711	174,840	12.5
Asia	143,062	111,650	28.1
Europe	35,052	20,167	73.8
Total Retail	374,825	306,657	22.2
Internet:			
Americas	63,153	59,175	6.7
Asia	15,999	11,012	45.3
Europe	23,465	25,707	(8.7)
Total Internet	102,617	95,894	7.0
Total revenues:	$ 1,123,301	$ 1,000,903	12.2%

Source: 2012 Form 10K, p. 28.

By Channel

As indicated in Exhibit 3, Crocs' revenue increased nicely in 2012 in all channels. Note in Exhibit 4 that Crocs reduced its number of kiosks in 2012 to 121 from 158 the prior year, but increased its number of retail stores and outlet stores to 287 and 129 respectively.

Finance

Crocs' stock price recently jumped 9 percent in one day after Goldman Sachs analyst Taposh Bari gave the creator of those colorful plastic shoes a "Buy" rating, saying that investors have misinterpreted the shoe brand as a fad. "We see Crocs as a lifestyle brand with global appeal that appears both proven and sustainable," he wrote in a note to investors. Crocs' stock hit a 52-week low price of $12 on November 15, 2012, but since then has increased to $18 in mid-2013. Crocs, Inc. has little debt and has more than $315 million in total cash, and a price-to-earnings to growth (PEG) ratio of only 0.90. All these factors indicate a stock that is undervalued. The company has never paid a cash dividend on shares of its stock.

As revealed in Exhibit 5, 2012 was the best year ever for Crocs with the company reporting revenues up 12.2 percent percent from 2011 to an all-time record of $1.12 billion and net income rose 17 percent to $131 million. The record growth was fueled by all three geographic operating segments and Crocs attention to focusing on selling prices, new product styles, forming new contracts with existing and new wholesale customers and a strong expansion of new Crocs stores. In addition, Crocs increased marketing efforts of Ocean Minded products to provide Crocs footwear options for all four seasons.

The balance sheets in Exhibit 6 reveal that Crocs' stockholders' equity increased 30 percent from 2011 to 2010 and an impressive 71 percent more than the two-year period ending in 2011. Crocs has acquired other firms over the years, but to their credit, the company has $0 goodwill on their balance sheet.

EXHIBIT 3 Crocs Income by Segment

($ thousands)	Year Ended December 31, 2012	Year Ended December 31, 2011	Change %
Revenues:			
Americas	$ 495,852	$ 448,077	10.7%
Asia	457,411	381,766	19.8
Europe	169,464	170,869	(0.8)
Total segment revenues	1,122,727	1,000,712	12.2
Other businesses	574	191	200.5
Total consolidated revenues	**$ 1,123,301**	**$ 1,000,903**	**12.2%**
Operating income:			
Americas	$ 85,538	$ 70,532	21.3%
Asia	140,828	123,918	13.6
Europe	21,678	37,106	(41.6)
Total segment operating income	248,044	231,556	7.1
Other businesses	(10,805)	(14,128)	(23.5)
Intersegment eliminations	60	66	(9.1)
Unallocated corporate and other	(91,125)	(86,415)	5.5
Total consolidated operating income	**$ 146,174**	**$ 131,079**	**11.5%**

Source: 2012 *Form 10K*, p. 33.

EXHIBIT 4 Crocs' Company-Owned Stores

	December 31, 2012	Opened	Closed	December 31, 2011
Type:				
Kiosk/Store in Store	121	39	(76)	158
Retail Stores	287	120	(13)	180
Outlet Stores	129	42	(5)	92
Total	**537**	**201**	**(94)**	**430**
Geography:				
Americas	199	44	(42)	197
Asia	241	94	(51)	198
Europe	97	63	(1)	35
Total	**537**	**201**	**(94)**	**430**

Source: 2012 *Form 10K*, p. 28.

Strategy

A competitive advantage for Crocs is the absence of any type of box packaging, saving millions on costs. Although revolutionary, Croslite remains cheaper to purchase and manufacture than other shoe materials like leather. Rival firms such as Deckers Outdoor and Timberland report cost of sales around 55 percent, whereas Crocs' cost of sales are about 42 percent.

One of the biggest changes Crocs undertook in the aftermath of the 99-percent stock depreciation was that the firm began producing their own footwear in their own facilities in Mexico, Italy, and China. Ultimately this reduced costs, provided Crocs with better quality control and enabled the company to significantly speed up production and delivery of products to customers. Crocs also expanded away from their traditional clog-style shoe into beachwear, hiking shoes, boats shoes, and other more casual and fashionable options.

EXHIBIT 5 Crocs' Income Statement

($ thousands, except share data)	For the Year Ended December 31,		
	2012	2011	2010
Consolidated Statements of Operations Data			
Revenues	**$ 1,123,301**	**$ 1,000,903**	**$ 789,695**
Cost of sales	515,324	464,493	364,631
Restructuring charges	—	—	1,300
Gross profit	607,977	536,410	423,764
Selling, general and administrative expenses	460,393	404,803	342,961
Restructuring charges	—	—	2,539
Asset impairments	1,410	528	141
Income (loss) from operations	146,174	131,079	78,123
Foreign currency transaction (gains) losses, net	2,500	(4,886)	(2,325)
Other income, net	(2,711)	(1,578)	(1,001)
Interest expense	837	853	657
Income (loss) before income taxes	145,548	136,690	80,792
Income tax (benefit) expense	14,205	23,902	13,066
Net income (loss) attributable to common stockholders	**$ 131,343**	**$ 112,788**	**$ 67,726**
Income (loss) per common share:			
Basic	$ 1.46	$ 1.27	$ 0.78
Weighted average common shares:			
Basic	89,571,105	88,317,898	85,482,055
Footwear unit sales	49,947	47,736	—
Average footwear selling price	21.55	20.04	—

Source: 2012 *Form 10K,* p. 24.

Crocs continues to expand globally. The company's unique products match well with consumer demand around the world, so there are numerous countries yet that Crocs can enter.

External Issues

The footwear industry is quite fragmented in the USA and Western Europe. Total footwear sales rose just under 5 percent in 2011 to $50.5 billion in the USA. Out of the main categories of footwear, fashion represented 48 percent, performance 27 percent, sports and leisure 13 percent, outdoor 8 percent, and work and occupational 4 percent. It is expected the leading area for growth the footwear industry in the USA and Western Europe resides in the fashion category. Markets in Asia and Eastern Europe are less developed and offer a wider range of product development and penetration strategies for firms to explore. Firms competing in the industry are increasingly expanding their product offerings. Nike, for example, is now well entrenched in the apparel business and more recently has expanded into producing golf clubs, watches, yoga mats, and other products in an attempt to grow revenues.

Shoe Composition: Health Concerns

The Swedish Society for Nature Conservation found in 2009 alarming concentrations of toxic chemicals in many popular plastic-based shoes, including flip flips, sandals, clogs, and other similar style shoes. Out of 27 shoes tested originating from the Philippines, India, Indonesia, South Africa, and other nations, 17 or 63 percent of the shoes tested contained high levels of phthalates. Although Crocs does not manufacture their shoes in any of the tested nations, many fake crocs illegally using Croc logos have historically been produced in the Philippines. The growing awareness of toxic chemicals in shoe production is of potential concern for all shoe manufacturers, including Crocs. But Crocs conceivably could turn this issue into a competitive

EXHIBIT 6 Consolidated Balance Sheets

($ thousands, except number of shares)	December 31, 2012	December 31, 2011
ASSETS		
Current assets:		
Cash and cash equivalents	$ 294,348	$ 257,587
Accounts receivable, net of allowances of $13,315 and $15,508, respectively	92,278	84,760
Inventories	164,804	129,627
Deferred tax assets, net	6,284	7,047
Income tax receivable	5,613	5,828
Other receivables	24,821	20,295
Prepaid expenses and other current assets	24,967	20,199
Total current assets	613,115	525,343
Property and equipment, net	82,241	67,684
Intangible assets, net	59,931	48,641
Deferred tax assets, net	34,112	30,375
Other assets	40,239	23,410
Total assets	**$ 829,638**	**$ 695,453**
LIABILITIES AND STOCKHOLDERS' EQUITY		
Current liabilities:		
Accounts payable	$ 63,976	$ 66,517
Accrued expenses and other current liabilities	81,371	76,506
Deferred tax liabilities, net	2,405	2,889
Income taxes payable	8,147	8,273
Current portion of long-term borrowings and capital lease obligations	2,039	1,118
Total current liabilities	157,938	155,303
Long term income tax payable	36,343	41,665
Long-term borrowings and capital lease obligations	4,596	—
Other liabilities	13,361	6,705
Total liabilities	**212,238**	**203,673**
Commitments and contingencies		
Stockholders' equity:		
Preferred shares, par value $0.001 per share, 5,000,000 shares authorized, none outstanding	—	—
Common shares, par value $0.001 per share, 250,000,000 shares authorized, 91,047,297 and 88,662,845 shares issued and outstanding, respectively, at December 31,2012 and 90,306,432 and 89,807,146 shares issued and outstanding, respectively, at December 31,2011	91	90
Treasury stock, at cost, 2,384,452 and 499,286 shares, respectively	(44,214)	(19,759)
Additional paid-in capital	307,823	293,959
Retained earnings	334,012	202,669
Accumulated other comprehensive income	19,688	14,821
Total stockholders' equity	617,400	491,780
Total liabilities and stockholders' equity	**$ 829,638**	**$ 695,453**

Source: Crocs 2012 *Form 10K,* p. F-4.

advantage by educating consumers because crocs are made of Croslite, which is a proprietary blend of materials the company does not disclose. Lack of transparency by Crocs in this regard could be a major problem for the firm. The chemicals associated with phthalates and PVC are believed to cause health complications including infertility, testicular problems, endocrine disorders, and possibly even cancer.

The Swedish Society for Nature Conservation has advised consumers to demand full disclosure of product information and to avoid products derived from PVC and phthalates. These chemicals are also currently used in many household products such as baby milk bottles, pacifiers, printer inks, nail polish, adhesives, and perfumes just to name a few. The USA and European Union have passed laws banning phthalate rich children toys. Walmart and Target are phasing out PVC in their packaging, as are various companies, including Nike. China and the Philippians still do not have laws in place regarding acceptable levels of these containments. It remains to be seen how companies such as Crocs will fare when their shoes possibly contain these pollutants, and even if they do not contain them, public perception may steer customers away, especially parents of young kids who are a primary target of Crocs.

Demographic and Economic Factors

China, Vietnam, Brazil, Nigeria, Nambia, and Chile are just a few among many countries in which Crocs shoes could be well received. Those countries have rapidly growing middle-class consumers looking for new and innovative products. As consumers worldwide become more health conscious and more interested in style and convenience, Crocs could take advantage of demographic trends. World economies are in general improving, which also bodes well for firms such as Crocs.

Competition

Crocs competes with Foot Locker, Timberland, Decker, Adidas, Columbia Sportswear (COLM), Skechers USA, Inc. (SKX), Wolverine World Wide (WWW), and Nike, as well as numerous smaller firms. Croc-off companies that produce and market imitation crocs are the company's primary competitors. It is difficult to determine names of firms producing the knock-off crocs that sell for less than $10, whereas authentic crocs sell for over $20 per pair.

Among competitors' price-to-earnings ratios in December 2012, Deckers was low at 10.2, compared to Nike at 17.4, and Wolverine World Wide and Adidas both above 15. Columbia Sportswear was nearly 17. Crocs had the lowest price earnings ratio at 8.8. Note in Exhibit 7 that Crocs' earnings per share (EPS) and revenue per employee lag far behind both Deckers and Nike. The latter ratio indicates that Crocs may have some internal efficiency problems, perhaps even too many employees. Note that Decker has less than one-half the employees of Crocs, but generates 27 percent more revenue.

Deckers Outdoor Corp.

Headquartered in Goleta, California, Deckers is publically traded on the NASDAQ and has enjoyed 35-percent increases in profits from 2009 to 2010 and 2010 to 2011. Deckers' acquisition of Sanuk in 2011 inflated company goodwill from $6 million to $120 million. Deckers

EXHIBIT 7 Crocs, Inc. versus Deckers Outdoor and Nike

	Crocs	Deckers	Nike
Price earnings ratio	8.8	10.2	17.4
Number of employees	4,157	1,900	44,000
Revenue ($)	1.1B	1.4B	43.8B
Revenue per employee	264K	736K	995K
Net income	140M	156M	2.14B
EPS	1.54	4.06	4.60
Book value	1.21B	1.34B	43.8B

EPS, earnings per share.
Source: Company documents.

designs, manufactures, and markets footwear and accessory luxury items ranging apparel to handbags. Deckers designs products for cold weather applications, hiking, amphibious footwear, and more. Deckers' popular UGG brand, accounted for 87 percent of 2011 revenues. Under the firm's Teva brand, Deckers offers what the company calls, rugged outdoor travel shoes. Other brands offered include Sanuk, TSUBO, Ahnu, and MOZO. These brands produce items ranging from high-end casual footwear to amphibious footwear products. To reduce Deckers' dependence on their UGG brand for revenue, Sanuk was purchased in 2011 for $120 million plus future payments for five years based on revenues the brand generates.

Deckers sells its products mainly through third-party retail stores, but they also own outlet stores, and in addition sell from the company website. Deckers' products are available worldwide in the United States, Europe, Canada, Australia, Asia, and Latin America. Deckers UGG brand, made with luxury sheepskin, is currently the company's most popular product. To maintain strong sales, Deckers introduces a consistent flow of new product variations in the fall and spring seasons, along with year-round styles. To expand the UGG Brand, Deckers is targeting men, expanding the brand globally, and creating additional products such as handbags to supplement the shoe sales. Pricing for the UGG brand is considered mid- to upper-priced luxury.

Teva and Sanuk are the two other principle brands offered by Deckers. The Teva brand has evolved from sports scandals to also include open- and closed-toe outdoor-themed footwear. In addition, the Teva brand has evolved to include light hiking, amphibious footwear, and travel shoes. Most recently, Deckers introduced an insulated boot under the Teva brand. Sanuk revolves almost entirely around the surf community.

Deckers' stock price hit its all-time closing high of $117.66 on October 28, 2011, but from there it has been a steep and rapid decline, down to its lowest level in three years, $28.63 on October 31, 2012. Since then, though, Deckers' stock has been increasing nicely.

Nike

Headquartered in Beaverton, Oregon, Nike specializes in the design and development of footwear, apparel, sports equipment, and accessories for men, women, and children worldwide. The company also markets their products to college and professional sports teams. Nike distributes products under the Converse, Chuck Taylor, All Star, Hurley, and One Star trademarks, among others.

The Hurley brand produces sandals and shoes designed for the surf boarding community, competes directly with Crocs Ocean Minded products. Nike's Cole Haan brand designs reflective shoes for night life and other evening outings best competing with the more stylish brands of shoes Crocs develops. Nike and Crocs both develop and market shoes for golfers.

Nike sells its products mainly through retail stores and the company website, but Nike has its own retail stores and outlet stores. To its credit and financial soundness, Nike has goodwill of only $201 million despite numerous acquisitions in Nike's history. Of late, however, Nike has been divesting brands. In late 2012, Nike sold its Cole Haan handbag and shoe brand to private equity firm Apax Partners for $570 million and also sold its Umbro football brand to Iconix Brand Group for $225 million.

Skechers USA

Headquartered in Manhattan Beach, California, Skechers' Chief Executive Officer Robert Greenberg leads this firm that designs and sells more than 3,000 styles of lifestyle and athletic footwear (oxfords, boots, sandals, sneakers, training shoes, and semi-dressy shoes) for men, women, and children. Skechers also offers fashion and street-focused footwear under the Marc Ecko, Zoo York, and Mark Nason brands. Its shoes are sold through department and specialty stores in more than 100 countries, as well as in some 330 company-owned concept and outlet stores and on its website. Sketchers footwear is manufactured primarily by Chinese contractors.

For the third quarter of 2012, Skechers sales grew 4.2 percent to $429.4 million from the prior-year quarter, reflecting excellent performance across company-owned retail businesses, domestic wholesale, and international distributors. The company's domestic wholesale sales were up 7.2 percent, reflecting a 9.1-percent increase in pairs shipped, coupled with a strong growth across kids and performance divisions. Sales grew 10.9 percent in the quarter for the company's international distributor, reflecting strong growth across Pan-Asian distributors, Middle East, Indonesia, Philippines, South Korea, Taiwan, New Zealand, and Australia.

However, international subsidiary sales declined 14.6 percent. On a combined basis, Skechers' retail business sales grew 13.9 percent. Domestic retail sales grew 13.2 percent, and the company added 23 new domestic and 4 new outside-U.S. stores.

The Future

If Croslite is indeed free of phthalates, then (a) a huge marketing campaign by Crocs may be worthwhile in the future to educate consumers, and (b) numerous health-related specialty areas exist for Crocs to develop new products. If Croslite is not free of phthalates, Crocs, Inc. should correct this problem as quickly as possible while the exact composition of its shoes is a secret.

Crocs could in some manner follow the lead of Nike and Deckers regarding (a) diversification into accessory items, (b) expansion into other countries, and (c) development of new products. There is nothing wrong with being a fast follower, as evidenced by firms such as Samsung doing quite well following Apple's first-mover advantage strategy. The Croslite material perhaps has many undiscovered, marketable applications, so the company could devote more resources to research and development to develop innovative new products.

It may be in Crocs' best interest to take legal action against croc-off imitation shoes, especially against firms that produce nearly identical-looking shoes. Despite this and other external threats, Crocs has performed admirably in recent years, but a clear strategic plan is still needed help assure continued success. Crocs plans to open about 90 new stores in 2013 but analysts question whether this is a desired strategy.

Develop a three-year strategic plan for Crocs based on sound strategic-management tools and techniques.

Snyder's-Lance, Inc., 2013

www.snyderslance.com, LNCE

Headquartered in Charlotte, North Carolina, Snyder's-Lance (LNCE) is the second largest salty snack maker in the USA behind PepsiCo's Frito-Lay. LNCE manufactures and markets snack foods throughout the USA and Canada, including pretzels, sandwich crackers, potato chips, cookies, tortilla chips, restaurant style crackers, nuts, and other snacks. LNCE brands include Snyder's of Hanover, Lance, Krunchers!, Cape Cod, EatSmart Naturals, Jays, Tom's, Archway, O-Ke-Doke, and Stella D'oro, along with a number of private label and third party brands. LNCE revenues for 2012 declined one percent to $1.618 billion, while the firm's long-term debt doubled to over $500 million.

LNCE products are distributed widely through grocery and mass merchandisers, convenience stores, club stores, food service outlets, and other channels. LNCE has about 5,900 employees and over $1.6 billion in annual sales. No LNCE employees are covered by a collective bargaining agreement.

In fiscal 2013, LNCE completed its new 60,000 square foot R&D center in Hanover, Pennsylvania. The company reported revenue for Q2 of 2013 of $439 million, up 9.9 percent compared to prior year, and net income of $16.9 million, up from $15.0 million the prior year. The company declared a quarterly cash dividend of $0.16 per share on the company's common stock, payable on August 30, 2013 to stockholders of record at the close of business on August 21, 2013. At that time, LNCE reported that its net revenue for the full year 2013 would be up 10 to 12 percent, with 2013 capital expenditures projected to be between $78 and $83 million.

LNCE has manufacturing operations in Charlotte, as well as in Hanover, Pennsylvania; Goodyear, Arizona; Burlington, Iowa; Columbus, Georgia; Jeffersonville, Indiana; Hyannis, Massachusetts; Perry, Florida; Ashland, Ohio; Cambridge, Ontario; and Guelph, Ontario. In late 2012, LNCE opened a new distribution facility in Southaven, Mississippi and acquired Snack Factory, LLC for $343 million. That company develops and markets snacks under the Pretzel Crisps brand name.

LNCE does not have a stated vision or mission statement, but on many LNCE packages, the following phrase appears and perhaps is the firm's mission: "We make, sell, and deliver the most irresistible specialty snacks in the world."

Copyright by Fred David Books LLC. (Written by Forest R. David)

History

Snyder's of Hanover is a bit older than Lance, but both firms have a rich history dating back to the early 1900s.

Snyder's of Hanover

Business began in 1909 when Harry Warehime, founder of Hanover Canning Company (the firm's parent company until 1980), began producing OldeTyme Pretzels for the Hanover Pretzel Company. In the 1920s, Grandma Eda and Edward Snyder II began frying potato chips in a kettle at their home and selling the home cooked snack door-to-door and to fairs and farmers' markets. William Snyder in 1940 constructed a new plant in Hanover, PA. To extend the shelf life of his product for distant markets, William began to use aluminum foil bags, becoming the first chipper to implement this creative, yet practical innovation. Eleven years later, William's son, William "Billy" L. Snyder, sold the Hanover plant to Hanover Canning, headed by Alan R. Warehime. Company sales in 1961 were about $400,000.

In 1963, the Bechtel Pretzel Company, founded by Bill and Helen Bechtel in 1947, was purchased and incorporated into Snyder's Bakery. Bill developed the original recipe for the Sourdough Hard Pretzel that is still enjoyed by consumers today. In 1980, nineteen years after Snyder's was purchased, the Warehime family decided to "spin off" Snyder's of Hanover Snack Operation from Hanover Brands, enabling the companies to focus on their respective industries of snacks and vegetables. Snyder's sales in 1980 were $15.8 million. After the split, both companies began growing faster than industry averages.

Lance

Business began in 1913 when Phillip Lance, a food broker in Charlotte, obtained 500 pounds of raw peanuts for a customer. When the customer backed out of the deal, Mr. Lance kept the peanuts and began roasting them and selling them on the streets of Charlotte for a nickel a bag. Mr. Lance was later joined in business by his son-in-law, S. A. Van Every, and together they formed Lance Packing Company. Mr. Lance's wife and daughter added to the product line when they developed a peanut butter sandwich cracker. It is believed that this was the first such combination sandwich cracker offered for sale. Incorporated in 1926, Lance continued to grow as better methods of preparing peanuts and making peanut butter candy were developed. In 1935, Lance reached one million dollars in sales, and then two million in 1939 when the company's name was officially changed to Lance, Inc. By 1960, annual sales volume had grown to $26 million.

In 1979, Lance greatly expanded its product offerings with the acquisition of Midwest Biscuit Company in Burlington, Iowa. Midwest, the predecessor to Vista Bakery and Lance Private Brands, gave Lance a solid foothold in the rapidly growing private label cookie and cracker market. Lance continued to grow throughout the 1980s and 1990s and in 1999 made two acquisitions, Cape Cod Potato Chip Company and Tamming Foods. Based in Ontario, Canada, Tammong is a manufacturer of private label sugar wafers. Cape Cod is one of the nation's leaders in kettle-cooked potato chips. Sales of Cape Cod snack products grew rapidly as Lance leveraged the power of its company-owned direct-store-delivery system to increase distribution.

Since 2005, Lance experienced rapid revenue growth as the Company augmented organic growth with a series of strategic acquisitions. In 2005, Lance acquired the assets of Tom's Foods, a well-established company with a product line and distribution system very similar to Lance's. In 2008, Lance acquired Brent and Sam's Inc., a manufacturer of premium private label cookies. That same year the company acquired the Archway bakery in Ashland, Ohio. With Archway, Lance was able to add a well-known brand of cookies to its snack portfolio and increase its presence in the supermarket trade channel. In late 2009, Lance acquired the Stella D'oro brand. Stella D'oro is well-known in the Northeast and offers consumers a number of lightly sweet Italian-style cookies.

The Merger

LNCE was formed in 2010 when Lance, Inc. and Snyder's of Hanover merged. In late 2011, LNCE acquired George Greer Co., a snack food distributor, for $15.0 million in cash. Goodwill recorded as part of the purchase price allocation was $10.1 million, and identifiable intangible assets acquired as part of the acquisition were $8.4 million.

In late 2012, LNCE acquired the brand Pretzel Crisps, owned by Snack Factory, for $340 million and thus entered the fast growing deli-bakery section of grocery stores. Pretzel Crisps (http://pretzelcrisps.com/) are a thin and crunchy pretzel cracker,

Brands

LNCE contracts with other branded food manufacturers to produce their products. However, LNCE branded products represent about 59 percent of total revenue and non-branded products about 41 percent. LNCE sales are almost all within the USA, with the largest customer being Walmart, which comprises about 18 percent of revenue.

LNCE has many famous brands of its own as described below:

Snyder's of Hanover (www.snydersofhanover.com)—OldeTyme pretzels are made from wholesome ingredients, individually twisted and slow-baked to seal in the flavor.

Lance (www.lance.com)—Lance sandwich crackers are baked fresh with real peanut butter or cheese, and no preservatives, trans fat or high-fructose corn syrup.

Cape Cod (www.capecodchips.com)—Cape Cod Potato Chips are high quality, all natural, hand-stirred, kettle-cooked chips with a classic legendary, crisp, crunch.

Krunchers! (www.krunchers.net)—Krunchers is a kettle chip produced from hand picked premium potatoes, sliced to the ideal thickness, and seasoned with the finest spices.

Tom's (www.toms-snacks.com)—Tom's snacks come in unique shapes and textures, and offer exceptional freshness and quality.

Archway (www.archwaycookies.com)—Archway produces fresh-baked cookies made with high-quality ingredients.

EatSmart Naturals (www.eatsmartnaturals.com)—EatSmart Naturals are unique interesting snacks packed with wholesome ingredients made without artificial preservatives and additives.

Organizational Structure

LNCE appears to operate using a functional structure since the company's *Form 10K* lists only six top executives, as indicated in Exhibit 1. Apparently COO Carl Lee, Jr. oversees all the company's brands and operations. Most analysts contend that LNCE is too large to operate from a functional design. Thus, in the design given in Exhibit 1, note that a strategic business unit (SBU) executive is proposed for the Snyder's-Lance Brands and another for Private Brands—but certainly other alternative designs could be utilized.

Code of Ethics

Snyder's Lance has an elaborate code of ethics posted on its website. An excerpt from the code is given below:

"It is up to each of us no matter what our position or length of service with the Company to be responsible for ensuring that we operate with integrity and treat one another with professionalism and respect. Our Code of Ethics will provide clarity about what is expected from each of us." (Source: Corporate website)

Sustainability

LNCE was recently recognized as one of the top 20 companies in the USA for utilizing solar energy capacity at their facilities. LNCE ranked No. 17 with 3.5 megawatts of installed solar capacity, anchored by a 26-acre solar farm in Pennsylvania that supplies energy for its manufacturing facility in nearby.

EXHIBIT 1 The Synder's-Lance Organizational Structure

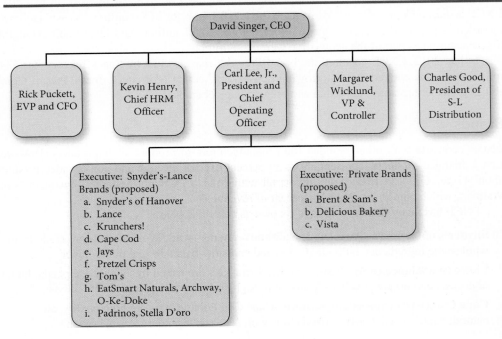

LNCE's Cape Cod Potato Chips, Snyder's of Hanover Pretzels, and EatSmart Naturals recently received the following awards for being healthy.

- Cape Cod's newest variety, *Waffle Cut Sea Salt,* was selected as the potato chip winner for the 2012 *SHAPE Snack Awards* in the "Best for Parties" category. The *SHAPE Snack Awards* recognizes the best low-calorie snacks of the year and products must meet strict nutritional guidelines to be considered by editors. The awards are listed in the July 2012 issue of *SHAPE* magazine, which reaches more than 2 million readers through its print and online editions.
- Snyder's of Hanover Organic Honey Whole Wheat Pretzel Sticks were selected as a better-for-you snack option in Rodale's "*Eat This, Not That!*" list of the 21 Best Organic Snacks. Rodale is a publisher of health and wellness magazines, books, and digital properties, including *Men's Health, Women's Health, Prevention,* and *Runner's World.* The publisher reaches more than 70 million people around the world.
- Snyder's of Hanover Bacon Cheddar Pretzel Pieces and EatSmart Naturals Potato Crisps were selected by *Progressive Grocer* for the 2012 "Editors' Picks." Both snacks were recognized, out of a pool of more than 300 entries, as two of the best new consumer products introduced in 2012. They were honored as "Editors' Picks" in the August 2012 print issue of *Progressive Grocer* as well as on the *Progressive Grocer* website. The supermarket industry publication reaches more than 50,000 people each month through its print and online versions.

LNCE strives to reduce, reuse, and recycle extensively. The company recycles corrugated cardboard, shipping cartons, metal and plastic drums, office paper, stretch film, plastic jugs and buckets, meal bags, dry waste, salt, pretzel pieces, burnt chips, oil, petroleum, scrap metal, iron, potato starch, and potato peels. The company website gives the following information:

Reduce

- We use low wattage high efficiency light bulbs.
- Motion sensors have been added to areas with low traffic.
- Meters have been installed on our ovens to control gas usage.
- We've reduced the size and thickness of our cartons.
- Water meters have been installed to control usage.
- Our delivery system has been optimized to use less fuel.

Reuse

- Bulk material is delivered in reusable bags.
- Office printer paper is used for scrap paper or recycled.

Recycle

- We now use 100% renewable corn based film for our new Variety Packs.
- Our shipping cartons contain up to 50% recycled materials.
- We use 100% recycled paperboard in our Lunch Packs.
- Plastic drums and barrels are recyclable plastic.
- We repair and recycle damaged shipping pallets.
- Office and printer paper is recycled or reused.

Segment Data

LNCE owns four core brands: 1) Snyder's of Hanover Pretzels, 2) Lance Sandwich Crackers, 3) Cape Cod Potato Chips, and 4) Pretzel Crisps. The company provides of revenue breakdown of its brands versus its revenues from other brands, as indicated in Exhibit 2. Note that LNCE revenues are increasing nicely. Exhibit 3 provides a geographic breakdown of LNCE revenues. Note that almost all LNCE sales are in the USA.

Finance

LNCE has consistently paid dividends of 16 cents per quarter to its shareholders since 2000. LNCE stock offers a healthy dividend yield of 2.52 percent, compared to a snacks industry average dividend yield of only 1.55 percent.

EXHIBIT 2   LNCE Revenues by Brand Category (in millions)

	2012	2011	2010	2009
Branded Products	$ 955.5	943.2	569.5	533.6
Non-Branded Products	663.1	691.8	410.3	384.6
Total	1,618.6	1,635.0	979.8	918.2

Source: 2012 *Form 10K*, p. 28.

EXHIBIT 3   LNCE Revenues by Region (in thousands)

	2012	2011	2010	2009
USA	$ 1,564,338	1,582,967	929,633	871,964
Canada	54,296	52,069	50,182	46,199
Total	1,618,634	1,635,036	979,835	918,163

Source: 2012 *Form 10K*, p. 45.

Michael Warehime and his wife Patricia, own about 16 percent of the outstanding common stock of LNCE. Mr. and Mrs. Warehime serve as directors of LNCE, with Mr. Warehime serving as the Chairman of the Board.

LNCE's recent income statements and balance sheets are provided in Exhibits 4 and 5 respectively. Note in Exhibit 4 the company's dramatic increase in both revenues and net income in 2011. Note in Exhibit 5 the dramatic increase in number of shares outstanding in 2011.

Competitors

Major competitors of LNCE in the snack foods industry include Frito-Lay North America, a subsidiary of PepsiCo, and the U.S. Snacks Division of Kellogg. Other LNCE competitors include General Mills and Mondelez International. A summary of key competitive information is given in Exhibit 6. Note that LNCE has the least revenue per employee among the four firms featured.

Frito-Lay

Frito-Lay North America (FLNA), as PepsiCo refers to this business they own, produces Lay's potato chips, Cheetos, Quaker-brand cereals, Doritos, Tostitos, Ruffles, Fritos, SunChips, and Santitas. For the second quarter of 2012, Frito-Lay recorded revenue growth of 2.5 percent to

EXHIBIT 4   LNCE's Income Statements (in millions)

(in millions)	2012	2011	2009
Net revenue	**$ 1,618.6**	**$ 1,635.0**	**$ 979.8**
Cost of sales	1,079.7	1,065.1	601.0
Gross margin	538.9	569.9	378.8
Selling, general and administrative	440.6	495.2	359.6
Impairment charges	11.9	12.7	0.6
Gain on sale of route businesses, net	(22.3)	(9.4)	—
Other (income)/expense, net	(0.4)	1.0	6.5
Income before interest and income taxes	109.1	70.4	12.1
Interest expense, net	9.5	10.6	3.9
Income tax expense	40.1	21.1	5.6
Net income	**$ 59.5**	**$ 38.7**	**$ 2.6**

Source: 2012 *Form 10K*, p. 28.

EXHIBIT 5 LNCE's Balance Sheets

(in thousands, except share data)	2012	2011
ASSETS		
Current assets:		
Cash and cash equivalents	$ 9,276	$ 20,841
Accounts receivable, net of allowances of $2,159 and $1,884, respectively	141,862	143,238
Inventories	118,256	106,261
Income tax receivable	—	18,119
Deferred income taxes	11,625	21,042
Assets held for sale	11,038	57,822
Prepaid expenses and other current assets	28,676	20,705
Total current assets	320,733	388,028
Noncurrent assets:		
Fixed assets, net	331,385	313,043
Goodwill	540,389	367,853
Other intangible assets, net	531,735	376,062
Other noncurrent assets	22,490	21,804
Total assets	$ 1,746,732	$ 1,466,790
LIABILITIES AND STOCKHOLDERS' EQUITY		
Current liabilities:		
Current portion of long-term debt	$ 20,462	$ 4,256
Accounts payable	52,753	52,930
Accrued compensation	31,037	29,248
Accrued profit-sharing and retirement plans	354	9,249
Accrual for casualty insurance claims	4,779	6,957
Accrued selling and promotional costs	16,240	21,465
Income tax payable	1,263	—
Other payables and accrued liabilities	27,735	31,041
Total current liabilities	154,623	155,146
Noncurrent liabilities:		
Long-term debt	514,587	253,939
Deferred income taxes	176,037	196,244
Accrual for casualty insurance claims	9,759	7,724
Other noncurrent liabilities	19,551	15,146
Total liabilities	874,557	628,199
Stockholders' equity:		
Common stock, $0.83 1/3 par value. Authorized 75,000,000 shares; 68,863,974 and 67,820,798 shares outstanding, respectively	57,384	56,515
Preferred stock, $1.00 par value. Authorized 5,000,000 shares; no shares outstanding	—	—
Additional paid-in capital	746,155	730,338
Retained earnings	50,847	35,539
Accumulated other comprehensive income	15,118	13,719
Total Snyder's-Lance, Inc. stockholders' equity	869,504	836,111
Noncontrolling interests	2,671	2,480
Total stockholders' equity	872,175	838,591
Total liabilities and stockholders' equity	$ 1,746,732	$ 1,466,790

Source: 2012 *Form 10K,* p. 45–46.

EXHIBIT 6 Comparative Information for Various Snack Food Companies

	LNCE	Mondelez	General Mills	Kellogg
# of Employees	6.1K	126K	35K	31K
$ Net Income	41.6M	3.59B	1.71B	1.19B
$ Revenue	1.64B	54.3B	16.9B	13.6B
$ Revenue/Employee	270K	430K	482K	438K
$ EPS Ratio	0.61	2.01	2.56	3.31

Source: Company documents.

$5.77 billion—obviously a huge company compared to LNCE. A global company in all respects, Frito-Lay's operating profit declined 1 percent to $1.33 billion in a recent quarter. FLNA's revenue was $13.3 billion in 2011, up from $12.6 billion the prior year.

Kellogg

Kellogg, the world's largest cereal maker well known for Frosted Flakes, Pop-Tarts, and Eggo waffles, acquired Pringles chips in 2012. The deal instantly made Kellogg the world's second-biggest salty snack food maker, behind only Frito-Lay. Based in Battle Creek, Michigan, Kellogg said Pringles sales rose by 10 percent in a recent quarter. A major competitor to LNCE, Pringles has only two major manufacturing plants in the world. Those plants—in Tennessee and Belgium—are running around the clock at full capacity, and Kellogg plans to expand Pringles' production capacity. Because Pringles derives two-thirds of its revenue from overseas, Kellogg is also hoping Pringles can give it inroads into the emerging markets where the number of people with disposable income is growing. Kellogg's stable of other salty snacks include Cheez-Its and Special K crackers.

Mondelez

In October 2012, the former Kraft Foods Inc. changed its name to Mondelez International and spun-off some brands into a new company called Kraft Foods Group. Kraft Foods Group focuses on the North American foods business. Mondelez International focuses on the global snacks business, including the former Cadbury businesses, plus global brands including Dairylea and Philadelphia. Mondelez makes some of the best-known snacks brands around the globe, including cookies and crackers such as Oreo, Nabisco, Chips Ahoy!, TUC, Belvita, Club Social, and Barni. Headquartered in Deerfield Township, Illinois, near Chicago, Mondelez also produces chocolate, biscuits, gum, confectionery, coffee, and powdered beverages. Mondelez has operations in more than 80 countries. Based in Mississauga, Ontario with primary operations in Scarborough, Mondelez Canada controls the rights to Christie Brown and Company, which consists of brands like Mr. Christie and Dad's Cookies.

General Mills

Headquartered in Golden Valley, Minnesota, General Mills produces and markets many well-known brands, such as Betty Crocker, Yoplait, Colombo, Totinos, Jeno's, Pillsbury, Green Giant, Old El Paso, Haagen-Dazs, Cheerios, and Lucky Charms. The company's grain-snack brands that compete more with LNCE products include Bugles, Cascadian Farms, Chex Mix, Gardetto's, Nature Valley, and Fiber One bars. General Mills' brand portfolio includes more than 100 leading brands in the USA and more around the world.

External Issues

Industry Consolidation

Snack foods industry consolidation has resulted in intense price competition, discounting, and other techniques by competitors who generally are significantly larger and have greater resources and economies of scale than LNCE. This size disadvantage could result in LNCE losing one or more major customers, losing existing product authorizations at customer locations, losing market share and/or shelf space, and/or having to lower prices below breakeven, which could have an adverse impact on LNCE's financial results.

LNCE is exposed to risks resulting from several large customers that account for a significant portion of the firm's revenue. LNCE's top ten customers account for about 48 percent of the firm's revenue, with their largest customer, Walmart, representing about 18 percent of their 2011 revenue. The loss of one or more of these large customers could adversely affect LNCE's financial results. LNCE hopes that their large distributors (customers), such as Walmart or Kroger, do not cut deals with rival firms that could limit or even prohibit exposure of LNCE products. Exclusivity activity routinely occurs in some industries, such as PepsiCo or Coca-Cola products being exclusively available in various fast food restaurant chains.

Social/Cultural/Demographic Issues

Consumer preferences and tastes change, which requires companies to continuously monitor trends and innovate accordingly. For example, concerns of consumers regarding health and wellness and obesity affect perceptions about product attributes and ingredients. In addition, changing consumer demographics could result in reduced demand for LNCE products, such as aging of the general population; changes in social trends; changes in travel, vacation, or leisure activity patterns; weather; or negative publicity resulting from regulatory action or litigation against companies in the snack food industry. Good and bad news as well as opinions about LNCE or their rival firms products and services travels instantly on social media outlets.

Consumers are trying to eat fresher, healthier snacks, beverages, and food. The volume of packaged food consumed is declining while the volume of fresh food is increasing. Firms like PepsiCo are actively developing a variety of healthier foods and beverages that focus on such areas as nutrition, weight management, improved digestion, disease prevention, and allergy remedies. These new products generally contain fewer calories, less fat, low carbohydrates, and/or less sugar and sodium. Many new products are gluten-free and/or whole-fiber.

Future

Since Snyder's-Lance is very small compared to its major rivals, yet is performing quite well, should the company expand its manufacturing and distribution operations further penetrating Canada, and even venturing out into Mexico and Latin America and beyond? Economies of scale are critical in this business due to increasing price competition. The snack foods business is global, so to remain solely a domestic player in such an industry could be ineffective long term. In this light, the dilemma for LNCE is how, where, when, and to what extent to engage in geographic expansion. Since its largest customers, such as Walmart, are global, would it not be advantageous for the firm to negotiate deals with those firms to offer their products in other countries. Surely customers worldwide would enjoy eating the firm's snacks just as much as Americans.

Prepare a three-year strategic plan for Snyder's-Lance that will grow the firm globally.

Netgear, Inc., 2013

www.netgear.com, NTGR

Headquartered in San Jose, California, Netgear develops and markets Ethernet switches, wireless controllers, storage devices, routers, media services, and other products associated with connecting users with the Internet. All Netgear products are produced through third-party manufacturers and marketed through thousands of retailers worldwide. Netgear prides itself on developing and marketing high performance devices that are dependable and easy to operate in homes. But this "desired competitive advantage" is difficult to maintain because consumers widely believe such products are a commodity (like gasoline). For businesses, Netgear provides networking, storage, and security devices that are cheaper and easier to use than comparable products offered by rival firms. Netgear products are sold in more than 28,000 retail locations around the world and through about 42,000 resellers. Netgear has operations in 25 nations and has 850 employees, of which 352 are in sales, marketing and technical support, 251 in research and development (R&D), 128 in finance, and 119 in operations.

Netgear's revenues for 2012 were $1.27 billion, up 7.6 percent from 2011. The company reported revenue for Q2 of 2013 of $357.7 million, up from $320.7 million the prior year when the company's new acquisition, AirCard, was not in the numbers. Q2 2013 net income was $14.0 million, down from $21.5 million the prior year. During Q2, Netgear grew its Retail Business Unit (RBU), led by its 802.11ac upgrade cycle, as well as the rollout of the Smart Home for developed markets. The integration of the AirCard business into the company's Service Provider Business Unit (SPBU) went well. On a year-over-year basis, Netgear's RBU revenue was up 3 percent. The company's strong Q2 2013 year-on-year growth for RBU in North America and Asia was offset by weakness in the European region. The company's SPBU revenue was up 58 percent sequentially, and up 20 percent over the prior year quarter. The company's Commercial Business Unit (CBU) revenue was up 25 percent sequentially, and up 10 percent over the prior year quarter.

Copyright by Fred David Books LLC. (Written by Forest R. David)

History

Netgear was incorporated in 1996 as a subsidiary of Bay Networks and was purchased by Nortel in 1998. The company became fully independent from Nortel in 2002 and remains independent today. Back in 1996, the Internet was in its infancy, especially high speed and wireless devices. As an industry pioneer, Netgear has kept tight inventory controls and used off-the-shelf hardware and software products from existing companies. Founder, chairman, and CEO Patrick Lo was quoted in 2004 as saying: "We do the system integration and let the contracted firms do the grunt work of designing circuit boards." Netgear went public in 2003. Since then, the company has grown into a $1.2 billion in sales firm. In 2011, Netgear combined its North, Central, and South U.S. salesforces to form a new Americas territory as a means to increase operational efficiencies. Today, the company operates in three distinct geographic territories: (1) Americas, (2) Europe, and (3) Middle East and Asia Pacific.

To get a flavor of what Netgear develops and markets, in late 2012, the company introduced its CG4500TM Voice/Data Gateway that received the CableLabs® DOCSIS® 3.0 certification. This unit has the capability for 24 × 4-channel bonding and is the firm's most advanced DOCSIS 3.0 Voice/Data Gateway integrating in one device. The new product allows concurrent 802.11n dual-band wireless networking that provides up to 900 Mbps (450 + 450 Mbps) aggregate speed and with simultaneous dual-band technology helps mitigate interference ensuring sustained throughput and reliable connections. With integrated MoCA, the CG4500TM Gateway enables seamless data and video distribution over the in-home coax network.

Internal Issues

Vision and Mission

Netgear's mission statement is: "To be the innovative leader in connecting the world to the Internet," recently changed from, "To be the preferred customer-driven provider of innovative networking solutions for small businesses and homes." There is a statement on the company's website that may be their vision: "Our goal is to be the leading provider of innovative networking products to the consumer, business, and service provider markets."

Location

Netgear's primary administrative, sales, marketing, and R&D facilities consist of 142,700 square feet in an office complex in San Jose, California, under a lease that expires in 2018. Netgear's international headquarters comprise 10,000 square feet of office space in Cork, Ireland, under a lease that expires in 2026. Netgear's international salespersons are based out of local sales offices or home offices in Austria, Australia, Brazil, Canada, China, Czech Republic, Denmark, France, Germany, Hong Kong, India, Italy, Japan, Korea, Mexico, New Zealand, Poland, Russia, Singapore, Spain, Sweden, Switzerland, the Netherlands, the United Arab Emirates, and the United Kingdom. Netgear has operations personnel in Hong Kong, and R&D facilities in Atlanta, Chicago, Beijing, Guangzhou, Nanjing, and Shanghai, China, and in Taipei, Taiwan.

Organizational Structure

Netgear is managed in three specific business units: (1) retail, (2) commercial, and (3) service provider. The retail business unit consists of home networking, storage, and digital media products to connect users with the Internet and their content and devices. The commercial business unit consists of relatively low-cost business networking, storage, and security solutions. The service provider business unit consists of made-to-order and retail proven, whole-home networking solutions sold to service providers for sale to their customers.

Netgear recently combined their North American, Central American, and South American sales forces to form the Americas territory. Thus, the firm is today organized into the following three geographic territories: (1) Americas, (2) Europe, Middle-East, and Africa (EMEA) and (3) Asia, Pacific (APAC).

Exhibit 1 provides a diagram of Netgear's existing organizational structure. Note there is no Chief Operations Officer. Some analysts contend that the company is too dependent on Lo, with no other person being groomed as an eventual successor.

EXHIBIT 1 Organizational Chart

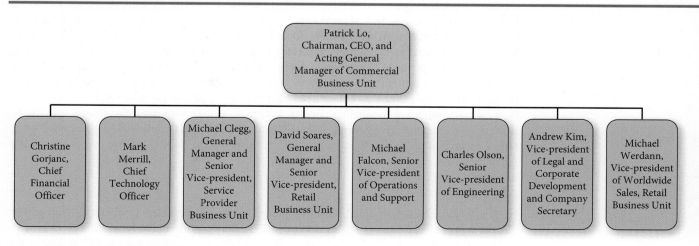

Source: Based on company documents.

Products

Netgear products that target businesses are designed with metal cases and are capable of faster speeds, up to 10 gigabits per second, and higher port counts to allow more users. Products targeting homes are designed with more pleasing aesthetics and are often offered at much lower prices than the more robust higher security business models. Netgear plans to develop a home network that will enable all devices to be connected to the Internet at all times.

Netgear's products can be grouped into three categories: (1) commercial business networking, (2) broadband access, and (3) network connectivity. Commercial business networking products include (a) Ethernet switches and wireless controllers such as routers used in WiFi applications, (b) Internet security appliances that enable Internet access with capabilities such as anti-virus and firewalls, and (c) network-attached storage, which provides file sharing with multiple PCs over a businesses own local area network.

Netgear's broadband access enables customers to move digital content over high-speed networks rather than traditional low-speed telephone lines. Products in this segment include: (a) routers, which allow the home or office networks to connect wireless to the Internet via a broadband modem, (b) gateways, which are routers integrated into a modem, (c) Internet Protocol (IP) telephony products, which enable voice communications over a network, and (d) media servers, which store multimedia content for use on PCs laptops, smartphones, and other devices.

Netgear's connectivity products enable resource sharing and include wireless access points, wireless network interface cards, Ethernet network interface cards, media adapters, and power line adapters.

R&D

High technology firms spend anywhere from 5 to 15 percent of revenue on R&D. In 2012, Netgear spent $61 million, up 25.5 percent, on R&D to develop new and improved products and respond to changing technology in a timely manner. The $61 million was 4.8 percent of Netgear's revenues, up from 4.1 percent the prior year. Netgear works closely with their technology suppliers to develop products using a methodology such as Original Design Manufacturer (ODM) or In-House Development. Under ODM, Netgear defines the product and specifications and coordinates with suppliers who develop the product. On development of a prototype, debugging and testing begins, and the product is ultimately released for production after passing final measures. The In-House Development model is similar to ODM, except entire development is coordinated by Netgear engineers.

Manufacturing

Like Apple, Inc., Netgear outsources all of their manufacturing to third parties, such as Cameo Communications, Delta Networks, Hon Hai Precision (more commonly known as Foxconn Corporation), and several others. Almost all Netgear products are manufactured on mainland China or in Vietnam. Products are sometimes tested in a pilot basis in Taiwan. Netgear component parts such as connector jacks, plastic casings, and physical layer transceivers are all purchased from a few sources, making reliance on a few suppliers a threat. If any third-party manufacturers experience any delay, disruption, or quality control problems in their operations, Netgear could lose market share and the Netgear brand could suffer. Netgear outsources warehousing and distribution logistics to five third-party providers, located in California, Hong Kong, Netherlands, and Australia. Netgear does not have long-term contracts with any of their third-party manufacturers, some of whom produce products for competitors.

Marketing

Netgear's global sales channel includes thousands of value added resellers (VARs), direct market resellers (DMRs), such as CDW, and 37,000 traditional retailers worldwide, such as Best Buy, Walmart, Fry's Electronics, and Staples in North America; PC World in the United Kingdom; and MediaMarket in Germany, as well as online retailers such as Amazon.

com, Dell.com, and NewEgg.com. Netgear also sells its products through broadband service providers such as BSkyB, Virgin Media UK, YouSee Denmark, Telecom Denmark, Time-Warner Cable, Comcast, TV Cabo Portugal, Telkom South Africa, J:Com of Japan, and Comhem of Sweden.

Best Buy and Ingram Micro each account for 10 percent or greater of Netgear revenues. Netgear works closely with customers on market development activities, such as co-advertising, in-store promotions and demonstrations, instant rebate programs, event sponsorship, and sales associate training. It also participates in major industry trade shows and marketing events. Netgear marketing managers work closely with the company's sales and R&D people to align product development roadmaps to meet customer technology demands.

Finance

Netgear's net income declined in 2012 to $86.5 million from the year before value of $91.4 million.

Income Statements

Netgear's recent income statements are provided in Exhibit 2. Note the steady increases in revenues but recent drop in net income.

EXHIBIT 2

NETGEAR, INC.
STATEMENTS OF OPERATIONS
(In thousands, except per share data)

	Year Ended December 31,		
	2012	2011	2010
Net revenue	**$1,271,921**	**$1,181,018**	**$902,052**
Cost of revenue	888,368	811,572	602,805
Gross profit	383,553	369,446	299,247
Operating expenses:			
Research and development	61,066	48,699	39,972
Sales and marketing	149,766	154,562	131,570
General and administrative	45,027	39,423	36,220
Restructuring and other charges	1,190	2,094	(88)
Litigation reserves, net	390	(201)	211
Total operating expenses	257,439	244,577	207,885
Income from operations	126,114	124,869	91,362
Interest income	498	477	426
Other income (expense), net	2,670	(1,136)	(564)
Income before income taxes	129,282	124,210	91,224
Provision for income taxes	42,743	32,842	40,315
Net income	**$86,539**	**$91,368**	**$50,909**
Net income per share:			
Basic	$2.27	$2.46	$1.44
Diluted	$2.23	$2.41	$1.41
Weighted average shares outstanding used to compute net income per share:			
Basic	38,057	37,121	35,385
Diluted	38,747	37,932	36,124

Source: 2012 *Form 10K*, p. 54.

Balance Sheets

Netgear's recent balance sheets are provided in Exhibit 3. Note the zero long-term debt.

Segments

Netgear reports operating income by geographic region. Before 2011, the company's operations in Central and South America were categorized under the APAC segment. Note in Exhibit 4 that Netgear's APAC segment was the largest gainer in 2012 versus the prior year, whereas EMEA reported a decline in revenues.

EXHIBIT 3 Netgear's Balance Sheet

NETGEAR, INC.
BALANCE SHEETS
(In thousands, except per share data)

	December 31, 2012	December 31, 2011
ASSETS		
Current assets:		
Cash and cash equivalents	$149,032	$208,898
Short-term investments	227,845	144,797
Accounts receivable, net	256,014	261,307
Inventories	174,903	163,724
Deferred income taxes	22,691	23,088
Prepaid expenses and other current assets	33,724	32,415
Total current assets	**864,209**	**834,229**
Property and equipment, net	19,025	15,884
Intangibles, net	27,621	20,956
Goodwill	100,880	85,944
Other non-current assets	22,834	14,357
Total assets	**$1,034,569**	**$971,370**
LIABILITIES AND STOCKHOLDERS' EQUITY		
Current liabilities:		
Accounts payable	$87,310	$117,285
Accrued employee compensation	18,338	26,896
Other accrued liabilities	126,255	120,480
Deferred revenue	27,645	40,093
Income taxes payable	1,382	4,207
Total current liabilities	**260,930**	**308,961**
Non-current income taxes payable	13,735	18,657
Other non-current liabilities	5,293	4,995
Total liabilities	**279,958**	**332,613**
Commitments and contingencies		
Stockholders' equity:		
Preferred stock: $0.001 par value; 5,000,000 shares authorized; none issued or outstanding	—	—
Common stock: $0.001 par value; 200,000,000 shares authorized; shared issued and outstanding:		
38,341,644 and 37,646,872 at December 31, 2012 and 2011, respectively	38	38
Additional paid-in capital	394,427	364,243
Cumulative other comprehensive income	4	23
Retained earnings	360,142	274,453
Total stockholders' equity	**754,611**	**638,757**
Total liabilities and stockholders' equity	**$1,034,569**	**$971,370**

Source: 2012 Form 10K, p. 53.

EXHIBIT 4 Revenues by Geographic Segment

| | Year End December (in thousands) | | | | | | | |
| | 2012 | | 2011 | | 2010 | | Percent Change | |
	$	%	$	%	$	%	2012	2011
Americas	$679,419	53.4	$587,056	49.7	$466,542	51.7	15.7	25.8
EMEA	$457,724	36%	$477,713	40.4	$340,249	37.7	(4.2)	40.4
APAC	$134,778	10.6	$116,249	9.9	$95,261	10.6	15.9	22.0
Total	$1,271,921	100%	$1,181,018	100%	$902,052	100%		

APAC, Asia Pacific; EMEA, Europe, Middle East, Africa.
Source: 2012 *Form 10K*, page 41.

Competition

Netgear operates in an extremely competitive industry, with many products being viewed by consumers as commodities, proper position on store floors being critically important, and competitive pricing being essential. Many Netgear products, such as media adapters, Ethernet, and routers, are also made by rivals Cisco Systems, Roku, Western Digital, and Apple in the USA, and by many foreign competitors such as AVM in Europe, Corega in Japan, and TP-Link in China. Netgear also develops and markets networking and streaming products, competing against rivals LG, Microsoft, Samsung, and Sony. Also competing against Netgear are many cable companies that now provide modems, and those companies may soon provide their own routers as part of their service offerings. If Netgear cannot form contracts with various cable providers, then those firms may also become competitors.

Netgear's principal competitors in the commercial business market include Allied Telesys, Barracuda, Buffalo, Data Robotics, Dell, D-Link, Fortinet, Hewlett-Packard, Huawei, Cisco Systems, the Linksys division of Cisco Systems, QNAP Systems, Seagate Technology, SonicWALL, Synology, WatchGuard, and Western Digital. Netgear's principal competitors in the home market for networking devices and television connectivity products include Apple, Belkin, D-Link, the Linksys division of Cisco Systems, Roku, and Western Digital. Netgear's principal competitors in the broadband service provider market include Actiontec, ARRIS, Comtrend, D-Link, Hitron, Huawei, Motorola, Pace, Sagem, Scientific Atlanta (a Cisco company), SMC Networks, TechniColor, Ubee, Compal Broadband, ZTE, and ZyXEL. Other current and potential competitors that Netgear considers include numerous local vendors such as Devolo, LEA, and AVM in Europe; Corega and Melco in Japan; and TP-Link in China. Even consumer electronics vendors are rivals, including LG Electronics, Microsoft, Panasonic, Samsung, Sony, Toshiba, and Vizio, who could integrate networking and streaming capabilities into their line of products, such as televisions, set top boxes, and gaming consoles.

Exhibit 5 provides a comparative summary of Netgear versus four leading competitors. Note that Netgear is a bit larger than D-Link, but much smaller than most rival firms.

EXHIBIT 5 Comparative Data for Netgear versus Rival Firms

	Netgear	Cisco Systems	D-Link	Alcatel Lucent	Western Digital
Number of Employees	791	71.8K	500	76K	103K
Net Income ($)	95.3M	7.36B	41.5M	1.4B	1.9B
Revenue ($)	1.23B	45.6B	1.15B	19.8B	13.8B
Revenue ($)/Employee	1,554K	635K	2,300K	260.5K	134K
EPS Ratio ($)	2.49	1.36	0.06	0.54	7.61
Market Capitalization	1.26B	87.64B	—	—	10.1B
Headquarters	California	California	Taiwan	France	California

EPS, earnings per share.
Source: Based on company information.

Cisco Systems, Inc.

Nearly 40 times the size of Netgear, Cisco is headquartered in the same city as Netgear, San Jose, California. Like Netgear, Cisco structures its operations in the same three geographic segments, with its European and Middle East headquarters in the Netherlands and the Asia Pacific headquarters in Singapore. Also like Netgear, Cisco produces Internet protocol networking and other related devices to support communications and information technology. Cisco's sales by geographic region reported in its fiscal year end June 2012 were 65, 21, and 14 percent respectively for Americas, EMEA, and APAC. Also like Netgear, Cisco produces cable modems, video software, encoders, decoders, and many more products. Cisco's Linksys wireless routers compete directly with Netgear routers. As of year-end 2012, Cisco had 66,000 employees, annual revenues of $46 billion, and net income of $8 billion. Also like Netgear, Cisco relies exclusively on contract manufacturers for all their manufacturing needs.

Cisco spends about 12 percent of net sales on R&D compared to only 4 percent for Netgear. Cisco contains around $17 billion in goodwill on the balance sheet resulting in approximately 40 percent of total stockholders' equity residing from intangible assets, which is not good, versus Netgear's 17 percent.

Western Digital Corporation

Headquartered in Irvine, California, Western Digital creates and markets storage devices, home entertainment devices, and networking devices, similar to Netgear. Western Digital is known for their 2.5- and 3.5-inch form factor hard drives under the Ultrastart, XE, WD, and SiliconDrive brand names. Western Digital also produces a wide range of external hard drives in 500-gb sizes, FireWire, and Ethernet connections.

Western Digital is structured based on the same geographic regions both Netgear and Cisco. One notable exception, Western Digital, with $12.5 billion of revenue in fiscal 2012 that ended June 2012, reported that about 58 percent of their revenues come from Asian markets with 23 and 19 percent coming from the Americas and EMEA, respectively, providing the company a significantly more Asian presence than both Netgear and Cisco. The company currently spends 8 percent of revenues on R&D. The firm has $2 billion in goodwill and around 37 percent of all current assets are in inventory.

As of December 2012, Western Digital has a price-to-earnings (P/E) ratio of five, below the S&P 500 P/E ratio of 17.7, and its stock price was up 22.9 percent year-to-date. Western Digital has numerous strengths, such as robust revenue growth, reasonable debt levels, solid stock price performance, impressive record of earnings per share growth, and compelling growth in net income. Western Digital has no glaring weaknesses.

Western Digital recently acquired the hard disk drive operations of Hitachi, greatly increasing its capacity and sales volume. Like rival Seagate Technology, Western Digital has been targeting some acquisitions upstream to better control input costs. Seagate recently acquired the hard disk operations of Samsung.

D-Link Corporation

Headquartered in Taipei, Taiwan, D-Link develops, produces, and markets networking, connectivity, and data communications hardware, offering hubs and switches, adapters, print servers, routers, and transceivers. Other D-Link products include broadband modems, virtual private network/firewall devices, data-storage systems, videoconferencing equipment, Web cameras, and business phones. D-Link sells to individuals and businesses, but the firm specializes in wi-fi and Ethernet components for the small to medium-sized office market. D-Link sells its products through distributors in more than 100 countries, but generates most of its sales in Asia.

The Future

In July 2012, Netgear acquired AVAAK, Inc., a privately-held company that develops wire-free video networking products for a total purchase consideration of $24.0 million in cash. This acquisition bolstered the company's retail business unit product offerings and expanded their presence in the smart home market. Some analysts however contend that the fate of Netgear's industry is inexorably tied to the PC and that PCs are in decline as users switch to tablets, which will not need hard disk drives. But there are external storage needs for hard-disk drives that seem to be growing and conventional storage is still cheaper than flash memory.

Every few months or so, Netgear introduces a new or improved product, including the recently introduced Netgear ProSecure® UTM25S Unified Threat Management Firewall, which provides two modular slots that fit optional interface cards, enabling IT administrators to custom tailor the firewall to their specific connectivity requirements. In addition, like other members of the ProSecure UTM family of security appliances, the UTM25S integrates with Netgear ReadyNAS® network-attached storage systems, giving businesses almost unlimited activity log and quarantine capacity for forensic, regulatory and legal requirements.

Netgear also recently introduced the CentriaTM, a powerful, all-in-one automatic backup/media server and high-speed wi-fi router. Centria is a dual-band high-performance router with the added convenience of automatic data backup for both PCs and Macs. The backup capability of the Centria router gives a consumer peace of mind knowing that data is always backed up. If a PC or Mac goes down or is lost, a consumer can still access data from Centria using another computer. Routers are excellent for data backup because they are always on and are the central point of connection for all computers in the home. Centria can also be used as a storage repository for photos, media, and documents that may take up too much space on your computer. Centria uses an internal SATA drive or external USB drives to backup and store data.

There are companies such as Western Digital or Cisco that may be interested in acquiring Netgear. Even D-Link desires a greater market share in the USA. And Netgear itself has a history of making acquisitions. What would be some good acquisition targets for Netgear, to help solidify its competitive position and gain economies of scale.

To remain attractive in this rapidly changing industry, Netgear needs a clear strategic plan going forward.

Polaris Industries, Inc., 2013

www.polaris.com, PII

Headquartered in Medina, Minnesota, Polaris (named after the North Star) designs, engineers, manufactures, and markets off-road vehicles (ORVs), snowmobiles, motorcycles, and electric on-road vehicles primarily in the USA, Canada, and Europe, with 70 percent of revenue coming from the USA. Polaris also produces On-Road Vehicles (ORV), which are predominantly Victory motorcycles. Their ORV sales grew 64 percent in 2012 to $240 million.

Polaris does business in more than 130 different nations and outside; U.S. sales were up 21 percent in 2012 and net income was up 37 percent. Completion of a 425,000-square foot manufacturing facility in Monterrey, Mexico, in 2011 serves as a platform for better Polaris penetration in Latin and South America. Polaris also produces replacement parts and other accessories such as oils, chrome accessories, electric starters, covers, cargo box accessories, and much more.

Polaris has a defense (military) segment that recently reported excellent sales of the electric Ranger and the unmanned mine roller. Sixty-nine percent of Polaris's sales came from ORVs, a 22-percent increase from the prior year. Nine percent of sales comes from snowmobiles, and 8 percent comes from on-road vehicles. Polaris is the North American leader in total power sports sales with around 20-percent market share, above rivals Harley Davidson, Honda, and Yamaha. In December 2012, Polaris acquired Teton Outfitters, LLC, a privately owned, Rigby, Idaho-based company that designs, develops and distributes KLIM Technical Riding Gear. This acquisition adds KLIM to Polaris' growing parts, garments, and accessories (PG&A) business.

For the six months that ended 6-30-13, Polaris' sales were up 12 percent overall, including Off-Road Vehicles (+7%), Snowmobiles (71%), Motorcycles (−6%), Small Vehicles (+109%), and Parts, Garments & Accessories (+30%). The company's Small Vechicles division includes its GEM and Goupil electric vehicles as well as Aixam. For Q2 of 2013, Polaris reported record second quarter net income of $80.0 million, up 15 percent from the prior year's second quarter net income of $69.8 million. Sales for the second quarter 2013 totaled a record $844.8 million, up for last year's second quarter sales of $755.4 million.

Copyright by Fred David Books LLC. (Written by Forest R. David)

History

The father of the snowmobile is considered to be Edgar Hetteen, who in 1955, with employees David Johnson, Paul Knochenmus, and Orlen Johnson, created a vehicle to ride through the snow. The primary use of the craft was to access better hunting areas that traditionally had required wearing snowshoes. An early Polaris snowmobile was called the Polaris Sno Traveler that rolled off the assembly line in Minnesota in 1956. Edgar displayed his snowmobile on a 1,200-mile trek across Alaska in 1960. However, unhappy with the performance of his Polaris vehicle, Edgar soon left the company, and started Polar Manufacturing, that later changed its name to Artic Enterprises, which ultimately went bankrupt in the 1980s. Artic emerged from bankruptcy and continues today under the Arctic Cat Brand, one of Polaris's major competitors in the snowmobile market. For the next 50 years, without Edgar, Polaris developed snowmobiles, all-terrain vehicles (ATVs), side-by-side vehicles (ORVs), and motorcycles.

Polaris began developing a smaller consumer-sized, front-engine snowmobile to compete with the SkiDoo in the early 1960s. In 1964, Polaris released the Comet, and then in 1965 the Mustang, which became a hit as a family snowmobile. In the early 1980s, Polaris created an Indy style snowmobile with a wider stance. In 1985, Polaris introduced the Trailboss, considered to be the first U.S.-made ATV. ATVs are a one-seat variation of ORVs. Today, Polaris is one of the top-selling ATV brands. In the 1990s, Polaris entered the motorcycle market and the watercraft market, producing jet skis, but exited the jet-ski market in 2004. In 2010, Polaris moved its parts plant from Wisconsin to Monterrey, Mexico, saving the company about $30 million annually in lower labor costs.

In 2011, Polaris announced an investment in Brammo, an electric vehicle company based in Ashland, Oregon. Its first production electric motorcycle, the Brammo Enertia, is assembled in Ashland and sold at dealerships. Polaris participated in the $13 million opening tranche of Brammo's Series C funding in July 2012. Polaris had been showing interest in electric propulsion, producing an electric version of its Ranger Side-by-Side and more recently buying Global Electric Motorcars (GEM) from Chrysler. As one publication put it, "This latest move likely signals the addition of clean and quiet drivetrains to ATVs and motorcycles under the global giant's brand umbrella—snowmobiles may have to wait on battery breakthroughs before they become commercially feasible."

Polaris purchased GEM from Chrysler in 2012 and also purchased France-based Goupil. Polaris recently restarted production on its Indy-named sleds (stopped in 2004 with the Indy 500) with the release of the 2013 Indy 600 and Indy 600 SP.

Internal Issues

Strategy

Polaris is a testament to the benefits of strategic planning. Led by Chief Executive Officer (CEO) Scott Wine, the company is in the mist of a 10-year strategic plan that is broken down into stated objectives, three- to five-year goals for each, annual actions for each, and last three-year results for each objective—all provided on the company website (http://phx.corporate-ir.net/phoenix.zhtml?c=108235&p=irol-progress). Polaris's overall objective is to increase sales to $5 billion and obtain a 10-percent net income margin by completion of its strategic plan in 2018. CEO Scott at the front of the company's 2011 *Annual Report* says:

> We again achieved record performance in a down market. Our success is the result of being extremely focused on our strategic plan and executing against it meticulously. Our disciplined approach has made us the best in Powersports and it's how we'll continue to deliver shareholder value well into the future.

Polaris has a history of successfully acquiring and divesting businesses to continue on a path of strategic improvement. Yet to its credit, Polaris reports minimal goodwill on its balance sheet. Some recent notable divestures include exiting the jet-ski market in 2004 after a 12-year stint. Polaris ceased production of its Breeze line of on-road vehicles in 2011 and acquired GEM and Goupil to fill this void. Currently, Polaris is producing more side-by-side ORVs because customers are favoring them over the traditional ATV style, single-driver, four-wheeler product.

Vision and Mission

Despite placing great emphasis on strategic planning, Polaris does not have a clearly stated vision or mission statement, but various statements on the company's elaborate website could be construed to represent those statements.

Organizational Structure

Polaris has a hybrid divisional-by-product-by-region organizational structure as illustrated in Exhibit 1. Note in the diagram it is somewhat unusual for the Vice-president of Sales and Marketing (a staff officer) to also be a line executive. It is also unclear who in the hierarchy has command and control over the U.S. operations analogously to the two other geographic vice-presidents. For example, who would be responsible for motorcycle sales in Texas, or for that matter, motorcycle sales in Germany? Also, notice that there is only one female in the corporate hierarchy.

Production

Polaris assembles products in Minnesota, Iowa, Wisconsin, and Mexico. To save costs and improve component part quality, many of the firm's product lines are vertically integrated. Plastic injection molding, welding, clutch assembly, and painting are all produced in house. Items such as fuel tank, tires, seats, and instruments are purchased from third-party vendors.

Polaris has an effective inventory management process called Maximum Velocity program (MVP) in which ORV orders can be placed in two-week intervals for high-volume dealers.

EXHIBIT 1 The Polaris Organizational Structure

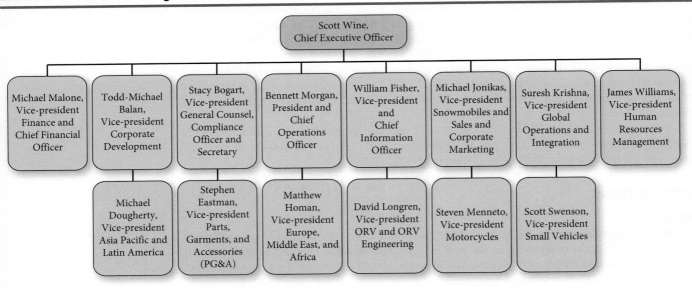

Source: Based on company documents.

Smaller dealers can use a similar process. The new process helps to keep costs down and inventories at manageable levels. Although ORV orders can be placed at any time, snowmobile orders must be placed in the spring and secured by deposit. Victory motorcycle orders are currently under MVP testing.

Sales and Marketing

Polaris has a network of about 1,650 independent dealers in North America and 15 subsidiaries and 80 distributors in over 100 countries outside of North America. The company's brands include RZR and Ranger ATVs, Indian and Victory motorcycles, and Polaris Rush snowmobiles. Snowmobiles are sold to dealers in the USA and Canada; many dealers also carry Polaris ORVs. A little more than half of all Polaris dealers in North America sell snowmobiles. ORVs are also sold through lawn and garden dealers in North America, but outside of North America, ORVs are generally handled through independent distributors. Polaris is shifting this strategy to wholly owned subsidiaries, which are now operating in Spain, China, Brazil, and India.

The Polaris Victory and Indian motorcycles are distributed through independently owned dealers outside the USA, with Melbourne and Sydney, Australia, being exceptions, in which Polaris has company owned dealers. As of 2012, Polaris had 400 dealers of Victory brand motorcycles in North America and 20 dealers of Indian motorcycles. The Polaris GEM business has around 130 dealers, and Groupil sells direct to customers in France and to dealers outside of France. The firm's military products are sold directly to the military and other government agencies.

Polaris uses group publications, billboards, and traditional television and radio for advertising. Product brochures, leaflets, posters, dealer signs, and other items are also used to help dealers market the products. Polaris spent $210 million in marketing in 2012, up from $179 million the prior year.

Research and Development (R&D)

Polaris has about 550 employees in R&D that concentrate on improving production techniques and developing new and improved products. R&D has a long tradition at Polaris because the company claims to have produced the first snowmobile with liquid cooled brakes, hydraulic breaks, three cylinder engines, and recently the MacPherson strut front suspension and Concentric Drive System in ORVs. Many of the R&D employees work in the 127,000-square foot R&D facility in Minnesota. Polaris spent about $127 million on R&D in 2012, up from $106 million the prior year.

Segments

Polaris competes in four distinct product segments: (1) ORVs, (2) snowmobiles, (3) on-road, and (4) PG&A. ORVs include side-by-side and ATV vehicles. Total revenues, as well as percent share each segment, are provided in Exhibit 2. Note that ORVs overwhelmingly are Polaris's best selling segment.

ORVs

As illustrated on the corporate website, Polaris produces 7 ORV models designed for the military, ranging in price from $7,000 to $35,000. The full line of ORVs, excluding military, consist of 35 vehicles in two-, four-, and six-wheel designs ranging in price from $7,000 to $35,000. A nice feature of most Polaris ORVs is that they offer a variable transmission, resulting in no manual shifting, and several models come with the MacPherson strut front suspension, enabling better control and stability. ORV sales increased 22 percent in 2012.

Snowmobiles

Although snowmobiles are where Polaris got its start, snowmobiles today account for about 9 percent of all sales, but the company's snowmobile sales increased 1.0 percent in 2012. Polaris today produces 28 different models of snowmobiles, including youth models, utility models to performance, and competition models used in racing. In 2012, U.S. retail prices for snowmobiles averaged $2,700 to $12,300 and are sold in Canada, Europe, and Russia. The company has a history of snowmobile innovation.

On-Road Vehicles

Polaris offers many options of its Victory brand motorcycles and many designed for cross-country trips. Acquired by Polaris in 2011, the Indian Motorcycle Company was the first motorcycle company in the USA, even predating Harley Davidson. Founded in 1901, Indian Motorcycle has earned distinction as one of the most legendary and iconic brands in the USA through unrivaled racing dominance, engineering prowess, and countless innovations and industry firsts (see www.indianmotorcycle.com). In total, Polaris makes 20 different motorcycle options available ranging in price from $12,500 to $36,000. Prices on the Polaris GEM range from $7,600 to $13,500, and the higher-end Goupil has 2012 prices ranging from $25,000 to $35,000.

PG&A

Polaris's PG&A segment is used to supply replacement parts and provide accessories for Polaris product lines. Items included in this category for ORVs include winches, bumper guards, plows, racks, mowers, tires, cargo box accessories, and many more. Snowmobile accessories include covers, traction products, electric starters, bags, and windshields. Motorcycle accessories include saddle bags, backrests, windshields, seats, and various chrome accessories. In addition to parts designed for use with specific products, the Polaris also produces apparel, including helmets, jackets, bibs, and pants.

By Region

Polaris provides a geographic breakdown of its revenues. Polaris sells products worldwide, but as revealed in Exhibit 3, 72 percent of all revenues in 2012 came from the USA and 14 percent from Canada. Polaris is trying to further expand into Western Europe and Russia, especially with its ORV and Victory motorcycle lines of products. Not revealed in Exhibit 3, Latin America and

EXHIBIT 2 Revenues by Product Category (in millions)

Year	ORV		Snowmobiles		On Road		PG&A	
2012	$2,225	69%	$283	9%	$240	8%	$408	14%
2011	1,822	69	280	11	146	5	408	15
2010	1,376	69	189	10	82	4	344	17
2009	1,021	65	179	12	53	3	313	20

Source: Based on 2012 *Form 10K*, page 30.

EXHIBIT 3 Revenues by Geographic Region (in millions)

Year	USA		Canada		Other Nations	
2012	$2,311	72%	$438	14%	460	16%
2011	1,864	70	369	14	424	16
2010	1,406	71	279	14	306	15
2009	1,074	69	239	15	252	16

Source: Based on 2012 *Form 10K*, page 31.

Asia Pacific sales grew 21 percent, respectively in 2012. However, these regions remain a negligible contribution to total revenues. With the new manufacturing plant in Mexico, Polaris hopes to improve on this weakness.

Finance

Polaris reported sales of $3.21 billion in 2012, up 21 percent from the prior year. In early 2012, Polaris announced a 14 percent increase in its quarterly cash dividend of $0.42 per a share.

Income Statements

Note in the income statements in Exhibit 4 that the company's revenue and net income have increased nicely in recent years.

EXHIBIT 4

POLARIS INDUSTRIES INC.
CONSOLIDATED STATEMENTS OF INCOME
(In thousands, except per share data)

	For the Years Ended December 31,		
	2012	**2011**	**2010**
Sales	$3,209,782	$2,656,949	$1,991,139
Cost of sales	2,284,485	1,916,366	1,460,926
Gross profit	925,297	740,583	530,213
Operating expenses:			
Selling and marketing	210,367	178,725	142,353
Research and development	127,361	105,631	84,940
General and administrative	143,064	130,395	99,055
Total operating expenses	480,792	414,751	326,348
Income from financial services	33,920	24,092	16,856
Operating income	478,425	349,924	220,721
Non-operating expense (income):			
Interest expense	5,932	3,987	2,680
Gain on securities available for sale	—	—	(825)
Equity in loss of other affiliates	179	—	—
Other (income) expense, net	(7,529)	(689)	325
Income before income taxes	479,843	346,626	218,541
Provision for income taxes	167,533	119,051	71,403
Net income	**$312,310**	**$227,575**	**$147,138**
Basic net income per share	$ 4.54	$ 3.31	$ 2.20
Diluted net income per share	$ 4.40	$ 3,20	$ 2.14
Weighted average shares outstanding:			
Basic	68,849	68,792	66,900
Diluted	71,005	71,057	68,765

Source: 2012 *Form 10K*, p. 48.

Balance Sheets

Note in the balance sheets provided in Exhibit 5 that the company's long-term debt is relatively low and the firm is in good financial shape.

EXHIBIT 5 The Polaris Balance Sheets

POLARIS INDUSTRIES INC.
CONSOLIDATED BALANCE SHEETS
(In thousands, except per share data)

	December 31, 2012	December 31, 2011
ASSETS		
Current Assets:		
Cash and cash equivalents	$417,015	$325,336
Trade receivables net	119,769	115,302
Inventories, net	344,996	298,042
Prepaid expenses and other	34,039	33,969
Income taxes receivable	15,730	24,723
Deferred tax assets	86,292	77,665
Total current assets	**1,017,841**	**875,037**
Property and Equipment:		
Land, buildings and improvements	133,688	123,771
Equipment and tooling	557,880	524,382
	691,568	648,153
Less accumulated depreciation	(438,199)	(434,375)
Property and equipment net	253,369	213,778
Investment in finance affiliate	56,988	42,251
Investment in other affiliates	12,817	5,000
Deferred tax assets	22,389	10,601
Goodwill and other intangible assets net	107,216	77,718
Other long-term assets	15,872	3,639
Total Assets	**$1,486,492**	**$1,228,024**
LIABILITIES AND SHAREHOLDERS' EQUITY		
Current Liabilities:		
Current portion of capital lease obligations	$2,887	$2,653
Accounts payable	169,036	146,743
Accrued expenses:		
Compensation	139,140	165,347
Warranties	47,723	44,355
Sales promotions and incentives	107,008	81,228
Dealer holdback	86,733	76,512
Other	73,529	68,856
Income taxes payable	4,973	639
Total current liabilities	631,029	586,333
Long term income taxes payable	7,063	7,837
Capital lease obligations	4,292	4,600
Long-term debt	100,000	100,000
Other long-term liabilities	53,578	29,198
Total liabilities	**795,962**	**727,968**
Shareholders' Equity:		
Preferred stock $0.01 par value, 20,000 shares authorized, no shares issued and outstanding	—	—
Common stock $0.01 par value, 160,000 shares authorized, 68,647 and 68,430 shares issued and outstanding	686	684
Additional paid-in capital	268,515	165,518
Retained earnings	409,091	321,831
Accumulated other comprehensive income, net	12,238	12,023
Total shareholders' equity	**690,530**	**500,056**
Total Liabilities and Shareholders' Equity	**$1,486,492**	**$1,228,024**

Source: 2012 Form 10K, p. 47

External Issues

The recreational vehicle industry has been one of the most consistent performers in terms of stock price over the last five years, which is pretty amazing for what some analysts say is a bunch of companies selling expensive toys. According to Morningstar, the recreational vehicle industry achieved an annualized total return of 10 percent over the past five years, which is 610 basis points higher than the S&P 500. In fact, the stocks in that sector performed in the top quartile over the last five-year, three-year, one-year, and year-to-date periods. Many analysts think that an improving economy should keep the party going for some time.

Industry Background

ORVs are designed for traversing through rough terrain such as swamps and marshlands and can often carry two to six passengers depending on the model. Their main purpose is for hunting and fishing, but they are also used on farms and ranches, in the military, and for mud riding or other rough-riding activities. ORVs were introduced in the USA in 1970 by Honda, followed later by Yamaha, Kawasaki, and Suzuki. Polaris entered the ATV market in 1985 followed by Artic Cat in 1995 and Bombardier in 1998. Both the USA and Western Europe, also a primary market for ATVs, have experienced a sales decline as customers prefer side-by-side ORVs. Polaris estimates during 2012, worldwide sales of ATVS increased 2 percent to 419,000 ATVs sold, whereas the side-by-side ORV sales increased 13 percent during the same period with around 353,000 units sold worldwide. Currently, the main competitors of Polaris in the side-by-side market are Deere & Company, Kawasaki, Yamaha, and Artic Cat.

Snowmobiles have been produced in the USA since at least the early 1950s and under the Polaris name since 1954. Originally, their designed purpose was for work in northern and snow-covered rural environments, however, like the ATV, many recreational fans have arisen providing additional markets for manufacturers. The novelty of snowmobiles peaked in the 1960s with more than 100 producers and 495,000 units produced in 1971. Today, the only makers of snowmobiles are Yamaha, BRP, Artic Cat, and Polaris. Industry-wide sales were around 131,000 units in 2012.

The on-road vehicle market consists of motorcycles and small electric vehicles. Polaris makes both the Victory and Indian motorcycles and a brand of small electric vehicles. There are generally four segments of motorcycles: (1) cruisers, (2) touring, (3) sports bikes, and (4) standard. Entering the motorcycle market in 1998 in the cruiser segment, Polaris enjoyed an overall industry doubling in sales from 1996 to 2006, but sales declined from 2007 to 2010 with the weakening economic conditions. Polaris entered the cruiser and touring market (defined as a bike with 1,400 cc and above) in 2010, and estimates this brand of bike had industry-wide sales of about 173,000 units in 2012 in North America, up 2 percent from the prior year.

Safety Regulations

Polaris products can be dangerous, especially because they are often used by youth. Both the federal and state governments continually promulgate laws to increase product safety and awareness in regard to ORVs, ATVs, snowmobiles, and motorcycles. International governments have taken similar measures. Two key commissions in the USA are the Consumer Product Safety Commission (CPSC), which has oversight on ATVs, snowmobiles, and side-by-side vehicles. The National Highway Transportation Safety Administration (NHTSA) has oversight on motorcycles and other small electric vehicles that Polaris produces. In 1988, for example, the CPSC forced Polaris and five of its competitors to recall all three- and four-wheel ATVS sold that could be used by youth younger than 16 years of age. The government is constantly imposing better suspension, breaks, and handing of vehicles. As recently as 2006, the U.S. government banned the sale of all three-wheel ATVs. Governmental oversight puts increased pressure on Polaris to closely monitor its dealers and ensure all dealers are in compliance with safety regulations.

Environmental Concerns

Recent governmental oversight has restricted the amount of lead paint that can be used on products aimed at youth 12 years of age and younger. In addition, to better protect the environment, the federal government and many state governments have restricted the use or banned all together the use of ATVs, ORVs, and snowmobiles from some national parks, federal lands, and state lands. It is unclear how these bans will impact sales.

The Environmental Protection Agency (EPA) continues to adopt and revise more stringent emission regulations for ATVs and ORVs. The laws require firms in the industry to increase its R&D expenditures to improve on emission technologies to meet not only current regulations but also future regulations. With Polaris products being sold in many different nations, it often results in all products being developed for the most stringent set of laws regarding emissions, further adding to costs.

Competition

Polaris competes in an industry that is fiercely competitive based on price, perceived quality, reliability, style, service, and warranties. In addition, dealers compete on financing, local advertising, and location of stores. Major Polaris competitors are Arctic Cat, Honda, Harley-Davidson, and Kawasaki, with John Deere also entering the side-by-side market. Note in Exhibit 6 that Honda is more than 30 times larger than Polaris, but Polaris is four times larger than Arctic Cat.

Arctic Cat

Headquartered in Plymouth, Minnesota, Arctic Cat designs, engineers, and produces snow-mobiles, side-by-sides, and ATVs under the Arctic Cat brand name. Arctic Cat's fiscal year ends March 31. With 1,300 employees, Arctic Cat also makes garments and accessories for its products. As noted previously, one of the founders of Polaris also founded rival Arctic Cat after leaving Polaris. The two companies make similar products, are structured similarly, and are located in the same region of the USA. Arctic Cat does business in the USA, Canada, and Europe through independent dealers, whereas customers in South America, the Middle East, and Asia can purchase products through third-party distributers.

For reporting purposes, Arctic Cat combines its ATVs, ORVs, and snowmobiles into one segment and lists its PGA in a separate segment. In fiscal 2013, Arctic Cat reported revenues of $250 million for snowmobiles, $227 million for its ATVs and ORVs, and $108 million for PGA. As revealed in Exhibit 6, Arctic Cat reported revenues of $671 million in fiscal 2013 and spent $37 million on marketing and $21 million on R&D.

The Arctic Cat brand is well respected in the recreational vehicles (RV) industry and controls 23 percent of the North American snowmobile market, about the same as larger rival Polaris. On the ATV side in North America, Artic Cat has just a 7.5-percent market share but recently introduced a side-by-side product line. Arctic Cat's Wildcat 4 1000 is especially popular. The company's stock's performance over the past five years is spectacular, up nearly 25 percent on an annualized basis.

Honda

Founded in 1946 and headquartered in Tokyo, Japan, Honda develops and sells motorcycles, ATVs, automobiles, and other power products such snow blowers, lawn mowers, weed eaters, generators, among many other power products. Honda is the world's largest motorcycle company and one of the world's largest automakers. Honda has recently initiated a new strategy with

EXHIBIT 6 Polaris versus Rival Firms (in millions except for debt/equity and EPS)

	Polaris	Arctic Cat	Honda
Sales	$3,028	$671	$98,090
Income	$327	$40	$3,650
Debt/Equity	0.15	0.00	0.98
EPS	4.62	3.24	1.92
Market Cap.	6,570	520	68,420
Shares Outstanding	69	13.19	1,810

EPS, earnings per share.
Source: Based on year-end 2012 company information.

its motorcycles to target the "fun segment." Honda's research reveals there is a growing demand for motorcycles in the smaller 125-cc and 700-cc sizes used for leisure, enjoyment, and everyday use. These products cost less and are cheaper to operate, having excellent fuel economy. The 125-cc size is targeted primarily at Asian and Indian customers.

In fiscal 2012, Honda reported that 17 percent of all its revenue was derived from motorcycles and ATVs, with total revenues of around 1,400 billion yen or approximately $16 billion. Like Honda's other divisions, the motorcycle and ATV division has experienced declining sales over the last five years. Sales in this division are down since 2008 in Japan, North America, and Europe with sales down around 60 percent in both the North America and European markets since 2008. Sales in Asia, South America, and the Middle East however are up 11 percent collectively since 2008. In 2012, Honda reported sales of 7,948 billion yen or around U.S. $93 billion.

The Future

In mid-2013, Polaris raised guidance for its full year 2013 earnings to a range of $5.20 to $5.30 per diluted share, up 19 percent over 2012 based on expected full year 2013 sales growth of 14 percent. Polaris acquired Indian Motorcycle Company in 2011 and has been focusing on re-launching the Indian brand. The company will soon compete directly with Harley Davidson in the 1400cc heavyweight motorcycle segment, which has a global addressable market of around 214,000 units. However, Polaris has less than one percent global market share in this segment, or just 428 units in 2012. The company is planning to increase Indian's dealer base from 20 in 2012 to nearly 140 by year-end 2013.

Develop a clear strategic plan for Polaris Industries.

Under Armour, Inc., 2013

www.ua.com, UA

Headquartered in Baltimore, Maryland, Under Armour (UA) was founded in 1996 by a former University of Maryland football player who desired a t-shirt that would whisk away perspiration rather than get soggy wet. The company has grown to be one of the most sought after brands among athletes around the world, being worn by some of the largest U.S. college football and European soccer teams. Colleges such as the Maryland Terrapins, Auburn Tigers, South Carolina Gamecocks, and many more have contracts with UA to outfit their teams. English soccer team Tottenham Hotspur, Greek team Aris F.C., and Mexican club Deportivo Toluca F.C. all are out-fitted by UA. Mega stars such as Tom Brady, Cam Newton, Bryce Harper, Michael Phelps, and many more, all sponsor and market UA products.

UA designs, develops, markets, and distributes apparel, footwear, and accessories for men, women, and children worldwide. The company offers apparel in three styles: compression, fitted, and loose and designed to be worn in hot, cold, or normal weather. Footwear products include cleats for most all sports, running and basketball shoes, and even hunting boots. Accessories include gloves for football, baseball, golf, socks, and team uniforms. UA's moisture-wicking fabrications are engineered in many different designs and styles for wear in nearly every climate to provide a performance alternative to traditional products. Its products are sold worldwide and worn by athletes at all levels, from youth to professional, on playing fields around the globe. UA's European headquarters are in Amsterdam's Olympic Stadium, with additional offices in Denver, Hong Kong, Toronto, and Guangzhou, China. With about 1,800 employees, UA distrib-utes its products through specialty retailers, department stores, outlet stores, and institutional athletic departments.

For the second quarter of 2013 that ended June 30, 2013, UA reported that revenues increased 23 percent to $455 million while the company's net income increased 163 percent to $18 million compared to the prior year's period. The company's apparel revenues increased 23 percent to $310 million, primarily driven by a new baselayer product and the expansion of the Storm and Charged Cotton products. The company's second quarter footwear revenues increased 21 percent to $82 million, spurred by the Highlight football cleat and the UA Spine platform. UA's Q2 2013 accessories revenues increased 30 percent to $51 million, primarily driven by headwear. For the quarter, UA's Direct-to-Consumer revenues represented 30 percent of total net revenues and grew 29 percent year-over-year. The company's Women's category is doing well with its new Studio and ArmourBra products, and the Spine running footwear is doing well.

Copyright by Fred David Books LLC. (Written by Forest R. David)

History

At age 23, Kevin Plank developed a new t-shirt in his grandmother's basement in Washington D.C. after noticing that his compression shorts always stayed dry, but t-shirts had to be changed frequently because they became sweat soaked. This observation led Plank to create a new compression t-shirt that whisked away sweat. After graduating, Plank provided this t-shirt to his former teammates who were playing in the National Football League (NFL). After positive reviews, UA had t-shirt orders totaling $100,000 in 1997. UA's first big break came when *USA Today* pictured Oakland Raiders quarterback Jeff George wearing UA apparel. In late 1997, Georgia Tech asked for 10 shirts, ultimately leading to deals with Georgia Tech, Arizona State, and North Carolina State universities.

In the 2000s, UA expanded rapidly after outfitting Warner Brothers with apparel for two films, and an advertisement placed in *ESPN Magazine* generated $750,000 in sales. In 2003, UA became the outfitter of the now defunct XFL football league and launched its first TV advertise-ment with the motto "Protect this House."

UA recently opened specialty stores, including a 6,000-square foot store in Illinois and has opened factory outlet stores in 34 states. In 2011, the company purchased 400,000 square feet of office space for $60.5 million. UA has new contracts with the NFL, National Basketball Association (NBA), and Major League Baseball (MLB) to produce footwear, apparel, and accessories. Many European football teams such as Trottenham Hotspur and other rugby teams are outfitted with UA products. None of UA's 5,900 employees are members of a union, and 1,900 are full-time.

Internal Issues

UA owns no fabric or process patents. Thus, UA competitors can manufacture and sell products very similar to UA products. UA's success thus hinges a lot on their brand image, trademarks, and copyrights.

Vision and Mission

Regarding UA's vision, CEO Plank recently said:

> Our investments illustrate our commitment to realizing our long-term vision of one day having our Women's business larger than Men's, Footwear larger than Apparel, and our International business larger than our U.S. business.

Organizational Structure

UA reportedly operates under four geographic segments: (1) North America, (2) Europe, the Middle East, and Africa (EMEA), (3) Asia, and (4) Latin America. However, from its organization structure revealed in Exhibit 1, it appears the company is structured divisionally by product.

Marketing

UA's marketing expenses were $205.4 million in 2012, up from $167.9 million the prior year. But these marketing expenses were 11.2 percent of revenues, down from 11.4 percent the prior year. UA's advertising expenditures in 2012 and 2011 were $205.4 million and $167.9 million respectively. UA develops and markets products primarily for use in athletics, fitness, and any outdoor activities. UA attempts to drive demand through brand equity and increasing consumer awareness of its superior product. UA's growth is largely dependent on sales from Dick's Sporting Goods, The Sports Authority, and Foot Locker, which have store-within-a-store sales

EXHIBIT 1 Under Armour's Organizational Structure

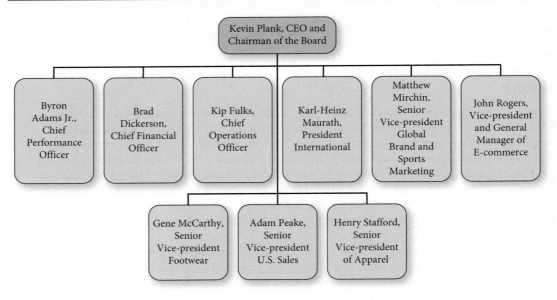

Source: Based on company documents.

channels. However, UA has been making great strides selling its products directly to consumers, with 29 percent of revenue in 2012 coming from direct sales. UA has the brand strength to attract many consumers to more profitable channels. However, 69 percent of 2012 revenue was from wholesale, and 2 percent from licenses.

A key strategy for UA is securing endorsement of its products from high-performing athletes who have significant influence in the NFL, NBA, MLB, and even high school teams. Many sports stars such as Cam Newton and Tom Brady endorse and wear UA products. It is UA's belief that this strategy is the best possible way to advertise its products because many fans become familiar with UA products seeing them worn by high-performing athletes on a year round basis. In addition to focusing on the large-market leagues, UA also focuses on brand authenticity from a more grassroots level. By hosting camps, clinics, and other activities for young athletes, it is able to gain a firsthand appreciation for UA's product quality and brand equity.

UA uses broadcast, print, and social media outlets to promote the firm's product. UA also engages in acquiring prime real estate in the 25,000 major retail stores worldwide in which their products are sold, as well as operating outlet stores in 34 different states. UA products are sold throughout the world. New UA products in 2012 included UA Studio line, the Armour Bra, cold-back technology, UA Spine footwear, and UA scent control technology.

"The biggest, baddest brand on the planet, bar none." That's how founder and CEO Plank likes to describe his vision for what UA can ultimately become. Plank and his team are excellent marketers; the company's blood-pumping ads resonate with athletes and those who aspire to become athletes. UA's bold logo and brash and edgy marketing campaigns inspire movement and physical fitness, positioning the company well within the healthier lifestyle megatrend. Plank and his team relish their underdog image versus big rival firms; they love to operate within and promote an "us-versus-them" philosophy. This competitive fire has served UA well and has encapsulated many athletes and fans.

UA has 102 factory house stores in North America, mostly located in the eastern USA. UA opened its first factory house store in Canada in 2012.

Finance

In late 2012, UA has an impressive annual growth rate of 34 percent since 2005, has a market cap of $4.32 billion, and a price-to-earnings (P/E) ratio of 49.4, above the S&P 500 P/E ratio of 17.7. UA shares were up 44.6 percent year-to-date as of December 20, 2012. Strong financially, UA has used zero of its $300 million revolving credit facility at the end of September 2012. UA's debt-to-equity ratio is low at 0.10. UA has a quick ratio of 1.84 and has improved its earnings per share by 22.7 percent in the most recent quarter compared to the same quarter a year ago. UA does not pay dividends, preferring to reinvest all earnings back into the firm.

UA expects 2012 net revenues of approximately $1.82 billion, representing growth of 24 percent over 2011, and 2012 operating income of approximately $207 million, representing growth of 27 percent over 2011. Plank says: "I am proud of what our team has accomplished so far this year and we are well positioned for growth in 2013 and beyond. I emphasize 'team', as we continue to make great strides with the additions of seasoned leadership in Supply Chain, Women's, and International."

UA revenues increased 24 percent in the third quarter of 2012 to $575 million compared with net revenues of $466 million in the previous year's period. Net income increased 25 percent. UA's recent income statements and balance sheets are provided in Exhibits 2 and 3, respectively. Note that the company pays no dividends and is performing in an excellent manner.

Segment Data By-Product

Exhibit 4 provides a breakdown of UA's revenues by product. Note that apparel continues to be the strongest product offered based on net revenues, but footwear and accessories such as bags, hats, and gloves experienced higher percent increases over the most recent fiscal year. License revenues decreased as a result partly of less orders of hats and bags. Seventy-six percent of company revenues are derived from apparel in 2012. Followed by footwear at 13 percent and accessories at 9 percent.

EXHIBIT 2

Under Armour Statements of Income
(In thousands, except per share amounts)

	Year Ended December 31,		
	2012	2011	2010
Net revenues	$1,834,921	$1,472,684	$1,063,927
Cost of goods sold	955,624	759,848	533,420
Gross profit	**879,297**	**712,836**	**530,507**
Selling, general and administrative expenses	670,602	550,069	418,152
Income from operations	208,695	162,767	112,355
Interest expense, net	(5,183)	(3,841)	(2,258)
Other expense, net	(73)	(2,064)	(1,178)
Income before income taxes	203,439	156,862	108,919
Provision for income taxes	74,661	59,943	40,442
Net income	**$128,778**	**$96,919**	**$68,477**
Net income available per common share			
Basic	$1.23	$0.94	$0.67
Diluted	$1.21	$0.92	$0.67
Weighted average common shares outstanding			
Basic	104,343	103,140	101,595
Diluted	106,380	105,052	102,563

Source: 2012 Form 10K, p. 49.

EXHIBIT 3 Under Armour Balance Sheets

Under Armour, Balance Sheets
(In thousands, except share data)

	December 31, 2012	December 31, 2011
Assets		
Current assets		
Cash and cash equivalents	$341,841	$175,384
Accounts receivable, net	175,524	134,043
Inventories	319,286	324,409
Prepaid expenses and other current assets	43,896	39,643
Deferred income taxes	23,051	16,184
Total current assets	**903,598**	**689,663**
Property and equipment, net	180,850	159,135
Intangible assets, net	4,483	5,535
Deferred income taxes	22,606	15,885
Other long-term assets	45,546	48,992
Total assets	**$1,157,083**	**$919,210**
Liabilities and Stockholders' Equity		
Current liabilities		
Accounts payable	$143,689	$100,527
Accrued expenses	85,077	69,285
Current maturities of long-term debt	9,132	6,882
Other current liabilities	14,330	6,913
Total current liabilities	**252,228**	**183,607**
Long-term debt, net of current maturities	52,757	70,842
Other long-term liabilities	35,176	28,329
Total liabilities	**340,161**	**282,778**

EXHIBIT 3 Continued

	December 31, 2012	December 31, 2011
Commitments and contingencies		
Stockholders' equity		
Class A Common Stock, $0.0003 1/3 par value; 200,000,000 shares authorized as of December 31, 2012 and 2011; 83,461,106 shares issued and outstanding as of December 31, 2012 and 80,992,252 shares issued and outstanding as of December 31, 2011.	28	27
Class B Convertible Common Stock, $0.0003 1/3 par value; 21,300,000 shares authorized, issued and outstanding as of December 31,2012 and 22,500,000 shares authorized, issued and outstanding as of December 31, 2011.	7	7
Additional paid-in capital	321,338	268,206
Retained earnings	493,181	366,164
Accumulated other comprehensive income	2,368	2,028
Total stockholders' equity	**816,922**	**636,432**
Total liabilities and stockholders' equity	**$1,157,083**	**$919,210**

Source: 2012 Form 10K, p. 48

Apparel is offered in many styles and fits to cover most any environment condition. Apparel is specifically engineered to replace traditional nonperformance fabrics and replace them with the most cutting edge products available. UA currently has three gear lines that achieve the designed purpose of having a sophisticated apparel option for all weather conditions. The three products are marketed under HEATGEAR, designed for hot weather, COLDGEAR, designed for cold temperatures, and ALLSEASONGEAR, designed for between the extremes. In addition to the three temperature ratings, all products also come in three fit types: compression (tight fit), fitted (athletic fit), and loose (relaxed). All UA appeal products are designed to whisk water away from the wearer to keep them as dry and comfortable as possible in any temperature or type of activity.

UA expanded into offering footwear in 2006 and today makes footwear for virtually all sports including running and even hunting boots. Like the traditional shirts, footwear offerings are designed to cushion and manage moisture. In 2011, UA began to sell hats and bags in house; these products were previously provided by a licensee. Other accessories developed and now marketed by UA include gloves for football, baseball, golf, and running as well as mouth guards, socks, and eye wear.

Segment Data By Region

Exhibit 5 reveals UA's recent revenues and operating profits for the North American and international markets. UA reports revenues in four distinct geographic regions: (1) North America, (2) EMEA, (3) Asia, and (4) Latin America. Each geographic segment operates in the same

EXHIBIT 4 UA Segment Data by Product

	Year Ended December 31 (in Thousands),			Percent Change	
	2012	2011	2010	2012	2011
Apparel	$1,385,350	$1,122,031	$853,493	23.5%	31.5%
Footwear	238,955	181,684	127,175	31.5	42.9
Accessories	165,835	132,400	43,882	25.3	201
Total net sales	1,790,140	1,436,115	1,024,550	24.7	40.2
License revenues	44,781	36,569	39,377	22.5	(7.1)
Total revenues	1,834,921	$1,472,684	$1,063,927	24.6%	38.4%

Source: 2012 Form 10K, p. 29.

manner, to design, develop, market, and distribute UA products. Note that only 6 percent of UA revenues were derived from international markets so the company combines all these countries into one segment for reporting reasons. UA acknowledges that the trend in performance products is becoming increasingly global with a bright future, but 6 percent so far leaves tremendous upside for the company.

UA's North American segment includes about 18,000 retail stores; UA also owns 80 outlet stores located in 34 different states. The company's two largest customers are Dick's Sporting Goods and The Sports Authority. In addition to selling to the public, UA earns income from the sale of uniforms and practice gear to high school, college, and professional teams.

In EMEA, UA products are sold in approximately 4,000 retail outlet stores. European football teams that wear UA gear reside in many European nations including the United Kingdom, France, Germany, Greece, Italy, and Spain among others. First division rugby clubs in France, Ireland Italy, and the United Kingdom also wear UA products. Products in Europe are currently distributed out of The Netherlands.

Since 2002, UA has enjoyed a licensing agreement with Dome Corp., which produces and sells UA products in Japan, which are all tailored for Japanese consumers' specific taste. Products are sold in more than 2,500 specialty stores in Japan, as well as to several professional soccer and baseball games in Japan. Also in Asia, products are sold in both Australia and New Zealand, and in 2011, UA's first specialty store opened in Shanghai, China. Latin American customers are provided UA products through independent distributors but more commonly are served through distribution facilities in the USA. Only 6 percent of UA's 2012 revenues were generated from outside North America. The company does have two specialty stores in Shanghai, China. About 55 percent of the fabric used in UA products comes from suppliers in China, Malaysia, Mexico, Taiwan, and Vietnam. UA has 27 manufacturers in 14 countries.

Competition

UA has unique branding of a fabric to whisk away water from the body, but competitors such as Nike and Adidas have copied UA's designs and technology. The fabrics UA uses are not unique to them, and it does not control any patents on fabrics or processes. It is all about branding for UA. Because firms such as Nike and Adidas have much larger resources to draw on, competing long term may be difficult for UA, but so far the firm is doing well. In addition, competing for floor space at large retailers is difficult because many stores have their own store brands, in addition to private label brands, all competing for floor space.

Exhibit 6 provides some comparative information for UA and rival firms. Note that in terms of revenue UA is about the size of Columbia Sportswear, but Nike and Adidas are both more

EXHIBIT 5 UA Segment Data by Geographic Region

	Year Ended December 31 (in Thousands),				
	2012	2011	2010	Percent Change	
Net Revenues					
North America	$1,726,733	$1,383,346	$997,816	38.6%	
Other Foreign Countries	108,188	89,338	66,111	35.1%	
Total Net Revenues	1,834,921	1,472,684	1,063,927	38.4%	
Operating Profits				2012	2011
North America	$197,194	$150,559	$102,806	31.0%	46.4%
Other Foreign Countries	11,501	12,208	9,549	(5.8)	27.8
Total Operating Profit	208,695	162,767	112,355	28.2	44.9

Source: 2012 Form 10K, p. 33.

EXHIBIT 6 Comparative Information for Sports Apparel Firms

	Under Armour	Adidas	Columbia Sportswear	Nike
Number of Employees	1.9K	39.9K	4.1K	40K
Net Income ($)	98.9M	922M	94.6M	2.2B
Revenue ($)	1.54B	17.1B	1.7B	24B
Revenue ($)/Employee	855K	429K	414K	600K
EPS Ratio ($)	0.95	2.20	2.78	4.73
Market Cap.	5.2B	15.3B	1.8B	42.6B

EPS, earnings per share.
Source: Based on company documents.

than 10 times the size of UA. Note also that UA is exceptionally efficient as indicated by its high revenue per employee ratio.

Nike

Headquartered in Beaverton, Oregon, Nike is the largest apparel and footwear provider for men, women, and children worldwide. Nike outfits athletes globally in virtually every sport, including running, basketball, football, soccer, golf, and many more. In addition to apparel and footwear, Nike also produces golf clubs, athletic bags, gloves, footballs, bats, and much more. Nike owns brands such as Converse, Chuck Taylor, and All Star to name a few.

Nike reported in 2011 that 42 percent of revenues derived from U.S. operations, where the company sells its products in a wide range of mediums from retail stores, its Internet site, 156 Nike factory stores, and tens of thousands of other stores, such as Foot Locker. Nike's international sales accounted for 58 percent of revenues in 2011 and products are sold in similar ways as in the USA. Nike currently operates 308 factory stores outside the USA. Approximately 67 percent of all Nike North American revenues are derived from footwear, 28 percent from appeal, and only 5 percent from equipment. Nike's operations in international markets have a similar revenue breakdown by product, making Nike's primary revenue generator footwear, as opposed to UA being primarily an apparel producer.

Like UA, Nike outfits many professional and major U.S. college teams with their gear. Notable teams wearing Nike gear include the University of Oregon, Penn State University, and The University of Alabama. Nike has stars such as Michael Jordan, LeBron James, and Tiger Woods serving as spokespersons to help in promoting the brand. Late in 2012, Nike sold its Cole Haan handbag and shoe brand to private equity firm Apax Partners for $570 million and also sold its Umbro football brand to Iconix Brand Group for $225 million.

Adidas AG

Headquartered in Herzogenaurach, Germany, Adidas AG develops and produces a wide range of athletic appear, footwear, and accessories and operates in six business segments: wholesale, retail, TaylorMade-Adidas Golf, Rockport, Reebok-CCM Hockey, as well as other brands. Adidas sells its products through retail stores, the Internet, and through 2,401 company-owned stores worldwide. The company most closely competes with UA with its sport performance line of apparel that is modeled after UA fabrics to help keep athletes dry and comfortable for the duration of their activity.

Adidas currently has a contract with the NBA to outfit all teams with apparel, and in addition, Adidas outfits some or the largest European football clubs with apparel. Adidas employs many of soccer's biggest starts to market their products, such as Frank Lampard, Steven Gerrard, and Micheal Ballack. Tennis stars endorsing Adidas include Andy Murray, Justine Henin, Marcos Baghdatis, and many more. Andy Murray is Adidas's highest paid spokesman with a five-year contract worth $24.5 million.

Adidas had sales of more than 13 billion euros in 2011, an 11-percent increase from the previous year, with every reporting segment enjoying larger revenues than the previous fiscal year.

The retail and TaylorMade-Adidas Golf segments enjoyed the largest percent increases at 20 and 16 percent, respectively.

Columbia Sportswear Company

Headquartered in Portland, Oregon, Columbia's trademark Bugaboo parka with weatherproof shell competes with some UA products, as does Columbia's performance apparel for a variety of activities and Columbia's sportswear accessories, boots, and rugged footwear, sold under brands Columbia, Mountain Hardwear, Sorel, and Montrail. Columbia brands are used globally during outdoor activities, such as skiing, snowboarding, hiking, climbing, camping, hunting, fishing, running, and the like. Columbia operates about 50 outlet retail stores and 10 branded retail stores in the USA, as well as 10 in Europe, 2 outlet stores in Canada, and about 300 stores in Japan and Korea. Thousands of other stores sell Columbia products globally, including even Dick's Sporting Goods and The Sports Authority that UA counts on most.

External Issues

Economic Factors

The apparel industry has a mediocre outlook given weak economies in which consumers are faced with less discretionary income. Items expected to maintain strong sales are those that are well differentiated from competing products, where consumers value the extra features and are less price sensitive to products they deem necessary. More luxury items in both sporting activities are expected to have modest growth. In 2011, the apparel industry reported sales up 5.9 percent over 2010, however much of this gain was the result of inflation and the rising prices of commodities such as cotton, increased labor wages overseas, and increased freight fees. Nevertheless, the S&P Apparel Retail Index rose 22 percent versus a 12-percent increase for the S&P 1500 Index from March 2011 to March 2012. The S&P Footwear Index rose only 11.5 percent during this same time frame.

Apparel sales totaling $77.7 billion was imported into the USA in 2011, up nearly 9 percent from 2010. Approximately 38 percent of all apparel imported came from China. The apparel industry is extremely fragmented with many firms competing for the same customers. For example, the top 10 national brands only account for 16 percent of wholesale apparel sales in the USA with 84 percent of apparel distributed coming from smaller brands and store brand goods. Women's segment has traditionally accounted for significantly more sales at 55 percent. Men only accounted for 28 percent and children 17 percent of apparel sales in 2011.

The footwear industry grew at a slower rate than apparel in 2011. Fashion footwear accounted for 48 percent of total footwear sales, with performance footwear accounting for 27 percent, sports footwear 13 percent, outdoor footwear 8 percent, and work and safety footwear 4 percent. Fashion and sports footwear are expected to be the most significant areas of growth moving forward as people look to improve their fashion looks and the growing health-minded concerns of the public.

Technological Changes

Nike was one of the first companies to understand the importance of producing better sporting apparel and footwear for athletes, when Phillip Knight and his track coach Bill Bowerman developed a better shoe for members of the University of Oregon track team. Since the 1960s, there have been many developments and improvements in shoe and apparel design away from the traditional cotton sweat suit and basic tennis shoe. Today, apparel hugs the body and insulates the wearer from cold and keeps them cool from hot. Shoes can be synced to computers to determine performance and impact points for the runner and t-shirt fabrics can even help manage odors. These types of technological offerings keep customers purchasing new items and can create intense competition and brand loyalty.

Where to Produce

China has historically been the low-cost alternative for apparel firms when selection a nation for the production of their products. In 2011 alone, 38 percent of all apparel imports and 74 percent of all footwear imports into the USA came from China. However, with rising production costs, higher wages in China, increased transportation costs and less control over quality, Chinese imports may be waning in the eyes of large U.S. apparel corporations in favor of facilities in Mexico and the Caribbean. UA currently produces many of their items in Mexico and enjoys quicker turnaround and more quality control than some rival firms who import a large percentage of their inventory from China.

The Future

UA needs considerably more global presence to gain economies of scale versus its large rival firms. Increasing downward pressure on prices could necessitate that UA effectively expand globally. The primary strategic issue facing UA therefore is how and when and where to expand globally. Other secondary strategic issues facing UA include whether to diversify into other accessory items to reduce the firm's reliance on apparel and whether to increase its expenditures on R&D to keep pace with changing technological advancements in the apparel industry. UA is strong financially, which does enable the firm to make strategic acquisitions as needed, so the firm should identify potential acquisition candidates around the world. Effective global expansion is an important key to UA's growth and prosperity in the future. Even South America, Central America, Mexico, and Australia are all sports-minded areas in which UA products should be well received. Perhaps what UA needs most is to fulfill CEO Plank's vision: "Our long-term vision is to one day have our Women's business larger than Men's, our Footwear business larger than Apparel, and our International business larger than our USA business."

Prepare a five-year strategic plan for CEO Plank to fulfill his vision for UA.

Avon Products, Inc., 2013

www.avon.com, AVP

Headquartered in New York City, Avon is one of the world's largest direct-seller firms, and is by far the largest direct seller of cosmetics and beauty-related items. Avon is the fifth-largest cosmetics and fragrance firm in the world. The company receives sales from catalogs and a website, but the vast majority of its sales come from its 6.4 million independent sales representatives in some 110 countries. These women are all independent contractors. Avon has 39,100 employees, but only 4,800 are employed in the USA. Since 1892, Avon has been on the forefront of empowering women to be their own boss and be independent and become leaders in communities and business.

Avon products include cosmetics, fragrances, toiletries, jewelry, apparel, home furnishings, watches, footwear, children's products, skin care, and gift and decorative products, nutritional products, housewares, and entertainment and leisure products. Avon owns and sells Silpada jewelry. A few well-recognized company brand names include Avon Color, ANEW, Skin-So-Soft, Advance Techniques, and *mark*. Although a large U.S. iconic corporation, Avon is struggling today to recover from poor management strategies that led to CEO Jung resigning over global bribery investigations. The direct-selling business model has waned in the USA, but it is effective in many emerging economies globally. Avon obtains 85 percent of its revenue from outside the USA. Millions of motivated direct sellers in many countries is Avon's key competitive advantage going forward, but the company needs a clear strategic plan.

Avon reported a loss of $38.2 million in 2012 compared to a net income of $517.8 million the prior year. Avon's second-quarter 2013 net income declined 48 percent but that was above Wall Street expectations and so Avon's stock price hit a new high for the year. Avon has made an offer to settle its overseas bribery allegations for $12 million; the offer has been rejected by U.S. authorities. Avon's beauty products earned $31.9 million for Q2, down from $61.6 million a year ago. Revenue slipped 2 percent to $2.51 billion due to currency rates and North American sales. Avon's sales in North America during Q2 2013 declined 12 percent, hurt by a 13 percent drop in the number of active sales representatives. Avon's Asia-Pacific sales fell 9 percent, but the company's sales in Latin America and Europe, the Middle East and Africa rose. For the quarter, Avon's prices rose and their average order size increased.

Copyright by Fred David Books LLC. (Written by Forest R. David)

History

David McConnell started a business in 1886 that eventually came to be named Avon Products. A traveling book salesman, McConnell did not originally intend to create a beauty company, but he realized that his female customers were far more interested in the free perfume samples he offered than in his books. McConnell had also noticed that many of his female customers were isolated at home while their husbands went off to work. So, McConnell purposely recruited female sales representatives and believed they had a natural ability to network with and market to other women. At a time of limited employment options for women, the Avon earnings opportunity for women historically was a revolutionary concept for mankind. It marked the start of the company's long and rich history of empowering women around the globe.

In 1892, McConnell changed the company name when his business partner, who was living in California, suggested that he name his business the California Perfume Company, because of the great abundance of flowers in California. In 1916, the California Perfume Company was incorporated in the state of New York and filed its first trademark application for Avon on June 3, 1932. The document described the company's goods and services as perfumes, toilet waters, powder and rouge compacts, lipsticks, and other toiletry products.

Avon entered the Chinese market in 1990, but legal changes in 1998 forced Avon to sell only through physical stores called Beauty Boutiques. The company received China's first license for direct selling in 2006. Avon purchased Silpada, a direct seller of silver jewelry, in 2010 for $650 million. Brazil is the company's largest market, passing the USA in 2010. Avon closed its Atlanta distribution center in 2013 and is closing its Pasadena distribution center in 2014. Avon's revenue dropped 5 percent to $10.72 billion in 2012.

Internal Issues

Vision and Mission

Avon has stated vision and mission statements on its corporate website. Avon's vision is: "To be the company that best understands and satisfies the product, service and self-fulfillment needs of women—globally." Avon's mission statement is quite lengthy, but in summary it says: Avon's mission is focused on six core aspirations the company continually strives to achieve: (1) leader in global beauty, (2) women's choice for buying, (3) premier direct-selling company, (4) most-admired company, (5) best place to work, and (6) to have the largest foundation dedicated to women's causes.

Marketing and R&D

Avon uses both door-to-door sales people ("Avon ladies," primarily, but a growing number of men) and brochures to advertise its products. Avon training centers help women who want to become Avon representatives selling beauty products, jewelry, accessories, and clothing. The Avon training centers have a small retail section with skin care products, such as creams, serums, makeup, and washes. There are classroom areas in which the representatives learn about the products and sales techniques. Avon representative are each independent sole proprietors running their own business.

Avon spent $253.6 million on advertising in 2012, down from $311.2 million the prior year. Avon spent $75.2 million on R&D in 2012, down from $77.7 million the prior year. Avon's primary R&D facility is located in Suffern, New York.

Sustainability and Philanthropy

Avon has extensive information on its corporate website about its sustainability and philanthropy programs and operations. Avon is a huge advocate for women's rights and works tirelessly through its Foundation for Women to combat violence against women, breast cancer, and more. For example the recent 10th Annual New York Avon Walk for Breast Cancer raised more than $8.3 million. Avon is also on a mission to help prevent deforestation worldwide.

Founded in 1955, the Avon Foundation for Women is the largest corporate-affiliated philanthropic organization for women in the world. Avon has always been committed to helping women achieve their highest potential of economic opportunity and self-fulfillment by empowering them through scholarships and support for other forms of educational and occupational training and advancement. The Avon Foundation awards scholarships for Avon Sales Representatives and their families, as well as for the children of Avon associates. The Avon Foundation is currently focused on two key causes: breast cancer and domestic violence. The foundation approved $38 million in grants in 2011. In 2012, Avon launched its first global fundraising drive.

Organizational Structure

Avon's CEO is Sheri McCoy, who previously was a top executive at Johnson & Johnson. The former Avon CEO, Andrea Jung, was the longest-tenured female CEO among *Fortune* 500 companies. Jung stepped down as CEO in April 2012 and relinquished her Avon board seat at year-end 2012.

As indicated in Exhibit 1, Avon operates from a divisional-by-geographic region organizational structure. Note there is no chief operations officer (COO) so apparently all top executives report to the CEO. In fact, there has been no COO at Avon since 2006, a potential strategic mistake by CEO Jung (and McCoy).

EXHIBIT 1 Avon's Organizational Chart

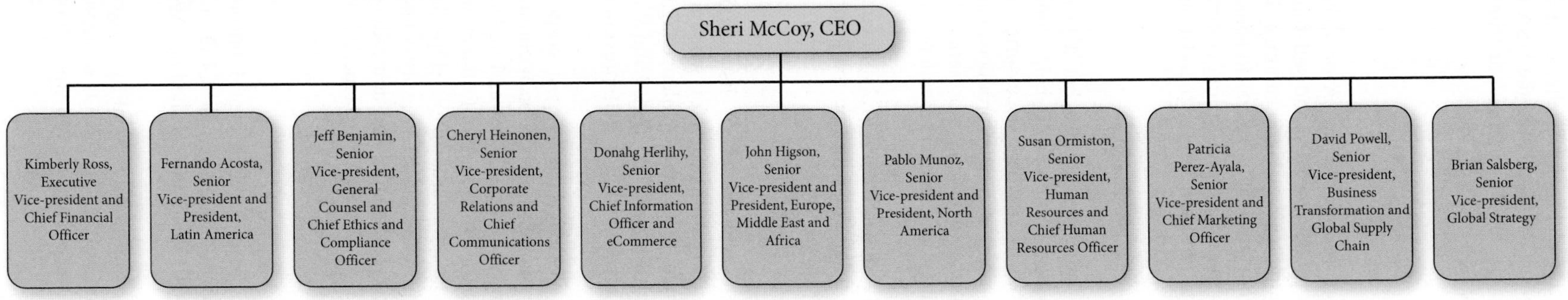

Sheri McCoy, CEO

Kimberly Ross, Executive Vice-president and Chief Financial Officer

Fernando Acosta, Senior Vice-president and President, Latin America

Jeff Benjamin, Senior Vice-president, General Counsel and Chief Ethics and Compliance Officer

Cheryl Heinonen, Senior Vice-president, Corporate Relations and Chief Communications Officer

Donahg Herlihy, Senior Vice-president, Chief Information Officer and eCommerce

John Higson, Senior Vice-president and President, Europe, Middle East and Africa

Pablo Munoz, Senior Vice-president and President, North America

Susan Ormiston, Senior Vice-president, Human Resources and Chief Human Resources Officer

Patricia Perez-Ayala, Senior Vice-president and Chief Marketing Officer

David Powell, Senior Vice-president, Business Transformation and Global Supply Chain

Brian Salsberg, Senior Vice-president, Global Strategy

Source: Based on company information.

EXHIBIT 2 Avon's Revenue and Profits By Region

Years ended December 31	2012		2011		2010	
	Total Revenue	Operating Profit (Loss)	Total Revenue	Operating Profit (Loss)	Total Revenue	Operating Profit
Latin America	$4,993.7	$443.9	$5,161.8	$634.0	$4,640.0	$613.3
Europe, Middle East & Africa	2,914.2	312.8	3,122.8	478.9	3,047.9	474.3
North America	1,906.8	(214.9)	2,064.6	(188.0)	2,193.5	147.3
Asia Pacific	902.4	5.1	942.4	81.4	981.4	82.6
Total from operations	10,717.1	546.9	11,291.6	1,006.3	10,862.8	1,317.5
Global and other expenses	–	(232.1)	–	(151.7)	–	(244.4)
Total	**$10,717.1**	**$314.8**	**$11,291.6**	**$854.6**	**$10,862.8**	**$1,073.1**

Source: 2012 *Annual Report,* p. 33.

Segments

Comparing 2012 to 2011, Avon's geographic results are provided in Exhibit 2. Note the percent revenue decline in every geographic region, although a few particular countries with regions reported increases.

Avon's reportable segments are sometimes noted to be: (a) beauty, (b) fashion, and (c) home. Beauty consists of color cosmetics, fragrances, skin care, and personal care. Fashion consists of fashion jewelry, watches, apparel, footwear, accessories, and children's products. Home consists of gift and decorative products, housewares, entertainment and leisure products, and nutritional products. Avon's sales in its Beauty, Fashion, and Home segments decreased 5, 5, and 4 percent respectively in 2012 from the prior year. For 2012, the Beauty segment accounted for 72 percent of company sales, followed by Fashion at 18 percent and Home at 10 percent. Specifically within the Beauty segment, 2012 Fragrance, Color, Skincare, and Personal Care revenues were down 4, 6, 7, and 6 percent respectively.

Finance

Avon's cash dividends paid out dropped to $0.75 per share in 2012 from $0.92 the prior year. The company's long-term debt increased to $2.62 billion from $2.45 billion the prior year.

Avon's recent income statements and balance sheets are provided in Exhibits 3 and 4, respectively. Note that Avon's revenue and net income decreased in 2012.

Competitors

As indicated in Exhibit 3, Avon's earnings per share (EPS) and profit margin are negative. L'Oreal leads the beauty industry, but other firms also compete with Avon, especially Mary Kay, Revlon, Estee Lauder, Coty, and Procter & Gamble. A synopsis of some of these rival firms is provided.

EXHIBIT 3 Avon versus Rival Firms

	Avon	L'Oreal	Revlon
Number of Employees	39.1K	68.3K	5.2K
Revenue ($)	10.7B	27.7B	1.4B
Net income ($)	(42.5)M	3.36B	40.6M
Profit Margin (%)	—	12.1	2.9
Revenue ($)/employee	273K	406K	269K
EPS	—	1.12	0.78
Market capitalization	10.5B	83.1B	775.9M

EPS, earnings per share.

L'Oreal SA

Headquartered in France, L'Oreal is a large, global, cosmetic conglomerate with annual sales of about $30 billion and net income of about $3.5 billion. L'Oreal is structured into three segments: (1) Cosmetics, (2) The Body Shop, and (3) Dermatology. The Cosmetics unit is divided into four sectors: Consumer Products, Professional Products, Luxury Products, and Active Cosmetics. Consumer Products are marketed under L'Oreal Paris, Garnier, Maybelline New York (Maybelline NY), and Softsheen-Carson brands. Professional Products, including hair care products for use by professional hairdressers, are marketed under Kerastase, Redken, Matrix, and L'Oreal Professionnel. Luxury Products are sold under such international brands as Lancome, Diesel, Giorgio Armani, and Cacharel among others. Active Cosmetics, which consists of products under Vichy and La Roche Posay brands, are for sale mainly in pharmacies. The Body Shop segment is focused on cosmetics on the basis of natural ingredients. The Dermatology segment consists of Galderma, a joint venture between L'Oreal and Nestle.

Mary Kay, Inc.

Headquartered in Addison (outside of Dallas), Texas, Mary Kay is a privately-owned cosmetic and fragrance direct-selling company. Mary Kay is the sixth-largest direct selling company in the world, with annual sales of about $3 billion. Mary Kay's business model is similar to the Avon business model. Founded by Mary Kay Ash in 1963, the company is famous for its pink Cadillacs, given to high-selling representatives. Richard Rogers, Mary Kay's son, is the chairman of the board. Mary Kay products are sold in more than 35 markets worldwide, and the global Mary Kay independent sales force exceeds 2.4 million women.

In 1968, Mary Kay Ash purchased the first pink Cadillac and had it repainted to match the Mountain Laurel Blush in the Mary Kay compact. Since the Cadillac program's inception, more than 100,000 independent sales force members have qualified for the use of a Career Car or elected the cash compensation option. GM estimates that it has built 100,000 pink Cadillacs for Mary Kay. For 2012, high-sellers may select other Career Cars, including the Chevrolet Malibu, Chevrolet Equinox, Toyota Camry, and the Cadillac CTS, SRX, and Escalade Hybrid—or most recently, a black Ford Mustang.

Estee Lauder Companies, Inc.

Headquartered in New York City, Estee Lauder has sales of about $10 billion annually and income of about $1 billion. Estee Lauder manufactures and markets skin care, makeup, fragrance, and hair care products. The company's products are sold in more than 150 countries and territories under a number of brand names, including Estee Lauder, Aramis, Clinique, Origins, M.A.C, Bobbi Brown, La Mer, and Aveda. The company is also the global licensee for fragrances or cosmetics sold under brand names, such as Tommy Hilfiger, Donna Karan, Michael Kors, Tom Ford, and Coach. The company sells its products at more than 30,000 points of sale, consisting of upscale department stores, specialty retailers, upscale perfumeries and pharmacies, and prestige salons and spas.

Revlon, Inc.

Headquartered in New York City, Revlon is a cosmetics leader with brands such as Almay and Revlon ColorSilk hair color, Mitchum antiperspirants and deodorants, Charlie and Jean Naté fragrances, and Ultima II and Gatineau skin care products. Revlon's beauty aids are distributed in more than 100 countries, though the USA is its largest market, generating about 55 percent of sales. Walmart is Revlon's biggest single customer, accounting for some 22 percent of sales.

Revlon manufactures, markets, and sells cosmetics, women's hair color, beauty tools, antiperspirant deodorants, fragrances, skin care, and other beauty care products. Revlon products are sold and marketed under brand names, such as Revlon, including the Revlon ColorStay, Revlon Super Lustrous, and Revlon Age Defying franchises; Almay, including the Almay Intense i-Color and Almay Smart Shade franchises; Sinful Colors in cosmetics; Revlon ColorSilk in women's hair color; Revlon in beauty tools; Mitchum in antiperspirant deodorants; Charlie and Jean Nate in fragrances, and Ultima II and Gatineau. Revlon also owns certain assets of Sinful Colors cosmetics, Wild and Crazy cosmetics, freshMinerals cosmetics, and freshcover cosmetics.

Coty, Inc.

Headquartered in New York City, Coty is one of the world's leading makers of beauty products for men and women. Led by CEO Bernd Beetz, Coty is a $4.1 billion beauty company, and the biggest seller of nail care, nail polish, and fragrances in the USA. Sarah Jessica Parker, Jennifer Lopez, Celine Dion, Gwen Stefani, Katy Perry, and Thomas Dutronc are several celebrities that promote Coty. Founder of the company, François Coty created his first perfume, La Rose Jacqueminot, in 1904.

Coty's product lineup today ranges from moderately priced scents sold globally by mass retailers to prestige fragrances and nail polishes found in department stores. Coty's brands include adidas, philosophy, Rimmel, and Sally Hansen. Cody's prestige perfume labels are led by Calvin Klein. Coty's shimmery blue nail polish and Lady Gaga's perfume are high-selling products. Thomas Dutronc is the face of Coty's new Cerruti fragrance for men that was launched in the Spring 2013.

Coty's Rimmel Scandaleyes mascara, which debuted in early 2012, is another big seller. Over-the-top lashes are hot these days because false eye lashes have made a comeback and are "almost mainstream." Promotional material for Scandaleyes urges women to "ditch those falsies." Mascara makers today compete with eyelash lengthening drugs such as Latisse.

Nail care generated $735 million in sales in U.S. discount stores, pharmacy chains, and supermarkets in 2011, up 6.5 percent from 2010. Lipstick sales rise even as a nation's economy falters, partly because the economy has put the consumer in charge of her own beauty treatments without having to go to the nail bar. Sally Hansen Salon Effects nail polish strips also brings "nail art," which has been trending at beauty salons nationwide, to everyday drugstore shoppers at a mere $8 to $10. Vivienne Rudd, head of beauty and personal care for market research firm Mintel, says "the nail-art trend is largely being driven by younger shoppers; it takes a little courage to wear stripes and spots." Still, women of all ages are experimenting with the strips as they look for inexpensive fun.

Overall, nail care product sales have been booming in today's shaky economic climate. Women have been skipping the salon and playing at-home manicurist, whereas consumer products companies have been injecting innovation into the business with products like Salon Effects and the hologram, crackle, and magnetic nail finishes on the market, analysts say. The strips are available in funky prints and patterns such as leopard, florals, and tie dye.

EXHIBIT 4 Avon's Recent Income Statement (in millions)

				%Change	
				2012 vs.	2011 vs.
	2012	2011	2010	2011	2010
Total revenue	$10,717.1	$11,291.6	$10,862.8	(5)%	4%
Cost of sales	4,169.3	4,148.6	4,041.3	–%	3%
Selling, general and administrative expenses	5,980.0	6,025.4	5,748.4	(1)%	5%
Impairment of goodwill and intangible asset	253.0	263.0	–	(4)%	*
Operating profit	314.8	854.6	1,073.1	(63)%	(20)%
Interest expense	104.3	92.9	87.1	12%	7%
Interest income	(15.1)	(16.5)	(14.0)	(8)%	18%
Other expense, net	7.0	35.6	54.6	(80)%	(35)%
Net (loss) income attributable to Avon	(42.5)	513.6	606.3	(108)%	(15)%
Diluted (loss) earnings per share attributable to Avon	$(.10)	$1.18	$1.39	(108)%	(15)%
Advertising expenses	$253.6	$311.2	$400.4	(19)%	(22)%
Gross margin	61.1%	63.3%	62.8%	(2.2)	.5

Source: 2012 *Annual Report,* p. 29.

The Future

Avon announced in late 2012 that it is cutting about 1,500 jobs globally and will exit the South Korea and Vietnam markets as part of a turnaround plan. The global beauty industry is growing at the rate of 6 percent, good news for Avon. The company's current ratio and debt service coverage ratios indicate that it has enough liquidity to survive in the near future, but a clear strategic plan is needed to survive.

The general feeling about Avon is negative because of the sliding profits, four-year pending legal probe related to bribery and ineffective business strategies. However, Avon has a popular global brand with a high market share in emerging markets. Although door-to-door selling may be an outdated business model in the USA, direct selling remains effective in emerging markets such as Brazil. Direct selling grew about 30 percent between 2006 and 2012 into a $150 billion global market. Many of the more than 100 countries in which Avon competes do not have good retail infrastructure, so Avon's 6.5 million person global sales force is its biggest advantage over its competitors. Avon's stock price hit a 52-week high in June 2013 of $24.30.

EXHIBIT 5 Avon's Balance Sheets

	December 31,	
(In millions, except per share data)	2012	2011
Assets		
Current Assets		
Cash, including cash equivalents of $762.9 and $623.7	$ 1,209.6	$ 1,245.1
Accounts receivable (less allowances of $161.4 and $174.5)	751.9	761.5
Inventories	1,135.4	1,161.3
Prepaid expenses and other	832.0	930.9
Total current assets	**$ 3,928.9**	**$ 4,098.8**
Property, plant and equipment, at cost		
Land	66.6	65.4
Buildings and improvements	1,165.9	1,150.4
Equipment	1,479.3	1,493.0
	2,711.8	2,708.8
Less accumulated depreciation	(1,161.6)	(1,137.3)
	1,550.2	1,571.5
Goodwill	374.9	473.1
Other intangible assets, net	120.3	279.9
Other assets	1,408.2	1,311.7
Total assets	**$ 7,382.5**	**$ 7,735.0**
Liabilities and Shareholders' Equity		
Current Liabilities		
Debt maturing within one year	$ 572.0	$ 849.3
Accounts payable	920.0	850.2
Accrued compensation	266.6	217.1
Other accrued liabilities	661.0	663.6
Sales and taxes other than income	211.4	212.4
Income taxes	73.6	98.4
Total current liabilities	**2,704.6**	**2,891.0**
Long-term debt	2,623.9	2,459.1
Employee benefit plans	637.6	603.0
Long-term income taxes	52.0	67.0
Other liabilities	131.1	129.7
Total liabilities	**$ 6,149.2**	**$ 6,149.8**

EXHIBIT 5 Continued

(In millions, except per share data)	December 31,	
	2012	2011
Commitments and contingencies		
Shareholders' Equity		
Common stock, par value $.25 – authorized 1,500 shares; issued 746.7 and 744.9 shares	$ 188.3	$ 187.3
Additional paid-in capital	2,119.6	2,077.7
Retained earnings	4,357.8	4,726.1
Accumulated other comprehensive loss	(876.7)	(854.4)
Treasury stock, at cost (314.5 and 314.1 shares)	(4,571.9)	(4,566.3)
Total Avon shareholders' equity	1,217.1	1,570.4
Noncontrolling interests	16.2	14.8
Total shareholders' equity	**$ 1,233.3**	**$ 1,585.2**
Total liabilities and shareholders' equity	**$ 7,382.5**	**$ 7,735.0**

Source: 2012 *Annual Report*, p. F5.

Exxon Mobil Corporation, 2013

www.exxonmobil.com, XOM

Headquartered in Irving, Texas, ExxonMobil is by some measures the largest corporation in the world. ExxonMobil produces and markets crude oil, natural gas, petroleum products, chemicals, plastics, and much more under brand names that include Exxon, Mobil, Esso, and in Canada, Imperial Oil. Exxon produces about 6.3 million barrels of oil daily by operating more than 37,000 oil wells in 21 different countries, but the firm also has huge interests in electric power generation. With more than 77,000 employees worldwide, ExxonMobil has annual revenues of about $500 billion. In 2012, Apache Corp. acquired ExxonMobil's North Sea Limited assets including the Beryl field. Exxon has ownership interests in 32 refineries in 17 countries.

In August 2013, ExxonMobil released its estimated second quarter 2013 results saying its total revenues and other income would be down 16.4 percent year-over-year to $106.5 billion; the company's Q2 2013 net income will be down 56.9 percent to $6.9 billion. Weaker refining margins and volumes associated with planned refinery turnaround and maintenance activities negatively impacted the company's Downstream earnings.

Copyright by Fred David Books LLC. (Written by Forest R. David)

History

ExxonMobil began when John D. Rockefeller's Standard Oil was established in 1870. The name Standard was used to denote high, uniform quality. The federal government forced Standard Oil to separate into 34 companies in 1911, and two of these companies eventually became Exxon and Mobil. The Mobil Oil trademark was first used in 1920 when gasoline eclipsed kerosene production because the automobile industry was growing. In 1972, Jersey Standard changed its name to Exxon Corporation. The worst company accident in Exxon's history occurred on March 24, 1989, when the tanker Exxon Valdez ran aground in Prince William Sound in Alaska.

Exxon acquired Mobil in 1998 for $73.7 billion and formed a new corporation called Exxon Mobil Corporation. The merger reunited the two largest companies of Rockefeller's Standard Oil after nearly a century of operating independently. In 2005, ExxonMobil passed General Electric as the largest company in the world based on market capitalization and reported record profits of $36 billion the same year, up 42 percent from 2004. ExxonMobil announced in 2008 plans to transition out of company-owned gas stations, but the brand names Exxon and Mobil are still be used by operators, who compensate ExxonMobil for use of its name. A complete, elaborate interactive history of ExxonMobil is provided on the corporate website.

Internal Issues

Vision and Mission

Exxon does not report a mission or vision statement, but the company has a statement of guiding principles:

> Exxon Mobil Corporation is committed to being the world's premier petroleum and petrochemical company. To that end, we must continuously achieve superior financial and operating results while simultaneously adhering to high ethical standards.

Organizational Structure

ExxonMobil appears to operate from a strategic business unit (SBU) organizational structure, with the groups being Upstream, Downstream, Chemical, and Other. Upstream is the term that refers to the search, recovery, and production of crude oil and natural gas, also commonly called *oil exploration*. Underground and underwater drilling for oil and gas is an upstream activity. Downstream operations include the refining, selling, and distribution of natural gas and products derived from crude oil such as gasoline, diesel, asphalt, plastics, antifreeze, and by-products such as sulfur. There are literally thousands of products that derive from oil that the consumer can purchase in retail stores.

As indicated in Exhibit 1, there apparently is no chief operations officer (COO) or chief accounting officer (CAO) in the Exxon hierarchy, nor an SBU head for each group. In addition, note that ExxonMobil has virtually zero women, Hispanics, or African Americans among its top corporate executives. Perhaps that is why the company's *Form 10K* lists executives' names only by first and middle initials, rather than providing first names, which would more clearly reveal the lack of diversity.

Exxon Oil Spills

Exxon has had several notable spills over its history with the worst being the Exxon Valdez, an oil tanker that spilled more than 11 million gallons of crude oil into Prince William Sound, Alaska. The spill resulted in Congress passing the Oil Pollution Act of 1990 and initially rewarded $5 billion of punitive damages, although that amount was later reduced. Exxon endured criticism to its slow response time to the spill and the use of single-hull ships. As of 2009, Exxon still employed more single-hull oil tankers than the next 10 largest oil companies combined. In 2007, there was a major Exxon oil spill in Brooklyn, New York, that spilled 17 to 30 million gallons of petroleum. In 2011, Exxon was responsible for a spill in the Yellowstone River that leaked up to 40,000 gallons of oil before the refinery was shut down. In 2012, a crude pipeline in Baton Rouge, Louisiana, burst and spilled around 80,000 gallons into the nearby rivers and creeks.

Environmental Record

Exxon's Sakhalin-I oil and gas project in eastern Russia has been claimed by scientists to threaten the western gray whale population, and they have called for a moratorium on all oil activities in the area. Scientists claimed Exxon's activities discouraged the whales in their summer and fall feeding areas and sighted a decline in whales as evidence. Similarly, Exxon's Alaskan pipeline is oftentimes criticized for possibly harming migration routes of Alaskan animals, especially caribou. Exxon also endures criticism at times regarding its impact on global warming and climate change. ExxonMobil was recently accused of paying for TV advertisements and programs that generate skepticism that global warming is principally the result of greenhouse gasses caused by burning of coal and petroleum-based fuels. *Mother Jones Magazine* says Exxon has paid more than $8 million to 40 different organizations that challenge the scientific evidence of global warming. Exxon was a member of the Global Climate Coalition, a skeptic group on the possible destructive nature of greenhouse gasses.

Segments

The oil and gas industry is commonly divided into two segments: (1) upstream and (2) downstream. Exhibit 2 reveals ExxonMobil's earnings broken down by source and geographic location. Note that the vast majority of Exxon's earnings derive from upstream processes outside the USA.

Upstream

ExxonMobil's upstream business accounted for 67 percent of all earnings after tax in 2012, down from 84 percent from 2011. Exxon continues to expand its diverse portfolio in this segment through global exploration, development, production, and marketing activities. Between now and 2016, oil and natural gas output in North America is expected to increase dramatically. About 30 percent of Exxon's production comes from North America, but by 2016 this number is expected to grow to 35 percent. Arctic technology, deepwater drilling, and oil sands recovery are expected to grow from 45 percent to 50 percent also by 2016. Melting of the Artic ice cap as a result of global warming is spurring additional drilling as well as rising disputes among Russia, Canada, and the USA regarding even ownership of new "unfrozen" areas.

In 2013, ExxonMobil and its partners began developing the Herbron oil field offshore of Newfoundland on Canada's east coast. The gravity-based structure used is expected to cost $14 billion and to recover 700 million barrels of oil or 150,000 barrels per day. Production is expected to begin toward the end of 2017. Exxon operates the Herbron facility but controls only

EXHIBIT 1 Exxon's Organizational Structure

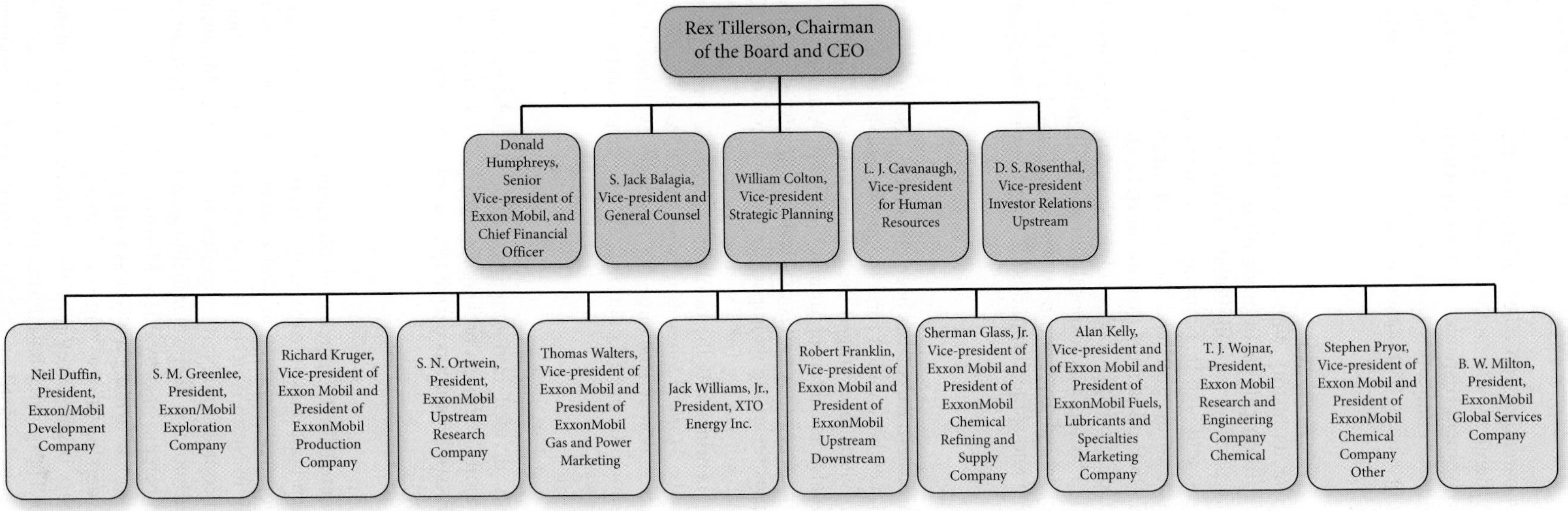

Rex Tillerson, Chairman of the Board and CEO

- Donald Humphreys, Senior Vice-president of Exxon Mobil, and Chief Financial Officer
- S. Jack Balagia, Vice-president and General Counsel
- William Colton, Vice-president Strategic Planning
- L. J. Cavanaugh, Vice-president for Human Resources
- D. S. Rosenthal, Vice-president Investor Relations Upstream

- Neil Duffin, President, Exxon/Mobil Development Company
- S. M. Greenlee, President, Exxon/Mobil Exploration Company
- Richard Kruger, Vice-president of Exxon Mobil and President of ExxonMobil Production Company
- S. N. Ortwein, President, ExxonMobil Upstream Research Company
- Thomas Walters, Vice-president of Exxon Mobil and President of ExxonMobil Gas and Power Marketing
- Jack Williams, Jr., President, XTO Energy Inc.
- Robert Franklin, Vice-president of Exxon Mobil and President of ExxonMobil Upstream Downstream
- Sherman Glass, Jr. Vice-president of Exxon Mobil and President of ExxonMobil Chemical Refining and Supply Company
- Alan Kelly, Vice-president and of Exxon Mobil and President of ExxonMobil Fuels, Lubricants and Specialties Marketing Company
- T. J. Wojnar, President, Exxon Mobil Research and Engineering Company Chemical
- Stephen Pryor, Vice-president of Exxon Mobil and President of ExxonMobil Chemical Company Other
- B. W. Milton, President, ExxonMobil Global Services Company

Source: Based on company information.

EXHIBIT 2 ExxonMobil's Earnings by Segment

Segment	Revenue 2012	Earnings 2012	Earnings After Tax (in millions)	
			2011	2010
Upstream				
United States	$11,472	$3,925	$5,096	$4,272
Non-United States	28,854	25,970	29,343	19,825
Total	**$40,326**	**$29,895**	**$34,439**	**$24,097**
Downstream				
United States	$125,088	$3,575	$2,268	$770
Non-United States	248,959	9,615	2,191	2,797
Total	**$374,047**	**$13,190**	**$4,459**	**$3,567**
Chemical				
United States	$14,723	$2,220	$2,215	$2,422
Non-United States	24,003	1,678	2,168	2,491
Total	**$38,726**	**$3,898**	**$4,383**	**$4,913**
Corporate and Financing				
Total	$24	$(2,103)	$(2,221)	$(2,117)
Total	$453,123	$44,880	$41,060	$30,460

Source: Based on company information at 2012 *Annual Report*, page 35.

a 36 percent interest. Chevron and Suncor control 27 and 23 percent respectively, and two other firms control the remaining 14 percent.

Exxon strengthened its presence in the upstream area with the purchase of XTO Energy for $41 billion in 2009. XTO specializes in natural gas, but natural gas prices have fallen to historic lows even though this gas burns cleaner than oil. Exxon forecasts a long-term growing demand for natural gas, and the company has the extra cash to withstand the lower prices at present. Natural gas is for Exxon a hedge or diversification away from crude because the prices are not strongly correlated with each other and can even trade opposite of each other. In addition, the crude business is becoming more competitive, and there is an increased difficulty in finding oil.

Downstream

Exxon is the largest global refiner of oil in the world with downstream operations refining and distributing products derived from crude oil to customers around the world. Products are marketed to customers through retail service stations and three business-to-business segments: (1) industrial and wholesale, (2) aviation, and (3) marine. Three of Exxon's largest service stations in the USA are Exxon, Mobil, and Esso. Delivering Exxon Mobil's downstream revenues are ownership interests in 36 refineries located in 21 countries that contain a distillation capacity of more than 6 million barrels of crude per day, plus a lubricant base stock capacity of 131 thousand barrels per day. Exhibit 3 provides a breakdown of how Exxon Mobil uses a barrel of crude oil. Note that gasoline and then diesel are the two largest uses.

The USA accounts for slightly more than 50 percent of Exxon's earnings, and Exxon's entire downstream business only attributes about 11 percent of companywide earnings. The company's downstream business is not as profitable as upstream operations even with the downstream industry improving. Over the prior 20-year period, inflation-adjusted refining margins have been flat, and ExxonMobil's long-term outlook in refining margins will likely remain weak because competition grows and capacity additions grow quicker than global demand. Increased governmental regulations regarding pollution and a growth in biofuels also hinder growth in the refining business.

One of the weaker segments in the downstream industry for ExxonMobil is its dealer and company operated retail gas stations in the USA. Starting in 2008, Exxon began transitioning these stores into a branded distributor model, allowing distributors to use the Exxon and Mobil names. This transition was competed in 2012.

Exxon's lubricants business in the downstream market continues to grow, and Exxon is the current market leader in high value synthetic lubricants in many key markets such as

EXHIBIT 3 How Exxon Uses a Barrel of Crude Oil

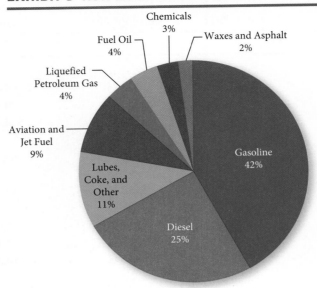

Source: Data from company website

China, India, and Russia. Despite the success in lubricants, overall the downstream business remains weak, and Exxon recently divested their downstream businesses in Argentina, Uruguay, Paraguay, Central America, Malaysia, and Switzerland. In 2012, Exxon announced restructuring of their downstream holdings in Japan.

Exxon is nearing completion of new units and improvements of existing facilities in Thailand to refine lower sulfur diesel and gasoline to meet new Thailand specifications. New plans are also in the construction phase in Singapore, Saudi Arabia, and China.

Chemical

ExxonMobil is one of the largest petrochemical companies in the world, providing materials for use in products including plastic bottles, synthetic rubber, solvents, and countless other goods. The company is the largest global manufacturer of paraxylene and benzene. Exxon is also a large producer of ethylene and propylene which, like many of the chemicals Exxon produces, are considered feedstock, meaning they are the basic ingredients used to help produce many of the products we use today such as different fuels, fibers, packaging film, automotive parts, and more. ExxonMobil's chemical business experienced modest demand growth in 2011, but its overall chemical earnings after tax declined 11 percent in 2011 from the prior year. Exxon in 2012 completed construction of its Singapore petrochemical project.

Finance

Note in the income statements provided in Exhibit 5 that the company's revenues and profits are increasing nicely.

Geographic

ExxonMobil also reports revenues by country. Note in Exhibit 4 that about 66 percent of company revenues are made outside the USA.

Note in the balance sheets provided in Exhibit 5 that Exxon has zero goodwill, which is excellent.

Competitors

ExxonMobil ranks third on the S&P Global Oil Industry Classification Standard, behind Saudi Aramco of Saudi Arabia and National Iran Oil Company (NIOC). ExxonMobil sells more than $6.4 million barrels a day, far more than the Saudi and Iran state-owned operations that dominate in reserves. However, Saudi Aramco controls liquid reserves of 24 times that of ExxonMobil and

EXHIBIT 4 ExxonMobil's Revenues by Region (in millions)

Geographic Sales and other operating revenue	2012	2011
United States	151,298	150,343
Non-U.S.	301,825	316,686
Total	**453,123**	**467,029**
Significant non-U.S. revenue sources include:		
Canada	34,325	34,626
United Kingdom	34,134	34,833
Belgium	23,567	26,926
France	19,601	18,510
Italy	18,228	16,288
Germany	16,451	17,034
Singapore	14,606	14,400
Japan	14,162	31,925

Source: 2012 *Annual Report*, p. 122.

EXHIBIT 5 ExxonMobil's Recent Income Statements (000,000 omitted)

	2012	2011
Revenues and other income		
Sales and other operating revenue	453,123	467,029
Income from equity affiliates	15,010	15,289
Other income	14,162	4,111
Total revenues and other income	**482,295**	**486,429**
Costs and other deductions		
Crude oil and product purchases	265,149	266,534
Production and manufacturing expenses	38,521	40,268
Selling, general and administrative expenses	13,877	14,983
Depreciation and depletion	15,888	15,583
Exploration expenses, including dry holes	1,840	2,081
Interest expense	327	247
Sales-based taxes	32,409	33,503
Other taxes and duties	35,558	39,973
Total costs and other deductions	**403,569**	**413,172**
Income before income taxes	78,726	73,257
Income taxes	31,045	31,051
Net income including noncontrolling interests	47,681	42,206
Net income attributable to noncontrolling interests	2,801	1,146
Net income attributable to ExxonMobil	**44,880**	**41,060**
Earnings per common share (dollars)	**9.70**	**8.43**

Source: 2012 *Annual Report*, p. 61.

has gas reserves 3.6 times greater. Iran-based and state-owned NIOC controls 14 times the liquid reserves and 15 times the gas reserves than ExxonMobil controls.

Acquisitions and joint ventures are common in the oil industry. Notable recent acquisitions include CNOOC Canada paying $19 billion for Nexen, Energy Transfer Partners paying $8.7 billion for Sunoco, several firms purchasing EP Energy for $8 billion, and 16 other purchases with each totaling over $1.5 billion, all in 2012 alone.

ExxonMobil is the top refiner in the world and has a significant edge on both Saudi Aramco and NIOC on refining. In 2011, ExxonMobil refined 5.8 million barrels per day, Royal Dutch

Petroleum refined 4.1 million, Sinopec refined 3.9 billion, and BP refined 3.3 billion. Saudi Aramco was 10th and NIOC was 14th. The results are not surprising because the USA alone controls approximately 19 percent of the world's refineries, whereas Saudi Arabia and Iran control around 1 percent each. For comparison, China has 8 percent of the world's refineries and Russia and Japan control 6 and 4.5 percent, respectively.

Exhibit 6 provides a financial comparison of ExxonMobil with two competitors, BP and Chevron. Other large publically-traded competitors include Royal Dutch Shell, Eni SpA, Total S.A., and ConocoPhillips. Note in Exhibit 7 that Exxon generates more revenue per employee than BP or Chevron.

EXHIBIT 6 ExxonMobil's Balance Sheets (in millions)

	Dec. 31, 2012
Assets	
Current assets	
Cash and cash equivalents	9,582
Cash and cash equivalents—restricted	341
Notes and accounts receivable, less estimated doubtful amounts	34,987
Inventories	
Crude oil, products and merchandise	10,836
Materials and supplies	3,706
Other current assets	5,008
Total current assets	**64,460**
Investments, advances and long-term receivables	34,718
Property, plant and equipment, at cost, less accumulated depreciation and depletion	226,949
Other assets, including intangibles, net	7,668
Total assets	**333,795**
Liabilities	
Current liabilities	
Notes and loans payable	3,653
Accounts payable and accrued liabilities	50,728
Income taxes payable	9,758
Total current liabilities	**64,139**
Long-term debt	7,928
Postretirement benefits reserves	25,267
Deferred income tax liabilities	37,570
Long-term obligations to equity companies	3,555
Other long-term obligations	23,676
Total liabilities	**162,135**
Commitments and contingencies	
Equity	
Common stock without par value (9,000 million shares authorized, 8,019 million shares issued)	9,653
Earnings reinvested	365,727
Accumulated other comprehensive income	(12,184)
Common stock held in treasury (3,517 million shares in 2012 and 3,285 million shares in 2011)	(197,333)
ExxonMobil share of equity	165,863
Noncontrolling interests	5,797
Total equity	**171,660**
Total liabilities and equity	**333,795**

Source: 2012 *Annual Report,* p. 84.

EXHIBIT 7 Comparing ExxonMobil to BP and Chevron

	ExxonMobil	BP	Chevron
Number of employees	82,000	83,000	61,000
Revenue ($)	$488	$381	$241
Net Income ($)	$44	$17.6	$24
Net Profit Margin	9.64%	4.70%	10%
Revenue ($)/Employee	$5.9 M	$4.6 M	$3.9 M
EPS	$9.47	$5.51	$12.19
Market Capitalization	403 B	138 B	213 B
Shares Outstanding	4.56 B	3.19 B	1.96 B

EPS, earnings per share.
Source: Based on company documents.

Royal Dutch Shell

Headquartered in the Netherlands, Royal Dutch Shell plc (Shell) is a huge oil and gas producer and marketer and also has interests in chemicals and other energy-related businesses. Shell operates in three segments: (1) Upstream, (2) Downstream, and (3) Corporate. Shell has a market capitalization above $220 billion, a P/E ratio of 8, and a dividend yield of 5.3 percent. Shell's stock price has increased 18 percent since 2010. However, Shell's third quarter in 2012 cash flow from operations dropped 18 percent year-over-year. Through the first nine months of 2012, Shell's income dropped 18 percent, although the company raised its dividend by 2 percent.

Eni

Headquartered in Italy, Eni SpA is a large oil and gas company that operates under seven segments: (1) refining and marketing focuses on refining and marketing of petroleum products; (2) trading covers group services in commodity trading, shipping, and derivatives; (3) petrochemicals covers the production and sale of petrochemical products; (4) engineering and construction includes the services for the oil and gas industry; (5) exploration and production focuses on exploration, development and production of oil and natural gas; (6) gas and power covers the supply, regasification, transport, storage, distribution, and marketing of natural gas, power generation, and electricity sales; (7) other activities handles the corporate, financial, and service components. Eni sells oil and gas in 85 countries and operates numerous subsidiaries and affiliates in Nigeria, Poland, and Germany, among others.

Eni has a market value of $90 billion and trades at a P/E ratio of slightly greater than 9 with a dividend yield of about 4.5 percent. Eni's stock price recently rebounded to a 52-week high of $50 per share, after plunging to $37 during the summer of 2012. For the first nine months of 2012, Eni's operating profit was up nearly 14 percent versus the same period in 2011, and its oil and natural gas production was up 8 percent. Eni's new licenses in Liberia and its expanded presence in Asia is spurring growth.

ConocoPhillips

Headquartered in Houston, Texas, Conoco explores for, produces, transports, and markets crude oil, natural gas, natural gas liquids, liquefied natural gas, and bitumen on a worldwide basis. In May 2012, the company separated into two stand-alone, publicly traded corporations, (1) Upstream and (2) Downstream. All the firm's midstream, downstream, marketing, and chemical operations were separated into a new company named Phillips 66. As a result, ConocoPhillips continued its operations as an exploration and production company.

In April 2012, ConocoPhillips sold its Trainer Refinery to Monroe Energy LLC. As of January 1, 2012, Conoco conducted exploration activities in 19 countries and produced hydrocarbons in 13 countries, with proved reserves located in 15 countries. The company's production averaged 1.57 million billion barrels of oil equivalent (BOE) per day for the nine months ending on September 30, 2012, and proved reserves were 8.4 BOE. In August 2012, Conoco closed a transaction with LUKOIL for the sale of ConocoPhillips's indirect 30 percent interest in NaryanMarNefteGaz (NMNG).

Total S.A.

Headquartered in France, Total S.A. is a huge oil and gas company with operations in more than 130 countries, Total engages in all aspects of the petroleum industry, including (1) Upstream operations (oil and gas exploration, development and production, liquefied natural gas [LNG]) and (2) Downstream operations (refining, marketing, and the trading and shipping of crude oil and petroleum products). It also produces base chemicals (petrochemicals and fertilizers) and specialty chemicals for the industrial and consumer markets. Total has interests in coal mining and power generation and is active in solar-photovoltaic power, both in Upstream and Downstream activities. Total has subsidiaries, including Elf Aquitaine, Total Venezuela, Total E&P Nigeria SAS, and Total E&P USA, Inc., among others. For the first half of 2012, Total's sales increased 10 percent and cash flow from operations increased 6 percent year-over-year (as measured in euros). Return on equity for the first six months of the year was 17.5 percent. Total is executing on new initiatives in Thailand, the Norwegian Sea, and Italy, which should drive future production growth.

Chevron

Headquartered in San Ramon, California, and the second-largest U.S. oil company by market capitalization (behind ExxonMobil), Chevron in December 2012 reported that its upstream operations oil and natural gas production averaged 2.662 million BOE per day, 0.8 percent above the fourth quarter in 2011 level. Production for the fourth quarter in 2012 was up by about 5.8 percent from the third quarter of 2012. In the first two months of the fourth quarter, Chevron's total domestic oil production rose 39,000 barrels per day from third-quarter levels, primarily as a result of volume gains from its recently acquired Permian Basin (Texas) assets. Net international oil production was 1,986,000 barrels per day, up 107,000 barrels from the third quarter in 2012. The upsurge was driven by the completion of planned repair work in Kazakhstan and the United Kingdom.

Regarding Chevron's downstream operations, its U.S. refinery crude input fell 77,000 barrels per day, affected largely by the shutdown of its Richmond, California, refinery crude unit after a fire in August. Refinery crude-input volumes outside the USA was up slightly by 9,000 barrels per day.

In 2013, Chevron discovered two new offshore natural gas sites, Pinhoe-1 and Arnhem-1, in Western Australia's Carnarvon Basin. The discoveries, the 18th and 19th by Chevron off the Australian coast since mid-2009, adds to Chevron's leading position in this area. Drilled to a total depth of 13,396 feet (4,083 meters), the Pinhoe-1 well encountered 197 feet (60 meters) of net gas pay. The find is situated in the WA-383-P permit area, approximately 124 miles (200 kilometers) north of Exmouth Plateau area of the Carnarvon Basin. Similarly, the Arnhem-1 discovery—that lies in the WA-364-P permit area, roughly 180 miles (290 kilometers) north of Exmouth—was drilled to a total depth of 9,557 feet (2913 meters). The well came across 149 feet (45.5 meters) of net gas pay. Chevron Australia has a 50-percent operated interest in both the prospects, with the other partner being the subsidiary of Royal Dutch Shell Plc.

External Issues

The world's population is expected to grow to 8.7 billion by 2040, an increase of 28 percent from today's population and accompanied by an economic growth rate of about 3 percent per year. Energy demand is expected to increase about 35 percent by 2040. However, with increasingly energy-efficient technologies, energy consumption per unit is expected to decrease. For example, by 2040, energy for cars, trucks, ships, trains, and airplanes is likely to increase only around 45 percent. Liquid fuel is still expected to be the fuel of choice to power the world's transportation fleets by 2040.

Natural gas demand is expected to enjoy larger gains and the largest market share percent gain by 2040, although geothermal, solar, and wind may eclipse in percent gain but they are not significant players. Once thought of as unprofitable to collect, many natural gas sources found in shale and other rock formations will help supply demand for this product. Coal, despite environmental concerns, is expected to continue to be the leading choice of power generation for a number of years, but it could lose its status as the number-2 source of energy to natural gas by 2025. Nuclear power and renewables, such as wind, geothermal, and solar, are also expected to grow in their use over the next 30 years. The demand for electricity globally will increase 85 percent by 2040, while the demand for natural gas increases 65 percent.

Energy Prices

Energy prices tend to be highly volatile and are expected to continue their volatile nature in the future. Economic problems in Europe, the USA, and other areas resulted in the price of oil falling to as low as $78 dollars a barrel in May 2012, but then that price increased to more than $100 by year-end 2012. Crude demand in the USA, which accounts for 21 percent of global demand, declined around 2.6 percent in the first half of 2012. Demand in Europe, which accounts for 16 percent of the world's use of oil, has declined as well. China, the world's second largest consumer of oil, reported in mid-2012 the slowest growth for oil in more than 20 months.

For ExxonMobil, a $1 change in the price of oil produces a weighted average effect of $350 million in annual after-tax earnings on upstream production. A $0.10 change in gas would have a $200 million annual after-tax effect on upstream production. Some of the cited concerns for the current volatility in the price of oil include the USA, Europe, and China offering extra stimulus packages to spur the economy; sanctions on Iran, which has threatened to close the Strait of Hormuz where 20 percent of the world's petroleum is shipped; concerns about Iran and Israel's geopolitical relationship; and reduced production concerns in the North Sea. The Organization of the Petroleum Exporting Countries (OPEC), which accounts for nearly 80 percent of the world's oil reserves, has kept production unchanged recently, but Saudi Arabia is trying to negate the impact or the embargo on Iran by increasing its own output. Possibly reducing some oil volatility in the future is the fact that the largest non-OPEC area currently is in onshore shale in the USA and Canada along with traditional drilling in North America. Given the current price of oil, extracting oil from shale sand remains expensive and produces lower margins than traditional drilling, but this problem is fading as increased technologies emerge and oil and gas prices resume their upward trends.

Unconventional Fuel Sources

Accessing so-called unconventional resources such as shale, rock, and sands for oil was impracticable for years because of lower demand and unprofitable because of lower oil prices and the expense of extracting the product. However, with increasing demand, rising oil prices, improved technology, and competition for traditional oil fields, tapping such energy sources is a new avenue for growth among petroleum companies today. One of the largest sources of this energy is in North America, with natural gas being derived at a high rate in recent years that current prices of gas have plummeted as a result of oversupply. Many firms have engaged in mergers and acquisitions for shale, with Exxon's acquisition of XTO energy being a notable example. Currently however, with the low prices for natural gas, many companies are drilling the same shale, rock, and sands areas for liquid oil instead of natural gas.

Notable hotbeds for exploration include the Eagle Ford, Bakken, and Permian Basin. Eagle Ford is located in south Texas and is considered the hottest area in North America producing higher liquid content than traditional shale. Competition in Eagle Ford remains high with Norway's Statioil ASA, India's Reliance Industries, and China National Offshore Oil Corp. all entered with billion-dollar deals in 2011. As of 2012, there were 211 rigs operating in Eagle Ford.

Located in Montana, North Dakota, and Saskatchewan, the Bakken Shale formation is the second-most concentrated shale region in North America. The U.S. Geologic Survey estimates the region is capable of producing up to 4.3 billion barrels of oil. Companies such as Hess and Marathon are increasing their presence in the region. As of 2012, there were 160 active rigs in the Bakken formation.

The Canadian oil sands have also been economically feasible in recent years and could potentially make Canada one of the world's largest oil producers. French-based Total SA has invested $3 billion in the Athabasca oil sands in Alberta, and Devon Energy and BP have a joint venture to develop properties in the region. Sinopec and China National Offshore also have invested in the area with Sinopec investing more than $8 billion alone to acquire rights to sand deposits.

U.S. Natural Gas

Recent discoveries and advances in drilling and hydraulic fracturing are making natural gas drilling in North America increasingly assessable. If technologies developed in the United States can be applied to shale, rock, and oil sands in Europe and Asia, the results would be revolutionary. Developments in the USA include Exxon's acquisition of XTO Energy and Chevron's merger with Atlas Energy to acquire Atlas's Marcellus Shale holdings in the Appalachian Basin.

Natural gas exposes companies to less public backlash than conventional fuel options such as coal, gasoline, and diesel because it is a clean-burning low-carbon fuel.

OPEC

The largest single player in the oil market is OPEC, controlling 73 percent of the world's oil reserves. As of 2012, OPEC maintained its output level of 30 million barrels a day, helping to fix the price of oil for consumers around the world. Member nations have been quite compliant in sticking to the agreed-on output levels over the last few years, but as the price of oil has increased, compliance dropped from 83 to 80 percent. Analysts expect member nations to violate their agreements and produce more oil than agreed on, thus tempering the price appreciation of a barrel of oil. The top five OPEC nations in order of oil reserves are (1) Venezuela, (2) Saudi Arabia, (3) Iran, (4) Iraq, and (5) Kuwait. Venezuela controls approximately 25 percent of OPEC's oil, whereas Saudi Arabia controls 22 percent. All other nations control less than 13 percent each.

U.S. Refining

The USA leads the world with 125 of the world's 655 refineries, but the trend is toward fewer but larger refineries as a result of competition and the economies of scale the larger refineries offer. In 1981, considered the peak of the refining business, there were 324 refineries in the USA. This downstream product is less profitable than upstream operations, so many firms including Exxon are attempting to reduce their exposure to this market.

Argentina Reserves

In South America, everybody knows about Venezuela with Hugo Chavez and the country's Orinoco Valley. Many people also know about the numerous discoveries during the past five years in Brazil's prolific deepwater Santos Basin. However, Argentina is South America's largest natural gas producer and its oil production registers something less than 750,000 barrels per day (or about a third of Venezuela's output). ExxonMobil and Chevron of late have been excitedly pursuing shale-drilling opportunities in Argentina's Neuquen Basin. The Basin's Vaca Muerta (dead cow) shale is fast gaining worldwide attention. Including Vaca Muerta's 23 billion BOE, Argentina likely holds the world's third-largest deposits of shale gas, behind only the USA and China.

Of all the energy companies involved in Argentina, Apache is the largest with that company owning about 3.7 million acres and being active in the country's four primary producing basins: Neuquen, Austral, Cuyo, and Noroeste. But in late 2012, Chevron reached an agreement with Argentina's nationalized oil company YPF to form a $1 billion partnership to develop shale oil reserves in the Vaca Muerta. YPF is also holding talks with Norway's Statoil for the development of Argentinean properties.

The Future

ExxonMobil just acquired Plano, Texas-based Denbury Resources' Bakken Shale assets in North Dakota and Montana for $1.3 billion, along with property in Wyoming and Texas. The company now controls 50 percent of the Bakken Shale region.

A number of analysts contend that Exxon should spin-off its refining business because the refining and production business are at odds with each other; oil-refining companies look to buy oil at the lowest possible cost while production companies look to sell oil at the highest possible cost. ConocoPhillips and Marathon Oil Corp. (MRO) recently separated their refining operations into separate companies.

Exxon is trying to sell its stake in the giant southern oilfield in Iraq after clashing with the central government in Baghdad over exploration contracts it had signed with the autonomous Kurdistan region in the north. The CNPC unit of Petrochina is currently negotiating for Exxon's 60 percent in the $50 billion West Qurna-1 project. Iraq has the world's fourth-largest oil reserves and wants to at least double its production in the next few years, and ultimately challenge Russia and Saudi Arabia as the world's biggest oil nation. Exxon's departure would all but wipe out the U.S. presence in Iraq's southern oilfields. Occidental Petroleum has a small stake in the Zubair oilfield development project.

Prepare a three-year strategic plan for ExxonMobil's CEO Rex Tillerson.

Microsoft Corporation, 2013

www.microsoft.com, MSFT

Headquartered in Redmond, Washington, Microsoft is the world's largest software company and had record revenues of $73 billion in fiscal year 2012 that ended on June 30, 2012. Microsoft develops a variety of software and hardware products and services for customers around the world, including its Windows Office, Windows 8 operating system for personal computers (PCs), Windows Phone 7 operating systems for mobile phones, Windows Server operating systems, Windows Azure, Microsoft SQL, Visual Studio, Silverlight, and the popular Xbox gaming and entertainment console. Many PC makers such as Acer, Lenovo, Dell, Hewlett-Packard, and Toshiba pre-install Microsoft software on devices. The firm also offers consulting services, cloud-based services, and training certifications as well as online products such as Bing, MSN, adCenter, and Atlas. Microsoft has strategic alliances with Nokia, NIIT, and Dominion Enterprises. The company owns Skype and recently introduced a Windows Phone and a Windows tablet computer named "Surface."

Microsoft's third quarter of fiscal 2013 results reported April 2013 were outstanding, with its Business Division's revenues up 8 percent to $6.32 billion, its Server and Tools' revenues of $5.04 billion up 11 percent, its Windows' division revenues of $5.07 billion up 23 percent, its Online Services segment revenues up 18 percent to $832 million, and its Entertainment and Devices segment revenues up 56 percent to $2.53 billion.

In August 2013, CEO Ballmer announced he would resign from Microsoft within 12 months, so the firm is scurrying to determine who will be a good replacement. The month prior, Microsoft revamped its organizational structure, dissolving its eight business lines up in favour of four new segments to focus on engineering and encourage collaboration across the company. Basically the company is now structured as a division-by-function type of structure. The divisions are expected to focus on operating systems, apps, cloud technology and devices. The move largely reversed the strategy and structure put in place by CEO Ballmer in 2005. Microsoft's stock price jumped in response the Ballmer announcing that he would resign soon.

Copyright by Fred David Books LLC. (Written by Forest R. David)

History

Founded by Bill Gates and Paul Allen in 1975, Microsoft was established to develop and sell BASIC Interpreters for the Altair 8800. The company rose to dominate the PC operating system market in the mid-1980s with their MS-DOS software, followed by the Microsoft Windows operating system, which was a graphical extension of MS-DOS. Microsoft went public in 1986, instantly creating three billionaires and 12,000 millionaires from Microsoft employees. In 1990, Microsoft introduced its software office suite, Microsoft Office that bundled MS Word and MS Excel together.

Microsoft acquired Skype Technologies for $8.6 billion in 2011 in its largest-ever acquisition. Following the release of Windows Phone 7, Microsoft underwent a gradual rebranding of its product range throughout 2011 and 2012. Its logos, products, services, and websites adopted the principles and concepts of the Metro design language. Microsoft in early 2012 introduced Windows 8, an operating system designed to power both PCs and tablet computers. Then in May 2012, Microsoft introduced its own tablet computer, the Microsoft Surface. As the company continued to diversify away from operating systems, it paid $1.2 billion to buy the social network firm Yammer and then launched its Windows Phone 8. To cope with the potential increase in demand for products and services, Microsoft is slowly but surely opening its own Microsoft Stores across the USA. Bill and Melinda Gates are today one of the richest couples on the planet, and one of the most giving couples in terms of philanthropic endeavors through the Bill and Melinda Gates Foundation.

Internal Issues

Vision and Mission

A statement at the corporate website says: "At Microsoft, our mission and values are to help people and businesses throughout the world realize their full potential."

Organizational Structure

Among the 17 executives listed in Exhibit 1, there are three women in Microsoft's management hierarchy. Note in Exhibit 1 that Microsoft uses a division-by-product organizational structure, with Steve Ballmer being chief executive officer (CEO) and Kevin Turner being chief operations officer (COO). Some analysts say that executive titles could be more effectively named. For example, President of Microsoft Corp. versus President of Microsoft Business is unclear to some observers. It is unclear from the structure where Microsoft Phone and Microsoft Tablet and Microsoft Stores reports. Such items would ideally be clear in executive titles. Perhaps a strategic business unit (SBU) structure would be more effective.

The Surface Tablet

Sales of Microsoft's Surface tablet are not good; analysts expect the company to sell between 500,000 and 600,000 Surface tablets in their second quarter of fiscal 2013, much lower than the company's original estimate of 1 to 2 million. Introducing a tablet is a good idea for three reasons: (1) Microsoft has the cash to invest heavily in research and development (R&D) for its own tablet; (2) the tablet market has been booming; and (3) the PC market is declining. But the problem perhaps is that Microsoft priced the Surface too high at $499 and up, roughly the same price as the competing Apple iPad. Microsoft likely should compete on price, not luxury, when up against Apple products. Microsoft could undercut Apple's price, and even if it *loses money* on Surface, the initial loss could be worth it if it revitalizes sales of other company products. The success of Windows 8 largely hinges on widespread adoption of the Surface tablet. The whole

EXHIBIT 1 Organizational Chart

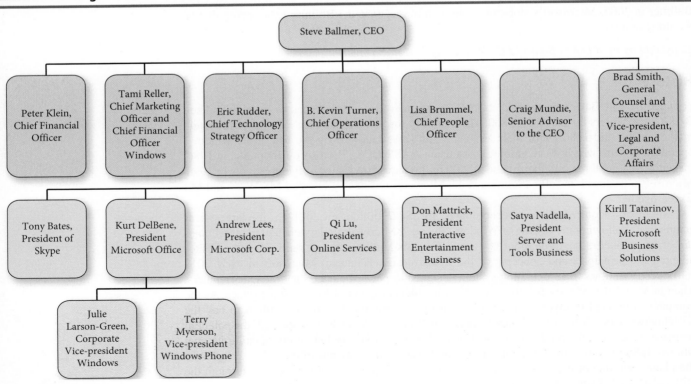

Source: Based on company documents.

point of Windows 8 was to launch Microsoft into the world of tablet computing, and with weak sales of its tablet, Microsoft's transition away from the faltering PC market may be a difficult one. Microsoft should perhaps consider McDonald's successful strategy of offering and heavily marketing inexpensive products (for example, the Dollar Menu) and by promoting low-grade items.

Segments

Microsoft has five reportable business segments as listed in Exhibit 2. Note that Microsoft Business is the largest segment in both revenues and operating income, whereas both the Windows and Windows Line (called Windows Division from here on), and Server and Tools segment, contribute greatly to the company's financial position. A sixth segment, titled Corporate Level Activity, includes all financial dealings not allocated to specific segments. The division includes costs related to marketing, product support services, legal, finance, and other business activities. Some analysts contend that the company's segments could be more effectively named to reveal their nature.

The Windows Division receives approximately 75 percent of its revenue from the Windows operating system, with the bulk of this revenue coming from equipment manufacturers such as Dell, Sony, Toshiba, and others pre-installing Windows on their machines for customers. The division in addition to providing Windows also provides related software, online services, and PC hardware products. This division could be vulnerable if worldwide PC sales continue to slump, as they did in 2012 with a 3.2-percent decline. Windows 8, launched in October 2012, provides better communication with cloud services and enables tablets and phones to run with near PC power. The whole world is becoming less dependent on traditional PCs, which historically has been Microsoft's bread and butter and is a key reason why the firm is looking to diversify.

Microsoft's Server and Tools Division is Microsoft's third most profitable division, producing name brand products such as Windows Server, Microsoft SQL, Windows Azure, Visual Studio, Enterprise Services, and others. Enterprise Services include product support and consulting services and account for 20 percent of the division's revenues. The division also offers developer tools, training, and certifications. Around 55 percent of Server and Tools revenues are derived from multiyear licensing agreements, with the remaining 25 percent coming from transactional volume licensing programs. In 2012, revenues increased by 12 percent in the division mainly attributed to growth in the SQL and Windows servers, although Enterprise

EXHIBIT 2 Microsoft's Revenues by Segment (in millions)

	2012	2011	2010
Windows Division			
Revenues	$18,373	$19,033	$19,491
Operating Income	11,460	12,211	12,895
Server and Tools			
Revenues	18,686	16,680	15,109
Operating Income	7,431	6,290	5,381
Online Services			
Revenues	2,867	2,607	2,294
Operating Income	(8,121)	(2,657)	(2,408)
Microsoft Business			
Revenues	23,991	22,514	19,256
Operating Income	15,719	14,657	11,849
Entertainment and Devices			
Revenues	9,593	8,915	6,079
Operating Income	364	1,257	517
Corporate Level Activity	(5,090)	(4,597)	(4,136)

Source: Based on 2012 *Annual Report*, p. 21–25.

Services grew 18 percent over the same period from an increase in both product support and consulting services. Overall operating income still increased 17 percent.

The company's Online Services Division designs products that aid customers in simplifying tasks and making more informed decisions online. Products include Bing and MSN, which generate sales through advertising. In fiscal year 2012, advertising revenues grew 13 percent in this segment to $2.6 billion. Online advertising revenues grew 13 percent over the fiscal year to $2.6 billion; however, operating losses totaled $8 billion resulting from $6 billion in goodwill impairment from fourth quarter of fiscal year 2012, resulting from the 2007 acquisition of aQuantive. Expectations of future sales growth and profitability are significantly lower for aQuantive than anticipated.

The company's Microsoft Business Division produced 32 percent of total companywide revenues and 72 percent of operating income in fiscal year 2012. The segment derives revenues from software and online servers that help to increase personal team and organizational productivity. Microsoft's most notable product, its Microsoft Office System, makes up more than 90 percent of this division's revenues. However, future reliance on this segment is somewhat tenuous because Google and other competitors are now offering Web-based products that work much the same as Microsoft Office products work.

The company's Entertainment and Devices Division generated 13 percent of total revenues in fiscal year 2012, led by the Xbox 360 entertainment platform. The division includes Xbox, Skype, and Windows Phone. Skype is a free popular video chat platform and for-pay phone service. Sales from Skype and Windows Phone increased 6.5 percent in fiscal year 2012, but Xbox sales declined $113 million even though Xbox LIVE revenue increased. Skype reported revenues of $860 million, net losses of $7 million, and long-term debt of $686 million in 2011, leading some analysts to say Microsoft paid too much for Skype. Overall, Microsoft has a history of using poor judgments in acquisitions, as indicated by the company's goodwill being more than $13 billion. Skype does overlap considerable with Windows Live Messenger in that both offer free chat, voice chat, and video chat. Windows Messenger though has around three times the users as Skype, but Skype offers a more refined platform for video chats. The one key difference between Microsoft's existing products and Skype is that about 8 million Skype users pay for the service through telephone connectivity, making it easy for many customers across the globe to buy phone numbers in foreign markets affordably. With the purchase price of $8.5 billion, Microsoft is in essence paying around $1,000 for each customer who is worth around $30 each, assuming most of Skype's income is from call charges, leaving much to be made up on possible advertisements or some synergy with existing Microsoft products. Compounding problems for Skype, it is estimated a large percentage of their customers come from emerging markets and do not have much money to spend. However for Microsoft, preventing Google and Facebook from obtaining Skype also played a role in the purchase.

Exhibit 3 reveals that approximately 52 percent of Microsoft's 2012 revenues are derived from the USA. Note that international revenues have increased as a percent of total revenues in each of the three years provided.

Finance

Microsoft's fiscal year ends on June 30 of each year. As indicated in the financial statements provided in Exhibits 4 and 5, Microsoft's revenues have been growing annually in recent years, a good thing. However, note in Exhibit 4 that the company's net income dropped 26.7 percent in

EXHIBIT 3 Microsoft's Revenues by Geographic Region (in millions)

	2012	2011	2010
USA	$38,846	$38,008	$36,173
Outside USA	$34,877	$31,935	$26,311
Total	$73,723	$69,943	$62,484

Source: Based on 2012 *Annual Report*, p. 80.

EXHIBIT 4 Microsoft's Income Statements (in millions)

	2012	2011	2010
Revenue	73,723.0	69,943.0	62,484.0
Other Revenue, Total	0.0	0.0	0.0
Total Revenue	73,723.0	69,943.0	62,484.0
Cost of Revenue, Total	17,530.0	15,577.0	12,395.0
Gross Profit	56,193.0	54,366.0	50,089.0
Selling/General/Administrative Expenses, Total	18,426.0	18,162.0	17,218.0
Research and Development	9,811.0	9,043.0	8,714.0
Depreciation and Amortization	0.0	0.0	0.0
Interest Expense (Income), Net Operating	0.0	0.0	0.0
Unusual Expense (Income)	5,895.0	-80.0	-10.0
Other Operating Expenses, Total	0.0	0.0	0.0
Operating Income	22,061.0	27,241.0	24,167.0
Interest Income (Expense),	0.0	0.0	0.0
Gain (Loss) on Sale of Assets	0.0	0.0	0.0
Other, Net	1.0	-31.0	14.0
Income Before Tax	22,267.0	28,071.0	25,013.0
Income Tax, Total	5,289.0	4,921.0	6,253.0
Income After Tax	16,978.0	23,150.0	18,760.0
Minority Interest	0.0	0.0	0.0
Equity in Affiliates	0.0	0.0	0.0
U.S. GAAP Adjustment	0.0	0.0	0.0
Net Income Before Extraordinary Items	16,978.0	23,150.0	18,760.0
Total Extraordinary Items	0.0	0.0	0.0
Net Income	**16,978.0**	**23,150.0**	**18,760.0**
Total Adjustments to Net Income	0.0	0.0	0.0
Basic Weighted Average Shares	8,396.0	8,490.0	8,813.0
Basic EPS Excluding Extraordinary Items	2.02	2.73	2.13
Basic EPS Including Extraordinary Items	2.02	2.73	2.13

EPS, earnings per share; GAAP, generally accepted accounting procedures.
Source: Based on company documents.

fiscal year 2012 and that the company's R&D expenditures have held at 13 percent of revenue for the last three years. Microsoft's sales and marketing expenditures for the last three years have dropped from 21 to 20 to 19 percent of revenues.

Note in Exhibit 5 that Microsoft's goodwill increased another $900 million to $13.4 billion in fiscal year 2012. Goodwill represents the cumulative amount the company has historically paid "above book value" for acquisitions, so such a high number is not good.

EXHIBIT 5 Microsoft's Balance Sheets (in millions)

	2012	2011	2010
Assets			
Cash and Short-Term Investments	63,040.0	52,772.0	36,788.0
Total Receivables, Net	15,780.0	14,987.0	13,014.0
Total Inventory	1,137.0	1,372.0	740.0
Prepaid Expenses	0.0	0.0	0.0
Other Current Assets, Total	5,127.0	5,787.0	5,134.0
Total Current Assets	**85,084.0**	**74,918.0**	**55,676.0**

(continued)

EXHIBIT 5 Continued

	2012	2011	2010
Property, Plant, and Equipment	8,269.0	8,162.0	7,630.0
Goodwill, Net	13,452.0	12,581.0	12,394.0
Intangibles, Net	3,170.0	744.0	1,158.0
Long-Term Investments	9,776.0	10,865.0	7,754.0
Note Receivable, Long Term	0.0	0.0	0.0
Other Long-Term Assets, Total	1,520.0	1,434.0	1,501.0
Other Assets, Total	0.0	0.0	0.0
Total Assets	**121,271.0**	**108,704.0**	**86,113.0**
Liabilities and Shareholders' Equity			
Accounts Payable	4,175.0	4,197.0	4,025.0
Payable/Accrued	0.0	0.0	0.0
Accrued Expenses	3,875.0	3,575.0	3,283.0
Notes Payable and Short-Term Debt	0.0	0.0	1,000.0
Current Portability of Long-Term Debt Capital Leases	1,231.0	0.0	0.0
Other Current Liabilities, Total	23,407.0	21,002.0	17,839.0
Total Current Liabilities	32,688.0	28,774.0	26,147.0
Total Long-Term Debt	10,713.0	11,921.0	4,939.0
Deferred Income Tax	1,893.0	1,456.0	229.0
Minority Interest	0.0	0.0	0.0
Other Liabilities, Total	9,614.0	9,470.0	8,623.0
Total Liabilities	54,908.0	51,621.0	39,938.0
Redeemable Preferred Stock	0.0	0.0	0.0
Preferred Stock, Nonredeemable, Net	0.0	0.0	0.0
Common Stock	65,797.0	63,415.0	62,856.0
Additional Paid-In Capital	0.0	0.0	0.0
Retained Earnings (Accumulated Deficit)	−856.0	−8,195.0	−17,736.0
Treasury Stock, Common	0.0	0.0	0.0
ESOP Debt Guarantee	0.0	0.0	0.0
Unrealized Gain (Loss)	1,523.0	1,658.0	1,231.0
Other Equity, Total	−101.0	205.0	−176.0
Total Equity	**66,363.0**	**57,083.0**	**46,175.0**
Total Liabilities and Shareholders' Equity	**121,271.0**	**108,704.0**	**86,113.0**

ESOP, employee stock ownership plan.
Source: Based on company documents.

Competition

Being so diversified, Microsoft has different competitors in different segments. The company's Windows Operating System faces competition from Apple and Google who have their own operating systems. Microsoft's server products face stiff competition from Hewlett-Packard, IBM, and Oracle, who all offer preinstalled operating systems on their server hardware. Microsoft's cloud-based services compete with Amazon, Google, and Salesforce.com, whereas Microsoft's SQL Azure faces intense competition from IBM, Oracle, and many other firms.

The Microsoft Office package (Word, Excel, Access, and other products) faces heavy competition from Adobe, Apple, Cisco, Google, SAP, and many other Web-based competitors offering word processing, spreadsheets, and databases. The company's Entertainment and Devices segment, producer of Xbox360, faces intense competition from heavyweights Nintendo and Sony. The average life of an entertainment console is surprisingly long at 5+ years, and game selection is one of the largest factors in deterring the success of a gaming console.

EXHIBIT 6 A Financial Comparison of Microsoft to Rival Companies

	Microsoft	Apple	Google	Oracle
Number of employees	94,000	72,800	53,546	115,000
Revenue	$72.4B	$156.5B	$47.5B	$37B
Net Income	$15.7B	$41.7B	$10.6B	$10.6B
Net Profit Margin	21.7%	26.7%	22.2%	28.7%
EPS	$1.85	$44.15	$31.91	$2.13
Market Capitalization	228B	457M	237.9B	$164B
Shares Outstanding	8.42B	940M	228M	4.7B

EPS, earnings per share.
Source: Based on company documents.

Microsoft's new Windows Phone competes with market share leader Apple with their iPhone and Google with their Android platform powering Samsung and other phones. Also, Research in Motion is revitalizing their once-popular Blackberry. Microsoft's alliance with Nokia to power Nokia phones with Windows 8 hopes to inch away at market share in the phone industry.

Exhibit 6 provides a financial comparison of Microsoft with three competitors. Note that Microsoft has the lowest earnings per share (EPS) among the firms included, partly as a result of having by far the most shares of stock outstanding.

Apple

Headquartered in Cupertino, California, Apple produces PCs, digital music players, iPhones, and other communication media to customers around the world. Some of their most popular products include the iPhone, iPad, MacBook Pro, and iPod. Apple has their own operating system for all of their products. The iPhone is the world leader in market share for all mobile phones, but Samsung is the world leader in smartphone unit volume (most phones sold) because they produce multiple options for customers, rather then a one-size-fits-all as Apple does with their current iPhone. In addition, Google's Android platform, which Samsung and other phone manufacturers use on their phones, powers more phones than Apple's operating system, which is only used to power Apple iPhones.

Apple also provides many software products with their operating system such as iLife, iWork, Final Cut Pro, Logic Studio, and of late Apple TV. Apple provides their products through online stores, retail stores such as Walmart, Best Buy, Apple Stores, and others. Apple operates about 250 Apple Stores in the USA and 140 stores internationally.

Apple's stock price fell from $700 around the launch of iPhone 5 in 2012 to $485 in early 2013. Some analysts suggest products by Samsung powered by Google's Android software are taking significant market share away from Apple. Apple launched a new phone in the middle of 2013 called the iPhone 5S, reportedly to sell at a significant discount to the iPhone 5. To be targeted at large emerging markets in which many customers have no phone and less money, the 5S phone is likely to have a polycarbonate construction instead of the glass and aluminum the iPhone 5 sports. In addition, there will be no retina display and the phone will not be compatible with newer LTE markets and will thus run on 3G. Running on 3G however, is adequate because many emerging markets will not have LTE for a number of years into the future. The iPhone 5S follows the line of thinking of the iPad Mini, providing a discounted item for customers on a limited budget. Although the 5S may hurt profit margins, producing the phone is an attempt to win market share in emerging markets before Samsung, Dell, Nokia, and other competitors win legions of fans over to their products.

Google

Headquartered in Mountain View, California, Google provides the world's most popular search engine as well as cloud computing, Google Chrome, Google Maps for GPS users, Google Earth, Google Analytics for keeping track of hits and traffic on websites, and YouTube. Many of Google's products are supported by heavy advertisements, helping to produce record revenues of $38 billion for year end 2011. Google produces Android, the world's most popular smartphone platform.

About 96 percent of all Google revenues are derived from advertising programs, with the balance coming predominantly from licensing agreements. Using technology from a firm named DoubleClick, Google can better determine user interest and effectively target advertisements, thus enabling Google to charge more for their service.

Google's Android operating system used for touch-screen smartphones and tablets currently enjoys a 75-percent market share in the smartphone marketplace. One of the key benefits of using Android products is that they are open source, meaning the software can be modified and distributed to anyone. Phone manufacturers such as Samsung or wireless carriers such as Verizon can alter the software to meet their specific needs. In addition, enthusiasts who enjoy developing applications for use in mobile devices can also alter the platform to fit their needs. The popularity and open source nature of Android has led it to becoming the top choice in the world for smartphones and tablets. The future of Android's use may eventually extend away from solely phones and tablets into television, games, and consoles and virtually any electronic device. This could potentially put further pressure on Microsoft with their Windows 8 operating system and Xbox consoles.

Oracle Corp.

Headquartered in Redwood City, California, Oracle is a producer of middleware software, application software, application server and cloud application, data integration, development tools, Java, and much more. Oracle also provides consulting services in business and information technology (IT), strategy alignment, and ongoing product enhancements. In 2012, Oracle acquired RightNow Technologies, Inc. (RightNow) and Taleo Corporation (Taleo). Oracle's stock hit a new 52-week high of $35 in January 2013.

As an example of Oracle's software products that compete with Microsoft, one of the largest Australian Supermarket chains is Coles with more than 100,000 employees and 2,000 stores throughout Australia. Coles recently installed Oracle's Exadata Database Machine and Oracle Enterprise Manager 12c running on Oracle Linux to enable critical trend reporting during retail seasonal spikes. By implementing the Oracle Exadata Database Machine, Coles's processes improved three to four times out of the box, with four to six times faster query performance so that Coles's can now meet SLAs and drive customer satisfaction. With the Oracle software, Coles can now also store 20+ TB of trending historical data, enabling new, complex analytical reports to help better predict the needs and potential issues for Coles's stores.

Nintendo

Headquartered in Kyoto, Japan, Nintendo is the world's largest video game company by revenues. Translated into English the company name is: "leave luck to heaven." Nintendo is Japan's third most valuable publically traded company and has a market value of more than $85 billion and revenues of more than $12 billion. Based in Redmond, Washington, near Microsoft's headquarters, Nintendo North America is the majority owner of the Seattle Mariners Major League Baseball team. Nintendo is a market share leader position with products such as the Nintendo 3DS and Nintendo's Wii products including the new Wii U, which features touch-screen controllers. Nintendo's European division is based in Frankfurt, Germany. Nintendo has a joint venture in China now produces and markets the iQue Player, a modified version of the Nintendo 64.

External

Smartphone Growth

Smartphone shipments have risen dramatically since 2005 from 50 million phones shipped worldwide to more than 650 million phones shipped in 2012. Shipments by 2016 are expected to be more than 1,200 million phones. Most of the growth is expected to come from emerging markets, with China leading the way. In 2012, China surpassed the USA as the world's largest smartphone market, yet there are millions of untapped customers remaining in China. India, Brazil, and other emerging markets offer millions of customers. Aside from traditional phone providers, companies such as Apple, Dell, and others are all continually offering new products and features to differentiate their handsets. Google and Microsoft are teaming up with existing phone producers to provide new and better operating systems for their respective phones.

Nokia Migrates to Windows 8

Nokia unveiled in late 2012 their latest Lumia 920 and 820 model smartphones, Nokia's first set of smartphones to run off the new Windows 8 operating system. A main advantage gained for Nokia using Windows 8 resides in the compatibility of file-sharing capabilities because both the 920 and 820 devices will sync with PCs and tablets with Windows 8. Nokia hopes the switch to Windows 8 will differentiate its products and aid in improving sales which declined 37 percent from the second quarter 2011 to the second quarter 2012.

Cloud Computing

Cloud computing, supplying computing services via the Internet without having to use hardware or platform support, continues to grow in its use and offerings. Many businesses employ the technology to save on costs because they can lease data storage and computing capacity from web-based providers. Advantages for businesses using cloud technology include reduced capital investments in equipment and software, while allowing for payments only for the capacity needed. Traditionally, firms would buy their own in-house capacity and have to forecast future needs, often resulting in purchasing more capacity than was needed. Google is the lead company using cloud technology to support many of their offerings. However, there is still some concern among businesses that cloud computing offers less security, and increased dependability on a third-party vender such as Google to continually provide the service at an appropriate network speed is questionable. Nevertheless, cloud services are expected to yield revenues of $100 billion in 2016, up from $40 billion in 2011.

The Future

Microsoft is developing technologies that increasingly enable touch screen and voice to be more readily understood by PCs, tablets, and phones. Microsoft CEO Ballmer envisions that technology will soon act on people's behalf rather than at their command, so he has directed Microsoft R&D staff to develop cloud services that enhance the experience for both businesses and individuals. Microsoft plans to better align the communication between PCs, tablets, phones, and servers by developing improved operating systems with Windows 8 delivering preliminary results in this arena.

High-definition TVs and tablets of today are expected to soon lose market share to gadgets than can read human emotions and to eye gaze technology that will allow for automatic scrolling and opening of apps. Even "skin stretch feedback" on devices will take into account people's emotions. Tom Wilson, CEO of emotions3D, for example recently remarked that such devices will "interpret moods and give consumers a more helpful and rewarding experience." Some analysts predict that the audio quality alone on smartphones will increase 16 times from 2013 to 2018. Also, as the tablet's video gaming experience increases and becomes closer to the experience on an Xbox, PlayStation or Nintendo's market share for traditional gaming consoles may decline. More useable devices for people on the go are being developed in part to reduce accidents while driving and using mobile devices.

Microsoft in early 2013 introduced its new Office 365 product, a subscription service for $99.99 or $9.99 per month pay-as-you-go option. Office 365 constantly updates itself every time you open a program. The product works great on Apple Macs and virtually all companies' computers, tablets, smartphones, and more.

Microsoft's $2 billion investment to finance part of Dell computer's buyout in early 2013 is an attempt by the firm to support the ailing PC industry—which saw shipments fall 14 percent in the first quarter of 2013 alone. Millions of consumers globally are skipping over PCs altogether and going straight to mobile devices.

Technology is changing so rapidly everyday, and new rival firms arising globally in the industry, that Microsoft needs a clear strategic plan going forward.

Develop a new strategic plan for the upcoming new CEO of Microsoft.

The Emirates Group, 2014

www.theemiratesgroup.com

Based in Dubai, United Arab Emirates (UAE), Emirates Group (Emirates) includes (a) Emirates (the airlines) and (b) Dnata, a company specializing in aviation ground-handling services and operating at 20 airports. The largest airline in the Middle East, Emirates flies to more than 130 destinations in 70 countries on six continents and offers direct flights from Dubai to Washington, DC, San Francisco, Los Angeles, and Seattle. Emirates services the world from Beijing to San Francisco and more than 100 markets in between. More than 1,200 Emirates flights depart Dubai each week, accounting for about 40 percent of all air traffic out of Dubai International Airport.

Emirates carries 40 million passengers and 2.0 million tons of cargo annually, using a fleet of more than 170 aircraft. The company has another 230 aircraft on order (worth about $84 billion) and is the world's largest operator of both the Airbus 380 and Boeing 777. Using large planes such as the Airbus 380 and Boeing 777 provides extra space and luxury for wealthy and business passengers alike. Most of the company's planes even include spacious private suites, and some planes provide a spa with showers. Emirates is well known for providing excellent service for high-end passengers in first class, but it also provides excellent service in business class and economy class. Economy-class customers receive well-thought-out meals consisting of many courses, e-mail, SMS services, telephone, and personal TV monitors with more than 1,400 channel options. Singapore Air is considered the closest competitor based on overall business model of top service at a premium price and markets served.

Emirates has more than 67,000 employees and annual revenues of more than 73.1 billion Dirham (the United Arab Emirates currency). The Dirham is pegged to the U.S. dollar so currency fluctuations are not significant. Emirates is owned by the government of Dubai operating under the Investment Corporation of Dubai name, but the company and the government of Dubai are quick to point out the airline has grown in scale not by way of protectionism but through competition. The government of Dubai treats Emirates as a wholly independent business entity on its own and attributes this to the firm's success. Dubai has an open-skies policy and more than 60 percent of all flights in Dubai are by companies other than Emirates.

In August 2013, Emirates became the first airline in the Middle East to provide Google Now cards for their passengers who book via Emirates.com. A feature of the Google Search app, Google Now is available and fully integrated for Android (devices running Android 4.1 and above) and iOS (iPhones and iPads). This new product enables Emirates' customers to see and monitor their upcoming flight, providing flight times and departure terminal. Google Now gives passengers relevant information on their destination (for example weather conditions locally, currency, local landmarks, accommodations, and attractions).

Copyright by Fred David Books LLC. (Written by Forest R. David)

History

Dubai is a city-state in the UAE, located within the emirate of the same name, one of the seven emirates that make up the UAE. Dubai has the largest population in the UAE (2,104,895) and the second-largest land territory by area (4,114 km^2) after Abu Dhabi. Dubai and Abu Dhabi, the national capital, are the only two emirates to have veto power over critical matters of national importance in the UAE legislature. The city of Dubai is located on the emirate's northern coastline and is often misperceived as a country or city-state and, in some cases, the UAE as a whole has been described as Dubai.

When the British pulled out of Dubai in the late 1950s, Sheikh Saeed bin Maktoum (the current CEO of Emirates) decreed open-seas, open-skies, and open-trade policies to develop the country. He also required that all government agencies make a profit. Dubai was aiming to eliminate its dependence on its finite oil reserves within 50 years and thus has operated under a free market society for decades. Emirates Group started in 1959 as the Dubai National Air

Transport Association (Dnata), with Dnata airport operations, Dnata cargo, and Dnata agencies as segments. After Gulf Air began cutting back service to Dubai in the 1980s, Dubai's royal family provided funding for Dnata to obtain two planes and the company became known as Emirates Group. The company's first flight was in 1985 on a leased Airbus plane. After being in operation for four years, Emeritus was serving 12 destinations, and by 1994 the airline was serving 32 destinations but still only operated 15 aircraft and was the sixth largest airline in the Middle East. During this time, 92 rival firms were serving Dubai Airport, which provided intense competition for Emirates.

The late 1990s was a time of rapid expansion for Emirates; it ordered 16 Airbus 330-200s at a cost of $2 billion, and in 1997, it ordered an additional six Boeing 777-200s. The company followed that by opening a $65-million training center with simulators for training pilots and crew. The company continued to expand, ordering an additional 22 Airbus A380s, the largest plane in the world, and six additional Boeing 777s in 2001. The 2000s saw considerable expansion in the number of planes operated and destinations served, including new flights being added every month to various places around the world. Emirates received 22 new aircraft in fiscal year 2012, the most ever obtained in a single year by the company. Emirates is perhaps the world's fastest growing and most profitable airline in the industry.

Dubai is one of the fastest-growing countries in the world because thousands of people migrate to Dubai monthly, often because there is no tax on the personal wages in Dubai. The living standard is great, the climate is great, the infrastructure is impressive, business is growing leaps and bounds, and the schools in Dubai are international and provide a great learning environment for kids of all nationalities. However, an expatriate (foreigner) may work in Dubai only if sponsored by an employer.

Internal Issues

Mission and Vision
Emirates' mission is "to become one of the top lifestyle brands in the world."

Organizational Structure
As indicated in Exhibit 1, Emirates operates from a divisional-by-product organizational design. Note that no women are among the company's top management team, which comes as no surprise given Middle Eastern culture. However, Emirates could set an example soon by promoting

EXHIBIT 1 Emirates' Organizational Structure

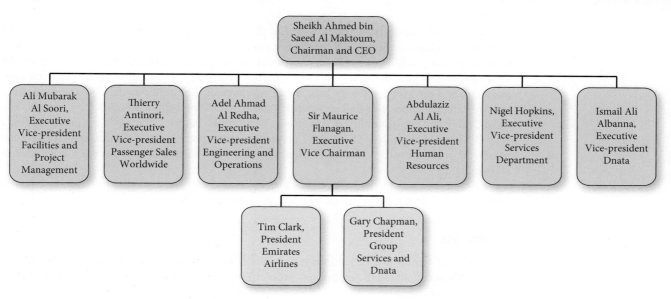

Source: Based on company documents.

one or more women to top management, to exemplify that women are as capable as men to manage business operations. The Executive Vice Chairman position perhaps is analogous to the traditional Chief Operations Officer.

Emirates Luxury

First-class passengers on Emirates flights enjoy their own private suites on Airbus 380, Airbus 350, and Boeing 777 planes. The Emirates first-class experience starts with a personal chauffeur picking up a passenger and driving him or her to the airport for a seamless check in. Customers are then able to enjoy the first-class lounge while they wait for the plane to arrive before the boarding process begins. First-class passengers have an allowance for two carry on items totaling 25 pounds combined and unlimited checked bags up to 170 pounds total weight. Once on board, the customer enjoys suites that include a personal mini-bar, vanity table, mirror, wardrobe, 23-inch TV with more than 1,400 channels including the latest movies, sliding door for extra privacy, SMS, Internet, and much more. If desired, the flight crew can covert the seat to a fully flat bed with mattress. To complement the bed, pajamas, slippers, and toiletries with Bulgari lotions are provided. First-class customers have exquisite free food and drink options, including Dom Perignon, martinis, Iranian caviar, stir-fried lobster, glazed duck breast, Arabic mezze (appetizers), and much more. First-class customers have access to the first-class lounge to mingle with other first-class passengers and enjoy hors d'oeuvres prepared by some of the world's best chefs. First-class customers can enjoy one of the two onboard shower spas as part of their experience on the Emirates Airbus 380. The spas are marketed as having walnut and marble designs with fine linens and provide complimentary massages in addition to a shower. The price in 2009 for a first-class ticket from Dubai to Melbourne, Australia was around $16,000.

Business-class travel on Emirates is possibly the best in the world. Business-class passengers enjoy many amenities, such as seats turning into a 79-inch flat bed at the push of a button, power supply for laptops, extra large tables, large screen TVs with more than 1,400 channels, SMS, Internet, mini-bar built into every seat, and privacy dividers. These amenities are provided on A380 and most Boeing 777 aircraft. Business-class passengers also enjoy delicious food and many drink options. Complimentary champagne and vintage wines are the norm, and all food is presented on Royal Doulton fine-bone china. Business-class customers also have access to the business-class lounge on the second level of all A380 aircraft where chefs fix snacks and hors d'oeuvres. Emirates' economy-class customers enjoy more than 1,400 channels on their personal TV, meals, and Internet, phone, and SMS capabilities at their seats.

Finance

Emirates' fiscal year ends on March 31st, and all financial statements are prepared in accordance with the International Financial Reporting Standards (IFRS) and are reviewed by an unaffiliated institution as any publicly traded company would be subject to. Emirates reported a profit for the 25th consecutive year in fiscal year 2013 with revenues up 17.4 percent from the previous year, and the best year ever for Dnata, which had revenues of 6.62 million AED. Rising fuel prices hurt overall profits because fuel accounts for more than 40 percent of all costs for Emirates. The Arab Spring and the instability in Africa also hurt profits, but the company's net profit for fiscal year 2013 was 7.83 billion AED, up 57 percent from the previous year. Emirates increased total passenger volume by 15.9 percent in fiscal year 2013 and maintained a passenger seat factor of 80 percent.

Emirates' recent income statements and balance sheets are provided in Exhibits 2 and 3, respectively. Note the strong financial position of this company.

Segments

The Emirates Group has two primary divisions, Emirates and Dnata. Emirates is the airline, whereas Dnata includes (a) cargo and ground handing, (b) travel services, (c) catering, and (d) freight forwarding.

EXHIBIT 2 Emirates' Income Statement (in millions of AED)

	2013 AED m	2012 AED m	2011 AED m
Revenue	71,159	61,508	52,945
Other operating income	1,954	779	1,286
Operating costs	(70,274)	(60,474)	(48,788)
Operating profit	**2,839**	**1,813**	**5,443**
Other gains and losses	—	—	(4)
Finance income	406	414	521
Finance costs	(900)	(657)	(506)
Share of results in associates and joint ventures	127	103	91
Profit before income tax	**2,472**	**1,673**	**5,545**
Income tax expense	(64)	(53)	(78)
Profit for the year	**2,408**	**1,620**	**5,467**
Profit attributable to non-controlling interests	**125**	**118**	**92**
Profit attributable to Emirates' owner	**2,283**	**1,502**	**5,375**
Profit for the year	**2,408**	**1,620**	**5,467**
Currency translation differences	9	(9)	38
Cash flow hedges	56	(259)	(282)
Actuarial losses on retirement benefit obligations	(70)	(116)	(57)
Other comprehensive income	**(5)**	**(384)**	**(301)**
Total comprehensive income for the year	**2,403**	**1,236**	**5,166**
Total comprehensive income attributable to non-controlling interests	**125**	**118**	**92**
Total comprehensive income attributable to Emirates' Owner	**2,278**	**1,118**	**5,074**

Source: Based on page 8, 2013 *Annual Report.*

EXHIBIT 3 Emirates' Balance Sheets (in millions of AED)

	2013 AED m	2012 AED m	2011 AED m
ASSETS			
Non-current assets			
Property, plant and equipment	57,039	49,198	39,848
Intangible assets	910	902	901
Investments in associates and joint ventures	485	430	386
Advance lease rentals	807	370	384
Loans and other receivables	508	917	1,704
Derivative financial instruments	92	69	—
Deferred income tax asset	15	10	—
		51,896	43,223
Current assets			
Inventories	1,564	1,469	1,290
Trade and other receivables	8,744	8,126	6,481
Derivative financial instruments	67	8	123
Short term bank deposits	18,048	8,055	3,777
Cash and cash equivalents	6,524	7,532	10,196
	34,447	25,190	21,867
Total assets	**94,803**	**77,086**	**65,090**

(continued)

EXHIBIT 3 Continued

	2013 AED m	2012 AED m	2011 AED m
EQUITY AND LIABILITIES			
Capital and reserves			
Capital	17	801	801
Retained earnings	22,729	21,256	20,370
Other reserves	(768)	(833)	(565)
Attributable to Emirates' owner	**22,762**	**21,224**	**20,606**
Non-controlling interests	**270**	**242**	**207**
Total equity	**23,032**	**21,466**	**20,813**
Non-current liabilities			
Borrowings and lease liabilities	35,752	26,843	20,502
Retirement benefit obligations	—	631	479
Deferred revenue	1,460	1,074	930
Deferred credits	294	350	401
Deferred income tax liability	—	—	2
Trade and other payables	—	—	31
Derivative financial instruments	1,016	957	642
		29,855	**22,987**
Current liabilities			
Trade and other payables	25,013	20,601	17,551
Income tax liabilities	24	36	22
Borrowings and lease liabilities	5,042	4,037	2,728
Deferred revenue	1,147	915	792
Deferred credits	87	136	136
Derivative financial instruments	6	40	61
	31,319	25,765	21,290
Total liabilities	**71,771**	**55,620**	**44,277**
Total equity and liabilities	**94,803**	**77,086**	**65,090**

Source: Based on page 9, 2013, *Annual Report.*

Emirates

Passenger revenue is the largest overall revenue generator as revealed in Exhibit 4. Substantial revenue also is derived from cargo, which produces 15 percent of the segment's total revenue, whereas sale of goods produces 3 percent. All other sources contribute less than 1 percent of the segment's revenues. This segment includes several maritime and mercantile holdings,

EXHIBIT 4 Emirates Revenues by Segment (in millions of AED)

REVENUE			
	2013 AED m	2011–12 AED m	2010–11 AED m
Passenger	57,477	48,950	41,415
Cargo	10,346	9,546	8,803
Excess baggage	388	332	293
Other	767		
Transport revenue	**68,978**	**58,828**	**50,511**
Sale of goods	1,196	2,017	1,774
Food	502	245	226
Other	483	418	434
Total	**71,159**	**61,508**	**52,945**

Source: Page 13, 2013, *Annual Report.*

a 49 percent ownership in a wine and spirit business in Thailand, and hotels in UAE, Australia, and Seychelles.

This segment operates more than 180 aircraft with approximately 120 on operating lease, 55 on financial lease, and 6 being fully owned by Emirates. Out of the 180 planes the company operates, 98 are Boeing's 777, one of Boeing's largest planes and the largest twin-engine plane in the world. An additional 21 aircraft are Airbus 380s, the four-engine double-decker plane that is the largest in the world. Emirates is the largest operator of Airbus 380 aircraft in the world. The company has on order 223 additional aircraft broken down to 84 Boeing 777s, 69 Airbus 380s, and 70 Airbus 350-900s. The Airbus 350s are wide-bodied, long-range planes designed to compete with Boeing's Dreamliner. Although the 350s are considered large capacity, they hold significantly less passengers than the 777 and 380 models. On average, Emirates wide-body planes are 77 months old compared to the industry average of 136 months. With 223 new planes on order, the average age of planes in the fleet should drop substantially.

More than 40 percent of all expenses are related to jet fuel. Employment expenses account for 13 percent of revenue and operating leases account for 8 percent. Maybe surprising to some, aircraft maintenance only amounted for AED 1,296 million or 2 percent of total revenues, about the same as parking and landing fees. Exhibit 4 details a revenue breakdown within the Emirates segment.

Exhibit 5 reveals the geographic breakdown of Emirates' flights. No single market accounts for more than 30 percent of revenues, creating a well-diversified company with respect to regions served. The Americas market grew at the highest rate in the most recent fiscal year, but East Asia and Australasia regions had the largest overall AED growth. Note that the Americas segment grew from last place to fourth place.

Dnata

Dnata's profits and revenues for fiscal year-end March 31, 2013 were at all time records of 6.5 billion AED and 815 million AED respectively, as revealed in Exhibit 6. Much of the revenue growth can be attributed to recent acquisitions Dnata made including Travel Republic Ltd., the largest privately-held online travel company in the United Kingdom, in 2011.

EXHIBIT 5 Geographic Breakdown of Emirates' Revenues (in millions of AED)

Year	East Asia and Australasia	Europe	West Asia and Indian Ocean	Americas	Middle East	Africa	Total
2012–2013	20,884	20,140	8,031	8,275	7,117	6,712	71,159
2011–12	18,227	17,058	7,083	6,696	6,314	6,130	61,508
2010–11	15,503	14,433	6,405	5,518	5,488	5,598	52,945

Source: Page 14, 2012–2013 *Annual Report.*

EXHIBIT 6 Dnata's Revenues by Segment (in millions of AED)

Revenue

	2012–2013 AED m	2011–12 AED m	2010–11 AED m	% change
In-flight Catering	1,686	2,452	576	325.7
Airport operations	2,474	2,321	1,980	17.2
Cargo	1,077	993	882	12.6
Information Technology	755	649	546	18.9
Travel services	544	319	243	31.3
Other	—	173	100	73.0
Total	6,536	6,907	4,327	59.6

Source: Based on company documents.

EXHIBIT 7 Geographical Revenue in Percent

	2011–2012	2010–2011	2009–2010
UAE	77%	62%	45%
International	23%	38%	55%

Source: Based on page 54, 2012 *Annual Report.*

In late 2010, Dnata acquired Alpha Flight Group's in-flight catering business. This is why the segment's revenues increased so much in 2011–2012 because Travel Republic's revenues first appeared on the income statement.

In-flight catering was both the largest revenue gainer and the largest revenue percent increase by 325 percent; however, the 2010–2011 fiscal year represents only three months of providing this service in house, resulting in the large percent increase. In-flight catering through the acquisition of Alpha Flight Group provided more than 48 million meals to customers in fiscal year 2012. Note all revenue streams in the Dnata segment experienced significant increases over the two years reported. Exhibit 7 provides a breakdown of Dnata services in UAE and internationally. For the first time ever, revenues in international markets were greater than domestic revenues.

Competition

Factors impacting the airline industry include global unrest, volatility of fuel prices, mergers and acquisitions, strategic alliances, video conferencing, and entry of discount airlines such as Ryanair. More than 100 different airlines provide service to Dubai International Airport, which is projected to become the world's busiest airport by 2016. Opening for passenger travel by the end of 2013 will be the new Al Maktoum Airport in Dubai. In fiscal year 2012 alone, Emirates started long-haul flights to Seattle, Dallas–Fort Worth, Rio de Janeiro, Buenos Aries, Washington DC, Geneva, Baghdad, and St. Petersburg (Russia), among others. Emirates' largest direct competitors are Singapore Airlines, British Airways, Delta, Middle East Airlines, and flydubai. Dubai is located eight hours by air from 75 percent of the world's population.

Singapore Airlines Group
Singapore Air dates back to1947 when the company was known as Malayan Airways Limited, operating flights to cities in and around Singapore. But in 1971 Malayan Airways split into Singapore Airlines and Malaysian Airline System, and the Singapore Airlines brand took off. Singapore Air now operates 101 planes that average six years and seven months and have 30 more planes on order. Like Emirates, Singapore Air operates the Airbus 380 (19 in operation) and the Boeing 777 (58 in operation). The Group operates 20 subsidiaries within the air travel industry, including SIA Cargo, SIA Engineering Company, SilkAir, Scoot, and Tradewinds Tours and Travel. Both SilkAir and Scoot are airlines that compliment the service of Singapore Air. Singapore Air predominantly serves Europe, Asia, and Australia, but it also flies to four cities in the United States and three in Africa.

Singapore Airline Group's fiscal year, like Emirates', ends on March 31. For fiscal year 2012, the company's profits were down $756 million to $336 million or 69 percent reduction, whereas revenues grew by $333 million to $14.8 billion, up 2 percent from the previous year. Both Singapore Air and Emirates are luxury airlines using Suites (separate from first class), first class, business class, and economy class. First-class passengers can enjoy 23-inch TVs, dining with food served on tableware designed by Givenchy, wines, and champagne. Singapore Air markets that they are the only airline to offer a stand-alone bed, not a converted seat. To complement the stand-alone bed, a sleeper suit, bedroom slippers, and linens also designed by Givenchy are provided. Soft lighting options and premium skin care products and toiletries are also provided.

Customers in first, business, and economy classes also enjoy amenities that exceed most all competing airlines. Hot, moist, hand towels are provided after meals to customers, even those in economy class. Serving all passengers since 1972 is the distinguished "Singapore Girl" that according to the company "is an enduring symbol of our impeccable service standards."

flydubai

flydubai was started by the government of Dubai in 2008 and was supported by Emirates during the firm's establishing phase, but flydubai is not part of the Emirates Group. With the backing of the Dubai government, flydubai ordered 50 Boeing 737-800s at a total price of $3.74 billion. The first planes were delivered in 2009, and flydubai was air bound for Beirut, the first market served. The company quickly grew as additional planes on order arrived. As of early 2013, the company served 52 markets, mostly in the Middle East but also a few select markets in Eastern Europe and India. In contrast to Emirates, flydubai is a discount airline provider much like a Spirit Airlines or AirTran in the USA or Ryanair or easyJet in Europe. flydubai operates 28 planes and 800 flights per week. The average age of aircraft is less than two years. The company does not currently provide financial information to the public.

Middle East Airlines

Middle East Airlines (MEA) began in 1945 in Beirut and served cities in Syria, Cyprus, Egypt, and later Saudi Arabia. The airline provides a local alternative for customers in the Middle East. In 1963, MEA merged with Air Liban and added destinations in the Middle East, West Africa, and Europe. In 2010, MEA accepted delivery of two new Airbus 320 aircrafts and resumed flights to Berlin and Brussels. In 2012, MEA joined SkyTeam and currently serves Europe, Persian Gulf, Middle East, and Africa. Notable destinations include four flights a day to Paris, London, Frankfurt, and Brussels; they also have flights to Rome, Milan, Athens, Geneva, Istanbul, and others in Europe and flights to several cities in Saudi Arabia, Amman, Iraq, Cairo, and Sharm el Sheikh. In total, MEA operates 19 aircraft with an average age of less than four years, has 10 planes on order, and serves 31 markets. The company offers Cedar Class (first class) and economy class. In 2011, MEA had revenues of $637 million with profits of $62 million.

British Airways

British Airways is a member of the Oneworld Alliance and is the largest carrier based on fleet size in the United Kingdom. The airline currently operates more than 250 aircraft with 50 more on order and serves the entire world. The airline has alliances with several airlines including Comair of South Africa and Sun Air of Scandinavia. The company had revenues of $14.8 billion in 2011. British Airways offers economy class, premium-economy class, business clas, and first class.

Delta

Headquartered in Atlanta and a member of the Sky Team Alliance, Delta is a major U.S. airline. Delta has hubs in several U.S. cities as well as in Amsterdam, Tokyo, and Paris. Operating more than 5,000 flights a day and an additional 2,500 flights through Delta Connection, Delta is one of the largest airlines in the world, and one of only a select few to provide service to all six inhabited continents. The airline provides business elite, first class, economy comfort, and economy class. Delta reported revenues of $14 billion and net income of $854 million in 2011.

Strategic Alliances

Airlines started forming strategic alliances in the 1990s to better compete with rival firms. Historically, if an airline did not serve a select market, a customer would either find an airline that did or be forced to purchase two separate tickets. Alliances largely resolve this problem because airlines can jointly benefit having a competitor (now also an alliance member) provide service for that leg of the flight. Other benefits of alliances are more efficient marketing and advertising exposure and frequent-flier programs, which attempt to hook passengers on to one particular airline for all their flying needs.

Three of the largest alliances in the world are SkyTeam, Star Alliance, and Oneworld. SkyTeam is based out of Amsterdam and was created in 2000 by founding members: Delta, Air France, Aeromexico, and Korean Air. The Sky Team Alliance consists of 19 carriers from five continents and carries more than 550 million passengers each year. Based out of New York City, Oneworld was formed in 1999 with founding members: American Airlines, British Airways, Canadian Airlines, Cathay Pacific, and Qantas. Today, 11 airlines operate within the Oneworld alliance and carry more than 335 million passengers annually. The Star Alliance was founded in 1997 by Air Canada, Lufthansa, Scandinavian Airlines, Thai Airways International, and United Airlines.

Based in Frankfurt, Germany, the Star Alliance has 28 member airlines and serves 193 different countries with annual passenger numbers more than 670 million, making Star Alliance the largest alliance in terms of passengers served.

Alliance with Quantas

Emirates is not a member of any airline alliance, whereas Quantas is a member of Oneworld. However in January 2013, Emirates and Quantas, two rival firms, formally entered into a partnership allowing Quantas Airbus 380 customers to depart from Concourse A at Dubai Airport, the world's only concourse designed for the Airbus 380. Quantas customers can enjoy the concourse, while waiting for their connecting flights to Europe. In exchange, Quantas moved their hub for European flights from Singapore to Dubai. Neither airline owns shares of the other, but they work together to better coordinate price, sales, and schedules. Quantas CEO Alan Joyce believes the partnership is a first of its kind and different from traditional alliances.

Dubai Business Culture

To be successful in business in Dubai, their culture and religion must be respected and rules must be followed. For example, a colleague should never be embarrassed or criticized in public. Women in Dubai should dress conservatively. Alcohol should never be consumed on the street, and it should be taken home only if one has a license to purchase it. Singles of the opposite sex may not live together in Dubai; gay marriages and relationships are not accepted in Dubai. If an unmarried woman becomes pregnant, then she must leave the country immediately. Other important rules to follow in Dubai include: do not cross your legs in front of someone of higher authority because it is seen as disrespectful; do not hold onto a handshake for a long time because it signifies a brotherly bond instead of a friendly gesture; do not use your left hand because it is considered dirty so use only the right hand to offer drinks, food, and so on; do not turn down a drink offer because it might insult the host; do not engage in friendly talk in pubic with any females; do not shake hands with women unless they come forward to do so; do not flirt, hug, and have other physical contact with a member of the opposite sex; do not make eye contact with women; do not ask a male Arab about any female because that is bad manners; do not point the soles of shoes at an Arab because the soles are dirty; do not refuse any gifts (if offered) but open them in private not in public; do not express a desire to communicate with any member of the opposite sex.

In Dubai, the workday starts at 8 A.M. until 1 P.M., but employees return at 7 P.M. to work more. During the Muslim Festival Ramadan, working hours in offices become shorter by two hours. In Arab cultures, clothes should be worn on all body parts including limbs. On Friday, Muslims pray and rest, so business should not be conducted on that day. During the month of Ramadan, Muslims avoid eating, smoking. and drinking during daylight.

The Future

Ironically for Emirates, the flydubai discount airline may pose the largest threat to the firm because demand for low price flights is growing rapidly globally. Flying with Emirates is high dollar, and competitors see great potential to take market share from Emirates with lower prices. It is important, therefore, for Emirates' Chairman and CEO, Sheikh Ahmed bin Saeed Al Maktoum, to have a clear strategic plan for the next three years.

Design a business strategy for the Emirates Group for the next three years.

Royal Bank of Canada, 2013

www.rbcbank.com, RY

Headquartered in Toronto, Ontario, Canada, Royal Bank of Canada (RBC) is the largest bank in Canada, providing a full range of services from commercial banking and wealth management to insurance and capital markets services. Also known as RBC Financial Group, RBC has more than 1,000 locations in Canada and additional operations in 49 other countries. In the USA, RBC owns investment bank RBC Dominion Securities and RBC Wealth Management, but the company sold its RBC Bank in the Southeast USA to PNC Financial in 2012 for $3.62 billion. RBC's bank's asset management operations are among the largest in the world. RBC has about 75,000 employees who serve more than 15 million personal, business, public sector, and institutional clients.

Some RBC highlights for their fiscal year 2012 that ended October 31 were as follows:

1. Earnings increased by 9 percent with return on equity (ROE) of 31.5 percent
2. Net interest margin (NIM) of 2.86 percent
3. Volume growth (loans and deposits) in Canadian Banking of 8.4 percent from last year and well ahead of peer average
4. Efficiency ratio of 46.9 percent, improved from 47.3 percent last year in Canadian banking
5. Named "Best Retail Bank in North America" (2012 Retail Banker International Awards)
6. Highest cross-sell among Canadian peers (Ipsos-Reid)
7. Announced agreement to acquire Canadian auto finance and deposit business of Ally Financial, Inc.

For the bank's third quarter that ended July 31, 2013, RBC reported record net income of $2,304 million, up $64 million or 3 percent from the prior year, and up $368 million or 19 percent from the prior quarter. Two of the bank's segments, 1) Personal & Commercial Banking and 2) Wealth Management, did especially well for the period. Specifically, Personal & Commercial Banking's net income was a record $1,180 million, up $78 million or 7 percent compared to last year, largely due to solid volume growth across all businesses in Canada as well as the company's acquisition of Ally Canada. RBC's Wealth Management segment reported record net income of $236 million, up $80 million or 51 percent compared to last year, mainly due to higher average fee-based client assets. However for the quarter, RBC's Insurance segment reported net income of $160 million, down $19 million or 11 percent from a year ago, largely due to higher claims costs of $14 million related to severe weather in Alberta and Ontario.

Copyright by Fred David Books LLC. (Written by Forest R. David)

History

The Merchants' Bank of Halifax was incorporated in 1869 when 134 Halifax businessmen became shareholders of a new progressive bank started to support their various businesses. The new bank was renamed The Royal Bank of Canada in 1901. The history of RBC closely parallels the growth of Canada. Between 1921 and 1940, RBC regularly traded top ranking with Bank of Montreal, until 1941 when it became Canada's largest bank. Under the leadership of John E. Cleghorn (1995–2001), RBC completed its transformation from a traditional commercial bank to a broad-based financial services group. Today, many, if not most, Canadians own shares in RBC through pension funds and mutual fund holdings and close to 90 percent of RBC's employees are shareholders in the bank.

On March 2, 2012, RBC sold its U.S. regional retail banking operations to PNC Financial Services Group, Inc. On May 31, 2012, RBC acquired the Latin American, Caribbean, and African private banking business of Coutts, the wealth division of The Royal Bank of Scotland Group PLC., with client assets of approximately U.S. $2 billion. That acquisition gave RBC many clients in Latin America, the Caribbean, and Africa, as well as key private banking staff based primarily in Geneva, Switzerland, along with a team in the Cayman Islands.

On July 27, 2012, RBC acquired the remaining 50 percent stake in the joint venture RBC Dexia from Banque Internationale à Luxembourg S.A. (formerly Dexia Banque Internationale à Luxembourg S.A.) for €837.5 million ($1 billion) in cash. RBC thus now owns 100 percent of RBC Dexia, which has been rebranded RBC Investor Services.

Internal Issues

Vision and Mission

RBC's vision statement is given on the firm's website as: "Always earning the right to be our clients' first choice." There is no mention of a mission statement on the RBC website, but the company has an Aspiration Statement as follows: "To be a top performing diversified financial institution." In what could be mission statements, RBC has several Strategy Statements, as follows: For Canada: "to be the undisputed leader in financial services." For the bank's Global Operations: "to be a leading provider of capital markets and wealth management solutions." For what RBC calls its targeted markets: "to be a leading provider of select financial services complementary to our core strengths."

Segments

RBC operates in five segments:

1. **RBC Royal Bank** provides a broad suite of products and financial services in Canada through the largest national distribution network.
2. **RBC Wealth Management** provides services to affluent, high and ultra-high net worth clients globally with a full range of investment, trust, credit, and insurance solutions; provides asset management solutions through RBC Global Asset Management. RBC is the largest asset manager in Canada and number one in retail mutual funds.
3. **RBC Insurance** provides a wide range of travel, life, health, home, auto, wealth, and reinsurance products and solutions, as well as creditor and business insurance services.
4. **RBC International Banking** provides banking offices in the Caribbean; includes U.S. cross-border banking operations and RBC Dexia Investor Services. Note: RBC does business in 20 Caribbean countries and territories, stretching from the Bahamas in the north to Suriname in the south, with 121 combined branches, and more than 6,400 employees serving more than one million clients. RBC's Caribbean headquarters are based in Port-of-Spain, Trinidad.
5. **RBC Capital Markets** provides global investment bank services to institutions, corporations, governments, and high net worth clients around the world. Leading all firms in Canada in 2012, RBC advised on 102 announced merger and acquisition (M&A) deals worth $76 billion. The deals advised on in 2012 included Chinese state-owned company CNOOC Ltd's $15.1 billion takeover of Canadian oil and gas producer Nexen Inc., and Glencore International PLC's C$6 billion purchase of Canadian grain handler Viterra, Inc. In total, the number of M&A deals with Canadian advisors involved fell by 13.1 percent from 2011, but the value rose by 38.7 percent. In addition, RBC accounted for 34.9 percent share of the equity-advising market, finishing ahead of Goldman Sachs Group, Inc., which advised on 21 deals worth $49.2 billion, and BMO Capital Markets, which advised on 63 deals worth $47.5 billion. In equity issuance, RBC raised C$5.5 billion ($5.58 billion) in 68 transactions, taking the top spot from 2011 leader TD Securities, which finished third in 2012 with C$3.7 billion. BMO finished second with C$4.7 billion. Also in 2012, RBC led in debt issuance, raising C$39.9 billion in 131 issues, and in initial public offerings, advising on C$367.5 million worth of deals in a slow year for new issues.

Effective at the end of October 2012, RBC eliminated its international banking segment and created a new Investor & Treasury Services segment that includes RBC Investor Services, formerly a business under international banking. RBC moved correspondent banking and treasury services from capital markets into this new segment. In addition on that date, RBC created a Personal & Commercial Banking segment that includes the former Canadian banking segment and expanded it to include the company's businesses in the Caribbean and the USA.

Exhibit 1 provides a summary of RBC's segment performance in fiscal year 2012. Note that their Insurance segment had the highest ROE (46.8 percent) whereas their Investor & Treasury

Services has the lowest (4.3 percent). Exhibit 2 provides information on RBC's geographic operations. Note in Exhibit 2 that Canadian operations comprised 79.6 percent of the bank's net income in 2012.

EXHIBIT 1 RBC's 2012 Segment Results by Product (in millions of Canadian dollars)

	Personal and Commercial Banking	Wealth Management	Insurance	Investor and Treasury Services	Capital Markets
Net interest income	9,061	393	—	668	2,559
Non interest income	3,582	4,442	4,897	657	3,629
Total Revenue	12,643	4,835	4,897	1,325	6,188
Non interest expense	5,932	3,796	515	1,134	3,746
Net income before taxes	5,544	1,040	761	191	2,307
Income tax	1,456	277	47	106	726
Net income	4,088	763	714	85	1,581
ROE	31.5%	14.1%	46.8%	4.3%	13.6%
Average Assets	33.4K	20.9K	11.5K	563.6K	349.2K

ROE, return-on-equity.
Source: Based on company information.

EXHIBIT 2 RBC's 2012 Segment Results by Region (in millions of Canadian dollars)

	Canada	USA	Other	Total
Net interest income	10,413	1,308	777	12,498
Non interest income	9,378	3,564	4,332	17,274
Total revenue	19,791	4,872	5,109	29,772
Noninterest expense	8,809	3,404	2,947	15,160
Income taxes	1,600	519	(19)	2,100
Net income before taxes	6,041	843	706	7,590

Source: Based on company information.

Organizational Structure

RBC operates from a strategic business unit organizational structure, having three group head positions, with various product divisions reporting to those group heads. The company's organizational structure is illustrated in Exhibit 3. Note in Exhibit 3 that the only female in the corporate hierarchy serves both as the company's Chief Financial Officer (CFO) and Chief Accounting Officer (CAO); basically she is the Chief Operations Officer (COO) for the firm. It is a bit unusual for the COO, or CAO in this case, to also be the CFO in a company.

Finance

For the first time ever in 2012, RBC provided their Annual Consolidated Financial Statements in accordance with International Financial Reporting Standards (IFRS) as issued by the International Accounting Standards Board (IASB) with corresponding comparative IFRS financial information presented for the prior year. All amounts for 2010 and before are based on Canadian generally accepted accounting principles (GAAP).

For fiscal year 2012, RBC reported record net income of $7.5 billion, up $1.1 billion or 17 percent from the prior year. The results reflected record earnings in Personal & Commercial Banking, Capital Markets, and Insurance. Note in Exhibit 4 that RBC's revenue in 2012 jumped $2.1 billion to $29.7 billion. Note in Exhibit 5 that RBC's total deposits increased $29 billion in 2012 to a total of $508 billion.

EXHIBIT 3 RBC's Organizational Chart

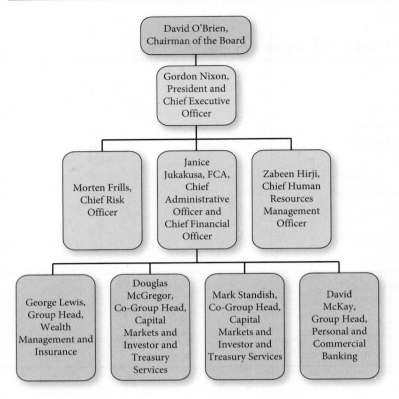

Source: Based on company information.

EXHIBIT 4 RBC's Income Statements (in millions of Canadian dollars)

	2012	2011	2010
Interest Income, Bank	20,852.0	20,813.0	17,746.0
Total Interest Expense	8,354.0	9,456.0	7,408.0
Noninterest Income, Bank	17,274.0	16,281.0	15,744.0
Total Revenue	**29,772.0**	**27,638.0**	**26,082.0**
Loan Loss Provision	1,301.0	1,133.0	1,240.0
Noninterest Expense, Bank	18,781.0	17,525.0	17,015.0
Income Before Tax	9,690.0	8,980.0	7,827.0
Income Tax, Total	2,100.0	2,010.0	1,996.0
Income After Tax	7,590.0	6,970.0	5,831.0
Minority Interest	–97.0	–101.0	–99.0
Equity in Affiliates	0.0	0.0	0.0
U.S. GAAP Adjustment	0.0	0.0	–59.0
Net Income Before Extraordinary Items	7,493.0	6,869.0	5,673.0
Total Extraordinary Items	–51.0	–526.0	–509.0
Net Income	**7,442.0**	**6,343.0**	**5,164.0**

GAAP, generally accepted accounting principles.
Source: Based on company documents.

EXHIBIT 5 RBC's Balance Sheets (in millions of Canadian dollars)

	2012	2011	2010
Assets			
Cash and Due From Banks	12,617.0	12,428.0	8,440.0
Other Earning Assets, Total	295,511.0	267,939.0	278,288.0
Net Loans	378,244.0	347,530.0	273,006.0
Property, Plant, Equipment, Total (Net)	2,691.0	2,490.0	2,139.0
Goodwill, Net	7,485.0	7,610.0	6,660.0
Intangibles, Net	2,686.0	2,115.0	1,710.0
Long-Term Investments	125.0	142.0	171.0
Other Long-Term Assets, Total	2,756.0	29,357.0	35,181.0
Other Assets, Total	122,985.0	124,222.0	120,611.0
Total Assets	**825,100.0**	**793,833.0**	**726,206.0**
Liabilities and Shareholders' Equity			
Accounts Payable	0.0	0.0	1,877.0
Payable/Accrued	5,242.0	3,954.0	0.0
Accrued Expenses	6,880.0	6,285.0	7,179.0
Total Deposits	508,219.0	479,102.0	414,561.0
Other Bearing Liabilities, Total	9,385.0	7,689.0	7,371.0
Total Short-Term Borrowings	64,032.0	42,735.0	42,066.0
Policy Liabilities	0.0	0.0	0.0
Notes Payable, Short-Term Debt	0.0	0.0	0.0
Current Portability of Long-Term Debt and Capital Leases	0.0	0.0	0.0
Other Current Liabilities, Total	2,244.0	2,172.0	929.0
Total Long-Term Debt	8,515.0	9,643.0	7,408.0
Deferred Income Tax	176.0	266.0	0.0
Minority Interest	1,761.0	1,761.0	2,256.0
Other Liabilities, Total	174,379.0	200,524.0	203,608.0
Total Liabilities	**780,833.0**	**754,131.0**	**687,255.0**
Redeemable Preferred Stock	0.0	0.0	0.0
Preferred Stock, Nonredeemable, Net	4,814.0	4,813.0	4,811.0
Common Stock	14,323.0	14,010.0	13,378.0
Additional Paid-In Capital	0.0	0.0	236.0
Retained Earnings (Accumulated Deficit)	24,270.0	20,381.0	22,706.0
Treasury Stock, Common	30.0	8.0	−81.0
ESOP Debt Guarantee	0.0	0.0	0.0
Unrealized Gain (Loss)	0.0	0.0	0.0
Other Equity, Total	830.0	490.0	−2,099.0
Total Equity	**44,267.0**	**39,702.0**	**38,951.0**
Total Liabilities and Shareholders' Equity	**825,100.0**	**793,833.0**	**726,206.0**

ESOP, employee stock ownership plan.
Source: Based on company documents.

External Issues

Canada's banks weathered recent economic woes in the USA and around the world quite well, having no housing bubble issues in Canada. That is partly why all six of Canada's biggest banks made the Global Finance list of the world's 50 Safest Banks for 2012. RBC expects the Canadian economy to grow by 2.4 percent in 2013, mainly driven by consumer spending, business investment, and improved net exports. However, given the continued global uncertainty, RBC plans to maintain the overnight rate at 1.0 percent until global factors restraining the Canadian economy ease. Modest and gradual withdrawal of the Canadian stimulus measures is expected to begin in the second half of 2013.

RBC expects the U.S. economy to grow by 2.3 percent in 2013, mainly driven by slightly higher consumer spending, continued business investment, and improvement in the housing market. RBC expects U.S. growth in 2013 to be restrained by fiscal policy tightening, with the Federal Reserve holding interest rates at historically low levels through mid-2015.

RBC expects Eurozone economic growth to improve to 0.1 percent in 2013 as governments implement policy measures to address the Eurozone structural issues and restore confidence. Consumer and government spending are expected to further decrease in Europe, reflecting weak labor market conditions and fiscal austerity measures implemented to ensure sovereign debt sustainability. Although inflation remains elevated, RBC expects interest rates in Europe to be maintained at 0.75 percent in 2013 to provide continued stimulus to the economy.

Basel Committee

The Basel Committee on Banking Supervision Global Standards for Capital and Liquidity Reform (Basel III) provides new standards for capital and liquidity, establishes minimum requirements for common equity, and increases capital requirements for counterparty credit exposures, a new global leverage ratio, and measures to promote the build up of capital that can be drawn down in periods of stress. Banks around the world are preparing to implement these new standards (commonly referred to as Basel III). In Canada, the Office of the Superintendent of Financial Institutions Canada (OSFI) expects deposit-taking institutions to meet the minimum 2019 Basel III capital requirements for Common Equity Tier 1 (CET 1) in the first quarter of 2013. RBC continues to be well capitalized by global standards, with excellent capital ratios.

Domestic-Systemically Important Banks (D-SIBs)

The Financial Stability Board and the Basel Committee on Banking Supervision have finalized a principles-based framework to guide national authorities in establishing principles for dealing with D-SIBs. OSFI has not communicated formally on a Canadian D-SIB regime, but RBC expects one to be put forward. The implementation of a D-SIB regime in Canada may result in RBC being subject to additional capital and disclosure requirements.

Over-the-Counter Derivatives Reform

Reforms in the over-the-counter (OTC) derivatives markets continue on a global basis, with the governments of the G20 nations proceeding with plans to transform the capital regimes, national regulatory frameworks, and infrastructures that RBC operates. Thus, RBC anticipates changes in their wholesale banking business, some of which will impact their client- and trading-related derivatives revenues in capital markets. In July 2012, the U.S. Commodity Futures Trading Commission (CFTC) released proposed cross-border guidance regarding the application of U.S. swaps rules to international banks, including requirements to register with the CFTC as a swap dealer.

Competitors

The banking business is intensely competitive, with rival companies having branches within close proximity of each other, and online banking taking a greater and greater share of the market each day. Exhibit 6 shows that RBC's major rival firms are Canadian Imperial Bank of Commerce (CIBC), the Toronto-Dominion Bank (TD), and the Bank of Nova Scotia (BNS). Note that RBC has the lowest profit margin, a respectable 27.87 percent, but is the leader in most categories.

Canadian Imperial Bank of Commerce (CIBC)

Headquartered in Toronto, Ontario, Canada, CIBC has more than 1,000 branches in Canada, offering a wide range of services, including deposits, loans, investments, and insurance. With a stock symbol of CM, CIBC operates in two main segments: (1) CIBC Retail Markets (consumer

EXHIBIT 6 **A Financial Synopsis of RBC versus Rival Banks in Canada (as of 10-30-13)**

Stock Ticker Symbols	RY	CM	TD	BNS
Market Capitalization	93.03B	33.60B	83.89B	73.00B
Revenue	29.70B	11.79B	22.38B	19.88B
Net Income	7.44B	3.37B	6.47B	6.15B
Profit Margin	27.87%	29.49%	29.75%	32.04%
Total Debt	157B	48.54B	156B	126.52B
EPS Ratio	5.50	8.37	6.47	5.13
Price/Earnings Ratio	12.21	10.13	12.98	11.83

Note: B = billions of Canadian dollars RY = RBC; CM = Canadian Imperial Bank of Commerce; TD = Toronto-Dominion Bank; BNS = Bank of Nova Scotia.
Source: Based on company information.

and small-business banking, credit cards, wealth management) and wholesale banking arm (2) CIBC World Markets (merchant and investment banking, capital markets services, and research for corporate, institutional, and government clients). Outside of Canada, CIBC owns a majority of First Caribbean International Bank.

The Toronto-Dominion Bank (TD)

Headquartered in Toronto, Ontario, Canada, TD is also known as TD Bank that owns 45 percent of U.S. discount brokerage TD Ameritrade. Sometimes called TD Financial, the company ranks among the world's top online financial services firms and is one of the largest banks in Canada, where it operates more than 1,100 branches under the TD Trust banner. U.S. subsidiary TD Bank, N.A., has another 1,300 branches in about 15 eastern states. TD also offers commercial financial and advisory services. Other segments of TD include TD Insurance, TD Asset Management (mutual funds), TD Securities (investment banking, equities, and foreign exchange), and TD Waterhouse, the largest online brokerage in the United Kingdom and Canada.

The Bank of Nova Scotia (BNS)

Headquartered in Toronto, Ontario, Canada (rather than Nova Scotia), BNS, or ScotiaBank, has about 1,000 branches in Canada and 1,700 offices in more than 50 other countries, mainly in the Caribbean, Central America, and South America. Services include deposit accounts, loans, insurance, brokerage, asset management, mutual funds, and trust accounts.

The Future

RBC paid its employees bonuses of 11 percent in 2012, compared for example to JPMorgan that cut its bonus by 2 percent. RBC also shares its wealth with investors, paying out a dividend of $0.67 per share for Q3 of 2013, up 6 percent or 4 cents from Q2 of 2013. RBC is aggressively looking to expand outside of Canada, from where most of its current income originates. In comments regarding future plans, the CEO Gordon Nixon noted in the company's third-quarter report that he would "like to see at least half of RBC's revenue come from outside of Canada." To this end, the bank's wealth management arm has been actively pursuing business around the world. With the recent purchase of Ally Financial's Canadian unit, RBC has become a strong presence in the auto-lending sector, and the unit is expected to bring in around $120 million in its first year.

Anytime a firm is the leader in any industry, as RBC is in banking in Canada, that firm is the target of rival firms who imitate and duplicate the leading firm's strategies. RBC shareholders have come to expect high returns. The company's top management team needs a clear strategic plan going forward.

Develop a three-year strategic plan for RBC.

Embraer S.A., 2013

www.embraer.com, (Sao Paulo Stock Exchange and ticker ERJ on NYSE)

Headquartered in Sao Jose dos Campos, Brazil, Embraer specializes in developing and manufacturing civilian and military aircraft as well as providing aeronautical services. Embraer has more than 18,032 full-time workers (16,325 in Brazil) and more than $15 billion worth of aircraft on back order. One of the largest aerospace firms in the world, Embraer has carved its niche on what many airline companies are calling "right-sized" aircraft. To date, Embraer commercial jets are produced with seating options generally between 70 and 124 seats on the E-Jets and 37 to 50 passengers on the ERJ jets. By producing quality jets, sized right at affordable prices, Embraer is one of the largest exporting firms in Brazil. Both Delta and JetBlue use Embraer jets to shuttle passengers between New York, Boston, Atlanta, Washington, and similarly distanced locations. Since 1969, Embraer has delivered more than 5,000 aircraft to airlines or militaries in more than 100 countries on five continents. In mid-2013, SkyWest places an order for 200 Embraer 175 aircraft worth about $4.1 billion to begin being delivered in Q2 of 2014. SkyWest is headquartered in Utah and is the largest regional airline in the world operating such companies as United Express, USAir Express, Delta Connection, American Eagle, and ExpressJet.

On 8-27-13, RBC Capital Markets published an initiation report on Embraer S.A. (ERJ) with a stock price target of $42. Embraer had last traded in New York at $33.37, representing a 25 percent upside. There were two main reasons for RBC's Buy recommendation. First, RBC projected strong demand for regional jets and Embraer has been gaining market share from rival Bombardier, from 29 percent in 2003 to 76 percent in 2013. RBC forecasted a 17 percent year-on-year Embraer earnings growth in 2014. Second, Embraer at the time was trading at a 20 percent discount compared to rival firms, even though the company reported the second fastest earnings growth at 14.3 percent for 2012–2015 (estimated), versus its commercial aircraft rival firms at 6.1 percent and its defense peers at 1.2 percent.

Copyright by Fred David Books LLC. (Written by Forest R. David)

History

Embraer was founded in 1969 as a state-owned civilian and military aviation company known at the time as Empresa Brasileira de Aeronautica. Brazil's Aeronautics Ministry signed a contract for the purchase of 80 Bandeirante aircraft that were produced in a hanger capable of producing two planes per month with a workforce of 500 employees. After growing during the 1970s, Empresa Brasileria de Aernonautica obtained an office in Florida and formed a subsidiary named the Embraer Aircraft Company to better serve the U.S. market. In 1983, the company started Embraer Aviation International in Paris to better serve European markets and markets in the Middle East and Africa. Despite growth, macroeconomic conditions and the burden of being state-run culminated in the company struggling and facing possible bankruptcy by 1990. To avoid bankruptcy, and to cash in on revenues received from the demand for smaller aircraft in the early 1990s, the company was privatized in 1994 with a handful of financial institutions acquiring ownership in the company. The company name was also officially changed to Embraer S.A. in 1994.

After rapid growth for 15 years, Embraer opened its first plant in the USA in Melbourne, Florida, in 2011. The hanger was 7,500 square feet and designed for final assembly and included a modern paint booth. Also in 2011, Embraer's Defense and Security segment backward integrated by purchasing 64 percent of the shares of OrbiSat da Amazonia SA's radar division and created Harpia Sistemas SA to focus on unmanned aerial vehicles research. Embraer holds a 51 percent stake in Harpia with AEL Sistemas owning the remaining 49 percent.

In January 2013, Embraer and Republic Airways Holdings Inc., operator of the largest E-jets fleet in the world, revealed a contract for the sale of 47 embraer 175 jets, with options for an additional 47 aircraft, providing a potential for 94 E175s, which could reach a total value of approximately U.S. $4 billion, in 2013 economic conditions, at list price. The new aircraft will be operated by Republic Airlines, a Republic subsidiary, under the American Eagle brand in the American Airlines' regional network. The deal was approved in early 2013. The E175 is a dual-row layout, seating up to 76 passengers; the first delivery was in mid-2013.

"It is significant that our long-time, valued customer Republic Airways—a true innovator in the regional transport business—is the first customer for the enhanced E175," said Paulo Cesar Silva, President and CEO, Embraer Commercial Aviation. "The E175 is the most comfortable, technologically advanced and efficient aircraft in its class and it represents the best value for airlines because it also delivers the lowest total operating cost."

Internal Issues

Vision and Mission

Embraer in late 2012 developed a vision statement as follows: "Embraer will continue to consolidate its position as one of the primary powers in the global aeronautics and defense security industries, with market-leading positions in the segments in which it operates, and a reputation for excellence." The company's mission statement is as follows: "Embraer's business is to generate value for its shareholders by fully satisfying its customers in the global aviation market. By 'generate value,' we mean maximizing the Company's value and ensuring its perpetuity, acting with integrity and social environmental awareness."

Organizational Structure

As indicated in Exhibit 1, Embraer has two primary segments (1) Defense and Security and (2) Commercial Aviation. Instead of a Chief Operations Officer, note that the company has an Executive Vice-president of Operations.

Finance

Embraer's EPS increased 336 percent in 2012 to 0.96 as the company delivered 221 aircraft that year. Among the 221 were 106 commercial jets, 99 executive jets, 14 Super Tucanos, and 2 EMB 145 jets. Embraer's revenues increased 6 percent from 2011 to 2012, and net income increased 212 percent. American Airlines filed Chapter 11 bankruptcy protection in 2011, and they utilized ERJ 145 jets, forcing Embraer to lose up to $293 million.

Embraer's income statements and balance sheets are provided in Exhibits 2 and 3, respectively. Note in Exhibit 3 the zero goodwill, which is good.

EXHIBIT 1 Embraer's Organization Chart

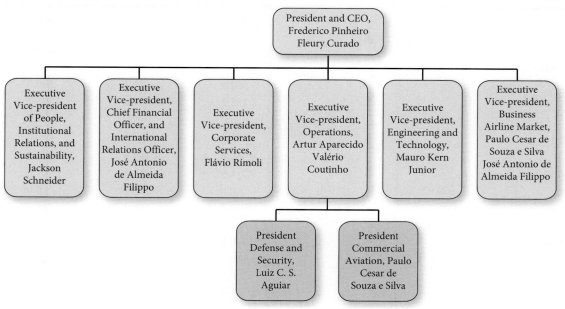

Source: Based on company documents.

EXHIBIT 2 Embraer's Income Statement (in millions of $)

	2012	2011	2010
Revenue	6,177.9	5,802.95	5,364.1
Other Revenue, Total	0.0	0.0	0.0
Total Revenue	**6,177.9**	**5,802.95**	**5,364.1**
Cost of Revenue, Total	4,683.0	4,495.86	4,338.1
Gross Profit	**1,494.9**	**1,307.1**	**1,026.0**
Selling/General/Administrative Expenses, Total	762.5	681.83	571.6
Research & Development	77.3	85.25	72.1
Depreciation/Amortization	0.0	0.0	0.0
Interest Expense (Income), Net Operating	0.0	0.0	0.0
Unusual Expense (Income)	11.4	0.0	0.0
Other Operating Expenses, Total	33.3	221.43	−9.4
Operating Income	**610.2**	**318.24**	**391.7**
Interest Income (Expense), Net Non-Operating	0.0	0.0	0.0
Gain (Loss) on Sale of Assets	0.0	0.0	0.0
Other, Net	−30.6	−143.72	−32.0
Income Before Tax	**614.1**	**247.55**	**408.1**
Income Tax - Total	265.5	127.12	62.7
Income After Tax	348.6	120.42	345.4
Minority Interest	−0.8	−8.82	−15.2
Equity In Affiliates	0.0	0.0	0.0
U.S. GAAP Adjustment	0.0	0.0	0.0
Net Income Before Extra. Items	**347.8**	**111.61**	**330.2**
Total Extraordinary Items	0.0	0.0	0.0
Net Income	**347.8**	**111.61**	**330.2**

Source: Based on company documents.

EXHIBIT 3 Embraer's Balance Sheet (in millions of $)

	2012	2011	2010
Assets	2,379.4	2,103.8	2,126.6
Cash and Short-Term Investments			
Total Receivables, Net	564.9	532.7	380.6
Total Inventory	2,155.3	2,283.4	2,193.4
Prepaid Expenses	0.0	0.0	0.0
Other Current Assets, Total	266.3	249.5	282.2
Total Current Assets	**5,365.9**	**5,169.4**	**4,982.8**
Property/Plant/Equipment, Total – Net	1,738.5	1,450.4	1,201.0
Goodwill, Net	0.0	0.0	0.0
Intangibles, Net	958.9	808.3	716.3
Long-Term Investments	51.3	57.5	52.1
Note Receivable - Long Term	509.8	563.1	577.4
Other Long-Term Assets, Total	866.0	809.6	861.4
Other Assets, Total	0.0	0.0	0.0
Total Assets	**9,490.4**	**8,858.3**	**8,391.0**

EXHIBIT 3 Continued

	2012	2011	2010
Liabilities and Shareholders' Equity			
Accounts Payable	758.9	829.9	750.2
Payable/Accrued	0.0	0.0	0.0
Accrued Expenses	65.4	89.2	79.5
Notes Payable/Short-Term Debt	0.0	0.0	0.0
Current Port. of LT Debt/Capital Leases	348.2	564.6	184.4
Other Current Liabilities, Total	1,619.9	1,358.0	1,374.6
Total Current Liabilities	**2,792.4**	**2,841.7**	**2,388.7**
Total Long-Term Debt	2,118.5	1,556.1	1,721.7
Deferred Income Tax	26.5	23.0	11.4
Minority Interest	92.0	110.5	103.1
Other Liabilities, Total	1,202.7	1,319.7	1,137.7
Total Liabilities	**6,232.1**	**5,851.0**	**5,362.6**
Redeemable Preferred Stock	0.0	0.0	0.0
Preferred Stock - Non Redeemable, Net	0.0	0.0	0.0
Common Stock	1,438.0	1,438.0	1,438.0
Additional Paid-In Capital	0.0	0.0	0.0
Retained Earnings (Accumulated Deficit)	1,980.3	1,737.3	1,759.8
Treasury Stock – Common	−154.2	−183.7	−183.7
ESOP Debt Guarantee	0.0	0.0	0.0
Unrealized Gain (Loss)	0.0	0.0	0.0
Other Equity, Total	−5.8	15.7	14.3
Total Equity	**3,258.3**	**3,007.3**	**3,028.4**
Total Liabilities & Shareholders' Equity	**9,490.4**	**8,858.3**	**8,391.0**
Total Common Shares Outstanding	740.47	723.67	740.47

Source: Based on company documents.

Segments

Commercial Aviation

Embraer's commercial aviation segment accounts for more than 60 percent of all company revenues. Embraer has more than 90 customers, including 30 of which are airline companies on five continents. To date, more than 900 regional jets from the ERJ 145 family are in service. ERJ planes typically offer 37 to 50 seats and are designed to carry passengers from small cities to larger airports for connecting flights. United Airlines uses the 50-seat ERJ from the USA to Mexican cities such as Torreon, Queretaro, and Veracruz. Despite rapid growth in this segment, it is Embraer's belief that this segment has reached maturity in the current markets where they operate.

To create new market share in the commercial aviation segment, Embraer is now producing a larger E-jet in four different models. The E170 and E175 models are designed for 70 to 88 passengers whereas the E190 and E195 jets are designed for 93 to 124 passengers. The company likes to promote the E-jet as a product that "taps the gap" between regional and larger aircraft. For example, a flight from Atlanta to Boston could easily be accommodated by an E-jet around noon when demand is lower because most flight demand is during the morning and afternoon hours. Advantages to the E-jet is there is no middle seat and they are large enough to stand up as a passenger walks down the aisle, just as one would be able to on a Boeing 737 or Airbus 320, unlike competitor Bombardier's planes where many people have to bend over as they make their way to their seat. A drawback with the E-jet is that it does not have the fuel capacity to fly across the USA. But forecasts indicate that demand will grow for E-jets, as indicated by Republic Airlines paying Embraer to $4 billion to provide E175 jets.

Executive Aviation

Embraer's second most profitable segment is the executive aviation, accounting for 19 percent of all revenues. Embraer entered this market in 2000 and rolled out the first plane, a Legacy 600, in 2002. Currently, Embraer provides seven different executive jet options, including the Phenom, Legacy, and Lineage models. The Phenom 100 is the smallest jet offered in the segment and carries 4 passengers up to 1,200 nautical miles. That plane retails for just under $4 million. Larger than the Phenoms are Embraer's Legacy line of jets. The Legacy 500 can carry 12 passengers up to 2,800 nautical miles and costs around $18 million. The larger Legacy 600 and 650 aircraft are capable of carrying 13 passengers over 3,000 nautical miles at altitudes of 41,000 feet. Purchase price is around $27 million.

The Lineage is a variation of the commercial Embraer 190 and is designed with an executive floor plan and additional range by adding a fuel tank. The aircraft can carry 19 passengers upward of 4,500 nautical miles with a price tag of more than $50 million. Currently less than 20 of these aircraft have been built, compared to more than 200 Legacy 600-style planes. All Embraer executive jets can be customized to include showers, bedrooms, or standard commercial jet seating layouts.

Defense and Security

Revenues from Embraer's Defense and Security segment increased 44 percent in 2012. Embraer's Defense and Security segment accounts for 15 percent of revenues. Embraer provides 48 different nations with services and products contained under the Defense and Security's umbrella, including supplying the Brazilian Air Force with more than 70 percent of its fleet. In addition to traditional manned aircraft, Embraer is also engaged in unmanned aerial vehicles and public security systems. These new endeavors were acquired through acquisitions and partnerships with existing firms.

One of Embraer's newer crafts, the Super Tucano, replaced the Tucano that was first produced in 2003 and continues to be produced today. The plane is a single-engine turbo propeller that resembles a World War II fighter plane to the untrained eye. The plane is designed for light attack and aerial reconnaissance in low-threat environments as well as serving a role in pilot training. The Embraer 99 is the military version of the ERJ 145 used in early warning and control. The plane differs mainly from the ERJ 145 in that it provides 20 percent more thrust. The firm also provides several variations of the Embraer 99, all with slightly different features and purposes. The Embraer KC-390 is a twin-engine military jet aircraft designed for troop transport. That plane's first flight is scheduled for 2014 with introduction scheduled for 2016. The company currently does not produce a fighter jet or bomber.

Agricultural

The Embraer EMB 202 Ipanema is a small single-engine plane designed for use in crop dusting. The cost is around $250,000. The agricultural segment makes up less than 2 percent of total revenues and is not separated by Embraer into its on distinct segment, just listed as "other revenues." Since 1969, more than 1,200 aircraft have been built. In 2012, 66 Ipanerna aircraft were sold in Brazil and Mercosur, up 15 percent over 2011.

The Segment Numbers

Note in Exhibit 4 the drop in Embraer aircraft deliveries in 2011 versus 2010. Exhibit 5 shows the company's percentage of revenue provided by each segment. Exhibit 6 details the geographic breakdown of Embraer's revenues. Currently North America accounts for 20 percent of total revenues, a number that is expected to increase as the company continues to provide aircraft to large U.S. carriers and additionally increases production of the executive jets such as the Phenom produced in Melbourne, Florida. The USA comprises 40 percent of the aviation world market share.

EXHIBIT 4 Embraer Aircraft Deliveries

	2012	2011	2010	2009
Commercial Aviation	106	105	100	122
Executive Aviation	99	99	144	115
Defense and Security	16	0	2	7
Total Jets	221	204	246	244

Source: Based on company documents.

EXHIBIT 5 Revenue Percent by Segment

	2012	2011	2010	2009
Commercial Aviation (%)	61	64	61	69
Executive Aviation (%)	21	19	23	17
Defense and Security (%)	17	15	15	12
Others (%)	1	2	1	2

Source: Based on company documents.

EXHIBIT 6 Geographic Revenues

	2012	2011	2010	2009
North America (%)	24	20	13	22
Europe (%)	31	25	33	33
Latin America (%)	3	11	15	7
Brazil (%)	14	17	13	11
Asia Pacific (%)	19	23	22	21
Others (%)	9	4	4	6

Source: Based on company documents.

Competitors

Embraer's three primary competitors are Bombardier, Boeing, and Airbus. But, up-and-coming aircraft manufacturing rivals such as Japan's Mitsubishi Heavy Industries, Russia's Sukhoi, and even China's COMAC are aiming to drive down prices in coming years. This industry is already highly competitive and getting more so every day.

Bombardier virtually invented the regional-jet segment when its CRJ100 entered service in 1992. Embraer broke into the space with its ERJ145 in 1996. Embraer today controls slightly more than 50 percent of the regional aircraft market, including turboprop planes, but the landscape is fluid.

Exhibit 7 shows that Embraer is only one-third of the size of Bombardier and one-tenth of the size of Boeing, which hurts Embraer in terms of economies of scale. Note in Exhibit 7 that Boeing is by far the most efficient and most profitable. However, in the 61 to 120 seat size jets, Embraer leads all rivals in producing these planes—holding a 43-percent market share.

Bombardier

Based in Montreal, Canada, Bombardier is the world's only producer of both aircraft and trains. With customers in more than 60 nations and a workforce of 70,000 employees, Bombardier is a world leader in transportation services. The company trades publicly on the Toronto Stock Exchange under ticker symbol BBD and is also listed on the Dow Jones Sustainability World and North American indexes.

About half of the total workforce at Bombardier is devoted to working in the aerospace segment. Products produced include planes for business and commercial purposes and

EXHIBIT 7   Aircraft Manufacturer Competitor Comparison

	Embraer	Bombardier	Boeing
Number of employees	18,000	61,900	171,000
Revenue	$6.2B	$18.3B	$78.9B
Net Income	$347M	$837M	$4.3B
Net Profit Margin	5.59%	4.89%	5.46%
Revenue per Employee	$344K	$295K	461K
EPS	$0.73	$0.44	5.67
Market Capitalization	5.93B	$7.02B	55.8
Shares Outstanding	185M	1.75B	754M

EPS, earnings per share.
Source: Derived from a variety of sources.

specialized amphibious aircraft. Bombardier is currently the number-one producer of business and regional aircraft in the world and the third-largest aircraft manufacturer behind Boeing and Airbus. Bombardier products in the business aircraft segment include: Learjet, Challenger, and Global aircraft. Commercial aircraft include the C-Series program, CRJ series, and Q-Series. Amphibious aircraft include the Bombardier 415 and Bombardier 415 MP.

Headquartered in Wichita, Kansas, Learjet is part of Bombardier; Learjet offers four variations of planes that range in capacity from 7 to 10 passengers and have ranges between 2,000 and 3,000 nautical miles. All Learjets have a top speed of around 540 miles per hour. The Learjet 60, a midsize Learjet, costs $13.5 million. Bombardier's Challenger series business jets come in three sizes with capacities ranging from 10 passengers to 14 passengers. The Challenger crafts have a longer range, 2,800 nautical miles to more than 4,000 nautical miles, making nonstop flights across the USA or Europe possible. Speeds are comparable with the Learjet family. The Global family of jets is available in four different models with passenger volume either 17 or 19. Top speed is around 590 miles per hour, making the Challenge series the fastest jet Bombardier manufactures. Total range varies by model ranging from 5,200 to 7,900 nautical miles making transocean travel possible.

Bombardier's commercial series of craft includes the Q-Series propeller planes and the CRJ and C-Series jets. Q-series prop planes offer seating for 60 to 90 passengers. The prop planes are designed for short haul flights but offer jetlike speed. The CRJ planes offer seating options ranging from 40 to 100 passengers depending on the model and are designed for short to midrange flights. The larger C-Series plane accommodates either 100 or 149 passengers depending on the model and are designed for midrange flights. Bombardier also offers special aircraft for surveillance and fire fighting.

Boeing

Headquartered in Chicago, Illinois, Boeing is the world's largest manufacturer of commercial jets and military aircraft combined. The company also designs and manufactures rotorcraft, missiles, satellites, launch vehicles, and much more. Boeing is the principle contractor for the International Space Station, a major provider to NASA, and serves customers in more than 150 nations.

Boeing's commercial jets range in size from the 737, with total capacity ranging from 110 to 220 seats, to the 747, with capacity of up to 550 passengers. The 737 family most closely competes with Embraer's commercial aircraft. With fuel capacity of up to 6,875 gallons, the 737 can fly 3,000 nautical miles and is rated for a maximum altitude of 41,000 feet. Prices in 2012 ranged from $71 million to $107 million for the Boeing 737. Boeing produces a wide range of business craft as well, but these planes are similarly reconfigured versions of existing passenger aircraft and not smaller business planes like Embraer and Bombardier produce.

Demand for commercial air transportation globally increased 5.3 percent in 2012, but profitability of airline companies declined from $8.8 billion (in 2011) to $6.7 billion in 2012. That profitability number is expected to increase to $8.4 billion in 2013.

Airbus

Headquartered in Toulouse, France, Airbus is a subsidiary of the European Aeronautic Defense and Space Company and produces around half of the world's commercial jet airliners. Airbus employs more than 63,000 people and has annual revenues of about $43 billion. Airbus produces a wide array of aircraft including commercial jets, business jets, freighters, and military planes. The military jets are limited to cargo and surveillance and are not designed for attacking military operations. Competing principally with Embraer is Airbus's 320 line of commercial craft and a wide array of business aircraft.

Airbus's 320 is available in four different models, with the A318 and A319 competing most closely with Embraer. The A318 is capable of carrying up to 107 passengers in two-class layouts with maximum range of 1,500 nautical miles. The A319 has a capacity between 124, which is the same capacity as one version of Embraer's E-jet, and 156 seats. The A319 has a range of 2,000 nautical miles and is the widest single-isle fuselage on the market. There are 1,352 A319s in service and another 1,526 on order. The A318 is not as popular, with 78 planes in operation and 81 on order.

Airbus also manufactures eight versions of business-class aircraft. The ACJ318 is the smallest version with total capacity of 8 passengers and an impressive range of more than 4,200 nautical miles. The largest plane offered is the ACJ380 with capacity up to 50 passengers and range more than 9,500 nautical miles. Like Boeing, Airbus business craft are virtually the same as their respective passenger craft, just reconfigured with office space, conference tables, and larger seats for business travelers.

External Issues

Growth in the Middle Class

Although many discuss the U.S. shrinking middle class, worldwide there is a rapid growth in the middle class. The middle class in Eastern Europe, China, and Latin America is expected to grow substantially over the next 20 years as a redistribution of wealth created from increasing gross domestic product (GDP) in these regions. By 2030, it is expected that emerging market cities will have more middle and high-end residents than developed cities. The size of the middle class will grow from 1.8 billion to 3.2 billion by 2022 resulting in a larger population of middle class than poor. By 2030, the number of middle-class people is expected to be 4.9 billion. Total economic benefit is expected to increase from $21 trillion to $56 trillion by 2030, all of which posits increasing demand for airlines and thus consistent demand for aircraft makers such as Embraer.

In addition, Africa is a new frontier that corporations are turning to for business. Historically, the African economy has been largely dependent on natural resources and as recently as 2010, around 67 percent of all exports were related to natural resources. Kenya, South Africa, and the Ivory Coast are three of the leading markets in Africa and overall around 33 percent of the population in Africa has grown into the middle class. The African economy is expected to outpace the world average over the next 20 years and with an increasing amount of middle-class citizens and reduction in the dependence of exports, more and more businesses and citizens will come to depend on air travel to conduct business throughout the continent. European and Middle Eastern airlines have begun to expand their routes into Africa, forcing African airline companies to respond because more than 50 percent of their planes are 10 years or older and cannot operate as efficiently as the new aircraft. In addition, most African-based aircraft offer seating configurations of 120 seats or more, although most flights contain less than 100 passengers. This limits markets served and frequency of air service. It is Embraer's expectation their smaller-sized jets will fit the bill in the new revitalizing Africa.

Business Culture in Brazil

Home to Embraer, Brazil is the largest nation in South America and fifth largest in the world in both land area and population. Brazil has a population of 146 million with more than 15 million living in the Sao Paulo and Rio de Janeiro areas. Approximately 55 percent of all Brazilians are of Portuguese descent with 38 percent a mixture of several cultures. Around 6 percent of the population is of African decent. Portuguese is the official language, and although there is no official religion, about 90 percent of the population consider themselves Roman Catholics.

Currently around 50 percent of the population of Brazil is younger than 20 years of age, and despite economic problems, Brazil has much potential to become a rich nation with its strong industrial, agricultural, and natural resource operations.

Workers in Brazil, like other areas of Latin America, hold a higher concern for rules, controls, and career security than in the USA or Europe. Brazilian society tends to be risk-adverse and reluctant to accept change, and this has contributed to a growing inequality between rich and poor in Brazil. However, the reluctance for change is complimented by a strong respect for tradition, including a strong work ethic. Employees believe in long-term rewards for a hard day's work. New ideas or ways of doing business are often met with great skepticism in Brazil.

Brazilians dress formal at work with executives wearing three-piece suits and office workers often wearing two-piece suits. Women are expected to dress conservatively and have their nails well manicured. Appointments in Brazil should be made with at least two weeks notice; last-minute appointments with either businesses or government agencies should not be attempted. Although parts of Brazil may not be the most punctual in regard to meetings starting on time, meetings in Sao Paulo and Rio De Janerio are much like those in the USA or Europe because they start on time. However, even in these two cities, casual chit chat should start the meeting and only when the host moves to the business at hand should the conversation turn to more serious matters. It is also common courtesy to purchase lunch or dinner for a host but not to provide a gift.

The Future

In a market that some analysts consider to be a duopoly, the short-hop, narrow-body jets manufactured by Embraer have outsold those from Bombardier for nearly a decade. But Bombardier is not conceding ground, especially in its traditional North American stronghold. United Airlines and smaller rival US Airways are both expected to announce airplane purchases in 2013. Bombardier received a December 2012 order worth up to $3.29 billion from Delta Air Lines. That order almost matches Embraer's deal worth up to $4 billion to supply the regional network of AMR Corp's (AAMRQ.PK) American Airlines. More orders for somebody will follow soon because U.S. carriers need new short-haul planes, to the tune of 250 to 400 planes in the next 18 months. American Eagle already has a large mixed fleet of Embraers and Bombardiers, so neither suppliers has exclusive rights.

Bombardier's market share in the regional-jet market has fallen below 30 percent, from 72 percent in 2003, but the company has a strategic plan to regain its dominance. Airlines are often hesitant to switch fleets from one supplier to another because additional training and maintenance costs can outweigh savings on the purchase. Unfortunately for Embraer, Delta, US Airways, and their regional flying partners already operate more Bombardier CRJs, whereas American and United and their partners use more Embraer jets. Embraer needs a clear strategic plan to maintain (or increase) its current market share. Perhaps Embraer needs to shift some focus to trying to supply firms such as Ryanair, Emirates, Singapore Air, and flydubai.

Bayerische Motoren Werke (BMW) Group, 2013

www.bmwgroup.com, BMW.DE

Headquartered in Munich, Bavaria, Germany, BMW Group is a world famous German automobile-, motorcycle-, and engine-manufacturing company. In June 2012, BMW was listed in *Forbes* magazine as the number-one most reputable company in the world. Rankings were based on aspects such as "people's willingness to buy, recommend, work for, and invest in a company." The rankings were based 60 percent on public perceptions of the company and 40 on public perceptions of their products.

BMW owns and produces the Mini marque and is the parent company of Rolls-Royce Motor Cars. BMW produces motorcycles under the Motorrad and Husqvarna brands led by the K 1200 GT, R 1200 RT, and F 800 S models. BMW Group operates 29 production and assembly facilities in 14 countries and has a global dealer network in more than 140 countries. BMW's premium lineup includes sedans, coupés, convertibles, and sport wagons in the 1, 3, 5, 6, and 7 Series, as well as the M3 coupe and convertible, the X5 sport active, and the Z4 roadster. BMW has a profitable financial services segment that provides purchase financing and leasing, asset management, dealer financing, and corporate fleets. About 3,000 dealers worldwide sell BMWs.

In calendar year 2012, BMW Group sold 1.85 million cars and nearly 117,000 motorcycles worldwide, the highest annual total ever for the company and an increase of 10.6 percent over the previous record year in 2011. BMW sales in the month of January 2013 were the highest ever in a January for the company; sales grew 11.5 percent to 107,276 units and it was the first time that more than 100,000 BMW vehicles were delivered worldwide to customers in that month.

In early 2013, BMW Group and Toyota Motor Corporation extended their long-term collaboration agreement for the joint development of a fuel-cell system, joint development of architecture and components for a sports vehicle, joint research and development of lightweight technologies, and collaborative research on lithium-air batteries with a post-lithium-battery solution. BMW Group had a workforce of approximately 105,000 employees.

BMW Group reported the best-ever May 2013 sales with 166,397 BMW, MINI, and Rolls-Royce automobiles delivered to customers worldwide, up 5.8 percent from the previous May. BMW Motorrad also had a successful May 2013 with sales up 14.2 percent to 13,081 vehicles delivered. However, in August 2013, BMW customers around the world were complaining intensely about not being able to obtain spare parts for their BMW. The world's biggest maker of luxury cars, BMW has struggled from June to September 2013 to ship components on time because of a new supply-management system being introduced in its central warehouse in Germany. BMW's 40 parts-distribution centers originate at the main warehouse in Dingolfing that also directly supplies about 300 repair shops in Germany. Raimund Nestler—who lives in Ingolstadt, Germany, the home base of rival Audi AG (NSU)—has been waiting six weeks for a new part that controls engine speed. "I have always been a die-hard BMW driver and am currently driving my seventh BMW, but will consider which brand I'll buy the next time," he said by phone. "For a premium carmaker like BMW, this is particularly disappointing." BMW's stock has declined 2.5 percent in 2013 through August, valuing the company at 45.7 billion euros ($61 billion).

Copyright by Fred David Books LLC. (Written by Forest R. David)

History

BMW was established in 1917 following a restructuring of the Rapp Motorenwerke aircraft manufacturing company. At the end of World War I, BMW was forced to cease aircraft engine production by the terms of the Versailles Armistice Treaty. The company shifted to motorcycle production in 1923 and once the restrictions of the treaty started to be lifted, began producing automobiles in 1928–1929. The first car produced by BMW was the Dixi, a vehicle whose design was based on the Austin 7, from the Austin Motor Company in Birmingham, England.

BMW's circular blue and white logo, or roundel, evolved from the circular Rapp Motorenwerke logo, but as BMW grew, that emblem was combined with the blue and white colors of the flag of Bavaria. The BMW logo has also been portrayed as the movement of an aircraft propeller with the white blades cutting through a blue sky—first used in a BMW advertisement in 1929, 12 years after the roundel was created.

BMW's first significant aircraft engine was the BMW IIIa inline-six liquid-cooled engine of 1918, much preferred for its high-altitude World War I performance. With German rearmament in the 1930s, the company again began producing aircraft engines for the Luftwaffe. Especially successful World War II aircraft engines were the BMW 132 and BMW 801 air-cooled radial engine, and eventually the BMW 003 axial-flow turbojet that powered Germany's 1944- and 1945-era jets, such as the Heinkel He 162 and eventually the Messerschmitt Me 262.

After outselling Lexus in 2011 and 2012, BMW and Mercedes are vying to be the top luxury auto brand in the USA. Lexus was the top-selling luxury car brand in the USA from 1999 to 2010. Sales of the Toyota Lexus rose 32 percent to 16,211 in January 2013, led by the ES sedan, which more than doubled to 5,186 deliveries.

Internal Issues

Year 2012

In calendar year 2012, BMW sales rose 11.6 percent to 1,540,085 vehicles, the best sales level in the history of the company. Success was led by the highly successful BMW 1 Series, with a total of 226,829 vehicles sold in 2012, an increase of 28.6 percent over the previous year. The BMW X1 also did great in 2012 with a total of 147,776 vehicles sold, up 16.9 percent over the prior year. The BMW 3 Series Sedan did best with 294,039 vehicles delivered, an increase of 22.4 percent over 2011. Sales of the BMW X3 grew 27.1 percent to 149,853 units sold, whereas the BMW 5 Series reported that 337,929 vehicles were delivered to customers in 2012, up 9.0 percent from the prior year. Even sales of the BMW 6 Series grew 146.8 percent, with 23,193 vehicles being delivered to customers.

Also for 2012, global sales of the BMW MINI were a record 301,526 vehicles, up 5.8 percent. The USA remained the largest market for the MINI, with a record-breaking 66,123 cars sold in 2012, followed by the United Kingdom, with 50,367 cars sold. In the ultra-luxury-class segment, Rolls-Royce sales for the full year 2012 reached record sales result of 3,575 motor cars, the highest annual sales in the 108-year history of Rolls-Royce and the third consecutive record.

Additionally, a record total of 106,358 BMW Motorrad motorcycles were sold in 2012.

Organizational Structure

BMW operates using an autocratic, functional structure with no apparent Chief Executive Officer or Chief Operations Officer and divisional presidents. As indicated in Exhibit 1, if executives with these titles exist, they are neither listed on the corporate website nor in the *Annual Report*.

EXHIBIT 1 BMW's Organizational Structure

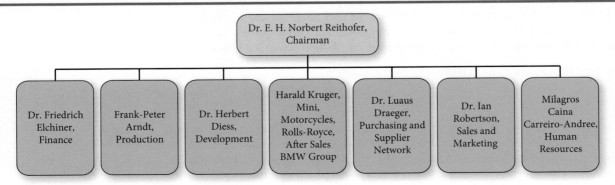

Source: Based on company documents

Segments

BMW reports their revenues by region and by brand and is doing exceptionally well in all regions and brands. For example, BMW reported its strongest January ever as sales climbed 11.5 percent to 107,276 units for January 2013, the first time ever that more than 100,000 BMW vehicles were delivered worldwide to customers in a January. There were 29,053 BMW 3 Series sold, up 27.9 percent, as well as 11,753 BMW X1 vehicles sold, up 57.8 percent. The BMW X3 continued to be popular with 10,230 vehicles delivered to customers, up 9.4 percent. Sales of the BMW 1 Series were up 8.8 percent to 14,222 units sold, and the BMW 5 Series sales grew 6.4 percent to 23,049. Sales of the BMW 6 Series grew 22.4 percent to 1,354 units. Also in January 2013, worldwide sales of the MINI reached 15,864 vehicles, up 0.6 percent, which was a new all-time high for any January ever.

As indicated in Exhibits 2 and 3, BMW's sales in January 2013 increased in all regions and all brands, except Motorrad motorcycles. Despite BMW's record January 2013, rival Audi (owned by Volkswagen AG) beat BMW in 2013 luxury-car market January sales, propelled by a 39-percent jump in Audi deliveries in China, its biggest national market. Audi sold 111,750 cars and sport utility vehicles (SUVs) worldwide in January, a 16-percent increase from a year prior, compared to BMW brand's 12-percent gain to 107,276 deliveries. Global sales at Mercedes (owned by Daimler AG) rose 9 percent in January 2013 to 94,895 vehicles, helped by demand for the A- and B-class compacts and its SUV line-up.

Exhibit 4 reveals BMW's 2012 year-end segment data by region for automobiles. Note the 2.8 percent decline in motorcycle revenues, and the decline in United Kingdom revenues.

EXHIBIT 2 BMW's January 2013 Sales by Region (units sold)

	2013	2012	Change (%)
Asia	43,114	36,422	+ 18.4
China	30,397	26,505	+ 14.7
Japan	3,250	—	+ 19.0
South Korea	2,790	—	+ 32.9
Americas	25,021	24,419	+ 2.5
United States	20,195	19,739	+ 2.3
Europe	50,594	46,831	+ 8.0
Germany	18,709	17,028	+ 9.9
Russia	2,311	1,653	+ 39.8
Africa*	37,649	32,890	+ 14.5
Oceania*	23,000	21,297	+ 8.0

*For all of 2012

Source: Based on company documents.

EXHIBIT 3 BMW's January 2013 Sales by Brand (units sold)

	2013	2012	Change (%)
BMW Group Automobiles	123,276	112,164	+ 9.9
BMW	107,276	96,184	+11.5
MINI	15,864	15,768	+ 0.6
BMW Motorrad	4,818	5,237	− 8.0
Husqvarna Motorcycles	587	544	+ 7.9

Source: Based on company documents.

EXHIBIT 4 BMW's Revenues By Segment

Revenues

in € million	2012	2011
Automobiles	50,165	46,681
Motorcycles	980	1,008
Other revenues	7,660	7,318
	58,805	55,007
Germany	11,974	12,494
United Kingdom	4,059	4,061
Rest of Europe	12,303	12,766
North America	12,991	10,903
Asia	14,436	12,042
Other markets	3,042	2,741
	58,805	55,007

Source: Company documents.

Finance

Exhibit 5 shows the income statement for BMW Group.

EXHIBIT 5 BMW's Income Statements

(in € million)	2012	2011
Revenues	58,805	55,007
Cost of sales	−46,252	−43,320
Gross profit	**12,553**	**11,687**
Selling expenses	−3,684	−3,381
Administrative expenses	−1,701	−1,410
Research and development expenses	−3,573	−3,045
Other operating income and expenses	703	670
Result on investments	598	181
Financial result	−99	−665
Profit from ordinary activities	**4,797**	**4,037**
Extraordinary income	—	29
Income taxes	−1,635	−2,073
Other taxes	−31	−23
Net profit	**3,131**	**1,970**
Transfer to revenue reserves.	−1,491	−462
Unappropriated profit available for distribution	**1,640**	**1,508**

Source: Company documents

EXHIBIT 6 BMW's Balance Sheets

(in € million)	2012	2011
Assets		
Intangible assets	178	161
Property, plant and equipment	7,806	6,679
Investments	3,094	2,823
Tangible, intangible and investment assets	**11,078**	**9,663**

EXHIBIT 6 Continued

(in € million)	2012	2011
Inventories	3,749	3,755
Trade receivables	858	729
Receivables from subsidiaries	6,297	5,827
Other receivables and other assets	2,061	1,479
Marketable securities	2,514	3,028
Cash and cash equivalents	4,618	2,864
Current assets	**20,097**	**17,682**
Prepayments	118	120
Surplus of pension and similar plan assets over liabilities	672	43
Total assets	**31,965**	**27,508**
Equity and liabilities		
Subscribed capital	656	655
Capital reserves	2,053	2,035
Revenue reserves	5,515	4,024
Unappropriated profit available for distribution	1,640	1,508
Equity	**9,864**	**8,222**
Registered profit-sharing certificates	32	32
Pension provisions	56	84
Other provisions	7,406	7,651
Provisions	**7,462**	**7,735**
Liabilities to banks	1,408	911
Trade payables	3,900	2,940
Liabilities to subsidiaries	8,451	6,923
Other liabilities	800	741
Liabilities	**14,559**	**11,515**
Deferred income	48	4
Total equity and liabilities	**31,965**	**27,508**

Source: Based on company documents.

Competitors

The combined sales for Toyota's Lexus, Daimler's Mercedes-Benz, BMW, Honda's Acura, GM's Cadillac, Volkswagen's Audi, and Nissan's Infiniti, which are the seven best-selling luxury brands automobiles in the world, rose 15 percent in the USA in 2012 through November. Growth in sales of luxury vehicles exceeds growth in all other automobile categories, and these brands are fiercely competitive globally.

Exhibit 7 provides a financial summary of leading luxury-car manufacturers. Note that BMW is the smallest firm in terms of number of employees, but it has the second highest earnings per share (EPS).

Volkswagen

Headquartered in Wolfsburg, Lower Saxony, Germany, Volkswagen (VW) is the largest German automobile manufacturer and the second- or third-largest automaker in the world behind GM or Toyota. The word *volkswagen* means "people's car" in German and is pronounced *folks wagen*. VW aims to double its U.S. market share from 2 percent to 4 percent by 2014 and aims to be the world's largest carmaker by 2018. VW introduced diesel-electric hybrid versions of its most popular models in 2012, including the Jetta, followed by the Golf Hybrid and the Passat. VW also owns Porsche.

Mercedes-Benz

Headquartered in Stuttgart, Baden-Wuttemberg, Germany, Mercedes-Benz is a division of the German automobile manufacturer Daimler AG. Mercedes-Benz is active in three forms of motorsport racing: Formula Three, DTM, and Formula One. The parent, Daimler AG, holds

EXHIBIT 7 A Financial Comparison of BMW with Rival Firms (in U.S. dollars)

	BMW	VW	Daimler	GM	Toyota	Nissan
Revenue ($)	76.1B	251B	153B	151B	243B	102B
Net Income ($)	5.1B	30B	7.5B	4.5B	8.3B	3.3B
Profit Margin (%)	6.65	11.9	4.9	3.0	3.4	3.2
Debt-to-Equity Ratio	1.47	1.24	1.85	0.40	1.15	1.45
EPS ($)	7.27	12.82	7.03	2.67	2.60	0.79
Number of Employees	106K	549K	275K	213K	325K	157K
Revenue per Employee ($)	717K	457K	556K	708K	747K	680K

EPS, earnings per share.
Source: Based on company information.

a 60 percent stake in Formula One team Mercedes-Benz Grand Prix, as well as a 22 percent stake in aerospace and defense consortium EADS. Daimler sells its vehicles in 40 countries, but Europe represents 40 percent of its sales.

Mercedes-Benz's U.S. sales surged 11 percent in January 2013, in its effort to overtake BMW in luxury-auto deliveries for all of 2013. Mercedes sold 22,501 vehicles in January 2013, its best January ever, and helped the C-Class sedan's 11 percent climb to 7,214 units sold. In comparison, sales for BMW increased 0.7 percent to 16,513 units, boosted by a 56 percent gain for its X5 SUV.

Toyota Motor Corporation

Headquartered in Toyota, Aichi, Japan, Toyota runs neck and neck with GM as the largest automobile company in the world. Toyota's U.S. operations are headquartered in Torrence, California. Popular Toyota models include the Camry, Corolla, Land Cruiser, and Lexus, as well as the Tundra truck. The Lexus competes directly with BMW. Lexus sales were up 23 percent in the USA in 2012 through November and are expected to gain at least 10 percent in 2013.

Volvo Car Corporation

Headquartered in Gothenburg, Sweden, Volvo, or *Volvo Personvagnar AB*, is owned by Zhejiang Geely Holding Group China, headquartered in Hangzhou, China. Geely acquired Volvo in 2010 from Ford Motor Company. Volvo manufactures and markets a wide range of vehicles, some that compete with BMW. With approximately 2,300 local dealers from around 100 national sales companies worldwide, Volvo's largest markets are the USA, Sweden, China, Germany, the United Kingdom, and Belgium. In 2011, Volvo recorded global sales of 449,255 cars, an increase of 20.3 percent compared to 2010. In 2012, Volvo signed NBA star Jeremy Lin to an endorsement agreement. Over the next two years Lin will participate in Volvo's corporate and marketing activities as a "brand ambassador" for Volvo.

Audi

Headquartered in Ingolstadt, Bavaria, Germany, Audi Aktiengesellschaft (Audi) designs, engineers, manufactures, and markets automobiles and motorcycles. Audi-branded vehicles are produced in seven production facilities worldwide. AUDI AG has been a majority owned (99.55 percent) subsidiary of VW since 1966. In September 2012, Audi began construction of its first North American manufacturing plant in Puebla, Mexico, expected to be operative in 2016 and produce the successor to the Q5.

In 2012, Audi again won the 24 Hours of Le Mans, a historic first Le Mans victory for a hybrid, which was captured by Audi's R18 e-tron quattro. Audi's other R18 hybrid took second, whereas R18 ultras took third and fifth. This sports car racing success followed Audi R18's victory at the 2011 24 Hours of Le Mans. The Audis finished in front of three Peugeot 908s by 13.8 seconds to claim victory.

Audi offers a computerized control system for its cars, called multimedia interface (MMI). This advancement came amid criticism of BMW's iDrive control, a rotating control knob and "segment" buttons—designed to control all in-car entertainment devices (radio, CD changer, iPod, TV tuner), satellite navigation, heating and ventilation, and other car controls with a screen. Some believe MMI is a considerable improvement on BMW's iDrive, although BMW has since improved their iDrive.

Business Culture in Germany

Germany survived the 2008 recession in good position thanks to their strong economy and manufacturing base. Unemployment in Germany is lower now than it was in 2008. German companies are generally run by individuals specializing in various technical areas. For example, a car company is more likely to be run by an expert mechanical engineer in Germany than an expert accountant or finance individual. This technical nature often extends down the chain of command for other key positions as well. For example, responsibility is often delegated to another technically sound individual, who then expects his or her manager to leave them alone to perform the task with little oversight. People from other cultures often view this approach as distant and cold. In addition, socializing is much more common at the peer level than up or down the hierarchy in Germany.

Meetings in Germany generally start on time with all members in attendance having well researched any aspects of the meeting that touch on their area of expertise. It is often assumed by people outside Germany that "German businesspeople have their minds made up before the meeting even starts," but this is not the case. Germans take a sense of pride in their subject matter and want to be as well prepared as possible, so they can contribute and make key points during the meeting. During a meeting, it is expected that individuals will contribute when the discussion touches on their area of expertise. This is an overriding theme in German business, where well-prepared specialists are groomed and preferred to generalists. This line of thinking also extends into teamwork in Germany. Each team member answers to the leader, but each tends to focus on his or her individual technical task, with little overlapping conversations, at least in technical nature, with other team members.

Communication in Germany tends to be direct and to the point. Supervisors tend not to sugarcoat their reviews or requirements for subordinates, instead informing them in direct words their performance reviews, expectations, and so forth. In addition, when interviewing a German worker for a job, they will tend to describe in clear terms what they are capable of doing, rather than speaking in vague terms like in other cultures. German workers tend not to oversell themselves in an interview; if they claim they are capable of a task, you can generally bet they are capable.

Dress in Germany is professional but not as clearly defined as in the United Kingdom, USA, or many Asian nations. Women often wear dress pants, rather than dresses or skirts, and men often wear sport jackets, as opposed to black or blue suits. Despite having a woman president as leader of Germany, women in Germany still lag behind women in other European nations in securing top-level management opportunities, partly because women are not majoring in the technical fields as commonly as men; senior-level jobs generally go to individuals heavily trained in key technical areas.

The Future

China overtook the USA in 2012 as BMW's biggest international market, with the company's sales in China rising 14 percent to 28,597 automobiles and motorcycles. "Looking ahead, we expect the headwinds in Europe to remain," said Ian Robertson, BMW's head of sales and marketing. "However, we are confident of healthy sales growth in other regions, especially Asia and the Americas."

BMW borrowed a new retail concept from Apple stores, which was tested in the United Kingdom, by rolling out its version on the Apple "Genius Bar" across Europe. The iPad-equipped, specially trained "BMW Genius Everywhere" staff will give customers information about vehicles and features, but they will not sell cars. The new BMW employees wear a white polo shirt that says "BMW Genius," but they are paid a salary, not a commission on sales. A pilot program for the "BMW Genius Everywhere" program will began in the USA in late 2013, with a full launch by early 2014, which is when the new BMW i3 electric car is set to go on sale.

Davide Campari-Milano S.p.A., 2013

www.camparigroup.com, DVDCF

Headquartered in Milan, Italy, Gruppo Campari (Campari) is the sixth-largest beverage company in the world with operations in more than 190 nations, including being the self-proclaimed leader in Italy and Brazil and a top-tier presence in the USA, Germany and Switzerland. Campari is growing and expanding its international footprint. The company is a subsidiary of the parent company Davide Campari-Milano, but most all company operations are referred to in respect to Campari, including the financial statements.

Campari produces a wide array of spirits, wines, and even a few soft drinks that are limited solely to the Italian market. The company is structured into four segments: spirits, wines, soft drinks, and other. Some notable spirit products include: Wild Turkey, Campari, Appleton Estate Rum, Skyy Vodka, Cynar, Ouzo 12, Zedda Piras, and Drury's. Campari wines include include Cinzano, Liebfraumilch, Mondoro, Riccadonna, Sella & Mosca, and Teruzzi & Puthod. Campari soft drinks include Crodino and Lemonsoda.

Campari has more than 2,200 employees, annual sales of more than €1.5 billion, and 12 manufacturing plants: 4 located in Italy, 1 in Greece, 1 in Scotland, 1 in Ukraine, 1 in the USA, 1 in Argentina, 2 in Brazil, and 1 in Mexico. Gruppo Campari also owns four wineries: three in in Italy (Sella & Mosca, Teruzzi & Puthod, and Enrico Serafino) and one in France (Lamargue).

Effective March 2013, Campari disposed of its Punch Barbieri brand to Distillerie Moccia, for €4.45 million, thus relinquishing its Aperol, Aperol Soda, Mondoro Asti, and Enrico Serafino still wines. Punch Barbieri is a medium alcohol-content liqueur that specializes in the tastes of rum, mandarin, and orange, with Italy as its main market. For Q1 of 2013, Campari's sales totaled €315.2 million, up 12.9 percent from the prior year's Q1. For that Q1 of 2013, Campari's sales in the Americas (45.1% of company total) were up 66.7 percent led partly by selling Wild Turkey in the United States. Q1 of 2013 sales in Italy were down 26.2 percent while sales in Europe were down 2.8 percent.

For the first half of 2013, Campari Group's sales totaled €698.6 million, up 13.0 percent driven by the newly-acquired LdM. The company's gross margin was €373.4 million, up by +2.8 percent (–6.8% organic change), or 53.4 percent of sales. Advertising and promotion spending was up by +11.7 percent to €115.4 million, or 16.5 percent of sales (16.7% of sales in the first half of 2012). The company's earnings before taxes and interest (EBIT) for the first half of 2013 reached €140.7 million, a decrease of –11.7 percent, or 20.1% of sales. The company's pre-tax profit was €92.2 million, down by –24.9 percent, while the Group's net profit reached €57.6 million, down by –26.1 percent.

Copyright by Fred David Books LLC. (Written by Forest R. David)

History

Campari was founded in 1860 by Gaspare Campari with the creation and marketing of a bright red, mid-proof aperitif, he named *Campari*. In addition to this signature wine, Campari also had several dozen other products (vermouth, champagne, amontillado, sherry) he sold from his downtown café in Milan, Italy. After several decades of selling various beverages in Italy, Gaspare's son, Davide, began producing only the firm's strongest brand beverages as he expanded the firm globally. Davide led Campari brands to being distributed in more than 80 countries. By the 1960s, Campari products were sold in more than 190 nations.

After impressive growth from the 1960s to the 1990s, the group found itself competing with huge firms such as PepsiCo, Coca-Cola, InBev, Constelletation Brands, Diageo, and others. Consolidation among firms in the beverage industry forced Campari into two strategically viable options: (1) grow through acquisitions or (2) defend a niche market. The firm chose the acquisition process and in 1996 acquired rights to distribute and produce many foreign products in Brazil and Italy. Two of the more notable brands were the Scotch whiskey brand Glenfiddich and Germany's world famous Jagermeister. Two years later in 1998, Campari obtained world distribution rights, except for the USA, of Skyy Spirits who owns Skyy Vodka. Skyy Spirits, through the alliance, became the distributer for the entire Campari portfolio in the USA. In addition to spirits, Campari became the Italian distributer of Lipton Ice Tea. In 1999, Campari acquired Ouzo 12, a Greek spirit famous especially in Greece and Germany. Also acquired was Cinzano, one of the most well-known Italian sparkling wines (champagne). During the next decade, Campari continued to acquire many firms and obtain distribution rights to many other products. In 2009, the company completed the largest acquisition in its history with the acquisition of the world's most popular Kentucky bourbon whiskey, Wild Turkey. With that deal, Campari acquired the Wild Turkey distillery in Lawrenceburg, Kentucky.

Campari's full year 2012 sales were €1.34 billion, up 5.2 percent from the prior year, but company profits were €156.7 million, down 1.6 percent.

Internal Issues

Vision and Mission

Campari does not have a written vision or mission statement. The company does have an elaborate Code of Ethics and a commitment to responsible drinking posted on their website. But there is no statement of purpose, or guiding vision, in the firm's *Annual Report*.

Organizational Structure

As is typical in many companies in Italy, there are no females among the top 16 executives and no minorities, as indicated in Exhibit 1. Note in the diagram that Campari operates from a divisional-by-geographic-region structure. Note also there is no chief operations officer (COO) or chief strategy officer (CSO). It is unclear who all the segment executives report to, perhaps to the chief executive officer (CEO).

Segments

Campari is structured into four segments related to the products produced: spirits, wine, soft drinks, and other. In 2012, sales were up 5.2 percent across the board with spirits accounting for 76 percent of all sales and up 5.4 percent. Wines, the second-largest segment with

EXHIBIT 1 Campari's Organizational Chart

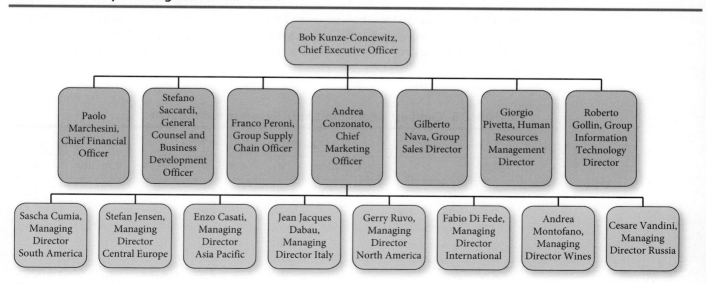

Source: Based on company information.

EXHIBIT 2 Campari's Product Revenue Comparison

	2012		2011		2010	
	€ million	%	€ million	%	€ million	%
Spirits	1,028.5	76.7	975.1	76.6%	876.4	75.4%
Wines	196.4	14.6	185.1	45.5%	175.0	15.0%
Soft drinks	99.5	7.4	98.2	7.7%	98.5	8.5%
Other sales	16.4	1.3	15.8	1.2%	13.1	1.1%
Total	1,340.8	100.0	1,274.2	100.0%	1,163.0	100.0%

Source: Page 18, 2012 *Annual Report.*

14.6 percent of sales, increased 5.9 percent. Soft drinks accounted for 7.4 percent of total revenue in 2012. Other sales made up only 1 percent of total revenues in 2012, as indicated in Exhibit 2.

Spirits

In September 2012, Campari purchased Lascelles for $414 million. Lascelles is the producer of Appleton Estate, a Jamaican rum, along with Wray & Nephew and Coruba brands. Campari hopes the addition of Lascelles will help to solidify Campari's presence in the North American and Caribbean markets with their previous purchases of Skyy and Wild Turkey.

Wine

Wine sales totaled €196.4 million in 2012, with Cinzano vermouth sales increasing nearly, mainly from strong sales in Argentina and Russia. Germany remains the largest market for Cinzano with potential market development opportunities in both the USA and Sweden.

Soft Drinks

Accounting for about 7.4 percent of Campari's total revenues, soft-drink sales were up slightly in 2012. The soft-drink market derives around 95 percent of its revenues from sales in Italy. Popular drinks include Crodino, a nonalcoholic aperitifs, Lemonsoda, Lemonsoda Zero, Mojito Soda, and mineral waters. Lemonsoda drinks are growing the fastest with nearly 10-percent growth. Most other drinks in the segment are declining in sales.

Even though Campari is a global company, Italy still represents around 32 percent of worldwide revenues, practically tied with the Americas, representing North, South, and Central America. The U.S. wine market is saturated with wines particularly from California. The two main players in the Americas market, accounting for 33 percent of all sales, were the USA and Brazil. The USA accounted for 60 percent of sales and Brazil accounted for 25 percent. Although the rest of the Americas only accounted for 15 percent of the region's sales, these nations experienced a 41 percent growth rate. Exhibit 3 provides Campari revenue data by region.

EXHIBIT 3 Campari Geographic EBIT Revenue Breakdown

EBIT		2012		2011		2010	
		€ million	%	€ million	%	€ million	%
75.9	Italy	391.1	29.2	402.6	31.6%	397.3	34.2%
90.8	Rest of Europe	345.3	25.8	328.1	25.7%	276.7	23.8%
102.5	Americas	464.8	34.7	427.0	33.5%	405.3	34.8%
35.4	Rest of the world and duty free	139.5	10.3	116.5	9.2%	83.7	7.2%
304.6	Total	1,340.7	100.0	1,274.2	100.0%	1,163.0	100.0%

Source: 2012 *Annual Report,* page 19.

Finance

Campari pays a modest dividend of around €0.07 per share with a stock price around €5.80. Major owners of the firm's stock include Alicros S.p.A with 51 percent of the stock and Cedar Rock Capital with 18 percent. Exhibit 4 provides recent income statements for Campari. Sales increased 9.6 percent whereas profits were only up 1.9 percent.

Campari's balance sheets in Exhibit 5 reveal that about 50 percent of the company's assets are goodwill—not a good thing. Campari has a history of acquiring too much goodwill with acquisitions; but sometimes such acquisitions are vital to obtaining distribution rights. For example, Campari's 2011 80 percent acquisition of Moscow-based Vasco (CIS) OOO, a distributer of wines and spirits to the Russian market, for €8.2 million, resulted in net assets of €4.5 million and goodwill of €3.7 million. Campari's rationale to justify the goodwill was "to serve their products directly to the Russian market without going through a third party distributer." Likewise the 100 percent acquisition of Sagatiba Brazil S.A., the production and owner of the Cachaça market in Brazil, resulted in net assets of €5.7 and goodwill of €17.1 Here again, Campari described the goodwill as necessary to obtain synergies in the Brazilian market as well as 100 percent of the goodwill associated with the transaction being tax deductible.

EXHIBIT 4 Campari's Recent Income Statements (in millions €)

	2012	2011	2010	2009
Revenue	1,340.8	1,274.2	1,163.0	1,008.4
Other Revenue, Total	0.0	0.0	0.0	0.0
Total Revenue	**1,340.8**	**1,274.2**	**1,163.0**	**1,008.4**
Cost of Revenue, Total	**571.3**	**539.6**	**496.2**	**435.6**
Gross Profit	**769.5**	**734.6**	**666.8**	**572.8**
Selling, General, Administrative Expenses, Total	464.9	427.9	386.5	327.1
Research and Development	0.0	0.0	0.0	0.0
Depreciation and Amortization	10.0	8.1	7.5	6.0
Interest Expense (Income), Net Operating	0.0	0.0	0.0	0.0
Unusual Expense (Income)	0.0	5.0	1.4	11.8
Other Operating Expenses, Total	0.0	0.0	0.0	(–0.1)
Operating Income	**294.6**	**293.6**	**271.4**	**228.0**
Interest Income (Expense), Net Nonoperating	0.0	0.0	0.0	0.0
Gain (Loss) on Sale of Assets	0.0	0.0	0.0	0.0
Other, Net	58.4	(–0.7)	(–0.5)	(–3.8)
Income Before Tax	**236.2**	**250.7**	**232.9**	**198.3**
Income Tax, Total	**79.0**	90.9	**76.2**	60.8
Income After Tax	157.2	159.8	156.7	137.5
Minority Interest	(–0.5)	(–0.6)	(–0.5)	(–0.4)
Equity In Affiliates	0.0	0.0	0.0	0.0
U.S. GAAP Adjustment	0.0	0.0	0.0	0.0
Net Income Before Extra. Items	**156.7**	**159.2**	**156.2**	**137.1**
Total Extraordinary Items	0.0	0.0	0.0	0.0
Net Income	**156.7**	**159.2**	**156.2**	**137.1**

GAAP, generally accepted accounting principles.
Source: Based on company documents.

EXHIBIT 5 Campari's Balance Sheets

(€ million)	December 31, 2012	December 31, 2011	Change
ASSETS			
Non-current assets			
Net tangible fixed assets	392.6	320.6	72.0
Biological assets	17.2	17.4	(0.2)
Investment property	0.5	0.6	(0.1)
Goodwill and trademarks	1,631.2	1,448.6	182.6
Intangible assets with a finite life	20.5	21.0	(0.5)
Investment in affiliated companies and joint ventures	0.2	0.0	0.2
Deferred tax assets	11.5	6.5	5.0
Other non-current assets	52.6	17.1	35.5
Total non-current assets	**2,126.2**	**1,831.8**	**294.4**
Current assets			
Inventories	446.5	331.3	115.2
Current biological assets	4.9		4.9
Trade receivables	312.4	278.0	34.4
Financial receivables	42.4	1.8	40.6
Cash and cash equivalents	442.5	414.2	28.3
Receivables for income taxes	9.4	17.8	(8.4)
Other receivables	24.2	23.9	0.3
Total current assets	**1,282.3**	**1,066.9**	**215.4**
Non-current assets held for sale	1.0	2.3	(1.3)
Total assets	**3,409.5**	**2,901.0**	**508.5**
Shareholders' equity			
Share capital	58.1	58.1	0.0
Reserves	1,370.8	1,305.6	65.2
Group's shareholders' equity	1,428.9	1,363.7	65.2
Minority interests	4.2	3.7	0.5
Total shareholders' equity	**1,433.1**	**1,367.5**	**65.6**
LIABILITIES			
Non-current liabilities			
Bonds	1,178.2	787.8	390.4
Other non-current financial liabilities	36.2	37.1	(0.9)
Staff severance fund and other personnel-related funds	13.0	8.8	4.2
Provisions for risks and future liabilities	39.6	7.1	32.5
Deferred tax	198.8	144.4	54.3
Total non-current liabilities	1,465.7	985.2	480.6
Current liabilities			
Short term debt banks	121.0	144.9	(23.9)
Other financial liabilities	34.9	103.2	(68.3)
Payables to suppliers	201.4	166.8	34.6
Payables for taxes	17.8	34.6	(16.8)
Other current liabilitles	135.6	98.9	36.7
Total current liabilities	**510.7**	**548.4**	**(37.7)**
Total liabilities and stockholders' equity	**3,409.5**	**2,901.0**	**508.5**

Source: 2012 *Annual Report,* p. 58.

Competitors

Barriers to entry are high in the beverage industry, at least for smaller start-up firms. To start a winery of any size in the USA it is estimated requires a $1 million investment after accounting for the vineyard, equipment, government regulation, a tremendous amount of knowledge, and many other variables. On average, assuming a successful wine product, it would still take more than three years to return a profit. Despite protection from the high barriers to entry, many of the bigger players in the industry are competing fiercely with one another. Three major rivals to Campari are Constellation Brands, Beam Inc., and Diageo plc.

The beverage industry has experienced many acquisitions over the last decade as well as joint ventures for distribution rights in select markets. The aim usually is to gain or limit or prohibit the distribution of a firm's products in select markets. Campari and rivals are concerned about having their products shut out of select markets, so distributors often have the upper hand and consequently often sell their business for values in excess of a fair price, thus inflating the purchasing firm's goodwill on the respective balance sheets. Often this goodwill ends up being written off as goodwill impairment when it is finally determined the transaction is not going to produce the expected revenues.

Constellation Brands (STZ)

Headquartered in Victor, New York, Constellation Brands has grown into one of the largest wine and sprit companies in the world. In fact, the company claims to be the "world leader in premium wine" with its portfolio of more than 100 wines, beers, and spirits. Through its Crown Imports segment, Constellation has rights to import, distribute and sell the full line of products produced by Mexican based Grupo Modelo. Constellation has 4,300 employees and has sales in 125 nations. Constellation reported total revenues of $2.6 billion for their fiscal year ending February 2012.

Constellation has two primary business segments: Constellation Wines North America (CWNA) and Crown Imports. The CWNA segment also includes sales to New Zealand and Australia despite the misleading name. CWNA has the leading market position in the USA, Canada, and New Zealand and is the leading producer of premium wines in the USA. CWNA sells 14 of the top 100 table wine brands in the USA. Premium wines is a special classification of wine and not simply a generic term. CWNA produces all four wine price points (popular, premium, super-premium, and fine). The company also sells a wide variety of wines including table wine, sparking wine, and dessert wine. CWNA uses vineyards around the world particularly in the USA, Canada, New Zealand, and Italy. Some of the more notable Constellation wine brands sold are: Robert Mondavi Brands, Clos du Bois, Blackstone, Arbor Mist, Ruffino, and many more. In addition to wines, the segment also sells spirits including: SVEDKA Vodka, Black Velvet Canadian Whiskey, and Paul Masson Grande Amber Brandy.

The Crown Imports segment, through a joint venture with Grupo Modelo whereby both firms hold equal interest in Crown Imports, provides Constellation Brands exclusive rights to import, market, and sell Modelo Brands. Popular products include: Corona Extra, Corona Light, Modelo Especial, Pacifico, Negra Modelo, and Victoria. In total, Crown Imports sells 6 of the top 25 imported beers in the USA with Corona Extra being the best selling of Crown Imports mix and the sixth best-selling imported beer in the USA overall. About 80 percent of Crown Imports' revenues were derived from the USA, 16 percent from Canada, 3 percent from New Zealnd, and 1 percent from Australia.

Like many firms in the beverage industry, Constellation Brands has acquired many rival firms over the last decade and has accumulated over $2.6 billion in goodwill with their acquisition strategy. In fact, after removing goodwill and other intangible assets from stockholders' equity results in net tangible assets of negative $823 million in 2012. One notable recent acquisition was the 2011 acquisition of the remaining 50.1 percent interest in Ruffino for $68.6 million. Two notable divestitures were the selling of 80 percent of CWAE, Australian, and U.K. business resulting in cash proceeds' of $193 million, and the 2010 divestiture of its U.K. cider business for $71 million.

Beam, Inc. (BEAM)

Headquartered in Deerfield, Illinois, Beam was known as Fortune Brands before a name change in 2011 to Beam. The company produces and sells distilled spirits worldwide. Generic product lines include: bourbon whiskey, Scotch whisky, Canadian whisky, tequila, cognac, rum, and many ready-to-drink cocktails. Notable brand names include: Jim Beam, Maker's Mark, Canadian Club, Knob Creek, Cruzan, Skinnygirl, Pinnacle, Calico Jack, and many others. Products are sold through direct sales and also through joint ventures around the world. The company operates in the three following business segments: North America, Europe/Middle East/Africa (EMEA), and Asia-Pacific/South America (APSA). Segment revenues in 2011 were $1,271; $506; and $487 million; respectively. Total revenues were $2.3 billion. Recent Beam acquisitions include (a) the 2012 acquisition of Cooley Distillery, a popular Irish whiskey and (b) the 2011 acquisition of Skinnygirl, a ready-to-drink cocktail.

Diageo PLC (DEO)

Based in London, England, Diageo produces, distills, brews, bottles, and distributes their spirits, beer, wine, and ready-to-drink beverages worldwide. Popular spirit brands include Johnnie Walker Scotch whiskey, Crown Royal, Buchanan's Scotch whisky, Bushmills Irish whisky, Smirnoff vodka, Kettle One vodka, Captain Morgan rum, Baileys Irish Cream, Jose Cuervo, and Seagram's 7. Notable beer brands include Guinness stout, Harp lager, Tusker lager, and Red Stripe. Wines include Blossom Hill, Sterling Vineyards, and Beaulieu Vineyard. Ready-to-drink products are derivatives off of the spirits and include Smirnoff Ice, Bundaberg, and Jose Cuervo cocktails. Diageo has 28,000 employees, annual revenues of $16.8 billion, and unlike many competitors, zero goodwill. Diageo also sells Guinness beer.

About 29 percent of all Diageo sales come from its scotch brands. Beer is the firm's second-largest revenue generator, producing 21 percent of sales, and vodka is third with 12 percent of sales. Five other sprits all contributed between 3 and 7 percent of total sales. Ready-to-drink products accounted for 7 percent of total sales and wine accounts for 4 percent. Diageo's sales by geographic region were also remarkably well diversified. The North American market is the largest producer of sales accounting for 33 percent of sales in 2012, followed by European markets at 28 percent of sales. Asia Pacific, Africa, and Latin America/Caribbean all produced between 12 and 14 percent of total sales.

Central European Distribution Corp. (CEDC)

Headquartered in Mount Laurel, New Jersey, the Central European produces, imports, and sells alcoholic beverages in Poland, Hungary, and the Russian Federation. Notable vodka products include Absolwent, Zubrówka, Talka, and several other brand names. The company also serves as importer of products such as E&J Gallo wines, Sutter Home, Corona, Budweiser, Jose Cuervo, Jim Beam, Jagermeister, and others. Two products made by Campari that are distributed by the firm are Cinzano and Campari. Central European has about 4,500 employees, but incurred a net loss of $1.3 billion for 2011. As of early 2013, the stock price fell from more than $75 per share in 2008 to $1.70, making the company ripe perhaps to be acquired.

External Issues

Over the past several years, there has been a modest increase in the consumption of alcoholic-based drinks around the world, and firms in the industry have mostly done well. For example, in 2011, all European alcoholic companies outperformed most broad-based indexes and the DJ Stoxx 600 Index's Food and Beverage benchmark outperformed the DJ Stoxx 600 index by more than 16 percent. Much of this can be explained by a poor economy and food and beverage stocks, including alcoholic stocks, being viewed by investors as safer havens than broad-based investments.

Factors that could possibly contribute to reducing overall sales in the industry include (a) a substantial decline in economic or geopolitical conditions, (b) increasing health concerns and consequences as new data becomes available regarding alcohol consumption and various health problems, (c) stricter laws in respect to drinking and driving, (d) smoking bans at restaurants around the world may reduce drinking, (e) consumers preferring lower-calorie beverages such as water, or diet soft drinks, and (f) increased regulatory pressures from governments and anti-alcohol groups. Governmental groups could start impose additional excise taxes and import duties and limit the manner in which products can be advertised, such as the tobacco business experienced.

Weather and Diseases

Potential problems facing all producers of alcohol, especially wines, are weather and diseases. To illustrate just how impactful droughts, or warmer-than-normal summers can be take the price of cabernet sauvignon grapes that are grown in the Napa Valley, California, versus the same species of grapes grown in Fresno, California. Typically the grapes from the Napa Valley fetch up to 15 times more than their counterpart grapes in Fresno. The principle reason cited is the 5-degree Fahrenheit temperate difference between the two locations. Attributing this price difference around the world, any small changes in weather patterns for a season could drastically impact grape prices and resulting wine prices. The risk of disease, insects growing resistance to currently allowed pesticides, concern for bird safety (which feed on grapes) all jointly increase the risk of weather- and disease-related issues.

Business Culture in Italy

To this day, Italy is still in a recovery period from the global economic crisis of 2008–2010 and has one of the highest levels of debt of all EU members. Some experts suggest the level of debt is compounded by Italy's complex demographics. Italians are known around the world for their close families and the importance they put on family life. Within many Italian firms, the chain of command on paper may be less impactful than personality, loyalty, and respect. Although high-ranking job titles might have formal authority, this is no assurance the position will have the practical power someone in a lower-ranking position might possess.

In addition to unclear corporate structures in Italy, many businesses still hold a high degree of nationalized industries, much more so than other EU members. Italy has one of the least mobile management populations in the world, making it difficult for outside companies to have corresponding offices and programs in different Italian cities. Nevertheless, Italy is the world's seventh-largest economy and home to some of the most luxurious textile, automobile, and fashion companies in the world.

Punctionality in Italy is expected but exceptions are often made for personal reasons. Small meetings tend to be informal with larger meetings taking on a more formal aspect. With the informal nature, side conversations and people taking breaks to answer mobile phone calls are common in some Italian meetings. If working as a team, it is generally a good strategy to have a respected figure lead the team and assign each individual their own task. If not, individuals could possibly work on whatever they feel is best, often at the expense of the macroplan. Italians believe in talking and using the power of persuasion to prove their points. Italians tend to not like formal presentations and meetings because they are viewed as stiff and academic. This feature is in contrast to normal meeting in the USA or United Kingdom.

Although a member of the EU, women in Italy comprise a large percentage of the workforce but struggle to advance into upper-management roles. Women have made better inroads into upper management in smaller corporations. When high-ranking women from outside Italy do business with Italian firms, it is not uncommon for them to receive compliments on their style or personal appearance. Although these compliments may constitute harassment in the USA or United Kingdom, in Italy it is considered an honest compliment. With Italy known around the world for many famous fashion designers and high-end leather goods it is no surprise that dressing well for work is important. In Italy it is often said, if you want to be taken seriously, dress seriously.

Tequila

Campari owns a premium tequila brand, Cabo Wabo. Tequila is distilled from the roasted hearts, or pinas, of the spiky blue agave plant in Mexico. Tequila is gaining in popularity, especially in the USA, its biggest market. U.S. consumption rose at an average annual rate of 4.1 percent from 2006 to 2011, according to International Wine & Spirit Research (IWSR), almost double the growth of the total U.S. liquor market. Pricier, premium varieties are expanding the fastest. Tequilas that sell for more than $20 a bottle increased more than 10 percent over the last five years, IWSR reports. The majority of tequila drunk is in cocktails such as margaritas, according to Kevin Vanegas, Master of Tequila at Wirtz Beverage.

The high-end tequila market is dominated by Patron, part-owned by Bacardi Ltd. Patron sold 1.66 million cases in the USA in 2011, double that of its next competitor, Grupo Cuervo's

1800 brand, IWSR estimates. There are more than 150 tequila distilleries in Mexico, producing more than 1,500 brands. Like Cognac, Bourbon, or single malt scotch, tequilas vary by how long they're aged. So-called anejo varieties, sold by most brands at a premium, must spend at least a year in wooden barrels. High-end tequila should be sipped "like a fine whiskey," not downed in shot glasses alongside a lime wedge and a lick of salt, as is often the case in U.S. bars.

Diageo in 2013 terminated its tequila distribution deal with Jose Cuervo. Cuervo is the world's top-selling tequila, but Cuervo is not a premium brand. Diageo wants to focus on premium tequila because cheaper tequilas priced under $20, which make up more than half of the U.S. market by volume and the bulk of Cuervo's sales, have slid 1.1 percent over the past 5 years. Cuervo's market share in the USA has fallen to 34 percent from 45 percent over the same period, Liberum Research estimates. Some analysts believe that Diageo is planning to acquire Beam, which makes Sauza, the third-biggest tequila brand in the USA. Diageo owns half of a premium tequila called Don Julio, alongside the Beckmann family, Cuervo's owners. The brand saw sales growth of 26 percent in 2011 versus a 5-percent decline for Jose Cuervo.

The Future

Campari is being adversely impacted by high unemployment, higher taxation, and increasing political uncertainty in Italy. Given this environment, Campari needs a clear strategic plan going forward that will enable the firm to aggressively grow outside Italy. There are more than 180 countries in the world that have consumers that would enjoy Campari products, but distribution rights are a key to obtaining market share in those lands.

L'Oréal SA, 2013

www.loréal.com, LRLCF or LRLCY or OR (Paris Exchange)

Headquartered in Clichy, France, just outside Paris, L'Oréal is the world's largest beauty products company, with brands that include L'Oréal Paris and Maybelline (mass-market), Lancôme (luxury), and Redken and SoftSheen/Carson (retail and salon). L'Oréal owns Dallas-based SkinCeuticals that conducts cosmetology and dermatology research. With more than 50 percent of sales generated outside Europe, L'Oréal has focused on acquiring brands globally. L'Oréal owns UK-based natural cosmetics retailer The Body Shop International, which has about 2,550 retail stores worldwide. L'Oréal's dermatology unit, Galderma S.A., is a joint venture with Nestlé.

L'Oréal SA is structured into three branches: (1) Cosmetics, (2) The Body Shop, and (3) Dermatology. The Cosmetics branch is divided into four sectors: Consumer Products, Professional Products, Luxury Products, and Active Cosmetics. Consumer Products are marketed under L'Oréal Paris, Garnier, Maybelline, Softsheen, and Carson brands. The company's Professional Products segment includes hair care products for use by professional hairdressers, such as Kerastase, Redken, and Matrix. L'Oréal's Luxury Products are sold globally under such brands as Lancome, Diesel, Giorgio Armani, and Cacharel. The firm's Active Cosmetics division, which consists of products under Vichy and La Roche Posay brands, are for sale mainly in pharmacies.

L'Oréal has a portfolio of 27 international, diverse, and complementary brands. With sales amounting to 22.5 billion euros in 2012, L'Oréal employs 72,600 people worldwide, has 43 production plants worldwide, 146 distribution centers, more than 20,000 employees in industrial operations worldwide, and 5.8 billion units produced. The world's largest cosmetics firm by sales, L'Oréal in August 2013 offered to buy a Chinese facial mask company for about US $840m. The company, Magic Holdings International, a Hong Kong-listed cosmetics producer based in Guangzhou, is known for its facial masks, one of the fastest-growing segments in China's cosmetics market. Magic Holdings generated revenues of about €150m in 2012, up 29 percent from the previous year. L'Oréal, which makes Lancôme creams and Garnier shampoo, said it would offer $HKD6.3 (HKD = Hong Kong Dollar) per share for the Chinese company. The offer represents a 25 percent premium on the previous day's closing price. L'Oréal already has won approval from six shareholders representing 62.3 percent of Magic Holding's shares. The deal requires approval from Chinese authorities.

History

In 1907, Eugene Schueller, a young French chemist, working with La Cagoule, developed a hair dye formula called *Auréale*. Schueller formulated and manufactured his own products, which he then sold to Parisian hairdressers. In 1919, Schueller registered his company as the French Society of Inoffensive Tinctures for Hair, which became L'Oréal. The guiding principles of the company were research and innovation in the field of beauty. In 1920, L'Oréal employed three chemists. By 1950, the research teams were 100 strong; that number reached 1,000 by 1984 and is nearly 2,000 today.

L'Oréal got its start in the hair-color business, but the company soon branched out into other cleansing and beauty products. L'Oréal currently markets more than 500 brands and many thousands of individual products in all sectors of the beauty business: hair color, permanents, hair styling, body and skin care, cleansers, makeup and fragrances. The company's products are found in a wide variety of distribution channels, from hair salons and perfumeries to hyper- and supermarkets, health/beauty outlets, pharmacies, and direct mail.

L'Oréal today has five worldwide research and development centers located in: (1) Aulnay, France, (2) Chevilly, France, (3) Clark, New Jersey, (4) Kawasaki, Japan, and (5) Shanghai, China. A future facility in the USA will be in Berkeley Heights, New Jersey.

L'Oréal has recently faced discrimination lawsuits in France related to the hiring of various spokespersons and institutional racism. In the United Kingdom, L'Oréal has faced widespread condemnation from the Office of Communications regarding truth in their advertising and marketing campaigns concerning the product performance of one of their mascara brands.

Protest group Naturewatch states that L'Oréal continues to test new ingredients on animals. L'Oréal has the largest factory in the Jababeka Industrial Park, Cikarang, Indonesia. L'Oréal does significant business in Indonesia.

Financially, L'Oréal is strong and is excelling globally in developing, producing, and marketing cosmetics, fragrances, and personal care products. For Q1 of 2013, L'Oréal reported sales of 5.93 billion euros, up 6.5 percent overall, including 8.5 percent up in North America and 11.8 percent up in Africa and the Middle East.

Internal Issues

Vision and Mission

L'Oréal does not have a vision statement, but the company's mission statement is provided on the corporate website, as follows:

> Beauty for all—For more than a century, L'Oréal has devoted itself solely to one business: beauty. It is a business rich in meaning, as it enables all individuals to express their personalities, gain self-confidence and open up to others.
>
> Beauty is a language—L'Oréal has set itself the mission of offering all women and men worldwide the best of cosmetics innovation in terms of quality, efficacy and safety. It pursues this goal by meeting the infinite diversity of beauty needs and desires all over the world.
>
> Beauty is universal. Since its creation by a researcher, the group has been pushing back the frontiers of knowledge. Its unique Research arm enables it to continually explore new territories and invent the products of the future, while drawing inspiration from beauty rituals the world over.
>
> Beauty is a science. Providing access to products that enhance well-being, mobilizing its innovative strength to preserve the beauty of the planet and supporting local communities. These are exacting challenges, which are a source of inspiration and creativity for L'Oréal.
>
> Beauty is a commitment. By drawing on the diversity of its teams, and the richness and the complementarity of its brand portfolio, L'Oréal has made the universalisation of beauty its project for the years to come.
>
> L'Oréal, offering beauty for all.

Sustainability

Regarding sustainable development, Corporate Knights, a Global Responsible Investment Network, has selected L'Oréal for its 2012 ranking of the Global 100 Most Sustainable Corporations in the World. L'Oréal has received this distinction for the fifth consecutive year. L'Oréal has more than 84 percent of its production globally being manufactured in compliance with the ISO 9001 (quality), ISO 14001 (environment), OHSAS 18001 (safety) certifications.

In San Luis Potosi, Mexico, L'Oréal opened the largest hair color production plant in the world in 2012, the firm's second plant in Mexico. L'Oréal views Mexico as the gateway between both North and South America. The new plant is in the process of becoming LEED certified and features advanced technologies for water treatment and solar-powered equipment. L'Oréal Mexico has reduced water consumption per unit by 60 percent and carbon dioxide emissions per unit by 60 percent in recent years.

On November 12, 2012, for its 10th anniversary, Vigeo European rating agency revealed a new range of environmental-social-governance (ESG) indices measuring companies' corporate and social responsibility on a global or European level, and more specifically in France and the United Kingdom. Vigeo's France index ranks L'Oréal as "the leading company in social responsibility" among 20 companies. The France index is based on 35 criteria, consolidated in an overall score covering six areas of social responsibility: human rights, human resources, environment, business behavior, corporate governance, and community involvement. L'Oréal ranks fourth in Vigeo's Europe index (120 companies) and fifth in Vigeo's World index (120 companies).

Organizational Structure

L'Oréal's organizational chart is provided in Exhibit 1. Note there is no chief operations officer (COO), but perhaps Jean-Philippe Blanpain serves that role. Note the divisional-by-geographic-region structure in conjunction with divisional-by-product. This could prove problematic in the sense that, for example, professional products operations in the Africa, Middle East Zone could report to either Geoff Skinsley or An Verbulst-Santos.

Advertising

L'Oréal's famous advertising slogan was "Because I'm worth it." In the mid-2000s, this slogan was replaced by "Because you're worth it." In late 2009, the slogan was changed again to "Because we're worth it." The shift to "we" was made to create stronger consumer involvement in L'Oréal philosophy and lifestyle and provide more consumer satisfaction with L'Oréal products. L'Oréal owns a Hair and Body products line for kids called L'Oréal Kids, the slogan for which is "Because we're worth it too."

Segments

L'Oréal has five product groupings:

1. L'Oréal LUXE (Luxury): Lancome, Giorgio Armani, YSL Beaute, Biotherm, Kiehl's, Ralph Lauren, Shu Uemura, Cacharel, Helena Rubinstein, Diesel, Viktod&Rolf, Stella McCartney, and Maison Martin Margiela. As indicated in Exhibit 2, L'Oréal Luxe sales grew in the first quarter of 2013 by 8.1 percent, largely as a result of the acquisition of *Clarisonic*. In a market that has slowed slightly, L'Oréal Luxe is continuing to increase market share worldwide.

EXHIBIT 1 L'Oréal's Organizational Structure

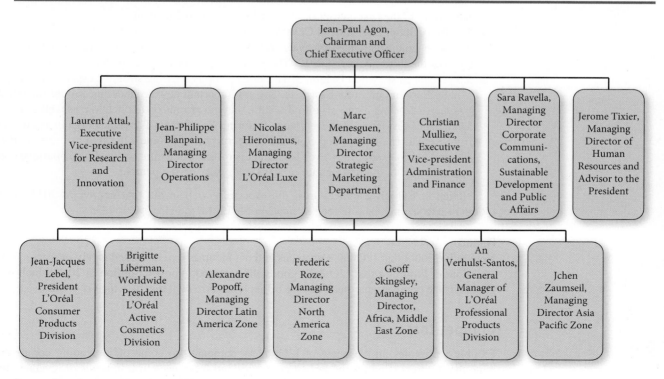

Source: Based on company documents.

EXHIBIT 2 L'Oréal's Sales by Operational Division and Geographic Zone (000,000 euros omitted)

By division	Q1 2012	Q1 2013	% Change
Professional Products	755.6	752.6	−0.4%
Consumer Products	2,769.5	2,920.8	5.5%
L'Oréal Luxe	1,315.5	1,422.0	8.1%
Active Cosmetics	468.6	497.6	6.2%
Cosmetics total	**5,309.1**	**5,593.0**	**5.3%**
BY GEOGRAPHIC ZONE			
Western Europe	1,953.9	1,990.4	1.9%
North America	1,263.4	1,371.4	8.5%
New Markets, of which:	2,091.7	2,231.1	6.7%
- Asia, Pacific	*1,124.3*	*1,188.4*	*5.7%*
- Latin America	*433.5*	*458.7*	*5.8%*
- Eastern Europe	*360.0*	*389.7*	*8.2%*
- Africa, Middle East	*173.8*	*194.3*	*11.8%*
Cosmetics total	**5,309.1**	**5,593.0**	**5.3%**
The Body Shop	180.4	181.9	0.8%
Dermatology	153.5	156.7	2.1%
Group total	**5,643.0**	**5,931.6**	**5.1%**

Source: Company documents.

2. Consumer Products: L'Oréal Paris, Garnier, Maybelline New York, Le Club Des Createurs, and Essie. In the first quarter of 2013, sales were up 5.5 percent.
3. Professional Products: L'Oréal Professionnel, INOA, Serie Expert, Serie Nature, L'Oréal Prefessionnel Homme, Tecni.art, Play ball, and Texture Expert. In quarter one of 2013, sales were down 0.4 percent.
4. Active Cosmetics: Vichy, La Roche Posay, Skinceuticals, Inmeov, Roger&Gallet, and Sanoflore. In the first quarter of 2013, sales were up 6.2 percent.
5. The Body Shop: Dermablend Coverage Cosmetics are sensitivity tested, non-comedogenic, non-acnegenic, fragrance free, water-resistant, smudge-resistant, long lasting and easy to use. For the third quarter of 2012, The Body Shop recorded like-for-like sales growth at 5.3 percent as shown in Exhibit 3. The Body Shop is growing strongly, especially in the Middle East and in South East Asia. Several important new product innovations include *BB Cream All-in-One*, a one-of-a-kind texture that transforms on application, as well as *Pore Minimiser* in its iconic *Tea Tree* range featuring Community Fair Trade organic tea tree oil from Kenya. The Body Shop continues to recruit new customers through its e-commerce channel, with 20 sites now live. The brand is rolling out its innovative Pulse boutique concept globally. In the first quarter of 2013 sales were up 0.8 percent.

Notice in Exhibit 2 that L'Oréal did especially well in the first quarter of 2013 in their L'Oréal Luxe segment and in their Africa/Middle East region.

Finance

Note in Exhibit 3 that L'Oréal's revenues and net income have increased nicely in recent years.

Note in Exhibit 4 that L'Oréal's goodwill increased almost €5 billion in 2011 which is not good, but the company has been paying off its long-term debt nicely, which is good.

Competitors

Exhibit 5 provides an overview of L'Oréal as compared to some of its leading competitors. Note that L'Oréal is by far the largest cosmetics and fragrances firm in terms of revenue, number of employees, and net income. L'Oréal also has the highest profit margin and revenue per

EXHIBIT 3 L'Oréal's Income Statement (000,000 euros omitted)

	2012	2011	2010	2009
Revenue	22,462.7	20,343.1	19,495.8	17,472.6
Other Revenue, Total	0.0	0.0	0.0	0.0
Total Revenue	**22,462.7**	**20,343.1**	**19,495.8**	**17,472.6**
Cost of Revenue, Total	6,587.7	5,851.5	5,696.5	5,161.6
Gross Profit	**15,875.0**	**14,491.6**	**13,799.3**	**12,311.0**
Selling, General, Administrative Expenses, Total	11,387.2	10,478.5	10,077.7	9,124.2
Research and Development	790.5	720.5	664.7	609.2
Depreciation and Amortization	0.0	0.0	0.0	0.0
Interest Expense (Income), Net Operating	0.0	0.0	0.0	0.0
Unusual Expense (Income)	93.7	108.1	74.0	277.6
Other Operating Expenses, Total	30.1	−11.8	79.2	0.0
Operating Income	**3,753**	**3,196.3**	**2,903.7**	**2,300.0**
Interest Income (Expense), Net Nonoperating	0.0	0.0	0.0	0.0
Gain (Loss) on Sale of Assets	0.0	0.0	0.0	0.0
Other, Net	−7.8	−5.6	−9.0	−13.1
Income Before Tax	**3,875.9**	**3,466.7**	**3,151.9**	**2,471.0**
Income Tax, Total	1,005.5	1,025.8	909.9	676.1
Income After Tax	**2,870.4**	**2,440.9**	**2,242.0**	**1,794.9**
Minority Interest	−2.7	−2.5	−2.3	−2.7
Equity In Affiliates	0.0	0.0	0.0	0.0
U.S. GAAP Adjustment	0.0	0.0	0.0	0.0
Net Income Before Extraordinary Items	**2,867.7**	**2,438.4**	**2,239.7**	**1,792.2**
Total Extraordinary Items	0.0	0.0	0.0	0.0
Net Income	**2,867.7**	**2,438.4**	**2,239.7**	**1,792.2**

GAAP, generally accepted accounting principles.
Source: Based on company documents.

employee. But every day is another day, and all of these rivals strive to overtake L'Oréal anywhere and everywhere they can.

Estée Lauder Companies, Inc.

Headquartered in New York City, Estée Lauder has annual sales of about $10 billion and net income of about $1 billion. Estée Lauder manufactures and markets skin care, makeup, fragrance, and hair care products. The company's products are sold in more than 150 countries and territories under a number of brand names, including Estee Lauder, Aramis, Clinique, Origins, M.A.C, Bobbi Brown, La Mer, and Aveda. The company is also the global licensee for fragrances or cosmetics sold under brand names, such as Tommy Hilfiger, Donna Karan, Michael Kors, Tom Ford, and Coach. The company sells its products in more than 30,000 points of sale, consisting of upscale department stores, specialty retailers, upscale perfumeries and pharmacies, and prestige salons and spas.

Avon

Headquartered in New York City, Avon Products is the world's largest direct-seller firm, and by far the largest direct seller of cosmetics and beauty-related items. Avon is the fifth-largest cosmetics and fragrance firm in the world. The company receives sales from catalogs and a website, but the vast majority of its sales come from its 6.4 million independent sales representatives in some 110 countries. Since 1892, Avon has been on the forefront of empowering women to be their own boss and be independent and become leaders in communities and business.

Avon products include cosmetics, fragrances, toiletries, jewelry, apparel, home furnishings, watches, footwear, children's products, skin care, and gift and decorative products, nutritional

EXHIBIT 4 L'Oréal's Balance Sheets (000,000 euros omitted)

	2012	2011	2010	2009
Assets				
Cash and Short-Term Investments	1,823.2	1,652.2	1,550.4	1,173.1
Total Receivables, Net	3,682.8	3,423.3	3,100.7	2,826.8
Total Inventory	2,033.8	2,052.0	1,810.1	1,476.7
Prepaid Expenses	234.3	231.3	208.9	168.1
Other Current Assets, Total	435.5	363.6	326.2	296.4
Total Current Assets	**8,209.6**	**7,722.4**	**6,996.3**	**5,941.1**
Property, Plant, and Equipment, Total (Net)	2,962.9	2,880.8	2,677.5	2,599.0
Goodwill, Net	6,478.2	6,204.6	5,729.6	5,466.0
Intangibles, Net	2,625.4	2,477.3	2,177.4	2,042.4
Long-Term Investments	8,445.3	6,901.0	5,837.5	6,672.2
Note Receivable, Long Term	86.0	0.0	0.0	0.0
Other Long-Term Assets, Total	717.8	671.5	626.2	570.8
Other Assets, Total	0.0	0.0	0.0	0.0
Total Assets	**29,525.2**	**26,857.6**	**24,044.5**	**23,291.5**
Liabilities and Shareholders' Equity				
Accounts Payable	3,318.0	3,247.7	3,153.5	2,603.1
Payable/Accrued	0.0	0.0	0.0	0.0
Accrued Expenses	0.0	1,039.0	986.8	918.2
Notes Payable and Short-Term Debt	20.8	806.0	119.0	151.5
Current Portability of Long-Term Debt and Capital Leases	180.3	284.8	648.0	238.2
Other Current Liabilities, Total	2,850.4	1,752.4	1,674.8	1,475.5
Total Current Liabilities	**6,369.5**	**7,129.9**	**6,582.1**	**5,386.5**
Total Long-Term Debt	46.9	57.5	824.3	2,741.6
Deferred Income Tax	764.4	677.7	462.0	418.0
Minority Interest	4.8	3.1	2.9	3.1
Other Liabilities, Total	1,407.9	1,355.0	1,310.3	1,147.1
Total Liabilities	**8,593.5**	**9,223.2**	**9,181.6**	**9,696.3**
Redeemable Preferred Stock	0.0	0.0	0.0	0.0
Preferred Stock, Nonredeemable, Net	0.0	0.0	0.0	0.0
Common Stock	121.8	120.6	120.2	119.8
Additional Paid-In Capital	1,679.0	1,271.4	1,148.3	996.5
Retained Earnings (Accumulated Deficit)	20,035.3	16,886.8	14,445.3	13,550.5
Treasury Stock, Common	−904.5	−644.4	−850.9	−1,071.6
ESOP Debt Guarantee	0.0	0.0	0.0	0.0
Unrealized Gain (Loss)	0.0	0.0	0.0	0.0
Other Equity, Total	0.0	0.0	0.0	0.0
Total Equity	**20,931.6**	**17,634.4**	**14,862.9**	**13,595.2**
Total Liabilities and Shareholders' Equity	**29,525.1**	**26,857.6**	**24,044.5**	**23,291.5**
Total Common Shares Outstanding	598.36	594.39	589.66	584.74
Total Preferred Shares Outstanding	0.0	0.0	0.0	0.0

ESOP, employee stock option plan.
Source: Based on company documents.

products, housewares, and entertainment and leisure products. Avon owns and sells Silpada jewelry. A few well-recognized company brand names include Avon Color, ANEW, Skin-So-Soft, Advance Techniques, Avon Naturals, and *mark*. Although a large U.S. iconic corporation, Avon is today struggling to recover from poor management strategies that led to CEO Jung resigning amid global bribery investigations. The direct-selling business model has waned in the USA, but

EXHIBIT 5 **L'Oréal versus Rival Firms (in U.S. dollars)**

	L'Oréal	Revlon	Avon	Estée Lauder
Number employees	72.6K	5.2K	40.6K	38.5K
Revenue ($)	27.7B	1.4B	10.7B	9.8B
Net income ($)	3.36B	40.6M	115.5M	877M
Profit Margin (%)	12.1	2.9	1.1	8.9
Revenue per employee	406K	269K	263K	255K
EPS	1.12	0.78	0.27	2.22
Market capitalization	83.3B	775.9M	6.35B	23.2B

EPS, earnings per share.
Source: Based on company documents.

it is effective in many emerging economies globally. Millions of motivated direct sellers in many countries are Avon's key competitive advantage going forward, but the company needs a clear strategic plan.

Mary Kay, Inc.

Headquartered in Addison, Texas, (outside Dallas) Mary Kay is a privately-owned cosmetic and fragrance direct-selling company. Mary Kay is the sixth-largest direct-selling company in the world, with annual sales of about $3.0 billion. Mary Kay's business model is similar to the Avon business model. Founded by Mary Kay Ash in 1963, the company is famous for the pink Cadillacs, given to high-selling representatives. Richard Rogers, Mary Kay's son, is the chairman of the board. Mary Kay products are sold in more than 35 markets worldwide, and the global Mary Kay independent sales force exceeds 2.4 million women.

In 1968, Mary Kay Ash purchased the first pink Cadillac and had it repainted to match the Mountain Laurel Blush in the Mary Kay compact. Since the Cadillac program's inception, more than 100,000 independent sales force members have qualified for the use of a Career Car or elected the cash compensation option. GM estimates that it has built 100,000 pink Cadillacs for Mary Kay. For 2012, high-sellers may select other Career Cars, including the Chevrolet Malibu, Chevrolet Equinox, Toyota Camry, and the Cadillac CTS, SRX & Escalade Hybrid, or most recently, a black Ford Mustang.

Revlon, Inc.

Headquartered in New York City, Revlon is a cosmetics leader with brands such as Almay and Revlon ColorSilk hair color, Mitchum antiperspirants and deodorants, Charlie and Jean Naté fragrances, and Ultima II and Gatineau skincare products. Revlon's beauty aids are distributed in more than 100 countries, though the USA is its largest market, generating about 55 percent of sales. Walmart is Revlon's biggest single customer, accounting for some 22 percent of sales.

Revlon manufactures, markets, and sells cosmetics, women's hair color, beauty tools, antiperspirant deodorants, fragrances, skincare, and other beauty care products. Revlon products are sold and marketed under brand names, such as Revlon, including the Revlon ColorStay, Revlon Super Lustrous, and Revlon Age Defying franchises; Almay, including the Almay Intense i-Color and Almay Smart Shade franchises; Sinful Colors in cosmetics; Revlon ColorSilk in women's hair color; Revlon in beauty tools; Mitchum in antiperspirant deodorants; Charlie and Jean Nate in fragrances, and Ultima II and Gatineau. Revlon also owns certain assets of Sinful Colors cosmetics, Wild and Crazy cosmetics, freshMinerals cosmetics, and freshcover cosmetics.

Coty, Inc.

Headquartered in New York City, Coty is one of the world's leading makers of beauty products for men and women. Led by CEO Michele Scannavini, Coty is a $4.1 billion beauty company, and the biggest seller of nail care, nail polish, and fragrances in the USA. Sarah Jessica Parker, Jennifer Lopez, Celine Dion, Gwen Stefani, Katy Perry, and Thomas Dutronc are several celebrities that promote Coty. Founder of the company, François Coty created his first perfume, La Rose Jacqueminot, in 1904.

Coty's product lineup today ranges from moderately-priced scents sold globally by mass retailers to prestige fragrances and nail polishes found in department stores. Coty's brands include Adidas, Philosophy, Rimmel, and Sally Hansen. Cody's prestige perfume labels are led by Calvin Klein. Coty's shimmery blue nail polish and Lady Gaga's perfume are high-selling products. Thomas Dutronc is the face of Coty's new Cerruti fragrance for men, which launched in 2013.

Coty's Rimmel Scandaleyes mascara, which debuted in early 2012, is another big seller. Over-the-top lashes are hot these days because false eye lashes have made a comeback and are "almost mainstream." Promotional material for Scandaleyes urges women to "ditch those fals-ies." Mascara makers today compete with eyelash lengthening drugs such as Latisse.

The Future

On November 14, 2012, in the Kingdom of Saudi Arabia, L'Oréal created L'Oréal KSA, a new subsidiary based on a joint venture with Al Naghi Group. L'Oréal brands have been distributed in the Kingdom of Saudi Arabia for two decades and since 2000, Al Naghi Group has been the company's sole distributor for its Consumer Products, Active Cosmetics, and Professional Products Divisions. However, L'Oréal KSA will manage a portfolio of brands including, among others, L'Oréal Professional, Kerastase, L'Oréal Paris, Garnier, Maybelline New York, and Vichy. L'Oréal KSA's will enable the company to better understand and to meet needs of woman in one of the most male-dominated countries in the world. There are other countries globally, especially in Africa and South America, that L'Oréal could engage in a similar manner. Brazil, for example, is where Avon derives most of its revenue, more even that from the USA.

There are numerous firms that could be acquired by L'Oréal to further expand and penetrate globally. Even a firm such as Avon that is struggling financially, but has a business model that is especially suited to emerging economies, may be interested in an offer from L'Oréal. Another firm could be Coty, Inc. that could fit well with the L'Oréal portfolio. And then there are cosmetic and fragrance divisions of large firms such as Procter & Gamble that could be available if L'Oréal deemed that to be attractive.

L'Oréal needs a clear strategic plan for the future. Perhaps the firm could vastly improve its selling operations online. Being the biggest and the best at year-end 2012 does not guarantee prosperity in the years to come.

Develop an effective three-year strategic plan for L'Oréal.

Nikon Corporation, 2013

www.nikon.com, NINOY

Headquartered in Tokyo, Japan, Nikon is known worldwide for its digital and film cameras, binoculars, microscopes, and ophthalmic lenses. Nikon's major competitor is Canon, also headquartered in Tokyo. In January 2013, Nikon introduced two new cameras, the COOLPIX S9500, a multifunctional, high-power zoom model offering 22× optical zoom and equipped with wi-fi connectivity and GPS functions, and the COOLPIX S9400, a high-performance model equipped with an 18× optical zoom lens. Nikon Vision Co., Ltd. recently released the new ACULON A211 binoculars, designed for a wide range of outdoor activities, such as bird watching, nature observation, boating, and hiking. The compact digital camera market globally is shrinking and prices are falling with the proliferation of smartphones with built-in cameras. This is a major problem for Nikon going forward, as is the shrinking global market for their liquid crystal display (LCD) steppers and scanners. Nikon's fiscal year ends on March 31.

The top three digital camera producers, Canon, Nikon, and Sony, are facing potential disaster because excellent technology in smartphones today allows people to take high quality pictures without buying a high quality camera. According to International Data Corp. (IDC), in the first five months of 2013, global shipments of compact digital cameras declined 43 percent. Canon is trying to maintain its 23 percent share of the global camera market, followed by Nikon with a 21 percent and Sony with 15 percent. IDC reports that the global digital camera market peaked in 2010 and will likely endure a 30 percent drop in revenue in 2013 alone. For Nikon, digital cameras are part of its imaging products segment, a segment that generates 91.8 percent of revenues. In contrast, Canon's imaging systems segment, which includes sales of digital cameras, accounts for 39.4 percent of the company's sales.

Copyright by Fred David Books LLC. (Written by Forest R. David)

History

The company that became Nikon was founded in 1917 as part of the huge Mitsubishi *keiretsu*, a group of businesses linked by cross-ownership. Originally the company name was Nippon Kogaku, but the name changed to Nikon in 1988. During World War II, the company grew to 19 factories and 23,000 employees, supplying binoculars, lenses, bomber sights, and submarine periscopes to the Japanese military. After the war, Nippon Kogaku reverted to producing civilian products in a single factory. In 1948, the first Nikon-branded camera, the Nikon I, was released. Nikon lenses became popular during the Korean War because U.S. photojournalist, David Duncan, popularized them. Nikon also designs and manufactures precision equipment for use in semiconductor and LCD fabrication, inspection, and measurement.

Over its long history, Nikon has developed and sold millions of photographic lenses under the Nikkor name, including projection lenses for LCD's and scanners, as well as lenses for both film and digital cameras. The Nikkor history began in 1933 with shipments of Aero-Nikkor lenses for aerial photography.

Nikon Middle East FZE started operations in Dubai, United Arab Emirates (UAE) in 2012, and in Brazil and Thailand the year before. In January 2013, to tell the story of the company, Nikon released its second movie, *The Day*, telling about the Nikon brand (http://nikonimaging.tumblr.com). That movie followed *Tears*, released by Nikon in late 2012, to personify the ultimate human emotion (tears). *The Day* reveals the fun of manipulating light with Nikon digital cameras and Nikkor lenses, using various scenes such as the morning sun, a vibrant flower, and the natural smile of a child.

Internal Issues

Vision and Mission

Nikon's vision statement is: "Our Aspirations—Meeting needs. Exceeding expectations."

Nikon's mission statement is: "Trustworthiness & Creativity."

Organizational Structure

There are no females among Nikon's top executive team. Note in Exhibit 1 that Nobuyoshi Gokyu is in essence the chief operations officer (COO) of the company, although his official title does not include that designation. Nikon operates from a strategic business unit (SBU) organizational structure by product because many subsidiaries and divisions report to the three unit executives (Ushida, Masai, and Okamoto).

Segments

Nikon operates in four business segments: (1) Precision Equipment, (2) Imaging, (3) Instruments, and (4) Other. Nikon has 86 subsidiaries and 11 associated companies that report under these four segments. Exhibit 2 reveals the various products offered with each Nikon segment. Note that digital and film cameras dominate its Imaging division, whereas microscopes dominate its Instruments division. The Imaging segment is nearly four times larger than the other segments combined, so Nikon is primary a camera company.

Note in Exhibit 3 that Nikon's sales in fiscal 2013 increased 10.0 percent to 1.01 trillion yen, but the company's precision equipment sales decreased 28 percent, Instruments decreased 3.5 percent, and Other decreased 3.7 percent. These declines were offset by the company's 29 percent in Imaging Products sales to 751 billion yen.

Strategy

As cameras in smartphones become increasingly effective, Nikon's compact camera business is a low-to-no-growth proposition, so Nikon is trying to diversify into other, more profitable areas. But this process at Nikon has perhaps been too little too late, and some analysts are concerned

EXHIBIT 1 Nikon's Organizational Chart

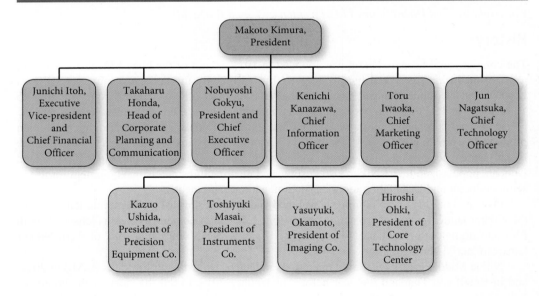

EXHIBIT 2 Nikon Products by Segment

Precision Equipment: Steppers and scanners for LCDs
Imaging: Digital and film cameras, lenses, speed lights, film scanners, software, and sport optics
Instruments: Biological, industrial, and stereoscopic microscopes, measuring instruments, semiconductor inspection equipment, and surveying instruments
Other: Ophthalmic lenses, glass, and encoders

Source: Based on company documents.

EXHIBIT 3 Nikon's Segment Sales (in millions of yen)

Fiscal Year-Ended (March 31)	2011	2012	2013
Net Sales	887,512	918,651	1,010,493
Net Sales by Industry Segment			
Precision Equipment	208,613	248,145	179,013
Imaging Products	596,375	587,127	751,240
Instruments	57,451	56,000	53,877
Other	25,071	27,379	26,363
Net Sales in Japan and Export Sales by Region[1]			
Japan	127,162	130,517	144,417
Overseas	760,350	788,134	866,075
USA	237,611	221,768	271,459
Europe	202,854	225,739	260,038
China	96,956	126,302	118,162
Other Areas	222,927	214,325	216,416
North America	—	—	—
Asia & Oceania[2]	—	—	—

[1] From the year ended March 2011, "North America" and "Asia" area has been changed to "Other Areas".
[2] From the year ended March 2008 to the year ended March 2010, "Asia" area had been changed to "Asia & Oceania" area.

Source: Based on company documents.

that Nikon may eventually go the way of Eastman Kodak. But Nikon has great name recognition, which the firm could parlay into other endeavors, such as perhaps "smartphones with wonderful cameras," but Nikon has not indicated interest in that business. Rivals Canon and Sony have diversified into numerous related products, so their camera business contributes only a small part of overall revenue. Nikon definitely needs a clear strategic plan going forward; the firm at present is stable.

Ethics

Nikon's website reveals that the company is quite giving. For example, Nikon gave money and support for the victims of Hurricane Sandy in the U.S. Northeast and similarly to victims of Typhoon Bopha in the Philippines. Many such activities are described at the corporate website. Nikon also has an effective Environmental Management System (EMS) and Policy and works hard to be a good steward of the natural environment, as elaborated on at the company website.

Finance

As indicated in Exhibit 4, Nikon's revenues increased 10.0 percent in fiscal 2013, but net income decreased 28.5 percent. The balance sheet in Exhibit 5 reveals a continued drop in the company's goodwill in 2013.

Competitors

Nikon's competitors include Canon, Casio, Eastman Kodak, Sony, Pentax, Fujifilm, Olympus, and Netherlands-based ASML Holding. Canon is Nikon's biggest and most worrisome competitor, followed by Sony. Note in Exhibit 6 that Canon is four times larger than Nikon and dramatically more profitable than any company featured in the analysis. Pentax is a brand name used by Pentax Ricoh Imaging Company for cameras and binoculars that compete with Nikon products. In late October 2011, Ricoh renamed the subsidiary Pentax Ricoh Imaging Company, Ltd.

EXHIBIT 4 Nikon's Income Statement (in millions of yen)

Fiscal Year-Ended (March 31)	2011	2012	2013
Net sales	**887,512**	**918,651**	**1,010,493**
Cost of sales	575,535	567,000	663,509
Gross profit	311,977	351,651	346,984
Selling, general and administrative expenses	257,924	271,570	295,982
Operating income	**54,052**	**80,080**	**51,001**
Non-operating income	9,860	11,917	7,849
Non-operating expenses	8,101	2,614	10,506
Other non-operating expenses	21,729	16,107	20,260
Ordinary income (loss)	**55,811**	**89,383**	**48,344**
Extraordinary gains	121	16,144	14,299
Gain on sales of property, plant and equipment	91	159	302
Gain on sales of investment securities	30	65	5,132
Extraordinary losses	9,427	19,360	788
Loss on disposals of property, plant and equipment	1,000	250	—
Loss on sales of property, plant and equipment	47	4	57
Non-recurring depreciation on noncurrent assets	—	—	—
Impairment losses	397	6,502	663
Loss on sales of investment securities	82	96	31
Losses on devaluation of investment securities	4,512	0	35
Loss on restructuring of business	—	—	—
Environmental expenses	—	—	—
Effect of application in accounting standard for asset retirement obligations	1,073	—	—
Loss on disaster	2,313	12,505	—
Income (loss) before income taxes	46,505	86,168	61,856
Current	13,096	26,627	12,081
Deferred	6,097	235	7,316
Income taxes	19,193	26,862	19,397
Income (loss) before minority interests	**27,312**	**59,305**	**42,459**
Net income (loss)	**27,312**	**59,305**	**42,459**

Source: Company documents.

EXHIBIT 5 Nikon's Balance Sheet (in millions of yen)

Fiscal Year-Ended (March 31)	2011	2012	2013
Assets			
Current assets			
Cash and time deposits	181,077	132,404	110,281
Notes and accounts receivable-trade	123,077	137,533	134,225
Inventories	236,407	263,033	269,411
Deferred tax assets	42,640	47,110	43,959
Other current assets	15,118	34,061	21,563
Allowance for doubtful receivables	(7,365)	(4,667)	(3,795)
Total current assets	**590,954**	**609,474**	**575,647**
Fixed assets			
Tangible fixed assets			
Buildings and structures	43,362	37,807	45,774
Machinery, equipment and vehicles	34,003	35,200	57,551
Land	14,777	14,609	15,025
Lease Assets, net	5,794	4,901	3,878
Construction in progress	7,566	23,809	15,935
Other	13,511	14,615	23,439

EXHIBIT 5 Continued

Total tangible fixed assets	**119,016**	**130,943**	161,605
Intangible fixed assets			
Software	26,237	27,927	27,826
Goodwil	13,235	5,157	4,443
Total intangible fixed assets	39,473	33,085	32,270
Investments and other assets			
Investment securities	56,303	55,355	66,859
Deferred tax assets	17,604	13,293	7,317
Other	6,817	18,284	21,551
Allowance for doubtful receivables	(260)	(207)	(231)
Total investments and other assets	80,465	86,727	95,496
Total fixed assets	238,954	250,755	289,371
Total assets	**829,909**	**860,230**	**865,019**
Liabilities and Net Assets			
Liabilities			
Current liabilities			
Notes and accounts payable-trade	171,735	155,338	124,676
Short-term borrowings	16,732	18,350	18,739
Commercial paper	—	—	—
Current portion of bonds	—	—	—
Lease obligations	2,422	2,163	1,703
Accrued expenses	54,545	54,751	54,505
Accrued income taxes	2,520	15,076	1,395
Advances received	63,626	54,214	50,799
Warranty reserve	7,296	7,594	8,096
Other current liabilities	23,415	34,519	39,270
Total current liabilities	**342,295**	**342,009**	**299,186**
Long-term liabilities			
Bonds	40,000	40,000	40,000
Long-term debt	24,700	22,900	22,600
Lease obligations	3,620	2,953	2,305
Liability for employees' retirement benefits	14,951	3,700	2,876
Retirement allowances for directors and corporate auditors	606	—	—
Asset retirement obligations	2,324	2,365	2,512
Other long-term liabilities	12,191	12,684	4,214
Total long-term liabilities	98,393	84,604	74,508
Total liabilities	**440,069**	**426,613**	**373,695**
Net assets			
Shareholders' equity			
Common stock	65,475	65,475	65,475
Capital surplus	80,711	80,711	80,711
Retained earnings	272,227	319,823	345,692
Treasury stock	(13,173)	(12,992)	(12,804)
Total Shareholders' equity	405,241	453,017	479,076
Valuation and translation adjustments			
Unrealized gains on available-for-sale securities	4,450	3,061	9,482
Deferred gains or losses on hedges	(696)	(1,592)	(216)
Foreign currency translation adjustments	(20,201)	(21,474)	2,187
Total Valuation and translation adjustments	(16,448)	(20,005)	11,452
Share subscription rights	427	604	795
Total net assets	389,220	433,616	491,324
Total liabilities and net assets	**829,909**	**860,230**	**865,019**

Source: Based on company documents.

EXHIBIT 6 A Financial Comparison of Nikon vs. Rival Firms (in yen)

	Nikon	Canon	Sony
Sales	1 T	3.5 T	6.8 T
Net Income	42 B	225 B	43 B
Profit Margin	4.2 %	6.5%	0.6%
Number of Employees	24 K	201 K	163 K
Debt-to-Equity Ratio	0.18	0.01	0.68
Market Capitalization	733 B	4.1 T	1.7 T
EPS	105	173	43

EPS, earnings per share.
Source: Based on information at a variety of sources on February 10, 2013.

Canon, Inc.

Headquartered within a few miles of Nikon in Tokyo, Japan, Canon makes cameras, LCD projectors, lenses, LCDs, and binoculars—competing against Nikon on all these products. But Canon has diversified and also manufactures printers, multifunction document equipment, and other computer peripherals for home and office use. Canon generates only 20 percent of its revenues in Japan. Canon manufactures digital single-lens reflex cameras, compact digital cameras, interchangeable lens, digital video cameras, ink-jet multifunction devices, single-function ink-jet printers, image scanners, television lens for broadcasting use, office network, color network and personal multifunction devices, office, color and personal copy machines, laser printers, large-sized ink-jet printers and digital production printers, exposure equipment used in semiconductor and LCDs, medical image recording equipment, ophthalmic instruments, magnetic heads, micro motors, computers, handy terminals, and document scanners.

In early 2013, Canon released three stylish, feature-packed PowerShot Digital Cameras: the PowerShot ELPH 330 HS, ELPH 115 IS, and A2500. These new models offer great photo quality and excellent video performance in compact, powerful point-and-shoot designs while providing advanced wireless connectivity for easy sharing and great performance in dimly lit situations. With about $45.6 billion in global revenue, Canon's U.S. parent company, Canon, Inc., ranked third overall in U.S. patents registered in 2011 and was one of *Fortune* Magazine's World's Most Admired Companies in 2012.

September 30, 2013 Revenue was 913 billion yen ($9.3 billion U.S. Dollars) and June 30, 2013 Revenue was 967 billion yen ($9.8 billion U.S. Dollars) for a 5.6% decline.

Sony Corporation

Headquartered within a few miles of Nikon (and Canon) in Tokyo, Japan, Sony manufactures LCD televisions, cameras, audio and video equipment, personal computers (PCs), personal navigation systems, game consoles and software, audio, videos and monitors for broadcast and commercial use, image sensors and other semiconductors, optical pickups, batteries, data recording media and systems, movie software, and animation works. Sony also has a Finance segment that provides life and nonlife insurance, banking services and credit finance services, and a new Sony Mobile segment provides that mobile phones.

Sony recently sold its U.S. headquarters for $685 million and has benefited lately from the weak Japanese currency, the yen. In fact, for each one-yen slide against the euro helps to boost Sony's annual operating profit by 6 billion yen. Nikon, too, is benefiting from the weak yen because much of its revenue comes from outside Japan. Sony recently lowered its sales forecasts for LCD television sets, Blu-ray disc players, digital cameras, camcorders, personal computers, and portable videogame machines. Smartphones have crept into all of these other consumer electronic domains, especially cameras, to the dismay of Nikon.

For the quarter ending September 2013, net loss of 19.3 billion yen ($195 million U.S. Dollars) (Note is 98.8 yen to 1.0 Dollars on November 4, 2013). Sony's new smartphone, the Xperia Z, became available in Japan in early February 2013, but Samsung's Galaxy and Apple's iPhone dominate the smartphone industry globally. Sony recently dissolved its capital-intensive LCD-panel joint ventures with rivals Samsung and Sharp.

The Future

Even though Nikon benefits from a weak yen, Nikon's Precision Equipment segment is reporting falling revenues as a result of the semiconductor-related and LCD panel-related markets shrinking. In the Imaging Products segment, the compact digital camera market continues to shrink, but the interchangeable lens digital camera market is growing. In Nikon's Instruments segment, the bioscience-related market has worsened as a result of reductions and execution deferments in government budgets in countries such as Japan and the USA, and the industrial instruments-related markets contracting resulting from restrained capital investment in the semiconductor and electronics fields. The company is suffering from the proliferation of cameras in smartphones because consumers increasingly find those cameras sufficient for their everyday needs.

Nikon needs a clear strategic plan for the future. Perhaps the firm needs to make key acquisitions to move into other areas that offer higher growth in revenues. Or perhaps the firm needs to establish cooperative agreements with Samsung, Nokia, or even Apple to offer Nikon's camera quality smartphone cameras. But that strategy could further curtail Nikon's mainstream revenue source from compact digital cameras.

A thorough strategic analysis is needed to determine the best path forward for Nikon.

Grupo Modelo S.A.B, 2013

www.grupomodelo.mx, GPMCF or GMODELOC

Headquartered in Mexico City, Grupo Modelo is the leading beer producer in Mexico, brewing 13 brands in 8 breweries, including Corona Extra, the top-selling Mexican beer in the world. Other brands include Modelo Especial, Victoria, Pacifico, Corona Light, and Negra Modelo. Six brands are exported outside of Mexico, with Corona Extra being sold in more than 180 countries. Negra Modelo is available in 34 nations, Modelo Especial in 23, Pacifico in 12, and Corona Light in 11.

On June 4, 2013, Anheuser-Busch InBev (NYSE: BUD) formally completed its acquisition of Grupo Modelo, S.A.B. de C.V. in a transaction valued at $20.1 billion. AB InBev says Grupo Modelo will continue to operate as an independent entity and thus has mandated that the firm develop a clear strategic plan for the future. Grupo Modelo's headquarters remain in Mexico City and the company continues to have a local board. Carlos Fernandez, Maria Asuncion Aramburuzabala and Valentin Diez Morodo both continue to play an important role on Grupo Modelo's Board of Directors.

AB InBev desires to introduce AB InBev brands through Modelo's distribution network. The combined company leads the global beer industry with roughly 400 million hectoliters of beer volume annually, bringing together five of the top six most valuable beer brands in the world. Mexico is the world's fourth largest profit country for beer. AB InBev desires to own approximately 95 percent of Grupo Modelo's outstanding common shares.

Modelo produces bottled water and operates 960 convenience stores in Mexico under the Extra name. With more than a 60-percent share of the Mexican beer market, Modelo is 50 percent owned by Anheuser-Busch (AB) InBev. Modelo imports of AB InBev products, such as Budweiser, into Mexico and also imports Chinese Tsingtao and the Danish brand Carlsberg. Through an alliance with Nestlé, Modelo distributes several Nestlé water brands in Mexico. Through an alliance with Constellation Brands, Modelo established Crown Imports as a vehicle for Modelo's products to be sold in the USA.

Modelo is vertically integrated with operations ranging from producing the base ingredients needed in beer production all the way to owning convenience stores. The company has more than 37,000 employees and annual revenues in excess of $91 billion Mexican Pesos (U.S. $7.2 billion). Modelo stock trades on the Mexican Stock Exchange under the ticker symbol GMODELOC and also trades in Spain under the ticket XGMD.

Of the six Modelo brands marketed and sold in the USA, volumes are at all-time highs. Modelo's chief executive officer (CEO) attributes much of the gains in the USA to Crown Imports.

Copyrighted by Fred David Books LLC. (Written by Forest R. David)

History

Founded in 1925, Grupo Modelo opened their first brewery in Mexico City, and by 1928, sales of Modelo and Corona brands reached 8 million bottles. In 1930, Negro Modelo was produced with limited exports to the USA starting in 1933. In 1935, the company acquired a rival Mexican company that produced the Victoria and Pilsner brands. In 1954, Modelo acquired the Mexican rival that produced Pacifico and several other brands.

Modelo spent the 1980s building and updating existing breweries and founding companies that supply the base ingredients for beer such as barley and malt. With the new capacity, Grupo Modelo for the first time ever exported beer to Japan, Australia, New Zealand, and several nations in Europe in 1985. The next year, Corona was the second most commonly imported beer in the USA. By 1990, Corona was available in traditional beer nations such as Germany, the Netherlands, and Belgium.

Grupo Modelo was listed for the first time in 1994 on the Mexican Stock Exchange, allowing the company to finance through equity more easily. With the extra capital, Modelo built additional breweries and by 1997, Corona was the number-one imported beer in the USA, a distinction it still holds today. In 2003, construction on a malting facility in Idaho began to help supply the growing firm's need for raw ingredients. One of the larger joint ventures in the company's history took place in 2006 with the agreement between Grupo Modelo and U.S.-based Constellation Brands to form Crown Imports LLC to export Modelo products more efficiently into the USA.

By 2013, AB was trying to purchase the remaining 50 percent of Modelo that it did not own. The U.S. federal government resisted this acquisition over concerns about potential price fixing of Corona versus Budweiser and other factors.

Internal Issues

Vision and Mission

Modelo's vision is "to obtain more than half of our revenue from international markets by 2015, and to consistently strengthen our leadership in the domestic market, while maintaining profitability." Modelo's mission is "to grow as a multinational competitor in the beverage market, inspiring pride, passion and commitment, and generating value for our stakeholders."

Organizational Chart

Neither Modelo's *Annual Report* nor their corporate website reveal the top executives of the firm, except for the CEO and two vice-presidents. No clue is provided at either source regarding whether the firm operates from a divisional-by-product or divisional-by-region structure. Exhibit 1 reveals the chart as best as can be construed.

Marketing

From marketing (in 1966) "the first beer sold in a can," to using catchy slogans such as "how can 20 million Mexicans be wrong," Modelo is always marketing. The company's advertising theme in the USA is to "find your beach" that portrays people enjoying Corona in a relaxing place, whether that be an actual beach, the mountains, or somewhere else. Modelo promotes the principle that the best option for success is to provide the best service in the industry by being a strategic partner with clients. The company's Ruta Modelo program helps facilitate better distribution planning systems and installs subzero refrigerators for all clients. The CEO of Modelo believes that extra cold beer is a key component to a brand's success and wants to ensure restaurants, grocery stores, and other mediums only offer Modelo products as cold as possible.

Borrowing from Coors Light, cans of Modelo Light and Pacifico Light now incorporate ink that changes colors to inform customers when their beer is the ideal temperature. The Ruta Modelo program currently includes 4,500 routes and serves 500,000 clients in Mexico. Through

EXHIBIT 1 Modelo's Organizational Chart

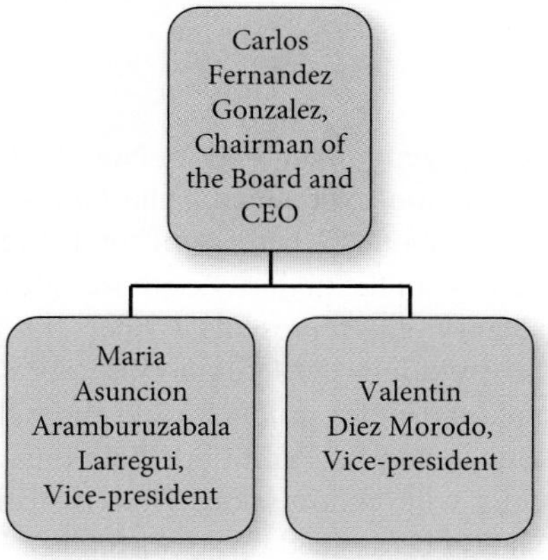

Source: Based on company documents.

the Extra convenience stores, Modelo provides a means of advertising at little additional cost and test markets different beers in different regions of Mexico.

Corona Extra provides the largest incremental volume gain among Modelo's portfolio of beers. Corona Extra is the most popular imported beer in the USA; further, Corona is a popular beer in Mexico City with a metropolitan population of more than 21 million. Advertisements showing the pride of the Mexican people for Corona Extra as a global brand and ads related to LA passion manda, a campaign pertaining to Mexican soccer, have attributed to the success of Corona. In addition to soccer, Modelo promotes its name through projects that finance Mexican youth who have aspirations in boxing and wrestling.

Modelo's Especial brand uses a campaign called *Con dedicacion especial* to reinforce the importance of dedication and quality. U.S. football legend, Joe Montana serves as a Modelo sponsor because U.S. football is extremely popular in Mexico. In addition, Modelo began a campaign for Bud Light in which the logos of the U.S. Major League Baseball teams were added to the cans. Additional sports-related marketing includes a tour by U.S. country music singer Kenny Chesney whereby more than 1 million Corona Extra consumers were reached. Corona Extra has sponsored 12 Association of Tennis Professionals tournaments. Other developments include offering Corona Light in the iconic glass bottle in Mexico and providing Coronita Extra in a can.

In Oceania, Modelo uses the "from where you'd rather be" campaign, and in Australia, where Corona leads the next import beer by a factor of three, Modelo sponsors the Quicksilver Pro world surfing tour year round. Customers in New Zealand have classified Corona Extra as the "most adored" brand, and the launch of Pacifico is expected soon in this market. A "save the beach" marketing strategy was enacted in Spain promoting trash pickup on Spanish beaches, resulting in extensive media coverage for Modelo.

Sustainability

Grupo Modelo maintains their strategy of being a good corporate citizen by exceeding the minimal standards required by the governments where they operate, primarily through their foundation Fundacton Grupo Modelo. One of the notable activities of the foundation is its Juntos en la Conservacion program where for more than 10 years, restoration projects have been enacted and performed at Iztaccihuatl-Popocatepetl national park where Modelo has captured around 1,400 tons of carbon dioxide annually. In addition, there are several other national parks in Mexico where Modelo performs restoration and environmental education programs. Modelo has also teamed up with several other firms to better use waste and by-products from the beer production process. Modelo also engages in and promotes programs geared toward preventing child abuse. For their efforts, Modelo is included in the Mexican Stock Market's Sustainability Index.

Finance

Modelo's income statements are provided in Exhibit 2, followed by the company's balance sheets in Exhibit 3. Note the 10.6-percent increase in beer sales in 2011 and the 14.4 percent increase in net income.

Segments

Exhibit 4 reveals Modelo's sales by geographic region. Note that company revenues increased 9.1 percent, with the domestic division experiencing the largest total peso and percent gain. The domestic division accounts for about 52 percent of total revenues and the export (outside Mexico) segment about 40 percent, with the majority of those sales being derived from the USA. Note that Modelo's "Other" category only represents 7.9 percent of total sales but that segment includes royalties from nations, excluding the USA and Europe, as well as from sales of soft drinks, water, wine, liquor, food, and other products sold through the 960 Extra convenience stores. In addition, sales of Tsingtao and St. Pauli Girl (both a part of Crown Imports) are also included in Other segments along with commissions from distributing Nestlé water products. (The Others segment perhaps should be divided up strategically). Bud Light is the top imported beer in Mexico with O'Doul's leading the alcohol-free category. Carlsberg reported the highest percent growth of any brand in Grupo's portfolio.

EXHIBIT 2 Modelo's Income Statement (in thousands of Mexican pesos)

FOR THE YEARS ENDING
ON DECEMBER 31, 2012 AND 2011
(Amounts in thousands of Mexican pesos)

	2012	2011
Net beer sales	$91,403,937	$84,011,703
Other regular revenue	7,893,525	6.994,277
	99,297,462	**91.005,980**
Cost of sales	46,831,150	43,410,766
Gross profit	**52,466,312**	**47,595,214**
Operating expenses		
Sales and distribution	20.595,001	19,499,251
Administrative	7,054,973	6.464,604
	27,649,974	**25,963,855**
Share of profit of associates	1,025,629	890,000
Other expenses	(736,370)	(494,601)
Operating profit	**25,105,597**	**22,026,758**
Financial income	1,558,952	1,505,297
Financial costs	(592,428)	(560,276)
Foreign exchange rate (loss) gain - Net	(568,464)	786,864
Financial income - Net	**398,060**	**1,731,885**
Profit before taxes to income	25,503,657	23,758,643
Taxes to income	6,588,340	5,473,561
Consolidated net income for the year	**$18,915,317**	**$18,285,082**
OTHER ITEMS OF COMPREHENSIVE INCOME:		
Remeasurement of employee benefits, net of taxes	(773,850)	(155,810)
Cash flow hedge	152,022	(41,648)
Consolidated comprehensive income	**$18,293,489**	**$18,087,624**
Net income attributable to:		
Controlling sharing	$12,343,656	$11,825,699
Non-controlling sharing:		
Anheuser-Busch Companies, Inc.	3,690,122	3,564,536
Other investors	2,881,539	2,894,847
	6,571,661	**6,459,383**
Consolidated net income for the year	**$18,915,317**	**$18,285,082**
Consolidated comprehensive income attributable to:		
Controlling sharing	$11,869,069	$11,674,151
Non-controlling sharing:		
Anheuser-Busch Companies, Inc.	3,542,881	3,518,626
Other investors	2,881,539	2,894,847
Consolidated comprehensive income	**$18,293,489**	**$18,087,624**
Basic and diluted earnings per share (Amounts in Mexican pesos attributable to controlling sharing)	**$3.8147**	**$3.6567**

Source: Company documents

EXHIBIT 3 Modelo's Balance Sheets (in thousands of Mexican pesos)

AS OF DECEMBER 31, 2012 AND 2011 AND JANUARY 1, 2011
(Amounts expressed in thousands of Mexican pesos)

	2012	2011	2010
CURRENT:			
Cash and cash equivalents	$29,118,774	$32,271,175	$23,813,706
Accounts and notes receivable - Net	6,360,662	7,333,382	6,734,595
Taxes to income recoverable	955,238	892,044	1,751,570
Inventories	10,201,658	8,614,389	10,028,272
Derivative financial instruments	24,222	—	—
Prepaid advertising and others	2,397,991	2,677,254	3,038,048
Assets available for sale	595,052	579,749	716,907
Total current assets	**49,653,597**	**52,367,993**	**46,083.098**
NON-CURRENT:			
Long-term accounts and notes receivable	933,846	953,574	1,274,630
Investments in associates	6,800,193	6,155,929	5,695,130
Property, plant and equipment - Net	59,045,264	59,431,154	60,821,611
Prepaid advertising and others	1,186,070	1,807,979	954,796
Intangible assets - Net	7,076,704	7,092.074	6,872,551
Total non-current assets	75,042,077	75,440,710	75,618,718
Total assets	**$124,695,674**	**$127,808,703**	**$121,701,816**
CURRENT:			
Suppliers and other payables	8,024,082	8,490,694	8,210,999
Provisions	130,000	60,000	—
Excise tax on production and services payable	1,693,520	1,619,247	1,554,187
Employee profit sharing	1,185,877	1,153,955	1,083,369
Derivative financial instruments	—	111,419	—
Income taxes payable	—	95,826	55,019
Total current liabilities	**11,033,479**	**11,531,141**	**10,903,574**
NON-CURRENT:			
Deferred taxes	5,305,889	5,975,126	6,464,562
Controlling company liability under tax consolidation	1.129,188	1,157,454	1,313,340
Employee benefits	1,753,806	686,258	473,713
Financial liability due to non-controlling sharing in subsidiaries	475,562	497,703	530,326
Total non-current liabilities	8,669,445	8,316,541	8,781,941
Total liabilities	**$19,702,924**	**$19,847,682**	**$19,685,515**
Capital stock	9,925,397	9,923,819	9,938,119
Premium on share subscription	1,090,698	1,090,698	1,090,698
RETAINED EARNINGS:			
To apply	52,727,384	55,547,525	62,902,339
Current period	12,343,656	11,825,699	—
	65,071,040	67,373,224	62,902,339
Reserves	3,294,637	3,177,961	3,209,925
Total stockholders' equity of controlling sharing	79,381,772	81,565,702	77,141,081
NON-CONTROLLING SHARING:			
Anheuser-Busch Companies, Inc.	23,959,963	24,684,423	23,350,314
Other investors	1,651,015	1.710,896	1,524,906
Total stockholders' equity of non-controlling sharing	25,610,978	26,395,319	24,875,220
Total stockholders' equity	**$104.992.750**	**$107,961,021**	**$102,016,301**
Total liabilities and stockholders' equity	**$124,695,674**	**$127,808,703**	**$121,701,816**

Source: Company documents.

EXHIBIT 4   Modelo's Sales by Geographic Region (in millions of pesos)

Sales Millions of pesos	2012	2011	2010	2012 Change	2011 Change
Domestic	51,628	48,521	43,896	6.5%	10.5%
Export	39,776	35,540	33,929	11.9%	4.7%
Other income	7,894	7,142	7,194	12.99%	−0.7%
Total net sales	**99,298**	**91,203**	**85,019**	**9.1%**	**7.3%**

Source: Company documents.

For the second straight year, Crown Imports in 2012 was the only major distributor (out of four distributors) to post-positive growth in the USA. Considering the decline in beer consumption in the USA, Modelo believes the results are good. Corona Extra and Corona Light were the top two brands in the USA, with Modelo Especial ranked third and being awarded the "Hot Brands" prize by *Impact Magazine* for the brands growth. The Victoria brand continues to grow in popularity in the markets it serves and was awarded the "Leaders Choice Award" by *Market Watch* magazine in 2011 as the best new product.

Modelo reports rising sales in markets outside Mexico and the USA. In 2011, Australia became the second-largest export market behind the USA, with Corona Extra being the best-selling premium imported beer, with an impressive market share of 38 percent among imports. Building on the demand in Australia for its products, Modelo introduced Pacifico and Negra Modelo in late 2011. Europe, much like the USA, has endured several years of decreased beer consumption, but export volumes for Modelo had a growth rate of 10 percent in Europe in 2011. Modelo's sales in Asia were sluggish from changes in key importers. Sales in Latin America and the Caribbean were not as good as desired by the company.

External

Exhibit 5 reveals the top beer brands in the world based on volume sold. The relatively unknown Snow beer is a Chinese beer resembling a U.S. lager in nature and is sold almost exclusively in China. Possibly surprising to some, Bud Light and Budweiser rank second and third by a rather comfortable margin. Modelo's Corona Extra was the fourth and experienced a 9 percent gain over the pervious year, in an environment where most beer sales were declining. Three of the top five in the list are products of AB InBev, including Brahma, a Brazilan beer also owned by AB InBev that is the ninth most popular.

Beer Drinking Trends

More and more Americans are drinking less and less mass-produced beers because demand is shifting toward higher alcohol alternatives. Statistics reveal that beer drinking in the USA has dropped 11 percent over the last decade. Beer consumption in the USA was down every year from 2007 through 2011. However in contrast, craft beer sales grew by as much as 15 percent per year in the USA over that time period. That trend continued through at least the first half of 2012, when craft beer sales were up 14 percent, according to the Brewers Association.

EXHIBIT 5   World's Most Popular Beers (millions of barrels sold)

Brand	2011	2010	Percent Change (%)
Snow	50.8	52.0	(2.4)
Bud Light	45.4	47.4	(4.4)
Budweiser	38.7	37.0	4.5
Corona Extra	30.4	27.9	9.0
Skol	29.5	30.2	(2.3)

Based on information at http://www.huffingtonpost.com/2012/09/26/worlds-most-popular-beer_n_1914327.html.

As a nation's economy improves, historically consumers shift away from beer (cheaper) to wine, liquor, and spirits (more expensive). The taste for more alcohol in their drinks has also meant that beer drinkers are generally shifting to small batch, locally made, craft beers, which have higher alcohol content. This trend has benefited beer companies such as Boston Beer Company (NYSE: SAM) that produces Sam Adams. Although not a die-hard locally made craft beer, Sam Adams enjoys the middle ground between the mass-produced beers from AB and Molson Coors and the specialty brews found in top-notch liquor stores. Sam Adams's sales jumped 50 percent in the 2011–2012 period. Sam Adams's shipments in the third quarter in 2012 grew 17 percent over the third quarter in 2011. Samuel Adams's introduction a few years ago helped redefine beer and launched the craft beer revolution in the USA.

The major threat that AB InBev, Heineken, and Molson Coors pose to brewers like Boston Beer, Craft Brew, and more than 2,000 privately owned small brewers lies in distribution clout. All beer companies fight for shelf space at stores and tap handles at bars and restaurants. Big brewers have far greater influence over distributors in deciding which beers win those spots. About 94 percent of noncraft beer brands are owned by the three, so as AB InBev, Molson Coors and SAB Miller continue to grow their lines of craft-style offerings, those beers crowd out beers made by the smaller craft brewers. So the big three's craft brands such as Shock Top, Goose Island, Blue Moon, and Franciscan Well, have a huge upper hand over companies such as Sam Adams and privately held brewers.

Business Culture in Mexico

Even though many Mexicans are also Americans, and about 80 percent of Mexican exports are bound for the USA, there are quite a few differences in the two countries' business culture. Mexican companies tend to be much more hierarchical (autocratic) with respect to how the firm is structured with important decisions being made by a few key individuals in high ranks. When collaborating with management, it is suggested to match levels of seniority as closely as possible, and when dealing with subordinates, it is important to keep a human touch, much more so than in the USA. Mexican managers tend to offer detailed instructions to subordinates to aid them in performing their tasks. Meetings in Mexico often start late and run late; so be careful when scheduling multiple meetings for the same day. Business lunches tend to start later than they do in the USA and often can run 2 hours in length.

Dress is formal in Mexico, and visiting women executives are treated with respect. However, Mexico still has a glass-ceiling problem regarding women having opportunities in business. Management style in Mexico is more authoritative and less participative as compared to the USA. Mexicans in general work hard for low wages, and for this reason many companies that departed Mexico 10 years ago to take advantage of lower wages in China, are now returning to Mexico. Mexico likely has a bright future for doing business globally and attracting businesses.

A Pending Anheuser-Busch InBev Takeover of Modelo

In fall 2012, all appeared well for AB InBev to buy the remaining 50 percent of Grupo Modelo for $20 billion and acquire the firm's 50 percent stake in Crown Imports. But the U.S. government has delayed this acquisition, suing in February 2013 to block the acquisition for fear that AB InBev would have too much power in setting beer prices in the U.S. market. AB InBev's home country of Belgium, claims the U.S. government has no grounds for such tactics and points out that Corona only has 7 percent of the current market share. In addition, AB InBev argues that Crown Imports sets the prices for Grupo Modelo products in the USA, and as part of the agreement they would be selling the acquired 50 percent share of Crown Imports to Constellation Brands with an option to buy their stake back in 10 years. Constellation Brands currently owns the remaining 50 percent of Crown Imports.

Despite AB InBev's arguments, company documents cite one of the main reasons for the acquisition is Corona putting increasing price pressure on AB InBev products. The weak Mexican peso is much to blame. AB InBev vows to continue to fight and work every possible angle to salvage the deal. Analysts point out that the deal is actually more advantageous for AB to gain access to the Mexican beer market than for AB InBev to squeeze out a little extra profit in the USA, where the company already has a 48-percent market share. If true, it is likely AB InBev will negotiate a settlement with the U.S. Department of Justice, giving up some provisions in the USA to enable the firm to gain full access to the Mexican market. However, if the acquisition is approved, according to Exhibit 5, AB InBev will control four of the top five beer brands in the world, with the top brand not even readily available outside of China.

The 2013 Super Bowl

The cost for a 30-second Super Bowl ad in January 2013 was $4 million, following the average $3.6 million price the prior year. Demand for craft-style beer accelerated after the 2012 Super Bowl when AB InBev released its Bud Light Platinum ads. With a 6 percent alcohol content, that brand was a more upscale version of Bud Light, although it as not really a craft beer, the ad was successful. After those 2012 Super Bowl ads, Platinum sold more than 1 million barrels in just seven months, pushing up AB stock 42 percent. Those ads also helped portray Bud Light as a beer that could be enjoyed rather than guzzled.

During the 2013 Super Bowl, Budweiser rolled out Black Crown, a golden amber lager with the same 6 percent alcohol content as Platinum. This is more relatable to original Budweiser in terms of brewing style and heaviness, which probably makes it riskier than Platinum because of the beer's strength. The two Super Bowl ads portrayed Black Crown beer as a classy, sexy, sophisticated beer, rather than Platinum's hip, cool vibe. Interestingly, Molson Coors did not have a commercial during the 2013 Super Bowl. Their thought was that so many people have smartphones now that these people may be more plugged into their phones than the television, so they placed cheaper ads on the Internet. Over the last three years though, Miller has reported a 35-percent drop in sales of their Genuine Draft, Milwaukee's Best, and High Life brands.

Competitors

Anheuser-Busch InBev SA/NV

Headquartered in Leuven, Belgium, AB InBev is the world's largest beer brewer with a 25-percent global market share. AB InBev has four of the top 5 beer brands sold in the world and more than 200 brands total, 14 of which generate more than U.S. $1 billion annually. Popular AB InBev brands include Bud Light, Budweiser, Stella Artois, Beck's, Brahma, Skol, and Natural Light. As of May 1, AB InBev owns 50 percent of Grupo Modelo and is desperately trying to buy the remaining stake. AB InBev has 116,000 employees in 30 nations and reports their financial results in U.S. dollars. The company trades on the Euronext Brussels Index as well as on the NYSE under the ticker symbol BUD. Sales in 2011 totaled $39 billion.

Heineken N.V.

Headquartered in Amsterdam, Netherlands, Heineken is a global brewing giant with more than €17 billion in sales in 2012. The company claims to have the most extensive global reach of any beer company, with products available in more than 178 countries, operations in 71 countries, and a workforce of more than 70,000. Heineken was founded in 1864 and currently markets more than 250 different brands of beer, including Heineken, Amstel, New Castle, Murphys Irish Stout, Tiger, Fosters, and many more. Perhaps Grupo Modelo's largest competitors, Heineken owns 100 percent of Cerveceria Cuauhtemoc Moctezuma that produces well-known Mexican beers such as Tecate, Sol, Dos Equis, Bohemia, Indio, and Carta Blanca. The company operates breweries in seven different Mexican cities and sponsors many soccer teams in Mexico.

Cuauhtémoc Moctezuma Holding, S.A. de C.V. (www.cuamoc.com)

A subsidiary of Heineken and headquartered in Monterrey, Mexico, Cuauhtémoc Moctezuma Holding produces and distributes beer from six breweries in Mexico, including the branded beers Carta Blanca, Dos Equis, Tecate, Bohemia, and Sol. The Heineken label was added to the lineup in 2010 when Heineken acquired Cuauhtémoc Moctezuma (formerly Fomento Económico Mexicano Cerveza) from FEMSA. Cuauhtémoc Moctezuma controls more than 40 percent of Mexico's beer market but also produces glass bottles, aluminum cans, and crown caps through its subsidiaries Fábricas Monterrey (FAMOSA) and Sílices de Veracruz (SIVESA).

Fomento Económico Mexicano, S.A.B. de C.V. (www.femsa.com)

Headquartered in Monterrey, Mexico, FEMSA is a leading soft-drink bottler and convenience store operator in Latin America. FEMSA's Coca-Cola FEMSA subsidiary is the world's largest Coca-Cola bottler. FEMSA bottles Coca-Cola, Sprite, other soft drinks, juices, and water in nine Latin American countries. Competing with Modelo's 960 Extra convenience stores, FEMSA owns 9,000 OXXO convenience stores in 31 Mexican states, primarily in the northern part of the country, through its FEMSA Comercio subsidiary.

Before being sold to Heineken in 2010, FEMSA was a major beer brewer in Mexico and Brazil, through its former FEMSA Cerveza subsidiary. It brewed Carta Blanca, Indio, Sol, and Tecate beer. Heineken changed the name of FEMSA Cerveza to Cuauhtémoc Moctezuma Holding, S.A. de C.V.

Molson Coors Brewing Company (TAP)

Headquartered in Denver, Colorado, Coors and Molson joined forces in 2005 to create Molson Coors that manufactures and sells beers around the world. Popular brands include Coors Light, Molson Canadian, Keystone, Cobra, Miller Light, Miller High Life, and Blue Moon. Molson Coors produces some 19 million hectoliters (502 million U.S. gallons) of beer a year and dominates the Canadian market, accounting for 40 percent of the beer sold in that country. In the USA, Molson Coors does business through MillerCoors, a joint venture that is 58 percent owned by SABMiller. MillerCoors, the second-largest U.S. brewer by volume, markets Coors, Coors Light, and Molson brands. Miller won nine awards at the 2012 World Beer Cup, but not advertising during the 2013 Super Bowl is widely seen as a sign of weakness.

Molson Coors operates in the United Kingdom and as Molson Coors International (MCI) in developing markets. In mid-2011, Molson Coors finalized a joint venture in India with Cobra India, whereby the company has a 51 percent interest and operational control of the Molson Coors Cobra India. In mid-2012, the company acquired StarBev. In January 2013, Molson Coors acquired Ireland's Franciscan Well brewery, a small Irish craft brewery. Although Franciscan Well brews only about 1,700 barrels a year, Molson Coors' strategy is to further tap into the fast-growing craft brew market, which is still small at just 6 percent in the USA. Molson Coors' plans for Franciscan Well include a sizable expansion in brewing capacity—from 1,700 barrels to more than 62,000—as well as the exploration of the export market for Franciscan's beers.

SABMiller plc

Headquartered in London, England, SABMiller is one of the world's largest brewers, producing more than 200 international, national, and local beer brands. Popular brands include Grolsch, Miller, Peroni Nastro, and Pilsner Urquell, and many local favorites, such as Castle Lager, the number-one beer in Africa. In Latin America, SABMiller owns Bavaria and Cervecería Nacional. In the USA, SABMiller owns 58 percent of MillerCoors, a joint venture with Molson Coors. SABMiller acquired Australian rival Foster's in 2011. In addition to brewing, SABMiller is one of the world's top bottlers of Coca-Cola products. Altria owns more than 25 percent of SABMiller and Colombia-based Santo Domingo Group almost 15 percent. In 2012, SABMiller acquired (a) the remaining 50 percent interest in Pacific Beverages Pty Ltd., (b) a 27.5 percent interest in BIH Brasseries Internationales Holding (Angola) Ltd., (c) a 33 percent interest in International Breweries plc, and (4) an additional 2.9 percent interest in Tanzania Breweries Ltd.

The Future

Big beer companies all over the globe are constantly making acquisitions to gain distribution rights and market share. Grupo Modelo needs a clear strategic plan to garner the best deal for its shareholders given the pending AB InBev acquisition. The beer industry is intensely competitive with acquisitions occurring quarterly. The overall demand for beer is declining, further fueling price competition and distribution battles. There are thousands of local craft breweries that could be acquired given that segment beer is growing, and the Far East remains virtually untapped for growth for Mexican beers.

Develop a three-year strategic plan for the CEO of Grupo Modelo.

Pearson PLC, 2013

www.pearson.com, PSORF or PSON (London exchange)

Headquartered in London, United Kingdom, Pearson is the largest education company and the largest book publisher in the world. Pearson is organized into three main business groupings: (1) Pearson Education (digital learning, education publishing and services including Poptropica and eCollege; (2) Financial Times (FT) Group (business information, including the *Financial Times* newspaper); and (3) Penguin Group (consumer publishing, including the Dorling Kindersley and Penquin Classics imprints). In late 2011, Pearson acquired Global Education and Technology Group. In 2012, Pearson acquired Certiport, Inc., Author Solutions, Inc. (ASI), and EmbanetCompass.

In late 2012, Pearson agreed to merge its Penguin Books division with Bertelsmann's Random House to create the world's biggest book publisher, a newly created joint venture named Penguin Random House. Bertelsmann will own 53 percent of the joint venture and Pearson will own 47 percent. The joint venture excludes Bertelsmann's trade publishing business in Germany and Pearson retains rights to use the Penguin brand in education markets worldwide. The newly formed company is subject to customary regulatory and other approvals but is expected to complete in the second half of 2013.

In October 2013, Harish Manwani joined the board of directors of Pearson. Harish is Chief Operating Officer of the global consumer products company Unilever. Harish is a graduate from Bombay University and holds a Masters degree in management studies. Pearson chairman Glen Moreno said: "Harish brings to Pearson a deep knowledge of emerging markets, an understanding of the rapidly growing middle class in those countries, and senior experience in a successful global organization. This background is very relevant to our transformation of Pearson into the world's leading learning company." Harish replaces Dr. Susan Fuhrman on the Pearson board; Susan is President of Teachers College, Columbia University. Pearson also recently announced another appointment to its board, Linda Lorimer, Vice President of Yale University.

History

Founded by Samuel Pearson in 1844, Pearson originally was a building and engineering firm operating under the name of *S. Pearson & Son*. In 1880, control passed to grandson Weetman Pearson, an engineer later known as Lord Cowdray, who in 1890 moved the business to London and turned it into one of the world's largest construction companies. Pearson was listed on the London Stock Exchange in 1969. Pearson acquired Penguin Books in 1970 and Ladybird Books in 1972.

During the 1990s, Pearson acquired a number of TV production and broadcasting assets and sold most of its nonmedia assets, under the leadership of future U.S. Congressman Bob Turner. Pearson acquired the education division of Simon & Schuster in 1998 from Viacom and merged it with its own education unit, Addison-Wesley Longman, to form Pearson Education.

In 2000, Pearson acquired National Computer Systems and entered the educational assessment and school management systems market in the United States. That same year, Pearson acquired Dorling Kindersley, the illustrated reference publisher and integrated it within Penguin. In 2006, Pearson acquired National Evaluation Systems, Inc. (NES; Amherst, MA), a provider of customized state assessments for teacher certification in the USA. Pearson completed the acquisition of Harcourt Assessment in 2008, merging the acquired businesses into Pearson Assessment & Information. In that same year, Pearson acquired eCollege, a digital learning technology group for $477M. In 2011, Pearson created the Pearson College, a British degree provider based in London and Manchester. Also that year, Pearson acquired Connections Education.

In late 2012, Pearson acquired KEV Group, the North American leader in the management and accounting of school activity funds and online payments. KEV Group's *School Cash Suite* of products manage all aspects of every dollar that comes into secondary schools. Whether cash, check, or an online transaction, KEV's products help more than 4,000 schools reduce fraud and significantly decrease their workload. Limiting cash in a school system and increasing transparency of cash that does come in decreases the risk of bullying, reduces classroom distractions, and ensures maximum efficiency for all users.

Internal Issues

Vision and Mission

Pearson has no clearly stated vision or mission statement. However, there is a statement at the Pearson website, under the Strategy icon, that may be the firm's mission statement. It reads: "Pearson's goal is to help people make progress in their lives through learning. We aim to be the world's leading learning company, serving the citizens of a brain-based economy wherever and whenever they are learning."

Strategy

Pearson's strategy, as stated on the company website, consists of four initiatives, paraphrased as follows to focus on:

1. Long-term organic investment in content,
2. Digital products and services businesses—Add services to our content, usually enabled by technology; Pearson's digital revenues were £2bn or 33 percent of total sales.
3. International expansion—Pearson sells in more than 70 countries, but desires new particular emphasis on fast-growing markets in China, India, Africa and Latin America. In 2011, Pearson generated $1bn of revenue in developing markets for the first time, accounting for 11 percent of total sales and 22 percent of employees.
4. Efficiency—Pearson profit margins have increased to 16.1 percent and the ratio of average working capital to sales has improved from 20.1 percent to 16.9 percent.

Organizational Structure

On the Pearson website, the top management team is listed under the Board of Directors icon. Pearson's organizational chart is provided in Exhibit 1. Chief executive officer (CEO) John Fallon replaced CEO Marjorie Scardino on January 1, 2013.

Segments

Pearson is organized into four main business groupings: (1) Pearson International Education, (2) Pearson North American Education, and (3) Professional Education and FT Group. In 2012 Pearson generated total revenues of £5.059 billion, as indicated in Exhibit 2. £2.658

EXHIBIT 1 Pearson's Organizational Structure

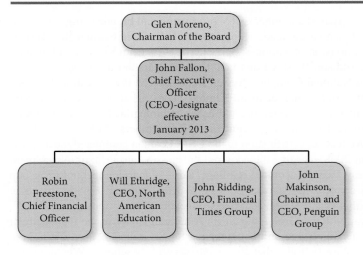

Source: Based on company documents.

EXHIBIT 2 Pearson's Segment

All figures in £ millions	North American Education	International Education	Professional	FT Group	Corporate	Discontinued operations	Group
			2012				
Continuing operations							
Sales (external)	2,658	1,568	390	443	—	—	5,059
Sales (inter-segment)	5	1	12	—	—	—	18
Adjusted operating profit	536	216	37	49	—	—	838
Intangible charges	(66)	(73)	(37)	(4)	—	—	(180)
Acquisition costs	(7)	(8)	(1)	(4)	—	—	(20)
Other net gains and losses	—	—	(123)	—	—	—	(123)
Operating profit	**463**	**135**	**(124)**	**41**	**—**	**—**	**515**

All figures in £ millions	North American Education	International Education	Professional Education	FT Group	Corporate	Discontinued Operations	Group
			2011				
Continuing operations							
Sales (external)	2,584	1,424	382	427	—	—	4,817
Sales (inter-segment)	3	—	9	—	—	—	12
Adjusted operating profit	493	196	66	76	—	—	831
Intangible charges	(57)	(60)	(11)	(8)	—	—	(136)
Acquisition costs	(2)	(9)	—	(1)	—	—	(12)
Other net gains and losses	29	(6)	—	412	—	—	435
Operating profit	**463**	**121**	**55**	**479**	**—**	**—**	**1,118**

billion were from North America, £1.568 billion from International, £390 million were from Professional, and £443 million from Financial Times (FT) Group—as indicated in Exhibit 2. Note in Exhibit 3 that Pearson had 2012 revenue declines in three regions, but sales were up in the USA slightly.

Pearson Education

Pearson Education provides textbooks and digital technologies to teachers and students across all ages. Pearson's education brands include Bug Club, Edexcel, Financial Times Publishing, Fronter, MyEnglishLab, and BBC Active. Pearson's education brands in North America include eCollege, Poptropica, FT Press, MyLabs/Mastering, SAMS Publishing, and Que Publishing. Pearson generates about 60 percent of its education sales in North America but operates in more than 70 countries. Pearson publishes across the curriculum under a range of brand names including Scott Foresman, Prentice Hall, Addison-Wesley, Allyn and Bacon, Benjamin Cummings, and Longman.

Pearson's Prentice Hall division is the market leader in higher education publishing across all discipline areas; Pearson's Addison Wesley and Benjamin Cummings are premier publishers in computing, economics, finance, mathematics, science, and statistics; Pearson's Longman brand focuses on materials in English, history, philosophy, political science, and religion; and Allyn and Bacon focuses on the social sciences, humanities, and education disciplines.

In 2013, Pearson Education reorganized into three main divisions: Pearson International Education, Pearson North American Education, and Professional Education. Pearson International is headquartered in London, with offices across Europe, Asia, and South America. Pearson North America is headquartered in Upper Saddle River, New Jersey, with major business units based

EXHIBIT 3 Pearson's Revenues By Region

All figures in £ millions	Sales	
	2012	2011
Continuing operations		
UK	705	713
Other European countries	391	394
USA	2,800	2,707
Canada	145	150
Asia Pacific	647	514
Other countries	371	339
Total continuing	**5,059**	**4,817**
Discontinued operations		
UK	160	152
Other European countries	78	77
USA	603	606
Canada	56	59
Asia Pacific	139	132
Other countries	17	19
Total discontinued	**1,053**	**1,045**
Total	**6,112**	**5,862**

in San Francisco, Boston, Columbus, Indianapolis, and Chandler (Arizona). In 2012, Pearson International Education had revenues of £1,568 million, Pearson North American Education had revenues of £2,658 million, and Professional Education had revenues of £443 million.

The North American segment had 2012 operating profits of £536 million. Student registration for MyLab grew 11 percent to almost 10 million. Student registrations in 2012 at Pearson's eCollege grew 3 percent to 8.7 million. Also in North America, Pearson's Connection Education, which operates online K-12 schools in 22 states, served more than 43,000 students, up 31 percent from 2011.

Pearson's International Education segment reported 2012 operating profits of £216 million, partly due to student enrollments in China at Wall Street English (WSE), increasing 15 percent to 61,000. WSE is Pearson's worldwide chain of English language centers for professionals with 11 new WSE centers opened in 2012. Pearson did especially well in 2012 in India with its TutorVista program and in Mexico with the launch of UTEL, a new university enabling Mexicans to enroll in online business courses. Also in the International segment, Pearson VUE test volumes grew 7 percent in 2012 to almost 8 million.

Financial Times Group

The FT Group provides business and financial news, data, comment, and analysis in print and online. FT Publishing includes: the *Financial Times* newspaper and FT.com website; a range of specialist financial magazines and online services; and Mergermarket, a financial data vendor. The FT Group also has shareholdings in *Business Day* and *Financial Mail* (BDFM) of South Africa (50 percent stake) and *The Economist* (50 percent stake). Pearson's FT group reported 2012 operating profits of £49 million, with digital subscriptions increasing 18 percent to almost 316,000 and with 3.5 million FT web app users. The *Economist* (50% owned by Pearson) reported in 2012 a 2 percent increase in worldwide printed digital circulation.

Penguin Group

Penguin Group is an international consumer publisher, which includes imprints such as Allen Lane, Avery, Berkley Books, dial, Dutton, Dorling Kindersley, Grosset & Dunlap, Hamish Hamilton, Ladybird, Plume, Puffin, Penguin, Putnam, Michael Joseph, Riverhead, rough Guides, and Viking. Penguin publishes around 4,000 titles every year and its range of titles includes classics, reference volumes, and children's titles. In October 2012, Pearson agreed to merge Penguin Group with Bertelsmann's Random House to create the world's biggest trade book publisher—Penguin Random House. Bertelsmann will own 53 percent and Pearson will own 47 percent. Penguin reported 2012 revenue of £1,053 million and operating profits of £98 million. E-book revenue grew strongly and accounted for 17 percent of Penguin's global revenue.

Pearson now owns 47 percent of the new Penguin/Random House publishing company. In 2012, Penguin published 255 *New York Times* bestsellers.

Finance

Note in the income statements in Exhibit 4 that Pearson reported increasing revenues but declining profits in 2012. The decline in earnings resulted in a decline in 2012 retained earnings on the Pearson balance sheets, as shown in Exhibit 5.

External

Total U.S. college enrollments declined 2 percent in 2012 while the overall higher education publishing market declined 6 percent, according to the Association of American Publishers (AAP). AAP also reported a 15 percent decline in the textbook publishing market in 2012.

Competitors

The world of book publishing is changing rapidly as e-books, renting books, sharing books, avoiding books, photocopying books, scanning books, creating custom books, using e-readers

EXHIBIT 4   Pearson's Income Statements

All figures in £ millions	Year ended 31 December 2012	
	2012	2011
Sales	5,059	4,817
Cost of goods sold	(2,224)	(2,072)
Gross profit	2,835	2,745
Operating expenses	(2,216)	(2,072)
Profit on sale of associate	—	412
Loss on closure of subsidiary	(113)	—
Share of results of joint ventures and associates	9	33
Operating profit	515	1,118
Finance costs	(113)	(96)
Finance income	32	25
Profit before tax	434	1,047
Income tax	(148)	(162)
Profit for the year from continuing operations	286	885
Profit for the year from discontinued operations	43	71
Profit for the year	329	956
Attributable to:		
Equity holders of the company	326	957
Non-controlling interest	3	(1)
Earnings per share for profit from continuing and discontinued operations attributable to equity holders of the company during the year (expressed in pence per share)		
Basic	40.5p	119.6p
Diluted	40.5p	119.3p

EXHIBIT 5 Pearson's Balance Sheets

As of 31 December 2012

All figures in £ millions	2012	2011
Assets		
Non-current assets		
Property, plant and equipment	327	383
Intangible assets	6,218	6,342
Investments in joint ventures and associates	15	32
Deferred income tax assets	229	287
Financial assets–Derivative financial instruments	174	177
Retirement benefit assets	—	25
Other financial assets	31	26
Trade and other receivables	79	151
	7,073	7,423
Current assets		
Intangible assets–Pre-publication	666	650
Inventories	261	407
Trade and other receivables	1,104	1,386
Financial assets–Derivative financial instruments	4	—
Financial assets–Marketable securities	6	9
Cash and cash equivalents (excluding overdrafts)	1,062	1,369
	3,103	3,821
Assets classified as held for sale	1,172	—
Total assets	**11,348**	**11,244**
Liabilities		
Non-current liabilities		
Financial liabilities–Borrowings	(2,010)	(1,964)
Financial liabilities–Derivative financial instruments	—	(2)
Deferred income tax liabilities	(601)	(620)
Retirement benefit obligations	(172)	(166)
Provisions for other liabilities and charges	(110)	(115)
Other liabilities	(282)	(325)
	(3,175)	(3,192)
Current liabilities		
Trade and other liabilities	(1,556)	(1,741)
Financial liabilities–Borrowings	(262)	(87)
Financial liabilities–Derivative financial instruments	—	(1)
Current income tax liabilities	(291)	(213)
Provisions for other liabilities and charges	(38)	(48)
	(2,147)	(2,090)
Liabilities directly associated with assets classified as held for sale	(316)	—
Total liabilities	**(5,638)**	**(5.282)**
Net assets	**5,710**	**5,962**

EXHIBIT 5 Continued

All figures in £ millions	2012	2011
Equity		
Share capital	204	204
Share premium	2,555	2,544
Treasury shares	(103)	(149)
Translation reserve	128	364
Retained earnings	2,902	2,980
Total equity attributable to equity holders of the company	**5,686**	**5,943**
Non-controlling interest	24	19
Total equity	**5,710**	**5,962**
Total Liabilities and Equity	**11,348**	**11,244**

permeate today's publishing landscape. The historical day of students carrying around encyclopedic size books is drawing to an end. Although great news for students and customers, this changing environment makes book publishing much more risky for both publishers and authors.

The situation described leads to increased competition daily on many fronts such as price, e-commerce, new entrants, ancillary offerings, acquisitions, divestitures, and weakened players. A few of Pearson's major rivals in this turbulent environment are McGraw-Hill, John Wiley, Houghton Mifflin, and Thomson Reuters, but even online book publishers such as iUniverse are attacking from new directions. Pearson is the largest and most profitable book publisher, which in a sense makes Pearson most vulnerable to competitor's duplicating and imitating their product offerings, and continually examining Pearson for potential weaknesses that can be exploited.

A financial comparison of each rival firm is provided in Exhibit 6, followed by a brief overview of each firm. Note in Exhibit 4 that Pearson's earnings per share (EPS) is lower than both McGraw-Hill and John Wiley.

McGraw-Hill Companies, Inc. (NYSE: MPH)

Headquartered in New York City, McGraw-Hill is a leading producer of textbooks, tests, and related materials, serving the elementary, secondary, and higher education markets through McGraw-Hill Education (MHE). Other businesses include S&P Ratings (indexes and credit ratings); S&P Capital IQ and S&P Indices (financial and business information); and Commodities and Commercial (Platts, J.D. Power and Associates, McGraw-Hill Construction, and Aviation Week).

EXHIBIT 6 A Comparison of Publishers

	Pearson	McGraw-Hill	John Wiley	Thomson Reuters
Sales ($)	5.09B£	6.35B	1.75B	13.45B
Net Income ($)	329M£	789M	190M	–877M
Profit Margin (%)	6.46	13.01	10.89	–6.45
Debt-to-Equity Ratio	0.41	0.67	0.64	0.43
EPS ($)	0.40£	3.03	3.14	–1.06
Market Capitalization ($)	10.6B£	14.97B	2.27B	23.83B
Number of Shares Out	817M	277M	60.15M	826M

EPS, earnings per share.
Source: Based on company documents.

McGraw-Hill announced in late 2012 that it is divesting its education division for $2.5 billion to Apollo Global Management LLC (APO). McGraw-Hill's education division had been reporting shrinking revenues over recent years, partly as a result of reduced spending on textbooks by the government (and students). Also, McGraw-Hill was facing difficulty with its plans to develop its education division into a subscription-based model through digital delivery. The new McGraw-Hill, without the education division, is being renamed McGraw-Hill Financial and will primarily focus on capital and commodities markets and include iconic brands like S&P Ratings, S&P Capital IQ, and S&P Indices. McGraw-Hill Companies expected revenues of approximately $4.4 billion from McGraw-Hill Financial in 2012, with approximately 40 percent of it coming from international avenues.

John Wiley & Sons (NYSE: JW-A)

Headquartered in Hoboken, New Jersey, John Wiley publishes scientific, technical, and medical works, including journals and reference works such as *Current Protocols* and *Kirk-Othmer Encyclopedia of Chemical Technology*. Wiley publishes more than 1,600 journal titles, produces professional and nonfiction trade books, and is a publisher of college textbooks. Wiley also publishes the *For Dummies* how-to series, the travel guide brand Frommer's, and CliffsNotes study guides, as well. Wiley has publishing, marketing, and distribution centers on four continents: North America, Europe, Asia, and Australia. For second quarter of 2012 that ended October 31, 2012, Wiley reported a slight decline in revenue compared to the same period in the previous fiscal year, and a 15-percent decrease in net income. Wiley has a market capitalization of $2.3 billion.

Houghton Mifflin Harcourt Publishing Company

Headquartered in Boston Massachusetts, Houghton Mifflin is a publisher of pre-K through grade 12 educational material, as well as textbooks and printed materials. The company provides digital content online and via CD-ROM and publishes fiction (including J. R. R. Tolkien's *The Lord of the Rings* series), as well as nonfiction titles and reference materials, and offers professional resources and educational services to teachers. Although founded back in 1832, Houghton Mifflin today is owned by private-equity concerns, including hedge fund Paulson & Co. The company filed for bankruptcy in 2012.

Thomson Reuters (NYSE: TRI)

Headquartered in New York City, Thomson Reuters is the market leader in financial data (ahead of rival information provider Bloomberg), providing electronic information and services to businesses and professionals worldwide, serving the financial services, media, legal, tax and accounting, and science markets. Nearly all Thomson Reuters' revenues come from subscription sales to its plethora of offerings.

For the third quarter of 2012, Thomson Reuters reported revenues of $3.2 billion, a 7-percent decline from the same period last year. Its net profit rose, however, by 24 percent, to $474 million. Thomson Reuters' best performing division is tax and accounting, but the firm reports flat or declining revenues in all its other divisions. Rumors circulated in 2012 that Thomson Reuters was maneuvering to buy Pearson's *Financial Times* newspaper.

The Future

The digital world is rapidly eroding Pearson's traditional book publishing business model. Luyen Chou, chief product officer for Pearson's K–12 technology group, summed it up best, when he recently said: "Pearson needs to become an 'Electronic Arts' [EA] for education. To keep up with the changing environment, we can't just digitize the static textbooks of the past; we need to excel at producing high-quality, interactive digital learning experiences and get them into the hands of students. That includes digital studios, animators, illustrators, producers, and 3-D artists. We need to build that capacity from within and we need the whole supply chain to take that from the studio to the actual users. The folks that have done that well are the Electronic Arts type companies of the world, digital studios. That's not a core competency for companies like Pearson. We have to make sure that we're complementing our data and platform with high-quality interactive learning content."

In late 2012, Blackboard Inc. and Pearson reached an agreement to expand the availability of Pearson's leading learning solution—MyLab & Mastering—with Blackboard Learn, the market-leading learning management system (LMS). Previously available in North America, the integration is now available in most markets worldwide.

The systems integration includes state-of-the-art web services that enable instructors to find and access MyLab & Mastering within their Blackboard learning system. For example, faculty can synchronize grade books, transfer information and create corresponding links in both systems, and customize courses by choosing content and rearranging items in the content area and course navigation bar. For example, Dr. Salim M. Salim, head of the Mathematics Department at Qatar University said: "The integration of MyLab & Mastering and Blackboard Learn has created not only a more enriched teaching and learning experience, but it also makes my job much more convenient. The single sign on, grade book synchronization, personalized study paths and real-time evaluations allow me and my students to easily benefit from the powerful tools both systems offer."

Given the changing world of textbook publishing and publishing in general, Pearson is engaged is a competitive fight with rival McGraw-Hill for market share in the USA and indeed globally. McGraw-Hill's Connect software competes fiercely with Pearson's MyLab. Prepare a three-year strategic plan for Pearson.

Lenovo Group Limited, 2013

www.lenovo.com, LNVGY

Headquartered in Beijing, China, Lenovo designs, produces, and markets ThinkPad personal computers, notebook computers, tablet computers, desktop computers, mobile phones, workstations, servers, electronic storage, information technology (IT) management software, and smart televisions. Lenovo is the world's second-largest PC vendor (behind Hewlett-Packard [HP]), and markets the ThinkPad line of notebook computers and ThinkCentre line of desktops. Lenovo's U.S. headquarters is in Morrisville, North Carolina, and its registered office is in Hong Kong. Lenovo has operations in more than 60 countries and sells its products in around 160 countries. Lenovo ranks fourth in the global tablet market by volume. Lenovo's fiscal year ends on March 31 every year. For fiscal 2012/2013 ending March 31, 2013, Lenovo's revenues increased 14.5 percent to $33.8 billion while net income increased 33 percent to $631 million.

Lenovo sells directly to consumers and businesses through online sales, company-owned stores, chain retailers, and other distributors. Lenovo's principal facilities are in Beijing, Morrisville, and Singapore, with research centers in those locations, as well as Shanghai, Shenzhen, Xiamen, and Chengdu in China, and Yamato in Kanagawa Prefecture, Japan. Lenovo operates factories in Chengdu and Hefei, China and recently started production in Argentina.

In July 2012, Lenovo and the National Football League (NFL) announced that Lenovo had become the NFL's "Official Laptop, Desktop and Workstation Sponsor." Lenovo said that this was its largest sponsorship deal ever in the United States. Lenovo will receive advertising space in NFL venues and events and be allowed to use the NFL logo on its products and ads. Lenovo said that this sponsorship would boost its efforts to market to the key 18-to-35-year-old male demographic.

Lenovo entered the smartphone market in 2012 and quickly became a huge vendor of smartphones in the Chinese market. Entry into the smartphone market was accompanied by a change of strategy from "the one-size-fits-all LePhone strategy" to a diverse portfolio of devices. In 2012, Lenovo passed Apple to become the number 2 provider of smartphones in China with about a 15-percent market share, behind Xiaomi. In late 2013, Xiaomi was a growing smartphone rival to Lenovo, both firms being valued at $10 billion. Chinese-made smartphones are becoming serious competitors to Apple and Samsung both at home and overseas. In the second quarter of 2013, Xiaomi overtook Apple within China and became the sixth-largest smartphone maker globally with 5 percent market share compared to Apple's 18 percent. Xiaomi also derives revenue from its own digital game platform and social messaging app, MiLiao. Lenovo is contemplating making a move to acquire Xiaomi—or it could it be the other way around if Lenovo falters?

Lenovo has invested U.S. $793 million in the construction of a mobile phone manufacturing and research-and-development facility in Wuhan, China. Lenovo has expanded sales of its smartphones into Russia, Indonesia, and India, with further expansion intended. The LePhone smartphone is offered at a low price point and is customized for the Chinese market. It has benefited from strong support from Chinese mobile phone companies and content providers such as Baidu, Alibaba, and Tencent.

A 7,500-square foot flagship Lenovo store opened in Beijing in February 2013. At the same time in the USA, Lenovo introduced the ThinkPad X131e Chromebook—a rugged PC designed for K–12 education. This product simplifies software and security management for school administrators and provides students and teachers with quick access to thousands of apps, education resources, and storage.

Copyright by Fred David Books LLC. (Written by Forest R. David)

History

Liu Chuanzhi founded Lenovo in 1984 with a group of 10 engineers in Beijing. For the first 20 years of its existence, the company's English name was "Legend" but in April 2003, the company publicly announced its new name, "Lenovo," with a large media campaign involving huge outdoor billboards and primetime television advertisements. Lenovo's first successful product was the Han-card, an add-on card for PCs that allowed them to efficiently process Chinese characters. Lenovo became a publicly traded company after listing in Hong Kong in 1994, raising nearly $30 million.

Lenovo acquired IBM's PC business in 2005 amid a backlash in Congress against Chinese companies trying to purchase U.S. businesses. Lenovo's acquisition of IBM's PC division accelerated access to foreign markets while improving both its branding and technology. Lenovo paid $1.25 billion for IBM's computer business and assumed an additional U.S. $500 million of IBM's debt. This acquisition made Lenovo the third largest computer maker worldwide by volume.

In January 2011, Lenovo formed a PC joint venture with NEC, a Japanese IT company. The venture is named Lenovo NEC Holdings B.V., which is registered in the Netherlands. Lenovo owns a 51 percent stake in the joint venture, whereas NEC holds a 49 percent stake. Lenovo has a five-year option to expand its stake in the joint venture. This joint venture is intended to boost Lenovo's worldwide sales by expanding its presence in Japan, a key market for PCs. NEC spun off its PC business into the joint venture, so Lenovo is now the largest PC seller in Japan.

Lenovo recently acquired Medion, a German electronics manufacturing company, doubling its share of the German computer market to 14 percent and making it the third-largest vendor by sales after Acer and HP. The deal was the first in which a Chinese company acquired a well-known German company.

The Year 2012: Expanding Globally

Lenovo had acquired the Brazil-based electronics company CCE that sells products under the brand name Digibras for a base price of 300 million reais (U.S. $148 million) in a combination of stock and cash and an additional 400 million reais dependent on performance benchmarks. Before this acquisition, Lenovo already established a $30 million factory in Brazil, but Lenovo desired a local partner to maximize regional growth. Lenovo realizes that the 2014 World Cup that will be hosted by Brazil as well as the 2016 Summer Olympics and CCE has a reputation for quality.

Lenovo acquired the U.S.-based software company Stoneware, in its first software acquisition to date. Lenovo desires to improve and expand its cloud-computing services. For the two years before its acquisition, Stoneware partnered with Lenovo to sell its software. During this period, Stoneware's sales doubled. Stoneware was founded in 2000. Stoneware is based in Carmel, Indiana, and has 67 employees.

Lenovo has made an investment in Vertex, a technology-oriented venture capital firm in Israel. Lenovo's Chief Executive Officer (CEO), Yang Yuanging, said that this investment was just the beginning. He said, "Definitely we are interested in Israel's technology, to grow our company, to grow our business."

Lenovo recently introduced the more powerful desktop computer IdeaCentre A720, with a 27-inch touch-screen display and running Windows 8. With a TV tuner and HDMI, the A720 is also a multimedia hub of sorts. In 2013, Lenovo added a table computer to the IdeaCentre line. Lenovo sells tablet computers under the IdeaPad and ThinkPad product lines abroad and as the LePad in Mainland China. The LePad is part of an effort by Lenovo in the market for mobile Internet devices. Lenovo has established a Mobile Internet and Digital Home Business Group to compete in this space.

Lenovo is developing a new smart television product called LeTV. The PC, communications, and TV industries are currently undergoing a "smart" transformation. Lenovo recently offered a new cloud computing service that will allow users to share content between multiple devices, in addition to managing their personal information and social networking.

Internal Issues

Vision and Mission

Lenovo's vision statement reads as follows: "To create personal devices more people are inspired to own, a culture more people aspire to join and an enduring, trusted business that is well respected around the world."

Lenovo's mission statement reads as follows: "To become one of the world's great personal technology companies."

Organizational Structure

Lenovo's organizational chart is depicted in Exhibit 1. Note that there is no chief operations officer (COO), and the structure appears to be divisional by region because the only two presidents head geographic regions. There are three females among the top 13 executives. Lenovo's

EXHIBIT 1 Lenovo's Organizational Chart

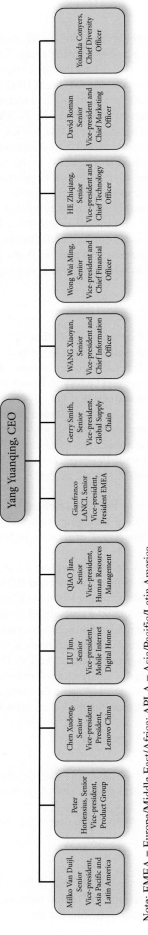

Note: EMEA = Europe/Middle East/Africa; APLA = Asia/Pacific/Latin America

Source: Based on company information provided at the corporate website.

new geographic based structure became effective in April 2012 with the creation of new reporting business units as follows: (1) China, (2) Asia-Pacific/Latin America (APLA), (3) Europe-Middle East-Africa (EMEA), and (4) North America. The new geographical structure, according to Lenovo, enables the firm to stay as close to its customers as possible.

Strategy

Lenovo is still primarily a PC company, but demand for PCs is falling; however, demand for smartphones is rapidly growing, so Lenovo is shifting gears. In smartphones, Lenovo is competing with Chinese rivals, such as Huawei Technologies Co Ltd. and ZTE Corp., that are already among the top-five smartphone companies globally. Although the second-biggest smartphone vendor in China, Lenovo has begun selling smartphones in Russia, Indonesia, the Philippines, and Vietnam, but the company faces stiff competition globally from Samsung Electronics Co. Ltd. and Apple Inc.

Lenovo's manufacturing operations are a departure from the usual industry practice of outsourcing to contract manufacturers. Lenovo instead focuses on vertical integration to avoid excessive reliance on suppliers and to keep down costs. Speaking on this topic, Yuanqing said, "Selling PCs is like selling fresh fruit. The speed of innovation is very fast, so you must know how to keep up with the pace, control inventory, to match supply with demand and handle very fast turnover." Lenovo benefited from its vertical integration after flooding affected hard-drive manufacturers in Thailand in 2011 because the company could continue manufacturing operations by shifting production toward products for which hard drives were still available.

Lenovo began to accentuate vertical integration after a meeting in 2009 in which Yuanqing, and the head of Lenovo's supply chain, analyzed the costs versus the benefits of in-house manufacturing and decided to make at least 50 percent of Lenovo's manufacturing in-house. Lenovo Chief Technology Officer George He said that vertical integration has an important role in product development. He stated, "If you look at the industry trends, most innovations for PCs, smartphones, tablets and smart TVs are related to innovation of key components—display, battery and storage. Differentiation of key parts is so important. So we started investing more … and working very closely with key parts suppliers."

Lenovo has partially moved production of its ThinkPad line of computers to Japan. ThinkPads are produced by NEC in Yamagata Prefecture. Akaemi Watanabe, president of Lenovo Japan, said, "As a Japanese, I am glad to see the return to domestic production and the goal is to realize full-scale production as this will improve our image and make the products more acceptable to Japanese customers." Lenovo recently started manufacturing computers in Whitsett, North Carolina.

For Lenovo's third quarter of 2012 that ending December 2012, the company reported a quarterly profit of $200.0 million, up 30 percent from a year previously. That amount exceeded its previous record of $163 million, on strong sales of smartphones and tablet computers. For the third quarter, Lenovo's revenue grew 12 percent from a year previously to $9.4 billion, but the bulk of that still came from its PC business. Lenovo shipped 9.4 million smartphones in the third quarter, all but about 400,000 of them however in China. CEO Yang says "the smartphone business outside China is 'still in the first stage' and Lenovo needs to invest to gain market share before focusing on profitability." The company's third-quarter revenues in the bigger but slower-growing PC market rose 7 percent to $7.9 billion.

Lenovo's global market share in PCs increased to 15.9 percent in the third quarter, trailing HP's 17.0 percent, but well ahead of both Dell and Acer. Lenovo's 15.9 percent was the average of their 11.1 percent market share in EMEA, 9 percent in North America, and 36.7 percent in China. Lenovo has rapidly gained market share in the PC sector and in early 2013 trails HP only by a slim margin in PC shipments. However, as PC demand growth slows, Lenovo has been diversifying into the mobile device sector to tap robust demand for smartphones and tablets, particularly at home in China, the world's biggest market for mobile phones and PCs.

About a one-tenth of Lenovo's third-quarter revenues in 2012 came from its mobile Internet and digital home (MIDH) business—mainly consisting of its smartphone sales in China, which jumped 77 percent to $998 million, although that was only 11 percent of total revenue. The company's third-quarter shipments of media tablets rose 77 percent to 800,000 units. MIDH now contributes 11 percent of Lenovo's overall revenue. At the end of the third quarter in 2012, Lenovo is number-three worldwide in Smart Connected Devices (PC's, tablets, and smartphones).

Lenovo basically has what it calls a two prong strategy: (1) Protect its commercial global PC business and its China business and (2) attack three high-growth opportunities in emerging markets with smartphones, tablets, and smart TVs. For quarter ending January 31, 2013, Lenovo's "attack" businesses delivered 50 percent of the company's revenues, a significant increase from four years ago when the company first launched the strategy and attack revenues were 32 percent. Lenovo's MIDH revenues include its smartphone, tablet, and smart TV businesses and accounted for a record 11 percent of total Lenovo revenue in the third quarter, up 77 percent year-over-year. And for the first time ever, Lenovo's smartphone business in China became profitable in third quarter.

Ethics
In fiscal 2012, Lenovo CEO Yang received a $3 million bonus as a reward for record profits, which he in-turn redistributed to about 10,000 Lenovo's employees. According to Lenovo spokesman, Jeffrey Shafer, Yang felt that it would be the right thing to "redirect [the money] to the employees as a real tangible gesture for what they done." Shafer also said that Yang, who owns about eight percent of Lenovo's stock, "felt that he was rewarded well simply as the owner of the company." The bonuses were mostly distributed among staff working in positions such as production and reception who received an average of 2,000 yuan or about U.S. $314. This was almost equivalent to a month's pay for the typical Lenovo worker in China. According to Lenovo's annual report, Yang earned $14 million, including $5.2 million in bonuses, during the fiscal year that ended in March 2012.

Finance
Lenovo's recent income statements and balance sheets are provided in Exhibits 2 and 3, respectively. Note in Exhibit 2 the 14.6 percent increase in revenues for fiscal 2012/2013, as well as the 33 percent increase in net income.

EXHIBIT 2 Lenovo's Income Statements (U.S. $ 000,000 omitted)

	FY2012/13	FY2011/12
Revenue	33,873	29,574
Cost of sates	(29,800)	(26,128)
Gross profit	**4,073**	**3,446**
Other income, net	20	1
Selling and distribution expenses	(1,888)	(1,691)
Administrative expenses	(847)	(730)
Research and development expenses	(623)	(453)
Other operating income - net	65	11
Operating profit	**800**	**584**
Finance income	44	43
Finance costs	(42)	(44)
Share of losses of associated companies	(1)	(1)
Profit before taxation	801	582
Taxation	(170)	(107)
Profit for the period	631	475
Profit attributable to:		
Equity holders of the company	635	473
Non-controlling interests	(4)	2
Dividend	248	183
Earnings per share (U.S. cents)		
Basic	**6.16**	**4.67**
Diluted	**6.07**	**4.57**

Source: Based on company documents.

EXHIBIT 3 Lenovo Balance Sheet (in millions of U.S. dollars)

	As of Mar 31, 2013	As of Mar 31, 2012
Non-current assets	4,492	4,040
Property, plant and equipment	480	392
Intangible assets	3,326	3,092
Others	686	556
Current assets	12,390	11,820
Bank deposits and cash	3,573	4,172
Trade, notes and other receivables	6,694	6,297
Inventories	1,965	1,218
Others	158	133
Current liabilities	12,091	11,809
Short-term bank loans	176	63
Trade, notes and other payables	10,576	11,251
Others	1,339	495
Net current assets	299	11
Non-current liabilities	2,111	1,603
Total equity	**2,680**	**2,448**

Source: Based on company documents.

Segments

Lenovo does an excellent job of reporting segment financial information both by geographic region and by product. Exhibit 4 reveals geographic segment information for Lenovo's 2012/2013 fiscal year that ended March 31, 2013. Note the high revenue growth in Europe/Middle East/Africa (EMEA) and the high profit margin in China. At March 31, 2013, Lenovo's worldwide personal computer (PC) market share grew from 13.0 percent to 15.3 percent, trailing only HP's 15.7 percent, and above Dell's 13.2 percent.

Competitors

A financial comparison of various Lenovo competitors is provided in Exhibit 5. Note that Apple crushes all competitors, including Lenovo, on profit margin and earnings per share (EPS). Note that HP is struggling and that Lenovo does not have that many shares outstanding versus most rival firms. Apple is the second-largest publicly traded corporation in the world by market capitalization with its $424 billion figure. Lenovo is also concerned about China's ZTE Corp., which plans to become one of the world's top-three smartphone brands. ZTE was struggling financially as 2012 ended, but the company has aggressive plans and a good product.

Apple, Inc.

Headquartered in Cupertino, California, Apple's best-known products are the Mac line of computers, the iPod, iPhone, iPad, iTunes, iLife, and iWork. Apple software includes the OS X and iOS operating systems and the Safari web browser. Apple is the world's second-largest information technology company by revenue after Samsung Electronics. Apple is also the world's third-largest mobile phone make after Samsung and Nokia. As of November 2012, Apple has 394 retail stores in 14 countries and an online Apple Store and iTunes Store. For its fiscal year that ended in September 2012, Apple posted revenue of $22.5 billion in China, Taiwan, and Hong Kong, nearly double the amount from the prior year. However, partly as a result of Lenovo, Apple's market share dropped to 4.2 percent of the China smartphone market in the quarter ended September 2012, from 5.8 percent the prior year. Another problem for Apple in China is that the China's largest mobile carrier, China Mobile Ltd., does not sell the iPhone, although that company had 87.9 million subscribers to high-cost, third-generation mobile services at year end 2012.

EXHIBIT 4 Lenovo's Sales and Profit by Region (in U.S. dollars)

Including MIDH and non-PC revenue & results	Revenue US$ Million		Segment Operating Profit/ (Loss) US$ Million		Segment Operating Profit Margin	
	FY13	Y/Y	FY13	FY12^	FY13	FY12^
China	14,539	17%	678	569	4.7%	4.6%
China - PC	11,751	6%	733	638	6.2%	5.8%
APLA	6,860	8%	24	0	0.3%	0.0%
EMEA	7,535	20%	147	83	2.0%	1.3%
North America	4,939	9%	168	161	3.4%	3.5%

Note: EMEA = Europe/Middle East/Africa; APLA = Asia/Pacific/Latin America.

EXHIBIT 5 A Financial Comparison of Lenovo with Rival Firms (in U.S. dollars)

	Lenovo	Apple	Dell	HP	Toshiba	Fujitsu
Sales ($)	34 B	165 B	58 B	120 B	63 B	49 B
Income ($)	631 M	42 B	2.7B	–12.6 B	1.3 B	279 M
Profit Margin	1.86%	25.35%	4.44%	–10.5%	2.27%	0.55%
Market Capitalization ($)	11.07 B	424 B	24 B	32.5 B	18.5 B	8.5 B
Shares Outstanding	518 M	939 B	1.75 B	1.95 B	4.25 B	414 M
EPS ($)	1.10	44.10	1.47	–6.45	0.30	0.64

Note: EPS, earnings per share.
Source: Developed in February 2013 from a variety of sources.

An increasing number of companies are interested in purchasing Mac computers for all or part of their global operations. Apple focuses its business toward consumers and does not aggressively develop products and services for global enterprise customers. Organizations that have multiple-country operations oftentimes have to make separate arrangements in each region, with local partners making global deployments more complex. Apple has outstanding product design and innovation as well as financial stability, but the company lacks consistent global service and support. In September 2012, Apple unveiled the iPhone5, featuring an enlarged screen, more powerful processors, and running iOS6. The phone also includes a new mapping application (replacing Google Maps) that has attracted some criticism.

Dell, Inc.

Headquartered in Round Rock, Texas, Dell is the third-largest PC vendor in the world after HP and Lenovo. Dell employs more than 103,300 people worldwide and is a strong corporate PC supplier with good global coverage and capabilities. Dell is positioning itself beyond its PC roots however and as such is becoming less competitive on PC pricing. To diversify away from PCs—although that product, like Lenovo, is still Dell's best seller—Dell in 2012 acquired Wyse Technology and Quest Software and Gale Technologies and Credant Technologies. These acquired firms produce and market other high-technology products and services, but not PCs, smartphones, or tablets.

Fujitsu

Headquartered in Tokyo, Japan, Fujitsu is the world's third-largest IT services provider measured by revenues after IBM and HP. Fujitsu executes on a global basis and provides a good option for corporate purchasing for many organizations. Although its U.S. operations are still weak, Fujitsu has added desktops and bolstered its North American capabilities. Fujitsu is also a strong supplier of pen tablet PCs, an important segment with Windows 8. Fujitsu has a good desktop service portfolio across Europe and is strong in the Middle East, Africa, and Japan. In May 2011, Fujitsu entered the mobile phone market again and released various Windows Phone devices. Fujitsu offers a public cloud service delivered from data centers in Japan, Australia, Singapore, the United States, the United Kingdom, and Germany based on its Global Cloud Platform strategy. The platform delivers Infrastructure-as-a-Service (IaaS) virtual information and communication technology (ICT) infrastructure, such as servers and storage functionality.

Hewlett-Packard

Headquartered in Palo Alto, California, HP has a strong global PC presence and portfolio of services and products and is a viable supplier for global enterprise customers, regardless of business size. In May 2012, HP announced plans to lay off approximately 27,000 employees, after posting a profit decline of 31 percent in the second quarter of 2012. The profit decline is largely as a result of the growing popularity of smartphones, tablets, and other mobile devices that have slowed the sale of PCs. HP recently merged its printing and PC businesses under one executive, Todd Bradley. In November 2012, HP recorded a write down of around $8.8 billion related to its $11.3 billion acquisition of the U.K.-based software maker Autonomy Corp. HP accused Autonomy of deliberately inflating the value of the company before its takeover, but Autonomy flatly rejected the charge. The FBI is investigating but HP's stock has fallen to a decades' low.

Toshiba Corporation

Headquartered in Tokyo, Japan, Toshiba provides a wide range of notebook computers targeted at businesses, but its global focus has shifted increasingly toward the consumer and small-business markets. Toshiba remains strong in Canada and Australia in commercial sales, but a lack of desktop offerings makes Toshiba inappropriate if a sole PC vendor is desired for a company. Toshiba's focus has shifted toward the nonenterprise notebook market. Toshiba is no longer a major concern for Lenovo because the two firms' product lines overlap less and less every day.

Acer

Headquartered in Taiwan, Acer plans to build up its smartphone business, raising sales from 500,000 units in 2012 to 1.5 million in 2013, and 5 million in 2014. Acer is targeting specific operators individually instead of trying to offer models across entire markets. Acer has suffered two consecutive (2011 and 2012) annual losses, still struggling from its bad acquisitions of Gateway, Packard Bell, and eMachines. Of late however, Acer has posted strong sales of note-books using Google's Chrome platform.

Nokia Corporation

Nokia is a communications and IT corporation headquartered in Keilaniemi, Espoo, Finland. Its principal products are mobile phones and portable IT devices. Nokia was the world's largest vendor of mobile phones from 1998 to 2012 but over the past five years, the company has suffered declining market share as a result of the growing use of smartphones from other vendors, principally the Apple iPhone and devices running on Google's Android operating system. As a result, its share price has fallen from a high of U.S. $40 in 2007 to under U.S. $3 in 2012. Since February 2011, Nokia has had a strategic partnership with Microsoft whereby Nokia smartphones will incorporate Microsoft's Windows Phone operating system (replacing Symbian). Nokia unveiled its first Windows Phone handsets, the Lumia 710 and 800 in October 2011 but sales subsequently dropped and Nokia made six consecutive loss-making quarters from second quarter 2011 to third quarter 2012.. The fourth quarter of 2012 saw Nokia return to profit after strong sales of its new Windows Phone 8 handsets, particularly the high-end Lumia 920. In October 2012, Nokia said its high-end Lumia 820 and 920 phones, which will run on Windows Phone 8 software, will soon be available across Europe and in Russia. In December 2012, Nokia introduced two new smartphones, the Lumia 620 and 920T. In January 2013, Nokia reported 6.6 million smartphone sales for the fourth quarter in 2012, consisting of 2.2 million Symbian and 4.4 million sales of Lumia devices (Windows Phone 7 and 8). In North America, only 700,000 mobile phones have been sold including smartphones.

Samsung Electronics

Based in Seoul, South Korea, Samsung makes the popular Galaxy smartphone. Samsung also makes DVD players, digital TVs, and digital still cameras; computers, color monitors, LCD panels, and printers; semiconductors such as DRAMs, static RAMs, flash memory, and display drivers; and communications devices ranging from wireless handsets and smartphones to networking gear; microwave ovens, refrigerators, air conditioners, and washing machines. Galaxy runs on Google's android mobile-operating software.

The Future

Lenovo's diverse product brands overlap more and more, which is becoming confusing to many customers. The company's current aggressive pricing may not be profitable in future years. The differentiation provided by Lenovo's ThinkVantage software tools is eroding. Alternative offerings from Microsoft and third parties are improving, and are often free, reducing the value of Lenovo's unique tools. Even for a strong firm such as Lenovo, rivals await at every turn to seize market share and customer loyalty. The global smartphone market increased by 39 percent in 2012 in terms of units shipped, according to International Data Corporation.

In the summer of 2013, Lenovo introduced another new product, a table PC that weighs 17 pounds and runs off Windows 8 and is called the Lenovo Idea Centre Horizon Table PC. The new product does everything and features a 27-inch high-definition display panel. Hundreds of fun games and educational apps come preloaded on the new product. Lenovo is engaged in discussions to acquire the maker of the BlackBerry smartphone, but a larger concern for the company perhaps is Xiaomi.

Develop a clear strategic plan for Lenovo that will enable the company to continue its historical success.

Glossary

Acquisition   When a large organization purchases (acquires) a smaller firm; a merger.

Actionable factors   Meaningful in terms of having strategic implications; reveal potential strategies to capitalize or compensate.

Activity ratios   Inventory turnover and average collection period measure how effectively a firm is using its resources.

Advantage   A way to evaluate strategies, i.e. to determine if a particular strategy creates or extends a firm's competitive superiority in a selected area of activity.

Aggressive quadrant   In a SPACE matrix analysis, when the firm's directional vector points in the upper right quadrant, the firm should pursue aggressive strategies.

Annual objectives   Desired targets to achieve; used to focus/direct/channel efforts and activities of organization members. They (1) represent the basis for allocating resources; (2) are a primary mechanism for evaluating managers; (3) are the major instrument for monitoring progress toward achieving long-term objectives; and (4) establish organizational, divisional, and departmental priorities.

Annual objectives   Short-term milestones, usually one year, that organizations must achieve to reach long-term targets/goals.

Attractiveness scores (AS)   In a QSPM, the numerical value (rating) that indicates the relative attractiveness of each strategy given a single internal or external factor.

Auditing   The accounting process that firms undertake to have their financial statements reviewed for accuracy in order to assure compliance with the law and IRS code.

Avoidance   A method for reducing conflict through such actions as ignoring the problem in hopes that the conflict will resolve itself or physically separating the conflicting individuals (or groups).

Backward integration   A strategy seeking ownership or increased control of a firm's suppliers, such as a manufacturer acquiring its raw material source firms.

Balanced scorecard   A framework of desired objectives; derives its name from the need of firms to "balance" quantitative (such as financial ratios and percentages) with qualitative (such as for employee morale and business ethics) objectives that are oftentimes used in strategy evaluation.

Balanced Scorecard   A strategy evaluation tool utilized to establish, monitor, and evaluate both qualitative and quantitative (hence the word balanced) objectives in order to improve organizational effectiveness and performance.

Bankruptcy   A legal document that allows a firm to avoid major debt obligations and void union contracts in order to survive and regroup as a firm. There are five major types: Chapter 7, Chapter 9, Chapter 11, Chapter 12, and Chapter 13.

Benchmarking   A management technique associated with value chain analysis, whereby a firm compares itself on a wide variety of performance-related criteria against the best firms in the industry, thus establishing standards of excellence.

Benchmarking   An analytical tool used to determine how a firm's value chain activities compare to rival firms in order to better gain and sustain competitive advantages.

Board of directors   A group of individuals above the CEO, who have oversight and guidance over management and who care for shareholders' interests.

Bonus system   A form of incentive compensation whereby employees and/or managers receive a year-end or period-end reward, usually cash, based on some organizational performance criteria such as sales, profit, production efficiency, quality, and safety; used to motivate individuals to support strategy-implementation efforts.

Book value   Number of shares outstanding times stock price.

Boston Consulting Group (BCG) Matrix   A four quadrant, strategic planning analytical tool that places an organization's various divisions as circles in a display (similar to the IE Matrix) based on two key dimensions: 1) relative market share position and 2) industry growth rate. The diagram's four quadrants (Stars, Question Marks, Cash Cows, Question Marks) each have different strategy implications.

Breakeven (BE) point   The quantity of units that a firm must sell in order for its total revenues (TR) to equal its total costs (TC).

Bribe   A gift bestowed to influence a recipient's conduct.

Bribery   Offering, giving, receiving, or soliciting of any item of value to influence the actions of an official or other person in discharge of a public or legal duty.

Business analytics   An MIS technique designed to analyze huge volumes of data to help executives make decisions; sometimes called predictive analytics or data mining.

Business ethics   Principles of behavior/conduct a firm may institute to minimize wrongdoing among employees/managers.

Business portfolio   Autonomous divisions (or profit centers or segments) of an organization as represented by circles in a BCG and IE matrices.

Business-Process Outsourcing (BPO)   When a firm contracts with an outside firm(s) to take over some of their functional operations, such as human resources, information systems, payroll, accounting, or customer service.

Capacity utilization   The extent to which a manufacturing plant's output reaches its potential output; the higher the capacity utilization the better, because otherwise equipment may sit idle.

Capital budgeting   A basic function of finance; the allocation and reallocation of capital and resources to projects, products, assets, and divisions of an organization.

Cash budget   The most common type of financial budget; developed to forecast future receipts and disbursements of cash in operations, investments, and financing.

Cash cows   A quadrant in the BCG Matrix for divisions that have a high relative market share position but compete in a low-growth industry; they generate cash in excess of their needs, they are often milked, this is the lower left quadrant.

Champions   Individuals most strongly identified with a firm's new idea/product/service, and whose futures are linked to its success.

Chief Information Officer (CIO)   Is more an external manager compared to a CTO; focuses on the firm's technical, information gathering, and social media relationship with diverse external stakeholders.

Chief Technology Officer (CTO)   Is more of an internal manager than the CIO; focuses on technical issues such as data acquisition, data processing, decision-support systems, and software and hardware acquisition.

Code of business ethics   A written document specifying expected employee/manager behavior/conduct in an organization.

Combination strategy   The pursuit of a combination of two or more strategies simultaneously.

Communication   Perhaps the most important word in strategic management, because gathering, assimilating, and evaluating information in an interactive, effective manner can lead to enhanced understanding and commitment so vital in strategic planning.

Competitive advantage   Anything a firm does especially well, compared to rival firms. For example, when a firm can do something that rival firms cannot do, or owns something that rival firms desire, that can represent a competitive advantage.

Competitive analysis   The process of gathering and analyzing data about competitors and disseminating the data (intelligence) on a timely basis to who needs to know in order to gain and sustain a firm's competitive advantages.

Competitive Intelligence (CI)   "A systematic and ethical process for gathering and analyzing information about the competition's activities and general business trends to further a business's own goals" (SCIP website).

Competitive Position (CP)   One of four dimensions/axes of the SPACE Matrix; determines an organization's competitiveness, using such factors as market share, product quality, product life cycle, customer loyalty, capacity utilization, technological know-how and control over suppliers and distributors.

Competitive Profile Matrix (CPM)   A widely used strategic planning analytical tool designed to identify a firm's major competitors and its particular strengths and weaknesses in relation to a sample firm's strategic position.

Competitive quadrant   In a SPACE Matrix analysis, when the firm's directional vector points in the lower right quadrant it suggests that the firm should pursue competitive strategies such as horizontal integration.

Concern for employees   A component of the mission statement; are employees a valuable asset to the firm?

Concern for public image   A component of the mission statement; is the firm responsive to social, community, and environmental concerns?

Concern for survival, growth, and profitability   A component of the mission statement; does the firm strive to survive, grow, and (if for-profit) be profitable?

Conflict   A disagreement between two or more parties on one or more issues.

Confrontation   A method for reducing conflict exemplified by exchanging members of conflicting parties so that each can gain an appreciation of the other's point of view, or holding a meeting at which conflicting parties present their views and work through their differences.

Conservative quadrant   In a SPACE Matrix analysis, when the firm's directional vector points in the upper left quadrant it suggests that the firm should pursue conservative strategies such as market penetration.

Consistency   A way to evaluate strategies, i.e. to determine if a particular strategy is supportive of overall strategies/objectives/policies of the firm.

Consonance   Refers to the need for strategists to examine sets of trends, as well as individual trends, in evaluating strategies.

Contingency plans   Alternative plans that can be put into effect if certain key events do not occur as expected.

Controlling   A basic function of management; includes all of those activities undertaken to ensure that actual operations conform to planned operations.

Cooperative arrangements   Includes joint ventures, research and development partnerships, cross-distribution agreements, cross-licensing agreements, cross-manufacturing agreements, and joint-bidding consortia.

Core competence   A value chain activity that a firm performs especially well.

Cost leadership   One of Michael Porter's strategy dimensions that involves a firm producing standardized products at a very low per-unit cost for consumers who are price-sensitive.

Cost/benefit analysis   An activity that involves assessing the costs, benefits, and risks associated with marketing decisions. Three steps are required to perform this: (1) compute the total costs associated with a decision, (2) estimate the total benefits from the decision, and (3) compare the total costs with the total benefits.

Creed statement Another name for mission statement; a declaration of an organization's "reason for being." It answers the pivotal question, "What is our business?"

Cultural products Include values, beliefs, rites, rituals, ceremonies, myths, stories, legends, sagas, language, metaphors, symbols, heroes, and heroines. These products are levers that strategists can use to influence and direct strategy formulation, implementation, and evaluation activities.

Culture The set of shared values, beliefs, attitudes, customs, norms, personalities, heroes, and heroines that describe a firm.

Culture The set of shared values, beliefs, attitudes, customs, norms, personalities, heroes, and heroines that describe a firm. Strategists should strive to preserve, emphasize, and build upon these aspects.

Customer analysis Examination and evaluation of consumer needs, desires, and wants; involves administering customer surveys, analyzing consumer information, evaluating market positioning strategies, developing customer profiles, and determining optimal market segmentation strategies.

Customers A component of the mission statement; individuals who purchase a firm's products/services.

Data mining Analyzing huge volumes of information in order to determine trends and garner information to make decision making more effective.

Data Raw facts and figures; "data" becomes "information" only when they are evaluated, filtered, condensed, analyzed, and organized for a specific purpose, problem, individual, or time.

De-integration Reducing the pursuit of backward integration; instead of owning suppliers, companies negotiate with several outside suppliers.

Decentralized structure Also called a divisional structure, this type of organizational design is based on having various profit centers or segments by geographic area, by product or service, by customer, or by process. With a divisional structure, functional activities are performed both centrally and in each separate division.

Decision stage Stage 3 of the strategy formulation analytical framework that involves development of the Quantitative Strategic Planning Matrix (QSPM). A QSPM uses input information from Stage 1 to objectively evaluate feasible alternative strategies identified in Stage 2. A QSPM reveals the relative attractiveness of alternative strategies and thus provides objective basis for selecting specific strategies.

Defensive quadrant In a SPACE Matrix analysis, when the firm's directional vector into the lower left quadrant it suggests that the firm should pursue defensive strategies such as retrenchment.

Defusion A method for reducing conflict includes playing down differences between conflicting parties while accentuating similarities and common interests, or compromising so that there is neither a clear winner nor loser, or resorting to majority rule, or appealing to a higher authority, or redesigning present positions.

Delayering Reducing the number of divisions or units or hierarchical levels in a firm's organizational structure.

Demand void Areas in a perceptual map where there is not a cluster of ideal points indicating an unattractive group of potential customers.

Differentiation One of Michael Porter's strategy dimensions that involves a firm producing products and services considered unique industry-wide and directed at consumers who are relatively price-insensitive.

Directional vector In a SPACE Matrix analysis, this line begins at the origin and goes into one of four quadrants, revealing the type of strategies recommended for the organization: aggressive, competitive, defensive, or conservative.

Director of competitive analysis The person who gathers and analyzes data about competitors, and disseminates data (intelligence) on a timely basis to who needs to know in order to gain and sustain a firm's competitive advantages.

Discount If an acquiring firm pays less for another firm than the firm's stock price times its # of shares of stock outstanding (book value or market value), then that # less the actual purchase price is called a discount.

Distinctive competencies A firm's strengths that cannot be easily matched or imitated by competitors.

Distribution The process of getting goods and services to market; includes warehousing, distribution channels, distribution coverage, retail site locations, sales territories, inventory levels and location, transportation carriers, wholesaling, and retailing.

Diversification strategies When a firm enters a new business/industry, either related and unrelated to their existing business/industry. Related diversification is when the old vs. new business value chains possesses competitively valuable cross-business strategic fits; unrelated diversification is when the old vs. new business value chains are so dissimilar that no competitively valuable cross-business relationships exist.

Divestiture Selling a division or part of an organization.

Dividend decision A basic function of finance; concerns issues such as the percentage of earnings paid to stockholders, the stability of dividends paid over time, and the repurchase or issuance of stock.

Dividend recapitalizations When private-equity firms especially, but other firms also, borrow money to fund dividend payouts to themselves.

Divisional structure This type of organizational design is based on having various profit centers or segments by geographic area, by product or service, by customer, or by process. With a divisional structure, functional activities are performed both centrally and in each separate division.

Dogs A quadrant in the BCG Matrix for divisions that have a low relative market share position and compete in a low-growth industry, this is the lower right quadrant.

Downsizing Reducing the number of employees, number of divisions or units, and/or number of hierarchical levels in the firm's organizational structure.

Educative change strategy A management technique to facilitate a firm adapting to new strategies/policies/situations by presenting to employees/managers information that reveals why the firm needs to do what is to be done; this approach can be slow but oftentimes yields high commitment.

Empirical indicators Refers to three characteristics of resources (rare, hard to imitate, not easily substitutable) that enable a firm to gain and sustain competitive advantage.

Employee Stock Ownership Plans (ESOP) A tax-qualified, defined-contribution, employee-benefit plan whereby employees purchase stock of the company through borrowed money or cash contributions.

Empowerment The act of strengthening employees' sense of shared ownership by encouraging them to participate in decision making and rewarding them for doing so.

Environment The surroundings in which an organization operates, including air, water, land, natural resources, flora, fauna, humans, and their interrelation.

Environmental Management System (EMS) When a firm or municipality operates utilizing "green" policies/practices/procedures as outlined by ISO 14001.

Environmental scanning Another term for external audit; conducting research to gather and assimilate external information.

Environmental scanning Process of conducting research and gathering and assimilating external information.

EPS/EBIT analysis A financial technique to determine whether debt, stock, or a combination of debt and stock is the best alternative for raising capital to implement strategies.

Establishing annual objectives The managerial activity that determines appropriate/desired targets to achieve by region/product/service.

External audit Process of identifying and evaluating trends and events beyond the control of a single firm, in areas such as social, cultural, demographic technology, economic, political, and competition; reveals key opportunities and threats confronting an organization, so managers can better formulate strategies.

External Factor Evaluation (EFE) Matrix A widely used strategic planning analytical tool designed to summarize and evaluate economic, social, cultural, demographic, environmental, political, governmental, legal, technological, and competitive information.

External forces (1) Economic forces; (2) social, cultural, demographic, and natural environment forces; (3) political, governmental, and legal forces; (4) technological forces; and (5) competitive forces.

External opportunities Economic, social, cultural, demographic, environmental, political, legal, governmental, technological, and competitive trends/events/facts that could significantly benefit an organization in the future.

External threats Economic, social, cultural, demographic, environmental, political, legal, governmental, technological, and competitive trends/events/facts that could significantly harm an organization in the future.

Feasibility A way to evaluate strategies, i.e. to determine if a strategy is capable of being carried out within the physical, human, and financial resources of the firm.

Feng shui In China, this term refers to the practice of harnessing natural forces, which can impact how you arrange office furniture.

Financial budget A financial document that details/reveals how funds will be obtained and spent for a specified period of time in the future.

Financial objectives Include desired results growth in revenues, growth in earnings, higher dividends, larger profit margins, greater return on investment, higher earnings per share, a rising stock price, improved cash flow, and so on.

Financial Position (FP) One of four dimensions/axes of the SPACE Matrix that determines an organization's financial strength, considering such factors as return on investment, leverage, liquidity, working capital, and cash flow.

Financial ratio analysis Quantitative calculations that reveal the financial condition of a firm and exemplify the complexity of relationships among the functional areas of business. For example, a declining return on investment or profit margin ratio could be the result of ineffective marketing, poor management policies, research and development errors, or a weak management information system. Ratios are usually compared to industry averages, or to prior time periods, or to rival firms.

Financing decision A basic function of finance; determines the best capital structure for the firm and includes examining various methods by which the firm can raise capital (for example, by issuing stock, increasing debt, selling assets, or using a combination of these approaches).

First mover advantages The benefits a firm may achieve by entering a new market or developing a new product or service before rival firms.

Fixed Costs (FC) A key variable in breakeven analysis; includes costs such as plant, equipment, stores, advertising, and land.

Focus One of Michael Porter's strategy dimensions that involves a firm producing products and services that fulfill the needs of small groups of consumers.

Force change strategy A management technique to facilitate a firm adapting to new strategies/policies/situations by simply giving orders and enforcing those orders; this approach has the advantage of being fast, but it is plagued by low commitment.

Forward integration A strategy that involves gaining ownership or increased control over distributors or retailers, such as a manufacturer opening its own chain of stores.

Franchising An effective means of implementing forward integration whereby a franchisee purchases the right to own one or more stores/restaurants of a chain firm.

Friendly merger If the merger/acquisition is desired by both firms.

Functional structure A type of organizational design that groups tasks and activities by business function, such as production/operations, marketing, finance/accounting, research and development, and management information systems.

Functions of finance/accounting The basic activities performed by finance managers; consists of three decisions: the investment decision, the financing decision, and the dividend decision.

Functions of management Consist of five basic activities: planning, organizing, motivating, staffing, and controlling.

Functions of marketing The basic activities performed by marketing managers, including (1) customer analysis, (2) selling products/services, (3) product and service planning, (4) pricing, (5) distribution, (6) marketing research, and (7) opportunity analysis.

Furloughs Temporary layoffs.

Future shock High anxiety that results when the nature, types, and speed of changes overpower an individual's or organization's ability and capacity to adapt.

GAAS, GAAP, and IFRS Generally accepted auditing standards, generally accepted accounting principles, and international financial reporting standards.

Gain sharing A form of incentive compensation whereby employees and/or managers receive bonuses when actual results exceed some pre-determined performance targets.

Generic strategies Michael Porter's strategy breakdown; consists of three strategies: cost leadership, differentiation, and focus.

Glass ceiling A term used to refer to the artificial barrier that women and minorities face in moving into upper levels of management.

Global strategy Designing, producing, and marketing products with global needs in mind, instead of solely considering individual countries.

Globalization A process of doing business worldwide, so strategic decisions are made based on global profitability of the firm rather than just domestic considerations.

Goodwill If a firm acquires another firm and pays more than the book value (market value), then the additional amount paid is called a premium, and becomes goodwill, which is a line item on the assets portion of a balance sheet.

Governance The act of oversight and direction, especially in association with the duties of a board of directors.

Grand Strategy Matrix A four-quadrant, two axis tool for formulating alternative strategies. All organizations can be positioned in one of this matrix's four strategy quadrants, based on their position on two evaluative dimensions: competitive position and market (industry) growth. Strategy suggestions ensue depending on which quadrant the firm is located.

Growth ratios Measures such as the percent increase/decrease in revenue or profit from one period to the next are important comparisons.

Guanxi In China, business behavior is based on "personal relations".

Halo error The human tendency to put too much weight on a single factor.

Horizontal consistency of objectives Objectives need to be compatible across functions; for example if marketing wants to sell 10% more than production must produce 10% more.

Horizontal integration Acquiring a rival firm.

Hostile takeover If the merger/acquisition is not desired by both firms.

Human resource management Also called personnel management; a basic function of management; includes activities such as recruiting, interviewing, testing, selecting, orienting, training, developing, caring for, evaluating, rewarding, disciplining, promoting, transferring, demoting, and dismissing employees, as well as managing union relations.

Industrial Organization (I/O) An approach to competitive advantage that advocates that external (industry) factors are more important than internal factors for a firm in striving to achieve competitive advantage.

Industry analysis Another term for external audit; conducting research to gather and assimilate external information.

Industry Position (IP) One of four dimensions/axes of the SPACE Matrix that determines how strong/weak a firm's industry is, considering such factors as growth potential, profit potential, financial stability, extent leveraged, resource utilization, ease of entry into market, productivity and capacity utilization.

Information Technology (IT) The development, maintenance, and use of computer systems, software, and networks for the processing and distribution of data.

Information Data that has been evaluated, filtered, condensed, analyzed, and organized for a specific purpose, problem, individual, or time.

Inhwa A South Korean term for activities that involve concern for harmony based on respect of hierarchical relationships, including obedience to authority.

Initial public offering When a private firm goes public by selling its shares of stock to the public in order to raise capital.

Input stage Stage 1 of the strategy-formulation analytical framework that summarizes the basic input information needed to formulate strategies; consists of an EFEM, CPM, and IFEM.

Integration strategies Includes forward integration, backward integration, and horizontal integration (sometimes collectively referred to as vertical integration strategies).

Intensive strategies Includes market development, market penetration, and product development.

Internal audit The process of gathering and assimilating information about the firm's management, marketing, finance/accounting, production/operations, R&D, and MIS operations. The purpose is to identify/evaluate/prioritize a firm's strengths and weaknesses.

Internal Factor Evaluation (IFE) Matrix A strategy-formulation tool that summarizes and evaluates a firm's major strengths and weaknesses in the functional areas of a business, and provides a basis for identifying and evaluating relationships among those areas.

Internal strengths An organization's controllable activities that are performed especially well, such as in areas that include finance, marketing, management, accounting, MIS, across a firm's products/regions/stores/facilities.

Internal weaknesses An organization's controllable activities that are performed especially poorly, such as in areas that include finance, marketing, management, accounting, MIS, across a firm's products/regions/stores/facilities.

Internal-External (IE) Matrix A nine quadrant, strategic planning analytical tool that places an organization's various divisions as circles in a display (similar to the BCG Matrix) based on two key dimensions: 1) the segment's IFE total weighted scores on the x-axis and 2) the segment's EFE total weighted scores on the y-axis. The diagram is divided into three major regions that have different strategy implications: 1) grow and build or 2) hold and maintain, or 3) harvest or divest.

International firms Firms that conduct business outside their own country.

Internet A global system of interconnected computers that serve billions of users worldwide; provides a vast range of information resources and services; enables billions of businesses and individuals globally to communicate instantly with each other by email, tweets, etc.

Intuition Using one's cognition without evident rational thought or analysis; based on past experience, judgment, and feelings; essential to making good strategic decisions but must not relied upon heavily in lieu of objective analysis.

Investment decision Also called capital budgeting; a basic function of finance; the allocation and reallocation of capital and resources to projects, products, assets, and divisions of an organization.

ISO 14000 A series of voluntary standards in the environmental field whereby a firm minimizes harmful effects on the environment caused by its activities and continually monitors and improves its own environmental performance.

ISO 14001 A set of standards adopted by thousands of firms worldwide to certify to their constituencies that they are conducting business in an environmentally friendly manner. These standards offer a universal technical standard for environmental compliance that more and more firms are requiring not only of themselves but also of their suppliers and distributors.

Joint venture A strategy that occurs when two or more companies form a temporary partnership/consortium/business for the purpose of capitalizing on some opportunity.

Just-In-Time (JIT) A production approach in which parts and materials are delivered to a production site just as they are needed, rather than being stockpiled as a hedge against late deliveries.

Leverage ratios The debt-to-equity ratio and debt-to-total assets ratio measure the extent to which a firm has been financed by debt.

Leveraged Buyout (LBO) When the outstanding shares of a corporation are bought by the company's management and other private investors using borrowed funds.

Linear regression A quantitative statistical technique often used for forecasting, but based on the assumption that the future will be just like the past. To the extent that historical relationships are unstable, linear regression is less accurate.

Liquidation Selling all of a company's assets, in parts, for their tangible worth.

Liquidity ratios The current ratio and quick ratio measure a firm's ability to meet short-term cash obligations.

Long-range planning Deciding upon future actions/objectives/policies with the aim to optimize for tomorrow the trends of today; less effective and comprehensive than strategic planning.

Long-term objectives Specific results that an organization seeks to achieve (in more than one year) in pursuing its basic vision/mission/strategy.

Long-term objectives The specific results expected from pursuing various strategies.

Management by wandering around A part of strategy evaluation whereby managers simply walk around facilities and operations in order to observe and talk with employees, thus garnering information useful in evaluating strategies.

Management Information System (MIS) A system that gathers, assimilates, and evaluates external and internal information to facilitate decision-making.

Management information system A computer-based process for obtaining and utilizing external and internal facts/figures/trends to support managerial decision-making. Includes gathering and utilizing data about marketing, finance, production, and personnel matters internally, and social, cultural, demographic, environmental, economic, political, governmental, legal, technological, and competitive factors externally.

Market capitalization   Number of shares outstanding times stock price.

Market commonality   The number and significance of markets that a firm competes in with rivals.

Market development   Introducing present products or services into new geographic areas.

Market penetration   Increasing market share for present products or services in present markets through greater marketing efforts.

Market segment   Areas in a perceptual map where there is a cluster of ideal points indicating an attractive group of potential customers to target.

Market segmentation   The marketing technique of subdividing consumers into distinct subsets according to needs and buying habits in order to more effectively and economically direct marketing efforts.

Market value   Number of shares outstanding times stock price.

Marketing research   The systematic gathering, recording, and analyzing of data about problems/practices/issues related to the marketing of goods and services.

Markets   A component of the mission statement; geographic locations where a firm competes.

Marking mix variables   Product, place, promotion, and price.

Matching stage   Stage 2 of the strategy-formulation framework that focuses upon generating feasible alternative strategies by aligning internal with external factors by utilizing five matrices: BCG, IE, SWOT, GRAND, SPACE.

Matching   When an organization matches its internal strengths and weaknesses with its external opportunities and threats using, for example, the SWOT, SPACE, BCG, IE, or GRAND Matrices.

Matrix structure   This type of organizational design places functional activities along the top row and divisional projects/units along the left side to create a rubric where managers have two bosses – both a functional boss and a project boss, thus creating the need for extensive vertical and horizontal flows of authority and communication.

Measuring organizational performance   Activity # 2 in the strategy evaluation process; includes comparing expected results to actual results, investigating deviations from plans, evaluating individual performance, and examining progress being made toward meeting stated objectives.

Merger   When two organizations of about equal size unite to form one enterprise; an acquisition.

Mission statement components   1) Customers, 2) products and services, 3) markets, 4) technology, 5) concern for survival, growth, and profitability, 6) philosophy, 7) self-concept, 8) concern for public image, 9) concern for employees.

Mission statement   A declaration of an organization's "reason for being." It answers the pivotal question, "What is our business?" Is essential for effectively establishing objectives and formulating strategies; consists of nine components.

Mission statement   An enduring statement of purpose that distinguish one business from other similar firms; several sentence statement that identifies the scope of a firm's operations in product and market terms and addresses the question "What is our business?"

Motivating   A basic function of management; the process of influencing and leading people to accomplish specific objectives.

Multidimensional scaling   The same as product positioning (perceptual mapping), except encompasses three or more evaluative criteria simultaneously.

Multinational corporations   Firms that conduct business outside their own country.

Nemaswashio   U.S. managers in Japan have to be careful about this phenomenon, whereby Japanese workers expect supervisors to alert them privately of changes rather than informing them in a meeting.

Organizational culture   A pattern of behavior developed by an organization over time as it learns to cope with its problem of external adaptation and internal integration, and that has worked well enough to be considered valid and to be taught to new members as the correct way to perceive, think, and feel in the firm.

Organizing   A basic function of management; the process of arranging duties and responsibilities in a coherent manner in order to determine who does what and who reports to whom.

Outstanding shares method   A method for determining the cash worth of a firm by multiplying the number of shares outstanding by the market price per share; also called book value, market value, or market capitalization.

Perceptual map   Also called product-positioning map; a two-dimensional, four quadrant marketing tool designed to position a firm vs. its rival firms in a schematic diagram in order to better determine effective marketing strategies.

Personnel management   Also called human resource management; a basic function of management; includes activities such as recruiting, interviewing, testing, selecting, orienting, training, developing, caring for, evaluating, rewarding, disciplining, promoting, transferring, demoting, and dismissing employees, as well as managing union relations.

Philosophy   A component of the mission statement; the basic beliefs, values, aspirations, and ethical priorities of the firm.

Planning   A basic function of management; the process of deciding ahead of time strategies to be pursued and actions to be taken in the future.

Policies   The means by which annual objectives will be achieved. Policies include guidelines, rules, and procedures established to support efforts to achieve stated objectives. Policies are guides to decision making and address repetitive or recurring situations.

Policy   Specific guidelines, methods, procedures, rules, forms, and administrative practices established to support and encourage work toward stated goals.

Porter's Five-Forces Model   A theoretical model devised by Michael Porter, who suggests that the nature of competitiveness in a given industry can be viewed as a composite of five forces: 1) Rivalry among competing firms, 2) Potential entry of new competitors, 3) Potential development of substitute products, 4) Bargaining power of suppliers, and 5) Bargaining power of consumers.

Premium   If an acquiring firm pays more for another firm than that firm's stock price times its # of shares of stock outstanding (book value or market value), then the overage is called a premium.

Price-earnings ratio method   This method involves dividing the market price of the firm's common stock by the annual earnings per share and multiplying this number by the firm's average net income for the past five years.

Pricing   A basic function of marketing; determining the appropriate value for products and services to be charged to customers, given associated costs and competitor's prices.

Product and service planning   A basic function of marketing; includes activities such as test marketing; product and brand positioning; devising warranties; packaging; determining product options, features, style, and quality; deleting old products; and providing for customer service.

Product development   Increased sales by improving or modifying present products or services.

Product positioning   Also called perceptual mapping; a two-dimensional, four quadrant marketing tool designed to position a firm vs. its rival firms in a schematic diagram in order to better determine effective marketing strategies.

Production/operations function   Consists of all those activities that transform inputs into goods and services; including issues such as inventory control and capacity utilization.

Products or services   A component of the mission statement; commodities or benefits provided by a firm.

Profit sharing   A form of incentive compensation whereby some of a firm's earnings are distributed to employees/managers based on some pre-determined formula; used to motivate individuals to support strategy-implementation efforts.

Profitability ratios   The profit margin ratio and return on investment ratio measure the profitability of a firm's operations.

Projected financial statement analysis   A financial technique that enables a firm to forecast the expected financial results of various strategies and approaches; involves developing income statements and balance sheets for future periods of time.

Protectionism   When countries impose tariffs, taxes, and regulations on firms outside the country to favor their own companies and people.

Quantitative Strategic Planning Matrix (QSPM)   An analytical technique designed to determine the relative attractiveness of feasible alternative actions. This technique comprises Stage 3 of the strategy-formulation analytical framework; it objectively indicates which alternative strategies are best.

Question marks   A quadrant in the BCG Matrix for divisions that have a low relative market share position but compete in a high-growth industry; this is the upper right quadrant; firm's generally must decide whether to strengthen such divisions or sell them (hence a question is at hand).

Rational change strategy   A management technique to facilitate a firm adapting to new strategies/policies/situations, whereby employees/managers are given incentives to be supportive while at the same time are educated as to the need to change.

Reconciliatory   In regard to mission statements, the need for the statement to be sufficiently broad to "reconcile" differences effectively among diverse stakeholders, ie appeal to a firm's customers, employees, shareholders, creditors – rather than alienate any group.

Reengineering   Reconfiguring or redesigning work, jobs, and processes in a firm, for the purpose of improving cost, quality, service, and speed.

Related diversification   When a firm acquires a new business whose value chain possesses competitively valuable cross-business strategic fits.

Relative market share position   It is the horizontal axis in a BCG Matrix, which is the firm's particular segment's market share (or revenues or #stores) divided by the industry leader's analogous number

Research and Development (R&D)   Spending money to develop new and improved products and services.

Research and development   Monies spent by firms to enhance existing products/services and/or create new and improved ones.

Reshoring   Refers to American companies planning to move some of their manufacturing back to the USA.

Resistance to change   A natural human tendency to be wary of new policies/strategies due to potential negative consequences; if not managed then this could result in sabotaging production machines, absenteeism, filing unfounded grievances, and an unwillingness to cooperate.

Resource allocation   A central strategy implementation activity that entails distributing financial, physical, human, and technological assets to allow for strategy execution.

Resource similarity   The extent to which the type and amount of a firm's internal resources are comparable to a rival.

Resource-Based View (RBV)   An approach that suggests internal resources to be more important for a firm than external factors in achieving and sustaining competitive advantage.

Restructuring   Modifying the firm's chain of command and reporting channels to improve efficiency and effectiveness.

Retreats   Formal meetings commonly held off-premises to discuss and update a firm's strategic plan; done away from the work site to encourage more creativity and candor from participants.

Retrenchment   When an organization regroups through cost and asset reduction to reverse declining sales and profits.

Reviewing the underlying bases of an organization's strategy   Activity #1 in the strategy evaluation process; entails a firm developing a revised EFE Matrix and IFE Matrix to determine if corrective actions are needed.

Revised EFE Matrix   Part of activity #1 in the strategy evaluation process whereby a firm reassesses its previously determined external opportunities and threats.

Revised IFE Matrix   Part of activity #1 in the strategy evaluation process whereby a firm reassesses its previously determined internal strengths and weaknesses.

Rightsizing   Reducing the number of employees, number of divisions or units, and/or number of hierarchical levels in the firm's organizational structure; also called downsizing.

Secondary buyouts   When private-equity firms buying companies from other private-equity firms.

Self-concept   A component of the mission statement; the firm's distinctive competence or major competitive advantage.

Self-interest change strategy   A management technique to facilitate a firm adapting to new strategies/policies/situations by attempts to convince individuals that the change is to their personal advantage. When this appeal is successful, strategy implementation can be relatively easy. However, implementation changes are seldom to everyone's advantage.

Selling   A basic function of marketing; includes activities such as advertising, sales promotion, publicity, personal selling, sales force management, customer relations, and dealer relations.

Sexual harassment (and discrimination)   Unwelcome sexual advances, requests for sexual favors, and other verbal or physical conduct of a sexual nature; this activity is illegal, unethical, and detrimental to any organization, and can result in expensive lawsuits, lower morale, and reduced productivity.

Six Sigma   A quality-boosting process improvement technique that entails training several key persons in techniques to monitor, measure, and improve processes and eliminate defects in a firm; trained persons can earn black belts.

SO strategies   Strategies that result from matching a firm's internal strengths with its external opportunities.

Social policy   Guidelines and practices a firm may institute to guide its behavior towards employees, consumers, environmentalists, minorities, communities, shareholders, and other groups.

Social responsibility   Refers to actions an organization takes beyond what is legally required to protect or enhance the well-being of living things

ST strategies   Strategies that result from matching a firm's internal strengths with its external threats.

Stability position (SP)   One of four dimensions/axes of the SPACE Matrix that determines how stable/unstable a firm's industry is, considering such factors as technological changes, rate of inflation, demand of variability, price range of competing products, barriers to entry into market, competitive pressure, ease of exit from market, price elasticity of demand and risk involved in business.

Staffing   Includes activities such a recruiting, interviewing, testing, selecting, orienting, training, developing, caring for, evaluating, rewarding, disciplining, promoting, transferring, demoting, and dismissing employees.

Stakeholders   The individuals and groups of individuals who have a special stake or claim on the company, such as a firm's customers, employees, shareholders, and creditors.

Stars   A quadrant in the BCG Matrix for divisions that have a high relative market share position and compete in a high-growth industry; this is the upper left quadrant.

Strategic Business Unit (SBU) Structure   This type of organizational design groups similar divisions together into units; widely used when a firm has many divisions/segments in order to reduce span of control reporting to a COO.

Strategic management   The art and science of formulating, implementing, and evaluating cross-functional decisions that enable an organization to achieve its objectives.

Strategic objectives   Desired results such as a larger market share, quicker on-time delivery than rivals, shorter design-to-market times than rivals, lower costs than rivals, higher product quality than rivals, wider geographic coverage than rivals, achieving technological leadership, consistently getting new or improved products to market ahead of rivals.

Strategic planning   The process of formulating an organization's game plan; in a corporate setting, this term may refer to the whole strategic-management process.

Strategic Position and Action Evaluation (SPACE) Matrix   Indicates whether aggressive, conservative, defensive, or competitive strategies are most appropriate for a given organization. The axes of this matrix represent two internal dimensions (financial position [FP] and competitive position [CP]) and two external dimensions (stability position [SP] and industry position [IP]). These four factors are perhaps the most important determinants of an organization's overall strategic position.

Strategic-management model A framework or illustration of the strategic-management process; a clear and practical approach for formulating, implementing, and evaluating strategies.

Strategic-management process The process of formulating, implementing, and evaluating strategies as revealed in the comprehensive model, that begins with vision/mission development and ends with strategy evaluation and feedback.

Strategies The means by which long-term objectives will be achieved. Business strategies may include geographic expansion, diversification, acquisition, product development, market penetration, retrenchment, divestiture, liquidation, and joint ventures.

Strategists The person(s) responsible for formulating and implementing a firm's strategic plan, including the CEO, President, Owner of a Business, Head Coach, Governor, Chancellor, and/or the top management team in a firm.

Strategy evaluation Stage 3 in the strategic-management process. The three fundamental strategy-evaluation activities are (1) review external and internal factors that are the bases for current strategies, (2) measure performance, and (3) take corrective actions; strategies need to be evaluated regularly because external and internal factors constantly change.

Strategy formulation Stage 1 in the strategic-management process; includes developing a vision/mission, identifying an organization's external opportunities/threats, determining internal strengths/weaknesses, establishing long-term objectives, generating alternative strategies, and choosing particular strategies to pursue.

Strategy implementation Stage 2 of the strategic-management process. Activities include establish annual objectives, devise policies, motivate employees, allocating resources, developing a strategy-supportive culture, creating an effective organizational structure, redirecting marketing efforts, preparing budgets, developing and utilizing information systems, and linking employee compensation to organizational performance.

Strategy-formulation analytical framework A three stage, nine matrix, array of tools widely used for strategic planning as a guide: (stage 1: input stage; stage 2: matching stage; stage 3: decision stage).

Strengths-Weaknesses Opportunities-Threats (SWOT) Matrix The most widely used of all strategic planning matrices; matches a firm's internal strengths/weaknesses with its external opportunities/threats to generate four types of strategies: SO (strengths-opportunities) Strategies, WO (weaknesses-opportunities) Strategies, ST (strengths-threats) Strategies, and WT (weaknesses-threats) Strategies.

Sum Total Attractiveness Scores (STAS) In a QSPM, this is the sum of the Total Attractiveness Scores in each strategy column; value reveals which strategy is most attractive in each set of alternatives.

Sustainability The extent that an organization's operations and actions protect, mend, and preserve, rather than harm or destroy, the natural environment.

Sustained competitive advantage Maintaining what a firm does especially well, compared to rival firms – by (1) continually adapting to changes in external trends and events and internal capabilities, competencies, and resources; and (2) effectively formulating, implementing, and evaluating strategies that capitalize upon those factors.

Synergy The $1 + 1 = 3$ effect; when everyone pulls together as a team, the results can exceed individuals working separately.

Takeover If the merger/acquisition is not desired by both firms.

Taking corrective actions Activity # three in the strategy evaluation process; involves a firm making changes to competitively reposition a firm for the future.

Technology A component of the mission statement; the firm technologically current?

Test marketing An activity to determine ahead of time whether a certain product or service or selling approach will be cost effective; also used to forecast future sales of new products.

Total Attractiveness Scores (TAS) In a QSPM, the product of multiplying the weights by the Attractiveness Scores in each row. The values indicate the relative attractiveness of each alternative strategy, considering only the impact of the adjacent external or internal critical success factor.

Treasury stock An item in the equity portion of a balance sheet that reveals the dollar amount of the firm's common stock owned by the company itself.

Turbulent, high-velocity markets Industries that are changing very fast, such as telecommunications, medical, biotechnology, pharmaceuticals, computer hardware, software, and virtually all Internet-based industries).

Tweet Posted messages of 140 characters or less on Twitter.com.

Unrelated diversification When a firm acquires a new business whose value chains are so dissimilar that no competitively valuable cross-business relationships exist.

Vacant niche In product/market positioning (perceptual map), this is an area in the perceptual map that reveals a customer segment not being served by the firm or rival firms.

Value Chain Analysis (VCA) The process whereby a firm determines the costs associated with organizational activities from purchasing raw materials to manufacturing product(s) to marketing those products, and compares these costs to rival firms using benchmarking.

Value chain The business of a firm, where total revenues minus total costs of all activities undertaken to develop, produce, and market a product or service yields value.

Variable Costs (VC) A key variable in breakeven analysis; includes costs such as labor and materials.

Vertical consistency of objectives   Compatibility of objectives from the CEO (corporate level) down to the Presidents (divisional level) on down to the Managers (functional level).

Vertical integration   A combination of three strategies: backward, forward, and horizontal integration, allowing a firm to gain control over distributors, suppliers, and/or competitors respectively.

Vision statement   A one sentence statement that answers the question, "What do we want to become?"

Vision statement   Answers the question, "What do we want to become?"

Wa   In Japan, this stresses group harmony and social cohesion.

Whistle-blowing   The act of telling authorities about some unethical or illegal activities occurring within an organization of which you are aware.

White knight   When a firm agrees to acquire another firm at a point in time when that other firm is facing a hostile takeover by some company.

Wikis   Websites that allows users to add, delete, and edit content regarding frequently asked questions and information across the firm's whole value chain of activities.

WO strategies   Strategies that result from matching a firm's internal weaknesses with its external opportunities.

Workplace romance   An intimate relationship between two truly consenting employees, as opposed to sexual harassment, which the EEOC defines broadly as unwelcome sexual advances, requests for sexual favors, and other verbal or physical conduct of a sexual nature.

WT strategies   Strategies that result from matching a firm's internal weaknesses with its external threats.

Name Index

Subject Index

Comprehensive Model of the

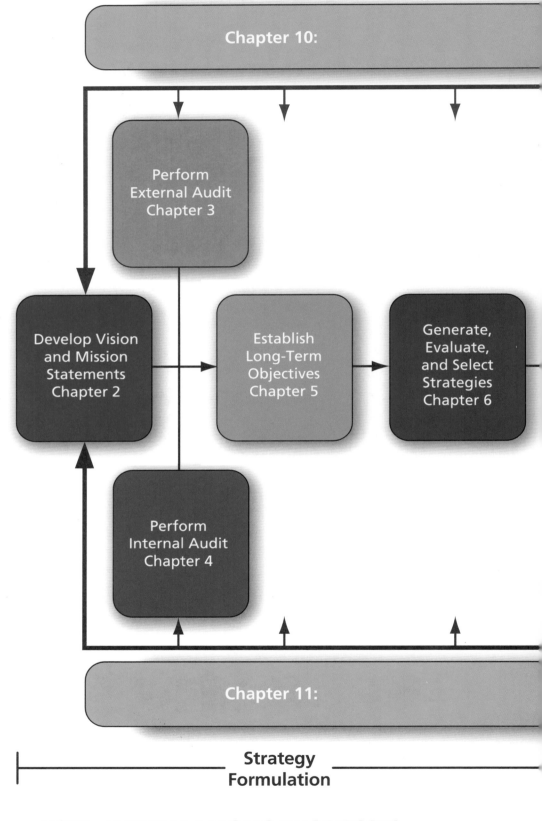

## Chapter 10

Perform
External Audit
Chapter 3

Develop Vision
and Mission
Statements
Chapter 2

Establish
Long-Term
Objectives
Chapter 5

Generate,
Evaluate,
and Select
Strategies
Chapter 6

Perform
Internal Audit
Chapter 4

Strategy
Formulation

USED WIDELY AMONG BUSINESSES
AND ACADEMIA WORLDWIDE